# The Legal Foundation and Borders of Israel under International Law

*by*

Howard Grief

Mazo Publishers

Jerusalem, Israel

The term "Israel" appearing in the title of this book is used to denote all areas of the historical Land of Israel, including both Cisjordan and Transjordan that were part of the mandated area of Palestine. It also includes those parts of the historical Land of Israel that were illegally excluded when the boundaries of Palestine were determined by Great Britain and France in 1920 and 1922: Southern Lebanon up to the bend of the Litani River, the Bashan (including the Golan) north of the Yarmuk River, and at least half of the Sinai Peninsula.

*(HG)*

**The Legal Foundation and Borders of Israel under International Law**



ISBN 978-1-936778-55-3

*Published by:*

Mazo Publishers

Chaim Mazo, Publisher

P.O. Box 36084

Jerusalem 91360 Israel

*Israel Tel:* +972-2-652-3877

*USA Tel:* 1-815-301-3559

*Website:* www.mazopublishers.com

*Email:* mazopublishers@gmail.com

*This work is dedicated*

*To the memory of my loving mother, Jenny Leah Grief (née Frankel),*
*who surpassed me in her devotion to and enthusiasm for Israel,*
*and to the memory of my dear father, Samuel Shlomo Grief,*
*whose untimely death preceded my own eighth birthday;*

*It is dedicated also*
*To my wonderful sons, Ariel and Elad, both Israeli-educated,*
*whose future awaits them;*

*To my beautiful and devoted wife, Ilana,*
*who has borne with patience and understanding the time I have not spent with her*
*in writing this book;*

*and it is dedicated finally*
*To all who support Israel in their daily lives, wherever they may live,*
*with the hope that the information contained in this book will be*
*of great use and value in advocating Israel's cause.*

*(HG)*

# TABLE OF CONTENTS

# About The Author

Howard Grief was born and educated in the city of Montreal where he attended and graduated from Baron Byng High School, McGill University and McGill Law School, obtaining degrees in Arts and Law. He became a member of the Bar of the Province of Quebec in 1966 and was a self-employed practicing attorney for 23 years, principally in the fields of civil and commercial law. A fervent Zionist and advocate of the Land of Israel all his life, he was appointed in 1980 the representative in Canada of the newly formed *Tehiya* Party. After a hard struggle, he gained recognition for *Tehiya* as a separate grouping in the Canadian Zionist Federation, the first official branch outside Israel to receive such recognition. As *Tehiya's* representative in Canada, he arranged trips and speaking engagements for Professor Yuval Ne'eman, Moshe Shamir, Shmuel Katz and Professor Edward Teller.

In August 1989, Grief left Canada to settle in Israel to fulfil his own personal vision of Zionism, together with his Jerusalem-born wife, Ilana, and their two sons, Ariel and Elad. In May 1991, he was admitted to the Bar of Israel and subsequently became a notary. On December 29, 1991 he was formally appointed by Professor Ne'eman, then the Minister of Energy and Infrastructure in the Yitzhak Shamir Government, to be his legal adviser in international law on matters pertaining to the Land of Israel.

In the wake of the Israel-PLO agreements, Howard Grief filed several petitions and applications before the Israel Supreme Court based on substantive constitutional and criminal grounds, challenging the legality of those disastrous agreements, the aim of which was to partition the Land of Israel once again, a step he strongly opposed. In this respect, he was the first to call for a state commission of inquiry to investigate all the illegalities committed by the Rabin Government in concluding secretly the Declaration of Principles with the terrorist and criminal organization, the Palestine Liberation Organization.

He has authored many articles on legal topics that have appeared in the Hebrew language journal, *Nativ*, and several position papers of his have been published by the Ariel Center for Policy Research. In the mid-1980s, Howard Grief formulated the original thesis never previously voiced that de jure sovereignty over the entire Land of Israel and Palestine was vested in the Jewish People as a result of the San Remo Resolution adopted at the San Remo Peace

Conference in April 1920 and it was from that moment that the State of Israel derives its legal existence. Grief was the person who first formulated and used the term "San Remo Resolution" that has now become widespread, to identify the extremely significant base document that laid the legal foundation for the State of Israel under international law.

His legal work, analysis and conclusions have drawn the praise of several prominent jurists, including inter alia Eliezer Dembitz, Dr. Haim Misgav, the late Professor Ya'akov Meron and the late Justice Asher Felix Landau. In elucidating Jewish legal rights to the Land of Israel ever since he first began work on this subject, he has made, in the words of a former President of the Jerusalem District Court, "a cardinal contribution to Israeli constitutional law", as well as international law. This book is the culmination of his life work.

# Introduction

This book is the culmination of 25 years of serious study and analysis of Israel's legal foundation and rights to the Land of Israel under international law. My researches on this subject began in 1982 after I had met in New York with the late Dr. Paul Riebenfeld, a legal scholar on the subject of Transjordan, with whom I had subsequently, throughout the 1980s, many discussions on Israel's legal rights and status in regard to Judea, Samaria and Gaza. Prior to my first meeting with Dr. Riebenfeld, I had followed intensely from my home city of Montreal the events unfolding in Israel ever since my teenage years when the Sinai War of 1956 was headline world news. Between 1956 and 1982, I had acquired a considerable store of knowledge of the politics, history and geography of Israel through voracious reading of newspapers and books and attending lectures, both at McGill University and in public forums. Some of the books I read that captured my interest on Israel were ones written by Leon Uris – "Exodus", Richard Meinertzhagen – "Middle East Diary", and Shmuel Katz – "Days of Fire", all of which made an indelible impression on me. Another book, not surprisingly, was the Hebrew Bible, the root and backbone of Judaism and the Jewish People. The stories of the Bible always fascinated and inspired me, ever since my days as a schoolchild. In 1980, I was asked to become the representative in Canada of the newly-formed *Tehiya* party of Israel, a task I gladly accepted. I then proceeded to form a group to represent it in the Canadian Zionist Federation, which had the distinction of being the first official branch outside Israel.

As a practicing attorney in Montreal since 1966, it was natural for me, sooner or later, to interest myself in Israel's legal foundation and in the rights of the Jewish People to Palestine and the Land of Israel. This became a matter that required great attention after the Six-Day War of June 1967, since Israel's legal position in Judea, Samaria, Gaza, the Golan and Sinai were topics of daily debate and acrimony. Israel was constantly being assailed in the 1970s, as it still is today, for its "occupation" of Arab territories, the implication being that it had no right to the territories it had repossessed or liberated from enemy occupation in the Six-Day War. To my sorrow, no satisfying legal rebuttal was forthcoming to offset this false accusation, even by committed advocates of Israel's cause. The best response offered was that either Israel had a better "claim" to these territories than did the surrounding Arab states, or that in any case everything would be eventually settled in future peace agreements and that in the meantime the *status quo* could continue. Not a single jurist ever voiced the opinion, with supporting evidence, that Israel, as the agent and assignee of the Jewish People, was the actual sovereign of Judea, Samaria and Gaza or that the Golan was really an historical part of the Land of Israel rather than of Syria illegally ceded to France in a 1922 agreement that took effect the following year or finally that the Jewish People's long connection with Sinai dating back to the days of Moses, as confirmed in the Torah, gave Israel a right to retain Sinai, a territory which historically was never a part of Egypt except by virtue of conquest during various periods in history.

In addition, the true importance of the Balfour Declaration of November 2, 1917 as encapsulated in the San Remo Resolution of April 25, 1920 was not understood or realized. In fact, no single book contained an organized and systematic presentation of Israel's legal rights to the entire Land of Israel, not just the area included in the State of Israel, but to all the land east and west of the Jordan, north and south of the Yarmuk, and, separately, to Sinai and the territory of what is today Southern Lebanon. The latter is geographically an extension of Upper Galilee, that historically was part of ancient Israel and therefore should have been included in the boundaries of Mandated Palestine, had it not been for French obstinacy and imperial designs. It was to rectify this glaring omission that I set myself the task of composing the present book. I devoted day and night to writing it from October 2001 to March 2003, and in the succeeding years made constant additions, revisions and updates to reach the point of publication. The book thus required seven years before it was ripe for publication.

I had for more than a decade prior to writing this book prepared the ground for it by composing a series of articles and papers on legal questions affecting the Land of Israel. Many of these articles appeared in the Hebrew bi-monthly publication of *Nativ*, where I stressed the San Remo Resolution as the principal founding document of the State of Israel. My thesis was that the Jewish People were recognized under international law as the *de jure* sovereign over Mandated Palestine ever since the adoption of the San Remo Resolution. This view contrasted sharply with that of other jurists who propagated the theory that there existed a "sovereignty vacuum" for Judea, Samaria and Gaza or that these regions had the legal status of unallocated (or unallotted) territories of the Mandate for Palestine. At the time this view was propounded, it appeared to many to favour Israel's interest. However, it actually damaged Israel's legal case, since not only did it ignore the importance of the San Remo Resolution, which had created Palestine for the exclusive national benefit of the Jewish People, but also opened the door to the local Arab inhabitants of the Land of Israel to claim ownership of the so-called "unallocated territories" for themselves and thereby acquire national and political rights over them that they were never meant to have under the San Remo Resolution and the Mandate for Palestine. I came to the conclusion that since all of Palestine had already been allocated to the Jewish People at the San Remo Peace Conference that issued the San Remo Resolution, the Arabs therefore had no national rights whatever to any part of the territory of formerly mandated Palestine under international law, though they, together with the other inhabitants of the country, naturally enjoyed civil and religious rights. It was in the mid-1980s that I began to formulate my view that *de jure* sovereignty had already been vested in the Jewish People over all of the Land of Israel dating from the 1920 San Remo Resolution and then devolved upon the State of Israel upon its re-establishment. I then explained this view to Dr. Paul Riebenfeld of New York. He advised me that no one had previously expressed this position. I also mentioned my view in an article I wrote in 1989, published in *The Jewish Press* of Brooklyn, New York, on "the Question of Sovereignty and Final Status of Judea, Samaria and Gaza" (August 4, 1989, p.4). In that article I stated that at a meeting of the Supreme Council of the victorious Allied Powers at San Remo, Italy, on April 25, 1920 "Palestine was specifically set aside and given to the Jewish People for the establishment of a National Home… The establishment of a Jewish homeland meant eventual statehood and hence the transfer to the Jewish People of sovereignty to all parts of the homeland including Judea, Samaria and Gaza".

Over a year after I made *aliya* in August 1989, I was appointed by Professor Yuval Ne'eman, leader of the *Tehiya* party, then serving as Minister of Energy and Infrastructure in the Yitzhak Shamir Government, to be his legal adviser on Eretz-Israel. In January 1991, he asked me to prepare a paper for him on Israel's legal foundation and rights to the country, since he was scheduled to deliver a speech in a month's time on this subject at the Carnegie Foundation in the United States. I compiled a 93 page paper for this purpose. Professor Ne'eman not only accepted my thesis, he used what I wrote for him to very good advantage on his speaking tour before American audiences and followed this up with an article published in the journal *Global Affairs* (Fall 1992, Vol. VII, No. 4). In his article, he cited my work as the legal authority for his statement that "it is… at San Remo that the State of Israel draws its legal existence" and that "sovereignty over an area that would later be defined as the Palestine mandate was thereby bestowed on the Jewish People".

The briefing paper I had authored for Professor Ne'eman became the impetus for the present book. However, I could not undertake this task immediately, because as a new *oleh* still new to the country, I had to seek employment in order to provide for my family. I was obliged to leave the Ministry of Energy when *Tehiya* lost its Knesset representation and Professor Ne'eman resigned his position as Minister even before the June 1992 elections and the Labour Party's assumption of power. With the signing of several accords between Israel and "Palestine Liberation" Organization, I felt compelled to challenge the legality of these accords in the Israel Supreme Court, and for that purpose I filed a total of five petitions or applications on behalf of distinguished Israeli citizens. The Court, however, always refused to hear these petitions on their merits, because of what it determined to be the political nature of the agreements made with the PLO, as if the question of the legality of such agreements was outside the scope of its jurisdiction, thus giving the Government of Israel a blank cheque to do whatever it desired, regardless of several existing Israeli laws that prohibited the ceding of territory to any foreign state whatsover, and by natural deduction to any lesser entity, particularly to a criminal and terrorist organization.

Finally, in 2001, I started to compose the present book at the urging of my good friend, Mr. Yoel Lerner, an educator and linguist in Jerusalem, who recognized the importance of putting down in writing the legal knowledge I had gained over the years on the subject of Israel's legal rights to the Land of Israel. It was a proverbial "labour of love" from beginning to end. To present Israel's legal case I have relied on all the basic documents, agreements and acts formulated in the critical period between the years 1915-1925 that shaped the modern Middle East as it is today. As already indicated, the base document for the founding of Israel was the San Remo Resolution, as it was also for Syria and Iraq. I take pride in the fact that I have preached this point for the last two decades and that it has now become a widespread and accepted idea, directly attributable to myself as confirmed by Professor Yuval Ne'eman himself.

I sincerely hope that this book will be used in the future as a teaching and educational tool to inform those who know little of the depth and strength of Israel's legal case for retaining in its possession the territories liberated in 1967 that still remain under its rule and even for the recovery – one day – of those territories already illegally given away. Arguments based on legal facts and evidence are needed to counter the enormous lies and mis-information put out by Israel's detractors, both at home and abroad, who urge the State "to end its occupation" of territories that rightfully belong to Israel. Such facts and evidence are provided in this book. The State of Israel is entitled to rule all the lands encompassing the Land of Israel with which it has incomparable historical, geographical, religious, economic and security links.

A concise summary of the main points of this book has been published by the Ariel Center for Policy Research in its Policy Paper No. 147, entitled "Legal Rights and Title of Sovereignty of the Jewish People to the Land of Israel and Palestine under International Law" (ACPR Publishers, April 2003). To that source I refer interested readers who may wish to have a quick review of the main points of this book. I have also discussed the approach I have taken in presenting Israel's legal case, as compared to that of others, in two letters I sent to Professor Ne'eman in 2004, which are reprinted *infra* in Appendix III.

Professor Ne'eman had originally intended to write his own introduction to the book, but his untimely decease in 2007 has made that impossible. However, the letter he wrote to a prospective publisher expressing his enthusiastic endorsement of the book is reproduced in that appendix as a substitute for the intended introduction. I have also included in Appendix IV a juridical assessment of the book composed by the late Dr. Ya'akov Meron, Professor of Moslem Law and Adviser on the Law of Arab Countries at the Ministry of Justice, who sadly passed away in the spring of 2008. He read this book in its entirety and characterized it as "a forceful and erudite pleading for the respecting of the letter and spirit of the law, not only Israeli law but also international law that came into existence in the wake of World War I". It is certainly a great honour to receive the support of such eminent figures as Professors Ne'eman and Meron for the book as now finally published.

Finally, I have included in Appendix V the correspondence I had with the late Joel Carmichael, the celebrated long-time editor of *Midstream*, a monthly Jewish review based in New York. I had written to him concerning a article penned by one of his contributors. This article was based on my original thesis as stated above, that *de jure* sovereignty over all of Palestine had been vested in the Jewish People as a result of the decision taken at the San Remo Peace Conference to create the new mandated state of Palestine in accordance with the Balfour Declaration and Article 22 of the Covenant of the League of Nations, though the writer of the article, having learned of this thesis directly from me, neglected to attribute it to me, nor was he authorized to make it public until I had done so in a systematic manner. Nevertheless he posted it on the internet, thus giving it widespread publicity. Mr. Carmichael accepted my analysis most eagerly, and in follow-up correspondence even requested that I submit an article for publication in *Midstream*, which he said he would publish as the leading article in a future issue. Unfortunately, Mr. Carmichael retired from his position as Editor of *Midstream* before the article was ready. The article, never published in its original format to this day, is included in Appendix V. The penning of the article marked the precipitate cause that set me on the path to the compilation of the present book, the idea and contents of which having been swirling around in my mind ever since I first presented my legal paper to Professor Ne'eman in 1991. The book is thus the final rendition of that long chain of thoughts.

The comments I have received on my earlier writings on the subject, as expressed in various letters and articles, give me cause to hope that the book may prove in the long run to be of actual benefit to the Jewish People and the State of Israel in their on-going process of reclaiming and repossessing all of the Jewish National Home and the remaining parts of the Land of Israel*.

Howard Grief,
Jerusalem, June 2008

*The Jewish National Home and Mandated Palestine were originally meant to be synonymous terms under international law, and were supposed to correspond to the historical or biblical frontiers of the Land of Israel in the First and Second Temple Periods. However, when the borders of Mandated Palestine were finally drawn in 1920 and 1922 by Britain and France, they illegally excluded various areas comprising the Land of Israel in the definition of Palestine, thus creating an unwarranted distinction between what became Palestine and what historically was the Land of Israel. Paradoxically, the distinction between Palestine and the historical Land of Israel was not reflected in the law of Palestine during the period of the Mandate, since the term used in Hebrew to designate the country was *Eretz-Israel*, even though certain historical parts of it were not included.

# Acknowledgments

This book could not have seen the light of day without the invaluable help of several persons that made it possible. The person I am most indebted to in this regard is the late Professor Yuval Ne'eman of Tel-Aviv University, who served as Israel's Minister of Energy and Infrastructure, as well as its first Minister of Science. It was he who first provided me with the opportunity to set down my thoughts on Jewish legal rights to the Land of Israel when he requested that I compose a paper on this subject for his use, prior to his going to the United States on a speaking tour. That paper was the spark that led to the eventual composition of the present volume, the fulfillment of the work I began at the Ministry of Energy under Minister Yuval Ne'eman. Before I managed to complete the book, Professor Ne'eman kindly provided me with a grant to defray the cost of its publication, without which this book may not have appeared in print.

As someone who had frequent contact with Professor Ne'eman ever since I first met him in 1980 in Montreal and learned greatly from his unrivaled insights about Israel, no person ever impressed me more than he did. Not all his amazing achievements are well known to the public. Without him, Israel would never have achieved the stunning success it did in the Six Day War of June 1967. Without him, Israel's nuclear program would never have gotten off the ground, nor would Israel have made such great progress in space exploration and satellite launching. In sum, he was Israel's greatest scientist and defense specialist, including military intelligence. It is an underestimation to say that he was one of Israel's most important figures in ensuring Israel's continued existence as a state. Though he did not have a legal education, I can attest to the fact that he also had a very deep awareness of Israel's legal rights to all of the Land of Israel, including Sinai, and strongly advocated its retention, since in his eyes Sinai rightfully belonged to Israel rather than to Egypt, a view he enunciated to Prime Minister David Ben-Gurion even before Operation Kadesh in 1956. Ben-Gurion adopted Ne'eman's view on Sinai, but superpower intervention and threats compelled Israel to relinquish this valuable territory in favour of Egypt. After Israel regained it in 1967, it was illegally ceded by a Prime Minister who did not realize it was really a part of the Land of Israel, rather than a part of the land of Egypt.

To serve as legal adviser on Eretz-Israel to a man of Professor Yuval

Ne'eman's stature and intelligence was the greatest honour to ever befall me.

This book also owes its existence to my honoured friend, Mr. Yoel Lerner, an expert linguist and educator living in Jerusalem, who not only strongly encouraged me to undertake the writing of the book, but spent countless hours typing out the entire manuscript and made many valuable comments and editorial improvements in the book's text and style. Without his devoted and untiring efforts, this book would likely never have been published. It was also Mr. Lerner who was instrumental in finding a suitable publisher for the book, the most practical contribution to be made that ended a frustrating quest to bring this work to light.

I am also very grateful to the late Law Professor, Ya'akov Meron, who kindly read through the original manuscript and made critical comments to improve the text. His own legal scholarship on Eretz-Israel was of the highest quality, and I was indeed fortunate to benefit from his thorough assessment of my work. His untimely death in the spring of 2008 was a great loss not only to his family and friends, but also to the cause of Eretz-Israel.

Ever since I first met Mr. Eliezer Dembitz, a former military court judge in Judea and Samaria, who worked for many years as the chief legal draftsman in the Ministry of Justice and then in the Knesset as legal adviser to the Finance Committee, I have benefited greatly from innumerable discussions with him on points of Israeli law and international law. Mr. Dembitz is one of Israel's prominent jurists and I am fortunate to have had constant access to his legal views and superb logic.

The person with whom I first discussed Israel's legal right to all of the Land of Israel was the late Dr. Paul Riebenfeld of New York. He was a treasured source of information about Transjordan and the Mandate period in general. It was in talking to him that I first began to formulate my own views on how newly-created Mandated Palestine in 1920 came under the *de jure* sovereignty of World Jewry as a result of the San Remo Resolution, a view that, as he informed me, had never before been advanced by any other jurist.

I also wish to acknowledge the encouragement and moral support I received from several friends, both prior to and during the time my book was being written. Among them was the late Yehudit Ben-Zion, a professor of education and a great advocate of Eretz-Israel. She truly fitted the definition of an *eshet hayil*, a woman of valour, in the Jewish tradition. She blessed me with her heartfelt friendship and never-ending good wishes.

Another woman of valour of the same spirit is Jenny Grigg of Kfar Sava, who has seen to it on her own initiative, without any urging on my part, that various articles of mine expressing ideas more fully developed in this book were made available to many people.

I also wish to acknowledge the encouragement and moral support I have received from my good friend, Attorney David Heimowitz, a specialist in Israeli labour law, who believes that my legal thesis as presented in this book will constitute a very important contribution to the people and State of Israel.

David has set a personal example for all diaspora Jews to follow. He came to Israel as a young lawyer to fulfil the vision of Zionism as preached by the late revered Rabbi Meir Kahane, a path he urges every Jew to emulate to preserve the strength and destiny of Israel. We have worked together in filing several petitions and applications to the Supreme Court of Israel to annul the disastrous and illegal Israel-PLO agreements.

To my brother Nathan of San Francisco and his wife, Penny, I am grateful for their generous financial support in making this book a reality. My brother shares my views on Eretz-Israel and presents Israel's case with invincible logic and an irrepressible, one-of-a-kind, sense of humour. It was he, as well as my late brother Louis, who directed me to enter McGill University Law School and become a lawyer, a profession I practiced for twenty-three years in Montreal before coming on *aliya.*

Finally, I could not have embarked on a seven-year task of producing a work of this magnitude without the love and forbearance of my wife Ilana, who has been my faithful companion ever since our marriage in 1982 in Jerusalem. She provided extraordinary support and care during a period of grave illness in 2004-2005. To her, I owe my life and well-being, as well as the completion of this book.

# Testimonials

"I have now had a chance to go through your book, and have learned a great deal from it. Your book throws important light on tremendously important issues."

– The Rt. Hon. Sir Martin Gilbert,
renowned author, historian, biographer of Winston Churchill.

"The subject of the book (*The Legal Foundation and Borders of Israel under International Law*) is important. Those using the Supreme Court Library, first and foremost, the Honourable Justices, will find it extremely interesting."

– L. Bork, Director of the
Supreme Court Library, Jerusalem.

"*The Legal Foundation and Borders of Israel under International Law* will be useful to people who frequent the Jerusalem Bar Library."

– A. Axelrod, Chairman, Jerusalem District.

"Grief's work must be part of the international legal library on the Arab-Israeli conflict."

– Prof. Sanford R. Silverburg (in AJL Newsletter),
Catawba College, Salisbury, North Carolina.

"This excellent detailed study by Howard Grief addressing both Israel's legal foundation and borders is an absolute must read… This is a book that desperately needs to be read and re-read."

– M.D. Roberts,
(in Amazon Customer Review), Gwent, U.K.

"Howard Grief's book lays to rest… some of the biggest and most pervasive myths of the modern day, myths like 'Israel is illegal, there's an occupation, settlements are illegal'. All discussed, all definitively disproven… This book should be read by everybody. Everybody… An amazing book… Absolutely highest recommendation."

– Gemi (in Amazon Customer Review).

"Howard Grief has given us a book that shatters every myth, lie, misrepresentation and distortion… to negate the sovereign rights of the Jewish People to their national home."

– Bill Mehlman (in Mideast Outpost).

"Mr. Grief's treatise… is a fantastic work, and one of the most important books written in decades. Every Jew – and non-Jew – should take the time to read and digest the information in this work."

– Stephen Allen,
VP Bio Vision Technology Inc., Montreal, Canada.

*Section One*

# Origin of The Legal Title

*Chapter 1*

# The San Remo Peace Conference and the San Remo Resolution on Palestine

The legal title of the Jewish People to the mandated territory of Palestine in all of its historical parts and dimensions was first acknowledged and recognized under modern international law on April 24, 1920. That is when the Supreme Council of the Principal Allied Powers, consisting of Great Britain, France, Italy and Japan, after a heated debate between the highest British and French representatives, decided to approve the Balfour Declaration of November 2, 1917, and thereby give international legal effect to its provisions. This decision was taken at a session of the San Remo Peace Conference, convoked to complete the work of the earlier Conference of London in February 1920[1] to prepare a treaty of peace with the shattered Ottoman Empire and make an authoritative settlement for the ex-Turkish territories in Asia. By virtue of this decision, known as the San Remo Resolution on Palestine, the Balfour Declaration was to constitute and became the legal basis for administering Palestine, in conjunction with the general provisions of the newly-established Mandates System.

The Allied Supreme Council decision taken on April 24, 1920 converted the Balfour Declaration, which until then had only been a statement of British Government policy or one of future intentions, into a binding legal document. That was accomplished by changing significantly the nature and wording of Britain's pledge or promise to the Jewish People from one of only using "their best endeavours to facilitate the achievement of the object" to establish in Palestine a national home for the Jewish People to one which legally made Britain "responsible for putting into effect" this declared object.

Thus, until April 24, 1920, Britain's promise was not legally binding, but after April 24, 1920 it was. As a direct consequence of this decision, Britain committed herself to establish or more precisely to reconstitute the Jewish National Home in Palestine for an ancient nation most of whose members then lived outside Palestine and only for that specific objective was a mandate

[1] The London Conference, which opened on February 17, 1920, adopted a proposal four days later, on February 21st, that Palestine would be defined in accordance with its ancient limits of Dan to Beersheba and be under British Mandate. However, no decision was then taken to approve the Balfour Declaration although it was alluded to in a preliminary discussion.

then conferred upon it the following day, on April 25, 1920.

The establishment of a Jewish National Home in Palestine simultaneously meant creating the state and country of Palestine which then did not officially exist as a legal entity under international law. That in turn meant Palestine in its entirety was reserved exclusively for the self-determination of the Jewish People. These two new entities in international law, the Jewish National Home and Palestine, were therefore synonymous since they were both created at the very same time and for the very same purpose. The Jewish National Home was to be housed in Palestine and Palestine was to be the Jewish National Home, i.e., the Jewish State – otherwise, Palestine would never have been legally created on April 24, 1920 as a separate country. It must always be borne in mind and emphasized that Palestine was not created to satisfy Arab national aspirations in any part of the country, whether east or west of the Jordan. Those aspirations were duly taken into account at the San Remo Peace Conference in a different paragraph of the San Remo Resolution, but it was decided that they would be satisfied in the adjoining territories of Mesopotamia and Syria, in addition to the already existing state of the Hedjaz in the Arabian Peninsula. Hence the idea of the partition of Palestine into Jewish and Arab States shortly to be introduced by the British in regard to Transjordan and still later in Cis-Jordanian Palestine, was a foreign idea that was never contemplated when Palestine was originally created on April 24, 1920.

As a direct result of the Allied Supreme Council decision on April 24, 1920, the title of sovereignty over Palestine was exclusively vested in the Jewish People and not in any other nation, state or entity, a conclusion which will be more fully discussed in the following pages. The decisions taken by the Allies at the San Remo Peace Conference concerning Palestine, Mesopotamia and Syria were first embodied in a Draft Resolution on April 24, 1920. This Draft Resolution was then submitted to the Supreme Council for final approval at the very next session on April 25, 1920, which was given unanimously by the four Powers who made up the Supreme Council. Both the Draft Resolution and the Final Resolution were duly recorded in the minutes of the Peace Conference and can be lumped together as the San Remo Resolution. This Resolution in regard to Palestine stands on its own merit as an act of basic international law which was the legal source of British power of government in Palestine under the Mandates System. It was, as agreed at the Conference of San Remo, subsequently inserted in the Treaty of Sèvres on August 10, 1920 and then in the Preamble of the Mandate Charter, which was itself approved by 52 nations in 1922, and by additional nations that subsequently joined the League of Nations. Because it was an independent act of binding international law, the San Remo Resolution on Palestine was not diminished in any way by the fact that the Treaty of Sèvres was later replaced by the Treaty of Lausanne which did not mention the Resolution in any way.

As a further consequence of the San Remo Resolution, the secret Sykes-Picot Treaty of May 9 and 16, 1916 – the dates on which it was formally ratified by Britain and France – was officially replaced and terminated. This treaty was an inter-Allied agreement on the future disposition of the territories of the Ottoman Empire in the Middle East, based on Turkey's expected defeat in World War I. Under the treaty, these territories were to be divided into different zones or spheres of influence amongst the Allied Powers, Britain, France and Russia, and placed under their direct or indirect administration or control. In the case of Russia, some regions of the Ottoman Empire (Kurdistan and parts of Armenia) would be annexed or ceded to it. The treaty was named after its two principal negotiators, Mark Sykes and Charles François Georges-Picot. Sykes, a Conservative Member of Parliament who was then Lord Kitchener's Middle East adviser at the War Office, acted on behalf of Prime Minister Herbert Henry Asquith's coalition government. Picot, a diplomat who had been his country's Consul in Beirut and was then appointed First Secretary at the French Embassy in London, represented the government of Aristide Briand, who served as both Prime Minister and Foreign Minister throughout the negotiations leading to the Sykes-Picot Treaty. Those negotiations had begun in London on November 23, 1915 when Arthur Nicholson, the Permanent Under-Secretary at the Foreign Office, was the British negotiator prior to his replacement by Sykes a month later, and ended with an agreement approved by Britain in January 1916 and by France a month later.

During the negotiations France had made a determined effort to secure Palestine's inclusion in Syria which was to come under French control, but that effort failed because of resistance from both Britain and Russia. British policy on Palestine at that time was guided by the recently released Report of the Committee on Asiatic Turkey (known as the De Bunsen Committee after its chairman of that name) of June 30, 1915. Without offering any concrete suggestions as to the type of regime Palestine should have nor stating the Zionist or Jewish interest in it, the Committee's Report ruled out any separate claims to the country either by France or by Britain, concluding that:

> Palestine must be recognized as a country whose destiny must be the subject of special negotiations, in which both belligerents and neutrals are alike interested.[2]

Russian opposition to French dominance over Palestine sprang from a different reason. Russia considered itself the Protector of the Orthodox Church in Palestine, which made the Imperial Government of Czar Nicholas II unwilling to accept the French position to be the sole ruler in the Holy Land. The position of Russia recalled the past dispute between it and France about 60 years earlier, when each contended to be the guardian of the Palestinian Holy Places, a dispute that ignited the Crimean War (1853-1856). Faced with British

---

[2] *British Desiderata in Turkey In Asia. Report, Proceedings and Appendices*, Cab. 27/1; paragraph 96, page 28. See also Leonard Stein, *The Balfour Declaration*, the Magnes Press, Jerusalem (1983), p. 247.

and Russian refusal to accept its designs on Palestine, France reluctantly gave up its claim to become the exclusive ruler of the country, a claim it based on the French historical connection with the Holy Land, dating back to the Crusader Era, and agreed to its internationalization. Though Palestine was an object of intense interest to the negotiating parties, neither it nor Jerusalem was even mentioned in the agreement itself, nor was there any reference or allusion to Jews and Judaism in regard to their ancient homeland and most venerated city.[3] One result insofar as the future status of Palestine was concerned, was that the agreement confirmed the distinction already made by Britain in the 1915 De Bunsen Committee Report, that the area of Palestine, though limited in scope in the Treaty to the core central part of the country, would be separate and apart from Syria, unlike France's aforesaid position that was subsequently adopted by Arab nationalists who referred to Palestine as Southern Syria.

In support of the French position was the fact that the Treaty of London of July 15, 1840 had indeed recognized Palestine as an integral part of Syria. Furthermore, in 1878, at the Berlin Congress, Lord Salisbury, then the Secretary for Foreign Affairs in the Disraeli Government and later British Prime Minister, agreed to recognize the whole of Syria, which then included the area of Palestine, as a French sphere of interest.[4]

Once Britain and France came to an agreement on the future attribution of the Ottoman Empire, they had to obtain the approval of Russia pursuant to the Declaration of London, signed in September 1914, obliging all three Allied Powers to consult each other on peace terms to end the Great War. Russia had already received British and French backing early in 1915 for its claim to Constantinople and the Straits as its share of the anticipated Turkish spoils. Russian consent to the Anglo-French arrangements was given through a diplomatic exchange of letters with France (April 13/26, 1916) and subsequently with Britain (May 23, 1916; September 1, 1916; and October 23, 1916). The Sykes-Picot Treaty was now a tripartite agreement aligning three European Allies known as the Triple Entente against the Central Powers consisting of Germany,

---

[3] The correspondence embodying the Sykes-Picot Treaty is reprinted in the 1952 publication of *Documents on British Foreign Policy*, First Series, Volume 4, pp. 241-51, edited by E.L. Woodward and Rohan Butler. In a letter dated May 16, 1916 sent by British Foreign Secretary Edward Grey to the French Ambassador at London, Paul Cambon, which conforms to Cambon's earlier letter of May 9, 1916 sent to Grey in French, there is no reference to Palestine as such, but only to the "brown area" which embraced only the core central area of historical Palestine. However, in an information paper published earlier by The Royal Institute of International Affairs in 1946 under the title *Great Britain and Palestine*, 1915-1945, 3rd edition, London, p. 7, it is affirmed, contrary to the text given in the above-cited Documents, that Palestine was mentioned in the Sykes-Picot Treaty together with the "Holy Places".

[4] V. *Notes on the Diplomatic History of the Jewish Question*, by Lucien Wolf, printed for the Jewish Historical Society of England by Spottiswoode, Ballantyne & Co., Ltd., London (1919), pp. 106-107.

Austria-Hungary, Bulgaria and the Ottoman Empire. This treaty anticipated the final break-up of the Ottoman Empire to be divided amongst themselves.

The most important aspect of the Sykes-Picot Treaty for the future of the Middle East was that it envisaged the creation of an Arab State or Confederation of Arab States that would be independent, though not immediately, embracing Syria (excluding the area of the Mediterranean coast), Transjordan and strips of territory in northern and southern Mesopotamia. The establishment of this State or Confederation of States, to contain French and British spheres of influence, was made conditional by the Allied Powers upon securing Arab cooperation in the war against Turkey and also upon their conquest of the towns of Damascus, Homs, Hama and Aleppo. This condition was specifically mentioned in the French-British as well as in the British-Russian exchange of notes ratifying the Sykes-Picot Treaty. The latter also stated that neither Britain nor France nor any third Power were to acquire territorial possessions in the Arabian Peninsula.

In British eyes, the Sykes-Picot Treaty was in harmony with the McMahon-Hussein Correspondence that had just been concluded, in which the Arabs were promised independence over a wide area of the Middle East, but which did not include Palestine. This British belief was evident in the reaction to the treaty by Gilbert Clayton, then serving as Director of Military Intelligence in Cairo and one of Henry McMahon's principal advisers who had made the preliminary drafts of all the letters sent to Hussein Ibn-Ali, the Sherif of Mecca. In a telegraphed dispatch to the War Office on May 3, 1916 Clayton stated:[5]

> The present arrangement seems the best possible. It does not clash with any engagements which have been given to the Sherif and has the advantage of clearly defining our position vis-à-vis other parties.
>
> ...Although the agreement does not clash with our engagements to him, it is difficult to foresee the interpretation he might place on the two spheres of influence.

It may be assumed, judging from Clayton's above remarks, that Britain would never have concluded the 1916 treaty with its allies, France and Russia, had the British truly believed that it was in direct conflict with their secret promise given the year before to Hussein to establish an independent Arab state which excluded Palestine from its ambit, without harming French interests in Syria. That was an assumption made not only by Clayton at the time, but by Sykes himself and by Edward Grey, the Foreign Secretary, who was in office when both the Correspondence and the Treaty were approved. It is most likely that Hussein actually knew from the very moment the British first assured him of their support for a projected independent Arab state under his rule, that

---

5 Elie Kedourie, *In the Anglo-Arab Labyrinth, The McMahon-Husayn Correspondence and its Interpretations*, 1914-1939, London (1976), Cambridge University Press, p. 124.

Palestine was not to be included in that state. The probability that he knew of its exclusion derives not only from the Correspondence itself, but also from the fact that the Sherif received messages about British intentions in Arabia from General Reginald Wingate, the British Commander of the Egyptian Army (the sirdar), who also filled the position of Governor-General of the Sudan and was one of the chief proponents of the Arab cause and of Hussein himself. The person who acted as intermediary for the messages sent by Wingate to Hussein was Sayyid Ali al-Marghani, Grand Kadi of the Sudan. Wingate told Marghani on November 1, 1915 that in regard to British support of an independent Arab state contained in the letter dated October 24, 1915, sent to Hussein by Henry McMahon, the British High Commissioner in Egypt, Britain had made certain reservations in Syria, Palestine and Mesopotamia concerning the Sherif's suggested borders for the state.[6] It can be safely presumed that such an important statement directly affecting Hussein's personal aspirations of ruling such a state, coming from a high-ranking British official in the region several days after the dispatch of the McMahon letter, was immediately made known to the Sherif by Marghani. This presumption corroborates McMahon's testimony given at a later period (in 1922 and again in 1937), when the question of Palestine's inclusion in the area of Arab independence became a subject of dispute, that Hussein well understood that Palestine was excluded from independent Arabia. This exclusion is moreover confirmed by the easily verifiable fact that in the entire Hussein-McMahon Correspondence, the Sherif never once asserted the claim that Palestine was "Arab territory", as he explicitly did for the Turkish vilayats of Beirut and Aleppo, as well as those in Mesopotamia. It bears noting that the lack of any contradiction insofar as the British promise to Hussein is concerned and the Sykes-Picot Treaty was current in British thinking prior to the Balfour Declaration in 1917 and before the Arabs claimed, several years later, that there did in fact exist a contradiction.[7]

The most justified complaint that could have been made against the Sykes-Picot Treaty, apart from its apparent illegality as discussed below, should have come not from the Arab side that stood to gain immensely from the Allied recognition of its national claims, but from the Zionist quarter. While catering to Arab ambitions, the Sykes-Picot Treaty completely ignored Zionist aspirations to Palestine, despite the fact that Zionism was already at that time a worldwide movement for the restoration of the Jewish homeland, which attracted much attention and support. The Treaty as it stood in 1916 decapitated Palestine by removing from its historical borders such integral regions as Upper Galilee, the Negev and all of Transjordan, north and south of the Yarmuk. This shabby treatment of Zionism drew a sharp rebuke from Captain (later Admiral) William Reginald Hall, head of the Intelligence Department at the Admiralty.

[6] Isaiah Friedman, *The Question of Palestine, 1914-1918*, Routledge & Kegan Paul, London (1973), p. 90. Friedman's source is a letter from Wingate to Clayton dated November 1, 1915, contained in the Wingate Papers, Box 135/5.

[7] Stein, *op. cit.*, pp. 268-269.

In a remarkable document he drew up in the form of a Memorandum on the Proposed Agreement with the French, dated January 12, 1916, he not only scorned the military value of the Arabs in the war against Turkey and the assumption that the Arabs desired unity under Franco-British aegis, but also raised the Jewish interest in the future of Palestine that was not addressed in the agreement reached by Sykes and Picot. Captain Hall's assessment of the situation is all the more interesting since it was arrived at independently of any contact with official Zionist representatives. As noted by the historian Isaiah Friedman:[8]

> Another point which Hall disputed concerned the Jews. In contrast to Sykes and Picot, who assumed them to have only a sentimental attachment to Palestine, Hall pointed out that 'the Jews have a strong *material*, and a very strong *political*, interest in the future of the country'. He envisaged opposition on their part 'throughout the world, to any scheme recognizing Arab independence and foreshadowing Arab predominance in the southern Near East' but hoped that they 'may be partly placated by the status proposed for the "*Brown Area*"'. He added:
>
> In the *Brown Area* the question of Zionism, and also of British control of all Palestinian railways... [will] have to be considered. It would be more satisfactory if the line of demarcation between French and British spheres of influence was drawn *straight* from [Tyre to] the Sea of Galilee [and] to Tadmor (Palmyra). As the line curves at present, our area of influence is almost entirely sheer desert. (All italics and square brackets are in the original.)

Under the Sykes-Picot Treaty, the historical Land of Israel was divided into five parts, comprising three colour areas and two letter zones as follows:

***Red Area:*** The ports of Haifa and Acre under British rule, as were also the provinces of Basra and Baghdad;

***Blue Area:*** Upper Galilee under French rule, joined to coastal Syria (i.e., Lebanon) and the province of Cilicia in Asia Minor;

***Area (A):*** Hauran north of the Yarmuk, including the Golan, to be in a projected semi-independent Arab State under French protection. Area (A)

[8] Isaiah Friedman, *op. cit.* p. 111. Friedman adds in a footnote (n. 50, p. 364) that the First Sea Lord, Admiral Jackson, approved of this memorandum, but there is no indication whether Balfour, at that time First Lord of the Admiralty, consulted it. The same quotations from Captain William Reginald Hall are found in an earlier acclaimed article on the background to the Balfour Declaration written by Mayir Verité, "The Balfour Declaration and its Makers", published in the journal *Middle East Studies*, Volume VI:1 (1970), pp. 48-76; reprinted in the book *Palestine and Israel in the Nineteenth and Twentieth Centuries*, edited by Elie Kedourie and Sylvia G. Haim, Frank Cass & Company Ltd., London (1982), p. 60. Hall's remarks are reported in the text on p. 72 and much more fully in n. 5, p. 81.

embraced the interior of Syria, including the cities of Damascus, Homs, Hama and Aleppo and extending to Mosul up to the Persian border.

***Area (B):*** The Negev and Transjordan, south of the Yarmuk, was also destined for inclusion in the projected Arab State, but under British protection. Area (B), like Area (A) also included a portion of Mesopotamia in the north, to the border of Persia, as well as a portion of Mesopotamia in the south, descending toward the Persian Gulf, but excluded the area from Baghdad to Basra.

***Brown Area:*** A truncated area of central Palestine bounded roughly by a line north from Acre on the Mediterranean coast to the northwestern shore of Lake Tiberias, southward along the Jordan to the Dead Sea and then westward to Gaza. This area was to be governed by an international condominium made up of Britain, France and Russia in consultation with other Allies and the representatives of the Sherif of Mecca. The Allies who were to be consulted were Italy and Japan, as appears from the last two paragraphs of the British diplomatic note dated May 16, 1916, dispatched by Foreign Secretary Grey to the French Ambassador at London, Paul Cambon. This note contained the precise terms of the agreement negotiated by Sykes and Picot.

Italy subsequently adhered to the Sykes-Picot Treaty by virtue of the Saint Jean de Maurienne Agreement named after a small mountain village in Savoy on the French-Italian frontier where a tri-lateral conference between Britain, France and Italy took place on April 19, 1917. On that date, a tentative agreement was reached but the final text of the agreement with Italy was not set out until August 18, 1917 when a letter containing the details of the agreement was sent by Foreign Secretary Balfour to the Italian ambassador in London, the Marquis Imperiali di Francavilla. In addition to satisfying Italian demands in southwestern Anatolia (in the province of Antalya, previously known as Adalia and Attalia), Italy acquired the right to share in the international administration of the brown area comprising central Palestine. However, the Agreement of Saint Jean de Maurienne had been made conditional upon Russian assent, which was never given. Russia repudiated the Sykes-Picot Treaty after the Bolsheviks seized power on November 7, 1917 and thus Italy's right to share in the administration of Palestine could no longer be sustained. The Sykes-Picot Treaty now became an Anglo-French bilateral agreement, and its terms were then substantially revised after a visit made by French Premier Georges Clemenceau to London on November 30, 1918. In a conversation he held the next day – December 1, 1918 – with his British counterpart, David Lloyd George, the two leaders agreed that Palestine "from Dan to Beersheba[9]" would be placed under British control, as well as Mosul with its oil fields, which the Sykes-Picot Treaty had assigned to the French sphere of influence. In return, Britain agreed to give France a just share of the petroleum resources in Mosul and to support French rights in Syria. Though the Lloyd George – Clemenceau Agreement was only a

[9] The phrase "Dan to Beersheba" appears in several books of the Bible, as for example, in Judges (20:1), etc.

verbal understanding for which no written protocol existed, it was nonetheless generally adhered to by both Britain and France in subsequent negotiations with the revised arrangements agreed to being recorded in other documents.[10] The Palestine aspect of this new arrangement with France was first set down in the San Remo Resolution, while the change relating to Mosul was dealt with in three separate Anglo-French oil agreements, the last of which was initialed at the San Remo Peace Conference on April 24, 1920 by Philippe Berthelot and John Cadman and confirmed by the French and British Prime Ministers. This latter oil agreement is sometimes confusingly called the San Remo Agreement and should be distinguished from the San Remo Resolution dealing with the creation and government of the mandated states of Palestine, Mesopotamia and Syria. Upon the adoption of the San Remo Resolution in its final version on April 25, 1920, the Sykes-Picot Treaty came to an official end though its effect lingered on in the matter of Palestine's ultimate boundaries in the north and northeast with Syria and Lebanon, as discussed further below.

Whenever the Sykes-Picot Treaty is discussed, one point is never mentioned, namely, whether it was a legal and binding agreement under international law. There is little doubt that this treaty did not meet the test of legality even when it was made, though it had a very important and lasting effect in the eventual configuration of the modern Middle East. The idea that the lands comprising what remained of the dying Ottoman Empire could be secretly attributed to Britain, France, Russia and Italy even before the Empire was defeated and subjugated in World War I was contrary to international law. That attribution could have been made only at the Peace Conferences which followed the War in the event of an Allied triumph and not by secret negotiations between the Entente Powers in anticipation of such a triumph.

During the years 1915-1917, Britain entered into four[11] main undertakings of a secret nature with its European allies concerning the attribution of Turkish territory in Asia Minor while the war was still being fiercely fought and its outcome uncertain. These were the Constantinople Agreement of March-April 1915 with France and Russia; the Treaty of London of April 26, 1915 with France and Italy; the Sykes-Picot Treaty of May 9 and 16, 1916 subsequently adhered to by Russia; and the Agreement of Saint Jean de Maurienne of April 1917 with France and Italy. A fifth secret undertaking that Britain entered into during the War was the McMahon Pledge made to the Sherif of Mecca, Hussein Ibn-Ali, on October 24, 1915, to win Arab support against Turkey. The cooperation of Hussein needed for this British overture was in effect an act of rebellion and treason on his part against Turkey, even though this rebellion did

[10] See the book by Jukka Nevakivi, Britain, *France and the Arab Middle East, 1914-1920*, University of London, The Athlone Press, 1969, pp. 91-93, citing the work of David Lloyd George, *The Truth About the Peace Treaties*, Vol. II, p. 1038.

[11] *Documents on British Foreign Policy 1919-1939*, First Series, Volume IV, Chapter III, p. 635.

not in fact take place as the British had hoped. Unlike the Jews of Palestine, the Arabs living in the Ottoman Empire were not oppressed, but were largely content with their lot as subjects of a Moslem Empire. The Arabs in general harboured no enmity towards Turkish rule which was not regarded as alien to their life.[12]

When U.S. President Woodrow Wilson learned about the secret agreements made by the Entente Powers, he was shocked and greatly displeased. He wanted the Allies to repudiate all such agreements and strove to usher in a new era of open diplomacy where secret agreements would never be made again. His deeply-held conviction on the matter is reflected in the very first point of the Fourteen Points peace program he outlined in an address delivered before both Houses of the U.S. Congress on January 8, 1918, when he proclaimed the virtue of:

> open covenants of peace, openly arrived at, after which there shall be no private international understandings of any kind, but diplomacy shall always proceed frankly and in the public view.

President Wilson's vision was written into the Covenant of the League of Nations in the Treaty of Versailles (Article 18) which declared:

> Every treaty or international engagement entered into hereafter by any Member of the League shall be forthwith registered with the Secretariat and shall as soon as possible be published by it. No such treaty or international engagement shall be binding until so registered.

A similar provision is contained in the United Nations Charter (Article 102). The Vienna Convention on the Law of Treaties of 1969 also requires treaties to be transmitted to the Secretariat of the United Nations for registration and publication (Article 80).

It is therefore evident that the rules of international law now make it impossible for secret treaties and agreements to ever again become a tool or means of international diplomacy as they did in World War I in regard to the disintegration of the Ottoman Empire.

### *Further Elaboration On The San Remo Resolution*

The Supreme Council of the Principal Allied Powers represented the victorious coalition of countries of Great Britain, France, Italy and Japan who fought in World War I against the Central Powers, who were also banded together in a military alliance consisting of Germany, the Dual Hapsburg Monarchy of Austria-Hungary dominated by German-ethnic Austrians, Bulgaria and the Ottoman Turkish Empire. At the peace conference held in the Italian resort city of San Remo in the Villa De Vachan, which opened on April 18 and lasted

[12] Isaiah Friedman, *op. cit.*, pp. 98-99 and 222-224.

until April 26, 1920, the Supreme Council decided during two days of hectic discussions[13] (April 24-25, 1920) the future fate of all of Turkey's ex-territorial possessions lying outside Anatolia (also called Asia Minor or Asiatic Turkey) which, as a consequence of World War I, had ceased to be under the sovereignty of the Ottoman Turkish Empire which formerly governed them, as specifically stated in the Treaty of Versailles concluded with Germany on June 28, 1919, and were now in the joint hands of the four Allied Powers. These territories embraced all of the historical region today known as the Middle East but then called the Fertile Crescent, which originally comprised the trio of countries from the Persian Gulf to the Sinai Peninsula along the northern edge of the Arabian peninsula, namely Palestine, Syria (including Lebanon) and Mesopotamia (the classical Greek name of the country – "between two rivers" – was changed to the Arabic term of Iraq when it became a kingdom governed by the mandate regime in 1921), before any substantial alterations were made to their intended boundaries.[14]

The major participants in the discussions at the Interallied Conference were, on the British side, Prime Minister David Lloyd George and Foreign Affairs Secretary George Nathaniel Curzon, while the French position was represented by Prime Minister Alexandre Millerand who was also the Foreign Minister and successor of Prime Minister Georges Clemenceau since his resignation in January 1920, actively assisted by Philippe Berthelot, then the director of political affairs in the Ministry of Foreign Affairs and soon afterwards, its Secretary-General. Italy was represented by Prime Minister Francesco Nitti and Senator Vittorio Scialoja. Japan sent its ambassador to Paris, K. Matsui, to attend the

[13] All of the source material about what was said in these discussions can be found in the British Secretary's Notes of a Meeting of the Supreme Council held at the Villa De Vachan, San Remo on April 24, 1920 at 4 P.M. and on Sunday, April 25, 1920 at 11 A.M. The citation in the Public Record Office is: Secret I.C.P. 105, Cab 29/86/03/38 and Secret I.C.P. 106, Cab 29/86/03/38. In addition, there is also a French version of the Minutes of the San Remo Peace Conference for the session on April 24, 1920 which is found in the records of the Foreign Office. See Fo 371/5244; 9220; E 5636/4164/44. The minutes in English have been edited by Rohan Butler and J.P.T. Bury and are reproduced in *Documents on British Foreign Policy, 1919 – 1939*, London, Her Majesty's Stationery Office, 1958, First Series, Volume VIII, pp. 156 ff, and are also printed in *The Rise of Israel*, "San Remo Conference, April 1920", edited by Isaiah Friedman, Garland Publishing Inc., New York and London, 1987, Volume 12,, Document 36, pp. 199-211.

[14] The name of al-Iraq in Classical Arabic was applied only to the portion of the country from Takrit to the Persian Gulf. From Takrit northwards it was called al-Jazira, the Arabic word for island or peninsula. The region of al-Jazira is a tongue of higher land lying between the Euphrates (Perat in the Hebrew Bible and al-Furat in Arabic) and the Tigris (Hiddekel in the Bible and Dijlah in Arabic), bounded on the north by the Sinjar mountain. This mountain is peopled by the Kurdish-speaking Yezidis. In 1921, with the British installation of Emir Feisal as King in Mesopotamia after his eviction from Syria, the entire country he ruled was re-named Iraq, covering both the northern and southern regions of the country.

Conference. U.S. President Wilson deputed the American ambassador to Rome, Robert Underwood Johnson, to be an observer so that he could receive a full report on the proceedings of the Conference of San Remo.

The question of Palestine took up most of the time of the session held on April 24, 1920 allotted to the subject of what to do with the freed former Turkish territories in Asia. Britain and France each introduced their own written draft resolution for the consideration of the Supreme Council. The discussion on that day centered on whether to accept the British draft proposal or the French version which considerably extended the meaning of the first proviso in the Balfour Declaration to include also "political rights" and "existing traditional rights".

The British resolution, which was ultimately adopted, provisionally recognized Syria and Mesopotamia as independent States, in accordance with the fourth paragraph of Article 22, Part I, of the Treaty of Versailles, dealing with the Mandates System contained in the Covenant of the League of Nations, subject to the rendering of administrative advice and assistance by a Mandatory until such time as they were able to stand alone. By contrast, Palestine was to be administered by a Mandatory in conformity with the overall spirit and general provisions of Article 22.

No real differences emerged with respect to Syria and Mesopotamia concerning their future as Mandated states where native governments were to be installed, who would be tutored by a Great Power before gaining independence. It was the question of Palestine that engaged the top-level British and French representatives in sharp exchanges of opinion. The French wanted to change the first proviso of the Balfour Declaration on the ground that the Declaration was not an official document, but only a semi-official communication or unofficial declaration that should not be put into the formal Treaty of Peace with Turkey, which would give it an official status. At one point in the discussion, Philippe Berthelot even said that the Balfour Declaration "had long been a dead letter" and therefore disputed the necessity of referring to it. Despite this open derision of the Balfour Declaration, that was hotly contested by Lord Curzon, the French, after some spirited discussion, finally accepted the concept of the Jewish National Home subject to the first proviso of the Declaration. However, they did not want to surrender their position as the protector of the religious rights or what they called the "existing traditional rights" of the French and Latin Catholic Community in Palestine. France also wanted to broaden the concept of "civil rights" by adding "political rights" to the rights to be awarded to the "existing non-Jewish communities in Palestine" referred to in the Declaration, which France said were also part of the "existing traditional rights" of the Catholic religious community. The French believed that if the Balfour Declaration in its original rendition of November 2, 1917 (whose date was constantly misstated as November 8, 1917) was made part of the Peace Treaty with Turkey, only the Jews would have "political rights", which is why they opposed inserting the Declaration into the treaty.

At the end of the protracted debate, the French consented to give up their religious protectorate, because Lloyd George, with Italian support, absolutely rejected a dual British-French administration of Palestine, pointing out that the British, unlike the Turks, could be counted upon to respect the religious rights of all the existing non-Jewish communities. However, as a gesture of goodwill, the British agreed to set up a special commission as soon as possible to study and regulate all questions and claims relating to the different religious communities, to be presided over by a chairman appointed by the Council of the League of Nations.

As regards the important question concerning "civil rights" and "political rights" contained in the first proviso of the Balfour Declaration, the French argued that the former rights did not include the latter rights under French law, while Lord Curzon maintained that British law, on the contrary, did include them. Millerand explained that what he conceived to be "political rights" were really only "electoral rights" – such as the right to vote and to take part in elections. The "political rights" the French had in mind were thus limited to individual political rights of the members of the religious communities concerned, which did not mean collective political rights for the communities themselves as separate national entities. This ruled out any kind of political and national autonomy or self-determination for the Arabs living in Palestine.

Lord Curzon insisted that the first proviso in the Balfour Declaration could not be changed, as the French demanded, because that would violate the promise the British Government made to the Jewish People, who "regarded the Declaration of Mr. Balfour in its entirety as the charter of their rights" or as stated in the French version of the minutes of the Conference, "the Charter which recognized their freedom" ("la carte qui reconnait leur liberté"). He had met with Zionist representatives just prior to the Conference and had personally undertaken to preserve the original text of the Declaration. If he gave way in this matter he felt that he might be charged with a breach of good faith. However, to placate the French, Curzon agreed to consult them as to the precise form of the Mandate for Palestine before it was submitted for approval to the Council of the League of Nations.

The French backed down from the strong stand they took on continuing to be the foreign protector of the individual political and traditional rights of the Christian inhabitants of Palestine, particularly those of the Roman Catholic community in Palestine, saying they would be satisfied to record the French claim in the procès-verbal of the Conference which would represent its official position on the matter. They therefore accepted the British proposal to include the Balfour Declaration in the Peace Treaty with Turkey based on the firm understanding that none of the agreed-upon existing rights of the non-Jewish communities in Palestine mentioned in the first proviso of the Declaration would be curtailed.

On the next day – April 25, 1920 – the Allied Powers discussed two very important matters. The first dealt with the selection of the Mandatory Powers for Palestine, Mesopotamia and Syria and the second concerned the fixing of the boundaries of the Mandated countries or states created by the San Remo Resolution. In regard to the first question, Lord Curzon pointed out that the names of the Mandatory Powers had not been inserted in the corresponding peace treaty with Germany for its colonies in Africa (those colonies specifically mentioned were Togoland, Cameroons, and German East Africa; the latter today consists of Tanzania, Rwanda and Burundi), but rather in a separate act, and he suggested that the Supreme Council follow the same course for the territories to be severed from Turkey. Curzon voiced his opinion in opposition to Philippe Berthelot who desired that the names of the Mandatory Powers be given in the peace treaty with Turkey. Upon hearing the opinion of the British Foreign Secretary, Berthelot then agreed that it was logical to follow the precedent of the German treaty and that the Supreme Council should take a separate decision in regard to the nomination of the Mandatory Powers, provided that the decision was taken as soon as possible and without any unnecessary delay. However, a little later in the discussion he backtracked and declared that he was not in favour of Lord Curzon's suggestion that the best thing to do would be to settle the question of naming the Mandatory Powers in an Act separate from the Treaty. The deadlock on this question ended when French Prime Minister Millerand said he was anxious that the decision should be reached that day, if possible, and he enquired whether they could not decide now that the British be given a mandate for Mesopotamia and separately for Palestine, while the French would receive a mandate for Syria. The Chairman of the meeting, Italian Prime Minister Nitti, thought that a formal decision could be taken that morning. An agreement was then reached that the assignment of the Mandates as proposed by Millerand be recorded in the minutes of the meeting only and not to have this decision naming the Mandatories appear in the Peace Treaty with Turkey. The decision of the Supreme Council on the Mandates was made subject to a reservation requested by Italy that it was not obliged to accept the conferment of these Mandates as recorded in the San Remo Resolution until it was satisfied that its extensive economic interests in Asia Minor would not be prejudiced. Those interests were previously recognized in a secret agreement Italy made with the Entente Powers (Britain, France and Russia) to enter the War on their side against the Central Powers, known as the London Agreement of April 26, 1915, and were reiterated in the defunct Agreement of Saint Jean de Maurienne.

This reservation in the San Remo Resolution was later invoked by Italy to hold up needlessly the confirmation of these mandates and later their entry into legal force until its interests were properly safeguarded, as it demanded.

On the question of boundaries, Philippe Berthelot outlined the French position for the northern, eastern and southern frontiers of Syria. As regards Palestine, he said her frontiers would conform to the definition advocated by Lloyd George, who favoured the ancient boundaries of Dan and Beersheba, as previously discussed at the first London Conference of February 1920. This biblical formula was based on the historical connection of the Jewish People with the entire Land of Israel and was not to be construed literally from Dan to Beersheba, but rather referred in effect to those areas of the Promised Land that had been conquered, settled and ruled by the Twelve Tribes of Israel and their descendants, in both the First and Second Temple periods.[15] Lord Curzon did not want the exact boundaries of Syria and Palestine to be fixed during the Conference because while there was agreement on Palestine's northern boundary with Syria, the Supreme Council had not yet settled what the eastern frontier was to be and he thought it was impossible to settle only one boundary without the other.

In addition, he thought that the boundaries of Syria and Palestine should not be demarcated in the absence of Emir Feisal, otherwise a violent Arab reaction would occur. Berthelot was not convinced by Curzon's arguments to delay the fixing of boundaries and said that France did not want to prolong indefinitely coming to a decision about them. He thought that Great Britain and France should be in complete agreement before the Emir was admitted to their counsels. He did not see any difficulty about the eastern frontier of Palestine which he suggested should be the line fixed in the Sykes-Picot Treaty. Berthelot warned that if no agreement was reached on all the frontiers, France might later on seek something further, which in fact proved to be the case.

Lloyd George came to Curzon's aid by citing the Treaty of Peace with Germany to back the contention that the boundaries of the Mandated countries did not have to be settled then and now for inclusion in the Peace Treaty with Turkey, and he also agreed with Lord Curzon that the Supreme Council should not dispose of the countries under discussion without giving Emir Feisal a chance to state his case.

In his remarks Lloyd George recalled that former French Prime Minister Georges Clemenceau, when he was in London on December 1, 1918, had agreed to his suggestion that the limits of Palestine should be fixed by the ancient towns of Dan and Beersheba. The French had not favoured this suggestion, he said, but they had agreed to it and were loyally standing by it. The British Government also had many objections to it, but were equally prepared to stand

[15] The minutes of the San Remo Peace Conference drawn up at the session held on April 25, 1920 make it clear that this is what Lloyd George actually meant when he defined Palestine according to the biblical formula "Dan to Beersheba", as appears from his documented reliance on George Adam Smith's scholarly works to determine the exact territorial extent of ancient Israelite habitation and rule. He included in Palestine all the land historically settled or occupied by Jews in the First and Second Temple Periods. This is confirmed by the third recital in the Preamble of the Mandate, which refers to the historical connection of the Jewish People with Palestine and is further evidenced by Colonel Richard Meinertzhagen who recalled, in his book, the statement made by Lloyd George in Paris in 1919 regarding the true meaning of "Palestine": "The area occupied by the twelve tribes of Israel, from Dan to Beersheba". *Middle East Diary*, Thomas Yoseloff, Publisher, New York, p. 355.

by it. He said it was not a good arrangement for Palestine because the head waters of the Jordan would be outside its control, but in any case, they had never been under the control of "the men who had been inhabiting Palestine" at any time in history, a reference to Israelite settlement in the First Temple period and to Judean rule in the Second Temple period.[16] Under the agreed formula of Dan and Beersheba there would be no extension of Palestine's northern frontiers as the Zionists wanted, because, according to Lloyd George, that would have meant adding Tyre and Sidon to Palestine, which had never been within her historical boundaries.

To substantiate his statements, Lloyd George relied on a book written by the Scottish Biblical scholar, Rev. George Adam Smith, which he regarded as the ablest book on Palestine ever written.[17] He had given copies to British military experts who had taken it practically as a text-book. It was finally decided in light of Lloyd George's remarks to defer the question of determining the exact boundaries between Palestine, Syria and Mesopotamia to a later date.

All the various points agreed upon by the Supreme Council during two days of intensive discussion were set down in a final resolution printed in the minutes of the meeting on April 25, 1920, accurately called the San Remo Resolution, even though one will look in vain for the exact name of this most important document in subsequent political, diplomatic and legal reports about the proceedings and decisions taken at the Conference of San Remo. It was also called the "Mandates Article" of the Treaty of Peace with Turkey, that was signed at Sèvres on August 10, 1920, the same name that was applied to Article 22 of the League of Nations Covenant.

The legal results of the San Remo Resolution on Palestine may be summarized as follows:

1. It made the Balfour Declaration, as of April 24, 1920, the date of its

---

[16] This statement by Lloyd George is both mystifying and factually incorrect. It contradicted his own previously stated position and also that of the British negotiators in the 1920 boundary negotiations with France to determine Palestine's northern border. During the Biblical First Temple period, the head waters of the Jordan River were indeed under the control of the Israelite monarchy, and thus should have been included in Mandated Palestine, in accordance with the "Dan to Beersheba" historical formula.

[17] George Adam Smith was an ordained Scottish Minister and scholar of the Bible, as well as the principal of the University of Aberdeen (1909-35). He wrote a book about the topography, economics and history of Jerusalem from the earliest times to 70 A.D. and several commentaries on books of the Bible. His main works which the British consulted for determining Palestine's borders and which won high praise from Lloyd George were *The Historical Geography of the Holy Land* which appeared in 25 editions beginning in 1894, followed by the publication of an *Atlas of the Historical Geography of the Holy Land* in 1915. These books were the outcome of detailed observation and investigation made in Palestine. They also proved invaluable to General Edmund Allenby in the Palestine campaign in World War I.

official acceptance by the Principal Allied Powers, a binding act of international law rather than a mere policy statement of the British Government supported by its wartime allies. Henceforth, Britain was under an obligation of result (or specific performance) to secure the establishment of a Jewish state in Palestine, not under a reduced obligation merely to use its best endeavours to achieve that object. The Balfour Declaration, by virtue of the San Remo Resolution, henceforth became the constitutional basis for administering Palestine, under the Mandatory regime created by Article 22 of the League of Nations Covenant, in the place and stead of the international condominium visualized in the Sykes-Picot Agreement.

2. It officially established on April 24, 1920 the country of Palestine as one of the new mandated states in the Middle East that emerged from the breakup of the Ottoman Turkish Empire, despite the fact that its boundaries were not immediately demarcated, as was also the case for Mesopotamia and Syria. However, as noted above, it was agreed in principle that the frontiers should be defined according to the historical formula, extending from Dan to Beersheba, as thrice agreed to previously by Britain and France. The first time was in the Lloyd George – Clemenceau agreement of December 1, 1918. Secondly, these frontiers were re-affirmed in a British aide-memoire dated September 13, 1919, drawn up in the wake of Anglo-French negotiations at Deauville, France and handed over to France on that date, and also presented to the Supreme Council on September 15, 1919. The aide-memoire dealt with the military occupation of Syria, Cilicia, Palestine and Mesopotamia pending the decision in regard to the Mandates. It defined Palestine in accordance with the aforementioned historical formula. A third time this formula had been accepted was in a decision taken at the London Conference on February 21, 1920.

Until the official creation of Palestine, the territory that formerly comprised it had been included in the following Ottoman Turkish administrative divisions, in whole or in part:

***(One)*** The independent sanjak or Mutasarriflik of Jerusalem, that stretched from the Egyptian frontier across central Sinai to just north of Jaffa.

***(Two)*** Those areas of the province or Vilayet of Beirut which embraced three separate counties or sanjaks known as Balqa (Nablus), Acre and Beirut. The sanjak of Balqa once covered both sides of the Jordan until 1888. These sanjaks were subdivided into qadas or districts, made up of several villages.[18]

***(Three)*** Those areas of the province or vilayet of Syria which took in all of Transjordan, including the portion north of the Yarmuk known as Bashan or Hauran. This province was also called Damascus, which caused a lot of confusion, since there was also a smaller administrative division of that same name – the sanjak of Damascus. The two sanjaks in the province of Syria which were historically connected with Palestine were Hauran and Ma'an. When Transjordan was later separated from Cisjordanian Palestine during the Mandate

[18] See *Palestine Royal Commission Report*, Command 5479, p. 150.

period, it was divided into the four districts of Ajlun (ancient Gilead), Belqa (ancient Ammon), Kerak (ancient Moab) and Ma'an (ancient Edom).

Most of these administrative names were used in earlier periods, particularly during the time of Mameluk and Crusader rule.[19]

3. The San Remo Resolution designated Palestine as a whole to be the Jewish National Home and Jewish State. This is apparent from the statement by Lord Curzon "that Palestine was in the future to be the National Home of the Jews throughout the world". Prime Minister Lloyd George also made a statement to that effect, as recorded in the minutes of the meeting of April 24, 1920. It will be obvious to anyone reading the minutes in the English and French versions of the San Remo Peace Conference for April 24, 1920 that the country of Palestine was carved out of Ottoman lands only for the purpose of creating the Jewish State and homeland and for no other reason. France based its objection to inserting the Balfour Declaration in the Peace Treaty with Turkey precisely on the ground that doing so meant the actual establishment of a Jewish State which it strongly opposed but which it implicitly conceded to be the case after it was agreed by the Supreme Council to insert an obligatory version of the Balfour Declaration into the provisions of the Treaty of Sèvres. Philippe Berthelot is quoted in the French procès-verbal of the meeting as saying that "it would be an error to put the Jews in a situation different from that of other communities who are found in Palestine [because] that would be equivalent to creating a sort of Jewish State whose establishment is not what the French Government thinks should be done" (author's translation from the French). In the English minutes, Berthelot referred to "this new projected state" and asked whether it was "to have an entirely different administration from other States". It may also be noted that in the French procès-verbal, Lord Curzon spoke about a future state of Palestine that was promised to the Jews in the Balfour Declaration, but the term "state" is absent from the English version of the minutes of that meeting.

4. The San Remo Resolution on Palestine named the Jewish People as the national beneficiary of the principle of self-determination in the Mandate Charter, for the purpose of applying the general provisions of Article 22 of the Covenant of the League of Nations. The dual or joint application of the Balfour Declaration with Article 22 conclusively meant that Palestine was reserved for the Jewish People as a whole, not merely for the approximate 60,000 Jews living in Palestine at the end of the Great War. Nor was Palestine reserved for the estimated half-million Arabs then living there, even though they comprised the great majority of the relatively small population of the country. Prime Minister Lloyd George could not have made the identity of the national beneficiary any clearer than when he stated, as reported in the English version of the minutes:[20]

---

[19] See maps on pp. 277 and 283, *Encyclopaedia Judaica*, (1971) Volume 9.

[20] *The Rise of Israel*, Garland Publishing Inc., New York & London (1987),

> ...the task of governing Palestine would not be an easy one, and it would not be rendered less difficult by the fact that *it was to be the national home of the Jews* (emphasis added), who were an extraordinary intelligent race, but not easy to govern.

By becoming the beneficiary of the right of national independence under Article 22 in conjunction with the Balfour Declaration, the Jewish People were given a recognized international status. The Arabs were mentioned only once in the English version of the minutes (though not in the French version) by Lord Curzon in regard to safeguarding the rights of religious minorities under the first proviso of the Balfour Declaration that applied to the existing non-Jewish communities in Palestine. His reported reference to "Arabs" was completely out of sync with the fact that the whole discussion that took place on April 24, 1920, about the "existing non-Jewish communities" centered on religious communities only and did not deal with national communities. In the context of the San Remo discussion, it may be justly assumed that Curzon was actually referring to Moslems, rather than Arabs. Curzon's confusion of these two terms is also evident from the addition made to the British text of the mandates article in the Treaty of Peace with Turkey. The addition which became the second paragraph of Article 95 of the Treaty of Sèvres provided for the appointment of a special commission to study and regulate all questions and claims relating to the different religious communities. The communities that were specifically mentioned in the minutes of the meeting on April 24, 1920 were those whose members belonged to the Roman Catholic Church (particularly French Roman Catholics, Franciscans and others), the Protestant Churches and the Orthodox Church of Russia, the largest of the Eastern Orthodox churches.

5. As a direct result of naming the Jewish People as the national beneficiary of the Mandate for Palestine and basing the future administration of the country upon both the Balfour Declaration and Article 22 of the League Covenant, *de jure* sovereignty or legal title over Palestine was implicitly transferred to the Jewish People by the Supreme Council of the Principal Allied Powers who acted as the disposing agent under international law, by virtue of their military victory over the Central Powers. The Jewish People received this devolution of sovereignty or legal title from the very same source that the inhabitants of Syria and Mesopotamia also received it, by the considered decision of the Supreme Council of the Principal Allied Powers. No valid complaint can therefore be seriously made by Arab spokesmen that the Supreme Council had no right to grant to the Jewish People what it also granted to the new Arab states who were, in fact, the greatest recipients of Allied munificence. This kind of argument is inconsistent and illogical, without any merit in light of their own acceptance of the global political and legal settlement devised by the Council. It is also an

---

Volume 12, Document 36, p. 206.

act of supreme ingratitude to their benefactors who suffered huge human and material losses in World War I in defeating the Central Powers.

Once international law in the form of the San Remo Resolution recognized that *de jure* sovereignty over all regions of historical Palestine and the Land of Israel had been vested in the Jewish People, neither the Supreme Council of the Principal Allied Powers nor the Council of the League of Nations nor its successor, the United Nations, could thereafter revoke or alter Jewish sovereignty by a new decision. Legal ownership or title to Palestine had been permanently transferred to the Jewish People and any right the Principal Allied Powers previously had in regard to this country had disappeared after its official creation. In the case of the League of Nations, it never had any right in its Covenant to deprive the Jewish People of its sovereignty over any part of Palestine, the designated Jewish State under Mandate. Nor does the United Nations possess this right in its Charter. If either of these bodies really had such a right in regard to Palestine and the Land of Israel, the sovereignty of every state in the world over its own territory would be put in jeopardy.

6. The responsibility for ensuring that Jewish legal rights to Palestine under the Mandate would be respected and culminate in the establishment of an independent Jewish State was placed on the shoulders of the British Government, who undertook this obligation as the Mandatory, Tutelary and Trusteeship Power. It is true that Lord Curzon stated that "Great Britain was in no way anxious to accept this charge",[21] and Lloyd George referred to the hard task facing Britain in governing Jews, but it is also evident that Britain would never have accepted this onerous responsibility if it had not been in its national interests to do so at the time. By contrast, neither Britain nor France would accept a proposed mandate for Armenia after the U.S. Senate refused to advise ratification of the Treaty of Versailles, but both of them aspired very much to be directly involved in the administration of Palestine, with France only reluctantly giving up its idea to maintain a legal role or foothold in Palestine as the protector of the interests of French Catholics. The Mandate for Palestine was committed to Britain in accordance with a previous unwritten understanding reached between Clemenceau and Lloyd George on December 1, 1918, and was the natural outcome of the fact that Britain had conquered Palestine virtually by itself. France and Italy had only contributed small contingents to the military campaign in Palestine undertaken by General Edmund Allenby as commander of the Egyptian Expeditionary Force.[22]

7. The official name of the country where the Jewish National Home and Jewish State would be established was to be Palestine. During the period of British military and civil administration, this name was rendered in Hebrew in all legal documents and postage stamps as Palastina followed by the letters aleph, yod in brackets, which was a recognized abbreviation for Eretz-Israel or the

---

[21] Ibid., p. 209.

[22] These were the reasons cited in the minutes of the Conference, *ibid.*, p. 204.

Land of Israel, thereby giving it an official status. The choice of Palestine as the official name was not surprising because it was generally used in the Christian world to denote the land where Jesus was born, alternating at times with the names "Holy Land" and Judea. Palestine was also the unofficial name of the independent sanjak of Jerusalem in the Ottoman Turkish Empire, though it was not officially known by that name. However, in light of the later Arab appropriation of this name in the late 1960's, it would no doubt have been much better from a psychological perspective, as Professor Yuval Ne'eman[23] has stated to the author, if the historical name of Judea had been chosen. The Zionists themselves used the name "Palestine" in the Basle Program adopted at the First Zionist Congress in August 1897 and again when submitting their own formula for the Balfour Declaration in July 1917. In the early drafts of the Mandate prepared by Zionist and British officials, the words "Eretz Israel" appeared in full in brackets next to the name of Palestine in the preamble of the document. However, these two words were deleted in a unilateral British revision of the Draft Mandate of March 15, 1920 that elicited no objection from Chaim Weizmann when he became aware of the change.[24]

The importance of the San Remo Resolution on Palestine cannot be overestimated. It is the starting point of Jewish legal rights under international law to all of the mandated territory of Palestine, particularly the rights of sovereignty and legal title. It is the base document upon which the Mandate for Palestine was constructed and to which it had to conform. It is no less than the foundation document of the State of Israel, the legal existence of which is directly traceable from that document and not, as commonly believed, from the U.N. General Assembly Partition Resolution of November 29, 1947. It represented the crowning achievement of Herzlian Zionism that aimed to reconstruct the ancient Jewish state.

The San Remo Resolution determined that Palestine would be a Jewish State, first under mandatory rule, then as an independent entity in frontiers embracing all of the historical Land of Israel in accordance with the formula "Dan to Beersheba". The San Remo Resolution was placed in the Treaty of Sèvres

---

[23] Professor Yuval Ne'eman was Israel's Minister of Science and Development (1981-1984) and Minister of Energy and Infrastructure (1990-1992), and subsequently chairman of the Israel Space Agency.

[24] Weizmann's approval for the deletion of the words "Eretz Israel" from the text of the Mandate is mentioned in a letter sent by Hubert Young to Robert Vansittart, dated June 30, 1920. The citation for this letter in the Public Record Office is: E 7369/4164/44, which is included among the Foreign Office documents bearing the numbers 371/5244:9220. Before the deletion was made, the words "Eretz Israel" appeared with provisional British approval in the Draft Mandates of December 11, 1919 and March 15, 1920. The relevant text read as follows: "Recognizing the historical connection of the Jewish people with Palestine and the claim which this gives them to reconstitute Palestine as their national home (Erez Israel)". *Documents on British Foreign Policy 1919-1939*, First Series, Volume IV, Document 397, p. 571.

signed on August 10, 1920. Though the latter was never ratified, the San Remo Resolution remained as a binding legal document standing on its own merit, because it was encapsulated into the first three recitals of the Preamble of the Mandate for Palestine, and was reinforced by the Franco-British Convention of December 23, 1920, which delineated the original borders of what was meant to be the Jewish State of Palestine. The Resolution is in effect an inter-Allied agreement between the four Principal Allied Powers that created the modern Middle East. Its status as an independent act of international law that was not merely one of the articles of the Treaty of Sèvres is further evidenced by the fact that it contained two provisions not found in any other document. First was the naming of the Mandatory Powers for the three Middle East Mandates concerning which the treaty of peace with Turkey is silent, and second was the right accorded to Italy to refuse to approve the terms of those Mandates if their rights in Southern Anatolia were thereby prejudiced. Italy subsequently took advantage of this right to delay the legal implementation of both the Mandates for Palestine and Syria.

The San Remo Resolution in regard to Mesopotamia and Syria was executed in full. The tragedy of the Jewish People in the ensuing years after the Resolution's adoption resulted from the fact that it was decapitated in practice, by successive Governments of Great Britain who distorted it beyond recognition and failed to properly carry out its true meaning in accordance with the international legal obligations they had undertaken.[25]

The San Remo Resolution, which gave binding legal force to the Balfour Declaration under international law, was no less than the Magna Carta of the Jewish People, as Lord Curzon aptly called it. It can justifiably be seen as the charter that eluded Theodor Herzl, the greatest of all Zionist leaders, despite his attempts to obtain it from the Turkish Sultan, Abdul Hamid II, in order "to establish a home (i.e., a Jewish State) for the Jewish People under public law" as formulated in the Basle Program, that required mass Jewish immigration and dense settlement by Jews in the Land of Israel. After the Zionist Movement obtained this Charter of Freedom, Curzon told Weizmann that "the San Remo decision definitely fixed the status of Palestine and nothing more was required", which is why he turned down Weizmann's request to insert a clause in the Preamble of the Mandate for Palestine which would have explicitly recognized the historical connection of the Jewish People with Palestine.[26] Weizmann replied to Curzon that what he said "is of course true from the purely legal point of view", but justified its inclusion in order "to seek from the Jews of the world the sacrifice and treasure required to make Palestine again a healthful and happy land".[27] Weizmann's persistence angered Curzon. In a letter dated October 29, 1920, to Lloyd George he wrote:[28]

---

[25] The writer treats this subject in greater detail in Section 3 below.

[26] *Documents on British Foreign Policy*, Volume XIII, Document 331, p. 375.

[27] *Ibid.*, p. 376.

[28] *Ibid.*, p. 376.

> The Zionists rest their claim to have this sentence introduced upon the plea that it will enable them to raise more money in America for the development of Palestine. I may say, in passing, that I attach very little importance to this plea. The important thing is that we got the Balfour Declaration – you will remember how hard a fight I made for it – into the Treaty [of Peace with Turkey] at San Remo, and that is the Magna Charta of the Zionists. What they really want this particular clause in the Mandate for is, not in order to get money now, but in order that this sentence may be the foundation on which, at every stage, they may hold a claim for preferential treatment in Palestine, and ultimately for the complete government of the country.

Weizmann was right to seek explicit recognition of the Jewish historical connection with Palestine, but he based his demand on the wrong reason. He should have linked it to the underlying reason of the San Remo Resolution, which recognized implicitly what he wanted to be explicitly stated. Curzon therefore rightfully condemned the reason Weizmann gave for his demand – financial or philanthropic – but he contradicted himself in complaining that the Zionists would use the "historical connection" to establish a Jewish Government in Palestine, which is exactly what the San Remo Resolution was intended to do as a natural consequence of setting up a Jewish State. He was therefore not loyal to his own words in characterizing the San Remo Resolution as being the "Charter of Jewish Rights or Freedom", while Weizmann on his side did not fully grasp the true meaning of the San Remo Resolution.

The only Zionist leader at the time who properly understood the natural consequences of the legal recognition of the Balfour Declaration as embodied in the San Remo Resolution was U.S. Supreme Court Justice, Louis Dembitz Brandeis. He realized that the political and legal battle to obtain the Charter that was the central goal of Herzlian Zionism had been won and that practical measures could now be taken by the Zionist Movement to re-build the ancient Jewish State and Homeland, concentrating mainly on economic policy and promoting investments to make the Jews of Palestine self-reliant and self-supporting. He saw no further need for more political action in the international arena to secure over again what had just been so marvelously secured by the extraordinary efforts of Weizmann and many others, including Brandeis himself. He clashed with Weizmann and his supporters who wanted the Zionist Movement to continue unabated its political work, as if the San Remo Resolution, the crowning achievement of pre-State Zionism, never existed. Brandeis thought that such work should be left principally in the hands of the Jewish community in Palestine. When Weizmann's view gained the upper hand, Brandeis withdrew in 1921 from the ranks of leadership of both American and world Zionism.

One can only lament the fact that the brilliant legal mind of Brandeis was subsequently absent in Zionist counsels when it was most needed to defeat ignoble British attempts to undermine Jewish legal rights and title of sovereignty over Palestine that began immediately after the San Remo Resolution was adopted by the Supreme Council of the Principal Allied Powers. Had he been in charge of the Zionist Movement instead of Weizmann, for which he was much better qualified by reason of his peerless intellect and legal understanding of the true meaning of the San Remo Resolution, there is little doubt that he would have successfully halted Britain's gross violations of its obligations to the Jewish People to rebuild the Jewish State. The constitutional structure of Palestine would have been solidly laid down in an efficient manner and better understood by one and all, without the rampant confusion and entanglements that resulted during the period of the Mandate arising from British deceit, false Arab claims and inadequate Jewish responses.

There is still very little awareness of the great importance of the San Remo Resolution on Palestine. Anyone who does not know and understand the real meaning and legal consequences of this Resolution as detailed above cannot truly know and understand Jewish legal rights and title of sovereignty over Palestine and the Land of Israel under international law. Even though it is sometimes briefly alluded to, it is mainly uncited or ignored in political, diplomatic and legal circles today. With one solitary exception,[29] the San Remo Resolution does not appear in any of the modern collections of legal documents concerning the Arab-Jewish Question under its actual name, although some older collections place it in the context of the aborted Treaty of Sèvres which hides its significance. It was almost entirely forgotten despite the fact that it is the best proof that the whole country of Palestine and the Land of Israel belong exclusively to the Jewish People under international law. By way of contrast, the Sykes-Picot Treaty, which was secretly made and superceded by the San Remo Resolution, is well known and frequently quoted. A partial explanation lies in the fact that the minutes in English of the San Remo Peace Conference for the sessions held on April 24 and 25, 1920 were not published until 1958 when they appeared in a British Government publication entitled *Documents on British Foreign Policy* (Volume 8). But the real reason for the widespread ignorance of the importance of the San Remo Resolution – representing the international law approval of the Balfour Declaration – is that it was undermined by the fact that the Treaty of Sèvres which incorporated it, never entered into legal force as a ratified treaty, as further discussed in Section 3 of this work. This, combined with British refusal to implement the San Remo Resolution according to what it really meant in regard to Palestine, led to its *de facto* erasure as an independent

---

[29] See C.L. Geddes, *A Documentary History of the Arab-Israeli Conflict*, Praeger Publishers, New York (1991), p. 13 ff. In this book, the San Remo Resolution is referred to by the similar term "the San Remo Agreement". In his reproduction of the resolution, Geddes omitted the important reservation made by Italy in paragraph (C) thereof, a reservation later cited by Italy to delay the confirmation of the Mandate until Italian economic interests in southern Anatolia were satisfied. This book was brought to the author's attention by Elon B. Magill, founder of the website *Israel White Paper*.

act of international law, though it still remains the preeminent foundation document of the State of Israel.

*The Mandates System And The Global Peace Settlement*

The Mandates System was principally the work of the South African statesman, Jan Christiaan Smuts, who was a member of the British Imperial War Cabinet in 1917-18, serving as a minister without portfolio. Under the plan that he proposed, the colonies and territories conquered from the Central Powers by the Principal Allied and Associated Powers in World War I would not be directly annexed, but would be created as new states under the Mandates System to be administered by Mandatories or trustees chosen from among the Allied Powers. The Mandates plan was joined to President Wilson's proposal to create a League of Nations. On January 25, 1919, the Paris Peace Conference approved the creation of a League of Nations and appointed a committee to draft its constitution. On January 30, 1919, the Mandates System was endorsed by the Allied Supreme Council in a provisional resolution that soon became Article 22 of the Covenant of the League of Nations. The Covenant, with the Mandates article appearing in it, was then adopted by the Peace Conference on April 28, 1919 and placed in the first part of the Treaty of Versailles of June 28, 1919, as well as in four other peace treaties signed to conclude World War I. The Mandates System as well as the League of Nations, which was given the task of supervising it, both began to operate as soon as the Treaty of Versailles was ratified on January 10, 1920.

The various peoples and communities in the former German and Turkish territories were put under the tutelage of advanced nations until such time as they were able to stand by themselves, whereupon they would gain the right of national self-determination as envisaged by President Woodrow Wilson in his Fourteen Points of January 8, 1918. Three different types of mandates were created, "A", "B" and "C", that varied according to the stage of development of the people involved, the geographical situation of the territory, its economic conditions and other similar circumstances. The Mandates were conferred by the Allied Supreme Council upon advanced nations acting in the combined role as Mandatories, Trustees and Tutors, and it was the duty of the Council of the League of Nations to supervise the observance of the mandates committed to their charge. The League Council did this through a body of eleven members called the Permanent Mandates Commission which received the annual reports of the Mandatories.

Three "A" Mandates were created out of former Turkish territories consisting of Palestine, Mesopotamia and Syria. The terms of those Mandates were formulated by the Principal Allied Powers and submitted to the Council of the League of Nations for confirmation. Six "B" Mandates were established from former German colonies in Africa. These were for Ruanda and Urundi (today the independent states of Rwanda and Burundi) – to Belgium; Tanganyika – to Britain; French Cameroon, British Cameroon, French Togoland, British

Togoland. In addition, five "C" Mandates were granted as follows: South-West Africa was entrusted to the Union of South Africa; the North Pacific Islands comprising the Marshalls, the Marianas and the Carolines (including Palau and Yap – today one of the four federated states of Micronesia) – to Japan; New Guinea and certain adjacent South Pacific Islands – to Australia; Nauru (Pleasant Island) to Australia and the British Empire; Western Samoa – to New Zealand.

Altogether, 14 mandates were distributed to advanced nations by the Allied Powers of World War I. The terms of the "B" and "C" Mandates were formulated by a committee appointed by the Allied Supreme Council on June 28, 1919 under the chairmanship of Lord Alfred Milner and those terms also needed confirmation by the League Council. The Mandatories administered the mandated territories entrusted to them on behalf of the League of Nations.

The rationale for dividing the Mandates into three classes was explained in blunt and colorful language by British Prime Minister David Lloyd George on January 30, 1919 at the Paris Peace Conference.[30]

> It had been decided to accept the doctrine of a Mandatory for all conquests in the late Turkish Empire and in the German colonies. But three classes of mandates would have to be recognized, namely:
>
> Firstly: Mandates applicable to countries where the population was civilized but not yet organized – where a century might elapse before the people could be properly organized; for example, Arabia. In such cases it would be impossible to give full self-government and at the same time prevent the various tribes or units from fighting each other. It was obvious that the system to be applied to these territories must be different from that which would have to be applied to cannibal colonies, where people were eating each other.
>
> Secondly: Mandates applicable to tropical Colonies situated a long way from the country of the possible Mandatory. In other words, territories which did not form an integral part of any particular Mandatory country: for example, New Guinea. In these Colonies the full principle of a Mandatory would be applied, including the "open door".[31]
>
> Thirdly: Mandates applicable to countries which formed almost a part of the organization of an adjoining Power, who would have to be

[30] The spoken words of Lloyd George are taken from the "Secretary's Notes of a Conversation Held at M. Pichon's Room at the Quai d'Orsay, Paris on Thursday, January 30, 1919 at 11 A.M. The Secretary's Notes are presented as Document 18 in the book entitled *The Drafting of the Covenant* by David Hunter Miller, G.P. Putnam's Sons, New York (1928), Volume 2, pp. 194-95.

[31] The policy of the "open door" meant that the Mandatory was bound to ensure to the nationals of all states members of the League the same rights or equality in treatment in respect of trade and commerce as were open to the nationals of the Mandatory.

appointed the Mandatory.

Finally, he wished to emphasize the fact that the memorandum[32] was intended to deal only with those parts of the Turkish Empire and of the German Empire which had actually been conquered. Districts such as Smyrna, Adalia, the North of Anatolia were purposely excluded. Such territories would have to be considered separately on their merits.

In the case of certain Asiatic and North African possessions freed earlier from Turkish rule and *de facto* sovereignty, it was decided to exclude those areas from being part of the new system of mandatory government, particularly the Hedjaz and the rest of the Arabian Peninsula, as well as Egypt, which remained for the time being under British protection or control.

The global political and legal settlement made after World War I in regard to the disposition of former Turkish territories bestowed enormous benefits on the Arabic-speaking world. The Arabs received the lion's share of these territories. As a result of this favouritism they hold today lands equal to twice the area of the USA, as the late Editor of Midstream, Mr. Joel Carmichael, has keenly observed in a letter to the author.[33]

Other peoples who were originally included in this global settlement fared very badly. Kurds and Armenians were supposed to get their own autonomous homelands or states, and the Assyro-Chaldeans, who were a Christian community centered in Mosul or northern Iraq, were also promised protection and safeguards for their rights. However, in the final outcome, none of the promises made to them by the Allied Powers were fulfilled, because their claims and aspirations, although explicitly recognized in the abortive Treaty of Sèvres of August 10, 1920, were subsequently disregarded by both the British and French who turned over their designated areas to the complete control of both Arabs and Turks who then cruelly deprived the aforesaid communities of their projected national rights and status within those areas.

When the global settlement and division of Ottoman lands was devised at the San Remo Peace Conference, it was clear to all concerned parties, Arab and Jew alike and to all European, American and Japanese statesmen, that Palestine, within its historical frontiers according to the biblical formula, from Dan to Beersheba, but which still needed to be marked out in a separate treaty, was exclusively reserved for the benefit of the Jewish People all over the world, of which only a fraction then actually lived in the ancient Jewish country. What this obviously meant to one and all was an independent Jewish State in all of the historical territory of Palestine.

---

32 A reference to a document drawn up by General Jan Christiaan Smuts approved by the Council of Ten on January 30, 1919.

33 See Appendix V, letter dated February 27, 2001.

*Chapter 2*

# The Franco-British Boundary Convention and the Demarcation Agreement

Pursuant to the adoption of the San Remo Resolution on April 24-25, 1920, which declared that the boundaries of Palestine shall be determined by the Principal Allied Powers of Britain, France, Italy and Japan, an assertion reiterated twice more in the Treaty of Sèvres and the Draft Mandate of December 6, 1920, Britain and France proceeded to negotiate a treaty for that explicit purpose, called the Franco-British Boundary Convention of December 23, 1920, also known as the Convention of Paris of that date. As a direct result of this Convention, Jewish legal rights and title of sovereignty over most of what had constituted the historical Land of Israel were formally recognized under international law. This recognition specifically covered what is today wrongly called "the occupied territories" or "disputed territories" of Judea, Samaria and Gaza, as well as the whole of Transjordan south of the Yarmuk, whose eastern boundary with Mesopotamia still awaited final determination. What was glaringly excluded from Palestine was the fertile area of the southern Litani Valley comprising present-day southern Lebanon, and most of ancient Bashan, containing the headwaters of both the Jordan and the Yarmuk Rivers and covering the area north of the Yarmuk until Mount Hermon and extending from the city of Dan in the west to that of Salchah (Salcah) in the east.

The convention or treaty between Britain and France involved arduous negotiations in which the British, urged on by Chaim Weizmann and his Zionist colleagues, with important assistance from Justice Louis Dembitz Brandeis, tried to convince the French to provide the Jewish National Home with the best possible boundaries for its economic, political and commercial development. These boundaries had to be entirely different from the defunct Sykes-Picot Treaty of May 9 and 16, 1916, which was ratified four years before the Balfour Declaration was adopted by the Principal Allied Powers at the San Remo Peace Conference and represented the physical and economic mutilation of Palestine. The realization of Zionist goals required the whole of the historical Land of Israel for rebuilding a prosperous, self-sustaining and secure Jewish National Home. This meant, according to a Statement of the Zionist Organization dated February 3, 1919, submitted to the Paris Peace Conference, that most of the Litani valley at the lower reaches of the Litani (Leontes) River and all of the headwaters or sources of the Jordan on Mount Hermon, the highest peak in the Land of Israel, would be included inside the borders of Mandated Palestine. This mountain, known to the Arabs as Jebel al-Sheikh (Mountain of the Elder) and called in the Bible variously by the names of Sion (in Hebrew), Sirion by the Sidonians (Phoenicians) and Senir by the Amorites, is mentioned there as the northern boundary of the Promised Land, being the extreme northern limit of Transjordan. Under the Zionist Plan for Palestine, the northern border would begin from a point south of Sidon up to Rashiya – land that was basically a natural extension of Upper Galilee. The border would proceed further east along the Hermon ridge incorporating the Golan and Hauran and the Yarmuk valley, all of which constituted ancient Bashan. The border would then continue southward, along the Hedjaz Railroad, down to the Gulf of Aqaba.

Support for Zionist boundary aspirations as outlined in the statement submitted to the Paris Peace Conference came surprisingly from the anti-Zionist Foreign Secretary, Lord Curzon, who conveyed to the French negotiating representative, Philippe Berthelot, what Prime Minister David Lloyd George had in mind for determining the northern frontier of Palestine with Syria and Lebanon. At an Anglo-French meeting held at the British Foreign Office in London on December 23, 1919, Curzon said that "the Sykes-Picot line should be taken north so as to include the Litani bend, the headwaters of the Jordan, and the streams flowing south from Mount Hermon in Palestine".[1] Curzon cited two reasons to support the British position. The first was that the war against Turkey had been fought almost entirely by Great Britain at great cost to its Treasury, while France did not contribute an equivalent effort, either in men or in money, contrary to the hypothesis of the Sykes-Picot Treaty which required equal efforts on the part of both countries in conquering Turkey. The second reason was that Lloyd George had publicly committed himself on more than one occasion to the inclusion in Palestine of all its ancient territories according to the Biblical formula "from Dan to Beersheba", and he could not back down. Curzon's statement to Berthelot constitutes strong evidence that when Lloyd George defined Palestine according to the "Dan to Beersheba" formula, he meant by that not just the territory lying between those two towns, but a much wider area that extended northwards up to the bend of the Litani and included also the headwaters of the Jordan and the streams of Mount Hermon in the Biblical region of Bashan that embraced all of the present-day Golan Heights.

Zionist boundary aspirations received important support from President Woodrow Wilson as well, whose aid in this matter was enlisted by Justice Brandeis. In a remarkable telegraph message sent by the U.S. State Department on February 10, 1920 to the American Ambassador to Paris on the instructions of President Wilson, the Ambassador was ordered to inform both the British and French Governments what Wilson believed Palestine's boundary in the North and the East should be:[2]

---

[1] *Documents on British Foreign Policy*, First Series, Vol. IV, no. 405, p. 599.

[2] *Documents on British Foreign Policy*, First Series, Vol. IV, no. 425, p. 634.

> Palestine should have rational boundaries in the North and the East, [extending to] the Litani River, the watershed of the Hermon and the Hauran [mispelled as Haulon] and Golan [mispelled as Yaulon], and that it was to be hoped that the French and British Governments were not carrying out the Sykes-Picot Agreement to the detriment of Mr. Balfour's Declaration as to the Palestine of the future.

As shown by Lord Curzon's northern boundary proposal to Philippe Berthelot on December 23, 1919, the initial British reaction to the Zionist boundary plan was favourable but they later changed their mind and rejected the extended northern frontier for Palestine, most of which was part of the historical Land of Israel and therefore should have been included in Palestine, as implicitly required by the adoption of the historical formula "Dan to Beersheba" at the San Remo Peace Conference. Feisal, on behalf of the Hedjaz Delegation at the earlier Paris Peace Conference, did not oppose the Zionist-proposed borders – calling them moderate and proper since they did not include the Hedjaz Railway which had special relevance for Moslems.[3] Curzon agreed that the foundation of a National Home for Jews in Palestine "largely depends for its success on the future utilization of the waters of the Litani and Yarmuk",[4] echoing President Wilson's sentiments. Weizmann told Curzon in a letter dated October 30, 1920:[5]

> ...If Palestine were cut off from the Litany, Upper Jordan and Yarmuk, to say nothing of the eastern shore of Galilee, she could not be economically independent.

However, soon thereafter, Curzon wrote to Weizmann on November 8, 1920 to inform him that the French Government had refused to have the eastern frontier of Palestine extended either north of the Yarmuk or east of the Sea of Galilee, nor were they willing to conclude any formal agreement as to the utilization by Palestine of the waters of the Yarmuk, North Jordan or Litani.[6] France considered the area of Transjordan north of the Yarmuk as one

---

This entry contains not the actual text of the U.S. State Department telegraph message, but the paraphrased version of it sent in a letter by George Grahame, a minister of the British Embassy at Paris, to Lord Curzon informing him of the message conveyed by the U.S. Ambassador from President Wilson regarding the future boundaries of Palestine.

[3] See pp. 35 and 38 in the Political Report of the Executive of the Zionist Organization to the 12th Zionist Congress, reproduced in *The Rise of Israel*, Volume 8, Document 57, pages 190 and 193.

[4] *Documents on British Foreign Policy*, First Series, Vol. XIII, No. 328, p. 359: Curzon's letter to Vansittart, dated October 16, 1920.

[5] *Op. cit.*, Vol. XIII, Number 331, p. 375.

[6] *Op. cit.*, Vol. XIII, Number 333, p. 381.

of special interest to itself, because a French company had laid a railroad line there at the end of the 19th century. This French attitude was not only a slap in the face of the Zionist Organization, but also represented a total disregard of and contempt for the considered opinion of the U.S. President.

France adopted an anti-Zionist position which was based on a return to the expired Sykes-Picot Treaty, contrary to Lord Curzon's and President Wilson's exhortations, ignoring the fact that this treaty had already been superceded by the San Remo Resolution and in any event could never have been relied upon from a legal point of view since it had been conceived secretly *prior* to the break-up of the Ottoman Empire and was never publicly announced by Britain and France even after they ratified it. Consequently it had no validity under international law. France also ignored its own proposal of March 16, 1920, known as the Berthelot line, which offered Palestine a much more generous boundary to the north than was eventually adopted on December 23, 1920. The Berthelot line began at Ras-al-Ein, south of Tyre, on the Mediterranean, extended across southern Lebanon and lay about 6 kilometers north of Banias (ancient Dan and ancient Laish, also called Caesarea Philippi in the Herodian age). The suggested boundary included most of the Golan, lying well east of Lake Huleh and Lake Tiberias.[7] However, France retracted its proposal in June 1920, not long after the end of the San Remo Peace Conference, on the flimsy ground that it had been made conditional on the consent of Prime Minister Alexandre Millerand who also served as his own Foreign Minister. Millerand was certainly well aware of what Philippe Berthelot, the Secretary-General of the French Ministry of Foreign Affairs, had earlier proposed when the matter of Palestine's future borders arose at the Conference session on April 25, 1920, at which both Millerand and Berthelot were in attendance. Berthelot advocated deciding then and there the final boundaries between the mandated territories of Palestine and Syria, a move he would have never made, if he had not had the prior consent of Millerand to whom he was clearly subservient. British refusal to immediately accept Berthelot's suggested boundary line served as a weak pretext for France to later retract the Berthelot offer of March 16, 1920 and introduce a new line in June 1920 that was much less favourable to Zionist aims. France acted selfishly, erratically and illegally in trying to force on Britain an inaccurate determination of Palestine's historical frontiers, seemingly motivated by the fantasy that the enlargement of Syria beyond its historical limits at Palestine's expense was, in effect, an enlargement of French sovereign territory. The British eventually succumbed to French hostility to the Zionist border proposals and accepted the French position, to the great detriment of the Jewish National Home. It was apparently more important for Britain to have harmonious relations with its ally, France, than to protect the interests of the Zionist Organization and of the Jewish State in the making.

---

[7] See FO 371/5244: E 7691/4164/44.

The French change of attitude towards Zionism was well noted by Robert Vansittart, one of the key officials dealing with Palestine in the British Foreign Office. In a confidential letter from Paris dated June 21, 1920, Vansittart reported to the Foreign Office as follows:[8]

> As to the Palestine mandate, [Berthelot] said that Millerand had nearly jumped out of his skin when he had shown it to him. Berthelot added that, frankly, he himself was both surprised and alarmed by it. They both think it too judaised and judaising – full of red flags indeed. Bethelot said, however, that if we liked to run ourselves into trouble, that seemed our affair, and spoke as if he hoped to get M. Millerand to adopt this view and to leave him (Berthelot) to agree with me.

It is clear from Vansittart's report on the malevolent French attitude towards the Mandate for Palestine (then still in draft form), that France irrationally wanted to limit the size of the Jewish National Home regardless of the historical formula it had just agreed to at the San Remo Peace Conference. France succeeded in its nefarious aim, thus depriving Palestine and the future independent Jewish State of the northern boundary it was legally entitled to. In a follow-up letter to Curzon dated November 13, 1920, he informed him of the strongly negative attitude of the French Government to Weizmann's demands for the Jewish National Home, which they characterized as extravagant:[9]

> [The French Government] had agreed to a Jewish National Home, not to a Jewish State. They considered we [the British Government] were steering straight upon the latter, and the very last thing they would do was to enlarge that State, for they totally disapproved our policy. They might eventually have to make representations to us on this point, as the policy was full of dangers for them too. For the present they contented themselves with saying, *'Vous barbotterez si vous le voulez, mais vous ne barbotterez pas à nos frais'* [you will flounder if you like, but you will not flounder at our expense].

Vansittart added:

> The claims of the Zionists went far beyond the ground on which the British Prime Minister had always placed himself, and on which the French Government considers they had met him – *the historic formula,*

[8] Registry Number E7033/4164/44, Letter from Mr. Vansittart to Major Young, dated June 21, 1920, Eastern 7033, June 23, 1920, p. 175.

[9] *Documents on British Foreign Policy*, First Series, Vol. XIII, Number 337, p. 387.

> *Dan to Beersheba* (emphasis added). To make the bigger Jewish State, of which the French disapproved, the Zionists continued to claim territory to which the historic argument did not apply.

On November 16, 1920, Vansittart told Curzon in still another revealing letter:[10]

> The French are increasingly anti-Zionist. They mistrust and fear our whole policy in Palestine... They believe we are in a direct train of making an all-Jewish State, as opposed to a National Home... [The French] remain obstinately convinced that they are going to have a Bolshevik colony on their flank... The French are therefore determined that this "Bolshevik colony" shall be as small as possible, and conceive this necessary for their own safety.

In a letter[11] dated December 21, 1920 sent by John Tilley, the Assistant Under-Secretary of State in Curzon's Foreign Office, to Wyndham Deedes, the Chief Secretary of Palestine, he explained the French and British positions on the historical frontiers of Palestine as follows:

> The question of Palestine came up at a meeting with the French and British Prime Ministers at No. 10, Downing Street on December 4th...
>
> We understand that at the meeting the French took the line that they had fully met the Prime Minister's plea for a Palestine with the historical frontiers stretching from Dan to Beersheba by conceding the Safed, Huleh, Metullah and Banias (Dan) strip of territory and that, for the rest, provided the needs of Syrian territory were first met, they were ready to share in a liberal spirit with Palestine the rest of the waters of the Upper Jordan and Yarmuk and their tributaries. As our case for extended Palestine frontiers had always been argued at the Supreme Council [of the Principal Allied Powers] generally on the 'historical' ground and in particular (however unfortunate it may now seem) on the basis of plate No. 34 ('Palestine under David and Solomon') of [George] Adam Smith's *Atlas of the Historical Geography of the Holy Land*, you will readily understand how difficult it was to meet the French argument as regards the inclusion in Palestine of territory east of the Jordan and north of the Yarmuk [i.e., the entire area of Bashan or Turkish Hauran]. It would not have been so difficult, if the above plate be taken as the test, to argue for a frontier including part of the Litani but, as I have said, the course of the discussion at San

[10] *Op. cit.*, Vol. XIII, Number 340, p. 391.

[11] *Op. cit.*, Vol. XIII, Number 353, p. 419.

> Remo practically excluded that point being again taken up. In the end it was decided that the French offer as to sharing the surplus waters of the northern Jordan and Yarmuk should be turned into a clause for insertion in the convention providing for an expert examination. You will have seen the actual wording of the clause. [All ( ) in the original; all [ ] my additions – H.G.].

There may have existed some uncertainty in the British mind about the exact location of the historical border of Palestine in the north, but it was definitely not congruent with the border finally chosen in the Franco-British Boundary Convention of December 23, 1920. To the extent that this Convention did not include all historical areas of the Land of Israel that had once been under Israelite or Jewish rule, it was in violation of the San Remo Resolution of April 25, 1920 whose definition of Palestine was dependent on the historical argument, or intimately tied to it. This Resolution which embodied an agreement between the four Principal Allied Powers of Britain, France, Italy and Japan as to the dismemberment of the Ottoman Empire after its defeat in World War I had to be adhered to in fixing the northern boundary of Palestine because it was a fundamental document of international law for the Middle East that had created not only Palestine but also Syria and Iraq and was incorporated in both the Treaty of Sèvres and in the first three recitals of the Preamble of the Mandate for Palestine. The pending Mandate recognized the historical connection of the Jewish People with Palestine, which implied that the reconstituted Jewish National Home and State would have the approximate historical frontiers of those of ancient Judea (Judah) and ancient Israel when they existed as independent states.

In regard to the Zionist claim that the northern border of Palestine should extend northwards up to the bend of the Litani River, including Sidon and Tyre on the Mediterranean coast, the British had, for all practical purposes, abandoned this claim in the course of their discussion with the French at the San Remo Peace Conference on April 25, 1920, as pointed out by Tilley in his letter to Deedes, quoted above. At the Conference, Prime Minister David Lloyd George had stated that the whole of this region, today embracing Southern Lebanon, had never been included in the boundaries of Palestine, a statement that contradicted the map 'Palestine under David and Solomon' produced by George Adam Smith on whom he had always theretofore relied. The British Prime Minister's statement was not true historically respecting most of the southern Litani Valley, since it had definitely been a part of the United Kingdom of David and Solomon (circa 1010-930 B.C.E.) and had earlier been settled by the Israelite tribes of Asher, Naphtali and Dan. However, it was true, as Lloyd George alleged, that Sidon and Tyre had never been part of Palestine since these towns had never been conquered by the Israelites and brought under their dominion. On the other hand, they were specifically included in the inheritance of the tribe of Asher according to the Book of Joshua (19:28-31), and the

Asherites lived there among the Canaanite inhabitants (Judges 1:31-32). They were thus part of the Promised Land and the Land of Canaan that yet remained to be conquered by the Israelite tribes (Joshua 13:1-6; Judges 3:1-3). In time, strong Jewish communities took root in these Phoenician cities and flourished until the close of the Second Temple Period in the Roman era. Based on the foregoing Biblical evidence, it may be concluded that the Zionist claim to most of the Litani Valley was well conceived, not only economically but historically as well. However, the claim affecting Sidon and Tyre, though not altogether unfounded, was nevertheless problematic. The British should therefore have unswervingly maintained their initial demand in their boundary negotiations with the French that the southern Litani Valley, except for Sidon and Tyre, be included in Palestine and the Jewish National Home, as Lloyd George, Balfour and Curzon all originally sought,[12] and which was also supported by President Wilson.

The place name or geographical term of Lebo-Hammath (or simply Hammath) is frequently mentioned in the Bible as the northern boundary mark of the Land of Israel.[13] It is identified with modern Lebweh (Labwa) situated in a fertile region near one of the sources of the Orontes River (Nahr al-Asi), in the northern Lebanese Beqa. Moreover, Ijon (Iyon), today called Marj al-Ayun, lying due north of Metulla and northwest of Dan, was an Israelite city in the southernmost part of the Lebanese Beqa, included in the historical territory of Naphtali. The area of southern Lebanon also included the petty kingdom of Chalcis, ruled briefly in the first century by Herod, brother of Agrippa I, then by his nephew, Agrippa II. This knowledge, had it then been relied upon, should have been enough to convince the British and French negotiators to include *most of* the southern Litani Valley in the northern border of Palestine under the historical formula. Had these negotiators truly abided by this formula as the governments of their respective countries had committed themselves to do, the waters of the Litani might well have become a principal source for irrigating semi-arid Palestine and also used for the production of hydro-electric power, exactly as the Zionists were hoping.

In addition, other historical areas of the Land of Israel were excluded from the Jewish National Home. Only the northwestern part of the Golan, which forms the western section of Bashan, was included in the 1920 boundaries for Palestine. The rest of Bashan[14] north of the Yarmuk was placed outside

---

[12] Colonel Richard Meinertzhagen, *Middle East Diary – 1917-1956*, published by Thomas Yoseloff, New York (1960), pp. 25, 355.

[13] See the entry *Lebo*-Hammath in the *Encyclopaedia Judaica*, (1971) Volume 10, column 1551, written by Professor Benjamin Mazar.

[14] Bashan has been part of the historical Land of Israel since the time Moses allotted it to the half-tribe of Menasseh as their inheritance, after the Israelites defeated the Amorite King Og, the ruler of this territory. Bashan formed part of the dominions of David and Solomon and the Israelite kings Joash (Jehoash) and his son Jeroboam II. In the Second Temple Period, all of Bashan was included in Herod's kingdom and that of his heirs, Herod Philip and Agrippa I and II, until

Palestine, including Mount Hermon, except for the southern portion of the mountain that borders on the edge of the basalt tableland of the Golan. This exclusion from Palestine of most of Mount Hermon whose snows and rains feed the headstreams of the Jordan River[15] was a severe blow to Zionist plans to utilize these waters for the benefit of the country. As in the case of the lower Litani Valley, this too represented a clear violation of the historical formula, "Dan to Beersheba", for fixing Palestine's boundaries, decided upon at the Conferences of London and San Remo. Moreover, the eastern half of Lake Kinneret (also known as Lake Tiberias or, in the New Testament, the Sea of Galilee) was left on the French-Syrian side of the frontier.

A contemporary account of the northern boundary settlement between Palestine and Syria, written by the distinguished English archeologist and oriental scholar, Commander David George Hogarth, supported in principle the Zionist position for borders that met the historical criterion and economic needs of the Jewish National Home, although he also believed that France would never have agreed to these borders since they did not correspond to those assigned to France in the Sykes-Picot Treaty and closely affected what he said were their supposedly "vital interests". He wrote:[16]

> The frontier between Syria and British mandated territory in the south involved various contentious questions, and was not so easily settled. The successful economic development of Palestine in the future depended on water-supply, both for power and irrigation. Water adequate for these purposes and at sufficient elevation existed only in streams flowing through the border districts between Syria and Palestine – in the Litani River, the Upper Jordan, the Yarmuk River, itself the chief tributary of the Jordan from the East. But these streams, either in whole or in part, lay within the Syrian area provisionally assigned to France by the Sykes-Picot Agreement – Palestine then not having been envisaged as a possible area of industrial development and closely

about 100 C.E. It was divided into four separate regions: 1) the Golan, which included Mt. Hermon and the ancient kingdoms of Ma'acah and Geshur; 2) Batanea, lying east of the Golan; 3) Trachonitis, first known by the name of Argob, representing the easternmost part of Bashan, and 4) Auranitis, south of Batanea and Trachonitis. *Encyclopaedia Judaica*, (1971) Volume 4, columns 291-293.

[15] The Jordan, the largest river in Palestine, has its source in three headstreams which are Nahal Senir (al-Hazbani in Arabic) originating in Lebanon; Nahal Hermon (al-Banias) originating in Syria; and Nahal Dan (al-Liddhan) which lies within the territory of the State of Israel. The Senir is the largest of the sources of the Jordan. The Yarmuk, the second largest river in the Land of Israel after the Jordan, is also the largest tributary of the Jordan. *Encyclopaedia Judaica*, (1971) Volume 10, column 192; Volume 16, column 718.

[16] *A History of the Peace Conference of Paris*, Volume VI, pp. 164-165, edited by H.W.V. Temperley, Oxford University Press. First published in 1924, reprinted in 1969.

> settled population.
>
> At the Peace Conference, indeed, Mr. Lloyd George had asked for a Palestine restored to its ancient confines of 'Dan unto Beersheba', and M. Clemenceau is understood to have conceded the claim in principle. But just what, geographically, did the name Dan imply? Doubtless Dan of old included the basin of the Upper Jordan, very likely of the Litani, too. With the future of the Jewish National Home before them the Zionist Organization rightly pleaded that Palestine should include not only the basins of the Upper Jordan and the Litani, as part of Dan, but the northern half of the basin of the Yarmuk – all of which areas fell within the territory claimed by France under the Sykes-Picot Agreement. The attainment of such advantageous frontiers for Palestine was, however, out of the question at this time. On all Syrian questions the French had ever been difficult and uncompromising, as on matters closely affecting vital French interests. They now declined to make any concession of Syrian territory except a small extension which brought the northern extremity of Palestine up to (but not including) the town of Beisan[17] – which of old was Dan...

Hogarth admitted that the borders of Palestine should have rightfully included the basins of the Upper Jordan and the Litani, which he saw as part of the territory of Dan, as well as the northern half of the basin of the Yarmuk. However, he erred in saying that the territory encompassing these streams, in whole or in part, was "Syrian territory". It may have been decided in the Sykes-Picot Treaty that the riverine territory would be part of a projected Arab state, but historically such territory was part of the domains conquered, settled and ruled by the Israelites and their descendants and thus fit the exact definition of "Palestine territory" contemplated by the Allied-approved "Dan to Beersheba" formula for determining Palestine's borders.

The British must be condemned and held liable, together with France, for abandoning the historical formula they originally adopted as the legal criterion to fix the northern border of Palestine and for not taking strong enough exception to vicious anti-Zionist and anti-Semitic statements made by French officials during the course of the negotiations on the boundaries. They gave in much too easily to France's untenable arguments on the frontier issue, allowing it to disregard the historical formula and illegally exploit the discredited and defunct Sykes-Picot Treaty to gain an unnecessary territorial addition to French-administered Syria and Lebanon at the expense of Palestine and the Jewish National Home, which were treated as and assumed to be identical entities

---

[17] In referring to "Beisan – which of old was Dan", Hogarth actually meant and should have written "Banias", located at the foot of Mt. Hermon on the Hermon Brook, one of the sources of the Jordan River. "Beisan", more accurately called Beth Shean, lies in the Beith Shean valley, south of Lake Kinneret. In Hellenistic times, the city was called Scythopolis (the city of the Scythians).

during the boundary negotiations. As a result, Palestine and the Jewish National Home were denied direct access to or control of the precious waters of the Litani as well as those of the northern Yarmuk and most of those of the Upper Jordan, including their tributaries, all of which except for the Dan River lay within the French-mandated area and were considered vital to Palestine's economic growth and prosperity. However, as a concession to Palestine, the French agreed that it could use the surplus waters of the Upper Jordan and the northern Yarmuk, but not the waters of the Litani, for purposes of irrigation and the production of hydro-electric power.

Britain and France agreed on the boundaries separating Syria-Lebanon and Palestine at a second conference in London on December 4, 1920 when the new French Prime Minister Georges Leygues met his British counterpart, David Lloyd George. Their agreement came at the very moment when the British and French Governments submitted their respective mandates for Palestine, Mesopotamia, Syria and Lebanon for approval to the Council of the League of Nations. Without such a prior boundary agreement between the two Powers, the terms of these Mandates would have been incomplete and could not have been submitted as aforesaid. The timing of their submission and the reaching of a boundary agreement on December 4, 1920 were therefore not accidental, but coordinated. The Franco-British Boundary Convention was only formally signed about three weeks later, on December 23, 1920 at Paris, by the French Prime Minister and the British Ambassador, Charles Hardinge of Penhurst, based on a draft of the Convention that had been prepared as early as July 27, 1920. [18] In addition to the primary objective of fixing the boundaries to separate the aforementioned French and British mandated territories, the Convention also dealt with other points of an ancillary nature. These points, among others, were the construction of a British railway and pipeline, the maintenance for the benefit of France of the provisions of the Franco-British Agreement of San Remo regarding Mosul oil, the employment, as noted above, of the surplus waters of the Upper Jordan and the northern Yarmuk for the benefit of Palestine, and finally the continuation of existing French and British administered schools in the mandatory area of the other.

In a legal sense, this Convention, insofar as it defined the northern boundary of Palestine with Syria and Lebanon, must be considered an integral part of the terms of the Mandate for Palestine, specifically Article 5, even though it was technically a separate act of international law. The intention of Britain and the Zionist Organization had always been to define the country's borders in the Mandate Charter itself, but because this required extensive negotiations between Britain and France, they were omitted, in conformity with a decision taken at the San Remo Peace Conference.

These borders were originally meant by Britain to be the final borders

[18] See: Projet De Convention Franco-Britannique, *Au Sujet des Mandats de Syrie et Liban, de Palestine et de Mesopotamia* – enclosed in a letter from Vensittart to Curzon on July 27, 1920; cited as FO 371/5245; 9220; E 9125.

between Palestine and Syria-Lebanon, not subject to further change, because the British were anxious to have the Mandate for Palestine approved in a hurry in time for the December 1920 session at Geneva of the Council of the League of Nations after having submitted their request for approval on December 6, 1920 in tandem with the French. In the covering letter bearing that date which Balfour sent to the Secretary of the League of Nations with copies of the texts of the mandates for Mesopotamia and Palestine, he stated:[19]

> ... in the interest of the native inhabitants of Mesopotamia and Palestine and with the object of conferring upon them with the least possible delay the benefits of a system based on the stipulations of the Pact [i.e., Article 22 of the Covenant of the League of Nations], His Majesty's Government desire to draw the attention of the Council to the advisability of bringing to an early close the temporary arrangements at present in force.

But then a very detrimental delay arose in confirming all the Middle East Mandates which had nothing to do with the question of Palestine's borders. Had no such delay occurred, the borders for Palestine, fixed in the Convention of December 23, 1920, including the northwestern part of the Golan and Transjordan south of the Yarmuk, would have been final with no further revision, except as regards the right given only to Britain under Article 5, paragraph 3 of the Convention,

> to readjust the frontier line in the valley of the Yarmuk as far as Nasib [on the Hedjaz Railway] in such a manner as to render possible the construction of a British railway and pipe line connecting Palestine with the Hedjaz Railway and the valley of the Euphrates, and running entirely within the limits of the areas under the British Mandate.

The delay was caused by three factors. First, Italy had not been consulted by Britain and France in formulating the terms of the Mandates as specifically stipulated in the San Remo Resolution and Treaty of Sèvres. Italy wanted a specific assurance from France prior to the confirmation of the Mandate for Syria, that their economic interests in southwestern Anatolia would not be jeopardized once this Mandate went into force. The Italian demand stemmed originally from the right Italy was given to the Turkish province of Antalya (Adalia) in Asia Minor, as recognized in the secret Treaty of London (April 26, 1915) with its allies France and Britain and later upon the reservation it had made in the San Remo Resolution (April 25, 1920) that its approval for the Resolution was made subject to the settlement of the great economic interests it had as a Mediterranean power in the aforementioned province. The lack of

---

[19] See FO 371/5248; E 15390/4164/44.

French consultation with Italy about this matter understandably angered the Italians and they decided not to give their approval to any of the Mandates until the ratification of the Treaty of Sèvres. Second, the U.S., without the same justification as Italy had, also delayed the confirmation of the remaining Mandates to ensure that it and its nationals would get equal treatment in regard to the rights accorded in the Mandates to all member-states of the League of Nations. Finally, a point of jurisdiction arose as to whether the Assembly in addition to the Council of the League of Nations could also deal with the whole subject of Mandates under Article 22, paragraph 8 of the League Covenant. The Council wished to retain exclusive control over the whole question.[20]

The first two factors led to an inordinate delay of a year and a half in the confirmation of the Mandate for Palestine, followed by an additional delay of fourteen months to bring the Mandate into legal force in the country. This twofold delay gave Britain and France an unexpected and accidental opportunity to make significant changes in the boundary between Syria and Palestine, including the Transjordanian part of Palestine, that deviated from what had just been agreed to in the Boundary Convention of December 23, 1920. These changes dealt a severe blow to the territorial integrity of the Jewish National Home and were illegal in nature insofar as they deprived the Jewish People of their rights to historical areas of the Land of Israel, contrary to the intention of the San Remo Resolution.

The illegal changes concerning Transjordan are dealt with in Section 3 below. The discussion here will focus on those boundary changes made to the northern and northeastern borders of Palestine that brought about its loss to Syria of that portion of the Golan included in Palestine in the 1920 Convention.

Under the Boundary Convention of December 23, 1920, provision was made in the first paragraph of Article 2 for the establishment of a Boundary Demarcation Commission consisting of four members whose duty was

> to trace on the spot the boundary laid down in Article 1 of the Convention

between the territories under the French Mandate of Syria and Lebanon, on the one hand, and those of the British Mandates of Palestine and Mesopotamia, on the other. It was further stipulated in the last paragraph of Article 2 that

> [the] final reports by the Commission shall give the definite description of the boundary as it has been actually demarcated on the ground; the necessary maps shall be annexed thereto and signed by the Commission. The reports, with their annexes, shall be made in triplicate; one copy shall be deposited in the archives of the League of Nations, one copy shall be kept by the Mandatory, and one by the other Government concerned.

[20] See memorandum by Cecil Hurst dated December 10, 1920, found in Document FO 371/5248; 9220; E 15728.

As appears from the language of Article 2, referring to the obligation of the demarcators to trace the boundary "on the spot", or to give a definite description of its actual demarcation "on the ground", the Commission had no authority to make any deviations from the boundary prescribed in Article 1 of the Convention, apart from the exception in Article 5. The latter, as already noted, allowed for a readjustment of the frontier in the Yarmuk Valley as far as Nasib for the construction of the British railway and pipeline in order that these facilities should be wholly situated in British mandated territory. It was also stated in Article 5 that any agreement made between Britain and France for the joint use of the existing railway was subject to periodical revision, as the need arose, but that could hardly serve as a pretext for making substantial changes to the agreed boundary line of December 23, 1920.

In 1921 and 1922, the Boundary Commission demarcated the frontier from the Mediterranean to El-Hamma, an ancient site southeast of Lake Kinneret in the Lower Yarmuk Valley containing five thermal springs, today called Hammat Gader. The Commission marked the entire route from cairn to cairn, valley to valley, village to village. All the technical details of the actual demarcation *on the ground* were set down in a final report dated February 3, 1922, signed at Beirut, drawn up in both English and French. The English version was signed by Lieutenant-Colonel Stewart Francis Newcombe on behalf of Britain and the corresponding French version by Lieutenant-Colonel N. Paulet on behalf of France. Attached to the report were three signed maps which delimited the frontier in red. The Newcombe-Paulet Demarcation Report was not merely a report, but actually a new British-French frontier agreement that substantially amended the Boundary Convention of December 23, 1920, contrary to the injunction given to the members of Commission "to trace on the spot" or demarcate "on the ground" the boundary line between the British and French mandated territories.

Under the amended frontier agreement of February 3, 1922, (hereafter "the Demarcation Agreement") the area of the Golan previously included in Palestine, i.e., the northwestern part, was removed and placed in French-mandated Syria. Most ironically, so, too, was the village of Banias (the Arabic corruption of the Greek Panias) which, under its more famous Hebrew name of Dan, was earlier earmarked for inclusion in Palestine by Prime Minister Lloyd George when he adopted the historical formula "from Dan to Beersheba" to define the frontiers of the country. This formula meant that Palestine would have frontiers which approximated those of the First and Second Temple Periods, as indicated in the maps of George Adam Smith[21] which the British Government used as a guide to determine the exact frontiers of Palestine. Words to that effect were actually uttered by Lloyd George in discussing the northern limit of Palestine at the session of the San Remo Peace Conference dealing with the boundary question on April 25, 1920. The removal of the Golan and Banias from the Jewish

[21] Found in his *Atlas of the Historical Geography of the Holy Land* (1915)

National Home was therefore a clear violation of the San Remo Resolution on Palestine, based as it was on this historical or Biblical formula.

Not only was the village of Banias removed from Palestine, but also the Banias springs in Mount Hermon, one of the sources of the Jordan River, at the request of France. Britain agreed to the removal of this water source on a temporary basis only, until there were further negotiations leading to a final settlement. As it turned out, no negotiations on the subject ever took place, with the result that the Banias River remained in Syria until recovered by Israel in the Six-Day War.

In compensation for detaching the northwestern area of the Golan from the Jewish National Home, the Boundary Commission placed all of Lake Tiberias inside Palestine, in contrast to what had been done in 1920 when Syria had been allotted the eastern half of the lake with riparian rights. However, the Commission maintained fishing and navigation rights for the inhabitants of Syria and Lebanon on Lakes Huleh and Tiberias and on the River Jordan between the said lakes, the same as those enjoyed by the inhabitants of Palestine. Placing all of Lake Tiberias within the limits of the Jewish National Home may have seemed advantageous, but the frontier extended only several feet from the edge of the lake on its northeastern side to the Syrian border. This miniscule "distance" allowed Syria to exercise *de facto* control over that part of the lake. This, combined with the fact that Syria now also controlled the Golan overlooking the Galilean plain below, gave that country a great military advantage over Israel after the establishment of the Jewish State on May 15, 1948 which it used to repeatedly snipe at and bombard Jewish settlements in the area. Among the Jewish villages hardest hit were Ein Gev, Ha'On and Tel Katzir on the east shore of the lake. Syria's air and artillery attacks ended only when it was ousted from the Golan in the Six-Day War.

In addition to the boundary changes concerning the Golan Heights and Lake Kinneret, a wedge of land lying south of the lake, north of the Yarmuk River and extending to the spa of El-Hamma was transferred to Palestine in the British-French demarcation agreement of February 3, 1922. This created a point of contiguity between Palestine, Syria and Transjordan.

The Commission also made some minor deviations from the 1920 boundary line in regard to the Lebanese-Palestinian frontier between the Mediterranean coast and Metulla. The territory of Palestine was extended northward by one to three miles (two to five kilometers) with a total gain of nearly 70 square miles (200 square kilometers), particularly around the village of Sasa.[22]

The foregoing frontier changes were made while Winston Churchill, the Colonial Minister, was in charge of Palestine's affairs which had been taken out of the hands of the Foreign Office run by Lord Curzon, after the 1920 Boundary Convention was concluded. Those changes were not motivated by a desire to give the Jewish National Home a secure frontier, as is apparent from the result, but to avoid the division of Arab villages and their lands near Lake Tiberias between two states and also to safeguard the property rights of two influential Arab landowners. One was Mahmud el-Faour el-Fadl, who did not want to have his lands in the Golan divided. The other was Abbas Effendi (Knight of the British Empire), who owned land to the south of Lake Tiberias in what became the Yarmuk triangle. He lived in Haifa under British rule and he, too, like el-Fadl, did not want his lands situated in another state.[23]

The Demarcation Agreement of February 3, 1922 between the British and French Governments on behalf of Palestine and Syria-Lebanon to determine the borders between these mandated states from the Mediterranean to El-Hamma was not ratified until a year and a half after the Boundary Commission had presented its report. The ratification occurred on March 7, 1923, when the two countries exchanged diplomatic notes in the English and French languages for that purpose. Confusion has arisen as to the exact date of this revised frontier agreement. It was not March 7, 1923, the date of ratification, but rather February 3, 1922 when the report of the members of the Commission was drawn up at Beirut and contained the agreement of the two sides. This agreement took effect on March 10, 1923, three days after its ratification. The new Demarcation Agreement needed ratification since it changed the terms of the original Boundary Convention of December 23, 1920 which had gone into force upon its signing, without requiring ratification, as stated in articles 2 and 8 of the Convention. Despite the changes made in the original Boundary Convention of 1920, the latter remains very important not only because it determined the basic

---

[22] See *Encyclopaedia Judaica*, (1971) Volume 9, columns 312-313, in the item dealing with Frontiers and Boundaries of Mandatory Palestine by Moshe Brawer, Professor of Geography, Tel-Aviv University. This item is subsumed within the comprehensive Historical Survey of the State of Israel. See also the technical details of the Newcombe-Paulet Demarcation Report of February 3, 1922 respecting the Boundary Line between Syria-Lebanon and Palestine from the Mediterranean to El-Hamma, Command 1910, in Volume 13 of *The Rise of Israel*, Document 6, p. 44. All the territorial changes made are shown in three maps printed in the book *Israel's Boundaries, Past, Present and Future, A Study in Political Geography* by Moshe Brawer, on pp. 108, 114 and 116, Yavneh Publishing House Ltd., Tel-Aviv (1988).

[23] See the article by Professor Ya'akov Meron, "The Golan Heights, 1918-1967", in: Meir Shamgar (ed.), *Military Government in the Territories Administered by Israel, 1967-1980: The Legal Aspects*, Hebrew University, Jerusalem, Hemed Press (1982; reprinted 1988), p. 85.

boundaries separating the mandated territories of Palestine and Syria-Lebanon, but also because Britain and France became bound by the Draft Mandate as it existed on December 6, 1920 by virtue of its being incorporated by direct reference in both the title and text of that Convention, despite the fact that the Mandate did not go into general legal force in Palestine itself until September 29, 1923.

The reason that the Draft Mandate for Palestine of December 6, 1920 (as well as those for Mesopotamia and for Syria and Lebanon) was specifically mentioned in the Boundary Convention of December 23, 1920 despite the fact that it was only in draft form was because it was confidently assumed on the date of its submission that all the Middle East Mandates would be confirmed immediately by the League Council and so enter into force without further revision. That hope was quickly dashed by the delays caused by the United States and Italy, which gave the new Colonial Secretary Winston Churchill the opportunity to revise the Mandate for Palestine with respect to Transjordan, the Golan and certain other points and to replace the Mandate for Mesopotamia with a treaty. Churchill did not act in the spirit of the Balfour Declaration and the San Remo Resolution, to which he paid lip service, but strictly in the imperial interests of Britain, contrary to its fiduciary obligation under the Mandate to preserve the integrity of the territory of Palestine for the benefit of the Jewish National Home and State.

The incorporation of the Draft Mandate in the 1920 Convention had important consequences concerning the legality of the Demarcation Agreement of February 3, 1922, especially when weighed against the bulk of those provisions of the Mandate that had already assumed final shape or virtually so. While it is true that the Boundary Demarcation Commission established under the Convention did deviate from the boundary line laid down in Article 1 of the Convention, it is not for that reason that the 1922 Demarcation Agreement was an illegal amendment of the Convention insofar as the loss of Palestine territory was concerned. If there had not existed any restraints to the contrary, Britain and France as sovereign states would have been entitled to amend the Convention in whatever way they saw fit, but such restraints did in fact exist. They were both under an obligation not to leave out of Palestine any regions or areas that were clearly part of the historical Land of Israel as a result of the adoption of the historical formula "Dan to Beersheba" at the San Remo Peace Conference of April 25, 1920, which implicitly underlay the definition of Palestine in the San Remo Resolution. Moreover, under Article 5 of the Draft Mandate of December 6, 1920, which was then awaiting confirmation by the League Council and which bound Britain and France as mentioned above,

> no *Palestine territory* shall be ceded or leased to or in any way placed under the control of, the Government of any foreign Power (emphasis added).

Finally, under what became Article 27 of the Mandate, no modification of the terms of the Mandate could be made without the consent of the Council of the League of Nations.

In light of both the San Remo Resolution and the Draft Mandate of December 6, 1920, it was therefore illegal for Britain and France to remove the northwestern section of the Golan from Palestine and the Jewish National Home, since there was no question that that area constituted part of the historical *Palestine territory* to which both Articles 5 and 27 of the Draft Mandate were applicable. What the 1922 Demarcation Agreement did in effect was to exchange one piece of historical *Palestine territory* for other *Palestine territory*, all of which should have been originally included in Mandated Palestine when the boundary was being officially determined in 1920. There was a corresponding provision in the Mandate for Syria and Lebanon which also made the Mandatory responsible for seeing that "no part of the territory of Syria and Lebanon is ceded or leased or in any way placed under the control of a foreign Power". However, none of the territory involved in the 1922 exchange was by definition "the territory of Syria and Lebanon" in the historical sense as distinguished from "Palestine territory" in the historical sense, otherwise known as the Land of Israel. The surrender of historical *Palestine territory* to French-Mandated Syria in the 1922 Demarcation Agreement was thus by its very nature illegal, while the restoration of historical *Palestine territory* to the Jewish National Home, achieved by the 1922 Demarcation Agreement, was perfectly legal and even to be welcomed.

An additional legal question has been raised as to whether or not the consent of the League Council was required for both the 1920 Boundary Convention and the 1922 Demarcation Agreement. Logically, if the consent of the Council was needed for the approval of the Mandate as a whole, than *a fortiori* that consent was also necessary for the fixing of the boundaries of the mandated territory, especially when it is realized that the boundaries were in fact an integral part of the terms of the Mandate Charter implicit in the use of the term "Palestine". Britain and France assumed it was definitely needed, because in the Convention there are two references to the Council, once in regard to having it decide any dispute that arose in connection with the work of the Boundary Commission and once in regard to sending it a copy of the report of the Commission (Article 2 of the Convention). There is an additional reference in the ratification documents of the Demarcation Agreement in which Britain and France undertook to send to the League of Nations a copy of the Demarcation Report, together with a copy of their exchange of notes. There would logically have been no such references, had there been no need to obtain Council consent.

The same conclusion can be drawn from the fact that the Council had supervisory power over the Mandatories in regard to their actions respecting their Mandates in the territories committed to their charge and hence a self-evident right to verify if those actions complied with the terms of their Mandates. This would perforce apply to so fundamental a matter as a boundary revision affecting the definition of Palestine. In the case of the 1920 Boundary Convention, it may be assumed that when the Council finally confirmed the Middle East Mandates on July 24, 1922, it by that very act also confirmed the Boundary Convention that was an inseparable part of these Mandates. However, the same cannot be said for the 1922 Demarcation Agreement which was not brought to the attention of the Council at the time it was made, as required by the references contained in the aforementioned documents, and in any event that agreement did not take effect until after the confirmation of the Mandates by the Council.

Once the Mandates were confirmed, Britain and France were no longer free to act as they saw fit – their position in this regard was analogous to that of states signing a treaty awaiting ratification. During the interim period from signing to ratification, no changes are allowed in the treaty unless all signatories have given their consent. The same was equally true for the period from the confirmation of the Middle East Mandates (July 24, 1922) to their entry into legal force (September 29, 1923). However, in these cases, there were no signatories as such, since the Mandates did not take the form of treaties, but rather the form of decisions of the Council of the League of Nations. Modification of the boundaries of the mandated territories was a subject of concern not only to the Mandatories themselves, but also to Italy and Japan (the other two Principal Allied Powers) and especially the League Council as soon as Articles 5 and 27 of the Mandate for Palestine (and the corresponding articles of the Mandate for Syria and Lebanon) became applicable to the Mandatories. The date of applicability, as discussed above, was actually from the moment Britain and France signed their Boundary Convention on December 23, 1920 and certainly by no later than the confirmation of the Mandates on July 24, 1922.

Normally, the Mandate for Palestine would have gone into legal force immediately after its confirmation by the League Council on July 24, 1922, but because a dispute had arisen between Italy and France regarding the Mandate for Syria-Lebanon, a dispute which had nothing whatsoever to do with the Mandate for Palestine, it was decided at the request of France, who wanted its Mandate to go into force simultaneously with the British Mandate for Palestine, to postpone the date of legal commencement of both Mandates until the resolution of the Italian-French dispute which occurred on September 29, 1923. In this light, it is patently absurd to adduce a legal argument that because the Demarcation Agreement of February 3, 1922 was ratified only on March 7, 1923 (i.e., *after* July 24, 1922, but *prior to* September 29, 1923), Britain therefore had the right to make any changes in Palestine's borders it pleased on the ground that the Mandate for Palestine had not yet gone into legal force. The fact that Britain agreed to the postponement of the date of legal commencement of the Mandate in deference to its ally, France, and for that reason only, and both then persuaded the League Council to agree to the postponement, should not serve as a quasi-legal pretext for Britain making illegal changes in the borders of Palestine that would have otherwise been prohibited by Articles 5 and 27 of the Mandate, had the latter already been in force as originally planned. If Britain had really wanted to delay the confirmation process to effect boundary changes, it need not have sought confirmation of the Mandate on the date it was given. In any event, all these frontier changes that were detrimental to the integrity of Palestine and the Jewish National Home were prohibited by the historical formula for determining Palestine's borders as intended by the San Remo Resolution.

The necessity for Council consent for the boundary changes effected by the Demarcation Agreement of February 3, 1922 is demonstrated also by analogy to what was done in the case of Transjordan, which was administratively separated from the rest of Palestine on September 16, 1922, one year before the Mandate went into general legal force in Palestine on September 29, 1923. In that case the consent of the Council was considered to be absolutely necessary before the administrative separation could be considered legally valid, even though the Mandate was not yet in force. What applied to Transjordan also applied to any other boundary changes modifying the terms of the Mandate, otherwise Articles 5 and 27 of the Mandate would have been meaningless. If the date of September 29, 1923 had been the crucial date to determine whether Council consent was needed for the boundary changes made in 1922 in respect to the Golan and other areas, the British Government would not have bothered to ask the Council for its approval on September 16, 1922 for the administrative separation of Transjordan from the rest of Palestine and the Jewish National Home. In regard to the Golan, it was not until 1935, long after it had been detached from Palestine and handed over to Syria, that the Council, acting on a British request, finally approved the boundary changes made in 1922.[24]

One final question that arises is whether Palestine and the Jewish National Home could be deprived of any part of its historical territory even if the Mandatory and the League Council jointly agreed on the matter. In this context, it must be remembered that neither Britain as the Mandatory nor the League of Nations as the supervising body enjoyed sovereignty or ownership over the territory that comprised Mandated Palestine. Therefore neither had had the right, even if they had acted in unison, to cede any area of Palestine to another foreign Power as if it were their own sovereign territory to be disposed of as they pleased. Put simply, they could not give away land governed by the Mandate, which did not belong to either of them and which was only temporarily in British possession as Mandatory, Trustee and Tutor.

The prohibition on ceding any mandated or trust territory also follows from the rules governing a trust. Where a trust exists, the property to be administered by the Trustee must always be preserved or kept intact during the entire period of the trust. Applying this principle to the Mandate for Palestine, the "property in trust" meant all the land or patrimony of Palestine in its historical dimensions. None of that land constituting the trust could therefore be ceded or exchanged,

---

[24] See article by Professor Ya'akov Meron, *op. cit.*, p. 93 and n. 34 cited therein.

otherwise the legal basis for creating the trust would either be undermined or cease to exist altogether.

In consequence of these restrictions placed on both Britain and the League of Nations by the concept of sovereignty and the legal definition of a trust, the only way to reconcile Articles 5 and 27 of the Mandate for Palestine which allowed for amendments to be made to the Mandate is to assume that the text of Article 5 may be modified only in some procedural way which does not change the substance of the text dealing with the prohibition on the cession of territory. Alternatively, it is possible to assume that Article 27 did not apply to certain terms of the Mandate which, if they were allowed to be modified, would prevent the implementation of the purpose of the Mandate for which it was issued or defeat or impair that purpose substantively. This was especially the case in regard to other fundamental terms of the Mandate that granted rights to the Jewish People. For example, Article 6 confirms the right of Jewish immigration under "suitable conditions". No amendment could have been made under Article 27, even if done with League Council consent, which would have legally altered or impeded that fundamental right of the Jewish People. However, a procedural modification could have been made in the conditions under which the right granted was exercised, without damaging the substance of the right. By further analogy, neither Britain nor the League could have legally abolished the obligation set down in Article 2 to establish the Jewish National Home or weaken it in any respect, for that would have been contrary to the intentions of the Allied Supreme Council in conferring the Mandate on a Mandatory, but procedural modifications designed to assist its establishment were possible.

Based on the foregoing reasoning, it can be seen that Britain had no right to cede the northwestern part of the Golan to French-mandated Syria even if it had obtained the prior consent of the League Council under Article 27 of the Mandate. Its hands were legally tied not only by the terms of the Mandate for Palestine, but also by the principles of the Mandates System contained in the Treaty of Versailles (Article 22 of the Covenant of the League of Nations) which embodied the rules governing a trust as well as the concept of sovereignty in favour of the national beneficiary of the Mandate. In this context, it did not matter, as already noted, that the Mandate for Palestine only went into effect on September 29, 1923 and that the cession of the British-administered part of the Golan to Syria occurred before that date. The date of entry into force of the Mandate was not the determining factor in deciding whether the cession of territory was legal or illegal. Nor, too, was the date of the signing of the Treaty of Lausanne on July 24, 1923 or the date of its ratification on August 6, 1924 relevant to the question, since Turkey had already lost its sovereignty over Palestine four years prior to this Treaty, as further discussed below. The dates that were most important in determining the legality of the British move were January 10, 1920, April 24, 1920 and April 25, 1920 – the first date when the Treaty of Versailles was ratified, by virtue of which the Mandates System took effect with the above rules and concepts that it embodied, the second date when the Balfour Declaration was accepted by all four Principal Allied Powers as the reason for creating the new mandated state of Palestine, and the third date when the San Remo Resolution was adopted in its final form containing the obligatory version of the Balfour Declaration which sanctified the frontiers of Palestine based on the Jewish historical connection as the criterion of what those of Mandated Palestine ought to have been. Also relevant was the date of December 23, 1920, which expressly defined Palestine's borders under international law in the north and northeastern sections, even though those borders diverged significantly from the historical borders of the Land of Israel. In addition, the date of July 24, 1922 is important because it confirmed the terms of the Mandate for Palestine that was officially granted to His Britannic Majesty on April 25, 1920, at the San Remo Peace Conference.

In sum, the borders of Palestine were not something to be determined or trifled with in a haphazard or capricious manner dictated by the Mandatory or any other government involved without regard to the rules established for their determination, by the historical formula, the San Remo Resolution, the Treaty of Sèvres and the Mandate. The borders of Palestine and the Jewish National Home should have conformed as closely as possible to those constituting the Land of Israel in its historical dimensions and should also have been compatible with its economic, political and strategic requirements. What was done in 1920 and 1922 achieved none of these basic goals.

*Chapter 3*

# Pillars Of Support Underlying Jewish Legal Title (Sovereignty) To Palestine Under International Law

Jewish legal rights and title of sovereignty to the country of Palestine under international law were founded on three basic pillars of support, which consisted of:

1) the historical connection of the Jewish People with Palestine and the Land of Israel;

2) the principle of self-determination for the benefit of peoples and territories that were to be governed by the Mandates System under Article 22 of the Covenant of the League of Nations in the Treaty of Versailles, and

3) the designation of the Jewish People as the sole national beneficiary of the principle of self-determination in regard to the Mandate for Palestine. These three pillars of support may be summarized as follows:

### *The Historical Connection*

The historical connection of the Jewish People with Palestine in its entirety is the first and most important pillar of support for founding the Jewish legal title to Palestine under international law. Without this acknowledgment by the Principal Allied Powers of the country's storied Jewish past, there would have been no Balfour Declaration, no San Remo Resolution on Palestine, no Mandate and no Jewish National Home. The historical connection dates back to the Israelite and Judean periods, which are recounted in the Hebrew Bible, known as the Tanakh, consisting of three separate sections, the Pentateuch, Prophets and Hagiographa (Holy Writings). These historical periods in Jewish and world history cover the Period of the Patriarchs and the Judges, the First Temple Period of the Kingdoms of Israel and Judah, the Second Temple Period beginning with Persian governance, followed by Macedonian, Ptolemaic and Seleucid occupation, the Hasmonean restoration of Jewish rule in the Land of Israel and the Herodian Era. Those deeply ingrained periods in the national memory in which either Jewish rule existed in some form, whether as an independent state or as a vassal state under external control or where a Jewish population was predominant in the Land of Israel gave way to an extended period of foreign rule of the Jewish homeland, in which the Jewish population was greatly reduced in ranks, submerged or displaced. The long night of foreign subjugation and oppression ranged from Roman, Byzantine, Arab Ummayyad, all the Abbasid rulers, Egyptian Fatamid, Seljuk Turk, French Crusader, Kurdish Ayubid, Khwarazm (or Khorezmian) Turk, Mongol (Tartar), Turkish and Circassian Mameluke to Ottoman Turkish conquerors until the start of the British Mandatory Administration and renewed Jewish immigration and independence. During this extended period of subjugation and oppression, the Jews or People of Israel in Exile always maintained a physical presence and strong longing for their destroyed homeland, with the ineradicable hope of rebuilding it. In general, the historical connection refers to the unbroken chain of links which Jews of every generation had always maintained with the Land of Israel from the very first days of the Patriarchs, Abraham, Isaac and Jacob, right up to the present day, embracing a continuous history of approximately 3800 years, unmatched in human history for any other country or nation in the world.

### *The Principle Of Self-Determination In Article 22 Of The Covenant Of The League Of Nations, In The Treaty Of Versailles*

The second pillar of support for Jewish legal rights and title of sovereignty to Palestine is implicitly enshrined in Article 22 of the Covenant of the League of Nations in the Treaty of Versailles of June 28, 1919 which provided for eventual national independence or self-determination under the Mandates System for those peoples, inhabitants and communities living in the colonies and territories formerly under Turkish and German sovereignty.

The principle of self-determination was expressly mentioned in the early drafts of the proposed Covenant or Constitution of the League of Nations by President Wilson in accordance with his Fourteen Points of January 8, 1918. But in the final version of the Covenant, such express mention was eliminated, though the principle remained implicit in Article 22 of the Covenant. The Allied Powers considered that the immediate application of this principle to the severed territories of the German Empire would be impossible to realize in the African territories because the peoples or inhabitants were still in a state of savagery, while the islands in the Pacific were sparsely populated, too small in size or remote from the centers of civilization. On the other hand, it was believed that this principle could be better applied to certain communities formerly belonging to the Turkish Empire, whose development was more advanced. The unit specifically earmarked for self-determination or self-government in paragraph 1 of Article 22 was either a people (nation or community) or a territory (colony). It stated as follows:

> To those colonies and territories which as a consequence of the late war have ceased to be under the sovereignty of the States which formerly governed them and which are inhabited by peoples not yet able

> to stand by themselves under the strenuous conditions of the modern world, there should be applied the principle that the well-being and development of such peoples form a sacred trust of civilization and that securities for the performance of this trust should be embodied in this Covenant.

It was intended that the peoples and/or territories mentioned in Article 22(1) would be tutored by advanced nations acting as Mandatories until they were sufficiently capable and well-organized to obtain national independence. Article 22(1) did not name which peoples or territories would be the beneficiaries of the "sacred trust of civilization" or be the subjects of tutelage. That lack of specificity was deliberate, because it was decided by the Allied Powers that Article 22 as a whole should state only general principles and not name the peoples or territories which would benefit from the application of these general principles.

However, an important document does exist which was the forerunner of Article 22, that does specify the territories to which this article of the Covenant would apply. This is the "Smuts Resolution" named after General Jan Christiaan Smuts who, at the time he drafted the Resolution bearing his name, was a member of the British Delegation to the Paris Peace Conference, as well as a Minister without Portfolio in the Imperial War Cabinet of Prime Minister David Lloyd George. The Smuts Resolution is important because it was adopted by the Council of Ten (one of the alternate names used for the Supreme Council of the Allied and Associated Powers[1]) at a meeting of the Peace Conference on January 30, 1919 and thereupon became the basis of Article 22 of the Covenant. The Resolution details the names of six territories severed from the Turkish Empire which would be governed by Article 22, including Palestine. In regard to the former territories of the Turkish Empire it stated:[2]

> ...because of the historic misgovernment by the Turks of the subject peoples and the terrible massacres of Armenians and others in recent years the Allied and Associated Powers are agreed that Armenia, Syria, Mesopotamia, and Kurdistan, Palestine and Arabia must be completely severed from the Turkish Empire. This is without prejudice to the settlement of other parts of the Turkish Empire.

---

[1] The Council of Ten derived its name from the fact that the five Great Powers of Britain, France, Italy, Japan and the United States each had two representatives present at their meetings during the Paris Peace Conference (January 1919 to January 1920). The meetings of the four heads of state, excluding Japan, were referred to as the Council of Four. All of these meetings were called meetings of the Supreme Council.

[2] The text of the Smuts Resolution is found in the book by David Hunter Miller, *The Drafting of the Covenant*, G.P. Putnam's Sons, New York, The Knickerbocker Press (1928), Volume I, p. 109.

The names of the six countries in the Smuts Resolution were then included in President Wilson's Fourth Draft of the Covenant (his third at the Conference), dated February 2, 1919.[3]

The Allied and Associated Powers had already appointed a special committee on January 25, 1919, called the Commission on the League of Nations, to take charge of the drafting of the Covenant, and one of its tasks was to incorporate the Smuts Resolution as approved by the Peace Conference into the Covenant. At the meeting of the Commission which took place for that purpose on February 8, 1919, the Italian Prime Minister Vittorio Emanuele Orlando and the French representative, Leon Bourgeois, who was a former Premier of France, both proposed that no territories be specifically mentioned, as that would be adding too much precision. The only reason offered for not mentioning any specific territories as had been done in the Smuts Resolution was that the list of countries would inevitably be incomplete. Their proposal was adopted at the meeting in the form that became Article 22 of the Covenant, whose language was almost identical to the Smuts Resolution except for the first two paragraphs and several slight changes. The entire Covenant was accepted by the Peace Conference on April 28, 1919 for inclusion in the Treaty of Versailles which was signed on June 28, 1919.

Even though the specific names of ex-Turkish territories were not included in the final text of Article 22 as they had been in both the Smuts Resolution and Wilson's Fourth Draft of the Covenant, those territories mentioned by Smuts and Wilson can still be read into the text of that article as actual examples of territories that were originally meant to be governed by Article 22. Their names were removed not because they were rejected for future application, but only because Orlando and Bourgeois thought it would be unwise to provide a precise enumeration. Insofar as Kurdistan and Armenia were concerned, their omission from the text of Article 22 proved very costly for the Kurdish and Armenian peoples, for it allowed Britain and France to subsequently renege on the promises made to them in the Treaty of Sèvres of August 10, 1920 for independent statehood, self-government or self- determination. Those who profited from such a disastrous development for an independent Kurdistan and Armenia were Turkey, Iraq and Syria, which were enlarged at the expense of the Kurds and the Armenians who were shamefully betrayed by the European allies. In regard to Arabia, one of the six territories mentioned in the Smuts Resolution, it did not matter that its name was left out of the text of Article 22, because its future status was placed in British hands outside the framework of the Mandates System. In the case of Palestine, the omission of its name in Article 22(1) did not affect its status as a mandated territory governed by the general provisions of Article 22, but it caused much confusion over the following years as to whether the Arabs of Palestine also had a right to national independence in a partitioned state. The Arab leaders also raised the fallacious argument that

[3] David Hunter Miller, *op. cit.*, pp. 151-152.

the Mandate for Palestine which accorded the right of self-determination to the Jewish People violated Article 22 as well as Article 20 of the Covenant, which banned members of the League of Nations from undertaking obligations inconsistent with the terms of the Covenant. In light of the fact that the progenitor of the Smuts Resolution was General Jan Christiaan Smuts, who was a strong advocate of Palestine becoming a great Jewish State, a belief he shared with Lloyd George and Balfour, both of whom were serving as Prime Minister and Foreign Minister of Britain respectively when the Smuts Resolution was approved by the Peace Conference, it was a foregone conclusion that Palestine was always intended to be the country for Jewish self-determination and not Arab self-determination under Article 22 of the Covenant, and therefore the Mandate for Palestine could not be inconsistent with the Covenant, as the Arabs alleged. That conclusion is further substantiated by the world approval given to the Balfour Declaration after its public announcement in November 1917, and then to the San Remo Resolution of April 25, 1920, and finally to the Mandate for Palestine on July 24, 1922. This also included Arab approval, as evidenced by the Feisal-Weizmann Agreement of January 3, 1919, expressly stipulated in Article 3 thereof.

### *Naming The Jewish People As The National Beneficiary Of The Mandate For Palestine In Application Of The Principle Of Self-Determination Under Article 22 Of The Covenant Of The League Of Nations*

The first two pillars of support for Jewish legal rights to Palestine under international law, important as they were, did not by themselves create a title of sovereignty. It was only when the first pillar, the historical connection of the Jewish People with Palestine, and the second pillar, the principle of self-determination, were both united with the third pillar that the title of sovereignty of the Jewish People over Palestine became an established fact under international law. The joining together of all three pillars or components meant that the principle of self-determination embedded in Article 22 of the Covenant would apply to World Jewry rather than to the Arabs of Palestine, who were then the preponderant majority, outnumbering the Jews in the country by a ratio of about 6 to 1.

The principle of self-determination in the case of Palestine engendered much confusion because normally it applied to the inhabitants of a country who formed the majority of the population as the Arabs did on January 30, 1919 when the Smuts Resolution was adopted by the Council of Ten at the Paris Peace Conference and became the basis for Article 22 of the Covenant in the Treaty of Versailles. However, the normal rule for self-determination was set aside when it came to determining the fate of Palestine as Foreign Secretary Balfour made clear in a memorandum he sent to Prime Minister Lloyd George on February 19, 1919, and again in a meeting in Paris with U.S. Supreme Court Justice Louis Dembitz Brandeis on June 26, 1919 (see *infra*, Chapter 4). Instead of numerical self-determination limited to the population within Palestine, this principle would be applied on a wider basis to encompass world Jewry because of the long historical connection the Jewish People had with the country and the expectation that one day they would again become the majority of the population and the Arabs would then become the minority. This is what Balfour meant when he wrote to Lloyd George on February 19, 1919 and said:[4]

> The weak point of our position is that in the case of Palestine we deliberately and rightly decline to accept the principle of self-determination. [The author would add the words "as normally applied: to the inhabitants within a particular territory" – H.G.] If the present inhabitants were consulted they would unquestionably give an anti-Jewish verdict. Our justification for our policy is that we regard Palestine as being absolutely exceptional; that we consider the question of the Jews outside Palestine as one of world importance, and that we conceive the Jews to have an historic claim to a home in their ancient land; provided that home can be given them without either dispossessing or oppressing the present inhabitants.

Balfour amplified what he meant by self-determination in regard to Palestine when he had a friendly conversation in Paris with Colonel Richard Meinertzhagen on July 30, 1919 upon the latter's appointment as Chief Political Officer for Palestine and Syria on General Allenby's Staff. According to Meinertzhagen's diary entry for that date, Balfour spoke the following words:

> He said he was an ardent Zionist and that His Majesty's Government [H.M.G.] was committed to Zionism as our policy in Palestine…
>
> He defined the policy of H.M.G. as follows: All development, industrial schemes of all kinds, and financial assistance must be based on the principle that Zionists are the Most-favoured Nation in Palestine…
>
> He agreed in principle to the creed of self-determination, but it could not be indiscriminately applied to the whole world, and Palestine was a case in point, and a most exceptional one. To those who argued that the fate of Palestine should be decided by a Plebiscite, in which case the Arabs would have an overwhelming majority, he would reply that in any Palestine Plebiscite, the Jews of the world must be consulted; in which case he sincerely believed that an overwhelming majority would declare for Zionism under a British Mandate.[5]

---

[4] Isaiah Friedman, *op. cit.*, p. 325. The document he cites is F.O. 371/4179/2117, Balfour to the Prime Minister, 19 February 1919.

[5] Colonel Richard Meinertzhagen, *Middle East Diary – 1917-1956*. Published by Thomas Yoseloff, New York (1960), pp. 24-25. See also Isaiah Friedman, *op. cit.*, p. 326.

By applying the principle of self-determination to the Jews of the world for the reasons noted above, World Jewry indisputably became the national beneficiary of the Mandate for Palestine under paragraph 1 of Article 22. In technical legal parlance, the Jewish People were the equivalent in civil law of the person who is called *cestui que trust* (Old French: "He who trusts"): a person for whom another is appointed trustee, i.e., the beneficiary of a trust.

The decisive event to make the Jewish People the *cestui que trust* occurred when the Balfour Declaration was adopted by the Allied Supreme Council consisting of Britain, France, Italy and Japan at the session of the San Remo Peace Conference on April 24, 1920. This was followed by a decision to grant a Mandate to Britain on the next day, to implement the Balfour Declaration in application of Article 22 of the Covenant. The two decisions taken on April 24 and April 25, 1920 were together embodied in the San Remo Resolution, then in the Treaty of Sèvres and finally in the Mandate for Palestine. The result of these two decisions was to make the Jewish People not only the national beneficiary of the Mandate or Trust being set up, but also the sovereign owner of Palestine, because the country was created specifically to be the Jewish National Home and a future independent Jewish State.

As a further result of naming the Jewish People as the national beneficiary of the Mandate for Palestine, to whom the principle of self-determination would be applied, rather than to the local Arabs, the country could not be governed in the short run by the democratic requirements of representative and responsible government. Had Herbert Samuel's attempts to impose this kind of democracy at the onset of Mandatory rule been successful, newly-created Palestine would have become an Arab state instead of a Jewish one. This non-democratic feature made the Mandate for Palestine the most unique of all the mandates conferred under the provisions of Article 22 of the League Covenant.

*Chapter Four*

# Meaning of the Balfour Declaration

It is important to clarify the usage of certain terms or language in the Balfour Declaration in order to fully understand its true meaning. Prior to its adoption by the Principal Allied Powers on April 24, 1920 at the San Remo Peace Conference, the Declaration of November 2, 1917 constituted only a statement of British policy in sympathy with "Jewish Zionist aspirations", as stated in the letter containing the Balfour Declaration that was addressed to Lord Lionel Walter Rothschild, the honourary president of the English Zionist Federation, who was asked to bring it to the knowledge of the Zionist Federation of England, under the presidency of Chaim Weizmann. In its operative and affirmative part, it declared:

> "His Majesty's Government view with favour the establishment in Palestine of a national home for the Jewish People, and will use their best endeavours to facilitate the achievement of this object..."

The intent was clear enough, namely to create a Jewish State in Palestine, as proved conclusively by the Cabinet discussions on the matter, when it was finally presented for approval on October 31, 1917, but those who sought to deliberately obfuscate and sabotage the true meaning of the Declaration found ammunition in three terms used in the Declaration, the first being the word "home", the second being the phrase "in Palestine", and the third being the expression "communities" as used in the first proviso of the Balfour Declaration (as further discussed below). The first two of these terms had a strong Zionist pedigree. They were both taken from the Basle Program of the Zionist Organization approved by the First Zionist Congress on August 30, 1897, and had been used extensively in Zionist literature and work, prior to their being reproduced in the Balfour Declaration and the Mandate for Palestine.

The Basle Program which set out the aim of Zionism – "to create (or establish) for the Jewish People a home in Palestine, secured by public law" – and outlined four separate means to achieve that aim, was the product of a seven-member Program Committee chaired by Dr. Max Nordau, the celebrated author, physician and co-founder of the Zionist Organization. Most of the members of this Committee were lawyers, among whom were Dr. Max Bodenheimer, Dr.

Saul Raphael Landau, Dr. Alexander Mintz and Adam Rosenberg.

The Committee members were instructed to draw up a formula that would not only succinctly express the aim of Zionism and its means, but avoid antagonizing the Turkish Sultan and his Government, from whom Herzl hoped to obtain a charter to advance the Jewish settlement of Palestine and overcome the ban on Jewish immigration into the country. The Turkish Government even sent an official to Basle to report on the proceedings unfolding at the First Zionist Congress, which was attended by about 200 delegates, the first national assembly convened by the Jewish People themselves since the Exile began.[1] In drafting the Basle Program in three very long sessions, the Committee members subjected every word contained in the draft to the most ingenious and searching analytical criticism, according to Nordau. Guided by the instructions they had received, they deliberately omitted any reference to either a Jewish State or to international law to keep the door open for future negotiations with the Sultan. With this purpose in mind, the word "home" (*Heimstaette* in the original German) was substituted for "state" and the term "public law" (*Oeffentlich-rechtlich*) for "international law" (*voelkerrechtlich*).

Nordau is credited with formulating the classic definition of Zionism's ultimate goal in the Basle Program, originally stated to be "the creation for the Jewish People of a home in Palestine secured by law", to which Herzl in a compromise gesture added the word "public" before the word "law". This change from "law" to "public law" satisfied those delegates at the Congress who called for a direct reference to international law, which – had that been done – would likely have aroused the opposition of Turkey as constituting an infringement of its sovereignty over Palestine. As a result of this opportune change, it became apparent to all delegates that in the context of the Basle Program the reference to public law actually denoted "international law", made even more obvious by the fourth clause in the program, which spoke of the need to obtain the consent of governments [of foreign states] for the attainment of the aim of Zionism. It was likewise apparent that the formula adopted at Basle, the forerunner of the Balfour Declaration, which was carried by acclamation, definitely meant a Jewish State even though there was intentionally no specific mention of that term in the text, so as not to offend the ever-suspicious Turkish government of the Sultan, a point that was stressed by Dr. Alexander Mintz of Vienna, one of the legal experts serving on the Program Committee.[2]

Anyone doubting the true meaning of the word "home" as an alternative for "state" need only read what Herzl wrote in his diary two days after the formal closing of the First Zionist Congress to be convinced of this truth:[3]

---

[1] Nahum Sokolow, *History of Zionism 1600-1918*, Volume 1, p. 268, published by Longmans, Green and Co., London, 1919.

[2] *The Jewish Chronicle*, September 3, 1897, p. 13, at the bottom of the first column.

[3] See the booklet, *The Jubilee of the First Zionist Congress 1897-1947*, published by the Organization Department of the Executive of the Zionist Organization

> If I were to sum up the Basle Congress in a single phrase – which I would not dare to make public – I would say: In Basle I created the Jewish state. Were I to say this aloud I would be greeted by universal laughter. But perhaps five years hence, certainly fifty years hence, everybody will perceive it. The State is basically founded by the will-to-a-State of the people, even by the will of a single person who is powerful enough. Territory is only the concrete basis; the state, even when it has territory, is always something abstract.
>
> In Basle, therefore, I created this abstraction which, as such, is invisible to the great majority. Actually with infinitely small means I gradually incite the feeling for a State and impart the feeling that the National Assembly exists. – Vienna, 3rd September, 1897.

Additional evidence that the Basle Program was a blueprint for a Jewish State was the message inscribed within a red border on an azure blue Zionist Badge issued in conjunction with the Congress, which read as follows: "The organization of a Jewish State is the only possible solution of the Jewish Question".[4]

One of the means in the Basle Program for the attainment of the aim of Zionism was the strengthening and fostering of *Jewish national* sentiment and consciousness. The adjective "national" was later appended to the word "home" by Nahum Sokolow, a co-leader with Weizmann in the Zionist Movement, when he oversaw the drafting of an internal Zionist document setting forth the aim and means of Zionism towards the end of 1916 at the urging of James de Rothschild,[5] son of the famous benefactor of Jewish settlement in Eretz-Israel, the French baron Edmond de Rothschild. Sokolow had participated in the First Zionist Congress as the correspondent of the Warsaw Hebrew newspaper, *Ha-Zefirah* ("The Dawn"), which he edited and was deputed to look after the press contingent to the Congress, that numbered 25, mainly non-Jewish. During the debate on the expressions used in the Basle Program relating to the aim of Zionism, Fabius Schach, a delegate from Cologne, stated:[6]

> We want to express here the basic thoughts of Zionism. It is therefore essential that in the program we say quite plainly for what we are striving. *A national Jewish Home* (emphasis added – H.G.) – that is

through the Publishing Department of the Jewish Agency for Palestine, October 1947, Jerusalem. Herzl's diary entry quoted above is on page 5.

4 *The Jewish Chronicle*, Sept. 3, 1897, p. 15, first column. The words on the badge are a translation from German. The badge had twelve stars representing the Twelve Tribes, surrounding a Shield of David in the center of which was a lion to denote the crest of Judah.

5 See the book by Leonard Stein, *The Balfour Declaration*, new edition (1983), by the Magnes Press, Israel, pages 297 and 369.

6 *The Jubilee of the First Zionist Congress, 1897-1947*, *op. cit.*, p. 74.

> the object of our desires, not a charitable refuge. We want to make the land of our fathers into the land of our future. It is self-evident that we do not want to conquer it with the sword, but by friendly negotiations with the Sultan, through the mediation of European Powers. But without guarantees based on *international law* our *National Home* can never obtain security.

Fabius Schach, one of the drafters of the Basle Program and one of the founding members of the Zionist Movement in Germany, was thus the first person to coin the famous phrase "a National Home" in Palestine as the basic aim of Zionism, to be achieved under international law. The exact words Schach spoke at the Zionist Congress did not appear in the Basle Program formulated in August 1897 which, as already noted, referred only to "a home in Palestine secured by public law", but they likely served as a precedent 19 years later for Nahum Sokolow.

After Sokolow's revival of the expression "national home" in the internal Zionist document prepared in November 1916 concerning the Zionist program, it then appeared in most of the successive drafts of the Balfour Declaration and in the final text. The word "national" is derived from the word "nation" or "nationality". The word "nationality" also connotes the meaning of citizenship, but only if a state already exists or is intended to be established. In the case of the Balfour Declaration, that intention was clearly shown by the two provisos in the Declaration referring to the safeguards to be accorded to both the "existing non-Jewish communities in Palestine" and to "Jews in any other country". In the former case the civil and religious rights of the existing non-Jewish communities in Palestine would be maintained. In the latter case, the rights and political status of Jews outside Palestine would not be prejudiced. These two provisos would never have been inserted in the Balfour Declaration or made any sense at all if no Jewish State was intended or assumed. Hence the word "national" in the expression "national home" referred not only to Jewish nationhood or nationality in the ethnological and anthropological sense of the term, but also to future Jewish statehood and citizenship. Citizenship automatically implies statehood since only a state can confer citizenship on its residents or inhabitants. A "national home" for the Jewish People was therefore a home for the Jewish nation exclusively who would also enjoy the benefits of both statehood and citizenship.

The significant phrase "national home" should have dispelled any doubt as to what the ultimate goal of the Zionist Organization was, namely the establishment of a "Jewish State", as Herzl himself explicitly said in the book he wrote under that name, *Der Judenstaat* ("The State of the Jews", often translated "The Jewish State"), in 1896. It is further evidenced by what he wrote afterwards on the subject in his diaries, as well as in his 1902 Zionist novel *Altneuland* ("Old-New Land"), the motto of which being "If you will it, it is no fable (legend, fairytale)".

On February 7, 1917, several important Zionist leaders including Nahum Sokolow and Chaim Weizmann met with Sir Mark Sykes, the British diplomat who had negotiated the Sykes-Picot Treaty, at the home of Rabbi Moses Gaster, in London, to discuss the question of Palestine and the revival of Jewish national life there. This was an important step in the chain of events leading up to the Balfour Declaration. Two of the participants expressed their full sympathy for the establishment of a Jewish State: Lord Lionel Walter Rothschild, the person to whom Balfour communicated the Declaration later that year, and Harry Sacher, a lawyer and adviser to the Zionist leadership. Weizmann said that Jews going to Palestine would constitute a Jewish nation, which in effect meant a Jewish State. Rabbi Gaster, the Hakham of the London Sephardic community, declared that Jews should be given full rights to develop a national life and be recognized as a nation. This, too, meant an autonomous Jewish Commonwealth, as he later made clear in a speech at the London Opera House on December 2, 1917 celebrating the issuance of the Balfour Declaration.

It was well understood at the highest political level in the British Government that the phrase "National Home" as used by the Zionists and which was inserted in the Balfour Declaration meant that a Jewish State would one day come into existence. With this meaning known beforehand, the Government of Prime Minister David Lloyd George approved the wording of the Balfour Declaration. This appears from the minutes of a meeting of the Imperial War Cabinet held on October 31, 1917 convoked to consider the Balfour Declaration. At the Cabinet meeting, the British Secretary of State for Foreign Affairs, Arthur James Balfour, explained to his Cabinet colleagues the exact meaning of this term:[7]

> As to the meaning of the words "national home", to which the Zionists attach so much importance, he understood it to mean some form of British, American or other protectorate, under which full facilities would be given to the Jews to work out their own salvation and to build up, by means of education, agriculture and industry, a real centre of national culture and focus of national life. It did not necessarily involve the early establishment of an independent Jewish State, which was a matter for gradual development in accordance with the ordinary laws of political evolution.

The wording of the Balfour Declaration with the meaning and interpretation thus given to it by the Foreign Secretary on behalf of the Government was then unanimously approved by the Cabinet and formally issued on November 2, 1917.[8] Two Cabinet ministers had earlier expressed strong, and pointed

---

[7] The minutes of the War Cabinet are reproduced in *The Rise of Israel*, Volume 8, "Britain Enters into a Compact with Zionism", Part II, Document number 48, p. 138, published by Garland Publishing Inc., New York or London, 1987.

[8] News of the issuance of the Balfour Declaration was not published in the

opposition to the Declaration, Lord George Nathaniel Curzon and Edwin Samuel Montagu, but when it came to the actual vote, the former accepted it, while the latter was abroad at the time.

The British initially had two principal reasons for wanting to issue the Balfour Declaration, though other reasons also emerged during the course of the year 1917. The first immediate reason was that they sought to find a convenient and persuasive excuse for breaking loose from their recently-made commitment to France under the Sykes-Picot Treaty to jointly administer Palestine after the War with Turkey ended, in consultation with their allies Russia and Italy in an international condominium. For this purpose, they needed the invaluable aid of the Zionist leaders to convince the French as well as the Russians and Italians to abandon their projected role in Palestine, which would then allow Britain to become the sole protecting Power. Seen from this perspective, the Balfour Declaration was at the very outset a British initiative and not a Zionist one, though it was in conformity with the declared aim of Zionism to re-establish a Jewish State in Palestine with the support of European Powers, as visualized by Herzl and the delegates at the First Zionist Congress.

A second principal reason that motivated the British to issue the Balfour Declaration was that unilateral British control of Palestine enhanced their strategic position in two important areas: Egypt where since 1875 the administration of the Suez Canal was in British hands, and in all of Arabia and the Persian Gulf area, where the British had extensive economic and political interests. Palestine was also an important junction in the system of imperial communications to India and the East; it was therefore a focal point for preserving strategic British interests that would certainly be jeopardized if the country came under the rule of any other foreign power but itself, whether Germany or even their ally, France. The foregoing reasons led Britain to approach the Zionists and initiate negotiations with them, rather than the other way around, and propose the issuance of a declaration expressing open support for Jewish-Zionist aspirations in Palestine, which Britain considered vital for the protection of its far-flung Empire and to meet the danger of a possible military attack on Mesopotamia.

Beginning in June 1917 and gaining momentum in the following months, the British Foreign Office learned that Germany had made its own overtures to the Zionist Executive then located in Berlin and was planning to issue a declaration of sympathy with Zionism. To forestall any such move, which would have united Zionism with Germany and seriously undermined the support of world Jewry for the Allied cause in the world war then raging, the British Government was further strongly motivated to promise the Jews a national home in Palestine. Moreover, the issuance of a pro-Zionist declaration served another important

---

press until a week later, on November 9, 1917. The almost certain reason for the one-week delay, according to Leonard Stein, was to allow the *Jewish Chronicle*, a weekly newspaper that appeared on Fridays, to be first with the news before the British dailies. See Stein's book on *The Balfour Declaration*, The Magnes Press, The Hebrew University, Jerusalem (1983), pp. 559-560.

purpose, that of rallying all of Jewry, especially the large communities in the U.S. and Russia, to the side of the Allied and Associated Powers at a critical time in their war against the Central Powers. This aim was, in fact, the major one cited by Prime Minister David Lloyd George for the Balfour Declaration. He said that both the Allies and their enemy, the German Empire, "offered to the Jewish leaders, as the reward for their support, that in the event of victory they would secure for Israel the realization of its dreams, the restoration... of a home in the land... of their ancestors... The Jews accepted our word in preference to that given to them by the Germans. The famous Balfour Declaration... was a bargain in return for a valuable consideration given to us – the effective support of the Jews of the world to the Allied cause, notably in America, Russia and Central Europe."[9]

Other reasons that have been advanced for the issuing of the Balfour Declaration certainly existed but were not of overriding importance. One was a deep-seated religious sentiment or empathy felt by some British leaders and religious segments of the British people in favour of the Jewish restoration in Palestine. It must be noted that Balfour's own religious and Zionist sentiments were genuine and did influence his thinking, as it also did for some others. Another ancillary reason was Weizmann's great contribution in helping Britain manufacture its own explosives for productive use in World War I, which undoubtedly created a favourable atmosphere for the cause of Zionism but did not in itself explain British plans to support the Zionist program in 1917.

Nahum Sokolow, the Zionist diplomat *par excellence* was more aware than any other Zionist leader in Great Britain of what the "Jewish National Home" truly meant, based on his own deep knowledge of the origin and history of Zionism and his important role in helping to prepare a memorandum of the Zionist program, completed by November 25, 1916, as well as drafts of the Balfour Declaration, while working with Foreign Office officials Mark Sykes, Harold Nicolson and William Dunlop in 1917 during Balfour's tenure as Foreign Secretary. Sokolow used that expression for the first time in the above-mentioned memorandum containing the Zionist Program, sent to Mark Sykes on February 1, 1917 prior to a meeting with him held at Moses Gaster's house on February 7, 1917. Two earlier versions of the Zionist Program had referred to the "recognition of a separate Jewish nationality or national unit in Palestine".[10] Therefore it defies imagination and belief that it was none other than this dedicated leader who made outstanding contributions[11] to the realization of the

[9] Mr. Lloyd George's Broadcast on the White Paper, May 23, 1939, reprinted as Appendix 6 in the book *Britain Opens a Gateway*, by Silas S. Perry, Museum Press Limited, London (1944), pp. 94-95.

[10] Leonard Stein, *op. cit.*, p. 369.

[11] Among Nahum Sokolow's outstanding contributions to the cause of Zionism was his diplomatic accomplishment in obtaining from France the first official pro-Zionist pronouncement made by any of the Allied Powers. That came in the form of a letter dated June 4, 1917, from Jules Cambon, the Secretary-General of

aim of Zionism was the one who actually laid the basis and gave credence to the scandalous misinterpretation of the term "home" by the British Government after the Mandate began to be implemented on July 1, 1920 with the changeover to civilian administration. The meaning attributed to this term in the Churchill White Paper of June 3, 1922 written by Herbert Louis Samuel, was that the Jewish National Home in Palestine would only be a "centre of interest and pride" for the Jewish People, but definitely not a "state".

Samuel's false interpretation of the meaning of the word "home" in the White Paper was undoubtedly helped along by Sokolow's own statement appearing in the author's introduction to his two-volume commendable work, *History of Zionism*, published in 1919, which also featured introductions by Arthur James Balfour, still serving then as the British Foreign Secretary, and Stéphen Pichon[12], Minister of Foreign Affairs for France in the Georges Clemenceau Government. Samuel was well acquainted with Sokolow's views since both worked closely together during 1918 and 1919 when Samuel was a senior adviser of the Zionist Organization on economic and political matters and chaired the Committee that drafted the Zionist proposals to the Paris Peace Conference of 1919.

In composing the White Paper of June 3, 1922, which radically played down the true aim of Zionism, Samuel simply had to borrow Sokolow's tactically deceptive interpretation of the word "home" to determine what would be henceforth the official British interpretation of the expression, "Jewish National Home". The exact words of Sokolow as they appear in Volume I of his book are:

> It has been said and is still being obstinately repeated by anti-Zionists again and again, that Zionism aims at the creation of an independent "Jewish State" [quotation marks in the original]. But this

---

the French Foreign Ministry, expressing the sympathy of the French Government for what it called the "renaissance of the Jewish nationality in that Land from which the people of Israel were exiled so many centuries ago". The Cambon letter, not revealed at the time, also assured the support of France for the Zionist project the object of which, according to the letter, was "the development of Jewish colonization in Palestine". France's assurances as expressed in this letter to Sokolow could only have meant its approval of the rebirth of a Jewish state, though this was not explicitly stated. British Foreign Minister Balfour subsequently used the Cambon letter at a meeting of the War Cabinet on October 4, 1917 as evidence that its ally would support a similar kind of declaration to be issued by Great Britain.

[12] Three months after the issuance of the Balfour Declaration, French Foreign Minister Stéphen Pichon, at the urging of Prime Minister Clemenceau, issued a communiqué (February 1918) stating that "there is complete agreement between the French and British Governments in matters concerning the question of a Jewish establishment [*un établissement juif*] in Palestine". This appeared to constitute an official French endorsement of the Balfour Declaration, but at the San Remo Peace Conference two years later France, under a new French Prime Minister, objected to that interpretation.

> is wholly fallacious. The "Jewish State" was never part of the Zionist programme. The "Jewish State" was the title of Herzl's first pamphlet, which had the supreme merit of forcing people to think. This pamphlet was followed by the first Zionist Congress, which accepted the Basle Programme – the only programme in existence.[13]

That statement in the introduction of his acclaimed work completely overshadowed and undermined a less resolute statement to the contrary appearing in the last chapter of Volume I, where he wrote:[14]

> Happily, the stage of action has been entered in Palestine; we need only action on a larger scale. And for this enlargement and extension of its activities, for this colonization work which means the reopening and regeneration of a neglected country, Zionism needs such special facilities and protective measures as the Basle Programme contemplates when it speaks of a home for the Jewish People secured by public law. The formula may be varied, but the sense is abundantly clear: it means such rights and assurances as will, in existing conditions, help to lay the foundations of *a modern Commonwealth* for the Jewish people (emphasis added).

Sokolow's use of the term "a modern Commonwealth" echoed the same language used by Theodor Herzl in his book *Altneuland* where the phrase denoted a new model society built by Jews in Palestine, based on modern technology with a flourishing economy. However, Sokolow's absurd denial of the true intended meaning of the word "home", which he blamed on "anti-Zionists", was itself an incredible anti-Zionist statement that was an unnecessary and inane deception that no longer served the original purpose for which it was used vis-à-vis the Ottoman Turkish Government. That statement by Sokolow which soon reverberated in the Churchill White Paper immensely helped the British to sabotage the implementation of the Mandate for Palestine. It caused enormous and permanent damage to the program of Zionism, achieving the exact opposite effect of what Sokolow intended. He should have known that Jewish statehood could not be achieved by stealth and disguise.

---

[13] *Op. cit.*, page xxv of the Author's Introduction. In Chapter XLVII of Volume 1, Sokolow devotes a scant five pages to the First Zionist Congress, without discussing or analyzing the meaning of the Basle Program or reporting on the actual debates that occurred concerning it. He merely quotes the text of the Program and then deals with some of the personalities who attended the Congress and the letters received from the Grand Rabbin of France, Zadoc Kahn, and the Hakham of the Spanish and Portuguese Jewish community of London, Dr. Moses Gaster. Though Sokolow does not mention it, Kahn rejected the idea of a Jewish State while Gaster supported it.

[14] *Op. cit.*, Vol. I, Chapter LIII, p. 312.

The refutation of Sokolow's strange disavowal of a Jewish State being the true meaning of the Balfour Declaration came simultaneously from a source least expected by Sokolow, namely, the very person whom he requested to write the preface to his book, the distinguished British statesman, Arthur James Balfour. The latter's opinion on what the Declaration named after him actually meant was not given in the Introduction he wrote to Sokolow's book, but in a private letter dated September 19, 1918 which he sent before its publication to Alfred Zimmern, an authority on international relations and an adviser to the British Foreign Office. Sokolow, of course, never knew about this confidential communication between the two men. Had he known what Balfour confided to Zimmern, it would have caused him great embarrassment, since Sokolow's definition of an anti-Zionist would have included Balfour himself, one of the most outstanding and convinced Christian supporters of the cause of Zionism.

Zimmern was asked by Balfour to make corrections to the draft of the preface he had just written for Sokolow's book. The Foreign Secretary had originally intended to insert in the preface the phrase "the eventual Jewish State", but as Isaiah Friedman writes, he was forewarned by Zimmern not to do so because of the adverse repercussions this might have among the Arabs of Palestine, who had already begun to demonstrate their fierce opposition to the Balfour Declaration, aided and abetted by the British military personnel administering Palestine at the time. In reply Balfour told Zimmern:

> I am sure you are right in your warning about "the eventual Jewish State". Personally, this is what I should like to see. But it may prove impossible, and in any case it is not likely to become more possible if it is prematurely discussed.[15]

Balfour was circumspect and purposely restrained in publicly expressing his personal belief which, as noted above, was also the Cabinet interpretation given on October 31, 1917, when the Balfour Declaration was laid down as official British policy that the Jewish National Home would eventually develop into an independent Jewish State. His public reticence on the subject was wrong in light of subsequent British evasions and outright denials that no such state was

---

[15] Balfour's quotation is taken from *The Middle East Journal*, Volume XXII, 1968, pages 340 to 345, where it is found in the section entitled *Documents: Lord Balfour's Personal Position on the Balfour Declaration*. The text of Balfour's important letter is reproduced in full, as well as a comment about it by Carroll Quigley, professor of history at Georgetown University, Washington, D.C. The forewarning given by Zimmern to Balfour is cited in the book written by Isaiah Friedman, *The Question of Palestine, 1914-1918,* published by Routledge and Kegan Paul (1973), London, p. 319. It is based on a document found in the British Foreign Office FO 800/210, Balfour's Private Papers, Zimmern to Balfour, 16 September 1918, and Balfour to Zimmern, 19 September 1918.

ever intended. Public disclosure by Balfour when he was Foreign Secretary that the Jewish National Home really meant a Jewish State would have prevented such evasions and denials. However, in private, he was much more frank. For instance, he told Paul Cambon, the French Ambassador to London, on December 30, 1917 "that it would be an interesting experiment to reconstitute a Jewish kingdom".[16]

Balfour's hope for the emergence of an eventual, independent Jewish State was even more clearly enunciated in answering a question posed to him by Colonel Richard Meinertzhagen during a luncheon they attended with others on February 7, 1918, as recorded in the latter's diary. Meinertzhagen's question was:

> Do you regard this declaration as a charter for ultimate Jewish sovereignty in Palestine or are you trying to graft a Jewish population on to an Arab Palestine?

To which Balfour gave the following answer:[17]

> My personal hope is that the Jews will make good in Palestine and eventually found a Jewish State. It is up to them now; we have given them their great opportunity.

A year later, when Meinertzhagen was in Paris at the Peace Conference and about to leave for official duty in Palestine, to become the Chief Political Officer to the Military Administration, he asked both Balfour and Lloyd George what their own interpretation of the Declaration and their view of the ultimate goal of political Zionism was. They both answered that "they envisaged a Jewish sovereign State emerging from the Jewish National Home promised under the terms of the Balfour Declaration".[18]

In a conversation with American Reform Rabbi and Zionist leader, Stephen Samuel Wise, that took place in London shortly after Wise was elected by the American Jewish Congress on December 15, 1918 as one of the representatives of American Jewry to the Paris Peace Conference, Balfour defined for Wise the meaning of a "national home for the Jewish People", as used in his Declaration,

---

[16] Isaiah Friedman, *op. cit.*, p. 319. Friedman's source for Balfour's "Jewish kingdom" remark is *The Diary of Lord Bertie of Thame*, 2, p. 233. Lord Francis Bertie was the British Ambassador to Paris and was evidently repulsed by the whole idea of Zionism, since he referred to it as "rot" in his diary, as reported by Leonard Stein, *op. cit.*, p. 316.

[17] Meinertzhagen's sharp question and Balfour's frank answer appear in Colonel Richard Meinertzhagen's book, *Middle East Diary, 1917-1956*, p. 9 for the entry in the diary dated February 7, 1918, and also in Isaiah Friedman's book, *op. cit.*, p. 319.

[18] Meinertzhagen, *op. cit.*, Diary Entry of November 14, 1945, p. 205.

in the following words:[19]

> I think of Palestine, not as a home of the limited number of Jews now in Palestine, but as the future home of millions of your people who may ultimately wish to make their permanent home in Palestine.

Millions of Jews populating Palestine, as Balfour prophesied, could only be interpreted as meaning a future, independent Jewish State – just as he had indicated previously to Alfred Zimmern, Paul Cambon and Richard Meinertzhagen. Moreover, in a later interview with Weizmann on February 15, 1919, which was recorded in a memorandum written by the Zionist leader, Balfour referred to the "national home" as the "Jewish Commonwealth".[20]

The reason Balfour did not want to discuss the true meaning of the Balfour Declaration in public was, according to the Royal Commission Report of 1937, the need to conciliate, as far as might be, Arab antagonism to the National Home, which it said "was still no more than an experiment" that would take a very long time before the Jews could become a majority in the country. This was one reason no public allusion was made to a State, either in the 1917 Declaration or the 1922 White Paper.[21] It was apparently also the reason that motivated Sokolow in saying that the expression "Jewish National Home" did not mean an independent Jewish State.

However, Balfour, unlike Sokolow, did in fact make public statements on occasion which indicated in a general way that he had in mind an eventual independent Jewish State as his vision for Palestine. Two examples may be cited. First was a speech he gave to the American Zionist Medical Unit, a body organized by Hadassah to provide emergency and regular health services in Palestine, which was reported in the Jewish Chronicle of June 26, 1918, where he said:[22]

> The destruction of Judea that occurred nineteen centuries ago was one of the great wrongs which the Allied Powers were trying to redress. This destruction was a national tragedy...

Redressing this destruction could only mean the reconstitution of a Jewish

---

[19] Rabbi Wise's recall of Balfour's words is found in an article that appears in the book *The Jewish National Home*, edited by Paul Goodman, London, J.M. Dent & Sons Ltd. (1943), p. 45.

[20] Isaiah Friedman, *op. cit.*, p. 319.

[21] Palestine Royal Commission Report, Command 5479, July 1937, page 33.

[22] Quoted in the Memorandum submitted to the Palestine Royal Commission on behalf of the Jewish Agency for Palestine, p. 13. It was originally published in 1936 in London, and reprinted in 1975 by Greenwood Press, Westport, Connecticut.

State in Judea to replace the one destroyed by Rome.

In a second eloquent and glowing speech indicating his desire to make the whole of Palestine into a Jewish State, he told a public demonstration held by the English Zionist Federation on July 12, 1920, at the Royal Albert Hall, London, to celebrate the conferment of the Mandate for Palestine upon Great Britain and the incorporation of the Balfour Declaration in the Treaty of Peace with Turkey:

> ...the Great Powers... most especially Great Britain, has freed them, the Arab race, from the tyranny of their brutal conqueror... I hope they will remember it is we who have established the independent Arab sovereignty of the Hedjaz. I hope they will remember that it is we who desire in Mesopotamia... a self-governing, autonomous Arab State, and I hope that, remembering all that, they will not grudge that small notch – for it is no more geographically, whatever it may be historically – that small notch in what are now Arab [populated] territories being *given* to the people who for all these hundreds of years have been separated from it – *but surely have a title to develop on their own lines in the land of their forefathers*, which ought to appeal to the sympathy of the Arab people as it, I am convinced, appeals to the great mass of my own Christian fellow-countrymen...
>
> The deep underlying principle of self-determination really points to a Zionist policy, however little in its strict technical interpretation it may seem to favour it...
>
> None but those who are blinded by [religious or racial bigotry] would deny for one instant that the case of the Jews is absolutely exceptional and must be treated by exceptional methods...
>
> We may look forward with a happy gaze to a future in which *Palestine will indeed*, and in the fullest measure and degree of success, *be made a home for the Jewish People* (emphasis added).[23]

Sokolow was not the only dissimulator who practiced the fine art of mendacity in order to disguise the true aim of Zionism shrouded under a false cover. His superior in this respect was Herbert Louis Samuel, his former working "partner" in furthering Zionist aspirations.

Samuel was the first Jew openly professing the Jewish faith ever to sit in a British Cabinet, that of Prime Minister Herbert Henry Asquith. Samuel occupied several different ministerial posts, including Postmaster General and Home Secretary. While in Asquith's Cabinet, he outlined a scheme to Edward Grey, the Foreign Secretary, for setting up a Jewish State in Palestine. In January

---

[23] The quotation above is taken from a book called *Speeches on Zionism* (pp.24ff) by the Right Honourable, the Earl of Balfour, edited by Israel Cohen, with a foreword by the Rt. Hon. Sir Herbert Samuel, published by Arrowsmith, London, 1928.

1915 he submitted a memorandum to Asquith on the future of Palestine and two months later, he circulated a second memorandum to the Cabinet in which he referred to the possibility of establishing an autonomous Jewish State in Palestine. Nothing came of his proposal because of the opposition of Asquith.

The idea of a Jewish State being eventually established in Palestine remained part of his thinking as late as November 2, 1919, when in a speech at the London Opera House he stated:[24]

> No responsible Zionist leader has suggested the *immediate* (emphasis added) establishment of a complete and purely Jewish State in Palestine... The policy propounded before the [Paris] Peace Conference, to which the Zionist leaders unshakably adhere is the promotion to the fullest degree that the conditions in the country allow of Jewish immigration and of Jewish land settlement... in order that with the minimum of delay the country may become a fully self-governing Commonwealth under the auspices of an established Jewish majority.

In the same speech, Samuel said that the ideal of Zionism will not be fully attained unless Palestine becomes a State in which all its inhabitants, with special reference to the Arabs, are helped to attain a higher standard of civilization. He referred to the creation of a "Zionist Palestine" – a code word for a Jewish State, with boundaries in the North to include the Litani River, "to secure for Palestine the water resources, without which it cannot fully prosper", and with regard to the Eastern boundary, he said:

> Every expert knows that for a prosperous Palestine, an adequate territory beyond the Jordan is indispensable.

As a result of his strong identification with the official British policy of the Jewish National Home, he was appointed the first High Commissioner for Palestine by Prime Minister Lloyd George, while present together with Sokolow and Weizmann in San Remo at the fateful time when deliberations were taking place by the Allied Supreme Council at the Peace Conference called to dispose of Turkey's ex-Middle Eastern territories, though not attending the secret diplomatic sessions. He thus became the first Jewish ruler in the Land of Israel since the days of Shimon Bar Kokhba and the later brief reign in Jerusalem of Nehemiah b. Hushiel (614-617) during the period of the Persian invasion. Samuel's appointment was naturally welcomed by Weizmann and Sokolow, both of whom he consulted before he accepted it. They naively believed he would loyally carry out the project of the Jewish National Home. For that very reason

[24] Taken from a pamphlet published by the Zionist Organization entitled *Zionism – Its Ideals and Practical Hopes*, London 1919.

his appointment was fiercely opposed by the Arabs, in particular by Emir Feisal who told Field Marshall Edmund Allenby in Cairo:[25]

> The news of [Samuel's appointment as High Commissioner for Palestine] had had [the] worst possible effect upon [the] Arab population, since Mr. Samuel is universally known to be a Zionist whose ideal is to found a Jewish State upon [the] ruins of a large part of Syria, i.e., Palestine.

Curzon, an avowed skeptic and opponent of Zionism who apparently knew the real character of Samuel better than Weizmann and Sokolow, telegraphed to Allenby:[26]

> You should reply to Feisal as follows: ... His Majesty's Government... are convinced that his high reputation and administrative experience render him peculiarly qualified for the task and because his authority with the Zionists, coupled with his well-known sympathy for the Arabs, will enable him to hold [the] scales even and to exercise a pacifying and moderating influence at the outset of [the] new system of civil administration... We believe that the Emir and the Arabs will find in him a sincere friend.

Curzon's words about Samuel would soon prove prophetic. Upon assuming his new position in Jerusalem, he turned his back on Zionism causing great despair among his former colleagues in the Movement and retracted the unreserved support he had previously expressed for the establishment of Palestine as a Jewish State in enlarged borders, including the Litani River in the North and Transjordan in the East. He assumed a new pro-Arab stance because he was anxious to appease vociferous Arab opposition to the implementation of the Balfour Declaration and its inherent idea of a Jewish State. In authoring the "Churchill" White Paper, he gave the most glaring misinterpretation of the meaning of the Jewish National Home. That misinterpretation had the most baleful consequences for the implementation of the Mandate for Palestine. It prevented the independent Jewish State from ever coming into being during the British Administration of the country and exacerbated Arab violence against the Jews of Palestine.

Samuel's hostile attitude toward establishing a Jewish State after he became High Commissioner never changed. On July 31, 1946, he stated in the House of Lords:

> "...the Jews must abandon their plan, their demand for all Palestine as a Jewish Commonwealth, which is utterly impracticable and could

[25] *Documents on British Foreign Policy*, Vol. 13, Document No. 257, p. 284.

[26] *Op. cit.*, No. 261, p. 287.

> never come about..." (Hansard, Situation In Palestine, HL Deb 31 July 1946, Vol 142, cc 1150-222.)

Contrary to what both Sokolow and Samuel wrote and said – and even Chaim Weizmann sometimes followed their lead – British and American and other statesmen of the same era when the global political and legal settlement in the Middle East was originally being devised in the years between 1917 and 1920 took a different and more honest position on the subject of a Jewish State, in particular Arthur James Balfour, David Lloyd George, General Jan Christiaan Smuts, U.S. President Woodrow Wilson and even Winston Churchill before he became Colonial Secretary.

Reference has already been made to Balfour's attitude. It will suffice now to quote what the American President said on the subject, as recorded in a statement he made on March 2, 1919 to a delegation of the American Jewish Congress composed of Julian Mack, Dr. Stephen Wise, Louis Marshall and Bernard Richards:

> As to representations touching Palestine, I have before expressed my personal approval of the Declaration of the British Government regarding Palestine.
>
> I am moreover persuaded that the Allied Nations with the fullest encouragement of our Government and people are agreed that in Palestine there shall be laid the foundations of a Jewish Commonwealth.[27]

Questioned later about the authenticity of these remarks by Secretary of State Robert Lansing, President Wilson explained to his intimate confidant and adviser, Colonel Edward Mandell House, "that while he did not use the direct words quoted, he did in substance say what was quoted, though the expression 'foundations of a Jewish Commonwealth' went a little further than his idea at the time. All that he meant was to corroborate his expressed acquiescence in the position of the British Government with regard to the future of Palestine.[28]

This explanation was not a disclaimer or denial of the original statement of March 2, 1919, though it superficially appeared to have lessened its clarity. However, any loss of clarity was restored soon afterwards when President Wilson reaffirmed that the Balfour Declaration promised or presaged a Jewish State, when at a meeting held at the Paris Peace Conference on May 3, 1919, he stated:[29]

---

[27] From the book *America and Palestine*, edited by Reuben Fink, 1944, page 33 and also quoted in the *New York Times*, March 3, 1919.

[28] Leonard Stein, in his book *The Balfour Declaration* citing the research article by Professor Selig Adler, "The Palestine Question in the Wilson Era". See p. 596 of Stein's book, *op. cit.*

[29] Leonard Stein quoting P. Mantoux, *Les Deliberations du Conseil des Quatre*

> ... the Palestine problem was difficult because the British and American Governments had promised the Jews a State, to which the Arabs strongly objected.

It is noteworthy that President Wilson referred not only to the promise made by the British Government to facilitate a Jewish State on November 2, 1917, but also to the American promise to the same effect. This was a clear and logical reference to the fact that the British Government did not issue the Balfour Declaration until it had obtained President Wilson's prior approval which was given on October 13, 1917 by the President to Colonel Edward Mandell House, and which he then passed on to the head of the British Military Intelligence in the U.S.A., William Wiseman, who in turn telegraphed the President's approval to Balfour's private secretary, Eric Drummond, on October 16, 1917.

President Wilson's endorsement of the draft Balfour Declaration, after an initial reluctance to do so, related to what Leonard Stein called the "Rothschild Formula" or "Zionist Draft" of the Balfour Declaration, which read as follows:[30]

> 1. His Majesty's Government accepts the principle that Palestine should be reconstituted as the National Home of the Jewish People.
> 2. His Majesty's Government will use its best endeavours to secure the achievement of this object and will discuss the necessary methods and means with the Zionist Organization.

It is most likely that Wilson's favourable attitude to the draft Balfour Declaration as embodied in the Rothschild Formula of July 18, 1917 was based on the advice of Supreme Court Justice, Louis Dembitz Brandeis, a trusted and highly esteemed adviser, though Leonard Stein gives the credit to Colonel House, whom he depicted as being anti-Semitic.[31] Had President Wilson not approved the Balfour Declaration in advance, Stein was of the opinion that it may have been "the end of the Declaration".[32] This certainly attested to the importance of securing President Wilson's advance approval of the contemplated pro-Zionist Declaration by the British Government, but this opinion of Stein is untenable in light of the fact that Britain was, in any event, intent on issuing the Balfour Declaration in favour of Jewish-Zionist aspirations for its own reasons, as noted above, and it would not have been dissuaded from doing so even had President Wilson withheld his endorsement for the draft Balfour Declaration.

---

(Paris, 1955), I, p. 482. See Stein's book, *The Balfour Declaration*, p. 596, n. 30.

[30] Leonard Stein, *op. cit.*, pp. 470, 471, 496, 506, 507, 518, 529, 530 and 664 concerning the "Rothschild Formula" of July 18, 1917 and President Wilson's sympathetic endorsement of it.

[31] *Ibid.*, pp. 508-509.

[32] *Ibid.*, p. 510.

Wilson's pronouncement that "in Palestine there shall be laid the foundations of a Jewish Commonwealth" was also earlier reflected in the Report and Recommendations of the Intelligence Section of the American Delegation to the Peace Conference in Versailles, which was drawn up on January 21, 1919 for the use of President Wilson and the delegation. In discussing the recommendation "to recognize Palestine as a Jewish State as soon as it is a Jewish state in fact", the Report of the Intelligence Section stated as follows:

> It is right that Palestine should become a Jewish state, if the Jews, being given the full opportunity, make it such. It was the cradle and *home* (emphasis added) of their vital race, which has made large spiritual contributions to mankind, and is their only land in which they can hope to find a *home* of their own; they being in this respect unique among significant peoples.[33]

As can be clearly seen from all the above quotations and statements made by the leading British and American public figures directly involved in the formulation and approval of the Balfour Declaration and by those who understood its significance, the term "home" meant a "Jewish State". Both "home" and "state" were used interchangeably by the British and American Governments, until the publication of the Churchill White Paper on June 3, 1922.

Aiding and abetting Sokolow and Samuel in their grand deception and greatly compounding the confusion was Ahad Ha'Am, the pompous pen-name used by Asher Ginsberg, a bitter foe of Herzl and the mentor of Weizmann who also took part in the discussions leading to the Balfour Declaration. After it was issued, he stated erroneously in a trouble-provoking exegesis that the words "in Palestine" did not mean that the whole country of Palestine would become the Jewish National Home.

His pedantic, narrow and anti-Zionist reading of what the Balfour Declaration stood for may be gleaned from the following excerpt from the introduction to his work, "Ten Essays of Zionism and Judaism":[34]

> Had the British Government accepted the version suggested to it – that *Palestine should be reconstructed as the national home* (emphasis added) of the Jewish People – its promise might have been interpreted as

[33] From the book by David Hunter Miller, *My Diary at the Conference at Paris*, Vol. IV, pp. 263-264. Reproduced in the Book of Documents submitted to the General Assembly of the United Nations by the Jewish Agency for Palestine, New York, May 1947, compiled by Abraham Tulin, p. 8.

[34] London, 1922, pp. xvi-xix. Cited in the Memorandum submitted to the Palestine Royal Commission on behalf of the Jewish Agency for Palestine, pp. 98 ff.

> meaning that Palestine, as it now is, was restored to the Jewish People on the ground of its historic right… without regard to the consent or non-consent of its present inhabitants… But the *British Government*, as it stated expressly in the Declaration itself, *was not willing to promise anything which would harm the present inhabitants of Palestine and therefore it changed the Zionist formula and gave it a more restricted form* (emphasis added)… When, then, the British Government promised to facilitate the establishment *in Palestine of a national home* (italics in the original) for the Jewish people – *and not*, as was suggested to it, the *reconstitution of Palestine as the national home* (emphasis added) of the Jewish People – that promise meant two things. It meant in the first place recognition of the historic right of the Jewish people to build its national home in Palestine, with a promise of assistance from the British Government, and it meant in the second place a negation of the power of that right to over-ride the right of the present inhabitants and to make the Jewish People sole ruler in the country.

The interpretation attributed by Ahad Ha'Am to the Balfour Declaration was artificial and groundless in two very important factual respects which have not been properly refuted to this very day. On the contrary, Ahad Ha'Am's interpretation has been an accepted article of faith embraced by many people ever since he first expounded it.

The first mistake of fact in Ahad Ha'Am's interpretation was that he said the British Government intentionally changed the Zionist formula of the draft Balfour Declaration from the Zionist proposal, i.e., that "Palestine should be reconstructed as the national home of the Jewish People" to "a more restricted form", i.e., the national home would be established "in Palestine", thus implying, according to his overworked imagination that the home would not include all of Palestine, but only a part of it. This change was made, he said, in order not to harm "the present inhabitants of Palestine", by which he meant not harming the alleged national rights of the Arabs of Palestine. This was a gross misstatement of fact because the "Zionist formula", also known as the "Rothschild formula" of July 18, 1917 which used the stylistic form "Palestine as" instead of the alternative form of "in Palestine", was changed for a different reason altogether that had nothing to do with harming the alleged national rights of the Arabs living in Palestine.

As noted above, the Rothschild or Zionist formula had been approved by Balfour and the British Foreign Office in a slightly amended form and also by U.S. President Woodrow Wilson on October 13, 1917. Leonard Stein, author of the acclaimed book, *The Balfour Declaration*,[35] says it is not clear whether the Rothschild formula had in fact been approved by Prime Minister Lloyd George, but it is highly unlikely that Balfour would have approved this formula without

---

[35] *Op. cit.*, p. 506, n.10.

informing the Prime Minister. Moreover, Stein cites Chaim Weizmann as saying in a telegram[36] he sent to Supreme Court Justice Louis Dembitz Brandeis that Lloyd George's approval had in fact been given to the Rothschild formula. When this formula was submitted for approval to the War Cabinet on September 3, 1917, it was discussed in the absence of both Prime Minister Lloyd George and Foreign Secretary Balfour. During the discussion the members present heard a scathing denunciation of the proposed draft Declaration from Edwin Montagu, a self-described "Jewish Englishman" and cousin of Herbert Samuel who had just been appointed to the Cabinet as Secretary of State for India. He was an uncompromising and vociferous opponent of Zionism, who followed in the footsteps of his father and grandfather – who were ennobled as the First and Second Barons Swaythling – both of whom also vigorously opposed Zionism. Montagu had been the private secretary of Herbert Asquith from 1906 to 1916, who as Prime Minister had absolutely no sympathy for Zionism and thought that its aim was just a fantasy, not to be taken seriously. In line with this thinking, Montagu rejected the concept that a "Jewish Englishman" like himself could have any allegiance or connection to a Jewish National Home in Palestine. He was afraid that the draft Declaration as already approved by Balfour and the Foreign Office, as well as by Lloyd George (according to Weizmann) would compromise his own rights and status to participate in the government of the British Empire. The immediate result of Montagu's fierce attack on Zionism was to postpone Cabinet approval of the Rothschild formula at the session of September 3, 1917, since it did not take into account the opposition to it from a number of wealthy, assimilated or half-assimilated English Jewish leaders, most of whom had forgotten their identity as Jews, that included not only Edwin Montagu but others such as Claude Montefiore, Leonard Cohen, Philip Magnus and Lucien Wolf. A new formula was thus needed to address the concerns of these smug and self-betraying anti-Zionist Jews who wanted nothing to do with the establishment of the incipient Jewish National Home and were anxious to demonstrate their obsequious loyalty to Great Britain as proud citizens of the Mosaic faith, whose mirror image was also found among Jews in Germany. The Rothschild formula was therefore rejected by the Cabinet not because of the wording of the formula "that Palestine should be reconstructed as the national home of the Jewish people" as falsely alleged by Ahad Ha'Am, nor because of any concern related to what he called "the negation of the right of the present inhabitants [to Palestine]", but only to allay the apprehensions of upper-crust English Jews who feared that the rights and political status they enjoyed in Britain would be adversely affected by issuing the draft Declaration as it was then formulated.

In his memoirs, written many years after the War Cabinet meeting of September 3, 1917, Leopold Stennet Amery, who served it as an assistant secretary and in 1924 was appointed Colonial Secretary, said he was asked

[36] *Ibid.*, p. 506.

by Lord Alfred Milner, an important member of that Cabinet who in 1918 became Secretary of State for War, to devise a new formula "which would go a reasonable distance to meeting the objections, both Jewish and pro-Arab, without impairing the substance of the proposed declaration".[37]

The new formula he drafted – known as the Milner-Amery formula – replaced the Rothschild version and became the one eventually approved by the War Cabinet on October 31, 1917. It contained two provisos, the first relating to "the existing non-Jewish communities in Palestine" and the second to "Jews in any other country".[38] Amery's belief that the first proviso related to the Arabs is not supported by any convincing evidence or documentation and is logically untenable, as discussed immediately below. It is really only a retrospective reflection or afterthought influenced by subsequent Arab opposition to the Balfour Declaration or a memory dimmed by lapse of time. Or it may simply be a mixup or confusion in Amery's mind of two separate terms, "Arab" and "Moslem". No one in the Cabinet except for Lord Curzon even raised the point dealing with the consequences the about-to-be-issued Balfour Declaration might have on the Arabs of Palestine. Curzon set out his views in a memorandum of October 26, 1917 circulated to the Cabinet, but in the actual discussion five days later on approving the Balfour Declaration, he abstained from any further mention of this particular point. Balfour, in stating the objections to issuing the Declaration at the Cabinet meeting on October 31, 1917, did not even consider the possible reaction of the Arabs of the country, which would certainly not have been the case had that been a serious matter of concern at the time. By contrast, he did take into account the Edwin Montagu argument against Zionism in regard to the future position of Jews in Western countries.[39] Therefore it is evident that the reference to the "existing non-Jewish communities in Palestine" was in fact not a reference to Arabs as such, and their alleged national rights, but rather to the various religious communities in Palestine, particularly those whose traditional rights were of special concern to the French, Italian and Russian Governments and to the Roman Catholic and Orthodox Churches, as will now be examined in greater detail.

The term "community" can mean either a people, nation or religious group. It has the meaning of a people or nation when referring to the whole populace of a country who are organized or grouped together as a nation and deserving of national independence as exemplified in paragraph 4 of Article 22 of the Covenant of the League of Nations which speaks of "certain communities formerly belonging to the Turkish Empire [which] have reached a stage of development where their existence as independent nations can be provisionally recognized...." In another sense, the term "community" denotes not a people or nation, but a religious group comprised of all the individuals belonging to

---

[37] Stein, *op. cit.*, p. 520.

[38] *Ibid.*, p. 522.

[39] *Ibid.*, p. 547.

a particular religion, as indicated by three explicit provisions in the Mandate for Palestine, namely, articles 14, 15 and 23. The term "communities", in the plural, as used in the first proviso of the Balfour Declaration cannot refer simultaneously both to a nation and a religious community, but can hold only one specific meaning. Upon logical analysis, it cannot mean a people or nation in the context of the Declaration for two reasons: First, a people or nation as a single entity cannot have "civil and religious rights", but only the individuals who belong to it. In stark contrast, a religious community existing as a body politic or corporate can possess such rights, as was the case with all the minority religious communities, excluding that of the Moslem faith, which existed in the Ottoman Empire at the time the Balfour Declaration was issued and enjoyed special rights and privileges or autonomy in matters of personal status under the Millet system. Second, the actual word used in the first proviso of the Declaration is "communities", in the plural; thus more than one community was envisaged. If this term meant peoples or nations, it would make no sense at all, since there were essentially only two separate peoples recognized as such, who then lived in what unofficially was Turkish "Palestine" which did not then exist as a separate territory or administrative unit, one being the Jews of the country, numbering about 85,000 at the start of the Great War and only 60,000 at its termination, and the other, the Arabs, numbering over a half-million. Since this proviso spoke about "existing non-Jewish communities", it could not have referred exclusively to the Arab people, when the term plainly applied to several different groups or communities apart from the Jews. For these two reasons, "the civil and religious rights of existing non-Jewish communities" could only have denoted all the various religious communities which then existed in Palestine, of which there were about a dozen.[40] This proviso was inserted in the Balfour Declaration in order to provide a firm and explicit guarantee to the various religious communities in Palestine that the rights and autonomy they always enjoyed under Ottoman Turkish rule would not be harmed or impaired in any way in a future independent Jewish State. This first proviso, far from detracting from the operative part of the Balfour Declaration aimed at the creation of such a state, only reinforces what was truly intended, as does the second proviso in the Declaration, to the effect that nothing shall be done which may prejudice "the rights and political status enjoyed by Jews in any other country".

If any further evidence is needed about the actual meaning of this term, it is supplied by the San Remo Resolution as adopted at the San Remo Peace Conference in April 1920. Britain was at pains to assure the French

---

[40] In a schedule added in 1939 to the Palestine Order-in-Council, 1922, the religious communities are listed as follows: the Eastern (Orthodox), the Latin (Catholics), the Gregorian Armenian, the Armenian (Catholic), the Syrian (Catholic), the Chaldean (Uniate), the Greek (Catholic) Melkite, the Maronite, and the Syrian Orthodox. Neither the Copts and Ethiopians nor the Anglicans and other Reformed Churches are mentioned in this list. *Encyclopaedia Judaica*, Jerusalem (1971), volume 9, Column 909.

representatives to the Conference, Prime Minister Millerand and Philippe Berthelot, Secretary-General of the Ministry of Foreign Affairs, that all the civil and religious rights of the Roman Catholic community in Palestine would be scrupulously respected, as provided for in the Balfour Declaration which they wanted inserted in the Treaty of Peace with Turkey. The French, after much reluctance, agreed to the British demand but only on the condition that Britain as the Mandatory Power of Palestine would ensure that in the Mandates article of the Treaty there would be a provision that "the rights hitherto enjoyed by the [existing] non-Jewish communities in Palestine" would not be surrendered, in deference to the religious protectorate which France had theretofore been exercising over the Roman Catholic or French Latin population in Palestine. The San Remo Resolution also provided for a special commission to be appointed by the Mandatory "pour étudier toute question et toute réclamation concernant les differentes communautes religieuses et en établir le règlement." Based upon these British assurances given by Prime Minister Lloyd George and Foreign Minister Lord Curzon, France accepted the British administration of Palestine under the Mandates system and agreed to abandon its religious protectorate for the Roman Catholic community. The use of the term "communautes religieuses" in the San Remo Resolution is thus irrebuttable proof that the words in the Balfour Declaration regarding "existing non-Jewish communities" referred not to a people or a nation, such as the Arab people residing in what became Mandated Palestine, but only to religious communities, in existence at the time the Declaration was announced.

In this connection, it must be emphasized that the rights enjoyed by these religious communities included neither national nor political rights, but strictly civil and religious rights. Civil rights within the British meaning of this term included "all ordinary rights" (the term used by Lord Curzon) and freedoms enjoyed by the inhabitants of a nation, such as the freedom of religion and of speech, the right to make contracts and hold property, to sue and be sued, etc. Civil rights includes individual political rights, such as the right to vote and to take part in elections that apply only to citizens and cannot by definition apply to national or religious entities or collectivities. Religious communities which exist as bodies politic or corporate therefore have no political rights, unlike the members of these communities which certainly have such rights. The absence of political rights attached to a religious community constitutes an additional reason for saying that the term "communities" in the first proviso did not refer to the Arab people or nation, even though the Arabs of Palestine comprised for the most part the actual members of these religious communities and enjoyed those rights on an individual basis.

There is also external evidence provided by Italy and the United States as to the intended meaning of the first proviso in the Balfour Declaration. In a letter dated six months after the Declaration was issued, May 9, 1918, and written to Nahum Sokolow, the Chairman of the Zionist Executive, by the Marquis Imperiali, the Italian Ambassador to London, on the direct instructions of the

Italian Foreign Minister, Baron Sidney Sonnino, it is significant that Imperiali, in endorsing the Balfour Declaration on behalf of his government, used the words "nothing shall be done to prejudice the existing juridical and political status of the existing religious communities", thus replacing the word "non-Jewish" with "religious". Similarly, in the Lodge-Fish Joint Resolution of both Houses of the U.S. Congress, signed by President Warren G. Harding on September 21, 1922, the proviso reads as follows: "it being clearly understood that nothing shall be done which may prejudice the civil and religious rights of Christian and other non-Jewish communities, and that the holy places and religious buildings and sites in Palestine shall be adequately protected."

To confuse the meaning of a nation with that of a religion is a serious error, except as regards the Jewish People, whose definition embraces both aspects. In the case of the Arab people and the Moslem religion, the two are distinct terms and should not be treated as synonymous or interchangeable. This mistake was made not only by Ahad Ha'Am and Leopold Amery, as already noted above, but surprisingly, also by Lloyd George and Lord Curzon. In his reaction to the Malcolm MacDonald White Paper of May 17, 1939, Lloyd George, in a radio broadcast denouncing the White Paper and expressing his dismay at "an act of national perfidy which will bring dishonour to the British name", also declared that Britain had fulfilled its promise to the Arabs that "nothing should be done which might prejudice the civil and religious rights of existing non-Jewish communities in Palestine.[41] This, however, was a promise to the Christian and Moslem communities in Palestine, and not to the Arab people as such. The only explanation for this gaffe was that Lloyd George, a staunch supporter of Zionism and the Jewish National Home, was really thinking not of the Balfour Declaration as he remembered it, but of the concluding part of Article 2 of the Mandate for Palestine. This article contains the exact promise mentioned by Lloyd George, which he mistakenly attributed to the Balfour Declaration, namely that the Mandatory shall safeguard "the civil and religious rights of all the inhabitants of Palestine, irrespective of race and religion". This promise in Article 2 did definitely apply to all Arab inhabitants of Palestine.

Two decades earlier, Lord Curzon made the same mistake as Lloyd George. In the minutes of the San Remo Peace Conference, it is recorded that he said the following:[42]

---

[41] A transcript of the broadcast is found in the book *Britain Opens a Gateway*, by Silas S. Perry, Museum Press Limited, London (1944), pp. 94-96. A similar comment about British pledges given to the Arabs was made by Lloyd George in his book, *The Truth about the Peace Treaties*, Gollancz (1939), Vol. II, pp. 1140-1142. He is quoted there as saying "that the establishment of a Jewish National Home would not in any way... affect the civil or religious rights of the general population of Palestine" nor "diminish the general prosperity of that population".

[42] British Secretary's Notes of a Meeting of the Supreme Council Held at the Villa Devachan, San Remo, Saturday, April 24, 1920 at 4 p.m., Secret I.C.P. – 105; Cab 29/86; 103138, p. 7 of the Secretary's Notes.

> ...the [Balfour] Declaration contemplated, first, the creation of a national home for the Jews, whose privileges and rights were to be safeguarded under a military Power. Secondly, it was of the highest importance to safeguard the rights of minorities: first the rights of the Arabs, and then of the Christian communities. Provision for this was made in the second part of the declaration...

Curzon, in foreseeing the day when the Arabs would be a minority in an independent Jewish State, mistook the rights accorded to non-Jewish communities, including the whole Moslem community, for rights accorded to the Arab people, as such, thereby confusing two separate entities, a religious community and a nation. Like Lloyd George, he may have mixed up what was said in Article 2 of the Mandate with the first proviso in the Balfour Declaration. At the time of the San Remo Peace Conference, the Mandate already existed in draft form and was being revised under his direction.

Returning now to Ahad Ha'Am's wrongful interpretation in regard to the Balfour Declaration, the second factual mistake made in his analysis was that in substituting the Milner-Amery formula for the Rothschild formula, the British Government gave the Balfour Declaration "a more restricted form", which thereby weakened it. This observation is also supported by Leonard Stein who says in his book, *The Balfour Declaration*, that "there was a progressive or noticeable watering down of the formula originally proposed for the Balfour Declaration by the Zionists as submitted by Rothschild in July and in substance approved by Balfour".[43] Stein even berated President Wilson for saying that the Balfour Declaration "laid the foundations of a Jewish Commonwealth". According to Stein's restricted interpretation of the Declaration, "Wilson allowed himself to be quoted as favouring even larger promises to the Zionists than those contained in the Balfour Declaration".[44] Ahad Ha'Am's assessment and Stein's support for it is belied by Amery's recollection that he was instructed by Milner not to impair the substance of the proposed Declaration as previously set out in the Rothschild formula. Though Amery's memory may have betrayed him in regard to his substitution of "Arabs" for "religious communities" in the first proviso of the Balfour Declaration, it did not betray him on the point of his not having to change its substance, because to have done so would have defeated the very purpose for which the Balfour Declaration had been issued. The British Government at the time was trying to win over world Jewish support for the war being waged by the Allied side against the Central Powers and also needed Jewish support to morally and legally justify its invasion and imminent conquest of Palestine and the unilateral setting up of a British administration, unhampered by any constraints imposed by its French, Russian and Italian

[43] Stein, *op. cit.*, read in combination with pp. 522, 626.

[44] Stein, *op. cit.*, pp. 595-96.

allies. These important objectives would have been frustrated if a pro-Zionist declaration did not envision a national home that would become a Jewish State. The Zionists wanted to look forward to something more than a national home that would have only been a cultural center as championed by Ahad Ha'Am. It was only because the Jewish National Home did in fact mean an eventual independent Jewish State that the Balfour Declaration excited the Jewish masses of the world and attracted enormous support. The Declaration was by no means restrictive in nature or any different in substance from the Zionist Draft of July 18, 1917, even with the two provisos in it, as wrongly alleged by Ahad Ha'Am, Stein and anti-Zionist detractors. Its true meaning was conveyed by Lord Robert Cecil, the assistant Foreign Secretary who in the critical months of 1917 was closely concerned with the handling of the Palestine question, and hence was well-versed on its future as seen by the British. In a memorable turn of phrase, he told a thanksgiving meeting organized by the English Zionist Federation held at the London Opera House on December 2nd:[45]

> Our wish is that Arabian countries shall be for the Arabs, Armenia for the Armenians, and Judea for the Jews.

"Judea for the Jews", whatever Cecil's alleged deviation from its plain message afterwards, as reported by Leonard Stein[46], clearly meant no recognition of Arab national rights to Palestine, just as Jews would likewise have no national rights in "Arabian countries" or in Armenia.

Cecil's pithy description of what was intended for Palestine, Arabia and Armenia matched perfectly the assessment given by Lloyd George to Colonel Edward Mandell House, President Wilson's closest adviser at the time, less than three weeks after the Declaration was issued. On November 20, 1917, the British Prime Minister told him:[47]

> P.M. and Lord Chief Justice took dinner with us... What Great Britain desires are [various gains in Africa and elsewhere]... Palestine to be given to the Zionists under British or, if desired by us, under American control.

The Balfour Declaration as finally approved by the Cabinet on October 31, 1917 meant in essence a British promise to help facilitate the establishment of an independent Jewish State in Palestine that naturally covered the whole country. The Zionist draft of July 18, 1917 which both Ahad Ha'Am and Stein said was later made more "restricted" or "watered down" had by the time the

[45] Stein, *op. cit.*, p. 565. See also p. 186.

[46] *Ibid.*, pp. 599-600.

[47] From an entry in Colonel Edward M. House's diary for November 20, 1917. See Stein, *op. cit.*, p. 599.

final text was formulated the same essential meaning. Moreover, the phraseology of the final text was a mere reiteration of the Basle Program which also meant a Jewish State, even without the adjective "national" in front of the word "home". Whether Palestine was to be established "as" a Jewish State or whether a Jewish State was to be established "in Palestine" was saying the very same thing in two different ways. The substance was not changed at all. In fact, the two provisos in the final text, as already noted above, provided additional proof that a Jewish State was to be established, since otherwise there would have been no need for tacking them onto the Milner-Amery draft.

All the emphasis placed by Ahad Ha'Am, a cultural Zionist, and Herbert Samuel, a renegade Zionist, on the phrase "in Palestine" was for the sole purpose of diminishing Jewish national rights to the whole country, while at the same time creating brand-new Arab national rights to the same country. Unfortunately, their false and tendentious interpretation of what "in Palestine" meant, succeeded in confusing everyone, causing a distinction to be made between two synonymous terms, the Jewish National Home and Palestine, that laid the theoretical justification for the partition of the country.

In light of the far-reaching consequences stemming from the phrase "in Palestine", it is worthwhile to take a closer look at the true meaning of that phrase. It originated from the same Zionist source as did the word "home", in the Basle Program of August 1897, which is why its usage in the Balfour Declaration was not contrary to the aim of Zionism. At the time those words "in Palestine" were inserted into the Balfour Declaration on November 2, 1917, the country of Palestine, as previously noted, did not yet officially exist. The latter was carved out of Ottoman Turkish territory by the coalition of Principal Allied Powers at the San Remo Peace Conference on April 24, 1920, for one purpose only, to create a Jewish State, that was euphemistically called a Jewish National Home in accordance with Zionist tradition and provenance. When Palestine was born as an embryonic Jewish State on this date, it was never imagined or believed by anyone it would then be re-divided or partitioned into separate Jewish and Arab States, since the Arabs received other territories elsewhere from the Allied Nations for the express purpose of setting up their own sovereign national states. Palestine as a whole was designated exclusively for the benefit of the Jewish People for the eventual establishment of an independent Jewish State, as Balfour made indisputably clear in his explanation to the War Cabinet on October 31, 1917 and in his Royal Albert Hall speech of July 12, 1920. This was also made clear in Lord Robert Cecil's aforementioned public pronouncement (Judea for the Jews) and Lloyd George's divulgence to Colonel House on November 12, 1917. The oft-heard statement that Palestine was a land promised to both Arabs and Jews by the British Government is as false as any deliberate lie can be. It contradicts completely the global political and legal settlement made by the Principal Allied Powers after World War I, which King Hussein of the Hedjaz and his son Feisal originally accepted – in the Weizmann-Feisal Agreement of January 3, 1919 before reneging on this agreement.

In this particular context, against the background of its genesis, the words "in Palestine" could have only a single meaning: the country as a whole, embracing both banks of the Jordan, which is exactly what Herbert Samuel said on November 2, 1919, and what Winston Churchill wrote in 1920.[48] Their statements were earlier confirmed by a person with first-hand knowledge of why Palestine was created, General Jan Christiaan Smuts, who was a member of Lloyd George's War Cabinet when the Balfour Declaration was approved by it and actively participated in the framing of the policy it expressed. On the first anniversary of the Declaration he wrote that among the most striking changes wrought by the War were "the liberation of Palestine and its recognition as the Home of Israel".[49] It was, therefore, Palestine as an integral entity, not one or more particular parts or regions of the country that was recognized by the British Government as the Jewish National Home in its policy pronouncement on November 2, 1917. To imply or warn, as did Ahad Ha'Am, that "in Palestine" meant only a part of the country was a flagrant untruth and misrepresentation.

A complete refutation of his argument emerges from the meeting held between Foreign Secretary Balfour and Justice Brandeis in Paris on June 24, 1919, as recorded in a memorandum prepared by Felix Frankfurter, who was also present, along with Lord Eustace Percy.[50] Brandeis told Balfour that for the realization of the Zionist program, three conditions were essential. The first condition was:

> That Palestine should be the Jewish homeland and not merely that there be a Jewish homeland in Palestine. That, he assumed, is the commitment of the Balfour Declaration and will, of course, be confirmed by the Peace Conference.

The second essential condition concerned the securing of adequate boundaries for a "Jewish Palestine", not merely "a small garden within Palestine", to ensure economic elbow-room and "self-sufficiency for a healthy social life". As regards the northern boundary of Palestine, Justice Brandeis said that Palestine needed to have "control of the waters".[51] This could only

---

[48] In: *Illustrated Sunday Herald*, London, Feb. 8, 1920.

[49] *The Zionist Review* (London), November 1918. Cited by Leonard Stein in his book on *Zionism*, p. 90, published by Kegan Paul Trench & Trubner & Co., Ltd. (London) 1930.

[50] The memorandum located in the private papers of Lord Balfour is printed in *Documents on British Foreign Policy 1919-1939*, First Series, Volume IV (1919), Appendix II, p. 1276. Lord Eustace Percy was, at that time, private secretary to Mr. Balfour.

[51] Justice Brandeis, who strongly believed that Palestine needed "control of the waters" for its northern boundary, as related to Balfour on June 26, 1919, had undoubtedly convinced President Wilson to make the same demand to

have been a reference to the waters of the Litani River, the headwaters of the Jordan River on Mount Hermon and those of the Yarmuk River in the region of Bashan (Turkish *Hauran*). Further, as regards Palestine's boundary on the east, Brandeis advocated the Transjordan line:[52]

> For there the land is largely unoccupied and settlement could be made without conflict with the Arabs much more easily than in the more settled portions of the North.
>
> Mr. Balfour pointed out that in the East there is the Hedjaz railroad which can rightly be called a Mohammedan railroad.
>
> The Justice replied that there is land right up to the railroad, and Mr. Balfour stated that he felt Feisul (*sic!*) would agree to having an eastern boundary of Palestine go up to the Hedjaz railroad.

The third essential condition was[53] "that the future Jewish Palestine must have control of the land and the natural resources, which are at the heart of a sound economic life. It was essential that the values which are being and will be created because of the cessation of Turkish rule and due to British occupation and Jewish settlement should go to the State and not into private hands."

In response, Balfour expressed entire agreement with the three conditions laid down by Brandeis. According to Frankfurter's memorandum:[54]

> No statesman could have been more sympathetic than Mr. Balfour was with the underlying philosophy and aims of Zionism as they were stated by Mr. Justice Brandeis, nor more eager that the necessary conditions should be secured at the hands of the Peace Conference and of Great Britain to assure the realisation of the Zionist program.

---

the British and French Governments that was transmitted to them by telegraph on February 10, 1920. See *supra,* Chapter 2. For his part, Balfour shared the same view as Brandeis and Wilson, as can be verified independently by two separate memoranda the Foreign Secretary composed, the first dated June 26, 1919 and the second on August 11, 1919 (*Documents on British Foreign Policy*, First Series, Vol. 4, no. 211, p. 302 and no. 242, p. 347). In addition, Balfour told Richard Meinertzhagen on the day he was appointed the Chief Political Officer for Palestine and Syria on General Allenby's Staff, that both the Litani and Mount Hermon should be included in Palestine. See Meinertzhagen's *Middle East Diary, op. cit.,* pp. 25, 355 and see also his map on p. 64, known as the Meinertzhagen Line, encompassing both the Litani and Mount Hermon, that was also approved by Prime Minister Lloyd George and later by Lord Curzon. Despite British and American unanimity on the question of Palestine's northern boundary, France's stubborn opposition proved to be an insurmountable obstacle, thus leaving Palestine in the end without "control of the waters".

[52] *Ibid.,* p. 1277.

[53] *Ibid.,* p. 1277.

[54] *Ibid.*, p. 1278.

On the key question of whether the principle of self-determination would apply to Palestine in which the wishes of the people in the country would be consulted as to its future in accordance with the norms of democracy, Balfour expressed his opinion and that of his government in the following manner:[55]

> The situation is further complicated by an agreement made early in November [1918] by the British and French, and brought to the president's [Woodrow Wilson's] attention, telling the people of the East that their wishes would be consulted in the disposition of their future. One day in the Council of Four, when the Syrian matter was under dispute, the President suggested the dispatch of a Commission[56] to find out what the people really wanted. It began with Syria, but the field of enquiry was extended over the whole East. Mr. Balfour wrote a memorandum to the Prime Minister [David Lloyd George] and he believed it went to the President, pointing out that Palestine

---

[55] *Ibid.*, p. 1277.

[56] In March 1919, President Woodrow Wilson proposed the setting-up of an Inter-Allied Commission to determine the wishes of the various peoples of the region on their political future. This Commission was opposed by both Britain and France. However, Wilson, acting under pressure from anti-Zionist groups, especially Christian missionary interests, appointed Henry C. King, President of Oberlin College, Ohio, and Charles R. Crane, a Chicago businessman who supported Christian missions in the Middle East, to visit the region for the intended purpose, a task they undertook in June 1919. In their report submitted in August 1919, first published in condensed form in December 1922 and officially published only in 1947, they advocated a single mandate for a united Syria comprising both Lebanon and Palestine to be entrusted to the United States, or if it declined, to Great Britain. The Commission further recommended "a serious modification of the extreme Zionist program for Palestine of unlimited immigration of Jews, looking finally to making Palestine distinctly a Jewish State." According to King and Crane, the governing principle for Palestine should be the one laid down by President Wilson on July 4, 1918: "The settlement of every question on the basis of the free acceptance of that settlement by the people immediately concerned". Since the non-Jewish population of Palestine – nearly 90% of the whole – were emphatically against the entire Zionist program, their wishes should be respected. Thus, they concluded that Jewish immigration to Palestine "should definitely be limited and the project for making Palestine distinctly a Jewish commonwealth should be given up".

The Commission's report, which ran completely counter to the Balfour Declaration and the Jewish historical connection with Palestine was never submitted either to the Paris Peace Conference or to the San Remo Peace Conference, and its recommendations were ignored by the Principal Allied Powers. See the article by Herbert Parzen in the *Encyclopedia of Zionism* under the entry "King-Crane Report", Herzl Press/McGraw-Hill, New York (1971), Vol. 2, p. 673 and see also the *Encyclopaedia Judaica* (1971) under the entry "Palestine, Inquiry Commissions", Vol. 13, cols. 30-31.

> should be excluded from the terms of reference because the Powers had committed themselves to the Zionist programme, which inevitably excluded *numerical self-determination. Palestine presented a unique situation. We are dealing not with the wishes of an existing community but are consciously seeking to re-constitute a new community and definitely building for a numerical majority in the future. He has great difficulty in seeing how the President can possibly reconcile his adherence to Zionism with any doctrine of self-determination, and he asked the Justice how he thinks the President will do it. The Justice replied that Mr. Balfour had already indicated the solution and pointed out that the whole conception of Zionism as the Jewish homeland, was a definite building up for the future as the means of dealing with a world problem*[57] *and not merely with the disposition of [an] existing community. Mr. Balfour stated he supposed that would be the President's line* (emphasis added).

Finally, on the question of the Sykes-Picot Treaty and on various other difficulties facing Great Britain in the Middle East, Balfour sagaciously noted:[58]

> He [Balfour] continued to point out the great difficulties that are now besetting Great Britain in the East, namely: the ferment in the whole Eastern world, the Mohammedan restlessness, *the new Arabic imperialism* and the relations with the French. Then there is also the Sykes-Picot Agreement; that is dead, but its ruins still encumber the earth. He was anxious that the Justice should know these difficulties for they all bear upon the Palestinian situation (emphasis added).

A year later, on July 12, 1920, when he was then Lord President of the Council, Balfour, no doubt remembering his Paris meeting with Brandeis, reiterated the meaning of the Declaration of November 2, 1917, before a public gathering at the Royal Albert Hall, London:[59]

---

[57] The "world problem" as Balfour saw it, as appears in the context of his discussion with Brandeis, was the solving of Jewish homelessness through the implementation of the Zionist program. This problem affected not merely the existing community in Palestine, but all of world Jewry then numbering about 14 million, the vast majority living in Russia and the rest of Eastern Europe. The Jews in those countries were leaders in the revolutionary movements occurring there, according to Justice Brandeis. He wanted these very same Jewish leaders to find other constructive channels for expression and make positive contributions to civilization, which led him to the conviction that Zionism was the answer to the Jewish problem. Balfour expressed his agreement, adding that, of course, these were the reasons that made both of them such ardent Zionists. *Ibid.*, pp. 1276, 1278.

[58] *Ibid.*, p. 1278.

[59] See footnote 23 of this Chapter.

> ...we may look forward with a happy gaze to a future in which *Palestine will indeed*, and in the fullest measure and degree of success, *be made a home for the Jewish People* (emphasis added).

Palestine in full, not merely a part of it, was therefore the area of the Home, as understood by Balfour, who had given the authoritative meaning of the Declaration named in his honour to the War Cabinet on October 31, 1917, when he submitted it for approval. There was no dissent or challenge to that meaning. Even the great adversary of the projected Home, Lord Curzon, in a memorandum of November 16, 1917, printed for the War Cabinet, entitled "Peace Negotiations with Turkey", affirmed:

> ...we have pledged ourselves, if successful, to secure *Palestine as a national home for the Jewish People* (emphasis added)...[60]

The foregoing reflections and convictions of Brandeis, Balfour and Curzon, three central figures who were intimately aware of the true meaning of the Balfour Declaration when it was being considered by the War Cabinet, should be sufficient to lay to rest Ahad Ha'Am's absurd and woolly contention that the phrase "in Palestine" meant that the Jewish National Home would not embrace all of Palestine. His interpretation of that phrase was so artificial and contrived it lacked any credibility except for those people such as Herbert Samuel who saw this innocent phrase as a handy weapon to distort the meaning of the Balfour Declaration and advocate the partition of Palestine.

In any case, Article 5 of the Mandate made it clear that Palestine could not be partitioned. It reads as follows:

> *Article 5.*
>
> The Mandatory shall be responsible for seeing that no Palestine territory shall be ceded or leased to, or in any way placed under the control of, the Government of any foreign Power.

Stripped of its natural meaning or context as used in the Balfour Declaration and Mandate for Palestine, it is possible in some cases or circumstances to conceive of the preposition "in" as contained in the phrase "in Palestine" to mean a part of something, rather than the whole of it. By way of illustration, it may be said that Palestine is "in Asia", France is "in Europe" and Canada is "in North America". Obviously, in this different context from that prevailing in the Balfour Declaration, Palestine is not equivalent to the whole of Asia, France is only a part of Europe, while Canada is smaller than North America.

However, it can be logically proven, not only from the political genesis of the Balfour Declaration, but also from an internal examination of the Mandate

[60] F.O. 800/214.

for Palestine which gave legal meaning to the whole of the Declaration that the phrase "in Palestine" in a geographical sense meant Palestine as a whole and not Palestine in a limited part.

The official title of the Mandate is the Mandate for "Palestine", which indicates the entire area. The Mandate is entrusted to a Mandatory to administer "the territory of Palestine", as the first recital of the Preamble states. This administration naturally applied to the whole country. The Principal Allied Powers selected His Brittanic Majesty (i.e., the British Government) to be the Mandatory for "Palestine" as stated in the fourth recital of the Preamble, which is another indication that the whole country was to be under Mandatory rule for the implementation of the Balfour Declaration. Article 2 of the Mandate says that the Mandatory shall be responsible for "placing the country" under such political, administrative and economic conditions as will secure the establishment of the Jewish National Home, as laid down in the Preamble…". The "country" referred to here by a combined reading of the first and fourth recitals of the Preamble together with Article 2 of the Mandate is necessarily the whole country of Palestine, not a mere part of it, and that country is also where the establishment of the Jewish National Home will be secured. Hence "Palestine", "Jewish National Home" and "country" must all be one and the same thing by the very language of these two recitals in the Preamble and Article 2 of the Mandate read together.

Furthermore, it is clear from the context of Article 2 that the Jewish National Home is intended to cover the whole of Palestine as an undivided land. There is no difference then in saying that the Jewish National Home is "in Palestine" or that "Palestine, as a whole," is the Jewish National Home. This also follows from the syllogism used in deductive logic where A is B, B is C, and therefore C is exactly equivalent to A and vice-versa. Substituting actual words for the letters in this equation of logic, we get the following syllogism: 1) The whole of Palestine is the country under Mandate, 2) this country shall be placed under various conditions to secure the establishment of the Jewish National Home, i.e., the country is the Jewish National Home, 3) therefore the Jewish National Home is the whole of Palestine under the Mandate.

In addition to the rules of deductive logic which can be invoked in this particular case to prove conclusively that the expression "in Palestine" refers to the whole country and not any particular section of it, there is also other internal evidence in both the Balfour Declaration and the Mandate for Palestine which proves the very same point.

In the Balfour Declaration, the words "in Palestine" appear twice, once in regard to the establishment "in Palestine" of a national home for the Jewish People and once in the double proviso which reads: "it being clearly understood that nothing shall be done which might prejudice the civil and religious rights of existing non-Jewish communities *'in Palestine'*, or the rights and political status enjoyed by Jews in any other country."

It is evident that in the latter usage concerning the civil and religious rights of existing non-Jewish communities "in Palestine", these words can only refer to the whole of Palestine and not one particular part or parts of it, as was fallaciously claimed to be the case for the corresponding usage of the same phrase ("in Palestine") in the operative and affirmative part of the Balfour Declaration. Those who sought to make this baseless distinction for only the opening half of the Balfour Declaration but not for its closing half containing the double proviso in what is a textbook case of syntactical parsing, did so only to derive a new, unintended meaning from the Balfour Declaration in order to allow the Arabs living in Palestine to also claim national and collective political rights to the country that were provided only for the Jewish People and hence to partition the country to satisfy the rights of both peoples.

Ahad Ha'Am's unfounded, polemical interpretation was gleefully adopted in the Churchill White Paper where Samuel wrote as follows:

> ...the terms of the [Balfour] Declaration referred to do not contemplate that *Palestine as* (emphasis added) a whole should be converted into a Jewish National Home, but that such a Home should be founded *in Palestine* (italics in the original).

This interpretation by Samuel and Churchill duplicitously allowed for the immediate detachment of Transjordan from the rest of Palestine, slicing away by sleight of hand a fertile and productive part of eastern Palestine that was considered absolutely essential for the economic viability of the Jewish National Home. This was more than ironic since Britain had argued in their boundary negotiations with France in 1919-1920 that the Sykes-Picot line needed considerable rectification in favour of the Zionists in order to give Palestine, i.e., the Jewish National Home, an eastern boundary that would encompass at least a part of Transjordan, namely, the fertile territory east of the Jordan but west of the Hedjaz Railway (or from a point south of Dar'a in Syria, near the Jordanian border – biblical Edre'i – across the desert to Abu Kamal).[61] It is true that Curzon and his Foreign Office team had wanted to exclude Transjordan from Palestine whatever may have been the legal requirements imposed by the acceptance of the "Dan to Beersheba" formula as confirmed in the minutes of the San Remo Peace Conference and previously in the Lloyd George-Clemenceau Agreement of December 1, 1918. But the determining factor in considering its legal status was not Curzon's desire or opinion, but the actual fact that as of December 23, 1920, the fertile portions of Transjordan became officially part of the Jewish National Home, as a direct consequence of the signing of the Franco-British Convention on that date. The Convention was an

---

[61] *Documents on British Foreign Policy*, First Series, Vol. 4, No. 338, pp. 577 ff. See the Comments of the Political Section of the British Peace Delegation, made by Foreign Office officials E.G. Forbes Adam and Robert Vansittart on December 18, 1919 concerning the note of M. Philippe Berthelot on December 12, 1919 [167432/15167/44].

international treaty, constituting a part of international law and therefore legally binding on both Britain and France, even though the Mandate had not yet been confirmed or entered into general legal force. As a result of the Samuel-Churchill concoction, both parts of Palestine, east and west of the Jordan, now had separate administrations. Relying not only on verbal and grammatical acrobatics, the counterfeiting team of Samuel and Churchill also justified the detachment of Trans-Jordan from the Jewish National Home by arguing in a roundabout way that a promise to recognize and support the independence of the Arabs made in a letter dated October 24, 1915 from Sir Henry McMahon, then British High Commissioner in Egypt, to the Sharif of Mecca, later King Hussein of the Hedjaz, did not include Palestine west of the Jordan. By means of this circular logic, Samuel and Churchill falsely stated that the promise made to Hussein therefore included Palestine east of the Jordan, which they promptly turned over to Abdullah, an emir of the Hedjaz and not an emir of Transjordan, which had not hitherto existed as a separate legal and political entity. Even Abdullah himself admitted in his memoirs that this territory was intended for inclusion in the Jewish National Home just prior to the time he began his long rule there.

It seems unlikely that either Samuel or Churchill really believed their own distorted logic or official pronouncements about Transjordan, since each had previously stated shortly before the publication of the 1922 White Paper the very contrary of what they now said was required – the separation of Transjordan from Palestine. If Samuel really believed that Transjordan was promised to Hussein in 1915, why then as a high Zionist official intimately associated with Weizmann and Sokolow did he advocate its inclusion in Jewish Palestine on November 2, 1919, when he spoke at a public rally to celebrate the second anniversary of the Balfour Declaration before he knew he would return to full-time British Government service on July 1, 1920? When he subsequently went to Palestine as High Commissioner, he suddenly changed his mind, in order to align himself fully with the anti-Zionist views of Curzon, his new superior, who sought to limit the physical dimensions of the Jewish National Home by subtracting three-fourths of it.[62] His change of opinion was an act of pure hypocrisy because as a member of Herbert Asquith's Cabinet in 1915-1916, he was fully cognizant of the McMahon-Hussein Correspondence and had he really believed Transjordan was excluded from the Jewish National Home because of that Correspondence, he would never have said what he said on November 2, 1919. He adopted his new view in the 1922 White Paper on the definition of Jewish Palestine only to suit the convenience of himself and be in harmony with the wishes and intentions of British policymakers in the Churchill Colonial

---

[62] According to the figures of Dr. Abraham Heller, the area of Transjordanian Palestine consisted of 84,530 square km. or 32,640 square miles, while Cisjordanian Palestine had an area of 27,020 square km. or 10,435 square miles. See the book *Whose Land?*, by Dr. Abraham Heller, translated by Artziah Hershberg, edited by Burton Ravins, published by Lifsha Jameson, Tel-Aviv.

Office and before that, in Curzon's Foreign Office, all of which were radically different from the original plan to make Transjordan up to the Hedjaz Railway a part of Jewish Palestine.

The years went by and Churchill out of office demonstrated very strong concern and support for the Jewish National Home, especially in his stirring reaction to the MacDonald White Paper of May 17, 1939. When he spoke in the House of Commons on May 23, 1939 denouncing this ignominious and illegal White Paper in the harshest language possible for a British parliamentarian, as being a betrayal of the pledge of a Jewish National Home in Palestine, he still stuck, however, to the distinction that was made in his name in the White Paper of 1922 "between making a Jewish National Home *in Palestine* and making *Palestine [as]* a Jewish National Home." (emphasis added).

Samuel, too, continued to make this untenable distinction as late as April 23, 1947 when he said in a debate on Palestine in the House of Lords that not a Jewish State was promised, but rather a Jewish National Home; not Palestine as a Jewish National Home, but a Jewish National Home in Palestine." (Hansard, Palestine, HL Deb 23 April 1947, Vol 147, cc 57-121).

That distinction was always completely wrong, whether from a legal, political or geographical point-of-view or simple common sense. Despite Churchill's fine oratory in defence of the Jewish National Home in Palestine, he was directly responsible, along with Samuel, for the great damage that pernicious distinction caused to the Jewish National Home. It was late in the day to make amends for his own betrayal of the Jewish People as Colonial Secretary in 1921-1922. The 1922 White Paper was always cited by succeeding British Governments as the "legal" justification to stunt the growth of Jewish Palestine not only in relation to Transjordan but in Cisjordan as well, and to diminish their obligations towards the Jewish People under the Mandate. The Churchill White Paper was without doubt the real reason why the Balfour Declaration and Mandate for Palestine were never implemented during the period of British Administration in the way it was originally intended, because it prescribed a different course of action in favour of the Arab population of Palestine, contrary to the explicit provisions of the Declaration and the Mandate.

As a final proof that the phrase "in Palestine" did not mean what Ahad Ha'Am, Samuel and Churchill all said it meant, it is only necessary to count the number of times this phrase is used in the Mandate for Palestine, to further understand its true meaning. The Mandate document contains a Preamble of seven recitals and 28 articles. The words "in Palestine" appear three time in the Preamble and 12 times in the text of the document, in Articles 4, 7, 8, 9, 13, 14, 16 (twice), 17, 18 (twice) and 23. Any objective reading of these provisions where the words "in Palestine" appear, leads only to one natural conclusion: they were intended to apply to the whole country to preserve intact the Jewish National Home on both sides of the Jordan.[63]

[63] It may be wry humour to note that Samuel's letter of appointment from the Foreign Office dated June 19, 1920 stated that he was to be High Commissioner

It is exasperating to note that what was set down in the Declaration as a clear statement of restoring Palestine to the Jewish People for the purpose of reconstituting a Jewish State became immediately entangled in a fog of grammatical ambiguity not caused by the words actually used in the Declaration, but by motivated and tendentious attempts to change the plain meaning of the Declaration to one different from the original one intended by its framers to suit new British policy considerations. Notwithstanding all the denials and obfuscations that followed in the wake of the 1922 White Paper, the Balfour Declaration was meant to create a Jewish State in Palestine embracing the whole country in the boundaries that were eventually fixed for it in the Franco-British Convention of December 23, 1920.

It was up to the Jewish leaders who led the Zionist Movement at the time to press upon the British Government the clear and unequivocal meaning of the Balfour Declaration, to establish the Jewish State without hindrance once the Balfour Declaration was adopted by the coalition of Principal Allied Powers at the San Remo Peace Conference on April 24, 1920. But those leaders were too timid and dependent upon the Government, which allowed the British to escape from the paramount obligation imposed upon them in Article 2 of the Mandate to place Palestine under the appropriate conditions that would secure the establishment of the Jewish State intended by the Balfour Declaration. Blame therefore rests squarely on Weizmann and Sokolow and those who supported their passive views in the face of British betrayals, or those like Ahad Ha'Am who did not even discern any betrayal but instead inspired it with his nonsensical and damaging interpretation of the Balfour Declaration. Blame, too, naturally rests on all the British leaders and responsible officials who refused to carry out the Balfour Declaration as originally intended and inverted or distorted its true meaning, with the exception of a few.

One of the persons who worked very closely with Weizmann while he was President of the Zionist Organization was Leonard Jacques Stein, who served as the legal adviser of the Organization from 1920 to 1929 and then as honourary legal adviser to the Jewish Agency from 1929 to 1939. He drafted the very thorough Zionist Memorandum submitted to the Palestine Royal Commission before which he also testified as an expert witness on the meaning of the Balfour Declaration and the legal intricacies of the Mandate for Palestine. He was without doubt the most important legal figure in the Zionist Movement during the Weizmann period of leadership, responsible for propounding the Zionist legal case to the British Government and its investigative bodies.

If there was a great failure by Weizmann and other Zionist leaders, as indeed there was, to correctly understand and discern the legal ramifications

---

and Commander in Chief *in Palestine* (emphasis added) and the phrase was even repeated a second time in the two-paragraph letter. If Samuel had followed his own logic in the 1922 White Paper, to limit the area of the Jewish National Home to Cisjordan by relying on the phrase "in Palestine", his appointment would not have included responsibility for the whole country, but only for a part of it.

of the Balfour Declaration from April 24, 1920 onwards and all that it signified for the recognition of the legal rights and title of sovereignty of the Jewish People to Mandated Palestine and Land of Israel under international law, that failure can be laid at the feet of Stein. He may have been a brilliant advocate in expounding the cause of Zionism in the understated spirit of Ahad Ha'Am, Nahum Sokolow and Chaim Weizmann, which may have won him plaudits as a cautious "moderate", but in reality he badly misjudged the whole legal picture and severely underestimated Jewish legal rights to the whole area of Palestine under international law created by the Balfour Declaration after its adoption at the Conference of San Remo and its elaboration in the Mandate for Palestine, as is evident from what he wrote during his career as a Zionist advocate.

For a long time, Stein did not believe that the expression "Jewish National Home" as used in the Balfour Declaration meant a Jewish State, changing his mind only when he appeared as a witness before the Peel Commission in 1936 when he affirmed that was the original conception before it was altered by the official interpretation given to it in the Churchill White Paper. In 1923, he stated what he thought it did not mean in a Note on the History and Aims of Zionism:

> A new situation was created by the Balfour Declaration of November 2, 1917. The significance of the Declaration is often misunderstood. It is hardly necessary to explain that it does not envisage the handing over of Palestine to a body vaguely known as "the Jews" (quotation marks in the original) for the purpose of creating what is described, not less vaguely, as a "Jewish State".[64]

In the same note, Stein stated what the Balfour Declaration and the Mandate supposedly gave the Jews, according to his interpretation:

> What the Declaration and the Mandate really gave them is primarily *a moral advantage* – the assurance that their *legitimate aspirations* have the sanction of international approval and the security of an international guarantee (emphasis added).[65]

What those "legitimate aspirations" were, Stein restrictively defined in a cultural sense in the same way Ahad Ha'Am conceived them to be: *a home for the Jewish spirit* (emphasis added) concerned with the revival of the Hebrew language, with the strengthening of education and undertaking the project of a Hebrew University, but strangely enough, Stein's "spiritual values" did not include those of the Jewish religion. Herzl by contrast used the word "home"

---

[64] See Appendix II, Note on the History and Aims of Zionism, by Mr. Leonard Stein, p. 168, in the book written by J. De V. Loder, *The Truth About Mesopotamia, Palestine and Syria* (1923), London: George Allen & Unwin Ltd.

[65] *Ibid.*, p. 167.

in a different sense altogether, to mean a budding Jewish State in Palestine, as detailed in his novel, *Altneuland* (Old New Land), published in October 1902, where Jews would control their own political destiny with autonomous rights, though Turkey would retain ultimate sovereignty over the territory. In the context of 1902, when the Ottoman Empire was still in full control of "Palestine", Herzl's plan was revolutionary.

The only special right for Jews that Stein found in the Balfour Declaration, apart from its "moral advantage", was the right to enter Palestine "within the limits of its capacity to absorb them", echoing the Churchill White Paper. But once they entered Palestine, the Jews were to receive no preferential treatment over other nationalities, each being on the same footing, without discrimination, a statement reportedly made by Lord Cecil to Walter Page, the U.S. ambassador in London, according to Page's dispatch to the U.S. State Department on December 21, 1917.[66]

While this was certainly true as regards individuals residing in Palestine, in which the principle of equality before the law applied to everyone, without distinction, it was absolutely false from the national perspective where Jews in their corporate life or as a body politic did enjoy special privileges no other people or ethnic community in Palestine had or was supposed to have, particularly the right of establishing exclusive Jewish settlements and obtaining land from the State for that specific purpose. Hence, in referring to Jews without any qualification in regard to their collective rights, Stein made the inexcusable mistake of not distinguishing clearly between the rights accorded to individual Jews which all other inhabitants of Palestine enjoyed and the rights accorded exclusively to the Jewish nation.[67]

In his *magnum opus* published in 1961 on the history and evolution of the Balfour Declaration, which is considered the most authoritative work on the subject, Stein viewed the Declaration as strictly a political act, having no legal

[66] Stein, *The Balfour Declaration*, p. 599.

[67] The same inexcusable mistake was made by the President of the Supreme Court of Israel, Mr. Justice Aharon Barak, and his two colleagues, Justices Theodor Or and Yitzhak Zamir, who were joined by Justices Mishael Cheshin with Justice Ya'akov Kedmi dissenting, in the landmark case of the communal settlement of Katzir in the Eron ('I-ron) River region decided on March 8, 2000. The Court held that the State of Israel could not allocate state land to the Jewish Agency to establish an exclusive Jewish settlement such as Katzir, since that discriminated between Jews and non-Jews. However, the Justices ignored the fact that this is exactly what was permitted by Articles 6 and 11 of the Mandate for Palestine, which is still part of the law of Israel today, notwithstanding the general clause in Article 15 of the Mandate banning discrimination among individual inhabitants on the grounds of race, religion or language. If Jews in their national corporate existence had not populated the land of Palestine in exclusive Jewish settlements some of which grew eventually into towns and cities where everyone can live, including Arabs, there would have been no Jewish State. When speaking of equality and discrimination, the distinction between individuals and nation must therefore always be borne in mind.

content. This was a mistaken perception. He did not realize the interlocking legal relationship existing between the Balfour Declaration, the San Remo Resolution, Article 22 of the Covenant of the League of Nations, and the Mandate for Palestine, all of which were inextricably intertwined. He actually belittled the cardinal legal importance of the Balfour Declaration when he summed up his thoughts on it, as follows:

> What the British Government did undertake was to use its best endeavours to 'facilitate' (no more) 'the establishment in Palestine of a national home for the Jewish People' – not as it had been put in the Zionist draft and as Balfour would, apparently, have been prepared to concede, the reconstitution of Palestine as the national home of the Jews. The Declaration was a political and not a legal document and the crucial words did not lead themselves to close analysis.[68]

This summary conclusion of Stein is widely off the mark. While it was true that on November 2, 1917, the Balfour Declaration was no more than what he said it was, it was transformed or converted less than three years later, on April 24, 1920, into a legal document when the Declaration was adopted by the Supreme Council of the Principal Allied Powers at the San Remo Peace Conference to be the legal basis of the future government of the new Mandated state of Palestine, in application of Article 22 of the League Covenant. By virtue of this collective decision of the Allied Supreme Council, first embodied in the San Remo Resolution and subsequently in the Treaty of Sèvres and the Mandate for Palestine, world Jewry was recognized as having the exclusive right of self-determination in Palestine. The obligation and function of Great Britain was thenceforward changed from one of merely `using its best endeavours to facilitate the establishment in Palestine of a national home for the Jewish People' to one for achieving a specific result, namely, making it legally responsible for putting into effect the Balfour Declaration in order to "secure" the establishment of the Jewish National Home. This in turn changed the whole nature of the British undertaking from one of facilitator bound by an obligation of means to one of guarantor bound by an obligation of result (or one of specific performance) based on the assumption that a sufficient number of Jews would in the years ahead immigrate to Palestine to reconstitute the Jewish State of yore, i.e. Judea (Judah).

In another curious conclusion, Stein says that the Balfour Declaration "avoided any suggestion that Palestine belonged to the Jews".[69] However, he then strangely avoids answering the critical question to whom Palestine actually belonged, if it did not belong to the Jews. Did it belong to the Arabs? To the British? To the League of Nations? To any combination of them, or to no one?

---

[68] *Op. cit.*, pp. 552-553.

[69] *Op. cit.*, p. 521.

He did not derive the natural conclusion arising from the fact that Palestine was created for one purpose only: to implement the Balfour Declaration for the establishment of a National Home for the Jewish People leading eventually to an independent Jewish State in the whole country. This could only mean that all of Palestine belonged to the Jews, under international law, otherwise there would have been no reason to create it and allow Jews to reconstitute their home and state there. Palestine and the Jewish National Home were therefore synonymous, but that basic fact was apparently never absorbed by Stein and those who thought like him. With all the deep knowledge he possessed about the Balfour Declaration, it is sad to note that he never came to the proper conclusions inherent in its words.

The Balfour Declaration was the lynch-pin or foundation stone in support of all Jewish legal rights and title of sovereignty to Palestine under international law, upon which additional building-blocks were soon thereafter erected, namely the San Remo Resolution which brought the Declaration within the confines of international law, certain provisions of the Treaty of Sèvres dealing with Palestine, Mesopotamia and Syria, which codified the San Remo Resolution in the Treaty itself, the Mandate for Palestine which implemented the San Remo Resolution on Palestine to its fullest extent, and the Franco-British Convention of December 23, 1920, which delineated the northern boundaries of Palestine with Syria-Lebanon as part of the existing terms of the Mandate for Palestine. Not to be excluded from this list are the Smuts Resolution of January 30, 1919 and Article 22 of the League of Nations Covenant, which, read in conjunction with the Feisal-Weizmann Agreement of January 3, 1919, signified that Palestine had been established and reserved exclusively for the national self-determination of the Jewish People, and not of the Arabs of the country. All these acts together formed one sturdy legal edifice and are the founding documents of the State of Israel under international law. In theory, all the legal groundwork for the Jewish State to be rebuilt had been meticulously laid, but its implementation was a different matter altogether that depended on the goodwill of the Mandatory Power, Great Britain, which floundered and disappeared as the years rolled by. Nevertheless, it may be said without any exaggeration that the Jewish State of Israel is the direct outgrowth and consequence of the Balfour Declaration as it evolved from a 1917 policy statement to an act of international law in 1920.

Those persons of great vision who were instrumental in giving birth to the Balfour Declaration are owed the everlasting gratitude of the Jewish People. They include both Jews and inspired Christian statesmen. Among the former who played a direct role were Chaim Weizmann, Louis Dembitz Brandeis and Nahum Sokolow, who were aided by many others. Another great figure who paved the way for the Balfour Declaration was Theodor Herzl, the great visionary who valiantly sought from Turkey and the European Powers a charter for the Jewish State he visualized, but passed away before his dream was realized. Nor should we forget Herzl's principal collaborator, Dr. Max Nordau, a co-founder of the Zionist Organization, who is given the main credit for formulating the famous Basle Program that set forth the aim of Zionism and the means to achieve it.

The Christian statesmen largely responsible for the Balfour Declaration were Prime Minister David Lloyd George and Foreign Secretary Arthur James Balfour, General Jan Christiaan Smuts, Lord Alfred Milner and President Woodrow Wilson, as well as several others who, at the critical time, supported the project of the Jewish National Home. It is true that Lloyd George and Balfour were preceded in their thinking of a Jewish State in Palestine by political and military officials during the last years in office of the Asquith Government, who thought that such a State might bring great advantage to Britain in pursuit of its imperial goals.[70] However, nothing concrete was done during Asquith's term as Prime Minister in this respect until the Lloyd George Government came to power in December 1916 and adopted a non-ambiguous pro-Zionist policy. Lloyd George and Balfour must therefore be given the chief credit for initiating the Balfour Declaration. Its eventual implementation was left largely to World Jewry in support of the Jews of Palestine which realized its two-thousand year old dream to resurrect the Jewish Commonwealth destroyed by Rome.

[70] On this point, see the well-researched and detailed scrutiny of the Balfour Declaration by Mayir Vereté, "The Balfour Declaration and its Makers", *Middle East Studies*, Vol. VI:1 (1970), pp. 48-76. Reprinted in: Elie Kedourie and Sylvia G. Haim (eds.), *Palestine and Israel in the 19th and 20th Centuries,* published by Frank Cass And Company Limited (1982), p. 60. In his article, Vereté minimized Balfour's personal role in having the Declaration issued, claiming it was "rather small", despite the fact that it came to fruition during his term as Foreign Secretary and that he was an avid proponent of it and actually presented it to the Cabinet for approval. Balfour, a self-described ardent Zionist, spent his subsequent years as Foreign Secretary actively promoting the Declaration among his colleagues, in contrast to other British officials who undermined it and even sought to nullify it.

*Chapter 5*

# The Mandate for Palestine

The Mandate for Palestine[1] was originally an agreement between the Principal Allied Powers of World War I – Britain, France, Italy and Japan – which was embodied in the San Remo Resolution of April 24-25, 1920, entrusting the administration of Palestine to Great Britain and making it responsible for putting into effect the Balfour Declaration in accordance with the general provisions of Article 22 of the Covenant of the League of Nations. It then took the shape of a detailed legal charter of 28 articles prefaced by a preamble of seven recitals. The Mandate may also be deemed an instrument of international constitutional law after it was confirmed by a decision of the Council of the League of Nations on July 24, 1922. The involvement of the League Council in confirming the terms of a mandate, previously conferred by the Principal Allied Powers, and then in supervising its observance sprang directly from the Mandates Article in the Covenant of the League of Nations – Article 22 – found in Part I of the Treaty of Versailles and in the other peace treaties that concluded World War I. This in effect meant that an agreement henceforth existed between the Mandatory Power and the Council of the League requiring the former to provide the latter with an annual report in reference to the territory committed to its charge and making it answerable for any violations in exercising the Mandate, as specified in paragraphs 7 and 9 of article 22 of the Covenant.

The Mandate for Palestine was drawn up to serve as a legal guide for the Mandatory – officially designated as His Britannic Majesty – in administering Palestine on behalf of the League of Nations which succeeded the Principal Allied Powers in the role of supervisor of the Mandatory and protector of the interests of the national beneficiary of the Mandate. It obliged the Mandatory to secure the establishment of a Jewish State, euphemistically called the

[1] This chapter is not intended to be an exhaustive review of all the individual articles of the Mandate, but rather a discussion of the development of those articles that determined the unfolding Jewish character of Palestine. Further discussion of various articles of importance, or the exact meaning of which was subject to dispute, is also elaborated upon in succeeding chapters.

Jewish National Home by placing Palestine under the appropriate political, administrative and economic conditions, as set out in article 2 of the Mandate. The necessary infrastructure required for the state would thus be created and the purpose of the Mandate fulfilled.

Like the San Remo Resolution, the Mandate also contained the same three sources or components of the Jewish legal title of sovereignty over Palestine, namely the afore-mentioned Article 22 of the Covenant, the Balfour Declaration and the recognition of the historical connection of the Jewish People with Palestine, all of which were specifically mentioned in the first three recitals of the Preamble of the Mandate, which epitomized its heart and soul together with articles 2 and 6 thereof. Henceforth, the Mandate would be the final resting place of the Jewish legal title to Palestine. Since the Mandatory was required by the San Remo Resolution on Palestine to put into effect the Balfour Declaration, the Resolution which embodied the Declaration was the base or core document upon which the Mandate had to be constructed and its terms interpreted, from which the Mandatory could not deviate, otherwise it would be in violation of its obligations under the Mandate. Thus the Balfour Declaration, the San Remo Resolution on Palestine and the Mandate for Palestine were all interrelated and aimed to achieve the same thing: the establishment of a Jewish State according to its historical boundaries, from Dan to Beersheba, which signified the whole of the Land of Israel i.e., all the land conquered, settled and governed by the Israelites and their descendants during the First and Second Temple Periods.

The interests of four separate parties were involved in the Mandate for Palestine. They were, first, the Mandator who conferred the Mandate on the Mandatory, made up of the Four Great Powers as a collective entity, consisting of Great Britain, France, Italy and Japan; second, the Mandatory selected by the Mandator to administer the mandated territory to secure the establishment of the Jewish National Home culminating in a Jewish State, i.e., His Britannic Majesty, represented by the British Government; third, the national beneficiary of the Mandate in whose favour it was established by the Mandator which gave effect to the principle of self-determination laid down in Article 22 of the Covenant, i.e., the Jewish People, most of whom were outside Palestine; and fourth, the party who confirmed the Mandate to whom the Mandatory reported on an annual basis and made sure it was being observed according to its stated terms, i.e., the Council of the League of Nations, assisted and advised by the Permanent Mandates Commission.

The Mandate for Palestine may also be seen as a legal trust because the Land of Israel or Palestine, which can be assimilated to the property of a trust, was transferred by the Principal Allied Powers to the British Government in its capacity as trustee so that it could then administer the whole country in accordance with the general provisions of Article 22 of the Covenant with the obligation imposed upon it to preserve intact the trust territory during the period of its administration while also securing the establishment of the Jewish State. The word "trust" was in fact used twice in the opening paragraph of

Article 22 indicating that the Mandate also had the features of a trust.

In addition, there were also characteristics of a tutorship involved in the Mandate for Palestine since Britain was also required by Article 22 of the Covenant to act as a tutor to the Jewish People to guide them over the course of years towards national independence which would be achieved as soon as they had become the majority of the population through an influx of a large number of immigrants and were then able to stand by themselves. In this particular sense, the Jewish People had the legal status equivalent to a minor or ward in civil law, until the Jews in Palestine gained independence under British tutelage.

The Charter or instrument containing the provisions of the Mandate for Palestine was drafted by the Zionist Organization in unison with the British Foreign Office. There was no participation or consultation with any Arab body or representatives, whether in Palestine or elsewhere, which was another confirmation of the fact that no Arab self-determination or self-government on the national level was intended by the Mandate. National rights to all of Palestine were conferred only upon the Jewish People and not upon the local Arab population as subsequently claimed by the British Government.

The actual drafting of the terms and conditions of the Mandate for Palestine was initiated by the Zionist Organization. It began unofficially in November 1918 with memoranda drawn up by Herbert Samuel and Julius Simon containing the Zionist proposals relating to the establishment of a Jewish National Home for presentation to the Paris Peace Conference which convened on January 18, 1919.[2] These proposals set down some of the basic principles of the Mandate for Palestine but were not drafted in the form of a legal document. The prototype of the Mandate was formulated by Felix Frankfurter, then a Harvard Law School Professor who attended the Paris Peace Conference as a member of the American Zionist Delegation, later becoming a renowned U.S. Supreme Court Justice. He drew up a tentative Draft Mandate, dated March 28, 1919, which was more detailed and precise than the Zionist proposals. He sent it to David Hunter Miller[3] together with a memorandum explaining the

---

[2] See 1) the memorandum of November 19, 1918 containing the "Proposals Relating to the Establishment of a Jewish National Home in Palestine", drawn up for the Zionist Organization by a special committee of Jewish leaders in London under the chairmanship of Herbert Samuel, M.P. – *Rise of Israel*, Volume 10, Document 17, n. 81; 2) Statement of the Zionist Organization Regarding Palestine, 3 February 1919, Proposals to be Presented to the Peace Conference, *Ibid.*, Volume 10, Document 57, p. 195; 3) Statement of the Zionist representatives to the Council of Ten in Paris, 27 February 1919, *Ibid.*, Volume 10, Document 61, p. 226; 4) Julius Simon: *Certain Days: Zionist Memoirs and Selected Papers*, edited by Evyatar Friesel, Israel Universities Press, Jerusalem 1971, p. 85.

[3] An American lawyer who was the legal adviser of the American Commission at the Paris Peace Conference. He assisted in drawing up the final draft of the Covenant of the League of Nations. He wrote two important books about the proceedings of the Peace Conference, the first entitled *My Diary at the Paris Peace Conference, 1918-1919,* the other *The Drafting of the Covenant.*

considerations which guided the Zionist drafters.[4]

The draft Palestine Mandate of Professor Frankfurter referred to the Principal Allied Powers as the Signatory Powers and stated specifically in the Preamble that sovereignty over the territory of Palestine "possessed, asserted or claimed by the Emperor of the Ottomans was ceded to the Signatory Powers". The Preamble of this Mandate also stated that the League of Nations and the Signatory Powers recognized:

> The historic title of the Jewish People to Palestine and the right of the Jews to reconstitute Palestine as their National Home: and there to establish the foundations of a Jewish Commonwealth.

The second article of this draft affirmed that the guiding purpose of the mandate was the establishment of Palestine as the Jewish National Home and its development into an autonomous commonwealth dedicated to the advancement of Social Justice. The Mandatory was required to adopt measures appropriate for the creation of political, administrative and economic conditions to realize this purpose. The first of these measures that had to be adopted was one to promote the immigration of Jews and their close settlement upon the land.

In formulating this draft Palestine mandate, Professor Frankfurter had the help of two American colleagues: Benjamin Victor Cohen and Howard Gans, and they all worked under the overall direction of U.S. Supreme Court Justice Louis Dembitz Brandeis in Washington. This document is an indispensable source for understanding the real purpose and meaning of the eventual Mandate which became a part of international law. Together with the Statement containing the Zionist proposals dated February 3, 1919, that were presented orally to the Supreme Council of the Paris Peace Conference on February 27, 1919, the prototype of the Mandate was firmly established.[5]

The British Delegation at the Conference made comments on each of the Zionist proposals that were recorded in the minutes of the meeting it held on March 21, 1919, and the next day.[6] This was followed up by separate draft mandates prepared by the Zionist Organization and the Political Section of the British Delegation in July and September 1919.[7] An agreed draft between the two sides was then worked out on December 11, 1919. During the period from July to December, the dominant roles in drafting the Mandate for Palestine were played by two young persons. The Zionist Organization was represented by the above-mentioned Benjamin Victor Cohen, an American lawyer and skillful legal

---

[4] *Rise of Israel*, Vol. 10, Document 77, p. 296 ff.

[5] See the reference to the Zionist Proposals and Frankfurter's Draft Mandate in the Palestine Royal Commission Report, *Rise of Israel*, Vol. 24, Document 2, p. 48.

[6] *The Rise of Israel*, Vol. 10, Document 60, p. 221.

[7] *Ibid.*, Volume 10, Document 81, p. 311 and Document 83, p. 322.

drafter, who later served President Franklin D. Roosevelt with great distinction in drafting much of the legislation that constituted the New Deal programs and still later helped write the United Nations Charter.[8]

Cohen's counterpart was Eric Graham Forbes Adam, a junior official in the British Foreign Office who was in Paris attending the Peace Conference on behalf of his country at the same time that Cohen was present in the American Zionist delegation. During the time he served in Lord Balfour's Foreign Office, he showed no anti-Zionist proclivities of the type prevailing amongst most of the British officials serving in Palestine, both military and civilian, and worked diligently to carry out the policy of the Jewish National Home as stated in the Balfour Declaration.

Lord Curzon replaced Arthur James Balfour as Foreign Minister on October 24, 1919 but he did not take an active role in monitoring the drafting of the Mandate until mid-March 1920. When he first saw the form of the Mandate as it then existed, he was horrified at the depth of British commitment to the cause of Zionism which now openly aimed for a Jewish State in Palestine as the final result of the Mandate. He ordered immediate revisions to be made to the Draft Mandate to water down the strong Zionist character of the document. The task fell primarily on Robert Vansittart and Hubert Young who, during the period from March to December 1920 under the rigorous scrutiny of Lord Curzon, made various modifications to particular provisions of the Draft Mandate. But in the end, Lord Curzon, who ironically was obliged to defend Zionism from the French onslaught against the Balfour Declaration at the San Remo Peace Conference in April 1920 and thereafter during the boundary negotiations did not succeed in watering down the Zionist Mandate as much as he had hoped. It was finally approved by the British Cabinet on November 29, 1920, and submitted to the Council of the League of Nations on December 6, 1920, for international confirmation.

When the Mandate was submitted to the League Council, it was presented in the form of a decision of this body, rather than a treaty (convention) or declaration signed by plenipotentiaries of the Principal Allied Powers, which, if that had been done, would have caused more delay by requiring the signatures of all the "High Contracting Parties". This was affirmed by the Legal Adviser of the British Foreign Office, Cecil J. B. Hurst, who subsequently became a judge of the Permanent Court of International Justice. Here is how Hurst put it:[9]

> Mr. Balfour has now forwarded [the] draft mandates [for Palestine and Mesopotamia] to the Secretary-General [of the League of Nations]. The only changes which were made in the text as the result of my

---

[8] See article on Benjamin Victor Cohen in *Encyclopaedia Judaica* (1971), Volume 5, column 667.

[9] FO 371/5248: 9220; E 15390/4164/44. See also the explanation given by Eric G. Forbes Adam in FO 371/5248: 9220; E 15728/4164/44.

> discussion with M. Fromageot[10] were the substitution of the formula: "The mandatory shall…" or "The mandatory will…", or some such formula, where the original draft had the words "The mandatory undertakes…". The French had made similar changes in the Syrian mandate, as they maintain it was a necessary consequence of putting the mandates into the form of a decision of the Council instead of a convention or declaration to be signed by the [Principal Allied] Powers. M. Fromageot therefore begged that we would do the same.

The assent of the two other Powers, Italy and Japan, who made up the rest of the coalition of the Principal Allied Powers, was also needed before any agreement on the terms of these mandates could be submitted to the Council of the League of Nations for final confirmation in accordance with Article 96 of the Treaty of Sèvres, whose observance was then obligatory, pending ratification of the treaty, signed on August 10, 1920. However, here too a different path was followed as noted by Hurst in a memorandum dated December 10, 1920.

The mandates were prepared and submitted to the League Council by France and Great Britain without the participation of Italy and Japan. The reason for excluding the other two Principal Allied Powers was explained by D. G. Osborne of the Foreign Office in a letter to Cabinet Secretary Maurice Hankey:[11]

> When the preparation of the Mandates [for Palestine and Mesopotamia] was nearing completion, it was found to be impossible to consult the Japanese and Italian Governments and obtain their formal consent within the time available before the end of the [League Council] meeting at Geneva. As however, both the Italian and Japanese Governments were represented on the Council, it was thought that their consent could most readily be obtained by submitting the mandates at once to the Council, thus affording those Powers full opportunity to consider and comment upon the terms of the draft instruments.

The confirmation of the Mandate for Palestine was then inordinately held up for a variety of reasons chiefly caused by the U.S. Government, thus allowing time for more revisions and amendments to the Draft Mandate until it was finally confirmed by the Council of the League of Nations on July 24, 1922 but the date of its entry into legal force was further delayed to September 29, 1923[12]

---

[10] The Legal Adviser of the French Foreign Office.

[11] The Hurst memorandum dated December 10, 1920 is found in FO 371/5248: 9220: E 15728, C13748/154/18 (also marked 172 RH) and Osborne's letter dated December 30, 1920 is found in E 15728/4164/44.

[12] The resolution of the Council of the League of Nations on September 29, 1923, which brought into operation the Mandate for Palestine, is found in the League of Nations Official Journal, 4th year, No. 11, November 1923, cited in the book *The Holy Land Under Mandate*, Volume 2, pp. 111-112, by Fannie

when the reservation of Italy contained in the San Remo Resolution, concerning its interests and rights in South-West Anatolia (in the province of Antalya) was finally settled to its satisfaction. Britain and France had previously agreed among themselves that their respective mandates over Palestine and Syria would only go into effect both at the same time. As noted above, the involvement of the League of Nations in the confirmation process of the Mandate for Palestine now meant that the Mandate was not only an agreement between the Principal Allied Powers themselves, as recorded in the San Remo Resolution, but also a legal agreement between Britain and the League of Nations, on whose behalf the Mandate was then exercised as stated in Article 22, paragraph 2 of the League Covenant. This created a contractual bond between all the parties involved. The Mandate for Palestine was accepted by 52 nations of the world in 1922, prior to going into legal force on September 29, 1923, and by additional nations (including the Arab states of Iraq and Egypt) when these joined the League of Nations subsequently. Though strictly speaking the Mandate for Palestine was a decision of the Council of the League of Nations, the document itself was not included in the peace treaty with Turkey, originally the Treaty of Sèvres and later its replacement, the Treaty of Lausanne. However, the Mandate for Palestine did eventually become part of a treaty when a convention was concluded between Britain and the United States on December 3, 1924, in which the latter consented to the Mandate undertaken by the former to administer Palestine.

Had the Mandate for Palestine been an integral part of the Turkish peace treaty, whose terms were set out therein, as was originally envisaged, there would have been no doubt that it could be called a treaty. But since that was not the actual case, it cannot be considered a treaty in the formal sense, although it still constituted a binding act of international law that is similar in status to a trusteeship agreement under the Charter of the United Nations.

As already noted, the importance of the reference to Article 22 of the Covenant of the League of Nations in the first recital of the Preamble of the Mandate for Palestine has been either overlooked or misconstrued as applying to the Arabs of Palestine. It was placed there to show that all the general provisions of Article 22 were applicable to the Mandate, none more important than the

---

Fern Andrews, published by Houghton Mifflin Company, 1931. See also Colonel Richard Meinertzhagen's book, *op. cit.*, p. 119; the book by D. F. W. van Rees, *Les Mandats Internationaux*, Paris, Librairie Arthur Rousseau, 1927, at p. 31. In regard to Mesopotamia, it was decided by Great Britain at the Cairo Conference of March 1921, even before King Feisal was enthroned as King of Iraq on August 23, 1921 to replace the Draft Mandate, already pending before the Council of the League of Nations since December 6, 1920, by a treaty signed with Iraq on October 10, 1922, together with some subsidiary agreements (one on April 30, 1923, and four more on March 25, 1924) which recognized its national sovereignty. However, Iraq still remained subject to the Mandatory regime, advised and assisted by the British High Commissioner in accordance with Article 22(4) of the Covenant of the League of Nations, until its independence in 1932, when it became a member of the League of Nations.

first paragraph of Article 22 which deals with the right of self-determination of peoples or territories. If Article 22 had been incompatible with the Mandate's plan to establish Palestine as a Jewish State, it would never have been mentioned in the Preamble of the Mandate. The right of national self-determination found in Article 22(1) was therefore meant to apply to the Jewish People exclusively insofar as Palestine was concerned, in combination with the Balfour Declaration of November 2, 1917.

This was certainly the assumption of Professor Frankfurter who had proposed in his Draft Mandate of March 28, 1919 that the Government of Palestine be administered by the Mandatory in accordance with the principles proclaimed in the Covenant. He thought this would lead to Palestine becoming a Jewish Commonwealth exactly as declared by President Wilson in Washington on March 2, 1919.

However, the direct opposite assumption about Article 22(1) was made by the Palestine Royal Commission who assumed that the reference to it in the Mandate meant that the Arabs of Palestine also had a right of self-determination. This assumption was a grave and cardinal mistake that was contrary to the essence and spirit of the Mandate for Palestine which did not deal with any Arab national rights at all, except in the matter of language which recognized Arabic as one of the three official languages of Palestine, together with English and Hebrew. However, for the Peel Commission, this false assumption provided the legal justification for its Partition Plan which proposed the setting up of an Arab state alongside a miniature Jewish State.[13]

Leonard Stein, the eminent legal adviser to the Zionist Organization and Jewish Agency, while not interpreting Article 22(1) in the same erroneous manner as found in the Peel Report, nevertheless believed that nothing turned on the allusion to Article 22 in the Preamble of the Mandate so far as the construction of the Mandate was concerned.[14] He simply failed to realize that Article 22 was a part of the threefold legal basis for Jewish independence in Palestine, not of course in and by itself, but when joined to the Balfour Declaration and the historical connection of the Jewish People with the country, as set forth in the Preamble of the Mandate. These three elements constituted the San Remo Resolution on Palestine.

The Mandate, whatever shortcomings it may have had in terms of clarity of language and despite deliberate British attempts to stifle its Jewish national character, still amounted in its final rendition to a blueprint for an independent Jewish State under British auspices. Had the Mandate been implemented according to its carefully laid out plan, the Jewish State would have been brought into being during the period of British administration and not as an independent act of the Jewish Agency for Palestine under U.N. guidelines after the British

---

[13] *Rise of Israel*, Volume 24, Document 2, pp. 61 and 382.

[14] See the Memorandum of the Jewish Agency submitted to the Palestine Royal Commission in 1936, which he authored, *op. cit.*, pp. 16 and 42.

decided to withdraw from the country. The latter did not discharge their primary obligation to create the Jewish State because the Mandate was never made part of the supreme or fundamental law within Palestine itself, notwithstanding several references to it in a new constitutional document known as the Palestine Order-in-Council enacted by the British Government on August 10, 1922, and went into legal force on September 1, 1922. It specifically provided that no law or ordinance could be passed or promulgated which could in any way be repugnant to or inconsistent with the provisions of the Mandate.[15]

The Mandate was in effect shunted aside in the internal administration of Palestine and replaced by the Palestine Order-in-Council. The latter was issued pursuant to an imperial statute called the Foreign Jurisdiction Act of 1890 which made it lawful for the British Sovereign ("His Britannic Majesty" or simply "His Majesty") to exercise jurisdiction within a foreign country such as Palestine as if such jurisdiction had been acquired by cession or conquest of territory.

The language of the Preamble of the Foreign Jurisdiction Act was inserted in the Preamble to the Palestine Order-in-Council, as follows:

> And whereas, by treaty, capitulation, grant, usage, sufferance and other lawful means, His Majesty has power and jurisdiction within Palestine.[16]

This reference to the Foreign Jurisdiction Act rather than to the Mandate for Palestine in the Palestine Order-in-Council as to the reason why "His Majesty" had power and jurisdiction within Palestine can only be described as a colossal deception perpetrated not only on the Jews of Palestine and the Jewish People at large, but also on the other Allied Powers and the League of Nations, since it was the Mandate and only the Mandate which gave "His Majesty" the right to govern Palestine under international law.

The alleged sources of power and jurisdiction which Britain invoked as justifying its governing of Palestine would, if factual, have conferred on Britain a right of sovereignty over Palestine. This, however, ran counter to the then newly-designed Mandates System and President Woodrow Wilson's Fourteen Points. Moreover, Britain actually acted in the name of the Principal Allied Powers rather than in its own name when General Allenby's forces conquered Palestine. Therefore, power and jurisdiction within Palestine was, prior to the issuance of the Mandate, vested in the Principal Allied Powers as a group, rather than in Britain alone.

The name of the treaty cited by the Foreign Jurisdiction Act in the Palestine Order-in-Council was not given, nor was any explanation offered for listing the

---

[15] These particular references were contained in articles 17(1)( c), 18, 85 and 89 of the Palestine Order-in-Council, 1922, as amended.

[16] "Capitulation" was another word for "surrender" under stipulated terms, while "sufferance" meant a "tacit assent" or acquiescence but without express permission.

other diverse sources of jurisdiction. In fact, none of these alleged sources of jurisdiction gave Britain the power under international law to govern Palestine except as a military occupying power for an interim period until peace was established. In this connection, it should be reiterated that technically the Mandate for Palestine was not a treaty but an international agreement. In addition, while it is true that Turkey capitulated to Britain in regard to Palestine, which decisively influenced the choice of Britain as Mandatory, that fact alone did not give Britain any legal rights to set up a civilian administration under international law, staffed by its own officials until British rule was sanctioned by the San Remo Resolution and the decision to confirm the Mandate by the Council of the League. The citation of all the sources in the Order-in-Council explaining why Britain had power and jurisdiction in Palestine was therefore nothing but legal gobbledygook to hide the true reason for British power and jurisdiction in Palestine, namely the Mandate for Palestine.

The only possible legal justification for British reliance on the Foreign Jurisdiction Act of 1890, adopted by the U.K. Parliament 30 years before the Mandates System was created, was to ensure the legality of all acts carried out by British officials in Palestine prior to the date of September 29, 1923 when the Mandate for Palestine took legal effect. The British had started to rule Palestine first under military administration in a part of the country beginning in October 1917 and then under a regime of civil administration from July 1, 1920 onwards, in accordance with the San Remo Resolution of April 24-25, 1920. To cover the short period of 3-1/4 years when the Mandate was already being exercised in practice, but had not yet gone into legal force, it may have been a cautionary measure in British eyes to cite the power and jurisdiction afforded Britain under its own laws pending confirmation of the Mandate to rule a foreign country such as Palestine that had been conquered primarily by its military forces, with the invaluable aid of Jewish intelligence provided by the NILI[17] underground. But that reason ceased to exist as soon as the Mandate went into legal force. Britain should have then forthwith amended the Order-in-Council to admit unequivocally that it now derived its legal authority in Palestine from the Mandate and not from the formulary sources enumerated in the Foreign Jurisdiction Act and simply repeated *ad nauseam* in the Order-in-Council of 1922.

The British Government actually admitted this in the case of Transjordanian Palestine. In an agreement it concluded with Emir Abdullah on February 20, 1928, the opening recital of the agreement stated as follows:

> Whereas His Brittanic Majesty in virtue of a Mandate entrusted to

---

[17] NILI was a clandestine pro-British espionage organization that operated in Palestine and Syria under Turkish rule during World War I, under the joint leadership of Aaron Aaronsohn, Avshalom Feinberg, Sarah Aaronsohn and Yosef Lishansky. The acronym NILI is a transliteration of the initial Hebrew letters of *Netzah Yisrael Lo Yeshakker*, translated "The Strength or Eternal One of Israel will not fail". *Encyclopaedia Judaica* (1971), Vol. 12, col. 1162.

him on the 24th of July 1922 has authority in the area covered thereby.

This recital was an official acknowledgment by Britain that it had power and jurisdiction in Transjordan by virtue of what was simply called "a Mandate" – without specifying that it was actually the Mandate for Palestine, though a reference to Britain being the Mandatory for Palestine was included in Article 2 of the agreement. This agreement then transferred British legislative and administrative authority over Transjordan to Abdullah. By contrast to what Britain acknowledged for Transjordan, it always refused to similarly acknowledge in regard to the rest of Palestine, i.e., Cisjordanian Palestine – because that would have automatically meant that the Mandate for Palestine, as an international instrument, was also an integral part of the constitutional and legal structure of Palestine – confirming it as the fundamental law upon which to judge the validity of all orders-in-council and other legislation Britain and the Administration of Palestine enacted for the country.

One looks in vain to find any mention of the Mandate for Palestine included in the laws of the country in force on the 31st day of December, 1933, in the three-volume authorized compendium, prepared by Robert Harry Drayton, the Solicitor General (1920-34) and Legal Draftsman to the Government of Palestine. As Professor Max M. Laserson so cogently pointed out in his book:[18]

> At once the most painful and most naive expression of this tendency [to abandon the Mandate or at least to deny its application as municipal law] is found in the elimination of the Mandate from the sources of public law in Palestine. In the authorized compilation of the Laws of Palestine, by Drayton, the Mandate is simply not printed. The citizen of Palestine… if he wishes to know the real substance of this so important and authoritative juridical source, the Mandate, he is not able to find it in the Laws of Palestine.

The practical consequences of this British deception denying the rightful place of the Mandate for Palestine in the laws of the country was that Britain could now govern Palestine not in obedience to the specific provisions of the Mandate Charter based as they were on a deep and pervading Jewish character, but according to the comparatively neutral provisions of the Palestine Order-in-Council which lacked any semblance of that character. The situation was then made irreversible by a series of tortuous-reasoned judgments, rendered in several cases by the Palestine Courts, which were headed by British judges who adjudicated as if the Mandate did not exist for them. Those judgments denied that the Mandate had the force of law in Palestine because it was never incorporated into the internal laws of the country, as required for all treaties.

---

[18] *On the Mandate, Documents, Statements, Laws and Judgments Relating to and Arising from the Mandate for Palestine*, compiled and with introduction by Prof. Max M. Laserson, Tel-Aviv (1937), "Igereth", p. xxxv of the Introduction.

Hence none of the Mandate's provisions were enforceable in Palestine, except for those isolated ones which had no prominent Jewish content that may have been expressly incorporated in the Palestine Order-in-Council.[19] The Mandate, which was designed to be the most important part of the constitutional law of the country, thereafter lost its juridical value inside Palestine as a result of British judicial denial – which was a staggering blow to the ongoing development of Palestine as the Jewish National Home and Jewish State.

Furthermore, without court enforcement of the Mandate, the British Government acting through the aegis of the High Commissioner of Palestine, who embodied in his person both the executive and legislative authority throughout the entire period of Mandatory rule, was released from any constraints forbidding passage of laws and ordinances which blatantly contradicted the provisions of the Mandate to secure the establishment of the Jewish National Home. The most famous example where this happened was the enactment of the Palestine Land Transfers Regulations in February 1940 that had retroactive effect to May 18, 1939, pursuant to the MacDonald White Paper released the day before. Those regulations prohibited or restricted the transfer of lands in certain designated zones of Palestine except to Palestinian Arabs. This was a clear violation of Article 6 of the Mandate because instead of encouraging "close settlement by Jews on the land" – where such land could be easily purchased on the open market or was otherwise readily available as State lands, the British not only discouraged the acquisition of land by Jews within certain areas in Palestine for purposes of settlement, but prohibited such acquisition altogether. These Regulations could never have been enacted had the Mandate been seen as an integral part of the law of Palestine.[20]

---

[19] The first judgment of this kind decided along these lines was *Jamal Husseini v. Government of Palestine* (High Court No. 55 of 1925) where it was held: "The terms of the Mandate are enforceable in the Courts only insofar as they are incorporated by the Palestine Order-in-Council, 1922 or any amendment thereof... Insofar as the Mandate is not incorporated into the law of Palestine by the Order-in-Council, its provisions have only the force of treaty obligations and cannot be enforced by the Courts." This case was followed by a judgment rendered in the Ramadan case (*Sharif Esh-Shanti v. Attorney-General*) where the District Court of Nablus, sitting as a Court of Appeal, held that the Mandate had no juridical value in the Courts of Palestine except so far as its provisions have been expressly incorporated into the law of Palestine. It further stated that the juridical position of Palestine is that of a dependency of the Crown in which the Sovereign had full power to legislate by means of Orders-in-Council which could not be challenged in the Courts even though their provisions went beyond the powers recognized by the Mandate. The Palestine Order-in- Council 1922-23 was not subject to nor governed by the terms of the Mandate except so far as it had itself expressly assimilated the language of the Mandate in its provisions. This judgment was confirmed by the Supreme Court of Palestine sitting as a Court of Appeal.

[20] See the case of Bernard Rosenblatt vs. Registrar of Lands, Haifa, in *Palestine Annotated Law Reports*, p. 499, High Court Number 19/47. The Supreme Court

The provisions of the Mandate Charter as it applied at the level of international law can be divided into four broad divisions concerning its grounds, purposes, means for achieving its purposes, and general provisions and safeguards. The grounds for establishing the Mandate were, as already noted, first, the Balfour Declaration which sought to rectify Jewish homelessness by reconstituting the ancient Jewish State of Judea; second, Article 22 of the League Covenant providing for the right of self-determination of peoples, communities, colonies and territories, including that of the Jewish People in the Land of Palestine; and third, the historical connection of the Jewish People with Palestine. These grounds are all found in the first three recitals of the Preamble of the Mandate.

There is really only one overriding purpose of the Mandate, rather than purposes, and that is to secure the establishment of the Jewish State in Palestine by the means provided in the Mandate. The purpose and the grounds are mutually interlocking, which is why Article 2 of the Mandate, which states what that purpose is, refers one back to the Preamble where the grounds are mentioned.

The means for achieving the paramount purpose of the Mandate to create Palestine as a Jewish State are enumerated in various articles of the Mandate. Article 2 requires the Mandatory to place the country under the appropriate conditions – political, administrative and economic – to achieve the purpose of the Mandate. The political and administrative conditions included the development of self-governing institutions for the Jewish State of Palestine and the encouragement of local autonomy as stipulated in Article 3.

The most important means that were explicitly spelled out to achieve

---

of Palestine sitting as a High Court of Justice dealt with the question of the legal validity of the Land Transfers Regulations made by the High Commissioner under Article 16 D of the Palestine (Amendment) Order-in-Council, which prohibited the transfer of land within a specific zone between Jews only. The Court ruled that the Regulations did not violate the fundamental principles of English law, but refused to consider whether they also contravened the terms of the Mandate. It held that the terms of the Mandate, being a covenant between Great Britain (as Mandatory) and the Principal Allied Powers, were not enforceable in the Municipal Courts of Palestine, save insofar as they were embodied in the Order-in-Council or in the laws made by the legislature of this country. Inasmuch as no such law or ordinance existed with this kind of provision incorporated in it, the terms of the Mandate were therefore declared by the Court to be unenforceable. This ruling was a prime example of judicial misfeasance or misconduct involving bad faith, because the court cited a rule concerning international treaties and their incorporation into the domestic law of Palestine which really had no application in Palestine in respect to the Mandate. Britain had no legal authority to civilly govern Palestine except by the very Mandate which the Supreme Court of Palestine said was inapplicable. The judgment of the court stripped the Mandate of any meaning or purpose. The Supreme Court of Israel has taken the opposite stand in regard to the applicability of the Mandate in the domestic law of Palestine, ruling that it indeed applied, even without any specific law of incorporation.

the purpose of the Mandate were found in Article 6 which required the Administration of Palestine – i.e., the Government – to facilitate Jewish immigration under suitable conditions and close settlement by Jews on the land, including State lands and waste lands not required for public purposes. This article in the Mandate was in essence the international recognition of the Jewish right of return to their ancestral homeland, combined with the accompanying right of those Jews who immigrated to the Land of Israel to settle anywhere in the country. This right of return always existed under Jewish law (*halakha*), but was denied by the Ottoman authorities from 1882 onwards, and during the period of British Mandatory rule was hemmed in by illegal British restrictions that resulted in so-called "illegal immigration", differentiated from what was described as "legal immigration". The quicker Jewish immigration could take place under suitable conditions, the quicker the purpose to establish the Jewish State could be realized. The suitable conditions for immigration should have meant the improvement of the conditions existing in Palestine to make it easier for Jewish immigrants to settle in the country by encouraging such things as its economic, health and transportation infrastructure and maintaining public order and security. Instead the British interpreted these "conditions" in Article 6 as a qualifying test on the kinds of Jewish immigrants who could enter the country, allowing in only those who had good employment prospects, were self-supporting or had sufficient capital, who met certain health requirements and were not considered Bolsheviks, among other conditions. The result was to drastically reduce the number of immigrants who were allowed entry, the opposite of what was intended.

One of the ways Jewish immigration could be facilitated was expressly mentioned in Article 7 which required the Government of Palestine to enact a nationality law to allow Jews who took up permanent residence in Palestine to acquire Palestinian citizenship. The granting of citizenship in the context of the Mandate represented an act of Palestinian Jewish statehood inasmuch as only existing states have the right and power to confer distinct citizenship on their residents. Hebrew was recognized as one of the official languages of Palestine which could be used on stamps or money under Article 22, and Jewish holy days were recognized as legal days of rest for members of the Jewish community under Article 23.

Other means to achieve the purpose of the Mandate were set out in Article 11, which referred to the development of the country's natural resources, the establishment of public works, services and utilities and the introduction of a land system appropriate to the needs of the country which would promote, among other things, close settlement and intensive cultivation of the land.

Another very important means to achieve the Mandate's purpose was provided for in Article 4: the recognition of an appropriate Jewish agency as a public body to advise and cooperate with the Administration of Palestine in economic, social and other matters affecting the Jewish National Home and to assist and take part in the development of the country. The original agency designated under Article 4 was the Zionist Organization and from 1929 onwards, this agency was the Jewish Agency, working in close cooperation with the Zionist Organization.

The general provisions of the Mandate referred to a host of matters such as defining the powers of the Mandatory, establishing a judicial system, maintaining democratic freedoms and safeguards for religious rights, including free access to Holy Places, religious buildings and sites, organizing the forces necessary for the preservation of peace and order and also for the defense of the country, regulating archaeological excavations and antiquities, dealing with the obligations of the Mandatory in regard to the Council of the League of Nations and resolving disputes relating to the interpretation or the application of the provisions of the mandate between the Mandatory and another member of the League of Nations. These general provisions were not meant to be seen as divorced from the "purely Jewish National Home provisions", as Britain falsely made it appear in invoking the article for separating Transjordan from the rest of Palestine and simultaneously dividing the Articles of the Mandate into those which were applicable to the Home and those that were not. This kind of division was completely alien to the whole spirit of the Mandate, since all its provisions were a coherent and indispensable whole related to the future independent Jewish State and not to an Arab state. The ironic result was that this false dichotomy came to be accepted by everyone, including Jews, which led to the misinterpretation of the Mandate. It was a perfect illustration of the way the British distorted the true meaning of the Mandate, without always arousing suspicion or protest.

The Mandate for Palestine must therefore be seen as a unified document, containing all the requirements and combining all the qualities and characteristics of an independent Jewish State in the making. Every article of the Mandate, with the exception of the one dealing with Transjordan, fulfilled that purpose of state-making, not just those which expressly mentioned the Jewish National Home. If one of the purposes of the Mandate had been to detail Arab national rights, then it could be justly said that the Mandate contained non-Jewish National Home provisions, but that was definitely not the case, as one will look in vain for such rights in the Mandate apart from the right to use Arabic.

The relationship of the Mandate to the Balfour Declaration was confusing to most people, and still is even today. Both came into being on separate dates, but were intimately connected with one another or interlocking. Each had the very same purpose in mind. The Balfour Declaration, in its new dress as the San Remo Resolution on Palestine where it is combined with Article 22 of the League Covenant, is the base document or skeleton for the establishment of the Jewish State, while the Mandate fills in all the details or covers it with flesh and blood for implementing the Declaration, including all the so-called "non-Jewish articles". However, we should not consider the Declaration or the Mandate as unrelated acts, completely distinct from one another or only partially related, but as component parts of the same building foundation to establish the independent Jewish State, each representing a different stage or building block in its establishment. The Mandate for Palestine is really, in essence, the Balfour Declaration writ large, or put another way, an enlarged written format of the Declaration, in completion of it.

The Mandate also includes the Franco-British Boundary Convention of December 23, 1920 as one of its implicit terms, insofar as this convention deals with the delineation of the boundaries of Palestine. The Convention also deals with other points which form no part of the Mandate for Palestine. A provision for setting forth the boundaries of Palestine was originally supposed to be included in the Mandate itself, and indeed a blank space was left open for their inclusion either in one of the articles or in an annex to the Mandate in its early drafts. However, the question of final boundaries raised too many difficulties with France who insisted on following the defunct and illegal Sykes-Picot Treaty to the great detriment of a united Jewish country embracing the historical limits of Palestine, from Dan to Beersheba, so it was decided to settle the whole matter in a separate boundary convention that was officially signed by Britain and France shortly after the Draft Mandate was submitted to the League Council for confirmation on December 6, 1920. Thus a string of international acts were all linked together, the Balfour Declaration as recognized under international law in the San Remo Resolution in conjunction with Article 22 of the Treaty of Versailles (the Covenant of the League of Nations), the Mandate for Palestine, and the Boundary Convention of December 23, 1920 respecting the northern boundary of Palestine with Syria-Lebanon. All these acts together formed a composite whole that comprised the founding documents of Palestine and the Jewish State of Israel under international law.

The Mandate as a legal document produced permanent legal rights for the Jewish People that did not end with the Mandate, when the latter expired at midnight of May 14-15, 1948. It is precisely those rights which give Israel today the title of sovereignty over all of Palestine and the Land of Israel. These rights are protected from the vicissitudes of material change by virtue of the principle of acquired legal rights and its flip side, the doctrine of Estoppel, as will be discussed below. Any attempt therefore, to give those rights to another entity – in particular, to the fictitious Palestinian people – in regard to Judea, Samaria and Gaza by creating new acts of so-called "international law" – through the medium of U.N. Resolutions adopted by the General Assembly, Security Council or any other organ of the United Nations or by American and European recognition of a so-called "Palestinian State" would be completely illegal – in violation of the acquired legal rights and title of sovereignty of the Jewish People over the same territory. If acquired legal rights belonging to the Jewish People over the territory comprising the Jewish National Home, could be so easily changed at will, by transferring them to Arabs who have transformed themselves into "Palestinians", there would be no value at all to international law as a body of respected law. The situation is no different in private civil law where a person may inherit the rights to family property and personal identity from his parents or antecedents after their decease. In the same manner, the State of Israel, as the assignee of the Jewish People, has inherited the national rights of the Jewish People under the aforementioned founding documents, even though the Mandate itself is no longer in operation, once the state was declared and established.

In addition, all the rights and obligations in the Mandate also continue to exist in Israeli constitutional law, save as they have been modified by Israeli legislation and by the re-birth of the State. This arises from Article 11 of the Law and Administration Ordinance of 1948, the first law adopted in the State of Israel, which provided for the continuation of the law previously existing in Palestine on the eve of the establishment of the State. The Supreme Court of Israel has in several judgments recognized the Mandate for Palestine as being part of the legal structure that existed during the Mandate period and hence it is still relevant today in dealing with such subjects as the right to establish Jewish settlements in any part of the Land of Israel under Israeli rule, and to claim any other rights granted in the Mandate unless they have been modified, as noted above.[21]

The right to establish Jewish civilian settlements anywhere in the Land of Israel, including Judea, Samaria and Gaza, is a continuing legal right of the Jewish People and hence of the State of Israel, derived directly from articles 6 and 11 of the Mandate for Palestine. This right remains in force today, since any right acquired under a legal instrument, such as the Mandate, does not expire with the execution of the instrument which gave birth to such right, as later codified in Article 70 (1)(b) of the 1969 Vienna Convention on the Law of Treaties, to which the Mandate for Palestine, though technically not a treaty, may be legally assimilated. In addition, as just noted above, the same right was incorporated into Israeli constitutional law by virtue of Article 11 of the Law and Administration Ordinance (1948), as well as by the Law of Return, enacted by the Knesset on July 5, 1950, which formalizes the pre-existing Jewish Right of Return that applies to all of the Land of Israel, not merely to the State of Israel.

Seen in perspective, the Mandate for Palestine was actually a job or a service to be performed by the Mandatory according to the agreed instructions of the Supreme Council of the Principal Allied Powers as originally set down in the San Remo Resolution. By virtue of those instructions, which were equivalent to a power of attorney from the Principal Allied Powers to Great Britain, the latter undertook the job to establish the Jewish State in all of Palestine on behalf of the League of Nations who then replaced those Powers as the body supervising the Mandatory. The Mandate also had the characteristics of a trust, in that the job also involved the management of the property of the Jewish People (i.e.,

[21] See Leon V. Gubernik (1948), I Piskei Din 58 (Law Reports of the Supreme Court), also found in *Selected Judgments of the Supreme Court* (English), Vol. I, p. 41; Al-Karbateli v. Minister of Defence (1949/50) 2 P.D. 5. See also National Groups v. Minister of Police (1970) 24(ii) P.D. 141 at 212.

the territory of Palestine or Land of Israel) by the Mandatory Power. As history recorded, Britain never succeeded in the job assigned to it by the Supreme Council of the Principal Allied Powers to create the Jewish State. When, in fact, Britain gave up the Mandate, which was followed immediately by the establishment of the Jewish State in a truncated part of Palestine, not only did the rights of the Mandatory or Trustee to perform the job cease upon its resignation, but also the very job itself, i.e, the Mandate, ceased. The Jewish People then took over directly the task formerly defined in the provisions of the Mandate and created by itself the Jewish State, without the help or intervention of any third party or nation. It is true that the State as proclaimed did not cover the entire patrimony of the Jewish People, which is the crux of the problem today, because substantial parts of the Jewish-designated lands under the Mandate were either given away illegally by the Mandatory to neighbouring States before the Jewish State came into being or were seized in acts of aggression during the War of Independence of 1948-49 by Transjordan and Egypt and even temporarily by Lebanon, that wanted to extend its boundaries to include western Upper Galilee that had been allotted to the Arab state proposed in the U.N. Partition Resolution of November 29, 1947. Syria captured land in eastern Upper Galilee (Mishmar HaYarden) but was required to return it in accordance with the Israel-Syria Armistice Agreement. There is therefore a job still to be done by the Jewish State that was left unfinished upon the termination of the Mandate – to recover all of its lost property or patrimony (i.e., the land illegally removed or transferred to other states) and then to incorporate the recovered land into the borders of Israel, as should have been done in June 1967, when Judea, Samaria and Gaza were repossessed.

This job, though, is no longer based on the Mandate instrument which officially expired at midnight on May 14-15, 1948, but rests squarely upon the need to implement the legal rights that were acquired by the State of Israel from the Jewish People under the Mandate instrument at the date of expiry. These rights continue to exist in full force and effect to this very day, and are the legal justification or basis for the existence of the State of Israel under international law.

A final point to consider concerning the Mandate for Palestine is the question of its alleged illegality. Arab spokesmen constantly raised this point throughout the period it was in force in Palestine. According to their oft-heard argument, the Mandate was illegal because it violated the League Covenant, specifically Article 20 and paragraphs 1 and 4 of Article 22. In so arguing, the Arabs were unintentionally and ironically acknowledging that the Mandate for Palestine was drawn up for the ultimate aim of securing Jewish independence, rather than for the benefit of the local Arab population, otherwise they would never have raised this legal argument. Their argument called into question the entire legal foundation for reconstituting the Jewish National Home in Palestine.

Article 20 provided that members of the League were obliged to abrogate all obligations or understandings inconsistent with the terms of the Covenant or not to enter into any engagements that were also inconsistent with those terms. It strains the imagination to believe that the authors of the Covenant, who gave their unqualified approval to the Mandate for Palestine, would find any inconsistency between the Covenant itself and what they intended for Palestine, as the Jewish National Home and future independent Jewish State. The Covenant was intended to produce a new world order to achieve international peace and security as well as justice for all peoples under international law. This included not only Arabs, but also Armenians, Kurds, Assyrians, Lebanese Christians and, of course, Jews, *inter alia.* In regard to Palestine, the Mandate sought to right the great injustice inflicted on the Jewish People nineteen centuries earlier by the brutal Roman destruction of the Jewish state of Judea. Under the intended new world order, the Arabs were rewarded with several countries of their own in Arabia, Syria and Mesopotamia that had not existed as independent states for many hundreds of years. It was only just and equitable that if the Arab peoples were entitled to renewed sovereignty in lands until recently occupied by the Turks, so were Jews entitled to revive their ancient homeland. Had there existed any inconsistency, as the Arabs argued, between the Covenant and the Mandate for Palestine, the Jewish claim to Palestine would never have been accepted and recognized by all the nations of the world who were members of the League of Nations.

As regards paragraph 1 of Article 22 of the Covenant, which referred to "the well-being and development of peoples" inhabiting territories no longer under the rule of their former sovereigns, this principle was never meant to apply to the Arab inhabitants in yet-to-be-created Palestine, but rather to the Jews of the world including about 80,000 [22] already settled in the land and the millions expected to arrive in the years ahead. Paragraph 1 of Article 22 was a general rule expressing the intention that various peoples formerly under the sovereignty of the Ottoman and German Empires were entitled to self-determination, this applying as much to the Jewish People by virtue of their historical connection with the Land of Israel as it did to the Arabs.

A more specific rule in regard to Arab self-determination was paragraph 4 of Article 22 which referred to "certain communities" formerly belonging to the Turkish Empire, whose existence as independent nations could be provisionally recognized. This paragraph was an implied reference to Syria and Mesopotamia (Iraq), but not to Palestine which, as already noted, had been set aside for the Jewish National Home. This was then made perfectly clear in articles 94 and 95 of the Treaty of Sèvres which specifically differentiated the Mandates for Syria and Mesopotamia, on the one hand, based on paragraph 4 of Article 22, from the Mandate for Palestine, on the other hand, based on Article 22 *treated as a whole*. In this sense, the Mandate for Palestine was *sui generis*, one of a kind, containing elements from all of the provisions of Article 22, but without falling

[22] The Churchill White Paper of June 3, 1922 confirmed that the Jewish population of Palestine in 1922 was 80,000, of whom 25,000 had entered the country since the British military occupation began four years earlier.

within any specific category as set out in paragraphs 4-6 of Article 22. While the Treaty of Sèvres was never ratified, it still remained valid as an inter-Allied agreement and is significant as indicating what the Allied Powers, as the creators of the Mandates System, had in mind in regard to the newly mandated states.

That no contradiction existed between the Mandate for Palestine and the League Covenant is further demonstrated by the adoption of the Smuts Resolution by the Allied Supreme Council on January 30, 1919. This resolution, which constituted the legal basis of Article 22 of the Covenant, listed Palestine among the countries for which Mandates would be conferred, it being clearly understood that Palestine was to be the Jewish National Home in accordance with the Balfour Declaration. Palestine thus indicated the Jewish People. This was further evidenced by the Feisal-Weizmann Agreement signed on January 3, 1919, under which Palestine was to remain separate from the projected Arab state (or states). President Woodrow Wilson, a leading progenitor of the League Covenant, personally endorsed both the Balfour Declaration and the Smuts Resolution, as well as the concept of a Jewish Commonwealth. Thus the very formulators of the Covenant and the Mandates System, Jan Christiaan Smuts and President Wilson, saw no inconsistency between the Covenant and the Mandate for Palestine. It would seem that only those animated by a deep sense of anti-Zionism perceived such inconsistency. All other international bodies that examined the Mandate for Palestine never found it to be illegal, contrary to the allegations made by Arab advocates. These included the Council of the League of Nations, which confirmed the Mandate on July 24, 1922; the Permanent Court of International Justice[23] and the United Nations Special Committee on Palestine.[24] In conclusion, the Arab case for the illegality of the Mandate for Palestine was without substance and constituted a crude attempt to prevent the Jewish National Home and State from being realized, while their own aspirations for national independence were being fully satisfied.

---

[23] The Permanent Court of International Justice heard a case brought by the Greek Government on behalf of its national, Euripides Mavrommatis, contesting the concession granted by the Government of Palestine to the Palestine Electric Corporation in 1921 – the Rutenberg concession – for the generation of electricity throughout the country. A previous concession had been granted to Mavrommatis by the Turkish Government in 1914 to supply electricity to Jerusalem. The Court, in upholding the validity of the Turkish concession to Mavrommatis, assumed the legality of the Mandate, the question of such legality not having been raised by any of the parties to the suit.

[24] The Report by the United Nations Special Committee on Palestine, submitted to the General Assembly on August 31, 1947, made the following appraisal of the Arab argument that the Mandate for Palestine was illegal: "There would seem to be no grounds for questioning the validity of the Mandate for the reason advanced by the Arab states. The terms of the Mandate for Palestine, formulated by the Supreme Council of the Principal Allied Powers as a part of the settlement of the First World War, were subsequently approved and confirmed by the Council of the League of Nations." See: Chapter II (D), "The Conflicting Claims", no. 179, p. 117 in the book, *Report on Palestine,* Somerset Books, Inc., New York City (1947).

*Chapter 6*

# Locus of Sovereignty over Palestine and the Land of Israel under the Mandate[1]

As a result of combining Article 22 of the Covenant of the League of Nations with the Balfour Declaration, originally in the San Remo Resolution of April 24-25, 1920, and subsequently in the Mandate for Palestine of July 24, 1922, *de jure* sovereignty in terms of ownership or title to the newly-created country or mandated state of Palestine was devolved upon the Jewish People under international law, and not on the community of local inhabitants, as happened in the new mandated states of Syria and Mesopotamia. Article 22 of the League Covenant was the source or well-spring of *de jure* sovereignty in favour of peoples or communities inhabiting the ex-German colonies and ex-Turkish territories that became subject to the Mandates System, who were "not yet able to stand by themselves under the strenuous conditions of the modern world", as stated in the first paragraph of that article", and therefore needed the tutelage of advanced nations who would assume the joint functions of Mandatories, Trustees and Tutors in regard to such peoples or communities on behalf of the League of Nations.

Article 22 did not specifically mention the Jewish People in this context, but by linking this article with the Balfour Declaration to create Palestine at the San Remo Peace Conference on April 24-25, 1920, it became applicable to the Jewish People though the Jews of Palestine were then a distinct minority in the country. Therefore, in relating to the inhabitants, peoples or communities of the territories to be placed under mandate, Article 22 should not be construed as referring, in the case of Palestine, to the Arab inhabitants of the country at that time, but rather to World Jewry – including the approximately 80,000 Jews already living in Palestine, and those Jews expected to immigrate there in the future – clearly the national beneficiary of the Mandate for Palestine. This

[1] This chapter should be read in conjunction with Chapter 3, Pillars of Support Underlying Jewish Legal Title (Sovereignty) To Palestine Under International Law, as well as Chapter 12, Effecting a Transfer of Sovereignty without a Peace Treaty by Subjugation or Consent after a Simple Cessation of Hostilities.

exceptional arrangement in favour of the Jewish People was definitively decided on April 24, 1920 at the San Remo Peace Conference, as noted *supra*, when the Principal Allied Powers adopted the Balfour Declaration as the only reason for creating the new state of Palestine. Even before the San Remo Resolution, it should also be recalled that the earlier-discussed Smuts Resolution passed by the Council of Ten on January 30, 1919 at the Paris Peace Conference that formed the basis of Article 22 had Palestine in mind as one of the territories that would benefit from the principle of self-determination in accordance with the Balfour Declaration that was approved by various European nations, the U.S. and also by Emir Feisal representing the Hedjaz and the wider Arab national movement. However, the right of *de jure* sovereignty – as in other cases under the Mandates System – was held in abeyance for the Jewish People until Palestine could be fully developed as an independent Jewish State, a process that required as much time as it would take to enable the Jews to become a majority in Palestine through immigration and their recognized right of return. During this transitional period all rights or attributes of sovereignty were exercised not by the Jewish People, but by Great Britain in its tri-functional role as Mandatory, Trustee and Tutor or Guardian.

Article 1 of the Mandate for Palestine provided the British Government with full powers of legislation and of administration, save as they may be limited by the terms of the Mandate. The greatest limitation of British powers was that Britain as the Mandatory could take no action nor propose any modification in the text of the Mandate Charter which would change its nature or purpose to establish the Jewish National Home, meaning an eventual independent Jewish State. This limitation was derived both from the San Remo Resolution and the second recital in the Preamble of the Mandate which stated that the Principal Allied Powers, in addition to giving effect to Article 22 of the Covenant, "have also agreed that the Mandatory should be responsible for putting into effect the declaration originally made on November 2, 1917, by the Government of His Brittanic Majesty, and adopted by the said Powers, in favour of the establishment in Palestine of a national home for the Jewish People...". The limitation of British powers to legislate for and administer Palestine meant that the Mandatory could not extinguish or restrict the right of Jews to immigrate and settle in any part of the country under Article 6 of the Mandate because that would defeat the very purpose for which the Mandate existed, as well as the reason it was entrusted to Britain.

Another very important limitation was that the Mandatory could neither cede nor lease any part of the territory of the theoretical or embryonic Jewish State of Palestine to the Government of any foreign Power as enunciated in Article 5 of the Mandate, inasmuch as the land comprising Palestine did not belong to either the Mandatory or to the League of Nations. Nor for the same reason could Britain annex the whole or any part of the mandated territory or hold specific areas or zones in perpetuity under a permanent mandate as was actually proposed in the Peel Partition Plan of 1937. Under the Peel Plan, the

British zone under permanent mandate consisted of Jerusalem, Bethlehem and their environs, Nazareth, as well as a corridor to the coast at Jaffa. As a further limitation, the British administration of Palestine was subject to the oversight of the Council of the League of Nations, which was advised and assisted by the Permanent Mandates Commission. Under paragraphs 2 and 7 of Article 22 of the Covenant and as confirmed in the sixth recital of the Preamble of the Mandate for Palestine, Britain exercised the mandate on behalf of the League of Nations in conformity with the provisions of this article. Thus there was no doubt that Britain did not possess sovereignty over Palestine, otherwise it would have been free to disregard the terms of the Mandate at will and not make any annual report to the Council as it was required to do concerning the way it observed the Mandate.

The power to make laws and enforce them over a specific territory is one of the principal attributes of sovereignty, and so placing legal limits on what the Mandatory could do proved it did not have absolute legal authority over Palestine. Britain was granted delegated powers as the Mandatory, Trustee and Tutor for Palestine by the Supreme Council of the Principal Allied Powers, thus allowing it to exercise the attributes of sovereignty, without actually becoming the sovereign of Palestine. Britain acted in favour of a national beneficiary, the Jewish People, who held the legal status of a minor or ward in regard to the Mandate, Trusteeship and Tutorship conferred upon it.

There is a difference in international law between sovereignty as such and the exercise of the attributes of sovereignty by a foreign state over territory which is not its own but which comes under its administration.[2] It is also clear from the experience of trust territories under the U.N. Charter that the "administering authority", which is equivalent to the role of a Mandatory ruling over a mandated territory, did not possess sovereignty or unchallengeable supreme authority over

---

[2] On this point, see L. Oppenheim, *International Law*, Volume I, 6th edition, edited by Sir Hersch Lauterpacht, section 94n, pp. 235-236. The distinction between one state holding *de jure* sovereignty over a specific territory while another state actually exercises the attributes of sovereignty over the same territory was seen in the case of Smyrna (known today as Izmir) as spelled out in Articles 69 and 70 of the Treaty of Sèvres which read as follows: Article 69: "The city of Smyrna and the territory defined in Article 66 [the territory adjacent to the city of Smyrna] remain under Turkish sovereignty. Turkey, however, transfers to the Greek Government the exercise of her rights of sovereignty over the city of Smyrna and the said [adjacent] territory. In witness of such sovereignty the Turkish flag shall remain permanently hoisted over an outer fort in the town of Smyrna. The fort will be designated by the Principal Allied Powers." Article 70: "The Greek Government will be responsible for the administration of the city of Smyrna and the territory defined in Article 66, and will effect this administration by means of a body of officials which it will appoint specially for the purpose.." The Treaty of Lausanne restored Smyrna (Izmir) to Turkey and most of the Greeks living there left for Greece, after a separate convention was signed between the two countries providing for an exchange of populations which was carried out under the supervision of the League of Nations.

the trust territory, though it exercised all the rights and powers of sovereignty during the time it administered the trust territory. What essentially applied to trust territories as determined in the U.N. Charter applied also to mandated territories as set out in Article 22 of the Covenant of the League of Nations.[3]

The facts on the ground, however, in Palestine during the time Britain administered the country showed that despite the clear provisions of the Mandate, Britain acted as if it were the actual sovereign, unhampered by restrictions of any sort, rather than merely being the selected administrator of a Mandated territory. This development manifested itself as early as the Churchill White Paper of June 3, 1922, continued unabated up to the McDonald White Paper of May 17, 1939 and thereafter until the very end of the Mandate on May 14, 1948. Britain treated Palestine as a dependency or Crown colony, where the applicability of the provisions of the Mandate inside the country was denied by outrageous judgments of Palestine Courts dominated by British judges. It barred Jewish participation in the Government or Administration, restricted the right of return of Jews to their national home, as well as their right to acquire land, proposed illegal partition plans and adopted other measures in violation of the Mandate.

The situation of a Mandatory Power not having actual sovereignty over the territory it administered, though exercising the attributes of sovereignty, prevailed in all of the other mandated territories, except in the case of Iraq, whose national sovereignty was recognized almost from the start of King Feisal's rule over the country. The right of sovereignty or ownership of the mandated territory did not vest in the Mandatory, even where such territory was made an integral part of the Mandatory's own territory, as shown in the landmark case concerning the status of South-West Africa (subsequently renamed Namibia) and the Union of South Africa which acted as the Mandatory Power and had the same full powers of legislation and administration as Britain possessed over Palestine.

*A fortiori* no sovereignty could have been vested in Britain over Palestine which was territorially distant from Britain and separated from it by large bodies of water.

If Britain did not have sovereignty over Palestine, under international law, neither did the League of Nations, as an international organization or entity. The League was never more than the supervisor of Great Britain in administering the Mandate for Palestine to ensure that its terms were being fully observed. The League of Nations was assigned that role by the coalition of Principal Allied and Associated Powers when it was officially created by the Treaty of Versailles upon the latter's ratification on January 10, 1920.

Prior to the League's birth, there were proposals made to vest it with sovereignty over the mandated territories, but they were not adopted. The most important proposal of this kind came from President Wilson. It is found in

---

[3] See Oppenheim, *op. cit.*, pp. 235-236 and 459-460.

the Mandates Article of his second draft of the Covenant where he wrote as follows:[4]

> In respect of the peoples and territories which formerly belonged to Austria-Hungary and to Turkey, and in respect of the colonies formerly under the dominion of the German Empire, the League of Nations shall be regarded as the residuary trustee with sovereign right of ultimate disposal or of continued administration…

President Wilson's view that the League of Nations should have the "sovereign right of ultimate disposal" and be the "residuary trustee" corresponded with a statement he made on the way to the Paris Peace Conference on December 10, 1918 that the German colonies [and presumably, by extension, the Turkish Middle East territories] "should be declared the common property of the League of Nations…"[5]

However, in President Wilson's next draft of the Covenant all mention of the League's proposed sovereign right of disposal as regards the mandated territories was eliminated, although he still assigned it the role of residuary trustee. The new version now spoke only of the League's "right of oversight or administration".[6] In the final version of the Mandates article adopted by the Peace Conference on April 28, 1919, both the right of administration and its projected role as residuary trustee were omitted, leaving the nascent League only with a power of supervision.

Another proposal to grant sovereignty to the League of Nations before it actually came into existence was made by the Zionist Organization when it submitted several draft resolutions or proposals to the Peace Conference in Paris, first in a printed Statement dated February 3, 1919, and then in an oral presentation to the Council of Ten on February 27, 1919. The third resolution or proposal stated as follows:[7]

> The sovereign possession of Palestine shall be vested in the League of Nations and the Government entrusted to Great Britain as Mandatory of the League.

When Foreign Secretary Balfour saw the resolution, he amended it as follows:[8]

---

[4] David Hunter-Miller, *The Drafting of the Covenant*, Vol. 2, Doc. 7, p. 87.

[5] *Ibid.*, Vol. I, Chapter IV, p. 43. President Wilson's view was recorded in notes taken by one of his advisers, the geographer Dr. Isaiah Bowman, who was present with a dozen others en route to Paris when Wilson explained his ideas on the Peace Conference and the League of Nations.

[6] *Ibid.*, Document 9, Volume 2, p. 103.

[7] *The Rise of Israel*, Vol. 10, Document 57, p. 195 and Document 61, p. 228.

[8] *Ibid.*, Vol. 10, Document 60, p. 221.

> The sovereign possession of Palestine shall be vested in the League of Nations who shall select a Mandatory responsible for the Government of the Country.

Thus it is interesting to note that Balfour himself, so intimately involved in setting up the British administration of Palestine in its early stages and an extremely important minister in the Lloyd George Government, never believed that sovereignty over Palestine vested in Britain itself. It is equally intriguing to note that neither Balfour nor the Zionist Organization itself considered that sovereignty over Palestine vested in the Jewish People, the actual national beneficiary of the Mandate for Palestine.

Despite Balfour's seeming acceptance of the Zionist proposal on the question of sovereignty, second thoughts quickly emerged on the advisability of this proposal at a meeting of the British delegation in Paris that was held on March 21, 1919 and continued on the following day. According to the minutes of the two-day meeting, the proposal regarding sovereignty was not accepted. The minutes stated "that the sovereignty of Palestine would have to be vested in the Mandatory who would be responsible to the League of Nations".[9]

It is apparent from the foregoing that though the League of Nations was seen as a possible repository of sovereignty over mandated territories, it was not in fact given that function. It is true that all Mandatories acted on behalf of the League and had to render annual reports to the Council in reference to the territories committed to their charge but the League had no independent power to exercise direct rule over any mandated territory under Article 22 of the Covenant, nor the right to interfere in the affairs of the territory on its own volition, or even to initiate any proposed modifications in the terms of a Mandate. The role played by the League of Nations as supervisor of the Mandates System did not, therefore, make it the sovereign of the territories it supervised. That was clearly shown in regard to the Saar Territory (now called Saarland, a state or province of Germany), which is the only case where a European Mandate actually existed, but governed by special provisions found in the Treaty of Versailles rather than by Article 22 of the Covenant of the League of Nations. The Saar Basin, as it was styled in the Treaty, came under the direct administration of the League of Nations in the capacity of trustee for a period of 15 years (1920-1935), which allowed it to exercise the attributes of sovereignty without being the actual sovereign of the territory, as confirmed by Article 49 of the Treaty of Versailles.[10] If the League of Nations did not have sovereignty in a situation where it exercised direct administration or control of

---

[9] *Ibid.*, p. 223.

[10] Article 49 of the Treaty of Versailles reads: "Germany renounces in favour of the League of Nations, in the capacity of trustee, the government of the territory defined above. At the end of fifteen years from the coming into force of the present Treaty, the inhabitants of the said territory shall be called upon to indicate the sovereignty under which they desire to be placed.

a territory that was not placed under the sovereignty of any state or people, all the more reason why it did not have sovereignty when it only had a lesser power of supervision over the Mandatory, as in the case of Palestine.

To better understand that the League of Nations never had sovereignty over any mandated territory despite the fact that the Mandatory was accountable to it and could not modify the terms of a mandate without its consent, as provided in Article 27 of the Mandate for Palestine, it is relevant to quote what Lord Balfour said on the subject of Mandates and the exact role of the League of Nations, when he appeared at the 18th Session of the League:[11]

> The Mandates are neither made by the League nor can they in substance be altered by the League... Remember that *a Mandate is a self-imposed limitation by the conquerors*[12] *on the sovereignty which they obtained over conquered territories* (emphasis added). It is imposed by the [Principal] Allied and Associated Powers themselves in the interests of what they conceived to be the general welfare of mankind; and they have asked the League of Nations to assist them in seeing that this policy should be carried into effect. But the League of Nations is not the author of the policy but its instrument...

It is clear from what Lord Balfour told the League of Nations that sovereignty over mandated territories conquered from Germany and Turkey could have only vested in the Principal Allied and Associated Powers as a collective group who in that capacity were the conquerors referred to by Lord Balfour in the above quotation. The period of joint Allied sovereignty which included the United States only in regard to the ex-German territories, but not for the ex-Turkish territories, was only for an interim period that lasted from the time they first conquered the territories during the course of World War I until they devised and put into effect the Mandates System as part of the peace settlement reached after the war, which automatically led to the divesting of their sovereignty and its transfer to the national beneficiaries of each of the Mandates in whose favour they were established. As Balfour correctly noted, the League of Nations played no part in creating the Mandates System. It had no say or input in determining the fate or eventual disposition of the conquered territories specifically as to which of them would be part of that system and who would be selected as Mandatories. It served only as an instrument of the policy put in place by the Principal Allied and Associated Powers without enjoying any rights or attributes

---

[11] Charles H. Levermore, *Third Year Book of the League of Nations*, p. 137. Cited on p. 47 of the book *British Rule in Palestine* by Bernard Joseph, published by Public Affairs Press, Washington, D.C., 1948.

[12] In the case of Turkish "Palestine" and the rest of the ex-Turkish Middle East, the "conquerors", and hence the sovereigns, were deemed to be all four Principal Allied Powers collectively, rather than Britain alone, even though it was primarily Britain that conquered Palestine, Mesopotamia and Syria.

of sovereignty over the mandated territories. It should also be remembered that not all territories liberated from Turkey in World War I were placed under the Mandates System. At the behest of Britain, those countries excluded from the System were, most notably, Arabia, Cyprus and Egypt. In addition, no mandate was ever awarded over the proposed "national home" for Armenia, as originally envisaged.

Balfour's statement that sovereignty was placed in the joint hands of the Principal Allied and Associated Powers because they were the conquerors of German and Turkish territories was also assumed even earlier by Professor Felix Frankfurter when he made a tentative draft of a mandate for Palestine in March 1919. He declared in the Preamble to this draft that the Emperor of the Ottomans had ceded sovereignty over Palestine to the "Signatory Powers" who had signed a treaty of peace with him, which in the context of the situation could have only been the Principal Allied Powers who had fought against him in World War I.

The subjugation[13] of the Ottoman Empire in World War I was sufficient by itself to effect a short-term change of sovereignty from the defeated enemy to the subjugating victorious coalition of Great Powers, without the immediate need of a treaty to confirm the change of sovereignty and cession of territory, provided there existed an undisputed intention on the part of those Powers not to restore the rule of the Ottoman Empire in regard to the non-Turkish populated provinces of the Ottoman Empire and simultaneously to bring those provinces within the ambit of the Mandates System as a legal alternative to their annexation or establishment as protectorates. That is exactly what happened on January 30, 1919 at the Paris Peace Conference, when the Supreme Council of the Principal Allied and Associated Powers, sitting as the

---

[13] Subjugation as a mode of acquisition of territory is defined as the conquest of enemy territory through military force in time of war followed by annexation of it, in whole or in part. In the case of the ex-German and ex-Turkish territories of World War I, annexation and/or the establishment of protectorates was replaced by the Mandates System that included a form of trusteeship and tutelage for the peoples living there in accordance with the principles proclaimed in the Covenant of the League of Nations and even earlier in President Wilson's Fourteen Points of January 8, 1918. Subjugation takes place without any treaty. Where transfer of territory does occur in a treaty, it is not considered subjugation but cession. See: Oppenheim-Lauterpacht, *International Law, a Treatise*, 6th Edition, Sections 236 and 237, pp. 566-67.

One proof of the subjugation of the Ottoman Empire and the fact that this Empire ceased to exist is seen by the change of its name to, simply, Turkey. Prior to the Treaty of Sèvres of August 10, 1920, all treaties signed on behalf of the Ottoman Empire were done either in the name of the Imperial Ottoman Government or in the name of His Imperial Majesty the Sultan. But in the Treaty of Sèvres, the designation of the Ottoman Empire was suddenly dropped, though the Sultan was still serving as Head of State. The name of the State in whose name the treaty was signed by representatives of the Sultan's Government was now given only as Turkey.

Council of Ten, approved the Smuts Resolution as the basis of the Mandates Article in the Covenant of the League of Nations (Article 22) and decided that former German colonies in Africa and Oceania, as well as former Turkish territories in Asia, would be permanently severed from Germany and Turkey. The Allied decision was then made a formal part of the Treaty of Versailles, signed five months later on June 28, 1919, which incorporated all the provisions of the League Covenant, including the Mandates Article. It may be concluded that as of January 30, 1919, Ottoman sovereignty or supreme authority over Palestine, Syria and Mesopotamia ceased forever and passed into the hands of the Principal Allied Powers. These Powers did not divide up the conquered territories among themselves, as they originally planned to do under the secret Sykes-Picot Treaty of May 9 and 16, 1916 and supplemented by the equally secret St. Jean de Maurienne Agreement of August 18, 1917 in which Italy acceded to the Sykes-Picot Treaty and became a full partner to its provisions with Britain, France and Russia. Instead of annexing any of these territories, they acted, as Lord Balfour said, "in the interests of what they conceived to be the general welfare of mankind" by creating the Mandates System and transferring their collective title of sovereignty over each mandated territory to the national beneficiaries of the various Mandates created under that system. In the case of Palestine, the devolution of nominal sovereignty to the national beneficiary was made at the San Remo Peace Conference on April 24-25, 1920, in favour of the Jewish People. Henceforth, the Jewish People were vested with *de jure* sovereignty under international law over all areas of the Jewish National Home which also embraced Transjordan, but they did not exercise *de facto* sovereignty, inasmuch as the administration of Palestine was place in the hands of Britain, who exercised the attributes of sovereignty, particularly the power of enacting legislation, except as limited by the terms of the Mandate.

This sequence of events in regard to the transfer of sovereignty over Palestine is actually acknowledged in the Preamble to the Mandate for Palestine in the first three recitals.

Each of these recitals has already been discussed *supra*, but they bear reiteration because they specify the three components or pillars of the Jewish legal title to the country, and are therefore of very great significance in understanding the question of sovereignty over Palestine. The first Recital of the Preamble refers to Article 22 of the Covenant of the League of Nations, embodied in Part I of the Treaty of Versailles, which created the Mandates System under which Palestine became a mandated territory or state. This reference to Article 22 meant that the principle of national self-determination called there "the well-being and development of peoples" would also apply to Palestine and the people or nation who would be the national beneficiary of this principle. However, the first recital in the Preamble of the Mandate does not specifically identify the people who shall be the beneficiary to be placed under the tutelage of an advanced nation in order to achieve national independence, though no mystery existed as to who was meant since Palestine was already promised to the

Jewish People for their national home in the Balfour Declaration of November 2, 1917, as further evidenced by the Weizmann-Feisal Agreement of January 3, 1919 and the Smuts Resolution of January 30, 1919.

The second Recital incorporates the text of the Balfour Declaration as adopted by the Principal Allied Powers in the San Remo Resolution on Palestine on April 24-25, 1920 at the Peace Conference convoked to dispose of the non-Turkish Asiatic possessions of the Ottoman Empire. The text which was adopted changed the British role and nature of its obligation from one of "us[ing] their best endeavours to facilitate the achievement" of the object of the Declaration, namely, to establish in Palestine a national home for the Jewish People into an obligation in which Britain "should be responsible for putting into effect" the same object. The significance of this Recital lay in the official designation of the national beneficiary of the Mandate – namely, the Jewish People, most of whom were not yet settled in the country, a feature that made this Mandate the most unique of all the Mandates and made it the focus of heavy criticism from Arabs and their supporters. The designation of Jews to be the national beneficiary is also inversely shown by the fact, that the community of local Arab inhabitants were not mentioned directly by name in the entire document. No rights were accorded to Arabs as a collective national and political entity. They were, however, implicitly included as individuals only in all the references in the Mandate pertaining to the Moslem religious community and its religious institutions (*waqfs*), sacred shrines and schools, in the provisions dealing with the prohibition of discrimination based on race, religion or language, in the safeguarding and protection of their civil and religious rights, in not prejudicing their economic well-being and position and in the official recognition of the Arabic language. Apart from the last right, these were rights that were also accorded to all sections of the population of Palestine who would come under the rule of an eventual independent Jewish State. They were normal rights given to the citizens of any democratic state, but naturally excluded national rights to set up a separate state of their own or any form of political self-rule or national autonomy, which could lead to independence and the break-up of Palestine as a unitary state.

The third Recital of the Preamble has a two-fold importance. It mentions, first of all, the historical connection of the Jewish People with Palestine, which is why that country was chosen to be the Jewish National Home and awarded by the Principal Allied Powers to the Jewish People. The words "historical connection of the Jewish People with Palestine" which appeared in a July 1919 draft of the mandate originated with Foreign Secretary Balfour himself.[14] This

---

[14] See "The Palestine Mandate Negotiations, 1919-1921" contained in the *Reports of the Executive of the Zionist Organization to the 12th Zionist Congress*, printed in *The Rise of Israel*, Vol. 8, Document 57, p. 182. The first Zionist proposals to the Paris Peace Conference (February 3 and 27, 1919) originally stated that "the High Contracting Parties recognise *the historic title* of the Jewish People to Palestine and the right of the Jews to reconstitute in Palestine their National

Recital then provides the best proof confirming Jewish legal title to the country when it organically links together all three components of this title, by stating as follows:

> "...recognition has *thereby* been given... to the *grounds* for *reconstituting* their national home in that country" (emphasis added).

There are three key words in the third recital, which are of utmost importance; these are "thereby", "grounds" and "reconstituting". The word "thereby" does not refer only to the historical connection of the Jewish People with Palestine as it had in some of the earlier drafts of the Mandate, but also to the "grounds" in the plural for reconstituting their national home in that country. Both words ("thereby" and "grounds") join together the first three Recitals of the Preamble into one composite whole. These "grounds" in consecutive order were (1) the right of national self-determination for the "people" of Palestine, a term which in the context of the Mandate, particularly Articles 2 and 6, anticipated the millions of Jews expected to immigrate to the country and who would be tutored by an advanced nation until reaching the stage of Independence; (2) the designation of the Jewish People as the national beneficiary of the Mandate for Palestine; and (3) the historical connection of the Jewish People with Palestine. These "grounds" for reconstituting the Jewish State can be further summarized or broken down as references to (1) Article 22 of the Covenant of the League of Nations, (2) the international recognition and adoption of the Balfour Declaration contained in the San Remo Resolution on Palestine upon which the Mandate for Palestine was subsequently formulated and (3) the long and continuous history of the Jewish People with the Land of Israel spanning close to four millennia.

Added proof of the Jewish legal title to Palestine as given in the third Recital of the Preamble is the use of the words "reconstituting their national home in that country", which is a direct reference to the State of Judea which came to an end when the Second Temple was destroyed by the Roman general Titus in the year 70 C.E. It was the State of Judea, the last Jewish state in the Land of Israel, that was to be "reconstituted" by the implementation of the Mandate for Palestine, thereby putting an end to Jewish homelessness. Judea was the region of Palestine and the Land of Israel most intimately connected to the Jewish People by history and religion. The word "Judea" in Greek and Latin actually means "the Jewish country", further evidence of the Jewish historical connection with Palestine, and is ultimately derived from the name of the Jewish Kingdom of Yehuda (Judah) in the First Temple Period, which co-existed with the Northern Kingdom of Israel, after the breakup of the United Monarchy

---

Home". Balfour amended this proposal to read as follows: "The High Contracting Parties recognize *the historic connection* of the Jewish People with Palestine and the claim which this gives them to find a national home in that country." See *Rise of Israel,* Volume 10, Document 100, page 221. (Emphasis added)

under Kings Saul, David and Solomon.

The instrument containing the Mandate for Palestine is thus the final locus or resting place of Jewish legal rights of sovereignty and title to all of Palestine. However, it must be stressed, that although the Mandate for Palestine is of immense importance for asserting these national rights, it is not the starting-point of Jewish sovereignty over all of Palestine. That point occurred on April 24-25, 1920, when the Balfour Declaration was adopted by the Principal Allied Powers as the reason for creating "Palestine" (April 24, 1920), which until then did not formally exist, to be under British Mandatory administration (April 25, 1920) for the benefit of the Jewish People, who were defined as World Jewry or the Jewish People as a whole, rather than merely the Jews of Palestine.[15] It was then that Article 22 of the League of Nations Covenant became intertwined and integrated with the Balfour Declaration which together with it devolved sovereignty over Palestine to the Jewish People to reconstruct the Jewish National Home and establish an eventual independent Jewish State. This conclusion represents the only true and logical meaning to be derived from joining Article 22 with the Balfour Declaration and the historical connection – Jewish sovereignty over all of Palestine and the Land of Israel under international law – as reflected in the San Remo Resolution and the Mandate for Palestine.

[15] At the outbreak of World War I in 1914, the Jewish population in the Land of Israel numbered 85,000 persons constituting only 0.6% of world Jewry. By the end of the War in 1918, the Jewish population was reduced by 28,000 to 57,000, because of Turkish expulsions. Though tiny in comparison to the Arab population, the existing Jewish community served as a nucleus for its eventual expansion into a majority. See *Encyclopaedia Judaica* (1971), Vol. 9, p. 474.

*Section Two*

# Continuation of Jewish Legal Rights and Title of Sovereignty over Palestine upon the Termination of the Mandate for Palestine

*Chapter 7*

# The U.N. General Assembly Resolution 181 (II) on the Future Government of Palestine – The Partition Resolution of November 29, 1947

Jewish legal rights and title of sovereignty to Palestine, which were firmly and irrevocably established under international law by the global political and legal settlement worked out by the coalition of the Principal Allied Powers during and after World War I, were never altered afterwards by any other binding act or instrument of international law which met the test of legality. With the coming to power of the British Labour Party in July 1945, these legal rights and title came under increased jeopardy and testing under the Government of Prime Minister Clement Richard Attlee. Pursuant to a Cabinet decision made on February 14, 1947, Foreign Secretary, Ernest Bevin, announced in the British House of Commons four days later that the Government would submit the question of Palestine's future to the United Nations because it saw no prospect for a settlement to end the impasse between the Jewish and Arab positions. A request was officially made by letter dated April 2, 1947, submitted by the U.K. Delegation to the Acting Secretary-General of the United Nations to place the question on the agenda of the General Assembly based on Article 10 of the Charter under which the General Assembly is authorized to make "recommendations" to the members of the United Nations or to the Security Council on any questions or matters "within the scope of the Charter or relating to the powers and functions of any organs provided for in the Charter".

Just prior to referring the question of Palestine to the United Nations, the Attlee Labour Government had tried to find a solution of its own. It initially proposed the Morrison Plan to set up a provincial system of government leading either to outright partition or to federal unity in a bi-national state embodied in a trusteeship agreement for Palestine. This plan of provincial autonomy, also called the Morrison-Grady Plan, was devised by a committee headed by U.S. Ambassador Henry F. Grady and British Deputy Prime Minister Herbert Morrison. The latter presented it to the House of Commons on July 31, 1946. It proposed dividing Palestine into four cantons or autonomous provinces.

The Arab province was to get 40% of the area of Cisjordanian Palestine, and the Jewish province – 17%. The rest of Western Palestine comprising 43% of the territory would form two British provinces, one for the Jerusalem district, and the other for the Negev. A British central government in Palestine would have administered the whole plan under trusteeship. This plan was rejected by the Arab states and by the Jewish Agency for Palestine, as well as by the U.S. Government in a public statement issued by President Harry S. Truman on October 4, 1946. Speaking for the Jewish Agency for Palestine, as Chairman of the Executive, David Ben-Gurion stated:

> We oppose this Plan because it is merely a modification of the White Paper of 1939 and the changes are not always even to the advantage of the Jews. We oppose the Plan because it deprives the Jewish People of its rights in its homeland, as promised to it by the Balfour Declaration and the Mandate. We oppose it because it conflicts with the international obligations of Great Britain and all the promises of the Labour Party to the Jewish People for nearly thirty years…[1]

In his detailed criticism of the Plan, Ben-Gurion amplified on the meaning of the Balfour Declaration:

> The undertakings of the Balfour Declaration applied at the outset not to a tiny Jewish Province nor yet alone to western Palestine, but to the whole of the country in its full historical and geographical boundaries, to the East and West of the Jordan. To whittle away these obligations to this point is the height of betrayal of that principle of fair play of which the British people is so justly proud.[2]

In regard to the Morrison Plan on Jerusalem, which included Bethlehem and the surrounding Arab villages, Ben-Gurion said:

> [it] is not designed to protect [the] Holy Places but to tear out from the Jewish homeland its very heart, the eternal Jewish city of Jerusalem which is the religious, national, political and scientific centre of the Jewish People. Moreover, the Plan is calculated to deprive the Jewish majority of Jerusalem of its existing political rights.[3]

---

[1] *Book of Documents (1917-1947)* submitted to the General Assembly of the United Nations Relating to the Establishment of the National Home for the Jewish People, compiled by Abraham Tulin, for The Jewish Agency for Palestine, New York, May 1947, pp. 287-288.

[2] *Ibid.*, p. 291.

[3] *Ibid.*, p. 293.

And in reference to British control over the Jerusalem district and the Negev, Ben-Gurion also voiced his great displeasure:

> For more than three thousand years, Palestine has been the homeland of the Jewish People. During the past few decades the Arabs have begun to claim that Palestine is an Arab country, but we have never heard that England has any claim to this country, or to any part of it, and it is difficult to explain in what respect it is either fair or reasonable for Great Britain itself to assume control – even if only, as we are told – temporarily, of one third of the area of Western Palestine... To hand it over to the English is to steal away from the Jewish People – the only homeless and landless people in the world – a large part of the area which is completely open for immigration and settlement, and which is quite uninhabited; it is to condemn the Negev to everlasting desolation and to deprive the Jewish settlements which have already been established there at the cost of so much labour and devotion, to isolation and stagnation.[4]

Upon rejection of the Morrison-Grady scheme, Foreign Secretary Bevin presented new proposals on Palestine on February 7, 1947, known as the Bevin Plan, which amended the former scheme to meet some of the criticism it engendered. It proposed a five-year Trusteeship over Palestine, with the declared object of preparing the country for independence, in accordance with Article 76 of the U.N. Charter.[5] The country would not be partitioned under the proposed Trusteeship Agreement. The new plan suffered the same fate as its predecessor, rejected by both the Arab and Jewish sides. The Jewish Agency found the Bevin Plan to be incompatible with the existing Mandate in regard to Jewish immigration, land settlement and ultimate Jewish statehood. Faced with unbridgeable negative reactions to their unrealistic plans, the weary and frustrated British Government decided as a last resort to put the Palestine Question before the United Nations General Assembly on April 2, 1947. A statement explaining the purpose of the British step was made in the House of Commons:

> We are not going to surrender the Mandate. We are going to the United Nations setting out the problem and asking their advice as to how the Mandate can be administered. If the Mandate cannot be administered in its present form, we are asking how it can be amended.[6]

---

[4] *Ibid.*, p. 293-94.

[5] For the text of Article 76 of the U.N. Charter, see *infra* in the present chapter.

[6] See article on Zionism in *Encyclopaedia Judaica*, (1971) Volume 16, column

In reaction to the British request to the Secretary-General of the United Nations that the question of Palestine be placed on the agenda of the next regular session of the General Assembly, the latter set up the "United Nations Special Committee on Palestine", better known as UNSCOP. Its mission was to "investigate all questions and issues relevant to the problem of Palestine" and "to prepare a report to the General Assembly and submit such proposals as it may consider appropriate for the solution of the problem of Palestine", not later than September 1, 1947. The special committee was composed of eleven members representing Australia, Canada, Czechoslovakia, Guatemala, India, Iran, the Netherlands, Peru, Sweden, Uruguay and Yugoslavia, presided over by Swedish Chief Justice Emil Sandstrom as chairman and Alberto Ulloa of Peru as vice-chairman. None of the five permanent members of the Security Council or of the Arab states were represented on the special committee. In its report to the General Assembly on August 31, 1947, a majority of seven committee members recommended[7] dividing Cisjordanian Palestine into an Arab State and a Jewish State. The proposed Arab state was to embrace western Galilee, Judea, Samaria and the southern coastal plain from Ashdod to the Sinai frontier and a portion of the western Negev. The proposed Jewish state would include eastern Galilee, the Jezreel Valley, most of the coastal plain and the Negev. Jerusalem was to be placed under an international Trusteeship scheduled to last for at least ten years, upon the conclusion of a Trusteeship Agreement which would designate the United Nations as *the Administering Authority* in accordance with Article 81 of the Charter of the United Nations. An economic union was recommended for the two States, which would also include the city of Jerusalem. The minority plan concurred in by India, Iran and Yugoslavia favoured a united federal Palestine, in which Jews, though having the autonomy of a so-called "state", would remain in a minority position subordinate to the Arabs. The other member of the committee, Australia, refused to subscribe to either of the two plans, and abstained.

The UNSCOP majority report was adopted by the General Assembly on November 29, 1947, by means of Resolution 181 (II) with a two-thirds majority of those present and voting (33 in favour, 13 opposed and 10 abstentions including the United Kingdom). The General Assembly Resolution contained a number of territorial changes in the boundaries of the Jewish State as originally proposed by UNSCOP. These chiefly concerned the Negev and the city of Jaffa, then populated mostly by Arabs. The proposed Jewish state was now allotted a larger area of the Negev than previously, and was to extend all the way to Eilat. However, the town of Beersheba still remained outside the borders of the Jewish State under the approved U.N. plan. In the UNSCOP Plan, Jaffa was placed inside the proposed boundaries of the Jewish State, but in the General

1091, written by Moshe Medzini.

[7] Report on Palestine: Report to the General Assembly by the United Nations Special Committee on Palestine, Somerset Books (1947), pp. 176-177.

Assembly version, it was taken out, largely through American influence, and shifted to the Arab State as an enclave surrounded by the Jewish State. In terms of figures, the Jewish State was allotted 5,579 square miles out of 10,000 square miles of Cisjordanian Palestine. The area allotted to the Jewish State also had an Arab population of 397,000 representing 46.46 *per cent* of the total population living there.[8]

Britain accepted the unanimous opinion of UNSCOP that the Mandate be terminated, in contrast to its earlier stated position not to relinquish the Mandate, but it openly and actively campaigned against the Partition Plan prior to its adoption and abstained in the vote of the General Assembly on the plan, held on November 29, 1947. Having failed to block its approval, Britain then refused to cooperate with the General Assembly in the implementation of the plan.

The General Assembly had appointed a five-member U.N. Palestine Commission which intended to travel to Palestine to set up provisional government councils for the proposed Jewish and Arab states to effect an orderly transfer of power from Britain to the new authorities. Britain, however, refused to allow the Commission even to enter Palestine before May 1948, on the ground that it alone was responsible for the administration of Palestine until the end of the Mandate. This led to the eventual disbandment of the Commission. The ironic result was that despite having requested and receiving the recommendations of the General Assembly, the British did not allow it to implement those recommendations.

The position taken by the Jewish Agency for Palestine in regard to the Partition Plan was born out of pressing necessity, duress or *force majeure*, in order to solve the problem of Jewish homelessness and to provide a state, with all the powers and prerogatives attached to it, for the Jews already living in Mandated Palestine, regardless of its territorial dimensions, and also for the hundreds of thousands of Jewish displaced persons stranded in war-ravaged Europe who had survived the Holocaust and were hoping to come to Palestine. That position was formally enunciated by Reform Rabbi Dr. Abba Hillel Silver, the Chairman of the American section of the Jewish Agency and a powerful advocate of the Zionist cause, in a statement he presented on behalf of the Jewish Agency on October 2, 1947 to the U.N. Ad Hoc Committee on the Palestine Question. Dr. Silver told the Committee that the Jewish Agency for Palestine approved the Partition Plan as first proposed in the UNSCOP Report of August 31, 1947, even though the City of Jerusalem would be established as a separate unit and hence not included in the proposed Jewish State. Other areas of Western Palestine would also be excluded, particularly Judea and Samaria and the Western Galilee. Despite these grave omissions from the proposed Jewish State, Dr. Silver explained to the Ad Hoc Committee on the Palestine Question why the Jewish Agency was prepared to make such a heavy sacrifice. In the

[8] See the article on "United Nations and Palestine-Israel", *Encyclopedia of Zionism and Israel*, (1971) Volume 2, p. 1143 ff.

words of Dr. Silver:[9]

> If that heavy sacrifice [as regards Jerusalem and the other excluded areas of Palestine] was the inescapable condition of a final solution, if it made possible the immediate re-establishment of the Jewish State, that ideal for which a people had ceaselessly striven, if it allowed an immediate influx of immigrants, which would be possible only in a Jewish State, then the Jewish Agency was prepared to recommend the acceptance of the partition solution to the supreme organs of the [Zionist] movement, subject to further discussion of constitutional and territorial provisions. That sacrifice would be the Jewish contribution to the solution of a painful problem and would bear witness to the Jewish People's spirit of international co-operation and its desire for peace.

Dr. Silver, one of the leading Zionist political activists at the time, added a reservation to the Jewish Agency's acceptance of the Partition Plan:[10]

> If [our] offer of peace and friendship were not welcomed in the same spirit [by the Arab states, including the proposed Arab state of Palestine], the Jews would defend their rights to the end. In Palestine there had been built a nation which demanded its independence, and would not allow itself to be dislodged or deprived of its national status. It could not go, and it would not go, beyond the enormous sacrifice which had been asked of it.

In contrast to the Jewish acceptance of the Partition Plan, the Arab representative who spoke before the Ad Hoc Committee on the Palestine Question vociferously rejected the Plan. In a statement presented on September 29, 1947, Mr. Jamal al-Husseini of the Arab Higher Committee of Palestine enunciated the view of the Arabs in Palestine:[11]

> Regarding the manner and form of independence for Palestine, it was the view of the Arab Higher Committee that that was a matter for *the rightful owners of Palestine* to decide (emphasis added). Once Palestine was found to be entitled to independence, the United Nations was not legally competent to decide or impose the constitutional organization of Palestine, since such action would amount to interference with an

---

[9] The Arab-Israel Conflict and its Resolution: Selected Documents edited by Ruth Lapidoth and Moshe Hirsch, Martinus Nijhoff Publishers, Dordrecht, The Netherlands (1992), p. 55.

[10] *Op. cit.*, p. 56.

[11] *Op. cit.*, p. 57.

internal matter of an independent nation.

Al-Husseini then gave a grim warning that force would be used to prevent the implementation of the Partition Plan:[12]

> The Arabs of Palestine were solidly determined to oppose with all the means at their command any scheme which provided for the dissection, segregation or partition of their country or which gave to a minority special and preferential rights or status... the Arabs would lawfully defend with their life-blood every inch of the soil of their beloved country.

It is truly ironic that Arab spokesmen such as Jamal al-Husseini raised the illegality of the U.N. Partition Plan from the Arab perspective which was based on the completely false premise that the Arabs of Palestine were "the rightful owners of Palestine" and were thus entitled to national independence. In actual fact, it was the Jewish nation settled in Palestine that were "the rightful owners" of the country who were entitled to national independence, as duly decided under international law set down in 1919, 1920 and 1922 and embodied in the Smuts Resolution, article 22 of the Covenant of the League of Nations, the San Remo Resolution, the Franco-British Boundary Convention and the Mandate for Palestine. The Partition Plan was indeed illegal, as al-Husseini said, but from the perspective of international law and not from that of the Arab League states and the Arab Higher Committee. The Arab argument shamelessly and crassly inverted the true legal basis for calling the Partition Plan "illegal", since this Plan denied the Jewish People their recognized legal rights to the whole of Palestine while, on the contrary, attributing national rights to the Arabs to large segments of Palestine they were never intended to have under international law. As regards al-Husseini's further argument that the U.N. was not legally competent to decide or impose the constitutional organization of Palestine, this argument had merit only to the extent that the U.N. violated or substantively and improperly changed the actual provisions of the existing Mandate for Palestine formulated in favour of the Jewish People, and not for any Arab people. In fact, the U.N. did exactly what it was not supposed to do – namely, to provide the Arabs with a state and government in Western Palestine, contrary to what the Mandate itself prescribed. The provisions in the Partition Plan providing for self-governing institutions for the Jewish State was in complete accordance with Article 2 of the Mandate, while proposing the equivalent status for the proposed Arab state was not. In sum, the Arab side should have been very satisfied with the Partition Plan because they were slated to obtain rights under this Plan to a substantial portion of Palestine that was never contemplated by the Mandate when it was formulated, and which therefore violated it.

---

[12] *Op. cit.*, p. 58.

Important legal questions arose from the U.N. Partition Plan. Did the U.N. acting through the General Assembly have the power or authority to set aside Jewish legal rights and title of sovereignty to all of Palestine as established in the San Remo Resolution and the Mandate for Palestine? These rights and title were recognized by the U.N. as existing only for the areas of Palestine designated for the proposed Jewish State, but not in those areas reserved for the Arab State, nor in regard to Jerusalem, which was to be converted into a trust territory of the U.N., with its own Governor, as part of a "Special International Regime" also called a *corpus separatum,* under the direct administration of the United Nations rather than through the intermediary of one or more member-States. The idea of establishing a temporary international regime in Jerusalem was also proposed on the last day of the Mandate (May 14, 1948) by the U.S. and France, but it failed to get the necessary support.

Weighed against the legal principle of honouring the acquired legal rights of the Jewish People granted under previous acts of international law as already listed above, acts which could not be negated or overridden by the U.N. General Assembly, the Partition Plan must be considered illegal by any objective legal yardstick, even had the Arab side accepted it. The author here disagrees with Professor Julius Stone who maintained that Resolution 181 (II) would have acquired "binding force" under the principle of *pacta sunt servanda*[13] if the parties at variance had accepted it.[14] The U.N. had a duty imposed by the pre-existing international law to uphold and respect that law which recognized Jewish legal rights and title of sovereignty over the entire territory of Palestine, not merely the areas the U.N. designated for a Jewish State. The failure of the General Assembly to respect that law by proposing a Partition Plan for Palestine which removed recognized integral areas of the Jewish homeland and transferred them to a proposed foreign Arab entity as well as to the United Nations itself in regard to Jerusalem constituted a legal wrong against the Jewish People, that made the whole U.N. Partition Plan invalid from the very start. The General Assembly had no power vested in it under the U.N. Charter to change the legal status of Palestine which had already been irrevocably determined at the San Remo Peace Conference, 27 years before the passage of U.N. General Assembly Resolution 181 (II). It was then that international law first recognized Palestine in its entirety as the Jewish National Home, a legal status it never ceased having. Under one of the important provisions of that law, as spelled out specifically in Article 5 of the Mandate for Palestine, the entire territory was protected from the very partition or dismemberment envisaged in the U.N. Partition Plan. The proposed Plan also violated Article 2 of the Mandate, which provided for the development of self-governing institutions, not for the Arabs of Palestine, but for the Jewish National Home. Moreover, it illegally altered inviolable

---

[13] Agreements not contrary to the laws must be observed in all respects.

[14] *Israel and Palestine: Assault on the Law of Nations*, 1981, Johns Hopkins University Press, p. 101.

Jewish legal rights to all of mandated Palestine protected under Article 80 of the U.N. Charter. The Partition Plan was therefore in clear violation of established international law. In effect, this plan constituted a double violation of international law, one specifically directed against the existing rights of the Jewish People and one directed against the unity of a mandated territory.

The deleterious effect which the proposed U.N. Partition Plan had on acquired Jewish legal rights was noted by three of the most important Zionist leaders of the day, just before it was adopted. Dr. Abba Hillel Silver speaking on October 2, 1947 before the *ad hoc* Committee on Palestine said, in addition to what has already been noted above, that the proposals of the Committee "do not represent satisfaction of the rights of the Jewish People. They are a serious attenuation of those rights".[15]

Moshe Shertok (Sharett) stated on October 17, 1947:

> We took note of the rejection of our own plan; we took note of the unanimous recommendation that the Mandate must be terminated; we took note of the proposal of the majority of the Committee for the partition of Palestine and the establishment in it of two states. With a heavy heart but in full consciousness of the historic responsibility which the step involved, we decided to give this plan our full consideration. The sacrifices involved in *the partition plan* for the Jewish People cannot be exaggerated. It *entails giving up nearly one half of a country* on the regaining of the whole of which the hopes and prayers of countless generations had centered (emphasis added).

On October 18, 1947, Dr. Chaim Weizmann commented:

> It is not an easy compromise to envisage – least of all to one like myself who knows that the original purpose of the Mandate involved no such limitation as is now proposed. Nobody dreamed in those days that the processes of Jewish immigration and of development would have to be confined in *an eighth of the area in which the national home was to be established by international consent* (emphasis added).

The United Nations did not inherit any power from the League of Nations which would have given it the right by itself to change the terms of the Mandate for Palestine. The Mandate was conferred not by the League of Nations but by the Supreme Council of the Principal Allied Powers and as already noted in Section I, the principal function of the Council of the League in regard to mandated territories was to supervise the observance of all Mandates

---

[15] This and the next two quotations appear in the article written by Benjamin Akzin, "The United Nations and Palestine", the *Jewish Yearbook of International Law 1948*, published by Rubin Mass, Jerusalem 1949, contained in footnote 29 on pp. 101-102.

committed to the charge of Mandatories to ensure that all their terms were being faithfully carried out. The League of Nations had no sovereign authority over any mandated territory. It acted as the instrument of the Principal Allied Powers, who created the Mandates System, as Foreign Secretary Balfour stated (see *supra*, Chapter 6). The League of Nations was neither the maker of policy nor a law-making authority with sweeping powers. It is true that the League Council could define the terms of a mandate in certain cases, but that applied only where the Principal Allied Powers, whose four members were permanent Representatives on the Council, were unable to agree upon their formulation. Such disagreement which would have necessitated Council intervention never happened for any of the "A", "B" or "C" Mandates, though points of dispute did naturally arise during the drafting process in regard to the "A" Mandates.[16]

The Mandate for Palestine, in the last Recital of the Preamble, went so far as to state that the Council of the League of Nations, in confirming the said Mandate, was also "defining" its terms. This was a mere "clause de style" or formulaic expression, in imitation of the language used in Article 22 (Paragraph 8) of the Covenant of the League of Nations which envisaged the possibility of the whole Council defining the terms of the Mandate. In actual fact, the terms were defined not by the Council, but by the British Government working in close co-operation initially with the Zionist Organization and, at the end of the drafting process, with France.

The role attributed to the League Council in "defining" the terms of the Mandate for Palestine was thus only a facade to hide or obscure what actually occurred. It was instigated by the British to emphasize the importance of the League of Nations in confirming the Mandate, to impress the United States with whom it was engaged at the time in preliminary negotiations to conclude a treaty regarding the Mandate for Palestine and thereby confer on the U.S. and its nationals the same rights in regard to mandated territories that were conferred on all League members. The British wanted to cajole the Americans into joining the League which it refused to do as a consequence of not ratifying the Treaty of Versailles. The original Draft Mandate submitted to the Council on December 6, 1920 by Lord Balfour did not use the word "define" in regard to the Council's approval of the Mandate. Nor was it included in the one re-submitted in August 1921. This word was added only in a subsequent draft. The exact same change was made in the Mandate for Syria.[17]

---

[16] See Article 96 of the Treaty of Sèvres and Paragraph 8 of Article 22 of the Covenant of the League of Nations, Part I, Treaty of Versailles.

[17] The original draft Mandate for Palestine submitted by Lord Balfour on December 6, 1920 stated: "The Council of the League of Nations... hereby *approves* the terms of the Mandate as follows:..." The change appeared in the final version of the Mandate for Palestine dated July 24, 1922, which contained the following stylistic change: "The Council of the League of Nations... confirming the said Mandate, *defines* its terms as follows:...". In this context it is always worth remembering that the Mandate for Palestine, as in the case of all other

Once the terms of a mandate were formulated by the Principal Allied Powers – or more specifically, by those delegated to act in their name – and then confirmed and "defined" by the League Council in a stylistic but not real sense, the consent of the latter was henceforth required to make any modifications.[18] However, this did not mean that the Council could make the modifications on its own volition, as the United Nations General Assembly attempted to do in regard to the Partition Resolution of November 29, 1947. If the League had such power, it would have meant it was the superior authority for Palestine, contrary to Article 1 of the Mandate, which specifically gave full legislative authority and administration to the Mandatory. The League Council on its own initiative never attempted to make any modifications in the terms of the Mandate during the entire period the Mandate came under its supervisory jurisdiction, nor could it legally have done so because it was assumed that this power belonged exclusively to the Mandatory. The same inability of the League Council to change the existing terms of the Mandate held true with equal force regarding the United Nations General Assembly.

Another important legal question which arose in the wake of the adoption of the U.N. Partition Plan by the General Assembly was tracing the source of power, if any, in the U.N. Charter authorizing the Assembly to adopt the Plan, which did not conform to the existing terms of the Mandate for Palestine, nor to other acts of international law, nor even to Article 80 of the U.N. Charter whose text is given immediately below. After the formal dissolution of the League of Nations on April 18, 1946, the provisions of Article 22 of the Covenant of the League were replaced by Chapters XI, XII and XIII of the U.N. Charter, which dealt respectively with non-self-governing territories, the International Trusteeship System and the Trusteeship Council. The principal provisions in the Charter which affected the continuing implementation of the Mandate for Palestine and its possible replacement by a system of trusteeship were found in Articles 76, 77, 79, 80, 81 and 85, which read as follows:

*Article 76*

> The basic objectives of the Trusteeship system, in accordance with the purposes of the United Nations, shall be: a. ... b. to promote

Mandates that comprised the Mandates System were conferred or assigned by the Supreme Council of the Principal Allied Powers. The official title of the "Mandate for Palestine" is no more than that, without the addition of such epithets as "League of Nations" or "British". To describe any mandate as being a "League of Nations" Mandate is misleading, because it gives a false impression that it was the League of Nations, rather than the Allied Supreme Council that actually conferred the Mandates upon the Mandatories under Article 22 of the Treaty of Versailles and the other peace treaties which concluded the First World War. If a descriptive term is to be applied to indicate the origin of the Mandate or the party who conferred it, the words "Principal Allied Powers" or "Great Powers" or "Allied Supreme Council" or some similar variant should be employed.

[18] Article 27 of the Mandate for Palestine.

the political, economic, social and educational advancement of the inhabitants of the Trust territories, and their progressive development towards self-government or independence as may be appropriate to the particular circumstances of each territory and its peoples and the freely-expressed wishes of the peoples concerned, and as may be provided by the terms of each trusteeship agreement.

*Article 77*

The trusteeship system shall apply to such territories in the following categories as may be placed thereunder by means of trusteeship agreements (a) territories now held under mandate, (b)..., (c)....

2. It will be a matter for subsequent agreement as to which territories... will be brought under the trusteeship system and upon what terms.

*Article 79*

The terms of trusteeship for each territory to be placed under the trusteeship system, including any alteration or amendment, shall be agreed upon *by the states directly concerned,* including the Mandatory Powers in the case of territories held under mandate by a Member of the United Nations and shall be approved as provided for in articles 83 and 85 (emphasis added).

*Article 80*

*Except as may be agreed upon in individual trusteeship agreements*, made under Articles 77, 79, and 81, placing each territory under the trusteeship system, *and until such agreements have been concluded, nothing* in this Chapter[19] *shall be construed* in or of itself *to alter in any manner the rights whatsoever of any states or any peoples or the terms of existing international instruments* to which Members of the United Nations may respectively be parties... (emphasis added).

*Article 81*

The trusteeship agreement shall in each case include the terms under which the trust territory will be administered and designate the authority which will exercise the administration of the trust territory. Such authority, hereinafter called *the administering territory*, may be one or more states or the Organization itself (emphasis added).

*Article 85*

1. The functions of the United Nations with regard to trusteeship agreements for all areas not designated as strategic, including the approval

[19] Chapter XII dealing with the International Trusteeship System.

> of the terms of the trusteeship agreements and of their alteration or amendment, shall be exercised by the General Assembly....
>
> 2. The Trusteeship Council, operating under the authority of the General Assembly, shall assist the General Assembly in carrying out these functions.

The above articles of the Charter, particularly Article 80, show that the General Assembly had no power of its own to decide unilaterally to replace or terminate an existing Mandate under which a specific territory was governed and to place it under the international trusteeship system with the aim of establishing self-government or independence for the benefit of the people of a newly-created trust territory. This inability of the General Assembly or Trusteeship Council to act on its own initiative without the consent of the Mandatory Power was understood at the time to be the controlling rule. Barring exceptional circumstances, the United Nations could only act after an individual trusteeship agreement had been worked out by *the states directly concerned*, which then required the approval of the General Assembly. If no trusteeship agreement was made by *the states directly concerned*, the mandate continued in force. The probability of not being able to conclude a trusteeship agreement could explain why Britain did not originally expect to be called upon to surrender the Mandate, even after it submitted the Palestine Question to the United Nations on April 2, 1947 when it only sought U.N. advice on how the Mandate should be amended.

In the case of Palestine, *the states directly concerned* could have only been the states which comprised the coalition of Principal Allied Powers, i.e., Britain, France, Italy and Japan who collectively agreed to the creation of Palestine as a mandated state on April 24, 1920 and to entrust the administration of the country under the Mandates System to Britain on April 25, 1920 for the purpose of giving effect to the provisions of Article 22 of the Covenant of the League of Nations as well as the Balfour Declaration of November 2, 1917. Another state that was directly concerned with the Mandate for Palestine in the legal sense was the United States because of the treaty it signed with Britain on December 3, 1924 making it in effect a contracting party for the implementation of the terms of the Mandate. Altogether this represented five states who were directly concerned in the affairs of Palestine. But two states were disqualified, Italy and Japan, because of their responsibility for World War II, their defeat and their renunciation or forfeiture of all rights and claims deriving from the Mandates system in respect of any mandated territory.[20] In

---

[20] See article 40 of the Peace Treaty with Italy, quoted in the article "The Trusteeship System" by Duncan Hall, in the *British Yearbook of International Law*, 1947, p. 52, and also the statement by the United States about the forfeiture or extinction of Japan's right to be a Mandatory for the North Pacific Islands, because of its violation of the Mandate, on p. 53 of Hall's article, including footnote 2 found there. The Pacific Islands north and south of the equator consisted of various island groups. Those in the North Pacific Ocean that were mandated to Japan in

addition to the disqualification of Italy and Japan, a third country – France – voluntarily withdrew itself from involvement in the affairs of Palestine, leaving it to Britain and the United States to make the critical decisions about Palestine as the "states directly concerned".

It should be noted and emphasized that none of the Arab States were "directly concerned" in the legal sense with the resolution of the Palestine Question, though they falsely claimed to have this legal status.[21] Nor for that matter was the "Arab Higher Committee" who represented the interests of the Arabs of Palestine in the United Nations debate on Palestine in 1947, a true party to this question, since the Mandate for Palestine did not recognize Arab national rights in the country, except in the limited sense of language, as a matter of culture rather than national or collective political rights. The Arabs of Palestine were not one of the peoples contemplated by Article 80 of the Charter in regard to this Mandate, nor for that matter by Article 22(1) of the Covenant of the League of Nations, as incorrectly assumed in the report of the Palestine Royal Commission of 1937. In this context, the correspondence in October 1946 between President Truman and Abdul-Aziz Ibn Saud, the founder and first King of Saudi Arabia, was very revealing. The latter complained about opening the "floodgates of immigration" in support of the Jews in Palestine, whom he labeled "aggressors seeking to perpetuate a monstrous injustice" against the Arabs of the country, whose "natural rights" to it, he said, go back "thousands

---

1920 as "C" Mandates were the Caroline Islands (Yap and Palau), the Marshall Islands and the Mariana Islands. At the close of World War II, they were seized by U.S. forces and then became part of the U.S.-administered "Trust Territory of the Pacific Islands", under a strategic area Trust Agreement approved in 1947 by the U.N. Security Council, based on Articles 82 and 83 of the U.N. Charter. Yap became part of the independent state of Micronesia in 1986, while Palau and the Marshall Islands became separate independent political entities. The Northern Mariana Islands chose to become a U.S. Commonwealth.

[21] This issue came up for general discussion at the tenth meeting (August 5, 1937) and the eleventh meeting (Aug. 6, 1937) of the Thirty-Second (Extraordinary) Session of the Permanent Mandates Commission held at Geneva between June 30 and August 18, 1937. The Chairman of the Commission, Pierre Orts of Belgium, maintained that the Arab States led by Iraq and Saudi Arabia were third parties to the Question of Palestine, with no right to intervene in its internal affairs, which nonetheless both sought to do. Such intervention, he asserted, violated the principle of the territorial independence of Palestine under Article 5 of the Mandate which made the Mandatory "responsible for seeing that no Palestine territory shall be ... in any way placed under the control of the Government of any foreign Power". The intervention of the Arab States, he added, was transforming a local problem into a vast international problem. The British representative, John Hathorn Hall, Chief Secretary of Palestine (1932-1937), replied on Britain's behalf that their intervention was humanitarian to stop unnecessary suffering and loss of life, with no political motives involved. He conceded that Iraq had no right to be heard in the debate before the Commission. The minutes of the 32nd (Extraordinary) Session are published in Volume 25, *The Rise of Israel*, Document 4, beginning on p. 91. The relevant remarks of Orts and Hall are found on pp. 176-182.

of years" to ancient times. President Truman responded to Abdul-Aziz Ibn Saud in the following manner, explaining why he supported the immediate transfer and entry of 100,000 Jewish survivors of the displaced persons camps in Europe to Palestine:

> The Government and people of the United States have given support to the concept of a Jewish National Home in Palestine ever since the termination of the First World War, which resulted in the freeing of a large area of the Near East, including Palestine, and the establishment of a number of independent states which are now members of the United Nations. The United States, which contributed its blood and resources to the winning of that war, could not divest itself of a certain responsibility for the manner in which the freed territories were disposed of, or for the fate of the peoples liberated at that time. It took the position to which it still adheres, that these peoples should be prepared for self-government and also that a national home for the Jewish People should be established in Palestine. I am happy to note that most of the liberated peoples are now citizens of independent countries. The Jewish National Home, however, has not as yet been fully developed. It is only natural therefore, that this Government should favour at this time the entry into Palestine of considerable numbers of displaced Jews in Europe, not only that they may find shelter there, but also that they may contribute their talents and energies to the upbuilding of the Jewish National Home.[22]

It is clear from President Truman's remarkable words that he saw the Jewish People and not the Arab inhabitants of Palestine as the people for whose benefit the country was "freed" during World War I and which would be established as a Jewish National Home that was then still being developed. As Truman rightly observed, the same process that secured the establishment of a Jewish National

[22] *Book of Documents* submitted to the General Assembly of the United Nations, by the Jewish Agency for Palestine, *op. cit.*, pp. 299-303. The letter from King Ibn Saud to President Truman is dated October 15, 1946, and the response is dated October 28, 1946. Truman's desire to see Britain immediately admit 100,000 Jewish refugees was based on the recommendation of Earl G. Harrison, Dean of the University of Pennsylvania Law School and the American representative on the Intergovernmental Committee on Refugees, whom he appointed to investigate the situation of the Jewish displaced persons in Germany and Austria. Truman urged Prime Minister Attlee in a letter dated August 31, 1945 to adopt this proposal which he found to be a meritorious solution to the Jewish refugee problem. But instead of granting his request, Attlee advised the setting up of an Anglo-American committee of inquiry regarding the problems of European Jewry and Palestine. The report completed on April 20, 1946 made the same recommendation earlier proposed by Harrison, which Britain again refused to implement.

Home also led to the establishment of a number of independent Arab states, that had become members of the United Nations.

Britain and the United States alone could have therefore theoretically under the trusteeship provisions of the Charter concluded a trusteeship agreement that then had to be approved by the General Assembly, which would have allowed Britain to continue its administration of Palestine, or alternatively to designate some other state to take its place. The agreement could even have provided for the United Nations to become the administering authority, as permitted by Article 81 of the Charter, but until there was an actual agreement nothing could be done or construed to alter the rights of the Jewish People in Palestine as set down in the existing Mandate, which was the meaning attached to Article 80 and assumed by everyone, including the Arab States.

In 1947, with no prospect of a trusteeship agreement in sight after the failure of the Morrison-Grady Cantonization Scheme and its amended version, the Bevin Plan, a solution for Palestine needed to be urgently found, otherwise the country would have possibly slid into chaos, left without any government after the British departed – barring a possible move by the Jewish Agency for Palestine declaring Jewish independence and setting up its own government. This uncertain situation spurred intervention by the U.N. General Assembly, but in a practical sense such intervention could not be based on the provisions of the Charter relating to the Trusteeship System, since there needed to be a prior trusteeship agreement before the Trusteeship Council, operating under the authority of the General Assembly, could deal with the question of Palestine.[23] The functions of the Trusteeship Council in regard to monitoring the political, economic, social and educational advancement of the inhabitants of the trust territories and their progressive development toward self-government or independence were analogous to the functions of the Permanent Mandates Commission under the Mandates System.

By not being able to undertake any meaningful action under the provisions of the Trusteeship System, the only real option left open for U.N. intervention in the developing situation in Palestine was for the General Assembly to make recommendations for a solution, either on the basis of Article 10 of the Charter or, as it decided to do so, on the basis of Article 14, which reads as follows:

> Subject to the provisions of Article 12,[24] the General Assembly may

---

[23] A somewhat similar situation arose in the mandated territory of former German South-West Africa (a class "C" Mandate), where the Union of South Africa stopped fulfilling the terms of the Mandate, but, unlike Britain, refused to surrender it. In that case, too, the U.N. General Assembly was able to assert authority to terminate the Mandate and devise a plan leading to the eventual independence of the country, now known as Namibia.

[24] Article 12 stated in effect that the General Assembly would not deal with any matter relative to the maintenance of international peace and security while the Security Council also dealt with the same question.

> recommend measures for the peaceful adjustment of any situation, regardless of origin, which it deems likely to impair the general welfare or friendly relations among nations, including situations resulting from a violation of the provisions of the present Charter setting forth the Purposes and Principles of the United Nations.

Wherever the actual source of authority may have been in the Charter justifying U.N. involvement, it was widely accepted that the General Assembly could act to formulate a new plan for Palestine, once the British Government placed the Palestine Question on the U.N. Agenda. What was not acceptable in any legal sense was that it could adopt a partition plan that trampled on Jewish legal rights and title of sovereignty over all of Palestine specifically preserved from alteration by Article 80 in the interim period before a hypothetical trusteeship agreement could be made. This plan was in certain respects a replacement for the missing trusteeship agreement, but it was only a recommendation, with no binding force or self-execution, and therefore could not alter the existing Mandate for Palestine, Jewish rights thereunder. For that matter, neither the General Assembly nor any other organ of the U.N. had the power to abrogate or diminish those rights in any way, but it decided to do illegally exactly that by recognizing Arab national rights in major regions of Cisjordanian Palestine and in removing Jerusalem from Jewish rule to become a U.N. administered trust territory or *corpus separatum*. Those aspects of the Partition Plan contained in Resolution 181 (II) setting up both Arab and U.N. rule in Cisjordanian Palestine contravened *acquired Jewish legal rights* under international law to the entire country based, as already noted on Article 22 of the Covenant of the League of Nations, the San Remo Resolution, the Mandate for Palestine and the Franco-British Convention of December 23, 1920, and finally, the Anglo-American Convention of December 3, 1924 Respecting the Mandate for Palestine, all of which were still in force throughout the year 1947, and therefore made the U.N. Plan illegal, as did Article 80 of the Charter.

As it turned out, the Partition Plan was aborted at birth, both by the British refusal to allow for provisional implementation of the plan while they still governed Palestine as Mandatory and by the simultaneous Arab rejection of the plan and the war they launched to prevent its implementation. Five Arab states fought alongside the local Arab population of Palestine in a war to destroy the Jewish community known as the Yishuv, and thereby prevent the establishment of the projected Jewish State. As a result of this cruel aggression, Resolution 181 (II) had no legal effect, independently of its violation of acquired Jewish legal rights under the terms of existing international instruments made between 1919 and 1924 and preserved by Article 80 of the Charter.

The illegality of the Partition Plan, as well as its still-birth caused in part by lack of British co-operation, but primarily by Arab rejection and initiation of war, allowed the nascent Jewish State declared on May 14, 1948 to legally incorporate into the State all the territorial gains it made beyond the lines suggested by Resolution 181 (II). Had the newly proclaimed State taken complete control of all of the territory of Palestine, west of the Jordan, no legal objection could have been made by anyone, since all of the land was part of the Jewish National Home under international law by virtue of the aforementioned acts of international law concluded immediately after World War I, which are the true founding documents of the State of Israel, rather than Resolution 181 (II).

Another legal question that arose from the British referral of the Palestine Question to the U.N. and the adoption of General Assembly Resolution 181 (II) was whether the Jewish People, acting through its representative bodies, could have taken matters into its own hands and declared independence in Palestine not after but before the adoption of this Resolution. This was certainly a serious option considering the rise in numbers of the Jewish population in Palestine and the desperate straits of the remnant of Jews confined in refugee camps in Germany and Austria after the end of World War II. It is submitted that in the prevailing circumstances, the Jewish Agency for Palestine, which was the officially recognized public body representing the Jewish People in the country, could have legally exercised this option. The Jewish People were ripe for independence because, unlike the situation that existed at the start of the Mandate, it was now able to stand alone and exercise the powers of self-government, at least according to its own perception, which was the only requirement for terminating the Mandate under Article 22 of the Covenant of the League of Nations that was an integral part of the Mandate for Palestine. The consent of the League of Nations or the British Mandatory was not formally needed because declaring independence was not a "modification" of the terms of the Mandate but the realization or fulfillment of its purpose for which it existed. The Jewish People had in effect reached the age of majority and no longer needed an advanced nation to guide it to independence or act as its Tutor. A nation that had reached the age of majority was able to act without the consent of the Tutor or the international body supervising the Tutor, especially in the circumstance where the Tutor who also acted as the Mandatory had willfully violated the Mandate it had received and subverted and abandoned its paramount purpose to gradually bring about Jewish independence. By its own illegal conduct, Britain had thereby forfeited any right it had to continue governing Palestine, just as Japan was stripped of its right to govern the mandated territories in the North Pacific committed to its charge or the Union of South Africa in regard to South-West Africa (formerly German South-West Africa, and today – Namibia) for ignoring the terms of its Class "C" mandate. The fact that no corrective action was ever taken to overturn the Mandatory's wholesale violation of international law completely justified any planned move by the Jewish People to declare its own independence. Had the Jewish People taken this step even before the U.N. General Assembly recommended a Jewish State under its partition plan, this declaration would have been perfectly legal and proper in the prevailing circumstances. There was precedent both for and against this course of action. Iraq's independence in 1932 was approved formally by the League of Nations. However, both Syria and Lebanon declared their independence without the consent of the League of Nations.[25] Neither did Britain seek the prior *formal* consent of the United Nations in laying the groundwork for the independence of Transjordan, which anyhow could not have been legally given, since the detachment of this territory from Palestine violated Articles 2, 5 and 25 of the Mandate, as well as Article 80 of the U.N. Charter. While it was theoretically possible for the Jewish Agency for Palestine to declare independence without waiting for the stamp of approval from the U.N., it cautiously preferred to wait until the U.N. General Assembly submitted its own plan for the future government of Palestine, no doubt to see what kind of proposal would be made and what the world reaction would be.

It is true that the Jewish Agency accepted the concept of partition in August 1946, prior to the Resolution of November 29, 1947, and again on October 2, 1947, in regard to the UNSCOP Plan. It did so in response to the anti-Zionist policy of the British Government and acted under the necessity of obtaining American support for its key demand to establish a Jewish State, even if it covered only a part of Palestine where most Jews lived. Therefore, instead of asking for a Jewish State in the whole of Cisjordanian Palestine, in accordance with the Biltmore Program of May 9-11, 1942,[26] a program that was adopted by the World Zionist Congress (London, 1945) and the World Zionist Congress (Basle, 1946), the Jewish Agency, in contradiction to the official Zionist policy at the time, proposed a plan of its own that roughly excluded Judea and Samaria and the coastal enclave of Jaffa in favour of the Arabs where they constituted the large majority of the population, while Jerusalem, the eternal Jewish city, would be placed under international control but under no circumstances, would

---

[25] The process of terminating the Mandate for Syria and Lebanon included the following steps: (1) Free French General Georges Catroux's Proclamation to the Syrians and Lebanese, June 8, 1941; (2) General Catroux's Proclamation of Syrian Independence, September 28, 1941; (3) General Catroux's Proclamation of Lebanese Independence, November 26, 1941; (4) subsequent piecemeal recognition by various Powers; (5) admission as original members of the United Nations; (6) confirmation of independence made by the Anglo-French Agreement of December 13, 1945. The first three documents can be found in *Syria and Lebanon: A Political Essay*, by A. H. Hourani, Oxford University Press, London, 1946, pp. 308 ff. See also the article by H. Duncan Hall, "The Trusteeship System", in the *British Yearbook of International Law,* 1947, at p. 67, in footnote 3 of Hall's article.

[26] The Biltmore Program was an eight-point declaration adopted by the Extraordinary Conference of American Zionists held at the Biltmore Hotel in New York on May 9-11, 1942. The Program was drafted at the urging of David Ben-Gurion, Chairman of the Jewish Agency Executive, who attended the Conference to re-affirm the original intention of the Balfour Declaration and the Mandate for Palestine: to establish Palestine as an independent Jewish Commonwealth and thereby end Jewish homelessness. The Program became official Zionist policy when it was adopted by the Zionist General Council in October 1942 and later by the World Zionist Organization in August 1945.

it come under Arab rule.

In any event, the consent of the Jewish Agency to the partition of Palestine and the Land of Israel was of no legal effect since any plan based on partition, whether it was its own plan, the U.N. Plan, the Peel Plan or the Morrison-Grady Plan, was illegal *ab initio*, because all such plans violated Articles 2, 5 and 25 of the Mandate by proposing the permanent division of the Jewish National Home and ceding parts of it to the Government of an Arab state or foreign power, and accordingly, no consent, even if freely given, could validate an illegal plan. As already noted above, it should be recalled that the consent of the Jewish Agency for a partitioned Jewish State was born out of urgent concern to save what remained of Central and Eastern European Jewry who were languishing in displaced persons camps after the end of World War II. The immediate establishment of a Jewish State was vitally needed to give these Jewish displaced persons a place to live, where they would also be warmly welcomed, even if the State covered only a small area of Palestine. Jewish consent to a truncated Palestine was therefore equivalent to an act made under legal duress or *force majeure* that vitiated the consent once the immediate emergency had passed.

A third reason invalidating the consent of the Jewish Agency for the partition of Palestine was that so long as the Mandate was still in force, the Jewish population of Palestine and those acting on its behalf were, from a strict legal point-of-view, an unemancipated minor in regard to their legal status or capacity for achieving statehood under Article 22 of the Covenant. The Jewish Agency could, therefore, not validly surrender any of the acquired Jewish legal rights and title of sovereignty over the territory of Palestine and transfer them to the Arabs of Palestine, even if its consent was given without coercion.

The view that the legal status of a national beneficiary of a Mandate was equivalent to that of a legal minor was expressed by the French Government in regard to its Mandate for Syria and Lebanon. At a meeting of the Permanent Mandates Commission in February 1926, the accredited representative of the Government Robert de Caix told the Commission:[27]

> The idea which has governed, if not the whole exercise of the Mandate, at any rate all the efforts made to organize it, is the following: the Mandate is a provisional system designed to enable populations which, politically speaking, are still minors to educate themselves so as to arrive one day at full self-government...

Though de Caix referred to the Mandate in a political context, his observation applies equally to the legal sphere, inasmuch as the parties to a mandate and the national beneficiary thereof, including their rights, duties and capacities, are governed by law.

---

[27] Quoted in the book by A. H. Hourani, *Syria and Lebanon: A Political Essay*, published by Oxford University Press, London, 1946, p. 169.

As a legal minor before full self-government and statehood was achieved, the Jewish Agency, exercising the dual role as representative of World Jewry, as well as acting on behalf of the Jewish community in Palestine, could not validly consent to the U.N. Partition Plan. After the Jewish Agency set up the People's Council in April 1948 to prepare for Jewish independence, the legal status of the Jewish People and its agent, the Jewish Agency, changed, as regards the principles inherent in the Mandates System, from minor to adult. However, the consent to the U.N. Partition Plan given by the People's Council in the Proclamation of Independence that immediately thereafter became the Provisional State Council, was still of no avail since the Plan itself was illegal and the Arab side had rejected it *in toto,* and went to war to erase it. In addition, the Jewish Agency had no legal authority to waive Jewish rights to any part of Palestine, as David Ben-Gurion, Chairman of its executive, himself said in a famous speech in 1937 at the 20th Zionist Congress.[28] Finally, it should be recalled that Dr. Silver, representing the Jewish Agency before the United Nations Ad Hoc Committee on the Palestine Question, accepted the Partition Plan under a reservation that it would also be accepted by the Arab side and therefore, when no such Arab acceptance was ever forthcoming, the Jewish Agency approval of the Plan, already illegal because, *inter alia*, of its violation of Article 5 of the Mandate, automatically became legally null and void.

For all of the foregoing reasons, the Jewish Agency's initial approval of the Partition Plan, which was then reiterated in Israel's Proclamation of Independence, was stripped of all meaning and left without any legal force. That meant that the doctrine of estoppel applied neither to the State of Israel nor to the Jewish Agency, who were thus released from any obligation they may arguably have had to abide by the territorial provisions of the Partition Plan. This was soon reflected in new legislation enacted by the Provisional Government of Israel, namely, the Jerusalem Proclamation of August 2, 1948, the Land of Israel Proclamation of September 2, 1948 and the Area of Jurisdiction and Powers Ordinance adopted on September 16, 1948. All of these enactments[29] were made retroactive to May 15, 1948, the day on which the State of Israel came into being.

The Jewish State came into being as of midnight on May 14-15th, Israel time, or at six o'clock in the evening of May 14, 1948, Washington time. It is necessary

---

[28] See the text of this speech in the author's work, *A Petition to Annul the Interim Agreement*, Ariel Center for Policy Research, Policy Paper #77, p. 95.

[29] The Jerusalem Proclamation, formally known as the Israel Defense Forces Government in Jerusalem Proclamation No. 1, was promulgated in the *Official Gazette of the State of Israel*, Special Issue (August 2, 1948), No. 12, p. 66. The Land of Israel Proclamation, formally known as the Israel Defense Forces Government in the Land of Israel Proclamation No. 1, was promulgated in the *Official Gazette of the State of Israel*, Special Issue (September 3, 1948), no. 19, p. 114. The Area of Jurisdiction and Powers Ordinance may be found in the Official Gazette, No. 23 (September 22, 1948) and also in *Laws of the State of Israel*, Vol 1, Ordinances (1948), p. 64.

to stress that this date of May 14-15, 1948 at midnight marks the official end of the Mandate for Palestine and not November 29, 1947, since the British Government only relinquished its Mandate on the date of the establishment of the State of Israel and not on the date of the adoption of Resolution 181 (II).

The exact date for the termination of the Mandate for Palestine had not been explicitly provided for in the instrument itself, though it was foreseen in both Articles 8 and 28 of the Mandate.[30] As in the case of every other Mandate or trusteeship agreement, the end must come with the achievement of the object for which it was established. That object in regard to Palestine was the establishment of the Jewish National Home which by definition meant an eventual independent Jewish State as soon as the Jews formed a definite numerical majority of the population. This entailed a gradual process but the length of time it would take was unknown at the outset of the Mandate. That moment, which could have arrived much sooner, had it not been for illegal British moves to limit or block large-scale Jewish immigration, only came on May 14, 1948, when the Jews formed a very slight majority in the area of Palestine allotted for the Jewish State by the U.N. Partition Plan. It should also be kept in mind that the Jewish State could have been proclaimed even without a Jewish majority, upon the high expectation that such a majority would have emerged shortly after the proclamation of the State. The latter was not created by the U.N. General Assembly, which implicitly gave its consent for it in advance by the Partition Plan it adopted. The State was created by the independent action of the Jewish People acting through its representative bodies in Palestine, directed by the Jewish Agency.

In justification of this move, Israel's Declaration of Independence of May 14, 1948 cited the Balfour Declaration and Mandate as recognizing the right of the Jewish People to national rebirth in the Land of Israel which, in turn, was predicated upon the historical connection existing between the Jewish People and this country. The Declaration of Independence was right in referring to this historical connection for without it, there would not have been any Balfour

[30] Article 8 dealt with the privileges and immunities of foreigners formerly enjoyed by capitulation or usage in the Ottoman Empire and their possible re-establishment at the expiration of the mandate. Article 28 stated that in the event of its termination, the Council of the League of Nations shall make such arrangements as were necessary for safeguarding in perpetuity existing religious rights such as free access to the Holy Places. Article 28 also stipulated that the Government of Palestine will fully honour the financial obligations legitimately incurred by the Administration of Palestine during the period of the Mandate. Upon the birth of the State, these obligations were assumed by the Government of Israel. The obligations imposed by the Mandate upon its termination directly affected the sovereignty of the re-born Jewish State. Therefore they could only be carried out by the Government of Israel to the extent it deemed proper, without the interference of any foreign body or state. On that basis, it was inconceivable that the capitulatory regime that formerly prevailed in the Ottoman Empire prior to the establishment of the British administration in Palestine could again be applicable in the State of Israel.

Declaration, San Remo Resolution, or Mandate for Palestine in favour of the Jewish People which led directly to the revival of the Jewish State of Israel. However, it must be pointed out that the Declaration of Independence was imprecise in labeling the Jewish legal right to Palestine as an "historical right", since that was equating history with law. The historical connection was the principal reason or ground for claiming or obtaining the Jewish legal right and title of sovereignty to the country under international law, but not identical with it. Thus, the phrase "historical connection" is perfectly accurate, while the alternate phrase "historical right" is simply a misnomer. In addition to the historical factor, the Proclamation of Independence also cited "the natural right of the Jewish People to be masters of their own fate, like all other nations, in their own sovereign state".

The Partition Resolution did not bestow any legal rights or title of sovereignty on the Jewish People, since neither the United Nations nor its predecessor, the League of Nations, ever possessed such rights or title which they were able to bestow on a particular nation or territory, as was the case with the Principal Allied Powers of World War I when they created Palestine in 1920 at the San Remo Peace Conference and transferred to the Jewish People their rights and title over the country which they secured from their defeat of Ottoman Turkey in World War I. It was only then that international law and Jewish law, i.e., the law of Moses contained in the Torah and the Mishnah, intersected or overlapped in regard to the recognition of Jewish legal rights and title of sovereignty over the Land of Israel. Jewish Law, known also as *halacha*, always recognized the existence of such rights and title from the time of the Patriarchal Covenant made by Divine Providence with Abraham, Isaac and Jacob, even when there was no Jewish State in existence. On the other hand, international law, during the time that Palestine, or more properly speaking, Judea, disappeared from the world map, did not afford such recognition until April 24-25, 1920, the date of the San Remo Resolution, which determined that the Land of Israel would once again become a Jewish State in accordance with the Balfour Declaration and Article 22 of the Covenant of the League of Nations.

The Partition Resolution merely gave *additional* international recognition to the rights and title already vested in the Jewish People under the San Remo Resolution. This U.N. recognition was described as irrevocable by the Declaration of Independence. In regard to the Arabs of Palestine, the United Nations General Assembly acted in total disregard of existing international law when it decided to award about 45% of Western Palestine to them. The area of the Jewish State under the UNSCOP Plan was, as Chaim Weizmann pointed out, only one-eighth of the Jewish National Home as originally conceived, when Transjordan and the Golan are taken into account. The General Assembly had no right or authority to take what were in fact Jewish legal rights and transfer them to Palestinian Arabs, who were not the national beneficiary of the Mandate. This proposed illegal transfer of rights was inspired by the false interpretations of the Mandate given in several British White Papers issued between 1922 and 1939, beginning with the Churchill White Paper and ending with the Malcom MacDonald White Paper. The recognition of Arab national rights in Western Palestine, in addition to those illegally created in Transjordan, has now become so firmly planted in the consciousness of the world that it has become an accepted axiom of truth, even though there is not the slightest basis for that idea in the founding legal documents of Mandated Palestine and the State of Israel. That idea can only be overturned one day if Israel acts decisively and fearlessly to re-assert and exercise its own legally recognized rights and title of sovereignty over the whole of Palestine and the Land of Israel.

*Chapter 8*

# The Applicability of the Principle of Acquired Legal Rights in favour of the Jewish People over Palestine from 1948 Onwards

So long as the State of Israel remained within the borders demarcated in the Armistice Agreements made with Egypt, Lebanon, Jordan and Syria, the question of Israel's legal rights and title of sovereignty to the other parts of the Land of Israel that were not included within the State's borders remained dormant and was not publicly debated except by leaders of the Herut Party under Menachem Begin. With the outbreak of the Six-Day War on June 5, 1967 all that changed. As a result of that war, all the remaining territory of Cisjordanian Palestine, not previously ruled by Israel and which had always been integral parts of the Jewish National Home, was liberated from foreign Arab occupation, but by deliberate design was not incorporated into the State of Israel as its constitutional law required.[1] That provoked fierce and antagonistic arguments in the world concerning Israel's legal position in Judea, Samaria and Gaza, as well as the Golan and Sinai.

Israel was considered to be a belligerent occupier under international law not only by practically all of the world's governments, but surprisingly also by many political and legal figures within Israel itself. Very few of these figures really knew or properly understood that Israel had already acquired the pre-existing legal rights and title of sovereignty of the Jewish People over the re-possessed areas of the Jewish National Home that were now placed incongruously under Israel's military rule in obedience to the laws of war found in the Hague Regulations of 1907 and the Fourth Geneva Convention of 1949, instead of civilian rule, governed by the laws of the State. By applying international law to these regions, Israel demonstrated to everyone, including many of Israel's friends, that they were in fact "occupied territories" that did not belong to the Jewish People, and therefore had to be returned to their supposedly rightful owners. This represented a travesty of the true situation concerning Israel's

[1] The author has previously discussed the question of the non-incorporation of the freed territories of the Jewish National Home in the Six-Day War in the policy paper published by the Ariel Center for Policy Research (Number 77), entitled *A Petition to Annul the Interim Agreement* (January 1999) – See Chapter 4 of this policy paper, pages 54 to 58.

legal rights and title of sovereignty over all parts and regions of the Jewish National Home.

The devolution of legal rights under the Mandate for Palestine from the Jewish People to the State of Israel occurred automatically when the State was established on May 15, 1948. Until the founding of the State, the rights of the Jewish People to the country of Palestine were vested in the Zionist Organization (as of 1960, the World Zionist Organization) and its sister-organization, the Jewish Agency for Palestine, both acting as the official representative and assignee of the Jewish People. Legally, the Jewish State is a creation and an inherent part of the broader Jewish People who were recognized as an international legal entity in the various acts of international law constituting the founding documents of the State of Israel, discussed throughout this book.

As previously noted, those Jewish legal rights and title of sovereignty covered all of Mandated Palestine, on both sides of the Jordan, not just the tiny area in a part of Western Palestine held by the State of Israel before the Six-Day War began. However, the rights that existed over the areas outside Israel's pre-1967 borders could not of course be exercised in practice while Jordan, Syria and Egypt illegally occupied various regions of Mandated Palestine and the Jewish National Home.

The important question that arose in June 1967 was whether Jewish legal rights and title of sovereignty held by Israel to all of Palestine continued intact even after May 15, 1948 or whether they had lapsed during a nineteen year period of foreign rule. An immediate answer was provided by the 1949 armistice agreements which preserved those rights intact and the general recognition enunciated by most jurists who wrote on the subject that Jordan and Egypt which acquired different areas of the Jewish National Home in the 1948 War of Independence did not thereby gain any valid legal title of sovereignty over those areas they occupied by military aggression against the fledgling Jewish State. In the case of Jordan, the areas illegally seized and annexed were Judea and Samaria, while in the case of Egypt, the area illegally occupied was the Gaza Strip. Israel's re-acquisition of the Golan Heights from Syria involved different legal considerations, since this territory had been illegally included in Syria since 1923, though under the "Dan to Beersheba" formula it was really an integral part of historical Palestine that should not have been excluded from Palestine by the imperialist Powers, Britain and France, when they concluded a demarcation agreement that look legal effect in 1923, as already noted in Chapter 2 above. In a defensive war, in June 1967, Israel restored the Golan to its own rule and sovereignty.

The more substantive answer, however, as to whether Jewish legal rights over the foregoing territories remained intact after the end of the War of Independence should be based on the following points: (1) *the principle of acquired legal rights* which ensured that these fundamental rights of the Jewish People did not lapse with the international process or means which brought them into existence; and (2) the flip side of this principle known as *the doctrine of estoppel,* which further ensured that these acquired rights *under international law* could not simply be abrogated or denied by those states which previously recognized their existence.

The principle of acquired legal rights has been codified in international law in the Vienna Convention on the Law of Treaties (The "Treaty on Treaties") of May 23, 1969, which entered into force on January 27, 1980. The provision in this Treaty which enunciates this principle was merely declaratory, rather than constitutive, of general international law, reflecting an existing rule or practice. It is the definitive answer, when it is also joined with the doctrine of estoppel (discussed in the next chapter) to be made against anyone who claims that Jewish legal rights and title of sovereignty over all of Palestine and the Land of Israel did not continue after the end of the Mandate for Palestine on midnight May 14-15, 1948, except in the allotted boundaries of the U.N. Partition Plan. Article 70 (1)(b) of the Vienna Convention on the Law of Treaties reads as follows:

*Article 70*

*Consequences of the Termination of a Treaty*

> 1. Unless the treaty otherwise provides or the parties otherwise agree, the termination of a treaty under its provisions or in accordance with the present Convention:
>
> a)...
>
> b) does not affect any right, obligation or legal situation of the parties created through the execution of the treaty prior to its termination.

Though the terms of the Mandate for Palestine were framed in the form of a Decision issued by the Council of the League of Nations instead of a Treaty signed by the "High Contracting Powers", composed of the Principal Allied Powers of World War I, on the one hand, and Turkey, on the other, as envisaged prior to the Mandate's submission to the League Council for confirmation, the latter still resembled and was compared to a treaty having most of the characteristics of one.[2] This resemblance justifies the application of the principle of acquired legal rights concerning those rights, obligations or the legal situation created through the execution of the Mandate prior to its termination, exactly as stipulated in Article 70 (1)(b) of the Vienna Convention, even if such execution did not faithfully adhere to the terms of the Mandate. It should be kept in mind that the principle of Acquired Legal Rights already existed in international law *long before* its codification in this Convention. Though the Zionist Organization representing the Jewish People was not technically a party to the Mandate, although it initiated the formulation of the early drafts, the

[2] A treaty is defined in Article 2 (1) (a) of the Vienna Convention as meaning an international agreement concluded between states in written form and governed by international law, whether embodied in a single instrument or in two or more related instruments and whatever its particular designation.

Jewish People were in fact the national beneficiary of the Mandate, for whose benefit it was brought into existence, and therefore should be reckoned among the "parties", in a broader sense of the term. Hence all the legal rights and title of *de jure* sovereignty that inhered in the Jewish People under the Mandate for Palestine continued unabated in full force in favour of the State of Israel after the termination of the Mandate on midnight of May 14-15, 1948.

Moreover, Israel was the only legal successor of the rights formerly vested in Great Britain as the Mandatory Power under the Mandate for Palestine. From the standpoint of international law, all the states of the world which had previously recognized Jewish legal rights both when the Mandate was originally confirmed in 1922 and afterwards remained bound by their recognition of those rights from May 15, 1948 onwards in regard to the State of Israel. This fact has particular relevance today to the U.S. and the U.K. It is important to note also, that the territorial scope of acquired Jewish legal rights was definitely not limited to the part of Palestine that became a Jewish State on May 15, 1948 and those other parts re-conquered by it in the War of Independence of 1948. The actual territory covered by those rights encompassed the entire territory of Palestine and the Jewish National Home, on both sides of the Jordan, in accordance with the historical test of what constituted the Land of Israel, set out in the third recital of the Preamble of the Mandate. If only the historical test is used as a guideline without reference to the actual limits of the mandated territory of Palestine, then the Golan and much of Sinai are also included.[3]

In each armistice agreement a provision was inserted to the effect that the rights, claims and positions of either Israel or the Arab State which signed the agreement with it would not be prejudiced in the ultimate peaceful settlement of the Palestine question. This reservation was found in the Egyptian-Israel General Armistice Agreement signed at Rhodes on February 24, 1949, which also stated that "the Armistice Demarcation Line is not to be construed in any sense as a political or territorial boundary", a clause not found in any of the three other armistice agreements; the one with Lebanon signed at Ras-en-Naqura on March 23, 1949; the one with the Hashemite Kingdom of Jordan signed at Rhodes on April 3, 1949 and the final one, signed with Syria near Mahanayim on July 20, 1949. Thus, by virtue of these four armistice agreements concluded under the auspices of Ralph J. Bunche, the Acting United Nations Mediator for Palestine, who had succeeded the late Count Folke Bernadotte in this role, Israel specifically preserved its pre-existing legal rights and title of sovereignty over those areas of the Jewish National Home that came under foreign Arab domination between May 15, 1948 and June 10, 1967. Nor for that matter were any Arab national rights legally created by the Armistice Agreements over those

---

[3] Article 29 of the Vienna Convention reads: "Unless a different intention appears from the treaty or is otherwise established, a treaty is binding upon each party *in respect of its entire territory*" (emphasis added). This is further confirmation that the principle of acquired legal rights in favour of the Jewish People and later to the State of Israel applied to the whole mandated territory of Palestine.

parts of the Jewish National Home previously and illegally severed from it and ceded to the Arabic-speaking states of Transjordan, Syria and Egypt by Britain and France. The additional clause in the Egyptian Armistice Agreement that no political or territorial boundary was being permanently determined may have been intended by Israel to preserve not only its right to Gaza, which was part of Mandated Palestine, but also its claim to Sinai, the north-eastern parts of which Israel had captured in the War of Independence and then relinquished unconditionally after political pressure exerted by the United States and threats of British military intervention. Finally, it should be noted that no armistice agreement was ever signed with Iraq, even though that country had participated in the Arab aggression against the nascent Jewish State.

As regards the joint region of Judea and Samaria, illegally acquired by Jordan by attacking the new-born Jewish State in the War of Independence, Jordan never gained any valid legal rights and title of sovereignty over those territories under international law by its unlawful aggression and invasion of Palestine in 1948, which was in clear violation of Article 2 (4) of the U.N. Charter, which states that "all members shall refrain in their international relations from the threat or use of force against the territorial integrity or political independence of any State, or in any other manner inconsistent with the purposes of the United Nations". Accordingly, Jordan was an unlawful belligerent occupant of Judea and Samaria. The legal maxim which applied in these circumstances, as is often cited, is *jus ex iniuria non oritur* (a right does not arise from a wrong or unlawful act). However, the applicability of this legal maxim has not deterred Israeli Professor of Law Yoram Dinstein from believing that Jordan did in fact become sovereign of Judea and Samaria at the conclusion of the War of Independence because of the ostensible independent "decision" made by the Arab notables of these regions at various gatherings held in 1948, particularly one in Jericho, where they decided to transfer to Transjordan the alleged national rights vested in the Arab population under the U.N. Partition Resolution.[4]

[4] See the article by Professor (then Dr.) Yoram Dinstein entitled "Zion shall be Redeemed in International Law", which appeared in the journal *HaPraklit* (The Attorney), published by the Israel Bar, Vol. 27 (March 1971), No. 1, p. 5. In this initial article Prof. Dinstein does not explain why Jordan is the sovereign of eastern Jerusalem as well as the sovereign of Judea and Samaria, but only assumes or takes for granted that Jordan has this legal status. In consequence of this belief, he asserts that Israel's legal position in these areas resulted from its "belligerent occupation" of them in the Six-Day War of June 5-10, 1967. Therefore, as a "belligerent occupier", Israel cannot gain title or right of ownership to eastern Jerusalem through its own unilateral and arbitrary decision of annexation. According to Prof. Dinstein, it is only by means of a peace treaty with Jordan, the widely-accepted method under international law, that Israel could truly acquire title or right of legal ownership over eastern Jerusalem, Judea and Samaria. This reasoning, however, is invalid since it disregards the fact that Jordan could not bestow any title on Israel in the framework of a peace treaty inasmuch as it itself never possessed any recognized title under international law. Moreover, Israel had a prior existing legal right, which it chose not to exercise, to annex or, more

Professor Dinstein, a member of the Faculty of Law of Tel-Aviv University, who later became Dean of that Faculty and President of the University, engaged in "creative legal thinking" to discover or locate Arab national rights in Judea and Samaria under international law, where none ever existed before. His accompanying denial of Jewish national rights over the same joint region, particularly the right of sovereignty or ownership, as opposed to the right of possession which he generously conceded to Israel as a sop, marked a veritable demolition of legal reality and truth. His legal view has prevailed to this very day with the fictitious "Palestinian People" replacing the state of Jordan as the holder of the right of sovereignty over eastern Jerusalem, Judea, Samaria and Gaza.

It appears that in the mind of Professor Dinstein, the legal rights and title of sovereignty that were recognized as inhering in the Jewish People under several separate acts of international law pertaining to all parts of the Jewish National Home simply do not count. The acts which he believes are relevant to the legal situation as to who has the actual title of sovereignty or right of ownership were two in particular, one of which never came into legal force and was in any case illegal, namely, the U.N. Partition Resolution of November 29, 1947, while the other has been defunct since the outbreak of the Six-Day War on June 5, 1967, namely, the General Armistice Agreement made with Jordan on April 3, 1949 on the island of Rhodes, Greece. The Armistice Agreement ceased to exist after Jordan attacked Israel in alliance with Egypt and Syria, which constituted a serious violation of the armistice, thereby justifying the right of Israel to denounce it, in accordance with Article 40 of the Hague Regulations.[5]

What Professor Dinstein accomplished by his astonishing conclusions on the legal status of Israel in eastern Jerusalem, Judea and Samaria was to educate an entire generation of Israeli law students in the false belief that the Jewish State was a "belligerent occupier" of integral areas of the Jewish National

---

accurately, to incorporate any area of the Land of Israel, as soon as such area came under its military control, as in fact happened in the Six-Day War. In another article appearing in *HaPraklit*, Vol. 27 (1972), p. 519, entitled "And She [Zion] has not been Redeemed", or "Not Demonstrations but rather Deeds", Prof. Dinstein gives his reason for recognizing Jordan's alleged title or right of ownership over eastern Jerusalem, Judea and Samaria, based on the decision made by the Arab notables from these areas, who, at a gathering at Jericho, "transferred" this right to the Kingdom of Jordan, even though this "right" was non-existent and therefore could not be transferred. The first part of the title of Dinstein's article refers to the verse in Leviticus 19:20 which discusses the redemption of a female slave by giving her her freedom. The second part of the title refers to a speech delivered by Chaim Weizmann in 1927 in Czernowitz in the former Rumanian region of Bukovina, now the city of Chernovtsy, in the Ukraine.

[5] Article 40 of the Hague Regulations Respecting the Laws and Customs of War on Land reads as follows: "Any serious violation of the armistice by one of the parties gives the other party the right of denouncing it, and even, in cases of urgency, of recommencing hostilities immediately.

Home. According to him, they were therefore "occupied territories" under international law, belonging, first of all, to the Arab inhabitants who lived there, based on the Partition Resolution of November 29, 1947, then to Jordan to whom they were "transferred" by an assembly of notables convening in Jericho on December 1, 1948, who adopted a resolution to that effect.[6] He thereby contributed in no small measure, along with like-minded colleagues who teach in the law faculties of Tel-Aviv University and the Hebrew University in Jerusalem, to the widespread belief prevalent in the world today that Israel is in violation of international law by its continuing "occupation" of Judea, Samaria and Gaza and therefore must withdraw from all these areas.[7] In light of this professorial indoctrination that has put Israel on the defensive and rendered it subject to accusations that it violates international law, it is worthwhile to quote some important excerpts from one of Prof. Dinstein's principal articles on the subject to better understand his legal opinion and reasoning.[8] In that article, he expressed himself as follows:

---

[6] The resolution of the Jericho assembly is discussed by Joseph B. Schechtman, in his booklet *Jordan – A State That Never Was*, published by Cultural Publishing Co., Inc., New York (1968), pp. 59-60.

[7] The latest example of this pernicious approach adopted by law school professors to describe the legal status of Israel in the recovered areas of the Jewish National Home or what it ought to be can be found in a new book by David Kretzmer, Professor of International Law at the Hebrew University of Jerusalem: *The Occupation of Justice – The Supreme Court of Israel and the Occupied Territories*, published by State University of New York Press, Albany (2002). This book discusses the legal status of Judea, Samaria and Gaza and the legality of settlements without any substantive discussion of the relevancy of Article 22 of the Covenant of the League of Nations, the San Remo Resolution, the Mandate for Palestine and the Franco-British Boundary Convention of December 23, 1920, which, if taken into account, might have changed the conclusions reached by Prof. Kretzmer or at least given him pause to reconsider his dogmatic, unwarranted belief that these areas of the Jewish National Home are "occupied territories" under international law, a term he amazingly emphasizes in capital letters without let up throughout all the pages of his book. The supreme irony is that while Kretzmer ignores the foregoing acts of international law which conclusively determined Jewish legal rights to Judea, Samaria and Gaza, and are of cardinal importance in understanding the legal status of these areas, he relies heavily on other acts of international law that have no bearing or applicability on the question, namely the Fourth Geneva Convention of 1949 and the Hague Regulations of 1907, inasmuch as Israel is not occupying anyone else's land but its own. The question must be asked: Are Israeli professors teaching international law and constitutional law poisoning the susceptible minds of their young students against their own country when lecturing on this vital subject and, if that is the case, how long should this be allowed to go on without corrective steps being taken?

[8] See footnote 4 above. The excerpts are taken from the article in *HaPraklit*, entitled "And She [Zion] has not been Redeemed...", Vol. 27 (1972), p. 519 and translated from the Hebrew.

In the Armistice Agreement, Israel and Jordan confirmed in fact each other's rule within the borders that were fixed in the document. From the point of view of Israel these borders included areas which deviated considerably from what had been allotted to it in the Partition Resolution. ...if we ignore the decisive meaning of the Armistice Agreement, we are returning to the Partition borders...

The Armistice Agreement with Jordan created – by the delineation of armistice frontiers – a defined legal situation, which the parties lived and profited from, according to [its parameters] for 18 years. This situation is not automatically voided by the end of the agreement.[9] Anyone who claims that the armistice frontier (now called euphemistically "the Green Line") is null and void from a legal point of view is relying not on law, but rather on a slogan, similar to the slogan of the "Sun King", Louis XIV (which he was heard to utter when the Spanish Crown was handed over to the House of Bourbon), that "the Pyrenees [the mountains along the French-Spanish border] no longer exist".[10]

The claim that Jordan has no and has never had rights in eastern Jerusalem and the West Bank cannot pass the test or stand up to criticism. I will be content with making three short comments. First of all, a skeptical comment: if we assume that the coming of the Messiah is imminent and Jordan is ready to transfer to Israel in a peace treaty all of eastern Jerusalem; would we hear then from everybody that Jordan, too, has no right to transfer more than she has? Second, a procedural comment: in the Rhodes agreement – not only did Israel receive

---

[9] This is a reference by Prof. Dinstein to Article 70 (1)(b) of the Vienna Convention on the Law of Treaties – to the effect that the termination of a treaty does not affect the legal situation of the parties created through the execution of the treaty prior to its termination.

[10] The first Bourbon King of Spain was Philip V, a grandson of the Bourbon King of France, Louis XIV. Had the Spanish and French thrones ever been united under a single monarch, the Pyrenees would have ceased to be the international border between the two countries, and in that sense would "no longer have existed". For Dinstein, this statement by Louis XIV was "a slogan" that, in his opinion, was just as false as saying that the Armistice frontier between Israel and Jordan is null and void. However, Dinstein's reasoning is based on two false premises: (1) an international "border" existed between Israel and Jordan as a result of the General Armistice Agreement of April 3, 1949, and (2) that Article 70 (1)(b) of the Vienna Convention on the Law of Treaties applied to the situation. Prior to the 1994 peace treaty between Israel and Jordan, the only border ever delineated between the two countries was originally a provisional, administrative border as set out in the Memorandum presented by the British Government to the Council of the League of Nations on September 16, 1922, separating Transjordan from Cisjordan. This, however, was an internal border between two parts of Palestine, not an international border, until it was made permanent in 1946 when Jordan was recognized as an independent state.

approval or legitimization from Jordan for its rule on this side of the armistice line, but Jordan received from Israel [the same] approval or legitimization for its rule on the other side; it seems that it is much too late to argue today that it was forbidden for Jordan to exceed its rights at that time in Transjordan.[11] Third, and here is the chief weak point of the argument which is a substantive comment. Modern international law recognizes the right of self-determination of nations. *In the area of the Mandate there were in the main two peoples – a Jewish People and an Arab People – who were entitled to self-determination* (emphasis added). While the Jewish People made use of this right to establish the State of Israel, the majority of the Arabs of Palestine chose to waive or renounce Palestinian independence and to pin their hopes on – by joining their fate to – Jordan. They, who invited Jordanian armed forces to enter Palestine at the beginning of the War of Independence. They, who in a series of gatherings or conferences towards the end of the War of Independence (among them, the one which is especially well-known was the gathering of notables which took place in Jericho at the end of the year 1948) suggested to Abdullah, King of Transjordan, that the area of Judea and Samaria allotted to the proposed Arab state in the Partition Resolution of November 29, 1947, and later called "the West Bank" be annexed to his kingdom. And they who took part in elections that occurred in April 1950 on both sides of the Jordan River and authorized the two legislative houses of the Kingdom of Jordan to decide that same month on the annexation of the West Bank. Even today, after what could be called (in an inversion of Shakespeare) as "a tragedy of errors", the Arabs of the West Bank are not yet ready to publicly declare that they desire to cut themselves off from Jordan. In any case, in the year 1971, Jews can no longer repeat the sentence from the year 1897 (which is attributed by Amos Elon to Max Nordau – in his book, *The Israelis, Founders and Sons* [1971], p. 148): "But there are Arabs in Palestine! And I did not know."

---

[11] The change of name from Transjordan to Jordan took place officially on March 1, 1950 when the name of Jordan was gazetted. However, the new name of Abdullah's kingdom had already been used internally after March 22, 1946 when Britain recognized Transjordan as "a fully independent state" in a Treaty of Alliance it signed with Abdullah. The constitution adopted for the Kingdom on July 12, 1946 used the name "Jordan", as did the armistice agreement signed with Israel on April 3, 1949 at Rhodes. See the book by Dr. Uriel Dann, *Studies in the History of Transjordan 1920-1949*, Westview Press, the Dayan Center for Middle Eastern and African Studies (1984), p. 14; see also the book by Mary C. Wilson, *King Abdullah, Britain and the making of Jordan*, Cambridge Middle East Library, Cambridge University Press (1989), p. 190. Wilson, unlike Dann, says that the use of "Jordan" instead of "Transjordan" first appeared in the constitution of 1947 (p. 190 of her book), while Dann gives the date of the constitution as July 12, 1946 (p. 14 of his book).

> The fact that international law does not grant to Israel at this stage the *right of ownership* of eastern Jerusalem (or of any other part of the territories conquered in the Six-Day War) does not mean that Israel has no right whatsoever to it. Israel has a right, but it is at present – so long as the situation of occupation continues to exist in a time of war – merely *a right of possession* (emphasis added).

It is curious why Prof. Dinstein laid so much stress in his article on the importance of the General Armistice Agreement with Jordan, when at the time he wrote it, this agreement had already ceased to exist and never produced the permanent effects which he credited to it. The armistice agreement was always provisional in nature under Article 40 of the U.N. Charter, pending the making of a final peace treaty, as stated in the preamble of the agreement. It never created a permanent legal situation, fixing the rights of the parties for all time, as Prof. Dinstein seems to have believed when he cited Article 70 (1) (b) of the Vienna Convention on the Law of Treaties which in any case did not apply to the General Armistice Agreement with Jordan, since an armistice can hardly be described as a "treaty" in the formal sense of the word. Article II (2) of the armistice agreement, reflecting the language used in Article 40 of the U.N. Charter for a truce or armistice agreement, stated specifically that the rights, claims and positions of either Party would not be prejudiced in the ultimate peaceful settlement of the Palestine question – the provisions of this agreement being dictated exclusively by military considerations. No legitimacy was therefore given to Jordan's position in eastern Jerusalem, Judea and Samaria. Its position there simply reflected the military circumstances prevailing at the time the hostilities ceased on April 3, 1949. It did not change in any way the legal rights of the State of Israel to Judea, Samaria and Gaza which it inherited from the Jewish People on May 15, 1948 when the state was born. Jordan's rule crumbled on the third day of the Six-Day War and thereafter it had no justified claim based on the legal situation created by the armistice agreement as implied by Prof. Dinstein for the return of eastern Jerusalem, Judea and Samaria to which it never had any legal right recognized under international law. To assert or imply that these lands were "occupied Jordanian lands" and that Israel was the belligerent occupier of them, to which the laws of warfare were applicable was then and still is pure nonsense. In the same category is Prof. Dinstein's belief that only a treaty of peace with Jordan could give Israel the right of ownership to these "occupied territories", as opposed to the right of possession. That belief was mistaken on two counts: First, Jordan could not transfer to Israel any right of sovereignty over these territories since Jordan never possessed the title of sovereignty under international law. Second, no treaty was necessary because the State of Israel as noted had inherited all the rights over Palestine vested in the Jewish People, which included the right of *de jure* sovereignty implicitly accorded to it by the San Remo Resolution of April 25, 1920, in the same manner that the Arab peoples of Mesopotamia and Syria acquired their sovereignty from the very same Resolution.

The rights of the Jewish People to eastern Jerusalem, Judea and Samaria were not based on the Partition Resolution of November 29, 1947 which, on the contrary, illegally recommended the abrogation of those rights in favour of the United Nations, regarding Jerusalem in its entirety, and in favour of the Arabs of Palestine, regarding Judea and Samaria, in direct contravention of the Mandate (Articles 2, 5 and 25) and Article 80 of the U.N. Charter *inter alia*. Those rights were based in particular on the Franco-British Convention of December 23, 1920 which defined the borders of Palestine to include those very territories as part and parcel of the Jewish National Home. This Boundary Convention merely supplemented the terms of the Mandate for Palestine, which did not delineate the borders of the country as was originally intended to be done in that instrument. The importance of this Boundary Convention for Israel today is that it is not stuck with the borders set down in the Partition Resolution, as Prof. Dinstein feared would happen after the collapse of the General Armistice Agreement with Jordan, for the Convention provides the necessary legal support under international law for extending those borders to coincide with the limits of the Jewish National Home as fixed in that Convention supplementing the Draft Mandate for Palestine of December 6, 1920. When speaking of "modern international law" in regard to determining the rights and legal position of Israel vis-à-vis Jordan, Professor Dinstein should know that the 1920 Convention – together with the Mandate, the San Remo Resolution and Article 22 of the League Covenant read in conjunction with its precursor, the Smuts Resolution – should be the only international law he relies on, not the Partition Resolution or the Armistice Agreement. The latter did not determine the legal rights of any of the parties and expressly disclaimed doing so.

Prof. Dinstein falsely intimates that the Mandate for Palestine provided for the right of self-determination not only for the Jewish People, but also for the Arabs of Palestine. There is absolutely no legal basis for this intimation. The exclusive beneficiary of national rights to Palestine under the Mandate was the Jewish People which is why Article 22 of the Covenant of the League of Nations is mentioned in the first recital of the Preamble of the Mandate for Palestine. Article 22 was combined with the Balfour Declaration to produce the San Remo Resolution of April 25, 1920 as regards Palestine. There is no mention of the Arab people as such in the Mandate and no representatives of the Arabs living in Palestine or elsewhere participated in the drafting of the Mandate Charter, as did the representatives of the Zionist Organization, who actually initiated the drafting process. The right of self-determination was indeed provided for the Arabs, not in Palestine, but in Syria, Mesopotamia and Arabia. The allocation of former Turkish territories in the Middle East which reserved all of Palestine for Jewish self-determination rather than Arab self-determination can also be substantiated by the adoption of the Smuts Resolution on January 30, 1919 by the Council of Ten of the Principal Allied and Associated Powers at the Paris Peace Conference.

Finally, Prof. Dinstein stresses the role played by the Arabs of Judea and Samaria in granting Jordan the right of sovereignty over the territory designated for the Arab state in the Partition Resolution of November 29, 1947. It is hard to imagine a more far-fetched or bizarre idea than to believe that these Arabs could vest Jordan (then called Transjordan) with a right of sovereignty that they themselves did not have over this territory. Apart from any legal arguments about the validity of the Partition Resolution, it simply never came into operation, which is a crucial and overriding consideration, and therefore no territorial rights of any sort could accrue to the local Arab population that could then be transferred to Jordan, as the successor state of a non-existent, aborted Arab State that was contemplated in the Partition Resolution. This kind of legal argument to prove Jordanian ownership of territories belonging to the Jewish National Home is no better than building a castle in the air or on shifting sand, without any solid foundation or real existence.

In addition, Transjordan was an illegal creation of the British Government that became a quasi-independent state on March 22, 1946 as a result of a Treaty of Alliance between the two parties. It is ludicrous to assert, as does Professor Dinstein, that an Arab kingdom which itself was non-existent when the rights of the Jewish People to all of Palestine were first recognized in 1917 and 1920 could by some magical means usurp those Jewish national rights. Moreover, Transjordan was absolutely estopped from asserting such rights in consequence of a pledge by King Abdullah to Britain when he assumed the provisional administration of Transjordan (April 1921), not to interfere in the affairs of Cisjordan, as further discussed below (in Chapter 13). The annexation Transjordan purported to make of Judea and Samaria, on April 24, 1950, therefore had no legal validity under international law, regardless of partial British and full Pakistani recognition of it. Britain withheld recognition of the annexation by Transjordan of eastern Jerusalem, while even Pakistan's recognition has so far never been documented or truly proven. According to Professor Sanford R. Silverburg of Catawba College (Salisbury, North Carolina) "no original source for the Pakistani [diplomatic] action has come to light".[12] In any event, King Hussein of Jordan publicly announced on July 31, 1988 that his country was severing all existing legal and administrative links with Judea and Samaria. That ended any pretense of so-called rights being held by Jordan to these ancestral regions of the Jewish National Home. This left the pre-existing Jewish legal rights and title of sovereignty dating back to April 24-25, 1920 completely intact. Those rights had never been given up by the State of Israel during the 19-year period of Jordanian rule, as evidenced by Article II (2) of the General Armistice Agreement, and were now exercisable once again.

The strange fact and irony is that upon the liberation and repossession of these regions in June 1967, the Government of Israel decided not to exercise these rights by incorporating these regions immediately into the State, ostensibly,

---

12 See his article, "Pakistan and the West Bank: A Research Note, Middle East Studies, Vol. 19, No.2 (April 1983, pp. 261-263).

it was stated, to preserve an ephemeral hope for peace, but actually because of the demographic imbalance it would have created in the population of Israel regarding the relative numbers of Arabs and Jews.[13] Most surprising of all, not even Prime Minister Menachem Begin, the long-time leader of the Herut Party, incorporated Judea, Samaria and Gaza into the State of Israel, despite the fact that this was the main plank and *raison d'être* of Herut since its inception in 1948, as well as that of the newly-formed Likud Party (1973) which he led. In the 1977 election campaign, the Likud's platform stated:

> The right of the Jewish People to the Land of Israel is eternal and is an integral part of its right to security and peace. Judea and Samaria will therefore not be turned over to any foreign rule: between the sea and the Jordan [there] will be only Israel sovereignty. Any plan that involves surrender of part of Western Eretz Israel militates against our right to the Land, will inevitably lead to a Palestinian state, threatens the security of our civilian population, endangers the existence of the state and defeats all prospects for peace.

Upon Likud's assumption of power in May 1977, Begin, contrary to Likud's platform which he had personally approved, failed to apply Israel's sovereignty to all the re-possessed territory west of the Jordan, in deference to his Foreign Minister, Moshe Dayan, who conditioned his acceptance of the ministerial post offered him by Begin on preserving the territorial *status quo* so long as there remained a prospect for peace negotiations with the neighbouring Arab states. What Begin did instead was to leave the question of the final legal status of Judea, Samaria and Gaza open to possible negotiations and agreement with the elected representatives of the local Arab inhabitants and the Arab states of Jordan and Egypt.[14] Despite the Government of Israel's decision not to incorporate or annex Judea, Samaria and Gaza, Israel's own constitutional law had a special provision for this very purpose, which is found in Section 1 of the Area of Jurisdiction and Powers Ordinance. Eliezer Shostak of the Free Center Party was the only member of the Knesset to strongly protest the failure to invoke it.[15] The Law of Return also required their incorporation into the State.

---

[13] The opinion conveyed to the present author by the late Professor Yuval Ne'eman, former Minister of Energy and Infrastructure, as well as Minister of Science, that it was the demographic factor that prevented the immediate incorporation of Judea, Samaria and Gaza into the borders of the State by the Eshkol National Unity Government is undoubtedly correct.

[14] See Begin's 26-point plan of "Self-Rule for Palestinian Arabs" that he announced to the Knesset on December 28, 1977, which was formally submitted to President Anwar es-Sadat of Egypt. See also the "Camp David Framework Agreement for Peace in the Middle East", signed on September 17, 1978 at the White House.

[15] See the work of the author, *A Petition to Annul the Interim Agreement, op. cit.*, pp. 57-60.

The Government of Israel approved the establishment of civilian and military[16] Jewish settlements in the repossessed areas of the Jewish National Home immediately after the Six-Day War. The very first settlement was established on the Golan Heights in July 1967 by a group affiliated with *Ha-Kibbutz Ha-Me'uhad* (The United Kibbutz Movement) which founded the village Merom Ha-Golan under the impetus of Yehuda Har'el, a resident of Kibbutz Manara near the Israeli-Lebanese border, who later served in the Knesset as a member of the short-lived Third Way Party (1996-1999). In September 1967 the settlement of Kfar Etzion in the Hebron Hills south of Jerusalem, the first of the four villages formerly constituting the Etzion Bloc[17] founded prior to the establishment of the State of Israel, was rebuilt after it had been captured and destroyed by the Jordanian Arab Legion in the 1948 War of Independence. This religious kibbutz was renewed by a group which included the children of the defenders of the fallen village, most of whose members had been massacred after their surrender (May 14, 1948) by the Arab Legion assisted by irregular infantry forces from neighbouring Arab villages.

The first settlement that arose in Gaza after its recapture by the Israel Defense Forces in the Six-Day War was, appropriately enough, that of K'far Darom since it had been established prior to the creation of the State, but was evacuated on July 8, 1948 when Egyptian troops overran it in the War of Independence. This village was one of eleven that had been created by the Jewish National Fund on the night of October 6, 1946 to settle the Negev. The latter region has traditionally included the southern (Philistine) Plain up to Wadi el-Arish (the Brook of Egypt), of which Gaza is a physiographical part even though administratively it is treated separately from the Negev. At the first convention of the newly-formed Israel Labour Party that was held in August 1969 after the merger the year before of Mapai, Ahdut Ha'Avoda and Rafi, it was decided that the Gaza Strip should remain under Israeli rule.[18] In 1970, pursuant to a Government decision, a group of Nahal soldiers was sent to the original site of K'far Darom to resettle it.

The forerunner of seventeen new settlements set up in the unpopulated southwestern section of Gaza, called Gush Katif, was the settlement of Netzer Hazani. The latter began as a Nahal outpost in 1973 under the original name "Katif", but changed its name to Netzer Hazani in anticipation of its conversion into a civilian settlement which took place on February 17, 1977. The new name honoured the memory of Michael Ya'akov Hazani, a former Minister

---

[16] The military settlements were composed of young soldiers or cadets who combined army service with agricultural work in settlements that were known by the Hebrew acronym NAHAL from the Hebrew words *No'ar Halutzi Lohem* (Pioneering Combatant Youth). These military settlements were later converted into civilian settlements.

[17] In addition to Kfar Etzion, the other villages of the Etzion Bloc were Massu'ot Yitzhak, Ein Tsurim and Revadim.

[18] *Encyclopaedia Judaica* (1971), Vol. 9, col. 413.

of Welfare in Golda Meir's Government. Hazani enthusiastically supported the idea of Jewish renewal in the Gaza Strip and was known as "the father of the religious settlement movement". His efforts to settle Gaza with Jews was shared at the time by Prime Minister Rabin who attended the ceremony inaugurating the civilian settlement of Netzer Hazani and stated:[19]

> This is a great day for the State and the settlement movement, a day that symbolizes the consolidation of our grip in the region which, ever since the Six-Day War, has become an integral part of the State and its security.

The Government-sponsored establishment of all the new settlements in Judea, Samaria, Gaza, the Golan Heights and the Sinai in the wake of the Six-Day War constituted an assertion of Israeli sovereignty over these regions of the Land of Israel. None of these settlements would have been founded, had it not been taken for granted by the Government of Israel that the land on which they were situated was part and parcel of the Jewish National Home, recognized as such under international law in 1919, 1920 and 1922. This recognition allowed the State of Israel, the assignee and successor of all legal rights bestowed upon the Jewish People under international law, to proceed with the building of new settlements in the recovered areas of the Jewish National Home even before the passage of U.N. Security Council Resolution 242 on November 22, 1967. However, the failure of the Government of Israel to immediately incorporate the recovered areas of the Jewish National Home into the borders of the State, as it was required to do by its own constitutional law, engendered the false belief that is now universally prevalent, that these areas did not truly belong to the State of Israel and were therefore "occupied territories" under international law. This erroneous belief has constantly bedeviled the Jewish State ever since, and was further strengthened by the Government's ill-considered consent given to Resolution 242 which spoke about territories "occupied" by Israel in the Six-Day War, and its "withdrawal of armed forces" from such territories to "secure and recognized boundaries", even though Israel denied that this U.N. resolution applied, in particular, to Judea, Samaria and Gaza. Moreover, Israel's consent to this resolution was itself illegal in that it violated the constitutional law of the State, as embodied in the Area of Jurisdiction and Powers Ordinance, the Law of Return and Section 11B of the Law and Administration Ordinance, as amended on June 28, 1967, three laws which are based on the premise that Israel is the sovereign of the whole of the Land of Israel. In any event, no U.N. resolution could override Israel's existing legal rights and title of sovereignty over any region of the Land of Israel based on several earlier acts of international law: the Smuts Resolution of January 30, 1919, Article 22 of the Covenant of the League of Nations, included in the Treaty of Versailles of June 28, 1919, the

---

[19] http://www.katif.net/gush/city/14.htm

San Remo Resolution of April 25, 1920, the Mandate for Palestine as confirmed on July 24, 1922 and the Franco-British Convention of December 23, 1920, all of which recognized the historical connection of the Jewish People with the Land of Israel.

The argument centering around the missing article "the" before the word "territories" in the English-language version of this resolution is absolutely immaterial to the question of Israel's legal rights and title of sovereignty over all of the Land of Israel. To base Israel's legal case on the missing article "the" as the reason for not having to withdraw from Judea, Samaria and Gaza as many supporters of Israel have chosen to do is a flimsy basis for asserting Israel's rights in regard to them and is tantamount to disavowing or ignoring the real legal case based on the aforementioned acts of international law.

Insofar as Gaza alone is concerned, which historically always constituted an integral part of the Land of Israel and was at various times an important center of Jewish life since the Talmudic period, Egypt never claimed any national rights over this region, unlike what Jordan asserted for Judea and Samaria, but treated Gaza as foreign territory outside the borders of Egypt. During the period of Egyptian administration from 1948 to 1967, Gaza was ruled by a military Government which applied the law of Palestine, as it existed during the period of the Mandate, subject to Egyptian military regulations taking precedence over it. Israel's failure to annex Gaza promptly upon its liberation from Egypt led to the same false belief which followed its failure to annex Judea and Samaria. Everyone in the world considered it "occupied territory" and bewailed the Israeli "occupation", though there was no legal basis for holding this opinion, then or now.

A predisposition existed in the various organs of the United Nations to deny acquired Jewish legal rights not only in Judea, Samaria and Gaza, but most importantly to Jerusalem, the capital city of the Jewish People and the State of Israel. In the period that immediately followed the adoption of the U.N. Partition Resolution, the U.N. General Assembly passed another resolution[20] on December 9, 1949 to actually convert Jerusalem into a trust territory or *corpus separatum*, with its own Governor, legislative council, independent judiciary and special police force, under the jurisdiction of the Trusteeship Council of the United Nations. A so-called "statute" setting out these provisions in great detail was approved for Jerusalem by the Trusteeship Council on April 4, 1950, despite the fact that neither the Council nor the General Assembly nor any other U.N. organ had the legal authority to pass a legislative statute of this kind. Jerusalem was given extensive boundaries, embracing not only the present municipal boundaries, but also the surrounding Arab villages and towns. These presumptuous and blatantly illegal steps did not succeed, as neither Jordan nor Israel accepted them, though Israel did agree to a regime that concerned itself exclusively with the control and protection of Holy Places. In any event, as Prof.

---

[20] General Assembly Resolution 303 (IV).

Julius Stone observed: "the same facts that aborted the Partition Plan as a whole *ab initio* vitiated these subordinate delegated proceedings."[21] The Jerusalem *corpus separatum*, based as it was on illusory U.N. authority, never came into being.

With neither Jordan nor Egypt having any legal rights or authority within the former mandated territory of Palestine, it would have made good sense for Israel to act decisively and exercise its own rights and title of sovereignty. Israel did so only in regard to Jerusalem which it annexed on June 28, 1967, but, as already noted above, decided unwisely and illegally to leave the final legal status of Judea, Samaria and Gaza as an "open question", which therefore meant that sovereignty over these areas had never been decided. This self-defeating and self-denying policy was adopted, as already noted above, by the last person anyone expected to do so, Prime Minister Menachem Begin. His amazing turnabout contradicted the already existing Jewish legal rights and title of sovereignty over Palestine and the Land of Israel. [22] His program for Arab self-rule in Judea, Samaria and Gaza became the basis of the Camp David Framework Agreement for Peace in the Middle East signed on September 17, 1978 and 15 years later – of the infamous and illegal Israel-PLO accords begun at Oslo that have brought unprecedented terrorism to the Jewish State.

Begin's surprising statement of policy declaring that sovereignty over Judea, Samaria and Gaza was still an "open question" was aided and abetted by a number of American and Israeli jurists who advocated a nebulous and erroneous theory asserting that a sovereignty vacuum existed for these areas of the Jewish National Home which were falsely and unthinkingly called "unallocated territories" of the Mandate for Palestine.[23] This legal theory was unfounded because it, like Professor Dinstein's theory of Jordanian sovereignty over Judea and Samaria, was in direct contradiction to Israel's existing legal rights and title of sovereignty over these territories derived from the several acts of international

---

[21] See his observations and comments in his valuable book, *Israel and Palestine: Assault on the Law of Nations*, Johns Hopkins University Press, 1981, Chapter 7, pp. 98-108, in general and specifically at p. 101.

[22] Begin's description of the legal status of Judea, Samaria and Gaza being an "open question" was possibly based on the same description given by Cyrus Vance, when he was U.S. Secretary of State, at a press conference in Washington, D.C. on July 28, 1977, when he stated: "There is, I think, an *open question* as to who has [the] legal right to the West Bank." Quoted by Moshe Aumann, in his pamphlet "Jews in Judea: Israel's Right in Judea-Samaria." Published by Israel Academic Committee "On the Middle East", March 1981, p. 11.

[23] An example illustrating this point of view was given by William O'Brien, Professor of Government at Georgetown University in Washington, D.C., who wrote an article in the Washington Star of November 26, 1978, where he stated: "...the West Bank was not and is not clearly the sovereign territory of Jordan, from whom Israel took it in a war of self-defence in 1967. The West Bank is an integral part of the Palestine mandate within which a Jewish national home was to be created. In this sense, the territory must be considered today to be *unallocated* (emphasis added) territory."

law listed above. The theory of unallocated territories raised the real and awful possibility that these Jewish lands could be re-allocated to a non-Jewish entity which is what subsequently happened in the Israel-PLO agreements beginning on August 20, 1993 when about 42% of the so-called "unallocated territories" of Judea and Samaria and all of Gaza, as of August 2005, were placed under the control of the criminal and terrorist organization known as the "Palestine Liberation Organization" and its illegal progeny, the "Palestinian Authority". Still later, in January 2006, Gaza came under the terrorist rule of Hamas, whose charter calls for the State of Israel's unconditional destruction and its replacement with a Palestinian Islamic state in all of Cisjordan. The use of this expression "unallocated territories" showed deep and exasperating ignorance of the actual meaning of the fundamental acts of international law that gave birth to Jewish legal rights and title of sovereignty over Mandated Palestine as part of the global political and legal settlement made during and after World War I in regard to the disposition of the ex-Turkish territories in the Middle East. The most prominent jurists who represented this incongruous school of thought were Professor Eugene Rostow, former U.S. Undersecretary of State (1966-1969); Professor Elihu Lauterpacht of the University of Cambridge; Professor Stephen Schwebel, who later sat as a judge in the International Court of Justice; and Professor Yehuda Blum, Israel's former Ambassador to the United Nations. All of these renowned jurists posited the idea that Israel had the "best claim" or "better title" for sovereignty, but not the actual title itself. However, a claim or better title is only relative in nature and not equivalent to a legal right. It can at any time be easily withdrawn, compromised or supplanted, while a legal right is permanent and immune to attack or doubt, unless forfeited or extinguished by destructive circumstances or events, such as war, conquest or subjugation.

While existing Jewish legal rights and title of sovereignty over the Land of Israel can have no practical significance if they are not exercised by the Government of Israel, by incorporating Judea, Samaria and Gaza into the State of Israel, they can still be effectively invoked under the doctrine of estoppel against all the countries of the world who, having first recognized these rights under the San Remo Resolution and the Mandate for Palestine, denied their continuing validity in regard to the territories removed from the Jewish National Home under the Partition Resolution of November 29, 1947 even after Israel repossessed them in the Six-Day War of June 5-10, 1967. The non-exercise of Jewish legal rights and title of sovereignty over those parts of Judea and Samaria still remaining under Israel's control will not negate them, but will leave them open to challenge and doubt. Insofar as the Jewish People are concerned, their rights and title to the Land of Israel are imprescriptible, indefeasible and inalienable. They cannot be *permanently* lost, annulled or transferred either under Jewish Law, known in Hebrew as *halakha*, where the Land of Israel is the everlasting legacy of the Jewish People, or international law. Proof of this is seen in the fact that *de jure* sovereignty of the Jewish People over the Land of Israel under international law was resurrected after a lengthy period of *de facto* non-existence[24] lasting more than eighteen centuries. Thus international law explicitly recognized the pre-existing right of the Jewish People to the Land of Israel, first when the Principal Allied Powers decided in 1919 and 1920 to create Palestine as the national home of the Jewish People and second, when the Mandate for Palestine was confirmed for that very purpose in 1922. Had no such right, derived from the historical connection of the Jewish People with Palestine,[25] actually existed, there could have been no *recognition* of it under international law. Such recognition was therefore declarative in nature, rather than constitutive. *De jure* sovereignty over the Land of Israel extends today in favour of the Jewish people and its assignee, the State of Israel, as it once did in ancient times, during the First and Second Temple Periods, over all areas of the Land, whether incorporated into the State of Israel or lying outside its formal borders. By contrast, Israel's *de facto* sovereignty extends only to those areas of the Land of Israel under the State's direct and effective control.

---

[24] In *halakha* Jewish sovereignty over the Land of Israel has always existed in a theoretical or *de jure* sense, based on the idea of the Patriarchal Covenant as recorded in the Book of Genesis and reflected in present-day Israeli constitutional law, as embodied in the Area of Jurisdiction and Powers Ordinance of 1948 and the accompanying Land of Israel Proclamation. Jewish Law considers such sovereignty to be continuous and immutable from the time of Abraham, Isaac and Jacob, even after Rome subjugated Judea in the year 70, thus bringing an end to the Second Jewish Commonwealth. From that date onwards, during the long period when no Jewish State existed, international law relegated Jewish sovereignty over the country to a state of dormancy, considering it to be in abeyance until the adoption of the San Remo Resolution on April 25, 1920 which restored *de jure* sovereignty to the Jewish People. It was only then that the two views of sovereignty, one founded on Jewish law and the other on normative international law, merged once again and become one. See Appendix 1: *Summary Table of Sovereignty over Eretz-Israel from 1516 to the Present Day under International Law and Jewish Law (Halakha).*

[25] This historical connection is explicitly stated in the Third Recital of the Preamble to the Mandate.

*Chapter 9*

# The Doctrine of Estoppel and its Application to the Anglo-American Convention Respecting the Mandate for Palestine

To effectively counter unfounded, ignorant or plain hostile attacks emanating from the State Department of the United States Government and most of the countries of Europe as well as baseless Arab claims concerning Israel's legal presence in Judea, Samaria and Gaza, it is necessary to invoke against all of them the doctrine of estoppel, which applies as much in international law as it does in the internal law of a state. This doctrine or principle is considered to be one of the sources of international law implicitly included in Article 38(1)(c) of the Statute of the International Court of Justice, which states that the Court in adjudicating a case shall apply "the general principles of law recognized by civilized nations". One of these general principles of law is that of estoppel.

The use of estoppel in international law has been noted by the jurist Georg Schwarzenberger who, in his book on international law, has affirmed:[1]

> ...the principle of estoppel is certainly applicable to proceedings before international Courts. Parties are estopped from putting forward claims which are contrary to their own previous acts or which amount to an abuse of rights and they cannot derive benefits from their own violations of international law.

According to the British jurist Ian Brownlie, in his book, *Principles of Public International Law*:[2]

> The principle of estoppel or preclusion undoubtedly has a place in international law and it has played a significant role in territorial disputes which have come before international tribunals. Recognition,

[1] Georg Schwarzenberger, *International Law*, vol. 1: International Law as Applied by International Courts and Tribunals, 2nd edition, London, Stevens & Sons, Ltd. (1949), p. 436.

[2] Oxford University Press, 1966, pp. 151-153 and p. 330.

> acquiescence, admissions constituting a part of the evidence of sovereignty, and estoppel form an interrelated subject matter... It is clear that in appropriate conditions acquiescence will have the effect of estoppel...
>
> In many situations, acquiescence and express admissions are part of the evidence of sovereignty. Estoppel differs in that, if it exists, it suffices to settle the issue because of its unambiguous characterization of the situation...
>
> Express recognition in the treaty of the existence of title in the *other party* (italics in the original) to a dispute (as opposed to recognition by third states) creates an effect equivalent to that of estoppel.

To illustrate his above remarks, Brownlie cites the 1933 Eastern Greenland case where Norway was estopped or debarred from contesting Danish sovereignty over the whole of Greenland and from occupying any part of it because it had previously accepted bilateral and multilateral agreements containing provisions which expressly recognized that Greenland was a part of Denmark and therefore bound itself by this acceptance.

Estoppel in international law can be truly defined as a legal bar, impediment or limitation which prevents a state from denying or contradicting anything which it previously admitted or recognized either by its own actions or conduct or by making clear, voluntary and express statements or declarations, particularly as evidenced in an international agreement or treaty to which it was an original party or subsequently acceded or which it recognized.

As applied to the case of Palestine, the principle of estoppel will debar or impede any nation which expressly recognized the Balfour Declaration and Mandate for Palestine as well as the Franco-British Boundary Convention of December 23, 1920 from denying Jewish legal rights and title of sovereignty over the entire territory of Mandated Palestine. This principle can be invoked with great effect against the United States, which has advocated under President George W. Bush's Administration a new Arab state called "Palestine" inside the Jewish National Home territories of Judea, Samaria and Gaza, living side by side in peace with the State of Israel within secure and recognized borders.[3]

---

[3] President George W. Bush started using the term "Palestine" for the first time in an address to the U.N. General Assembly on November 10, 2001. Nine days later, on Nov. 19, 2001, came a speech by Secretary of State Colin Powell at the University of Louisville, in Kentucky, in which he said that the U.S. has "a vision of a region where two states, Israel and Palestine, live side by side within secure and recognized borders". In the same speech, Powell referred to "Israel's occupation of the West Bank and Gaza" that has lasted for over three decades. Then in a surprise move, the U.S. introduced Resolution 1397 in the U.N. Security Council that was adopted on March 12, 2002, affirming an American vision of a two-state solution in the Land of Israel, west of the Jordan. Later, in a speech on April 4, 2002, in Washington, President Bush spoke in favour of an independent state for the "Palestinian people" and called for an end to "occupation" and Israeli settlement

This new policy contradicted what the United States had accepted previously of its own volition and even made part of its internal law, namely, that Palestine was founded in April 1920 as the national home of the Jewish People and not as the homeland of a fictitious, non-existent entity, the so-called "Palestinian people".

The United States has apparently forgotten the fact that it signed a treaty with Great Britain on December 3, 1924 in London, generally called the Anglo-American Convention[4] respecting the Mandate for Palestine in which it assented to all the terms of the Mandate as the basis for the British administration of Palestine. The U.S. thereby expressly recognized in a treaty the right of the Jewish People, in conjunction with the obligation of the British Government, to reconstitute their national home in all of Mandated Palestine and the Land of Israel, which included every right associated with or incidental to that overarching right, in particular the twin rights of Jewish immigration and settlement in those areas of Palestine which President Bush and Secretary of State Colin Powell have wrongly labelled Israel's "occupied territories". The Convention or treaty was duly ratified by the U.S. Senate and proclaimed by President Calvin Coolidge on December 5, 1925, in the following words:[5]

---

activity in "occupied territories". President Bush's remarks were reiterated by Secretary Powell at a press conference in Jerusalem on April 17, 2002, where he said that Israel must "look beyond the destructive impact of settlements and occupation, both of which must end, consistent with the clear position taken by President Bush in his April 4 speech." President Bush returned to the same topic on June 24, 2002, announcing in a speech in Washington that the United States will support the creation of a "Palestinian State" as part of a final settlement in the Middle East, provided the alleged "Palestinian People" have new leaders who dismantle the infrastructure of the terrorists and create new institutions and security arrangements with their neighbours. President Bush also referred to Israel's presence in Judea, Samaria and Gaza as an "untenable occupation" that must end through a negotiated settlement based on U.N. Resolutions 242 and 338. He also said that Israeli settlement activity in the "occupied territories" must stop. The principle of estoppel can be effectively used to fight this dangerous American policy, founded on illegality insofar as it contradicts prior U.S. recognition of Jewish rights to the whole of Palestine. However, the Government of Israel under the direction of Prime Minister Sharon and his successor Ehud Olmert has perversely welcomed that policy. According to news reports, Shim'on Peres and Binyamin Ben-Eliezer, as members of the first Sharon Government, helped to devise the Bush Plan (Jerusalem Post, February 3, 2003, p.1).

[4] Also known as the American-British Palestine Mandate Convention or the Convention Between the United Kingdom and the United States of America Respecting the Rights of the Governments of the Two Countries and their Respective Nationals, or simply the Palestine Convention. See Command Paper 2559 and "Publications of the Department of State", *Near Eastern Series*, No. 1, entitled: *Mandate for Palestine*, U.S. Government Printing Office, Washington: 1931.

[5] "President Coolidge's Proclamation is found in: Reuben Fink, *America and Palestine: The Attitude of Official America and of the American People Toward the Rebuilding of Palestine as a Free and Democratic Jewish Commonwealth*,

> Now, therefore, be it known that I, Calvin Coolidge, President of the United States of America, have caused the said Convention to be made public, to the end that the same and every article and clause thereof may be observed and fulfilled with good faith by the United States and the citizens thereof.

Under the Anglo-American Convention respecting the Mandate for Palestine, American rights were summarized in a statement issued by Secretary of State Cordell Hull on October 14, 1938:[6]

> 1. non-discriminatory treatment in matters of commerce;
> 2. non-impairment of vested American property rights;
> 3. permission for American nationals to establish and maintain educational, philanthropic and religious institutions in Palestine;
> 4. safeguards with respect to the judiciary;
> 5. and in general, equality of treatment with all other foreign nationals.

The foregoing rights enumerated by Secretary Hull in his statement benefited not only American citizens, but also the U.S. Government. The latter was separately accorded rights under the treaty, as stated specifically in both its Preamble and operating terms of the Convention. The most important right of all granted to the U.S. Government under the Convention concerned the right it enjoyed to prevent any modification of the terms of the Mandate for Palestine, unless it agreed to such modification in advance, as further discussed below. Unfortunately and to the everlasting shame of the anti-Zionist U.S. State Department, the latter, in friendly collusion with the British Government, denied the very existence of this right, a position astonishingly accepted by President Franklin Delano Roosevelt. The denial of this right resulted in a situation that allowed the British Government a free hand unencumbered by any U.S. counteraction in trampling upon Jewish legal rights to Palestine under the new policy announced in the British White Paper of May 17, 1939 which severely limited Jewish immigration from Europe from the beginning of the Holocaust and very nearly aborted the Jewish National Home.

In return for the United States Government and its nationals having and enjoying what Article 2 of the Convention on Palestine stated was "*all* (emphasis

---

American Zionist Emergency Council, Herald Square Press, Inc., New York (1944), p. 487.

[6] The statement by Secretary Hull was published in the New York Times of October 15, 1938, p. 1, and is reprinted in the book *With Firmness in the Right – American Diplomatic Action Affecting Jews, 1840-1945,* by Cyrus Adler and Aaron M. Margalith, New York, The American Jewish Committee, (1946). See pp. 91-93. The same statement, bearing the date of Oct. 13, 1939, is also reprinted in Reuben Fink, *op. cit.* pp. 73-75.

added) the rights and benefits secured under the terms of the Mandate to the members of the League of Nations and their nationals", the United States consented in Article 1 of the Convention "to the administration of Palestine by His Britannic Majesty, pursuant to the Mandate" for Palestine, which was recited in full, word for word, in the Preamble of the Convention.[7] The recital of the whole Mandate, as well as the direct reference to it in Article 1, sufficed to make the terms of the Mandate an integral part of the *operating terms* of the Convention. As a direct consequence, the U.S. Government was required not only to fulfill in good faith every article and clause of the *Convention*, but equally to ensure that every article and clause of the *Mandate for Palestine* was observed by the Mandatory, in accordance with the meaning given to the treaty by President Coolidge in publicly proclaiming it. This gave the U.S. Government a direct interest in furthering the establishment of the Jewish National Home and in ensuring that the British Government would not deviate from this goal. The Convention therefore not only secured American rights in Palestine, but simultaneously recognized all the Jewish legal rights and title of sovereignty that constituted the warp and woof or essence of the Mandate for Palestine. The Convention was by its very nature an American legal guarantee of President Wilson's earlier statement on March 2, 1919 that "in Palestine shall be laid the foundations of a Jewish Commonwealth". In negotiating this treaty, the American Government understood that the expression "Jewish National Home" meant an eventual independent Jewish State, in the borders of Palestine as they existed at the time the Convention was signed and which were shown in all the maps of Palestine, including both Cisjordan and Transjordan. This understanding of what "Jewish National Home" meant to the Americans was revealed incidentally in a letter sent by U.S. Secretary of State Charles Evans Hughes to Lord Balfour on January 27, 1922, which contained the following excerpt:[8]

> ...with regard to the question of the revival of the capitulations... it will be necessary to provide for the revival of our original rights [granted in a U.S. treaty with the Ottoman Empire] upon the termination of the mandate regime. Even in case *a Jewish state* should survive, it would still be necessary for the United States to reach a decision for itself on the question at that time (emphasis added).

---

[7] The exact texts of Articles 1 and 2 of the Convention of December 3, 1924 read as follows:

*Article 1:* Subject to the provisions of the present convention the United States consents to the administration of Palestine by His Britannic Majesty, pursuant to the Mandate recited above.

*Article 2:* The United States and its nationals shall have and enjoy all the rights and benefits secured under the terms of the Mandate to members of the League of Nations and their nationals, notwithstanding the fact that the United States is not a member of the League of Nations.

[8] *The Rise of Israel*, Vol. 19, Document 38, pp. 546-547.

In concluding the Convention with Britain, the United States became in effect an additional contracting party to the Mandate for Palestine, alongside the four Principal Allied Powers of Britain, France, Italy and Japan, for the purpose of establishing a Jewish State in the entire country.

Furthermore, the Convention, being an international treaty, gave even greater meaning and legal force to the earlier Joint Resolution of the 67th Congress of the United States, which had been passed unanimously by both Houses of Congress and signed by President Warren Gamaliel Harding on September 21, 1922. The Joint Resolution, also known as the Lodge-Fish (or inversely the Fish-Lodge) Resolution after its initiators,[9] endorsed the essence of the Balfour Declaration, with slight changes in its wording. It stated as follows:

> *JOINT RESOLUTION*
> *Favouring the establishment in Palestine of*
> *a national home for the Jewish People*
>
> Resolved by the Senate and the House of Representatives of the United States of America in Congress assembled, That the United States of America favours the establishment in Palestine of a national home for the Jewish People, it being clearly understood that nothing shall be done which may prejudice the civil and religious rights of Christian and other non-Jewish communities in Palestine, and that the holy places and religious buildings and sites in Palestine shall be adequately protected.

Under American law, a Joint Resolution, when passed by both the Senate and House of Representatives in identical form and then signed by the President, becomes the law of the land, in contrast to a Concurrent Resolution which does not have the force of law and is not referred to the President for his signature. The Lodge-Fish Joint Resolution which recognized in effect a future Jewish State in the whole of Palestine thus became embedded in U.S. law and still

---

[9] The initiators of the Joint Resolution in the 67th Congress of the United States of America were Senator Henry Cabot Lodge of Massachusetts and Hamilton Fish, Jr., a Representative in Congress from the State of New York who was a member of the House Committee on Foreign Affairs and the original author of the Joint Resolution. The Resolution introduced by Fish in the House of Representatives and unanimously adopted by it had a preamble which did not appear in the final joint version. The preamble in the Fish Resolution stated: "Whereas the Jewish People have for many centuries believed in and yearned for the rebuilding of their ancient homeland; and whereas owing to the outcome of the World War and their part therein the Jewish People, under definite and adequate international guarantees are to be enabled, with due regard to the rights of all elements of the population of Palestine and to the sanctity of the Holy Places, to recreate and reorganize a national home in the land of their fathers."

remains a part of it today, never having been repealed. This Joint Resolution obligates the U.S. Government not to do anything which violates its plain meaning, namely, that Palestine is an integral whole where only one state was to be established, specifically a Jewish State, and not one or more Arab states in a partitioned country.

The same meaning found in the Joint Resolution but in more explicit detail was conveyed by the Anglo-American Convention on Palestine which incorporated the entire Mandate for Palestine and made it part of the supreme law of the United States. [10] In this context it should be remembered that the Mandate for Palestine as an act of international law was a constitution for the projected Jewish State that made no provision for an Arab State, and which explicitly prohibited the partition of the country. What the 1924 Convention connoted in terms of estoppel was that the United States has been barred ever since the adoption of the Joint Resolution and the signing of the 1924 Treaty, both by its own internal law and by international law, from taking any action that contradicted what it expressly recognized in the aforesaid documents in regard to Jewish legal rights and title of sovereignty to the whole of mandated Palestine. This applies today with particular relevance to U.S. opposition to Israeli civilian settlement activity in Judea, Samaria and Gaza and its advocacy of a new Arab state under the appropriated name of "Palestine". That shall remain the case, unless and until the U.S. Congress revokes the Lodge-Fish Joint Resolution and/or passes new legislation withdrawing the legal recognition the U.S. gave, by virtue of the 1924 Convention, to Jewish national rights in Palestine or supplants those rights in another international treaty. Even if that were to happen, as it may well have in the case of Transjordan, the United States could not legally rescind the State of Israel's acquired legal rights to the Land of Israel under international law, inasmuch as the doctrine of estoppel could still be applied against any American move to withdraw recognition of those rights. This is so because rights of this kind do not lapse with the implementation of the legal instrument creating them, a principle now codified, as mentioned above, in Article 70 (1)(b) of the Vienna Convention of the Law of Treaties.

The Government of Israel has the perfect right therefore to inform and sharply protest to the United States Government that it is legally estopped by virtue of the 1924 Convention respecting the Mandate for Palestine from condemning or taking any concrete measures against the establishment of Israeli

---

[10] The U.S. Senate advised ratification of the Convention on February 20, 1925. It was then ratified by President Coolidge on March 2, 1925. This was followed by U.K. ratification on March 18, 1925. Finally, the documents of ratification were exchanged in London on December 3, 1925. The figures who were principally involved in negotiating the Convention were the American Secretary of State, Charles Evans Hughes, who was later appointed Chief Justice of the United States, and his British counterparts, Foreign Secretary Lord Curzon in the early stage, and later, Foreign Secretary Austen Chamberlain. Lord Balfour also participated in the negotiations, as did Prime Minister James Ramsay MacDonald, who doubled as Secretary of State for Foreign Affairs in 1924.

civilian settlements by the Government of Israel in any region of the Jewish National Home. Nor can the U.S. Government press for a so-called "Palestinian State" to be born in favour of a fictitious nation falsely called "Palestinians", as it did in introducing U.N. Security Council Resolution 1397, passed on March 12, 2002 and as further amplified by President George W. Bush in an important speech delivered in Washington on June 24, 2002 that later inspired the Bush Road Map Peace Plan.

The U.S. Government is legally obligated to respect the fact that Israel is the *only Palestinian state* that has been legally established under international law by virtue of Article 22 of the League of Nations Covenant, based on the Smuts Resolution, the San Remo Resolution, the Mandate for Palestine and the Franco-British Boundary Convention of December 23, 1920. Any other Palestinian state to be established is a clear illegality and a terrible affront to the Jewish People, whose rights to all of Palestine would be gravely impaired by this new state, which would also be a significant security threat.

As a direct consequence of the 1924 Convention becoming U.S. law, the American Government was obliged to condemn any British violation of the terms of Mandate which denied or impugned any Jewish legal rights during the time the British Government was under an international obligation to implement those terms. Moreover, the American Government, in effect the guarantor of Jewish rights under the Mandate, had to take appropriate diplomatic and then legal steps – if this violation did not stop. This could have included seeking redress in the Permanent Court of International Justice, established under Article 14 of the League Covenant and as provided for by Article 26 of the Mandate for Palestine. The opportunity for doing exactly this, as noted above, came with the publication of the British White Paper of May 17, 1939 when the U.K. Government committed a wholesale and sweeping violation of the Mandate by severely limiting Jewish immigration and Jewish land acquisition and by declaring its intention to establish an Arab state in Palestine within ten years. But the official U.S. Government position under President Franklin Delano Roosevelt was far different from what it was supposed to be under its own law and international law.

In order to implement the British plan to create an Arab State of Palestine instead of a Jewish State of Palestine, the British Government needed to carry out far-reaching modifications in the terms of the Mandate that would have destroyed its very basis and hence were illegal. In any event such modifications required the prior consent of the League Council. A spirited debate then ensued in the two countries as to whether American consent, too, was really necessary.

There was no doubt about this being obligatory in the minds of many U.S. Representatives and Senators. The strongest protest made against the contemplated British plan to alter the original wording of the Mandate for Palestine came from the Committee of the House of Representatives on Foreign Affairs, headed by Chairman Sol Bloom, which issued the following statement on May 25, 1939, backed by 15 of the 25 members of the Committee:

> We, the undersigned members of the Committee on Foreign Affairs, desire to call to the attention of the House and the State Department a declaration of the British Government announced last Wednesday, May 17th, which is *a clear repudiation of the Convention between the United States and Great Britain with respect to Palestine, dated December 3, 1924* (emphasis added).
>
> . . .
>
> Last Wednesday's declaration of the British Government is a repudiation of the Balfour Declaration, the Mandate of the League of Nations, and of direct concern to us, *a violation of Article 7 of the Treaty between the United States and Great Britain*, in that the contemplated action of the British Government proposes to restrict further immigration of Jews into Palestine and to reduce the Jewish People in Palestine to a permanent minority status. *On neither of these matters has our Government been consulted as required by the Treaty* (emphasis added).
>
> . . .
>
> As members of the Foreign Affairs Committee, we respectfully request the State Department to advise the British Government that the contemplated action, if carried out, will be regarded as a violation of the British-American Convention and will be viewed with disfavour by the American People.

An earlier statement had been released by 28 senators on March 7, 1939, prior to the publication of the White Paper based on what it said were reliable reports that the British Government was "contemplating the liquidation of the Mandate for Palestine based on the Balfour Declaration". It declared that to reverse the process under which Palestine came to be a haven of refuge for thousands of homeless Jewish families would be "a tragic abandonment of a brave people in its hour of greatest need". It expressed the hope that the spirit and letter of the Balfour Declaration would be preserved in all its integrity.[11]

However, the U.S. Administration of President Roosevelt, while not explicitly approving what was done by Britain, said it could do nothing about the White Paper that "liquidated the Mandate for Palestine" – in the words of the 28 senators. Its official position on British modifications to the Mandate had been expressed in a State Department Memorandum issued on October 14, 1938 at the time a discussion was taking place on the report of the Palestine Partition Commission (known as the Woodhead Commission), which was set up to delineate boundaries for the proposed Jewish and Arab states recommended in the Peel Report of 1937. This Memorandum, endorsed by President Roosevelt, stated:

---

[11] The statements in full of the House Committee and the 28 Senators are found in the book edited by Reuben Fink, *op. cit.*, pp. 61-63.

> None of these articles (in the Convention of 1924) empower the Government of the United States to prevent the modification of the terms of any of the Mandates. Under their provisions, however, this government can decline to recognize the validity of the application to American interests of any modifications of the Mandates unless such modification has been assented to by the Government of the United States.[12]

The British position on whether or not U.S. consent was required in advance for any proposed modifications of the Mandate for Palestine, was originally addressed by British Foreign Secretary, Anthony Eden, after the U.K. Government decided to partition Palestine, in line with the Peel Report, which necessitated making modifications to the Mandate Charter. In a letter dated July 7, 1937 which Eden sent to the American Ambassador to London, Robert W. Bingham, he wrote as follows:

> The rights of the United States Government and their nationals as regards Palestine are those recited in Articles 2 to 6 of the Convention, and in Article 7 of the Convention these rights must remain intact whatever changes may be made in the Mandate for Palestine, unless the United States assent to such a change.
>
> In the view of His Majesty's Government, however, these rights are limited to those specified in the Articles of the Convention referred to above, and the consent of the United States Government will therefore not be required to any change in the Palestine mandate unless the specific rights in question are thereby affected. Indeed, the United States having assented, by Article 1 of the Convention, to the Mandate as a whole, it follows that the United States Government have accepted the provision in Article 27 of the Mandate which lays down that the Mandate may be altered with the consent of the Council of the League of Nations. His Majesty's Government in the United Kingdom propose to seek the consent of the Council of the League at its September session for any changes in the Mandate of Palestine which may be required as the result of the Royal Commission's Report; but, should any such changes affect any of the United States rights laid down in Articles 2 to 6 of the Convention referred to above, His Majesty's Government will immediately inform the United States Government and seek their consent thereto.[13]

---

[12] Quoted in: *Palestine: A Study of Jewish, Arab and British Policies*, ESCO Foundation, Yale University Press, Volume 2, p. 1111.

[13] *The Rise of Israel*, Volume 19, Document 40, pp. 681-682.

The explanation presented by Foreign Secretary Eden denying that the United States had a right to be consulted and give or withhold its consent before any modifications could be made in the terms of the *Mandate*, as distinct from the rights granted to it in the *Convention* itself, suffered from an inherent and glaring contradiction. As is the case in any contract, each of the parties to the Convention was obliged to uphold all the operating terms of the Convention contained therein, and as appears from Eden's own admission, Article 27 of the Mandate was included among those operating terms, when the U.S. assented by Article 1 of the Convention to the Mandate as a whole. This being the case for Article 27, then, by natural extension, so, too, were all the other articles of the Mandate part of the operating terms of the Convention. Therefore, if Britain unilaterally changed any terms of the Mandate without first obtaining American consent, it was *ipso facto* unilaterally changing the operating terms of the Convention, which would have been a gross violation of the sanctity of the Convention, agreed to by both parties, that was absolutely prohibited. The only logical conclusion that could be drawn was that Britain could not, by acting alone, modify the terms of the Mandate in any way, even if the modifications did not directly affect the rights of the United States Government specified in Articles 2 to 6 of the Convention. Therefore, Britain needed not only the consent of the Council of the League of Nations, but also the consent of the United States for changing any provision of the Mandate.

The contrary British view that they did in fact have a free hand to make any modifications they wanted in the terms of the Mandate, without American consent, so long as these changes did not affect any specific rights of the United States Government or those of its nationals, was not founded on a thorough examination and understanding of all the relevant articles of the Convention and those of the Mandate and the League Covenant, as listed immediately below, which had a bearing on the question. The British Government also ignored past statements made by the American and British negotiators of the Convention which shed light on whether or not American consent was needed.

The following dispositions contained in the Convention, Mandate and Covenant of the League of Nations were important in arriving at the proper answer:

> *Article 2 of the Convention:* The United States and its nationals shall have and enjoy *all* the rights and benefits secured under the terms of the Mandate to members of the League of Nations and their nationals, notwithstanding the fact that the United States is not a member of the League of Nations (emphasis added).

> *Article 7 of the Convention:* Nothing contained in the present convention shall be affected by any modifications which may be made in the terms of the Mandate, as recited above, unless such modification shall have been assented to by the United States.

> *Article 27 of the Mandate:* The consent of the Council of the League of Nations is required for any modification of the terms of this mandate.
>
> *Article 4 of the Covenant of the League of Nations:* The Council shall consist of Representatives of the Principal Allied and Associated Powers, together with Representatives of four other Members of the League…
>
> *Article 5 of the Covenant of the League of Nations:* Except where otherwise expressly provided in this Covenant or by the terms of the present Treaty [of Versailles] decisions at any meeting of the Assembly or of the Council shall require the agreement of *all* the Members of the League represented at the meeting… (emphasis added).

In light of the following premises which constituted indisputable facts based on the above dispositions:

> 1. that the 1924 Convention stated that the United State shall have not merely some but "all" the rights secured under the terms of the Mandate that were given to state members of the League of Nations, even without being an actual member;
> 2. that from among "all" those rights, one of them included the theoretical right given to "all" members to be represented on the Council of the League of Nations whether as a permanent or non-permanent member. In the case of the Principal Allied and Associated Powers of which the United States was the Associated Power, each of the members of this five-state select group had a guaranteed right to be represented on the Council;
> 3. that each of the states that had a right to sit on the Council whose decisions had to be approved unanimously, also had the individual right to give or withhold its consent for any modification of the terms of the Mandate at any meeting of the Council that would have had to be convened if Britain formally requested a modification in the terms of the Mandate;
> 4. that "all" rights held by state members of the Council who had joined the League were also held by the United States as a direct result of the 1924 Convention respecting the Mandate for Palestine.

The inevitable conclusion was that the United States had to be consulted in advance by Britain in order to obtain its specific approval for any change Britain proposed to make in the terms of the Mandate. This conclusion was the exact opposite of what Eden said it was, but the United States Government, acting upon erroneous and anti-Zionist State Department advice which was in perfect sympathy with the British interpretation and not wanting to get embroiled in a diplomatic and legal controversy with the British Government over the Mandate in support of the national rights of the Jewish People to Palestine, connivingly agreed to accept the wrong conclusion of Eden, rather than to press the British Government to retract the White Paper.[14]

It is indeed disappointing that at the crucial moment, when the American Government could have acted forcefully to forestall the publication of the British White Paper of May 17, 1939, it adopted a self-negating position as to whether its consent was necessary for the modification of the terms of the Mandate that was contrary to the position it had advocated in the negotiations leading up to the signing of the Convention of December 3, 1924 respecting the Mandate for Palestine. During those negotiations, it had always maintained the view that the consent of the United States was indeed necessary for any modification of the Mandate.[15] At that time the American Government went so far as to assert that its prior consent was necessary not only for modifications to the Mandate concerning Cisjordanian Palestine, but also for Transjordan. This understanding of United States rights pursuant to the Convention of December 3, 1924 was expressed in a letter dated April 30, 1924 sent by the American Ambassador to London, Frank B. Kellogg, to Prime Minister James Ramsay MacDonald, in which he stated:[16]

> Upon the conclusion of the Convention between the United States and Great Britain, it is my Government's understanding that the Convention will be applicable to such territory as may be under British

---

[14] This argument is also presented by Prof. Nathan Feinberg in a 1950 commentary on "The Interpretation of the Anglo-American Convention on Palestine, 1924", published originally in the *International Law Quarterly* and republished in *Studies in International Law, With Special Reference to the Arab-Israel Conflict* The Magnes Press, The Hebrew University, Jerusalem (1979) , pp. 414-429. An opposing view, that American consent was not required for modifications proposed by Britain in the terms of the Mandate for Palestine is given by Frank E. Manuel, Professor of History at Brandeis and New York University, in his book *The Realities of American-Palestine Relations*, Public Affairs Press, Washington, D.C. (1949), p. 279. Manuel did not properly understand the legal import of Articles 2 and 7 of the Convention. Others with an opposing view were Carl. J. Friedrich, in *American Policy toward Palestine*, American Council on Public Affairs, Washington 1944, p. 23, n. 1, and Quincy Wright, *Mandates under the League of Nations*, pp. 483 ff. A brief discussion of Friedrich's and Wright's views is found in *Palestine, A Study of Jewish, Arab and British Policies*, *op. cit.*, Volume I, pp. 253-255.

[15] See the memorandum on the position of the Government of the United States concerning Mandates, presented by the American Ambassador in London George Harvey to Lord Curzon, on August 24, 1921, in *The Rise of Israel*, Vol. 19, Document 38, p. 541. See also the letter sent by Secretary of State Charles Evans Hughes to Lord Balfour on January 27, 1922, *ibid.*, pp. 547-48.

[16] *Ibid.*, p. 577.

> mandate to the east, as well as to the west of the River Jordan, and that, in view of the provisions of Article 7 as proposed, no further change will be made with respect to the conditions of the British administration of the territory known as Transjordan without the previous assent of my Government. I am instructed to inquire whether the British Government is in accord with this view.

Prime Minister MacDonald replied on July 17, 1924 that the British Government agreed that the Convention applied to the east as well as the west of the River Jordan but it did not concur in the American interpretation as regards changes in the administration of what it called "Transjordania", saying:[17]

> It [is] essential that they be allowed latitude to make changes in the administration of that territory in such manner as may appear necessary, provided such action does not conflict with *the terms of the Mandate* (emphasis added).

The Prime Minister's statement, as recorded immediately above, was an explicit admission that Britain alone, without the concurrence of the United States, could not change the terms of the Mandate, by virtue of Article 7 of the Convention, except as regards changes deemed necessary in administering Transjordan. This admission conclusively refuted the contrary view pronounced thirteen years later by Foreign Secretary Eden that the U.K. did have the unilateral right to make whatever modifications in the terms of the Mandate it thought appropriate, so long as those modifications did not adversely affect the rights of the United States or those of its nationals, as set out in the Convention. It is almost inexplicable that the American Government never reminded the U.K. of the assurance given to it in 1924 that Britain needed to obtain the consent of the United States before modifying the terms of the Mandate. The only possible explanation for the lack of American protest at this brazen violation of the 1924 Treaty was that the U.S. State Department which advised the President on this matter supported and colluded with the British decision to issue the infamous White Paper of May 17, 1939 that was intended to kill the prospect of a Jewish State in Palestine and to substitute for it another Arab state.

In a further letter to Prime Minister MacDonald dated September 2, 1924, the U.S. Government through its Ambassador Frank B. Kellogg reiterated the American position that all states administering mandated territories had to consult with it, as a matter of general policy, as well as with the states represented on the Council of the League of Nations "in connection with any general changes in the form of the mandatory administration of Transjordania".[18] This

---

[17] *Ibid.*, p. 580.

[18] *Ibid.*, p. 581.

letter noted the British assurances given previously:[19]

> That the Palestine Convention shall be applicable to territory under British mandate to the east as well as to the west of the River Jordan and the further statement that the changes which may be made in the administration of the territory will not be of a character to conflict with *the terms of the Mandate* (emphasis added).

The American letter added that these British assurances appear to have safeguarded the essential points in which the American Government was interested, inasmuch as they "embody the undertaking that the changes which may be made in the administration of the territory [of Transjordan] will not be of such a character as to conflict with *the terms of the Convention*" (emphasis added).

As shown by the foregoing excerpts from the American and British correspondence respecting the 1924 Convention, the American Government assumed that "the terms of the Convention" included "the terms of the Mandate", a point that is decisive in the legal argument that any change made in the terms of the mandate by the British Government was *ipso facto* a change made in the operating terms of the Convention itself.

In the final letter on the subject of whether modifications to the terms of the Mandate required American consent, the British Secretary of State for Foreign Affairs, Austen Chamberlain, wrote to Ambassador Kellogg on November 10, 1924, that the assurance desired by the U.S. Government to be consulted on any alteration in the administration of Transjordania for which the British Government would seek the approval of the League Council is given without hesitation.[20]

It may be concluded that as a result of the exchange of correspondence between American and British negotiators regarding the Palestine Convention, that the British were under a legal obligation to consult with the United States and obtain its consent *before* any modifications could be made by the British Government in the terms of the Mandate Charter both as regards Cisjordanian Palestine and Transjordan in order to verify if such modifications were made in accordance with the Convention. This obligation the British Government failed to honour when it issued the White Paper of May 17, 1939, not long after the failure of the St. James Conference (also known as the Round Table Conference) in London called by the British to discuss the future of Palestine, which was attended by Arab and Jewish representatives between February 7 and March 17, 1939. The American Government accepted this breach of the Convention, thereby making it complicit with the British Government in the sabotage of the Mandate for Palestine and the fatal consequences that this entailed for Jewish

[19] *Ibid.*, p. 581

[20] *Ibid.*, p. 582.

immigration to Palestine from Hitler's Europe.

As already indicated above the very same conclusion that prior American consent was required before any proposed changes could be made by Britain in the terms of the Mandate for Palestine also sprang from Article 7 of the Palestine Convention. The words in this article stating that "nothing contained in the present Convention" included all the terms of the Mandate for Palestine which, it is important to stress, were an integral part of the operating terms of the Convention by virtue of Article I thereof and therefore those terms of the Mandate could not be changed unilaterally by Britain without also violating the Convention.

In the event, the British Government never bothered to change the actual terms of the Mandate, but still went ahead with the implementation of the White Paper of 1939 which continued in force until the termination of the Mandate. Such implementation had the same practical effect as if the terms of the Mandate had really been changed. This was clearly an illegal violation of the Mandate implemented through a White Paper procedure, without obtaining the consent either of the League Council or that of the United States Government. The British Government henceforth governed Palestine in complete and absolute violation of the Mandate with no shame, and was never brought to account at the Bar of Justice for its lawless conduct under international law, which overturned the entire basis of the Mandate as originally formulated.

The League Council never convened to consider the validity of the British White Paper because of the exigencies of World War II. However, the Permanent Mandates Commission, a body composed of international, generally impartial experts which advised the Council "on all matters related to the observance of the mandates" under Article 22, paragraph 9, of the Treaty of Versailles, did hold several meetings from June 15, 1939 to the end of the month to consider this important question. It came to the unanimous conclusion[21]

> That the policy set out in the White Paper was not in accordance with the interpretation which, in agreement with the Mandatory Power and the Council, the Commission had always placed upon the Palestine Mandate.

---

[21] See the *Report of the Permanent Mandates Commission of the League of Nations on the Policy Laid Down in the (MacDonald) White Paper of May 1939, Made at the Thirty-Sixth Session of the Permanent Mandates Commission, 1939*. This Report is published in *The Rise of Israel,* Volume 27, Document 29, pp. 338 ff. and as Document 17 in the *Book of Documents* submitted by the Jewish Agency for Palestine to the United Nations General Assembly, May 1947, pp. 176 ff. See also the article written by Benjamin Akzin, "The Palestine Mandate in Practice", *The Iowa Law Review*, Volume XXV, No. 1, November 1939, pp. 76-77. Reprinted in: *Seeds of Conflict*, Series 7, Palestine, The twice-promised land: The Jewish Cause, Part II, Volume 2, Paper No. 23, published by KTO Press (1978), a Division of Kraus-Thomson Organization, Ltd., Nendeln, Liechtenstein.

In considering whether the new interpretation given to the Mandate by the 1939 White Paper was in agreement with it, there were divergent views among the members of the Commission. The majority opinion of four members (Pierre Orts, the Chairman of the Commission from Belgium; Prof. William Rappard, the Vice-Chairman from Switzerland; Frederik Mari Baron van Asbeck from Holland; and Mlle. Valentine Dannevig from Norway) was that the White Paper did not conform to the Mandate, as shown by "the very terms of the Mandate and by the fundamental intentions of its authors". The minority view, advanced by the British, French and Portuguese members, gave a conditional acceptance to the White Paper, affirming that "existing circumstances would justify the policy of the White Paper, provided that the Council did not oppose it".

In complete contempt of the advisory opinion of the Permanent Mandates Commission, and without waiting for the Council of the League to pronounce on the matter, the British Government began to implement the White Paper as a *fait accompli*. Also amazing was the fact that even though the White Paper disemboweled the Mandate's paramount purpose to establish the Jewish National Home and State, Arab spokesmen rejected the White Paper since the Jewish nature of the Mandate Charter, which pervaded its most important provisions, could not be entirely erased despite the British re-interpretation of those provisions in favour of the Arab position. For the Arabs, the Jews simply had no right to be in Palestine at all, a right which the White Paper did not take away, though it limited the growth of the Jewish population to a third of the total. The radical result of this pro-Arab White Paper at the time it was released was summed up by Professor of Law Benjamin Akzin, who sagely noted:[22]

> ...the Jewish National Home, which in 1917 and for sometime afterwards [i.e, until the 1922 Churchill White Paper – H.G.] was interpreted as leading to a Jewish majority and to a Jewish State, is finally interpreted in the Statement of Policy of May 17, 1939, as meaning a State with a guaranteed two-thirds Arab majority.

The American Government by not protesting to the U.K. Government that the illegal White Paper violated not only the Mandate for Palestine, but also the Palestine Convention to which it was intricately joined, thereby abdicated its treaty obligation to ensure British compliance with the terms of the Mandate for Palestine, an obligation made even more important by the inability of the League Council to act during the period of World War II to redress the violation. It shamefully dishonoured the promise of President Coolidge's Proclamation of December 5, 1925, that the Convention including every Article and clause thereof would be observed and fulfilled with good faith by the United States. In not taking any active diplomatic or legal steps to overturn the flagrant British sabotage of the Mandate for Palestine and abort the implementation of the

---

[22] Akzin, *op. cit.*, p. 76.

disastrous White Paper, the United States became by its abject passivity a silent and collusive partner to British deceit and outright betrayal of the Jewish People regarding the latter's legal rights under the Mandate to a national and sovereign homeland, at the moment of its greatest peril, which soon resulted in the Holocaust of Six Million. Had there been no White Paper of 1939 and no ludicrous British restrictions placed on Jewish immigration to Palestine in 1939, aided and abetted by American inaction to scotch those restrictions, the tragedy of the Holocaust would certainly have been on a much lower scale. It is all the more difficult to comprehend that this occurred under President Roosevelt's Administration, who had declared his support for the project of the Jewish National Home which he himself knew meant a Jewish State. President Roosevelt's initial reaction to the White Paper of 1939 showed that he was acutely aware of Britain's violation of the Mandate for Palestine. He frankly commented at the time to Secretary of State Cordell Hull:[23]

> I have read with interest and a good deal of dismay the decisions of the British Government regarding its Palestine policy.
>
> I wish you would let me have a copy of the original Palestine Mandate. Frankly, I do not believe that the British are wholly correct in saying that the framers of the Palestine Mandate "could not have intended that Palestine should be converted into a Jewish state against the will of the Arab population of the country."
>
> My recollection is that this way of putting it is deceptive for the reason that while the Palestine Mandate undoubtedly did not intend to take away the right of citizenship and of taking part in the Government on the part of the Arab population, it nevertheless did intend to convert Palestine into a Jewish Home which might very possibly become preponderantly Jewish within a comparatively short time. Certainly that was the impression that was given to the whole world at the time of the Mandate…
>
> This new White Paper admits that the British Mandate is "to secure the development of self-governing institutions". Frankly I do not see how the British Government reads into the original Mandate or into the White Paper of 1922 any policy that would limit Jewish immigration.
>
> My offhand thought is that while there are some good ideas in regard to actual administration of government in this new White Paper, it is something that we cannot give approval to by the United States.
>
> … Arab immigration into Palestine since 1921 has vastly exceeded the total Jewish immigration during this whole period…

[23] Confidential Memorandum from President Roosevelt to Secretary of State Cordell Hull, May 17, 1939, questioning whether the new British White Paper conformed to the terms of the Palestine Mandate. See *The Rise of Israel*, Vol. 28, Document 2, pp. 5-6.

As appears from President Roosevelt's thoughts on the White Paper, the United States never formally accepted it, but did nothing to prevent its implementation, even though it was a flagrant violation of both the Mandate and the Palestine Convention, thus tacitly accepting it. He preferred to accept an erroneous interpretation which downplayed American rights under the Convention and found that no violation of its terms had occurred. This view was posited by the U.S. State Department whose Near East Division from 1929 until 1945 was headed by a domineering anti-Zionist personage, Wallace Murray, during the tenure of Secretary-of-State, Cordell Hull (1933-1944), who preferred not to involve himself in the affairs of Palestine. President Roosevelt therefore chose not to intervene with the British Government or even to consider taking any legal moves in the Permanent Court of International Justice, on the ground that the violation of the Mandate did not trample on any perceived American rights. The trampling of Jewish legal rights by the implementation of the White Paper policy which also impacted negatively on American Jews was apparently for President Roosevelt and his State Department an insufficient reason to warrant American intervention.

The Palestine Convention expired on May 14-15, 1948, when the British administration of Palestine ended and the State of Israel came into being. However, the rights accorded to the Jewish People under the Mandate that were recognized in U.S. law by the ratification of the Convention still retained legal force by virtue of the principle of acquired legal rights and the doctrine of estoppel. Both are facets of the same legal concept that work in tandem with one another, the only difference between them being that one facet is expressed in a positive sense, while the other in a negative and deterring manner. If these rights had truly expired under either international or U.S. law at the time the Mandate Charter terminated, there would not have been any legal foundation for reconstituting the Jewish State. Hence, the rights acquired by the Jewish People under international law and recognized by U.S. law survived the end of the Mandate and the 1924 Convention just as – by analogy – the rights of children from a legal marriage also survive its dissolution and can be invoked afterwards for their benefit. The principle of acquired legal rights and the doctrine of estoppel are integral parts of the American system of law, as they must be of every democratic country governed by the rule of law. As noted above, the principle of acquired legal rights is now codified in international law in Article 70 (1)(b) of the Vienna Convention on Treaties.

Jewish rights over all of Palestine were indivisible by reason of Article 5 of the Mandate. As a result, the United States cannot claim today that when it recognized the State of Israel, it only recognized those rights insofar as they applied to the frontiers of the Jewish State laid down in the U.N. Partition Resolution of November 29, 1947. At the time this resolution was approved, the U.S. was still bound by the terms of the Palestine Convention which had not yet terminated, and therefore could not legally recognize any Arab rights to statehood in any part of Palestine that were never contemplated in the

Mandate. The Partition Resolution which, contrary to the Mandate, provided for an Arab State in addition to a Jewish State in Western Palestine, was not only a violation of Jewish legal rights and title of sovereignty over all of Palestine under the Mandate, as discussed above, but equally, it was a violation of the 1924 Convention which had incorporated the Mandate into its operating terms. In any event, the Partition Resolution never came into effect, which negated the effect of any American recognition of Arab national rights in Western Palestine under this resolution. In these circumstances, American recognition of Jewish legal rights to statehood necessarily still applied to the whole country of undivided Palestine even though such rights could not be exercised over the areas of Judea, Samaria and Gaza at the time these areas of the Jewish National Home were occupied by Jordan and Egypt from 1948 to 1967. This is especially true in light of American rejection of any Jordanian or Egyptian rights in Western Palestine. It is useful to recall that the United States strongly denounced the seizure of Palestine lands by Jordan and Egypt in 1948 as the highest type of international violation of law.[24]

It is particularly in regard to the right of Jewish settlement in all regions of former Mandated Palestine that the doctrine of estoppel can be effectively invoked today to refute harsh American criticism directed against Jewish settlement anywhere in the Land of Israel under Israeli control. So long as the terms of the Anglo-American Convention on Palestine were being implemented, as well as those of the San Remo Resolution, the Mandate for Palestine and the Franco-British Boundary Convention of December 23, 1920, reliance was naturally placed on these acts of international law to secure the right of Jewish settlement, throughout the length and breadth of Palestine, to rebuild the Jewish National Home. Yet after the execution and expiry of the aforementioned acts at midnight, May 14-15, 1948, reliance ought to have been placed thenceforward on the principle of acquired legal rights and the doctrine of estoppel as the most appropriate legal vehicles to force a change of thinking or reassessment of the present negative American attitude toward the building of Jewish settlements in Judea, Samaria and Gaza.

The extant right of Jews to settle in the national home regions of Judea, Samaria and Gaza could only be resumed and exercised after Israel's sweeping victory in the Six-Day War of June 5-10, 1967, which freed these territories from illegal Jordanian and Egyptian occupation. Prior to this War – going back to the War of Independence of 1948 and even further, to the White Paper of May 17, 1939, Jews were prohibited from acquiring land there, which deprived them of their legal right to settle in these parts of their national home. When the prohibition was lifted by Israel's victory in the Six-Day War, hundreds of thousands of Jews established their homes in Judea, Samaria and Gaza to

---

[24] See the remarks of the American representative, Warren R. Austin, at the U.N. on May 22, 1948, quoted by Professor Yehuda Blum in his article: "The Missing Reversioner: Reflections on the Status of Judea and Samaria, 3 *Israel Law Review* 279 (1968).

exercise their right of settlement and to continue the process of reconstituting the Jewish National Home.

The return of Jews to their homeland in Judea, Samaria and Gaza did not violate any law – either international law or Israeli constitutional law. On the contrary, it is expressly sanctioned by both. The right of Jewish settlement anywhere in the national home in what was once Mandated Palestine is recognized under international law in Articles 6 and 11 of the Mandate for Palestine. The Mandate was made part of U.S. law, as noted above, both by the Joint Resolution of the U.S. Congress of September 21, 1922, in a general sense, and by the Anglo-American Convention of December 3, 1924 respecting the Mandate for Palestine, in a specific sense. The term "Palestine" embraced the areas of the Jewish National Home defined in the Franco-British Boundary Convention of December 23, 1920 (as subsequently amended in the Demarcation Agreement of February 3, 1922 that took effect on March 10, 1923) and thus indisputably included Judea, Samaria and Gaza. The reference in the third recital of the Preamble to the Mandate in regard to "the historical connection of the Jewish People with Palestine" extended the meaning of "Palestine" to include all of the Golan and the Bashan omitted from the final boundaries of Palestine and even the Sinai Peninsula, all of which were areas with which the Jewish People had a strong historical connection. The right of Jewish settlement continued to exist as an acquired Jewish legal right in the foregoing regions of the Land of Israel after the expiry of the Mandate. As previously noted in Chapter 5, this right was incorporated into Israeli constitutional law by virtue of section 11 of the Law and Administration Ordinance of 1948, the first law enacted by the legislature of the State of Israel. This right is also recognized by the Law of Return of July 5, 1950, the single most important law ever passed by Israel's Parliament, the Knesset. Under this law, Jews may immigrate to and hence settle anywhere in the Land of Israel – not merely to the State of Israel as such, but to wherever the State has effectively established its civilian and/or military rule in the Land of Israel. In realization of this recognized Jewish legal right, there were as of January 2008, according to statistics provided by the Israeli Interior Ministry, 130 Government-authorized settlements spread out in all parts of Judea and Samaria, with a current population of about 280,000, a figure constantly increasing. The largest communities are Modi'in Illit with over 37,000 and Ma'aleh Adumim with over 34,000.

Based upon the established principle of acquired legal rights existing in favour of the Jewish People and the State of Israel, there is no legal warrant or justification whatsoever for applying Article 49 of the Fourth Geneva Convention of 1949 in order to deny the right of Jewish settlement in the National Home regions of Judea, Samaria and Gaza, which are erroneously described as "occupied territories". Article 49, paragraph 6, states:

> The Occupying Power shall not deport or transfer part of its own civilian population into the territory it occupies.

The assumption behind Article 49(6) of the Convention is that an Occupying Power has no right to transfer its citizens to a foreign state whose territory it has occupied. Applying this Article to the case of Judea and Samaria on the hypothetical assumption that it is indeed applicable, would mean that Judea and Samaria were *legally* part of the State of Jordan prior to the Six Day War of June 5-10, 1967, that Israel was an Occupying Power when it took possession of these territories in the War, and that, as a consequence, Israel has always been forbidden, since the War, to transfer any of its own civilian population to that part of the occupied foreign state of Jordan. However, those assumptions have no true basis in international law. As has already been conclusively demonstrated, Jordan never had any legal right or title of sovereignty to Judea and Samaria, since it acquired them in a concerted Arab war of aggression in which it took an active part to prevent the emergence of the newborn State of Israel. The same analysis applies to Gaza, which Egypt itself concedes was never a part of its territory prior to 1967. Hence, it should be beyond doubt that Article 49(6) is not legally applicable to the case of Jews choosing to exercise their Right of Return to the Land of Israel, as recognized in Articles 6 and 11 of the Mandate, by moving to Judea, Samaria or Gaza and establishing their homes there. The actual movement of Jews from the State of Israel to these areas can best be described as a movement from one part to another part of the Jewish National Home, or as a movement within a single country, i.e., the Land of Israel, that from 1920 to 1948 was known as the Jewish land of Palestine. The resettlement of Jews in these areas of historical Palestine who voluntarily move there without government coercion does not constitute a transfer of Israel's civilian population from Israel to Jordan or from Israel to Egypt, and to characterize it as such in order to make Article 49(6) applicable to the situation is a legal travesty. While it is true that Judea, Samaria and Gaza were never incorporated into the State of Israel after the Six-Day War, this did not mean that the State of Israel and the Jewish People had no rights over these territories. What it did mean was simply that Israel illegally ignored its own constitutional law – the Area of Jurisdiction and Powers Ordinance and the two proclamations issued under its provisions, as well as the Law of Return – in not incorporating into its borders what were liberated or repossessed areas of the Land of Israel or the Jewish National Home. [25]

The question of "occupied territories" in relation to Judea, Samaria and Gaza is further discussed in the next chapter of this work and the question of the applicability of the Fourth Geneva Convention as a whole is further discussed below, in Chapter 20 of this book. It suffices to note here that the belief held by the critics of Israel's settlement policy that Article 49(6) of the Convention is applicable in this case would, if it were true, erase, negate and make a mockery of the entire legal basis and structure of the State of Israel under international law that derived from Article 22 of the League of Nations

[25] On this subject see the author's work: *A Petition to Annul the Interim Agreement*, Ariel Center for Policy Research, Policy Paper 77, January 1999.

Covenant, the Smuts Resolution, the San Remo Resolution, the Mandate for Palestine and the Franco-British Boundary Convention of December 23, 1920. It would expunge from memory the entire diplomatic history of the decade 1915-1925 (from the De Bunsen Committee Report to the ratification of the Anglo-American Convention) which witnessed the genesis of world recognition of the legal rights and title of sovereignty of the Jewish People over Palestine, created for that very purpose. Ironically, it would make the very lands which were the cradle of the Jewish People into *foreign territories* barred to Jewish presence and settlement. The falsity of this absurd belief, that Judea, Samaria and Gaza are occupied territories under international law, has not prevented the United States, perhaps in sheer ignorance of the true legal situation created by the aforementioned acts of international law, from vigorously and persistently condemning the establishment of Jewish settlements in these regions. This, it may be further noted, was in sharp contrast to the meek and dishonest approach it adopted towards the British White Paper of 1939 where it failed to protest the blatant violations committed against both the Mandate for Palestine and the Anglo-American Convention based upon it. During President Jimmy Carter's administration these settlements were denounced as "illegal". The Reagan Administration which followed it retracted this false charge, but still maintained they constituted "obstacles to peace". Under President Bill Clinton, his Secretary of State, Madeleine Albright, referred to Jewish settlements as a "destructive activity", as well as being "provocative". The scolding American attitude towards Jewish settlements has continued in the same vein under President George W. Bush who says they "must stop", "consistent with the recommendations of the Mitchell Committee".[26] Secretary of State Colin Powell has also repeated his predecessor's remark about the "destructive impact" of settlements.[27]

All of these prejudicial anti-Zionist statements on the subject of Israeli civilian settlements in Judea, Samaria and formerly Gaza made by the American Government, which threatens diplomatic and financial sanctions against the State of Israel if it does not refrain from building new settlements or expanding existing ones, are exactly what is precluded by the doctrine of estoppel. The U.S. cannot *legally* deny the rights of the Jewish People to any part of Palestine and the Jewish National Home which it expressly recognized in 1922 and 1924, unless new U.S. Congressional legislation says otherwise, and even then, as previously noted, the doctrine of estoppel would still apply. The Government of Israel should make it crystal clear to the American Government through diplomatic notes and explanations that it is indeed estopped from condemning Israeli settlements and should therefore cease doing so forthwith. If that does not succeed there is no reason why Jews living in these settlements, a fair number of whom are also dual American and Israeli citizens, who have been

[26] See President George W. Bush's speech of June 24, 2002 in Washington.

[27] Powell's comment about the destructive impact of settlements was made at a Jerusalem press conference at the conclusion of a ten-day visit to the Middle East in April 2002. See the Jerusalem Post, April 18, 2000, pages 1 and 11.

unjustly hurt and targeted as objects of derision and finger-pointing, cannot bring an action in American courts for an order against the U.S. Government to cease and desist from its unfounded criticism and to force it to abide by the still-existing American legal recognition of the right of Jewish settlement in all areas of the Jewish National Home and the Land of Israel of which it seems to be abysmally unaware. The post-Six-Day-War American position, which denounces that specific Jewish legal right, has blackened the name of Israel and all the Jewish pioneering and progressive communities established in the National Home regions of Judea, Samaria and, formerly, Gaza. It makes Israel appear as a lawbreaker, when the shoe is really on the other foot. The U.S. attitude has caused real prejudice to Israel's international relations and acts as a brake to further settlement activity, for fear of incurring American wrath and economic sanctions. If the U.S. continues along this troublesome and annoying path, and every sign points in that direction, the U.S. Government should be brought to legal account in an appropriate Court of law for all damages suffered by Israel and its citizens in Judea, Samaria and Gaza for its gross violation of the recognized right of the Jewish People to re-populate all parts of their homeland that are under their actual rule and control or which are subsequently recovered.

It is true that not all rights live forever and can certainly be extinguished by the passage of time if they are not asserted or are forefeited by illegal or vile conduct or by a change of circumstances, such as war. But in the case of the Jewish People and the State of Israel, so long as they continue to exist, their recognized legal rights and title of sovereignty to the Land of Israel remain intact under international law and cannot be terminated or *legally* transferred to another state or people. This, incidentally, is also the position of Jewish law (*halakha*) which regards Israel's rights to the land as eternal, provided the Jewish People faithfully observe the laws and judgments given to them by Divine Providence (*Leviticus* 25:18). The State of Israel as the assignee of the Jewish People and successor to the rights conferred upon them under international law thus has the fundamental right to establish new civilian settlements which also continue the process of building up and ensuring the survival of the Jewish State.

What applies to the United States regarding the Jewish right of settlement, applies as well to each of the Principal Allied Powers, Britain, France, Italy and Japan, all of whom were state parties to the Mandate Agreement which expressly recognized this right as essential for the rebuilding of the Jewish National Home. They are, in consequence, estopped by their previous concurrence or acquiescence from taking any action – such as condemning Israel in U.N. or other forums or imposing trade sanctions or an arms embargo on Israel to penalize it for having established Israeli civilian settlements in Judea, Samaria and Gaza, which comprise inseparable regions of the Jewish National Home under international law.

The same may even be said for the Central Powers of World War I, Germany,

Austria, Hungary, Bulgaria and Turkey, all of whom signed treaties with the Principal Allied Powers recognizing the Mandates System under which Palestine was governed. The doctrine of estoppel also applies to all other state members of the League of Nations who were bound by the League's confirmation of the Mandate for Palestine and the idea it espoused, namely, that Palestine was a country reserved for the benefit of the Jewish National Home and State. The doctrine of estoppel thus applied in addition to Turkey, to the Moslem Shi'ite state of Persia (Iran) and the Arab states of Iraq and Egypt, all of which had joined the League of Nations during its 26-year existence from January 10, 1920 to April 19, 1946.[28]

The doctrine of estoppel should also apply with equal validity to all of the Arab states created at or about the same time as Palestine because their own creation under international law derived from the very same global political and legal settlement which led to the establishment of the Jewish State. The Arabs cannot gleefully accept national rights accorded them under this binding international settlement, comparable to the terms of a contract or judicial settlement, which was approved by the Principal Allied Powers and embodied in the San Remo Resolution of April 25, 1920 and the Treaty of Sèvres of August 10, 1920, while simultaneously denying those very same rights to the Jewish People. This advice is exactly what Lord Balfour gave them in the speech he made at the Royal Albert Hall, London on July 12, 1920.[29] Lord Robert Cecil, who as Assistant Foreign Secretary and member of the British Delegation at the Paris Peace Conference in 1919 played an active role when both Jewish and Arab national rights in the Middle East were recognized, wrote in a foreword to a book written by J. De. V. Loder:[30]

> Only on one matter would I make some reserve – I am not sure that on the Palestine question I quite take his (Loder's) view. The Zionist policy seems to me of vital importance to the world. A nation without a country of its own is an anomaly, and anomalies bring trouble. *Nor has the Arab State any ground of complaint. The recognition of a Jewish national home was part of the terms on which the Arab State was brought into*

[28] All together 63 countries were members of the League of Nations at one time or another, between January 10, 1920 when the League of Nations came into existence and April 19, 1946, when it formally came to an end. Persia was an initial member of the League in 1920, while Turkey was admitted in July 1932, Iraq in October 1932 and Egypt in May 1937. For a complete listing of the Members of the League of Nations, see *The Guide to American Law*, West Publishing Company (1984), pp. 434-435.

[29] See above, Chapter 4.

[30] The book was entitled *The Truth about Mesopotamia, Palestine and Syria*, published by George Allen and Unwin, Ltd., London (1923), p. 7.

> *existence*, subject, of course, to the rights of individual Arabs being fully protected (emphasis added).

Lord Cecil's keen observation that the Arabs have no grounds for complaint as a result of the world's recognition of the Jewish National Home also exposes their attitude as one of blind and willful disobedience to international law, which is also plainly irrational and insufferable.

In tune with what Lord Cecil said is a remarkable comment made by an illustrious Belgian diplomat, Pierre Orts, who served on the Permanent Mandates Commission from 1923 to 1940, the last four years as Chairman of that important body which advised the Council of the League of Nations on the compliance of Mandatories with the terms of the mandates they administered. He was one of the four members of the Mandates Commission who found that the policy of the White Paper of May 17, 1939 as enunciated by Colonial Secretary Malcolm MacDonald did not conform to the Mandate. In his remarks delivered at the 36th session of the Mandates Commission, he pungently noted the ingratitude of the Arabs towards Britain and other Allied Powers for their current high position in the world which was accompanied by their selfish and relentless opposition to Jewish national rights over Palestine.

> Was not consent to the establishment of a Jewish National Home in Palestine the price – and a relatively small one – which the Arabs had paid for the liberation of their lands extending from the Red Sea to the borders of Cilicia on the one hand, Iran and the Mediterranean on the other, for the independence they are now winning or had already won, none of which they would ever have gained by their own efforts, and for all of which they had to thank the Allied Powers and particularly the British forces in the Near East? There were other peoples who, because they had failed to win independence by their own efforts, had paid for their independence by far heavier sacrifices, and in regard to whom the conscience of the world had nevertheless not been touched, even though the sacrifice demanded was not in any way designed to relieve [= deprive – H.G.] another people whose fate deserved equal attention.[31]

Despite later denials, Arab recognition of Jewish rights to Palestine under the Balfour Declaration was given by Emir Feisal, when he acted as the acknowledged spokesman for the Arab cause at the Paris Peace Conference of 1919. At a session of this Conference, held on February 6, 1919, Feisal presented to the Supreme Council of the Principal Allied Powers the Arab claim for the territories to be included in the area of Arab independence, but expressly

---

[31] *Book of Documents submitted to the General Assembly of the United Nations by the Jewish Agency for Palestine, op. cit., p. 183.*

excluded Palestine. As Professor Nathan Feinberg of the Hebrew University of Jerusalem well noted:[32]

> On his appearance before the Supreme Council of the Conference on 6 February 1919, the Emir Feisal, Chief of the Delegation of the Hedjaz... asked for the independence of all Arabic-speaking peoples in Asia from the line Alexandretta [now Iskenderun] – Diyarbakir [formerly Amida] southward...; while with regard to Palestine, we read in the official protocols of the Peace Conference as follows: "Palestine, for its universal character, he left on one side for the mutual consideration of all parties interested. With this exception, he asked for the independence of the Arabic areas enumerated in his memorandum." A second memorandum, also signed by the Emir Feisal, on 1 January 1919, serves to prove, in the words of UNSCOP, that "the special status of Palestine was recognized in Arab circles" (General Assembly Official Records, Second Session, Supplement No. 11, p. 34). In it, Feisal lists the "provinces of Arab Asia", as he calls them, whose unification he demands; Palestine is not included. Insofar as Palestine is concerned, he acknowledges the need for a special regime (See the full text of Feisal's memorandum in the book by David Hunter Miller, *My Diary of the Peace Conferenece, with Documents*, Vol. IV, pp. 297-299).

Prior to his appearance at the Paris Peace Conference, Emir Feisal signed an agreement with Chaim Weizmann on January 3, 1919 in his capacity as the representative of the Arab Kingdom of Hedjaz, in which he agreed that the future Constitution and Administration of Palestine "will afford the fullest guarantees for carrying into effect the British Government's Declaration of the 2nd of November 1917" (Article III of the Agreement), Moreover, he agreed that "all necessary measures shall be taken to encourage and stimulate immigration of Jews into Palestine on a large scale, and as quickly as possible to settle Jewish immigrants upon the land through closer settlement and intensive cultivation of the soil" (Article IV). The Agreement also distinguished in the Preamble between Arab national aspirations in the Arab State and Jewish national aspirations in Palestine, showing that Feisal was fully aware that Palestine would have a separate, Jewish destiny that differed from the anticipated Arab state. This is confirmed by the letter he sent to Felix Frankfurter, dated March 3, 1919, in which he told the future Supreme Court Justice that the proposals submitted on February 27, 1919 by Nahum Sokolow and Weizmann representing the Zionist Organization to the Council of Ten at the Paris Peace Conference calling for the creation of Palestine as an autonomous Jewish Commonwealth were "moderate and proper". The boundaries of Palestine which Feisal found satisfactory and

[32] Nathan Feinberg, *op. cit.* See Part IV, *A Critical Analysis of the Colloquium of Arab Jurists in Algiers*, pp. 454-455.

did not dispute embraced all of Cisjordanian Palestine. The northern boundary included what is today southern Lebanon up to Sidon, a share in using the waters of the Litani, complete control of the waters of the Hermon, and all of the Golan. The eastern border encompassed the fertile plains of Transjordan with the line drawn close to and west of the Hedjaz Railway, in order not to infringe on the Moslem interest in the railway. The southern frontier extended southward to the port of Aqaba to ensure that Palestine would have access to the Red Sea.

Feisal later said that he did "not remember having *written* anything of that kind with his knowledge", a statement conveyed in evidence to the 1929 Shaw Commission by Auni Abdul Hadi. This was a contrived attempt by Feisal to avoid admitting what he had previously told Frankfurter in the above letter. His words were literally true – he had not written the letter himself. That task was performed by his confidant, T.E. Lawrence, whom he authorized to put down in summary form in English the substance of his views on the Zionist proposals and their compatibility with the Arab national movement. Feisal signed the letter after it was read to him. It was then sent to Frankfurter in the name of the Hedjaz Delegation attending the Paris Peace Conference. The letter was reproduced in the *New York Times* on March 5, 1919. Frankfurter reaffirmed the letter's authenticity in a letter he wrote to Meyer W. Weisgal dated December 3, 1929 and again in a magazine column he wrote for *The Atlantic Monthly* of October 1930.[33]

In the Feisal-Weizmann Agreement of January 3, 1919, which legally was an agreement between the fledgling Kingdom of Hedjaz and the Zionist Organization, each represented by an authorized official, there was a reservation or proviso in Arabic, added by Feisal that read as follows, according to the English translation by George Antonius in his book *The Arab Awakening*:

> Provided the Arabs obtain their independence as demanded in my Memorandum dated the 4th of January 1919 to the Foreign Office of the Government of Great Britain, I shall concur in the above Articles [of the Agreement]. But if the slightest modification or departure were to be made, I shall not then be bound by a single word of the present Agreement, which shall be deemed void and of no account or validity, and I shall not be answerable in any way whatsoever.[34]

[33] See the references to Feisal's letter and Frankfurter's reaffirmation of it in the book *Palestine, A Study of Jewish, Arab and British Policies*, ESCO Foundation, Yale University Press, New Haven, Vol. I, pp. 142-143, 204-205, and in *The Rise of Israel*, Volume 10, Document 66, p. 252.

[34] Leonard Stein, *The Balfour Declaration*, The Magnes Press, The Hebrew University, Jerusalem (1983)pp. 641-642. The agreement was apparently signed after January 3, 1919 because the memorandum referred to in the proviso is dated January 4, 1919. See Paul Hanna, *British Policy in Palestine*, p. 178, n. 43.

The demands made by Feisal in his memorandum related to the immediate independence of Syria. At the time of the Agreement with Weizmann, Syria was a semi-independent country provisionally ruled by Feisal under British military protection, pending the final peace settlement then being hammered out at the year-long Paris Peace Conference of 1919 and shortly thereafter at the San Remo Peace Conference of April 1920.

Feisal's reservation appended to the Agreement was legally incapable of realization in the way he demanded and therefore invalid from the start, because it would have prevented France from lawfully exercising the Mandate for Syria it asked for as early as December 1, 1918 in talks French Prime Minister Clemenceau held in London with his British counterpart, Lloyd George,[35] and which was agreed to unofficially in further talks on March 7, 1919 at Paris[36] and then finally allocated at the Conference of St. Remo on April 25, 1920. Feisal's dislike of a French mandate over Syria was made known, but he did not have the right to decide the terms of the Peace Settlement made by the Principal Allied and Associated Powers. He foolishly chose to defy the French by accepting the "crown of Syria and Palestine" that was proffered to him by the "General Syrian Congress" on March 8, 1920, when it proclaimed the independence of Syria. This was an illicit action, so described by Lord Curzon at the San Remo Peace Conference, and led to the fall of his short-lived kingdom when French forces evicted him from Damascus on July 25, 1920. The non-fulfillment of the reservation he made to the Feisal-Weizmann Agreement was directly attributable to the fault of Feisal himself and no one else. As the author of his own misfortune, he could not profit from the fact that the reservation he appended to the agreement of January 3, 1919 could not be carried out in the way he desired. Thus he was still bound by the agreement he had made with Weizmann, nor could he retract the recognition he gave on behalf of the Arab Kingdom of the Hedjaz to the establishment of a Jewish National Home in Palestine in accordance with the Balfour Declaration. This is a highly relevant point when considering the universal Arab rejection of Jewish legal rights to Palestine that followed in the wake of Feisal's ouster from Syria. The agreement the Arab leader originally signed with Weizmann was a voluntary act that legally bound not only the Arab Kingdom of Hedjaz, in whose name he officially acted, but also the Arab national movement for which he was the acknowledged spokesman at the Paris Peace Conference.[37] As a result all subsequent Arab claims to Palestine

---

[35] Jukka Nevakivi, *Britain, France and the Arab Middle East, 1914-1920,* University of London, The Athlone Press (1969), p. 93.

[36] Leonard Stein, *op. cit.*, p. 617.

[37] Additional evidence that can be cited to show Arab acceptance of a future Jewish Palestine is Feisal's positive response to a proposal made by William Yale, a former U.S. Intelligence officer in Cairo and a member of the American Commission at the Paris Peace Conference, "to set up a separate political unit under the Mandate of Great Britain under whose guidance the Zionists will... be allowed to carry out these projects to make a National Home for the

can be legally dismissed by invoking the doctrine of estoppel, in particular as regards the false Arab claim that Palestine was intended to be included in the area set aside for Arab independence as allegedly promised by Henry McMahon, British High Commissioner in Egypt in correspondence he had in 1915 and 1916 with the Sherif of Mecca, King Hussein of Hedjaz. Feisal's recognition of Jewish legal rights to Palestine, as evidenced by his agreement with Weizmann and his letter to Frankfurter, occurred three years after the McMahon-Hussein correspondence and supercedes it, even if the supposed promise or pledge to include Palestine in the Arab State was true as the Arabs claimed, but emphatically denied by the author of that correspondence, McMahon himself, who also said that Palestine's non-inclusion was well understood by King Hussein.

Another question concerning estoppel is whether it can be invoked in Israel's favour against those countries which today refuse to grant recognition to Jerusalem as the capital city of Israel, when they previously recognized Jerusalem as the *de facto* administrative capital of Mandated Palestine. In the present discussion of estoppel, Palestine created as the Jewish National Home has been dealt with as a complete and unified territory to which Jewish legal rights and title of sovereignty apply, without distinguishing between different regions or locations. To limit such rights only to specific areas of the land is to commit a serious legal error, thereby producing a false dichotomy in the legal status of various parts of the country. This dichotomy was never meant to exist by the framers of the Mandate for Palestine, except in a limited, temporary sense with regard to Transjordan, as provided for in Article 25 of the Mandate. Paradoxically, Israel itself is responsible for making an unfounded distinction between Jerusalem and the rest of the territories liberated in the Six-Day War from Arab occupation: Israel did this by extending Israeli law, jurisdiction and administration to Jerusalem, and failing to do so for the rest of the liberated territories, contrary to the Area of Jurisdiction and Powers Ordinance, read in conjunction with the Land of Israel Proclamation.

To determine whether estoppel can be invoked in the case of Jerusalem, it must be recalled that every country formerly a member of the League of Nations recognized not only the Mandate for Palestine as such, but also the principal idea it embodied: that all areas of the country, including Jerusalem, were in the future to be subject to the sovereignty of the Jewish People as the sole national beneficiary of the Mandate under Article 22 of the League Covenant and the San Remo Resolution. The same assumption was true for the United States which in 1924 concluded a treaty with Great Britain recognizing the terms of the Mandate and all Jewish rights attached thereto, including the right to govern Jerusalem as an integral part of an eventual independent Jewish State.

---

Jewish People." Rustum Haidar, a member of the Arab Delegation at the Peace Conference and later the Chief Political Secretary to Feisal as King of Iraq, told Yale that with certain modifications with regard to Syria, Feisal would be ready to accept his solution. See Isaiah Friedman, Routledge & Kegan Paul, London (1973), p.92 and p.360, n. 158.

During the Mandate period, Jerusalem was the seat of the British Administration in Palestine. All the government departments were located in Jerusalem, including the office of the High Commissioner for Palestine who was the highest ranking executive official. Nobody could dispute the fact that Jerusalem was the administrative capital of the country, even if no mandatory law declared specifically that it was so. All those countries that approved the Mandate as members of the League of Nations and separately the United States by virtue of a treaty thus implicitly recognized Jerusalem as the capital city of Palestine which was legally synonymous with the Jewish National Home and State. As a consequence, these countries are subject to the limitations imposed by the doctrine of estoppel in regard to their present-day non-recognition of Jerusalem as Israel's capital city.

The reason for withholding such recognition derives from the U.N. Partition Plan of November 29, 1947 which intended Jerusalem to become a *corpus separatum* administered under a U.N. trusteeship. However, that is a poor rationale for denying recognition since the Partition Plan never went into legal effect and in any case, was not only of a non-binding character, but more importantly violated the terms of the Mandate for Palestine and the U.N. Charter, as previously discussed in Chapter 7. Another reason adduced for the non-recognition of Jerusalem as Israel's capital is that the legal status of Jerusalem has never been decided. That reason has no merit at all, since Jerusalem was part of the territory allotted to the Jewish National Home and State under the Franco-British Boundary Convention of December 23, 1920.

Aside from the fact that foreign countries, such as the U.S. and the U.K., treated Jerusalem as the capital of an eventual Jewish State during the Mandate period and are therefore estopped from asserting otherwise today, the decision of which city shall be the capital of a sovereign country is the prerogative of that country alone. For instance, Israel has no right to question whether or not Washington, D.C. should be the recognized capital of the United States. For the same reason, the latter cannot question Israel's choice of Jerusalem to serve as its capital. If it were otherwise, then any state would have an extra-territorial license to infringe or trespass upon the political independence and sovereignty of another state, contrary to Article 2 of the United Nations Charter.

As a final note on estoppel, it can only clearly apply where a state has contracted a valid international agreement or treaty by virtue of the laws prevailing in the state. Estoppel would therefore not apply to Israel's cession of territory to the "Palestine Liberation Organization" in the various agreements it made with that illegal body, and its offshoot, the "Palestinian Authority", since all these agreements were contrary to various provisions in the constitutional and criminal laws of Israel at the time they were made, apart from the fact that these agreements cannot be considered true international agreements within the meaning of that term, under international law.[38] The same may be said about

[38] See the author's work, *A Petition to Annul the Interim Agreement*, *op. cit.*, (January 1999).

the Road Map Peace Plan sponsored by the United States, the European Union, Russia and the United Nations. This plan, like the U.N. Partition Plan, seeks to nullify Jewish legal rights to Judea, Samaria and Gaza as established under international law in 1919, 1920 and 1922 and preserved from alteration in the U.N. Charter of 1945; these rights were then devolved upon the State of Israel upon its re-constitution on May 15, 1948. The Road Map Peace Plan is therefore an illegal invention designed to deprive the Jewish People and State of Israel of their recognized national rights to Judea, Samaria and Gaza and transfer them to the so-called "Palestinian People" in order to set up a second Arab state in what was formerly Mandated Palestine. In addition, the Road Map Peace Plan is illegal under Israeli law which does not recognize the national rights of any minority – including, first and foremost, the Arabs – to any part of the Land of Israel.

*Chapter 10*

# The Question of United Nations Jurisdiction over Mandated Palestine, the Land of Israel and the Middle East

## *(I) The Status Of The U.N. Regarding The Land Of Israel*

To examine the question of what powers the organs of the United Nations had as regards Mandated Palestine when the international organization began functioning in the period coinciding with the last two and a half years of the Mandate's existence and the powers these organs have today concerning events in the Land of Israel and the Middle East generally, one must start with the role of the League of Nations under the Mandates System.[1] Once a mandate had been confirmed by the League for a particular country, its role was basically limited to monitoring the actions of the Mandatory, who had been selected to administer the mandated territory, to verify that the latter was observing the terms of the Mandate conferred upon it. The League did not possess sovereignty over any mandated territory governed by the Mandates System, nor did it have any actual executive, legislative or judicial authority

[1] The United Nations was a name coined by President Roosevelt in 1941 to describe the countries fighting against the Axis Powers, headed by Germany, Italy and Japan. It was established by the Charter of the United Nations, a multilateral international agreement that was drafted at a founding conference which convened in San Francisco on April 25, 1945 attended by the representatives of 50 states. The U.N. Charter is considered to be a "law-making treaty", because it lays down new general rules for future conduct which the parties are bound to observe as "law", in the same way that a private contract constitutes the "law" for the contracting parties, even though the United Nations itself is not an international legislature that can make laws or pass legislation. The United Nations Conference on International Organization ended on June 26, 1945 with the signing of the Charter. It was then ratified by the required number of states on October 24, 1945. There were 51 founding members – the 50 participants at the Conference plus Poland. The General Assembly of the United Nations first met in London on January 10, 1946.

over the inhabitants of any mandated territory, who, however, had the right to petition the League to complain that the Mandatory was not fulfilling the terms of the Mandate. In accordance with Article 26 of the Mandate for Palestine, if any dispute arose between the Mandatory Power and another member of the League of Nations relating to the interpretation or the application of the provisions of the Mandate, such dispute, if not settled by negotiation, was to be submitted to the Permanent Court of International Justice, as provided for by Article 14 of the Covenant of the League of Nations.[2] When the League was officially disbanded by a resolution of its last Assembly in April 1946, it did not bequeath any special authority to the U.N. over Palestine, since it itself had no such authority, apart from its role of monitoring events in the mandated territory and receiving annual reports from the Mandatory as well as petitions containing complaints from the inhabitants of a mandated area.[3]

Under the U.N. Charter, the Trusteeship Council operating under the overall authority of the General Assembly was assigned responsibility for the remaining mandated territories such as Palestine, but theoretically it could not begin its task to administer or supervise these territories until individual trusteeship agreements were first made, which would have the effect of converting mandated territories into trust territories. Inasmuch as no trusteeship agreement by the states directly concerned placing Palestine under the trusteeship system at the time the British Government referred the question of Palestine to the U.N. on April 2, 1947, pursuant to the Cabinet decision of February 14, 1947, and in light of the fact that the U.N. Trusteeship Council had not yet commenced operations at the time of referral, Britain could not make use of the provisions of the Charter relating to the trusteeship system and the specific role assigned to the Trusteeship Council. It therefore turned to the General Assembly under Article 10 of the Charter to make recommendations concerning the future government of Palestine.[4] This article stated that the General Assembly may discuss any questions or matters within the scope of the Charter or relating

---

[2] Under Article 14 of the Covenant of the League of Nations, any dispute of an international character could be submitted by the parties thereto for hearing and determination to the Permanent Court of International Justice. The Court could also give an advisory opinion upon any dispute or question referred to it by the Council or by the Assembly.

[3] The right to submit Petitions to the League of Nations in regard to Mandated Palestine was recognized in Article 85 of the Palestine Order-in-Council of 1922. Article 85 read as follows: If any religious community or considerable section of the population in Palestine complains that the terms of the Mandate are not being fulfilled by the Government of Palestine, it shall be entitled to present a Memorandum through a member of the Legislative Council to the High Commissioner. Any Memorandum so submitted shall be dealt with in such manner as may be prescribed by His Majesty in conformity with the procedure recommended by the Council of the League of Nations.

[4] See Report of British Cabinet Meeting of February 14, 1947 in *The Rise of Israel*, Volume 36, Document 20, p. 134.

to the powers and functions of any organs provided for in the Charter, and may make recommendations to the members of the United Nations or to the Security Council or to both on any such questions or matters.

Though the General Assembly had a right to discuss any question within the scope of the Charter and to make recommendations, it had no power to enforce them. Therefore the British Government was not under any obligation to put into effect whatever solution the General Assembly might recommend.

In dealing with the question of Palestine, the General Assembly was restricted by Article 80 of the Charter not to alter the terms of the existing Mandate instrument or the rights of the Jewish People set down in it.[5] Despite the prohibition on the alteration of the Mandate, the General Assembly did exactly what it was not allowed to do, when it proposed a partition plan on November 29, 1947 to restrict Jewish national rights to only some regions of Palestine and called for an Arab state to be created alongside the Jewish State together with a plan to place the city of Jerusalem under trusteeship.

After the failure of its Partition Plan and the ancillary proposals that followed in its wake – the British Government took no steps to implement the Plan and the Arab states and the local Arab population of Palestine rejected it altogether – the General Assembly reverted to becoming, insofar as the Land of Israel and the Middle East were concerned, an international forum of general debate with the right only to make non-binding recommendations. The Assembly dropped all further pretence of being able to wield any constitutional or legal authority to determine the future course of the government of Palestine. In the ensuing years it has passed a great number of anti-Israel, pro-Arab resolutions sponsored by Arab states, supported by their allies in the Third World and the former Communist bloc of countries and, more recently, by the states comprising the European Union, which charged Israel with all kinds of baseless and invented misdeeds and violations of international law. These resolutions may have damaged Israel's image in the world, but they had no legal effect.

Under the Charter, the General Assembly has some important functions to perform, such as approving the budget of the U.N., apportioning expenses, admitting new members, suspending or expelling sitting members and making recommendations with respect to the maintenance of international peace and security. However, with regard to the Land of Israel and the Middle East it has no real power or substantive role to play. General Assembly resolutions in this regard do not constitute "international law", they have no binding or lasting effect, nor do they confer any "international legitimacy" on the Arab cause they always espouse, regardless of the facts or the rights and wrongs of any given dispute. In addition, these decisions have no value at all, especially from the moral point-of-view, when they are one-sided condemnations of Israel founded on blatant untruths.

---

[5] It was well understood that the word "peoples" mentioned in Article 80 was a reference to the Jewish People, in the particular case of Palestine, even though the word "Jewish" was naturally omitted from the text.

To determine whether the Security Council of the United Nations, as distinct from the General Assembly, has any jurisdiction in the Land of Israel, including Judea, Samaria and Gaza, a retroactive glance must be made to the Mandate period as well. When the Security Council started to function, the Mandate for Palestine was still being administered by Great Britain. The Security Council could not exercise any jurisdiction over Palestine since mandated territories were outside the scope of its area of concern under the explicit provisions of the Charter, except in the case of territory governed by a strategic area trusteeship agreement under Article 82 of the Charter.

Under Article 24 of the Charter, the Security Council was entrusted with primary responsibility for the maintenance of international peace and security, and under Article 39 it has the authority to decide which measures shall be taken where there exists any threat to the peace, breach of the peace or act of aggression. It was inconceivable to place the question of Mandated Palestine under any of these categories, since the implementation of the Mandate was required by several acts of international law, and therefore could not, by definition, be a threat to the peace, breach of the peace or an act of aggression, as Arab states sought to argue. Furthermore, while the Mandate was still in force, the Security Council could not assume jurisdiction over Palestine on the basis of Article 35 of the Charter upon the request of a member of the United Nations, since if foreign states intervened in or controlled the affairs of Palestine, apart from the Mandatory Power that was legally empowered to do so, this would have constituted a violation of the still-valid Article 5 of the Mandate, a provision which expressly banned all foreign intervention or control.

This limitation of the power to intervene was discussed at length at the tenth meeting of a session of the League of Nations Permanent Mandates Commission devoted to Palestine on August 5 and 6, 1937. Pierre Orts, the Chairman of the Commission, took strong exception to the reported intervention of Saudi Arabia and Iraq in the events then occurring in Palestine, viz., an Arab general strike as well as disorders throughout the country. Orts asked a pointed question[6] of the British representatives present, Colonial Secretary William Ormsby-Gore and former Chief Secretary to the Government of Palestine, John Hathorn Hall:

> ...how was it conceivable that foreign Powers could be allowed to intervene in the internal administration of [Palestine]... for which the Mandatory Power was solely responsible? It might be replied that they were Arab Powers; they were nonetheless foreign Powers in the same way as any other State outside Palestine, whether it was a member of

[6] See the Minutes of the Thirty-Second (Extraordinary) Session of the Permanent Mandates Commission, held at Geneva from July 30th to August 18th, 1937, in particular, the minutes of the 10th and 11th meetings, published in *The Rise of Israel*, Vol. 25, Document 4. The minutes of the tenth and eleventh meetings are found on pages 171 to 183.

> the League of Nations or not. The Chairman [Pierre Orts] had the impression that... Palestine, a separate political entity, had in a way been regarded already as an Arab province, as one of the members of a vast Arab confederation... Reverting to the part played by the Arab States, the Chairman asked whether in the study of the [Palestine] question now taking place between the Mandator, represented by the Mandates Commission, and the Mandatory, it was considered that a third intervening party had the right to be heard.

Mr. Hall replied on behalf of Britain that the Mandatory Power did not invite the intervention of any foreign Arab ruler, nor was any promise given "which might lead Arab rulers to think that they had been placed in any formal position to intervene in the affairs of Palestine." He attributed their intervention to humanitarian concerns, a desire to stop unnecessary suffering and loss of life, and that no political motives lay behind their intervention. At the end of this discussion, Hall conceded the point made by the Commission Chairman, that Iraq had no right to intervene in the debate on Palestine, except within the framework of the League and through the proper channels.

Two years later, however, Britain abandoned its position that Arab states could not formally intervene in the Palestine Question outside the League framework, when it convened the St. James Conference, held between February 7, 1939 and March 17, 1939. To this Conference they invited representatives of Egypt, Iraq, Saudi Arabia, Yemen and Transjordan to discuss the future of Palestine. Then, two months after the St. James Conference ended, Britain issued a White Paper which, *inter alia*, stated that it would consult with these same states in pursuit of its new policy on Palestine that was a radical departure from the existing terms of the Mandate and San Remo Resolution.

Hypothetically, had Britain referred the question of Palestine to the Security Council instead of the General Assembly on April 2, 1947, it would have been contrary to both the U.N. Charter as well as the still-existing Mandate. The Security Council had no power under the Charter to supervise or regulate mandated territories such as Palestine, nor any power to modify the terms of the Mandate. The Security Council would therefore have been duty-bound to decline acceptance of this referral. If, again hypothetically, the Security Council had in fact assumed jurisdiction, albeit illegally, it would have been under similar legal constraints as those which applied to the General Assembly. It would not have been able to recommend or impose any solution in regard to Palestine that altered or violated the existing terms of the Mandate and Jewish rights thereunder, as is clear from Article 80 of the Charter, as well as the principle of acquired legal rights and the doctrine of estoppel.

Once Israel became an independent state on May 15, 1948 and the Mandate ceased to exist, it then became possible for the Security Council to deal with pressing questions in the Middle East based on the primary responsibility it had under Article 24 of the Charter for the preservation of international peace and security. The most notable example came on November 22, 1967 in the wake of the Six-Day War when it passed Resolution 242 stating the principles of a just and lasting peace in the Middle East and again on October 22, 1973, in the wake of the Yom Kippur War when it passed Resolution 338 calling for a cease-fire and for the implementation of Resolution 242 in all of its parts.

In regard to all Security Council resolutions relating to the Middle East, it is important to examine the question if Israel is legally bound by any of these resolutions, particularly in regard to Israel having to withdraw its armed forces from "occupied territories", as indicated by Resolution 242.

Under Article 25, the members of the United Nations agree to accept and carry out the "decisions" (i.e., resolutions) of the Security Council in accordance with the present Charter. This provision means that Israel (as is the case with every member state) is obliged to accept Security Council "decisions" which are of a compulsory character provided they are consistent with other provisions of the Charter. As pointed out in a 1969 article by the jurist Amos Shapira, then a senior lecturer in Law at Tel-Aviv University, there is a fundamental distinction between decisions of the Security Council which are binding in nature and decisions which are only advisory and not compulsory.[7] His penetrating analysis makes clear that only those resolutions or decisions that impose legal obligations on the parties concerned, even without their consent, must be obeyed by all U.N. members unless they are inconsistent with other provisions in the Charter. On the other hand, those resolutions or decisions which are no more than recommendations do not have to be complied with by U.N. members unless they freely consent to implement them.

The principal decisions that are taken by the Security Council are those made under Chapters VI and VII of the Charter. All resolutions it adopts under Chapter VI, which deals with the pacific settlement of disputes are recommendations only, i.e., decisions of an advisory or hortatory nature which have no binding character and are therefore excluded from the scope of the word "decisions" as used in Article 25. The situation is different for resolutions adopted by the Council under Chapter VII, which deal with actions or enforcement measures concerning threats to the peace, breaches of the peace and acts of aggression. Resolutions which are adopted by the Security Council under Chapter VII may be either a recommendation or a binding decision depending on the wording of the resolution, the interpretation placed upon it, the reaction of the parties concerned and the action subsequently taken by the Council.[8] In this context there can be no doubt that all the Resolutions of the Council adopted by it under Articles 41 and 42 in Chapter VII of the Charter are binding decisions within the purview of Article 25, when their stated object is to maintain or

[7] See his valuable article, "The Security Council Resolution of November 22, 1967 – Its Legal Nature and Implications", *Israel Law Review*, Vol. 4, 1969, pp. 229-41, reprinted in Volume II, *The Arab-Israeli Conflict*, edited by John Norton Moore, Princeton University Press, 1974, pp. 566-578.

[8] Amos Shapira, *op. cit.*, p. 576, in John Norton Moore's *Arab-Israeli Conflict*.

restore international peace and security, since any failure to obey resolutions of this kind, may invite economic, diplomatic and military measures to be taken against the recalcitrant state.

Using the foregoing analysis as a guide to interpret the legal effect of U.N. Security Council Resolutions, it becomes possible to determine if Resolution 242 is binding or non-binding and whether Resolution 338 changed the situation in this respect.

Resolution 242 does not indicate the article of the U.N. Charter on which it was based. But as Amos Shapira pointed out in his insightful article, the language of the Resolution indicated that the Council relied upon Article 37 (2) in Chapter VI for its formulation. By virtue of this article, the Security Council can recommend "such terms of settlement as it may consider appropriate" to resolve any dispute whose continuation is likely to endanger international peace and security.[9] He adds that Article 36 (1) may also be applicable, since it allows the Council to recommend "appropriate procedures or methods of adjustment" to solve a dispute of this type.

On the assumption that Resolution 242 was based squarely on provisions in Chapter VI, it was a non-binding recommendation charting a course of action or establishing procedures, guideline and principles to be followed by every state in the area of the Middle East for the purpose of achieving a just and lasting peace, but which at the same time carried no orders or enforcement measures to ensure the resolution's implementation in the event of non-compliance. Israel chose to accept this non-binding resolution or decision, but it was not obliged to do so under Article 25.

Resolution 338 did not change the legal character of Resolution 242, even if it was adopted under Chapter VII of the Charter. Article 39 in this Chapter makes clear that certain resolutions adopted under the provisions of this chapter may be only recommendations, while others may be binding decisions, again depending on the wording of the resolution and the other factors noted above.

In addition to calling for a cease-fire in the Yom Kippur War, Resolution 338 also called upon the parties concerned to start immediately the implementation of Resolution 242 in all of its parts and furthermore decided that negotiations should get underway aimed at establishing a just and durable peace in the Middle East. This call and decision of the Security Council for the implementation of Resolution 242 and the start of negotiations did not constitute an order with penalties to be applied if any of the parties concerned did not abide by the resolution. The Council could neither force implementation of Resolution 242 nor make any of the parties affected by Resolution 338 enter into negotiations against their will. Resolution 338 was simply a reiteration of Resolution 242 that did not change its basic nature as a recommended course of action to be followed to achieve a just and lasting peace in which every State in the area can

---

[9] *Ibid.* (John Norton Moore), p. 572.

live in security. No binding obligations were therefore imposed on the parties to implement it or to start negotiations based on its recommended guidelines.

There has never been any agreed-upon definitive interpretation of Resolution 242, especially as to whether Israel has to withdraw from all or only some of the territories it re-conquered and repossessed from Jordan, Syria and Egypt in the Six-Day War on behalf of the Jewish People, though it is quite clear from the text of the resolution and also from statements made by its American and British formulators, that Israel was expected to withdraw only to secure and recognized boundaries. Statements to this effect were made by Arthur J. Goldberg, the then-U.S. Ambassador to the U.N., and by George Brown, the British Foreign Secretary in 1967, and finally by Lord Caradon, the British sponsor of Resolution 242 in the Security Council.[10] However, it can be stated without any qualification that any Security Council Resolution that aims to oblige Israel to withdraw from any land that was designated to be included in the Jewish National Home under the Mandate (or should have been part of it based on the test of historical connection) is *ipso facto* illegal, since such a resolution would be in direct conflict with Article 80 of the Charter and the acquired legal rights of the Jewish People secured under previous acts of international law, to which the doctrine of estoppel applies. Resolution 242 can therefore have no application to Judea, Samaria and Gaza, which were originally included in the Jewish National Home under the Mandate for Palestine. Nor should it be applied to the Golan Heights, which Israel captured in the Six-Day War of June 1967, since this territory is a part of historical Palestine rather than of historical Syria, though it was improperly and illegally excluded from the borders of mandated Palestine in the Demarcation Agreement of February 3, 1922. A separate reason that can be invoked by Israel for not withdrawing to the pre-war armistice lines is that since Israel fought a war of defense against its Arab neighbors, Egypt, Jordan and Syria, it is entitled to keep those areas it re-captured in the Six-Day War from the occupying countries that expressly threatened "to wipe Israel off the map" or participated in the joint Arab aggression.

Even the application of Resolution 242 to the Sinai cannot be sustained, because in 1967 when this resolution was passed, this territory did not belong to Egypt under international law, and so Israel was not obliged to make any withdrawal from Sinai since it did not constitute "occupied territory" within the meaning of Article 42 of the Hague Regulations. The question of sovereignty over Sinai is further discussed below in this chapter. One of the chief proponents of the view that Sinai was not Egypt but rather an extended part of the Land of Israel was Israel's first Prime Minister, David Ben-Gurion. After Israel's lightning capture of almost the entire Sinai Peninsula in a seven-day campaign code-named Operation Kadesh (October 29 – November 5, 1956), he addressed the Knesset on November 7, 1956 and announced in what is sometimes referred

---

[10] See: Yosef Tekoah, *In the Face of Nations*, edited by David Aphek, Simon and Shuster, New York (1976), pp. 257, 263 and 264.

to as his "Third Kingdom of Israel" speech:[11]

> Our army did not attack the area of the Land of Egypt and did not even try to attack it, and I hope that in the future as well, we will not be compelled by the Egyptian dictator to disobey the injunction enjoined upon us in going out of Egypt 3300 years ago – never to return to it. Our [military] operation limited itself solely to the area of the Sinai Peninsula.

Later on in his speech, Ben-Gurion reiterated the same idea that Israel never entered Egypt during Operation Kadesh:[12]

> As I said before, our army received a strict order not to cross the Suez Canal and not to attack the territory of the Land of Egypt and to remain only within the borders of the Sinai Peninsula.

A third and final reference in Ben-Gurion's speech that Sinai is not truly part of Egypt was his statement:[13]

> The flight of the officers of the Egyptian Army, as well as of the thousands of its soldiers, from Sinai proves clearly the fact that they had no interest or motive in fighting Israel *in a foreign desert* (emphasis added).

There exists clear-cut evidence that Ben-Gurion intended to annex Sinai to Israel, as well as the adjoining islands of Yotvata (Tiran) and Sanafir in the Red Sea, opposite Sharm-el-Sheikh, as soon as the situation following the war had stabilized. This emerges from a letter of Ben-Gurion that was read aloud by Chief-of-Staff Moshe Dayan at a ceremonial parade of Israeli troops of the Ninth Division at Sharm-el-Sheikh on November 6, 1956, in which he stated:[14]

> Yotvata (Tiran) which was an independent Hebrew state 1400 years ago, shall again be part of the Third Kingdom of Israel.

On the very next day, Ben-Gurion repeated the reference to Yotvata in the aforementioned speech to the Knesset, quoting the sixth-century Byzantine historian Procopius, as follows:[15]

---

[11] *Proceedings of the Knesset: The 182nd Session of the Third Knesset*, November 7, 1956, Vol. 21, p. 197.

[12] *Ibid.*, p. 198.

[13] *Ibid.*, p. 199.

[14] Mordechai Bar-On, *Gates of Gaza*, pp. 317-318.

[15] *Proceedings of the Knesset, op. cit.*, p. 197.

> Procopius, a Greek [Byzantine] historian of the sixth century, a native of Caesarea, in Eretz-Israel, in his book about the Wars of the Persians and the Byzantines, describes the island of Yotvata (now called Tiran) and says: "The Hebrews have been leading an autonomous existence there since ancient times, and only in the present reign of Justinian [527-565] have they become subjugated to the Romans" (i.e., the Byzantines). For the sake of the historical importance of this matter, I quoted the words of Procopius in their original form because several modern scholars who received these statements second- and third-hand distorted this hugely important historical evidence.

However, within one day after delivering his spirited address to the Knesset Ben-Gurion, under enormous foreign pressure amounting to duress, abandoned (November 8, 1956) his intention to annex Sinai and the two Red Sea islands. First came a direct Soviet threat to the very existence of Israel as a state when a sharply-worded letter was sent by Soviet Premier Nikolai Bulganin to Ben-Gurion on November 5, 1956, two days before Ben-Gurion's "Third Kingdom of Israel" speech. However, the decisive factor in causing Ben-Gurion not to proceed with the projected annexation of Sinai was an American warning that came from the U.S. State Department headed by John Foster Dulles and relayed to Israeli ambassador Reuven Shiloah, that if Israel did not withdraw from Sinai in accordance with the U.N. General Assembly resolution of November 2, 1956, there would be "serious consequences", such as cessation of all Government and private aid, U.N. sanctions and probable expulsion from the United Nations as well.[16]

The American warning conveyed to Shiloah was reinforced by a letter from President Dwight D. Eisenhower, dated November 7th but received only on the next day, firmly demanding Israel's withdrawal to the armistice lines which Ben-Gurion had already declared in his Knesset speech "expired together with the Armistice Agreement". Ben-Gurion sent an immediate reply whose key section read as follows:[17]

> Neither I nor any other authorized spokesman of the Government of Israel has stated that we plan to annex the Sinai Desert. In view of

---

[16] At a cabinet meeting on October 28, 1956, a day before the Sinai Campaign was launched, Ben-Gurion told Mordechai Bentov of the Mapam party: "I can conceive that there will be forces that will compel us to leave the Sinai Peninsula. There is America; there is Russia; there is the U.N.; there is Nehru; there are Asia and Africa. But most of all I fear the United States. America is capable of forcing us to withdraw. It need not send an army for that purpose. It has other means that are effective – and very serious". See Ben-Gurion's book, *Israel: a Personal History,* Funk & Wagnalls, Inc., New York; Sabra Books: New York, Tel-Aviv (1971), p. 505.

[17] *Op. cit.,* p. 511.

> the U.N. resolutions regarding the withdrawal of foreign troops from Egypt and the creation of an international force we will, upon the conclusion of satisfactory arrangements with the United Nations in connection with this international force entering the Suez Canal area, willingly withdraw our forces.[18]

Despite Israel's withdrawal from Sinai, completed in January 1957 except for the Sharm-el-Sheikh area which was evacuated two months later together with Gaza, there was never any admission by Israel that Sinai belonged as of right to Egypt. That was still the legal situation prevailing when Resolution 242 was passed on November 22, 1967. Bearing in mind the legal status of the territories

[18] The evidence, though, is overwhelming that Ben-Gurion did intend to annex the Sinai. Professor Yuval Ne'eman, then Deputy-Director of Military Intelligence who worked closely with Ben-Gurion at this time and who laid the groundwork for the secret connection with France in 1956 prior to the Sinai Campaign, and who also sat in on secret talks at Sèvres between Ben-Gurion and French leaders, Premier Guy Mollet, Foreign Minister Christian Pineau and others, at which British Foreign Minister Selwyn Lloyd and Permanent Undersecretary of State, Patrick Dean, also participated, told the present author in a letter dated September 8, 1996 (YN-6595 of his records): "In 1956, we conquered Sinai. Clearly, from the Briefing to Golda [Meir] and [Moshe] Carmel in September 1956, from Ben-Gurion's letter which Winky [Israel Medad] gave you, from BG's "Kingdom of Israel" speech and from my own witnessing of BG's argumentation at Sèvres (October 23, 1956) – he had every intention to incorporate Sinai – or in the worst case the islands of Tiran and Sanafir (which he kept describing as the Jewish Republic of Yotvata around 550 AD)…." Ben-Gurion was encouraged by Ne'eman, in a long conversation they had on November 1, 1956, at the Prime Minister's home, not to return Sinai to Egypt because of its military and economic importance to Israel and the weakness of Egypt's claim to sovereignty over it. It may be added that the term "Negev" which in Hebrew denotes the direction of South, also refers in a broad sense to the area of Sinai east of Wadi El-Arish ("Torrent of Egypt") where the Wilderness of Zin and Paran are located, and hence this area of Sinai, constituting about half of the peninsula, may be considered within the bounds of the Land of Israel. This was evidenced by the fact that the independent Sanjak of Jerusalem of the Ottoman Empire extended southward from El-Arish to Suez, across to Taba, covering upper-central Sinai, until the British forced a change in the provincial boundaries in 1906. Ne'eman's advice seems to have contributed considerably to Ben-Gurion's emerging policy to try to retain Sinai for Israel. Though Ben-Gurion was compelled under American-Russian duress to back down from his intention to annex the Sinai, his prior statements and his "Undivided Eretz-Israel Program" showed him, in the opinion of Professor Ne'eman, to have been "an Eretz-Israel loyalist on the pragmatic, though secret, level". See the latter's paper, "Partition Viewed as Incomplete Liberation of the National Territory", Proceedings of the International Conference [unpublished] in honour of Conor Cruise O'Brien, held at Haifa University in 1987 on the topic "Irish and Jewish Nationalism in the Twentieth Century: Politics, Religion and Terror". Ne'eman's paper was printed in Hebrew in Nativ Journal, June 1996, p. 29. See also Ne'eman's extraordinary article, "Ties with the French and the British during the Sinai Campaign" (in Hebrew), published in the IDF monthly journal, *Ma'arakhot*, Vol. 306-307 (Dec. 1986), pp. 28-37.

repossessed by Israel in 1967, at which Resolution 242 was undoubtedly aimed, the appropriateness of describing these territories as "occupied" under international law is not only challengeable but definitely wrong. It is therefore a travesty to affirm that Israel is obliged under international law to withdraw from territories that are deemed to be "occupied" when, in fact, they had been recognized internationally in 1919, 1920 and 1922 as being the patrimony of the Jewish People represented today by the State of Israel.

Israel's acceptance of this resolution was seen by the Levi Eshkol National Unity Government as beneficial because its text stated that "every State in the area", which naturally included Israel, had a "right to live in peace within secure and recognized boundaries free from threats or acts of force". The resolution affirmed further the necessity for guaranteeing the territorial inviolability and political independence of "every State in the area". An additional reference found in the Preamble of the Resolution stated that it was necessary "to work for a just and lasting peace in which *every State in the area* can live in security" (italics added). In order to achieve those purposes, Israel and the Arab States concerned would be required to conduct peace negotiations amongst themselves. That meant that every Arab State which accepted this resolution implicitly accepted the existence of Israel and its right to live in peace within "secure and recognized boundaries". In addition, it was understood from the language and context of Resolution 242 that Israel's withdrawal to "secure and recognized boundaries" did not entail a complete withdrawal from all the territories described in the resolution as occupied by Israel armed forces in the recent conflict. The clear understanding that Israel did not have to make a complete withdrawal to the 1949 cease-fire lines (known also as the Green Line or armistice borders) was reinforced by the fact that these lines could never be considered "secure" borders by reputable military experts, as attested to by the constant infiltration into Israel, prior to the war, by terrorists and marauders determined to wreak murder and havoc from both Egyptian-occupied Gaza and the Jordanian-occupied "West Bank".

Despite the language of Resolution 242 and its logical consequences, Arab states, aided and abetted by Russia and its Communist allies, as well as western European powers, interpreted Resolution 242 in another way, to mean Israel's full withdrawal to the armistice borders that existed on June 4, 1967, the day before the outbreak of the Six-Day War. Nor was the United States very different in this regard. Under the Rogers Plan of October 1969, presented by Secretary of State William Rogers, Israel had to withdraw to the armistice lines with Jordan with only insubstantial alterations, and to the boundary that existed with Egypt just prior to the outbreak of the war. The Rogers Plan did not deal with the fate of the Golan Heights.

The Rogers Plan was followed by President Ronald Reagan's Peace Initiative of September 1, 1982, conceived by Secretary of State George Shultz and others. It described U.N. Resolution 242 as "the foundation-stone of America's Middle East peace effort", which, it said, "applies to all fronts, including the West Bank and Gaza". The U.S. ruled out Israeli sovereignty or permanent control over Judea, Samaria and Gaza. More specifically, it interpreted U.N. Resolution 242 in the following manner:[19]

> It is our position that Resolution 242 applies to the West Bank and Gaza and requires Israel's withdrawal in return for peace. Negotiations must determine the borders. The U.S. position in these negotiations on the extent of the withdrawal will be significantly influenced by the extent and nature of the peace and security arrangements offered in return.

The U.S. position on Resolution 242 meant, in effect, that in return for full peace and security as evidenced by a binding treaty, Israel had to withdraw from nearly all of the territories it recaptured in the Six-Day War, except for some insubstantial changes to be made. The only redeeming feature for Israel under the Reagan Initiative was that it did not support the formation of a "Palestinian State" in Judea, Samaria and Gaza.

The U.S. interpretation of Resolution 242 regarding Israel's withdrawal from Judea, Samaria and Gaza has never essentially changed since the formulation of both the Rogers Plan and the Reagan Initiative. The U.S. has made that abundantly clear in various policy pronouncements enunciated over the years since the Six-Day War to resolve the Arab-Israel Question and by the votes it cast at the U.N. Under President Bill Clinton's plan of December 1999, Israel was expected to withdraw from practically all of these territories in return for peace with Arafat's "Palestinian Authority" and approve the setting up of a new Arab state. The U.S., under its 43rd President, George W. Bush, agreed to sponsor the Road Map Peace Plan with the same goal of Israeli withdrawal that it has always espoused.

Every foreign state or third party calling for Israel's total or near-total withdrawal to the 1949 armistice lines did not take into account the simple fact that these lines had already been obliterated by the Six-Day War, and in any case were never meant to be permanent borders as evidenced by the various Armistice agreements Israel signed with the Arab States in 1949. Furthermore, Judea, Samaria, Gaza, Golan and Sinai could never truly be called "occupied territories" since all of them, except for Sinai, had been part of the Jewish National Home during the mandate period and, as already noted above, Sinai in 1967 had never belonged to modern Egypt under international law, and about half of it was geographically and administratively considered part of Palestine, included until 1906 in the former independent sanjak of Jerusalem during the long period of Ottoman rule.

Under the definition given in Article 42 of the 1907 Hague Regulations

[19] *The Arab-Israel Conflict and its Resolution: Selected Documents*, edited by Ruth Lapidoth and Moshe Hirsch, published by Martinus Nijhoff Publishers, The Netherlands (1992), Document 60, p. 287.

Respecting the Laws and Customs of War on Land, "occupation" of territory only occurs when the territory of one state (called the "hostile state") is actually placed under the effective authority of the hostile army of another state (called the "occupying state" or "occupant").[20] That is the exact reason why the American and British formulators of Resolution 242 referred to Israel's "armed forces" in speaking about "territories occupied in the recent conflict", to make it conform to the customary definition of "occupation" enunciated in Article 42 of the Hague Regulations. The irresolvable problem with Resolution 242's use of the word "occupied" is that none of the territories Israeli "armed forces" are assumed in this resolution to have "occupied" as a result of the Six-Day War legally belonged as of that date under international law to any of the Arab states engaged in combat with Israel. Hence Resolution 242, which was meant to apply only to existing states at the time, is completely illogical on its face, without any true meaning, in addition to being illegal, because no territory can really be considered "occupied" in the international law sense if such territory was not previously under the sovereignty of any of the Arab states in question, as was in fact the case in 1967. Israel is therefore under no obligation to withdraw from any of the territories it allegedly "occupied" in the Six-Day War, since none of those territories meet the definition of "occupied territory" under Article 42 of the Hague Regulations.

A new incomprehensible phrase has come into general use since the late 1980's, namely, that of "occupied Palestinian territories", with the addition of the middle word "Palestinian". This phrase, too, has no logical meaning, since history knows of no Arab state called Palestine, nor of any Arab nation of Palestinians. The mandated state of Palestine was a Jewish State in legal theory, but it did not assume all the characteristics of a Jewish State in practice because of British malfeasance and betrayal of the Mandate for Palestine. That, however, does not detract from the fact that Israel is the only legal Palestinian state in the true sense of the term. Therefore the implication and impression conveyed by the usage of the term "occupied Palestinian territories" is a non-sequitur, devoid of any meaning or truth. Palestine was created on April 24, 1920 for the sole purpose of being the Jewish National Home. Thus, to say that Israel "occupies" Palestinian land as defined by Article 42 of the Hague Regulations is the same as saying Israel "occupies" or is the "occupier" of Jewish land, which is absurd on its face, but this is how terminology has become so misused, it is no longer intelligible.

---

20 The text of Article 42 of the 1907 Hague Regulations and the heading immediately above it reads as follows: "Section III – Military Authority [of the Occupying State] over the Territory of the Hostile State: Territory [of the hostile state] is considered occupied when it is actually placed under the authority of the hostile army [of the occupying state]. The occupation extends only to the territory where such authority has been established and can be exercised." The countervailing terms "occupying state" and "hostile state" are explicitly used in the English version of Article 55 of the Hague Regulations.

It is a measure of the lack of knowledge on this point on the part of Israel's legal and political elites, including the Supreme Court of Israel and professors of law at the country's academic institutions, that they so readily accepted the unfounded idea that Israel had no legal rights and title of sovereignty over Judea, Samaria and Gaza, and referred to them as if they were truly "occupied territories". If that were really so, then Judea, Samaria and Gaza are "foreign territories" for the Jewish People. It would require a great leap of imagination and complete amnesia to really believe that the Jewish People "occupy" in the international law sense "foreign territories" that were the cradle of the Jewish People, as recorded in almost four thousand years of history. To accept that assumption would mean that the long history of the Jewish People with the Land of Israel counts for nothing. It would also mean the retroactive erasure of the Balfour Declaration and the Mandate Charter and all the events associated with the rebirth of the Jewish State. Yet this belief has now become so universally implanted in the public mind, it is almost tilting at windmills today to assert the contrary. Even President George W. Bush now speaks of Israel's "occupation" of "Palestine" in referring to Judea, Samaria and Gaza. The worst part of this unfounded development is that most people in Israel have swallowed whole this travesty of international law. The only effective way to dispel this noxious notion is to make use of Israeli legislation passed in 1948 to immediately incorporate into the State of Israel those parts of Judea, Samaria and Gaza still remaining under Israeli military rule and at the same time to enforce the criminal laws of the State against those Israelis who publicly advocate the cession, surrender or unilateral abandonment of these sovereign areas of the State of Israel, which were never incorporated as required by the Area of Jurisdiction and Powers Ordinance of September 22, 1948 and the Land of Israel Proclamation validated by this Ordinance.[21] There is ample justification for taking corrective steps of this kind. Not only is it legally wrong to use the term "occupied territories" defined in Article 42 of the Hague Regulations as a synonymous term for any area of the Jewish National Home outside the bounds of the State of Israel under the control of the IDF, thus making a mockery of the founding documents of Mandated Palestine and the State of Israel, but the use of this term also induces "hatred or contempt or excites disaffection" for the Jewish State. Such usage can therefore be classified as an act of sedition in accordance with the definition given for this crime against the State in Article 136(1) of Israel's Penal Law, a crime which resembles an act of criminal libel against a private person. Moreover, the constant repetition of this term in news media outlets and publications impairs the sovereignty of the State over these areas, and may therefore be considered an act of treason, within the ambit of Article

[21] All the Israeli laws that bear on the subject of Israel's repossessed territories can be found in the author's work: *A Petition to Annul the Interim Agreement*, Supreme Court of Israel, HCJ 3414/96, Prof. Hillel Weiss vs The Government of Israel, published by the Ariel Center For Policy Research, Policy Paper 77, January 1999.

97(a) of the same law.

The U.N. Security Council and the General Assembly both pose a great danger to Israel's acquired legal rights and title of sovereignty to Judea, Samaria and Gaza. These two U.N. organs are constantly interfering directly in the events taking place there. A notorious example was the appointment of an investigating committee to determine if Israel perpetrated a "massacre" in Jenin[22] during eight days of fierce house-to-house fighting in April 2002 against Arab terrorists responsible for a wave of homicide-bombings in Israel.[23] In this respect, it should be noted that neither the Security Council nor the General Assembly have any actual authority over the internal affairs of all areas of the Jewish National Home, based on any specific legal document or act of international law. Article 2(7) of the U.N. Charter which deals with matters within the domestic jurisdiction of any state is actually a bar to U.N. intervention. This provision states:

> Nothing contained in the present Charter shall authorize the United Nations to intervene in matters which are essentially within the domestic jurisdiction of any state or shall require the Members to submit such matters to settlement under the present Charter; but this principle shall not prejudice the application of enforcement measures under Chapter VII.

Israel must take stronger measures to defeat persistent U.N. efforts to intrude on its domestic jurisdiction in reference to Judea, Samaria and Gaza. Arab states constantly introduce unbalanced and hostile resolutions in U.N. bodies, the only purpose of which is to censure, embarrass or to tie the hands of Israel in these regions of the Jewish National Home. To hinder or frustrate U.N. meddling in Israel's internal affairs, Israel should not allow any biased U.N. representatives

---

[22] Modern Jenin was an ancient Jewish town in the southern Jezreel Valley in Samaria. It is identified by some scholars with Ein-Ganim (Spring of the Gardens) or Beth-ha-Gan (House of the Garden). It is called Ginaea in the writings of Josephus and Gina in the El-Amarna correspondence in the list of Canaanite cities. See *Encyclopaedia Judaica* (1971), Volume 6, Column 741, under the entry of En-Ganim. See also Yohanan Aharoni, *The Land of the Bible, a Historical Geography,* translated by A.F.Rainey, the Westminister Press, Philadelphia (1967), pp. 159, 160 (Map 11), 163.

[23] The Arab claim of a massacre in the Jenin refugee camp was disproved by a U.N. report released on August 1, 2002, which had been requested by a General Assembly resolution of May 7, 2002. The 42-page report placed the death toll at no more than 52, which contrasted sharply with initial reports giving figures of 500 and even as high as thousands who had allegedly been killed by Israel. One such report came from a minister in the "Palestinian Authority", Saeb Erekat, who told the CNN world-wide television news network in the immediate aftermath of the military operation called "Defensive Shield", that Israel had killed 5,000 of the town's residents, a deliberate and malicious fabrication.

to enter the country to hear and record one-sided complaints and lies from Arab residents, who are often only too willing to besmirch the Jewish State with inflated and untruthful stories.

The legal position of Israel in regard to Judea, Samaria and Gaza is analogous to that of the United Kingdom in regard to the colony of the Falkland Islands which Argentina calls "Islas Malvinas". In neither case are the territories in question incorporated into the borders of the mother state, even though each state enjoys sovereignty over those respective territories. Israel's title of sovereignty over Judea, Samaria and Gaza is based squarely and irrefutably on the San Remo Resolution of April 24-25, 1920 (the combination of the Balfour Declaration with the general provisions of Article 22 of the Covenant of the League of Nations respecting mandated territories), the Mandate for Palestine and the Franco-British Boundary Convention of December 23, 1920 which indisputably included Judea, Samaria and Gaza within the borders of Palestine.

In the same manner that the United Nations could not intervene in the question of the future of the Falkland Islands, nor was it able to devise its own solution to put an end to the crisis between the U.K. and Argentina after the war of 1982, because of existing British sovereignty and jurisdiction over those islands, so it cannot intervene and impose any sort of solution it wishes in Judea, Samaria and Gaza, because of Israel's sovereignty and domestic jurisdiction over those regions. It has no right to challenge or impugn Israel's sovereignty, condemn the building of settlements or declare those lands to be "occupied territories". To do what the United Nations often resolves to do in regard to these lands is an unacceptable usurpation of authority it does not possess, and Israel should have made this clear to the United Nations and to everyone else long before it entered into pernicious agreements with the "Palestine Liberation Organization" and before talk started about setting up a new Arab state there. Israel's abject failure to act decisively in this matter has allowed the United Nations to intervene at will in the affairs of Judea, Samaria and Gaza, contrary to Article 2(7) of the Charter and to pass all kinds of resolutions as if it and not Israel really had legal authority and jurisdiction. Such intervention could have been forestalled or lessened, had Israel immediately exercised its legal rights to incorporate those National Home areas into the borders of the State after the Six-Day War ended, as it did for eastern Jerusalem and the Golan Heights. Instead, by following the opposite course and then foolishly accepting Security Council Resolution 242 five months later, it made these areas a subject for excessive U.N. intervention that continues to this day.

Thus, with Israel's unwitting help, the U.N. has brazenly asserted a non-existent right of jurisdiction over integral parts of the Land of Israel and the Jewish National Home, on the two-fold basis that the events taking place there constitute a threat to international peace and security and because they are deemed to be occupied territories belonging to another state or nation. If that can be done in the case of Israel as regards Judea, Samaria and Gaza, it could also be done in other places in the world where it is clear that the United Nations has no inherent right of direct intervention, or role to play, as in the instance of the Falkland Islands, as already noted, which from Argentina's slanted perspective constitutes "occupied territory", thus posing in its eyes a threat to international peace and security.

The same reasoning to justify U.N. intervention could also be used in the long and simmering dispute over the final disposition and fate of the Indian state of Jammu and Kashmir, which India rules despite the fact that the population of this state is overwhelmingly Moslem and wishes, according to what Pakistan argues, to be joined to that country rather than to Hindu India. Even in these unfavourable circumstances for India, the United Nations has no right to dictate the policy India must follow in regard to Jammu and Kashmir. It has already passed resolutions calling for a plebiscite to decide the future of this territory which India has annexed. However, it has no right to impose its will and decide that the territory should be ceded to Pakistan. It cannot declare that Jammu and Kashmir are "occupied Moslem Pakistan territory" as a pretext for intervention. Yet that is exactly the rationale the United Nations has adopted for intervening and deciding what should be done in Judea, Samaria and Gaza – asserting that there is either a threat to international peace and security and/or the areas in question are "occupied Arab or Palestinian territory" that does not belong to Israel under international law. It is quite curious that though these areas are always described as "occupied", no one who asserts that ever bothers to explain the origin of the Arab or "Palestinian" title, when it was bestowed or acquired and upon what document or provision of law it is based. That, in fact, can never be done because there is no such title, which is vested only with the Jewish People and the State of Israel based on the Smuts Resolution, Article 22 of the League Covenant, the San Remo Resolution, the Mandate for Palestine and the Franco-British Boundary Convention of December 23, 1920.

Another example can be cited to illustrate the principle of Article 2(7) of the Charter barring U.N. intervention in matters of domestic jurisdiction, which though theoretical in nature does have a sound basis in past historical events. This is the case of Puerto Rico, where one can easily imagine a dissident nationalist group stirring up trouble and launching a terrorist campaign against American rule in order to gain independence for this West Indies island, whose official status is that of a Commonwealth of the United States. Puerto Rico has been under American sovereignty ever since it was ceded by Spain to the United States in the Treaty of Paris of December 10, 1898, which ended the Spanish-American War. Despite the fact that the Commonwealth island is under American sovereignty, it is not counted among the states included in the United States of America and therefore lies outside the borders of the unified federal State of the United States, just as Judea, Samaria and Gaza lie outside the borders of the State of Israel, though under its *de jure* sovereignty.

In the event of a theoretical Puerto Rican revolt or uprising (in Arabic terms, a so-called *intifada*) against continued American rule, the United States would have the undisputed right to suppress it, without worrying about United Nations intervention on the pretended basis not only that the fighting constitutes a threat to both international and hemispheric peace and security, but is also a justified attempt to dislodge an "occupier" from the territory it allegedly occupies.

There is an exception embodied in Article 2(7) of the Charter, which does allow for U.N. intervention "in matters which are essentially within the domestic jurisdiction of any state," namely, that this rule of non-intervention shall not prejudice the application of enforcement measures under Chapter VII of the Charter. This exception to the rule does not apply to Israel's presence in Judea, Samaria and Gaza since there is no basis for the assumption that Israel's presence there constitutes a genuine threat to international peace and security, except in the fertile or overworked imaginations of Arab and Moslem leaders who strive to deprive Israel of its acquired legal rights and title of sovereignty over these territories. None of the Arab and Moslem states despite all their bluster and denunciations will go to war against Israel because of what it does or does not do there, whether in regard to the establishment of settlements, the exercise of Jewish rights of access and prayer on the Temple Mount in Jerusalem or the eviction of the "Palestine Liberation Organization" and its offshoot, the "Palestinian Authority" from the Land of Israel.

The best example of where the United Nations has had a plausible right to intervene and to take enforcement measures under Chapter VII of the Charter in order to preserve international peace and security despite the general principle of non-intervention in the domestic affairs of a country enunciated in Article 2(7) was the case of Saddam Hussein's Iraq. This country, it was widely believed prior to an American-led invasion in 2003, had either developed or was in the process of developing prohibited weapons of mass destruction, including chemical, biological and nuclear weapons, as well as ballistic missiles with a range greater than 150 kilometers. The right of U.N. intervention was assumed to exist because Iraq, after the Persian Gulf War of January-February 1991, had committed itself to disarm and destroy such weapons in its possession as part of the peace terms it accepted to end the war. The assumed continued possession and stockpiling of such weapons by Iraq, if confirmed by credible evidence, would have constituted a clear-cut violation of international conventions to which Iraq was a party, as well as many Security Council resolutions which required it to disclose all its weapons of mass destruction and destroy them[24] in accordance with the obligation it had undertaken. At it turned out, no such evidence has come to light, but in this matter, Iraq was already a notorious violator of international law. It had used chemical weapons or poison gas during its eight-year war with Iran (1980-1988), which killed about 15,000 Iranians, and then used them again against the Kurdish population of Northern Iraq where an estimated 5,000 to nearly 7,000 people died in Halabja and other Kurdish towns and villages in March, 1988.

---

[24] See Security Council Resolution 1441 passed on November 8, 2002 requiring Iraq to show that it had complied with its disarmament obligations or face serious consequences if it had not done so.

Arab states have laughably tried to place Israel in the same boat as Iraq, in order to urge the Security Council to take similar measures against Israel for non-compliance with U.N. resolutions, even though there is absolutely no comparison between the two cases. Israel never launched a war to illegally attack or subjugate neighboring states as Iraq has done, which would have made it subject to enforcement measures under Chapter VII of the Charter. On the contrary, it has always acted within the confines of its inherent right of self-defense, under Article 51 of the Charter and in accordance with its own legal rights and title of sovereignty over the Land of Israel. It has never used or threatened to use weapons of mass destruction for aggressive purposes, and has abided by all international conventions on the subject to which it previously adhered.

Inasmuch as Israel is always unjustly condemned by the United Nations as an occupier of "Arab land" in regard to Judea, Samaria and Gaza, a condemnation that has no basis in either fact or law, it is important to trace the origin of this pernicious myth. This myth has provided the world body with the necessary pretext to intervene constantly in the internal affairs of these Jewish lands. The myth originated and has persisted to this very day, astonishingly enough, with the aid of Israel's top legal echelon or coterie of eminent jurists ensconced in several centers of authority, notably (1) the Supreme Court of Israel; (2) the Attorney-General's Office; (3) the Ministry of Justice; (4) the International Law section of the Israel Defense Forces (IDF), operating under the Military Advocate-General's Command; and (5) the law faculties of Israel's universities. The individual who bore the greatest responsibility for this myth was Meir Shamgar, who was Military Advocate-General from 1961 to 1968, later the Attorney-General of Israel and the President of the Supreme Court. He was at the epicenter of the decision made by Prime Minister Levi Eshkol's National Unity Government during the Six-Day War to apply not Israeli law but the laws of war to all the liberated Jewish territories, in particular the provisions of the Hague Regulations of 1907 as well as the Fourth Geneva Convention of 1949. The latter convention was applied on a voluntary basis, in contrast to the Hague Regulations which were assumed to be obligatory as part of customary international law. This application was completely inappropriate to the situation considering the historical connection and sanctity of these territories to the Jewish People and their legal inseparability from the Jewish National Home.

What moved Meir Shamgar to invoke the laws of war? He described what he did without providing the rationale for doing so in an article he wrote called "Legal Concepts and Problems of the Israeli Military Government – the Initial Stage".[25] Shamgar did not conceal his belief that military government based on

---

[25] See the volume entitled *Military Government in the Territories Administered by Israel 1967-1980: The Legal Aspects*, edited by Meir Shamgar, Hebrew University Jerusalem – Faculty of Law, Harry Sacher Institute for Legislative Research and Comparative Law, Jerusalem (1982), Hemed Press, reprinted 1988, pp. 13-60.

international law relating to occupied territories was the proper course to follow in regard to Judea, Samaria, Gaza, Golan and Sinai. He referred in a general sense to these territories as "enemy territory" or "occupied enemy territory".[26] Elsewhere he called the same territories "occupied", "under military occupation" or "administered", but he never called them "liberated territories of the Jewish National Home", which was their true legal status under international law after their liberation from the illegal Jordanian and Egyptian occupation respectively lasting from May 15, 1948 to June 6-8, 1967.[27] In two revealing and significant footnotes Shamgar admitted that he had *planned* the entire legal framework for any territories Israel conquered in a future war with Arab states. He formulated his plan in the early 1960s before the Six-Day War was either foreseen or its results imagined. He did this to avoid the situation of a supposed legal vacuum that had prevailed in Sinai after Israel's lightning victory in the 1956 war (Operation Kadesh), when no plan existed for the legal administration of the peninsula during Israel's three-month stay there.

He supervised special courses for platoon officers belonging to the Military Advocate's Corps beginning in 1963 in Jerusalem. (Zvi Inbar, Law and Army [in Hebrew] Issue 16, 2002, p. 149.) All military advocates carried with them "movable emergency kits" which contained the laws of war (Hague 1907, Geneva IV 1949 etc.) and a large set of precedents of military government proclamations and orders, as well as detailed legal and organizational instructions and guidelines. In addition, Shamgar wrote and published a comprehensive *vade*-mecum which he called "Manual for the Military Advocate in Military Government".

As a direct result of Shamgar's ill-conceived plan and advice to the Government of what Israel was supposedly obliged to do under international law in the event that the IDF re-captured or liberated any territories of the Land of Israel in Arab hands, a regime of military government based upon the provisions of the Hague Regulations of 1907, specifically Articles 42 and 43, was immediately established in the wake of Israel's total victory on three fronts in the Six-Day War. Military Government was defined by Shamgar as "the form of government established by a country which has occupied enemy territory, whether the [occupied land] was formally under the sovereignty of such enemy or whether it could be regarded as former sovereign territory of the occupying power or any of its allies"[28]. Despite Shamgar's disclaimer that in establishing military government Israel was not necessarily occupying enemy territory that was truly under the sovereignty of the enemy state, especially in regard to Judea, Samaria and Gaza, that was in fact the general perception in the rest of the world, reinforced by the very application of the provisions of the Hague Regulations relating to "occupied territories".

---

[26] *Ibid.*, pp. 13, 28, 31.

[27] Shamgar did make one scant reference to "liberated areas" on p. 14 of his article, but this reference was not explicitly linked to the liberated areas of the Jewish National Home, but to liberated areas in a broader or general sense.

[28] *Ibid.*, p. 28.

The military government was made up of four regional entities covering 1) the Gaza Strip and Northern Sinai; 2) Central and Southern Sinai; 3) Judea and Samaria; and 4) the Golan Heights. The application of Articles 42 and 43 of the Hague Regulations meant that in the case of the single region of Judea and Samaria, Jordanian law as it existed on June 7, 1967 that included unrepealed provisions of Mandatory law and remnants of Ottoman law would continue to be enforced unless amended or repealed by new security enactments of the Military Government. In the case of Gaza, this meant that Egyptian military regulations that had been in force in the period from May 15, 1948 to June 6, 1967 would also continue to be applied, as well as unrepealed Mandatory provisions unless the law was also amended or repealed by the Military Government. In regard to northern Sinai, which was linked to Gaza to form a single administrative unit, the pre-1967 legal system remained in effect under the Military Government. Even Jerusalem came for a brief time under military government from June 7 to June 28, 1967, that ceased to exist only after "East" and "West" Jerusalem were finally reunited by virtue of a government order and proclamation.

The Golan Heights indeed presented a unique problem. As a result of the fighting that took place there in the Six-Day War, none of the judges or lawyers remained in the region after June 10, 1967 to administer the local Syrian law, nor were any Syrian law books available for use. With the breakdown of the previously-existing judicial administration, and in accordance with the accepted principles of international law applicable to occupied territories, Israel created new courts for both civil and criminal proceedings under military administration.[29] Security enactments were formulated setting out the substantive law, procedure and law of evidence in civil matters that followed the laws and practice in Israel, and this was also done for criminal offenses and trials. The military administration of the Golan Heights came to an abrupt end with the passage of a Knesset law on December 14, 1981, that henceforth applied the law, jurisdiction and administration of the State of Israel to this territory, thus in effect annexing it.

The setting up of a military government subject to the strictures of international law for all the liberated territories of the Land of Israel formerly under illegal Jordanian or Egyptian occupation was incredible in the extreme. Its effect, despite Shamgar's disclaimer, was to deny the rights of the Jewish People and its assignee, the State of Israel, to these ancestral Jewish lands and prevent their incorporation into the borders of the State, as well as to treat them illogically as foreign occupied territories that belonged under international law to the Arab states that previously and illegally occupied them. The person mainly responsible for this outrageous, ignorant and unforgivable legal conception that has caused untold damage to the Jewish Zionist case to this very day was Meir Shamgar, one of Israel's most eminent jurists.

The fatal flaw in Shamgar's plan that should have flashed a red light was that

[29] *Ibid.*, p. 55, and also p. 453 which contains the Court's Order for *Ramat HaGolan* (Order 273) issued by the Military Government.

there was never any true obligation incumbent upon Israel to apply international law to the areas of the Land of Israel recaptured in a defensive war by the Israel Defense Forces. This was because Judea, Samaria and Gaza were previously designated by international law in 1920 and 1922 as integral parts of the Jewish National Home under the Mandate for Palestine read in conjunction with the Franco-British Boundary Convention of December 23, 1920 and hence were being legally repossessed by Israel. The Golan Heights were also to be considered an integral part of the Jewish National Home, though illegally removed from the Home by Britain in a trade-off agreement with France dated February 3, 1922, which took effect only on March 10, 1923.

Sinai was illegally excluded from the Jewish National Home which was supposed to include all territories to which Jews had a proven historical connection and had settled or governed in the days of the First and Second Temple Periods, when Palestine's borders were first delineated on December 23, 1920. It was excluded because Britain had decided in 1906 to attach Sinai to Egypt to protect the Suez Canal which it controlled from possible Turkish attack. Egypt had been under the sovereignty of the Ottoman Empire since 1517, but in 1882 it was occupied by Britain which ruled it until Egypt attained provisional independence by a treaty concluded in 1922 and full independence by a second treaty concluded in 1936. The British were apprehensive about the earlier administrative border extending from Rafah (*Rafiah* in Hebrew) in the north to the city of Suez at the southern exit-point of the Suez Canal, since this border afforded the Turks easy access to the Canal, especially at the southern end. To change the administrative border between the Independent Sanjak of Jerusalem and the Province of Hedjaz, on the one hand, and the Sinai Peninsula, on the other, Britain deliberately fomented a crisis with Ottoman Turkey called the Aqaba Incident, in which they delivered an ultimatum to Sultan Abd-al-Hamid II on May 3, 1906, demanding a new border in Sinai from Rafah to the head of the Gulf of Aqaba (Gulf of Eilat), near Taba. The British backed up their ultimatum by sending military and naval forces to the area, one gunboat dropping anchor at Rafah and another off Taba. Under an imminent threat of war, the Sultan, acting under duress without the support of any foreign state, had no choice but to accede to the new administrative dividing line demanded by the British. An agreement was quickly negotiated and concluded on October 1, 1906. Colonel Richard Meinertzhagen, a military intelligence officer on the staff of General Allenby's army who also advised the Government of British Prime Minister David Lloyd George on Palestine, wrote a memorandum at Lloyd George's request on the question of the sovereignty of Sinai in which he stated that under the agreement "Egypt was granted *administrative rights* in Sinai up to a line drawn from Rafah to the head of the Gulf of Aqaba, Turkey expressly *retaining the right of sovereignty*"[30] (italics in the original). Meinertzhagen further observed in his diary that in 1917, "General Allenby, with British forces unaided

[30] See Colonel Richard Meinertzhagen's book, *Middle East Diary 1917-1956*, Thomas Yoseloff, Publisher, New York (1960), pp. 17-19.

by the Egyptian Army, conquered and occupied Turkish Sinai, which, by right of conquest, is at Britain's disposal". In actual fact, since Britain was then acting on behalf of the Principal Allied Powers (the wartime coalition of Britain, France, Italy and Japan), Sinai was at the disposal of these Powers as a group rather than of Britain alone, and since at least half of Sinai was part of the Land of Israel, it should have been attached to Palestine, i.e., the Jewish National Home, in accordance with the spirit and intent of the San Remo Resolution, which was based on the historical formula for determining the boundaries of Palestine, "from Dan to Beersheba", as confirmed in the April 25, 1920 minutes of the San Remo Peace Conference. Sinai was in fact administered by Ottoman Turkey until 1892 from what later came officially to be called Palestine, and about half of Sinai was included in the Independent Sanjak of Jerusalem until 1906. In any event, Egypt was never recognized as the sovereign of Sinai under international law, but at best only as its administrator. In fact, in 1906, the Egyptian National Movement under its leader Mustafa Kamil, opposed British attempts to annex Sinai to Egypt. Furthermore, until 1948, Egypt never claimed Sinai as part of its sovereign territory except for the northwestern, triangular area, which the Turkish Sultan had permitted Egypt to administer during the 19th century, to compensate it for relinquishing its administration of Crete and not because it was within Egypt's "ancient boundaries"[31]. The whole of Sinai was subsequently appropriated by Egypt before its exact status under international law could be ascertained, in order to prevent the emerging Jewish State from claiming or annexing it.

Prime Minister Menachem Begin erred grievously in 1978 when, during the peace negotiations with Egypt at Camp David, he did not challenge President Anwar Sadat's false assertion that Sinai was "sacred Egyptian soil" though it was nothing of the kind. Begin, the erstwhile champion of the Greater Land of Israel, let Israel's right to Sinai under the above-mentioned historical formula be lost by default. His costly blunder, which also constituted a violation of the law of treason under Section 97 of the Israeli Penal Code, resulted in Israel's complete and legally unnecessary withdrawal from Sinai that has had a long and important historical, geographical and religious connection with Israel and the Jewish People. Inasmuch as Israel's cession of the entire Sinai to Egypt in the 1979 Egypt-Israel Peace Treaty violated Israeli constitutional and criminal law, this treaty was illegal from that perspective. Moreover, Israel's withdrawal from Sinai completed in 1982 led eventually to Israel's "disengagement" from Gaza in August 2005.

The foregoing pertinent facts concerning Judea, Samaria, Gaza, Golan and Sinai should have been uppermost in the mind of anyone given the task of advising the Government of Israel whether to apply international law or Israeli law to these territories. This task was executed by Meir Shamgar, who tendered the wrong advice for reasons known only to himself. He was apparently not

[31] See *Myths and Facts 1978, A Concise Record of the Arab-Israeli Conflict*, published by Near East Report, Washington, D.C. (1978), pp. 41-42.

adequately familiar with some of the cardinal legal documents in the post World War I period, which affirmed Jewish legal rights and title of sovereignty to all of Palestine, as the Jewish National Home, particularly the Smuts Resolution of January 30, 1919 which became Article 22 of the Covenant of the League of Nations, the San Remo Resolution of April 25, 1920, the Franco-British Boundary Convention of December 23, 1920, the Mandate for Palestine confirmed on July 24, 1922 and finally, the Anglo-American Convention of December 3, 1924 respecting the Mandate for Palestine.

What is even more puzzling and legally very grave, which reflects badly on Shamgar's reputation as a jurist, was the manner in which he overlooked or neglected two fundamental Israeli constitutional laws that exclusively governed the post-Six-Day War situation before the enactment two and a half weeks later on June 27, 1967 of Section 11B of the Law and Administration Ordinance. This was not only bad legal advice, but also constituted a gross violation of the Rule of Law. Had he better evaluated the true significance of these constitutional laws, they would undoubtedly have steered him in the right direction, or at least warned him against the application of international law pertaining to the rules of warfare to the liberated Jewish territories of Judea, Samaria, Gaza, Golan and Sinai. The first of these laws was the Area of Jurisdiction and Powers Ordinance and the two proclamations issued by Prime Minister and Defense Minister David Ben-Gurion on August 2, 1948 and September 2, 1948 as the legislative means to apply the corpus of law of the State of Israel to territories of the Land of Israel beyond the U.N. Partition lines, repossessed by the IDF in the War of Independence. The other important law that was applicable to the new situation that arose after the Six-Day War was the ubiquitous Law of Return, which entitled Jews to settle in all parts of the Land of Israel under Israel's effective control. Had the proper laws been invoked and legal procedure followed, then all of the liberated territories comprising parts of the Land of Israel would have immediately been incorporated into the State. It is really dumfounding that Shamgar who was so preoccupied with observing international precedents and guidelines regarding the procedure to be followed after the effective conquest of what he perceived was "enemy territory", failed at the appropriate moment to advise the application of the existing Israeli laws on Eretz-Israel – the precedent established by Ben-Gurion during the War of Independence. The above facts and precedent were simply ignored or not discussed by Shamgar and the military advocates who participated in his training program. In several conversations the present writer has had with the jurist Eliezer Dembitz, a military court judge appointed by Shamgar himself, who attended the training courses organized by Shamgar and served as a Justice Ministry official, as well as a senior legal adviser to the Knesset Finance Committee, Dembitz has confirmed that, to his knowledge, no one who attended these courses ever propounded the argument that there was no legal necessity to apply the laws of war to the territories liberated in the Six-Day War. By his unwise advice that resulted in the application of the norms of international law to these territories, Shamgar entangled Israel in the morass and endless dispute about the applicability of the Fourth Geneva Convention and the Hague Regulations, and moreover, gave credence to the mislabeling of the territories as being "occupied" and the consequent libeling of Israel as an "occupier" of "Arab land". This proved to be an enormous propaganda coup for the Arab cause, while severely undermining Israel's legal argument that the liberated territories were the national patrimony of the Jewish People as enunciated in the Biblical record and confirmed in several post-World War I documents.[32]

Subsequently, Shamgar seems to have had some second thoughts about what he had planned and overseen to fruition. While he concurred in the application of the Hague Regulations, which he viewed as customary international law that was always binding on Israel, in regard to the conquest of "enemy territory", he did not accept the false claim that Israel was likewise bound by the Fourth Geneva Convention since the latter represented conventional international law that the Knesset had never introduced into Israel's legal system and in any case applied only to "occupied territories" over which neither Jordan nor Egypt had been recognized sovereigns with a valid title. Nevertheless, Shamgar's second thoughts on the subject were of no avail since he had already created the mould of a military administrative framework that (except in the cases of Jerusalem and the Golan Heights) was never subsequently repudiated or converted into Israeli civilian administration governed in all cases by Knesset statutory law. The first two military proclamations issued on June 7, 1967 by Brigadier-General Chaim Herzog, the future sixth President of the State, regarding the region of Judea and Samaria that resulted in the application of Jordanian law and drafted[33] by the Director-General of the Ministry of Justice, Zvi Terlo, based on the legal guidelines and forms compiled by Shamgar in the aforementioned *vade mecum*, resulted in the application of Jordanian law to this region. These proclamations, illegal and improper though they may be in relation to Ben-Gurion's precedent of 1948, are still in effect in those parts of Judea and Samaria not governed by the "Palestinian Authority".

The fact that Israel never incorporated Judea, Samaria and Gaza into the State, which since 1967 has been viewed by foreign opinion and most jurists in Israel as "occupied territory", is directly traceable to the Government's implementation of Shamgar's plan, guidelines and arrangements. The "Manual for the Military Advocate in Military Government" written and expanded by Shamgar proves beyond reasonable doubt that he is the one most responsible both for the

---

32 For further elaboration, see the author's *The Howard Grief Eretz-Israel Letters to Meir Shamgar, 2005-2007 on Eretz-Israel and Israeli Constitutional Law*, edited by Yoel Lerner, published by the Office for Israeli Constitutional Law, May 2007.

33 The information regarding the drafting of the first two military proclamations for Judea and Samaria was conveyed to the present writer by Professor Ya'akov Meron, an accomplished legal expert and jurist who served in the Ministry of Justice for thirty years as the adviser on Muslim Law in Arab countries.

establishment of military government in Judea, Samaria and Gaza and the pernicious notion that Israel is an occupying power, that so bedevils it today.

The tragic mistake and violation of law committed by Shamgar has been made immeasurably worse by two recent Supreme Court judgments,[34] rendered by the President of the Supreme Court and former Attorney-General, Aharon Barak, who decided, without reference to any of the aforementioned laws or international documents that indicated otherwise, that Judea, Samaria and Gaza are indeed territories held by Israel under "belligerent occupation". Barak, in his off-the-mark judgments, did not specify the states or people whose land Israel has been occupying or when such states or people were recognized under international law as having the sovereign right to Judea, Samaria and Gaza.

His judgments which bind the Government of Israel, unless overturned by legislation, and give great comfort to Israel's enemies and detractors both within and without, are even more damaging than the non-binding, non-enforceable advisory opinion of the International Court of Justice (ICJ) in the case involving the legality of Israel's security fence being constructed in Judea and Samaria. The Court, sitting in the Hague, established under Article 92 of the Charter of the United Nations as the principal judicial organ of the U.N., in a biased, legally unsupportable opinion delivered on July 9, 2004, declared the security fence illegal under a false reading of international law. It disregarded the cardinal fact that the whole of Palestine was set aside by international law in 1919, 1920 and 1922 as the Jewish National Home. The relevant documents of international law noted above were either completely ignored or, in the case of the Mandate for Palestine, while mentioned, its purpose and principal provisions were not discussed at all. At the same time, the ICJ recognized the national and political rights of a fictitious nation that calls itself "the Palestinians", a term that earlier identified the Jews of Palestine prior to 1948 and was scornfully rejected by the Arabs of the country. The ICJ further stated that Judea and Samaria are "Occupied Palestinian Territory" and that Israel has the status of an "Occupying Power". This opinion gives the Arabs a public-relations bonanza, but has absolutely no legal merit or validity. It reflects only the twisted, baseless views of the Arab League and the "Palestinian Authority" as well as the dozens of Islamic nations represented at the United Nations. The ICJ opinion proves how some respected jurists who had not already committed themselves to favouring the Arab cause prior to giving their opinion can be hoodwinked into swallowing nonsensical, illogical arguments, based on irrelevant U.N. resolutions and data that lack the force of law in deciding the issue at hand. Yet this senseless advisory opinion has been praised by none other than the most revered figure in Israel's judiciary, Aharon Barak, who found that the ICJ opinion "also contains many things that are favourable to Israel". He added, "I can definitely see the possibility

---

[34] See the case of Beit Sourik Village Council v. the Government of Israel, HCJ 2056/04 (judgment rendered on June 30, 2004); see also the case of Gaza Coast Regional Council v. Knesset of Israel, HCJ 1661/05 (judgment rendered on June 9, 2005).

in the not-too-distant future when the State will base many of its arguments [apparently concerning the route of the fence] on this opinion".[35] Never has Shamgar's 1967 folly reached such heights of absurdity! If Israel's leading jurists treat Judea, Samaria and Gaza as "occupied territories" and discount Jewish legal rights and title of sovereignty over them, or believe such rights do not exist at all, little can be expected from foreign governments, political leaders or media figures who have expressed themselves in a similar manner or have maliciously accused Israel of "stealing" the land of another people. The tremendous legal and political harm which these jurists have caused to the Jewish legal case cannot be rectified or reversed in a single stroke. However, a beginning can certainly be made to overcome this damage by having the Knesset pass a special law declaring that Judea, Samaria and Gaza are definitely not occupied territories under international law, but rather the national patrimony of the Jewish People in whose name the State of Israel acts.

Israel's legal and political standing in Judea, Samaria and Gaza was further undermined and became even weaker by the signing of the Israel-PLO accords in 1993 – which led to the transfer of substantial areas of the Jewish National Home to the "Palestine Liberation Organization" which in turn placed them under the civil administration of the "Palestinian Authority" established by the Declaration of Principles originally initialed on August 20, 1993 and ceremonially signed at the White House on September 13, 1993. This produced an anomalous situation in which international law affecting Judea, Samaria and Gaza was inverted or turned upside down. The new reality created by the various Israel-PLO agreements allowed the so-called "Palestinians", to assert and gain Israeli government recognition of national and political rights in the ancient Jewish homeland, supported by U.N. resolutions ungrounded in international law.

Unless the Government of Israel officially declares invalid all agreements it has made with the PLO since August 20, 1993 and forthwith ceases to apply the laws of war to the remainder of the liberated territories still in Israeli hands and replaces them with Israeli law, the Security Council may try to impose its own self-declared authority on the false ground that they are "occupied Palestinian territories" outside Israel's sovereign jurisdiction. This has become all the more likely now that the United States under the George W. Bush Administration is supporting an independent state of "Palestine" living side-by-side with Israel, as part of its "vision for peace" in the Middle East. Steps are already being taken in this direction by the joint action of the so-called Quartet, a combined name for the U.S., the U.N., the European Union and Russia. This artificial grouping that lacks any common basis or structure except for its pro-Arab slant and anti-Israel posture has devised a so-called "roadmap" which aims to illegally transfer Israel's national rights over all of Judea, Samaria and Gaza to the Arabic-speaking medley of Gentiles living in these regions. In these circumstances, it is conceivable that

---

[35] The Jerusalem Post, May 10, 2005.

the Security Council may one day pass a resolution that will contain one or more of the following orders or demands directed against Israel:

1. an order or demand for the complete withdrawal of Israel from the lands it allegedly occupies;
2. an order or demand for the dismantling of all Israeli settlements in these areas and the transfer of their residents to pre-Six-Day War Israel;
3. an order or demand for the establishment of an Arab State called "Palestine" in the heart of the Jewish National Home, with eastern Jerusalem as its capital and the Temple Mount under its control;
4. an order to Israel to accept the mass "return" of millions of Arab "refugees" and their descendants at least to the region of Judea and Samaria.

Upon the passage of this kind of hypothetical resolution, the sponsors of it will then say that Israel is obliged by Article 25 of the Charter to comply with the orders or demands it contains. Israel, however, would be on safe ground in refusing to obey such blatantly illegal orders or demands that were *ultra vires* the Security Council, because they deprived Israel of its inherited legal rights and title of sovereignty over all areas of the Jewish National Home secured under international law in the global political and legal settlement made after World War I. In addition, these U.N. orders or demands would jeopardize Israel's political independence or territorial integrity, interfere with its domestic jurisdiction and compromise its inherent right of self-defence.[36]

---

[36] Among the provisions of the Charter that would be violated by a resolution containing such orders or demands, the following may be cited:

1. Article 1(2), Article 2(4) and Article 80 in regard to the right of self-determination of the Jewish People, which was meant to apply to all of former Mandated Palestine, including Judea, Samaria and Gaza; Israel's political independence and territorial integrity would be put in jeopardy by the loss of areas that rightfully belong to the State of Israel as the assignee of the Jewish People under international law;
2. Article 2(7) in the case of interference with Israel's domestic jurisdiction that theoretically extends to all of Judea, Samaria and Gaza, though Israel has refrained from exercising its civilian jurisdiction over these areas;
3. Article 51 in regard to impairing Israel's right of individual or collective self-defense;
4. The third recital in the Preamble of the U.N. Charter concerning "justice and respect for the obligations arising from treaties and other sources of international law" – which can be cited as a firm support for those acts of international law that were the foundation of Israel's existence as a Jewish State: the San Remo Resolution (the marriage of the Balfour Declaration with the general provisions of Article 22 of the Covenant of the League of Nations), the Mandate for Palestine, the Franco-British Boundary Convention of December 23, 1920, all of which were reinforced by the American-British Convention of December 3, 1924 respecting the Mandate for Palestine.

The United States tacitly and sometimes overtly uses the threat of possible passage of U.N. Security Council Resolutions inimical to Israel's presence in Judea and Samaria as an effective diplomatic lever to apply pressure and extract concessions from Israel to further the American objective of setting up a so-called "Palestinian State", a step calculated also to appease the 21 Arab League states. The U.S. wants to prevent Israel from recovering the parts of those ancient Jewish lands that were illegally placed in the hands of the "Palestinian Authority" by the Yitzhak Rabin Government of 1992-1995 and all succeeding Israeli Governments. The only effective counter-response of Israel is to forcefully remind the United States through diplomatic channels and then by legal proceedings in American courts if necessary, of its treaty recognition of Jewish legal rights to all of the areas of Mandated Palestine under the American-British Convention of December 3, 1924 respecting the Mandate for Palestine. This recognition was never altered or disavowed by any subsequent legal act, and therefore these rights are still unimpaired and remain ingrained in U.S. law[37] by virtue of the principle of acquired legal rights to which the doctrine of estoppel applies, preventing the United States from denying their continued existence and validity.

Similarly, the rights enjoyed by the Jewish People and the State of Israel over all areas of former Mandated Palestine and the Land of Israel have never ceased to be part of true international law and cannot be overturned today by any resolutions, decisions or orders of the U.N. Security Council or General Assembly. These resolutions have no application to Israel's own constitutional law, just as they are inapplicable to the laws of the United States. In particular, U.N. Security Council resolutions apply only on the international level in regard to the maintenance of international peace and security where there is a genuine threat to peace or breaches of the peace, or where the party against whom enforcement measures are taken is an aggressor who has violated international conventions or agreements. Those resolutions do not apply to states such as Israel which act to protect their legal rights, previously granted or recognized under international law. In the context of Chapter VII of the U.N. Charter, the Security Council can impose obligations on all members of the U.N., as well as sanctions for the non-observance of its resolutions, provided as always the Council's Resolutions are in accordance with other provisions of the Charter, especially Articles 2(7) and 80, which when taken together preserve Israel's national rights and domestic jurisdiction over all parts of the Jewish National Home and the Land of Israel.

In the final analysis, Security Council Resolutions are not laws in the traditional sense of the term, which are passed by an international legislature and are capable of self-enforcement by the body which passed them. The Security Council lacks the powers of a state, a government or a legislature to enforce its

[37] See the chapter on the doctrine of estoppel *supra* dealing with its application to the U.S. Government in the matter of Jewish national rights to the whole of Palestine.

own resolutions, which is why they are called "resolutions" and not "laws". All enforcement measures of the U.N. depend on the volition of individual member states to carry them out. It is true that some Security Council Resolutions or even some General Assembly Resolutions may constitute a general consensus of international opinion on a particular matter that will eventually lead to the creation of new customs having the force of law. But that consensus of opinion is a gradual process over many years and does not elevate U.N. resolutions when they are originally passed to the level or status of international law, especially when many of the countries who are parties to this consensus are governed by tyrannical or totalitarian regimes which do not represent the free choice of their citizens. To pretend otherwise or to act on the assumption that the Security Council is a law-making body is to sow deliberate confusion or engage in a gross deception for whatever the purpose to be served. Resolutions of the Security Council which deal with real threats to international peace and security under Chapter VII of the Charter are binding and have to be obeyed by member states of the U.N. not because they are laws, but for the reason that these states have signed a treaty or adhered to its provisions subsequently – the U.N. Charter – in which they have agreed to accept and carry out the decisions of the Security Council made in accordance with the Charter. Such resolutions will indeed create legal obligations upon all members of the United Nations, but they do not at the same time constitute international law in the traditional sense of that term.

In this context, any U.N. Security Council resolution, governed by Article 25 of the Charter, can be compared to the making of a contract in civil law. Both will create binding obligations on the parties affected by the resolution or contract, but neither has the qualities of an actual "law" passed by a recognized sovereign authority with its own independent enforcement mechanism or capability, and therefore neither merits the appellation of "law", except in a metaphorical sense.

In summary, insofar as Israel is concerned, the resolutions of the Security Council do not have to be complied with when they are not made in accordance with other provisions of the United Nations Charter, when they flout Israel's acquired legal rights and title of sovereignty to all regions of the Jewish National Home under its rule, when they presume to dictate to the Government of Israel what should or should not be done inside the Land of Israel and, finally, when they endanger Israel's existence as a Jewish State and its inherent right of individual and collective self-defence and security.

## *(II) Article 80 Of The U.N. Charter*

The continuing validity of previously granted Jewish rights to Palestine and title of sovereignty is vouched for and protected both by the principle of acquired legal rights and the doctrine of estoppel. There is therefore no real need today nor was there ever such a need to rely on Article 80 of the U.N. Charter for this purpose, which in any case is now inapplicable to former mandated Palestine, in the sense of converting Judea and Samaria and, formerly, Gaza, as well as the City of Jerusalem, into a trust territory administered by the United Nations. However, this article is very useful for another purpose, not originally intended, and which is ancillary to the principal purpose of preserving from alteration "the rights of any states or any peoples or the terms of existing international instruments" before placing mandated territories under the trusteeship system. Article 80 may now serve as a test to judge the legality of "decisions" taken in regard to the Land of Israel by the Security Council under Article 25 of the Charter and in general to determine the legality of all resolutions passed by any organ of the U.N.. In this context Article 80 may be cited as support to show that the aborted Partition Resolution of November 29, 1947 was illegally adopted by the General Assembly because it constituted a direct violation of the very terms of the Charter itself, as well as violating the acquired Jewish legal rights and title of sovereignty over Palestine and the Land of Israel.

In its intended application to Palestine, Article 80 meant that until the country was placed under the trusteeship system, were it decided to do so, by means of an individual trusteeship agreement, which would take the place of the existing Mandate for Palestine, nothing would be done in the meanwhile *to alter* the rights of the Jewish People already contained in the terms of the Mandate. By the very language of Article 80, it was a transitional or stop-gap measure designed to safeguard existing rights of peoples in the mandated territories to be placed under trusteeship. Until a trusteeship agreement was actually reached by the states directly concerned, the "rights of peoples" continued in full force and were safe from any alteration. In one respect Article 80 is similar to Article 27 of the Mandate since both articles theoretically provided for the alteration or modification of the terms of an existing international instrument. This did not mean, however, that even if a trusteeship agreement were to be made, all kinds of alterations or modifications could then be freely introduced in order to change fundamental aspects of the Mandate, such as its purpose to establish the Jewish National Home and State and the means to achieve it. If such alterations were permitted, the reason for conferring a mandate on the Mandatory Power would have been defeated, the acquired legal rights of the Jewish People to Palestine would be put in jeopardy and the doctrine of estoppel would lose its deterrent effect. Alterations were possible only if they did not affect the heart and soul of the mandate which dealt with these acquired legal rights. Examples of what changes could be made in a Mandate being converted into a trusteeship would be the appointment or substitution of a new Mandatory for the current one and setting down new guidelines to bring about the accomplishment of the object intended in the original Mandate within a new time framework.

The Jewish Agency and the American Jewish Conference were responsible for getting the word "peoples" inserted into the text of Article 80, which was missing from the original draft. They made a proposal to this effect, which was accepted by the delegates representing various Governments who assembled in San Francisco for the United Nations Conference on International Organization held between April 25 and June 26, 1945. Everyone who participated in the discussions at the U.N. Conference knew that the word "peoples" was intended as a reference to the Jewish People living in Palestine even though no specific mention was made of that fact in the records of the Conference. This is why Article 80 came to be called the Palestine Clause.[38]

Thus, Article 80 was an extra guarantee given to the Jewish People in regard to its already existing legal rights to Palestine and the Land of Israel deriving from the San Remo Resolution, the Mandate for Palestine and the Franco-British Boundary Convention of December 23, 1920 during the short period of time this article was applicable to the country for converting the existing Mandate into a trusteeship, which lasted from the time the U.N. Charter came into force on October 24, 1945, until the date the State of Israel was proclaimed on May 14, 1948. During this 29-month span, it was possible to substitute a trusteeship agreement for the existing Mandate regime, without at the same time affecting or altering Jewish legal rights to the whole country as set out in that instrument. Attempts were indeed made by Britain to conclude a trusteeship agreement prior to submitting the Palestine Question to the judgment of the General Assembly of the United Nations on April 2, 1947 and later by the United States, after it appeared to reverse its position on the Partition Resolution of November 29, 1947 and supported a temporary United Nations trusteeship for Palestine to ensure that there would still be a government fully operating in the country to keep the peace after Britain departed Palestine.[39] A great danger would have arisen regarding the continuation of Jewish legal rights, particularly the rights regarding Jewish immigration and settlement, contained in the Mandate for Palestine had the American attempt succeeded. The very act of making a trusteeship agreement to provide for the future government of Palestine, which had to be approved by the General Assembly, would have inevitably opened the door or provided a golden opportunity for adverse changes being made to the aforementioned rights because of the pressure tactics certain to be used

---

[38] On this point, see the account on Article 80 given by I.L. Kenen, in the book, *Israel's Defence Line*, published by Prometheus Books, 1981, Chapter 3, pp. 20-25, as well as the book by Jacob Robinson, *Palestine and the United Nations*, Greenwood Press, 1947, reprinted in 1971, pp. 3-6.

[39] See President Truman's Press Statement on Palestine, March 25, 1948 urging adoption of a temporary United Nations Trusteeship for Palestine, to provide a government to keep the peace: *The Rise of Israel*, Volume 38, Document 33, pp. 155-157. President Truman emphasized that the United States had not reversed its position or that he personally had not done so. He added that he still favoured partition, but that the trusteeship proposed by the U.S. was only a temporary move to prevent continued bloodshed in Palestine, that could also affect the peace of the world. Trusteeship would fill the vacuum created by the termination of the Mandate on May 15, 1948, by providing a public authority in Palestine on that date capable of preserving law and order.

by the Arab and Moslem States who formed a cohesive bloc of ten nations at the United Nations, with the added support of India at the time. This danger looming in the background was averted in the nick of time by the Declaration for the Establishment of the State of Israel issued on May 14, 1948 by the National Council, the provisional legislature of the Jewish State, thereafter called the Provisional Council of State. This brought an end to the possibility of placing the whole country under the trusteeship system by means of a trusteeship agreement or a U.N.-imposed "statute" or resolution in substitution for a trusteeship agreement. Once the Mandate for Palestine terminated at midnight, May 14-15, 1948, with the departure of the British Mandatory Government, without a trusteeship agreement having been made, Article 80 was no longer needed to prevent the alteration of its terms. In that sense, Article 80 is no longer applicable to Palestine and has become a dead letter.

However, even though no trusteeship agreement was ever concluded for Palestine as a whole, the United Nations continued to attempt to set up a separate trusteeship for the city of Jerusalem as originally proposed in the UNSCOP report of August 31, 1947 and the Partition Resolution of November 29, 1947. Under the envisaged plan, the city of Jerusalem was to be, as already noted, a *corpus separatum* under a special international regime, administered by the United Nations, in accordance with Article 81 of the Charter. The General Assembly designated the Trusteeship Council to discharge the responsibilities of the Administering Authority on behalf of the world body. To carry out the ancillary plan for Jerusalem, the Trusteeship Council prepared a Draft Statute, dated April 21, 1948, to govern the city and its environs, including Abu Dis in the east, Bethlehem in the south, Ein Karim and Motza in the west and Shu'fat in the north. There was to be a Governor of the City in whom executive authority was vested; a Legislative Council, an independent judicial system and a special police force. The statute as formulated was to remain in force for a period of ten years, after which a referendum would be held for the residents of the City to ascertain their wishes regarding possible modifications of the international regime governing Jerusalem.

On December 11, 1948, the General Assembly adopted Resolution 194 (III) that Jerusalem should be accorded special treatment separate from that accorded to the rest of Palestine and placed under effective United Nations control. On December 9, 1949, the General Assembly restated "its intention that Jerusalem should be placed under a permanent international regime, which should envisage appropriate guarantees for the protection of the Holy Places, both within and outside Jerusalem" and requested the Trusteeship Council "to complete the preparation of the Statute of Jerusalem". Pursuant to the General Assembly Resolutions of December 11, 1948 and December 9, 1949, the Trusteeship Council presented a new updated version of the Statute for the City of Jerusalem, which it approved on April 4, 1950.

However, this new statute never went into effect as both Jordan and Israel strenuously opposed the proposed internationalization of Jerusalem. Jordan showed its disapproval when it annexed what it called the "West Bank" including the area of eastern Jerusalem which it had captured in the War of 1948. Though Israel originally accepted the Partition Resolution which recommended that Jerusalem be internationalized under the Trusteeship System, it withdrew its assent after it was invaded by five Arab states in the War of 1948.

In a statement to the Knesset on December 5, 1949, Prime Minister David Ben-Gurion presented Israel's new position on Jerusalem, that differed completely from its original acceptance of Resolution 181 (II) which he now stated was null and void. This was already evident from his isssuance of the Jerusalem Proclamation of August 2, 1948 and the Land of Israel Proclamation of September 2, 1948, two separate proclamations that incorporated into the borders of the State all the areas that had been repossessed by the IDF beyond the lines of the U.N. Partition Plan. Ben-Gurion stated:[40]

> ...Jewish Jerusalem is an organic and separate part of the State of Israel, as it is an inseparable part of the history and religion of Israel.
> ...We cannot conceive that the United Nations will try to tear Jerusalem from Israel or to impair the sovereignty of Israel *in its eternal capital* (emphasis added).
> ...We did not admit for one minute that the United Nations will try to take Jerusalem by force from Israel. We declare that Israel will not give up Jerusalem of its own free will just as throughout thousands of years it has not surrendered its faith, its national identity, and its hope to return to Jerusalem and Zion despite persecutions which have no parallel in history.
> ...We cannot likely regard the decision of 29 November 1947 as being possessed of any further moral force since the United Nations did not succeed in implementing its own decisions. In our view, the decision of 29 November about Jerusalem is null and void.

In a second statement to the Knesset on December 13, 1949, Ben-Gurion reiterated what he had declared the week before:[41]

> ...In the stress of war, when Jerusalem was under siege, we were compelled to establish the seat of Government in the Kirya at Tel-Aviv. But for the State of Israel there has always been and always will be one capital city – Jerusalem the Eternal. Thus it was 3,000 years ago – and thus it will be, we believe, until the end of time.

Faced with the united opposition of both Jordan and Israel to its plan to impose a U.N. Trusteeship on Jerusalem, the General Assembly took no

[40] *The Arab-Israel Conflict and its Resolution: Selected Documents*, edited by: Ruth Lapidoth and Moshe Hirsch, Martinus Nijhoff Publishers (1972), Document 16, p. 104 ff.

[41] *Ibid.*, p. 106.

further steps after 1952 to implement this plan. In light of Article 80 of the U.N. Charter and the acquired rights of the Jewish People under the Mandate and other acts of international law cited above, which contained no provision at all for the internationalization of Jerusalem, nor, for that matter, for the permanent partition of Palestine, the U.N. Trusteeship Statute for Jerusalem was not only unrealistic, but most important of all, an illegal intrusion in the governance of Palestine. Jerusalem was always meant, as Ben-Gurion stated, to be the capital of a Jewish State and not a city divided between Jews and Arabs and governed by the United Nations, as would have taken place had Jerusalem been internationalized.

Though Article 80 no longer applies to Palestine for the original purpose it was intended to serve, it has now taken on a different function directly related to the U.N. itself, namely, preventing the alteration of the legal rights of the Jewish People by the world organization. The U.N., under the influence of numerous Arab and Moslem states, frequently, through its various organs and agencies, adopts anti-Israel resolutions to deny or diminish Jewish rights to all of former Mandated Palestine in favour of alien Arabic-speaking Gentiles who are falsely called "Palestinians" and pretend to be the indigenous inhabitants of the country. All such resolutions are in violation of Article 80 and therefore illegal.

Another side of the coin in looking at Article 80 of the Charter was that until the Mandate ceased, it also maintained the rights of Great Britain as the Mandatory Power during the interim period prior to the making of a possible trusteeship agreement, since Article 80 also spoke of the "rights of states" charged with implementing a mandate, in addition to the "rights of peoples". The "rights of states" went hand in hand with all the obligations imposed upon states governing mandated territories. These rights and obligations permanently ended for Britain – unlike the rights accorded to the beneficiary nation, the Jewish People – when it voluntarily relinquished the Mandate for Palestine on May 15, 1948 signified by the departure from Haifa of the last High Commissioner for Palestine, Alan Gordon Cunningham.

What has been generally overlooked in examining the importance of Article 80 in regard to the Mandatory is the gross British violation of its obligation not to cede "Palestine territory" before Britain officially resigned its position as Mandatory. That violation first took place on January 17, 1946, three months after Article 80 had already been made applicable to Great Britain in regard to all of Palestine, when in an address on that date to the U.N. General Assembly at its first session in London, Foreign Secretary Ernest Bevin announced that Transjordan would soon be granted independence as a sovereign state as if there had existed a separate mandate for Transjordan in favour of the Arabs that was not subject to the strictures of Articles 2, 5 and 25 of the Mandate for Palestine which prevented that territory's permanent detachment from Palestine. In making this announcement, Bevin simply ignored Article 80 of the U.N. Charter which forbade Britain to alter the acquired legal rights of the

Jewish People to all parts of Mandated Palestine, which up to then still officially included Transjordan. No delegate attending this first session made any protest about the impending British move to sever the eastern part of Palestine from its historical frontiers. On February 9, 1946 the U.N. General Assembly unanimously expressed its approval of an independent Transjordan. In the last session of the Assembly of the League of Nations held at Geneva before its dissolution on April 18, 1946, it passed a farewell resolution approving and welcoming the termination of the mandated status of Transjordan.

However, it was the Permanent Mandates Commission and the League Council that were required to approve a step involving the modification of the Mandate for Palestine and not the League Assembly, whose approval was therefore legally irrelevant.

A second British violation occurred on March 22, 1946, when Bevin and Arthur Creech Jones, shortly to become Colonial Secretary, signed on behalf of the U.K. Government a 25-year Treaty of Alliance with Abdullah of Transjordan in which Britain recognized him as the sovereign of "a fully independent state". The treaty made no direct reference to the Mandate for Palestine and gave no reason for the permanent severance of Transjordan from Palestine. The British action was a glaring violation of both the Mandate for Palestine, particularly Articles 2, 5 and 25, and the U.N. Charter in regard to preserving Jewish rights and the terms of the existing Mandate, under Article 80 of the Charter. It was also a glaring violation of the Anglo-American Convention of December 3, 1924 respecting the Mandate for Palestine, in which Britain bound itself to consult with the United States Government and obtain its consent before any modification was made to the terms of the Mandate. These legal points were raised by Reform Rabbis Abba Hillel Silver and Stephen S. Wise, joint chairmen of the American Zionist Emergency Council, who sent a telegram to President Harry S. Truman on January 25, 1946 alleging "disregard" of the 1924 Convention and "defiance of American rights". It also stated that British policy was "an attempt... to avoid placing under [U.N.] trusteeship an area which Britain seeks as her exclusive influence", in defiance of Article 80 of the U.N. Charter.[42]

Britain was never brought to account for its illegal action in not restoring to the Jewish People on the day it surrendered the Mandate, all of the territory of Palestine which was originally placed in its hands in trust, to implement the Mandate granted to it on April 25, 1920 by the four-member Supreme Council of the Principal Allied Powers of World War I. The permanent detachment of Transjordan greatly prejudiced the legal rights of the Jewish People to a land with which it had an important historical connection in all periods of its history, dating from the time of Moses and his apportionment of land east of the Jordan to the tribes of Reuben, Gad and half the tribe of Menasseh.

Serious Jewish settlement projects were contemplated for Transjordan

[42] *Studies in the History of Transjordan, 1920-1949*, The Making of a State, Uriel Dann, Westview Press, Boulder, Colorado, p. 101.

as late as the mid-1930's, which were blocked by unflinching opposition of the British Government who even acted in this regard against the wishes of Abdullah himself, who favoured leasing land to Jews to foster its development and inaugurate a new era in Arab-Jewish relations. A plan to settle millions of Jews in Transjordan, which Article 25 of the Mandate called "the eastern boundary of Palestine", was proposed by a U.S. Senator from Delaware, Daniel O. Hastings, in a series of six articles published in the *New York American* newspaper between October 22 and November 2, 1936. To emphasize his plan he wrote the following capitalized sentence in the body of the sixth and final article of the series:[43]

> SEVERAL MILLION ADDITIONAL JEWISH FUGITIVES COULD BE PROVIDED FOR IF THEY COULD CROSS THE JORDAN AND BE ALLOWED TO SETTLE IN TRANSJORDAN.

He added:

> If Transjordan could be opened to the Jews through a change of policy on the part of the British Government which controls it, it would soon become a rich country. If the British Government could work out some plan of peace and good-will between the Arabs in Palestine and in Transjordan, and have the Mandate modified accordingly, it would not only go a long way in solving the problem of the Jews, but it would make out of these two countries rich and prosperous States

Despite Senator Hastings' strong urgings and the concurrent and separate efforts of the Jewish Agency to realize a project of this kind, the British Government refused to budge from its *Judenrein* policy for Transjordan and thus blocked any chance that this territory could still be developed to become a flourishing part of the Jewish National Home, as originally envisaged in the San Remo Resolution, the Mandate for Palestine and the Franco-British Boundary Convention of December 23, 1920 all of which assumed that Transjordan constituted part of the historical frontiers of Palestine. Britain thus illegally deprived the Jewish People of a major part of its homeland by working behind the scenes to squelch or foil any Jewish initiatives to settle Transjordan.

The attitude of the U.S. Administration regarding the granting by Britain of independence to Transjordan was not much different from that of the U.N. General Assembly (as exhibited on January 17, 1946 and February 9, 1946) or the League of Nations Assembly (as expressed on April 18, 1946). To the relief of Britain, the U.S. found no legal grounds for opposing the independence of Transjordan. In a memorandum dated February 26, 1946 prepared by Mrs.

---

[43] Senator Hastings' statements were printed in the Reports of the Hearst Unofficial Senatorial Commission under the title *The Crisis in Palestine*; reproduced in *The Rise of Israel*, Vol. 19, Document 39, p. 602 ff., at pp. 672-673.

Christina P. Grant, then the area specialist in the Division of Near Eastern Affairs, it was stated:[44]

> In the past the Government of the United States has taken the position that it is not empowered, under the articles of the American-British Convention of December 3, 1924, to prevent the modification of the terms of any of the mandates... The United States could not take any obstructive position with respect to the proposed independence of Transjordan without jeopardizing its relations with the whole Arab world ...It is our present policy, subject to the approval of the Secretary [James Francis Byrnes] to recognize the independence of Transjordan, as in the case of the Levant States [Syria and Lebanon], on securing a satisfactory assurance of the continuation of the rights guaranteed the United States under the American-British Convention of 1924. Formal termination of the Mandate with respect to Transjordan would be generally recognized upon the admission of the latter into the United Nations as a fully independent country...

On April 23, 1946 Secretary Byrnes set out the American policy in regard to the independence of Transjordan in a press release issued by the State Department:[45]

> After a careful study of the matter, the Department has found nothing which would justify it in taking the position that the recent steps taken by Great Britain with regard to Transjordan violate any treaties existing between Great Britain and the United States, including the Convention of December 3, 1924 or deprive the United States of any rights or interests which the United States may have with respect to Transjordan. The Department considers, however, that it would be premature for this government to take any decision at the present time with respect to the question of its recognition of Transjordan as an independent state".

Instead of Britain being severely reprimanded or condemned by the United States for illegally partitioning Palestine, whose territorial integrity both countries were legally obliged to preserve under Articles 2, 5 and 25 of the Mandate and Article 80 of the U.N. Charter, the American Government refused to see the independence of Transjordan in that light. It adopted the very same position towards the Anglo-Transjordanian Treaty of March 22, 1946 as it did towards the British White Paper of May 17, 1939, i.e., that the U.S. had no power to prevent any modification in the terms of the Mandate that did not prejudice its

---

[44] Uriel Dann, *op. cit.*, pp. 94-95. See also *Foreign Relations of the United States, 1946*, Vol. VII, p.798.

[45] Uriel Dann, *op. cit.*, p. 98.

rights and interests under the articles of the American-British Convention of December 3, 1924. This was a self-imposed restriction of its prerogatives under the Convention that was untenable, as previously discussed in Chapter 9. In addition, the U.S. was reluctant to block the independence of Transjordan out of fear of harming its interests in the wider Arab world. In the event, all the U.S. actually did was to defer recognition of the new kingdom of Transjordan until it received an assurance of the economic, commercial and cultural rights it had under the 1924 Convention. It also wanted to make sure that Transjordan was in fact truly independent and was not a continuing British dependency. As a result of this last consideration, it was not until January 31, 1949 that the White House announced *de jure* recognition of Transjordan concurrently with that of Israel.

The only substantial protests made that questioned the legal validity of Transjordan's independence, apart from Zionist sources,[46] came from the United States Congress. Two resolutions were passed in the House of Representatives on April 9 and July 1, 1946 and one in the United States Senate on July 2, 1946. These resolutions condemned the British action and requested the U.S. Government not to recognize "the Transjordan area of Palestine as a separate or independent state". The Senate resolution stated that the international status of Transjordan should not be settled "until such time as the future status of Palestine as a whole should be determined".[47]

In retrospect, it may be said that Article 80, after its incorporation into the U.N. Charter, did serve as an additional safeguard for protecting Jewish

---

[46] In addition to the protest made by the representatives of the American Zionist Emergency Council with regard to Transjordan's permanent removal from Palestine, an exceptional and well-formulated protest came from Dr. Paul Riebenfeld, Chairman of the New Zionist Organization in London. He issued a statement on behalf of his organization to express "opposition to the imminent independence of Transjordan on the ground that the territory was an integral part of Mandated Palestine". "Mr. Bevin's announcement must be fought not only on a purely political level, but also on a legal plane," he said. Dr. Riebenfeld further stated that Bevin's announcement flouted the authority of the U.N. because the termination of the Mandate will in the future be the concern of the Trusteeship Council. Britain had acted "when the League of Nations is defunct and when its functions with regard to the Mandate have not yet been properly taken over by the U.N....". See the report of the *Jewish Telegraphic Agency*, Daily News Bulletin, Vol. XIII, No. 15, Friday, January 18, 1946. Another strong protest came from Peter Bergson (born Hillel Kook), Chairman of the Hebrew Committee of National Liberation as well as the American League for a Free Palestine. He dispatched a letter on January 19, 1946 to Dean Acheson, then the Undersecretary of State, in which he stated that the British intention to grant independence to Transjordan would "deprive the Hebrew people of three-fourths of their national territory which is theirs from time immemorial by the will of God and which has been recognized as such in modern times by the Mandate of the League of Nations". Quoted in Uriel Dann, *op. cit.*, p. 100. A similar appeal but without any reference to God was made by the New Zionist [Revisionist] Organization of America [NZO] in a letter sent by its president, Colonel Morris J. Mendelsohn, to President Truman.

[47] *Ibid.*, p.103.

legal rights to Palestine during the entire time it was applicable to the country in regard to converting the Mandate regime into a possible trusteeship. On the other hand, it failed dismally to prevent the permanent detachment of Transjordan from Palestine and the Jewish National Home or the violation of acquired Jewish legal rights and title of sovereignty to the rest of the country engendered by the Partition Resolution of November 29, 1947. Neither the British nor the Americans heeded the strict requirements of Article 80. Had they done so, Transjordan would not have been permanently detached from Palestine.

Today it would be wiser for three separate reasons not to rely upon Article 80 at all except for the purpose of denouncing as illegal any U.N. resolutions which seek to alter Jewish rights and title to the Land of Israel. First, because all provisions of the Charter relating to the Trusteeship System for the conversion of mandated territories to trust territories have lapsed in a practical sense with the independence of all countries that were once either mandated or trust territories. Second, because Jewish rights under international law are better protected or ensured by invoking the principle of acquired legal rights as codified in Article 70 (1)(b) of the Vienna Convention on the Law of Treaties and the doctrine of estoppel rather than by relying on Article 80, which was originally meant to be only for a temporary and transitional purpose, until a trusteeship agreement was made to replace a mandate.

Third and finally, if Article 80 were still in effect today in regard to Palestine for converting any part of the country into a trust territory, particularly in regard to Judea, Samaria and Gaza, the U.N. could then likely try to forcefully intervene in the affairs of these areas of the Jewish National Home by advocating that they become "trust territories" in the same manner it once attempted to do with regard to Jerusalem. This inimical idea has already been advocated by a number of anti-nationalist Israelis, counting among them former Prime Minister Shim'on Peres and former Meretz party leader, Yossi Sarid, as well as by foreign public figures who wish to see these National Home territories ruled by the "Palestine Liberation Organization" and its offshoot, the "Palestinian Authority". U.N. intervention in the form of a trusteeship for Judea, Samaria and Gaza would be illegal on its face, and if allowed to be consummated, would create a whole new disaster for the State of Israel.

From the foregoing, it should be evident that Article 80 of the U.N. Charter did not create or even serve to confirm in a positive sense Jewish legal rights to the Land of Israel under international law. Its function was to prevent the alteration of or tampering with Jewish legal rights that already existed under international law from the moment the U.N. Charter was ratified until the time a trusteeship agreement could be concluded to replace the Mandate. It therefore preserved the *status quo* for a limited period of time that long ago expired. Those Jewish legal rights were originally created by the San Remo Resolution acting as a base document, in conjunction with Article 22 of the League Covenant and the Smuts Resolution, and then confirmed by the Mandate for Palestine and the Franco-British Boundary Convention of December 23, 1920. They were reinforced by the Anglo-American Convention of December 3, 1924. They continue to have legal force today not by virtue of Article 80, but by virtue of the principle of acquired legal rights and the doctrine of estoppel, two sides of the same coin, the former affirming them while the latter prevents their denial by states which previously recognized their existence as members of the League of Nations or, in the case of the United States, by an international treaty. Article 80 remains of value only as a potential shield or defence to block U.N. infringement of Jewish national rights in the recovered possessions of Judea, Samaria and, formerly, Gaza. For this exclusive purpose it should be invoked by the State of Israel.

*Section Three*

# Why Jewish Legal Rights and Title of Sovereignty over Palestine and the Land of Israel Became Obscured and Forgotten

*Chapter 11*

# Kemal Ataturk's Overthrow of the Ottoman Empire and the Consequent Replacement of the Treaty of Sèvres by the Treaty of Lausanne

What was clearly and precisely established in regard to Jewish legal rights and title to all of Palestine under international law, as evidenced by five separate acts of international law: the Smuts Resolution, the forerunner of Article 22 of the Covenant of the League of Nations; the San Remo Resolution on Palestine; the Mandate for Palestine; and the Franco-British Boundary Convention of December 23, 1920, soon became subject to ambiguity and obfuscation. That occurred when the global political and legal settlement contained in the Treaty of Sèvres, which carved up the remnants of the Ottoman Empire covering the Middle East and parts of southeastern Europe,[1] partly fell apart by the coming to power of General Mustafa Kemal, later called Kemal Ataturk ("Father of Turks"), who overthrew the last Ottoman sultan, Muhammad VI, and created the modern state of Turkey as a secular republic. To meet the changed situation brought about by Ataturk, whose military forces ousted the Armenians, Georgians, Italians, French and Greeks from Anatolia and dashed any hopes for an autonomous or independent Kurdistan, the British Government negotiated a new armistice agreement with Nationalist Turkey, signed at Mudania on October 11, 1922. This was followed by the negotiation of a formal peace treaty, the Treaty of Lausanne, that superceded the Treaty of Sèvres.

Ambiguity and obfuscation occurred in Jewish legal rights and title of sovereignty over Palestine despite the fact that Ataturk did not contest the provisions in the Treaty of Sèvres relating to the disposition of Palestine, nor those relating to the disposition of the Arabic-speaking countries in Asia and North Africa, except as regards Mosul held by Iraq and Alexandretta (now Iskenderun) included in French-administered Syria. What upset him most of all were the territorial losses Turkey suffered in Asia Minor or Anatolia, particularly in Smyrna, Antalya, Cilicia and the Armenian and Kurdish areas in the east of the

[1] In the Balkan Wars of 1912-13 just prior to World War I, Turkey lost all of its territories in Europe to Bulgaria, Serbia, Greece and newly independent Albania, except for the area of Constantinople. It had also lost its former possessions in North Africa.

peninsula, as well as in European Turkey (Eastern Thrace), which dismembered the country in its core parts.[2]

Dissatisfied with these territorial dispositions in regard to Anatolia and Eastern Thrace, Ataturk campaigned vigorously against the Allied settlement contained in the Treaty of Sèvres, which reduced the once proud Ottoman Empire to the rump of a small state. He set up a unified committee called "the Society for the Defence of Rights in Anatolia and Rumelia", to preserve the unity of the Turkish fatherland in defiance of the victorious Allies.[3] It was therefore no surprise that after he seized power in what remained of the Ottoman Empire, he refused to ratify the Treaty of Sèvres, which had already been signed by three representatives of the deposed Sultan's government. This prevented the treaty as a whole, with its clear and precise provisions on Palestine, which left no doubt about Jewish legal rights and title of sovereignty to the country, from ever coming into legal force. These provisions were not included again in the succeeding Treaty of Lausanne of July 24, 1923 (ratified on August 6, 1924) which restored to Turkey almost all of the territories in Anatolia and Eastern Thrace which the Sultan's Government had conceded in the Treaty of Sèvres, including the waterways which separated the Gallipoli peninsula of European Turkey from Asian Turkey.

To understand more fully how this change in the global settlement created ambiguity in Jewish legal rights and title of sovereignty to Palestine, one need only examine and compare the respective provisions of the two peace treaties. In the Treaty of Sèvres, Palestine is specifically dealt with together with Syria and Mesopotamia under Section VII. The relevant clauses for these three countries are found in Articles 94 to 97 inclusively, as well as Article 132. They read as follows:

---

[2] Under articles 70 and 83 of the Treaty of Sèvres, Turkey was obliged to accept temporary Greek administration of the Smyrna (Izmir) district though it remained under Turkish sovereignty, pending a plebiscite to determine its permanent status. It ceded most of Eastern Thrace to Greece, retaining only Constantinople and part of the Zone of the Straits, (Dardanelles; Bosporus), which was to be internationalised and demilitarised to ensure the freedom of navigation for the ships of all states. The Straits extended from the Aegean outlet of the Dardanelles, the Sea of Marmora up to the Black Sea outlet of the Bosporus. The Zone included the European and Asian banks of these waterways. The Treaty of Sèvres also provided for an autonomous Kurdistan to be set up in the predominantly Kurdish areas of Anatolia, which lay east of the Euphrates and north of the frontier of Turkey with Syria and Mesopotamia. Finally it provided for an Armenian state in north-eastern Anatolia, embracing four Turkish provinces (Erzurum, Trebizond, Van and Bitlis) with access to the Black Sea. This state was to comprise a Russian part as well.

[3] Rumelia is an area of the Balkan Peninsula that refers particularly to Thrace and the region of Macedonia of the Ottoman Empire. Thrace is today part of three countries, comprising North-east Greece, Southern Bulgaria and European Turkey.

*Article 94*

The High Contracting Parties agree that Syria and Mesopotamia, in accordance with the fourth paragraph of Article 22, Part I (Covenant of the League of Nations), be provisionally recognized as independent states subject to the rendering of administrative advice and assistance by a Mandatory until such time as they are able to stand alone…

*Article 95*

The High Contracting Parties agree to entrust, by application of the provisions of Article 22, the administration of Palestine, within such boundaries as may be determined by the Principal Allied Powers, to a Mandatory to be selected by the said Powers. The Mandatory will be responsible for putting into effect the declaration originally made on November 2, 1917, by the British Government, and adopted by the other Allied Powers, in favour of the establishment in Palestine of a national home for the Jewish people, it being clearly understood that nothing shall be done which may prejudice the civil and religious rights of existing non-Jewish communities in Palestine, or the rights and political status enjoyed by Jews in any other country.

The Mandatory undertakes to appoint as soon as possible a special Commission to study and regulate all questions and claims relating to the different religious communities. In the composition of the Commission the religious interests concerned will be taken into account. The Chairman of the Commission will be appointed by the Council of the League of Nations.

*Article 96*

The terms of the mandates in respect of the above territories will be formulated by the Principal Allied Powers and submitted to the Council of the League of Nations for approval.

*Article 97*

Turkey hereby undertakes, in accordance with the provisions of Article 132, to accept any decisions which may be taken in relation to the questions dealt with in this Section.

*Article 132*

Outside her frontier as fixed by the present Treaty, Turkey *hereby renounces in favour of the Principal Allied Powers* (emphasis added) all rights and title which she could claim on any ground over or *concerning any territories outside Europe which are not otherwise disposed of by the present Treaty* (emphasis added).

Turkey undertakes to recognize and conform to the measures which may be taken now or in the future by the Principal Allied Powers, in agreement where necessary with third Powers, in order to carry the above stipulation into effect.

The foregoing provisions of the Treaty of Sèvres should make it obvious that Palestine was created as a separate state or territory for one reason only by the Supreme Council of the Principal Allied Powers: to put into effect the Balfour Declaration in order to satisfy Jewish Zionist aspirations which would eventually make Palestine into an independent Jewish State, in accordance with the *general* provisions and principles of Article 22 of the Covenant of the League of Nations, rather than the specific provisions of that same Article as found in paragraphs 4 to 6 thereof which applied to all other mandated territories that formerly were either included in the Ottoman Empire or were German colonies in Central Africa, South-West Africa and certain of the Pacific Ocean Islands, both north and south of the Equator. Palestine, when it was created as a mandated territory on April 24-25, 1920 at the San Remo Peace Conference, was never meant to satisfy Arab national aspirations in any part of the country, either east or west of the Jordan. These aspirations were to be satisfied under the Mandates System in Syria and Mesopotamia. The Arab peoples destined for independence under the Mandates System were referred to as "certain communities" in paragraph 4 of Article 22 of the Covenant and were specifically identified as Syria and Mesopotamia in Article 94 of the Treaty of Sèvres. By way of contrast, Article 95 of the Treaty of Sèvres, in providing for the administration of Palestine, deliberately refrained from expressly mentioning paragraph 4 of Article 22 of the Covenant or any other particular paragraph of that article, but simply alluded to the provisions of Article 22 in general, which constitutes ample proof as to what the Principal Allied Powers intended to do. Syria and Mesopotamia were reserved for the Arabs, as provided for by paragraph 4, while the whole of Palestine was exclusively allocated to the Jewish People, as provided for by the general provisions of Article 22 without anyone then ever imagining that it would one day be further partitioned into Jewish and Arab parts.[4] The two Arab-populated mandated territories (Syria and Mesopotamia) were provisionally recognized as independent states, while Palestine, even though it too had a preponderant majority Arab population,[5] was set aside in favour of the establishment of a national home for the Jewish People. It was expected, before Britain introduced illegal restrictions, that the

[4] The same distinction made in the Treaty of Sèvres that Palestine was to be governed in the general spirit and principles of Article 22 of the League Covenant without specifying any exact paragraph thereof, while both Mesopotamia and Syria would be governed in accordance with the specific provision of paragraph 4 of Article 22 of the Covenant can also be deduced by comparing the Mandate for Palestine with the Draft Mandate for Mesopotamia and the officially adopted Mandate for Syria and Lebanon of July 24, 1922.

[5] The figures given in the Peel Report are half-a-million Arabs and 65,000 Jews in 1919; *The Rise of Israel*, Vol. 24, Document 2, p.60.

home would over the course of time evolve into an independent Jewish State through the anticipated influx of millions of Jewish immigrants and their close settlement on the land under the auspices of a Mandatory appointed for this purpose. In accordance with Articles 94, 95 and 132 of the Treaty of Sèvres, that was how the territories of Turkey outside Europe, namely Palestine, Mesopotamia and Syria, were "disposed of" under the Mandates System.

In a legal opinion, William Finlay, K.C. (later Justice Finlay) commented on the major points of difference between Palestine and the other Mandates:[6]

> The provisions of Article 22 are to be applied, but for the purposes laid down in the Treaty of Sèvres and, if there were any inconsistency between Article 95 of the Treaty of Sèvres and the Mandate on the one hand and Article 22 on the other (which, in my opinion… there is not) Article 95 would prevail. That this is the real position is, I think, shown by the fact that Palestine does not really fall within any of the three categories laid down in Article 22 and the validity of the Mandate depends upon Article 95 of the Treaty of Sèvres, *which applies to the special case of Palestine the provisions of Article 22*. …My attention was called in conference to the last sentence of the fourth paragraph. But I do not think this sentence is relevant to the matter I have to consider (1) because I do not think this paragraph applicable to Palestine; (2) because it *is only in the selection of the Mandatory* that the wishes of the community must be a principal consideration; (3) because the words are "*a* principal consideration" and not "*the* principal consideration"…
>
> I now turn to the draft Mandate for Palestine. This Mandate lays down the general principles upon which the administration is to be conducted and it appears to me that it is in complete accord with the general principles laid down in Article 22 (all the italics in the original).

It should be noted that Article 95 of the Treaty of Sèvres (mentioned by William Finlay in his legal opinion) was nothing other than the re-production of the text of the fundamental juridical act of international law, the San Remo Resolution on Palestine that was agreed to at the San Remo Peace Conference only four months earlier, on April 24-25, 1920. The Treaty of Sèvres also made it clear that the coalition of Principal Allied Powers (consisting of Britain, France, Italy and Japan) were the disposing sovereign authority in effecting this orderly allocation of mandated territories in the Middle East, as can be verified by Article 132 of the Treaty. It was in favour of these Great Powers that Turkey

---

[6] Finlay's opinion was printed in the official Journal of the League of Nations for August 1921 and also as Appendix II attached to the Memorandum submitted by the Jewish Agency for Palestine on November 20, 1936 for the consideration of the Palestine Royal Commission. The Memorandum was reprinted by Greenwood Press, Westport, Connecticut in 1975. Finlay's opinion, dated April 8, 1921, is on pp. 293-295.

renounced all rights and title to Palestine, Mesopotamia and Syria.

The only point in Finlay's well-founded expert opinion that may be somewhat misleading is his statement that "Palestine does not really fall within any of the three categories laid down in Article 22 [of the League Covenant]. It is true that Palestine did not have the same kind of administration as Syria and Mesopotamia, that were – together with Palestine – classified as "A" Mandates. Palestine was thus considered to have its own special characteristics differing from those of the other two "A" Mandates. On this particular point, the Chairman of the Permanent Mandates Commission, Pierre Orts of Belgium, voiced his opinion on August 5, 1937 when he stated:[7]

> For the Mandates Commission, Palestine had never ceased to constitute a separate entity. It was one of those territories which, under the terms of the Covenant, might be regarded as "provisionally independent". The country was administered under an "A" mandate by the United Kingdom, subject to certain conditions and particularly to the condition appearing in Article 5: "The Mandatory shall be responsible to see that no Palestine territory shall be… in any way placed under the control of the Government of any foreign Power."

The easily understood provisions of the Treaty of Sèvres regarding Palestine and other Middle Eastern territories were replaced three years later by a single provision in the Treaty of Lausanne following the revolutionary change of regime in Turkey from sultanate to republic, under the leadership of Mustafa Kemal. That single provision contained in Article 16 of the Treaty was too brief and vague to give a full understanding of the recognition of Jewish legal rights and title of sovereignty over Palestine, that was the unmistakable message of the relevant provisions of the earlier Treaty of Sèvres quoted above. It reads as follows:

> *Article 16*
>
> Turkey *hereby renounces* (emphasis added) all rights and title whatsoever over or respecting the territories situated outside the frontiers laid down in the present Treaty and the islands other than those over which her sovereignty is recognized by the said Treaty, the future of these territories and islands *being settled or to be settled by the parties concerned* (emphasis added).
>
> The provisions of the present article do not prejudice any special arrangements arising from neighbourly relations which have been or may be concluded between Turkey and any limitrophe countries.

A comparison of Article 16 of the Treaty of Lausanne with the articles of

[7] See: *The Rise of Israel*, Vol. 25, Document 4, p. 176.

the earlier Treaty of Sèvres reveals significant changes. First, the party in favour of whom Turkey renounced "all rights and title whatsoever over or respecting the territories situated outside the [newly-drawn] frontiers [of Turkey"' is not identified in the Treaty of Lausanne, as it was in the Treaty of Sèvres. However, this identification was unnecessary because the mandated territories had already been disposed of by the Principal Allied Powers three years earlier at the San Remo Peace Conference of 1920, thus making it redundant to designate once again those same Powers as the legal successor to Turkish sovereignty over those territories that were no longer in Turkish hands. This is evidenced by the fact that the Principal Allied Powers were listed in the Treaty of Lausanne simply by their individual names, in sharp contrast to the style adopted in the by-now-defunct Treaty of Sèvres where this designation – "the Principal Allied Powers" – was actually used. It is also interesting to note that the Treaty of Sèvres was concluded not with the Ottoman Empire, which was by then no longer functioning, but with Turkey, though represented by the Government of Sultan Muhammad VI at Constantinople. The Treaty of Lausanne was also concluded with Turkey, but this time the country was represented by the nationalist government of Kemal Ataturk at Ankara, formally styled the "Government of the Grand National Assembly of Turkey".

Second, the new treaty of 1923 omitted all reference to the Middle East Mandates conferred on Mandatories, contrary to what had been provided for in the Treaty of Sèvres. These two changes arose because of the rapid pace of events taking place in the governance of the mandated territories from Ottoman Turkish rule to a short interim period of collective Allied *military* government ("collective" more in theory than in practice) to Mandatory *civilian* administration. At the time the Treaty of Sèvres was signed, on August 10, 1920, civilian administration had barely begun in those territories, whereas by the time the Treaty of Lausanne was signed on July 24, 1923, a civilian regime under overall Mandatory control had already been in continuous operation for three years, with the terms of the Mandates for Palestine, Syria and Lebanon having already been confirmed. Moreover, the Draft Mandate for Mesopotamia had been replaced by a Treaty of Alliance between Great Britain and Iraq. However, a final settlement still had to be achieved between Italy and France with regard to Italian commercial rights and interests in southern Anatolia, before legal force was attributed to the French and British Mandates for Syria, Lebanon and Palestine. Inasmuch as the settlement in regard to these countries was still being negotiated or worked out and had not yet gone into legal force at the time the Treaty of Lausanne was signed with Nationalist Turkey, the situation then prevailing was correctly described as *being settled by the parties concerned* in Article 16 of the treaty. In addition, another bone of contention still *to be settled* was the rectification of boundaries involving Turkey, Syria and Iraq.

A third significant difference between the Treaty of Sèvres and the Treaty of Lausanne was that the former contained all of the twenty-six articles pertaining to the League Covenant and the Mandates system, while those same articles were not reproduced in the Treaty of Lausanne. The League Covenant was excluded because its provisions had already been put into effect after the ratification of the Treaty of Versailles on January 10, 1920, and upon the ratification of several other peace treaties with the Central Powers. There was, therefore, no need to include the Covenant once again in the Treaty of Lausanne.

In sum, by 1923 there was no longer any compelling reason, as there had been in 1920, to spell out in the new peace treaty with Turkey all the exact details or arrangements for the "A" Mandates that were already being implemented. The result of all these developments between 1920 and 1923 was the insertion of a lone article in the Treaty of Lausanne devoted to the newly-created mandated territories, rather than several articles as characterised the Treaty of Sèvres. The language of that lone article did, however, resemble that of Articles 97 and 132 of the earlier treaty in that both of those articles referred to the decisions or measures "which may be taken now or in the future by the Principal Allied Powers", which was hardly different in meaning from the content of Article 16.

In reading the text of Article 16 of the Treaty of Lausanne, it can be seen that no express mention of Palestine or of the Jewish National Home was made in that provision, nor for that matter was there any mention of Syria, Mesopotamia and the Hedjaz.[8] All of these four states or countries were included implicitly in the reference to "the territories situated outside the frontiers of Turkey laid down in the Treaty". Both Palestine and the Hedjaz were already completely outside the orbit of concern of Turkey; hence there was no need to mention either of them in the Treaty of Lausanne. After the Ottoman Empire had agreed to the Treaty of Sèvres that disposed of Palestine and the Hedjaz and in light of the fact that the new national government of Turkey under Ataturk never questioned the loss of these two countries, it may be concluded that Turkey had implictly consented to all of the previous decisions made by the Allied Powers concerning their new status. It was necessary to allude to Syria and Iraq in other provisions of the Treaty of Lausanne only in connection with the delineation of their common frontiers with Turkey but not in reference to their new legal status as provisionally recognized independent states detached from the Ottoman Empire, subject to the rendering of administrative advice and assistance by a Mandatory, in accordance with paragraph 4 of Article 22 of the League Covenant.

*The parties concerned*, as mentioned in the text of Article 16, who were responsible

---

[8] The Hedjaz was recognized as a sovereign state by Britain and its allies when Hussein ibn Ali, the Emir of Mecca, proclaimed himself "King of the Arabs" on October 30, 1916. In Article 98 of the Treaty of Sèvres, Turkey, in accordance with the action already taken by the Allied Powers, recognized the Hedjaz as a free and independent State and renounced in favour of the Hedjaz all rights and titles over the territories of the former Turkish Empire comprised within the boundaries of the Hedjaz as ultimately fixed. This provision was omitted in the Treaty of Lausanne. The Hedjaz was one of the states that signed the Treaty of Versailles on June 28, 1919, but refused to ratify it. It was designated as a state party to the Treaty of Sèvres but did not sign it. It was not a party to the Treaty of Lausanne.

for making and implementing a comprehensive settlement for the future of these territories could have only been, at the time this article was drafted, the alliance or group of states that comprised the Principal Allied Powers, namely Great Britain, France, Italy and Japan. The Zionist Organization representing the Jewish People, the national beneficiary of the Mandate for Palestine, was not a state party to the overall settlement, but in fact worked with Britain to help draft the Mandate as part of this settlement, which was natural considering that Palestine was specifically created to be the Jewish National Home. That made the Zionists, in effect, one of *the parties concerned* in determining the future of Palestine. By contrast, neither the Arabs of Palestine nor any Arab State were one of *the parties concerned* in this matter. They were not consulted in the formulation of the draft Mandate for Palestine and only learned of its terms after it had already been submitted to the Council of the League of Nations for confirmation. It was only then – in 1921 and 1922, at the time Winston Churchill was the Colonial Secretary – that the Arabs of Palestine represented by a body calling itself The Palestine Arab Delegation, led by Moussa Kazim el-Husseini, expressed very strong opposition to the proposed Mandate Charter and lobbied unsuccessfully in various European countries against its confirmation. The Arabs of Palestine also submitted many memoranda, appeals and letters to the Permanent Mandates Commission and the British Government protesting the terms of the Mandate for Palestine.

Finally, it should be noted that the United States was not one of the parties concerned at this juncture, since it was not a member of the coalition of powers that had declared war and fought against the Ottoman Empire though diplomatic relations between them were severed by the Imperial Turkish Government on April 20, 1917, after the U.S. declared itself to be in a state of war with Germany, the ally of the Ottoman Government. And by the time the U.S. concluded a treaty with Britain on December 3, 1924, regarding the Mandate for Palestine, the settlement referred to in Article 16 of the Treaty of Lausanne had already been completed and made final.

The limitrophe or bordering countries mentioned in the second paragraph of Article 16, with whom Turkey had already concluded "special arrangements" or may have needed to do so in the future, referred to several different border rectifications. One concerned the unresolved Turkish-Iraqi dispute over Mosul,[9] another was the unresolved Turkish-Syrian dispute over Alexandretta. Still other "special arrangements" that were either made or needed to be made in regard to the limitrophe or adjoining countries of Turkey involved Greece and Bulgaria on the European side of Turkey and with Soviet Russia concerning Armenia on the northeastern border of Turkey.[10]

---

[9] Specific mention of the arrangement that needed to be made for Mosul was provided for in Article 3(2) of the Treaty of Lausanne which said: "The frontier between Turkey and Iraq shall be laid down in friendly arrangement to be concluded between Turkey and Great Britain within nine months".

[10] The fate and fortune of Armenia waxed and waned from 1917 onwards. After

Despite the fact that the Treaty of Sèvres which incorporated the San Remo Resolution on Palestine was replaced by the Treaty of Lausanne, without any explicit provisions on the Jewish National Home, the Treaty of Sèvres, while not in legal force, still remained valid as an Inter-Allied Agreement between the four Great Powers of World War I, Britain, France, Italy and Japan, indicating what the Allied intentions were in regard to Palestine. This is attested to by the fact that all of the former provisions of the Treaty of Sèvres on Palestine were subsequently implemented in the Mandate conferred on Great Britain, and confirmed by the League of Nations. In effect, the provisions of the Treaty of Sèvres relating to Palestine were simply transferred to the Mandate Charter where they found expression in the first three recitals of the Preamble of the Mandate, thus making those provisions containing the San Remo Resolution a part of international law. Insofar as Palestine was concerned, Ataturk's refusal to ratify the Treaty of Sèvres did not affect the legal rights and title of sovereignty of the Jewish People to Palestine, but did succeed in obscuring them, since they were not explicitly enunciated in the Treaty of Lausanne.

---

the 1917 Bolshevik Revolution, it joined a short-lived anti-Bolshevik federation with Azerbaijan and Georgia known as the Transcaucasian Federation. In May 1918, the federation broke up when each of the constituent components declared its own independence. Armenia became independent under German auspices as a result of the Brest-Litovsk Treaty of March 3, 1918 concluded between Soviet Russia and Germany and the other Central Powers. This treaty restored the old boundaries between Russia and Turkey as they existed prior to the Treaty of Berlin (1878), which meant the exclusion of the Armenian districts of Kars and Ardahan from the State of Armenia. These districts had been recaptured by Turkey from Russia in World War I. In the wake of the general armistice of November 11, 1918 which ended military operations, Germany was obliged to renounce the Brest-Litovsk Treaty and Russia also declared it null and void. Under the Armistice of Mudros with Turkey of October 30, 1918, the Allied Powers reserved the right to occupy or take control of Transcaucasia including the Turkish-Armenian provinces. The Armenians then received a big boost from the Treaty of Sèvres of August 10, 1920 which created a free and independent Armenia, comprising Turkish and Russian areas. The state of Armenia soon collapsed – the Russian part became a Soviet republic and the Turkish part reverted to Turkish sovereignty. The end came with the signing of a Russo-Turkish Friendship Treaty on March 16, 1921. From 1922 to 1936, a smaller Armenia was again combined with Azerbaijan and Georgia, but this time as the Soviet federated socialist republic of Transcaucasia. It was dissolved in 1936 and Armenia then became a separate constituent republic of the USSR until 1991, when it declared itself independent. The fate of Armenia had an impact on Palestine because the removal of areas of northeastern Anatolia from Turkey and their joinder to the state of Armenia as laid out in the Treaty of Sèvres was one of the contributing factors which impelled the Kemalist Government to refuse the ratification of this treaty which also contained the San Remo Resolution, the basis of Jewish legal rights and title of sovereignty over Palestine under international law. As discussed in this chapter, the scrapping of the Treaty of Sèvres was a major reason in obscuring or dimming Jewish national rights over Palestine.

*Chapter 12*

# Effecting a Transfer of Sovereignty without A Peace Treaty by Subjugation or Consent after a Simple Cessation of Hostilities

The Treaty of Lausanne which replaced the clear and unambiguous terms of the Treaty of Sèvres in regard to the disposition of the ex-Turkish provinces in the Middle East caused a lot of confusion in the following years about the question of sovereignty over the mandated territories, specifically as regards the party or parties upon whom sovereignty was devolved or vested as well as the date of actual transfer of sovereignty. In an earlier chapter it was shown that sovereignty could not have been vested in either the League of Nations or the Mandatory Power, but was placed in the collective hands of the Principal Allied Powers who then transferred this right to the designated national beneficiaries of the mandated territories. In this Chapter, the concept of sovereignty will be further discussed in terms of all the peace treaties concluded after World War I, which created the Mandates System, the exact dates for the two-step transfer of sovereignty over the mandated territories and the reasons therefor under the applicable rules of international law.

The problem of ascertaining the locus of sovereignty for territories subject to a mandate, particularly in reference to Palestine, Mesopotamia and Syria, arose because the details about it were not to be found explicitly in any of the provisions of the Treaty of Lausanne, but rather in the provisions of the unratified Treaty of Sèvres and the other peace treaties made with Germany, Austria, Hungary and Bulgaria. Without reference to these treaties, it is impossible to have a clear understanding of how the title of sovereignty devolved from the Ottoman Empire to the Principal Allied Powers and then to the national beneficiary of the Mandate for each particular mandated territory and the date this devolution occurred. For this purpose a comparative look at the relevant provisions in all of these peace treaties needs to be made.

Starting with the Treaty of Sèvres, the question of sovereignty as noted in the preceding chapter is addressed in Article 132 of the treaty, where it is clearly stated that Turkey renounced in favour of the Principal Allied Powers all rights and title over or concerning any territories outside Europe which are not otherwise disposed of by that treaty. This provision by its sweeping language covered all the territories that were outside Turkey's newly-drawn national frontiers, whether they were under mandate, such as Palestine, Mesopotamia and Syria, or other countries not under mandate but also destined for self-determination, including, *inter alia*, the Hedjaz, Egypt, Cyprus and Libya. Article 132 was in effect a catch-all provision that eliminated any trace or claim of lingering Turkish sovereignty over any of its former territories in Asia and Africa that were once included in the Ottoman Empire.

Article 132 undoubtedly applied to the Sinai Peninsula, which was then neither included in the borders of Mandated Palestine nor those of Egypt, but which was administered by Great Britain under an agreement with the Turkish Sultan dating from October 1, 1906. A dividing line extending from Rafah to Aqaba[1] was drawn between three internal administrative units of the Ottoman Empire, which thenceforward separated the Ottoman vilayet or province of the Hedjaz, together with the independent sanjak or governorate of Jerusalem, from the Sinai Peninsula. This line, constituting an internal administrative border between sovereign parts of the Ottoman Empire, was forced upon the Turks by the British under threat of war in a classic case of gunboat diplomacy. This administrative arrangement was designed to transform the Sinai Peninsula into a buffer zone from which only Britain could benefit insofar as it kept the Turks as far away as possible from the Suez Canal, thereby providing an extra measure of security against possible attack. These administrative borders foisted on the Ottoman Empire by Britain had no historical antecedent, were purely arbitrary and did not establish any recognized international boundary between Turkish-ruled "Palestine" and Egypt, still under nominal Turkish sovereignty. Neither Britain nor its protectorate – Egypt were considered the actual sovereigns of the Sinai Peninsula, with the exception of a territorial wedge in North-Western Sinai, running from Suez to El-Arish, previously awarded to Egypt by a *firman* or royal decree of the Sultan, issued in 1841 and renewed in 1892. Under the prevailing rules of international law, the rights of administration over a territory were clearly distinguished from the rights of sovereignty, as exemplified in Article 1 of the Mandate for Palestine and Articles 70 and 83 of the Treaty of Sèvres with regard to Smyrna and its surroundings. When the borders of Palestine were first demarcated in the Franco-British Convention of December 23, 1920, Sinai, whose name may derive from the Hebrew word *sin* (סין), should have been properly attached to the Jewish National Home, because of its close historical connection with the Jewish People, the principal criterion for fixing the frontiers of Palestine. Its exclusion from Palestine may therefore be considered a violation of the San Remo Resolution and the Mandate, both of which implicitly assumed that all areas of historical Palestine or Judea would be made part of the country.

Special provisions were also inserted in the Treaty of Sèvres for new states

[1] Aqaba is the Arabic name for the ancient site of Elath or Ezion-Geber, also called Aila in the Roman and Byzantine period.

that came into existence, such as Armenia and the Hedjaz where Turkey recognized their free and independent status. In the cases of countries and islands formerly under the nominal sovereignty of Turkey, such as Egypt, Tunisia, Libya, Cyprus and the Italian group of Aegean Islands, Turkey agreed to respect the dispositions already made regarding their legal status. On the other hand, in the case of Kurdistan comprising the predominant Kurdish areas of south-eastern Anatolia, to the east of the Euphrates between Mesopotamia and the proposed state of Armenia, sovereignty remained vested in the hands of Turkey until the Kurdish inhabitants of that area decided, subject to the approval of the Council of the League of Nations, and within one year of the coming into force of the Treaty of Sèvres, if they wanted independence from Turkey. In the event of an independent Kurdish state being created, it would have also covered that part of Kurdistan which was included in the vilayet of Mosul which the British not long thereafter annexed to Iraq..

The dispositions in the Treaty of Sèvres for the ex-Turkish territories in Asia which related to Palestine, Mesopotamia and Syria (including Lebanon) that were contained in Articles 94-97 respectively and Article 132 found expression in the recitals of each of the draft Mandates for those countries. In the draft Mandate for Palestine submitted to the League of Nations on December 6, 1920 and in the revised version of August 1921, the opening recital in the Preamble of the Mandate stated as follows:

> Whereas by Article 132 of the Treaty of Peace signed at Sèvres on the tenth day of August 1920, Turkey renounced in favour of the Principal Allied Powers all rights and title over Palestine.

The foregoing recital confirmed very clearly that sovereignty over the country had already been transferred from Turkey to the Principal Allied Powers long before the Treaty of Lausanne was concluded in 1923. The statement about Turkey's renunciation of sovereignty contained in the recital of the draft Mandate was declaratory rather than constitutive, since this loss of sovereignty, to be discussed below, occurred even earlier than the date of the draft Mandate.

The loss of Turkish sovereignty over Palestine is alluded to also in the final version of the Mandate confirmed by the Council of the League of Nations, on July 24, 1922, where the following words appear in the first Recital of the Preamble:

> ...the territory of Palestine which *formerly* belonged to the Turkish Empire... (emphasis added)

The Mandate for Palestine went into legal force on September 29, 1923 before the Treaty of Lausanne was ratified on August 6, 1924, which is yet another indication that a transfer of sovereignty had already occurred before the

Treaty of Lausanne, that established the terms of final peace with Turkey, took effect. In the Preamble of the two successive draft mandates for Mesopotamia which were submitted to the League of Nations at the same time as the two successive draft mandates for Palestine, the exact same wording concerning Turkey's renunciation of "all rights and title" over the country is used.

A similar allusion to Turkey's loss of sovereignty also appears in the first Recital of the Preamble of the Mandate for Syria and Lebanon approved by the League Council which reads as follows:

> Whereas the Principal Allied Powers have agreed that the territory of Syria and the Lebanon, which *formerly* belonged to the Turkish Empire... (emphasis added)

With the conclusion of an armistice agreement (the Mudania Convention of October 11, 1922) between the Allied Powers and the Nationalist Government of Turkey headed by Mustafa Kemal, which in effect voided the Treaty of Sèvres and necessitated the negotiation of a new formal peace treaty, the reference to Article 132 of the defunct treaty in the Preamble of the Mandate for Palestine had to be deleted. However, that deletion did not change the basic fact that it was in favour of the Principal Allied Powers that Turkey had originally renounced all rights and title of sovereignty over the mandated territories. In the cases of non-mandated territories, such as the Hedjaz and Egypt, Turkey's renunciation of sovereignty was not in favour of the Principal Allied Powers, but directly to the individual states themselves. Despite the non-ratification of the Treaty of Sèvres, the validity of the renunciation of sovereignty by Turkey remained unaffected, as can be verified by analogy to what occurred in the four other peace treaties concluded in or near Paris with Turkey's wartime allies, comprising the rest of the Central Powers, that formally ended World War I. Those treaties were:

> 1. The Treaty of Versailles, signed with Germany on June 28, 1919.
> 2. The Treaty of St. Germain-en-Laye, signed with Austria on September 10, 1919.
> 3. The Treaty of Neuilly-sur-Seine, signed with Bulgaria on November 27, 1919.
> 4. The Treaty of Trianon, signed with Hungary on June 4, 1920.

All these other peace treaties contained provisions similar in nature to Article 132 of the Treaty of Sèvres. In the Treaty of Versailles, for example, it was stated in Article 119, as follows:

> *Article 119*
>
> Germany renounces in favour of the Principal Allied and Associated

Powers all her rights and titles over her oversea possessions.

The difference between Article 119 of the Treaty of Versailles and Article 132 of the Treaty of Sèvres was that, in the former case, the renunciation of sovereignty by Germany over her overseas possessions was in favour of the "Principal Allied and Associated Powers", which included the United States, while in the latter case, the renunciation of sovereignty by Turkey over her Middle-East territories was in favour of the "Principal Allied Powers" which did not include the United States. In this context it should be remembered that while the United States had declared war against Germany, it did not do so against Turkey and was therefore not included in the designation of "Principal Allied Powers". It was the "Associated Power" in the other designation.

Corresponding provisions were found in Article 91 of the Treaty of St. Germain-en-Laye, Article 75 of the Treaty of Trianon, and Article 48 read in conjunction with Article 27(3) of the Treaty of Neuilly where, after specific allocations of territories had been made by the Allied and Associated Powers in favour of specific states, previously existing or newly created, there was also a catch-all provision concerning those territories which had not been assigned to any state. In such a case, sovereignty over the territories in question was placed in the collective hands of the coalition of Principal Allied and Associated Powers pending their final settlement or disposition.[2]

Another very strong indication that joint sovereignty was initially vested in the Principal Allied Powers over the mandated territories detached from the Ottoman Empire or in the Principal Allied and Associated Powers in the case of those detached from the German Empire before being transferred to the Mandate's national beneficiary lay in the fact that the Great Powers, the winners of World War I, assumed they had the authority to dispose of the vast areas of both Empires whose populations were non-Turkish or non-German, and also to decide the exact boundaries of all the new national states that emerged in Europe, Asia and Africa as a result of the global political and legal settlement that was made. It is self-evident that a nation or a group of nations with the undisputed power to determine the final boundaries of any newly-created entity in an international treaty or to delegate this authority to a subordinate body is certain to be the holder of sovereignty under international law. That was indeed the case with the Principal Allied Powers as a group, vis-à-vis Turkey, and the Principal Allied and Associated Powers vis-à-vis Germany.

The initial vesting of joint sovereignty in the Principal Allied Powers over former Turkish territories leads to the further question as to when it actually

[2] Two examples where the Principal Allied and Associated Powers held joint sovereignty over territories detached from Germany and Hungary until their final settlement or disposition was made concerned the territories of Memel and Fiume. As regards Memel, now known as Klaipeda in Lithuania, see Article 99 of the Treaty of Versailles. In the case of Fiume, a city today in Croatia called Rijeka, see Articles 53 and 74 of the Treaty of Trianon.

occurred. Despite the language of Article 16 of the Treaty of Lausanne which says that "Turkey hereby renounces all rights and title whatsoever over or respecting territories situated outside the frontiers laid down in the present Treaty", the date of vesting sovereignty was not – as other jurists have asserted – upon the signing of the Treaty (July 24, 1923) nor upon its ratification (August 6, 1924).

In a well-researched article[3], Carol Farhi, formerly assistant to the Attorney-General of Israel, cites the remarks of Elihu Lauterpacht of the University of Cambridge in favour of the view that prior to the coming into force of the Treaty of Lausanne, the Gaza Strip in particular and Palestine generally was still formally Turkish territory:

> "...It is true that Palestine had in fact already on July 24, 1922 been placed under the British Mandate but applying the doctrine that an enemy cannot be deprived of territory *pendente bello*, it is clear that Turkey did not validly lose her title to the area until she renounced it in terms of Article 16 of the Treaty of Lausanne".

In looking at Lauterpacht's statement as quoted by Farhi, it must be first noted that Palestine was officially placed under British Mandate by the Principal Allied Powers at the San Remo Peace Conference on April 25, 1920 and not on July 24, 1922. The Council of the League of Nations only confirmed a pre-existing fact on July 24, 1922 and did not have the power to change the award of the Mandate to Britain on its own volition. As regards the gist of his remarks, Lauterpacht assumed that a state of war still existed in Palestine until the signing of the Treaty of Lausanne on July 24, 1923. This assumption was incorrect, which makes his conclusion also incorrect. A *cessation of hostilities* with Turkey had already occurred by virtue of an Armistice Agreement signed at Mudros on the Greek Island of Lemnos on October 30, 1918 by British Admiral Sir Somerset A. Gough-Calthorpe, in the name of the Allied Powers, that took effect the following day. Under the terms of that agreement, Turkey surrendered all its garrisons in Syria, Mesopotamia, Hedjaz, Asir and Yemen. It no longer had any military outposts or troops stationed in Palestine. While it is certainly true that a general armistice by itself does not end a war – this is also true of conquest by itself, as distinct from subjugation – the situation where there is an actual cessation of hostilities between the belligerents that persists over time does in fact terminate a war, even without a peace treaty,[4]

[3] This article is found in the book *Military Government in the Territories Administered by Israel, 1967-1980: The Legal Aspects*, Volume I, ed. Meir Shamgar, Hemed Press, reprinted 1988. The quotation by Elihu Lauterpacht is found in a note on "State Territory" (1957), 6 *International Comparative Law Quarterly* 513.

[4] See the treatise by L. Oppenheim and H. Lauterpacht on *International Law*, Seventh Edition, Volume II, Section 262, p. 597, where the authors state: "The

The cessation of hostilities did, in fact, persist over time in regard to Palestine, Mesopotamia and Syria which led to a termination of the war in those theaters, especially after the Sultan's Government at Constantinople signed the Treaty of Sèvres on August 10, 1920. Even the Nationalist Government at Ankara under the leadership of Mustafa Kemal accepted the loss of these three Middle Eastern territories without a protest of any kind. It is wrong, therefore, to speak of a situation of *pendente bello* in regard to Palestine that lasted until the Treaty of Lausanne was signed on July 24, 1923, as Elihu Lauterpacht does.[5] By way of contrast, the cessation of hostilities which took effect in Syria, Mesopotamia and Palestine did not hold up in Anatolia and Eastern Thrace where fierce fighting broke out anew between the Greeks and the Turks during the two-year period from June 1920 to September 1922. When the Turks approached in a threatening way a small contingent of British troops stationed at Chanak on the Asian side of the Dardanelles, war appeared to be imminent and was only averted by a new armistice convention signed at Mudania on October 11, 1922, which led directly to the peace treaty of Lausanne.

In the statement by Elihu Lauterpacht as quoted by Carol Farhi, he states emphatically that it is clear that Turkey did not validly lose her title to Palestine until she renounced it in terms of Article 16 of the Treaty of Lausanne. This incorrectly implies that a treaty of peace is absolutely necessary for a transfer of sovereignty to take place. A treaty is indeed the usual method to bring about a transfer of sovereignty, but this can also be effected without a peace treaty by the joint process of *subjugation and annexation*, and even by consent or acquiescence after a period of simple cessation of hostilities that leads to a termination of war. In the case of post-World War I Turkey, the potential annexation of three of its Middle Eastern territories (Palestine, Syria and Mesopotamia) by the conquering Allied Powers was replaced by the introduction of the Mandates System in fulfillment of the principle of eventual national self-determination for the designated beneficiaries. This process was well described in the Palestine Royal Commission Report which stated:[6]

---

regular modes of termination of war are treaties of peace or subjugation; but cases have occurred in which simple cessation of all acts of war on the part of both belligerents has actually and informally brought the war to an end. Thus ended in 1716 the war between Sweden and Poland, in 1720 the war between Spain and France, in 1801 the war between Russia and Persia, in 1867 the war between France and Mexico, and in the same year the war between Spain and Chile.

[5] See the pamphlet by Elihu Lauterpacht, *Jerusalem and the Holy Places*, published by the Anglo-Israel Association, London (October 1968, reprinted December 1980), pp. 49-50. Lauterpacht states that the rule of *pendente bello* is "[that] for so long as the technical condition of war lasted, a belligerent was not entitled to annex enemy territory, which he might have occupied. A transfer of title to territory in consequence of war could take place only as a result of the cession of the territory in the treaty of peace."

[6] *The Rise of Israel*, Vol. 24, Document 2, p. 60 (para. 45, 46 of the Palestine

> While the British tradition of trusteeship for backward peoples had a good deal to do with it, the Mandate System was mainly the outcome of American ideas. From the moment that the United States entered the War, President Wilson made it clear that in his view such territorial readjustments [author's note: "territorial readjustments" in this context is simply another way of describing the transfer of sovereignty from one state to another] as might result from victory should be made on different principles from those which had been followed at the close of previous wars. There were to be "no annexations" against the wishes of the people concerned. The principle of "national self-determination" should be applied as far as possible. "Peoples and provinces are not to be bartered about from sovereignty to sovereignty as if they were mere chattels and pawns in a game."
>
> It was in order to apply these principles to the disposition of the ex-German colonies and ex-Turkish provinces that the Mandate System was established. In earlier days the simple annexation of such "prizes of war" had been a matter of course. Now they were to be governed not as the "possessions" of this or that victorious Power, but as a "sacred trust of civilization" under regulations laid down by the League of Nations and under its constant supervision (All quotation marks are in the original).

On the subject of subjugation of enemy territory, the following comment from the joint work of Professors Oppenheim and Sir Hersch Lauterpacht is highly relevant:[7]

> Conquest is the taking of possession of enemy territory through military force in time of war. Conquest alone does not *ipso facto* make the conquering state the sovereign of the conquered territory... Conquest is only a mode of acquisition if the conqueror, after having firmly established the conquest, formally annexes the territory. Such annexation makes the enemy State cease to exist and thereby brings the war to an end. And as such ending of war is named subjugation, it is conquest followed by subjugation and not conquest alone which gives a title and is a mode of acquiring territory... Annexation turns the conquest into subjugation. It is the very annexation which *uno actu* [by a unilateral act] makes the vanquished State cease to exist and brings the territory under the conqueror's sovereignty. Thus the subjugated territory has not for one moment been no state's land, but passes from the enemy to the conqueror, not through cession, but through annexation.

---

Royal Commission Report).

[7] This comment is found in L. Oppenheim, *A Treatise of International Law,* 6th Edition, edited by Sir Hersch Lauterpacht, Vol. I, sections 236 and 237, pp. 566-568.

The above quotation from Oppenheim-Lauterpacht lays down the rule that three conditions must exist in order for a conqueror to acquire a title over enemy territory by the method of subjugation, without the necessity of a peace treaty. First, there must be a firmly-established conquest and effective possession of enemy territory. Second, there must be annexation which follows the conquest of enemy territory. Third, the annexation should cause the extinction of the enemy state, thereby rendering the signing of a peace treaty impractical and, nonetheless, bringing the war to an end. When all of these conditions are fulfilled, subjugation or what is called in Latin *de bellatio*[8] has then taken place. It is only then that the conqueror acquires sovereignty over the enemy territory.[9]

---

[8] *De bellatio*, in the opinion of many jurists, signifies the complete annihilation of the enemy armed forces, total occupation of the enemy state and the permanent destruction of its government resulting in the extinction of the enemy state. When this takes place, the victorious state may or may not annex the territory of the former enemy state. For these jurists, the act of annexation is not a legal necessity, though usually occurring. On the other hand, other jurists, including the author, hold that *de bellatio* arises only when annexation of the conquered enemy territory, or an equivalent such as the imposition by the conqueror of a mandatory administration or a trusteeship, actually takes place, thus rendering *de bellatio* synonymous with subjugation. A recent example of *de bellatio* that lasted only five months occurred when Iraq invaded and conquered Kuwait in August 1990, destroyed its government, extinguished the independent state of Kuwait and annexed its territory to Iraq (the famed "nineteenth province"). Similar cases existed in ancient days, regarding the subjugation of the Northern Kingdom of Israel by Assyria c. 722 B.C.E. and, almost a century and a half later, of the Southern Kingdom of Judah by Babylonia in 586 B.C.E. After the re-emergence of the Second Jewish Commonwealth, the legions of the Roman Empire subjugated Judea at the time of the Great Revolt (66-70 C.E.). Earlier, in the second century B.C.E., Rome subjugated Carthage in the Third Punic War, and then made it part of the Roman Empire.

[9] Oppenheim-Lauterpacht illustrates the difference between conquest and occupation, on the one hand, and subjugation and *de bellatio*, on the other hand, in the case of Germany after its defeat in World War II. Germany had been conquered and occupied by Britain, the U.S., Russia and France. In a joint declaration issued on June 5, 1945, the four Allies assumed "supreme authority" (i.e., sovereignty) over all of Germany, but expressly disclaimed that Germany was being annexed. Had there been no such disclaimer, according to Oppenheim-Lauterpacht, Germany would have been considered subjugated and hence no longer in existence. In addition, the war would have been considered to have automatically ended. What happened from a legal point-of-view was that the international personality of Germany and its sovereignty were deemed to be only suspended, not permanently lost or extinguished. Germany therefore continued to exist as a state, even though its sovereignty was temporarily placed in the hands of the four Allied Powers. There was therefore no subjugation or *de bellatio* – again, according to the authors – within the legal meaning of this term. In sum, only conquest and occupation had taken place, without annexation.

The present author, however, holds that subjugation and *de bellatio* had indeed taken place, as evidenced by the fact that Germany was divided into four military zones, each controlled by one of the Allied Powers, thus replacing the

However, subjugation which causes a transfer of sovereignty without a peace treaty does not have to take place over the entire territory of an enemy state, but can apply only to a part of the whole territory of that state, in which case the enemy state can continue to exist in those areas which were not subjugated. Here is how Oppenheim-Lauterpacht describes this unique situation:

> Subjugation is, as a rule, a mode of acquiring the entire enemy territory. But it is possible for a state to conquer and annex *a part* (italics in original) of enemy territory, either when the war ends by a treaty of peace in which the vanquished State, without ceding the conquered territory, *submits silently* to the annexation, or by simple cessation of hostilities (emphasis added).
>
> It must, however, be emphasized that such a mode of acquiring a part of enemy territory is totally different from forcibly taking possession of a part thereof during the continuance of war. Such a conquest, although the conqueror may intend to keep the conquered territory and therefore to annex it, does not confer a title so long as the war has not terminated either through simple cessation of hostilities or by a treaty of peace. Therefore, the practice, which sometimes prevails, of annexing during a war a conquered part of enemy territory cannot be approved. For annexation of conquered enemy territory, whether of the whole or of part, confers a title only after a *firmly established* (italics in original) conquest, and so long as war continues conquest is not firmly established.[10]

---

Third Reich (Hitler's dictatorial empire that grew out of the Weimar Republic). Three of the zones were controlled by the Western Powers and were subsequently consolidated into a new state called the Federal Republic of Germany (West Germany), while in the Soviet zone another new state was formed, namely, the German Democratic Republic (East Germany) – all these arrangements being themselves yet another equivalent of annexation. See previous footnote. As Germany was truly under Allied subjugation, rather than mere occupation, the Hague Regulations of 1907, being applicable only to occupied territories, were not applied in regard to the laws enacted by Nazi Germany and the Hitler regime. Such laws and others which discriminated on grounds of race, nationality, creed or political opinions were abrogated or rendered inoperative by the Allied Powers (See *Directive to General Eisenhower on the Military Government of Germany*, April 1945; the Directive is reprinted in *Documents and Readings in the History of Europe since 1918*, compiled by Walter Consuelo Langsam with the assistance of James Michael Egan, Kraus Reprint Co., New York (1969), Document 293, p. 1003, at p. 1008.

[10] *Ibid.*, pp. 570-571. In the case of post-World War II Germany, the Allied Powers decided at the Potsdam Conference held near Berlin from July 17 to August 2, 1945, to allocate parts of pre-war German territory to Poland and the Soviet Union. Most of former East Prussia was henceforth administered by Poland, except for North East Prussia, which was awarded to the USSR, and, in addition, Poland was given more German territory east of the Oder and western

As enunciated above the transfer of sovereignty over a part of the territory of an enemy state can occur not only through the instrument of a peace treaty, the usual method, but also through the method of subjugation, which is what actually happened in part to the Ottoman Turkish Empire after World War I ended, when it re-emerged as a smaller national state, shedding all its foreign possessions populated by non-Turks. The territories detached from Turkey that became mandated territories may have been initially considered as "occupied territories", which is what they were officially called by the British Government after they were conquered by the forces of General Edmund Allenby. The administration of these territories was organized at first into three separate zones, to which a fourth zone was later added, each zone designated as Occupied Enemy Territory Administration, abbreviated to OETA, followed by its geographical location.[11] However, the legal status of these territories then changed from one of "occupation" to "subjugation", except for Cilicia located in southern Anatolia which Ataturk re-captured from France. It had already been decided on January 30, 1919 by the Supreme Council of the Principal Allied and Associated Powers at the Paris Peace Conference not to return the non-Anatolian territories to Turkey, but to place them under a Mandatory regime administered by Britain and France on behalf of the League of Nations in accordance with the Smuts Resolution which became the basis of Article 22 of the Covenant. This was confirmed by the Palestine Royal Commission Report which said:

> On the 30th of January 1919, the Supreme Council of the Peace Conference had decided that the conquered Arab provinces were not to be restored to Turkish rule.[12]

In the above quotation, it would have been more accurate to describe the

---

Niesse rivers, including Upper and Lower Silesia. Germany thus lost about 10 percent of its former territory to Poland. The Allied decisions at the Potsdam Conference were eventually accepted by the Federal Republic of Germany. In retrospect, this constituted further evidence for the subjugation (and *de bellatio*) of post-World War II Germany by the temporary sovereigns of Germany, the four Allied Powers.

[11] These zones were: 1) OETA (East), covering the interior of Syria and Transjordan; 2) OETA (West), for the coast of Syria, including Lebanon; 3) OETA (South), covering Palestine north to Acre and east to the Jordan River; 4) OETA (North), covering the area of Cilicia in Anatolia, occupied by the French in December 1918 – January 1919. The zone OETA (West) was originally designated OETA (North), but when Cilicia came under French rule, this zone became OETA (West), while Cilicia was henceforth referred to as OETA (North). See: Paul L. Hanna, *British Policy in Palestine* (1942), p. 40 and note 4, p. 176. See also: Fannie Fern Andrews, *The Holy Land Under Mandate* (1931), Volume II, p. 47, note 2.

[12] *The Rise of Israel,* Vol. 24, Document 2, p. 48.

conquered territories of the Ottoman Empire not as "Arab provinces", but rather as the Middle-Eastern provinces of that Empire that ethnically comprised not only Arabs, but also Jews, Kurds, Assyrians, Maronite Christians and other peoples. The Allied subjugation of these provinces meant that until Mandatories were actually appointed to govern these territories under the Mandates System, they were to remain under the joint sovereignty of the Principal Allied Powers. At the meeting of the Supreme Council on January 30, 1919, Prime Minister Lloyd George had suggested that it act immediately to assign the Mandates, but President Wilson opposed his suggestion on the ground that the League of Nations had not yet been constituted. As a result, the Mandates for the former Ottoman Middle Eastern territories were granted only a year later on April 25, 1920 at the San Remo Peace Conference.

In fact, as noted by Attorney-General Meir Shamgar,[13] who later became President of the Supreme Court of Israel, a conquered territory which goes through a process of subjugation ceases to be "occupied territory" in the legal sense, to which the Hague Regulations of 1907 or the Fourth Geneva Convention of 1949 would now no longer apply. Had the doctrine of subjugation been duly applied to Palestine instead of the law of occupation, then the internal laws of Ottoman Turkey would have ceased to have legal force. However, that step was not taken, and hence certain immoral Ottoman laws, such as those prohibiting the immigration of Jews into the country, were kept in force by the British military administration. This caused Russian Jews a great disadvantage, for many of them were anxious to emigrate to Palestine to escape the chaos then prevailing in Russia after the Bolshevik Revolution. After the Bolsheviks consolidated their power in Russia, Jews were no longer free to leave.

In addition to subjugation as a possible mode to transfer sovereignty over a territory without a peace treaty being necessary, this can also be achieved by simple consent. On this point Ian Brownlie writes:[14]

> If an actual transfer (of territory) has taken place and a change of sovereignty is accepted by the interested parties, the validity or otherwise of the treaty is irrelevant (author's note: this applies particularly in the case of the Treaty of Sèvres). *Informal expression of consent* is not far removed from *consent implied from conduct* (emphasis added)...

In the specific context of Palestine, Mesopotamia and Syria, the transfer of these territories from the Ottoman Empire to the coalition of Principal Allied Powers had already taken place on January 30, 1919 by the process of subjugation or *de bellatio* (conquest followed by the conversion of the "occupied

---

[13] See his article on "The Observance of International Law in the Administered Territories", *Israel Yearbook on Human Rights*, Volume I (1971), Tel-Aviv University, p. 263.

[14] *Principles of Public International Law* by Ian Brownlie, Clarendon Press, Oxford (1966), p.124.

territories" into "mandated territories" under the internationally sanctioned Mandates System) prior to the signing of the Treaty of Sèvres and the Treaty of Lausanne. Turkey accepted all the dispositions that were made by the Principal Allied Powers concerning all the Middle Eastern territories that were once integral parts of its far-flung Empire including the Hedjaz, when it signed the Treaty of Sèvres on August 10, 1920. It never contested afterwards what was done, except for the disputed areas of Alexandretta and Mosul on the borders with Syria and Iraq respectively (subjugation, in any case, did not require Turkish consent). This contrasted with the utter rejection by the Ankara-based Nationalist Government of the detachment from Turkey of various portions of Anatolia and Eastern Thrace as set out in the Treaty of Sèvres. Turkish acceptance of the dispositions made by the Principal Allied Powers concerning the subjugated provinces of the Ottoman Empire outside Anatolia which had non-Turkish populations was sufficient in itself to constitute a transfer of sovereignty either by *silent submission* (Oppenheim-Lauterpacht) or by *informal expression of consent* (Brownlie) or by *consent implied from conduct* (Brownlie) even before the Treaty of Lausanne was concluded on July 24, 1923 and ratified on August 6, 1924. That explains why neither Palestine nor the Hedjaz is mentioned in the Treaty of Lausanne. Their final detachment from the Ottoman Empire had already been accepted by both the Sultan's Government at Constantinople and Mustafa Kemal's nationalist Government at Ankara regardless of the failure of the latter to ratify the Treaty of Sèvres.

Article 16 of the Treaty of Lausanne, despite the misleading impression given by the opening words "Turkey hereby renounces", only confirmed a pre-existing fact that the date on which the Ottoman Empire lost its sovereignty over the mandated territories in the Middle East to the Principal Allied Powers was much earlier than the conclusion of the Treaty of Lausanne, which was supported by the diplomatic and political arrangements already made and felt on the ground that took shape after the military defeat of the Ottoman Empire in World War I. This fact was evidenced by the Treaty of Versailles with Germany, the other peace treaties with Austria, Hungary and Bulgaria, and the San Remo Resolution which created the new states of Palestine, Mesopotamia and Syria, under separate Mandates.

Article 22, Part I of the Treaty of Versailles, which contains the Covenant of the League of Nations, states clearly and emphatically in the opening words of the first paragraph of this article:

> *Article 22*
>
> To those colonies and territories which as a consequence of the late war have *ceased* to be under the sovereignty of the States which *formerly* governed them… (emphasis added)

Again in the fourth paragraph of Article 22, in regard to Syria and Mesopotamia being under mandate, it states in the opening of this paragraph:

> Certain communities *formerly* belonging to the Turkish Empire…

The word "ceased" in paragraph 1 of Article 22 and the word "formerly" as used in both paragraph 1 and paragraph 4 of the same article, which appear in the Treaty of Versailles signed on June 28, 1919, indicate a loss of Turkish sovereignty over Palestine, Mesopotamia and Syria that preceded the signing of this treaty. Turkey's loss of sovereignty in favour of the Principal Allied Powers could therefore have only occurred on January 30, 1919 when it was definitively decided that these territories would never be returned to Turkish sovereignty, as spelled out in the Smuts Resolution, the forerunner of Article 22 adopted by the Allied Council of Ten (Supreme Council) at the Paris Peace Conference. That date is therefore the key date in denoting loss of Turkish sovereignty over Palestine, Mesopotamia and Syria, which five months later found express confirmation in the Treaty of Versailles, in paragraphs 1 and 4 of Article 22.

If the objection is raised that Turkey never signed any of the treaties which the other Central Powers made with the Principal Allied and Associated Powers, that objection can be easily overcome by citing the text of Article 25 of the Treaty of Lausanne signed with Mustafa Kemal's Turkey, which stated:

> *Article 25*
>
> Turkey undertakes to recognize the full force of the Treaties of Peace and additional Conventions by the other Contracting Parties with the Powers who fought on the side of Turkey, and the new states within their frontiers as there laid down.

By virtue of Article 25 of the Treaty of Lausanne, Turkey thereby retroactively recognized and accepted as binding the provisions in Article 22 of the Treaty of Versailles creating the Mandates System, specifically paragraphs 1 and 4 thereof, which positively affirm that Turkey and Germany both lost their sovereignty over the territories they formerly governed as a consequence of the late war. By virtue of the same Article 25, Turkey also recognized and accepted as binding the other peace treaties made with Austria (the Treaty of St. Germain-en-Laye), Hungary (the Treaty of Trianon) and Bulgaria (the Treaty of Neuilly-sur-Seine), all of which repeat the very same article found in Part I of the Treaty of Versailles.

In addition, when the Mandates System came into official existence on January 10, 1920, upon the ratification of the Treaty of Versailles, Turkey had knowledge of the fact that its former Middle East territories were being administered by mandatories and did not protest this fact thereafter. It even gave its express approval to the Mandates System when three representatives of the Ottoman Government of Sultan Muhammad VI signed the Treaty of Sèvres seven months later on August 10, 1920. During this period Turkey's behaviour constituted both a tacit and explicit renunciation of its sovereignty over those mandated territories, regardless of the fact that Mustafa Kemal, after assuming power in Turkey, refused to ratify the Treaty of Sèvres. Hence, Turkey's renunciation of sovereignty took place even before it expressly agreed in Article 25 of the Treaty of Lausanne, to recognize for a second time the Mandates System established by the Covenant of the League of Nations.

It may even be said that by virtue of Article 25 of the Treaty of Lausanne, Turkey ratified the League of Nations Covenant contained in the Treaty of Sèvres, which was produced verbatim in every one of the peace treaties signed with the Central Powers, except in the Treaty of Lausanne itself. To that extent, Ataturk's Turkey ratified the first 26 articles of the Treaty of Sèvres in a roundabout way. By thus ratifying the Covenant of the League of Nations and recognizing the Mandates System created by it, Turkey in effect retroactively acknowledged the loss of its sovereignty over the mandated states of Palestine, Mesopotamia and Syria as of January 30, 1919 in accordance with the Smuts Resolution of that date.

If it is argued that sovereignty over mandated territories had not already been transferred to the Principal Allied Powers by the time the Treaty of Versailles was signed on June 28, 1919 as specifically stated in Article 22 of the Covenant, then the League of Nations, when it began formal operations in 1920, would not have been able to exercise legally the supervisory authority it was assumed to have over such territories as soon as they were formally created on April 24-25, 1920 at the San Remo Peace Conference, without first obtaining the consent of Turkey. In compliance with Article 22(7) of the Treaty of Versailles, Britain began submitting its annual reports on Palestine beginning in 1921 even before the Mandate was formally confirmed by the Council of the League of Nations. The first report was an interim one covering the period July 1, 1920 to June 30, 1921, followed by another report that extended this period to December 1921. This confirms that the Council began its oversight on Palestine right from the start of the actual operation of the Mandate on July 1, 1920 with the changeover from a military administration to a civilian regime, in accordance with the San Remo Resolution of April 25, 1920. The changeover to civilian rule which occurred in all three Class "A" mandated territories would not have taken place if sovereignty had not already been transferred.

As a result of the foregoing analysis, it must be concluded that Article 16 of the Treaty of Lausanne was not constitutive in nature that created a new situation or departure point insofar as the transfer of sovereignty was concerned. Rather, Article 16 of the Treaty was declarative of a pre-existing *fait accompli*, which simply reiterated what had already taken place on January 30, 1919, and which was confirmed in the Treaty of Versailles and the other peace treaties, as well as in the San Remo Resolution.

After being vested with joint or collective sovereignty over the territories to be mandated, the Principal Allied Powers then transferred it to the peoples or communities *inhabiting* the territories that were being assisted or governed by a Mandatory Power or Trustee or Tutelary State representing an Advanced Nation under the provisions of Article 22 of the Covenant. That is exactly what happened with regard to Mesopotamia and Syria, but not in the special case of Palestine. In the latter instance, the title of sovereignty over the mandated territories was transferred not to the local inhabitants, i.e., the Arabs of the country, but to the Jews of the world, most of whom were not then living in Palestine. This made the Jewish People as a whole the national beneficiary of the Mandate for Palestine, in whom *de jure* sovereignty was vested. In this sense, the Jewish People were deemed to be the people or "inhabitants" of Palestine, for whose "well-being and development" the Mandatory, who accepted what was called "a sacred trust of civilization", would be responsible for the administration of Palestine under Paragraph 1 of Article 22 of the Covenant of the League of Nations in conformity with the Balfour Declaration. The term "inhabitants" was intended to embrace not only the Jews actually living in Palestine on April 25, 1920 when the Mandate was granted to Britain, but also all the Jewish immigrants who were expected to arrive in large numbers during the period of the implementation of the Mandate. That was the real reason for Article 22 being mentioned in the first Recital of the Preamble to the Mandate for Palestine. Had the intention been for the local Arab inhabitants to be the national beneficiary of the Mandate, they would have been similarly mentioned in this document. However, until the Jewish People had become a definite majority of the inhabitants of Palestine and could stand by themselves as an independent nation, all the powers or attributes of sovereignty were exercised by the Mandatory, while nominal or theoretical sovereignty (i.e., *de jure* sovereignty) remained with the Jewish People during the period of tutorship. This unique situation for a Class "A" Mandate was reflected in Article 1 of the instrument, which granted the Mandatory "full powers of legislation and of administration, save as they may be limited by the terms of this Mandate". The Mandatory was thus the Administering Authority of the mandated territory, entrusted with its administration rather than being its actual sovereign. This state of affairs also illustrates the difference under international law between the legal concepts of sovereignty, on the one hand, and administration, on the other.

The date when the actual transfer of *de jure* sovereignty to the Jewish People took place could have only been April 24, 1920 when the Balfour Declaration was originally accepted by the Supreme Council of the Principal Allied Powers as the basis for creating Palestine as a new mandated state to which would be applied the general provisions of Article 22 of the Covenant for the exclusive purpose of establishing Palestine as the Jewish National Home, the whole as embodied in the San Remo Resolution. In the same Resolution, as well as under Paragraph 4 of Article 22 of the Covenant, the Arabic-speaking national communities of Syria and Mesopotamia were provisionally recognized as independent states under the Mandates System, subject to the rendering of administrative advice and assistance by a Mandatory until they were ready for full independence. Palestine, too, according to Pierre Orts, chairman of the Permanent Mandates Commission, was provisionally independent, but such independence could only have been realized when Jews constituted a majority of the population of Palestine, an objective which the British, after Balfour's departure as Foreign Secretary in October 1919, worked deviously to subvert and delay.

The San Remo Resolution was reproduced in articles 94-97 inclusively of the Treaty of Sèvres, as well as in article 132, and had clearly identified the national beneficiaries of the mandates for Palestine, Mesopotamia and Syria, upon whom the title of sovereignty was being conferred over these respective mandated territories. Strangely, this devolution of *de jure* sovereignty upon the Jewish People over all of Palestine has never been acknowledged by foreign countries, especially those which were instrumental in creating Palestine as the Jewish National Home at the San Remo Peace Conference. Nor has Jewish sovereignty over all of former Mandated Palestine ever been acknowledged by international courts, nor even Israeli courts. Most surprising of all, such sovereignty was never claimed even by the State of Israel. For this reason the territories of Judea, Samaria and Gaza were treated by Israel itself as being under occupation after their liberation in the Six-Day War; thus Israel decided to apply foreign, rather than Israeli, law in violation of Israeli constitutional law. All of these consequences were derived from the fact that Treaty of Sèvres was never ratified and that, subsequently, the British sabotaged the true meaning of the Mandate for Palestine, as elaborated upon in succeeding chapters of this book.

Even though the Treaty of Sèvres was never ratified, it still had probative legal value as an agreement between the four Principal Allied Powers, showing exactly what they had intended to do in disposing of the ex-Turkish territories in the Middle East. Furthermore, articles 94-97 and 132 became part of the fabric of international law even without the ratification of the Treaty of Sèvres by their subsequent incorporation in the respective mandate instruments for Palestine and Syria and their confirmation by 52 member states of the League of Nations in 1922 and by additional states that subsequently joined the League of Nations.

The legal rights and title of sovereignty of the Jewish People recognized in the San Remo Resolution and Mandate for Palestine survived the end of the Mandate and afterwards inhered in the State of Israel over the whole Land of Israel, not just the portion of it that was made part of the State's boundaries on May 15, 1948. In this regard, those jurists who argue that the conquest of Judea, Samaria and Gaza by Israel in the Six-Day War of June 1967 did not give it any title of sovereignty over these areas under international law fail to realize that, while it is true that conquest alone does not confer any title, Israel's legal status there did not derive from the conquest of "enemy territory" through military force in time of war, but is based solely on the rights it inherited from the Jewish People, that were laid down in various by-now-familiar acts of international law: the Smuts Resolution, Article 22 of the League Covenant, both of which are to be read in conjunction with the Feisal-Weizmann Agreement, the San Remo Resolution, the Mandate for Palestine and the Franco-British Boundary Convention of December 23, 1920. The act of conquest and the rules applicable to it under international law, particularly as regards occupation of enemy territory, are therefore not relevant when it comes to understanding Israel's legal rights and title of sovereignty over all parts of the Jewish National Home and the Land of Israel. In this context, it was bizarre that the principle of "the inadmissibility of acquiring territory by war" was inserted in the preamble of United Nations Security Council Resolution 242 of November 22, 1967 to make this principle applicable to Israel in regard to its recovery of illegally removed areas of the Jewish National Home. The passage of this Resolution which called for the "withdrawal of Israeli armed forces from territories occupied in the recent conflict" was a denial of Israel's true legal position based on the founding documents of its existence under the acts of international law mentioned above.

Upon closer examination of the Treaty of Lausanne, it will be seen that it recognized that Mandated Palestine was already a state governed by the Mandates System and, to be even more precise, it implicitly recognized that the country was, theoretically, *a Jewish State* since that, after all, was the ultimate purpose of the Mandate. This recognition of statehood may be deduced from various articles in the Treaty. For example, Article 46 of the Treaty of Lausanne (Part II, Section I) and the articles immediately thereafter dealing with the payment of the Ottoman Public Debt, declare that the burden had to be shared by:

> ...the *States* newly created in territories in Asia which are detached from the Ottoman Empire under the present Treaty. All the above *States* shall also participate, under the conditions laid down in the present section, in the annual charges for the service of the Ottoman Public Debt from the dates referred to in Article 53 (emphasis added).

Among the *states* called upon to pay its share of the Ottoman Public Debt was Palestine. This constituted a definite treaty recognition under international law that Palestine was already a state, something which the British generally refused to admit publicly until the time the Peel Royal Commission Report of 1937 recommended statehood for both Jews and Arabs in western Palestine.[15]

The same conclusion that Palestine was a state and not just an amorphous "territory" can be drawn from two other Articles in the Treaty of Lausanne. One was Article 60 which stated that the property and possessions of the Ottoman Empire situated in states detached from it by the present treaty shall be acquired by those states without any payment to be made. Palestine was considered one of the states to which Article 60 applied.[16] Even more important evidence that Palestine was a recognized state under international law was Article 30 of the

---

[15] The Treaty of Sèvres had a provision similar to the one in the Treaty of Lausanne for the annual payment of a proportionate share of the Ottoman Public Debt to be made by newly created states in Asia, such as Palestine. See Article 241 of the Treaty of Sèvres.

[16] See *Digest of International Law*, by Marjorie Whiteman, Vol. 2, p. 650.

Treaty of Lausanne which provided:

> *Article 30*
>
> Turkish subjects habitually resident in territory which in accordance with the provisions of the present Treaty is detached from Turkey will become *ipso facto*, in the conditions laid down in the local law, nationals of the State to which such territory is transferred.

The existence of a distinct Palestinian nationality or citizenship, in conformity with Article 7 of the Mandate and Article 30 of the Treaty of Lausanne meant that Palestine was indeed a separate state under international law.

In light of the fact that Palestine was recognized as a state under the Treaty of Lausanne, and since Palestine was synonymous with the Jewish National Home under the Balfour Declaration and the Mandate for Palestine, as discussed above, then logically Palestine was already a Jewish state in the legal sense of the term during the whole period of the Mandate, under British administration, even before that state became independent on May 15, 1948 in only a part of Palestine. This conclusion is supported by the astute view taken by the British delegation in regard to recognizing the Jewish nationality in the Polish Minority Treaty, which it opposed on the ground "that if there was to be a Jewish nationality, it could only be by giving the Jews a local habitation and enabling them to found in Palestine a Jewish State".[17] This view does not deny that Jews are a part of a separate nation including those living in the Diaspora, but it equates the concept of nationality with citizenship, which can only be an attribute of a state. One can conclude then that Palestine became a Jewish State from the moment the Mandate for Palestine began to be implemented, that is, from the date of July 1, 1920, when the British military government ended and Palestine came under civilian Mandatory rule, with the arrival of Herbert Samuel in the country as High Commissioner. The name of the country then officially changed from "Occupied Enemy Territory Administration, South" to "Palestine" or translated into Hebrew as "Palestina", which was the English rendition for the Hebrew designation of the country, "Eretz Israel". This change of regime in Palestine was additional proof that the country would never be returned to Turkish sovereignty as first made clear by the decision of the Paris Peace Conference on January 30, 1919, i.e., the Smuts Resolution, approving the Mandates System. The switchover to civilian rule was carried out not as a unilateral step by the British Government, but as a result of the fundamental Allied Supreme Council decision taken on April 24, 1920 at the San Remo Peace Conference by the Principal Allied Powers to create Palestine as a Jewish State in implementation of the Balfour Declaration.

The implementation of the Balfour Declaration was carried a step further

[17] This quotation is found in *A History of the Peace Conference of Paris*, edited by H.W.V. Temperly, Vol. V, pp. 136-137, appearing in the work by Fannie Fern Andrews, *The Holy Land Under Mandate*, Vol. I, p. 349.

on December 23, 1920 when Britain made a treaty with France to determine the common frontiers between Palestine on both sides of the Jordan with the countries of Syria, Lebanon and Mesopotamia. If any of these Mandated territories or states had still been under Turkish *de jure* sovereignty, before the Treaty of Lausanne was concluded, then all the terms and provisions of the Franco-British Convention would have been considered null and void *ab initio*, under international law, since Britain and France would not have had the legal authority to fix boundaries for their mandated territories if these were still under the sovereignty of Turkey. The latter never officially contested the right of Britain and France to make this treaty which was amended on February 3, 1922, prior to the signing of the Treaty of Lausanne on July 24, 1923. This is further proof that Turkey had already lost its sovereignty over Palestine, Mesopotamia and Syria under international law *before* the conclusion of the Treaty of Lausanne, and also confirms the fact that Article 16 of that treaty was merely declaratory and reflective of a pre-existing situation insofar as Turkey's loss of sovereignty was concerned.

A final observation in regard to the loss of Turkish sovereignty concerns President Woodrow Wilson's Fourteen Points for assuring world peace, which were outlined in an address he delivered at a joint session of the U.S. Congress on January 8, 1918 before the end of the War. According to Felix Frankfurter, it was Walter Lippman who "drafted more or less the Fourteen Points".[18] The Twelfth Point of his program for world peace stated:

> The Turkish portions of the present Ottoman Empire should be assured a secure sovereignty, but the other nationalities which are now under Turkish rule should be assured an undoubted security of life and an absolutely unmolested opportunity of autonomous development,

[18] Cited in the book *Felix Frankfurter Reminisces*, recorded in talks with Dr. Harlan B. Phillips, published by Reynal and Company, New York (1960), p. 160. How the Fourteen Points came to be written is discussed in the book by Ronald Steel, *Walter Lippmann and the American Century*, published by Random House, New York. See Chapter 11 of this book, entitled "The Inquiry", pp. 128 ff. Lippmann was asked by Colonel Edward M. House, President Wilson's closest adviser, to participate in a project called "The Inquiry" that had a five-man directorate and a staff of experts to draw up material for the eventual peace conference. Lippmann served as general secretary of the group. His job was "to coordinate the work of the specialists, put their data into readable reports for Colonel House and President Wilson and give an overall political direction to the project." Lippmann organized the conclusions of the Inquiry into a series of points contained in a document entitled "The War Aims and Peace Terms It Suggests" that was presented to Colonel House on December 22, 1917. Upon a request for clarification, the document was revised and resubmitted to House on January 2, 1918. President Wilson made some changes but accepted most of the Inquiry's recommendations. He added six general principles of his own to the territorial points – the first five points and the fourteenth, while the other eight were formulated by Lippmann and his Inquiry team.

> and the Dardanelles should be permanently opened as a free passage to the ships and commerce of all nations under international guarantees.

All of the Allied Powers and the Central Powers, including Turkey, accepted the Fourteen Points program as a basis of peace and it was reflected in the provisions of the Armistice of Mudros of October 30, 1918, under which Turkey withdrew all its troops from its territories outside of Anatolia. The Arabs interpreted the twelfth point of President Wilson's Program as granting only them a promise of independence throughout the entire Middle East, without reference to the rights of the Jewish People despite the well-publicized fact that the American President had expressly endorsed the Balfour Declaration which he himself interpreted to mean an eventual independent Jewish state, both before and after the announcement of his Fourteen Points. Though it was wrong and selfish for the Arabs to believe that they alone would be the national beneficiaries, the twelfth point did envisage their eventual independence, as well as that of other aspiring nations, all of whom were to be given "an absolutely unmolested opportunity of autonomous development" in contrast to the strictly Turkish-populated portions of the Ottoman Empire which were assured of a secure sovereignty. This meant in effect that the Turkish nation in its defined area of habitation (basically, in the northern half of the Anatolian Peninsula and the Zone of the Straits) would still have a sovereign state of its own, while other nations, in particular, the Arabs, Armenians, Kurds and the Jewish People would have unfettered political autonomy which could only lead to eventual statehood and sovereignty in their designated areas.[19] This was buttressed by the fact that the Anglo-French Statement of November 7, 1918, which did not apply to Palestine in light of the Balfour Declaration of November 2, 1917, that set it aside for the exclusive benefit of the Jewish People, stated that the aim of France and Great Britain was the complete and final liberation of the peoples so long oppressed by the Turks and the establishment of native governments and administrations in Syria and Mesopotamia deriving their authority from the initiative and free choice of the native populations. Although the Imperial Ottoman Government originally accepted without condition the Twelfth Point as a basis for peace negotiations, which definitely implied and meant the loss

[19] Point 12 of Wilson's Fourteen Points was similar in language and spirit to Point 10, the former dealing with the Ottoman Empire while the latter was concerned with the Austro-Hungarian Monarchy or Dual Monarchy. Both of these points envisioned the independence of subject-nations included in a crumbling multi-national empire. Point 10 read as follows: "The peoples of Austria-Hungary, whose place among the nations we wish to see safeguarded and assured, should be accorded the freest opportunity of autonomous development." Point 10 was a harbinger of the new, separate sovereign states which would soon come into being: German Austria; Hungary – confined to Magyar areas only; Poland; Czechoslovakia; the Kingdom of the Serbs, Croats and Slovenes, whose name was changed in 1929 to Yugoslavia. The Romanians of Transylvania, which had been part of Hungary inside the Dual Monarchy, were joined to Romania.

of their sovereignty over their Middle East territories where the Turks did not constitute the dominant element of the population, it later backtracked from its initial position when it sent a delegation to submit its own proposals to the Paris Peace Conference. At a meeting before the Allied Supreme Council on June 23, 1919 the delegation pleaded for retention of Turkish sovereignty over all territories in the Empire, while at the same time conceding that administrative autonomy would be given to those territories that comprised "Arabia", which for the Sublime Porte also included Palestine.[20] A memorandum containing the Ottoman viewpoint was submitted to the Conference, which stated:[21]

> The Arab provinces lying to the south of the Turkish countries [sic], and including Syria, Palestine, the Hedjaz, the Asyr [Asir], the Yemen, Irak, and all the other regions which were recognized as forming an integral part of the Ottoman Empire before the war, would have a large measure of administrative autonomy, under the *sovereignty* of His Imperial Majesty the Sultan… (emphasis added)
>
> Nobody in Turkey is unaware of the gravity of the moment. The ideas of the Ottoman people are however well defined: it will not accept the dismemberment of the Empire or its division under different mandates…

This plea to maintain Ottoman sovereignty over "Arabia" and to preserve the unity of the Ottoman Empire had already been unambiguously rejected in advance by the Allied Powers, first by their decision to set up indigenous governments in Syria and Mesopotamia under the Mandates System in the Treaty of Versailles that was about to be signed, second by their intention to establish a Jewish National Home in Palestine under the same system in accordance with the Balfour Declaration and third by their recognition of an independent Hedjaz in the Arabian Peninsula.[22]

---

[20] Turkey's acceptance of President Wilson's program laid down in his message to Congress on January 8, 1918 and in his subsequent declarations, was communicated by the Charge d'Affaires of Turkey to the Minister for Foreign Affairs of Spain on October 12, 1918 at Madrid. A note to that effect was then relayed by the Ambassador of Spain to President Wilson on October 14, 1918. A reply acknowledging the Turkish communication was given by Robert Lansing, the U.S. Secretary of State. The relevant documents are found in the book entitled *Official Statements of War Aims and Peace Proposals* from December 1916 to November 1918, prepared under the supervision of James Brown Scott, 1921, Carnegie Endowment For International Peace, Washington D.C., pp. 419, 443.

[21] The Ottoman Memorandum to the Supreme Council of the Paris Peace Conference, June 23, 1919, is printed in Volume 2 of *The Middle East and North Africa in World Politics*, edited by J.C. Hurewitz, Yale University Press (1979), pp. 174-176.

[22] The last Turkish Sultan, Muhammad VI, had as much chance to maintain his vast empire intact as Wilhelm II had for the German Empire and Karl (Charles) for

A little over a year later, the Sultan's representatives expressly agreed to the loss of Turkish sovereignty over those territories they had referred to as Arabia in their memorandum of June 23, 1919, when they signed the Treaty of Sèvres on August 10, 1920. The loss of Turkish sovereignty was also accepted by Mustafa Kemal's nationalist movement when members of the newly-elected Ottoman Chamber of Deputies adopted the Turkish National Pact on January 28, 1920, setting forth its program of principles. This Pact recognized the idea that the Arab majority residing in the portions of the Ottoman Empire under Allied military occupation since the signing of the Mudros Armistrice on October 30, 1918 and situated south of the Armistice line could choose its own destiny, while at the same time it aimed to defend Turkish sovereignty north of this line embracing Anatolia, Eastern Thrace and Southern Kurdistan, all of which were areas with a non-Arab "Ottoman Muslim" majority, i.e., composed of ethnic Turks and Kurds, "who were united in religion, in race and in aim, imbued with sentiments of mutual respect for each other and of sacrifice, and wholly respectful of each other's racial and social rights and surrounding conditions...".[23] The National Pact reaffirmed the principles earlier set down in the Declaration of the Congress of Sivas on September 9, 1919 concerning those territories of the Ottoman Empire which the Kemalists definitely wanted included in a new Turkish State and those that could be left out.[24]

Thus, by the time of the signing of the Treaty of Sèvres, both the Imperial Ottoman Government at Constantinople and the Nationalist Government of Mustafa Kemal set up in April 1920 at Angora [Ankara] had acquiesced in the permanent separation from Turkey of Palestine, Mesopotamia, Syria and all of the Arabian Peninsula, three years before the signing of the Treaty of Lausanne on July 24, 1923. This Turkish acquiescence in the loss of its sovereignty over all those territories allowed the coalition of Principal Allied Powers as the sovereign disposing agent to proceed unhampered with its plans to create three new Mandated States at the San Remo Peace Conference on April 24, 1920 and to assign Mandatories for them on April 25, 1920.

Seen in this context and perspective, the transfer of *de jure* sovereignty

---

the Austro-Hungarian Monarchy, which was no chance whatever.

[23] See Article 1 of The Turkish National Pact (also called the Angora Pact), adopted by certain Turkish deputies in Constantinople, January 28, 1920, and by the Angora National or Kemalist Assembly early in 1921. A translation of the Preamble and the six articles of the National Pact, as published in the Official Gazette, is printed in *A History of the Peace Conference of Paris*, edited by Harold W. V. Temperley, Vol. VI, Oxford University Press, first published 1924, reprinted 1969, Appendix II, Part IIA, pp. 605-606. The text of the National Pact can also be found in *The Middle East and North Africa in World Politics*, *op. cit.*, pp. 210-211.

[24] According to the decision of the Congress of Sivas: "All of the Turkish territory within the frontier outlined October 30, 1918 [date of signing of the Mudros Armistice Agreement] between the Ottoman Government and the Allies, and inhabited by a preponderant majority of Turk population, will form an undivided and inseparable whole."

over Palestine, Mesopotamia and Syria from Ottoman Turkey to the Principal Allied Powers on January 30, 1919 and then to the national beneficiaries of the Mandates on April 24-25, 1920 had already occurred, either by the process of subjugation or, alternatively, by acts of express or tacit consent during the period of cessation of hostilities dating from the Armistice of Mudros (October 30, 1918) until the two aforementioned dates. The transfer of sovereignty was thus not hindered or affected by the lack of ratification of the Treaty of Sèvres and the necessity to negotiate a new peace treaty with Turkey.[25]

It is important to appreciate the sequence of events and dates involving the foregoing transfer of *de jure* sovereignty from Turkey to the Principal Allied Powers to the national beneficiaries of the individual Mandates, otherwise the entire new structure of world order created by the Principal Allied Powers and the United States after World War I, as evidenced by the Treaty of Versailles and other peace treaties, would have no logical meaning or connection. If Turkey had not lost its sovereignty over its Middle East territories that were composed of non-ethnic Turks, prior to the Treaty of Versailles containing the Covenant of the League of Nations, then the Mandates System could not have been legally constructed in 1919 and the disposition of those territories at the San Remo Peace Conference in 1920 could not have been legally undertaken.

The sequence of events and dates for Turkey's loss of sovereignty over its Middle Eastern territories mirrored the case of Germany's loss of sovereignty over its colonies and possessions in Africa and the Pacific Islands. Here, too, there was a two-step procedure for the change of sovereignty that was designed by the Principal Allied and Associated Powers: sovereignty was first removed from the defeated German Empire by the decision of the Allied Council of Ten on January 30, 1919 to establish the Mandates System to govern the conquered German territories. Prior to the date of selecting the various Mandatories to administer these territories which were classified as "B" and "C" Mandates, sovereignty over them was provisionally held by the Principal Allied and

[25] As noted by the Cambridge University historian, Harold W. V. Temperley, in the work he edited, *A History of the Peace Conference of Paris*, Vol. VI, p. 37: "The view was apparently now advanced that, despite the non-ratification of the Treaty of Sèvres, these areas [a reference to Mesopotamia, Syria and Palestine] had ceased to be under Turkish sovereignty". Temperley had earlier noted (*ibid.*, p. 25) that when the territorial arrangements were made for the areas of Arabia, Mesopotamia, Palestine and Syria, *in the period between the Armistice with the Turks* (October 30, 1918) and the Peace Conference (1919-20), it was accepted by *all* parties that they had been severed from Turkish sovereignty. By contrast, this was not the view of the Turkish nationalists for other areas of the Ottoman Empire north of the armistice line where there was a non-Arab Muslim majority, whose fate was then being decided by the Principal Allied Powers, namely Smyrna, Constantinople and the Straits, Thrace, the Armenian provinces (Erzerum, Trebizond, Van and Bitlis) and Kurdistan. The impending detachment of all or some of these areas from Turkey gave rise to a strong Turkish national movement organized by Mustafa Kemal, whose aim was to prevent the country's dismemberment.

Associated Powers with the United States included in this group. Upon the selection of the Mandatory Powers, the right of *de jure* sovereignty was then vested in the peoples of those areas in a nominal and theoretical sense. However, such sovereignty could not be exercised by them until they were deemed able to stand by themselves and achieve full independence, a process that could take many years and even decades.

The foregoing explanations for the transfer and vesting of sovereignty over diverse territories detached from the Turkish and German Empires provide a satisfactory answer to the question which has vexed many jurists since the creation of the Mandates System, as to exactly when sovereignty was transferred, the explanations therefor under international law and to whom it was given both in the interim stage and ultimately.

In sum, there was never any *sovereignty vacuum* or suspension over Mandated Palestine, whether in the country as a whole or in specific regions such as Judea, Samaria and Gaza. Consequently, there were no *unallocated territories*, as alleged by many jurists. Once the Balfour Declaration was adopted on April 24, 1920 by the Principal Allied Powers to be the basis for governing the country, *de jure* sovereignty over Palestine could have logically vested only in the Jewish People, while at the same time the Mandatory Power, the United Kingdom, exercised the attributes of sovereignty on their behalf for the purpose of implementing the Balfour Declaration.

*Chapter 13*

# The Separation of Transjordan from the Jewish National Home

## *(I) Background and Legal Issues*

The story of why the British Government deviously detached Transjordan from the Jewish National Home, first only temporarily and then permanently, is known by many people. It bears repeating because in the process of doing so, the British Government severely obscured Jewish legal rights and title of sovereignty not merely in regard to Transjordan, but over Cisjordanian Palestine as well. It began with the unilateral action taken by the 135 delegates of the General Syrian Congress who had assembled in Damascus on March 8, 1920, proclaiming the independence of Syria, including Palestine and Lebanon, and offering Feisal, son of King Hussein of the Hedjaz (in the western part of the Arabian Peninsula), the "throne" of Syria, which he agreed to accept.[1] The Congress also declared the end of the individual military governments set up in the three occupied zones known as OETA (Occupied Enemy Territory Administration) East, OETA South and OETA West. The Syrian proclamation of independence was intended to preempt the global political and legal settlement which the Principal Allied Powers had formulated for these Middle Eastern territories formerly belonging to the Ottoman Empire and which was subsequently adopted at the peace conference that convened in San Remo, Italy in the following month. The proclamation by the Syrian delegates also constituted a rejection of the incipient Mandates System that was already a part of international law but not yet fully operational. Both Britain and France refused to recognize this illegal act by an Arab body that had no legal authority to determine the fate of these territories. Such authority was vested exclusively in the hands of the Principal Allied Powers who fought and defeated

---

[1] Paul L. Hanna, *British Policy in Palestine,* American Council on Public Affairs, Washington, D.C. (1942), pp. 43 and 56. A program for the complete political independence of a united Syria, including Palestine, was earlier presented by the General Syrian Congress to the American "King-Crane Commission" on July 2, 1919. This program declared its opposition to "the pretensions of the Zionists to create a Jewish Commonwealth in the southern part of Syria, known as Palestine". It added that the Congress opposed "Zionist migration" to any part of their country and considered this to be a "grave peril".

the Ottoman Empire with only minimal Arab assistance.

By the third week in July 1920, the French felt compelled to take military action against Feisal's "United Kingdom of Syria" to restore law and order and enforce their mandate over Syria entrusted to them by the San Remo Peace Conference on April 25, 1920. General Henri Joseph Gouraud, who had been appointed as French High Commissioner in Syria and Cilicia and as Chef de l'Armee au Levant (Commander-in-Chief of the Army of the Levant)[2] on October 9, 1919, replacing the previous High Commissioner, Georges Picot, dispatched troops to Damascus and ousted the Feisal Government on July 25, 1920.[3] Abdullah, the older brother of Feisal, threatened military retaliation against French forces in Syria to restore his brother to power. It was little more than a bluff or an opera-bouffe "invasion", as Joseph B. Schechtman called it,[4] but that sufficed to impel the British Colonial Office under Churchill's ministerial responsibility to seek a solution to compensate Feisal for the loss of his throne and placate the anger of Abdullah and the Sherifian/Hashemite family. This solution came at the expense of the right of the Jewish People to reconstitute its homeland in historical Palestine on both sides of the Jordan. A new throne was found for Feisal in Iraq, which ironically had first been offered to Abdullah at the suggestion of Feisal himself by an Iraqi Congress convening in Damascus at the same time and working in collusion with the General Syrian Congress. Under the British offer, Abdullah would instead get the provisional administration of Transjordan that had already been included in the Jewish National Home by virtue of the Franco-British Boundary Convention of December 23, 1920 pursuant to the Draft Mandate of December 6, 1920 and the San Remo Resolution of April 25, 1920. The Boundary Convention signed by French Prime Minister Georges Leygues and British Ambassador to Paris, Charles Hardinge, gave official recognition to the Draft Mandate of December 6, 1920 *as between the parties themselves* by various references to it in the Convention which should have been sufficient to prevent subsequent illegal British tampering, especially as regards the question of detaching Palestine territory (i.e., Transjordan) from the Jewish National Home, even on a temporary basis.

As noted above, the make-shift British solution was devised as a result of Abdullah's advance into Transjordan from his home in the Hedjaz en route to Damascus with the announced goal of expelling the French from Syria and reestablishing Feisal as "King". Receiving permission for his mission from King

---

[2] The term "Levant" (from which the adjective "Levantine" is derived) is used today in a limited sense to denote the states of Syria and Lebanon, but formerly it applied to all the countries of the eastern shore of the Mediterranean, from Egypt to Turkey, including Palestine.

[3] Feisal remained in Syria until August 1, 1920, when he departed for Haifa. See the book by Zeine N. Zeine, *The Struggle for Arab Independence*, Caravan Books, New York (1977), p. 169.

[4] Joseph B. Schechtman, *Jordan – A State That Never Was*, Cultural Publishing Co., Inc., New York (1968), p. 22.

Hussein of the Hedjaz but not acting officially in the name of the Kingdom, he left Mecca for Medina and thence to Ma'an, arriving there in November, 1920 with a combined Bedouin and Syrian nationalist force of nearly two thousand men. The district of Ma'an was located in the northern outskirts of Hussein's kingdom even since it had been taken over from the Ottomans by Feisal's "Northern Army" in 1917-1918. Abdullah remained in Ma'an with his forces and did not leave until the approach of spring 1921. He then set out northwards to Kerak (Kir-Hareseth, the ancient capital of Moab) into the British mandated territory of Transjordanian Palestine, which had come under the overall civilian authority of the High Commissioner in Jerusalem, Herbert Samuel, and the Foreign Office in London under George Nathaniel Curzon ever since the collapse of Feisal's short-lived kingdom in July 1920. Feisal had ruled over Transjordan on a provisional basis, pending the decision of the Peace Conference as to its final disposition. The resident British military-political officer in charge of the district of Kerak, Alec Seath Kirkbride, who was also the head of the self-styled National Government of Moab, not having received any firm instructions from his superiors in Jerusalem and London and with only fifty policemen at his disposal to resist the advance of Abdullah, decided on his own initiative that the best course to follow was to welcome Abdullah to the territory under the control of the local Council. Abdullah in turn displayed no hostile intention towards the British presence in Transjordan but, on the contrary, eagerly sought British support and advice.

From Kerak, Abdullah proceeded to Amman on March 2, 1921 where he established his headquarters. He had by this time taken *de facto* control of the entire territory of present-day Jordan, south of the Yarmuk, just before the Cairo Middle East Conference called by Churchill got under way. When the future fate of Transjordan was first discussed at the Conference on March 17, 1921, the British civilian and military officials in attendance recommended converting this Palestine territory into an Arab province under an Arab governor, responsible to the High Commissioner. They also recommended the immediate military garrisoning of Transjordan, without which they believed it would be impossible to secure a settled government there or to stop anti-French action initiated in the British zone. However, it should be well noted that even before Abdullah came upon the scene, Transjordan was already looked upon by the British as part of Palestine, constituting its eastern boundary as ultimately determined. This is evidenced by the fact that the civilian jurisdiction of the High Commissioner who headed the Government of Palestine extended to Transjordan, upon assuming the duties of his office on July 1, 1920, one symbolic expression of which was the use of Palestine postage stamps for franking letters sent from Moab and Edom. What constituted a new course of policy was the British decision to exclude Transjordan from the Jewish National Home, that previously was only bruited about by the Curzon Foreign Office and to place this territory under provisional Sherifian/Hashemite rule.

The recommendations adopted at the Conference had been well prepared in advance by high-ranking officials of the newly-formed Middle East Department in the Colonial Office. They proposed the creation of a separate Arab administration for Transjordan, as laid out in a memorandum drafted by John Evelyn Shuckburgh during the last week of February 1921 (hereafter the Shuckburgh Memorandum).[5] The memorandum represented the collective view of Shuckburgh, who was the Head of the Department, Major Hubert Young and Colonel Thomas Edward Lawrence, better known as "Lawrence of Arabia". It sought to reconcile the Balfour Declaration with the British pledge given in the McMahon-Hussein Correspondence to recognize and support Arab independence in Arabia, although there was no actual legal or moral imperative to do so, since Palestine was excluded from that pledge, including the fertile part of Transjordan up to the Hedjaz Railway.

Churchill gave his full approval to the advice proffered to him by his departmental officials. It was not the first time he had heard the proposal to transfer Transjordan to Arab rule. General Walter Norris Congreve had made exactly that proposal in a letter he sent to Churchill on November 15, 1920 when the latter was Secretary of State for War and Air. Congreve was one of the participants at the Cairo Conference, holding the official title of General Officer Commanding the Troops in Egypt and Palestine (1921-1923). Having accepted the recommendations of the Shuckburgh Memorandum, Churchill turned a deaf ear to Weizmann's stirring appeal conveyed in a letter dated March 1, 1921, to save Transjordan for the Jewish National Home.

The legal justification for setting up a political system in Transjordan different from that in force in Cisjordan was explained in the Shuckburgh Memorandum which formed part of the official report on the Cairo Conference. According to the Memorandum, Britain could justify the Transjordanian plan by relying on two separate references in the Mandate then awaiting confirmation by the Council of the League of Nations:[6]

> 1. The second recital in the Preamble of the Mandate which referred to the Balfour Declaration and declared in a proviso "that nothing should be done which might prejudice the civil and religious rights of existing non-Jewish communities in Palestine;"
> 2. Article 3 of the Mandate which encouraged the widest measure of self-government for localities consistent with the prevailing conditions.

However, the foregoing two-fold justification for the administrative separation of Transjordan from the rest of Palestine was faulty because the

[5] See the biography of Winston S. Churchill by Martin Gilbert, Volume IV, 1917-1922, pp. 537-38, published by Heinemann: London (1975).

[6] See the "Report on the Middle East Conference held in Cairo and Jerusalem, March 12-30, 1921", found in *The Rise of Israel*, Volume 13, Document 26, p. 200. See also Gilbert, *op. cit.*, Volume IV, p. 538.

phrase "civil and religious rights" as used in the Balfour Declaration and the Mandate did not contemplate collective political rights for the Arabs of Palestine as a nation, and, moreover, Article 3 of the Mandate favouring local autonomy basically applied to a limited municipal area, not to a territory as large in size as Transjordan, over three times that of Cisjordan. Therefore, contrary to what was first believed by the British, there was simply nothing in the existing Draft Mandate to justify the far-reaching step of removing Transjordan from the Jewish National Home. That is why the British officials, seeing the futility of what they had tried to do, finally decided to revise the terms of the Mandate before its confirmation by inserting a tailor-made provision (Article 25 – see below) to accomplish their devious and injurious intention to wrest this territory from the Jewish National Home.

When Prime Minister Lloyd George and his Cabinet were appraised of the recommendations of the Cairo Conference, he dispatched a very urgent letter to Churchill on March 22, 1921 to advise him of the Cabinet's concerns and misgivings. The letter stated:

> Cabinet then discussed your proposals for Transjordan, as to which considerable misgivings were entertained. It was felt that almost simultaneous installation of the two brothers [Feisal and Abdullah] in regions contiguous to French sphere of influence would be regarded with great suspicion by them and would be interpreted as a menace to their position in Syria, deliberately plotted by ourselves. Further, while reasons for your recommendation of British military occupation of Transjordan as a guarantee against these perils were appreciated, it was urged by our military advisers that this occupation would involve a military commitment, the extension and duration of which it was impossible to forecast. Nor was it clear that Abdullah would accept such a position as that suggested, in a territory too small for a Kingdom and *subject to conditions identical with those which it is proposed to exact from Feisal as regards the Mandate and no intrigue against the French* (emphasis added).
>
> Presence of Abdullah in Transjordan from which he may be reluctant to go and general desire of His Majesty's Government to fulfill earlier promises to King Hussein about independence of Arab territories, undoubtedly favour an Arab rather than a Palestinian [i.e. Jewish - H.G.] solution. But the price to be paid for these advantages seems to be high and the results doubtful.
>
> The Cabinet was of opinion that you ought to be acquainted with these misgivings before you see Abdullah, and that you should not exclude other plans from your mind. It might, for instance, be possible, while preserving Arab character of the area and administration, to treat it as an Arab province or adjunct of Palestine.[7]

[7] *The Rise of Israel*, Volume 13, Document 12, p. 99.

It should be noted from the above remarks of Lloyd George to Churchill that the British proposals to Abdullah were subject to a double condition that also applied to his brother Feisal in Iraq. He had to accept the terms of the Mandate and not utilize his position to intrigue against the French in Syria.[8] As to the first condition imposed upon Abdullah regarding his obligation to accept the Mandate, if he was given the opportunity to administer the part of Palestine east of the Jordan, then all of Palestine west of the Jordan would be reserved exclusively for the Jewish National Home. He would thus be forever barred or estopped from claiming any rights over any area of Western Palestine. Jumping many years ahead, the installation of Abdullah in Transjordan, predicated on the aforementioned condition, rendered illegal, by this fact alone, his subsequent annexation of Judea and Samaria to Transjordan on April 24, 1950, which occurred only one year and three months before his assassination on July 20, 1951. It also made nonsense of the argument that was repeated endlessly after the Six-Day War of June 5-10, 1967 that Israel, in repossessing Judea and Samaria for the Jewish People, was "occupying Jordanian territory", i.e., the "West Bank" of Abdullah's enlarged kingdom, since the British had extracted a promise from Abdullah never to interfere in this territory, an undertaking he brazenly violated when he invaded and captured Judea and Samaria..

After the end of the Cairo Conference on March 22, 1921, Churchill visited Jerusalem and invited Abdullah to meet him at another conference that began on March 28, and ended two days later. It was arranged by Lawrence, who was then serving as an adviser on Arab Affairs to the Colonial Secretary. The participants also included Herbert Samuel, Wyndham Deedes and Major Hubert Young on the British side while Abdullah was assisted by Auni Abdul Hadi. At the first formal meeting of the Jerusalem Conference, Churchill informed Abdullah of what had just been decided at the Cairo Conference and approved by the Lloyd George cabinet, namely, that Transjordan would become an Arab province of mandated Palestine administered by an Arab Governor who would recognize British control over his administration. The Arab Governor was to be appointed by the High Commissioner for Palestine, but only after he had first obtained the prior agreement of Abdullah representing the Hashemite/Sherifian family. Churchill further stated to Abdullah that none of the Zionist clauses of the Mandate would apply in Transjordan. This arrangement was made contingent on Abdullah accepting the two preliminary conditions noted above: first, his repression of all anti-French activities in Transjordan, and second, his non-interference with Zionist activity in western Palestine where all the provisions of the Mandate would be in full operation. Churchill's proposals to Abdullah were accepted at their last meeting on March 30, 1921. In a letter from Churchill to Samuel, dated April 2, 1921, the Colonial Secretary informed the High Commissioner of the procedure to be adopted during the first six months

---

[8] These two British conditions imposed upon Abdullah are also mentioned by Sir Alec Seath Kirkbride in his book *A Crackle of Thorns: Experiences in the Middle East,* John Murray (Publishers), Ltd. (1956), p. 27.

of Abdullah's rule that began on April 1, 1921. The letter stated in part:

> The Emir Abdullah has promised to work with us and for us to do his best to restrain the people from anti-French action and to form, with our assistance, a local administration which can later on be handed over to a native Governor of less consequence. His position will be informal and no question of governorship or sovereignty is raised.[9]

The British concoction for Transjordan was a shameless betrayal of the Jewish People whose Zionist leaders had been induced to believe, in the just-concluded boundary negotiations with France, that this territory would indeed be a part of the Jewish National Home. Evidence for this belief is found in a letter written by Weizmann to the Under-Secretary of State at the Foreign Office dated January 5, 1921 and a nearly-identical letter to Winston Churchill on March 1, 1921, in which he reminded them about the assumption made in those negotiations that, as regards the territory in the east, "the needs of the Jewish National Home would be fully satisfied".

The following excerpt from Weizmann's letter to Churchill exposes the British betrayal:[10]

> May I bring to your attention *a matter of vital importance to the economic future of Palestine and the upbuilding of the Jewish National Home. It is the question of the eastern and southern frontiers.* The question has become especially critical in view of the agreement reached with France regarding the northern boundary which cut Palestine off from access to the Litani, deprived her of possession of the Upper Jordan and the Yarmuk and took from her the fertile plains east of the Tiberias which had heretofore been regarded as one of the most promising outlets for Jewish settlement on a large scale.
>
> During the discussions with the French, it may be recalled, *very little was said specifically of the eastern boundary south of the Hermon. It was for political purposes assumed that so far as the territory in the east was brought within the British sphere, the needs of the Jewish National Home would be fully satisfied.* Were this not the case, of course, *there would have been little purpose in the*

[9] Letter from Churchill to Samuel, at sea, April 2, 1921. Taken from "Appendix 19 – Transjordania", found in a Report on the Middle East Conference, held in Cairo and Jerusalem, March 12th to 30th, 1921. *The Rise of Israel*, Volume 13, Document 11, p. 98. The minutes of the conversations that took place in Jerusalem from March 28-30, 1921 between Churchill and Abdullah are found on pp. 90-97 of the foregoing citation. See also Gilbert's biography of Churchill, Volume IV, chapter 32, p. 558, entitled "Visit to Jerusalem". Abdullah's promise not to interfere in Zionist activity in Western Palestine is mentioned on pp. 561, 572 and 576.

[10] *The Letters and Papers of Chaim Weizmann,* Volume X, Series A, July 1920-December 1921, Letter 135, pp. 159-162.

> *struggle to secure for Palestine the right to use the Yarmuk, as the rights secured would be in large part valueless if the territory to the south also were to be taken from her jurisdiction and control. That territory must, it is clear, be settled with a fixed population* in order to give physical security and economic value to the extensive engineering works contemplated.
>
> ...*The opening of eastern Palestine to Jewish colonization* would consequently, far from aggravating the military burden of the Mandatory, offer the most promising prospect of its gradual reduction and ultimate surcease, for it is only through a permanent settlement of a peaceful population upon the Transjordanian plateaux that the problem of the defence of the whole Jordan Valley can be satisfactorily solved (emphasis added).

As pointed out by Weizmann in the above letter, it was assumed in 1920 by both the Zionist leadership and the British, prior to Abdullah's appearance in the region, that Transjordan (south of the Hermon: the Golan plateau; south of the Yarmuk: Gilead, Moab-Ammon and Edom) was of vital importance to the economic future of Palestine and the upbuilding of the Jewish National Home. This assumption was first made in the Zionist proposals submitted to the Paris Peace Conference, thereafter at the San Remo Peace Conference with the adoption of the historical formula for determining Palestine's borders, and finally by all the British negotiators in their boundary discussions with the French, where the Zionist leaders were in constant touch with the British team acting on their behalf. In light of this all-pervasive assumption that British-administered Transjordan would be an intrinsic part of the Jewish National Home, and the fact that Transjordan was an undeniable part of historical Palestine, Britain had no right to award the Arabian Emir Abdullah, at the expense of the Jewish National Home, a territorial and political plum in the form of the administration of Transjordan and a subsidy to boot. Instead of following a policy of appeasement, the British should have ejected the interloper Abdullah forthwith from Transjordan, just as the French did to his brother Feisal, for willfully preempting the legal decisions of the Peace Conference.

Churchill's proposals on Transjordan were contrary also to the Draft Mandate of December 6, 1920 because the latter, which had been pending before the League of Nations Council since that date after having received preliminary approval from the British Cabinet on November 29, 1920, did not contain any provision for setting up a separate administration for Transjordan. The appointment of Abdullah as Governor or Administrator of the so-called "Arab province of Palestine" was illegal in that it constituted a serious violation of the San Remo Resolution of April 24-25, 1920 and also article 95 of the Treaty of Sèvres, whose legal status as a treaty awaiting ratification was then not yet in serious doubt. While it is true that neither the San Remo Resolution nor the Treaty of Sèvres explicitly defined Palestine – the Jewish National Home – within specific boundaries, nevertheless they were assumed to be co-extensive with the historical frontiers of Palestine in accordance with the Lloyd George formula "from Dan to Beersheba" which undoubtedly included all or portions of Transjordan, extending north and south of the Yarmuk.[11] Exactly how much of Transjordan was to be included in the Home was discussed by Weizmann in his letter to Churchill of March 1, 1921. He recalled that the Zionists originally suggested in February 1919 at the Paris Peace Conference that the eastern border of Palestine be drawn close to, but west of the railway. This proposal was made at the time to accommodate Feisal, to give him a corridor along the railway, so as to connect the Hedjaz Kingdom with Damascus. However, after the fall of Feisal, this reason no longer existed. Weizmann now proposed to Churchill in the letter cited above:[12]

> In view of the French occupation of Damascus, His Majesty's Government may now consider... that it could be better for the present at least, to draw no definite eastern frontier short of the desert,

---

[11] Transjordan has been historically connected to the Jewish People since the time of Moses and the Exodus when the Israelite tribes, having left Egypt on the way to the Promised Land, conquered Gilead from Sihon, the Amorite king of Heshbon, and Bashan from Og, the Amorite king whose capitals were in Ashtarot and Edre'i. In later times, embracing the Periods of the Judges and the First Temple, the various regions comprising Transjordan changed hands a number of times, slipping in and out of Jewish control. In the Persian period, the area of Ammon was ruled by the Jewish family of the Tobiads. Large areas of Transjordan were conquered by the Hasmoneans. The Herodian kingdom included the Transjordanian territories of Perea, Gaulanitis, Batanaea, Trachonitis and Auranitis. During this time the territory of Transjordan also included the Greek-speaking league of cities known as the Decapolis and the kingdom of the Nabateans in the southern part. The Roman Emperor Trajan united all the different regions of Transjordan into the Province of Arabia in 106 C.E. Later, the Emperor Diocletian annexed the province of Arabia to Palestine, but in 358 C.E., this territory was detached and called Palestina Salutaris. In 425, two additional provinces of Palestine were created, Palestina Prima and Palestina Secunda. The name of the third province was changed from Palestina Salutaris to Palestina Tertia. Each province of Palestine included a specific area of Transjordan: Perea in Palestina Prima; the Decapolis and Golan in Palestina Secunda; and southern Transjordan down to Aila (Elath) in Palestina Tertia. The Arab conquerors of Palestine in the 7th century continued this administrative division of Palestine. Palestina Prima became the *jund* or district of Filastin and Palestina Secunda – the *jund* of Urdunn (Jordan), but Palestina Tertia was abandoned to the Bedouins and ceased to exist as an independent unit. The 12th century Crusader principality of Oultre Jourdain included Gilead (Ajlun), Kerak (Le Crac) and Shawbak (Montreal), down to the Red Sea. See article on Transjordan in *Encyclopaedia Judaica (1971)*, Vol. 15, cols. 1315-1318; see also the entry on the Land of Israel (Geographical Survey), Vol. 9, col. 121 and (History) cols. 254, 261, 269. Finally, see the article by Gideon Biger, "The Names and Boundaries of Eretz-Israel (Palestine) as Reflections of Stages in its History", p. 1, in the book entitled *The Land That Became Israel*, Studies in Historical Geography, edited by Ruth Kark, Yale University Press, New Haven (1990).

[12] See note 10 *supra*, Letter 135.

> but simply to provide special safeguards for the Moslem interests in the Hedjaz Railway.

In addition to violating the San Remo Resolution and the Treaty of Sèvres, Churchill's offer to Abdullah was illegal under Article 1 of the Boundary Convention of December 23, 1920 which fixed the northern and northeastern frontier lines between Palestine on one side and those of Syria and Lebanon on the other side. There was no territory in this Convention that was separately and formally designated as Transjordan. The newly-created frontier lines fundamentally assumed that all the territory that would constitute the Mandated State of Palestine would be assigned solely for the purpose of establishing the Jewish National Home and not for the purpose of forming a new Arab entity inside the Home, east of the Jordan, that was bigger than the Home itself. "Palestine territory" as set out in Article 5 of the Draft Mandate of December 6, 1920 and delineated in Article 1 of the Franco-British Boundary Convention of December 23, 1920 therefore meant "Jewish National Home territory" – or simply "Jewish territory". Hence, there was no difference between the two kinds of territory – whether it was called "Palestinian" or "Jewish" or by the combined name of "Jewish Palestine". Creating a difference between them or converting what was Palestinian-Jewish territory into Palestinian-Arab territory in regard to Transjordan was foreign to the legal structure, fabric and logic of both the Draft Mandate and the Boundary Convention seen as a whole.

Propelled by Churchill, Lawrence, Shuckburgh, Young and Samuel, the British Government proceeded with a plan to tear asunder the generally accepted concept that Palestine and the Jewish National Home were one and the same – by introducing in August 1921 an illegal revision to the Draft Mandate for Palestine in order to "legalize" an illegal offer to Abdullah to administer Jewish-designated territory in the wide expanse of Transjordan. This illegal amendment took the form of a new text for Article 25 in the Draft Mandate of December 6, 1920. It read as follows:

> In the territories lying between the Jordan and the eastern boundary of Palestine as ultimately determined, the Mandatory shall be entitled, *with the consent of the Council of the League of Nations*, to postpone or withhold application of such provisions of this Mandate as he [i.e., His Britannic Majesty, named as the Mandatory for Palestine in the Mandate] may consider inapplicable to *the existing local conditions*, and to make such provision for the territories as he may consider suitable to those *conditions*, provided no action shall be taken which is inconsistent with the provisions of Articles 15, 16 and 18 (emphasis added).

Article 25 of the Mandate acknowledged that Transjordan was "the eastern boundary of Palestine" and hence of the Jewish National Home, but then immediately provided for its provisional detachment from the Home because of the "inapplicability" of the pro-Zionist "provisions of this Mandate... to the existing local conditions" which mysteriously were never specified in the Article itself. The unsettled conditions existing locally in Transjordan in 1922 that justified its administrative separation from the rest of Palestine were comparatively speaking no more serious than those in Cisjordan, where fierce riots broke out in 1920 and 1921 that resulted in the deaths of many Jews and Arabs.

Transjordan was sparsely populated, one of the *existing local conditions* of this extensive territory which should have made it favourable for large-scale Jewish settlement. At the beginning of World War I, its population was only 141,982, not including the nomadic tribes, according to official Turkish sources.[13] For 1922 a new figure was arrived at by one researcher by including the people of these tribes in the overall count. The population was calculated to be 225,380, consisting of a settled population of 122,430 (54% of the total) and a nomadic population of 102,950 (46%).[14] The ethnic composition of the population of Transjordan was mainly Arab or Bedouin, with about 20,000 Circassians and Chechens from the Caucasus, who had been settled there since the 1870's by the Ottoman authorities.[15]

In a speech in the House of Commons on June 14, 1921, Churchill described the bad security situation in Transjordan which constituted the "existing local conditions" referred to in Article 25, as follows:

> Lastly, I must deal with the question of Transjordan. This is one of the most valuable parts of Palestine and comprises the ancient regions of Moab, Edom and Gilead. We have no troops of any kind in this district, and a state of continuous disorder has prevailed there for the last two years. The normal trade between Eastern and Western Palestine has been interrupted, and raiding parties of Arabs from Transjordan have repeatedly crossed the Jordan to kill and steal on the western side of the river. It was necessary to bring Transjordan under some form of settled government. This was necessary not only from our point of view but from that of the French, whose Syrian northern mandatory sphere marches with the northern boundaries of Transjordan. All

[13] See article by Joseph B. Schechtman in the *Encyclopedia of Zionism and Israel*, edited by Raphael Patai, Herzl Press/McGraw-Hill, New York (1971), Vol. 2, p. 1128.

[14] Mary C. Wilson, *King Abdullah, Britain and the making of Jordan*, Cambridge University Press (1987), p. 56, and footnotes 69-71 of her book on p. 229. Wilson's figure of 225,380 excludes the district of Ma'an and Aqaba, because, she states, it did not become officially a part of Transjordan until 1925. In any event, the population of this district was no more than 10,000, according to the figures she presented in her footnote number 70 on p. 229.

[15] Uriel Dann, *Studies in the History of Transjordan, 1920-1949: The Making of a State*, Westview Press, Boulder, Colorado (1984), p. 4.

> the discontented elements who were driven out of Damascus by the French in the recent trouble… had gathered in Transjordan, and had begun to raid northwards into French territory, blowing up bridges, etc., and taking other aggressive action. The French naturally objected to this state of things.
>
> It was clear that we ought to keep order ourselves, otherwise it was difficult to deny them the right to enter and to carry out operations in our territory. On the other hand, we were very reluctant to face the expense of maintaining two or three battalions in Transjordan and, worse than expense, the risk of getting them isolated and cut off by risings of the tribes. In these circumstances, we had recourse to the good offices of the Emir Abdullah, the elder brother of Emir Feisal, as part of our general policy of acting in accordance with Sherifian influence. I had a long conference with the Emir Abdullah at Jerusalem. He has undertaken to maintain order in Transjordan and to prevent any hostile action against the French. That was the indispensable stipulation which I made. We are assisting him to maintain local levies for the purpose of maintaining internal order…
>
> The general policy which we are pursuing of work with the Sherifian family is in no way opposed to the interests of France. On the contrary, it is the surest method open to us of securing France from disturbance in Syria by Arab influences with which she has unhappily disagreed…. It would be deeply injurious to both of us if France and Great Britain should be unable to act together in the Middle East. It would be absolutely fatal to our joint interests if the impression were to continue, as it has done during the last two years, that one country was indifferent to Arab aspirations and the other was especially opposed to the Turks. That would be disastrous. In such a way we should unite all the forces in these lands in hostility against us at the very time when we wish to reduce our military forces and the heavy expense to which both countries are put thereby. *If we wish to maintain our position and to discharge our responsibilities in the Middle East, England and France together must pursue a policy of appeasement and friendship towards both Turks and Arabs.*
>
> *The policy* which I have been endeavouring to explain to the Committee… *is animated throughout by a sincere desire to establish and consolidate a community of interest between the Arabs on one hand and Great Britain and her Allies on the other…*[16] (Italics added).

Churchill's comments about the lawless conditions prevailing in Transjordan for two years, even if true and which are not disputed, did not justify the removal of Transjordan from the Jewish National Home for that particular reason. The answer to the problem of disorder was to set up a better security apparatus to

[16] *The Rise of Israel*, Volume 13, Document 30, pp. 264-265.

control the situation and eliminate whatever lawlessness existed. That is exactly what Britain started to do in October 1923 when the "Arab Legion" was created under the command of Frederick Peake, by merging three security forces – the "Reserve Force", with the mounted gendarmerie and the urban police – into one new force. In 1926, the Transjordan Frontier Force was created with the duty of controlling raiding Beduin tribesmen in Transjordan. In 1930, a desert force was established by John Bagot Glubb, as part of the Arab Legion.

The only reason that a revamped Article 25 was introduced into the Mandate instrument was not because of the "existing local conditions" as stated in that article, but as Churchill implicitly indicated in his House of Commons speech of June 14, 1921, "to pursue a policy of appeasement and friendship" or "to establish and consolidate a community of interest" with the Sherifian Arabs, necessitated by the ouster of Feisal from Damascus on July 25, 1920. There was a real British fear that the anti-French Syrian nationalists who fled to Transjordan in the wake of the French takeover of Syria would embroil Britain in an unwanted dispute with France. To prevent that, the British needed to appease Abdullah with the gift of Transjordan on condition that he maintain public order there, cease all agitation against the French and also prevent raids into Cisjordan.

The very use of the phrase "existing local conditions" in regard to Transjordan meant that the "conditions" alluded to were of a passing nature and would, after they finally ceased to exist, make possible the re-union of Transjordan with Palestine. This is implicit in the wording of Article 25 which spoke of the need to "postpone or withhold application of such provisions of this Mandate as the [Mandatory] may consider inapplicable to the existing local conditions". No time limit was mentioned in Article 25 as to how long the postponement or inapplicability would last, particularly with regard to the provisions dealing with Jewish settlement. However, it had to be within a reasonable period of time during which there would be a restoration of public order and/or when the security forces were capable enough to deal with any tribal acts of brigandage to which Transjordan was susceptible.

Prior to the insertion of the revised Article 25 in the Mandate, it was always assumed that no matter how vociferous Arab opposition might be to the policy of the Jewish National Home, that by itself would not be a decisive factor to hinder its establishment anywhere in Palestine. The invention of the test of "existing local conditions" as a handy pretext to delay or deny inclusion of Transjordan in the Jewish National Home was therefore a sham which contradicted the other two reasons given in the White Paper of June 3, 1922 for Transjordan's detachment from the Home, namely the McMahon Pledge to the Sherif of Mecca, Hussein, and the grammatical interpretation given to the phrase "in Palestine". Article 25 was a skillful and recondite piece of draftsmanship that cleverly hid the actual reason why it was introduced into the Mandate, namely, to satisfy, in particular, the pretentious ambitions of Abdullah and, in general, those of the Sherifian Arab family of Hussein ibn Ali to control as much of the Middle East as possible. Hussein proclaimed himself "King of the Arab Countries" (or "King of the Arabs") on October 30, 1916, but Britain and her allies would only recognize him as the King of the Hedjaz. He was forced to abdicate in the autumn of 1924 after suffering defeat at the hands of Abd el-Aziz ibn-Saud, who overran the entire Arabian kingdom of the Hedjaz by the end of 1925. Article 25 amounted to an illegal and fraudulent addition to the provisions of the Mandate that had no inherent logic to it and was out of kilter with the entire thrust of the Mandate whose exclusive aim was to create a Jewish National Home throughout all regions of Palestine, regardless of the "existing local conditions" prevailing in any one region.

As a result of the Transjordanian interpolation into the Draft Mandate of December 6, 1920, the previously-numbered Articles 25, 26 and 27 were renumbered to become Articles 26, 27 and 28. Britain then re-submitted to the League Council a revised version of the Mandate for Palestine in August 1921 containing the new text of Article 25. The Mandate was finally confirmed a year later by the League Council on July 24, 1922, with some additional changes in other provisions of the Mandate. Barely two months later, the British Government had the venerable Lord Balfour present a memorandum to the League Council on September 16, 1922 inviting it to pass a resolution to create a separate provisional administration for Transjordan in accordance with Article 25 under the general supervision of the Mandatory. The Memorandum defined the territory of Transjordan as comprising

> All territory lying to *the east of a line* drawn from a point two miles west of the town of Aqaba on the Gulf of that name up the center of the Wadi Araba, the Dead Sea and the River Jordan to its junction with the river Yarmuk; thence up the center of that river to the Syrian frontier.[17] (Emphasis added.)

The British request was duly approved by the Council on the same day it discussed the Memorandum. A note dated September 23, 1922 was then sent to members of the League by the Secretary-General attesting to that fact. As a result, the provisions of the Mandate specifically referring to the Jewish National Home were not made applicable to Transjordan, which was ironic since all provisions of the Mandate for Palestine related directly in one way or another

[17] The valley from the southern end of the Dead Sea to the Gulf of Aqaba is called in Hebrew *Nahal ha-Arava* and in Arabic *Wadi el-Araba*, whereas north of the Dead Sea, the Jordan Valley is now called *el-Ghor*, meaning "the depression". The Dead Sea which lies at the deepest part of the depression is also known as "the (Salt) Sea of the Araba". The Hebrew word *araba* means an arid steppe, desert or wilderness. See *Encyclopedic Dictionary of the Bible* by Louis F. Hartman, McGraw-Hill Book Company, Inc. (New York) 1963, under the entry *Araba*, p. 122. In defining "Palestine" after carrying out the administrative separation of Transjordan, the British Government simply substituted the word "west" for "east" of a line drawn from the same point.

to the establishment of the Jewish National Home, not merely those which mentioned it specifically or obviously applied to it. The new text of Article 25 now had a facade of legality after its approval by the League Council, but it still remained in essence a contradiction of Articles 2 and 5 of the Mandate which considered all "Palestine territory" to be exclusively "Jewish territory" in light of the paramount purpose of the Mandate to establish the Jewish National Home in all of Palestine on both sides of the Jordan. The area of Palestine east of the Jordan was henceforth brought under the control of a foreign government in direct violation of Article 5.

The original separation of Transjordan from the Jewish National Home was illegal on another ground, procedural in nature, because it was carried out in the first stage by an order of the High Commissioner – hereafter the Boundary Order – published on September 1, 1922, that was issued under Article 86 of the Palestine Order-in-Council of 1922, two weeks before the League Council actually approved the British memorandum of September 16, 1922. This approval, while allowing for such an order to be made was not made retroactive to the date of the Boundary Order.[18] This violated the correct procedure for implementing Article 25 of the Mandate to administratively separate Transjordan from the rest of Palestine. The boundary order stated that the Palestine Order-in-Council shall not apply to "the territories East of the Jordan and the Dead Sea", which had the effect of removing what then became Transjordan from the new constitutional arrangement of government being set up for Cisjordan. Article 86 of the Order-in-Council expressly mentioned that any action taken by the High Commissioner with regard to the administrative separation of these territories from Palestine was "subject to the provisions of Article 25 of the Mandate". This provision of the Order-in-Council made Article 25 of the Mandate indisputably part of the domestic law of Palestine, and therefore the stipulations of this Article of the Mandate had to be meticulously observed when the High Commissioner invoked it, regardless of the fact that the Mandate as a whole did not come into legal force at the level of international law until September 29, 1923. Accordingly, the prior consent of the League Council was absolutely necessary before any order setting up a separate administration in the territories East of the Jordan and the Dead Sea could be issued. However, when the boundary order was in fact issued, no such prior consent for that order

[18] This order is found in the Official Gazette of the Government of Palestine, September 1, 1922, called the "Order defining Boundaries of Territory to which the Palestine Order-in-Council does not apply". The text of the boundary order reads as follows: "Whereas it is provided in the Palestine Order-in-Council, 1922, that the said Order shall not apply to such part of the territories to the East of the Jordan and the Dead Sea as shall be defined by order of the High Commissioner – It is Hereby Ordered As Follows: The Palestine Order-in Council, 1922 shall not apply to the territory lying East of a line drawn from a point two miles West of the town of Akabah in the Gulf of Akabah up the centre of the Wady Arabah, the Dead Sea and the River Jordan to the junction of the latter with the River Yarmuk, thence up the centre of the River Yarmuk to the Syrian Frontier."

had been obtained from the League Council, in direct violation of Article 25 of the Mandate. Since the boundary order was issued prematurely, without the required permission of the League Council, it was illegal for that reason alone. No additional boundary order was ever issued after September 16, 1922 when the British request to the League Council to separate the administration of the Transjordanian territories from the rest of Palestine was approved by the League Council, which would have retroactively corrected the illegality of the original boundary order issued by the High Commissioner. As a result, the Palestine Order-in-Council still applied to these territories, henceforth collectively called Transjordan. In this respect it may be noted that the Palestine Order-in-Council was proclaimed only *after* the confirmation of the Mandate on July 24, 1922, while the boundary order in regard to Transjordan was proclaimed *prior* to the approval of the British memorandum to the League Council on September 16, 1922. Therefore, from the perspective of the local law of Palestine, the exemption of the Palestine Order-in-Council from being made applicable to Transjordan was illegal and non-enforceable and so, too, was the subsequent establishment of a separate administration for Transjordan, because no valid order of exemption was ever issued under Article 86 of the Palestine Order-in-Council.

Despite the inapplicability of certain Jewish National Home provisions of the Mandate to Transjordan, as a result of the illegal British action, this territory still remained a constituent part of Palestine under international law, representing its eastern boundary as affirmed by Article 25 of the Mandate and Article 86 of the Palestine Order-in-Council. Both sides of Palestine, east and west of the Jordan, had the same Mandatory – His Britannic Majesty, the same High Commissioner, the same currency and a free trade arrangement without barriers or customs duties on imports and exports.

The status of Transjordan under international law as a constituent part of Palestine contrasted sharply with its status under the municipal law of Palestine, where it was not included within the definition of Palestine for purposes of the law, as a direct result of the illegal Boundary Order of September 1, 1922. In the law of Palestine, the country so designated was henceforth limited to the area of Cisjordan.

Under the provisions of Article 25 of the Mandate, Transjordan was to remain outside the orbit of the Jewish National Home only so long as Britain decided it was necessary because of the "existing local conditions". A pertinent discussion as to what exactly those conditions were which justified Transjordan's continuing exemption from certain provisions of the Mandate in regard to the Jewish National Home arose at a meeting of the 23rd session of the Permanent Mandates Commission held at Geneva in 1933 when this body examined the possibility of opening up Transjordan to Jewish settlement. The idea gained currency that year when a large loan was offered to Emir Abdullah by the Jewish Agency for the general development of Transjordan if a scheme for settlement was approved by the British authorities. The offer was made after an emissary of Abdullah had approached two members of the Jewish Agency Executive, Yehoshua (Joshua) Heshel Farbstein and Emanuel Neumann, to finance the development of 67,000 dunams of land in Transjordan. An agreement was reached for an option on a lease of 33 years, renewable for two similar periods with an annual payment of 2,200 Palestine Pounds. But under strong pressure exerted by Britain and violent denunciations of Abdullah in newspapers controlled by the Mufti of Jerusalem, Hajj Amin al-Husseini, Abdullah was compelled to disown the agreement he had made with the Jewish Agency.[19]

At the above-mentioned meeting of the Permanent Mandates Commission, the accredited representative of Britain, Mark Aitchison Young, who was the Chief Secretary to the Government of Palestine, was asked by some members of the Commission to explain the negative British attitude toward the Jewish settlement project. He told them:[20]

> The Mandatory Power had given close consideration to this question and concluded that it was not desirable for general reasons of security to encourage Jewish settlement in Transjordan. There was no movement in favour of settlement by other races, and there were no vast spaces calling for colonists, although it was true that the country was not so thickly populated as Palestine.

> He added:

> It was true that there was nothing in the Mandate which prohibited the Jewish colonization of Transjordan, but His Majesty's Government in view of all the considerations, had concluded on the ground of local feeling and of the general question of security, that it was not practicable to facilitate such colonization.

In reply to transferring Arabs from Cisjordan to Transjordan, to relieve congestion and to facilitate the settlement of the "dispossessed" Arabs, the British official replied:

> [I know] of no objection, provided there was no attempt to transfer

---

[19] See article on Transjordan in *Encyclopedia of Zionism and Israel*, Herzl Press, New York (1971), Vol. 2, p. 1128.

[20] The members of the Permanent Mandates Commission who questioned Mr. Young were Lord Lugard, Count De Penha Garda and D.F.W. Van Rees. The relevant minutes of the discussion were presented in the Memorandum submitted to the Palestine Royal Commission on behalf of the Jewish Agency for Palestine. See: *The Rise of Israel*, Vol. 23, Document 1, Zionist Evidence before the Peel Commission, 1936-1937, edited by Aaron S. Kleiman, pp. 211, 243. The Memorandum was reprinted in 1975 in book form by Greenwood Press, Westport, Connecticut. See pp. 211-213, paragraphs 349 to 351.

> a larger number of Arabs to Transjordan than the country could receive. There were no great empty spaces, nor was there any strong movement to transfer a large number of Arabs.

Young's contrived reasons as to why Britain did not permit the settlement of Jews in Transjordan nor, for that matter, even the re-location of Cisjordanian Arabs were baseless. Security was a pressing problem everywhere in Palestine, not limited to the east of the Jordan River. Hence, that factor alone did not deter the establishment of new Jewish settlements because their residents took whatever measures were necessary to ensure their own security. Local feeling was also not a determining factor, since if that was the criterion, it would have frustrated Jewish settlement throughout Palestine, not just in Transjordan. In truth, the real reason the British government barred organized Jewish settlement in Transjordan had nothing to do with local feeling or the demands of security, but rather it was a cornerstone of British policy to keep all Jews out of Transjordan. A different policy allowing Jews to settle there in organized groups would inevitably have led to the rescinding of the application of Article 25 of the Mandate to Transjordan.

It was strange for Young to say there were no great empty spaces for organized Jewish settlement in Transjordan. This was an obvious falsehood which did not fool anybody. On the contrary, the "existing local conditions" actually favoured Jewish settlement – for sufficient space was certainly available, internal security was assured by the settlers themselves, just as it was in Cisjordan, and the local inhabitants would have greatly benefited from the economic development of the territory fostered by a growing Jewish population and the inflow of new investment capital to an undeveloped, sparsely populated region of Palestine that was historically, geographically and economically connected to the country. Instead of passively and meekly accepting Britain's *judenrein* policy for Transjordan, the Jewish Agency for Palestine should have pressed Britain much harder in a persistent no-holds-barred campaign, for as pointed out in a previous chapter, millions of Jews could have then come from Europe to escape the gathering threat of Hitler and settle in Jewish communities in Transjordan, as proposed by U.S. Senator Daniel O. Hastings in 1936 in a series of six newspaper articles on the subject. If this proved of no avail, the Jewish Agency should have appealed either to the League of Nations for a decision on the matter, while there was still time to save Europe's Jews from impending disaster, or directly to the United States Government or any other sympathetic Government of a state which was a member of the League of Nations, to launch a suit in the Permanent Court of International Justice for the abrogation of Article 25's continuing illegal application to this territory on the ground that the "existing local conditions" had indeed changed in favour of allowing large scale Jewish settlement. Unfortunately, nothing of the kind was done or even contemplated, and thus the ban on organized Jewish settlement in Transjordan persisted beyond the limits of normal reason, contrary to Article 25 which only disallowed such settlement in Transjordan for a temporary period.

In addition, the British Government was able to ignore Article 15 of the Mandate which provided that "no person shall be excluded from Palestine on the basis of his religious belief". Theoretically, this provision made it possible for Jews to immigrate and settle in Transjordan on an individual basis, as opposed to collective and organized Jewish immigration and settlement, but Article 15 clashed with the still-applied Ottoman Turkish law which prohibited individual Jews settling in Transjordan.[21] The British duplicitously cited this prohibition as another reason to ban the entry of Jews into that part of Palestine. Properly, Turkish law could not be legally invoked against the binding provisions of the Mandate which represented international constitutional law and was the *raison d'etre* for the British presence in both Cisjordan and Transjordan. However, inasmuch as the Courts in Palestine, under the sway of British judges, ruled that the Mandate for Palestine was not part of the domestic law of the country unless it had been specifically incorporated, it was conceivable that this Turkish prohibition on individual Jews going to live in Transjordan may have been upheld, had there been an actual legal action instituted in the courts of Palestine. On the other hand, if it could have been conclusively shown that Article 15 of the Mandate had indeed been incorporated into the municipal law of Transjordan, then it is likely that the judgment of the local Courts or any appeal to the British Privy Council, if allowed to take place, would have upheld the right of Jews to settle in Transjordan. There was evidence that such incorporation had indeed taken place, based on the following logic: the boundary order of the High Commissioner dated September 1, 1922, issued by him pursuant to the authority he received under Article 86 of the Palestine Order-in-Council, was, as noted above, made subject to observing the provisions of Article 25 of the Mandate, which in turn was subject to the strictures of Article 15 of the Mandate. This meant that no action could be taken by the Mandatory in administering Transjordan that would be inconsistent with the provisions of Articles 15, 16 and 18, all of which banned discrimination between the inhabitants of Palestine, including Transjordan, on the grounds of race, religion or language and was applied specifically to the immigration of Jews into the country, both west and east of the Jordan. Therefore, by virtue of Article 86 of the Palestine Order-in-Council, both Article 15 and Article 25 of the Mandate not only were incorporated into the domestic law of Palestine west of the Jordan upon the publication of the Order-in-Council, but also Article 15 was automatically incorporated into the municipal law of Transjordan when the boundary order of September 1, 1922 was issued by the High Commissioner, leaving aside the question of the legality of this order as discussed above. That being the case, a court in Palestine or the U.K. would have been obliged to apply the non-discriminatory provisions enshrined in Article 15 of the Mandate and

[21] See the reference to the Turkish law affecting Jewish settlement contained in the Memorandum submitted to the Palestine Royal Commission by the Jewish Agency for Palestine, pp. 211 and 243. See note 20 above.

allow individual Jews to immigrate and settle in Transjordan, regardless of what Ottoman Turkish law said on the matter.

Apart from the question of Jewish immigration and settlement in Transjordan, there was also something very strange in setting up a provisional Arab Government there while at the same time denying the same opportunity of self-government to the Jews in Western Palestine, for whose benefit the Mandate for Palestine was conferred on Britain. A joint British and Jewish Government or sharing arrangement of some sort was certainly possible under Article 2 of the Mandate which made Britain "responsible for placing the country under such political, administrative and economic conditions as will secure the establishment of the Jewish National Home... and the development of self-governing institutions...". But Britain, after Balfour left the active political scene as Foreign Secretary with ministerial responsibility for the establishment of the Jewish National Home, that he championed, was not interested in developing self-governing institutions for the National Home, which they falsely interpreted as being an obligation they had only towards the Arab population of Palestine, rather than to the Jews of the country. Nor were the British particularly interested in placing Zionists who were not lackeys to British imperialist interests in important administrative positions. What is surprising is that the official Zionist leadership supinely accepted the British deviation from Article 2's command, initiated by Lord Curzon several months after he succeeded Balfour as Foreign Secretary on October 24, 1919. During Balfour's tenure and for a short period afterwards, Foreign Office officials, still guided by his directives before they were abruptly changed by Curzon, actually accepted a clause in the Draft Mandates of September 26, 1919 and December 11, 1919 which recognized a proposed Provisional Council (later referred to as an appropriate Jewish agency) representing Jewish opinion both in Palestine and in the world generally, "with power to advise and cooperate with the British Government *in all administrative... matters affecting the establishment of the Jewish National Home* (emphasis added) and the interests of the Jewish population in Palestine".[22] This clause, had it remained in force, would have enabled an embryonic Jewish Government to be eventually created in Palestine. What appears to be a contradiction in Balfour's attitude concerning the establishment of a Jewish government in Palestine as a natural precursor of a Jewish State, comes from a reply he made to Lord Curzon on January 29, 1919, who bitterly

[22] See *Documents on British Foreign Policy,* First Series, Volume IV, p. 429 ff regarding separate British and Zionist Draft Mandates, both dated September 26, 1919, and p. 572 ff regarding a jointly drafted Mandate dated December 11, 1919. In the memorandum of Eric Graham Forbes Adam dated September 26, 1919, the Draft of the Political Section of the British Peace Delegation in Paris is shown side by side with the Draft of the Zionist Organization. A common draft was then formulated on December 11, 1919 between the British and Zionist representatives. Forbes Adam, a junior member of the Delegation, and William Malkin, a legal adviser, acted for the British Foreign Office while Benjamin V. Cohen, a young American lawyer, acted for the Zionist Organization.

complained that Weizmann sought exactly that:[23]

> ...As far as I know, Weizmann has never put forward a claim for the Jewish *Government* (italics in the original) of Palestine. Such a claim is, in my opinion, certainly inadmissible and personally I do not think we should go further than the original declaration which I sent to Lord Rothschild.

In all fairness to Balfour, what he really meant by the above-quoted words, consistent with his explanation to the War Cabinet on October 31, 1917, that approved the declaration bearing his name, as well as with later statements he made on the subject of a Jewish state, was that a Jewish government would not be set up *immediately*, but was the end goal that would be realized only when the Jewish people formed a majority of the population of Palestine, a prospect that he thought may well have taken decades. Until that day arrived, the Jews in the meantime would have an opportunity to participate in the administration of Palestine through the above-mentioned Provisional Council approved by Balfour. It was precisely to prevent that from happening that Curzon deleted the reference to the administrative power of the projected Jewish agency or council in what eventually became Article 4 of the Mandate after he took over the Foreign Office and began to personally supervise the ongoing drafting of the Mandate. Thus Curzon effectively scotched any budding attempt by Weizmann to begin the process of creating a future Palestinian Jewish Government or even to give Palestinian Jewry an important administrative role in the Government of Palestine, although that still remained a valid expectation under Article 2 of the Mandate. One important Zionist leader had actively pressed this point. Julius Simon, a member of the Zionist Executive, proposed in his own draft mandate of 1918 that the High Commissioner should always be a Jew and that the principal administrative functions in the Palestinian government should be held by Jews. Major William Ormsby-Gore (later Lord Harlech) who was shown Simon's Draft Mandate by Weizmann told the latter that such provisions would not be acceptable to the British Government, as was later made even more explicit in the Churchill White Paper of June 3, 1922.[24]

Once Abdullah's administration was in place in Transjordan, the original British plan that it would constitute only an informal and temporary arrangement was swiftly discarded. The six-month time limit expired and was conveniently forgotten. Abdullah traveled to London in October 1922 and his role as Administrator of Transjordan was confirmed. He was given a verbal assurance on October 28, 1922 by Gilbert F. Clayton, on behalf of the Colonial Office,

---

[23] *Palestine Papers 1917-1920, Seeds of Conflict*, compiled and annotated by Doreen Ingrams, published by John Murray (Publishers) Ltd., London (1972), p. 57. See also Martin Gilbert's biography, *Winston S. Churchill*, Volume IV, p. 621, n. 1.

[24] See Julius Simon's book *Certain Days: Zionist Memoirs and Selected Papers*, p. 86.

that Britain would recognize the establishment of an independent administration in Transjordan. This assurance came nine days after the resignation of Lloyd George on October 19, 1922 as Prime Minister, which led to the fall of his government, and the subsequent departure from office of Churchill who had earlier appointed Abdullah to his position.

Abdullah was never the Emir or Prince of Transjordan as is often stated, but rather the Hashemite Emir of the Arabian Hedjaz, who received this title from his father, Hussein ibn Ali, who was himself appointed the Emir or Grand Sherif of Mecca in 1908 and who then became the King of the Hedjaz by self-proclamation on October 30, 1916.[25] The Hashemites claimed descent from the Hashem clan of the Kuraish (Quraysh) Bedouin tribe in central Arabia, near Mecca, to which Muhammad belonged. Abdullah's title of Emir of the Hedjaz, which he held several years before he took over the administration of Transjordan, had led many people to wrongly conclude that Transjordan was created as an emirate on April 1, 1921 for his benefit, when legally it was simply a separately-administered territory or region of Palestine throughout the period of the Mandate. In March 1921 the British Government decided that Transjordan would become an Arab "province" of Palestine, but the use of the word "province" to describe this territory was inexact since Palestine, including its eastern expanse into the desert, was never officially divided into provincial administrative units. The Administration of Palestine divided Cisjordan into districts, the number of which varied from time to time. The only legal title which Abdullah derived from ruling Transjordan as part of Mandated Palestine from April 1, 1921 to March 22, 1946 was that of Administrator.[26] It was the British Government which nourished the false impression that Transjordan existed as an emirate by formally calling Abdullah "His Highness, the Emir of Transjordan" in several agreements it concluded with him in 1928, 1934, 1941 and 1946. That in turn led to the erroneous belief that Transjordan existed not only as an emirate, but also as a separate mandated territory disconnected from the Mandate for Palestine.

On May 25, 1923, Herbert Samuel, the High Commissioner of Palestine, accompanied by Clayton and St. John Philby, Britain's Chief Political Representative in Amman, announced that an *independent government* in Transjordan would be recognized by Great Britain, subject to the approval of the League of

---

[25] The Arabic word *emir* or *amir* denotes a prince or commander, and is a title of honour given to the descendants of Muhammad.

[26] In his summary report to Colonial Secretary Leopold Stennett Amery dated April 22, 1925 covering the five-year period of his Administration of Palestine, including Transjordan (1920-1925), Samuel wrote in reference to Abdullah: "...The Mandatory Power recognized him, for a period, as administrator of Transjordan...". He was also described in the same paragraph as an amir, but that designation indicated the royal title he had received from his father Hussein. It did not refer to his new position in Transjordan, as is evident from the context of that paragraph. See *The Rise of Israel*, Volume 13, Document 35, p. 544.

Nations and provided it was constitutional in nature and allowed the British Government to fulfill its international obligations in respect of the territory, as evidenced by an agreement to be concluded between the two governments. That agreement was not made until nearly five years later on February 20, 1928, known as the Anglo-Transjordanian Agreement. Article 2 of this agreement stated that the powers of legislation and of administration, entrusted to Britain under Article 1 of the Mandate, would be exercised in Transjordan by Abdullah under a regime of constitutional government to be defined in an organic law.

Prior to February 20, 1928, Abdullah had exercised a legally undefined power of administration over Transjordan on a limited and provisional basis, subject to strict British supervision. Henceforth this power was much broader in scope, no longer provisional but permanent or almost so, and anchored in a constitutional law. His Government had the right to make laws, though certain ones needed to be referred for the advice of the British Government before enactment, such as the annual budget law, any law affecting the currency of Transjordan, the jurisdiction of the civil courts over foreigners or amending the provisions of the Organic Law. The power to make laws is an attribute of statehood and sovereignty, particularly a law which creates a new nationality. The inhabitants of Transjordan, who were previously Ottoman subjects and had been living in the territory for six months or more since 1924, now received Transjordanian nationality, a legal anomaly because of the fact that under international law, Palestine was still one undivided country which meant that all its citizens had the same nationality. Moreover, the passage of a nationality law by Abdullah's administration was contrary to the intent of Article 7 of the Mandate for Palestine, which said that "the Administration of Palestine shall be responsible for enacting a nationality law".

The making of the 1928 agreement, together with the enactment of an Organic Law of Transjordan and a Nationality Law meant that Transjordan was in the process of being created as a new sovereign state with jurisdiction over its own affairs, though still subject to British advice, particularly in the field of foreign relations, tendered by a British Resident acting on behalf of the "High Commissioner for Transjordan". The reference to the person holding the supposed rank of High Commissioner for Transjordan, instead of High Commissioner for Palestine, was novel. It was another indication that Britain was planning to make Transjordan into an independent state. All communications between foreign Powers and Transjordan had to be made through the British Resident and the High Commissioner. Matters relating to the defence of the country were in the hands of the British Government, which also assisted Abdullah in preserving domestic peace and order.

The enormous change in the legal status of Transjordan wrought by the Anglo-Transjordanian Agreement of February 20, 1928, the Organic Law and the Nationality Law should have set off alarm bells about the blatant illegality of what Britain did in that part of Palestine, in violation of Articles 1,2,5,7 and 25 of the Mandate, as well as Article 1 of the Franco-British Boundary

Convention of December 23, 1920 and the San Remo Resolution on Palestine. The *de facto* partition of Palestine into Cisjordan and Transjordan was virtually an accomplished fact, although that step was not officially taken until March 22, 1946 when Britain signed a Treaty of Alliance with Abdullah recognizing him as a sovereign ruler. Transjordan formally declared itself a sovereign and independent kingdom on May 25, 1946.

The 1928 Agreement was scrutinized by the Permanent Mandates Commission who correctly thought it went beyond what was allowed by Article 25 of the Mandate. The Commission believed that the modifications to the Mandate made by Britain as a result of that Agreement required the formal consent of the Council of the League of Nations under Article 27 of the Mandate.

The Permanent Mandates Commission pointed out that Article 2 of the Agreement of February 20, 1928, which turned over to Abdullah the powers of legislation and administration entrusted by the Mandate to Britain, "does not seem to be compatible with the stipulations of the Mandate", especially Article 1.[27] The transfer of these powers to Abdullah made him the ruler of an independent Government, as explicitly stated in the third recital of the preamble of the Agreement. This transfer was clearly a modification of Article 1 of the Mandate for Palestine that was still in force in Transjordan even after Britain had applied Article 25 of the Mandate. It violated the legal maxim of *delegatus non potest delegare*, i.e., a delegate cannot delegate, signifying that a person or body in whose favour powers have been delegated cannot in turn delegate the same powers to another.

The 1928 Agreement was then referred by the Permanent Mandates Commission to the Council of the League for its consideration. The British representative, Lord Cushendun (Ronald John McNeill), answered the charge of the Agreement's incompatibility with the stipulations of the Mandate by drawing the attention of the Council to the Memorandum approved by it on September 16, 1922 in regard to Article 25, specifically in the last part of paragraph 2 of the Memorandum, which said:

> In the application of the Mandate to Transjordan, the action which in Palestine is taken by the Administration of the latter country will be taken by the Administration of Transjordan *under the general supervision of the Mandatory* (emphasis added).

Lord Cushendun argued that the Memorandum of September 16, 1922, as well as Article 25 of the Mandate which entitled Britain to administer Transjordan in the way it considered suitable under the "existing local conditions", gave it the right to delegate its administrative and legislative powers. This argument was incorrect inasmuch as these powers, delegated to Britain in the Mandate, were

[27] League of Nations – Official Journal, October 1928, p. 1574 and 1451-1453.

supposed to be exercised by the British themselves and not by an Arab prince not completely beholden to Britain and its binding international obligations under the Mandate. None of the functions and duties of the Administration of (Cisjordanian) Palestine were ever delegated to a Jewish Government, despite the implicit obligation of the British to do so under Article 2 of the Mandate, and by the same logic, neither should those of the Administration of Transjordan have been delegated to an Arab Government, even if the two administrations were to be separate and apart from each other by virtue of the application of Article 25. The delegation of government powers to an independent *Arab* Government in Transjordan was all the more illogical because the Mandate as a document contained no mention of the Arabs in any part of Palestine nor of any Arab national rights. Thus the language of Article 25 of the Mandate, so carefully drafted by the legal advisers of the British Government to provide for the administrative separation of Transjordan from the rest of Palestine in order *to set up an Arab Government there*, did not actually meet their intentions in introducing this new article. To accomplish the desired goal or at least furnish a legal pretext for creating an Arab Government in Transjordan, it would have been necessary for the drafters of Article 25 to make explicit reference to a future *Arab* administration of Transjordan, not merely to an administration "suitable to the existing local conditions". The failure to stipulate a government of this exact kind for Transjordan made Abdullah's Arab administration illegal from the start.

In addition, and contrary to the impression Lord Cushendun gave to the League Council, this was no ordinary delegation of functions and duties from one delegate to another. What the British carried out on February 20, 1928 was not a true delegation in the legal sense, but the near-permanent transfer of powers to what they themselves called an independent government headed by Abdullah. This, by definition, meant that Abdullah's Administration would not be relegated to a subordinate position as a mere delegate or agent of the British Government. "An independent government" signified that neither Abdullah nor his Administration would any longer be subject to *the general supervision* or restraint *of the Mandatory* as required by the British undertaking to the League Council upon the approval of the Memorandum of September 16, 1922.

The status of Abdullah was, in fact, being illegally changed by the 1928 Agreement and the Organic Law pursuant to it from that of a mere Administrator possessing powers delegated by the British Government to that of a ruler in his own right not yet fully independent because Britain still retained the right to advise and assist his government in various matters specified in the Agreement. The situation now prevailing east of the Jordan was akin to that which prevailed in Iraq in the years just before it gained complete independence from Britain in 1932 and became a member of the League of Nations. It was expected that Abdullah, too, following in the same path as his younger brother Feisal, would extend his newly acquired autonomy to eventual statehood, a process that became inevitable by the conclusion of the 1928 Agreement.

Despite the misgivings voiced by the Permanent Mandates Commission about the incompatibility of the agreement of February 20, 1928 with the binding stipulations of the Mandate, the League Council accepted the British argument that the agreement was in conformity with the principles of the Mandate. The following draft resolution was adopted by it:[28]

> As regards the Agreement of February 28th, 1928, between Great Britain and Transjordan, the Council takes note of the declaration of the representative of Great Britain according to which his Government regards itself as responsible to the Council of the League of Nations for the application in Transjordan of the Palestine Mandate, with the exception of the articles which, based on Article 25, are not applicable, and acknowledges that this Agreement is in conformity with the principles of the mandate, which remains fully in force.

The League Council acted wrongly in this matter for the reasons just noted, which only encouraged the British authorities to continue unhampered with their illegal separation of Transjordan from Cisjordan. The reassuring explanation presented by the British representative hid the truth of what Britain was doing. Article 25 of the Mandate gave Britain the right to set up a provisional administration for a limited period only in Transjordan. It did not give it the right to lay the foundation of an embryonic sovereign state in that territory administered by an independent Arab Government not fully under British supervision, which would inevitably lead in the years immediately afterwards to a permanent partition of Palestine. What Britain did in 1928 clearly went beyond the parameters of Article 25, as well as several other articles of the mandate mentioned above, especially Article 5 which prohibited the Mandatory from ceding "Palestine territory" or placing any part of it under the control of the Government of a foreign Power. In the words of that article, Transjordan was "Palestine territory" and Abdullah's administration of this territory was henceforth the Government of a foreign Power. As a result of the Anglo-Transjordanian Agreement, the possibility of Transjordan's reunion with Cisjordan and the Jewish National Home no longer existed, unless drastic steps to the contrary were subsequently taken to reverse the effects of the Agreement, but this was never done.

The Boundary Convention of December 23, 1920, known also as the Leygues-Hardinge Treaty, was also relevant in determining the validity of the Agreement of February 20, 1928, because it had confirmed Transjordan as an integral part of Palestine and the Jewish National Home. When tied to Article 5 of the Mandate, it constituted a legal bulwark against the British move in 1928 to create the new state of Transjordan.

Under the provisions of this 1920 treaty, Transjordan, south of the Yarmuk

---

[28] *Ibid.*, p. 1453.

and Jebel Druse, was formally placed within the borders of Palestine, even though the eastern boundary of Transjordanian Palestine with Iraq was left for future determination, as well as the southern frontier with Arabia. These borders were to be fixed in accordance with the decisions taken eight months earlier by the Principal Allied Powers at the San Remo Peace Conference that had granted mandates to Britain and France to separately administer Palestine, Mesopotamia and Syria. The eventual demarcation of boundaries was also provided for in Articles 94 and 95 of the Treaty of Sèvres of August 10, 1920. Article 1 of the Franco-British Boundary Convention of December 23, 1920, which completed the provisions of Article 5 of the Draft Mandate of December 6, 1920 regarding the definition of Palestine's northern boundary, marked the first *explicit* acknowledgement under international law, that Transjordan was a definite part of Palestine. That fact was already *implicitly* assumed in the San Remo Resolution of April 24-25, 1920 which created Palestine as a country based on its historical frontiers extending from "Dan to Beersheba" as first agreed to by Georges Clemenceau and Lloyd George in discussions held between them on December 1, 1918 and reaffirmed several times afterwards. The Biblical limits representing the whole of "historic Palestine" naturally included Transjordan, as confirmed by the Palestine Royal Commission Report.[29]

The Boundary Convention thus conclusively settled the question as to whether Transjordan would be joined to Palestine or excluded from it. Prior to December 23, 1920 there were different proposals, arrangements and documents which pointed in one direction or the other concerning the future of Transjordan. This occurred because the borders of Palestine had never been specifically defined or delineated in any binding act or treaty of international law despite the frequent usage of the name of Palestine as a historical and geographical term. The territory of Transjordan was assumed to be part of Palestine in the Report of the De Bunsen Committee of June 30, 1915, as shown in the map of Palestine affixed to its Report, and implicitly in the Balfour Declaration of November 2, 1917 and the San Remo Resolution on Palestine of April 24-25, 1920. As regards the McMahon Pledge of October 24, 1915, see below in Part II of this chapter. However, it was excluded from the limits of Palestine in the secret Sykes-Picot Treaty of May 9 and 16, 1916 and in General Allenby's division of occupied enemy territory in September 1919, based on the Deauville-Paris Agreement, which temporarily placed Transjordan under the rule of Feisal's Government in Damascus covering the zone designated as Occupied Enemy Territory Administration (East) until the final decision as to its fate was taken at the Peace Conference. Any doubt that may have existed because of any of the foregoing documents or arrangements concerning the ultimate disposition of Transjordan was dispelled by the 1920 Boundary Convention. Transjordan was henceforth to be made a part of Mandated Palestine in recognition of its long association with historical Palestine previously assumed in the San Remo

[29] *The Rise of Israel*, Vol. 24, Document 2, p. 58.

Resolution and the Balfour Declaration and moreover as distinctly evidenced in the map of the country in the De Bunsen Report.

It is significant that the British never relied upon the Sykes-Picot Treaty as the reason for separating Transjordan from Palestine and the Jewish National Home despite the fact that it specifically included this territory in a projected Arab State. The reason is that this agreement, being secretly conceived by the Allied Powers of Britain, France and Russia (later joined by Italy) prior to the dismemberment of the Ottoman Empire, was clearly illegal under international law. The apportionment of Ottoman lands in Asia could only be legally done by a treaty or other recognized means (see *supra*) subsequent to a Turkish defeat or concession, but not in anticipation of it – and then only in accordance with the evolving principles of international law, exemplified at the time by President Wilson's Fourteen Point Program, the Covenant of the League of Nations and the Mandates System. This evolution in international law found expression in the San Remo Resolution which bequeathed the former Ottoman Asiatic territories to the Arabic-speaking inhabitants in the two cases of Syria and Mesopotamia and recognized the right of the Jewish People to newly-created Palestine. Under that Resolution, Transjordan was destined for inclusion, by reason of its ancient Jewish links, not in an Arab state, as envisioned in the Sykes-Picot Treaty, but in an independent Jewish State. British intentions in regard to the final disposition of Transjordan must therefore be judged solely in light of the San Remo Resolution and the 1920 Boundary Convention, and not by what was illegally conceived either before or after these two documents.

## *(II) Did the McMahon Pledge of October 24, 1915 include Transjordan as a territory for future Arab Independence?*

After Britain had taken the decision to include the area east of the Jordan River within the boundaries of Mandated Palestine and the Jewish National Home, as evidenced both by the Franco-British Boundary Convention of December 23, 1920 and the Draft Mandate of December 6, 1920 (the latter was approved by a Cabinet decision of November 29, 1920), a countervailing decision was taken by the Lloyd George Government on March 22, 1921 (less than four months later) approving a recommendation made on March 17, 1921 at the Middle East Conference held in Cairo, to treat this area as an Arab province or adjunct of Palestine, separately administered by an Arab governor, who would be responsible to the High Commissioner and advised by a British Political Officer. The effect of this last decision was to create a new administration for a territorial entity known as Transjordan that had never existed before, for the benefit not of the Jewish People but rather of the relatively small Arab population living there. During 1920 and particularly since the adoption of the San Remo Resolution of April 25 of that year, this area was considered a part of Palestine and the Jewish National Home, without being legally differentiated from any other region of the country to which the Balfour Declaration was applicable. This is why the Boundary Convention and the Cabinet-approved Draft Mandate, both of December of that year, made no specific mention or even allusion to the wide expanse of Transjordan.

The justification Britain gave for removing Transjordan from the Jewish National Home and placing it in the hands of an Arab prince was, it will be recalled, the pledge given by Henry McMahon, the British High Commissioner in Egypt (1914-1916) to Hussein ibn Ali, the Emir of Mecca, in a letter dated October 24, 1915 on behalf of the British Government of Prime Minister Herbert Henry Asquith, to recognize and support Arab independence in Arabia.

The new British policy for Transjordan was then officially enunciated in the Churchill White Paper of June 3, 1922. In addition to citing the McMahon Pledge as the principal reason for excluding this territory from the Jewish National Home, the White Paper also implied (without explicitly stating so), that the Pledge was in complete conformity with the language used in the Balfour Declaration, that the Home would be founded "in Palestine", thereby falsely conveying the impression that not all of Palestine was intended for this purpose. However, there exists sufficient evidence that McMahon, when he composed the letter of October 24, 1915, never contemplated the exclusion of all of Transjordan from Jewish Palestine. This evidence may be summarized as follows:

1. The McMahon Pledge for Arab Independence was made subject to a general reservation that it would not apply to territories claimed by the Sherif of Mecca where Britain was not free to act, as of the date of the Pledge, without regard to the interests of her ally, France. The claim of France on October 24, 1915 extended over the entire area of Cisjordanian Palestine and also included a fertile part of Transjordan, from the River Jordan up to or parallel to the Hedjaz Railway. The wide extent of French interests in the Middle East was set out in a cable message from Mark Sykes, dated November 20, 1915, transmitted to Foreign Secretary Edward Grey by Henry McMahon[30], which defined Syria in French eyes as bounded by the Euphrates as far south as the town of Deir ez-Zor (Dayr az-Zawr), from there to the town of Dar'a near the Jordanian border and thence along the Hedjaz Railway to Ma'an. Dar'a is identified with biblical Edre'i, an ancient city in Bashan which, the Bible tells us, was captured by the Israelites from King Og towards the end of their forty-year trek to the

[30] F.O. 371/2767/23579. The cable message from Sykes to Grey, dated November 20, 1915 was based on a statement made to him by Muhammad Sherif al-Faruqi, a Staff officer in the Ottoman army and a member of a Young Arab secret society called al-Ahd ("The Covenant"), who deserted to the British in Gallipoli and was then taken to Cairo where he met Sykes and other British officials. Michael J. Cohen in his book *The Origins and Evolution of the Arab-Zionist Conflict* calls Al-Faruqi a Kurdish soldier rather than an Arab. University of California Press (1987), p. 16.

Promised Land under the leadership of Moses.

Sykes' report of the extensive French claim was corroborated 24 years later by the Lord High Chancellor of England, Lord Frederic Herbert Maugham, who was the chief British spokesman sitting on a committee set up on February 15, 1939, pursuant to a decision taken at a Conference on Palestine, held at St. James' Palace, to consider the McMahon-Hussein Correspondence of 1915 and 1916. In the Committee Report, Lord Maugham stated:

> As regards the interests of France, it is common knowledge that in 1915 France laid claim to the eventual exercise, if not of actual sovereignty, at any rate of a considerable degree of influence, over wide and to some extent undefined areas in the Middle East; and the existence of these claims must have been known to the Sherif of Mecca, as the result of information received from Arab nationalists in Syria with whom he had been in communication, if from no other source, even before the first mention of French interests in the Correspondence.[31]

Lord Maugham expounded on the same point, further on in his presentation, as follows:[32]

> Now if there is anything which is certain in this controversy it is that Great Britain was not free in October, 1915, to act in Palestine without regard to French interests. It may be perfectly true that under the influence of Lord Kitchener and others, His Majesty's Government before and after the outbreak of the war were anxious to restrict the French claims on the Levant coast if they could find a legitimate means of doing so. But there is a great difference between desiring an object and attaining it. It can be stated as a fact that at the time of the Correspondence, France claimed the Mediterranean littoral as far south as the Egyptian border and as far east as Damascus, and it was not until the spring of 1916 that these extreme claims were modified as the result of discussions culminating in the so-called "Sykes-Picot" Agreement.

When France finally gave up its claim to govern Palestine at the San Remo Peace Conference on April 24, 1920 it did so on the definite understanding that all of the territory of Palestine including Transjordan would become part of the Jewish National Home according to the terms of the Balfour Declaration, even

[31] Command 5974, p. 22, paragraph 10.

[32] *Ibid.*, p. 27, paragraph 33. Lord Maugham underestimated the French claim in the east, since it included not only Damascus, as he says, but extended to the Euphrates, as far south as the town of Deir-ez-Zor, as noted by Sykes in his cable message to Grey on November 20, 1915.

though the exact borders between Syria and Transjordanian Palestine were not delimited until December 23, 1920 when the Boundary Convention was signed by France and Britain, and subsequently amended on February 3, 1922.

2. In regard to the McMahon Pledge, two reservations relevant to Palestine were made by McMahon in his letter of October 24, 1915 concerning the question of boundaries intended for the proposed independent Arab state. The general reservation dealing with those regions where Britain was not free to act "without detriment to the interests of her ally, France" and the question whether this reservation also excluded Transjordan from the Arab state has been discussed in paragraph 1 above. There was also another more specific and contentious reservation made by McMahon whose exact meaning has been the subject of endless debate. This reservation will now be examined to see if it, too, excluded Transjordan from the area of Arab independence. It was composed by McMahon in the following words:

> The two districts of Mersina and Alexandretta [both in southern Turkey] and the portions of Syria lying to the *west* of the *districts* of Damascus, Homs, Hama and Aleppo cannot be said to be purely Arab and should be excluded from the limits demanded (emphasis added).

In the 1922 White Paper, Churchill and Samuel interpreted the abbreviated phrase "the district of Damascus" to mean the entire Turkish *vilayet* or province of Syria. Their interpretation was in turn based on a reading by Major Hubert Young of the Arabic text of McMahon's letter of October 24, 1915 (originally written in English). Young set forth his opinion in a Memorandum dated November 29, 1920 when he served in the Eastern Department of the Foreign Office under Lord Curzon, who authorized the circulation of his memorandum.[33] Under that interpretation, which conveniently furnished Britain with a handy pretext for detaching Transjordan from the Jewish National Home, only Cisjordan, which was *west* of this *vilayet* would be excluded from the area of Arab independence, while Transjordan fell squarely within the scope of that area. However, this Churchill-Samuel-Young interpretation of McMahon's reservation made in the 1922 White Paper was palpably false because the word *district* as used by McMahon was not equivalent to a "province" or *vilayet*, contrary to the basic assumption of the White Paper, but only indicated the area of a town and its immediate vicinity. McMahon was aware of the distinction between *viyalet* and *district* because in his letter of October 24, 1915 he correctly used the term *viyalet*, rather than *district*, to describe the Turkish administrative divisions of Baghdad and Basra. On the other hand, neither Homs nor Hama were Turkish *viyalet*s, and therefore it would have been contrary to standard usage for McMahon to have denoted such places by this term when speaking about "the districts of

[33] Isaiah Friedman, *The Question of Palestine, 1914-1918*, Rutledge & Kegan Paul Ltd., London (1973), p. 90 and his footnote 140 on p. 359.

Damascus, Homs, Hama and Aleppo".

The four Syrian towns mentioned in the reservation ran in *a line* extending northward from the south, from Damascus to Aleppo, the area "west" of which was not Cisjordan at all but what is today Lebanon, the Latakia area of Syria and Hatay province in southern Turkey, roughly from Sidon to Alexandretta. This untenable British interpretation given in the 1922 White Paper allowed proponents of the Arab cause,[34] who were unalterably opposed to a Jewish Palestine, to put forward an equally false proposition of their own, namely, that all of Palestine had been promised to Hussein by virtue of the McMahon Pledge, since none of the country designated for the Jewish National Home was "west" of the four Syrian towns. What the British and Arabs both overlooked in formulating their arguments for and against the exclusion of Palestine from the area of Arab independence was that *the line* that could be traced on the map between the four Syrian towns upwards in a northerly direction was also originally intended by McMahon to extend downwards in a southerly direction following a path not marked by the Jordan River as a dividing line but to the east of the river, which would have excluded at a minimum the fertile regions of the Jordan Valley from the projected independent Arab state. This is exactly what McMahon said was in his mind when he expressed his government's support for Arab independence "in all the regions within the limits demanded by the Sherif of Mecca". The only mistake McMahon made in not clarifying the British intention in the October 1915 letter was in not mentioning additional places further south of the town of Damascus, such as Dar'a, Amman or even Ma'an, the southernmost of these towns. The reason he gave for not doing so was his inability, at the time he composed the letter, to recall a place further south of equal importance to the Arabs as the four towns he did mention. He also did not think it was necessary at that stage to give a very detailed definition of the borders of the Arab state which was then only hypothetical, awaiting the results of World War I.

In an explanatory letter dated March 12, 1922 sent to John Evelyn Shuckburgh, the Head of the newly-established Middle East Department in the Colonial Office, McMahon made clear what Shuckburgh had called "the vexed question whether Palestine was or was not excluded from the scope of the McMahon pledge about the independence of the Arabs". Shuckburgh had earlier requested of McMahon a letter of clarification in order that "we should have *all the evidence* possible at our disposal in case we are definitely challenged on the

[34] The most prominent proponent of the Arab cause was George Antonius, an Egyptian-born Christian Arab, who had served in the Administration of Palestine in the Department of Education and authored a book setting out Arab pretensions called *The Arab Awakening*, published in 1938. In presenting their case to the British Government in 1939, the Arab side was assisted by Michael McDonnell, formerly Chief Justice of the Supreme Court of Palestine (1927-37) who submitted a brief in support of the Arab contentions, that the Asquith Government promised all of Palestine to the Arabs.

subject" (emphasis added). McMahon's letter to Shuckburgh read as follows: [35]

> With reference to our conversation on Friday (10th), I write you these few lines to place on record the fact that in my letter of the 24th October 1915 to the Sherif of Mecca, it was my intention to exclude Palestine from *independent Arabia*, and I hoped that I had so worded the letter as to make this sufficiently clear for all practical purposes.
>
> My reasons for restricting myself to specific mention of Damascus, Hama, Homs and Aleppo in that connection in my letter were 1) these were *places* to which the Arabs attached vital importance and 2) that there was no *place* I could think of at the time of sufficient importance for purposes of definition, further South of the above.
>
> It was fully my intention to exclude Palestine as it was to exclude the more Northern coastal tracts of Syria.
>
> I did not make use of the Jordan [River] to define the limits of the Southern area [McMahon is here referring to the limits of the southern area of the proposed independent Arab state which Britain promised to recognize and support in the letter of October 24, 1915 – H.G.] because I thought it might possible (*sic!*) be considered desirable at some later stage of negotiations to endeavour to find some more suitable *frontier line* East of the Jordan and between that river and the Hedjaz Railway. At that moment, moreover, very detailed definitions did not seem called for.
>
> I may mention that I have no recollection of ever having anything from the Sherif of Mecca, by letter or message, to make me suppose that he did not also understand Palestine to be excluded from *independent Arabia* (all emphasis added).

A close analysis of the foregoing letter of McMahon to Shuckburgh on March 12, 1922 (hereafter "the March letter"), written to explain what he meant by his letter of October 24, 1915 to Hussein, throws additional valuable light on the meaning to be ascribed to the geographical term "district" when used in regard to Damascus, Homs, Hama and Aleppo. In the March letter, he described the four Syrian towns as "places", a word much more appropriate for designating towns and their environs, rather than *viyalet*s, which are considerably larger in area. McMahon also used the term "frontier line" in the March letter to indicate what his intention was in expressly mentioning the four Syrian towns. His aim was to draw a frontier line to separate the proposed Arab state from the

[35] See *The Rise of Israel*, Vol. 6, Document 36, pp. 125-7 for the letter of March 12, 1922 from McMahon to John Evelyn Shuckburgh. See also Shuckburgh's letter to E.G. Forbes Adam of the Foreign Office, dated March 13, 1922, in which he spoke about "the vexed question" and the need to obtain "all the evidence" concerning it. Forbes Adam answered him on March 20, 1922 calling McMahon's letter "important and most useful".

territory that would not be included in it. That is best done through points on a map by using the coordinates of a town's latitude and longitude, and not those of a *viyalet*. No such line could have been drawn in the way McMahon envisaged had the word "district" been equivalent to *viyalet*, as assumed in the 1922 White Paper based on Hubert Young's erroneous conclusion.

McMahon's March letter was contemporaneous with the very time in 1920-1921 when King Hussein and his son Feisal were first alleging that Palestine was included in the "Arab lands" that McMahon had earmarked for independence in his October 1915 letter. This allegation was contrary to every statement they had previously made on the subject. For instance, on February 6, 1919 Feisal appeared before the Supreme Council of the Paris Peace Conference to present the Arab claims in the name of his father, King Hussein. In regard to Palestine, Feisal, basing himself on a memorandum he had already submitted to the Conference on January 29, 1919, stated:[36]

> On account of its universal character, I shall leave Palestine on one side for the mutual consideration of all parties interested. With this exception, I ask for the independence of the Arabic areas enumerated in the memorandum.

Feisal, the spokesman for Arab national aspirations, thus expressly excluded Palestine from the territory in Asia for which he demanded Arab independence. In an earlier memorandum,[37] the date of which is given by Professor Nathan Feinberg as January 1, 1919, circulated among the delegates at the Paris Peace Conference, that was personally signed by Feisal and published by David Hunter Miller, the legal adviser to the American Delegation, Feisal enumerated the various lands in Asia that he considered were "Arab". He mentioned Syria, Iraq, Jezireh, Hedjaz, Nejd, and Yemen, but deliberately omitted Palestine from his list. He placed it in a special category that required "the effective super-position of a great trustee".[38]

When Feisal signed an agreement with Weizmann on January 3, 1919, endorsing the Balfour Declaration, he was acting for and on behalf of his father,

---

[36] This quotation can be found in the work of Prof. Nathan Feinberg, *Studies in International Law*, The Magnes Press, The Hebrew University, Jerusalem (1979), p. 454, as well as in an earlier work of his entitled *Some Problems of the Palestine Mandate*, Tel-Aviv (1936), p. 38. See also his 1971 article published in pamphlet form, *On an Arab Jurist's Approach to Zionism and the State of Israel*, The Magnes Press, Jerusalem, p. 65. For his source, Prof. Feinberg cited *Papers Relating to the Foreign Relations of the United States*, Vol. III, p. 891, as well as David Hunter Miller, *My Diary of the Peace Conference, with Documents*, Volume XIV, New York (1922-1924), p. 230.

[37] *Studies in International Law, op. cit.*, p. 455, and see also *The Arab-Israel Conflict in International Law,* The Magnes Press, Jerusalem (1970), p. 37.

[38] Professor Feinberg, *Some Problems of the Palestine Mandate*, p. 42.

King Hussein of the Hedjaz. According to Hussein's second son, Abdullah, who in 1919 served as his father's Minister of Foreign Affairs, Hussein "*very unwillingly*... accepted Feisal's agreement with Dr. Weizmann on January 4th, 1919"[39] (emphasis added). Legally, it is unimportant that Hussein's acceptance of the agreement was given "very unwillingly" or otherwise. What counts is only the actual acceptance, so long as it was not given under duress, which by any reasonable standard meant that as of the date of the 1919 agreement, Hussein had accepted the fact that historical Palestine was excluded from the area of Arab independence. Furthermore, Hussein's acceptance of this agreement corroborates what McMahon always claimed – that at the time of their correspondence in 1915 and 1916 Hussein well understood the fact that Palestine was definitely excluded from his pledge.[40] If any more evidence is needed on this point, it comes from an article Hussein wrote or inspired, which appeared on March 23, 1918, in his own newspaper, *al-Qibla* ("The Direction"), published in Mecca, describing Palestine as "a sacred and beloved homeland... [of] its original sons", which from the content of the article could only have been referring to Jews, who it said were returning to their homeland from Russia, Germany, Austria, Spain and America.[41]

McMahon's recollections of what was truly intended by the pledge he made on behalf of Britain to recognize and support Arab independence, ably refuted the unfounded Hashemite/Sherifian contention that Palestine was also included among the countries designated for that purpose. This claim was not raised with British authorities until almost five years after the conclusion of the McMahon-Hussein correspondence upon which it was founded. However, Elie Kedourie, author of an important study on this Correspondence and its various interpretations up to the year 1939, professed a very negative opinion about the worth of McMahon's March letter to Shuckburgh. He said that it contained statements "which seem unsupported by any evidence, and which only serve needlessly to make the transactions of 1915-16 even more obscure and complicated".[42] He called McMahon's explanation that he could think of no place of sufficient importance for purposes of definition further south of the four Syrian towns "patently a feeble afterthought", and added the following words:[43]

> If exact definition had been McMahon's object in 1915, he would

[39] *Memoirs of King Abdullah of Transjordan*, edited by Philip P. Graves, published by Jonathan Cape, London (1950), p. 197.

[40] *Vide* McMahon's letter to Shuckburgh of March 12, 1922 and his letter to the [London] *Times* of July 23, 1937.

[41] Isaiah Friedman, *op. cit.*, p. 91, and see also Shmuel Katz, *Battleground: Fact and Fantasy* (new updated edition), Steimatzky (1985), p. 128.

[42] See his book *In the Anglo-Arab Labyrinth*, Cambridge University Press, Great Britain (1976), pp. 247-248 with additional references on pp. 276, 310.

[43] *Ibid.*, p. 248.

> have had no difficulty in indicating, somehow or another, what the boundary was to be. One fairly exact boundary, for instance, would have been the course of the River Jordan, but in his letter McMahon claimed that he had not made use of it 'because I thought it might possibly be considered desirable at some later stage of negotiations to endeavour to find some more suitable frontier line East of the Jordan and between that river and the Hedjaz Railway.' *There is no evidence that this was a preoccupation of McMahon's in 1915* (emphasis added). A possible explanation of this mystifying passage is that it confuses two separate episodes: the negotiations with Hussein, and the discussions which took place in Cairo a short time before over the [De] Bunsen Report. McMahon, it will be remembered, had then argued that 'the Palestine portion of British territory should be included in the dominion of the Sultan of Egypt'. If this was to be, then, of course, the more eastward the frontiers of Palestine extended, the better.

In the above quotation, Kedourie says there is no *evidence* concerning McMahon's "preoccupation" with how far east of the Jordan the border should be. This is strange in light of Kedourie's knowledge that McMahon, having been shown by Mark Sykes a draft copy of the Report of the De Bunsen Committee for his comment just prior to its submission on June 30, 1915, was thus cognizant of the fact that Palestine had been depicted in the map attached to the Report with a border east of the Jordan extending into the Syrian Desert, covering all of what is now the modern state of Jordan. It is therefore not surprising that McMahon did not use the Jordan River to demarcate the boundary of Palestine vis-à-vis the proposed Arab State, and Kedourie should have realized this.

Insofar as the question of evidence is concerned, what McMahon recollected in his March letter to Shuckburgh would certainly have constituted "evidence" within the meaning of that term, if its contents had been sworn to in an affidavit or given in testimony before a Court. The substance of what McMahon stated in regard to Cisjordanian Palestine's exclusion from the proposed Arab state has been corroborated by other British officials who were in a position to know.[44] While there is no similar corroboration from the same officials concerning McMahon's statement that the frontier-line of Palestine might at some later stage of negotiations be extended east of the Jordan, his statement is indeed

[44] On the exclusion of Cisjordanian Palestine from the McMahon Pledge, see the documentation presented in *The Rise of Israel*, Volume 6, Document 40, pp. 131-134, reprinting the following: a letter to the [London] *Times* by Colonial Secretary Ormsby-Gore that appeared on July 21, 1937; the statement of Gilbert Clayton in a note to Herbert Samuel, April 12, 1923; and the letter of Colonel C.E. Vickery to the *Times*, dated February 21, 1939. In his letter Vickery recalled that in a long interview he had with King Hussein in 1920 at Jedda, "the whole of the King's demands were centered round Syria and only round Syria. He stated most emphatically that he did not concern himself at all with Palestine and had no desire to have suzerainty over it for himself or for his successors".

confirmed by the map of Palestine in the aforementioned De Bunsen Report whose boundaries McMahon had in mind when he wrote his letter of October 24, 1915 to Hussein. It would thus be wrong to dismiss for lack of evidence McMahon's important clarification concerning the eastern frontier-line he foresaw for Palestine since such evidence does indeed exist. Moreover, the dismissal of his clarification would mean that McMahon was lying or being disingenuous, a presumptuous inference since he had nothing to gain by lying or distorting the facts. If anyone should have known what was really meant by his letter to Hussein, which subsequently sparked great controversy, it was McMahon himself, and if he said that Palestine, including at least a portion of Transjordan, was excluded, there was no just reason to impugn the truth of his account.

The fact that McMahon was unable to precisely mark the boundary east of the Jordan because he could not think of any prominent place as well known to the Arabs as the four Syrian towns he did mention, is not as "feeble" a reason as Kedourie believed it was. There was, after all, in 1915 no well known town of any considerable size worth mentioning that lay south of Damascus and east of the Jordan. Places such as Dar'a, Amman and Ma'an were then little known villages, particularly to foreigners and laymen.

It was also not an "afterthought" that McMahon gave this reason for his silence on this point. He had been asked by Shuckburgh pursuant to an earlier conversation they had to explain what he meant when he wrote Hussein on October 24, 1915. His letter to Shuckburgh coincided with Hussein's and Feisal's false claims concerning Palestine's inclusion in the proposed independent Arab state. McMahon's own counter-version to what they were saying could be hardly considered an "afterthought", but was a natural response of a responsible official to a gross lie then being widely circulated.

His letter to Shuckburgh, far from being obscure and adding more confusion to the situation, actually clarified the matter, contrary to Kedourie's assertion. E. G. Forbes Adam considered McMahon's letter of March 12, 1922, of which he had received a copy from Shuckburgh, to be "important and most useful if and when the matter is raised again" (see note 35 *supra*). It is without doubt a key piece of evidence in understanding the true meaning of the McMahon Pledge. However, the ironic result was that McMahon's letter to Shuckburgh was not published at the time for, as Kedourie points out, it put forward a different argument from that officially used in reply to a Palestine Arab delegation then in London to present the Arab case. In fact, McMahon's explanation directly contradicted the justification given by Churchill in the 1922 White Paper for detaching Transjordan from the Jewish National Home. That justification claimed to be the McMahon Pledge!

Oddly enough, Samuel pressed for the publication of McMahon's March letter to Shuckburgh, written less than three months prior to the issuance of the White Paper of June 3, 1922, perhaps not fully realizing how much it undermined the British position presented in the White Paper to exclude

Transjordan from the Jewish National Home or alternatively, simply to go along with Churchill's decision to place Transjordan under Arab rule. It is thus evident from McMahon's explanatory letter, which was in the hands of the Colonial Office prior to the issuance of the Churchill White Paper (June 3, 1922), that the exclusion of Palestine from *independent Arabia* related not only to Cisjordan, but to Transjordan as well, at least up to *the frontier line* of the Hedjaz Railway.

The exclusion of the fertile regions of Transjordan up to the Hedjaz Railway from the British-envisioned independent Arab state in the McMahon-Hussein Correspondence may also be deduced from the phrase McMahon used to describe all of the lands that would comprise the Arab state. That phrase was *independent Arabia* which, as appears from his controversial letter of October 24, 1915, excluded any land that was not "purely Arab", even if Arabs formed the dominant element of the population, as in the specific case of Palestine. The term *Arabia* was mentioned in McMahon's first letter to Hussein dated August 30, 1915, regarding Britain's desire to see it become independent. In a letter to Foreign Secretary Grey, dated October 26, 1915, explaining the meaning of his letter to Hussein of two days previously, he referred to "purely Arab territories", all of which he thought should be included in an independent Arabia.[45] In this respect, Palestine was never mentioned in the McMahon Pledge for the obvious reason that it neither fell within the definition of Arabia nor fit the description of "purely Arab territory". McMahon referred to Arabia in two subsequent letters he wrote to Hussein and finally in his explanatory letter to Shuckburgh quoted above.

McMahon's repeated use of the term *Arabia* was important because its modern definition not only excluded Palestine west of the Jordan but the fertile areas of Transjordan as well. The De Bunsen Report of June 30, 1915 defined Arabia as being south of Palestine, as follows:

> *Paragraph 36*
>
> ...a line starting from Aqaba, at the head of the Gulf of Aqaba, running thence to Ma'an on the Hedjaz Railway, thence eastwards in a northerly curve to the limits of Kuwait, would correspond roughly to a fair division between Arabia proper and those Arabs who belonged to the districts of Damascus and Mesopotamia.

At the time of the McMahon-Hussein Correspondence, the British considered Transjordan to be Eastern Palestine and not part of an expanded Arabia. This can be verified not only by the De Bunsen Report but also by the surveys undertaken by the Palestine Exploration Fund in the last part of the nineteenth century which referred to the area of exploration either as "Western Palestine" or "Eastern Palestine". It was only when the British negotiated a new agreement with France and Russia for the partition of the Ottoman

---

45 *The Rise of Israel,* Volume 6, Document 35, p. 121 ff.

Empire – the Sykes-Picot Treaty of May 9 and 16, 1916 – that Transjordan was incongruously placed within the borders of Arab independence. That happened because no account was taken in the agreement of Zionist aspirations to reconstitute Palestine as a Jewish State.

3. Three leading British government figures concerned with the fate and destiny of Palestine all thought on the eve of the Balfour Declaration or shortly afterwards that a national home for the Jewish People in Palestine would include at the very least a portion of Transjordan. These figures were Lord Balfour, Lord Curzon and Mark Sykes. Had they truly believed that all of Transjordan had already been included in the McMahon Pledge for Arab independence, they would hardly have voiced a conflicting opinion to the effect that the fertile regions of Transjordan should become integral parts of Palestine and the Jewish National Home governed by the Balfour Declaration.

Balfour wrote two memoranda in 1919 two months apart, dealing with the boundaries of Palestine, including the territory east of the Jordan. In the first memorandum, Balfour wrote:[46]

> In determining the Palestinian frontiers, the main thing to keep in mind is to make a Zionist policy possible by giving the fullest scope to economic development in Palestine. Thus the Northern frontier should give to Palestine a full command of the water power which geographically belongs to Palestine and not to Syria; while the Eastern frontier should be so drawn as to give the widest scope to agricultural development on the left bank of the Jordan, consistent with leaving the Hedjaz railway completely in Arab possession.

In the second memorandum dated August 11, 1919, when he was still Foreign Minister, Balfour defined Palestine as "essentially the valley of the Jordan, with the adjacent coast and plains." He then added:[47]

> If Zionism is to influence the Jewish problem throughout the world, Palestine must be made available for the largest number of Jewish immigrants. It is therefore eminently desirable that it should obtain the command of the water-power which naturally belongs to it, whether by extending its borders to the north, or by treaty with the mandatory of Syria, to whom the southward flowing waters of Hermon (misspelled "Hamon") could not in any event be of much value.
>
> For the same reason, Palestine should extend into the lands lying

[46] *Documents on British Foreign Policy*, edited by E. L. Woodward and Rohan Butler, First Series, Vol. IV (1919), Document No. 211, Balfour to Lloyd George, June 26, 1919 on the subject, "Disposal of Turkish Territories", pp. 301-302.

[47] Balfour's second memorandum is found in *Documents on British Foreign Policy, op. cit.*, p. 347.

east of the Jordan. It should not, however, be allowed to include the Hedjaz Railway, which is too distinctly bound up with exclusively Arab interests.

In addition to the foregoing Foreign Office memoranda revealing Balfour's inner thoughts on what the eastern boundary of Palestine should be in pursuit of Britain's Zionist policy as formulated in the Balfour Declaration, Balfour also told Justice Louis Dembitz Brandeis that he thought Emir Feisal would agree to having Palestine's boundary extend up to the Hedjaz Railway. Balfour limited the area of Transjordan to be included in Palestine to the lands lying west of the Hedjaz Railway in order to provide Feisal, so long as he ruled over Syria, with a direct link to his father's kingdom in the Hedjaz. However, as Weizmann noted, once Feisal was evicted from Syria by France in July 1920 and thereafter installed as the new ruler of Mesopotamia-Iraq, that reason was no longer valid, and so all of Transjordan was then made part of Palestine.

Surprisingly enough, Lord Curzon, a fierce opponent of Zionism, agreed with his predecessor, Lord Balfour, that Palestine, as the Jewish National Home, extended 4,000 square miles to the east of the Jordan River. He presented a memorandum to the War Cabinet on October 26, 1917 entitled "The Future of Palestine" prior to its approval of the Balfour Declaration on October 31, 1917. In it, he expressed great pessimism about the chances of successfully converting Palestine into the national home of the Jewish People and a revived Jewish State. He defined Palestine as meaning

> ....the old Scriptural Palestine extending from Dan to Beersheba, i.e., from Banias [Dan] to Bir Saba [Beersheba]. This is a country of less than 10,000 square miles including 4,000 *to the east of the Jordan* (emphasis added), i.e., it is a country which, excluding desert lands, is not much bigger than Wales, ...[which] only supports a population of 2,000,000 persons.

In making an analogy with Wales, Curzon argued that Palestine could not support an increased population and therefore that it could not be a national, material or even a spiritual home for any more than a very small section of the Jewish People.[48]

[48] *The Rise of Israel*, Volume 8, Document 46, p. 130. Before succeeding Balfour as Foreign Secretary on October 24, 1919, Curzon was sent a copy of Balfour's memorandum of June 26, 1919 that had originally been sent to the Prime Minister. In that memorandum, as already noted, Balfour discussed the need to give Palestine adequate frontiers "to make a Zionist policy possible". After studying this memorandum with its call for including the left bank of the Jordan up to the Hedjaz Railway into Palestine's frontiers, Curzon minuted: "The memo is generally, as it appears to me, on sound lines". Curzon thus indicated (see: *Documents on British Foreign Policy, op.cit,* p. 303) he had no disagreement with Balfour on the question of Palestine's eastern boundary. It was only a year later

Curzon's pessimistic outlook on the economic future of Palestine was challenged and refuted by Mark Sykes four days after his memorandum was presented to the War Cabinet. Mark Sykes was Prime Minister Lloyd George's expert on the Middle East and the War Cabinet's assistant secretary. He submitted his own memorandum on October 30, 1917 in which he extolled the Jordan valley as:[49]

> ...a gigantic natural hothouse, capable of producing tropic and sub-tropic vegetables and products as well as rice, tobacco, opium... Intensive cultivation in the Jordan valley would certainly produce three crops a year if cultivated. It produced that in the 13th century and has not altered climatically since that time.

He then referred to

> ...the immense area of beyond Jordan [that] is practically uninhabited and yet yields good crops wherever cultivation is attempted. Cereals, vines, olives. Climate excellent, no fever, no mosquitoes, good grazing for sheep and cattle.[50]

Sykes therefore clearly visualized Transjordan as being part of Palestine and the Jewish National Home, at the moment the Balfour Declaration was about to be approved and issued by the War Cabinet. He believed this territory was vital for Palestine's economic and agricultural development. His view contrasted sharply with the one he had held only one year before, when he envisaged Transjordan not as part of a future Palestine which was to become the Jewish National Home, but as part of the independent Arab state to be set up in the wide expanses of Areas "A" and "B" under the Sykes-Picot Treaty of May 9 and 16, 1916.

4. The territory of Transjordan was assumed from the beginning to have been included in Palestine by all spokesmen and leaders of Zionism, as expressed in the memoranda they prepared on Palestine's borders and in their negotiations with British officials. At the Paris Peace Conference on February 27, 1919, the Zionist Organization asked that the eastern frontier be drawn close to but west of the Hedjaz Railway. This modest proposal elicited a very favourable reaction from Emir Feisal, who attended the Peace Conference on behalf of his father, King Hussein, to present the Arab case. In explaining Feisal's reaction, the Report of the Executive of the Zionist Organization to the Twelfth Zionist

---

that he radically changed his position on this question. He then sought to exclude Transjordan from the Jewish National Home, to limit the size of the Home and also to provide autonomy for the Arabs living in Transjordan.

[49] *The Rise of Israel*, Volume 8, Document 47, p. 135.

[50] Ibid.

Congress stated:[51]

> It was always realized that the true boundary was the desert beyond the railway. Nevertheless, the Zionists, recognizing the special Moslem interests in the railway, drew their eastern frontier west of the Hedjaz line. The Emir Feisal, in publicly declaring the Zionist proposals were moderate and proper, had this fact chiefly in mind. At that time the French were not in Damascus, and it was thought to be a matter of justice and expediency that a small corridor along the railway should serve to unite the Hedjaz Kingdom with Damascus. In view of the French occupation of Damascus, the necessity of such a corridor no longer exists, at any rate for the present, and the proper eastern limit of Palestine is for practical purposes the natural boundary of the Arabian [i.e., Syrian] desert.

Feisal's words of endorsement for the "moderate and proper" eastern boundary proposal by the Zionist leaders were contained in a letter he sent to Professor Felix Frankfurter dated March 3, 1919. If he (and his father) had thought then that all of Transjordan would be part of an Arab state by virtue of the McMahon Pledge of October 24, 1915, he would never have spoken in so favourable a manner about the Zionist proposal contained in the memorandum submitted to the Paris Peace Conference to fix the eastern frontier of Palestine just west of the Hedjaz Railway.

5. The boundaries envisaged for the Jewish State in the Balfour Declaration, though not specified therein, were those set out in two maps of Palestine published prior to the Declaration, both of which included all of Transjordan. One map was attached to a Report of the Committee on Asiatic Turkey, submitted on June 30, 1915. The Committee was appointed by Prime Minister Herbert Henry Asquith to set forth "British Desiderata in Turkey in Asia", headed by Maurice de Bunsen, assistant Secretary of State at the Foreign Office. The map of Palestine presented by the De Bunsen Committee to the British Government showed the country having frontiers that corresponded with those later fixed for Mandated Palestine. It should also be noted that when this map was drawn in 1915 for the De Bunsen Committee there was not the slightest British consultation or coordination with the Zionist Organization, which showed that this map was truly a British conception. A second map of Palestine was attached to a Memorandum of October 1917 prepared by William George Tyrrel, who worked in the Foreign Office at the time of the Balfour Declaration. The map that was attached to his memorandum showed the same extensive frontiers of Palestine including Transjordan as the one that was previously attached to the De Bunsen Report.

These two maps of Palestine drawn prior to the British conquest of the

---

[51] *The Rise of Israel*, Volume 8, Document 57, p. 193.

country were based on scientific maps produced by the Palestine Exploration Fund, established in Britain (1865) to carry out a systematic survey of the Land of Israel "from Dan to Beersheba". The Fund published its "Great Map of Western Palestine" in 1880 in twenty-six sheets. However, it was able to make only a partial survey of Eastern Palestine in 1881, before the Turkish authorities intervened and brought its work to an end. The survey was then continued by the Fund's German counterpart called *Deutscher Palaestina Verein*, which mapped out Gilead. The eminent Scottish cartographer, John George Bartholomew, later designed an important map of Palestine based on the foregoing surveys of the British and German societies. His general map of the country covering both Western and Eastern Palestine was jacketed to the 1894 edition of George Adam Smith's book, *The Historical Geography of the Holy Land*. The foregoing cartographic evidence of what constituted Palestine is proof in itself that if Palestine was excluded from the independent Arab state, as McMahon and others stated, that exclusion applied not only to Cisjordan, but also to Transjordan.

The reason that Transjordan was finally removed from the Jewish National Home had nothing to do with the McMahon Pledge, as falsely claimed by Samuel and Churchill in the 1922 White Paper, but rather with the destabilizing events surrounding Feisal's ouster from Damascus on July 25, 1920 which resulted in a British need to placate the outraged Hashemite/Sherifian family for the loss of Syria. It was also the result of the negative, anti-Zionist attitude of Lord Curzon, the Foreign Secretary, who directed the affairs of Palestine from October 24, 1919 to February 14, 1921, before Churchill took over actual responsibility as Colonial Secretary. Curzon personally detested the very idea of the Jewish National Home and wanted to reduce its size. This is why he was determined to prevent Jewish settlement or land purchase in Transjordan, and why he initially opposed Herbert Samuel's call to have the British army occupy and secure this territory for Palestine after it ceased to be under Feisal's rule following the French military takeover of Syria. In discussing the status of Transjordan with his officials in the Foreign Office and with Samuel from late July to December 1920, Curzon simply ignored the fact that at the San Remo Peace Conference it was assumed, though unstated, that Palestine's eastern border would extend to Transjordan and be contiguous with the western border of Mesopotamia, with no thought then being given to the establishment of an enlarged independent Arab state under the rule of Feisal or anyone else separating the two mandated territories. The idea of such a state was indeed envisioned in the defunct Sykes-Picot Treaty, but that agreement had been repudiated or swept away by the San Remo Resolution and even before then by the adoption in the Treaty of Versailles (Covenant of the League of Nations) of the Mandates System for the ex-Ottoman territories in the Middle East.

Curzon was a key participant at the San Remo Peace Conference and he had heard Prime Minister David Lloyd George say words to the effect that Palestine's boundaries would coincide with those which had been under the control of "the men who had been inhabiting Palestine", i.e., wherever the Twelve Tribes of

Israel had permanently settled in the Promised Land, as was shown on maps in George Adam Smith's book cited by the British Prime Minister. Yet Curzon, in parallel with the French government, acted as if the Sykes-Picot Treaty was still a valid and binding document upon which the borders of Palestine were to be based, even after the San Remo Peace Conference. He propounded the notion that the British-designated part of Transjordan south of the Yarmuk, under the 1916 treaty, would become a separate entity under local Arab administration, not connected in any way to the Jewish National Home, which was in direct contradiction to the assumption inherent in the San Remo Resolution. His statements on the arrangement he espoused for Transjordan after Feisal fled Syria have led some scholars, particularly Bernard Wasserstein and Avraham P. Alsberg, to wrongly conclude that the British Government never intended this territory to be included within the borders of the Jewish National Home, as will be further discussed in the next part of this chapter. Curzon's policy favouring an Arab solution for Transjordan was originally urged upon him by Samuel, who has been falsely credited by the aforementioned scholars for "saving" Transjordan for Palestine or "expanding" the latter's borders, when he was in fact instrumental in having it excluded first from the Jewish National Home and eventually from Palestine altogether. The so-called "expansion of Palestine" said to be engineered by Samuel shortly after he became High Commissioner was in reality a deceitful appearance – Transjordan was already implicitly a part of Palestine under the San Remo Resolution even before Samuel arrived there – his efforts to convince Curzon to include it within the Mandate's area of jurisdiction resulted in a contraction of the Jewish National Home by the surrender of this territory to the Hedjazian Prince Abdullah. The Curzon-Samuel policy favouring an Arab-administered Transjordan was not officially accepted until Churchill also embraced it on March 17, 1921 at the Cairo Conference, based upon the earlier Shuckburgh Memorandum. The policy then received the reluctant blessing of the Lloyd George Cabinet on March 22, 1921. This pro-Sherifian demarche was subsequently confirmed in the White Paper of June 3, 1922. By setting up Abdullah as Provisional Administrator of Transjordan on April 1, 1921, Churchill, acting on Samuel's advice and that of other officials in the Colonial Office, completed the job Curzon undertook to exclude this vast territory from the Jewish National Home.

Had Feisal not been evicted by the French, he would have continued to rule Syria and Lebanon under a French Mandate and tutelage, but his "kingdom" would never have included Transjordan, south of the Yarmuk, because Prime Minister Lloyd George was unalterably opposed to French control over the British designated portion of Transjordan under the Sykes-Picot Treaty. The proposal to add Transjordan to a French-mandated Syria was rejected out-of-hand by Lloyd George in December 1919, as well as by Curzon.[52] There would then have been no reason for Abdullah to gather his followers and threaten to

[52] See Yitzhak Gil-Har's article, "The Separation of Transjordan from Palestine", in the Jerusalem Cathedra, Yad Izhak Ben-Zvi Institute, Jerusalem 1981, p. 294.

march from the Hedjaz to Damascus, as he intended, to avenge the eviction of his younger brother from Syria and restore Hashemite/Sherifian rule in that country, nor any need for the British to pacify Abdullah by detaching Transjordan from the Jewish National Home and placing it under his provisional administration as a reward for ceasing his threats and agitation against the French. The Draft Mandate which had already been submitted for confirmation to the Council of the League of Nations on December 6, 1920 would not have been suddenly revised by Britain in order to insert a new Article 25 providing for the separate administration of Transjordan on account of the alleged "existing local conditions". Transjordan would then have had the same kind of administration favouring the establishment of the Jewish National Home as the rest of Palestine, exactly as envisaged both in the Cabinet-approved Draft Mandate and in the Franco-British Boundary Convention of December 23, 1920.

British rule in Transjordan was legally justified only on the basis that it was an inseparable part of the Mandate for Palestine. The Supreme Council of the Principal Allied Powers had awarded a mandate to Britain as recorded in the San Remo Resolution of April 25, 1920 for the exclusive purpose that all of Palestine on both sides of the Jordan would be governed by the Balfour Declaration as well as Article 22 of the Covenant and hence be within the confines of the Jewish National Home, not part of an Arab entity of any sort. Therefore, the territory of Transjordan could under no circumstances be separated from either Palestine or the Jewish National Home if Britain was to retain its legal right to govern it under the Mandate, otherwise it would have reverted to the sovereignty of the Principal Allied Powers by virtue of Article 132 of the Treaty of Sèvres, who could then decide how to dispose of it. In March 1921, at the time of the Cairo Conference, this treaty was considered to be provisionally in force, pending ratification, having been signed by all the Allied Powers and Turkey. To avoid any legal entanglement that would have been caused by the exclusion of Transjordan from the area of Palestine, Britain had no choice but to keep it as part of Palestine under the Mandate. At the same time Britain wanted to prevent Abdullah from launching raids against the French in Syria, which would have incurred their wrath and undoubtedly led to a quick military response against Abdullah and a possible French occupation of Transjordan whence the attacks originated. The British solution was to provisionally divorce Transjordan from the Jewish National Home, while maintaining the fiction that it was still part of Palestine as a whole but administratively separated from it. The result was that Cisjordan and Transjordan became in reality two separate countries, one where the Balfour Declaration was fully applicable and the other where it was not. This in turn meant that the Mandate for Palestine was seemingly divided *de facto* into two, "the Mandate for Cisjordan", as it were, to establish the Jewish National Home and "the Mandate for Transjordan" to establish a Hashemite/Sherifian Arab state, contrary to the task the British were originally entrusted with by the Principal Allied Powers and also contrary to the pretence that all of

Palestine was still a single country under international law. However, insofar as the League of Nations was concerned, there remained only one official Mandate under which Britain was required to file annual reports with the League Council regarding the territory committed to its charge.

To implement this solution the British needed a convincing reason to justify their illegal scheme to deprive the Jewish National Home of its eastern Transjordanian boundary. That reason was the McMahon Pledge to Hussein, which promised the Sherifian Arabs independence in all lands considered "Arab", but excluded any territory where the French had a special interest or claim. Both the French and the Sherifian Arabs would gain by this solution, the former relieved of potential disturbances in their mandated territory of Syria emanating from Syrian nationalists angered by the overthrow of Feisal's government, while the Sherifian Arabs would have yet another territory added to their potentially extensive domains. The British did not fear any negative repercussions from the Zionists because the latter considered themselves dependent on British good-will and could be easily brow-beaten into accepting whatever course of action they chose, as in fact proved to be the case. Britain itself would be a major beneficiary of the scheme separating Transjordan from the Jewish National Home because it would henceforth be free from French pretensions concerning Transjordan and, at the same time, Abdullah or any successor of his would be under British influence or control. The basic elements or contours of the British scheme can be detected from the agenda of the Middle East Conference as shown in particular by the first item thereof, the text of which is reproduced herewith.[53]

## *Agenda*

> **Distinction to be drawn between Palestine and Transjordan under the Mandate**
>
> His Majesty's Government are responsible under the terms of the Mandate for establishing in Palestine a national home for the Jewish People. They are also pledged by the assurances given to the Sherif of Mecca in 1915 to recognize and support the independence of the Arabs in those portions of the (Turkish) *vilayet* of Damascus in which they are free to act without detriment to French interests. The western boundary of the Turkish *vilayet* of Damascus before the war was the River Jordan. *Palestine and Transjordan do not, therefore, stand upon quite the same footing.* At the same time, the two areas are economically

[53] The text of Item number 1 of the agenda is found in *The Rise of Israel*, Vol. 13, Document 26, p. 199. The agenda for the Middle East Conference was drafted by John Shuckburgh pursuant to the instructions given by Churchill. See letter from Winston Churchill to John Shuckburgh dated February 18, 1921 in Martin Gilbert's biography of *Winston S. Churchill,* Companion Volume IV, Part 2, pp. 1362-1363.

> interdependent, and their development must be considered as a single problem. Further, His Majesty's Government have been entrusted with the Mandate for "Palestine" (Quotation marks in the original). *If they wish to assert their claim to Transjordan and to avoid raising with other Powers the legal status of that area, they can only do so by proceeding upon the assumption that Transjordan forms part of the area covered by the Palestine Mandate. In default of this assumption Transjordan would be left, under Article 132 of the Treaty of Sèvres, to the disposal of the Principal Allied Powers* (emphasis added). Some means must be found of giving effect in Transjordan to the terms of the Mandate consistent with "recognition and support of the independence of the Arabs."

As can be seen from the foregoing quotation, the whole British justification for separating Transjordan from the Jewish National Home was supposedly based upon the McMahon Pledge, which they falsely considered equal in stature to the Balfour Declaration. This justification ironically was contrary to McMahon's 1922 statement that the pledge excluded the land up to the Hedjaz Railway from the area of independent Arabia. In comparing the two British undertakings, it is to be noted that the Balfour Declaration had been approved by all the Allied Powers, including the United States, as part of the global political and legal settlement they devised at the Paris and San Remo peace conferences in 1919 and 1920 respectively, and then received the assent of fifty-two nations in 1922 when the Mandate for Palestine was confirmed by the League of Nations and separately by the United States, as well as other states who subsequently joined the League. By contrast, the pledge given to Hussein had no comparable legal status under international law, nor was it ever submitted to the Peace Conference. In fact, this pledge was merely a statement of British policy that entailed no legal obligations, despite the implication of such obligations by the use of the word "pledge" to describe British assurances to Hussein to support and recognize Arab independence. This pledge was also conditional upon Arab assistance in the war against Turkey, a condition largely unfulfilled. McMahon himself drew attention to the worthlessness of his Pledge when he told Lord Charles Hardinge, the then-Viceroy of India, in a letter of December 4, 1915:[54]

> I do not for one moment go to the length of imagining that the present negotiations [with Hussein] will go far to shape the future form of *Arabia* or *to either establish our rights or to bind our hands in that country* (emphasis added). The situation and its elements are much too nebulous for that. What we have to arrive at now is to tempt the Arab people into the right path, detach them from the enemy and bring them on our side. This on our part is at present largely a matter of

[54] Kedourie, *op. cit.*, pp. 119-120.

> words, and to succeed we must use persuasive terms and abstain from haggling over conditions – whether about Baghdad or elsewhere.

At the time of the McMahon-Hussein Correspondence, the Sherif of Mecca had no official status as the Head of a State. He was recognized by the Turks as an emir of the Hedjaz, but this territory was not then independent, merely a province of the Ottoman Empire. Hence no international agreement or treaty was validly concluded between Britain and Hussein in 1915 and 1916 as a result of what was called "Correspondence". Thus there was no legal basis to support the British contention that because of the McMahon Pledge, *Palestine and Transjordan do not, therefore, stand upon quite the same footing*, as stated in the Agenda for the Middle East Conference in Cairo. As already noted, the fertile part of Transjordan up to the Hedjaz Railway was not covered by the McMahon Pledge because of the two reservations he had made to exclude from the Arab state:

> 1. The territory relating to France's claim over Syria which in October 1915 the French defined as including Palestine, extending from Dar'a to Ma'an, a line which embraced most of the major towns and sites of Transjordan, probably including Amman;
> 2. The portions of Syria lying to the west of the districts of Damascus, Homs, Hama and Aleppo, which in accordance with McMahon's explanation given in his letter to Shuckburgh (March 12, 1922) excluded all territory from the Arab state, that was west of the frontier line from Aleppo to Damascus, continuing in a southerly direction, a line roughly parallel to the Jordan River but not identical with it.

Independently of these territorial exclusions, the San Remo Resolution superceded the McMahon Pledge, just as it did for the illegal Sykes-Picot Treaty, and thus neither of the latter two documents could be legally relied upon to demarcate the historical frontiers of the Jewish National Home, which had always included much of Transjordan. The British justification to exclude all of Transjordan from the Jewish National Home by citing the McMahon Pledge was simply a clever ruse they used to deprive the Jewish People of precious territory needed for the economic and agricultural development of the Home and also as an area in which to settle millions of Jews.

Although the British action regarding Transjordan contradicted the San Remo Resolution as well as the Franco-British Boundary Convention of December 23, 1920 and the Draft Mandate of December 6, 1920, they adroitly managed to avoid being seen as a violator of the obligation they undertook under international law to establish all of Palestine, on both sides of the Jordan, as the Jewish National Home by introducing a new Article 25 in the Mandate and then disingenuously relying on it – specifically "the existing local conditions" mentioned therein – rather than on the McMahon Pledge, as the supposed reason to exclude Transjordan from the Home. They invoked this Article on September 16, 1922, a mere two months after the Mandate was confirmed by the Council of the League of Nations on July 24, 1922. Had they invoked Article 25 at the same time as the Mandate's confirmation, their clever ruse many have come under closer scrutiny and been exposed as the fraud it was.

## *(III) Was Transjordan included in the Balfour Declaration of November 2, 1917 as part of the Jewish National Home?*

The question of whether Britain intended to include the territory of Transjordan in Palestine as part of the Jewish National Home governed by the Balfour Declaration became an important issue after the ouster of Feisal from Damascus on July 25, 1920, followed by the arrival of Abdullah in Amman on March 2, 1921. As a result of these developments a decision was made at the Middle East Peace Conference in Cairo (March 12 to March 22, 1921) to create Transjordan as an Arab "province" separated from the Jewish National Home. The future status of Transjordan was further discussed by Herbert Samuel in the Churchill White Paper of June 3, 1922 he wrote, and after a brief analysis he concluded that "the whole of Palestine west of the Jordan was thus excluded from Sir H. McMahon's Pledge" given to the Sherif of Mecca, later King Hussein of the Hedjaz. This left the clear and unmistakable impression that Palestine east of the Jordan, i.e., Transjordan, would be excluded from the Jewish National Home.

The British scheme to partition Transjordan administratively from Palestine and the Jewish National Home from March 1921 onwards exposed the hypocrisy of Samuel, for it was he, as a high official of the Zionist Movement before becoming High Commissioner for Palestine, who helped formulate the Zionist boundary proposals for presentation to the Paris Peace Conference, which asked that the frontiers of a future Jewish State extend to Transjordan, just west of the Hedjaz Railway. Moreover, in a speech he made at the London Opera House on November 2, 1919, he stated as follows:[55]

> It is essential at the outset that the boundaries of Palestine should be rightly drawn. That is a problem which will engage the attention of Statesmen in the very near future…

Samuel then expounded on how the northern boundaries[56] should be

[55] Samuel, in line with the official Zionist position presented to the Paris Peace Conference in February 1919, said that the boundaries of Palestine in the North should extend to the Litani River and Mount Hermon "to secure for Palestine the water resources without which it cannot fully prosper".

[56] Samuel's speech of November 2, 1919 was published in the "Zionist

determined, after which he continued:

> With regard to the Eastern boundary, *the structure of a modern State*, the organization of a progressive community, demands a certain size of population. You must have a sufficient base on which to build, and you cannot have numbers without area and territory. Every expert knows that *for a prosperous Palestine an adequate territory beyond the Jordan is indispensable* (Applause). These are matters which are being actively pressed upon the attention of Ministers by the leaders of the Zionist Movement (emphasis added).

It is evident from Samuel's above remarks that in referring to "the structure of a modern state", that needs a sufficient base on which to build, he had in mind a modern Jewish State in Palestine whose boundaries should extend beyond the Jordan if it was to be prosperous. This conclusion derives from the association Samuel himself made between the kind of state he imagined and the lobbying of British ministers conducted by the leaders of the Zionist Movement. It was therefore the height of mendacity for him, less than a year later as the newly-appointed High Commissioner for Palestine, to abruptly adopt the opposite view, that Transjordan was always viewed by the British as a territory to be excluded from the terms of the Balfour Declaration governing the Jewish National Home, a view which he knew lacked merit and contradicted his own previously stated opinion. He performed this somersault in order to identify himself with a new British policy to place this territory under Arab rule and thereby deprive the future Jewish State of its historical Transjordanian boundary in the east. This policy was adopted by Curzon in 1920, though a year before he himself had tacitly approved the Zionist policy on Transjordan as enunciated by his predecessor, Lord Balfour, in his memoranda. However, the new British policy only achieved fruition under Colonial Secretary Winston Churchill during 1921 and 1922, when he assumed responsibility for the affairs of Palestine.

In a report on the political activities of the Zionist Organization, presented by Chaim Weizmann to the 12th Zionist Congress in the Czechoslovakian (Bohemian) resort city of Carlsbad (today "Karlovy Vary" in the Czech Republic) on September 1-14, 1921, the President of the Zionist Organization referred to the boundary negotiations that took place concerning Transjordan and stated:[57]

> In 1920 and 1921, representations were made on several occasions by the Zionist Organization to the British Government bearing on the importance of Transjordania for any extensive cultivation scheme.

---

Bulletin", London, November 5, 1919, by the Zionist Organization. See also *The Rise of Israel*, Vol. 27, Document 35, p. 391.

[57] *The Rise of Israel*, Vol. 8, Document 57, p. 193.

> It was pointed out to the statesmen concerned that Transjordania had formed an integral and vital part of Palestine ever since Reuben, Gad and Menasseh first pitched their tents there, that the fields of Gilead, Moab and Edom, the rivers Arnon and Jabbok, as well as the Yarmuk are historically, geographically and economically linked with Palestine, that while Western Palestine had greater religious and historical significance, Eastern Palestine might occupy a more important position in the economic future of the Jewish National Home, that the formerly fertile plateaux of Transjordania today lie neglected and uninhabited save for a few scattered settlements and a few nomad tribes. It was further pointed out that the economic growth of Western Palestine depends to a great extent upon the cultivation of the soil of Transjordania. Zionists have thought, and still think, that Transjordania falls under the provisions of the Palestine Mandate.

Weizmann had earlier presented the same arguments about the reasons why Transjordan needed to be included in the Jewish National Home in a letter he wrote to Churchill on March 1, 1921, shortly before the convening of the Cairo Conference on March 12. In that letter he had also notably remarked:[58]

> It is fully realized that His Majesty's Government must consider their pledges to the Arab people and the means of satisfying their legitimate aspirations. But the taking from Palestine of a few thousand square miles, scarcely inhabited and long derelict [Weizmann calculated the population of the regions of Transjordan within the British sphere to be considerably less than 200,000], would be scant satisfaction to Arab nationalism, while it would go far to frustrate the entire policy of His Majesty's Government regarding the Jewish National Home.
>
> ...The aspirations of Arab nationalism center about Damascus and Baghdad and do not lie in Transjordan.
>
> ...It is confidently hoped, therefore, that there will be no thought of any further dimunition of the legitimate claims of Palestine when the eastern and southern frontiers come under discussion. The unsatisfactory character of the settlement on the north makes it all the more vital that the Jewish National Home be generously dealt with on the east and south.

There can be no doubt that Transjordan was originally conceived as being

---

[58] *The Letters and Papers of Chaim Weizmann*, Vol. X, Series A, Letter 135, To Winston Churchill, London, March 1, 1921, pp. 159 ff. Editor: Bernard Wasserstein. Published by Transaction Books, Rutgers University, New Brunswick, N.J. 1977.

part of the project of the Jewish National Home having an eventual Jewish majority in the minds of those who framed the Balfour Declaration as approved by the War Cabinet on October 31, 1917 and issued on November 2, 1917. The evidence to prove this point comes not only from the two maps referred to in Part II above showing how a future Palestine with extensive borders should be demarcated upon its creation as a state, but also from the statements made by the key figures associated with the making of the Balfour Declaration. The statements of Balfour, Sykes and Curzon have already been noted there, all of whom envisaged that the future Jewish National Home governed by the Balfour Declaration would contain at least a part of the territory lying to the east of the Jordan. This was also the clear intent of Lloyd George, as confirmed by his constant references to Palestine's boundaries extending from Dan to Beersheba, by which he meant all of the historical limits of the country conquered, settled and ruled by the Twelve Tribes of Israel and their descendants in the First and Second Temple Periods.[59] Additional evidence comes from Leopold Stennett Amery, who, in his capacity as an assistant secretary to the War Cabinet and the drafter of the penultimate version of the Balfour Declaration which became the final version with certain amendments, knew from the long discussions held immediately preceding the issuance of the Balfour Declaration in which he was directly involved, what the approximate territorial dimensions for the proposed Jewish National Home were, even though they were not specifically spelled out in the Declaration itself, because Palestine had not yet been created as a defined country.

In a speech he made to the House of Commons on May 22, 1939 in which he strongly denounced the MacDonald White Paper issued five days earlier, Amery also referred to the settlement effected by the Churchill White Paper of June 3, 1922, which excluded Transjordan from the Jewish National Home. Thus began, he indicated, the process which led to the partitioning of Palestine. His exact words were:[60]

> Of that final settlement of 1922, I would only say that it marked the drastic scaling down of Jewish hopes. It began by taking out of Palestine the larger and better half, the half more suitable to large-scale colonization, namely, Transjordan. That was the first partition. It also made it clear to the Jews that there was no question of Palestine ever becoming a Jewish State or a Jewish country in the sense in which England is English….

---

[59] See the map containing the Meinertzhagen Line 1919, drawn up by Colonel Richard Meinertzhagen, according the biblical formula "from Dan to Beersheba", which was approved by Lloyd George and Balfour and which encompassed the Transjordan catchment area. See *Middle East Diary 1917-1956*, Thomas Yoseloff, Publisher, New York (1960), p. 45 and p. 355.

[60] *Book of Documents submitted to the General Assembly of the United Nations by the Jewish Agency for Palestine*, New York, May 1947, p. 123.

Amery had no doubt that Transjordan was included in the Jewish National Home as of November 2, 1917 under the terms of the Balfour Declaration. He repeated the essence of the statement he had first made in the House of Commons on May 22, 1939 when he appeared before the Anglo-American Committee of Inquiry on Palestine on June 30, 1946 and stated:

> To the best of my recollection, certainly at the time the Cabinet decided on the Balfour Declaration, they regarded Transjordan as being within Palestine. They also, I think, regarded it, as probably the whole thing was experimental, that there would be eventually a Jewish majority over the whole of Palestine...

Other public figures who have spoken about the question of whether or not Transjordan was included within the Jewish National Home as envisaged by the Balfour Declaration were Weizmann, Abdullah and Alec Seath Kirkbride, all of whom had the most intimate knowledge of that matter by virtue of their involvement in the unfolding developments affecting Palestine.

Weizmann told the Palestine Royal Commission at a session in Jerusalem on November 25, 1936 what his thoughts were about Transjordan:[61]

> I have mentioned Transjordan and I would like to make only one brief reference to it, and I would like to preface my remarks by saying that it will not enter my mind to discuss the present political status of Transjordan. No Jew in his senses would demand any alteration in it, but it should be made clear to the Commission that when this project was adumbrated, *when the Balfour Declaration was made, and almost five years subsequently when it began to work, Transjordan was part and parcel of Palestine* (emphasis added). For reasons into which I need not enter and which are not my business, it was thought wise to separate them, to truncate Palestine and to separate a country which is larger than Palestine...

It should be noted that in the above remarks of Weizmann, his reference to "Palestine" was also a reference to the "Jewish National Home" since the two geographical terms were used synonymously by the British Government between November 2, 1917 and March 22, 1921, the latter date being when Cabinet approval was given for Churchill's plan to create Transjordan as an Arab province of Palestine, as recommended at the session of the Cairo Conference held on March 17, 1921. However, it was not until June 3, 1922, the date of the Churchill White Paper, that the policy of an Arab Transjordan as opposed to a Jewish Cisjordan became publicly enunciated policy, and it was not until September 16, 1922 that such policy was officially implemented under the terms

[61] *The Rise of Israel*, Volume 22, Document 2, p. 26, and repeated in Document 3, p. 80 of the same volume.

of Article 25 of the Mandate for Palestine. By saying that Transjordan was part and parcel of Palestine when the Balfour Declaration was made, Weizmann therefore meant part and parcel of the Jewish National Home. The same applied to his reference to the truncation of Palestine, denoting the truncation of the Jewish National Home.

The comment by Weizmann "that no Jew in his senses would demand any alteration in [the present political status of Transjordan]" and that it was not his business to enter into the reason that caused its separation from Palestine was bizarre, in light of the still ongoing efforts at the time to obtain British approval for organized Jewish settlement in Transjordan. One such Jew who did demand such an alteration a month prior to Weizmann's appearance before the Palestine Royal Commission was Moshe Sharett, then the official head of the Jewish Agency in Palestine, who later became the second Prime Minister of Israel and ironically, was known as a close supporter of Weizmann in his tussles with David Ben-Gurion. Sharett is quoted in a newspaper article written by the U.S. Senator from Vermont, Warren R. Austin, as making the following statement about Transjordan:

> An agreement not to become a majority would be impossible. The Jews of the world are pressing to enter the country. If we entered into such an agreement, what would prevent the upsetting of the balance?
>
> Look at Transjordan. In the law, it does not exclude Jews. [But] in reality, Jews are not allowed there. Yet Transjordan was promised to both Jews and Arabs, and the British Government decided to reserve it for Arabs only.
>
> The present controversy on immigration would be settled if Transjordan were to be opened to our people. One hundred thousand Jews would gladly move there from this side of the Jordan. They would break ground and make room for more settlers.
>
> Politically, we Jews feel that a part of our body has been separated from us by cutting off Transjordan from Palestine. But behind the Arab claims is the dream to abrogate the mandate and to build an independent Arab empire.
>
> In such an event, the alleged fear of the Jewish majority is meaningless. Even if we did bring in 5,000,000 Jews into Palestine, we would still remain a minority among the 25,000,000 Arabs in their proposed confederation or kingdom.[62]

---

[62] The above statement attributed to Moshe Sharett appeared in the fifth article of a series of eleven articles by Senator Warren R. Austin, which were published in the *New York American* and other Hearst newspapers from October 11 to October 21, 1936. These articles formed part of a Report of an unofficial senatorial commission sent to Palestine in the summer of 1936 by the Hearst newspaper chain to parallel the inquiry of the Palestine Royal Commission established in the same year. The three members of the Hearst Unofficial Senatorial Commission

In his book of completed memoirs, Abdullah stated that the Balfour Declaration included Transjordan within its ambit. He recalled his good fortune in 1921, attributing to God what the British had deviously done to betray Zionism and the Jewish People:[63]

> God granted me success in creating the government of Transjordan by having it separated from the Balfour Declaration which included it.

Abdullah was certainly not privy to the original British intentions regarding Transjordan prior to his meeting with Churchill in Jerusalem on March 28, 1921, when he was first offered the position of provisional Administrator of Transjordan for a period of six months. Undoubtedly, however, he soon became fully informed of those intentions together with the new plan devised by the British Colonial Office under Churchill. Abdullah's testimony given in his completed Memoirs that Transjordan was originally linked to the Balfour Declaration and hence an integral part of the Jewish National Home has significant evidentiary weight.

It is interesting that when he visited London in October 1922 to confirm his role as Administrator of Transjordan, after the six-month period of his installation had expired, he demanded a public announcement that the Balfour Declaration did not apply to Transjordan.[64] Since the British had already received approval from the League Council to invoke Article 25 of the Mandate on September 16, 1922 excluding Transjordan from the provisions of the Balfour Declaration and the Jewish National Home, this demand may have appeared to be superfluous, but from his perspective, he knew that the administrative separation of Transjordan from the Jewish National Home in Cisjordan was only a provisional measure that could be revoked in the future if the existing local conditions in Transjordan were changed. The theoretical possibility of reabsorbing Transjordan into the Jewish National Home is what apparently motivated him to ask the British for a public announcement that the Balfour Declaration did not apply to Transjordan.

Further confirmation that Transjordan had originally been intended for inclusion in Palestine and the Jewish National Home at the time the Balfour

---

were New York Senator Royal S. Copeland, Vermont Senator Warren R. Austin and Delaware Senator Daniel O. Hastings. The full report of their findings entitled *The Crisis in Palestine* is reprinted in *The Rise of Israel,* Volume 19, Document 39, p. 602 ff. Sharett's statement appears on p. 647.

[63] Cited in an article by Dr. Paul Riebenfeld, "Israel, Jordan, Palestine", *Midstream – A Monthly Jewish Review*, March 1976, p. 39. The citation is from the book *King Abdullah of Jordan, My Memoirs Completed*, Near Eastern Translation Program, Washington (1954), pp. 96-97.

[64] Uriel Dann, *Studies in the History of Transjordan, 1920-1949*, p. 53. Abdullah made his demand on October 16, 1922 to Gilbert Clayton of the Colonial Office, formerly the Director of Military Intelligence in Cairo and one of the chief advisers to Henry McMahon when he was the High Commissioner there.

Declaration was issued on November 2, 1917 comes from a British official who had intimate knowledge of the origin of Transjordan as a separate state. This was Sir Alec Seath Kirkbride, whose record of diverse service in what was to become the Hashemite Kingdom of Jordan is unmatched by any other British official. He started as a security officer attached to the Arab army commanded by the Emir Feisal ibn Hussein, and in that capacity was subordinate to Colonel T.E. Lawrence. After the war ended, Kirkbride, while still in military service, was sent in July 1920, along with a small number of other Arabic-speaking British officers, to various centers east of the Jordan to establish local autonomous administrations. Kirkbride's political assignment was in Kerak, where he had previously spent some months during Feisal's brief rule of Syria. Acting with the presumed authority invested in him by the British Government, Kirkbride formed a regional government in the town of Kerak[65] which he called the National Government of Moab. It had a Council of Twelve Elders or Sheikhs, which Kirkbride likened to a cabinet, presided over by a President or a Chairman. By the unanimous decision of the tribal elders, he was chosen to head the Council, contrary to his express wishes. This so-called National Government, which Joseph B. Schechtman viewed as "hastily improvised and largely fictitious",[66] ruled a territory that embraced Moab and northern Edom for a period of nine months until Abdullah created, under British auspices, a central administration at Amman on April 1, 1921 to govern all of Transjordan. Kirkbride then worked closely with Abdullah over a period of thirty years, though six of those years were spent in Jerusalem serving the High Commissioner as a member of the Secretariat. Considering Kirkbride's extensive association with Transjordan, his observations regarding this territory's relationship with the rest of Palestine must be treated with the greatest respect and attention.

In his book, *A Crackle of Thorns*, Kirkbride stated that Palestine was "a geographical term which included Transjordan" and hence the latter was inevitably included in the promise of the Balfour Declaration to establish in Palestine a National Home for the Jewish People. He further described the way Transjordan was regarded by the British in relation to the rest of Palestine at the outset of the Mandate: [67]

> At the time of the issue of this mandate His Majesty's Government were too busy setting up a civil administration in Palestine proper, west

---

[65] Modern Al-Kerak is on the site of Kir-Hareseth (Heres) or Kir of Moab, the capital of ancient Moab, lying south of the Arnon (Wadi el-Mojeb) and north of the Zered (Wadi al-Hasa) on the eastern-southern side of the Dead Sea in Hashemite Jordan.

[66] Joseph B. Schechtman, *Jordan – A State That Never Was*, Cultural Publishing Co., Inc., New York (1968), p. 23.

[67] Alec Seath Kirkbride, *A Crackle of Thoms: Experiences in the Middle* East, John Murray (Publishers) Ltd., London (1956), p. 19-20. The opening words of this title are taken from the Bible: Ecclesiastes 7:6.

> of the River Jordan, to be bothered about the remote and undeveloped areas which lay to the east of the river and which were intended to serve as a reserve of land for use in the resettlement of Arabs once the National Home for the Jews in Palestine, which they were pledged to support, became an accomplished fact. There was no intention at that stage of forming the territory east of the River Jordan into an independent Arab state.

Continuing his narrative, Kirkbride makes a brilliantly sarcastic statement of immense importance divulging in effect that at the very beginning of the implementation of the Mandate in July 1920, Palestine and Transjordan were intended to be a unified, undivided whole:[68]

> *In due course, the remarkable discovery* was made that the clauses of the Mandate relating to the establishment of a National Home for the Jews had never been intended to apply to the mandated territory east of the [Jordan] river (emphasis added).

Kirkbride did not identify the "remarkable discovery" in the above passage that resulted in severing the link between Transjordan and the Jewish National Home which, until then, had included it. The only possible "discovery" he could have been hinting at that was relevant to the meaning of the Mandate was the McMahon Pledge of October 24, 1915, which promised British recognition and support for Arab independence in a wide area that supposedly placed all of Transjordan within its confines.

Inasmuch as the McMahon-Hussein Correspondence containing the McMahon Pledge was a well-known fact to all British statesmen and high officials at the time the Balfour Declaration was issued (1917) as well as at the time the Mandate for Palestine was being formulated (1919-1920), approved and first submitted to the Council of the League of Nations for confirmation (1920), there was nothing about the Pledge or Correspondence that required "discovery", whether in 1917, 1920 or, as Kirkbride facetiously put it, "in due course". The date of "discovery" presumably was in March 1921 at the Cairo Conference, presided over by Winston Churchill, where the McMahon Pledge was first offered as the reason for detaching Transjordan from the rest of Palestine. Such reason was reiterated the following year in the Churchill White Paper.

The most logical conclusion to be drawn from Kirkbride's subtle choice of language was that he engaged in classical British humour to ridicule the attempted cover-up of what was evidently a change of course in British Middle East policy, one that now re-embraced a pro-Sherifian/Hashemite Arab orientation to the detriment of Zionism and the Jewish National Home. This policy favouring

[68] *Ibid.*, p. 27.

Arab over Jewish rule in Transjordan had already been manifest under Lord Curzon, the Secretary of State for Foreign Affairs, but was never officially and publicly proclaimed until Churchill's ascension to the Colonial Office.

It is equally evident that Kirkbride's statement provides conclusive evidence to refute the claim made by various scholars, that Transjordan was always intended by the British to be outside the scope of the Jewish National Home. If that truly had been the case, *no remarkable discovery* would have been needed to be made *in due course* that the clauses of the Mandate had never been intended to apply to Transjordan, as was, on the contrary, originally assumed in the first official draft of the Mandate (December 6, 1920) and in the Franco-British Boundary Convention of December 23, 1920, where Palestine was defined to include Transjordan.

During the nine-month period from the initial implementation of the Mandate on July 1, 1920 until Abdullah began to administer Transjordan on April 1, 1921 on behalf of the British Government, Christopher Sykes, a prominent historian focusing on this period, described the situation that then prevailed in Transjordan: [69]

> The southern half of the former *vilayet* of Syria, due east across the Jordan from Palestine, had been under Feisal's rule. By the San Remo decisions [April 25, 1920] this territory came under the British Palestine Mandate… Now suddenly [i.e., from July 25, 1920, when Feisal was ejected from Damascus by the French: HG], the territory was left without any rule at all and the High Commissioner in Jerusalem had neither the monetary nor manpower resources to undertake reorganisation immediately. He acted with bold improvisation. After

[69] Christopher Sykes, *Cross Roads to Israel*, Collins Press, London (1965), pp. 60-62. In an undated petroleum agreement made between the National Government of Moab and the Anglo-Saxon Petroleum Co., the territories or districts administered by the Government of Moab were mentioned in the agreement as extending from the Wadi Mojeb on the north [this is the Arabic name for the Arnon River on the eastern side of the Dead Sea, opposite Ein Gedi] to the Wadi Musa on the south [the Valley of Moses is also called al-Siq in Arabic, a long, narrow and winding canyon or gorge, which is the only entrance to Petra, a rock-cut (or rose red) city once known as Sela Ha'Adom]; and bounded on the East by the Syrian desert and on the West by the Dead Sea. The text of this agreement is reproduced in Uriel Dann's book, *op. cit.*, pp.31-34. See also Dann's Observations concerning the boundaries of the National Government of Moab on p. 35, paragraph (b) where he states that the authority of the National Government never extended south of Tafile, located south of the Zered (Wadi el-Hasa) in Edom. The area between Tafile and Wadi Musa at Petra was part of the Ma'an district which belonged to the Hedjaz until 1925. In addition to the National Government of Moab, under the presidency of Alec Seath Kirkbride, an "Ammonite Government" was established under his younger brother, Alan L. Kirkbride. See *The Emergence of the Middle East: 1914-1924*, by Howard M. Sachar, published by Alfred A. Knopf, New York (1969), p. 402.

> a meeting of notables convened at es-Salt, Sir Herbert Samuel, after promising to promote self-government in the Eastern territory, sent a few Arabic-speaking officers with small detachments of police across the Jordan with general instructions to maintain order...; the people East of Jordan had learned to look after themselves in a crude manner, and on the collapse of Feisal's Kingdom they formed themselves *into minute independent states*. The main task of the British officers was to prevent these states waging war on each other. The most southern of them had its "capital" at Kerak where the town was then sited entirely within the walls of the ruined Crusader stronghold, Crac du Desert. The British adviser was Major Alec Kirkbride, and with a fine sense of history he named its administration, of which he was elected president, "The National Government of Moab."
>
> ...Within a few weeks [after Abdullah's arrival in Kerak and Amman early in 1921] the national Government of Moab and all its *little sister-autonomies* vanished as the Emir established something resembling a central administration in Amman (emphasis added).

Christopher Sykes's statement that after the collapse of Feisal's "Kingdom", the people east of the Jordan formed themselves into "minute, independent states" or "little sister autonomies", is a gross exaggeration. While these entities were certainly minute, as Sykes said, they were neither states, nor autonomies, nor independent. They were little more than momentary British creations that pretended to be governments, but lacked real powers and had neither money nor troops.[70]

The most authoritative statement concerning the exact status of Transjordan in relation to Palestine and the Jewish National Home was given in the Report issued by the Palestine Royal Commission, dated June 22, 1937. The Commission heard scores of witnesses at numerous public and private sessions held in 1936 and 1937 on all aspects of the problems besetting Palestine. On the subject of Transjordan which had come under complete British control by September 24, 1918,[71]

---

[70] Kirkbride, *op. cit.*, p. 20.

[71] Transjordan was liberated from Turkish rule with the indispensable assistance of Jewish soldiers serving in the Jewish Legion, a volunteer corps conceived and organized by Vladimir Ze'ev Jabotinsky to fight against Turkish forces remaining in Palestine, that consisted of three battalions in the British Army. The key military operation in the Transjordanian war theatre was the capture of a bridgehead at *Umm-es-Shert* located at a ford of the Jordan River in the malaria-producing salt-pan of the Jordan Valley, known in Arabic as the *Mellaha*, 1300 ft. below sea-level. This was a pivotal act carried out during the hottest and most unhealthy month of the year which paved the way not only for the capture of Transjordan, but of Damascus as well, as openly acknowledged by Major-General Edward Chaytor, the commander of the Australian Cavalry. No mention of this feat of Jewish valor and endurance was ever published in Palestine or Egypt, because of a deliberate policy emanating from the antisemitic atmosphere of Allenby's General

it stated:[72]

> The field in which the Jewish National Home was to be established was understood at the time of the Balfour Declaration, to be the whole of historic Palestine, and the Zionists were seriously disappointed when Transjordan was cut away from that field under Article 25.

An additional testimony as to whether or not Transjordan was included in the Jewish National Home prior to Churchill's decision at the Cairo Conference on March 17, 1921 to provisionally exclude it has been provided by William Yale, an American expert on Arab affairs who was an adviser to the American King-Crane Commission. In his book on *The Near East, A Modern History*, he wrote that Transjordan was definitely meant to be part of the Jewish National Home:[73]

> When the Supreme Council of the Allies at San Remo allocated the Mandate for Palestine to Great Britain, not only was Transjordan included in the Palestine Mandate but a rider was added "to the effect that the Mandatory Power should be responsible for giving effect to the Balfour Declaration".

Despite overwhelming evidence that Transjordan was originally meant to be an integral part of the Jewish National Home governed by the Balfour Declaration as confirmed in the Boundary Convention of December 23, 1920 and, moreover, by the omission of all mention of Transjordan in the Draft Mandate of December 6, 1920, there are those who have maintained that no partition took place in 1921-22 because Transjordan, in their opinion, was never actually included *earlier* (i.e., prior to the decision taken at the Cairo Conference of March 17, 1921) in either the Jewish National Home or Palestine. This school of thought is represented by History Professor and author, Bernard Wasserstein, who in a 1983 article called the idea of a 1921-22 Partition of Palestine "a popular myth", "a tale", "bad history" or a "rewrite of history". He

---

Headquarters in Cairo. See the account of the Jewish role in the liberation of Transjordan in the book by Shmuel Katz, *Lone Wolf, A Biography of Vladimir Ze'ev Jabotinsky,* published by Barricade Books Inc., New York (1996), chapters 15 and 16, pp. 371-392.

72 Palestine Royal Commission Report presented to Parliament, July 1937. Command 5479, p. 38. Reprinted in *The Rise of Israel*, Vol. 24, Document 2, p. 58.

73 *The Near East, A Modern History* by William Yale, published by the University of Michigan Press, New Edition, Revised and Enlarged, p. 381. Yale's statement is based on a citation from the book *Great Britain and Palestine 1915-1939* (London: Royal Institute of International Affairs, 1939), p. 13.

stated emphatically:[74]

> *There was no such "partition" of Palestine in 1921-1922* (Italics in original). Indeed, the best description of what happened is that territory was *added on to*, not lopped off from the Palestine Mandate. Rather than a "partition" of Palestine, there was *an expansion of the area under British mandatory control* (emphasis added).

He stressed the same point later on in his article, writing:

> What had happened was less a "partition" than *an annexation*. The area of the Palestine Mandate had been greatly enlarged to include the area east of the River Jordan up to the border with Iraq (emphasis added).

The basis or premise for this theory of Wasserstein's is that Britain never made any formal commitment to include Transjordan within the area of Palestine, prior to the alleged "expansion" or "annexation":

> Although there was some British support for Zionist territorial claims east of the Jordan, *no formal British commitment on the subject was ever made* (emphasis added). The Balfour Declaration of November 1917 had, of course, specified no particular area. And when in April 1920, the Allied Powers, meeting in conference at San Remo, assigned the Mandate for Palestine to Britain, the question of borders was left open.

Although the borders were not legally defined, according to Wasserstein, he further alleged:

> They were, however, defined for practical purposes by the *status quo* bequeathed by the military administration, namely, the border of OETA South, which extended eastward only up to the River Jordan.

Wasserstein's conclusion that no partition occurred in 1921-22 in regard to Transjordan is a deceptive and misleading half-truth that turns upside-down the real meaning of what actually happened. The only part of his conclusion with some particle of truth in it is the fact that the partition was not made final in those two years, and hence was not an absolute partition in the full sense of the term. While the British moves in 1921-22 to partition Palestine were at that stage still only tentative and reversible, they nevertheless heralded the moves that were to come in 1928 and 1946 which definitively partitioned the country

---

[74] See his article in the Jerusalem Post, Friday, June 17, 1983, entitled: "Is Jordan Really Palestine?"

and illegally created a new state out of the patrimony of the Jewish People.

Wasserstein evidently forgot, when he set out his contentious and unsupportable conclusion in the above-mentioned article, that he had written the very opposite in 1977 in the Introduction to Volume X of the *Letters and Papers of Chaim Weizmann*, dealing with the period July 1920 – December 1921, where he said (page xxi):

> In March 1921 a conference of British officials (headed by the Colonial Secretary, Churchill) met at Cairo to plan the political geography of the British Middle East. *Abdullah was established on his throne and Transjordan was separated from Palestine with Samuel as High Commissioner of both areas* (emphasis added).

If it was true, as Wasserstein correctly asserted in 1977, that *Transjordan was separated from Palestine at the Cairo Conference*, then, logically speaking, there could not have been any "expansion of the area under British mandatory control" or annexation of this territory to Palestine, contrary to his assertion in his 1983 article, and it is up to him to explain how such expansion or annexation could have occurred. In fact, his entire thesis of an alleged enlargement of Palestine engineered by Samuel is a figment of his overactive imagination and his evident desire to exculpate Samuel for contributing to the partition of Palestine. Moreover, there was no throne established for Abdullah in 1921, as Wasserstein mistakenly stated in his aforementioned Introduction.

The tentative administrative partition of 1921-22 is naturally founded on the assumption that Transjordan was a pre-existing part of Palestine – otherwise there could not have been any partition. It is exactly this basic assumption which Wasserstein denies to be true because he says no borders were fixed either in the Balfour Declaration of November 2, 1917 or in the San Remo Resolution two and a half years later. However, the assertion that Palestine as envisaged in the Balfour Declaration had no borders, while true in the literal sense, constitutes an egregious distortion of the evidence, considered against the background of the Declaration. Britain was not in any position when it issued the Declaration on November 2, 1917 to delineate any kind of borders for Palestine which was not yet in its military possession. Setting final borders at that stage, when Palestine had not even been formally created as a mandated territory, was obviously premature and even absurd. Still Britain definitely had an idea of what those borders should be, which were not for the obvious reason just mentioned written into the text of the Declaration that merely constituted a short statement of British intention, namely, to establish a Jewish National Home in Palestine which would eventually evolve into an independent Jewish State.

The promise Britain made to the Jewish People in the Balfour Declaration to use their best endeavours to facilitate the establishment of a Jewish National Home in Palestine was firmly premised on the Jewish historical connection with that country, which indicated that Palestine would be created in accordance with its historical borders, wherever the Twelve Tribes of Israel and their descendants had conquered, settled and governed the land. That in turn meant the definite inclusion of the various regions of Transjordan, including Bashan (with the Golan), Gilead, Moab-Ammon and Edom, which reflected the oft-stated opinion of all those who had participated in the making of the Balfour Declaration, from the Prime Minister to the Foreign Secretary and all the other members of the Imperial War Cabinet, who visualized a great Jewish State arising one day on both banks of the Jordan. This opinion has been documented in the testimonies and writings of all the leading British officials directly involved in the proposed establishment of the Jewish National Home in 1917. Not one of them ever asserted or imagined that as of the date of the Balfour Declaration, Transjordan would be excluded from the Jewish National Home. The Zionist leaders shared the same opinion, as did Feisal and Abdullah. Though the British did not formally delineate the borders of Palestine in the Balfour Declaration, they did delineate them in the map drawn for the De Bunsen Committee Report of June 30, 1915 and also in the Foreign Office map attached to the memorandum of William George Tyrell of October 1917 on the eve of the Balfour Declaration. Both of these maps included the large area of Transjordan squarely within the borders of Palestine and the Jewish National Home. The evidence is therefore irrefutable that Transjordan with all its historical Jewish regions was meant to be part of Palestine when the British Government originally issued the Balfour Declaration in sympathy with Jewish-Zionist aspirations.

When the Principal Allied Powers met at San Remo in April 1920 to carve up the Ottoman Middle East Empire and draft the Mandates articles for the Turkish peace treaty to be signed at Sèvres, they were not collectively ready to officially delineate the borders of Palestine, Mesopotamia and Syria. Alone among these powers France definitely wanted to do so, based on the illegal Sykes-Picot Treaty with certain modifications, but Britain balked at the idea because it required more detailed negotiations to fix the exact borders for these three countries. It also did not want the borders delineated in the absence of Feisal, then the provisional ruler of Syria, whose consent it felt was needed to avoid an explosion in the Arab world.

The borders were finally drawn between Syria and Palestine in the Franco-British Boundary Convention of December 23, 1920, that underwent some further modifications in 1922-23, especially as regards the Golan. This treaty marks the date when Transjordan was expressly and formally included in Palestine, with the latter now being a full-fledged mandated State with generally recognized borders that needed final demarcation in the east (with Mesopotamia) and in the south (with the Arabian peninsula). It also constituted the "formal commitment" "for Zionist territorial claims east of the Jordan" that Wasserstein says so confidently was never made by the British.

The formal commitment to include Transjordan in the Jewish National Home was indeed a consequence of the Boundary Convention, because all the negotiations to determine the boundaries between Syria and Palestine were premised on Prime Minister Lloyd George's idea – stated openly in the archival correspondence and documents relating to these negotiations – that all the territory to be included in Palestine was meant specifically for the establishment of the Jewish National Home, which is why the Atlas of George Adam Smith (*Atlas of the Historical Geography of the Holy Land*) was used as a basic guide by British officials to determine the exact extent of Israelite and Judean settlement in the days of the First and Second Temple Periods, particularly the era of the United Kingdom of Israel's first monarchs Saul, David and Solomon. Moreover, it bears repeating that both on November 2, 1917 (date of the Balfour Declaration) and on April 24, 1920 (date of the acceptance of the Balfour Declaration by the Principal Allied Powers at the San Remo Peace Conference), as well as on August 10, 1920 (date of the Treaty of Sèvres), it was an article of faith or an implicit understanding, that Palestine's future borders would encompass all the territory concerning which there was a Jewish historical connection, and that certainly included Transjordan.

In addition to this understanding that Transjordan was indeed included in the Jewish National Home as of the date of the Boundary Convention of December 23, 1920, prior to Churchill's intervention (from February 14, 1921 onwards), there is further evidence to support its inclusion in the Home derived from the Draft Mandate of December 6, 1920. The boundaries marked out for Palestine in Article 1 of the Boundary Convention were, in effect, an integral part of Article 5 of the aforementioned Draft Mandate. This version of the Mandate, approved by the British Cabinet on November 29, 1920, when Curzon was still in charge of its formulation, has special legal importance, because it was incorporated by reference in the Boundary Convention as even a cursory reading of the Convention will reveal. The official Curzon draft made no distinction between Transjordan and Cisjordan. All of Palestine was treated as one unified entity and all of its territory was reserved for the Jewish National Home. Thus when Churchill decided to "lop off" Transjordan from Palestine at the session of the Cairo Conference of March 17, 1921, it was in effect a true administrative partition, since all the territory east of the Jordan was literally being ripped away from the projected development of all of Palestine as a future independent Jewish state. The only solace for the Jewish People was that this administrative partition was not final, but only provisional, holding out a slender hope that it could still be reversed and the territory reunited one day with Cisjordan and the Jewish National Home.

Wasserstein's contention that the borders of Palestine were fixed *de facto* by General Allenby's military administration known as OETA South is also grossly misleading, like much of what he wrote in his 1983 article about the status of Transjordan. It was merely a matter of military and economic convenience for Allenby and the British Government to allow Feisal to govern

Syria and Transjordan during the interim period[75] which lasted less than two years (October 5, 1918 to July 25, 1920), prior to deciding the terms of a final settlement with Turkey at the San Remo Peace Conference. These terms were then incorporated into the Treaty of Sèvres of August 10, 1920. The military arrangement was thus entirely provisional in nature and did not in any way predetermine the definitive borders of Palestine, a fact well-known by both Feisal and Allenby. It was during this interim period when he ruled Transjordan, that Feisal explicitly accepted the Zionist proposals presented to the Paris Peace Conference in February 1919 which set aside the most fertile or habitable regions of Transjordan for inclusion in the Jewish National Home of Palestine up to the Hedjaz Railway. Moreover, Prime Minister Lloyd George stated he would never allow British-controlled Transjordan to become part of Syria under the French Mandate, even if Feisal had remained in that country as its King. Thus no reliance can ever be placed on the temporary military arrangement of General Allenby for asserting as Wasserstein does that the borders of Palestine were fixed *de facto* by that arrangement. The borders of Palestine were in fact to be fixed as mentioned above by the historical connection of the Jewish People with that country, as resolved at the San Remo Conference, and it was up to the British and French negotiators to determine which lands were embraced by the Jewish historical connection.

The region across the Jordan most closely connected historically with the Jewish People was Gilead (Ajlun)[76] from the Yarmuk to the Jabbok (whose

---

[75] The forces of General Allenby occupied Damascus on October 1, 1918, Beirut on October 8, 1918 and Homs, Hama and Aleppo on October 25, 1918. Both Allenby and Feisal entered Damascus on October 3, 1918. Allenby, acting on instructions from the British Government, summoned Feisal to a meeting on that very day and explained to him that according to the Sykes-Picot Treaty, France would assume direct control of the "blue" zone, representing Syria west of Damascus and Aleppo, and which included the chief town of Beirut and the geographical area of Lebanon. In zone "A" of that Agreement, including the four Syrian towns of Damascus, Homs, Hama and Aleppo, France would be the protecting power. Feisal, as the representative of his father, King Hussein, was permitted to set up an Arab administration that would also embrace the British designated part of Transjordan in zone "B" of the Agreement under Allenby's overall command. Feisal's rule would thus cover these four Syrian towns and the entire viyalet of Syria to which was added the area from Ma'an to Aqaba, claimed by his father as part of the Kingdom of the Hedjaz, who then consented to his son's administration of it. This military arrangement was to last until the peace settlement was made. In conformity with the guidelines and limitations set forth by Allenby, Feisal established in Damascus on October 5, 1918 an Arab Military Government for Syria and the area east of the Jordan. See Zeine N. Zeine, *The Struggle for Arab Independence*, Caravan Books, Delmar, New York (2nd edition), 1977, chapter 2, pp. 25-43.

[76] George Adam Smith in *The Historical Geography of the Holy Land*, 17th edition, p. 587, states that Ajlun may possibly be the same as Mahanaim, an important fortress city in Gilead whose site is still uncertain.

Arabic name is *nahr al-Zarqa*), and included the cities of Gerash (*Jarash*), Arbel (*Irbid*) and Gadera (*Umm-Qays*)[77]. In its broad meaning Gilead encompasses central Transjordan on both sides of the Jabbok. It corresponds roughly to Perea, a name used by Josephus which in Latin and Greek usage referred to the land east of the Jordan. North of Gilead was the Bashan, which broadly encompassed the land between the Yarmuk and Mount Hermon. The Golan is the western section of Bashan, all of which was conquered by the Israelites and settled by the tribe of Menasseh. This region was later overrun by the Arameans but was restored to Israelite possession under David and later Jeroboam II. It was also ruled at various times by Jewish kings in the Second Temple Period. As to Moab-Ammon and Edom, they too had been attached at one time or other to the Kingdoms of Israel and Judah and to the Hasmonean and Herodian state of Judea.

Joseph B. Schechtman has accurately described the historical link between Transjordan and the rest of Palestine:[78]

> The Left Bank of the Jordan always was an organic part of Palestine. Jewish history in that country began with the occupation and settlement there of the two and a half Hebrew tribes which became the cradle of the Jewish State. Time and again the Mishnah (e.g., Shevi'it 9:2; Ketubot 13:19; Bava Batra 3:2) lays down the rule that "the Land of Israel is divided into three provinces: Judea, Galilee and Transjordan".

Apart from Jewish sources, there can be no doubt at all that historical Palestine in British eyes meant both sides of the Jordan. This is evident not only from the writings of the Scottish Biblical scholar George Adam Smith and Lloyd George's reliance on the maps in his atlas to determine the borders of Palestine, but also from the publications and activities of the British society, the Palestine

---

[77] Concerning the Biblical sites of Gilead in Transjordan, about the location of which great uncertainty still exists, George Adam Smith wrote: "It is impossible for us to believe that *es-Salt* with its *Jebel Osha, Ajlun* with its equally famous view-point and fortress in the *Kula'at-er-Rubaad, Pella, Gadara, Irbid, Remtheh* were not famous in the history of Israel in Gilead. Surely they were not unused. It may only be the meagreness of geographical details in the Old Testament which prevents us from identifying Mizpeh with far-seeing *Kula'at-er-Rubaad,* Mahanaim with so worthy a capital for Gilead as *Ajlun* or with so historical a site as Pella; or from placing Ramoth-Gilead at *Reimun* (as Conder does) or at *es-Salt* or at the *Kula'at-er-Rubaad*, though as already said, it seems necessary from what the Old Testament tells us of the frequency with which Ramoth-Gilead was contested by Aram and Israel, to put it further north, near the Yarmuk. Irbid and Remtheh on the north-east, are both of them fairly strong sites; the former is today the capital of the district of *Ajlun,* the latter a station on the *Hajj* road, that immemorial line of traffic. Both of them must have been prominent places in ancient times", *ibid.*, p. 587-588.

[78] See: *Jordan – A State That Never Was*, Cultural Publishing Co. Inc., New York (1968), pp. 19-20.

Exploration Fund, that scientifically explored the Holy Land since its founding in 1865. It began a survey of Transjordan conducted by Claude Regnier Conder in 1881, as part of its acclaimed work to map the Holy Land. This survey was abruptly terminated by the Turkish authorities. Any exclusion of Transjordan from the area of Palestine would thus have been inconsistent with the historical meaning of Palestine, from both the Jewish and British perspectives.

Another adherent of the belief of certain Jewish historians and authors who propagated the erroneous view that Transjordan was never intended by the British Government to be an integral part of Palestine and the Jewish National Home but rather an eventual independent Arab state or included in one was Avraham P. Alsberg, the former archivist of the State of Israel. In a scholarly article[79] that appeared in 1981, two years prior to the barbed piece by Wasserstein, he stated that it was on December 23, 1920, when it was finally resolved to include Transjordan in the area of the Mandate for Palestine, while at the same time establishing a separate local Arab administration. On this very same date a Boundary Convention was formally signed between Britain and France to determine the boundaries between the territories under the French Mandate of Syria and Lebanon and the British Mandates of Palestine and Mesopotamia. Alsberg chose December 23, 1920 as the determination day for resolving Transjordan's legal status because it was also when Curzon advised Samuel by telegram of the following principles which would guide British policy on the disposition of the territory east of the Jordan in his forthcoming negotiations with Feisal, who was then in London.[80]

> ...in the event of Feisal raising the question of Transjordania, I propose to explain to him:
>
> 1. That we regard Transjordania as being under our Mandate;
>
> 2. That we are helping the people to set up a native administration;[81]
>
> 3. We are prepared to discuss with Hussein the frontier between the Hedjaz and Transjordan;
>
> 4. that all other matters, including the delimitation of the frontier between Palestine and Transjordan, are matters for His Majesty's

[79] Alsberg's article appeared in the journal *Zionism*, Spring 1981, Volume 2, No. 1, "Delimitation of the Eastern Border of Palestine", pp. 87-98.

[80] *Documents on British Foreign Policy 1919-1939*, First Series, Volume XIII, No. 356, p. 421. Reprinted in Alsberg's article, *op. cit.*, p. 94.

[81] The idea of setting up a native administration in the part of Transjordan up till the Hedjaz Railway had been suggested even earlier, by Samuel to Curzon. On August 7, 1920 Samuel sent a personal telegram to the Foreign Secretary recommending that this part of Transjordan be administered through tribal organization supervised by two British District Governors, while the railway and territory to the east be put under control of the King of Hedjaz, if it was undesirable to include it in the British sphere. See *Documents on British Foreign Policy*, Vol. XIII, pp. 333-334, which are also quoted in footnote 16 on page 92 of Alsberg's article.

Government to decide in consultation with the inhabitants;

5. that due regard will be paid to the wishes of the properly constituted local authorities regarding their future form of government.

Alsberg made a serious error in relying on Curzon's set of principles enumerated above for the purpose of ascertaining the legal status of Transjordan. British government correspondence which was secret and unknown to the general public had no official standing in international law, whereas the Boundary Convention was, in effect, an integral part of the Mandate for Palestine, especially Article 1 of the Convention dealing with the borders of that land. The text of the Boundary Convention did not provide any legal support for the principles enunciated by Curzon in his telegram to Samuel (of the very same date!). There was nothing contained in the Boundary Convention about establishing a native administration in Transjordan in consultation with its inhabitants, nor even any allusion to a territory called Transjordan, because on this date it did not yet exist as a separate political or legal entity. Its alleged separate existence was still only an abstract concept in the minds of Curzon and his Foreign Office officials. The Boundary Convention regarded all of the land to the east and to the west of the Jordan equally as belonging to Mandated Palestine and the Jewish National Home, and only confirmed the pre-existing premise adopted at the San Remo Conference that Transjordan, because of its historical Jewish connection, had already been included in the Jewish National Home. There was therefore no justification for Alsberg's belief that the status of Transjordan had remained undetermined and awaited further resolution, during the eight-month period from the adoption of the San Remo Resolution (April 25, 1920) to the signing of the Boundary Convention (December 23, 1920).

To determine the true legal status of Transjordan, Alsberg should therefore have based his conclusion only on the following documents: the San Remo Resolution, Article 95 of the Treaty of Sèvres, the Draft Mandate of December 6, 1920 and the Boundary Convention. In addition to these documents he should have been aware of the premises underlying them as expressed in the Minutes of the San Remo Peace Conference, which are crucial to a complete understanding of the San Remo Resolution. Curzon's aforesaid principles, foreign to those documents, were merely the result of his anti-Zionist bias to limit the size of the Jewish National Home by detaching Transjordan from the intended area of the Home.[82]

In addition to his mistaken reliance on Curzon's principles as discussed above, Alsberg also asserted that there were extant documents in support of what Curzon advocated. In this regard Alsberg stated:[83]

---

[82] The area of Transjordan measured about 34,000 square miles, as opposed to that of Cisjordan, which constituted only about 10,000 square miles.

[83] *Ibid.*, p. 90.

> When the Allied Powers decided at San Remo, on April 24, 1920, to entrust the Mandate over Palestine and Mesopotamia to Britain and the mandate over Syria to France, *Transjordan was considered part of an independent state* (emphasis added) whose northern region was to be under French influence and included in the French mandated territory. No precise borders were defined at San Remo.

Later on in his article, Alsberg reiterated the same point when he said:[84]

> The delineation in 1918 of the borders of the Occupied Enemy Territory Administration by Allenby caused disappointment and resentment among Zionists who could hardly disregard the political intentions of the [Balfour] declaration. The guarantees given to King Hussein provided the pretext for leaving the eastern area outside the borders of Palestine. The British concept which advocated an independent Arab state in the area between Mesopotamia and Palestine was at the root of the exclusion of Transjordan from the discussions of the San Remo Conference in April 1920, at which the principles of the Mandates were approved. The borders of Palestine were not delineated at San Remo, but the British attitude is clearly reflected in the *extant documents* (emphasis added).

The "extant documents" that Alsberg was referring to, although not explicitly identified by him, may well have included the following documents, apart from any internal British government correspondence cited in the footnotes of his article:

> 1. The British Pledge given to Hussein in the McMahon letter dated October 24, 1915;
> 2. The secret Sykes-Picot Treaty of May 9 and 16, 1916;
> 3. A new Anglo-French agreement signed on September 30, 1918 and confirmed on October 19, 1918 concerning the military administration to be set up in Palestine and Syria[85] following the complete occupation of these territories by General Allenby's forces. The new agreement was based on the original Sykes-Picot Treaty. It was negotiated in the summer of 1918 in London by the same Georges Picot and Mark Sykes that produced the 1916 agreement, the French diplomat aided by Ambassador Paul Cambon while Sykes was joined by Lord Robert Cecil. Under the terms of the 1918 agreement, there were to be three military administrative zones, each governed by a

---

[84] *Ibid.*, p. 98.

[85] See the book *Britain, France and the Arab Middle East, 1914-1920* by Jukka Nevakivi (1969), pp. 58, 73-78.

> Chief Administrator directly responsible to General Allenby, who communicated with them through his Chief Political Officer. The first zone to be governed in this fashion was Palestine, administered by Britain, called OETA (Occupied Enemy Territory Administration) South. It extended north to Acre and east to the Jordan River, but did not include the land beyond it. A second zone was set up under French administration for the area of coastal Syria, north of Palestine, called OETA West. A third zone encompassing the rest of Syria and all of the area east of the Jordan was to be administered by Feisal and called OETA East, which under the Sykes-Picot Treaty was part of Areas "A" and "B" destined for an independent Arab state. In December 1918, a fourth zone was created for the area of Cilicia, to be administered by the French, which became OETA North.

This provisional military arrangement, as originally set down in this 1918 Anglo-French agreement, was modified a year later by the Deauville or Paris Agreement of September 13, 1919 drawn up in the form of an *aide-memoire* which Lloyd George presented to Clemenceau. The British announced their intention to evacuate Syria and Cilicia, commencing November 1, 1919, where they were not responsible for the administration of these territories. This meant that Britain would also evacuate all of Transjordan, then ruled by Feisal, even that part of it that was to be under British influence by reason of the Sykes-Picot Treaty.

None of Alsberg's "extant documents" proved that Transjordan was already considered a permanent part of an independent Arab state at the time of the San Remo Peace Conference as he alleged in his 1981 article. Transjordan could hardly have formed part of an independent Arab state in Syria when both Transjordan and Syria were officially classified as "Occupied Enemy Territory East" under military administration. It was a gross exaggeration of the truth to call this whole territory an independent state under Feisal's rule when it was neither independent nor even a state under international law. The status of Feisal during the whole time he ruled in Syria was nothing more than a "Hashemite emir" and the Head of a Provisional Arab Government under the supreme authority of General Allenby as Commander-in-Chief of the Occupied Enemy Territories. This was the exact response given to Feisal by the British Government after it was informed by him of the action taken by the General Syrian Congress at Damascus on March 8, 1920 proclaiming the independence of Syria and naming Feisal as King of the "United Kingdom of Syria" that also included Lebanon and Palestine.[86] Moreover, under the Hague Convention of 1907 governing the military administration of an occupied territory, a convention Britain claimed it was strictly observing, it would have been contrary to the principle of the *status quo ante bellum* (Article 43 of the Hague Regulations) to allow Syria to become

[86] Lord Curzon's letter to Feisal is cited by Zeine N. Zeine in his book *The Struggle for Arab Independence* (2nd edition – 1977), p. 127.

an independent state while it was still legally under military administration, prior to the peace settlement. In fact, Syria had already been designated as a future mandated territory under the Smuts Resolution of January 30, 1919, though as of March 1920, this mandate had not yet been granted nor were its territorial limits fixed.

To further clarify the matter, which Alsberg buried under a cloud of ambiguity, it will suffice to note the following points: first, the McMahon Pledge did not include the fertile parts of Transjordan, as already discussed in Part II of this chapter; second, the secret Sykes-Picot Treaty had been supplanted by the San Remo Resolution and therefore cannot be relied upon, from a legal standpoint, to demonstrate the true status of Transjordan; third, the military borders that divided British-administered Cisjordan from Arab-administered Syria-Transjordan were from the very start only temporary or transitional lines based primarily on military considerations that did not prejudge or decide the eventual delineation of the peace-time borders. Alsberg was unduly influenced by what he perceived as the practical implications of these military borders. He said they were "in fact a political division based on the map delineated in the Sykes-Picot Agreement".[87] However, even if this were true, and without regard to legal considerations[88] which are paramount, that still would not detract from the undeniable fact that these borders, whether military or political, were still only of temporary duration and subject to be changed in the final peace settlement in regard to Palestine, as indeed they were.

The real reason Britain started to withdraw its troops from occupied Syria in November 1919, a move that continued until the first week of December 1919, in accordance with the Deauville-Paris Agreement was not to create a political division based on the Sykes-Picot Treaty, as Alsberg mistakenly believed. Rather, it was motivated by a strong British desire to reduce its military expenditures in the Middle East and thereby ease the heavy burden imposed on the British taxpayer. This was the reason given by Lord Curzon in a letter to Feisal dated October 9, 1919, explaining the Cabinet decision withdrawing the British troops from Syria.[89] To believe that this military evacuation determined the borders of the Jewish National Home, particularly in regard to the eastern frontier, is an exaggerated and unwarranted inference.[90] It is never advisable to read back into an earlier event later developments not conceived at the time of the earlier event; for example, to view as planned the political separation of Transjordan

[87] *Ibid.*, p. 87.

[88] The Sykes-Picot borders had no legal standing under international law, as discussed above in Section I. Furthermore, any derivative of an illegal agreement can itself only be illegal.

[89] See Zeine N. Zeine, *op. cit.*, p. 105.

[90] If Alsberg is correct, then there would have been no need at all for Britain and France to then negotiate the precise borders between their respective mandated territories, negotiations conducted throughout 1920 culminating in the Boundary Convention at the end of that year.

from the Jewish National Home (that occurred officially on September 16, 1922) on the basis of military moves (which took place in 1919) interpreted as preparing the stage for that subsequent separation, without there being sufficient unambiguous evidence to confirm this interpretation.

To recapitulate, what counted in determining the legal status of Transjordan in the year 1920 was not what may have been written in internal British communications, but only what appeared in the text of the documents setting out the terms of the global political and legal peace settlement, including the premises upon which these documents were founded. In that light, it was presumed that Transjordan, based on its historical connection with Cisjordan, would become not an independent Arab state but rather an integral part of the mandated State of Palestine, that was then identical with the Jewish National Home. The British concept of an independent Arab state in Transjordan began to take concrete shape not on December 23, 1920 as alleged by Alsberg, but only in the Churchill period (February 14, 1921 to October 25, 1922) after the territory had already been included in the Jewish National Home under international law. The initial step in this partition process was the Cairo Conference recommendation to administratively separate Transjordan from Cisjordan on March 17, 1921 (based upon the Shuckburgh Memorandum), followed by Cabinet approval several days later. Two additional steps were then taken: a revision of the Mandate instrument through the insertion of a revised Article 25 in the August 1921 draft, and then the application of this article on September 16, 1922, which gave apparent legal effect under international law to Transjordan's administrative separation. During the 18-month gestation period from March 17, 1921 until September 16, 1922, Transjordan was legally part of the Jewish National Home, still open theoretically to organized Jewish settlement under Article 6 of the Mandate, even after Abdullah took over its administration on April 1, 1921 on a provisional basis of six months. It may also be affirmed that even after September 16, 1922, the foreclosure of Jewish settlement activity in Transjordan represented only a provisional prohibition under the provisions of Article 25, that was, also theoretically, subject to revocation.

However, Jewish hopes for the lifting of the British ban on Jewish settlement in Transjordan were gradually dashed in succeeding years, first, by the mere passage of time which solidified the earlier steps of 1921-1922 and made them impervious to further change, despite many entreaties to Britain to change its policy on this question; second, by the signing of new British accords with Abdullah that strengthened his powers and grip over Transjordan. Britain thus succeeded by subterfuge and by what appeared superficially to be legal methods, but were not, to rob the Jewish People of their national patrimony in Transjordan, contrary to its original intentions. They managed to push through their illegal plan of partition with neither remorse nor accountability until it was a *fait accompli*. It was another illustration of British perfidy in which Wrong triumphed over Right and Illegality over Legality.

Though no realistic chance exists today for Israel's recovery of Transjordan, it is important to record the illegality of its detachment from Jewish Palestine in the expectation that one day new circumstances will arise to rectify the insidious British trick perpetrated at the start of the Mandate period which will permit the return of the ancient Jewish regions of Transjordan to their rightful owner.

## *(IV) The American Role in Causing the Separation of Transjordan from the Jewish National Home and its Harmful Effects on Cisjordanian Palestine*

What is not generally known about the Transjordanian developments is the American role which facilitated the British detachment of Transjordan from the Jewish National Home at the expense of the Jewish People. After the "A" Mandates were assigned at the San Remo Peace Conference on April 25, 1920, the United States began a campaign to secure equality of treatment and opportunity in all mandated territories that was afforded for the commerce, citizens and subjects of all states which were members of the League of Nations.

On November 20, 1920, the American Secretary of State, Bainbridge Colby, wrote Lord Curzon requesting that the draft mandate forms be communicated to the U.S. Government before their submission to the Council of the League of Nations in order that it have the fullest opportunity to consider their terms, which may affect its interests. The U.S. was particularly interested in the question of petroleum resources in both Mesopotamia and Palestine and the granting of concessions for their exploitation. It was known that the Standard Oil Company of New York before the War had bought seven concessions from Ottoman subjects to explore for oil in the Negev and various minerals in the area around the Dead Sea. One study even "claimed that along the Jordan Valley, between the Sea of Galilee and the Red Sea, the oil deposits were as rich as any in the world".[91]

A copy of Colby's letter to Lord Curzon was sent to the Governments of France and Italy with a request for their interpretation of the provisions of a tripartite agreement between Great Britain, Italy and France signed at Sèvres on August 10, 1920 (separate and apart from the Treaty of Sèvres signed on the same day) which recognized Italy's special interests in southwestern Anatolia (Antalya) and those of France in Cilicia (Adana), and provided the nationals of the Contracting Powers perfect equality in all matters relating to commerce, navigation, transit, customs and similar matters. The Americans then sent a letter on February 21, 1921 to the President and members of the League Council making the same request contained in the note they had sent earlier to

[91] See: Frank Manuel, *The Realities of American-Palestine Relations*, Public Affairs Press, Washington, D.C. (1949), p. 267. Standard Oil was created in 1870 by John D. Rockefeller and was subsequently split into 34 companies, that today include Exxon, Mobil, Chevron, Atlantic Richfield and Amoco.

Lord Curzon on November 20, 1920. The U.S. had not participated in the War against Turkey, and ratified neither the Treaty of Versailles nor the Covenant of the League of Nations that was an intrinsic part of it. Because of this, Lord Curzon did not initially accept the American request to be consulted in advance about the mandates for the territories under former Ottoman sovereignty before their submission to the League Council. The draft mandates for Palestine and Mesopotamia were submitted by Lord Balfour to the Council of the League of Nations for confirmation on December 6, 1920, without advance notification given to the U.S. Government. It was expected by the British Government that early approval would be forthcoming at the Geneva sittings of the Council, during its 11th session, in December 1920. That British expectation was in harmony with the League Council's own wish to have a speedy decision made for all Mandates.

The Council did approve the charters drawn up for the "C" Mandates on December 17, 1920, but did not take any decision on those for the "A" and "B" Mandates. One reason was that the Treaty of Peace with Turkey (the Treaty of Sèvres) had not yet entered into legal force, a point raised by Italy who also objected to the confirmation of the French Mandate for Syria and Lebanon until it received reassurance that its rights and interests in Antalya would not be prejudiced. The non-ratification of the Treaty of Sèvres was certainly a snag in the confirmation process, but not the chief reason for the Council's inaction at that exact moment. It was assumed that Turkey had already lost its sovereignty over the non-Turkish populated territories of its former Empire, either through subjugation, consent or acquiescence after a period of simple cessation of hostilities, or by its behaviour, even before its formal renunciation of sovereignty in the Treaty of Lausanne. In any event, the "A" Mandates, when they finally entered into legal force on September 29, 1923, did so before the new Treaty of Peace of Turkey was ratified on August 6, 1924, demonstrating that the question of sovereignty was not the key issue in holding up the confirmation of these Mandates.

The principal snag for delaying the confirmation process was the repeated American demand to first see and approve the drafts of the mandates before their confirmation by the Council. It was likely that the Mandate for Palestine would have been approved in February 1921, according to D.F.W. Van Rees, Vice-President of the Permanent Mandates Commission, had it not been for the intrusive American intervention.[92]

What Van Rees observed is supported by Paul L. Hanna, who writes:[93]

> Despite the absence of a treaty with Turkey, the Council… might have given provisional approval of the "A" Mandates in February or

[92] See his statement to this effect in *Les Mandats Internationaux*, Librairie Arthur Rousseau, Paris (1927), p. 32.

[93] Paul L. Hanna, *op. cit.*, p. 64.

> March 1921 had it not been for two unforeseen difficulties. First, the British representative requested deferment of action pending a visit to the East of Winston Churchill, who was assuming control of the Mandated territories, then being transferred from the Foreign to the Colonial Office. Second, the United States protested the assignment of Mandates without its assent and even asked the confirmation of those in the "C" category be reconsidered. In view of these developments the Council decided to postpone action on the "A" and "B" groups and to invite the United States to send a representative to the next Council meeting.

A Political Report compiled in 1921 by the Executive of the Zionist Organization for the 12th Zionist Congress supports the view that American opposition to the approval of all Mandates generally was an important reason why the Mandate for Palestine was not confirmed by the Council of the League of Nations at the December 1920 meeting.[94] In addition, the Palestine Royal Commission affirmed that the reason for the delay in confirming the Mandate for Palestine by the League Council "was largely due to the intervention of the United States Government."[95] A news report in the New York Times of February 28, 1921 mentioned "the protest lodged by the United States" to explain why no action was then being taken to confirm the Mandate.[96]

The demand that prior American approval was required for all the mandates of whatever category was based on the ground that American participation in the War against Germany contributed to her defeat and the defeat of her allies, including Ottoman Turkey, and to the renunciation of the rights and titles of her allies in the territory transferred by them.[97]

However, the U.S. desire to secure rights for itself in the mandated territories, which was the reason behind its demand to approve all mandate forms in advance, did not justify its irritating and uncalled for disruption of the confirmation process. It was unnecessary because that demand would have been accepted in any event, as it eventually was, without the accompanying need to delay the confirmation of all the "A" and "B" Mandates. By the time the Council met again at its 12th session on February 21, 1921 for the purpose of finally confirming the Mandate for Palestine and the other "A" and "B"

---

[94] *The Rise of Israel*, Vol. 8, Document 57, p. 188.

[95] Chapter 2 of the Report, paragraph 34, p. 31. Reproduced in *The Rise of Israel*, Vol. 24, Document No. 2, p. 51.

[96] "The Great Contemporary Issues: The Middle East", *The New York Times*, Arno Press, New York (1976), p. 52.

[97] See the preamble of the American-British Palestine Mandate Convention of December 3, 1924. See also the *Exchange of Notes* dated February 21, 1921 and March 1, 1921 between the U.S. Secretary of State Bainbridge Colby and the President of the Council of the League of Nations, Gastao da Cunha, in *The Rise of Israel*, Vol. 19, Document 38, pp. 533-536.

mandates, the British Government, represented by Winston S. Churchill, who had just assumed ministerial responsibility for Middle Eastern affairs from Lord Curzon, and now faced with a crisis caused by Abdullah's entry into Transjordan and his threat to take up arms against the French for ousting his younger brother Feisal from Damascus, found it expedient to defer confirmation until Churchill could resolve the problem with Abdullah. This contrasted sharply with the British attitude a mere two months before when they had urgently sought the Council's confirmation for the Mandate for Palestine which made no legal distinction between Transjordan and Cisjordan. Before Churchill's reassessment of the situation was completed, each of these two broad-based areas of Palestine separated by the Jordan River was to have the same kind of administration, governed in accordance with the Balfour Declaration.

In light of the new circumstances which motivated the British Government to compensate the Sherifian/Hashemite family for their loss of Syria, Churchill asked the Council to withdraw all the Near-Eastern Mandates from its agenda, until he, as the newly appointed Colonial Secretary, could study the situation on the spot relating to the British mandated territories before any final decision was taken by the Council.[98] The Council acceded to Churchill's request. Churchill's opportunistic move to defer confirmation of the Mandate for Palestine was the fatal blow which, in turn, brought about the loss of Transjordan from the Jewish National Home that would probably never have occurred, had the Mandate been confirmed earlier. That loss was actually the direct result of the U.S. Government's irksome intervention in the Mandate confirmation process, which caused a delay sufficient to allow the British Government to rethink and change the terms of the Draft Mandate. It proceeded to exploit this American-induced delay by inserting a new text in Article 25 of the Mandate for Palestine which allowed for the eventual breakaway of Transjordan from the Jewish National Home.

The American Government later gave tentative consent to the British-Zionist-formulated Mandate for Palestine in a letter sent from the American Embassy in London to Lord Curzon, dated May 10, 1922, but by that time Britain had already decided on the provisional separation of Transjordan from the Jewish National Home. The U.S. Government has never realized to this day the grave damage their untimely intervention had caused to Jewish rights and title of sovereignty to all of Palestine, on both sides of the Jordan, nor admitted to any wrong in delaying approval for the Mandate that amounted to selfish obstruction and careless disregard for the implementation of the Mandates System in which they never participated.

Once the Americans caused a delay in the confirmation of the Mandate for Palestine by making unnecessary demands for the recognition of rights that could easily have been settled without disrupting the process, that in turn incited other parties who felt aggrieved to raise new demands of their own

[98] *The Rise of Israel*, Vol. 8, Document 57, p. 188.

which further delayed its confirmation. The Vatican, not a participant in any of the Peace Conferences and therefore lacking standing to intervene, nevertheless demanded stronger protection for the religious rights of existing non-Jewish communities in Palestine, while also expressing sudden concern for the Arab inhabitants of the country who would be affected by the establishment of the Jewish National Home. Italy at the eleventh hour pressed once again for renewed assurances from the French regarding its special interests in Southern Anatolia (Antalya) that might be prejudiced by the French Mandate for Syria. The Italian demand prevented both the French and British Mandates from entering into legal force immediately after their confirmation by the League Council on July 24, 1922 because Britain and France had previously agreed that their respective Mandates would take effect only at the same time. In addition, both Italy and France were dissatisfied with Article 14 of the Mandate for Palestine which provided for the appointment of a Holy Places special commission. Until everything was finally resolved and all the assurances were given as demanded, the Mandate for Palestine only entered into legal force on September 29, 1923.

The unforeseen negative ramifications of delaying confirmation of the Mandate for Palestine were soon seen, not only in regard to Jewish national rights in Transjordan, but also even more tragically in the application of the Mandate to Cisjordanian Palestine. As a result of Britain adding a disjointed text in Article 25 of the Mandate, a new interpretation was soon given to Article 2 of the Mandate, the heart of the document, to the great detriment of establishing the Jewish National Home. That was no trifling matter, because this provision embodied the true purpose of the Mandate to create an eventual independent Jewish State. The text of Article 2 reads as follows:

> The Mandatory shall be responsible for placing the country under such political, administrative and economic conditions as will secure the establishment of the Jewish National Home, as laid down in the Preamble, and *the development of self-governing institutions* (emphasis added), and also for safeguarding the civil and religious rights of all the inhabitants of Palestine, irrespective of race and religion.

The British Government amended this key provision in regard to Transjordan by deleting the following words to make it applicable to this territory:

> "placing the country under such political, administrative and economic conditions as will secure the establishment of the Jewish National home, as laid down in the Preamble, and"

The text of Article 2 of the Mandate for Palestine now read as follows insofar as Transjordan was concerned:

> The Mandatory shall be responsible for the development of self-

> governing institutions, and also for safeguarding the civil and religious rights of all the inhabitants of Palestine, irrespective of race and religion.

The British audacity in making this amendment to Article 2 of the Mandate lay in the fact that the words "the development of self-governing institutions" was meant to apply exclusively to the Jewish National Home in order to convert it in the course of time into a self-governing Jewish State or commonwealth. These words were not put in the Mandate for Palestine to create an autonomous Arab administration anywhere in the country, east or west of the Jordan, but were inserted as a direct corollary of the provisions regarding the Jewish National Home contained in the first part of Article 2.[99] The origin of these words can be easily traced back to the printed "Statement of the Zionist Organization Regarding Palestine" bearing the date of February 3, 1919, which was submitted to the Allied Council of Ten at the Paris Peace Conference on February 27, 1919. An extract from the statement, read out to the Council of Ten by Nahum Sokolow, affirmed:[100]

> The mandate shall be subject also to the following special conditions:
>
> Palestine shall be placed under such political, administrative and economic conditions as will secure the establishment there of the Jewish National Home and ultimately render possible the creation of *an autonomous Commonwealth* … (emphasis added)

The phrase "an autonomous Commonwealth" in the Zionist Statement was later altered slightly in the early Zionist and British drafts of the Mandate Charter drawn up in 1919. The altered version spoke of the gradual development in Palestine of "a self-governing Commonwealth" instead of an autonomous Commonwealth, as the end result of the establishment of the Jewish National Home. This amounted to the very same thing. The last draft of the Mandate to have that particular phrasing was dated March 15, 1920 before Lord Curzon furiously intervened to water down its intended meaning. He high-handedly ordered this phrase removed in a note dated March 20, 1920, sent to his official, Robert Vansittart. He told him he preferred the less clear phraseology "the development of self-governing institutions", which left its meaning open to different interpretations in regard to the Jewish National Home. His explanation

---

[99] *Book of Documents submitted by the Jewish Agency for Palestine to the General Assembly of the United Nations Relating to the Establishment of the National Home for the Jewish People*, New York, May 1947. Document 16, p. 144.

[100] *The Rise of Israel, ibid.*, Volume 10, Document 57, p. 195-196 and Document 61, p. 107.

for expunging this phrase was:[101]

> It all turns on what we mean. The Zionists are after a Jewish State with the Arabs as hewers of wood and drawers of water. So are many British sympathizers with the Zionists. Whether you use the word Commonwealth or State, that is what it will be taken to mean.
>
> That is not my view. I want the Arabs to have a chance and *I don't want a Hebrew State.* (emphasis added.)
>
> I have no idea how far the case has been given away to the Zionists. If not *I would prefer 'self-governing institutions'.*

As a direct result of Curzon's anti-Zionist blast, "I don't want a Hebrew State" – "I would prefer *self-governing institutions*", the latter phrase came to be substituted for the term used earlier, "a self-governing Commonwealth", a change that obscured or rendered ambiguous the Mandate's objective of establishing the Jewish State – the State that both Lloyd George and Balfour always had in mind. Curzon's new phraseology sharply contrasted with that of the other two mandate instruments that were formulated at the same time: the Mandate for Syria and Lebanon and the Final Draft of the Mandate for Mesopotamia, both of which referred to these countries becoming "independent states".[102]

In another memo written by Curzon on the same date, he again betrayed his true feelings about the draft Mandate for Palestine as it existed on March 15, 1920:[103]

> I have never been consulted as to this Mandate at an earlier stage nor

---

[101] Curzon's note to Robert Vansittard is found in document FO 371/5199: 009220; E 1447 (1920).

[102] See, for example, Article 1 of the Mandate for Syria and Lebanon, as confirmed on July 24, 1922, which reads as follows: "The Mandatory shall frame, within a period of three years from the coming into force of this Mandate, an organic law for Syria and the Lebanon. This organic law shall be framed in consultation with the native authorities and shall take into account the rights, interests and wishes of all the population inhabiting the said territory. *The Mandatory shall further enact measures to facilitate the progressive development of Syria and the Lebanon as independent states.* (Italics added) Pending the coming into effect of the organic law, the Government of Syria and the Lebanon shall be conducted in accordance with the spirit of this mandate. The Mandatory shall, as far as circumstances permit, encourage local autonomy". A similar provision was found in Article 1 of the Final Draft of the Mandate for Mesopotamia.

[103] This note by Lord Curzon is also found in FO 371/5199: 009220; E 1447 (1920). His derisive allusion to the low Jewish population in Palestine in 1920 ignored the Jewish plight that existed there during World War I. Prior to the outbreak of war, the estimated Jewish population of the country was 85,000-100,000. It then took a dramatic dip during the War as the result of Turkish expulsions, emigrations, diseases and famines, which reduced the population to 57,000. See Isaiah Friedman, *The Question of Palestine, 1914-1918*, p. 356, n. 110 and see also the *Encyclopaedia Judaica,* Vol. 9, p. 474.

> do I know from what negotiations it springs or on what understandings it is based....
>
> But here I may say that I agree with Sir John Tilley and that I think the entire conception wrong. (Author's note: Tilley was the Assistant Under-Secretary of State in the Foreign Office during 1919-1920.)
>
> Here is a country with 580,000 Arabs and 30,000 or is it 60,000 Jews (by no means all Zionists) acting upon the noble principle of self-determination and ending with a splendid appeal to the League of Nations, we then proceed to draw up *a document which reeks of Judaism in every paragraph and is an avowed constitution for a Jewish State.*
>
> Even the poor Arabs are only allowed to look through the keyhole as a non-Jewish community. It is quite clear that this Mandate has been drawn up by someone reeling under the fumes of Zionism. If we are all to succumb to that intoxicant this draft is all right.
>
> Perhaps there is no alternative. But I confess I should like to see something worded differently.

Curzon's hostile and unbridled sentiments about Zionism did, however, reveal plainly and conclusively in very frank language the true intention of the framers of the Mandate for Palestine as originally conceived prior to Curzon's tenure at the Foreign Office, which was to establish a Jewish State in the whole area of historical Palestine, including Transjordan. This is why he became so upset upon reading the Draft Mandate of March 15, 1920 and why he then wanted to obfuscate this intention by ordering further revisions to the Mandate. It was meant to be, as Curzon said, the avowed Constitution for a Jewish State. There was definitely no plan at that time to create an Arab state in a partitioned Palestine, despite the stark fact that the Arabs greatly outnumbered the Jews and vehemently opposed the Balfour Declaration.

The changes ordered by Curzon were embodied in the next draft of the Mandate dated June 10, 1920. Weizmann immediately objected to the proposed change regarding the "self-government" clause which, despite Curzon's attempt at obfuscation, still provided for eventual statehood for the Jews living in Palestine rather than for the Arab population, even though this idea was not explicitly declared in the instrument. However, as the Zionist leader presciently observed, the substitution of "self-governing institutions" for "self-governing Commonwealth" was open to misconstruction.[104] In a letter he sent to Lord Curzon dated August 11, 1920 he further complained that changes were being made to the draft Mandate without prior consultation with the Zionist Organization which had always been the case throughout 1919 and early 1920, before Curzon personally stepped in to end the joint coordination of British and Zionist drafting of the Mandate. As to the "self-government" clause, he

[104] See FO 371/5745: 9220, containing the "Zionist Observations on Draft Mandate for Palestine" which were attached to a letter sent by Hubert Young to Robert Vansittart, dated June 30 1920.

stated:[105]

> The Zionist Organization views with deep regret the omission of any reference to the ultimate development of a self-governing Commonwealth. While Jewish opinion recognizes that responsible government in Palestine cannot be fully achieved for many years to come, it is thought that the Mandate ought to contemplate its gradual and eventual realization.

Weizmann strongly urged in his letter that the phrase "self-governing Commonwealth" be restored to the original text. However, it was intimated to him that the British Government might not accept the Mandate at all if the reference to a "Jewish Commonwealth" were insisted upon.[106] This intimation was no doubt a bluff on the part of Lord Curzon which should have been called by Weizmann had he been a more resolute and bold leader of Zionism in the mould of Theodor Herzl. It would have seriously harmed the economic and military interests of the British Empire to give up the Mandate at this particular time and allow either France or Italy to take its place. France, to be sure, was especially eager to assume this task particularly for religious reasons, as evidenced by what its highest officials said at the first session of the San Remo Peace Conference devoted to Palestine on April 24, 1920. Had the British really carried out their threat to disengage from Palestine, such a move could have even opened the door for a Zionist administered Mandate by allowing for a Jewish Government to be set up immediately. However, instead of seeing opportunity and courageously facing down the British threat, Weizmann meekly succumbed to British intimidation. Unfortunately, this same kind of scenario then repeated itself not long afterwards in regard to forcing the Zionist Executive to accept the very injurious Churchill White Paper under threat of British withdrawal from Palestine.

The phrase "self-governing institutions" as used in Article 2 boomeranged on the Jewish National Home as correctly foreseen by Weizmann after it was made applicable to Transjordan by the League Council on September 16, 1922. It then dawned on British officials who followed in the wake of Curzon that this phrase now divorced from its original context in regard to the Jewish National Home could also be made to work for the benefit of the Arab inhabitants in Western Palestine, to allow them to have "self-governing institutions" in the name of democracy.

Thus was born the erroneous idea that Article 2 of the Mandate provided for a dual obligation of equal weight, one in favour of Jews to secure the establishment of a Jewish National Home, and a separate obligation in favour of the Arab population for "self-governing institutions" which completely

---

105 The reference to this quotation is found in FO 371/5245: 9220.

106 *The Rise of Israel*, Volume 8, Document 57, p. 185.

negated the original intention of developing such institutions for the future independent Jewish State. This was an unforeseen development deriving from the dissection or slicing up of Article 2 to provide "self-governing institutions" for Transjordan and best illustrated the negative ramifications on Cisjordan resulting from the separate Arab administration of this historical Jewish territory. The development of self-governing institutions for the Arabs of Cisjordan, based upon proportional representation, would inevitably have led to their complete takeover of the country and the nullification of the Jewish National Home.

The great distortions in the Mandate for Palestine set in motion by the detachment of Transjordan from the Jewish National Home could probably have been avoided if all the "A" Mandates had been approved without U.S. obstruction on the date originally scheduled for that purpose (either December 17, 1920 or February 21, 1921). Had there been no delay in the Mandate confirmation process, the British Government may have found it impossible later to revise or amend the Mandate, in order to detach Transjordan from the Jewish National Home and, ultimately, from Palestine altogether. There would have also been less of a probability for misinterpreting Article 2 to provide "self-governing institutions" in favour of the general Arab population, which was never the intention of the original framers of that article. Without the presence of Article 25 in the Mandate in regard to Transjordan's detachment from the Jewish National Home, Churchill, Lawrence, Shuckburgh, Young and Samuel would have had to find a different solution for Feisal and Abdullah that was not at the expense of Jewish legal rights and title of sovereignty over all of Palestine on both sides of the Jordan.

## *(V) The Israel-Jordan Peace Treaty*

With the conclusion of a Treaty of Peace between the State of Israel and the Hashemite Kingdom of Jordan on October 26, 1994 and its subsequent ratification, Israel has foreclosed any prospect, for all practical purposes, of ever regaining any of the ancient Transjordanian areas that were historically and indelibly connected to the Jewish People. That prospect could change only as the result of a possible future disintegration of the Jordanian state precipitated by a Syrian takeover or by some other unforeseen calamitous event.

The treaty of peace was preceded by the Washington Declaration of July 25, 1994 and an Agreed Common Agenda of September 14, 1993, both designed to achieve peace between the two states, based on five underlying principles, including Security Council Resolutions 242 and 338, as set out more fully in these two preliminary documents. Among the general principles enumerated in the treaty of peace, Israel recognized Jordan's sovereignty, territorial integrity and political independence as well as that of every state in the region. An international boundary was established between Israel and Jordan, delimited in accordance with the boundary definition under the Mandate for Palestine comprising four sectors: the Jordan and Yarmuk Rivers; the Dead Sea; the Emek Ha'Arava or Wadi Araba; the Gulf of Aqaba. Article 3, paragraph 2 of the treaty describes this boundary as "permanent, secure and recognized", resembling the language of U.N. Security Council Resolution 242, and further stated that it is "without prejudice to the status of any territories that came under Israeli military government control in 1967", a proviso that appears also in the Agreed Common Agenda. Further elaboration of this proviso appears in an annex to the treaty, entitled "Israel-Jordan International Boundary Delimitation and Demarcation" where the following is stated in Article 2A, paragraph 7:

> The orthophoto maps and image maps showing the line separating Jordan from the West Bank shall have that line indicated in a different presentation and the legend shall carry on it the following disclaimer: "This line is the administrative boundary between Jordan and the territory which came under Israeli military government control in 1967. Any treatment of this line shall be without prejudice to the status of that territory". (Quotation marks in the original)

There are some pertinent observations to be made concerning the foregoing paragraph indicating the international boundary between Israel and Jordan. To begin with, Israel accepted the self-defeating and self-negating interpretation that the legal status of Judea and Samaria has never been decided under international law, an interpretation previously put forth by many renowned jurists, such as Professor Eugene Rostow and others. This Israeli position made a mockery of the fact that Judea and Samaria had indeed been allocated to the Jewish National Home and future independent Jewish State in the Franco-British Boundary Convention of December 23, 1920. Neither Jordan nor any other nation or entity, such as the Palestine Liberation Organization and its offshoot, the Palestinian Authority created by the Declaration of Principles of August 20, 1993 and September 13, 1993, had any legal right to these ancestral lands of the Jewish People.

The boundary between Jordan and Israel was described in the annex to the treaty not merely as an "international boundary" but also as an "administrative boundary" which clearly indicated that Israel enjoyed neither *de jure* sovereignty nor *de facto* sovereignty over the areas in question, "which came under Israeli military control in 1967". By endorsing this position, Israel did not acknowledge its own sovereignty over this area, exactly in line with the position adopted in December 1977 by Menachem Begin, that the question of sovereignty was still "open" for ultimate decision and had to be resolved by "final status" talks, as spelled out in the Camp David Framework Agreement for Peace in the Middle East. This position represented a complete negation or undermining of Israel's actual rights to Judea and Samaria, since it not only denied pre-existing *de jure* Jewish sovereignty over these areas, as implicitly recognized in 1920, it also endorses the false concept of a sovereignty vacuum existing for Judea and

Samaria and allows the Arabs to set forth their own claim to this territory for the purpose of establishing a second Arab state in former Mandated Palestine.

Moreover, the description in the treaty, that the region of Judea and Samaria has been under Israeli military government control since 1967, is a sad reminder of the terrible mistake made that was, moreover, a violation of Israeli constitutional law perpetrated by the Eshkol National Unity Government of 1967, based on the erroneous legal advice proferred by then-Military Advocate General Meir Shamgar during the Six-Day War to apply international law rather than Israeli law to the territories liberated in the Six-Day War. This led directly to the establishment of a military government for Judea and Samaria, governed by the laws of belligerent occupation, instead of incorporating this territory into the borders of the State of Israel as required by the Area of Jurisdiction and Powers Ordinance, as well as the Land of Israel Proclamation that was constructively issued under the provisions of this law.

Had there been no disclaimer made both in the text and in the annex to the treaty stating that the line separating Judea and Samaria from the state of Jordan is only an administrative rather than an international boundary, then, a valid argument could have been put forth that the international boundary between Israel and Jordan, which was to be demarcated not later than nine months after the signing of the treaty, recognized that Israel enjoyed sovereignty over Judea and Samaria. However, the disclaimer was inserted into the treaty for this very reason: to deny the existence of such sovereignty. The most that can be said about this boundary, whether it is international or administrative, is that Jordan, in harmony with King Hussein's statement of July 31, 1988, has formally renounced in a treaty any right to the territory it called the "West Bank" of the Hashemite Kingdom.

Article 2A, paragraph 7 of the Annex also used terminology that, by 1994 when the treaty was made, was already out of date and contrary to Israeli law. The term "West Bank" intimated Jordanian sovereignty over it, but, as just noted, Jordan had already renounced its presumed "right" to this territory. Moreover, it had been officially renamed by Israel as Judea and Samaria, in accordance with the names it had borne for thousands of years prior to the Jordanian conquest in 1948 and their annexation in 1950.

In the treaty, Israel not only renounced any lingering and dormant right to Transjordan, a renunciation that itself renders the entire document illegal, it also agreed to surrender approximately 360 square kilometers of territory located in the Arava Valley, adjacent to Kibbutz Zofar, as well as land located near the Yarmuk River, called Naharayim – Baqura.

Israelis who owned land or had rights of use to the land in these areas did not lose their rights. They remained in force for 25 years, with options to renew. Jordanian law now applied to both areas, except Jordanian criminal law involving only Israeli nationals. The treaty also stated in two separate annexes that "Israeli law applying to the extra territorial activities of Israel may be applied to Israelis and their activities in the area", comprising both the Naharayim/Baqura Area and the Zofar Area.

Furthermore, Israel agreed to give Jordan large quantities of already-scarce water from the Jordan and Yarmuk Rivers, despite the fact that Israel itself suffers from a chronic water shortage.

Finally, and most troubling to some Israelis, Israel recognized Jordan's so-called special role on the Temple Mount in the old city of Jerusalem in regard to the Moslem Holy Shrines [the al-Aqsa Mosque and the Dome of the Rock] built there in the 7th century by the Umayyad caliphs who ruled from Damascus. This recognition constituted an infringement of Israeli sovereignty over the Temple Mount contrary to article 97(a) of the Penal Code.

In all the excitement and celebration surrounding the treaty engendered in Israel, no prominent political leader spoke about the illegal creation of Jordan, nor did any leader mention the fact that the area that constitutes Jordan had been removed from the Jewish National Home for that purpose. This glaring omission was particularly noticeable in the Likud Party led by Binyamin Netanyahu, who supported the treaty despite being well aware of the illegitimate origin of the state of Jordan, as he himself recorded in his book, "A Place Among the Nations". In the Knesset debate on the treaty held on October 25, 1994, Netanyahu expressed a positive opinion on the subject:[107]

> This is fundamentally a good agreement, an agreement that will bring peace. It does not entail territorial concessions... it does not entail bringing in foreign soldiers.

The main component of the Likud party before the merger of its different factions was the Herut Party, which, throughout its history as an independent political faction, had always campaigned on the platform of the unification of the Land of Israel within its historical boundaries, advocating "a state of Israel on both banks of the Jordan". That remained its steadfast position for two decades, from 1948 to 1965. That, in turn, meant no peace treaty could ever be concluded with Jordan since all its territory was claimed for Israel by the Herut party. In 1965 a change occurred when Herut aligned itself with the Liberal Party to form Gahal. The new platform of the joint bloc omitted any specific mention of Transjordan, referring instead to maintaining the claim to the entire homeland (shleimut ha-moledet) which could still be interpreted as embracing Transjordan but which obscured this fact. When Likud was formed in 1973 as a new electoral bloc, under the prodding of General Ariel Sharon, the new entity adopted a correspondingly new platform that championed Israeli sovereignty "between the sea and the Jordan", thus implicitly abandoning the claim to the territory of Jordan. No longer was the ditty of Betar and the Herut party sung: "The Jordan has two banks, and both belong to us!"

This ditty was composed in the form of a poem by Ze'ev Jabotinsky,

---

[107] Jerusalem Post, October 26,1994, p. 2.

entitled "The Left Bank of the Jordan", while he was in Paris in 1929. In this poem, Jabotinsky expressed his deep-felt undying attachment to Transjordan, considering it an integral part of the future independent Jewish State. He called the Jordan River the axis of his country Israel, denoting a line which divides it into two symmetrical parts. He compared the river to the middle column of a bridge or the spinal cord of a human being. Thus, for Jabotinsky, the country of Israel stretched from the Mediterranean Sea to the Syrian desert with the Jordan River in the middle. He ended his poem with the moving saying that "if I forget the Left Bank of the Jordan, may my treacherous right hand forget [its cunning]".

In pre-state Israel, the Revisionist Organization, founded in 1925 by Vladimir Jabotinsky, and later the New Zionist Organization which he also founded in 1935, the uppermost rallying cry was their rejection of Transjordan's separation from the Jewish National Home. This, too, was the slogan of Betar (B'rit Trumpeldor), the Revisionist youth movement Jabotinsky established in 1923. The teachings and ideals of Jabotinsky insofar as Transjordan was concerned were also shared by the underground movements, Etzel[108] and Lehi[109]. All these organizations fought tenaciously for the establishment of a Jewish state with a Jewish majority in the entire territory of Palestine on both banks of the Jordan.

However, by the year 1994 when a peace treaty was signed with Jordan, the Likud party had long forgotten the cherished principles which had characterized all its predecessors. It now openly supported the peace treaty with Jordan, negotiated and formulated by the Yitzhak Rabin Government. Former Mossad Chief, Ephraim Halevy, is credited with laying the groundwork for the peace treaty. This put an end to the last slim hope that one day the Jewish People could recover some of their lost territory east of the Jordan, a hope that was once fervently nourished by none other than Menachem Begin in the early 1950's when, as the leader of the Herut party, he made speeches in the Knesset to that effect.

The Knesset approved the peace treaty with Jordan by a lopsided margin of 105 to 3. The negative votes were cast by the Moledet Party led by Rehav'am Ze'evi. Those who abstained on the vote were Hanan Porat of the National Religious Party, Ariel Sharon, Dov Shilansky, Michael Eitan, Limor Livnat and Ron Nachman of the Likud. It appears that for the Labour party and the Likud opposition, the advent of peace with the illegal state of Jordan trumped any other consideration. Both political parties were in a state of euphoria by the diplomatic recognition accorded Israel by another Arab state, even one that had been created at the expense of the Jewish National Home, contrary to

[108] The Hebrew acronym for the "National Military Organization" under the command of Menachem Begin from December 1943.

[109] The Hebrew acronym derived from the words "Fighters for the Freedom of Israel", originally led by Avraham Stern, shot dead (or murdered, as believed by his comrades-in-arms) by the British in 1942.

international law.

Formal peace with Jordan in 1994 was never a necessity and was actually an act of self-debasement. Israel was then under no immediate or long-term military threat from Jordan and had no reason to confer legitimacy on a state artificially brought into existence by British imperialism to appease the ambitions of a self-aggrandizing Arabian emir who had absolutely no valid claim to the territory that became Jordan. Since the conclusion of the treaty, Jordan acts almost no differently towards Israel than it did in the years prior to the signing of the treaty. Jordan still remains wedded to an attitude of anti-Israel hostility, as shown by its use of harsh rhetoric against the Jewish State in every international forum in which it participates, whether in the halls of the United Nations and its various organs or at the summit-meetings of the states of the Arab League. This hostility is also pronounced among Jordan's intelligentsia, especially its legal echelon. On the 10th anniversary of the signing of the treaty, the leader of the Jordan Bar Association, Hussein Mejali, stated:[110]

> [The 1994 Treaty is] null and void and it is not legally binding on us. Our duty is to carry out armed struggle, to fight the occupation and the aggression.

Jordan has been since its creation and remains today a land without Jews, stemming from the refusal of the British Mandatory Government to allow Jews to exercise their right to settle there, even on an individual basis, despite the fact that Article 15 of the Mandate clearly stated that "no person shall be excluded from Palestine on the sole ground of his religious belief", a provision which remained in effect even after Article 25 of the Mandate was applied on September 16, 1922, provisionally separating Transjordan from the rest of Palestine. If official Israel had a more developed sense of pride and self-respect, it would not have entered into this shameful peace treaty that brought international legitimacy to Jordan, not to Israel, despite popular belief to the contrary. The existence of Jordan is a continuing insufferable reminder of how the British Colonial Office under Winston Churchill, aided and abetted by the High Commissioner for Palestine, Herbert Samuel, concocted a fraudulent scheme to deprive the Jewish People of their rightful patrimony east of the Jordan River. By signing a peace treaty with Jordan, Israel retroactively sanctioned the illegal removal of that territory from the Jewish National Home, which initially drew the ire of even Chaim Weizmann before he passively accepted the British action due to a British threat to surrender its mandate for Palestine if the Zionist Executive refused to agree to this move.

No Israeli political leader ever had the right to *recognize* the illegal partition of the Land of Israel. The entire land, including the historical Jewish parts of Transjordan, belongs to the Jewish people regardless of the fact that Jordan is

[110] *The Jerusalem Post*, October 27, 2004, p. 5.

not under Jewish rule. David Ben-Gurion, in a 1937 speech at Basle, stated quite unambiguously that no Jew or Jewish body may cede any part of Eretz-Israel. That, however, is what was accomplished by Israel's recognition of Hashemite sovereignty, an act that could never have been imagined by the great Revisionist leader Ze'ev Jabotinsky who inspired all his disciples never to forget the great importance of Transjordan for the resurrection of the Jewish State. He envisioned millions of Jews living there together with Moslems and Christians in happiness and prosperity, a dream that has been ruled out by the existence of *Judenrein* Jordan and the illegal peace treaty with it. In consequence of this peace treaty, Israel's legal case and rights to all of the Land of Israel, based on international law and justice, has been dealt a shattering blow.

*Chapter 14*

# British Acts Sabotaging the Jewish National Home and the Mandate for Palestine

The various artifices which the British Government successfully used to deviate from or ignore its responsibilities in carrying out the Mandate for Palestine, which amounted to sabotaging it, have been frequently mentioned throughout this work. These deviations and acts of sabotage will therefore now only be summarized, with some new points added not previously mentioned. It must be observed that those deviations and acts were carried out with such consummate skill and artful execution by the British Government that most people were fooled at the time they were actually made or were resigned to accept them once they were already adopted and being executed. It was even hard to criticize some of these British maneuvers because on certain points they were based on Zionist antecedents, statements or thoughts or culled from such leading figures in the movement as Nahum Sokolow, Asher Ginsberg (Ahad Ha'Am) and even Chaim Weizmann at times. The most famous Zionist leader of his day did not usually protest strongly enough in the face of British betrayal of the Mandate, but did occasionally voice his disapproval.

An interesting illustration of Weizmann's contradictory attitude towards British moves to sabotage the central idea of the Mandate, which was to create a Jewish majority by means of immigration and hence to establish an independent Jewish State, is seen by the following remarks he himself uttered on this very topic.

On October 14, 1921, Herbert Samuel wrote Colonial Secretary Winston Churchill that the Zionists should make a formal declaration "that their purpose is not the establishment of a State in which Jews would enjoy a position of political privilege, but a Commonwealth built upon a democratic foundation".[1]

[1] Martin Gilbert, *Winston S. Churchill*, Volume IV, p. 636. Samuel's letter to Churchill is reproduced in Companion Volume IV, Part 3, p. 1650.

Samuel also wanted the Zionists to repudiate Weizmann's statement that Palestine would become "as Jewish as England is English" since this was incompatible with the fact that Jews shared a "common home" with the Arabs of Palestine, the upbuilding of which assured each of its peoples "an undisturbed national development". This meant, in effect, not a Jewish State but an Arab State, since Arabs greatly outnumbered Jews in Palestine at the time. The idea that the Zionists should renounce their aim of a Jewish State in Palestine where the Jews would be the majority was put to Weizmann by the Colonial Office, but he absolutely rejected it. In a letter to Wyndham Deedes, the Civil Secretary (later restyled "Chief Secretary") of the Government of Palestine, dated November 12, 1921, he insisted that the Zionists could not give up their goal for a Jewish majority in Palestine, saying:[2]

> ...What else are we striving for? Did not every Englishman or Frenchman or Jew, every British statesman, say that same thing publicly hundreds of times?[3] What other meaning is there to the National Home? It is no use hanging on now to a nebulous phraseology. What is all the struggle about? Is it to create a few more stray colonies or to settle two thousand more *halutzim*? What are we all working for? If there is not the ideal of building up a Jewish Commonwealth, then our *halutzim* could go at less cost and with more prospects for a material well-being to America, or Australia, or Argentine. They [referring to the British Colonial Office – H.G.] asked me to put in a phrase that the Zionists don't intend to create a Jewish State in Palestine. I refused to do so, and gave them as chief reason that we cannot forswear such a possibility, which might or might not arise in some future generation. I told them that at present we are building Palestine, but it may be that the Jews may be in the ascendancy there, that neither they nor anybody

[2] Weizmann's remarks to Deedes can be found in full in *The Letters and Papers of Chaim Weizmann*, Bernard Wasserstein (editor), Volume X – Series A, July 1920 – December 1921, (1977). Transaction Books: Rutgers University, Israel Universities Press, Jerusalem, Letter 278, pp. 281-283. See also the book, *The British in Palestine: The Mandatory Government and the Arab-Jewish Conflict 1917-1929*, by Bernard Wasserstein, London, Royal Historical Society 1978, p. 115.

[3] Weizmann was referring to a statement made by Dr. Montague David Eder, a member of the Zionist Commission for Palestine and later of the Zionist Executive that replaced it, who told the Haycraft Commission of Inquiry appointed by Herbert Samuel to investigate the May 1921 Arab riots, that the Zionist aim in Palestine was "Jewish predominance as soon as the numbers of that race are sufficiently increased". The Haycraft Commission's October 1921 report declared that Dr. Eder's view was "considerably at variance with the policy of the British Government". The Commission, which denounced the idea of future Jewish domination of the country, was headed by Thomas Haycraft, Chief Justice of Palestine.

> else have a right to stop us, and we argued this point in a *friendly* way. But the Haycraft report is *plus papiste que le pape* (italics in original).

Weizmann's response to the Colonial Office ploy spearheaded by Samuel and accepted by Churchill was justified and admirable. However, he eventually fell in line with British policy about the question of a Jewish majority, which was the *sine qua non* for an independent Jewish State in Palestine. At the 17th Zionist Congress held in Basle in July 1931, he gave an interview to the Jewish Telegraphic Agency in which he was quoted as saying the very opposite of what he once told Wyndham Deedes:[4]

> ... I strongly feel that agreement with the Arabs is obtainable on the basis of parity. If the Legislative Council should come, equal Arab and Jewish representation would afford an opportunity for satisfactory cooperation. We also demand equal distribution of funds for Arabs and Jews within the Palestine Development Scheme.
>
> I do not see how we can demand more. Parity does not mean a bi-national state, which is vague and does not necessarily imply parity. *I have no sympathy or understanding for the demand for a Jewish majority* (emphasis added). A majority does not necessarily guarantee security. We may have a majority and still be insecure. A majority is not required for the development of Jewish civilization and culture.
>
> The world will construe this demand only in one sense, that we want to acquire a majority in order to drive out the Arabs. Why should we raise a demand which can only make a provocative impression?...

Weizmann's denial of the Zionist goal to create a Jewish majority in Palestine which would lead to an independent Jewish State, "the most sacred article of Zionist faith",[5] was met with disbelief and great anger. His published remarks were read out to the Congress plenum and produced a furore causing him to resign or be dismissed as President of the Zionist Organization and Jewish Agency. He was succeeded by Nahum Sokolow, his longtime colleague who had the same or even more pronounced defeatist views. His ouster lasted for four years until he was returned to office in 1935.

Though Weizmann devoted prodigious efforts to his tasks on behalf of Zionism and at times gallantly fought the anti-Zionist moves of the British, most notably in nullifying features of the Passfield White Paper of 1930 and obtaining Prime Minister Ramsay MacDonald's letter of February 1931, which allowed for continued Jewish immigration and close or intensive settlement by Jews on the land, he also displayed great weaknesses as a Zionist leader

[4] *Ibid.* Volume I – Series B, August 1898 – July 1931; Editor: Barnet Litvinoff. 1983. Paper 124, pp. 641-642.

[5] *Ibid.*, p. XIII of the Introduction.

that proved very costly to the Zionist Movement he represented on the world stage.

His lifetime cooperation with the British Government ended in tatters after the Labour Government which assumed power in July 1945 failed to keep its pre-election promise to adopt a pro-Zionist policy. Weizmann was now perceived as out-of-touch with the realities of Palestine. As a result, he lost his position as President of the Zionist Organization once again when he failed to be re-elected at the 22nd Congress, held at Basle in December 1946. A more activist policy to achieve the goal of Zionism of an independent Jewish State was pursued by David Ben-Gurion, then the head of the Jewish Agency Executive, who now became the chief Zionist spokesman in place of Weizmann.

The generally feeble Zionist response by the whole official leadership as to what the British Government did during the Mandate period in failing to carry out its international obligations as Mandatory in favour of the Jewish People, a mission or charge it willingly accepted at the beginning of the Mandate, allowed the British Government to get away with its brazen undermining of the Mandate. Jabotinsky and the Revisionist Movement and, later, the Irgun Zvai Leumi and the Stern Group were unfortunately in the visionary Zionist minority without real power or authority in their struggle to halt the British betrayal of the Mandate and to replace their administration of the country with a Jewish Government and an independent state.

The British tactics that ridiculed the true spirit of the Mandate and evaded the "solemn international obligations "[6] imposed on them can be summarized as follows:

1) Changing the intended meaning of the words "the establishment in Palestine of a national home for the Jewish People" as found in the Balfour Declaration and Mandate for Palestine to connote a cultural or spiritual center, as advocated by both Ahad Ha'Am and Nahum Sokolow, rather than the establishment of an independent Jewish State. In the Malcolm MacDonald White Paper of May 17, 1939, the British Government of Prime Minister Neville Chamberlain falsely claimed that this expression was ambiguous and vague, when in fact, he and his government knew very well its exact meaning, but preferred to ignore it. Up to the time of the Peel Royal Commission Report and then again in the 1939 White Paper, the British Government in power deliberately refrained in all its official, public declarations and statements of policy from stating the true meaning of the Declaration of November 2, 1917 and the Mandate which elaborated and implemented it, based on the excuse that this would inflame Arab opinion. All British governments took this policy to such an extreme form that they seldom referred to Palestine officially as a state, let alone a Jewish State, but simply as a "territory" under mandate. One of the few exceptions was when King George

[6] This is the way Prime Minister Ramsay MacDonald characterized these obligations in his letter to Weizmann on February 13, 1931, which was communicated as an official document to the League of Nations and also embodied as an instruction to the High Commissioner.

V sent a message to the people of Palestine when the new Civil Administration was being inaugurated at assemblies of notables in both Jerusalem (July 7, 1920) and Haifa (July 8, 1920). The royal message was read out and translated into both Arabic and Hebrew and contained a reference to the development of Palestine as a state.[7] Not many other references were made in this direction until the Peel Report, despite the fact that Palestine was considered to be one of the three Class "A" Mandates for which this term was indeed appropriate, as confirmed by the Treaty of Lausanne in dealing with various questions such as the Ottoman Public Debt, Ottoman property and possessions left behind in Palestine and the acquisition of Palestinian nationality or citizenship.

2) Misrepresenting the Mandatory's solemn obligations under the Mandate to include not only obligations in favour of the Jewish People, but also undertakings of equal weight designed to satisfy Arab national and political aspirations for self-government in Palestine. This British policy was foreshadowed by Herbert Samuel when he told Emir Abdullah on March 28, 1921 that the Balfour Declaration and the Mandate contained two distinct promises, one to the Jews and one to the Arabs, both of which would be fulfilled. However, it was not until the Report of the Shaw Commission of Inquiry into the 1929 riots, published on March 31, 1930, that the theory of duality or equality of mandatory obligations began to figure more prominently in British thinking. The Report adopted the basic assumption that the Balfour Declaration and Mandate imposed on Britain two equal obligations in favour of both Jews and Arabs. This theory was embraced by the Government of Prime Minister Ramsay MacDonald as its official policy in a statement he made in the House of Commons on April 3, 1930. The Government then issued the Passfield White Paper on October 20, 1930 under the authority of Colonial Secretary Lord Passfield (Sidney Webb) which officially accepted the dual obligation theory. Neither obligation was subordinate to the other, according to this White Paper. It affirmed that the obligations imposed on Britain were to promote the interests of both Arabs and Jews equally, which it said was the path laid down in the Mandate.

In truth, the British undertook no obligations at all in the Mandate towards the Arabs of Palestine, in a national, political or collective sense, unlike their obligations in favour of the Jewish People as a whole. Nowhere in this document of international constitutional law are the Arabs of Palestine even mentioned as a separate people because they were not considered a party to the Mandate in any legal sense nor its beneficiary, it having been drafted without them in mind. Even though they were not singled out as such, they were implicitly included by their mere presence in Palestine in all those general expressions contained in the Mandate referring to non-Jews in Palestine as "other sections of the population" (Article 6 of the Mandate), and also in the general reference "to safeguard the interests of the community" in connection with the development

[7] See: *The Rise of Israel, Great Britain and Palestine 1920-1925*, Volume 13, Garland Publishing, Inc., New York and London, 1987, Document 23, pp. 152-156.

of the country and its natural resources, public works, services and utilities (Article 11 of the Mandate). Their rights as individuals, but not as a separate nation or entity, were certainly recognized, which included their civil and religious rights as well as their material interests. This recognition was not exclusive to the Arabs of Palestine but also applied to all the other inhabitants of the country (Article 2). Their rights and the economic position of those who were members of the non-Jewish population were not to be prejudiced by Jewish immigration (Article 6).

It must be stressed that "the civil and religious rights of existing non-Jewish communities in Palestine", as contained in the second Recital in the Preamble of the Mandate, which were to be safeguarded in an eventual independent Jewish State did not refer to political or national communities, but only to religious communities, namely, Christians (Roman Catholic, Greek Orthodox, etc.), Moslems and Druze. This was shown, for example, in the Italian version of the Balfour Declaration which actually translated the words "existing non-Jewish communities" as being a reference to religious communities – *esistenti communita religiose.* The framers of the Balfour Declaration and the Mandate for Palestine wanted to reassure the religious communities of Palestine that had been the protégés of the Allied Powers, particularly France, Italy and also Russia before the Czarist Government fell, that their civil and religious rights would not be prejudiced in an independent Jewish State.[8] This point was also made crystal clear in the Joint Resolution of the Congress of the United States, also known as the Lodge-Fish Resolution, signed by President Warren Harding on September 26, 1922, which declared in the proviso of the resolution:

> It being clearly understood that nothing shall be done which may prejudice *the civil and religious rights of Christian and other non-Jewish communities in Palestine* (emphasis added), and that the holy places and religious buildings and sites shall be adequately protected.

Hence, while the Mandate did impose a binding obligation to protect the civil and religious rights of the various religious communities and of all the inhabitants of Palestine, as well as ensuring the rights and economic position of the non-Jewish sections of the population, this did not mean or imply any double legal undertaking to Palestinian Jews and Arabs alike in the sense of two separate nations living side by side in the same country. The Mandate provided only for the establishment of the Jewish National Home in Palestine, and did not recognize the idea that the Arab population in Palestine constituted a separate national minority which had special collective rights conferred upon it, except for the recognition of linguistic rights that applied to the English language as well. Palestine was reserved exclusively for the Jewish People and under the

[8] See *Minutes of Evidence at Public Sessions*, Palestine Royal Commission, Dec. 31, 1936, Colonial No. 134, Examination of Leonard Stein, p. 247, reproduced in *The Rise of Israel*, Vol. 22, Document 3, p. 289 and before, at p. 253.

Mandate's terms, it was never considered to be an Arab National Home. The reason for excluding collective political and national rights in favour of the Arab population living in Palestine was because such rights were simultaneously accorded by the Principal Allied Powers to Arabs in the neighbouring countries of Syria, Iraq and Arabia. That was part of the global political and legal settlement made to satisfy Arab and Jewish national aspirations by setting up separate states for them to exercise their respective rights of self-determination. The British attempt to subsequently establish new Arab national rights in Palestine or rights of a collective political nature was a blatant violation of their obligations to the Jewish People under international law. They did this in a very subtle way, using grammatical means to accomplish their purpose as astutely noted by Paul L. Hanna:[9]

> It required, however, a transposition of secondary and subordinate clauses into primary positions to give a real duality to the [Mandate] instrument. The plain sense of the [Mandate] document was inescapable. It sought to foster the establishment of a Jewish National Home, while safeguarding, so far as might be compatible with that purpose, the rights and well-being of the non-Jewish population.

One of the critical errors made by the Palestine Royal Commission concerned this very question of Arab national rights in Palestine. The Commissioners apparently believed that such rights existed alongside Jewish national rights based on Article 22 of the Covenant of the League of Nations, the general provisions of which – excluding the specific provisions in paragraphs 4 to 6 inclusive not applicable to Palestine – had been incorporated into the Preamble of the Mandate for Palestine by a direct reference to it in the first recital of the Preamble which read as follows:[10]

> Whereas the Principal Allied Powers have agreed, *for the purpose of giving effect to the provisions of Article 22 of the Covenant of the League of Nations*, to entrust to a Mandatory selected by the said Powers the administration of the territory of Palestine, which formerly belonged to the Turkish Empire, within such boundaries as may be fixed by them; and… (emphasis added)

This reference to Article 22 of the League Covenant in the Preamble of the

[9] See Hanna, *op. cit.*, pp. 67-68.

[10] Paradoxically, though Paragraph 4 of the League Covenant applied specifically to Syria and Mesopotamia, its general features or tenor in denoting a Class A Mandate also applied to that extent to Palestine, in the opinion of Pierre Orts, a long-time member of the Permanent Mandates Commission, the body that supervised the Mandatories' compliance with their obligations under Article 22 of the League Covenant.

Mandate alluded to the principle stated in the first paragraph of this article, that the well-being and development of peoples who inhabited the former Turkish territories in the Middle East, and who were not yet able to stand by themselves under the strenuous conditions of the modern world, formed a sacred trust of civilization. Inasmuch as the Mandate for Palestine never mentioned the local Arab inhabitants by name in connection with it, representing a deliberate omission, and inasmuch as the Mandate was drafted in 1919 and 1920 by the Zionist Organization jointly with officials of the British Foreign Office for the purpose of giving effect to Jewish national rights to all of Palestine (the first drafts originated with the Zionist Organization before a common draft was formulated), it should have been obvious to the Palestine Royal Commission that the reference in the Mandate to Article 22 of the League Covenant, having due regard to the Mandate's overall context and preparatory works as well as its object or purpose, was meant to apply to Jews only as the national beneficiary – those already inhabiting the country and those expected to come in large numbers in the years ahead. It was immaterial to the framers of the Mandate for Palestine that the local Arabs then outnumbered Jews by a relatively wide margin, because they felt that the ratio would be gradually reversed by waves of Jewish immigration and the close settlement by Jews on the land, in accordance with Article 6 of the Mandate. Thus, it was a fundamental misconception of the terms of the Mandate and the assumptions upon which this document was drafted to believe, as did the Royal Commission, that the Arabs of Palestine were as much entitled to self-determination as the Jews in regard to this territory, a misconception that could have been easily dispelled or discerned, had the commissioners taken the time to study the relevant text of the Smuts Resolution of January 30, 1919 and its background, upon which Article 22 was based. The Smuts Resolution, in referring to "Palestine" in its text, did not mean what is today falsely denoted as the "nation" of Arab "Palestinians", but rather the Jewish People, as is evident from three preceding documents or agreements, namely, the Balfour Declaration, the Lloyd George-Clemenceau Agreement and the Weizmann-Feisal Agreement. The panel members would then have realized that the establishment of Arab sovereignty anywhere in Palestine was a concept totally foreign to the provisions of the Mandate for Palestine.

In justifying their position, the Commissioners said:[11]

> ...the international recognition of the right of the Jews to return to their old homeland did not involve the recognition of the right of the Jews to govern the Arabs in it against their will. The case stated by

---

[11] Chapter II, paragraph 51 of the Peel Report, p. 42. The references in the Peel Report stating that Paragraph 1 of Article 22 of the Covenant of the League of Nations applied to the Arab inhabitants of Palestine toward whom the Mandatory allegedly had "general and positive obligations" are found in Chapter II, paragraph 47, p. 40; Chapter II, paragraph 49, p. 41; and Chapter XVIII, paragraph 13, p. 362.

> Lord Milner against an Arab control of Palestine applies equally to a Jewish control.

The statement by the Commissioners that the Jews did not have the right to govern the Arabs of Palestine against their will, whether as individuals or collectively, was exactly opposite to what the Mandate actually provided for, namely, the right of the Jews to govern all the inhabitants of the country, while at the same time safeguarding their civil and religious rights. By adopting this incorrect view of what was originally intended by the Mandate, the Palestine Royal Commission set the stage for recommending a partition of Cisjordanian Palestine. The Commission's Report is generally considered to be a superior document in a class by itself, as compared to other British documents of that period, showing sympathy to both Jews and Arabs. Nevertheless, it laid the pseudo-legal framework for the infamous White Paper of May 17, 1939 by asserting the fictitious notion that the Arabs of Palestine had the same national and political right to a state of their own in Palestine as the Jewish People had.

3) Adopting the principle or concept of Partition to establish a Jewish State in only a part of Mandated Palestine, while parcelling out the rest of the country to either Arabs or a permanent British or international authority. The idea of partitioning Palestine territory had no legal basis in the Mandate. It was expressly prohibited as regards any territory defined historically as "Palestine" by Article 5 of the Mandate. The historical territory of Palestine, in addition to all of Cisjordan extending northward to the southern valley of the Litani River into what is today Southern Lebanon, included all of Transjordan north and south of the Yarmuk River, i.e., Bashan (Hauran) and the Golan, Gilead, Moab-Ammon and Edom. All of these territories came under Jewish rule at various times in their history, either in the First Temple period or preceding it, as well as in the Second Temple period, whether under Tobiad, Hasmonean or Herodian governance. The southern border of Mandatory Palestine should have also included the Sinai Peninsula whose historical connection with the Jewish People can be traced back to the time the Israelites, numbering about two million, trekked 40 years in the wilderness before finally reaching the Promised Land from Egypt. This area contains the revered site where Moses received the word of God at Mount Sinai, as recorded in the Torah. The southern boundary of the Land of Israel according to the Patriarchal description based on Genesis 15:18 extended to the River of Egypt (*nehar Mizrayim*) which, depending on its exact location – a matter of scholarly debate – covers either about half of the Sinai if Wadi el-Arish[12], also called the Egyptian Wadi (*nahal Mizrayim*, usually translated as the Brook or Torrent of Egypt), is the location (Numbers 34:5)

[12] *Wadi El-Arish* rises in the middle of Sinai, 80 miles southwest of the Dead Sea and meanders northward to the Mediterranean, exiting near the town of *El-Arish* 145 km east of the Suez Canal and 80 km west of Gaza. This town, known in Greek as *Rhinokoroura* from the 1st century, is mentioned by Josephus as being in Judea.

or all of the Sinai if the easternmost branch of the Nile, called the Shihor (Joshua 13:3; Jeremiah 2:18), is the location. A possible solution to this dilemma lies in appreciating that *nehar Mizrayim* refers to the southern extremity of the Promised Land, while *nahal Mizrayim* denotes the southern limit of Israelite conquest and settlement.

There is no doubt that much of Sinai is part of the Promised Land, which by general definition lies between the two great rivers, the Nile[13] and the Euphrates. Whether it is also part of the Land of Israel depends on whether it was settled and governed by the Israelites and their descendants between the time of Moses and the close of the Second Temple period. The answer is furnished by the Bible (I Kings 5:1,4), which affirms that Solomon's kingdom extended to the Egyptian border:

> And Solomon ruled over all the kingdoms from the River [i.e., the Euphrates] unto the land of the Philistines, and unto the border of Egypt... For he had dominion over all the region on this side of the River [i.e., the Euphrates], from Tiphsah even to Gaza, over all the kings on this side of the River…

A corresponding passage describing Solomon's borders appears in II Chronicles 9:26, where it says:

> And he ruled over all the kings from the River, even unto the land of the Philistines, and to the border of Egypt.

From the foregoing biblical references it is not entirely clear whether the "land of the Philistines" was or was not included in Solomon's kingdom, but it is clear that the border nevertheless extended to and encompassed a significant portion of Sinai to wherever the border of Egypt was fixed around the time Solomon reigned in Jerusalem over all of Israel. The great Jewish king who built the Holy Temple on Mount Moriah sat on the throne for a period of forty years, spanning the middle decades of the tenth century B.C.E. (circa 971-931 B.C.E.).

Israelite rule over the Sinai during Solomon's reign necessarily implied Israelite settlement there, as confirmed by the biblical report that Solomon's subjects flocked to the dedication of the Jerusalem Temple from as far away as the "Brook of Egypt" (i.e., Sinai; 1 Kings 8:65; II Chronicles 7:8). One site of settlement known from the Bible was at Kadesh Barnea, though its exact location is uncertain. It is believed to be in northeastern Sinai near the southern border of Canaan in the Wilderness of Zin, which was also part of

---

[13] The Nile is generally denoted in the Bible by the word *ye'or*, meaning a river or any water-course, whenever the subject-matter dealt with has a clear Egyptian context, as in the Joseph narrative and that of Moses. Elsewhere, the Nile is simply called by the name *nehar Mizrayim*.

the Wilderness of Paran, where two Israelite fortresses have been discovered, as well as various archaeological remains throughout the region.[14]

Looking at this question from the Egyptian side, it must be observed that historically and geographically Egypt consisted of only two areas, the northern part known as Lower Egypt (containing the flat, swampy land of the Nile Delta) and the southern part known as Upper Egypt.[15] In antiquity, Sinai was not considered an integral part of the land of the Pharaohs, as is apparent *inter alia* from the biblical narrative of Moses, who guided the Israelites, accompanied by a "mixed multitude" (*'erev rav*), out of Egypt on the 15th day of the month of Nisan by crossing the Sea of Reeds (*Yam Suf*) on their way to the Promised Land. It is true that Egypt, at various periods in history, extended its imperial rule to include the Sinai and Palestine, reaching once as far as the Orontes River in Syria. Despite that fact, Sinai, which was under Ottoman rule from 1517 to 1906, was not considered an actual part of Egypt, but rather of the Land of Israel or Palestine, on both historical and geographical grounds. In the mid-1940s Egypt suddenly asserted a right of sovereignty to all of Sinai to forestall any move to make it part of the emerging independent Jewish State. However, it was only by virtue of the Egypt-Israel Peace Treaty of March 26, 1979 that Egypt was finally acknowledged as the sovereign of Sinai in what constituted an illegal cession by Israel of its own right to Sinai.

Under Article II of this treaty, the "permanent boundary" between Egypt and Israel was determined to be what the article alleged was the "recognized international boundary" that had existed between Egypt and the former mandated territory of Palestine. This boundary was recognized as inviolable, with each state agreeing to respect the territorial integrity of the other, including their territorial waters and air space, without prejudice to the status of the Gaza Strip. This proviso meant that despite the existence of the international boundary, Egypt did not recognize Israeli sovereignty over the area of Gaza. The affirmation in the treaty that an international boundary had existed between the two states during the Mandate period and was even supposedly recognized under international law was completely untrue, and it is a wonder that the Begin Government agreed to such an erroneous formulation. This point was further elaborated upon in an appendix to the treaty, where it was noted that "Egypt will *resume* the exercise of its full sovereignty over evacuated parts of the Sinai upon Israeli withdrawal..." (emphasis added). However, prior to the conclusion of the treaty, Egypt did not enjoy sovereignty over the Sinai Peninsula, except for the relatively small area in the north-west corner extending from El-Arish to the port city of Suez. Thus Egypt was not "resuming" its sovereignty over Sinai, but actually gaining sovereignty over the entire peninsula for the first time

---

[14] *Encyclopaedia Judaica* (1971), Volume 10, col. 664.

[15] The dual composition of Egypt may be reflected in the fact that the Hebrew name for the country is *Mizrayim*, which has a dual ending (-*ayim*) and may thus denote "two Egypts". By contrast, the Arabic name for Egypt, *Misr*, is a singular form.

since it became a quasi-independent state in 1922 and a fully independent state in1936. As a direct consequence of the Egypt-Israel Peace Treaty, Israel gave an unwarranted stamp of approval to the manipulative changes the British brought about to the legal status of Sinai in favour of Egyptian administration of the area, both before and during the Mandate period. Rather than leaving Sinai under joint Egyptian-British administration from 1906 onwards, after it was detached from the Independent Sanjak of Jerusalem, Britain, when it became the governor of Palestine, should have rightfully included Sinai in the borders of Mandated Palestine, since as already noted above, it was historically, geographically as well as religiously connected to the Jewish People. Britain simply left the international boundary separating Palestine and Egypt undetermined for an indefinite period. It failed to act on this question because as the governor of both lands, it felt no pressing need to fix the international border. The latter was delineated only with the conclusion of the Egypt-Israel Peace Treaty to Israel's great disadvantage. Until then, what had separated the two countries was only an administrative line dating back to Turkish rule, not an international boundary.

It is most ironic that the cession of Sinai to Egypt was effected by Prime Minister Menachem Begin, considered a great proponent of the Land of Israel, who apparently did not believe Sinai was a part of it, despite the biblical evidence to that effect. He seems to have been influenced by the fact that the Betar emblem included a map of Mandated Palestine, which showed both banks of the Jordan, but not the Sinai. In this respect, Begin was completely eclipsed by David Ben-Gurion who proved to be a greater believer in the Land of Israel program than he was.

The basis for using history as the guiding principle or criterion for determining the borders of Palestine under international law derives from two sources: firstly, the definition given to Palestine by the Principal Allied Powers at the San Remo Peace Conference as extending "from Dan to Beersheba", which was recorded in the minutes of this conference, and secondly, the third Recital in the Preamble of the Mandate which recognized the historical connection of the Jewish People with Palestine. It is true that the boundaries of the ancient kingdoms of Judah and Israel in the First Temple Period, and, later, those of Judea in the Second Temple Period varied at different times in history, but what the framers of the Mandate instrument had in mind was to include in Palestine any territories which once came under Jewish rule for an extended period and/or were also recognized as having a special historical connection, identification or relationship with the Jewish People. This meant that adjoining lands or regions of the Promised Land, such as Moab-Ammon, Edom and Sinai were or should have been rightfully included in the mandated territory of Palestine.

The British Government evaded the legal prohibition of the partition of historical Palestine by a clever and resourceful tactic which had no logical basis in the context in which it was employed. That tactic was simply to re-define the phrase "in Palestine" to mean that not the whole of the country would be established as a Jewish National Home, but only that the Home would be founded "in Palestine", suggesting therefore that only a part of the country would be set aside or designated for that purpose. An innocuous English-language expression was thus transformed to give it a special, unintended and restrictive meaning in regard to the Jewish National Home to meet temporary British needs, first in regard to Transjordan and then later to Cisjordanian Palestine as well. As for Sinai, as already stated, Britain had Turkey detach it from what was to become officially the mandated state of Palestine, fourteen years before its actual creation. The phrase "in Palestine" was thus used as a linguistic weapon against the Jewish People to scale down the size of their Home, which was indeed originally intended to be synonymous with all of historical Palestine, not just a part thereof. In the specific case of Transjordan, the British combined this linguistic weapon with two other reasons to justify its detachment from the Jewish homeland: (1) the McMahon Pledge of October 24, 1915 to the Emir of Mecca and (2) the existing local conditions in that part of Palestine. However, in regard to partitioning Cisjordan, other justifications were found: 1) the irreconcilability of Arabs and Jews to live together and 2) the dual legal obligation or double undertaking which Britain allegedly undertook towards both of them in the articles of the Mandate. In this context, the Palestine Royal Commission stated[16]

> ...the problem [of Palestine] cannot be solved by giving either the Arabs or the Jews all they want... But, while neither race can justly rule all Palestine, we see no reason why, if it were practicable, each race should not rule part of it.

At the end of the Report, the Commissioners stated:[17]

> ...We are bound to honour to the utmost of our power the obligations we undertook in the exigencies of war towards the Arabs and the Jews. When those obligations were incorporated in the Mandate, we did not fully realize the difficulties of the task it laid on us... Partition offers a possibility of finding a way through them, a possibility of obtaining a final solution of the problem which does justice to the rights and aspirations of both the Arabs and the Jews and discharges the obligations we undertook towards them twenty years ago to the fullest extent that is practicable in the circumstances of the present time.

The Commissioners no doubt sincerely believed they were offering good advice to find a just solution for the problems which arose in Palestine and that partition would ultimately bring peace. It was not only that their expectations

---

[16] Palestine Royal Commission Report: Chapter XX, Paragraph 19, p. 375; the same sentiment is expressed in Chapter XXIII, paragraph 1, p. 394.

[17] *Op. cit.,* Chapter XXIII, paragraph 6, p. 395.

for peace proved false by ensuing events that needs to be borne in mind. More important is that their rationale for advocating partition in the first place had no legal or factual basis in the Mandate itself. They falsely interpreted the Mandate to include British obligations to the Arabs as a nation, where none in fact existed, as previously discussed above. They also disregarded the proscription of the partition of the country as set down in Article 5 of the Mandate. The only interesting aspect about their partition plan was its direct linkage to Transjordan based on the assumption they made that the latter was still part of Palestine to which the Commissioners wanted to add Arab-populated areas of Western Palestine to create a new and bigger Arab state out of the total territory of historical Palestine.

The Peel Partition Plan led to other British partition proposals, then to the U.N. Partition Plan and the Israel-PLO Agreements of today which have embraced the same concept of dividing the Land of Israel, under the false slogan "land for peace". The results have proven catastrophic. The concept of partition and its implementation illegally reduced the size of the Jewish National Home under the original UNSCOP Plan to about an eighth of historical Palestine when Transjordan and Bashan, including the Golan, are taken into account. Partition removed the ancient heartland of Judea and Samaria where the Jewish People was born as a nation and flourished in ancient times. In its current manifestation in the illegal "Oslo Peace Process", the principle of partition has attributed national rights over the Land of Israel to an amalgam of foreign conquering peoples – comprised of Arabic-speaking Gentiles or *nochrim* in Hebrew, who never had such rights in the territory reserved for the Jewish National Home during the whole Mandate period. The acceptance of the concept of partition has given the world a false impression that the areas of the Land of Israel recovered in the Six Day War of 1967 were "occupied territories" belonging to the so-called Palestinians who fraudulently appropriated the name from the Jewish People, a brazen lie which has reached its zenith today, repeated *ad nauseam* every day of the week. The end result of the application of the concept of partition has been war, not peace. It should never have been adopted as a solution for the festering and endemic Arab hatred of Israel and the Jewish People and their insatiable greed to control all of the Middle East for themselves.

4) Administering Palestine and enacting legislation to bring about an Arab Government for Palestine, while at the same time ruling out any Jewish administrative role, which was at total variance with what the British Government was charged by the Mandate to do. Article 2 of the Mandate, as explained above, obliged Britain to secure the development of self-governing institutions for the benefit of the Jewish National Home in all of Palestine as part of a plan to gradually establish a Jewish Commonwealth or State. But Britain gave these words – the development of self-governing institutions – a false interpretation to make them applicable not to the Home, but to the preponderant Arab population of Palestine. The introduction of representative democracy, based on majority rule, at the very outset of Mandatory rule was an illegal anti-Zionist

recipe for Palestine to become an Arab state, contrary to the whole framework of the Mandate. The first step in the development of self-governing institutions for Palestine came in October 1920 when an Advisory Council was inaugurated which consisted of ten British officials besides the High Commissioner and ten nominated non-officials, of whom four were Moslem Arabs, three Christians and three Jews. There was also an Executive Council of officials. No ordinances were promulgated until they received the approval of the Advisory Council and the Colonial Secretary. The Churchill White Paper of June 3, 1922 then proposed establishing an elected Legislative Council consisting of Moslem Arabs, Christian Arabs, Jews and officials presided over by the High Commissioner. Elections were held in 1923 to choose the proposed Legislative Council, but the great majority of Arabs refused to vote, which led to the abandonment of the scheme. Samuel then invited the Arabs to become members of a reconstituted enlarged Advisory Council whose members, apart from British officials, were nominated on the same representative basis as that of the proposed Legislative Council, but as before the lack of Arab cooperation aborted this plan. In consequence, the Advisory Council of British officials continued to function without democratic representation, headed by the High Commissioner, which together with the Executive Council constituted the Government of Palestine. A renewed attempt was made to develop self-governing institutions in 1932 and again in 1935, but it met the same fate as Samuel's earlier proposals. The Arabs of Palestine refused to cooperate in any proposals for self-government because they wanted to have a national government that was not bound in any way to the Balfour Declaration as elaborated in detail by the Mandate. Had the Arabs of Palestine accepted the various British offers and taken up the Government posts they were offered in the early years of Mandatory rule, they may have well achieved their aim to scuttle the Balfour Declaration and the Mandate. In the last decade of the Mandate's existence, the British Government succumbed to the persistent Arab demand to govern all of Palestine without the "encumbrance" of the Balfour Declaration when the MacDonald White Paper of May 17, 1939 was published. Under the constitutional arrangements it proposed, "the people of Palestine" – a British euphemism for the Arab majority – were to enjoy the same rights of self-government as were being exercised by the people of neighbouring countries. The British Government desired to see established within ten years an independent Palestine State in treaty relations with the United Kingdom, which would terminate the Mandate. Both Arabs and Jews would ostensibly share governmental authority in proportion to their respective populations. Gone was any notion of parity or equality of representation as earlier advocated by Weizmann. Since the Jews then numbered 450,000, constituting about a third of the total population, this meant in practice that the government of the future state of Palestine would be forever in Arab hands with Jews having no guaranteed voice in the government. There was no possibility of ever having a Jewish majority, because under another part of the plan, there would be no more Jewish immigration after a further 75,000

Jews were allowed to enter Palestine during the ensuing five years, unless the Arabs acquiesced in it. That was the equivalent of stopping Jewish immigration altogether and left the Mandate shorn of any meaning.

The White Paper of 1939 was the high water mark of outright British betrayal of the Mandate representing a culmination of their manifold violations of their obligations towards the Jewish People. Its timing came at the worst moment for the Jewish People, since millions of them found themselves trapped inside the inferno of Central and Eastern Europe that resulted in the Holocaust of Six Million. Many of those who perished could have found a welcome and natural refuge in Palestine and Transjordan, had Britain not shut the gates of the country to their entry, an action that was illegal under international law, unconscionable and unforgivable. It is not idle speculation to say that the Final Solution for European Jewry would never have occurred to the extent that it did, had Britain faithfully honoured the obligations imposed upon it by the Mandate for Palestine, the chief one of which was to create the necessary conditions – political, administrative and economic – which would secure the establishment of the Jewish National Home – the Jewish State – through large-scale Jewish immigration. By 1939, it had set its mind on doing the very opposite, hoping to appease or win points with the Arab states and princes it had spawned, by smothering the pregnancy of the Jewish State and planning instead for the emergence of an Arab State in the land belonging to the Jewish People.

No more fitting and moving a condemnation of the British proposals contained in the 1939 White Paper was pronounced than that which came from the lips of former British Prime Minister David Lloyd George. In a radio broadcast delivered six days after the White Paper was made public, he explained why it had to be seen as a betrayal of the British 1917 undertaking to the Jewish People and also as a stain on British honour. He said:[18]

> As I was Prime Minister at the date of the inception of the famous Balfour Declaration, I was naturally very closely associated with that eminent statesman in its preparation. We were actually assisted in our deliberations by Lord Milner, Mr. Bonar Law and Mr. Arthur Henderson; so that men of all Parties were engaged in the preparation of that document.
>
> It would be useful at this stage to give some of the facts that prompted us to pursue this policy. Twenty-five years ago the British Empire became engaged in a life-and-death struggle against the most formidable military empire in the world, for the vindication of international right. In 1917, that conflict reached a critical stage, when the issue appeared more than doubtful. The scales of victory seemed then to weigh down in favour of the German militarists. The leaders

[18] Lloyd George's Broadcast on the White Paper, Tuesday, May 23, 1939, appearing as Appendix 6 in the book by Silas S. Perry, *Britain Opens a Gateway*, Museum Press Limited, London (1944), pp. 94-96.

on both sides of this conflict were straining every effort to rally all available forces and resources, internal and neutral, on their side to achieve a decision. The Allies and their foes alike realized the undoubted influence and opportunities which the Jews, the descendants of the great dispersal, could exert at vital points in the vast battle area. The contestants entered, therefore, into a competition for the capture of that influence. Both Parties offered to the Jewish leaders, as the reward of their support, that in the event of victory they would secure for Israel the realization of its dreams, the restoration to its children of a home in the land which has been made immortal by the contribution there of their ancestors to all that is noblest in our civilization.

The Jews accepted our word in preference to that given to them by the Germans. The famous Balfour Declaration about the establishment of a homeland for the Jews in the land of Canaan was not offered by us out of our abundant grace. It is important that it should be realized that it was a bargain in return for a valuable consideration given to us – the effective support of the Jews of the world to the Allied cause, notably in America, Russia and Central Europe. Every Party – Conservative, Liberal, Socialist without exception and without protest – accepted this declaration not only in Britain but in every Allied and associated country.

The Jews have honourably kept their part of the bargain. We are now seeking to crawl out of our share of it…

The mischievous activities fostered by the Italians and the Germans in recent years amongst a small section of the Arabs have driven us into *an act of national perfidy* (emphasis added) which will bring dishonour to the British name. It has already antagonised the powerful communities of Jews, numbering in the aggregate seventeen millions, residing in every quarter of the globe. It will strengthen a deepening and a disastrous conviction that our word of honour can no longer be relied upon if good faith costs us anything.

Britain had until recently been held in esteem as a country which always stood by her word. She is in danger of losing that honourable fame. Most of our troubles in recent years have come from the fact that whenever our plighted word comes up against any difficulty, our "yea" is no longer a "yea" and our "nay" ceases to be "nay". Our trail from Pekin to Mount Zion is littered with broken pledges.[19] I end

[19] By the foregoing references to Peking and Mount Zion, Lloyd George was stressing Britain's failure to faithfully honour its international commitments. In regard to Peking, now called Beijing, Britain was a signatory to a Nine-Power Treaty (1921-2) guaranteeing China's territorial integrity but did not intervene when Japan invaded China in July 1937 and occupied Peking in the Second Sino-Japanese War. Mount Zion is a hill in Jerusalem symbolizing the Holy City with its ancient Temple, as well as the Promised Land of the Jewish People. By

> by quoting Mr. Eden's great saying, that we cannot build world peace except on a basis of international good faith.

The British administrative and legislative measures enacted in the wake of the 1939 White Paper could not have been carried out had there not also been a compliant Palestine judiciary which refused to overturn those unconstitutional measures as being repugnant to the Mandate and hence blatantly illegal. The judiciary moved in lockstep with the executive branch of government in Palestine. In a series of warped judgments both before and after the White Paper, the British-administered courts of Palestine prevented the enforcement of the Mandate's clear provisions favouring Jewish legal rights on the false ground that the Mandate had never been incorporated as a whole into the domestic law of the country. The Mandate Charter was explicitly designed by its British and Zionist authors to serve as the basic constitution of Palestine, and therefore did not require specific legislation to bring it into force in Palestine, once it had been confirmed by the League Council. The requirement of incorporation by British judges was a crude, judicial ruse to allow the British Government to completely disregard its mandatory obligations in favour of the Jewish People. The judiciary thus became a servile adjunct for the British maladministration of Palestine, which allowed the Mandate's provisions enshrining Jewish legal rights – particularly those dealing with free immigration and land acquisition – to be abandoned and to fall into desuetude.

5) Restricting, suspending and prohibiting Jewish immigration into Palestine by relying on spurious grounds to prevent a Jewish majority from ever coming into existence during the Mandate period. Large-scale Jewish immigration was the indispensable means provided in the Mandate to fulfill its paramount purpose, to secure the establishment of the Jewish National Home and State. Without it, there was no possibility that the Jewish State could be created and maintained. The British Government was acutely aware of the necessity of massive immigration to realize the purpose of the Mandate, as is evident from a Memorandum dated May 17, 1920, written by Major Hubert Winthrop Young, a member of the Eastern and Egyptian Department of the Foreign Office during the tenure of Lord Curzon and later a high-ranking official of the Middle East Department of the Colonial Office. He explained the British undertaking in Palestine as follows:[20]

> ...Over 80 percent of the population of Palestine are non-Jews, and hostile to the idea of a Jewish National Home. It appears from this that it is not intended to institute a representative government in Palestine, but to set up a British administration which shall make it

issuing the 1939 White Paper, Britain dashed any remaining Jewish hopes that it would honour the Mandate's promise of a Jewish State in Palestine.

[20] Major Young's memorandum is contained in *Documents on Foreign Policy, 1919-1939*, First Series, Volume XIII, No. 250, p. 260.

> possible for a Jewish National Home gradually to be formed there. The Zionists *imagine* that Palestine is to become eventually a Jewish state. This could only be reconciled with the Principle of self-government if the country were developed to an extent that would admit of *the immigration of Jews in such large numbers that they would form the majority of the population.* If this is the intention of His Majesty's Government, it will presumably be found necessary to control immigration and development in Palestine with a view to the eventual establishment of a Jewish majority. This will require direct British administration *for a considerable period of time*... (emphasis added).

The British Government did not fulfil its obligation to create suitable conditions for the purpose of facilitating large-scale Jewish immigration that would ensure the establishment of an independent Jewish State. The latter was "imagined" not only by the Zionists, as Young believed, but also by the Imperial War Cabinet when the Balfour Declaration was unanimously approved on October 31, 1917, and hence it was also "imagined" by the Mandate itself that was drafted to implement the Balfour Declaration. Instead, the Government continuously placed illegal obstacles in the way to impede Jewish immigration at the outset of military rule, then at the institution of civilian administration and particularly in the last decade of the Mandate. Had the British fulfilled their mandatory obligation to allow unhampered Jewish immigration into Palestine, in accordance with Article 6 of the Mandate, a Jewish majority in Palestine would very soon have arisen and the British Administration of Palestine would not have lasted, as Hubert Young stated, "for a considerable period of time." The independent Jewish State would then have emerged much sooner.

After the issuance of the Balfour Declaration on November 2, 1917, hundreds of thousands of Jews from Russia were ready and willing to come to Palestine before the complete Bolshevik takeover of that country. However, British military authorities who were overtly hostile to Zionism and the policy of the Jewish National Home immediately prohibited Jewish immigration except for a few cases involving mainly repatriations. The transfer of land to Jews was also forbidden during the period of British military occupation. The legal basis for restricting Jewish immigration and land transfer was based on the principle of international law respecting the *status quo ante bellum* – the state of affairs existing before the war. This kept the existing law of the Ottoman Empire in force during the period of military occupation of Palestine. Under this law, it was forbidden for Jewish immigrants to settle not only in the independent sanjak of Jerusalem, but also in other places that were considered to be part of the Land of Palestine. The ban, first proclaimed in 1882 and made progressively more severe in 1884 and 1909, was never rigorously enforced and could be evaded in practice by payments of bribery or *baksheesh*.

The Turkish edict banning Jewish immigration was discriminatory and illegal on its face, since Jews had always assumed they had a right to return to their ancient homeland, even without a Jewish State in existence, as David Ben-Gurion so vividly stated in introducing the bill for Knesset approval that became the Law of Return, enacted on July 5, 1950. In the words of Ben-Gurion explaining the proposed law, he said:[21]

> This law lays down not that the State accords the right of settlement to Jews abroad, but that this right is inherent in every Jew by virtue of his being a Jew if it but be his will to take part in settling the land. This right preceded the State of Israel, it is that which built the State.

Ben-Gurion's belief that every Jew has the right to settle in the Land of Israel was also expressed earlier by Chaim Weizmann in a letter to Wyndham Deedes, dated November 12, 1921. In reacting to a speech given by Herbert Samuel in Jerusalem on June 3, 1921 in which the latter placed limits on Jewish immigration to Palestine that were fixed by the numbers and interests of the Arab population, Weizmann told Deedes:[22]

> The fundamental difference between Palestine and any other country consists in the fact that every Jew feels he has an inalienable right to come to Palestine and make there his home – and, what is the chief point, help to make the Jewish National Home – whereas the man who goes to America hopes to build an American National Home. This right we had before the Balfour Declaration.

It was, however, the Turkish "law" which the British military authorities decided to enforce, acting on legal advice to keep the *status quo ante bellum* or existing conditions in place until the changeover to civilian rule was made on July 1, 1920, after which time changes in the law could be carried out.

The person who principally advised the British War Office about the *status quo* principle was the great Jewish jurist, Lassa Francis Lawrence Oppenheim, a professor of international law at Cambridge well versed on questions pertaining to military law and the application of the Hague Regulations of 1907. He worked with Colonel Edmonds to prepare a guide entitled "Land Warfare: an Exposition of the Laws and Usages of War on Land for the Guidance of Officers of His Majesty's Army", published in 1912 by the British War Office. In 1914 this guide was embodied in a new edition of the official *Manual of Military Law*. He also took a leading part during the war in preparing manuals for the Foreign Office on subjects of international law, used to enlighten British delegates at the Peace Conferences.[23] After the British capture of Jerusalem on

---

[21] See article on the "Law of Return" in *Encyclopaedia Judaica*, Keter Publishing House Ltd., Jerusalem (1971), Volume 10, col. 1486.

[22] See Volume X – Series A – of *The Letters and Papers of Chaim Weizmann*, Letter 278, p. 282.

[23] See article on Professor Oppenheim by E.A. Whittuck in *The British Year*

December 9, 1917, the British Government needed a plausible reason to prevent the civilian personnel of their French and Italian allies from participating in the day-to-day affairs of Palestine, as they hoped to do by virtue of the Sykes-Picot Treaty of May 9 and 16, 1916 (made with France and Russia) and the Saint-Jean De Maurienne Agreement of April 19, 1917 (made with Italy), which provided for an international government for Palestine. The British dodged the commitments they made to their Allies by informing them, based on Professor Oppenheim's information, that the Hague Regulations excluded their having any civilian role in the military administration of Palestine until there was a final peace settlement which could permit changes in the *status quo ante bellum.* In the meantime, there would be no departure from this principle except for military necessity.

As noted, this had deleterious consequences for Jewish immigration and the goal of the Jewish National Home. The hundreds of thousands of Russian Jews, who would have come to Palestine had their entry not been blocked or restricted by the orders of British military administrators, were left behind in Russia with no prospect of ever getting out after Bolshevik rule became entrenched. This outcome did not displease the military authorities under the overall command of General Edmund Allenby who were strongly antagonistic to the Balfour Declaration. They refused to acknowledge its very existence or officially publish it in Palestine until pressed to do so on May 1, 1920, just two months before the end of military rule. During this initial period of British military administration when the Declaration was not published, some military officials even encouraged the local Arab inhabitants to believe that it might not be implemented at all and they unashamedly incited Arab opposition against it, which became more and more pronounced as the military government continued.

While he headed Palestine's military administration, General Allenby himself was indifferent or unsympathetic to Zionist aspirations. Stationed in Cairo, he was the Commander-in-Chief of the Egyptian Expeditionary Force, the official title of the British Army in the Middle East. He appointed a provisional military administration to govern Palestine west of the Jordan, composed of the Chief Administrator, six Heads of Departments and a number of District Military Governors. The powers of the administration were defined and limited by the laws and usages of war, which required Britain, as the Occupying Power, not to make innovations in the laws of the country, until peace was made and the sovereignty of the country determined.[24] Among the military administrators appointed by Allenby to serve in Palestine who sought to derail the Balfour Declaration or were strongly opposed to it were General Arthur Money, Colonel

---

*Book of International Law, 1920-1921*, London, p. 1ff.

[24] See the article by Norman Bentwich, Chief Judicial Officer, Occupied Territories, Palestine, entitled "The Legal Administration of Palestine under the British Military Occupation", which appeared in *The British Year Book of International Law*, London 1920-1921, p. 139.

Ronald Storrs, Colonel Edmund Vivian Gabriel, Colonel Bertie Harry Waters-Taylor[25] and General Louis Jean Bols. Another military figure who expressed unbending opposition to the establishment of the Jewish National Home was General Walter Norris Congreve, who served as military commander in Palestine after the inauguration of civilian administration. In October 1921, he sent a circular to all British troops in the country, declaring that the sympathies of the Army "are rather obviously with the Arabs, who… have been the victims of an unjust policy… based on the Balfour Declaration."[26]

The British displayed or tolerated a double standard in regard to the principle respecting the *status quo ante bellum.* This principle was applied only in Palestine, to the great detriment of the Zionist Movement, but not in Syria where Feisal was able, with British consent, to set up a provisional Arab State that ruled the towns of Damascus, Homs, Hama and Aleppo, as well as the entire area of Transjordan, until his ouster by French General Henri Joseph Gouraud on July 25, 1920. The French also set up their own provisional administration in coastal Syria, including Lebanon, and separately in Cilicia, known respectively as O.E.T.A. West and O.E.T.A. North. Most hypocritically, the British disregarded the principle whenever they decided this suited their particular needs, but in the matter of prohibiting Jewish immigration into Palestine, the lifeblood of the Jewish National Home, they showed the most slavish respect for the existing Turkish law, much more so than the Ottoman Government ever did.

The advice of Professor Oppenheim about maintaining the *status quo ante bellum* until a peace treaty was concluded was inappropriate in regard to the former Ottoman-ruled territories of what became Palestine because it left in place a corrupt and discriminatory legal system. Had the same advice and principle been accepted in World War II, the Allied Powers who invaded and conquered Germany would have had to legally enforce the pre-existing laws of the Nazi Government of Adolph Hitler, an idea which was dismissed out of hand. The reasons for not applying the relevant Hague Regulations to Germany following the end of World War II and the unconditional surrender of the German armed forces in 1945, which led to the suspension of German sovereignty, both internally and externally, and hence its temporary subjugation until 1949, but without permanent annexation, are explained in the following

---

[25] Colonel Richard Meinertzhagen, then serving as Chief Political Officer on General Allenby's staff, reported to him on April 6, 1920 that both Ronald Storrs and Waters-Taylor were in close touch with *Hajj* Amin al-Husseini, a violent and dangerous opponent of Jewish settlement in Palestine who in 1921 became Mufti of Jerusalem. Waters-Taylor opposed Zionism so strongly that he had even advocated Arab anti-Jewish riots in Jerusalem to impress on the Administration the unpopularity of its pro-Zionist policy. Such riots took place in April 1920 and May 1921. Allenby was shocked, but took no action. See Meinertzhagen's *Middle East Diary, 1917-1956*, published by Thoman Yoseloff, New York (1960), p. 56.

[26] General Congreve's circular is published in *Companion Volume IV* of Martin Gilbert's biography of *Winston S. Churchill*, Part 3, pp. 1659-1660.

extracts from Oppenheim's classical work:[27]

> 1. ...the principle laid down in Article 43 to the effect that, subject to some qualifications, the occupant must respect the laws in force in the occupied territory could hardly apply to an occupied State the law of which denied fundamental legal rights and the very notion of legal order as developed in civilized society. The Hague Convention did not envisage – and was not therefore applicable to – any such perversions of the idea of law as manifested themselves in the practice of National Socialist Germany.
>
> 2. The Signatories of the Hague Convention did not intend to undertake the obligation to maintain, even temporarily, a legal system and institutions which were utterly repugnant to civilized conceptions of the law and the destruction of which had been proclaimed to constitute a major purpose of the War. Thus the first Proclamation issued by the Military Government of Germany (Supreme Commander's Area of Control) announced that 'we shall... abolish the cruel, oppressive and discriminating laws and institutions which the [Nazi] Party has created.' The Military Government Law No. 1, issued on September 18, 1944, laid down that 'in order to eliminate from German law and administration within the occupied territory the policies and doctrines of the National-Socialist Party and to restore to the German people the rule of justice and equality before the law' certain fundamental Nazi laws, together with subsidiary and supplement laws, 'are hereby deprived of effect within the occupied territory.'
>
> 3. Similar Proclamations and Laws were issued in Italy in 1943. Thus Proclamation No. 7 of the Allied Military Government provided in Article 4 that the 'Chief Civil Affairs Officer will by Order annul, amend, or render inoperative... any law which discriminates on the basis of race, colour or creed.'

The same kind of proclamation that was issued on September 18, 1944 by the Allied Military Government in Germany "to abolish the cruel, oppressive and discriminating laws and institutions" which the Nazi Party had created should have been taken by Britain when it replaced the Ottoman regime in Palestine, because Turkish law, like the law of National-Socialist Germany under Adolf Hitler, blatantly discriminated against Jews, especially in matters of immigration and settlement throughout Palestine. Turkish law was utterly repugnant to the policy of the Jewish National Home as set down in the Balfour Declaration, which was the only justification for the British presence in Palestine. However, it served the political purposes of Britain to keep the *status quo ante bellum* in place not only to prevent French and Italian interference with British rule in Palestine

[27] See: *International Law*, 7th edition, a treatise by L. Oppenheim, edited by H. Lauterpacht (1963), paragraph 265a, p. 602, and footnote 2 on pages 603-604.

but also to prevent the mass influx of Jewish immigrants into the country, principally from Russia before the new Bolshevik Government slammed shut the door of immigration.

Not long after the introduction of civilian rule, the British Government invented a new and effective means to limit Jewish immigration to Palestine, namely, the concept of "economic absorptive capacity". On this subject, the Churchill White Paper of June 3, 1922 declared:

> ...It is essential that [the Jewish People] should know that it is in Palestine as of right and not on sufferance. That is the reason why it is necessary that the existence of a Jewish National Home in Palestine should be internationally guaranteed, and that it should be formally recognized to rest upon ancient historic connection.
>
> ...For the fulfillment of this policy it is necessary that the Jewish community should be able to increase its numbers by immigration. This immigration cannot be so great in volume as to exceed whatever may be the economic capacity of the country at the time to absorb new arrivals. It is essential to ensure that the immigrants should not be a burden upon the people of Palestine as a whole and that they should not deprive any section of the present population of their employment.

The 1922 White Paper simultaneously affirmed the right of Jewish immigrants to enter Palestine under an international guarantee in accordance with Article 6 of the Mandate just prior to its confirmation by the League Council, while imposing an economic restriction on that right which was not found in this provision. Article 6 was in effect the international legal recognition of a Jewish right of return to all of Palestine designated as the Jewish National Home, and imposed a paramount legal obligation on the British officials of the Government of Palestine to honour that right. The part of Article 6 that applied directly to Jewish immigration reads as follows:

> The Administration of Palestine, while ensuring that the rights and position of other sections of the population are not prejudiced, shall *facilitate* Jewish immigration under suitable conditions... (emphasis added).

What this actually meant was well stated in the British House of Commons on May 22, 1939, by Leopold Stennett Amery, the former British Colonial Secretary, 1924-29, who as Secretary to the Lloyd George War Cabinet was very closely associated with the long discussions which preceded the Balfour

Declaration:[28]

> The Jews were to be in Palestine as of right, and not on sufferance, and no other consideration was to be allowed to prevent their *free entry and free settlement* (emphasis added) as long as that entry and that settlement did not inflict direct injury upon the existing community, Jew or Arab.

A close analysis of Article 6 inevitably leads to the conclusion, that despite the impression given in that article by the two subordinate phrases of narrowing the right of Jewish immigrants to enter Palestine, this did not in fact constitute legal restrictions on this right. The qualifying words in the proviso, "while ensuring that the rights and position of other sections of the population are not prejudiced", were in essence only a reaffirmation of the civil and religious rights of all non-Jewish inhabitants of Palestine, already set down in Article 2 of the Mandate. Those words in article 6 simply meant that the aforementioned rights of non-Jews would not be harmed no matter how many Jews immigrated to Palestine, even after they formed the majority of the population. Nor would their financial situation or standard of living, i.e., their "position", suffer by the large influx of Jews, as wrongly concluded in the 1930 Passfield White Paper (see *infra*). Jewish immigration to Palestine never deprived Arabs of their employment or ownership of land, or directly injured them. On the contrary, as borne out by actual events, the economic or material position of all inhabitants drastically improved with the rise in Jewish immigration. The proviso in Article 6 was therefore not a legal cause to restrict Jews from exercising their recognized right of return under international law.

In regard to the next qualifying phrase, "under suitable conditions", this was actually a positive injunction imposed on the British Government to facilitate Jewish immigration and not a stipulation to restrict or hinder it. It consisted of a two-fold obligation derived from Articles 2 and 6 of the Mandate. First, Britain was obliged to administratively process in a prompt and orderly way the large numbers of Jews who were expected to arrive as landed immigrants to augment the Jewish population of Palestine. Second, it had to create the necessary political, administrative and economic conditions for the development of the country to enable Jews to be successfully absorbed in Palestine as soon as possible, exactly as Hubert Young's Memorandum of May 17, 1920 had outlined.

---

[28] This quotation is taken from Amery's speech delivered in the House of Commons, May 22, 1939, *Parliamentary Debates*, Vol. 347, No. 107, Columns 2012-2026. He was reacting to the publication of the White Paper of May 17, 1939, which he said meant that Britain had accepted the Arab contention that Palestine is an Arab country, and the idea that after an interval the entry of Jews to the country is to be on sufferance, and no longer as of right. This was of course the reverse of Article 6 of the Mandate for Palestine. Amery's exact words are reprinted in the *Book of Documents submitted by the Jewish Agency for Palestine to the U.N. General Assembly, op. cit.*, p. 124.

What the British were not allowed to do by virtue of the foregoing Mandate provisions was to create onerous conditions which hindered rather than facilitated Jewish immigration – exactly what they did. From 1922 to 1939 they limited the number of Jews who could enter Palestine by artificially determining what the economic absorptive capacity was for any particular year. Then in 1939 a new condition was added: the necessity of obtaining Arab consent. Such economic, administrative and political conditions were legally incompatible with the Jewish right of return. The same incompatibility applied to the suspension of Jewish immigration for any reason whatsoever.

British curbs on Jewish immigration should have been fought tooth and nail because they unnecessarily delayed the growth of a Jewish majority to establish an independent Jewish State. Under the Immigration Ordinance and regulations, if potential Jewish immigrants did not come within any of several categories set down in the law to regulate Jewish immigration, they were not allowed into the country, contrary to the Mandate which did not provide for different categories of Jews allowed to enter the country. Entry was restricted to Jews who had independent means, were members of a profession, were assured support from members of their families already resident in Palestine, were able to find employment with specified employers or enterprises or were persons of religious occupation who could show they had means of support. In case a potential immigrant's application was rejected, there was no right of appeal. During Samuel's tenure as High Commissioner, some prospective Jewish immigrants from Eastern Europe who had already packed their bags en route to a new life in Palestine were left stranded in European ports or sent back to their countries of origin after they were deemed unfit for immigration, a very cruel and devastating blow to those affected by orders of this kind. It was intolerable that Jews who had a legally-recognized right to immigrate to Palestine under international law could be so easily deprived of their right, on the mere whim of a British immigration officer without having any legal recourse to appeal an unjust arbitrary decision. No legal system based on the rule of law and justice would have ever accepted such an abusive curtailment of a right. Samuel was responsible for this grave injustice, since he devised the original policy under which the immigration rules were drawn up.

Years later, in 1937, in testifying before the Palestine Royal Commission, Churchill disowned Samuel's policy of curtailing Jewish immigration based on the concept of economic absorptive capacity. Since Churchill's testimony was not included in the Commission's Report, it is necessary to rely on what his biographer, Martin Gilbert, reports on what he said:[29]

> Churchill was summoned as a witness before the Commissioners on March 12 (1937). As Colonial Secretary in 1922 he had been responsible for the original administration of the Mandate, and

[29] Martin Gilbert, *Winston S. Churchill*, Volume V, 1922-1939, Heinemann: London (1976), reprinted 1988, p. 847.

> was closely questioned about his intentions at that time. In answer to a question from Lord Peel, he declared that the Jewish right to immigration ought not to be curtailed by the "economic absorptive capacity" of Palestine...

In his reaction to the White Paper of 1939, which he denounced in the strongest terms, he deviated from the view he had presented to the Royal Commission about the concept of economic absorptive capacity. He now said in a more circumspect manner that there was a need to control immigration in general, not just on economic grounds, but with a view to doing what was best for Palestine and to promote the establishment of the Jewish National Home. He stated in the House of Commons on May 23, 1939:[30]

> There need be no dispute about this phrase "economic absorptive capacity". It represented the intentions of the Government and their desire to carry out the Palestinian Mandate in an efficient and in a prudent manner. As I am the author of the phrase, perhaps I may be allowed to state that economic absorptive capacity was never intended to rule without regard to any other consideration. It had always rested with the Mandatory Power to vary the influx of the Jews in accordance with what was best for Palestine and for the sincere fulfillment – one must presuppose the sincere fulfillment – of our purpose in establishing a Jewish National Home there.
>
> ...The Mandatory Power was entitled to control the flow of immigration, or even to suspend it in an emergency. What they are not entitled to do without reproach – grave, public and worldwide reproach, and I trust self-reproach as well – is to bring the immigration to an end so far as they are concerned, to wash their hands of it, to close the door. That they have no right whatever to do.

It was wrong for Churchill to imply that Britain had a free hand to control as it saw fit the flow of immigration or even to suspend it in an emergency since that meant it could arbitrarily overrule the Jewish right of return to Palestine or prevent its exercise. However, it appears more likely that he only wanted better administrative machinery to supervise Jewish immigration in the interest of the country as a whole, which did not completely rule out a mass influx of Jews if the economic conditions of Palestine favoured it. In the same speech, Churchill explained what was "best for Palestine" – by pointing out the benefits that accrued from Jewish immigration:[31]

---

[30] *Parliamentary Debates*, Vol. 347, No. 108, Columns 2177-2189.

[31] Martin Gilbert, *op. cit.*, Vol. V, p. 1092. Gilbert provides the exact figures for Churchill's statement. At the beginning of the British Mandate, there were 487,573 Arabs and 83,894 Jews in Palestine (1922 census). By 1937 the population had

> Yesterday, the Minister responsible descanted eloquently in glowing passages about the magnificent work which the Jewish colonists have done. They have made the desert bloom. They have started a score of thriving industries, he said. They have founded a great city on the barren shore. They have harnessed the Jordan and spread its electricity throughout the land. So far from being persecuted, *the Arabs have crowded into the country and multiplied till their population has increased more than even all world Jewry could lift up the Jewish population* (emphasis added).

Churchill's words make it clear that up to the time of the 1939 White Paper, the Arab population of Palestine increased more than the Jewish population in absolute numbers, a rise largely attributable to Arab infiltration from neighbouring countries, rather than by natural increase, although there has raged a scholarly dispute as to the real reason for the Arab increase. Nevertheless, it may be concluded that British immigration policy during the mandate period *facilitated* greater Arab immigration than Jewish immigration. This development was contrary to the letter and spirit of the Mandate as a whole and exacerbated to this very day the Arab demographic danger to the Jewish National Home and State.

The consequences of enforcing a restrictive Jewish immigration policy based on a policy of economic absorptive capacity were to severely limit the number of immigrants who came to Palestine and thus unnecessarily prolonging the period needed to establish the Jewish State. This happened at a time when there was still a large reservoir of Jews in central and eastern Europe who were eager to immigrate to the country before the Holocaust took place. The great mass of Jews were stranded there, even as their plight became more and more desperate, because too many obstacles were placed in their way by British immigration authorities who acted on the basis of an immigration ordinance and its regulations that blatantly conflicted with Articles 2 and 6 of the Mandate for Palestine.

The entire course of the Jewish National Home would have been dramatically improved had Weizmann and his fellow Zionist leaders accepted the plan for an immediate mass transfer of Jews from the Diaspora to Palestine, numbering in the hundreds of thousands, which was presciently advocated by both Davis Trietsch and Max Nordau in 1919 and 1920 respectively. Trietsch set out his ideas in a Berlin journal he founded and edited called *Volk und Land* (Folk and Land), while Nordau, who wanted to bring a half million or more Jews to Palestine within a matter of months to secure Jewish independence in conformity with the underlying assumption of an "A" Mandate like Palestine, pushed for the

---

increased by a further 350,000 Arabs and 340,000 Jews. Many of the Jews came from Eastern Europe and Russia, most of the Arabs from Syria and Transjordan. In June 1940, the population of Palestine was officially estimated at 1,521,005 persons, of whom 453,286 were Jews. See also *British Policy in Palestine* by Paul Hanna, p. 5.

same policy in the Paris Zionist journal *Le Peuple Juif* (The Jewish People) in a series of ten articles published between September 14 and November 20, 1920. Both Trietsch and Nordau also lobbied for this plan at Zionist conferences they attended at the time. But they were stymied in their efforts by myopic Zionist leaders who were unable to appreciate the significance of their advice. They thus failed to exploit the non-recurring opportunity offered by Trietsch's and Nordau's well-conceived transfer plans for Jews to decisively change the demographic situation in the Land of Israel, to create a Jewish majority right at the very beginning of the implementation of the Mandate in July 1920, before Britain applied more and more restrictive criteria to limit the number of Jews admitted into their homeland. Had the advice of Trietsch or Nordau been heeded when it was first given, a vibrant Jewish State could undoubtedly have been hastened and established before the eruption of World War II which entrapped the mass of European Jewry.[32] This would have averted not only the scope of the Holocaust, but also the unfolding British sabotage of the Mandate that had already begun to manifest itself in the malevolent military administration of Palestine and which continued unabated under civilian rule, reaching a crescendo in the White Paper of May 17, 1939 and remaining at that level until the establishment of the Jewish State.

The Zionist leaders, who trusted in British good faith and did not foresee the perilous events that soon came to pass, feared that a huge wave of immigration would overtax their meager resources. They therefore rejected the farseeing Trietsch-Nordau proposals as unrealistic without a second thought. Britain refused to underwrite any of the expenses associated with caring for a limited number of immigrants, let alone a much greater number. The financial burden was put strictly on the shoulders of the Zionist Organization. For that reason, Weizmann and his colleagues even welcomed on a temporary basis some of the restrictions on immigration imposed by Samuel, showing a complete absence of judgment at a critical moment in the Mandate Period. Weizmann, whom Nordau, a co-founder of the Zionist Movement, had described as "the person least of all fitted to lead a political movement",[33] threw away the only chance the Zionist Organization ever had to autonomously determine without British control or regulation just how many Jews could come to Palestine each year when Churchill actually offered to place responsibility for immigration in Zionist hands, at a meeting they had to discuss this question and other "burning problems", according to a report Weizmann submitted to the London Zionist Executive on August 3, 1921. In his book, M. Mossek describes what happened at this meeting:

---

[32] The wisdom of Nordau's plan to transfer a half a million or more European Jews to Palestine to create a Jewish majority there was belatedly acknowledged in 1936 by Ze'ev Jabotinsky who proposed a similar "evacuation" program which he appropriately called "The Max Nordau Plan".

[33] *Encyclopedia of Zionism and Israel*, Herzl Press (1971), Vol. 2, p. 841.

> Weizmann later met Churchill and discussed... lastly, the question of immigration. On this matter Churchill undoubtedly shocked Weizmann, by suggesting that complete control of Jewish immigration into Palestine be transferred to the Zionist Organization. Weizmann rejected this proposal as not "practical, so long as the Government of Palestine had the power to expel persons". It seems that in reality, it was Weizmann's skepticism about the ability of the Zionist Organization to control immigration efficiently which prevented him from accepting the proposal. Instead he suggested that the control should remain in the hands of the British authorities, but that cooperation with the Zionist Organization should be strengthened. Finally, Weizmann asked that "immigration must be restricted for the time being".
>
> Weizmann's objection to taking full control over immigration, and his demand to restrict it temporarily, represented the official policy of the Zionist Executive.[34]

In the ensuing years, it became apparent that not taking advantage of Churchill's unprecedented offer to allow the Zionist Organization to control immigration, an offer which, as noted above, would have realized the goal of an independent Jewish State much sooner than actually happened and largely avoided the British sabotage of the Mandate, was a terrible mistake. This was true especially after Britain issued four successive documents in 1930 and 1931, each dealing with the question of Jewish immigration in some aspect and its impact on the Arab population. First came a report of a commission of enquiry headed by Walter Sidney Shaw, a former Chief Justice in the colonial administration of Southeast Asia. The Commission was appointed by Colonial Secretary Lord Passfield on September 13, 1929 to investigate the Arab riots of that year. It attributed the real causes for the disturbances to Arab political and economic grievances, citing in particular Jewish immigration, and called for stricter regulations. One member of the Commission, Henry (later Lord) Snell did say, however, that too much credence was given to Arab claims of economic injuries resulting from Jewish immigration. A follow-up report was then made by John Hope-Simpson, published on October 20, 1930, who recommended putting a stop to Jewish labour immigrants entering Palestine until a solution was found for Arab unemployment, which he blamed on Jewish national institutions for employing only Jewish labour. All labour immigration into Palestine was then suspended while he prepared his report, and a temporary suspension of all immigration was also mooted. The conclusions of the Hope-Simpson Report were accepted in the accompanying Passfield White Paper announcing that more stringent controls would be placed on Jewish immigration by giving a wider interpretation to the policy of economic absorptive capacity. It said

---

[34] See M. Mossek, *Palestine Immigration Policy under Sir Herbert Samuel*, Frank Cass and Company Ltd. (1978), pp. 43-44.

that if Jewish immigration to Palestine prevented Arabs from obtaining work or if Jewish unemployment in the country was adversely affected, Britain had a duty under the Mandate to reduce or if necessary suspend further Jewish immigration until the unemployed obtained work.

The Passfield White Paper caused a storm of protest compelling Prime Minister Ramsay MacDonald to issue a clarifying letter to Weizmann on February 13, 1931 (known as the MacDonald Letter) which offset the negative recommendations of this White Paper. His letter reaffirmed the British obligation to facilitate Jewish immigration and stated that no stoppage or prohibition was contemplated in any of the categories of immigration. The MacDonald Letter further stated that Jewish immigration and settlement did not prejudice the rights and position of other sections of the population, as alleged in the Passfield White Paper.

Despite the retraction of the Passfield White Paper, it was a portent of worse things to come, which materialized eight and a half years later with the publication of the Malcolm MacDonald White Paper of May 17, 1939, that drastically curtailed Jewish immigration. As cogent evidence of the success of the cruel and illegal British suppression of Jewish immigration into Palestine during World War II, the number of Jews who actually used the immigration certificates available under the schedule of the 1939 White Paper was only about 44,000 out of a five-year quota of 75,000 (10,000 per year and a further 25,000 refugees over the same period). The White Paper produced the phenomenon of "illegal immigrants" or *ma'apilim* entering Palestine on decrepit refugee ships, some of which were sunk thus costing the lives of thousands of Jews. However, it was not the immigrants who should have been described as "illegal", but the 1939 White Paper itself, which illegally changed the meaning of Article 6 of the Mandate without having obtained the prior requisite consent of the Council of the League of Nations under Article 27 of the Mandate or that of the U.S. Government under the provisions of the Anglo-American Convention of December 3, 1924 respecting the Mandate for Palestine.

The last statement on Jewish immigration from an official investigative body during the Mandate period came on April 26, 1946 with the release of the Report of the joint Anglo-American Committee of Enquiry regarding the problems of European Jewry and Palestine. The twelve-member Committee, appointed by the governments of Britain and the United States on November 13, 1945, was jointly chaired by British Justice John E. Singleton and U.S. Judge Joseph C. Hutcheson. It recommended that 100,000 Jews who were the victims of Nazi and Fascist persecution be immediately admitted into Palestine. Future immigration would then be regulated according to the Mandate pending the execution of a trusteeship agreement under the U.N. Charter. It rejected the view of the 1939 White Paper that Jewish immigration needed Arab acquiescence, but at the same time rejected any unconditional Jewish right of return to Palestine. It commented on this point as follows:

> While we recognize that any Jew who enters Palestine in accordance with its laws is there of right, we expressly disapprove of the position taken in some Jewish quarters that Palestine has in some way been ceded or granted as their State to the Jews of the world, that every Jew is, merely because he is a Jew, a citizen of Palestine and therefore can enter Palestine as of right without regard to conditions imposed by the Government upon entry, and that therefore there can be no illegal immigration of Jews into Palestine. We declare and affirm that any immigrant Jew who enters Palestine contrary to its laws is an illegal immigrant.[35]

It was indicative of the lack of true understanding of the critical documents that emerged from the global political and legal settlement made at the Peace Conferences after World War I in dividing up the Ottoman Turkish Empire, that the two distinguished judges who presided over the Anglo-American Committee were utterly unable to appreciate the extent of Jewish legal rights over Palestine that derived from Article 22 of the League Covenant incorporating the Smuts Resolution, the San Remo Resolution, the Mandate and the Franco-British Boundary Convention of December 23, 1920, as amended on February 3, 1922. If they had understood those documents in their proper light and meaning, they would not have come to the erroneous conclusions they reached: i.e., the non-existence of any Jewish title of sovereignty over the land of Palestine or of any unconditional right possessed by all Jews to enter Palestine. Rather than focusing a spotlight on what they called illegal Jewish immigrants, they should have excoriated the British Government for enacting laws and executing a policy that illegally restricted Jewish immigration contrary to the superior law of the Mandate.

Of all the acts of British sabotage of the Mandate none caused greater damage and suffering to the Jewish People than the British stifling of Jewish immigration into Palestine. As already noted, the Jewish State would have arisen much sooner had the free entry of Jews been permitted, in accordance with the right of return as recognized in Article 6 of the Mandate. The Holocaust would not have taken on the same enormous dimensions as it did. The partition of the Land of Israel – at least in Cisjordanian Palestine – would have been prevented. Unfortunately, the British received unexpected assistance from weak Zionist leadership who foolishly placed their naive trust in the goodwill of the British, who had reneged on their earlier commitments to the Jewish People. It is easy to see now with hindsight that the British sabotage of the Mandate could never have happened had Weizmann and his colleagues taken the necessary steps to implement the Trietsch-Nordau proposals on immigration in 1919-1920, when the moment was propitious and the British had not yet solidified their restrictive immigration policy in the way it evolved during the three decades of

---

[35] The Report was published by His Majesty's Stationery Office, London, Command 6808, Miscellaneous No. 8 (1946).

their misrule in Palestine. The vision of a mass relocation of Jews to Palestine as proposed by Trietsch and Nordau was also the original vision of Herzl. This vision was subsequently adopted by Jabotinsky in 1936 when there no longer existed a possibility to realize such a vision under the British administration of the country. It required the establishment of the independent Jewish State for that vision to finally become a reality for Jews living in foreign lands under conditions of great distress.

Notwithstanding the British sabotage of the Mandate, which should forever be remembered as an act of national perfidy, for which proper atonement has still never been made or even deemed necessary, the gratitude of the Jewish People should not be withheld from two noble British leaders, Arthur James Balfour and David Lloyd George, who had the foresight, wisdom and courage to support the Zionist aim of a Jewish State at a critical moment. They faltered badly in 1921 and 1922 by supporting or, in any case, not opposing the provisional detachment of Transjordan from the Jewish National Home and their disappointing acceptance of the Churchill White Paper which significantly changed the meaning of the Balfour Declaration to the great detriment of Zionism even though they had no active role in the drafting and formulation of that White Paper. As regards the detachment of Transjordan, that was more the brainchild and work of Curzon, Churchill, Lawrence, Shuckburgh, Young and Samuel. Even on this point, the most important steps which led ultimately to an independent Arab Government in Transjordan that was incompatible with the original vision of the Balfour Declaration and the Mandate were taken in the twilight years of Lloyd George and Balfour and after they had left office. In any event, what occurred illegally in Transjordan cannot wholly detract from their immense role in laying the international political and legal groundwork for the eventual establishment of an independent Jewish State, though only in part of the Jewish National Home. The British failure to properly implement the terms of the Mandate is to be attributed to the work of their successors in office and what they did to undo or overturn the momentous contributions of Lloyd George and Balfour in reconstituting the Jewish State in the Land of Israel.

*Chapter 15*

# Weizmann's Deficient Leadership and the Duplicity of Curzon, Samuel and Churchill

Those British figures who were chiefly responsible for scuttling the Mandate for Palestine and in the process of doing so, obfuscating Jewish legal rights and title of sovereignty to all of the country are among the most revered personages in British and Zionist history, specifically George Nathaniel Curzon, Herbert Samuel and Winston Churchill.

Curzon was a leading member in Prime Minister Lloyd George's Imperial War Cabinet, who became Foreign Secretary on October 24, 1919 upon the retirement of the great Christian Zionist advocate, Arthur James Balfour. He was placed in charge of Palestine's affairs during the critical formative years of the Mandate, when its terms were still being formulated. He displayed a very hostile attitude to the Jewish People and to Zionism. He detested with his whole being the idea of creating a "Hebrew State", as he put it, and did his utmost to weaken and dissimulate its legal basis and to slow it down. He was ably aided by his officials who were much less hostile to Jewish Zionist aspirations, notable among whom were Eric Graham Forbes Adam, Robert Vansittart and Hubert Young. What Curzon managed successfully to do was to detrimentally change into ambiguous constructions many of the original clear-cut provisions of the Mandate for Palestine designed to secure its establishment as a Jewish State, which had already been approved earlier by Balfour when he was the minister in charge of overseeing the actual drafting of the Mandate for Palestine.

As already noted *supra*, Lord Curzon, in order to forestall the emergence of a Jewish State, personally saw to it, as Foreign Minister in charge of the Mandate drafting process, that the Jewish agency referred to in Article 4 of the Mandate, which in the first decade of the Mandate's existence was deemed to be the Zionist Organization, was deprived of any administrative role in the Government of Palestine. Preventing Jews from advising or cooperating with the Government of Palestine in administrative matters ran contrary to the preliminary drafts of the Mandate approved in 1919 when Lord Balfour was still the Foreign Secretary in charge of the formulation of the Mandate. Curzon's anti-Zionist and mean-spirited tactic thus prevented an embryonic Jewish Government from ever arising during the three decades of British rule over Palestine.

The earliest indication of the establishment of a Jewish Government for Palestine under British auspices dates back to Foreign Secretary Edward Grey, a member of the Asquith Government, who in reaction to two memoranda submitted by fellow cabinet minister, Herbert Samuel, in January and March 1915 advocating a Jewish State or British Protectorate for Palestine, in expectation of the defeat of the Ottoman Empire in the Great War, suggested to Samuel that the government of the country be vested "in some kind of Council to be established by the Jews.[1]

After David Lloyd George formed a new government in early December 1916, it showed a marked interest in supporting Zionist aspirations, and this, coupled with the impending British conquest of what was unofficially called Turkish Palestine, rendered possible for the first time the realization of Grey's conception of vesting the government of Palestine in a Jewish Council. It is interesting to note that the British then instinctively associated "Palestine" with Jews as the natural inheritors of the country if it were to be liberated from Turkish yoke. During the year 1917, when the British needed world-wide Jewish support for pursuing the war against the Central Powers and, in particular, to justify their planned invasion of Palestine, the idea that a possible Jewish government could emerge under British protection now seemed practical. Such a government as visualized by Grey may have arisen at the very inception of British rule had Chaim Weizmann been prescient enough or strongly determined to head it upon the arrival of General Allenby's forces in Jerusalem.

Already by April 1917, six months before the Balfour Declaration, the British were wedded to the idea of establishing a "Jewish Palestine", a term frequently used by Weizmann and the Zionists in their manifold contacts with British officials. The widespread use of this term inevitably meant a Jewish State and Jewish Government.

To further the plans for the British takeover of Palestine, Prime Minister Lloyd George appointed Sir Mark Sykes in April 1917 to the post of Chief Political Officer on the staff of the Commander-in-Chief of the British Army based in Egypt, then led by General Archibald Murray, who was later replaced by General Allenby after the Turks had briefly checked the British advance into Palestine. Prior to going to Egypt, Sykes was instructed by the Prime Minister and Lord Curzon (then serving as Lord President of the Council), at a meeting held on April 3, 1917 at 10 Downing Street, London, attended also by Sir Maurice Hankey, the secretary of the War Cabinet:[2]

---

[1] Leonard Stein, The Balfour Declaration, The Magnes Press, Jerusalem (1983), p. 110.

[2] Meyer W. Weisgal (General Editor), The Letters and Papers of Chaim Weizmann, Volume VII, Series A, August 1914 – November 1917; edited by Leonard Stein, Israel Universities Press, Jerusalem (1975); Letter 329, Stein's editorial note 6, pg. 351.

> Not [to] prejudice the Zionist movement and the possibility of its development under British auspices. The Prime Minister laid stress on the importance, if possible, of securing the addition of Palestine to the British area, and suggested that Sir Mark Sykes ought not to enter into any political pledges to the Arabs, and particular none in regard to Palestine.

According to the Cabinet note of this meeting,[3] Sir Mark Sykes responded:

> The Arabs probably realised that there was no prospect of their being allowed any control over Palestine.

Armed with these precise instructions that could only be interpreted as meaning that Palestine was to be reserved for the Jewish People under British auspices and not intended for the local Arab population, Sykes met with Weizmann several times, to persuade him to follow him to Egypt within a week to ten days.[4] According to Weizmann's biographer, Jehuda Reinharz, "over the next few weeks Sykes continued to press from Cairo to drop everything and rush to join him". One of the reasons which Sykes gave Weizmann for joining him in Egypt was to make "plans for political action against our advance [into Palestine]".[5] What Sykes meant by "plans for political action" can be deduced from what he told Dr. Moses Gaster, the Sephardi Chief Hakham (Rabbi) of London, on January 30, 1917, as reported by Leonard Stein:[6]

> Assuming that the British invasion of Palestine would before long have made substantial progress, he [Mark Sykes] gave the Zionists a prominent place in his picture of the events which he believed to be imminent. He told Gaster on January 30th [1917] that at his first meeting with Weizmann two days earlier he had insisted, as a matter of urgency, that the Zionists 'should be prepared... to have men on the spot, when the English entered Jerusalem, so as *to take effective part in the administration of at least the Jewish section of the population'* (emphasis added).

Sykes' use of the words "at least" strongly implied the possible administration of Palestine as a whole by Zionist leaders who would already be in the country.

On April 25, 1917 Weizmann met with Lord Robert Cecil, the Acting Foreign Secretary during Balfour's absence in the U.S.A., and discussed the future status

[3] Ibid., p. 351. The Cabinet note cited is found in P.R.O.-Cab. 24/9 (April 3, 1917); see also the book by Jehuda Reinharz, Chaim Weizmann, The Making of a Statesman, New York, Oxford University Press (1993), Volume 2, p. 133.

[4] Reinharz, *op. cit.*, p. 133.

[5] Reinharz, *op. cit.*, p.134.

[6] Leonard Stein, *op. cit.*, p. 329.

of Palestine with him. They agreed that when Weizmann travelled to Egypt and Palestine, "he would go on the clear understanding that he is to work for a Jewish Palestine under a British Protectorate".[7] Even Herbert Samuel advised him very strongly to go to Egypt to work for a "British Palestine" and mobilize Jewish opinion both in and outside Palestine for that purpose. Though Samuel used the expression "British Palestine", it was, at this juncture, interchangeable or synonymous with "Jewish Palestine under British protection". On May 1, 1917, Ronald Graham, the assistant undersecretary of state in the Foreign Office, whose jurisdiction concerned "Zionist affairs" and who was one of the strongest proponents of the Zionist cause, told Weizmann that his presence in Egypt was now essential, according to the message he had received from Aaron Aaronsohn and Mark Sykes.

Despite the urgings of Sykes, Aaronsohn and Samuel and the support of the British Foreign Office that he should join Sykes in Egypt, Weizmann preferred to take the counsel of Charles Prestwich Scott, the Editor of the Manchester Guardian and Weizmann's trusted friend, who told him not to go on "a fool's errand" and "that he would be merely wasting his time were he to go to Egypt".[8]

Scott's counsel to Weizmann was reinforced by Lord Lionel Walter Rothschild who likewise advised Weizmann against going to Egypt since "you are the only man who can keep the Prime Minister up to the mark".[9] This was gratuitous advice, since Lloyd George was already a staunch Zionist who did not need Weizmann to keep him "up to the mark".

In retrospect, there can be little doubt that Weizmann by not going to Egypt and entering Jerusalem with the British army missed a one-time opportunity of setting up a Jewish government apparatus for Palestine, with himself as Provisional Administrator, at the very moment when British officialdom was the most sympathetic to such a development, before attitudes suddenly changed. A Jewish Government, after all, was in broad conformity with the instructions of Lloyd George and Lord Curzon to Sykes "not to prejudice the Zionist movement and its development under British auspices" and "not to enter into any political pledges to the Arabs, and particularly none in regard to Palestine", and was moreover in conformity with Sykes' own thinking on the subject.

In 1917, when Britain needed Zionism to justify its invasion of Palestine in the eyes of the world and bring it under British rule, it is not far-fetched to say that Lloyd George, himself an enthusiastic Christian Zionist whose law firm once represented Herzl in the Uganda Scheme and who told Samuel as early as November 1914 that he "was very keen to see a Jewish state established in

---

[7] The Letters and Papers of Chaim Weizmann, *op. cit.*, Letter 356, p. 375 ff; also Letter 357, p. 378 ff.

[8] Reinharz, *op. cit.*, p. 136 and his footnote 142 on p. 449.

[9] Reinharz, *op. cit.*, p. 137.

Palestine",[10] would likely have agreed to a Jewish Government in Palestine the moment Jerusalem was safely in British hands, had Weizmann whom Lloyd George described rather exaggeratedly as "one of the greatest Hebrews of all time",[11] been on the spot to assume the reigns of government under British protection. An apt comparison to the situation as it could have unfolded, can be made with the Sherifian Emir Feisal, the Arab national leader, who at the very moment British forces under the command of General Allenby were about to occupy Syria on behalf of the Principal Allied Powers, after routing the Turks in battle, immediately entered Damascus to assume the role of Provisional Military Governor of Syria. Weizmann had the identical opportunity to do that in regard to Palestine, but instead chose to listen to the wrong counsel and was not present in the country to implement the "political plans" that Sykes had in mind for Palestine.

In early November 1917, after the Balfour Declaration had already been issued but prior to General Allenby's victorious march into Jerusalem, Weizmann proposed that a Zionist Commission be attached to Allenby's advancing army as an advisory body "in all matters relating to Jews or which may affect the establishment of a National Home for the Jewish People in accordance with the [Balfour] Declaration."[12]

The British Government accepted Weizmann's proposal on January 19, 1918, charging it with some general objectives of a limited, non-controversial nature concerned with establishing friendly relations between Jews and Arabs, forming a link between the British authorities and the Jewish population in Palestine, assisting in relief work and the repatriation of Jewish refugees exiled by the Turks during the war, developing Jewish colonies, reorganizing the Jewish population and reporting upon the possibilities of future Jewish developments in Palestine, including the establishment of a Jewish university. However, no specific administrative role in the government of the country was assigned to the Zionist Commission – significantly, the very function it should have had.

During this period of the still incomplete British takeover of all of Palestine, the British Government may very well have refused such a prominent role for the Zionist Commission, but Weizmann never even bothered to demand it, neither for himself personally nor for the Commission. In fact, he shunned the very idea that the Jews could then govern Palestine in some capacity under General Allenby's military administration.

During the enthusiastic celebrations that took place in England in the cities of London and Manchester following the publication of the Balfour

---

[10] *Encyclopaedia Judaica* (1971), Vol. 11, column 413.

[11] *Encyclopaedia of Zionism and Israel* (1971), Vol. 2, p. 727.

[12] Reinharz, *op. cit.*, p. 222. The quotation is taken from Weizmann's address to the English Zionist Federation, Annual Conference, Feb. 2, 1918. See *The Letters and Papers of Chaim Weizmann*, Volume 1, Series B, August 1898-July 1931, Editor: Barnet Litvinoff, Transaction Books, Rutgers University, New Brunswick, N.J. (1983), Paper 40, p. 175.

Declaration, the idea of creating a Jewish State, which necessarily also implied a Jewish Government, came to the fore. At a large public rally that took place on December 2, 1917 at the London Opera House, Lord Robert Cecil, then the Parliamentary Under-Secretary for Foreign Affairs and one of the high-ranking guest speakers, stated to a cheering crowd:[13]

> Our wish is that Arabian countries shall be for the Arabs, Armenia for the Armenians and Judea for the Jews. Yes, and let us add, if it can be so, let Turkey, real Turkey be for the Turks.

He continued:

> The [British] Empire has always striven to give to all the peoples that make it up the fullest measure of self-government of which they are capable. We have always striven to give all peoples within our bounds complete liberty and equality before the Law. We are adjured to respect the principle of self-administration; but I say that the British Empire was the first organization to teach that principle to the world, and one of the great causes for which we are in this war is to secure to all peoples the right to govern themselves and to work out their own destiny, irrespective of the threats and menaces of their greater neighbour.
>
> One of the greatest steps – in my judgment, in some ways the greatest step – we have taken in carrying out this principle is the recognition of Zionism... It is not only the recognition of a nationality – it is much more than that... It is indeed not the birth of a nation, for the Jewish nation through centuries of oppression and captivity have preserved their sentiment of nationality as few people could; but if it is not the birth of a nation, I believe we may say it is the re-birth of a nation.

It is clear from Lord Cecil's rousing pro-Zionist speech that he viewed the Balfour Declaration as paving the way for a Jewish State with a Jewish Government, based on the principle of self-determination for World Jewry, then numbering about 14 million. Such a prospect represented for Lord Cecil the revival of Jewish nationality in the country he aptly called Judea rather than Palestine. No stronger and more sympathetic support could have been voiced by a high British official of the Foreign Office in favour of Zionism. His words reflected what Lloyd George, Balfour and Sykes also thought at that point in time.

At the same rally where Lord Cecil spoke, another prominent guest speaker

[13] *Great Britain, Palestine and the Jews: Jewry's Celebration of its National Charter*, George H. Doran Company, New York (1918), p. 39 ff.

was Dr. Moses Gaster who declared that Jews[14] wanted to establish in Palestine an autonomous Jewish Commonwealth in the fullest sense of the word. They wanted Palestine to be Palestine of the Jews and not merely a Palestine for Jews. They wished the land to be again what it was in olden times and what it had been for Jews in their prayers and in their Bible – a land of Israel. The ground must be theirs.

Dr. Gaster, one of the leading figures of British Zionism, was in effect reiterating what Lord Cecil had just said, but in even stronger language. He wanted Palestine to be possessed by the Jews and governed by them to bring about the Jewish State as in the old days of the United Kingdom of Israel and Judah and, later, of Judea.

Also speaking at this rally was Israel Zangwill, a celebrated literary figure and President of the Jewish Territorial Organization. He hailed the Balfour Declaration as a pro-Jewish manifesto and made the following interesting suggestion about the name of the Jewish national home:

> To diminish the risks of confusion, let Palestine be called what Lord Robert Cecil called it, Judaea, and let the Jews who adopt its citizenship be called Judeans. Then all the others [outside Judea] will remain as before, Jews – Jews of whatever political allegiance they choose. A national home in Palestine – freedom and equal rights everywhere else; here surely is a platform that can unite all Israel, and so far as I can see it is uniting them (Zangwill was here referring to the stipulation in the Balfour Declaration that "nothing shall be done which might prejudice the rights and political status enjoyed by Jews in any other country".)

Weizmann spoke only briefly at the London rally, and made no controversial pronouncement. He merely stated that he hoped that the present generation of Jews would be worthy of "the greatest responsibility of the last 2,000 years"[15] that has been placed on their shoulders by the Balfour Declaration. He spoke again a week later at Manchester, at a new public demonstration in further celebration of that Declaration. Here he did touch on matters of great substance, but in a manner calculated to dampen the general enthusiasm. He warned his listeners not to expect an immediate Jewish State, having a Jewish Government. He dismissed out of hand the prospect of the mass immigration of Jews into Palestine and spoke about "the difficult task of colonizing and rejuvenating the old country". He summed up his thoughts in the following words:[16]

> An ancient and experienced people will prove their wisdom by restraining themselves at the right time. Let us remember that the

[14] *Ibid.*, p. 48 ff.

[15] *Ibid.*, p. 59.

[16] *Ibid.*, p. 70 ff.

> building of Palestine is a slow, gradual and laborious process, which will tax heavily our resources and our patience. Catchwords such as "We must have a Jewish state at once" will do us a great deal of harm. We cannot have masses of immigrants streaming into Palestine before the country is ready to receive them. I am fearing such a contingency more than any opposition which is at present shown to Zionism. We must never be afraid of our opponents. I am frightened sometimes by the zeal of some of our friends.

Here then was Weizmann dashing the expectant hope stirred up by the Balfour Declaration for the immediate establishment of a Jewish State and Government in Palestine at the most propitious time, in the year 1917, when the British Government was most ready to accommodate Jewish national aspirations, as evidenced by Lord Cecil's speech. Despite all the economic hardship that mass Jewish immigration might well have entailed, subsequent Israeli experience indicates that it would have been by far preferable to have the land inundated with Jews whatever the hardship, in order to realize as soon as possible the establishment of an autonomous Jewish State. In retrospect, it may be added that such a step would have, at least in large part, forestalled the satanic plans to annihilate the Jews of Europe under the Hitler regime that sprang up as a consequence of the disintegration of the German Empire and resulting failure of democracy in the Weimar Republic.

The rest of the Jewish world would have in time been persuaded to aid the fledgling Jewish State and helped provide the economic infrastructure for that state to survive and grow. With a large settled Jewish population, more industrial and other business activity would have been encouraged, but without such a population base, enterprise of that sort could not reasonably have been expected to develop. Weizmann's go-slow approach was the wrong prescription for realizing the aim of Zionism. It clashed with Herzlian Zionism, nor was it in accord even with what the British Government had already agreed to – the establishment of Palestine as a Jewish country as soon as the Jews took advantage of the opportunity afforded them by the Balfour Declaration. Delay was fatal, since British positions and attitudes were prone to change, as developments soon proved to be the case.

Weizmann should have appreciated that the only feasible means for achieving a Jewish State in the shortest possible time was through the massive immigration of Jews to Palestine. However, because he was unduly influenced by his mentor, Ahad Ha'Am, who advised against the immediate Jewish large-scale settlement of Palestine, he preferred, as he stated, "a slow, gradual and laborious process". This was a disastrous misjudgment which almost prevented the eventual emergence of a Jewish State, since Britain, once it was safely ensconced in Palestine after routing the Turks, reneged on its undertaking to work for a Jewish State. It is also ironic that Weizmann opposed the mass immigration of Jews to Palestine since at that precise moment in history a mass migration of Jews was actually taking place to the United States, where Jews were still permitted to enter freely without many restrictions. Between 1880 and 1925, almost two and a half million Jews emigrated to the United States from Eastern Europe. In one five-year period alone, from 1904 to 1908, over six hundred thousand actually came.[17] Had a reasonable fraction of these two and a half million Jews been encouraged to come to Palestine to establish the Jewish National Home, a *de facto* Jewish State could have arisen almost immediately, as Max Nordau and Davis Trietsch had indeed proposed. In not following the right course, Weizmann's delay set Zionism back for many decades.

In his travels as head of the Zionist Commission, he foolishly disavowed any intention to bring about an immediate Jewish State and government. At a meeting in Cairo, he assured members of the "Palestine Committee of Moslems and Christians" that the Zionist Commission "did not intend to control the administration or plan to establish a Jewish state immediately after the war".[18] Upon arriving in Palestine, in early April 1918, Weizmann met with General Allenby and other British officers. In these meetings he stressed that the Zionists "did not seek immediately to establish a Jewish government in Palestine", sometimes even omitting the qualifying word "immediately".[19] In a meeting with important Moslem leaders in Jerusalem on April 11, 1918, he reiterated "that it was not his aim to establish a Jewish state or Jewish government at the end of the war."[20] He preferred "a British administration under which Jews and Arabs could work harmoniously for the development of the country."[21] Finally, in a meeting with Emir Feisal on June 4, 1918, at Wadi Waheida, near Ma'an, "Weizmann told him that the Jews did not propose to set up a government of their own, but wished to work, under British protection, to colonize and develop Palestine without encroaching on any legitimate interests".[22]

The inescapable conclusion of Weizmann's pronouncements was that at a critical time when the liberation of Palestine from Ottoman Turkey was taking place before his very eyes, he did not meet the challenge of trying to implement the primary aim of Zionism to bring about as soon as possible Jewish administrative control over Palestine in pursuit of a *de facto* Jewish State. Rather than press for the paramount Zionist aim, as Herzl would likely have done had he been alive, Weizmann decided not to hurry vital things along, thus revealing a lack of strong leadership qualities. He showed too much deference and trust in British good will and intentions, not fully appreciating the perfidious anti-Jewish character of many of the British officials on the spot in Palestine who displayed their hostility and reluctance to implement the policy of the

---

[17] *Encyclopaedia Judaica* (1971), Vol. 15, col. 1608.

[18] Reinharz, *op. cit.*, p. 234.

[19] Reinharz, *op. cit.*, p. 246.

[20] Reinharz, *op. cit.*, p. 248.

[21] Reinharz, *op. cit.*, p. 250.

[22] Reinharz, *op. cit.*, p. 255.

Balfour Declaration and who actually favoured the local Arab inhabitants in their vociferous opposition to that policy. Weizmann contented himself with the honours he received from the same British representatives on visiting Palestine. He refused to make the country his real base of operations for the advancement of Zionism, preferring to do so from London. It would have been much more beneficial for the movement for him to have been stationed in Jerusalem at least when the new British administration was being established. Weizmann thus squandered the only chance that ever presented itself to set up a Jewish administration under British military auspices during the critical year of 1917 when basic decisions were being made and implemented. It is true that such an administration may have been blocked by the British, but had Weizmann been more assertive on playing an administrative role, the British, who at this time still needed Zionist support to ward off its rivals, France and Italy, from participating in the government of Palestine, may have acquiesced in this demand, in the same way, as already noted, they allowed Feisal in October 1918 to rule in Syria under the cover of General Allenby's military administration. Had Weizmann assumed an administrative role instead of returning to England, he may have avoided the subsequent British sabotage of the Jewish National Home.

Much praise has been heaped on Weizmann as the leader of the Zionist Movement and for his important role in securing the Balfour Declaration. That praise must, however, be tempered because of the unwise restraint and caution he displayed in not pursuing the achievable goal of establishing a Jewish State and government as soon as possible through mass immigration. In light of the timidity he evinced in this regard, it is fair to conclude that Zionism would have fared much better in the years following the Balfour Declaration had a bolder and less hesitant leader been in charge. Weizmann scorned and feared the zealous Jews who demanded the prompt implementation of the Balfour Declaration. During the next thirty years of British administration the broken promises of the British Government proved that the latter were entirely right and Weizmann entirely wrong.

In regard to Lord Curzon, it is interesting to note that he, too, in April 1917 endorsed the idea that Palestine was to be reserved for the Jewish People rather than placed under Arab control. However, a short time later, he radically changed his opinion and did his utmost when he became Foreign Minister to water down the Zionist character of the Mandate for Palestine.

Despite Curzon's best attempts to prevent a Jewish state from being seen as the real and most important objective of the Mandate for Palestine, he did not fully succeed in his evil design. That job was left to two others, who worked in tandem at the time, Herbert Samuel and Winston Churchill, though it was Samuel who concocted the plan and got Churchill's endorsement. The latter was put in charge of Palestine's affairs, replacing Lord Curzon, when jurisdiction over the affairs of Palestine, Mesopotamia and Aden was removed from the Foreign Office and transferred to a Middle East Department in the Colonial Office by virtue of a Cabinet decision on February 14, 1921 endorsing the recommendations of an interdepartmental committee to that effect.[23]

The nefarious work begun by Curzon was ironically taken over and completed by the erstwhile Zionist, Herbert Samuel, who in 1918 and 1919 worked hand in glove with Chaim Weizmann in London in furthering the cause of Zionism. He was the head of the committee which had prepared the Zionist proposals submitted to the Allied Council of Ten on February 27, 1919 at the Paris Peace Conference. These proposals, with which Samuel generally identified at the time, envisioned the establishment of the Jewish National Home as leading ultimately to "an autonomous Commonwealth", i.e., a Jewish State whose borders encompassed not only Transjordan up to the Hedjaz Railway, but also all of what is today Southern Lebanon up to Sidon, and embraced Western Bashan (Hauran), north of the Yarmuk, thus extending to the Litani River and covering all of the Golan. In his role as a Zionist emissary, Samuel even visited Ronald Graham, Assistant Under-Secretary in the Foreign Office, on July 2, 1919 to complain about the attitude of the British military authorities who took every opportunity, he said, to injure Zionist interests,[24] citing, in particular,

---

[23] The idea for the creation of a separate Middle Eastern Department in the Foreign Office (originally called the Eastern Department) was first raised by Hubert Young in his Memorandum of May 17, 1920. Curzon accepted Young's recommendations and prepared a memorandum for circulation to the Cabinet advising its creation. See *Documents on British Foreign Policy*, First Series, Volume XIII, Document No. 250, p. 269. On August 20, 1920, at a meeting of the Cabinet Finance Committee, Churchill recommended setting up a Department for Middle Eastern Affairs "to coordinate Government policy in Palestine, Mesopotamia and Arabia, and to effect substantial cuts in military expenditure throughout the Middle East". See Martin Gilbert's biography of *Winston S. Churchill*, Vol. IV, p. 507. On December 31, 1920, Churchill's suggestion was accepted by the full Cabinet. This put an end to the unwieldy situation in which various responsibilities over Middle Eastern territories that were not independent states were divided among four separate ministries: the War Office, the India Office, the Colonial Office and the Foreign Office. The new set-up consolidated these responsibilities under a single Minister. On New Year's Day 1921, Lloyd George asked Churchill, serving then as War and Air Secretary, to succeed the incumbent Colonial Secretary, Lord Alfred Milner, who had decided to leave government service. On January 4, 1921 Churchill accepted the new position offered him. An interdepartmental committee chaired by James Masterton Smith was appointed by the Prime Minister on January 10, 1921 to determine the precise nature of Churchill's new Middle-East responsibilities. Its recommendations were endorsed by the Cabinet on February 14, 1921 and on that very night, Churchill moved from the War Office to the Colonial Office and received the Seals of his new office, which marked his formal investiture as Colonial Secretary.

[24] See the letter by Sir Ronald Graham to Lord Curzon, reporting on Herbert Samuel's and Chaim Weizmann's complaints against the administration in Palestine, July 2, 1919. Reprinted in *The Rise of Israel*, Volume 11, Document 30, pp. 100-05. See also Bernard Wasserstein's book, *The British in Palestine: The Mandatory Government and the Arab-Jewish Conflict 1917-1929*, London, Royal Historical Society (1978), p. 50.

Colonel Ronald Storrs, then the Military Governor of Jerusalem. He traveled to San Remo, Italy, together with Weizmann and Sokolow, where the peace conference was taking place, to help press the Zionist case, though he did not actually attend the two sessions of the Allied Supreme Council that determined the future of Turkey's former territories in the Middle East. Considering all the different opinions and positions he adopted on Zionism, particularly about the establishment of a Jewish State and the delineation of its borders, from the time he served in Liberal Prime Minister Herbert Asquith's Government[25] until the rebirth of the State of Israel, he was – it must be concluded – a great poseur who held insincere and contradictory beliefs, without regard to true principles or loyalty. He may also be described not unfairly as a Zionist apostate or renegade. Judged solely by his record as High Commissioner for Palestine during a 5-year period in which he bent over backwards to curry favour with the Arabs of the country while shunning his Zionist past, he, more than any other person, wrecked beyond repair the implementation of the Mandate for Palestine and prevented the realization of its principal objective: creating an

[25] Herbert Louis Samuel, the first professing Jew to sit in a British Cabinet, held the following positions beginning in 1909 during Herbert Henry Asquith's eight-year tenure as Prime Minister (1908-1916): Chancellor of the Duchy of Lancaster, Postmaster General, President of the Local Government Board and Secretary of State for Home Affairs. In November 1914, after Turkey entered the Great War on the side of the Central Powers (October 30, 1914), he was suddenly drawn to the cause of Zionism that had never before attracted him "because the prospects of any practical outcome had seemed so remote". He now sensed for the first time that the Zionist aim of establishing a Jewish State in Palestine would become a possibility at the conclusion of the War. He discussed the subject with Foreign Secretary Edward Grey on November 11, 1914 and then prepared a memorandum in January 1915 on the future of Palestine in the event of the break-up of the Turkish Empire in Asia, which he circulated amongst some members of the Cabinet. Two months later, he revised his memorandum and this time had it circulated to all members of the Cabinet. Regarding the establishment of a Jewish State in Palestine, he stated that the time was not ripe for such a step because the Jews were then outnumbered by Arabs in a ratio of about 1:6. His initial ardour in November 1914 gave way to great pessimism for he now thought *it would be necessary to wait at least a century to allow the Jewish population to grow into a majority and be well settled in the land before a Jewish State could be established. To create the State sooner than that*, he incomprehensibly concluded, *would "throw back its actual realization for many centuries more*". In the meantime, he advocated that Palestine be made into a British Protectorate as the best alternative to a Jewish State. Samuel's initial proposal regarding the Jewish State drew a positive response from Grey. Later Grey even suggested that the future government of Palestine be placed in the hands of a Jewish Council. The proposal also elicited a sympathetic reaction from the Chancellor of the Exchequer David Lloyd George, as well as from another minister, Lord Haldane. However, Prime Minister Asquith thought that the idea of a Jewish State was a wild fantasy and dismissed it peremptorily. See *The Rise of Israel*, Vol. 6, Documents 10-20, pp. 32-65. See also Leonard Stein, *The Balfour Declaration*, pp. 103-116.

embryonic Jewish State east and west of the Jordan during the period of British administration. Among other "accomplishments" in which he played a major role, if not the most significant role, were changing the original meaning of the Balfour Declaration, restricting Jewish immigration to Palestine and greatly reducing the size of the Jewish National Home, to include no more than Cisjordan.

Samuel's undermining of what was the true intent of the Mandate for Palestine was recorded in the very harmful "Churchill" White Paper dated June 3, 1922 and published on July 1, 1922. It was the most significant of all the Statements of Policy issued by the British Government because it set the path for everything that followed afterwards in Palestine. Its most notorious effect was to radically re-define the term "Jewish National Home" to mean not an eventual independent Jewish State, but simply a cultural or spiritual center for the Jewish People. Samuel wrote the White Paper with the blessing and connivance of Winston Churchill and his top staff in the Colonial Office. He was largely responsible for persuading Churchill that the White Paper ought to be issued.[26] This White Paper was accepted under ominous circumstances by the official Zionist leadership on a take-it-or-leave-it basis. On this point, it suffices to quote the martyred Italian Zionist pioneer leader, Enzo Sereni, who wrote a brief historical survey of Palestine and stated as follows:[27]

> Under enormous political pressure and the threat that the Mandate would not otherwise be ratified, the Zionist Organization accepted the White Paper of Churchill-Samuel as a foundation for its future policy (June 19, 1922).

It was the 1922 White Paper which was really the turning point for the ultimate failure and downfall of the Mandate, which ruined the original British plan of 1917, reiterated in 1920 at the San Remo Peace Conference, to establish an independent Jewish State under their tutelage, though Balfour would have preferred the Americans assuming this role. Everything thereafter became muddled and unclear, and caused endless disputes as to what was really intended by the Mandate for Palestine. The reason is simple enough. After publication of this White Paper, which interpreted the meaning of the Mandate even before

[26] *The Rise of Israel*, Volume 22, Document 3, p. 301. In testimony given by Leonard Stein at the sitting of the Palestine Royal Commission on December 31, 1936, his exact remarks on the authorship of the 1922 White Paper were: "... as is well-known, one of the authors, or at any rate, one of the main instigators, of the White Paper, as he said himself – there is no secret about it – was Sir Herbert Samuel. He was very largely responsible for causing the White Paper to be issued, for persuading the Secretary of State that the White Paper ought to be issued."

[27] This quotation is found in the book Enzo Sereni edited with R. E. Ashery, entitled *Jews and Arabs in Palestine*, 1936, Hechalutz Press, p. 61a. The date for Zionist acceptance of the White Paper is given elsewhere as June 18, 1922.

its actual confirmation by the League Council, all British Governments which followed over the years implemented not the actual terms of the Mandate for Palestine but Samuel's (and Churchill's) false interpretation as to the precise meaning to be ascribed to the Jewish National Home and in determining what the British responsibilities and obligations under the Mandate were. The latter was a blueprint for a Jewish State, while Samuel's interpretation of the Jewish National Home in the Churchill White Paper negated any such state, despite Churchill's subsequent testimony fifteen years later (March 12, 1937) before the Peel Royal Commission that a Jewish State was not precluded by the definition of the Jewish National Home given by Samuel in the 1922 White Paper. It is instructive to note that both the Passfield White Paper of October 20, 1930 and the MacDonald White Paper of May 17, 1939 were defended by their proponents on the same ground – that they rested squarely upon the Churchill-Samuel Statement of Policy.[28] The MacDonald White Paper of May 17, 1939 said in that regard:

> That Palestine was not to be converted into a Jewish State might be held to be implied in the passage from the Command Paper of 1922 which reads as follows:
>
> "Unauthorized statements have been made to the effect that the purpose in view is to create a wholly Jewish Palestine. Phrases have been used such as that Palestine is to become as Jewish as England is English. His Majesty's Government regard any such expectation as impracticable and have no such aim in view. Nor have they at any time contemplated… the disappearance or the subordination of the Arabic population, language or culture in Palestine…"

The 1939 White Paper continued:

> But this statement has not removed doubts and His Majesty's Government therefore now declare unequivocally that it is not part of their policy that Palestine should become a Jewish State. They would indeed regard it as contrary to their obligations to the Arabs under the Mandate, as well as to the assurances which have been given to the Arab people in the past, that the Arab population of Palestine should be made the subjects of a Jewish State against their will.

The statements in this White Paper that the British government would regard the establishment of Palestine as a Jewish State "as [being] contrary to their obligations to the Arabs under the Mandate, as well as to the assurances which have been given to the Arab people in the past", thus making them "the subjects

---

[28] As regards the Passfield White Paper, see the remarks of Drummond Shiels in the House of Commons on Nov. 17, 1930.

of a Jewish State against their will", were actually taken from the general tenor of the Peel Royal Commission Report. According to the Report, the Mandatory had undertaken "general and positive obligations" towards the Arabs that were implicit in the first Recital of the Preamble of the Mandate and in the first paragraph of Article 22 of the Covenant. However, as has been repeatedly stressed in this book, there were no such obligations ever imposed upon Britain under the Mandate for Palestine in favour of the Arabs as a national entity, either explicitly or implicitly. Nor were any *legally valid assurances* given to the Arab people in the past in regard to Palestine, of the type mentioned in the 1939 White Paper. On the contrary, it was for the sole benefit of the Jewish People that Britain undertook to execute obligations of an international character which inevitably meant a Jewish State in which Arabs, like anyone else, could be law-abiding residents or citizens.

Both the 1922 and 1939 White Papers denounced the use of the phrase "Jewish Palestine", which implied a Jewish State and Jewish Government. It will be recalled that this term had been used widely by Weizmann in 1917, both before and after the Balfour Declaration, when plans were being drawn up by both the Prime Minister and Foreign Minister in conjunction with Zionist leaders in support of Zionism under British auspices. Weizmann would never have spoken so freely about creating a "Jewish Palestine" when he met British officials, had they expressed any relevant reservations. It was only with the publication of the 1922 White Paper that Britain formally disassociated itself from what this term implied, which greatly undermined the meaning of the Balfour Declaration. As regards the other so-called "unauthorized statement" mentioned in both White Papers to the effect that "Palestine is to become as Jewish as England is English", this statement was actually uttered by Chaim Weizmann when he appeared before the Allied Supreme Council on February 27, 1919 to present the Zionist Proposals for Palestine's future government, together with Nahum Sokolow, Menachem Ussishkin and André Spire.

In his Political Report to the 12th Zionist Congress held in September 1921 at Carlsbad, Bohemia (today called Karlovy Vary in the Czech Republic), Weizmann recounted what he had said at the 1919 Paris Peace Conference in the following words:[29]

---

[29] *The Rise of Israel*, Volume 8, Document 57, p. 177. Those present at the session of the Paris Peace Conference on February 27, 1919 who stayed to hear the Zionist case were A. J. Balfour and Lord Alfred Milner, representing Britain; André Tardieu and Stéphen Pichon for France; Robert Lansing and Henry White for the U.S.; Baron Sidney Sonnino for Italy; and a Japanese representative. See also *Palestine: A Study of Jewish, Arab and British Policies*, ESCO Foundation for Palestine, Inc., Volume 1, pp. 102, 162-163, where a note is added that the phrase "as Jewish as England is English" was anticipated in Herbert Sidebotham's proposed formulation of the Balfour Declaration, whose merits were discussed by the Political Committee of the Zionist Organization on July 13, 1917. Sidebotham was a British journalist on the editorial staff of the Manchester Guardian and a devoted friend of Zionism. His text stated: "His Majesty's Government accepts as

> Mr. [Robert] Lansing, the American representative [U.S. Secretary of State, 1915-20], who sat in a corner, and moved his chair further and further as [Sylvain] Levi[30] was speaking, asked me what we meant by a 'Jewish National Home'. This gave me an opportunity. I declared that by a 'Jewish National Home' we meant the creation in Palestine of such conditions as should enable us to establish between 50,000 and 60,000 Jews per annum there, and to settle them on the land. Further, that the conditions should be such that we should be allowed to develop our Institutions, our schools and the Hebrew language – that there should ultimately be such conditions that Palestine should be just as Jewish as America is American and England is English. Then I asked Lansing if I had made my point clear. He said: 'Perfectly.' Mr. Balfour was very pleased, so were the Italian representatives.

Weizmann reiterated the same remarks in a letter he wrote to Churchill in July 1921, but which he never sent:[31]

> I have been blamed for saying that what we want is a state in Palestine that is Jewish as England is English. I will so far amend that as to say that we want a Palestine that is Jewish in the sense that Great Britain is English, but that is the irreducible bedrock of our demands.

In light of Weizmann's well-publicized belief that the Balfour Declaration meant that a future Palestine would one day be as Jewish as Great Britain was predominantly English, it is obvious that Samuel, in writing the 1922 White Paper, was attacking Weizmann when he called that interpretation of the Balfour Declaration "exaggerated", "unauthorized" and "impracticable". But Weizmann was right to believe that was the actual meaning to be attributed to the Balfour Declaration and it was Samuel with the willing connivance of Churchill who changed the meaning of the Jewish National Home in the 1922 White Paper to being not a Jewish State but merely a cultural or spiritual center for Jews. That is why the 1939 White Paper was able to impute to the 1922 White Paper the idea that Britain never intended to establish a Jewish State, even

---

one of the chief aims of the war, the reconstitution of an integral Palestine as a Jewish State and as a National Home for the Jewish People. By a Jewish State is meant a state composed not only of Jews, but one whose dominant national character, after the realization of the hopes of its founders, shall be as Jewish as the dominant national character of England is English, of Canada, Canadian, and of Australia, Australian. Religious equality shall always be fundamental to the laws of this state." *Ibid.*, p. 102.

[30] A French Jew who opposed the Zionist program for Palestine because it ran counter to French interests in the Middle East.

[31] Quoted in *A Nation Reborn*, by Richard H.S. Crossman, Athenum Publishers, New York, 1960, pp. 37 and 157.

though it cautiously said that the Churchill-Samuel Statement did not entirely remove all doubts about that point.

Had the authors of the 1939 White Paper consulted a memorandum of November 7, 1921 written by John Shuckburgh, the head of the Middle East Department in the Colonial Office, not the slightest doubt would have existed in their minds about what was meant by the 1922 White Paper. In this Memorandum which Shuckburgh sent to Churchill, it was stated:[32]

> I do not know what may have been the original intention, but it was certainly the object of Sir H. Samuel and the Secretary of State [Churchill] to make it clear that a Jewish State was just what we did not mean. It is clearly useless for us to endeavour to lead Doctor Weizmann in one direction and to reconcile him to a more limited view of the Balfour pledge, if he is told quite a different story by the head of the Government. Nothing but confusion can result if His Majesty's Government do not speak with a single voice.

Shuckburgh's memorandum reveals in a shocking manner exactly what Churchill and Samuel were doing – apparently on their own initiative – they were acting contrary to what "the head of the Government" was telling Weizmann about the meaning of the Balfour Declaration. For Churchill and Samuel, the "Balfour pledge", as Shuckburgh called it, did not mean a Jewish State, but for the Prime Minister that is exactly what it did mean. It appears, therefore, that Churchill and Samuel were implementing a new British policy on Palestine, independent of the intention of the Prime Minister.

The 1939 Munich-like White Paper (that is how Churchill, now in the opposition and no longer responsible for Palestine's affairs, described it) was therefore correct in ascribing the origin of the false meaning of the Jewish National Home to the 1922 White Paper. The publication of the White Paper by the Neville Chamberlain Government infuriated Churchill because he wanted to disassociate himself from any responsibility for the utter British failure to properly implement the Mandate which his own Statement of Policy had actually brought about. The precluding or denial of a Jewish State by the 1922 White Paper is further confirmed by the devilish attempt of Churchill's Colonial Office staff to convince Weizmann to explicitly agree to this anti-Zionist document. Moreover, Samuel's own statements made the year before, on March 28, 1921 and June 3, 1921, themselves confirmed that no Jewish Government was intended to be established by the Balfour Declaration to rule over the Muslim and Christian majority. In a meeting with Abdullah in Jerusalem on March 28, 1921 attended by Churchill and Lawrence, that was a continuation of the Middle East Conference

[32] Martin Gilbert's biography of *Winston S. Churchill*, Volume IV, p. 638, and *Companion Volume* IV, Part 3, p. 1662.

begun in Cairo, Samuel explained British policy in Palestine:[33]

> There was no question of setting up a Jewish Government there... The Mandate embodied the terms of the Balfour Declaration in which two distinct promises were made – one to the Jews and the other to the Arabs. His Majesty's Government were resolutely determined to fulfill both these promises.

Samuel elaborated more fully on the exact meaning to be given to the Balfour Declaration in a speech delivered at Jerusalem on June 3, 1921. He stated then:[34]

> I turn now to the political situation. I am distressed that the harmony between the creeds and races of Palestine, which I have desired most earnestly to promote, has not yet been fully attained, and I have given anxious thought to the measures that are best calculated to secure it. Let me, in the first instance, refer once more to the unhappy misunderstanding that has existed with reference to the phrase in the Balfour Declaration, "the establishment in Palestine of a national home for the Jewish People". I hear it said in many quarters that the Arab population of Palestine will never agree to their country, their Holy Places and their lands being taken from them and given to strangers: that they will never agree to a Jewish Government being set up to rule over the Moslem and Christian majority. People say that they cannot understand how it is that the British Government, which is famous throughout the world for its justice, could ever have consented to such a policy. I answer that the British Government which does indeed care for justice above all things, has never consented and will never consent to such a policy. That is not the meaning of the Balfour Declaration. It may be that the translation of the English words into Arabic does not convey their real sense. They mean that the Jews, a people who are scattered throughout the world but whose hearts are always turned to Palestine, should be enabled to find here their home, and that some among them within the limits that are fixed by the numbers and interests of the present population should come to Palestine in order to help by their resources and efforts to develop the country to the advantage of all its inhabitants (emphasis added). If any measures are needed to convince the Moslem and Christian population that those principles will be observed in practice and that their rights are really safe, such measures will be taken. For the British Government, the trustee under the mandate for the happiness of the people of Palestine, would never

[33] *The Rise of Israel*, Vol. 13, Document 11, p. 94.

[34] *The Rise of Israel*, Vol. 13, Document 29, p. 261.

> impose upon them a policy which that people had reason to think was contrary to their religious, their political and their economic interests.

As appears from Samuel's aforementioned speeches in Jerusalem, he denied that Britain intended to set up a Jewish Government in Palestine, which he said was not the meaning of the Balfour Declaration. In Samuel's eyes, had a Jewish Government been immediately established when Arabs greatly outnumbered Jews, that would have meant placing a majority under the rule of a minority, contrary to the principles of democracy. On the other hand, if a representative government was established in accordance with those same principles of democracy, an Arab government would have emerged that would have prevented the realization of the Balfour Declaration, itself the actual policy adopted by the British Government to establish a Jewish National Home in Palestine, a policy that had also been approved by its allies, the United States, France, Italy and Japan. Samuel, therefore, was not accurately representing the view of the Government on whose behalf he spoke.

Inasmuch as the Balfour Declaration meant the eventual establishment of an independent Jewish State, as both Balfour and Lloyd George declared, its natural corollary was that a Jewish Government would also come into being. The way this would be brought about as originally foreseen by the framers of the Balfour Declaration was through a gradual process, to take place during a transitional period, whereby fifty to sixty thousand Jews would immigrate each year into Palestine, as Weizmann himself explicitly stated at the Paris Peace Conference on February 27, 1919, until they became a secure majority. At that point an independent Jewish State could be established with a Jewish Government. This, indeed, was the meaning of the Balfour Declaration, which Samuel preferred not to disclose to the Arabs of Palestine for fear of arousing even greater hostility to the policy of the Jewish National Home. Samuel was therefore telling the Arabs a half-truth when he ruled out a Jewish Government. His words were valid only for the moment, but not the future, when the Jews would become the majority in Palestine and establish an independent state with their own government, as in fact actually happened in only a part of the country.

It should be noted that had a Jewish Government been established immediately, in 1917, contrary to democratic norms but in accordance with the ultimate meaning of the Balfour Declaration, the transitional period needed to achieve the Jewish majority would have been considerably shortened. With an existing Jewish Government, Jewish immigration could have been accelerated and not made subject to various restrictions which the British Government imposed in order to allay the Arab fear of a Jewish takeover of the country.

In his speech of June 3, 1921, Samuel set forth the following points about Jewish immigration:[35]

---

[35] *The Rise of Israel*, Volume13, Document 29, p. 260.

> 1. its extent must be proportional to the "employment" available in the country; employment was defined as "new work and work of a permanent character";
> 2. all Jewish immigration to the country was to be suspended pending a review of the situation;
> 3. rules for the admission of Jews to Palestine were laid down, establishing five different classes of persons who were allowed to enter. The enforcement of these rules was in the hands of British consuls and of the Immigration and Travel Department of the Government of Palestine. All new arrivals who were "tainted with the pernicious doctrines of Bolshevism" were to be expelled forthwith from the country;
> 4. "the conditions of Palestine", Samuel said, were "such as not to permit anything in the nature of a mass immigration", an opinion shared by Weizmann and Ahad Ha'Am.

Samuel's remarks caused a severe and bitter reaction among Jews. Arthur Ruppin, considered the most moderate of Zionists who founded the Brit Shalom (Peace Association) Movement in 1925 that worked to establish a bi-national state in the whole of Palestine, made the following entry in his diary the day after Samuel's speech (June 4, 1921):[36]

> Since 1 May [1921] our situation in Palestine has grown very much worse. Herbert Samuel, who used to be so calm and self-assured, is no longer the same. He has lost his confidence and, I fear, his belief in the possibility of realizing the Zionist idea. While he used to believe that Arab opposition to Zionism was limited to the small upper class, he now believes that the entire Arab people is hostile to Zionism... He now believes that he can calm the Arabs by making concessions to them, and he offered them the prospect of enlarging the advisory council and restricting Jewish immigration. While this did not appease the Arabs, it allowed them to see his weakness and encouraged them to make further demands. They are now quite openly demanding his resignation. On the other hand, the Jews have been extremely embittered by the prohibition on immigration, which has so far resulted in many hundreds of Jewish immigrants being sent back from Palestine to Trieste. Herbert Samuel, who was a sort of God to the Jews in Palestine only yesterday, has now become a traitor to the Jewish cause in their eyes. I do not think that he will be able to hold out much longer between Scylla and Charybdis [this refers to a person who, trying to avoid one danger, encounters another, i.e., navigating between two hazardous alternatives – H.G.]. He will have to go, and the Jewish High

[36] Arthur Ruppin, *Memoirs, Diaries, Letters*, edited by Alex Bein. Published by Weidenfeld & Nicolson, London (1971), pp. 191-192.

Commissioner will soon belong to history 'and legend'...

The Jewish Chronicle of June 10, 1921 called Samuel's speech one of the blackest instances of political betrayal. Dr. Montague David Eder told the Zionist Executive it was similar to a speech to the Arabs that could have been entitled the "Jewish Peril in Palestine". As a leading British psychoanalyst and physician and devoted Zionist leader, Dr. Eder's assessment was correct and proven by the content of Samuel's speech and by subsequent developments which witnessed British perfidy.

Weizmann, too, was greatly vexed by Samuel's speech, deploring in private Samuel's interpretation of the Balfour Declaration in which he used as a criterion the religious, political and economic interests of the existing Arab population in Palestine to fix the amount of Jewish immigration that could be permitted. When Samuel's interpretation was coupled with his other proposal to establish representative institutions in Palestine, which would have resulted in a preponderance of Arab members having authority over the Jewish National Home, the latter would then be transformed into an Arab National Home, said Weizmann. He viewed Samuel's entire speech as a gesture to propitiate or appease the Arabs, which "whittles down the Balfour promise to nothing".[37] He even thought of trying to get Samuel replaced by General George MacDonogh, a former Director of Military Intelligence and a supporter of Zionism. However, in the end he balked at doing so, because he thought that causing Samuel to resign would at the same time fatally hurt the cause of Zionism, so he decided to defend him from further Zionist criticism, which only demonstrated Weizmann's bad judgment. Nevertheless, more than a month later he told Churchill at a meeting held in Lord Balfour's house on July 22, 1921 attended also by Lloyd George and others, that Samuel's speech "was a negation of the Balfour Declaration", since "the Declaration meant an ultimate Jewish majority – and this speech would never permit such a majority to eventuate".[38] Churchill demurred at this interpretation of Samuel's speech, according to the notes of Colonel Richard Meinertzhagen. At this point in the conversation, Weizmann was assured by both Lloyd George and Balfour that by the Declaration they had always meant an eventual Jewish State. Lloyd George told Churchill not to give representative Government to Palestine and advised Weizmann "to do a lot of propaganda. Samuel is rather weak," he said.[39]

---

[37] *A Nation Reborn* by Richard H.S. Crossman, p. 156.

[38] Notes on the conversation held at Balfour's house on July 22, 1921 are found in Richard Meinertzhagen's Diary Entry for that date. *Middle East Diary*, Thomas Yoseloff Publisher, New York (1960), pp. 103-104.

[39] Ibid., p. 105. In an earlier diary entry of July 5, 1921, Meinertzhagen wrote: "Sir Herbert Samuel has been weak. The moment the Jaffa rioting broke out, he and his staff seem to have been hypnotized by the danger and everything was done to placate the Arabs. Immigration was stopped, elective assemblies were discussed, whereas what the Arab wanted was good sound punishment for

Meinertzhagen's account of what was said at this high-level meeting is corroborated by Weizmann's own account which he set down in two separate letters he sent, one to Asher Ginsberg (Ahad Ha'Am) on July 30, 1921 and the other to Wyndham Deedes on July 31, 1921. In the letter to Ginsberg he wrote:[40]

> The conference I mentioned to you has taken place. We were able to get little truth out of Churchill. He supported the official views and everything said by Samuel, whom he quoted constantly. *Samuel's speech* [of June 3, 1921] *was discussed first of all. I pointed out that the speech was a repudiation of the Balfour Declaration.* Churchill defended the speech. Lloyd George and Balfour admitted that the speech was unfortunate and that they had always had a Jewish State in mind. This greatly astonished Churchill. He admitted that 9/10 of Englishmen in Palestine are against Zionism and that a section of the Jews are also against it. He further emphasized that it was essential to give Palestine an Elective Assembly, which Lloyd George opposed. It is obvious that Lloyd George does not respect Churchill too much… *Lloyd George remarked several times that Samuel is cowardly and weak, and that he knows him only too well.*
>
> …Everything depends on what will be done *by Samuel, who keeps*

breaking the peace and killing Jews. The Arab is fast learning that he can intimidate a British Administration. Samuel has not been able to stand up to the solid block of anti-Zionist feeling among his military advisers and civil subordinates". *Ibid.*, pp. 101-02. Meinertzhagen in another diary entry of August 4, 1921, quotes Jan Christiaan Smuts as saying that Samuel was "hopelessly weak". *Ibid.*, p. 108. In the same entry he noted that Samuel "defined the Balfour Declaration in language which watered that document down to such an extent as to make it meaningless". However, Meinertzhagen saw Samuel in a completely different light long after he retired as High Commissioner for Palestine. In an editorial note in his Middle East Diary, he called him "one of the best administrators which mandated Palestine had. Being a Jew, he naturally sympathized with the National Home, but on every occasion observed strict fairness, often slightly leaning against his own people. His was an extremely difficult position, but was carried out with success". He added: "Many critics of Samuel's Commissionership have referred to his weakness. I have done so myself. What I mistook for weakness was in reality *a determination to be just and impartial.*" *Ibid.*, pp. 133-134. Meinertzhagen's original assessment concerning Samuel's stewardship of Palestine as weak was right and even understated. His subsequent assessment was inconsistent and incorrect. Either the lapse of time or a forgiving spirit made him forget what Samuel did to the Balfour Declaration. Watering down that document to make it meaningless and restricting or suspending Jewish immigration to Palestine were not acts of "strict fairness" or "a determination to be just and impartial". Rather such acts were nothing less than the sabotage of the Balfour Declaration and hence the Mandate, as well as the betrayal of Zionism which he once so ardently espoused. (emphasis added)

[40] *The Letters and Papers of Chaim Weizmann*, Vol. X, Series A, Letter 227, pp. 233-234.

> *making promises to the Arabs.* [Harry] Sacher arrived yesterday, and he had a great deal to say about our *nonentity of a hero* (emphasis added).

In his letter to Deedes, Weizmann reiterated what he had just told Ahad Ha'Am:[41]

> I had an important Conference with the Prime Minister, Mr. Balfour, and Mr. Churchill. We went, I think, right to the root of the whole question. I have asked the gentlemen the following questions: (1) "What did you mean when you gave us the Balfour Declaration?" Mr. Churchill tried to maintain the view expressed in the speech of June 3rd. *My retort was that the interpretation given in the speech is a negation of the Balfour Declaration, to which the Prime Minister and Arthur James Balfour replied that they always meant and understood a Jewish State* (emphasis added)....

In defending Samuel from Weizmann's strong criticism of his speech, Colonial Secretary Churchill was in reality defending his own mistaken and anti-Zionist interpretation of the Balfour Declaration. This he expounded in Jerusalem on March 28, 1921 in replying to the pretensions of a deputation of the Executive Committee of the Arab Palestine Congress that he received at Government House after the Cairo Middle East Conference. In his remarks then, which presaged what Samuel would say on June 3, 1921, he told the deputation:[42]

> I would draw your attention to the second part of the Balfour Declaration, which solemnly and explicitly promises to *the inhabitants of Palestine* the fullest protection of their civil and *political rights* (sic!). I was sorry to hear in the paper which you have just read that you do not regard that promise as of value. It seems to be a vital matter for you, and one to which you should hold most firmly and for the exact fulfillment of which you should claim. If the one promise stands, so does the other; and we shall be judged as we faithfully fulfil both.
>
> After all, the British Government has a view of its own in this matter, and we have right to such a view. Our position in this country is based upon the events of the war, ratified, as they have been, by the treaties signed by the victorious Powers... The position of Great Britain in Palestine is one of trust, but it is also one of right. For the discharge of that trust and for the high purposes we have in view, supreme sacrifices were made by all these soldiers of the British Empire, who gave up their lives and their blood. Therefore I beg you

---

41 *Ibid.*, Letter 228, pp. 234-239.

42 *The Rise of Israel*, Volume 13, Document 27, Appendix 23, p. 248.

> to realize that we shall strive to be loyal to the promises we have made both to the Arab and to the Jewish People, and that we shall fail neither in the one nor in the other.
>
> I would also draw your attention to the very careful and exact nature of the words which were used by Mr. Balfour. He spoke of "the establishment in Palestine of *a* (italics in original) National Home for the Jews". He did not say he would make Palestine *the* National Home for the Jews. There is a difference between the two which is of great importance. The fact that Palestine shall contain a National Home for the Jews does not mean that it will cease to be the National Home of other people, or that a Jewish Government will be set up *to dominate* the Arab people (emphasis added).

In speaking of the "political rights" promised to "the inhabitants of Palestine" whom he identified as the Arabs of the country, Churchill revealed that he completely misunderstood or deliberately misinterpreted the meaning of the Balfour Declaration. He either simply chose to ignore the actual text of the Declaration to score a point with his Arab interlocutors, or was not fully conscious of the fact that what was promised in the Declaration was the preservation of "the civil and religious rights of existing non-Jewish communities in Palestine". There was no promise of collective "political rights" awarded to the Arabs as a nation, and the phrase "existing non-Jewish communities" in the Declaration applied not to Arabs as such, but to religious communities only, whether Christian or Moslem and whether or not their members were Arabs.

Furthermore, Churchill's distinction between "a" National Home for the Jews to be established in Palestine, on the one hand, and making Palestine "the" National Home for the Jews, on the other, was a pure fabrication made out of whole cloth that had absolutely no factual basis in the decision taken by the War Cabinet on October 31, 1917, when it unanimously approved the Balfour Declaration. This distinction brought grammatical parsing of a sentence to new depths of cynicism and duplicity to discern a meaning in the Declaration that was never in the minds of its framers. The result of Churchill's fanciful playing with the text of the Declaration was to cheapen or deny its meaning as the Magna Carta of the Jewish People only one year after its enshrinement in the San Remo Resolution and the Treaty of Sèvres. In this respect, Palestine, according to Churchill, would not only be "a National Home for the Jews", but would also continue to be a national home of "other people", which for him could only have meant an Arab National Home. Churchill's restrictive interpretation of the Balfour Declaration, undoubtedly deriving from Samuel whose advice on Palestine he rigorously followed, dovetailed perfectly with the distorted interpretation given by Ahad Ha'Am who had earlier reached a similar conclusion based on the phrase "in Palestine". Samuel and Ahad Ha'Am were former colleagues in the Zionist Organization in London, where the latter had resided from 1907 or 1908 to 1922. Samuel was by all indications aware of Ahad

Ha'Am's bizarre view that the Balfour Declaration carried a twofold meaning in its formulation. According to Ahad Ha'Am, while it was true that the British recognized the "historical right" of the Jewish People to rebuild its original National Home "in Palestine", that right did not encompass *all* of Palestine nor did it override or nullify the national right of the local Arab inhabitants to their "National Home" in Palestine, where they had lived for countless generations. Furthermore, since Palestine was the "joint possession" or National Home of two different nations, that meant that the Jews could not be the sole ruler in the land or harm the "National Home" of the rest of the inhabitants. To forestall any clash between the two "homeowners", a "foreign protector" was therefore needed to ensure that the national rights of neither were infringed upon. This erratic and unfounded view of the Balfour Declaration, which contradicted its real meaning, when finally adopted, effectively ruled out the establishment of an independent Jewish State in *all* of Palestine, as originally envisaged.

What Ahad Ha'Am essentially advocated and thought important, was not that Palestine should be created as a Jewish State but rather that it become a "national spiritual center" for a cultural and spiritual revitalization of the Jewish People living in the lands of the Diaspora. His vision of Palestine as a spiritual center for the Diaspora was paradoxical because he had long ago abandoned his belief in the Jewish religion, condemned *halakha* (Jewish Law) as a "petrified tradition", and considered himself to be an agnostic. He also thought that most of the Jewish People would continue to live in Exile and did not foresee or urge the mass ingathering of Jews to the Land of Israel, a cardinal principle of Herzlian Zionism. He even opposed the immediate settlement of the Land until it was preceded by a process of education and training to instill in those intending to settle a sense of self-sacrifice and strengthened national consciousness. That may have been wise for small groups of idealistic young Jews planning to permanently settle in the Land of Israel in order to prepare themselves for such a momentous step, but it was not a practical course to follow for masses of Jews who may suddenly have needed to find quick refuge in the ancient Jewish homeland in order to escape persecution in the countries of their birth and domicile – a situation that in fact developed at the time of the Bolshevik Revolution in Russia, then in the 1930s in Central and Eastern Europe with the rise of Adolf Hitler and Benito Mussolini, and finally in Moslem Arab countries both before and after the birth of the State of Israel. Ahad Ha'Am's plan of limited settlement, if strictly observed, would have slowed down inordinately the goal of achieving a Jewish majority in the Land of Israel and hence a Jewish State. His perverted interpretation of the Balfour Declaration, which downgraded its importance to Jews while emphasizing the continued existence of Arab "national rights", was first published in June 1920 in the Preface to the Third Edition of his Collected Essays, *At the Crossroads ('Al Parashat Derakhim)*, and was widely disseminated even before excerpts from the preface were subsequently translated from Hebrew into English by the English Zionist leader, Leon Simon, in a 1922 edition (*Ten Essays on Zionism and Judaism*, pp. xvi-xix). Ahad Ha'Am's exposition of the Balfour Declaration was an unexpected godsend for Samuel, who had already revised his own attitude towards Zionism now that he was the highest ranking representative of the British Government in Palestine, particularly anxious not to incur Arab displeasure or that of other British officials serving in the country, by supporting the goal of a future Jewish State. Samuel brought to Churchill's attention this novel interpretation of the Balfour Declaration, which served Churchill in good stead when he met the Arab deputation in Jerusalem on March 28, 1921 and preached it to them.

In light of Churchill's convoluted and absurd statement to the Arabs that the establishment in Palestine of "a" National Home for the Jews did not make it "the" National Home for the Jews, nor did it also mean that Palestine would cease to be the National Home of "other people", a pertinent question for Churchill on his discourse with the Arab deputation would have been: If Palestine is merely "a" National Home for the Jewish People (and not "the" National Home for the Jewish People), where then are the other National Homes of the Jewish People located? And, secondly, how many National Homes can a newly created country be expected to have within its borders? He overlooked the obvious fact that the only reason for creating Palestine out of the Ottoman Empire as a new and separate country on April 24, 1920 at the San Remo Peace Conference was to establish an exclusively Jewish National Home, which would naturally have eventually had a Jewish government, that would perforce rule over and – in Churchill's inapt description – dominate the Arab inhabitants, as it would likewise rule over all its citizens and residents. Moreover, before giving his own false definition of the Jewish National Home, Churchill was grossly derelict in neither reading the minutes of the Cabinet discussion on October 31, 1917 which defined this term as a future independent Jewish State in all of Palestine nor consulting Lloyd George and Balfour about what was truly intended. Ironically, it was barely four months after his meeting with the Arab deputation that he learned firsthand from Lloyd George and Balfour that what they had always meant by the Declaration issued on November 2, 1917 was an eventual independent Jewish State, as recorded in the notes taken by Colonel Richard Meinertzhagen of their conversation held at Balfour's house on July 22, 1921[43] and also in the above-noted letters dispatched by Chaim Weizmann to Ahad Ha'Am (July 30, 1921) and Wyndham Deedes (July 31, 1921). However, this information clarifying the true meaning of the Balfour Declaration from those who propounded and authorized it, of which Churchill was apparently unaware when he addressed the Arab deputation, did not suffice to deter him from radically redefining the term "Jewish National Home" one year later in the White Paper that bears his name, when he had already been apprised of its original connotation. This redefinition excluded an eventual Jewish State, while the original Lloyd George-Balfour intention prescribed it. Churchill thereby hoped to placate antagonistic Arab opinion and further British interests at the

[43] Meinertzhagen, *op. cit.*, pp. 105-106.

expense of Zionism, whose ultimate aim, of course, was an independent Jewish State. He must be held primarily responsible, as the Cabinet officer in charge of Middle Eastern affairs, for deliberately causing the British government to renege on its solemn commitment to the Jewish People. The official policy or guidelines he personally approved for implementing the Balfour Declaration represented the greatest deception of all perpetrated by a British leader in the Mandate period, though in later years he conveniently denied what he (and Samuel) had actually done, as further discussed below.

As regards the Churchill White Paper of June 3, 1922, the following quotations taken from it, given here in paraphrased form, show conclusively that a Jewish State was definitely foreclosed, regardless of whether it would be established in all or part of Palestine:

> 1. "The British Government had no aim in view to create a wholly Jewish Palestine or to make Palestine as Jewish as England is English." A Jewish Palestine was a synonym for a Jewish State and was therefore excluded by these words.
>
> 2. "The subordination of the Arabic population, language or culture in Palestine was not contemplated, nor its disappearance." The term "subordination" recalled the 1921 Report of the Haycraft Commission which stated that British policy did not envision Jewish "predominance" in Palestine, the obverse of which concept meant no subordination of the Arab population. However, in a Jewish State, the Jews and their language, religion and culture would naturally be predominant, as happens in all other states where a majority group sets the national tone and character, even if there was complete respect for the linguistic, religious and cultural rights or other freedoms of individuals belonging to minority groups.
>
> 3. "Palestine as a whole would not be converted into a Jewish National Home, but merely a Home was to be founded in Palestine." This interpretation meant that all of Palestine was not synonymous with a Jewish National Home and therefore a wholly Jewish Palestine, i.e., a Jewish State with a Jewish Government, was not contemplated. It echoed what Churchill told the Arab deputation in Jerusalem on March 28, 1921 quoted just above.
>
> 4. "The Zionist Organization was not entitled to share in any degree in the Government or general administration of the country." If there were to be no Jewish Government nor even Jewish participation in the Government of Palestine that was to be established, then naturally there could not be any Jewish State. That, too, was a reiteration of what both Samuel and Churchill said before.
>
> 5. "The Jewish nationality (in modern terms, Israeli citizenship) would not be imposed upon the inhabitants of Palestine as a whole." Since "nationality" in the sense of "citizenship" is derived from

statehood, no Jewish State could be established. In a Jewish State, the Arabs would normally have the nationality or citizenship of that state, unless the law of the state specifically determined otherwise or if the Arabs themselves rejected the citizenship granted by the Jewish State.[44]

6. "When it is asked what is meant by *the development of the Jewish National Home in Palestine*, it may be answered that it is *the further development of the existing Jewish community*, in order that it may become a centre of Jewish interest and pride" (emphasis added). These words were the epitome of trickery and subtlety, because they conveyed a meaning different from that of the Mandate Charter, that was almost unnoticeable. The latter spoke of the establishment of the Jewish National Home or, alternatively, its reconstitution (see Recitals 2 and 3 of the Preamble, Article 2 and Article 4 [twice]). It did not speak of *the development* of the national home, a word that was used in the Mandate not with regard to the Jewish National Home but to the country itself (see Articles 4 and 11). Why then was the word *development* substituted for the word *establishment* in the above question posed in the White Paper? The answer lay in the fact that *the establishment of a home* meant the creation of something not yet in existence, to be achieved sometime in the uncertain future. That "something" was an independent Jewish State. This is why the author of the White Paper, Samuel, with the connivance of Churchill and his officials in the Colonial Office, deliberately avoided using the word *establishment* and replaced it with the word *development*. This was not the end of the deceit regarding the interchange of these two words. There was still another aspect behind the deception. The word *development* was juxtaposed with the term "Jewish National Home" not for the purpose of equating the Home with a State, for if that had been done, it would have meant that the Jewish State was already in existence and only needed to be further assisted to become independent, akin to the situation in Iraq under the Mandatory regime. Instead, Samuel used the word *development* together with the term "Jewish National Home" to describe an existing Jewish

---

[44] The non-imposition of Jewish nationality upon the Arabs of Palestine, which could only be done if a Jewish State was established, was brought up in a discussion amongst the members of the Peel Royal Commission, that took place on January 21, 1937 at Helouan (Helwan), Egypt, where they had retreated for a few days. Professor Reginald Coupland, a historian and proponent of 'partition' for Palestine, remarked that the aim of the Jews was that "there should be somewhere in the world where they were not a minority". Horace Rumbold, the vice-chairman of the Commission and career diplomat, retorted: "the idea of an eventual [Jewish] majority [i.e., the Jewish State – H.G.] was inconsistent with the declaration in the Churchill statement (p. 19 of Command 1700) that the development of the National Home did not mean the imposition of Jewish nationality upon the inhabitants of Palestine as a whole". *The Rise of Israel*, Volume 24, Document 1, p. 4.

community in Palestine, which would become a centre of interest and pride to Jews everywhere. It was this community and centre which was to be *further developed* through an increase in its population, whose numbers, however, would be strictly controlled by the economic absorptive capacity of the country. By this subterfuge that was not easily detectable, the White Paper subtly changed the meaning of the Jewish National Home from an eventual independent State to only a community and centre alongside the Arab population of the country. The meaning of this term was thus rendered harmless for the White Paper made the Jewish National Home no different in fact from other Jewish communities and centres in other parts of the world, which also were sources of interest and pride to the Jewish people as a whole.

7. "The Balfour Declaration did not contain or imply anything which need cause alarm to the Arab population of Palestine." The premise that the Balfour Declaration would indeed harm the Arabs was based on their belief that it heralded a Jewish State that would drastically change their lives, especially with regard to the Islamic prohibition of such an entity replacing a formerly Moslem one. The establishment in Palestine of a Jewish National Home was also a death blow to nationalist Arab hopes of creating a unified Arab state consisting of Syria and Palestine or, failing that, Palestine alone. Since Churchill and Samuel were at pains to *assure* the Arabs of Palestine that the policy of the Balfour Declaration gave them no cause for alarm, that could only mean that no Jewish State was contemplated, because that prospect was the very cause of their alarm. This assurance in the Churchill White Paper, together with the other assurances paraphrased in the preceding paragraphs and those given individually by Churchill and Samuel in their various meetings with Arab leaders, were cited seventeen years later by the MacDonald White Paper to deny that it was part of the policy of the British Government "that Palestine should become a Jewish State", since that would be contrary not only to their alleged obligations to the Arabs under the Mandate, but "as well as to the assurances which have been given to the Arab people in the past, that the Arab population of Palestine should [not] be made the subjects of a Jewish State against their will". Contrary to the 1922 and 1939 White Papers, the Arabs of Mandated Palestine correctly perceived that the Balfour Declaration did in fact mean a Jewish State, but their anguish that its realization would necessarily harm them in a personal or individual way was unfounded. The Arabs, however, did not have the right to live everywhere in the Middle East as the majority and nowhere as a minority. If they had had such a right, the entire Middle East would have become an exclusively Arab domain, regardless of the existence of other nations or peoples who desired self-determination or autonomy in their ancestral homelands, particularly the Jews, the

> Kurds and the Assyrians. The Arab fear of becoming a minority in Palestine reflected national avarice and a lack of respect or tolerance for the national rights of others, since new Arab states were being created in most of the Middle East at the very time they were alarmed about the future establishment of an independent Jewish State in Palestine.

When the Churchill White Paper was adopted as official British Government policy for Palestine, it was also approved by the two leading proponents of Zionism in the Government, Prime Minister Lloyd George and the venerable A.J. Balfour who, after resigning as Foreign Minister in October 1919, continued to serve in the Cabinet as Lord President of the Council. Both statesmen had always explained that an eventual independent Jewish State was the ultimate goal of the Balfour Declaration and the Mandate. It is thus hard to understand how they could have approved a statement of policy which negated that very goal. A possible answer is that they naively believed that, despite the language and guidelines of the White Paper, the goal of Jewish statehood had not been precluded. That, after all, was the flippant claim of Churchill, who was given almost free rein to act as he saw fit in shaping Palestine policy during his two-year term as Colonial Secretary without their actual input or close supervision. In any event, there had been a change of circumstances or perspective by the time Churchill took control of Middle-Eastern affairs: Zionism was then no longer a priority for the Lloyd George Government in the waning days of its existence, as it had been in 1917 when the support of world Jewry was being actively sought for the British war effort. It therefore did not matter as much if the aim of Zionism, i.e., an independent Jewish State in the whole of Palestine, was now modified in favour of other policy considerations, such as seeking greater support among the Arabs of Palestine as British officials, both military and civilian, who were serving in the area, ardently desired. The result was the promulgation of the Churchill White Paper which overturned the true meaning of the Balfour Declaration, making it less troublesome in British eyes and easier to explain to the Arabs. The formal acceptance of the White Paper by the Zionist leaders after its publication undoubtedly made it much less difficult for Lloyd George and Balfour to give their consent to an anti-Zionist document that, in the years ahead, derailed the proper implementation of the Mandate and the establishment of a Jewish State. It may be said, in defence of Lloyd George and Balfour that they were unwitting accomplices to a policy change brought to the fore by Churchill, with the active participation of Samuel, that was not of their doing, and whose far-reaching negative consequences they probably did not fully realize at the time.

When Churchill was summoned as a witness to testify before the Peel Royal Commission on March 12, 1937, he distanced himself greatly from what the White Paper of 1922 had said about the Jewish National Home. As recounted by Martin Gilbert,[45] he declared:

> *The British Government had certainly committed itself to the idea that* some day, somehow, far off in the future, subject to justice and economic convenience, *there might well be a great Jewish State there*, numbered by millions, far exceeding the present inhabitants of the country... *We never committed ourselves to making Palestine a Jewish State*... but if more and more Jews gather to that Home and all is worked from age to age, from generation to generation, with justice and fair consideration to those displaced and so forth, certainly it was contemplated and intended that they might in the course of time become an overwhelmingly Jewish State (emphasis added).

Churchill's new explanation in 1937, when he was out of office, about what the phrase "Jewish National Home" actually meant sharply contrasted with the meaning he attributed to it in the 1922 White Paper. He now freely admitted that the British Government had committed itself to the idea of a Jewish State being established one day, when it undertook the administration of Palestine, and that the National Home therefore meant much more than a mere cultural and spiritual center of Jewish interest and pride, as earlier stated in his White Paper. However, while honestly acknowledging that the Jewish National Home really meant an eventual Jewish State, he erred badly in denying that Britain had ever committed itself to making Palestine a Jewish State. On the contrary, that was exactly what Article 2 of the Mandate said Britain must do, based on the assumption that a Jewish National Home and a Jewish State were synonymous terms, as Churchill had now conceded to be the case, and which is what was originally intended when the Balfour Declaration was approved by the War Cabinet on October 31, 1917. Article 2 stated that "*the Mandatory shall be responsible* for placing the country [of Palestine] under such political, administrative and economic conditions *as will secure* the establishment of the Jewish National Home... and the development of self-governing institutions..." (emphasis added). The above words in italics in Article 2 make it evident that the British Government was indeed committed under international law to making Palestine a Jewish State, but this was a commitment it never carried out and which Churchill either deliberately or ignorantly denied.

To a question from Horace Rumbold, the Vice-Chairman of the Royal Commission on Palestine, Churchill replied that even when the Jewish Home becomes all Palestine as it eventually would, there was no injustice.

> Why is there harsh injustice done if people come in and make a livelihood for more, and make the desert into palm groves and orange groves? Why is it injustice because there is more work and wealth for

[45] See Volume V, *Winston S. Churchill*, 1922-1939, published by Heinemann, London, reprinted 1988, pp. 847-848.

> everybody? There is no injustice. The injustice is when those who live in the country leave it to be desert for thousands of years.

Churchill disputed the idea that the indigenous population of Palestine had been subject to the invasion of a foreign race, as stated by Rumbold. To that false aspersion Churchill answered:

> The Arabs had come in after the Jews. It was the great hordes of Islam who smashed Palestine up… where the Arab goes, it is often desert.

Asked when the Jewish Home would be considered established, Churchill replied:

> When it was quite clear the Jewish *preponderance* in Palestine was very marked, decisive and when we were satisfied that we had no further duties to discharge to the Arab population, the Arab minority (emphasis added).

Churchill's evidence was not included in the Peel Commission's Report. He wrote to Lord Peel on March 16, 1937 requesting that nothing he said be printed in the Report, because:

> there are a few references to nationalities which would not be suited to appear in a permanent record.

When the Peel Report recommended a plan to partition Palestine into a Jewish and an Arab state, he opposed it, because it pitted the Jewish area – "a rich and small state more crowded than Germany against vast Arab regions stretching up to Baghdad".[46]

And he went on to warn of "this great Arab area confronting this new Jewish State".

There is no doubt that Churchill at this particular moment in 1937 sincerely felt remorse for the 1922 White Paper which had indeed foreclosed the legal expectation of the Jewish National Home becoming a Jewish State embracing the whole country of Palestine as defined in the Franco-British Boundary Convention of December 23, 1920, before the insertion of the new Article 25 of the Mandate. That foreclosure was abundantly clear from the following: the assurances which the White Paper gave to the Arabs of Palestine regarding their status in the country (no subordination of their language and culture and no imposition of Jewish nationality), the disclaimer or repudiation of the idea to impart a *predominantly* Jewish character to Palestine (to become as Jewish as England is English), the wrongful and scaled-down meaning it gave to the

[46] Gilbert's book, *ibid.*, p. 867.

term "Jewish National Home" (denying it meant a Jewish State and Jewish Government, but only a further-developed community) and finally his own prior statements and those of Samuel, whose advice he followed in attempting to allay the mounting and fierce opposition of Palestine's Arabs to the establishment of the Home.

Colonial Secretary Churchill's reliance on Samuel in formulating his policy on Palestine was made evident not only by the White Paper of June 3, 1922, but also by what he once told the new French President, Alexandre Millerand (formerly the Prime Minister and Minister for Foreign Affairs, who succeeded Georges Clemenceau in January 1920). At a meeting which Millerand requested when Churchill passed through Paris on January 11, 1921, the President directed strong criticism at the Balfour Declaration and Zionism which he hypocritically stated he favoured in principle but feared that in Palestine "the Jews would be very high-handed when they got together there". Churchill recounted how he fended off his criticism as follows:[47]

> I expatiated on the virtues and experience of Sir Herbert Samuel, and pointed out how evenly he was holding the balance between Arabs and Jews and how effectively he was restraining his own people, as perhaps only a Jewish administrator could do.

Churchill's dependence on Samuel's advice was further recorded in a telegram he sent to Lloyd George from Cairo on March 18, 1921 to inform him that the proposed arrangement with Abdullah to govern Transjordan was decided upon after hearing the case fully set out by Samuel, General Congreve and T.E. Lawrence.[48]

In another telegram Churchill sent to Lloyd George from Cairo on March 23, 1921, he stated that in regard to reducing British military commitments in Palestine, he relied "most particularly" on the opinion of Sir Herbert Samuel, being convinced by him and the political officers on the spot that "the restoration of stable conditions in Transjordan is an indispensably preliminary to further reduction". The "stable conditions" sought in Transjordan referred to the elimination of the military threat emanating from Abdullah's agitation from Amman against the French in Syria.[49]

To the complaint heard from the deputation of the Executive Committee of the Arab Palestine Congress about whether Samuel was first of all a Jew or an Englishman, Churchill responded:[50]

---

[47] See Volume IV of Martin Gilbert's biography of *Winston S. Churchill*, p. 513 and *Companion Volume* IV, Part 2, p. 1304.

[48] See *Companion Volume* IV, Part 2, pp. 1402-03.

[49] *The Rise of Israel*, Vol. 13, Document 12, p. 100.

[50] *Ibid.*, Vol. 13, Document 12, p. 248. Churchill's remarks are also reprinted in Gilbert's *Companion Volume* IV, Part 2, p. 1420.

> ...in selecting him we knew we had a trained and experienced man who would understand what ought to be done and what the full meaning and purpose of British policy was. *Moreover, he is himself a Jew, and therefore* we knew that in holding the balance even and securing fair treatment for all, *he could not be reproached for being hostile to his own people* (emphasis added), and he would be believed by them when he said that he was only doing what was just and fair; and I think this appointment [of Samuel as High Commissioner] has been vindicated and justified not only by what has been done but by its results.

Thus we have it from the mouth of Churchill himself that Samuel, being a Jew, was exactly the right person to be entrusted with the task of carrying out a "just and fair" (pro-Arab) policy in Palestine. No matter what he did: undermining the goal of a Jewish State, urging the administrative partition of the country and limiting Jewish immigration, "he could not be reproached for being hostile to his own people". In other words, he was the perfect person to implement an anti-Zionist policy in Palestine on behalf of the British Government, since he had a ready-made cover as a Jew and an unassailable disguise as a devoted Zionist. However, no one devoted to the cause of Zionism as Samuel was alleged to be by Churchill would ever have agreed at the Cairo Conference on March 17, 1921 to what he was reported in the minutes to have agreed to:[51]

> He concurred in the necessity of differentiating between the Administrations in Palestine and Transjordan and he had never suggested any other policy.

Samuel's concurrence came at the very moment that the President of the Zionist Organization, Chaim Weizmann, was desperately trying to ensure that this ancient Jewish territory of Transjordan remained in the hands of the Jewish People. Samuel justified his position on the ground that Britain had pledged its support to the Sherif of Mecca during the war and that therefore there could be no question of failing to honour its word. In light of this, it is most ironic that Lord Curzon initially suspected that Samuel harboured a pro-Zionist opinion on the subject. In a note dated February 12, 1921 to Eric Graham Forbes Adam, a British official instrumental in drafting the Mandate for Palestine, Curzon stated his misgivings:[52]

> I am very much concerned about Transjordan. Sir H. Samuel wants it as an annex of Palestine and an outlet for the Jews. There I am against him. But I am with him in thinking that we ought to have sent troops there from the start. If we had done so, I believe none of this

[51] *Ibid.*, p. 203.

[52] Gilbert's Biography of *Churchill*, *Companion Volume* IV, Part 2, p. 1347.

trouble would have occurred…

Curzon soon found out, to his relief and surprise, that Samuel stood four-square behind his own anti-Zionist policy to deprive the Jews of Transjordan and reserve it for the local Arabs, within the framework of the Mandate for Palestine.

Apart from Samuel's advice, Churchill was much influenced by the head of the Middle East Department of the Colonial Office, John Evelyn Shuckburgh, who prepared a memorandum for him dated November 7, 1921 in which he asserted that the British object was not to establish a state in which Jews will enjoy a position of political ascendancy, but a commonwealth built upon a democratic foundation and framed in the best interests of all sections of the population.[53] These words of Shuckburgh were nearly identical to those penned by Samuel in a report he sent to Churchill three weeks earlier, on October 14, 1921.[54] Shuckburgh also proposed that a "Palestine Constitution" be imposed on both the Arabs and Zionists. It is noteworthy that in writing the 1922 White Paper, Samuel based himself partly on Shuckburgh's memorandum of November 7, 1921,[55] which pointed to close collaboration between these two officials. Shuckburgh thought that the Balfour Declaration was "too meaningless to mean anything", an opinion he conveyed to Colonel Richard Meinertzhagen, the former Chief Political Officer to the Military Administration of Syria and Palestine (1919-20), who served in the Colonial Office as a military adviser to the Middle East Department from 1921 to 1924. Meinertzhagen said of him in his book *Middle East Diary*:[56]

> He is saturated with anti-Semitism, loathes Zionism and the Jews. The National Home for the Jews is the main plank in our Middle East policy and a violent anti-Semite is the worst person to be in charge of the department. In fact, in many ways Shuckburgh is responsible for deliberately sabotaging the National Home and naturally he and I have come into conflict on that account.

On the question of Churchill's own role on the severance of Transjordan, from the Jewish National Home, Meinertzhagen, who had direct contact with him at the time of his service in the Colonial Office, wrote an extraordinary letter dated January 10, 1964 to Samuel Landman, a lawyer and Zionist leader in Britain, three years before each of them died in 1967, in which he stated the following:

---

[53] Wasserstein, *op. cit.*, p. 116.

[54] Gilbert's *Companion Volume* IV, Part 3, p. 1654.

[55] Wasserstein, *ibid.*, p. 118.

[56] *Middle East Diary* 1917-1956, published by Thomas Yoseloff, New York 1960, pp. 116, 132. Diary Entries of June 14, 1922 and July 6, 1923.

> ...Both Lloyd George and Balfour told me that in giving the Jews their national home in Palestine they meant the whole of Biblical Palestine, that is to say, the whole of the country occupied by the Jewish tribes, including Moab and Ammon. But Churchill, encouraged by Lawrence, gave the whole of Transjordan to that miserable Abdullah, thus depriving Israel of a vital territory and allowing a complete encirclement of Israel by Arabs. At the time (1921) I was working in the Colonial Office (Churchill was Colonial Secretary) and I remonstrated. He put on that ridiculous bulldog expression but nothing could be done to remedy Churchill's stupidity.
>
> I do not share the general admiration for Churchill. No living man has done so much harm to this country as Churchill and yet he is venerated as a God.[57]

In regard to Transjordan's geographical and historical connection to Palestine and why it should never have been separated from it, Meinertzhagen wrote in his diary:[58]

> Geographically, Palestine and Transjordan are one. They should have never been separated nor was their present status ever intended. Transjordan was 'jumped' with the connivance of certain British officials, and Churchill. The artificial partitioning of the Holy Land must be repugnant to many, who, like myself, regard that country as something quite unique and indivisible.

In another diary entry, he wrote:[59]

> Transjordan should never have been severed from Palestine for *it is Palestine* (Italics in original). Abdullah is a mere upstart, a useless

[57] Meinertzhagen's letter was published in Ha'Aretz newspaper and a copy of it can be found in the Zionist Archives. As to his personal background, he was sometimes mistaken for a German Jew, because of his name, which is of Danish origin. He related in the preface of his book, *Middle East Diary, 1917-1956*, "there is no Jewish blood in my veins, nor has there ever been... Maybe if I had Jewish blood in my veins I might be more intelligent than I am; but there is none." Meinertzhagen had a close relationship with T.E. Lawrence. He said he knew him better than any living man, having worked in the same room in the Colonial Office for almost two years, a relationship that continued afterwards with Lawrence, frequently visiting him at his home in London. Op. cit, p. 42.

[58] *Op. cit.*, p. 164. Diary entry of July 23, 1937.

[59] *Op. cit.*, p. 189. Diary entry of July 23, 1943. See also the diary entries of June 14, 1922, p. 117; of June 20, 1922, p. 117; of May 2, 1946, p. 208 among others where he makes similar remarks concerning Transjordan's close connection to Palestine, and in the Epilogue on p. 355, where he gives a definition of Palestine.

> figurehead and could not maintain himself for an instant without British bayonets. He has no more right to Transjordan than I have.

Although Meinertzhagen strongly opposed the detachment of Transjordan first from the Jewish National Home and then from Palestine itself, as is evident from many of his diary references on the subject, a mysterious asterisked editorial note appears in his book[60] (though not in his actual diary) after he had just described Transjordan as "Jewish territory" in his diary entry of June 21, 1921 (see *infra*). The editorial note states:

> I think I was mistaken. Though Transjordan was included within Palestine Mandated Territory it was not part of the country allotted to the Jews for their National Home, the eastern boundary of which was the River Jordan.

This note appears to be an aberration or a momentary and sudden change of opinion, if indeed he wrote that note, that he later recanted by the letter dated June 10, 1964 that he sent to Samuel Landman. In any event, even if he did write it, it carries less weight and importance than the entries he made in his diary as to what Lloyd George and Balfour explicitly told him about the inclusion of Transjordan in the Jewish National Home.

In a luncheon interview with Balfour in Paris on July 30, 1919, a day after he was appointed Chief Political Officer for Palestine and Syria on General Allenby's Staff, Meinertzhagen records the Foreign Minister as stating:[61]

> in deciding the boundaries of Palestine, economic grounds must count much more than military or strategic considerations, and that if the water necessary for successful development lay as far north as the Litani and Hermon, then the Jews must include both these places in Palestine. The eastern boundary of Palestine must be up to, but excluding the Hedjaz Railway.

In another editorial note following a dispatch by Meinertzhagen to Curzon on November 17, 1919, that discussed the future boundaries of Palestine, he commented:[62]

> At the Paris Peace Conference in 1919, there was much discussion on the boundaries between Syria, Palestine, Egypt and Iraq. When asked what he considered the boundaries of Palestine, Lloyd George always answered: 'Biblical Palestine, from Dan to Beersheba'. But

---

[60] *Op. cit.*, Diary Entry of July 5, 1921, p. 100.

[61] *Ibid.*, p. 25.

[62] *Ibid.*, p. 63.

> nobody knew where Dan was. Small wonder, for Dan was a district and not a town. The present kibbutz called Dan is somewhere about where the District Dan was situated.

In the Epilogue of his book, Meinertzhagen returned to the subject of what Lloyd George and Balfour meant by "Palestine". He wrote:[63]

> There has been much confusion about the definition of Palestine. When asked in Paris in 1919 as to the meaning of Palestine, Mr. Lloyd George said: 'The area occupied by the twelve tribes of Israel, from Dan to Beersheba'. In the same year in Paris, Lloyd George asked me what I considered to be Palestine. I replied the land occupied by the Jews at the birth of Christ. Lloyd George stuck to his 'Dan to Beersheba', but Dan could not be found on any map. I explained that Dan was a district at the southern base of Mount Hermon and at the head of the waters of the River Jordan. I mapped the area which I regarded as biblical Palestine. This was bounded on the north by the Litani River and the whole of the catchment area of the River Jordan from the southern slopes of Hermon, south through Moab to the head of the Gulf of Aqaba and thence along the Egyptian-Turkish administrative frontier to Gaza. *Both Lloyd George and Balfour agreed to this boundary* but the French objected that the whole of Hermon must be included within Syria.
>
> So Palestine came to include from Dan to Beersheba and the Transjordan catchment area of the Jordan Valley. This was further whittled down in 1921 when Churchill presented the Emir Abdullah with Transjordan, thus depriving the Jews of a valuable expansion area (emphasis added).

There is one other contradiction in Meinertzhagen's *Middle East Diary* concerning his attitude on Transjordan's place in to the Jewish National Home, which he resolved by himself within a space of two weeks. In the diary entry for January 30, 1919, he wrote:[64]

> The historic title of the Jews to Palestine is indisputable, but I disagree with the boundary claims. The correct eastern boundary for Palestine is the Sea of Galilee, Jordan and Dead Sea, as judged on ethnical grounds. On economic grounds it may be desirable to go further east, but it is encroaching on purely Arab territory. Weizmann

[63] *Ibid.*, p. 355. The Meinertzhagen map depicting these boundaries is found on p. 64.

[64] *Ibid.*, p. 14. Meinertzhagen's use of the expression "historic title" refers, in fact, to the Jewish legal title to Palestine, based on their historical connection with the country.

> argues that if he cannot go east of Jordan, the many millions of Jews who eventually come to Palestine will be crowded out. I also disagree with the southern boundary going to Aqaba. If they want an outlet to the Red Sea, I should sooner cede Sinai to the east bank of the Suez Canal. After all, the Jews have considerable claims to Sinai, both on historic and religious grounds; they are the only people who have wandered about there for forty years and [Moses] received the ten commandments on Mount Sinai.

However, he expressed a new opinion on Palestine's eastern boundary on February 14, 1919:[65]

> I have also advised that the Palestine boundaries extend east to cover the whole of Moab and south to Aqaba. I should also give the Jews Sinai and compensate Egypt elsewhere.

Meinertzhagen's revelations in his *Middle East Diary*, which are complemented by his letter to Landman, emanate both from his personal contact with the key decision-makers of British Middle East policy, particularly Lloyd George and Balfour, and from being a witness to the actual events as they were taking place by virtue of the various positions he held in government service during the five critical years from 1917-1922. These positions included being head of General Allenby's Intelligence Section, working in the War Office, an assignment at the Paris Peace Conference, followed by a new appointment as Political Officer for all occupied territory, including Syria, Cisjordanian and Transjordanian Palestine, reporting directly to the Foreign Office, and finally as military adviser to the Middle East Department in the Colonial Office run by Churchill.

His revelations provide a unique and reliable source of contemporary evidence to confirm the original meaning of the Balfour Declaration and the Mandate for Palestine – namely, an eventual independent Jewish State in the borders of Biblical Palestine, defined as the areas conquered, settled and ruled by the Twelve Tribes of Israel and their descendants during the First and Second Temple periods, and also those required for the country's economic development. His revelations also expose the duplicity of British officials who were determined to nullify or diminish the effect of the Balfour Declaration and the Mandate for Palestine. In this respect he severely castigated Churchill, Lawrence and Shuckburgh for sabotaging the policy of the Jewish National Home but, surprisingly, was much more lenient with Samuel, though in truth the latter's culpability was even greater for it was at his perverse instigation that the damaging 1922 White Paper was composed, thus crippling the Mandate and derailing the establishment of the Jewish State during the period of British rule.

Upon learning of the severance of Transjordan from the area of the Jewish

---

[65] *Ibid.*, p. 15.

National Home, Meinertzhagen exploded in anger at what he rightly saw as an act of British appeasement of the Arabs and a broken promise to the Jewish People. He expressed his disgust in his diary entry of June 21, 1921:[66]

> The atmosphere in the Colonial Office is definitely hebraphobe, the worst offender being Shuckburgh who is head of the Middle East Department. Hubert Young and little Lawrence do their utmost to conceal their dislike and mistrust of the Jews, but both strongly support the official pro-Arab policy of Whitehall and frown on the equally official policy based on the Balfour Declaration; the latter is the only policy I recognize.
>
> I exploded on hearing that Churchill had severed Transjordan from Palestine in an interview in Jerusalem between him and Abdullah on March 27th this year. Apparently Abdullah was moving through Transjordan on his way to help Feisal's adherents in Damascus and make trouble for the French who turned Feisal out last year. Abdullah had to be placated and met Churchill in Jerusalem. Abdullah was placated at the expense of the Jewish National Home which embraces the whole of Biblical Palestine. Lawrence was of course with Churchill and influenced him. So Abdullah was made Emir of Transjordan, was given a British adviser and a subsidy. Of course, the man accepted at once. This reduces the Jewish National Home to one third of Biblical Palestine. The Colonial Office and the Palestine Administration have now declared that the articles of the Mandate relating to the Jewish Home are not applicable to Transjordan and that the severance of Transjordan from Palestine is in accordance with the terms of the McMahon pledge. *This discovery was not made until it became necessary to appease an Arab Emir.*
>
> I told Shuckburgh I wished to see Churchill on the question; he said it would be no good as the matter was settled; so I rang up Eddy Marsh [private secretary to Winston Churchill] and told him I must see the Secretary of State at once and down I went foaming at the mouth with anger and indignation. Churchill heard me out; I told him it was grossly unfair to the Jews, that it was yet another promise broken and that it was a most dishonest act, that the Balfour Declaration was being torn up by degrees and that the official policy of H.M.G. to establish a Home for the Jews in Biblical Palestine was being *sabotaged*; that I found the Middle East Department whose business it was to implement the Mandate, almost one hundred percent hebraphobe and could not the duration of Abdullah's *Emirate* in Transjordan be of a temporary

[66] *Ibid.*, pp. 99-100. In this important quotation, which had attached to it the afore-mentioned asterisked note, it must be pointed out that Meinertzhagen was wrong in calling Transjordan an emirate, when legally speaking it was still only a separately administered territory of Mandated Palestine.

> nature, say, for seven years, and a guarantee given that *Abdullah should not be given sovereign powers over what was in fact Jewish territory.*
>
> Churchill listened and said he saw the force of my argument and would consider the question. He thought it was too late to alter but a time limit to Abdullah's *Emirate* in Transjordan might work.
>
> I'm thoroughly disgusted (emphasis added).

In the above excerpt from Meinertzhagen's diary, it is interesting to note that he refers to the "discovery" made by the Colonial Office that the provisions of the Mandate for Palestine relating to the Jewish National Home were not applicable to Transjordan because of the 1915 McMahon Pledge to Sherif Hussein. The same "discovery", it will be recalled, was also mentioned by Alec Seath Kirkbride, the long-time British military and political officer serving in Transjordan, to explain the reason why this territory was severed from the Jewish National Home by a decision first taken at the Cairo Conference in March 1921, and later approved by the League Council in September 1922. That "discovery" was nothing more than a fabrication invented by the Colonial Office when it could find nothing else in the articles of the Mandate to justify the new policy engineered by Churchill, Samuel, Shuckburgh, Young and Lawrence to appease Abdullah by giving him three quarters of the land that had already been reserved for Palestine and the Jewish National Home.

In Meinertzhagen's diary entry of July 21, 1921, he lamented that Churchill did not care or know much about Zionism.[67] Two days later he wrote:[68]

> Here in the Colonial Office, Winston is not too sympathetic [towards Zionism] and I suspect he regards it as a nuisance. In the Middle East Department I am alone in my views, but I am rapidly infusing into both [Hubert] Young and [John] Shuckburgh some enthusiasm for the cause.

What Churchill said in 1937 before the Peel Commission and again in 1939 against the Government's new White Paper which he characterized as "the abandonment of the Balfour Declaration, the end of the vision, of the hope and of the dream" may have been a tremendous morale booster for the cause of Zionism which undoubtedly alleviated his guilty conscience for what he did as Colonial Secretary in the critical years of 1921 and 1922, when the meaning of the Jewish National Home was being distorted and deprived of its true significance and intention. His new reflections were certainly welcomed and redounded to his credit, but these could not undo the grave damage already caused to the Jewish National Home by the 1922 White Paper, which served as the principal document thereafter to guide British officials in mis-administering the Mandate.

It is also noteworthy that when Churchill became Prime Minister during

---

[67] *Ibid.*, p. 102.

[68] *Ibid.*, p. 103.

the War Years, 1940 to 1945, he did not take any remedial steps to abolish the White Paper of 1939, which he had condemned in the most eloquent way, despite various appeals to him to do so. In his Memoirs he later explained his omission to act by saying he had to give single-minded concentration to winning the war and that all other matters had to be temporarily shelved. However, his inaction greatly exacerbated the dire consequences stemming from the British abandonment of the Balfour Declaration and Mandate. Churchill's explanation was a lame excuse which carried no conviction. In light of the unfolding Jewish tragedy in Europe of which he had to be aware, it should have been a matter of utmost urgency for Churchill to remove all restrictions on Jewish immigration to Palestine. That would have been the only honest thing to do, to redress the "lamentable act of default" as he also described the 1939 White Paper. There would have been no distraction to the war effort if Churchill had ordered its cancellation, just as there was no distraction to the prosecution of the war in 1917 against Turkey and the other Central Powers when the Balfour Declaration was drawn up as a war measure to enlist valuable Jewish support. Many of the six million Jews who died horrible deaths in the Holocaust could have been saved had the doors of the National Home suddenly swung wide open under an order by Churchill. Alas, he excelled in rhetoric when he was out of office, but not deeds when he was in power and able to do something to implement the Mandate's commands for establishing the Jewish National Home and independent Jewish State. The White Paper of Malcolm MacDonald remained in effect all through Churchill's term as Prime Minister and afterwards until the end of the Mandate. No British political leader proved more hypocritical than Churchill in professing glowing support for Zionism, but in reality doing the very opposite when formulating and carrying out Government policy or exhibiting gross indifference when his help was urgently needed. Meinertzhagen's strong denunciations of Churchill for sabotaging the establishment of the Jewish National Home were undoubtedly correct.

One additional important source can be cited to corroborate the fact that the 1922 White Paper changed the conception of the Balfour Declaration and Mandate for Palestine from one that required the establishment of a Jewish State to one that precluded it. This source is Leonard Stein, a trusted associate of Chaim Weizmann, who appointed him political secretary and legal adviser of the Zionist Organization, a position he filled from 1920 to 1929. He drafted the well-documented, comprehensive Zionist Memorandum submitted to the Palestine Royal Commission on behalf of the Jewish Agency for Palestine. He was not a proponent of a Jewish State, which makes his testimony before the Peel Commission on January 5, 1937 all the more compelling concerning the effect the 1922 White Paper had on the meaning of the National Home, as shown by the following exchange from his testimony:[69]

---

[69] *Palestine Royal Commission: Minutes of Evidence Heard at Public Sessions*, Colonial No. 134. Reproduced in *The Rise of Israel*, Vol. 22, Document 3, p. 323.

> Harold Morris: Are you suggesting that the Balfour Declaration envisaged a Jewish State?
>
> Leonard Stein: Yes, I do suggest that.
>
> Morris: You suggest it envisaged a Jewish State?
>
> Stein: Yes, I have no doubt about it.
>
> Morris: Can you show me anything in the words of the preamble [of the Mandate] which alter that?
>
> Stein: No, I cannot show you anything in the words of the preamble which alter that.
>
> Morris: I am going to suggest to you the words of the preamble did not envisage a Jewish State, neither did the words of the Declaration?[70]
>
> Stein: The reason why the conception is altered is that before the Mandate was issued, the British Government was at pains in the 1922 White Paper to show exactly how it was going to give effect to the Balfour Declaration and how it then interpreted the Declaration…I should have no difficulty at all in showing that it was changed and that what was said at the time by the representatives of the Powers concerned did contemplate a Jewish State. I do not say they were right, but that is what was said.

A little later in his testimony, Stein added the following remarks:

> I should like to assure the Commission that I am not speaking without some knowledge of the matter or without some authority when I say there is a good deal of evidence that what was contemplated at that time was a Jewish State or a Jewish Commonwealth in Palestine… to finish my answer to Sir Harold Morris, my answer would be that between 1917 and 1922 when the Mandate was issued, just as many other things and conceptions changed in the flux of public affairs, so there was a change – I am not making any complaint of it – there was a change in the conception and reading of the Balfour Declaration. It was to some extent cut down. It may be a good thing that it was, but it was cut down by the time we reached 1922. *The British Government made it clear in their White Paper in that year they did not contemplate a Jewish State in the sense in which that word would commonly be used* (emphasis added).

It is remarkable that the British Government was able to change without much difficulty and at a very early stage the true meaning and purpose of the Balfour

[70] Morris was here referring to Churchill's fine distinction between "the establishment in Palestine of 'a' national home for the Jewish people", i.e., merely a home in Palestine, and the establishment of Palestine as "the" national home. The indefinite article "a" was used in both the Declaration and the second recital of the Preamble of the Mandate.

Declaration and the Mandate, even before the latter went into legal force. The explanation lies in the fact that the Mandate was never amended in accordance with the formal procedure set out in the instrument itself, which required the consent of the Council of the League of Nations. Instead, an easier and more convenient method was adopted to impart a new meaning to the Mandate to reflect the British Government's revised thinking on whatever it should be at any particular time. It simply issued a statement of policy, commonly known as a White Paper, to change the way the Mandate ought to be implemented, which was tantamount to an illegal amendment of it that avoided the necessity of altering any specific provision of the Mandate. The most notable example in this regard were the British restrictions imposed on the Jewish right of return to Palestine, in Article 6 of the Mandate which were introduced in both the 1922 and 1939 White Papers. These restrictions were added despite the fact that Article 6 was never formally amended to say that Jewish immigration could be restrained, either by the economic absorptive capacity of the country or, later, by the lack of Arab consent. It is true that the British Government generally presented their White Papers to both the U.K. Parliament and the Council of the League of Nations for their consideration and approval, but doing that was still a less rigorous procedure than formally requesting the Council to approve a modification of the text of a particular article or articles of the Mandate which would clarify the exact changes to be made. All together, there were six White Papers that were issued, and all of them must be considered illegal because they all proposed or dealt with possible changes to the Mandate Charter without going through the proper and obligatory amending procedure set up for that purpose. The order of their appearance was:

1. The Churchill White Paper of June 3, 1922;
2. The Passfield White Paper of October 20, 1930;
3. The White Paper of July 7, 1937, published simultaneously with the Peel Royal Commission Report;
4. The White Paper of December 23, 1937 appointing a technical commission headed by John Woodhead to submit proposals for a detailed scheme of partition;
5. The White Paper of November 9, 1938 on the Partition Commission Report;
6. The Malcolm MacDonald White Paper of May 17, 1939.

These White Papers were really deviations from the plain meaning of the actual terms of the Mandate, whether it involved the definition of the Jewish National Home, the purpose of the Mandate, the question of Partition, the alleged theory of the dual obligation by the Mandatory towards Jews and Arabs or restrictions placed on both Jewish immigration and the transfer of land from Arabs to Jews. None of these Papers should have ever seen the light of day. The duty of the British Government as the Mandatory Power was to assiduously implement the directives already contained in the Mandate and not to devise its own unique interpretation that went completely contrary to those directives. If it had carried out the Mandate in the way it was supposed to, by observing its actual terms, as the fundamental law of Palestine, the great problems that arose in the administration of the Mandate would have been averted and an independent Jewish State would have arisen long before it actually did.

The British circumvention of the Balfour Declaration continued throughout the entire period of Mandatory rule which lasted from July 1, 1920 to May 14, 1948. The wreckage of the Mandate originating in the false interpretation placed on it by the Churchill White Paper and all the other statements of policy that followed, has left most people ignorant of the actual existence of Jewish legal rights and title of sovereignty over the whole country of Palestine, a situation that lasted not only during the period of the Mandate but also generally prevails today. The cloud of abysmal ignorance which hovers over those rights and title of sovereignty can only be dissipated by appropriate remedial steps that will need to be taken one day if and when propitious circumstances arise to allow them to be taken by a Government of Israel courageous enough to assert and repossess what truly belongs to the Jewish People and the State of Israel under international law as originally defined in Article 22 of the League Covenant founded on the Smuts Resolution, the San Remo Resolution, the Mandate and the Franco-British Boundary Convention of December 23, 1920. Until now that kind of iron-willed, courageous and patriotic Government has never come to power. In fact, the very opposite has manifested itself, continuing until the present day.

All Israeli governments in power from 1967 onwards have made the legal situation worse, but none so surprisingly as Menachem Begin's Likud Government elected on May 17, 1977. He left the question of sovereignty "open" in the Camp David Framework Agreement for Peace in the Middle East which contradicted the already acquired Jewish legal rights and title of sovereignty over Palestine and the Land of Israel. The self-abnegation of rights has been greatly compounded by all the Israel-PLO Agreements concluded since August 20, 1993 as well as the unnecessary and harmful Treaty of Peace signed with Jordan on October 26, 1994 which gave an imprimatur of false legality to the British dirty trick of detaching Transjordan from the Jewish National Home 72 years earlier. All agreements with the fraudulently-named Palestine Liberation Organization and treaties with Egypt and Jordan which either renounced Jewish legal rights and title of sovereignty over various areas of the Land of Israel or recognized or conceded foreign sovereignty over them were illegal and unconstitutional *ab initio* under Israeli constitutional and criminal law.[71]

[71] See the author's work, A Petition to Annul the Interim Agreement, Policy Paper 77, The Ariel Center for Policy Research, January 1999.

*Section Four*

# The Switch Of National Identities And Names

*Chapter 16*

# The Name "Palestine" and the Meaning of Palestinian Nationality during the Mandate Period

After Palestine was specifically created at the San Remo Peace Conference on April 24-25, 1920 as a mandated state to be the Jewish National Home as set out in the Balfour Declaration, and officially placed under British mandatory administration on July 1, 1920, the name "Palestine" became intimately associated in the worldwide public mind with the Jewish People, certainly not with the local Arab inhabitants. The ethnological, legal and linguistic association between Palestine and the Jews in terms of nationality existed because both Palestine and the Jewish National Home were created for each other at the same time under international law, and both terms referred to the same geographical territory at the time of their official creation. It is true that the limits of the territory (Palestine and the Jewish National Home) were not then defined, but they were understood to include all territory historically conquered, settled and governed by the Twelve Tribes of Israel and their descendants in the first and second Jewish Commonwealths, i.e., "from Dan to Beersheba". As a result, the national designation of "Palestinians" was primarily attributed to the Jews of Palestine. This perception was supported by Article 7 of the Mandate for Palestine which read as follows:

> The Administration of Palestine shall be responsible for enacting a nationality law. There shall be included in this law provisions framed so as to facilitate the acquisition of *Palestinian citizenship by Jews* who take up their permanent residence in Palestine (emphasis added).

The foregoing article of the Mandate obliged Britain as the Administrator of Palestine to enact a nationality law containing provisions to facilitate (i.e., provide facilities for) the acquisition of Palestinian citizenship by Jews coming from abroad, who decided to take up their residence in the new mandated state of Palestine. As pointed out by the late Professor Nathan Feinberg of the Hebrew University in Jerusalem, this meant that foreign Jews who emigrated to Palestine had a right to claim Palestinian citizenship, and Britain had a corresponding international obligation to confer such citizenship upon them, without exercising any discretion in the matter.[1] No such right or obligation existed in favour of foreign Arabs. Article 7 of the Mandate thus confirmed the fact that Palestine was created for the sole purpose of establishing it as the National Home for the Jewish People in recognition of their historical connection with that country. Consequently, those Jews who lived in their Home which was being reconstituted, were designated "Palestinians" in terms of their citizenship.

None of the Zionist leaders assisting the British officials in drafting the Balfour Declaration in 1917 apparently considered the question of the proper name of the country. They simply assumed it would be called Palestine since this was the name already used in the 1897 Zionist program adopted by the first Zionist Congress in Basle – itself an indication of the unfortunate estrangement that had developed between Zionism and the Jewish tradition to which the name "Palestine" was foreign – and was the unofficial name of the country most prevalent at the time. In his book Der Judenstaat published in Vienna in 1896, Theodor Herzl also referred to Palestine as the place where the Jewish State would be created if the Turkish Sultan gave this land to the Jews. Herzl also used the term "the Promised Land" as a synonym for the Jewish State he envisioned. Israel Zangwill, a loyal supporter of Herzl, addressed this very question in December 1917 at the London Opera House rally in celebration of the Balfour Declaration. As noted in the previous chapter, he proposed that the country be called "Judea", exactly as Lord Robert Cecil had suggested when he said "Judea for the Jews", but nothing came of his wise proposal.

The early drafts of the Mandate for Palestine, prepared in close cooperation between British and Zionist representatives, did contain the Hebrew name "Eretz Israel" alongside the name Palestine in the Preamble. The use of this term originated with even earlier Zionist drafts and was then placed in a joint Zionist-British Draft Mandate dated December 11, 1919. This Draft Mandate included the following recital in its Preamble:[2]

> Recognizing the historical connection of the Jewish people with Palestine (Eretz Israel) and the claim which this gives them to *reconstitute Palestine as their national home* (italics in the original).

The very same recital then appeared in a revised draft mandate dated March 15, 1920. However, in the next revised draft dated June 10, 1920, the recital

---

[1] See Prof. Feinberg's article "The Principles of Palestinian Citizenship as Laid Down by International Law", in the booklet Some Problems of the Palestine Mandate, Tel-Aviv (1936), pp. 58-59.

[2] *Documents on British Foreign Policy, 1919-1939*, edited by E.L. Woodward and Rohan Butler, First Series, Volume IV, 1919, London, Document No. 397, p. 571.

recognizing the historical connection of the Jewish People with Palestine was omitted, as was the reference to Eretz-Israel, in compliance with Foreign Minister Lord Curzon's instructions to water down the Zionist character of the Mandate. An explanation for the omission of the references both to the "historical connection" and to "Eretz-Israel" in this draft was provided in an internal Foreign Office letter dated June 30, 1920, sent by Hubert Young to Robert Vansittart, two British officials involved in the drafting process. This letter, which also recounted Chaim Weizmann's reaction to these omissions, read in part:[3]

> My dear Vansittart,
>
> ...Lord Curzon made a long speech in the House of Lords yesterday in which the first attempt was made to define [= redefine, H.G.] what was meant by the Jewish National Home. He minuted on your letter:
>
> "I am quite willing to water the Palestine Mandate, which I cordially distrust."
>
> ...
>
> I enclose the Zionists' observations on the last revise, of which I understand you gave Weizmann a copy. He came to see me today and asked me most earnestly to restore the little sentence in the original preamble "recognizing the historical connection..." (but without the words, Eretz Israel, which he agreed to be undesirable). I see no objection to this, and it will enable us to cover our retreat when the further watering [of the Mandate] takes place...
>
> Yours ever,
> Hubert Young

As appears from Hubert Young's revealing letter, the removal of the name "Eretz Israel" from the Mandate's Preamble not only elicited no protest from Chaim Weizmann, representing the Zionist Organization, but the latter actually agreed that that term was "undesirable". Weizmann acted wisely in urging the British to restore the reference to the "historical connection", a reference that had originally been inserted by Lord Balfour himself when he served as Foreign Minister before being replaced by Lord Curzon. Weizmann, however, inexplicably felt no pressing need to act similarly on behalf of the equally important reference to Eretz-Israel. Despite numerous warnings by contemporary Zionist leaders not to rely so completely on British good intentions, he apparently failed to recognize that having this clearly Jewish name for the country included in the official English version of the Mandate might have avoided possible future misunderstandings concerning the true significance of the Mandate and later British attempts to change that meaning during their thirty-year administration

---

[3] Letter from Hubert Young to Robert Vansittart, June 30, 1920, Foreign Office 371/5244; (E7369/4164/44).

of Palestine.

The abbreviation "E.I." for Eretz-Israel did appear on postage stamps of Palestine as a result of a formal decision taken by the High Commissioner, Herbert Samuel, at a meeting of the Advisory Council held on November 9, 1920. This followed the usage introduced by General Allenby's Military Administration soon after the conquest of Palestine in the Great War. In making his decision Samuel was reported to have said:[4]

> He was aware that there was no other name in the Hebrew language for this land except 'Eretz-Israel'. At the same time he thought that if 'Eretz-Israel' only were used, it might not be regarded by the outside world as a correct rendering of the word 'Palestine', and in the case of passports or certificates of nationality, it might perhaps give rise to difficulties, so it was decided to print 'Palestine' in Hebrew letters and to add after it the letters 'Aleph' 'Yod' [in parentheses], which constitute a recognized abbreviation of the Hebrew name. His Excellency still thought this was a good compromise. Dr. [Habib] Salem wanted to omit 'Aleph' 'Yod' and Mr. [David] Yellin wanted to omit 'Palestine'. The right solution would be to retain both.

The official use in Hebrew of "Palestina (Aleph Yod)" on postage stamps was challenged in a famous court case in 1925: Jamal Eff. Hussein v. The Government of Palestine.[5]In that case, the Petitioner asked for an order to be issued against the Postmaster-General to withdraw from circulation certain postage stamps marked with the Hebrew lettering of "Palestina (Aleph Yod)". The Petitioner claimed that such stamps describing the country of Palestine as the Land of Israel, was "a moral injury" and "an offense to the national pride of the Arab Nation". The Supreme Court rejected the application of the Petitioner on both technical, legal grounds[6] and because it was a matter dealing with sentiment and politics that did not warrant the court's interference with a public department. In his judgment, Chief Justice Thomas W. Haycraft noted

---

[4] See Memorandum No. 33, "Use of the Name 'Eretz-Israel'," in the *Report by the Palestine Royal Commission*, 1937, Memoranda Prepared by the Government of Palestine, C.O. Colonial No. 133, reproduced as Document 26, *The Rise of Israel*, Garland Publishing, Inc., New York (1987), Volume 21, p. 235 at p. 394.

[5] High Court No. 55 of 1925, *The Law Reports of Palestine*, selected and edited by Michael McDonnell, London (1934), p. 50. See also: *The Rise of Israel*, Volume 21, p. 394-5.

[6] In the opinion of the Court, the existing law embodied in Article 82 of the Palestine Order-in Council, 1922, did not prescribe that the Hebrew words had to be a literal translation of the English and article 22 of the Mandate did not apply to "executive acts"; moreover, the provisions of the Mandate had not been incorporated into the Law of Palestine by Order-in-Council and was therefore unenforceable.

"that Palestine is not an Arabic word" and that "the Arabs call this country Southern Syria". "Nevertheless," he observed, "the Arabs are content to let the word 'Palestine' stand."[7]

The name "Palestine" remained the official designation of the country throughout the Mandate period. Had the country of Palestine been called, instead, Israel or Judea at the start of that period, which would have been more appropriate psychologically[8] and historically, the status of the country as a Jewish State in the making could not have been challenged, the Jewish residents would have been known as Israelis or Judeans, and non-Jewish citizens would have had the same designation. Then the Arabs of today would never have adopted the name "Judeans" or "Israelis" for themselves. Nor, of course, would they have called their terrorist organization the "Judea/Israel Liberation Organization".

The reference to a nationality law in Article 7 of the Mandate raises the question of the definition of nationality. The word "nationality" is susceptible of two separate meanings. In an anthropological or ethnological sense it refers to the quality or fact of belonging to a particular nation, people or ethnic group whose members are united by strong ties of common origin and destiny, religion, history, language, culture, traditions and customs. Nationality in this sense is not necessarily related to one specific state and can even exist without statehood. The Jews were a recognized nation or people from the time of Moses, about 3300 years ago, but existed for 1,848 years without an independent state, from the year 70 to the year 1948. When all or most members of any particular nation live in the same state, the latter is considered to be a nation-state. When members of a recognized nation live in a state not their own, they are considered to be a national minority and may enjoy collective (political and linguistic) rights if that is provided for in a law or constitution. When most members of a national group become assimilated in a foreign state, they lose their separate identity as an ethnic nationality as has happened to many Jews, inter alia, in the American melting-pot.

In its second and different meaning that is strictly legal in nature and also broader in scope, the word "nationality" is used to refer exclusively to the status or rights of citizenship conferred by a state on the permanent inhabitants of that state without any connection to an individual's ethnic, religious or cultural identity. In return for these rights, a person owes allegiance to the state of which he or she is a citizen. In this legal sense, nationality and citizenship mean exactly the same thing, as do their cognate words "national" and "citizen".

---

[7] *The Rise of Israel*, Volume 21, p. 395.

[8] Prof. Yuval Ne'eman was also of the opinion that Palestine was the wrong name given to the country at the start of the Mandate period. He told the author at his Tel-Aviv University office in 2004, upon receiving an early draft of the present book, that from a psychological point-of-view, the names "Judea" and "Israel" were more suitable and would have obviated the current problem arising from the use of the name "Palestinians" by Arabs who appropriated it despite its primary use to identify the Jews living in the country.

In the Balfour Declaration of November 2, 1917, the word "national" as used in the phrase "a national home for the Jewish People" was intended to convey the double meaning of both the limited, anthropological-ethnological sense of the definition of nationality, as well as the meaning inherent in its broader, legal sense. There would have been no logic in creating the mandated state of Palestine if not for the specific purpose of creating a home for the Jewish nation, and granting all Jews emigrating to Palestine the right to obtain the nationality (i.e., citizenship) of Palestine.

A provision concurrent with Article 7 of the Mandate was found in Article 129 of the Treaty of Sèvres. It stated:

> Jews of other than Turkish nationality who are habitually resident, on the coming into force of the present Treaty, within the boundaries of Palestine as determined in accordance with Article 95, will ipso facto become citizens of Palestine to the exclusion of any other nationality.

As can be seen from the text of Article 129 of the Treaty, it granted automatic citizenship without any period of waiting or other formality to all Jews who were not of Turkish nationality but who were habitually resident in Palestine. As for those Jews residing in Palestine who held Turkish nationality, they, too, automatically became Palestinian citizens under a separate provision of the Treaty of Sèvres (Article 123).[9]

The automatic grant of Palestinian citizenship to foreign Jews under Article 129 annulled the citizenship they previously possessed. This article, like Article 7 of the Mandate, was a natural consequence of the fact that Palestine was created to be the Jewish National Home and an eventual independent Jewish State. A "Palestinian" in terms of the Mandate and the Treaty of Sèvres thus originally designated a member of the Jewish nation living in Palestine, who had acquired Palestinian citizenship, as would normally be expected in a theoretical Jewish nation-state in the making. That is exactly what Weizmann meant when he spoke of Palestine one day becoming as Jewish as England is English, at the Paris Peace Conference on February 27, 1919. The fact that the term "Palestinians" also legally included Arabs residing in Palestine did not detract from the intended meaning of this term, that it was used primarily to designate Jews, in the same way the modern term "Israeli" is generally understood to refer to Jews, though legally the term applies to all citizens of Israel, whether Jewish or members of any other ethnic group.

Article 129 of the Treaty of Sèvres stated in positive terms what Article 125 of the same treaty confirmed in a negative or deductive form, that Palestine was set aside by the Principal Allied Powers to be the National Home of the Jewish

[9] Article 123 stated: "Turkish subjects habitually resident in territory which, in accordance with the provisions of the present Treaty, is detached from Turkey will become ipso facto, in the conditions laid down by the local law, nationals of the State to which such territory is transferred".

People. Article 125 deliberately did not mention Palestine when it declared:

> Persons over eighteen years of age habitually resident in territory detached from Turkey in accordance with the present Treaty and differing in race from the majority of the population of such territory shall within one year from the coming into force of the present Treaty be entitled to opt for Armenia, Azerbaijan, Georgia, Greece, the Hedjaz, Mesopotamia, Syria, Bulgaria or Turkey, if the majority of the population of the State selected is of the same race as the person exercising the right to opt.

The significance of this article in regard to Palestinian nationality was explained by Professor Nathan Feinberg in a penetrating analysis. He stated:[10]

> This provision was inspired by the same ideology as Articles 85 and 91 of the Treaty of Versailles, Article 40 of the Treaty of Neuilly, Article 80 of [the Treaty of] St. Germain and Article 64 of [the Treaty of] Trianon.
>
> It was the aim of these measures to make the nationality status of every person to coincide with the ethnological membership of the nation or people to which he belonged. The option was intended here to serve the "principle of nationalities".[11]
>
> The attentive reader has undoubtedly noticed that in Article 125 Palestine was not mentioned among the States for which the inhabitants of the territories detached from Turkey were entitled to opt. No right to opt for Palestinian citizenship has been granted to Arabs living outside the boundaries of Palestine, although the majority of its population was Arab. The Arab majority was not recognized as a permanent and decisive factor, and Palestine has – with total disregard of this majority – not been considered as an Arab country. The recognition of "the historical connection of the Jewish People with Palestine and of the grounds for reconstituting their National Home in that country" brought the Peace Conference to the conclusion that Palestine was to be excluded from the list of States for which Arabs were entitled to opt.

It is clear from the foregoing quotation that the global political and

---

[10] *Op. cit.*, pp. 55-56.

[11] The "principle of nationalities" identifies a particular state with a particular nation. This principle is also called the "principle of national self-determination". In regard to the mandated State of Palestine, the San Remo Peace Conference identified the country with the Jewish People, thus making Palestine, in theory, a Jewish country from the time it was officially created (on April 24, 1920) by the Principal Allied Powers upon their adoption of the Balfour Declaration.

legal settlement of 1919-1920 hammered out at the Paris and San Remo Peace Conferences recognized Palestine as a Jewish country or nation-state, notwithstanding the demographic fact that the population was at that time predominantly Arab. As Professor Feinberg clarified above, the Arabs living outside Palestine had no legal right to opt for Palestinian nationality or citizenship, but in any event were given this right in practice by the British, who did not prevent the illegal mass influx of hundreds of thousands of Arabs into the country during the years of their administration. This doubled the size of the Arab population from 565,000 in 1920 to approximately 1,225,000 in 1947.[12]

The principle of nationalities was thus applied to the Jewish People and not to the local Arab inhabitants in the specific case of Palestine. It followed that Palestinian nationality was congruent with Jewish nationality in the ethnological sense, as well as in the legal sense of citizenship. The dual meaning of Palestinian nationality in favour of the Jewish People as set out in the relevant provisions of the Treaty of Sèvres and Mandate for Palestine was abruptly changed in 1922 by the Churchill White Paper. The latter defined the term "nationality" as broadly as possible, not limited to a particular nation or ethnic group, but included all sections of the Palestinian population. On this point the White Paper said:

> It is contemplated that the status of all citizens of Palestine in the eyes of the law shall be Palestinian, and it has never been intended that they, or any section of them, should possess any other juridical status.

As a result of the aforesaid redefinition of Palestinian nationality, the connection formerly existing between Palestinian nationality and the Jewish nation was no longer recognized by Britain as the Mandatory Power. Henceforth the terms "Palestinian" or "a Palestinian national" denoted citizenship only, without regard to ethnological or racial identity, particularly Jewish nationality. That is the basis of the statement made in the Churchill White Paper that "the development of the Jewish National Home in Palestine" does not mean "the imposition of Jewish nationality upon the inhabitants of Palestine as a whole".

This in turn produced a re-interpretation of the Balfour Declaration which, as expounded by Herbert Samuel,[13] meant that Palestine in its entirety was no longer the exclusive Jewish National Home, but a home that had to be shared with the Arabs, exactly as Ahad Ha'Am had previously stated in the Preface of the Third Edition of his book, Al Parashat Derakhim (At the Crossroads).

---

[12] See: N. Feinberg, "On an Arab Jurist's Approach to Zionism and the State of Israel", republished in *Studies in International Law*, the Magnes Press, The Hebrew University, Jerusalem (1979), p.563, n. 206.

[13] See Samuel's Report dated April 22, 1925 to Colonial Secretary Leopold Stennett Amery on the administration of Palestine 1920-1925, summarizing the first period of British civilian rule, in *The Rise of Israel*, Volume 13, Document 35, p. 518.

This preface also appeared in his English work, "Ten Essays on Zionism and Judaism".[14] According to the political thinking of Ahad Ha'Am, a Jewish national home would be founded "in Palestine" (i.e., not in the whole country) alongside the existing Arab national home, and neither nation would be the sole ruler in the country. Palestine would thus be a state of all its citizens and not a nation-state for the Jewish People alone, a view which is exactly what the political leaders of the Arabs of present day Israel would like the Jewish State become. However, that view was completely contrary to what was originally contemplated when the Balfour Declaration was issued in 1917 and approved by the Principal Allied Powers in 1920, namely, that all of Palestine was created specifically to be the Jewish National Home.

Despite the British policy to disassociate Palestinian nationality, in the ethnological sense, from Jewish nationality, it was still the custom and tendency throughout the Mandate period to call all the Jews who lived in Palestine between April 24, 1920 and May 14, 1948 by the distinctive name of "Palestinians" or sometimes "Judeans" who were re-creating the Jewish State of old. Those who were Arabic-speaking gentiles were referred to generally as either Arabs or the Moslem and Christian inhabitants of Palestine rather than Palestinians, as the Jews were. Arab nationalists preferred to call themselves Syrians, as exemplified by an all-Palestine Arab Conference in February 1919 which supported the country's inclusion in an independent Syria. These nationalists believed in the oneness of Palestine and Syria, while denying any specific Palestinian national identity. That view was emphatically presented by their leading spokesman, George Antonius, when he appeared as a witness to give evidence before the Palestine Royal Commission on January 18, 1937. In his testimony, he recalled the discussions and preparations made by leading persons in Syria and Palestine in 1915, which preceded the outbreak of the "Arab Revolt" and the reprisals made by the Turks against them. He described the shared fate of all these people who struggled for the independence of one unified country embracing both Syria and Palestine:[15]

> It is very important to note that the sacrifices made and the penalties incurred were common and shared in common by Syrians and Palestinians, as well as by Iraqis. In particular, the Turks had hanged a great many people, most of them on suspicion of belonging to societies which were known or suspected to have entered into communication with the British or French. On various occasions, people belonging to the best-known families, Moslem and Christian, Syrian and Palestinian, were hanged in the public squares of Damascus or Beirut or Jerusalem,

[14] Ahad Ha'Am: *Ten Essays on Zionism and Judaism*, London (1922), pp. xvi-xix. The relevant text of what Ahad Ha'Am wrote is found in the Memorandum submitted to the Palestine Royal Commission on behalf of the Jewish Agency for Palestine, reprinted in 1975 by Greenwood Press, U.S.A., pp.98-100.

[15] *The Rise of Israel*, Vol. 22, Document 3, p. 401.

> irrespectively. *There was no distinction between Syrian and Palestinian. The country was one, it acted as one, its future was one*, and the sufferings and penalties were all born in common (emphasis added).

Later on in his testimony, Antonius expounded on the position taken by the Arabs of Palestine towards Syria. He affirmed that Palestine had always been an integral part of Syria and that there were no essential differences between them:

> If I may go on now to another point, I should like to speak about the feeling of the Arabs in regard to their position in this country. I said a moment ago that the Arab movement began as a cultural revival and that it was some time before it turned into a political movement of which the aim was national independence, but one or two points are worth noting in connection with that. The first is that that movement was never a regional movement in which Syria wanted independence for Syria, or Iraq wanted independence for Iraq. It was a movement of the whole Arab race working together to free themselves from Turkish rule and establish the Arab life, a life in which they would be able to feel masters in their own home and pursue their destiny on a basis of the development of their language and their cultural values and their traditions. It was not until after the War and the settlement which followed the War that we hear for the first time of a national movement in Syria and a national movement in Iraq working for certain definite ends in Iraq or in Syria, as the case may be. In actual fact, that movement was all the same. It only acquired regional characteristics in the days after the War because of the partitioning that had been imposed on the Arab nation by the post-War settlement. *I want to emphasize this, because in a good deal of what is written and said abroad, particularly in England, by serious writers and students, this fundamental aspect of the movement here in Palestine is lost sight of, that Palestine has always been an integral part of Syria and that what was common to Syria is common to Palestine. There are dialectical differences, certain small differences of customs, local differences, but on the whole the differences are trivial. For instance, I do not think the difference between Jerusalem and Damascus, from the point of view of dialect and customs is as great as the difference between, say, Yorkshire and Somerset.*[16] *The country is one in every way, it has always lived and worked and fought as one, and, at the present time, what we see in Palestine is not a local movement against the British Mandate, but the continuation of the powerful movement which arose in the whole of the Arab world which it followed in common without any distinction between its component parts* (emphasis added).

---

[16] *Ibid.*, p. 407. Yorkshire is in north England, while Somerset is in the southwest of the country.

It is true that the Arabs who lived in Palestine during the Mandate period were indeed called "Palestinians" in terms of their citizenship and place of residence, to distinguish them from the Arabs living in French-mandated Syria and British-administered Iraq. Even George Antonius made this geographical distinction when referring to the Arabs of these different countries, a distinction he blamed on Britain and France for partitioning the Middle East in the post-World War I settlement. But that distinction – legal and geographical in nature – did not mean there existed a separate Palestinian nation, merely a separate Palestinian citizenship. The Arab identification of Palestine with Syria, which George Antonius so strongly emphasized, still echoed as late as May 1956 when the founder of the Palestine Liberation Organization, Ahmed Shukeiry, told the U.N. Security Council eight years prior to the founding of that organization: "It is common knowledge that Palestine is nothing but southern Syria".

As will be recalled, the Mandate Charter itself made no mention of any national group other than the Jewish People. No reference can be found therein to a distinct nation called "Palestinians". The only place where the word "Palestinian" does occur in the text of this document is in Article 7 where it is used as an adjective in front of the word "citizenship" in regard not to Arabs, but to Jews. Both the Peel Royal Commission Report and the 1939 White Paper referred only to Arabs and never to "Palestinians" to indicate those who comprised most of the non-Jewish population of Palestine. The same practice of not denoting Arabs as "Palestinians" was followed in the Report of the United Nations Special Committee on Palestine, but the Committee also claimed, contrary to what George Antonius told the Palestine Royal Commission, that there existed a "Palestinian nationalism" which was distinct from "Arab nationalism", that developed it said after the settlement of the First World War.[17] This claim of the Committee was obviously made to justify their majority proposal to partition Palestine into an Arab State and a Jewish State, as adopted by the General Assembly on November 29, 1947. However, as noted, most Arab nationalists did not accept the concept of a separate "Palestinian" nation during the period of the Mandate, because they knew intuitively that the term "Palestinian" was generally associated with the Jews of Palestine, even if there were some isolated instances where reference was made to a "Palestinian people" to connote a separate ethno-national identity.

Palestinian nationality in the legal sense of citizenship ceased to exist with the expiration of the Mandate and the establishment of the Jewish State of Israel. In an extraordinary and ironic development marked by clever falsehood to deceive the world and gain its sympathy, a Palestinian nationality in the ethnological sense has been revived by self-styled leaders of the Arab population in the Land of Israel, this time to designate not those for whom it was originally intended – the Jewish People – but rather the Arabs for whom it was never intended and

[17] See paragraph 166 of the *Report to the General Assembly by the United Nations Special Committee on Palestine*, p. 112, published by Somerset Books, Inc., New York City, 1947.

who, for the most part, had specifically rejected this appellation for themselves during the Mandate period, as shown in the testimony offered by George Antonius. This ruse has worked so well and gained so much momentum that the existence of a Palestinian nation now constitutes a superficially incontrovertible and universal, though non-historical, "fact" that poses the greatest danger of all to existing Jewish legal rights and title of sovereignty over the Land of Israel, particularly the regions of Judea, Samaria and Gaza. Even the State of Israel and its highest political echelons ever since Menachem Begin have fallen into the trap of accepting this *deadly fiction.* They have recognized a non-existent "nation" of "Palestinians" having a right to self-determination in the very land reserved, with world approval, for the Jewish People for its own self-determination. Thus the question of Palestinian nationality has returned to its original meaning in the narrow, ethnological sense, but has been inverted to make it coincide with Arab, rather than Jewish, ethnicity. This has made a sheer mockery of the global political and legal settlement devised by the Principal Allied Powers in which Palestine was created under international law to be a Jewish country belonging to the Jewish People and not to the local Arabs, now disguised as the fictitious nation of "Palestinians".

*Chapter 17*

# The Arab Appropriation of the Name "Palestinians"

As noted in the concluding paragraphs of the previous chapter, a fraudulent and threatening development of great dimensions has insidiously entered the legal and political picture to further cloud and inversely affect the genuine legal rights and title of sovereignty of the Jewish People over all of Palestine and the Land of Israel. This development can only be described as a switch of national identities and names that has taken place since the end of the Six-Day War of June 5-10, 1967, which became more concrete and seeped into the general consciousness of the world sometime during 1969 and in the early 1970's when Golda Meir was Prime Minister of the State of Israel, by means of a skillful and clever propaganda campaign conducted by the misnamed "Palestine Liberation Organization".

The constant use of the word "Palestinian" to denote a separate Arab nation in the Land of Israel is fraudulent since no such nation has ever existed, either in the days of antiquity or in modern times. This is evidenced by the fact that not once in the literature of the ancient world does the word "Palestinian" ever appear as a proper noun to describe a nation of that name or an individual member of such a nation.[1] Moreover, the appropriation of this name by the Arabs of former Mandated Palestine is really bizarre, because the name is derived from a Hebrew root, with no apparent connection to Arabic,[2] and was used by the ancient Israelites to describe the invading Philistines with whom the Arabs never had any historical, cultural or ethnic (racial) affinity.

In light of the fierce Arab hatred of Israeli Jews and their desire to destroy the Jewish State, it is not only bizarre but actually ludicrous for the same Arabs

---

[1] See article by Louis H. Feldman, "Some Observations on the Name of Palestine", *Hebrew Union College Annual, Volume* LXI (1990), pp. 1, 14, 18, 19.

[2] The Hebrew and Arabic languages, being cognate languages belonging to the Semitic-Hamitic family, share many common roots. The Arabic language, however, does not make use of the Hebrew root פ-ל-ש though this root does appear in other Semitic tongues, including Ge'ez (Classical Ethiopic), in the form *falashas*, a name applied to the Jews of Ethiopia by other Ethiopians. The author has verified this point with Yoel Lerner, a linguist and translator from Jerusalem.

to adopt as their national name one that is directly traceable to a Hebrew source. On the other hand, considering the Arabic penchant to Arabize and Islamize early Israelite history and culture and convert or transform Hebrew Patriarchs, prophets, judges and kings into Arab ones, while at the same time denying their Jewish genealogy, the adoption of the name "Palestinians" that was applied both ethnologically and legally to the Jewish People of Palestine from 1920 to 1948 falls into the same pattern of inversion and plagiarism that characterizes the habits of the Arabs of Palestine. To legitimize themselves, they have imbibed and arrogated what does not belong to them: the memories and achievements of the Jewish People, both ancient and modern. Nothing has been left untouched by the Arab falsifiers and cultural embezzlers in their shameless quest to portray themselves as the indigenous inhabitants of Palestine who allegedly hold the title-deed to the Land of Israel despite the fact that the Arabs only appeared on the scene as an identifiable people two thousand years after the Jews were already settled on the land and contributing enormously to civilization. The Arabs even went to the extent, in some instances, of copying the very programs and texts of the Zionist Movement, using the very same language, as in the case of their so-called Declaration of Independence of November 15, 1988 issued by the Palestine National Council, which imitates the very words and style of the Israeli Declaration of Independence of May 14, 1948, proclaimed by the People's Council (Mo'etzet Ha'Am).

The lack of any Arab affinity to the ancient Philistines was noted by the late Professor Yehoshafat Harkabi of the Hebrew University of Jerusalem, in the Departments of International Relations and Middle Eastern Studies, who made the following observations about the identity of the Arabs of Palestine during the Mandate period:[3]

> The definition that 'Palestine is the homeland of the Palestinian Arab people' may give the impression that the existence of the Palestinian people is an incontestable historical fact, and as if Palestine has always been the homeland of such a people. This glosses over the need to discuss the problem of the historicity of the Palestinian people.
>
> Apart from the Israeli period, 'Palestine' has never been a political unit, in which a unique nationality could emerge. *Palestine was a geographical term*, not a political one. Previously, an Arab who lived in geographical Palestine tended to describe himself as a Moslem, as an Arab, an Ottoman or as a native of his home town or village. Palestine as a political unit was carved out by the British. *'A Palestinian' in the period of the British Mandate until 1948 meant a person who bore Palestinian citizenship*. During the Mandate period, the population of the country was divided into 'Palestinian Jews' and 'Palestinian Arabs' [Harkabi adds

[3] *The Palestinian Covenant and its Meaning*, Y. Harkabi, Vallentine, Mitchell, Great Britain (1979), second edition (1981), p. 29.

> here a footnote stating that the Palestine Royal Commission referred in their report (on p. 130) to the Arabs in Palestine only as 'Arabs' and summarized their claims under the heading of Arab nationalism, not Palestinian nationalism]. Similarly, in the U.N. Partition Resolution of 29 November 1947 Palestine was divided into 'a Jewish state' and 'an Arab state', and it dawned on nobody to call the latter a Palestinian state. The identification of Jews in Palestine as 'Israelis' left the adjective 'Palestinian' free so that the Palestinian Arabs could acquire it for themselves exclusively.
>
> Thus, this term that expressed nationality or citizenship developed into a national definition for a group of Arabs, who either lived in Palestine or originated from it and became a self-conscious collectivity by the events they lived through in recent decades, though the name Palestine is an ancient one and originates from the Philistines, living on islands in the Mediterranean Sea, who invaded and settled in the southern coastal plain. However, the Palestinian Arabs are not descended from them racially, nor do they derive any inspiration from them culturally (quotation marks in the original; all italics added for emphasis).

Harkabi is correct in his perceptive observations regarding the non-historicity of the Palestinian people, but he failed to note that the word used in English to describe the Philistines of ancient times, whence the term "Palestinian" is derived, is, ironically, Hebrew in origin, rather than Arabic, Greek or Latin. In the modern age, the only people called "Palestinians" in a ethno-national sense until the term was brazenly plagiarized by the "Palestine Liberation Organization" were Jews who returned to their ancient homeland, the land of Zion, to rebuild a new national life and state where they were once again in control of their own destiny. Apart from the aforementioned failure on Harkabi's part, there is also no justification for believing as he does that there now exists a Palestinian people, brought into being by "the events of recent decades", as will be further discussed below.

The change of name of most of the gentile residents living in the Land of Israel, who now called themselves "Palestinians" instead of "Arabs", was an act of identity theft of both the ancient name of the Philistines as well as past Jewish national identity established in the Mandate period – from the legal, ethnological, historical, or linguistic point-of-view. It was specifically in order to dispel the notion of Jewish historical connection and sovereign ownership over the Land of Israel, which embraced all of Mandated Palestine, that the Arabs of the country resorted to a public relations and psychological tactic beginning in 1964 to rename themselves "Palestinians". It has proven to be a very effective weapon in the continuing Arab struggle to erase the meaning and consequences of the San Remo Resolution, to overthrow the State of Israel and to elicit sympathy for the Arab cause by claiming that the indigenous

Palestinians were displaced by foreign Jews. By 1969, the new name for the Arabs of former Mandated Palestine began to be accepted by the world at large, even by universalist, self-abnegating Jews in the State of Israel, who either supported the idea or did not care what the Arabs chose to call themselves, despite the enormous damage and confusion this was to cause Israel's legal case to all of Palestine and the Land of Israel under international law. The current belief that these Arabs form a distinct nation known as "Palestinians" has become so widespread that it is presently impossible to debunk, unless serious remedial steps are taken by Israel, as outlined *infra* in the last two chapters of this book.

As just noted, the Arabs who lived in Palestine during the Mandate period were "Palestinians" only in the legal sense of citizenship, in the same way that most Arabs who live today in the State of Israel are "Israelis" in terms of their citizenship. There was no nation then of "Palestinians", just as there is no nation today of "Israelis", but only Arabs and Jews, although Jews are also called the "Nation of Israel". Hence the word "Palestinian" did not connote any national or ethnic identification, but only indicated citizenship and the geographical name of the state or country where Arabs and Jews and others were recognized as citizens. Inasmuch as Palestine had ceased to exist from May 15, 1948 onwards, the continued use of that word to designate citizenship is unjustified and without any logical meaning, except for those who once held that legal status and never acquired any other status. In addition there was no right to use the term "Palestinian" to designate a new Arab nation in view of the fact that it had formally been used in the national sense prior to the Churchill White Paper and afterwards in an informal way to designate the Jews of Mandated Palestine and not the Arabs who had rejected that national designation for themselves. In appropriating the term "Palestinians", the Arabs of Judea, Samaria and Gaza have contradicted both the meaning attributed to this term in the Churchill White Paper where it denoted citizenship rather than national origin and its intimate past association with the Jews of Palestine from 1920 to 1948.

Up to the time of the creation of the State of Israel on May 15, 1948, there was no distinct nation known as "Palestinians" in existence, nor is there truly such a nation even today. This is evidenced by the fact that three key components of nationhood are missing to validate the existence of a Palestinian nation: a past history, a common language and a distinctive culture with its own national literature, traditions and customs, which differ in any significant respect from the Arabs of Syria, Lebanon, Jordan and Iraq. The idea that resistance to Israel's alleged occupation of "Palestinian territories" has produced a distinct "Palestinian nation" is ludicrous from almost every perspective. On the contrary, the Arabs of former Mandated Palestine have not engaged so much in "resistance" as in outright terrorism, which began not with the alleged occupation of Judea, Samaria and Gaza, but ever since the late nineteenth century when Jews began returning in large numbers to their ancestral homeland, long before there existed the notion of a distinct nation of "Palestinians". Moreover, Israel cannot "occupy" lands which by definition are integral parts of the Jewish National Home under international law. A nation is not created by the criterion of "resistance to a foreign occupier", even if in the eyes of its perpetrators "terrorism" is the equivalent of "resistance" and even assuming Israel to be an "occupier" of "Arab lands". A nation is born only when a sizeable community of people sharing what they perceive to be a common origin, a common history, a common language and often faith as well, then form national institutions that weld this community together in a defined territory of their own. A nation does not come into existence on demand, by propaganda or by journalistic or literary invention; it generally requires centuries of evolution and development. As already noted, a distinct nation generally differs from other peoples in language and culture. The Arabs who now call themselves "Palestinians" hardly differ in these essentials from Syrians, Jordanians and other Arabs, particularly the Arabs residing in the State of Israel. However, in light of the widespread belief that there nevertheless exists today a new nation called "Palestinians" who were previously called the Arabs of Palestine, it is worthwhile to trace the chronological steps which led to this fabrication. No definitive date can be given exactly when this fictitious nation of "Palestinians" was supposedly born or crystallized, but it can be said with reasonable certainty to have happened during the year 1969 when Yasser Arafat became the Chairman of the Palestine Liberation Organization and the term "Palestinians" started to come into vogue.

Between May 15, 1948 when the State of Israel was established and November 22, 1967, the date of U.N. Security Council Resolution 242, there was no general acknowledgement outside the Arab world of the existence of a separate people called "Palestinians", otherwise the Arabs who fled their homes in former Palestine after the outbreak of the War of Independence and the Six Day War would not have been called "refugees" in Resolution 242, but referred to by this specific name, as they would soon be in a host of subsequent U.N. Resolutions. Prior to Resolution 242, an Arab Summit Conference at Khartoum, Sudan, on September 1, 1967, attended by eight Heads of State and four Prime Ministers passed a resolution "upholding the rights of the Palestinian people to their country", which was included in the same paragraph that also proclaimed and reiterated the existing Arab policy towards Israel: "No peace with Israel, no recognition of Israel, no negotiations with it."[4] The fact that the language of the Khartoum Resolution regarding "the rights of the Palestinian people to their country" did not find its way into the text of U.N. Security Council Resolution 242 adopted a little less than three months after the Khartoum Conference,

---

[4] A summary of the Khartoum Resolution can be found in: 1) *The Arab-Israeli Conflict*, Volume 3, Documents, edited by John Norton Moore, Princeton University Press, New Jersey (1974), p. 788; 2) *The Arab-Israel Conflict and its Resolution: Selected Documents*, edited by Ruth Lapidoth and Moshe Hirsch, Martinus Nijhoff Publishers, The Netherlands (1992), Document 28, p. 133; 3) *Arab-Israeli Conflict and Conciliation: A Documentary History*, edited by Bernard Reich, Praeger Publishers, Westport, Connecticut (1995), p. 101.

demonstrates that the Arabs living in Judea, Samaria and Gaza, as well as those who previously left the Land of Israel to reside in refugee camps, were not considered a nation by the formulators of Resolution 242. Shortly thereafter, however, the United Nations became the chief propagator of the concept of a "Palestinian nation", which led, in large part, to its universal acceptance.

Though the idea of the Palestinian nation distinct from other Arab nations did not fully solidify until 1969, the starting point for this eventual belief can be considered as June 2, 1964 when the Palestinian National Covenant was adopted and the Palestine Liberation Organization (PLO) founded with the blessing and cooperation of the states comprising the Arab League.[5] An extra-territorial national and organizational entity was visualized, but not a separate state or territorial unit.[6] The person who formulated the Covenant was Ahmed Shukeiry, who is also considered to be the founder of the PLO. He was a lawyer by profession from Mandated Palestine, later an ambassador for Saudi Arabia at the United Nations and then the representative of Palestinian Arabs at the Arab League. He served as the first leader of the PLO until December 1967, when he was dismissed and replaced by Yahya Hammuda and later by Yasser Arafat. Shukeiry was known for his vituperative speeches advocating the physical extermination of the Jews of Israel.

The Palestinian National Covenant was only a first tentative step in forging a new national identity for Arabs who had lived in Mandated Palestine, but did not assert the completely separate existence of a so-called "Palestinian nation", evoking also a Pan-Arab image. This can be seen from the introductory part of the Covenant which spoke several times of "We, the Palestinian Arab People", a phrasing which stressed the Arab connection as much as the Palestinian connection, and this point was further emphasized in the text of the Covenant by the definition of Palestine as an "Arab homeland" linked to a greater Arab homeland comprised of other Arab countries. It also stated that the "Palestinian Arab people… is an inseparable part of the Arab nation" (Article 3 of the Covenant).

The 1964 Covenant (Article 6) defined "Palestinians" in terms of their Palestinian citizenship under the Mandate for Palestine and referred to them both as Arabs and "Palestinians". The definition stated:

> The Palestinians are thus Arab citizens who were living normally in Palestine up to 1947, whether they remained or were expelled. Every child who was born to a Palestinian parent after this date whether in Palestine or outside is a Palestinian.

---

[5] The PLO was preceded by a body established in Gaza in 1958 known as a "Palestinian National Union". However, it neither took root nor developed a separate Palestinian national consciousness.

[6] See article by Yaacov Shimoni under the entry of "Palestine Arabs" in the *Political Dictionary of the Middle East in the 20th Century*, Jerusalem Publishing House, Ltd. (1972), p. 303.

Jews of Palestinian origin were also considered "Palestinians" under the 1964 Covenant if they were willing to live peacefully and loyally in "Palestine" (Article 7).

The circumstances which greatly facilitated the acceptance of the idea of a separate "Palestinian nation" originated as a consequence of the Six-Day War of June 5-10, 1967, when Israel recovered foreign occupied parts of the Jewish National Home in Judea, Samaria and Gaza where about a million Arabs lived at this time. Suddenly the Arabs in these areas found themselves cut off from their previous rulers. Their political and legal status now became uncertain and subject to change. Israel decided not to impose its law, jurisdiction and administration, which, had it been done, might have given these Arabs a new status as citizens similar to that of the Arabs of the State of Israel. Israeli constitutional law required the annexation of Judea, Samaria and Gaza, but fear of upsetting the demographic balance in the State of Israel between Jews and Arabs, as well as the hope that these Jewish ancestral lands could be used as a bargaining chip for possible peace with the neighbouring Arab states, prevented any annexation.

The 600,000 to 700,000 Arabs who lived in Judea and Samaria at the time were Jordanian citizens, ever since these areas were annexed on April 24, 1950 by the Hashemite Kingdom, but after the Six-Day War, with the rise to prominence of the al-Fatah organization under the leadership of its chairman, Yasser Arafat, in a restructured PLO, they preferred to be considered "Palestinians", rather than "Jordanians". The 350,000 Arabs of Gaza were never Egyptian citizens. They were considered stateless refugees and were more than ready to assume a new political and national identity as "Palestinians".

The favourable circumstances wrought by the Six-Day War for creating a new national identity for the Arabs living in Judea, Samaria and Gaza – no annexation of these three regions to Israel, an abrupt cut-off from the rule of both Jordan and Egypt and the takeover of the PLO by Arafat – gave new birth to the concept of the "Palestinian People". Formerly this concept had existed only in inchoate form in some limited circles, even during the Mandate period. This new national identity started to crystallize with the adoption of a different version of the Palestine National Charter by the Palestine National Assembly at Cairo on July 17, 1968. The revised Charter, while still referring as previously to the Palestinian Arab people, now spoke also of the people of Palestine, the Palestinian people, the Palestinian identity, the Palestinian masses and the Palestinians. Some of the articles in the Charter distinguished between the Palestinian people on the one hand and the broader Arab nation on the other, although it posited an interrelationship between the two, with the former acting as the vanguard to "liberate Palestine", the "homeland" of the Palestinian Arab people. The Palestinian people were, as in the 1964 Covenant, considered a part of the Arab nation, but now entitled to their own self-determination (Articles 1 and 3 of the 1968 Covenant). The aspiration for a separate state was evidenced by a change in terminology. In 1964, the word used was *qawm* (pan-Arab nationalism), while in 1968 the word was changed to *watan* (local or state nationalism). The distinction between the two concepts was well explained by Professor Yehoshafat Harkabi when he wrote the following:[7]

> The two concepts *qawmiyya* [pan-Arabism] and *wataniyya* [patriotism in regard to a specific homeland] are not on the same footing: ...the 'classic' conception of Arab nationalism is *qawmiyya*, while *wataniyya* is presented as something truncated and even transient, as a result of the splitting up of the Arab region into separate states carved out by the colonial powers. However, once Arab unity is achieved and the frontiers wiped out, or at least change their nature and become a kind of demarcation line between districts, *wataniyya* will fade away and *qawmiyya* will hold sole sway. *Qawmiyya* is generally represented as the manifestation of unreserved good, while excessive *wataniyya* is represented as adherence to narrow, local or provincial patriotism, which exists at the expense of pan-Arab nationalism. Generally, terms of opprobrium frequently qualify *wataniyya* such as *iqlimiyya* (regionalism), *qutriyya* (territorialism) and kiyaniyya (a derisive term used by Arab radicals condemning the emphasis on Palestinian entity at the expense of Arabism) (all italics in the original).

The definition of a "Palestinian" given in the 1964 Covenant was nearly identical to the one given in that of 1968, in Article 5 thereof, which read:

> Palestinians are Arab citizens who were normally resident in Palestine until 1947. This includes those who were forced to leave and who stayed in Palestine. Anyone born to a Palestinian father after that date, whether inside or outside Palestine, is a Palestinian.

The retention of the 1964 definition of what a Palestinian is, showed that the term was still being linked with the definition of a Palestinian given in the Churchill White Paper embracing citizenship only rather than nationality in the anthropological- ethnological sense of belonging to a distinct nation. The evolution to a unique national identity as "Palestinians" was therefore not yet complete, but was chronologically close to realization.

The 1968 Covenant amended retroactively the original 1964 version concerning whether Jews, too, could be considered "Palestinians". Now it stated, in Article 6 of the revised Covenant, that only

> The Jews who had normally resided in Palestine until the beginning of the Zionist invasion will be considered Palestinians.

---

[7] Y. Harkabi, *op. cit.*, pp. 31-32. See also *The Politics of Palestinian Nationalism*, William B. Quandt, Fuad Jabber, Ann Mosely Lesch, University of California Press Ltd., Berkeley, California (1973), p. 96, n. 2.

No date for the "Zionist invasion" was given in this Article, but it was generally taken to be the date of the Balfour Declaration – November 2, 1917, while others pushed it even earlier, to 1882. That was the year the first agricultural Jewish pioneers of Bilu[8] emigrated to Palestine from Russia, to resettle the Land of Zion, as they called it. The effective meaning of Article 6 of the Covenant was that all Jews and their descendants, who arrived in Palestine from 1917 onwards, were to be evicted. The idea of the mass transfer of Jews to their "countries of origin" was thus written into the very text of the "Palestinian National Covenant" (al-mithaq al-watani al-filastini). The purpose of this article was to make Palestine, according to Professor Harkabi:[9]

> an Arab land *purified* of the alien population. Otherwise it would not be Arab and the Palestinians could not be its full masters (italics in the original).

Harkabi's interpretation of Article 6 of the Covenant was based on that of various spokesmen for the PLO. Sabri Jiryis, formerly a leader of the banned Israeli Arab political group called Al-Ard (The Land), denounced this Jewish mass-transfer provision as harming the "Palestinian" cause. He wrote in Al-Nahar, a Beirut newspaper, on May 15, 1975:[10]

> The first thing that has to be done is to abolish or amend the famous Article 6 of the revised Covenant of 1968. The only possible interpretation of this article is the uprooting of 99% of the Jews who live in Palestine today; this causes great damage to the Palestinians in various progressive circles in the world. There is no need, nor logic in retaining this Article in its present form, which indicates an exaggerated toughening of our stand in comparison with the earlier Article in the original Covenant.

---

[8] The name "Bilu" is formed from the Hebrew initials of an incomplete verse appearing in Isaiah 2:5, which states: בית יעקב לכו ונלכה (House of Jacob, come, let us go!). The Bilu society was founded in 1882 in Kharkov, Ukraine, by a group of university students on the initiative of Israel Belkind after the outbreak of pogroms in Russia in the preceding two years. The Bilu Manifesto was issued in Constantinople that same year, stating its purpose as (1) a Home in our country. It was given to us by the mercy of God, it is ours as registered in the archives of history; (2) to beg it of the Sultan himself, and if it be impossible to obtain this, to beg that at least we may be allowed to possess it as a state within a larger state; the internal administration to be ours, to have our civil and political rights, and to act with the Turkish Empire only in foreign affairs, so as to help our brother Ishmael in his time of need. This manifesto is printed in the *History of Zionism* 1600-1918, by Nahum Sokolow, published by Longmans, Green and Co., London (1919), Vol. II, pp. 332-333.

[9] *Ibid.*, p. 47.

[10] *Ibid.*, p. 49.

As noted above, the year 1969 is the turning point in fashioning a separate identity for a new nation known simply as "Palestinians" rather than "Arabs". In February of that year, the al-Fatah group under the leadership of Yasser Arafat took control of the PLO, becoming the strongest and most important constituent in charge of its policy and future direction. Its name meant "conquest" in Arabic and was an acronym formed by reversing the order of the first letters of the Arabic name of the "Palestine Liberation Movement" – *Harakat at-Tahrir al-Filastini.*

Arafat was appointed as the chairman of the Executive Committee of the PLO. He was born in Cairo on August 24, 1929, according to an Egyptian birth certificate, though he himself claims to have been born in Jerusalem on a slightly different date (August 4, 1929) in a stone house that abutted the Western Wall of the Temple compound. His reason for pretending to have been born in Palestine is obvious. It would not fit his carefully nurtured image as the symbol of the "Palestinian People" to be depicted as an outsider, who was born, raised and educated as an engineer in Egypt. However, from a legal perspective, his birth certificate is convincing evidence of his place of birth that is further corroborated by his Egyptian accent, the fact that his parents and siblings all lived in Egypt at the time he was born and his well-known penchant to lie and deceive others.[11]

One month prior to Arafat's climb to the top rung of leadership, the Fatah published in January 1969 a program of seven points[12] which spoke about the "Palestinian people" having its own national identity, separate and apart from other Arab peoples. It categorically rejected U.N. Security Council Resolution 242 exactly because it ignored the "national rights of the Palestinian people".[13]

---

[11] Any person's birth certificate is an authentic document that constitutes prima facie evidence and a legal presumption of the veracity of its contents. To disprove or deny the authenticity of his own birth certificate, Arafat would have needed to take a legal action, called improbation, to show that the document attesting to his birth is false or forged, which he never did. It must therefore be taken as a proven legal fact that Arafat was born in Cairo and not in Jerusalem. He adopted the nom de guerre "Abu Amar" after one of the followers of Mohammad. The question of Arafat's place of birth is sympathetically discussed by Janet and John Wallach in their book, *Arafat in the Eyes of the Beholder*, Carol Publishing Group, New Jersey (1997), p. XVI in the preface to the first edition and in the text on pp. 25-27.

[12] The Seven Points, passed by the Central Committee of Al-Fatah in January 1969 is found in *The Israel-Arab Reader, A Documentary History of the Middle East Conflict*, revised and updated, Walter Laqueur and Barry Rubin, editors, Penguin Edition (1984), pp. 372-373. See also the entry written by Ehud Ya'ari on "Palestine-Arab Guerilla Organizations" in the *Political Dictionary of the Middle East in the 20th Century*, edited by Yaacov Shimoni and Evyatar Levin, pp. 306-307.

[13] The attitude of Al-Fatah rejecting UNSC Resolution 242 was then made the official position of the PLO. On June 9, 1974 the Palestinian National Council reaffirmed the PLO's opposition to this resolution when it met in Cairo to draw up

The U.N. Resolution only affirmed the necessity for achieving a just settlement of the refugee problem and did not refer at all to the existence of any nation called the "Palestinians". Although the Fatah program also said that Palestine formed part of the "Arab fatherland", this did not detract from its principal demand that the "Palestinians" be seen and treated as a distinct Arab nation entitled to its own state.

The final objective of Fatah was the establishment of an independent, democratic, secular, multi-religious State of Palestine. What the actual meaning would be for Jews living in a democratic State of Palestine in place of Israel, that also incorporated a "right of return" for so-called "Palestinians" is chillingly stated by Professor Harkabi:[14]

> Thus the establishment of the 'democratic' Palestinian state is bound up with a mass evacuation of Jews from their homes, and they will be thus forced to emigrate. *The 'democracy' that is allegedly intended to assure the rights of the Israeli Jews to live in the Palestinian state is also the instrument of dispossessing them.*
>
> 'The return' as a chief PLO slogan embodies at one and the same time the Arab objective and the means of achieving it. The very 'return' will change 'Israel' into 'Palestine' and the right of return for the Palestinians boils down to a euphemistic expression of a right to *subvert* the state of Israel.
>
> In presenting triumphantly the idea of the democratic state at the U.N., Arafat did not succeed in hiding its true meaning. It became obvious that the use of the term 'democratic state' was nothing but a euphemism for the demise of Israel and that such a state was meant to replace Israel (all italics in the original).

At about the same time as Arafat rose to undisputed power in the PLO, the identical view held by Fatah in regard to the existence of a distinctive "Palestinian people" among the Arab peoples started to be propagated in the State of Israel by a prominent member of the political establishment, Arieh Lova Eliav, who was then the Deputy Minister of Immigration and Absorption and later elected as Secretary-General of the Labour Party, on January 8, 1970. He published a series of three articles in November 1968 in the newspaper, *Davar*, in which he listed the following attributes of the "Palestinian people" to prove that they

---

a "Phased Plan" to restore the "Palestinians" to Palestine. In paragraph 1 of this Plan, the Council rejected Resolution 242 because it "obliterates the national right of our people and deals with the cause of our people as a problem of refugees". See Professor Harkabi's book, *op. cit.*, p. 147, Appendix E entitled: "Political Programme for the Present Stage of the Palestine Liberation Organization Drawn up by the Palestinian National Council, Cairo, June 9, 1974.

[14] *Op. cit.*, p. 56.

were a separate nation:[15]

> They have national consciousness. They have territorial continuity where most of the Palestinians live. They have *a Palestinian history of decades* (emphasis added), marked by struggle and wars. They have a diaspora with a strong affinity to their birthplace. They have national awareness of a common disaster, common victims, sufferings and heroes. The nation has a vision, its own literature and poetry. The Arab Palestinian nation is perhaps the nation with the most obvious signs of identity and the strongest national unity among the Arab nations. This nation consists of some two million Arabs, half of them in the occupied territories on the western bank of the Jordan and the other half on the eastern bank of the Jordan. Some of them are dispersed throughout the Arab world.

Eliav advocated the creation of a "Palestinian-Jordanian State", comprising Jordan, most of Judea and Samaria and parts of the Gaza Strip, which would recognize the "national-historical" rights of the Palestinian Arab nation. In Eretz-Israel, he said, "there ought to be set up two states for two nations".[16] In talking about "national-historical" rights, Eliav confused history with law. Rights can only be legal in nature even if they are derived from a historical claim. History produced legal rights for the Jewish People that are recorded in several international legal documents, particularly the Smuts Resoluction, the San Remo Resolution, the Mandate for Palestine and the Franco-British Boundary Convention of December 23, 1920. No such legal rights had been recognized in comparable documents for a nation called the "Palestinian People" at the time Eliav wrote his book. The birth of a nation takes far more than "decades" to develop, even in this age of "instant gratification". The existence of a Palestinian nation is certainly not based on history, as Eliav asserted.

In regard to the ancestry of the Palestinian Arabs he said:[17]

> It is very likely that these Arabs were the descendants of ancient settlers: Jews, Samaritans, Idumeans, Nabateans, Greeks, Romans, Byzantines, and members of many other tribes and nations that lived in this country. The country was conquered by the Muslim Arabs who swept up out of the desert, and the overwhelming majority of its population accepted Islam.

---

[15] See article by Amnon Barzilai in *Ha'Aretz* newspaper, June 11, 2002, entitled "Some saw the refugees as the key to peace". See also the book written by Arieh Lova Eliav, entitled *Land of the Hart*, Jewish Publication Society of America, Philadelphia [1974], p. 129.

[16] *Land of the Hart*, p. 143.

[17] *Ibid.*, p. 121.

> The pure Arabs – the people of the Arabian Peninsula – assimilated over the generations into the indigenous population, and the two became one Arab amalgam. The same thing happened in many of the other countries conquered by the Arabs. In each country, the Arab amalgam comprises different elements.

By this definition a Palestinian Arab could be descended from anyone, whether from Semitic forbears, such as Jews, Samaritans, Idumeans, Nabateans and "pure Arabs" or from non-Semitic forbears, including Greeks, Romans, Byzantines and assorted Europeans, notably the Bosnians who settled in the Land of Israel in the latter part of the 19th century. A Palestinian Arab therefore embraces a myriad of different peoples, and is hardly distinguishable from the Arabs who live in Jordan, Syria and Iraq. The slight differences that may exist between the Arabs of all these countries are not substantial enough to warrant a special national designation for those who assert a unique "Palestinian" identity.

It was also in 1969 when the United Nations suddenly began to change the terminology it had previously used to describe the Arab refugees living in Judea, Samaria and Gaza. Until that year, they were consistently referred to as "Palestine refugees" or simply by the word "refugees". That was the designation given, for example, in General Assembly Resolution 194 (III) of December 11, 1948, resolving that the refugees should be permitted to return to their homes, and again in Resolution 212 (III) of November 19, 1948, establishing a special fund for their relief. This latter resolution was followed by an important resolution on December 8, 1949, which created a special U.N. agency still operating today, known as the United Nations Relief and Works Agency for Palestine Refugees in the Near East (UNRWA). The general description of "refugees" was also used in Security Council Resolution 242 of November 22, 1967 stating the principles of a just and lasting peace in the Middle East.

As late as December 19, 1968 the General Assembly passed a resolution concerning the territories captured by Israel in the Six-Day War, in which no specific national designation was given to the local Arab inhabitants who lived there. This resolution (Resolution 2443 [XXIII]), which dealt with alleged Israeli violations of human rights in what it called the "Occupied Territories", denoted their inhabitants or cited references to them by other United Nations organs in six different ways without using the term "Palestinians" even once, as follows:

> 1. *inhabitants* who have fled the area of military operations since the outbreak of hostilities;
> 2. *the Arab civilian population* in areas occupied by Israel;
> 3. *the inhabitants* of the Arab territories under military occupation by Israel;
> 4. *the Arab civilian population* inhabiting areas occupied by Israel;
> 5. all *inhabitants* who have left their homes as a result of hostilities

in the Middle East;

6. *the population* of the Occupied Territories.

The big change in United Nations terminology regarding the designation of the Arab population of Judea, Samaria and Gaza came in a General Assembly Resolution of December 10, 1969,[18] when they were referred to for the first time as "the people of Palestine", whose "inalienable rights" were "reaffirmed" by the resolution. This marked a departure from the practice which had existed until then of using the term "refugees" in reference to this population. Henceforth they were recognized as a "people". Their "rights" primarily meant the right to return to their homes in Israeli-governed areas of former Palestine from which they fled and to resume their normal life. This was followed by a resolution of November 4, 1970 recognizing "that respect for the rights of the *Palestinians* is an indispensable element in the establishment of a just and lasting peace in the Middle East (emphasis added)."[19] In a quantum jump, these rights were extended on November 30, 1970 and December 8, 1970 to include the right of self-determination in accordance with the Charter of the United Nations, exactly as demanded by the Arafat-led "Palestine Liberation Organization".[20] The right of self-determination for the "people of Palestine" was reiterated in a General Assembly Resolution of December 6, 1971,[21] which also referred to them as "the Palestinian People" and thereafter it was enunciated in additional resolutions adopted by the General Assembly. One of the most notable was a resolution of November 22, 1974 which reaffirmed the inalienable rights of the Palestinian people in Palestine including:

a) the right to self-determination without external interference;
b) the right to national independence and sovereignty;
c) the inalienable right of the Palestinians to return to their homes and property from which they have been displaced and uprooted.[22]

This resolution also used the designation "Palestinians" interchangeably with that of the "Palestinian People". One more important step taken by the General Assembly was to pass another resolution[23] on the same day granting observer status to the Palestine Liberation Organization, which entitled it to participate in the sessions and work of the General Assembly and all international conferences convened under the auspices of the General Assembly or other organs of the

[18] Resolution 2535 A, B, C (xxiv).

[19] General Assembly Resolution 2628 (xxv).

[20] See General Assembly Resolution 2649 (xxv) of November 30, 1970 and Resolution 2672 A, B, C, D (xxv) of December 8, 1970.

[21] Resolution 2787 (xxvi).

[22] Resolution 3236 (xxix).

[23] Resolution 3237 (xxix).

United Nations. This latter resolution was preceded by one on October 14, 1974, which stated that the "Palestinian People is the principal party to the question of Palestine", and for that reason the General Assembly invited "the Palestine Liberation Organization, the representatives of the Palestinian people, to participate in the deliberations of the General Assembly on the question of Palestine in plenary meetings".[24]

All of the foregoing resolutions marked the triumph of the greatest lie and invention of the twentieth century, that Palestine belongs to a fictitious nation called "the Palestinian People", an Arab nation hitherto unknown in the written records of history, ancient, medieval or modern, but which by means of a magic wand in the form of General Assembly resolutions was now endowed with inalienable rights that nullified or replaced those that rightfully belonged to the Jewish People and its devolved assignee, the State of Israel. These falsifying resolutions which abounded over the ensuing years inverted and disregarded the real legal situation under international law in regard to the Land of Israel. This inversion of rights and identity theft should have been actively fought by Israel by taking the strongest possible diplomatic and legal steps – including appeals to American and British courts, based on the doctrine of acquired Jewish legal rights and the principle of estoppel. The U.N. resolutions which openly and shamelessly awarded the State of Israel's inherited rights and title of sovereignty over Judea, Samaria and Gaza to the "Palestinians" constituted a very grave affront and injury to what had previously been accomplished by the Principal Allied Powers of World War I, who, at the Peace Conferences held at Paris (1919) and San Remo (1920, had fashioned a definitive global political and legal settlement defining the rights of various peoples, the chief beneficiary of which were the Arabs. This settlement was then recorded in the peace treaties that were concluded, particularly the Treaty of Versailles and Treaty of Sèvres. The General Assembly resolutions were also a grave affront to the important work of the Permanent Mandates Commission which had advised the Council of the League of Nations on all matters relating to the observance of the Mandates. This body had cast a vigilant eye on the actions of the Mandatory Powers to ensure that they respected the legal rights of peoples who were the national beneficiaries of the mandates, including in particular the rights of the Jewish People to all of Palestine. In their thorough discussions and deliberations, the Permanent Mandates Commission never once spoke about the inalienable rights of a Palestinian nation or were aware that one even existed. The gross disregard shown by the General Assembly and other U.N. organs for all that had been previously done under the global peace settlement of 1919 and 1920 attached an indelible stamp of illegality to all these resolutions. Moreover, they also constituted a mark of deep shame and disgrace on the reputation of the United Nations, whose institutional bias regarding the State of Israel should disqualify it from any future role in the effort to bring peace to the Middle East,

---

[24] Resolution 3210 (xxix).

until such time as that bias is completely eradicated, if that is indeed possible under its current rules and voting procedures.

Adding more ignominy to the United Nations Organization was the resolution of November 10, 1975 which proclaimed that Zionism (spelled there with a small "z") was a form of racial discrimination. This evil resolution based on sheer hate of the Jewish People served no other purpose than to deny Jews the right to their national home in the Land of Israel that was realized only after the most valiant struggle was waged to overcome British betrayal and Arab aggression. It was a malicious attempt not only to discredit Zionism and its manifold achievements, but even to repudiate past U.N. recognition accorded to the Jewish State of Israel. The revocation of the Zionism is Racism Resolution on December 16, 1991 did not in any way atone for the hatred exhibited and the damage already caused by the original resolution, as well as that of all the other General Assembly resolutions which still falsely affirm and reaffirm the national rights of a fictitious nation and deny those of the Jewish People to their true patrimony, the entire Land of Israel.

All of the features of the aforementioned General Assembly Resolutions were also reflected in a resolution adopted by the Arab Summit Conference held at Rabat, Morocco on October 29, 1974. The Conference of the Arab Heads of State included King Hussein, who until then had refused to concede to the PLO the right it claimed for itself to be "the sole representative of the Palestinian People". This resolution had five points, the first two of which stated:

> In light of the victories achieved by the Palestinian struggle in the confrontation with the Zionist enemy, at the Arab and international levels, at the United Nations, and of the obligation imposed thereby to continue joint Arab action to develop and increase the scope of these victories; ...the Seventh Arab Summit Conference resolves the following:
>
> 1. To affirm the right of the Palestinian people to self-determination and to return to their homeland;
>
> 2. To affirm the right of the Palestinian people to establish an independent national authority under the command of the Palestine Liberation Organization, the sole legitimate representative of the Palestinian people, in any Palestinian territory that is liberated. This authority, once it is established, shall enjoy the support of the Arab states in all fields and at all levels.[25]

The gentile Arabic-speaking population of Judea, Samaria and Gaza, aided and abetted by a bevy of dictatorial Arab states, Communist totalitarian countries and so-called "non-aligned" states, mainly in Asia and Africa, were thus able to

---

[25] *The Arab-Israel Conflict and its Resolution: Selected Documents* (ed. Ruth Lapidoth and Moshe Hirsch), Document 37, p. 156.

attain, through a batch of illegal U.N. resolutions emanating principally from the General Assembly, universal recognition as a separate nation known as "Palestinians", whose alleged homeland was Palestine. The change of name from Arabs to "Palestinians" and the allegation that Palestine was the homeland of this nation was a public relations trick that was fraudulent and artificial because the name "Palestinians" had been applied all throughout the Mandate period to designate the Jews of Palestine and not the Arabs of the country whose true homeland lay outside its borders. The Arabs rejected that name for themselves because they rightfully associated "Palestine" with the Jewish National Home. Moreover, Palestine had ceased to exist as a country after the Mandate expired on May 14-15, 1948, replaced by the Jewish State of Israel, with other parts of the country illegally in the hands of various Arab states – Jordan, Egypt, Syria and Lebanon. The use of these terms – "Palestinians" and Palestine – for Arabs instead of for Jews was no less than an inversion of the legal and historical facts. It caught on partly because of Israel's foolishness in 1967 after the Six-Day War, of not incorporating Judea, Samaria and Gaza into the State, which left a vacuum that was quickly filled by the Arabs. The change of national identity was a planned tactic whose aim was to wrest the Jewish homeland from the Jewish People by convincing Christian nations that Palestine was really the homeland, not of Jews but of the mythical nation called "Palestinians". It was a hoax that won many believers, first of all among the Arab perpetrators of the hoax who swallowed their own lies and disseminated them to a receptive world. By changing their identity to a Palestinian one, the descendants of the Arabs of former Mandated Palestine were able to win more sympathy for their cause because it was no longer a case of the Jews of Israel valiantly struggling against twenty-one Arab States arrayed against them, but was now a one-on-one battle between an existing militarily-strong Jewish State and the "desperate homeless Palestinians" who were supposedly under "occupation" and being deprived of their rightful homeland "contrary to international law" that consisted of biased U.N. resolutions that cannot be classified as such. In truth, their homeland was not in the Land of Israel or former Mandated Palestine, but in Syria, Iraq, Arabia or Egypt whence the great majority of them originated. This blatant Arab lie of a homeless nation seeking its freedom and independence, patterned on the precedent of Jewish homelessness prior to the re-creation of the State of Israel, was henceforth deliberately pursued and nurtured, rather than the previous argument, that Palestine was part of the overall Arab fatherland (the *qawmiyya*, Pan-Arab approach) which had been taken away to benefit the Jews, thus causing the problem of Arab "refugees". This new Arab exercise in dissimulation eventually paid handsome dividends, resulting in the greatest victory ever achieved by deceitful Arab propaganda even though it did not serve the cause of pan-Arabism which sought to unite all Arab states into one huge entity stretching from the Persian Gulf to the Atlantic Ocean.

A further milestone on the road to gaining recognition for the mythical nation of "Palestinians" and their alleged rights to Palestine came with the establishment of a "U.N. Committee on the Inalienable Rights of the Palestine People", which issued a series of recommendations in 1977. It urged the Security Council to use the powers the latter supposedly possessed under the U.N. Charter to take appropriate action to facilitate the exercise of those rights.[26] It stressed in particular "the legitimate and inalienable rights of the Palestinian People to return to their homes and property and to achieve self-determination, national independence and sovereignty" as part of a comprehensive and final settlement of the Middle East crisis. The alleged right of return was based upon General Assembly Resolution 194 (III) of December 11, 1948, a resolution which the Arab states of Egypt, Iraq, Lebanon, Saudi Arabia, Syria and Yemen voted against. Apart from the fact that this resolution was a non-binding recommendation of the General Assembly, this so-called "right" has no foundation in law, since Palestine was juridically created on April 24, 1920 by the Principal Allied Powers to be the exclusive national home of the Jewish People in accordance with the Balfour Declaration that was based upon the historical connection of the Jewish People with the country. Furthermore, the General Assembly Resolution makes the return of refugees to their former homes in Palestine subject to the condition that they wish to "live at peace with their neighbours", a condition they refused to accept when the resolution was first adopted, as may be deduced from the fact that no Arab refugees ever sought "repatriation" to Israel under the terms of that specific resolution. In any event, Security Council Resolution 242, which superceded the General Assembly Resolution on the refugee question, never enunciated a right of return for Arab refugees to Israel. It spoke only of the necessity "for achieving a just settlement of the refugee problem", which could not mean the return of millions of Arabs to the State of Israel, for under such circumstances Israel could not "live in peace within secure and recognized boundaries, free from threats or acts of force", as affirmed in the same Resolution. The Security Council, in effect, abrogated the refugees' alleged right of return under General Assembly Resolution 194 (III). In the eventuality that there is one day "a just settlement of the entire refugee problem", the Arab refugees, no more or no less than the larger number of Jewish refugees from Arab countries, are entitled to equitable financial compensation for loss of their homes and property.

The right of return to Palestine and the Land of Israel exists only for the Jewish People under international law, officially recognized in Article 6 of the Mandate for Palestine and buttressed by the right of settlement in Articles 6 and 11 thereof. No similar national rights or historical connection were ever recognized by the Principal Allied Powers for the interloping Arabs of Palestine, most of whom stole into the country from neighbouring territories prior to the rebirth of the Jewish State and left largely on their own volition during Israel's War of Independence. Moreover, the falsely claimed Arab "right of return" to Palestine is also debunked by the fact that as early as 1944 in the case of Syrian

---

[26] The Committee's recommendations are reproduced *op. cit.*, Document 45, p. 179ff.

Jews and 1945 in the case of Libyan Jews, a de facto exchange of Arab and Jewish populations had already begun and was to continue without letup in the years immediately following. Jews from Yemen were exceptional in this regard because they began to immigrate to Palestine as early as 1882. By virtue of this reality, the Arabs who had moved to Palestine over the centuries returned in 1948 to their countries of origin to where they did in fact have an undisputed right of return, while Jews, even before this Arab migration, were being expelled from the Arab League states to return in large numbers to the birthplace of their nation. This sequence of population movements by both Jews and Arabs into and out of Palestine was actually acknowledged by some former Palestinian Arabs. One such figure was Sabri Jiryis, Director of the Institute of Palestine Studies in Beirut. He wrote an article in the Beirut Al-Nahar newspaper of May 15, 1975 in which he stated:[27]

> ...Israel's arguments will take approximately the following form: It is true that we Israelis brought about the exodus of the Arabs from their land in the war of 1948... and that we took control of their property. In return, however, you Arabs caused the expulsion of a like number of Jews from Arab countries since 1948 until today. Most of them went to Israel after you seized control of their property in one way or another. What happened, therefore, is merely a kind of 'population and property transfer', the consequences of which both sides have to bear. Thus, Israel gathers in the Jews from Arab countries and the Arab countries are obliged in turn to settle the Palestinians within their own borders and work towards a solution of the problem. Israel will undoubtedly advance these claims in the first real debate over the Palestinian problem.

The 1977 "U.N. Committee on the Inalienable Rights of Palestine People" called upon the Security Council to establish a time-table for the complete withdrawal by "Israeli occupation forces from those areas occupied in 1967" and to use, if necessary, "temporary peace-keeping forces in order to facilitate the process of withdrawal". It advised the Security Council to request that Israel "desist from the establishment of new settlements and to withdraw from settlements established since 1967 in the occupied territories". It wanted Israel to abide scrupulously by the provisions of the Fourth Geneva Convention of August 12, 1949 relative to the Protection of Civilian Persons in Time of

---

[27] See Prof. Ya'akov Meron's article entitled "The Expulsion of the Jews from the Arab Countries: The Palestinians' Attitude Towards It and Their Claims', in the book *The Forgotten Millions: The Modem Jewish Exodus from Arab Lands*, edited by Malka Hillel Shulewitz, published by Continuum, London and New York, Paperback Edition (2000). p. 96. As regards the dates for the emigration of Jews from Yemen, Syria and Libya, prior to the mass Arab departure from Palestine, see pp. 85, 90 and 91.

War, and to declare, pending its speedy withdrawal from these territories, its recognition of the applicability of that Convention. Finally, it recommended that after Israel completed its evacuation of the territories, the latter should be taken over by the United Nations and then handed over to the Palestine Liberation Organization as the representative of the Palestinian People.

The argument advanced by the "U.N. Committee on the Inalienable Rights of the Palestine People", that the Security Council was vested with the power under the U.N. Charter to intervene in the internal affairs of Judea, Samaria and Gaza was unfounded. No such power was ever given to it or to any other organ of the world organization. On the contrary, the Security Council had to abide by the principle of acquired Jewish legal rights and the doctrine of estoppel which prevented it from altering the global political and legal settlement that was made in 1919 and 1920 by the Principal Allied and Associated Powers. This settlement placed Judea, Samaria and Gaza within the confines of the Jewish National Home because of the Jewish historical connection to those ancient Jewish lands. No new "final settlement" could legally change their status under international law so long as the Jewish People and the State of Israel existed.

Israel must therefore strenuously oppose any attempt by the Security Council to transfer to the fictitious Palestinian People the acquired legal rights it itself inherited as the agent and assignee of the Jewish People. It must gird itself for the unpleasant possibility that it could be faced with illegal U.N. intervention one day in the future. This will require it to take a series of forceful steps to thwart or block a development of this kind. It should begin by implementing a program whose object would be to ensure its own inalienable rights over the Land of Israel, which have been falsely and maliciously attributed to Arabic-speaking gentiles who have brazenly committed identity theft by assumed the former Jewish identity as Palestinians during the Mandate period. This program is presented in the concluding section of this book.

Following the recommendations made by the U.N. Committee, the most unlikely development of all then occurred to give a tremendous boost to the false notion that the Arabs of the Land of Israel possess a unique national identity as "Palestinians" with rights to the land, different from that of other Arabs of the surrounding states. This was the making of "A Framework for Peace in the Middle East" at the Camp David Summit (September 5–17, 1978) and a parallel document, "Framework for the Conclusion of a Peace Treaty between Israel and Egypt". These two documents were both signed on September 17, 1978 at the White House by Menachem Begin for the Government of Israel, Anwar Sadat for Egypt, and witnessed by U.S. President Jimmy Carter. The first Framework Document provided that negotiations would be conducted among Egypt, Israel, Jordan and the elected representatives of the inhabitants of the "West Bank" and Gaza to determine the "final status" (a euphemism for sovereignty) of the "West Bank" and Gaza not later than the third year after the beginning of the transitional period of five years that was to begin with the establishment of the "self-governing authority". The negotiations were to be based on the provisions and principles of U.N. Security Council Resolution 242 and were expected to resolve the location of the boundaries and the nature of the security arrangements. It was also agreed that the final outcome of these negotiations to be conducted among four parties: Egypt, Israel, Jordan and the elected representatives of the inhabitants of the "West Bank" and Gaza, would recognize "the legitimate rights of the Palestinian People and their just requirements". This language resembled that used by the "U.N. Committee on the Inalienable Rights of the Palestine People" which had also used the expression "legitimate rights" as a substitute for "inalienable rights". What was really important was that the recognition of the rights of a people or nation, whether they were "legitimate" or "inalienable", could only mean their national and political rights, particularly the right of self-determination and national independence,[28] accompanied by a right of return, as postulated by the aforementioned U.N. committee.

This represented a shocking change of deeply-held conviction by Begin, as noted by his former colleague in the pre-State underground Irgun Zvai Leumi, Shmuel Katz.[29] All of Begin's past statements were to the effect that the Jewish People alone had national rights to the Land of Israel and the Jewish National Home. Now in an amazing turnabout from that long-standing position, he recognized that another nation called "Palestinians" not only existed but had "legitimate rights" to Judea, Samaria and Gaza, and that their "just requirements" had to be satisfied. This recognition of the "Palestinian nation" and their rights and requirements accorded by the Government of Israel in an official document ended any hope that the historical and legal fabrication this entailed could be easily overcome in the future, unless there was an immediate and complete repudiation of that view by the Prime Minister and the Government of Israel.

Five days after the conclusion of the Camp David Summit, Begin came to his senses and realized the grave error he had just committed in recognizing the existence of the "Palestinians" as a nation with "legitimate rights and just requirements". He tried to rectify the error of nomenclature by having President Carter send him a letter dated September 22, 1978, but left standing Israel's recognition of "Palestinian rights", the heart of the matter. The letter stated:

---

[28] In a letter from Anwar Sadat to Jimmy Carter dated September 17, 1978 setting forth the Egyptian position on Jerusalem, the President of Egypt referred to the "legitimate national rights" of the "Palestinian inhabitants" of "Arab Jerusalem". In a second letter to President Carter bearing the same date, President Sadat spoke of "the legitimate rights of the Palestinian people" in the "West Bank" and Gaza. The pretence that the "legitimate rights" of the "Palestinian people" did not necessarily mean political rights as some in Israeli had argued, was swept away a decade and a half later by the Israel-PLO Declaration of Principles (August 20, 1993 and September 13, 1993) which specifically referred to the "mutual, legitimate and political rights" of both the State of Israel and the "Palestinian people" as further discussed below.

[29] See *The Hollow Peace*, published by Dvir and The Jerusalem Post, p. 271.

> I hereby acknowledge that you have informed me as follows:
>
> a) In each paragraph of the agreed Framework Document, the expressions "Palestinians" or "Palestinian People" are being and will be construed and understood by you as "Palestinian Arabs".
>
> b) In each paragraph in which the expression "West Bank" appears, it is being, and will be, understood by the Government of Israel as Judea and Samaria.

This letter by Carter to Begin was of no avail since Begin's interpretation of these expressions in the agreed Framework Document did not bind the other signatory to the agreement, Egypt, nor change the mind of the United States which witnessed the Agreement. In order for Begin's reservation or disavowal of the plain meaning of these expressions to have had any legal effect, he would have needed either to renounce on the spot the "Framework for Peace in the Middle East" which he had just signed, a most embarrassing and unlikely choice which would have required great fortitude and courage, or obtain Egyptian consent to have the language of the document changed, by substituting the term "Arabs" for "Palestinians". Begin could not make the change unilaterally or through a third party intermediary in the form of a letter from Carter to him announcing his own interpretation of the expressions "Palestinians" or "Palestinian People". In the event, the official English text of the "Framework for Peace in the Middle East" remained intact and Begin was thus trapped by his own carelessness or failure to realize the implications of what he had actually agreed to, in his desire to conclude a peace agreement with Egypt and to curry favour with President Carter.

The recognition by the State of Israel of the nationhood of the "Palestinians" and their "legitimate rights" and "just requirements" grew firmer and gained majority support within Israel itself by the stunning revelation that Israel and the Palestine Liberation Organization had secretly concluded an agreement known as the Declaration of Principles (DOP) at Oslo on August 20, 1993. The agreement was initialed ad referendum and received cabinet approval by the Government of Yitzhak Rabin on August 30, 1993. It was then signed in an official ceremony on the south lawn of the White House on September 13, 1993. Under Israeli constitutional law there was actually no need for any further signing of the DOP once cabinet approval had been secured. However, the White House signing ceremony had a different purpose in mind: to ensure the irreversibility of the just-concluded "peace agreement" between Israel and the Palestine Liberation Organization and thus prevent any Israeli backtracking from its planned illegal withdrawals from parts of the Jewish National Home mandated by that agreement. An ancillary agreement was also made between the parties, called the Mutual Recognition Agreement of September 9, 1993, which consisted of three letters from Arafat to Rabin, Arafat to the Norwegian Foreign Minister (Johan Jorgen Holst) and from Rabin to Arafat. In this last letter, Rabin wrote to the PLO Chairman:

> In response to your letter of September 9, 1993, I wish to confirm to you, in light of the PLO commitments included in your letter, the Government of Israel has decided to recognize the PLO *as the representative of the Palestinian people* (emphasis added) and commence negotiations with the PLO within the Middle East peace process.

The Israel-PLO agreements of 1993 had the legal effect of transferring authority from the Israeli Military Government and its Civil Administration in Gaza and the Jericho area to the "authorized Palestinians" named by the PLO (Article VI of the DOP and Article VI[2] of the Agreed Minutes) who were to be installed as the first members of the "Palestinian Authority" until a Council was elected to serve the "Palestinian People in the West Bank and the Gaza Strip" (Articles 1 and 3 of the DOP). The aim of the agreement reached between the Government of Israel and the "PLO team",[30] representing the "Palestinian People" was stated in the Preamble of the DOP:

> …it is time to put an end to decades of confrontation and conflict, *recognize their mutual legitimate and political rights* (emphasis added), and strive to live in peaceful coexistence and mutual dignity and security and achieve a just, lasting and comprehensive peace settlement and historic reconciliation through the agreed political process.

The recognition of the "legitimate rights" and "just requirements" of the "Palestinian People" in the Land of Israel deepened the wrongful perception already current in world opinion that had also manifested itself in Israel particularly since Menachem Begin's days in power, that the nation of "Palestinians" indeed existed and moreover had sovereign rights, also described as "inalienable rights", to all of Judea, Samaria and Gaza, that soon began to take on the resurrected name of Palestine in public debate and consciousness. There were, in fact, no sovereign rights ever granted to the "Palestinian People" under any document of international law. However, this perception was firmly rooted in Article IV of the DOP which read as follows, with the author's notes in square brackets:

---

[30] When the DOP was first initialed at Oslo on August 20, 1993, the party representing the "Palestinian people" was simply called the "Palestinian team" in the Jordanian-Palestinian Delegation to the Middle East Peace Conference. This designation hid the fact that PLO members then living in Tunis, rather than Arabs from Judea, Samaria and Gaza, actually negotiated the DOP with Israeli officials, contrary to the Madrid Agreement of 1991 which excluded the PLO from any participation in the "Peace Process". The pretence as to who actually represented the "Palestinian people" was swept aside at the White House signing ceremony on September 13, 1993, when, at the demand of Arafat, the "Palestinian team" became the "PLO team".

*Article IV – Jurisdiction [a legal term equivalent to sovereignty]*

> Jurisdiction of the Council [a body that was synonymous with the "Palestinian Authority"] will cover West Bank [Judea and Samaria] and Gaza Strip territory, except for issues that will be negotiated in the permanent status negotiations.[31]
>
> The two sides view the West Bank [a term which originally acknowledged Jordan's alleged sovereignty over Judea and Samaria] and Gaza Strip as a single territorial unit, whose integrity will be preserved during the interim period.

Article IV, the most important article in the DOP, was in effect an agreement to illegally transfer Israel's sovereignty over all of Judea, Samaria and Gaza to the "Palestinian People" represented by the "PLO team" and the newly-created "Palestinian Authority" less the territory of all the Israeli settlements and less the territory needed for specified military locations. From a *halachic* (Jewish Law) viewpoint, which is also the premise of Israeli constitutional law, Israel can never give up its inalienable right of de jure sovereignty over any part of the Land of Israel. This premise underlies three constitutional laws of the State: the Area of Jurisdiction and Powers Ordinance of September 16, 1948; Section 11B of the Law and Administration Ordinance of May 19, 1948, as amended on June 28, 1967; and the Law of Return of July 5, 1950. What Israel actually did in the DOP was to illegally transfer to the 'Palestinian Authority' its *de facto* sovereignty or control over the aforementioned territories. The DOP was also an acknowledgment ironically of Israel's pre-existing sovereignty over Judea, Samaria and Gaza, despite the use of the term "West Bank", since under it, Israel was the disposing Power which was transferring its jurisdiction to the "Palestinian Authority". The total area to be transferred to this body after a five year transitional period and the signing of a permanent status agreement was equivalent to a figure of more than 90% based on the original expectation that less than 10% would be required for settlements and specified security locations.

The official recognition by Israel of the "legitimate rights" and "just requirements" of the "Palestinian People" and the intention to transfer to its representative, the PLO/Palestinian Authority, substantial areas of the Jewish National Home could be classified as falling within each of the following categories of treason, under the Penal Code of Israel:

---

[31] In article V (3) of the DOP, the permanent status negotiations embraced the following subjects: Jerusalem, refugees, settlements, security arrangements [which included Israeli military locations as stated in Article IV of the Agreed Minutes], borders, relations and cooperation with other neighbours [i.e., foreign relations], other items of common interest [e.g., the status of Israelis in Judea, Samaria and Gaza].

> 1) An act calculated to impair the sovereignty of the State of Israel, in violation of section 97(a) of the Penal Code, based upon the legal premise that Israel has full sovereignty, *de jure* and *de facto*, over all areas of the Jewish National Home in its possession. This premise is derived from and substantiated by the founding documents of the State of Israel under international law: Article 22 of the Covenant of the League of Nations, based on the Smuts Resolution of January 30, 1919, the San Remo Resolution of April 24-25, 1920, the Mandate for Palestine of July 24, 1922 and the Franco-British Boundary Convention of December 23, 1920. The same premise also exists under several constitutional laws enacted by the State of Israel as just noted above.
>
> 2) An act calculated to bring about, without lawful authority, the withdrawal of any area under the sovereignty of the State of Israel or the placing of such area under the sovereignty of a foreign state, in violation of Section 97(b) of the Penal Code.
>
> 3) Any act evincing the intention to commit one of the crimes of treason mentioned in either 97(a) or 97(b), in violation of section 100 of the Penal Code.

The DOP was followed by a number of other agreements, the most important of which was the Interim Agreement of September 28, 1995 under which Israel agreed to transfer its powers and responsibilities in Judea and Samaria to the "Palestinian Authority" in several stages, accompanied by the redeployment of its military forces. The first phase covered populated areas, i.e., cities, towns, villages, refugee camps and hamlets. Further redeployments were to be carried out in three additional phases, spaced six months apart. The land comprising the Jewish National Home under the Mandate for Palestine that was to be illegally transferred to the "Palestinian Authority" was divided into Areas A, B and C, with internal security in the hands of the Authority for Area A, but retained by Israel in Area B to protect Israelis and confront the threat of terrorism. In both these areas, the Authority was given full civilian and criminal jurisdiction. Area C represented the portions of Judea and Samaria not yet transferred to the civilian and criminal jurisdiction of the Authority, though designated for that purpose.

After the conclusion of the Wye River Agreement of October 23, 1998 and the Sharm-esh-Sheikh Memorandum of September 4, 1999, the transfer of land in Judea and Samaria from Israel to the "Palestinian Authority" climbed to a figure of 42%, of which 12% was Area A and the rest Area B. Then Israel, under the leadership of Prime Minister Ehud Barak, in close coordination with U.S. President William Jefferson Clinton, offered Yasser Arafat at talks held at Camp David (July 2000) and Taba (January 2001) nearly all of Judea and Samaria (comprising about 97% of that combined region, supplemented by the equivalent of 3% taken from Israel proper in the Negev – the Halutza area), all of Gaza, the Arab-inhabited neighbourhoods of Jerusalem and environs and even sovereignty over the surface of the Temple Mount, but excluding the subterranean levels. No official document detailing Barak's concessions to Arafat was ever published, though they were widely reported in the Israeli press and confirmed by several of the participants in the Camp David and Taba talks. This offer, had it been accepted by Arafat, would have meant the uprooting of about a hundred Jewish settlements in Judea, Samaria and Gaza, a brazen violation of Israel's Law of Return as well as the rights derived from Articles 6 and 11 of the Mandate for Palestine. These two acts of Israeli and international law authorized the settlement of Jews anywhere in the Land of Israel in the possession of the State of Israel. Once settled on the land with government approval, given either in advance or after the fact, the Jewish settlers cannot be legally forced by the government to disband their settlements, since even though the Mandate expired on May 15, 1948, the Jewish right of settlement in the Land of Israel has retained its full legal force under international law by virtue of the twin principles of acquired rights and estoppel. The right of settlement embodied in Articles 6 and 11 of the Mandate is in full force in Israeli constitutional law by virtue of Section 11 of the Law and Administration Ordinance.[32] Conversely, the uprooting of legally established settlements is strictly forbidden, because that would constitute an act impairing the sovereignty of the State of Israel over the Land of Israel in direct violation of Section 97(a) of the Penal Law.

The Attorney-General of the State of Israel, whose sworn duty it is to uphold the law and to advise the Government of Israel on the legality or illegality of all its actions, never warned the Government or any of its high-ranking ministers, that they would be violating the laws of the State by ceding parts of the Jewish National Home to the PLO/"Palestinian Authority" and that uprooting settlements for that purpose is illegal on its face. That was a grave dereliction of duty which has seriously damaged the Rule of Law in Israel and the fundamental requirement of the Jewish State to preserve all of the Land of Israel in its possession for the Jewish People for all generations to come, as David Ben-Gurion once said even before the State of Israel was reborn.[33] Had there been a strong-willed Attorney-General during the time Prime Minister Yitzhak Rabin was in power (1992-1995), who was intent on enforcing the rule of law as it applied to the integrity of the Land of Israel, the transfer of territory

[32] The Supreme Court of Israel decided, as noted *supra*, that the Mandate as a whole was part of the existing law of Palestine before the establishment of the State of Israel; it was thus carried over into the legal system of the State on May 15, 1948 under Section 11 of the Ordinance.

[33] In August 1937, at the 20th Zionist Congress convened in Zurich, a special session was held in Basle to commemorate the first Zionist Congress forty years earlier. At that session, David Ben-Gurion stated that "no Jew is entitled to give up the right of establishing [i.e., settling] the Jewish Nation in the Land of Israel". These words were not empty in meaning. They are the basis of the Area of Jurisdiction and Powers Ordinance and the Law of Return, enacted when Ben-Gurion was Prime Minister of the fledgling State of Israel."

to the PLO/"Palestinian Authority" would never have taken place.

The Government of Israel was not the only institution in the State responsible for the great disaster that resulted from the Oslo peace process which recognized the so-called "Palestinian People" and illegally empowered its representative, the PLO, a terrorist and criminal organization under the laws of the State of Israel, with various powers and responsibilities that violated the sovereignty of the Jewish State. The Supreme Court of Israel was petitioned several times to stop the illegal and criminal process of transferring Jewish National Home territory belonging to the Jewish People and its assignee, the State of Israel, to the PLO and its offshoot, the "Palestinian Authority", but the Court cowardly refused to intervene and examine the merits of the petitions under Israeli constitutional and criminal law on the spurious and convenient ground that the question at issue was "political" in character rather than "legal" and therefore non-justiciable, though almost every other matter, including military decisions, has been brought under the Court's judicial scrutiny. This outward lack of interest by the Court on a matter everyone else conceded to be of the highest import affecting the very existence of the Jewish State, both present and future, disregarded an obvious fact: all contracts which produce obligations on the parties directly involved, as did all of the Israel-PLO agreements, are by definition and common sense an area of law subject to judicial review by the courts of any country, if such contracts are alleged to be illegal and serious arguments are adduced to support this allegation. The distressing result of the Court's refusal to adjudicate the aforesaid petitions (or in deciding not to decide) was to give the Government a green light to continue a process that openly violated the constitutional and criminal laws of the State.[34] The Court must one day acknowledge and show contrition for its shameful role under the leadership of post-Zionist Justice Aharon Barak and his predecessor, Justice Meir Shamgar, who by their refusal to adjudicate well-founded applications for judicial intervention aided and abetted in a calculating manner this patently illegal process that has caused and continues to cause untold damage to the State of Israel.[35]

---

[34] The following Petitions and Applications for Further Hearings were drafted and filed by the present author on behalf of various public figures and professors to nullify the Declaration of Principles and the Interim Agreement: 1) Prof. Ariel Cohen and others vs. Government of Israel, HCJ 2805/94; filed May 20, 1994. 2) Application for Further Hearing 5259/94 (re HCJ 2805/94); filed September 13, 1994. 3) Prof. Hillel Weiss and others vs. Government of Israel and others, HCJ 3414/96; filed May 13, 1996. 4) Prof. Hillel Weiss and others vs. Government of Israel, HCJ 9063/96 (Resubmission of Petition #3 in abbreviated form); filed December 19, 1996. 5) Application for Further Hearing 2206/98 (re HCJ 9063/96); filed April 5, 1998.

[35] Justices Shamgar and Barak held the positions of President and Deputy President of the Supreme Court of Israel respectively when a Petition was filed on May 20, 1994 by 26 Israeli professors and public figures challenging the legality of the Declaration of Principles (see the preceding footnote). The Court, presided over by Justice Barak, dismissed the Petition mainly on the ground that it was

In light of Israeli recognition of the "Palestinian People" and their "legitimate rights" in official documents, it is hardly surprising that the U.S. Government has followed suit, but has gone much further, to a degree that jeopardizes Israel's future. It has undercut and disregarded Israel's legal rights and title of sovereignty over the entire area of Palestine and the Land of Israel established under several acts of international law, viz., the Smuts Resolution, Article 22 of

---

political in nature without discussing the merits of the legal questions that were raised. Upon receipt of an Application for Further Hearing which enumerated the important legal questions involved, Justice Shamgar dismissed it on a technical objection that evaded the issue concerning the alleged illegality of the DOP. The judgments rendered by both Barak and Shamgar are analyzed in the author's article entitled "The Supreme Court of Israel and the Declaration of Principles: Undermining the Rule of Law and the Juridical Basis of the Jewish State" (Nativ Journal, February 1995, p. 54 ff – in Hebrew). In regard to Justice Shamgar, he was chiefly responsible for the decision taken by the Government of Israel during the Six-Day War of June 1967, when he served as the Military Advocate-General, to voluntarily and wrongly apply to Judea, Samaria and Gaza the Hague Regulations of 1907 as well as the humanitarian provisions of the Fourth Geneva Convention of 1949, regarding the belligerent occupation of foreign territories, instead of advising the Government, as he should have, to apply the whole corpus of law of the State of Israel. This Government decision was contrary to the Area of Jurisdiction and Powers Ordinance of September 16, 1948 and the Land of Israel Proclamation of September 2, 1948, both of which required the incorporation of all repossessed areas of the Land of Israel into the State of Israel. This decision also violated the Law of Return and the provisions of treason found in the Penal Code (sections 97[a], 97[b] and 100). On this point, see the author's Petition to Annul the Interim Agreement, Policy Paper #77, Ariel Center for Policy Research, January 1999, pp. 38-67, 71-79 and 97-122. The Shamgar-inspired decision has become the bane of Israel: every country in the world now refers to Judea, Samaria and the Golan (as it also did until recently for Gaza and formerly for Sinai) as "the occupied territories", despite the fact that they are integral parts of the Jewish National Home and the Land of Israel. For his part, Justice Barak handed down a judgment on March 8, 2000 which held that the allocation to the Jewish Agency of state-owned land to build the Jewish-only community of Katzir in the Nahal Iron (Wadi Ara) region was illegal because it barred Arabs from also building or living there. Justice Barak based his judgment on the principle of Equality of Rights among citizens, that allows no discrimination between Arabs and Jews. He cited Israel's Declaration of Independence and various international conventions and U.S. case law, but ignored the most relevant legal document of all, namely, the Mandate for Palestine, whose provisions regarding acquired Jewish legal rights are still in force in Israeli constitutional law. The Mandate, it is true, outlawed discrimination between the inhabitants of Palestine on the grounds of race, religion or language (Article 15), but, most importantly, it permitted Jewish-only settlements to be established on State and waste lands not required for public purposes (Article 6), as well as the introduction of "a land system appropriate to the needs of the country, having regard, among other things, to the desirability of promoting the close settlement [by Jews] and intensive cultivation of the land" (Article 11). Without such settlements and an appropriate land system, the Jewish State of Israel could never have arisen or survived.

the League Covenant, the San Remo Resolution and the Mandate for Palestine, which itself endorsed in 1924 by concluding a treaty with the United Kingdom (the Anglo-American Convention respecting the Mandate for Palestine).

American recognition of the "Palestinian People" began with President Jimmy Carter as evidenced by the agreed Framework for Peace in the Middle East and has reached its apex under President George W. Bush who in several speeches has outlined a utopian, but unrealistic vision of a "Palestinian State" living side by side in peace with the State of Israel. Such recognition of an Arab homeland and state in any region of western Palestine is clearly inconsistent with the aforementioned legal rights and title of sovereignty. In addition, the U.S. and Israel signed a Memorandum of Understanding on September 1, 1975 in which the U.S. Government undertook not to support any "proposals which it and Israel agree are detrimental to the interests of Israel".[36] As pointed out by the American jurist, William M. Brinton, it would be impossible to imagine anything more "detrimental to the interests of Israel" than a proposal that "Palestine is the homeland of the Arab Palestinian people".[37] His perceptive observation applies with even greater force to President George W. Bush's very damaging vision of a two-state solution in western Palestine for reconciling Jewish national rights with baseless Arab claims for another state. Incomprehensibly, Israel by concluding the Declaration of Principles, the Mutual Recognition Agreement, the Interim Agreement of September 28, 1995 as well as other agreements with the PLO has insanely agreed to the same disastrous proposal as that envisioned by Bush. Most disappointing in this regard is that even Prime Minister Ariel Sharon, originally elected in February 2001 on what was assumed to be a nationalist platform, committed the State of Israel to accepting the pro-Arab Bush vision. This surprised many because when he was just an ordinary member of the Knesset representing the Likud Party after it lost power to Labour in the elections of June 23, 1992, Sharon strenuously opposed the establishment of a new Arab "Palestinian" state which was the unstated aim of the Declaration of Principles. In a 1994 newspaper article published under his name, he wrote:[38]

> Jordan is the existing Palestinian state, and there mustn't be another.

---

[36] See Section 9 of the *Memorandum of Agreement Between the Governments of Israel and the United States* under the heading "United States – Israeli Assurances". Section 9 reads as follows: "The United States Government will not join in and will seek to prevent efforts by others to bring about consideration of proposals which it and Israel agree are detrimental to the interest of Israel." The text of the Memorandum of Agreement can be found in *The Arab-Israel Conflict and its Resolution: Selected Documents*, Document 42, p.171. .

[37] William Brinton's article was published in the *Harvard Journal of Law and Public Policy*, Volume 2, 1979, entitled "Israel: What Is Occupied Territory? A Reply To The Legal Adviser".

[38] *The Jerusalem Post*, Nov. 2, 1994. The op-ed article was entitled "Things that are Sacred".

In adopting the same view as Bush, Sharon repudiated the most sacred tenet of Herut-Likud ideology, the integrity of the Land of Israel under Jewish rule, and thereby disqualified himself from leading either the party or the state. Until Israel gets a leader who utterly opposes any new division of the Land of Israel as an intolerable infringement of Jewish legal rights and title of sovereignty to all of the country and until all the agreements made by the Government of Israel with the PLO are formally declared null and void, the "Palestinian Authority" dismantled and its leaders expelled, it will be difficult for Israel to hold the U.S. Government legally accountable for proposing a new Arab "Palestinian State". In the meanwhile, it remains for others unsullied with dirty hands to vigorously protest and fight by political and legal means the American betrayal of Jewish legal rights to all of the Jewish National Home.

Not all past Israeli leaders accepted the gross fabrication that a nation of "Palestinians" existed. Golda Meir, Prime Minister of Israel from February 1969 to June 1974, told the London Sunday Times in remarks published on June 15, 1969:[39]

> It was not as though there was a Palestinian people in Palestine considering itself a Palestinian people and we came and threw them out and took their country away from them. They did not exist.

The plain and simple truth of her words, delivered without guile in a commendable effort to expose the enormous falsehood of a "Palestinian People" existing in Palestine, which so upset the proponents of an Arab Palestinian state in Judea, Samaria and Gaza made her the target of a campaign of ridicule and vilification launched by ignorant Jewish universalists, anti-nationalists and pro-Arab sympathizers among the Israeli Jewish population that predominate in the Israeli media, particularly the *Ha'Aretz* newspaper, in the universities and in the Labour Party itself that Golda Meir served so faithfully. Stung by ferocious criticism from these quarters, she responded to her critics with an article that was published in the *New York Times* on January 14, 1976 in which she further expounded on her original statement that the "Palestinian People" did not exist. She wrote:

> To be misquoted is an occupational hazard of political leadership; for this reason I should like to clarify my position in regard to the Palestinian issue. I have been charged with being rigidly insensitive to the question of the Palestinian Arabs. In evidence of this I am supposed to have said, "There are no Palestinians". My actual words were: "There is no Palestinian people. There are Palestinian refugees".

[39] This quotation of Prime Minister Golda Meir is reproduced in The Faithful Triangle: Israel, the United States and the Palestinians, by Noam Chomsky, Black Rose Books (1984), p. 51.

The distinction is not semantic. *My statement was based on a lifetime of debates with Arab nationalists who vehemently excluded a separatist Palestinian Arab nationalism from their formulations.*

When in 1921 I came to Palestine – until the end of World War I a barren, sparsely inhabited Turkish province – *we, the Jewish pioneers, were the avowed Palestinians. So we were named in the world. Arab nationalists on the other hand stridently rejected the designation. Arab spokesmen continued to insist that the land we had cherished for centuries was, like Lebanon, merely a fragment of Syria.* On the grounds that it dismembered an ideal unitary Arab state, they fought before the Anglo-American Committee of Inquiry and at the United Nations.

When the Arab historian Philip K. Hitti informed the Anglo-American Committee of Inquiry that "there is no such thing as Palestine in history", it was left to David Ben-Gurion to stress the central role of Palestine in Jewish, rather than [in the original: if not] Arab, history.

As late as May 1956, Ahmed Shukeiry, subsequently head of the Palestine Liberation Organization, declared to the United Nations Security Council, 'It is common knowledge that Palestine is nothing but southern Syria." In view of this, I believe I may be forgiven if *I took Arab spokesmen at their word.*

Until the 1960's attention was focused on the Arab refugees for whose plight the Arab states would allow no solution, though many constructive and far-reaching proposals were made by Israel and the world community.

I repeatedly expressed my sympathy for the needless sufferings of the refugees whose abnormal situation was created and exploited by the Arab states as a tactic in their campaign against Israel. *However, refugee status could not indefinitely be maintained for the original 550,000 Arabs who, in 1948, joined the exodus from the battle areas during the Arab attack on the new State of Israel.*

*When the refugee card began to wear thin, the Palestinian terrorist appeared on the scene flourishing [i.e., brandishing] not the arguable claims of displaced refugees but of a ghoulish nationalism that could only be sated on the corpse of Israel.*

...But though Israel is small and beset, I am not prepared to accede to the easy formula that in the Arab-Israeli conflict we witness two equal contending rights that demand further "flexibility" from Israel. Justice was not violated when in the huge territories liberated by the Allies from the Sultan, *1 per cent was set aside for the Jewish homeland on its ancestral site, while in a parallel settlement 99 per cent of the area was allotted for the establishment of independent Arab states.*

We successively accepted the truncation of Transjordan, three-fourths of the area of historic Palestine, and finally the painful compromise of the 1947 Partition Resolution. Yet though Israel arose

> in only one-fifth of the territory originally assigned for the Jewish homeland, the Arabs invaded the young state.
>
> ...Israel cannot by its presence, sanction the participation of the Palestine Liberation Organization at the Security Council, a participation in direct violation of Resolutions 242 and 338.
>
> We have no common language with exultant murderers of the innocent and with a terrorist movement ideologically committed to the liquidation of Jewish national independence.
>
> At no point has the PLO renounced its program for "the elimination of the Zionist entity". With startling effrontery PLO spokesmen admit that their proposed state on the West Bank would be merely a convenient "point of departure", a tactical "first stage" and finally, a combatant arsenal strategically situated for the easier penetration of Israel (emphasis added).

In the above newspaper article, Golda Meir's rightfully pointed out the fakery of the "Palestinian People" which she distinguished from the "Palestinian refugees" who did exist. She astutely noted that the concept of the "Palestinian People" was invented only "when the refugee card began to wear thin" and a new status was needed to replace it – that of a "nation" dispossessed by the State of Israel. Her lucid and revealing comments are as perfectly true today as when she originally made them in 1969 and again in 1976. Unfortunately, her brave truths and pearls of wisdom have, to Israel's great detriment, been cast aside by those who succeeded her, both at the state level and at the party level. As she herself indicated in the above excerpts from her article, she was not the first Labour Party leader of the old school of Labour Zionist pioneers who devoted their lives to rebuilding the Jewish National Home, to deny the existence of the "Palestinians" as a separate Arab nation. In a speech on October 12, 1936, Ben-Gurion stated that the "Palestinians are not a nation".[40]

He followed this up ten years later in a statement given in evidence to the Anglo-American Inquiry Committee that is as powerful and penetrating today as when it was first presented to the Committee. He convincingly explained why the Arabs have no real historical connection to Palestine, at least in the same manner as the Jewish People who alone considered it their National Home, and where they created an outstanding culture and heritage, both for themselves and for the whole of humanity. An extract from his engrossing statement reads:[41]

---

[40] Chomsky, *op. cit.*, p. 51, quoting Simcha Flapan's book, Zionism and the Palestinians, p. 134.

[41] Ben-Gurion's remarks are found in a special volume in the Hyperion reprint series dealing with "The Rise of Jewish Nationalism and the Middle East". The volume is entitled *The Jewish Case before the Anglo-American Committee of Inquiry on Palestine as presented by the Jewish Agency for Palestine – Statements and Memoranda*, published by Hyperion Press, Inc., Westport, Connecticut, Reprint Edition 1976, pp. 61-62.

In evidence given to you in America, an American Arab, I believe it was John Hassan, said there was never a Palestine as a political and geographical entity; and another American Arab, a great Arab historian, Dr. [Philip K.] Hitti, went even further and said, and I am quoting him: "There is no such thing as Palestine in history, absolutely not." And I agree with him. (This is not the only thing on which I agree with the Arabs.) I agree with him entirely; there is no such thing in history as Palestine, absolutely, but when Dr. Hitti speaks of history he means Arab history, he is a specialist in Arab history and he knows his business. *In Arab history there is no such thing as Palestine* (emphasis added). Arab history was made in Arabia, in Persia and in Spain and North Africa. You will not find Palestine in that history, nor was Arab history made in Palestine. There is not, however, only Arab history – there is world history and Jewish history and in that history there is a country by the name of Judea or, as we call it, Eretz Israel, the Land of Israel. We have called it Israel since the days of Joshua, the son of Nun.[42] There was such a country in history, there was and it is still there. It is a little country, a very little country, but that little country made a very deep impression on world history and on our history. This country made us a people; our people made this country. No other people in the world made this country; this country made no other people in the world. Now again we are beginning to make this country and again this country is beginning to make us. It is unique, but it is a fact. This country came into world history through many wars, fought for its sake by Egyptians, Babylonians, Assyrians, Persians, Greeks, Romans, Byzantines and others, but it was not these wars that gained it its place. It gained its own place in history. Our country won its place in world history as not many other countries have done, even bigger and richer countries, for one reason only: because our people created here, perhaps a limited but a very great civilisation, which became the heritage of the whole of humanity. That country shaped our people, the Jewish People, to make it what it has been from then until today: a very exclusive people on one side and a universal people on the other; very national and very international. Exclusive in its internal life and its attachment to its history, to its national and religious tradition; very universal in its religious, social and ethical ideas. We were told that there is one God in the entire world, that there is unity of the human race because every human being was created in the image of God, that there ought to be and will be universal brotherhood and social justice, peace between peoples. Those were our ideas, this was our culture; and this was what won this country its place in world history. We created here a book, many books; many were lost, many remained only in

[42] Author's note: this is a reference to the Book of Joshua in the Bible, Chapter 11, verse 22: Land of the Children of Israel.

> translations, but a considerable number, some twenty-four, remain in their original language. Hebrew, in the same language, Mr. Chairman, in which I am thinking now when I am talking to you in English, and which the Jews in this country are speaking now. We went into exile, we took that book with us and in that book, which was more to us than a book – it was ourselves, we took with us our country in our hearts, in our soul. There is such a thing as a soul, as well as a body, and these three – the land, the book and the people – are one for us forever. It is an indissoluble bond. There is no material power which can dissolve it except by destroying us physically.
>
> ...Sir, our rights and our attachment and our significance in this country you will find in a book, in one book alone. That book is binding upon us, and only that book. It is binding on us. Whether or not it is on anyone else is not for me to say – I know many Christian people who believe it is binding upon them too – but it is binding on us. You cannot conceive of our people without this book, neither in the far away past nor in the present, just as you cannot conceive of our people without this country, in the past, present or future.

The flimsy and insubstantial Arab link to Palestine was also pointed out by Dr. Ernst Frankenstein, a noted international law specialist who wrote a book in 1944 in which he said:[43]

> The importance of the Arab element in Palestine has been exaggerated. There has been exaggeration of their numbers, as well as of the length and closeness of their connection with the land. Connection with a land finds its most eloquent expression in the common achievements and the common ideals of a people. In non-Jewish Palestine we would look for them in vain. Apart from the Mosque of Omar [Dome of the Rock][44] which was built in the seventh century by Greek architects, for the entire duration of Arab life in Palestine, that is, for 1300 years, there was *not one single Arab achievement* (italics in the original), no work of art, of letters, of science, not one single new thought. Arabia proper, though mostly desert, created the religious movement of the Wahabites. Arabic Palestine, intellectually

---

[43] See the book by Dr. Ernst Frankenstein, *Justice for My People*, Dial Press, New York (1944), pp. 130-131.

[44] According to an entry in the *Encyclopaedia Judaica* (1971) written by Eliezer Bashan (Sternberg) of Bar-Ilan University, the Dome of the Rock was not built at the direction of Omar ibn al-Khattab, the second caliph (634-644), though he did clear the site on the Temple Mount where the Rock or World's Cornerstone (Even Shetiya) stood. This structure was actually built in the years 691-92, in the time of Abd-al-Malik (685-705) who also built the al-Aqsa Mosque. Vol. 12, col. 1382 and Vol. 15, col. 1529.

and spiritually, is a complete blank.

Dr. Frankenstein's view echoed the statement given in the Report by the Palestine Royal Commission which observed:[45]

> In the twelve centuries and more that had passed since the Arab conquest, Palestine had virtually dropped out of history. One chapter only is remembered – the not very noble romance of the Crusades. In economics as in politics, Palestine lay outside the main stream of the world's life. In the realm of thought, in science or in letters, it made no contribution to modern civilization. Its last state was worse than its first.

If any more corroborating evidence is needed that the alleged existence of a distinct Palestinian People is nothing but an absolute fiction and fabrication which has fooled practically the whole world, it came from one of the propagators of the lie, Zuhair Muhsin, formerly a member of the executive committee of the "Palestine Liberation Organization" and the leader of the Syrian-sponsored terrorist organization, *al-Sa'iqa* (Arabic: lightning). In an interview he gave to James Dorsey, the Middle East affairs expert of the Dutch daily, Trouw, on March 31, 1977, he confessed:[46]

> A Palestinian people does not exist. The establishment of a Palestinian state is just the means for continuing our struggle against Israel and for Arab unity. Since Golda Meir denies the existence of a Palestinian people, I claim that such a people does exist and that there is a difference between it and the Jordanian people. However, *in actual fact, there is no difference between Jordanians, Palestinians, Syrians and Lebanese… We all belong to the Arab people. It is only for political reasons that we carefully stress our Palestinian identity, for it is in the national interest of the Arabs to encourage a separate Palestinian identity to counter Zionism. Yes, the existence of a separate Palestinian identity serves only tactical purposes.*
>
> The founding of a Palestinian state is a new tool or expedient in the continuing battle against Israel and for Arab unity (emphasis added).

The recognition of mislabeled "national-historical rights" of a gentile people, plagiaristically and artificially called "Palestinians", to its so-called

[45] *Palestine Royal Commission Report*, Command 5479 (1937), p. 6.

[46] This quotation is taken from an article written by Prof. Yehuda Z. Blum that appeared in the Jerusalem Post on August 16, 1977, entitled "Are the Palestinians 'a people'?" It also appears in the book he wrote, *For Zion's Sake*, Rosemont Publishing and Printing Corporation, U.S.A. (1987), p. 53. A brief news report of what Zuhair Muhsen said can be found in the Jerusalem Post of April 6, 1977.

homeland, that is in the very heart of the internationally recognized Jewish National Home, where the Jewish People and Judaism were born and ensconced two millennia before the Arabs arrived in Palestine in the seventh century, can only be described as the greatest hoax of the 20th century or one of the most fabulous lies ever invented, which continues in the 21st century to dominate the minds of everyone concerned with the Arab-Jewish Question, now erroneously called the "Israeli-Palestinian Conflict".

To anyone who has objectively examined the diplomatic history leading up to the creation of Palestine in 1920, as well as the international law formulated in the immediate aftermath of World War I, it must inevitably be concluded that a nation of Palestinians simply did not exist at that time, nor in the decades that followed, even if occasionally some statements may have been uttered by Palestinian Arabs referring to a Palestinian people to differentiate themselves from the Arabs of Syria. Had such a nation truly existed, it would have been duly recognized in the global political and legal settlement made in 1919 and 1920 to satisfy the needs of homeless or subjugated nations and countries, such as the Arabs of Syria and of Iraq, the Jewish People in regard to Palestine, the Armenians in regard to Armenia, the Kurds in regard to Kurdistan and the Assyrians who were promised "full safeguards" and "protection" in the predominantly Kurdish areas. Such recognition was even extended to the Maronite Christian Arabs of Lebanon, who were given a share of governmental power under the French Mandate.

The whole idea of a separate Palestinian nationalism that is now alleged to have existed while the Great Powers were formulating their Middle East settlement is not found in the actual events of those days, but only in the minds of modern scholars, particularly Jewish scholars,[47] who have produced books of scholarship to document or affirm the existence of a Palestinian nationalism whose roots supposedly go back to the early 20th century or even to the 19th century. This is an invented, retroactive nationalism, more the product or construction of latter-day writers who seek to justify the claims made today by Arabs calling themselves "Palestinians", rather than a genuine nationalism based on actual fact. In truth, "Palestinian nationalism" is not a natural development, like other nationalisms, but merely an emulation of Zionism and a shrewd propaganda ploy that has become an accepted belief, not only among the Arab inhabitants of Judea, Samaria and Gaza but to most Israelis and the rest of the world.

The slogans mounted about the "Palestinians" and their alleged "legitimate

[47] The work of Arieh "Lova" Eliav, *Land of the Hart*, has already been discussed above, as well as that of Yehoshafat Harkabi, *The Palestinian Covenant and its Meaning*. See also the book by Yehoshua Porath, *The Emergence of the Palestinian-Arab National Movement 1918-1929*, published by Frank Cass: London (1974) and his subsequent volumes on the subject. The latest work of this kind is entitled *The Palestinian People: A History* by Baruch Kimmerling and Joel S. Migdal, Harvard University Press.

and inalienable rights" to Palestine are now parroted endlessly by the gullible, the ignorant and the mass of gentile Jew-haters who style themselves as humanitarians and liberals. A large part of the blame for this phenomenon lies at the doorstep of successive governments of Israel which have incredibly accepted these untruths and thereby lent greater validity to them. There has been cascading support for a so-called "Palestinian State" which defies every point or aspect of logic, law, history and linguistics. The very act of calling for the establishment of still another "Palestinian State" composed of alleged "indigenous Palestinians" is absurd on its face, an insult to truth and intelligence, a fraud which must one day be shattered. It should always be stressed and remembered that Palestine was created by the Principal Allied Powers at the San Remo Conference in April 1920 to be a Jewish country, not an Arab one, and therefore only Israel is the legal "Palestinian State" under international law. Jordan is an illegally created one, with other parts of historical Palestine and the Land of Israel reposing under the foreign rule of Lebanon (the region of Upper Galilee up to the southern bank of the Litani), Syria (the area of the Bashan) and Egypt (at least half the Sinai Peninsula) and, since May 1994, the Palestine Liberation Organization and the Palestinian Authority (about 42% of Judea and Samaria and all of the Gaza region). Any action taken to establish a new Arab Palestinian state must be strenuously opposed as an illegal and destructive imposition on the State of Israel, which impairs its legal rights and title of sovereignty to all of the Land of Israel as originally conceived and laid down in international law.

*Chapter 18*

# A Historical Refutation of Arab and Moslem Claims to the Land of Israel

There is no logical or just reason why Arabic-speaking gentiles should have 21 states and then be entitled to another on the basis of the existence of a fake nation of Palestinians who have been deprived of the right of self-determination. They never enjoyed that right in any part of the Jewish National Home and the Land of Israel under international law, and there is not a single document of international law even today that requires it. In this regard all U.N. resolutions, whether emanating from the Security Council or the General Assembly, that endorse the right of "Palestinian" self-determination are not classified as international law, despite numerous assertions to the contrary. The latest international plot to redivide the Land of Israel and establish a so-called "Palestinian state", known as the Road Map Peace Plan, is neither a treaty nor an international agreement nor even a legal document of any sort, but, as its name indicates, merely a plan, the contents of which have not been fully agreed to by one of the parties expected to carry it out – the State of Israel, as is evident from its fourteen reservations.

These reservations[1] constitute in effect substantive Israeli amendments of the Road Map, the non-fulfillment of which prevents its realization. The first reservation to be fulfilled as a condition for progress between the phases of the Road Map states that the "Palestinian Authority" will act to combat terror, violence and incitement and furthermore to dismantle all terrorist organizations, specifically naming Hamas, Islamic Jihad, the Popular Front, the Democratic Front, and the Al-Aqsa Brigades. Another important reservation to the Road Map is that direct references must be made in both the introductory statements and final settlement to: "Israel's right to exist as a Jewish State and to the waiver of any right of return for Palestinian refugees to the State of Israel". A third reservation requires the removal of references in the Road Map to other external "peace plans", particularly Security Council Resolution 1397[2] of March 12, 2002,

[1] For a list of these reservations, see *inter alia* on the internet: the Jewish Virtual Library (website: www.jewishvirtuallibrary.org/jsource/Peace/rad1.html).

[2] Resolution 1397 demands the immediate cessation of all acts of violence and calls for the implementation of the Tenet Work Plan and the Mitchell Report

the Saudi Initiative of then Crown Prince Abdullah and the Arab Peace Initiative adopted in Beirut.[3] However, the references to Security Council Resolutions 242 and 338 were not objected to, but were to remain "only as an outline for the conduct of future negotiations on a permanent settlement". The Israeli Cabinet communicated to the United States Administration all of the 14 reservations it formulated at the time (May 25, 2003) it "agreed to accept the steps set out in the Road Map". By so doing, the Government of Israel was officially accepting the concept of a new Arab "Palestinian State" in all parts of Judea, Samaria and Gaza to be evacuated in the final settlement. The vote in the Cabinet accepting the Road Map was 12 supporters to 7 opposed with 4 abstentions. [4] The Israeli

---

recommendations. The Tenet Cease-Fire Plan of June 2001 formulated by former CIA Director George Tenet, commits the Government of Israel and the Palestinian Authority to a mutual, comprehensive cease-fire and to taking a series of steps to immediately resume the security cooperation that was broken off on September 29, 2000 following an outbreak of Arab "Palestinian" violence against Israel – the so-called Al-Aqsa Intifada. For details of the Tenet Cease-Fire Plan, see Jewish Virtual Library (http://www.jewishvirtuallibrary.org/jsource/Peace/tenet.html. The Mitchell Report was released on May 4, 2001 in the name of former U.S. Senator George Mitchell, Chairman of a Fact-Finding Committee investigating the cause of violence in the Land of Israel that had begun in mid-2000. The Mitchell Report makes a series of recommendations to end what it called the "cycle of violence". It called upon the Government of Israel and the "Palestinian Authority" to implement "confidence-building measures" and return to serious negotiations "in a spirit of compromise, reconciliation and partnership". Among the chief recommendations, the "Palestinian Authority" was asked to make "a 100-percent effort to prevent terrorist operations and punish perpetrators". The Government of Israel was presumptuously told to "freeze all settlement activity, including the 'natural growth' of existing settlements". The final result of these negotiations was to be a "Palestinian State" in the "West Bank" and Gaza Strip having territorial contiguity. For the text of the Mitchell Report, see: http://www.jewishvirtuallibrary.org/jsource/Peace/Mitchellrep.html.

[3] The Saudi Initiative of March 2002 offered Israel a comprehensive peace and normal relations if it implemented a complete withdrawal from Judea, Samaria, Gaza and the Golan, as well as the remaining occupied Lebanese territories and, furthermore, accepted "an independent Palestinian State with east Jerusalem as its capital" and provided a just solution for Arab "refugees". The Arab League States, in a meeting at Beirut on March 28, 2002, amended the Saudi Initiative by requiring Israel to accept the return of Arab "refugees", in accordance with U.N. General Assembly Resolution 194. The Saudi Initiative was renamed the Arab Peace Initiative.

[4] Those voting for the Road Map and consequently for the establishment of an Arab "Palestinian" state and the ending of the alleged Israeli "occupation" were Prime Minister Ariel Sharon, Defense Minister Shaul Mofaz, Foreign Minister Silvan Shalom, and Ministers Ehud Olmert, Tzipi Livni, Gideon Ezra, Meir Sheetrit, Yosef Lapid, Avraham Poraz, Yosef Paritzky, Yehudit Naot and Eliezer Sandberg. Those abstaining were Finance Minister Benjamin Netanyahu, Education Minister Limor Livnat, Health Minister Dan Naveh and Internal Security Minister Tzahi Hanegbi. The proposal was opposed by Ministers Yisrael Katz,

reservations were not accepted by the "Palestinian Authority" nor by the four entities comprising the artificial grouping known as the Quartet comprising two conglomerates, the United Nations and the European Union, and two states, the Russian Federation and the United States. That fact alone means that no international agreement was concluded between the parties involved. In any case, the "Palestine Liberation Organization"/"Palestinian Authority" is not a state and therefore has no standing under international law to conclude a valid international agreement with the State of Israel or with any of the above-mentioned four sponsors of the Road Map Peace Plan. To characterize as legal obligations Israel's political promises under the plan which represents no more than the adopted policy of the government of Prime Minister Ariel Sharon and the successor government of Ehud Olmert is to change the nature of this peace plan, converting it into a binding international agreement or contract which it definitely is not. In this respect, it can be compared to the Balfour Declaration at the time it was approved by the British Government and issued on November 2, 1917. The latter was a government promise to use their best endeavours to establish in Palestine a National Home for the Jewish People. This promise had no legal status in 1917 – it was then only a policy pronouncement, rather than a binding undertaking. The Declaration achieved a legal status only in 1920 when it was adopted by the Principal Allied Powers at the San Remo Peace Conference and became part of international law. Moreover, any plan to redivide the Land of Israel and set up a new Arab Palestinian state in Judea, Samaria and Gaza alongside the Jewish Palestinian State of Israel, is contrary to established international law. The right to Palestine under international law was originally and exclusively vested in the Jewish People and not in an unknown nation called "Palestinians". As has been repeatedly stated in this book, this right is evidenced by several international instruments, specifically Article 22 of the Covenant of the League of Nations, ratified as part of the Treaty of Versailles on January 10, 1920, followed by the San Remo Resolution of April 25, 1920, the Mandate for Palestine as confirmed on July 24, 1922, the Franco-British Boundary Convention of December 23, 1920, and finally the Anglo-American Convention of December 3, 1924 respecting the Mandate for Palestine. As also previously stated, the foregoing Article 22 is to be interpreted in conjunction with the Smuts Resolution of January 30, 1919 and the Weizmann-Feisal Agreement of January 3, 1919 in regard to the meaning of the term "Palestine", as used in the Smuts Resolution. That term denoted the Jewish People rather than the local Arab inhabitants of Palestine.

The founding of a new Arab state in Cisjordan would also constitute a grave violation of Israel's own constitutional and criminal law, notably the Area of Jurisdiction and Powers Ordinance, Section 11B of the Law and Administration Ordinance, the Law of Return, and Sections 97(a) and 97(b) of the Penal Law. Israel is therefore legally barred by its own law from surrendering any area of

Uzi Landau, Natan Sharansky, Effi Eitam, Zevulun Orlev, Avigdor Lieberman and Benjamin Elon.

the Land of Israel to the "Palestinian Authority" under the envisaged Road Map Peace Plan.

Looking at the Arab-Jewish Question (wrongly renamed the "Palestinian"-Israeli Conflict) from a purely historical perspective in order to judge the merits of the respective claims of each party to the Land of Israel, parallel situations can be discerned in other cases which refute recurring Arab claims and perceived rights to the country, based on their exaggerated duration of occupation. In all these cases an invading army occupied a country not its own for long periods of time, the country then being settled by the compatriots of that army or other foreigners without any national rights accruing to them. The best example is Spain which was overrun by Moslem Berbers and Arabs, known as Moors, a nomadic people from Northern Africa originally the inhabitants of Mauritania. Under the Umayyad ruler Abd-ar-Rahman III, a western caliphate was established in Cordoba, which became the Moorish capital of Andalusia, the largest and most populous region of Spain. This caliphate dominated most of the Iberian Peninsula for about five centuries. One province of Andalusia, called Grenada, remained under Moorish rule from 711 to 1492, a period of 781 years or nearly eight centuries before it was reconquered from the last Moorish king, Muhammad XI (whom the Spanish called Boabdil), during the reign of the Roman-Catholic monarchs, King Ferdinand V and Queen Isabella I. The Moors also occupied the rocky peninsula of Gibraltar for 751 years, from 711 to 1462. Yet no one today, apart from some radical Islamists, would view Spain and Gibraltar as being part of a Berber or Arab homeland.

The example of Spain was cited by David Ben-Gurion when he told the Anglo-American Committee of Inquiry during a session held in Jerusalem in March 1946:[5]

> When the Arabs conquered Spain, didn't they create there a magnificent civilization? They did. They created a magnificent civilization in Spain and then they were driven out. Can they claim Spain for the Arabs? Have they a right to Spain? I know of no other objection which proves our case so forcibly as this one, and I am taking it up. Is there a single Arab in the entire world who dreams about Spain? Is there an Arab in Iraq or in Egypt or anywhere else who knows the rivers and mountains of Spain better than he knows his own country? Is there an Arab in the world who will give his money to Spain? What is Spain to him? What does he care about Spain? Is there a single Arab in the world who loves Spain? And is there a people other than the Jews that loves this country [Land of Israel/Palestine]? There are many peoples who want to conquer and possess all kinds of countries as well as this one – not because of love for this country, but

[5] *The Jewish Case Before the Anglo-American Committee of Inquiry on Palestine as Presented by the Jewish Agency for Palestine*. Hyperion Press, Inc., Westport, Connecticut (1976), p. 63.

> people who want power. This love is peculiar to our people alone, and you will find it among the Jewish People wherever they are, not only in countries of oppression like Germany and the Yemen, but also in free countries like England and Canada. Here are Jews who have been away for centuries, some of them many centuries, some of them thousands of years, like the Jews in Yemen. They have always carried Zion in their hearts, and they came back, and came back with love. In no other country in the world will you find people loving their country as the Jews love this country.

Arab control over Palestine lasted a much shorter time than Moorish rule in Moslem Spain. Therefore, just as modern Spain cannot be considered a homeland to which the Berbers or Arabs have a national right despite the longevity of their rule in that country, so Palestine or the Land of Israel cannot be considered an Arab homeland to which the Arabs in the false guise of being "Palestinians" have a similar right.

Besides Spain, other examples can be cited to disprove Arab claims to Palestine based, as noted above, on the longevity of their occupation of the country. The country of Slovakia provides an interesting parallel in terms of length of domination by a foreign conqueror. The area now constituting Slovakia became the home of Slavic tribes in the fifth and sixth centuries, but early in the tenth century the Magyars of Hungary conquered Slovakia, subsequently making it a land of the Hungarian Crown, and generally ruled it until 1918, a period of about ten centuries. Despite the very long Magyar rule over Slovakia, which by far exceeds the period of Arab domination of Palestine, no national rights vest in Hungary today over the Slovak Republic, which proclaimed its independence on January 1, 1993.

Another case of foreign conquest lasting an inordinately long time was Ottoman Turkish rule over various countries in the Balkan Peninsula – Greece, Bulgaria, Roumania, Serbia, a part of Montenegro, Macedonia, Albania, Bosnia and Hercegovina, as well as in the Middle East – Palestine, Syria, Iraq (consisting of three disparate provinces of Shi'ite Basra, Sunni Baghdad and Kurdish Mosul), Arabia, Yemen and Egypt. Ottoman domination over all these territories began in the 16th century and only ended in some cases in the 19th century and in other cases, in the first two decades of the 20th. None of these territories were ever considered part of the Turkish homeland despite the fact that the Ottoman Empire flourished in the entire area for three to four centuries. Therefore, the Turks today have no right to repossess or even lay claim to any of these territories that were formerly included in their far-flung Empire, nor would they even imagine that such a right exists for them.

The Turks also extended their rule to India under different dynasties which ruled over their own principalities or kingdoms in the Indian sub-continent. This included the Ghaznavids and Ghorids in the eleventh and twelfth centuries, followed by the Delhi Sultanate (1210-1526), a series of Moslem dynasties, and the Mughal or Mongol Empire (1526-1857) founded by Babur, a Turkish chieftain from Afghanistan descended from Timur (Tamerlane) and Jenghiz Khan. The Delhi Sultanate and Mughal Empire, covering a period of six centuries, were Moslem states which made Islam into a powerful force in India. However, Hinduism still remained the faith of the majority of the population. Though Turkish and Mongolian rule lasted for a long time in India, this gave no right to Turks or Mongols to claim India as part of their national patrimony.[6] In the parallel situation in Palestine, Arabs do claim such a right, disregarding the fact that historically and, since 1920, under international law it is the recognized Jewish homeland once conquered by an invading Arab army from the Arabian peninsula, whose rule prevailed for only a limited period of time.

To refute the exaggerated and unfounded Arab claims to Palestine, it is first necessary to determine the precise period of time they were the actual masters of the country and then to compare the duration of Arab rule with the number of years it was ruled by Turkish dynasties, on the one hand, and with the period of Jewish rule, on the other.

The period from 634, when Arab warriors surged northward out of the confines of Arabia to conquer Palestine and many other lands, until 1099, when the Crusaders captured Jerusalem from the Fatimids, is usually called the "Arab Period" of Palestine's history, one that endured 465 years. This length of time of Arab rule over the Land of Israel is a gross exaggeration which almost doubles the number of years the Arabs actually controlled the country, strangely and unquestioningly accepted even by Jewish and Israeli sources though it does not correspond to the truth.[7] The peoples and dynasties who ruled the country during this relatively long period were not only Arabs from Arabia, but also non-Arabs, particularly those of Turkish, Berber and native Egyptian-Coptic descent. The identity of these latter groups is concealed under the all-embracing rubric of "Arab". A more accurate name for this 465 year period would be one that took account of all the non-Arab rulers that governed Palestine from foreign lands during that period. The Arab-Turkish-Berber Period would be such a name. An alternative name would be the First Islamic Period, prior to Crusader rule which began in 1099, in contrast to the Second Islamic Period, dating from 1187. That year witnessed the collapse of the Latin Kingdom of

---

[6] The Mongols include large elements of Turkic-speaking peoples. After the conquests of Jenghiz Khan in the first quarter of the 13th century, Mongols and Turks merged and became known as Tatars (Tartars). See entries in the Columbia Encyclopedia, 6th edition (2000), under Mongols and Tatars.

[7] An instance of this untruth is found in the *Encyclopaedia Judaica* ([1971] Volume 9, col. 259) which, under the heading of "Land of Israel, History", lists the Arab period as extending from 634-1099. This period contrasts with the preceding one from 70 to 640 which witnessed Roman, Byzantine and the interlude of Persian rule and with the subsequent non-sequential Crusader Period from 1099 to 1291. The scholarly article surveying the Arab Period was authored by Rabbi Dr. Haim Z'ev Hirschberg, Professor of Jewish History, Bar Ilan University, Ramat Gan.

Jerusalem, thereby ending 88 years of continuous Crusader rule, though it briefly returned to Jerusalem and Nazareth in 1229 for another 15 years and persisted on the coast of Palestine until 1291, when Acre fell.

In the specific era of direct Arab rule over Palestine, there were three separate periods. The first was the non-hereditary rule of the four Caliphs who were the successors of Muhammad, the first three of whom governed from Medina (ancient Yathrib). This town apparently had a Jewish majority shortly before Muhammad fled there from Mecca in 622 (called the Hijra or Hegira which marks the beginning of the Islamic calendar) and where he lived the last ten years of his life. The four Caliphs were Abu-Bakr (632-634), Umar ibn al-Khattab (634-644), Uthman (644-656) and Ali (656-661). It was during Umar's reign that Palestine came under Arab rule, marking the only time in its long history that it was ruled, although rather loosely, from Arabia. During Ali's five-year tenure the capital of the caliphate was moved to Kufa (al-Kufa) on the Euphrates (Perath) in central Iraq.

The second phase of Arab establishment in Palestine came with the advent to power of Mu'awiya, the first of the Umayyad caliphs, following a battle for supremacy with Ali and his two sons, Hasan and Hussein. Mu'awiya had been the governor of Syria but had refused to recognize Ali as the legitimate caliph after the murder of Uthman by Ali's supporters. In 660, Mu'awiya had himself proclaimed the new caliph in Jerusalem, but only in the following year was he recognized as such after Ali's assassination in Kufa and Hasan's abdication. In 680, Ali's second son Hussein was defeated decisively and killed at Karbala, in central Iraq, after he led an insurrection to restore the caliphate to the Alid family. This sparked a lasting schism in early Islam between the Sunnites – the followers of what came to be the orthodox tradition who accepted Mu'awiya as caliph – and the Shi'ites – the adherents of Ali who refused to do so. The Shi'ites clung tenaciously to the belief that the right of succession to the caliphate established on the death of Muhammad (632) vested exclusively with the members of the Alid family, specifically the direct linear descendants of Hussein, upon whom the title of Imam or leader was conferred. Hussein is considered a martyr by Shi'ites, and the site of his tomb in Karbala has become a venerated holy place in their eyes, second in importance only to the Kaaba, the cubic stone structure in Mecca which Islamic tradition holds was built by Adam and rebuilt by Abraham together with his son Ishmael.

The Umayyads belonging to the Quraysh tribe were one of the leading families of great wealth in Mecca in the pre-Islamic period who had originally opposed Muhammad, but later, in 627 (629?), converted to Islam. After they emerged victorious in their struggle with the Alid family and took over the caliphate, they transferred the seat of government to Damascus (661). The Umayyad dynasty then governed Palestine as part of the Islamic state from their Syrian stronghold for the next 89 years, from 661 to 750. In 750 the dynasty was overthrown at the Battle of the Great Zab River (a tributary of the Tigris [or Hidekel] that rises along the present Turkish-Iranian border east of Lake

Van). In the wake of the battle, not only was the last Umayyad caliph, Marwan II, beheaded, but all members of the Umayyad house were hunted down and exterminated, with the exception of the youthful Abd-ar-Rahman who escaped to Spain, where he founded a new Umayyad dynasty.

The Abbasids, the dynasty established to rule the Islamic state after the overthrow of the last of the Damascene Umayyad caliphs, took their name from Abbas, the uncle of Muhammad, of the Hashemite clan of the Quraysh tribe in Mecca. This dynasty constituted, in the initial period of its rule only, the third and final phase of Arab governance of Palestine. The first Abbasid caliph, Abu-al-Abbas as-Saffah (Shedder of Blood), established his capital in Kufa, but during the reign of his successor, Al-Mansur (the Victorious), it was transferred to Baghdad, a city he founded in 762. In a later period lasting 56 years (836-892), the capital was moved to Samarra in north central Iraq before reverting to Baghdad. The greatest of the Abbasid caliphs was the fifth, Harun al-Rashid (Aaron the Upright), whose rule (786-809) marked the apogee and splendor of Abbasid power. Harun al-Rashid, who is chiefly remembered as the caliph of *A Thousand and One Nights*, was a contemporary of Charlemagne (Charles the Great), the Carolingian king of the Franks and Emperor of the West, with whom Harun had friendly relations.

After a century or so of Arab rule, the actual rulers of the Abbasid empire were Turks who had adopted the Sunni Moslem faith and were originally used as mercenaries by the Abbasids. The Shi'ite Persian Buyids or Buwayhids, operating from their capital of Shiraz in what is today the province of Fars, took control of the Abbasid empire from the middle of the tenth to the middle of the 11th century (945-1055), until overthrown by the Sunni Turkish Seljuks under Tughril Beg (Tughril the Prince) who conquered both Persia (1040-1044) and Iraq (1055). Professor Philip K. Hitti noted the loss of Arab predominance in the Abbasid empire when he wrote as follows:[8]

> The truly Arab period in the history of Islam had now passed and the first purely Arab phase of the Islamic empire began to move rapidly toward its close. The Abbasid government called itself dawlah, new era, and a new era it was... Khurasanians formed the caliphal bodyguard and Persians occupied the chief posts in the government. The original Arabian aristocracy was replaced by a hierarchy of officers drawn from the whole gamut of races under the caliphate. The old Arabian Moslems and the new foreign converts were beginning to coalesce and shade off into each other. Arabianism fell, but Islam continued, and, under the guise of international Islam, Iranianism marched triumphantly on.

[8] *History of the Arabs* by Philip K. Hitti, 5th edition revised, MacMillan Company, New York (1951), pp. 286-287.

Hitti further characterized the Abbasid empire as one "of neo-Moslems in which the Arabs formed only one of the many component races"[9].

The same characterization of the Abbasid empire was made by the distinguished British historian and theologian, the Reverend James William Parkes, who observed:[10]

> The Umayyads were the only dynasty which could be called purely Arab. For when they fell and power passed to the Abbasids, it was Islam and not Arab blood which formed the basis of unity; and little more than another century saw the passage of effective power to successive usurpers who were wholly or largely of Turkish and not even of Semitic origin. But while Arab control of the empire dwindled and passed, and the empire itself broke up into rival kingdoms, the unity of the Syrian, Arab, Egyptian and North African territories on the basis of Islam and of the Arabic language remained and became stronger with time, being scarcely affected by the two centuries of Crusader rule in the Holy Land, by the growing power of Christian Europe, or by the secularism of the modern world.

The initial period of Abbasid rule in Palestine, centered in Baghdad and temporarily in Samarra, ended in 878 when a Turkish dynasty, the Tulunids, named after its founder, Ahmad ibn-Tulun, set up an independent state in Egypt, Syria and Palestine. Hitti notes that this was "the first time since Ptolemaic days Egypt had become a sovereign state and the first time since Pharaonic days it ruled Syria" which it continued to rule for over six centuries thereafter.[11] The Tulunid regime supported by an army of 100,000[12] based on a core of Turkish and Negro slaves brought to an end the continuous Arab dominion over Palestine which had begun in 634, a period of exactly 244 years.

From the time of the Tulunids to the end of Ottoman power in Palestine (878-1917), the Turks, and not the Arabs, were the principal foreign rulers of Palestine under one dynasty or another, even though during this millennium and more, power also resided in the hands of non-Turkish rulers, ranging from the North African Fatimids, the chiefly French Roman Catholic Crusaders, the Kurdish Ayyubids and the Circassian Mamluks.

The Tulunid dynasty (878-905) was followed by a period of renewed Abbasid rule (905-935), but by this time the caliphs of the Empire were no longer the actual rulers. Political power was now held by Turkish soldiers and generals who

---

[9] *Ibid.*, p. 289.

[10] James William Parkes, *A History of Palestine from 135 A.D. to Modern Times*, Oxford University Press, New York (1949), p. 86.

[11] Hitti, *op. cit.*, p. 453.

[12] *Ibid.*, p. 453.

made and unmade caliphs at will.[13] The person who actually held the reins of secular government in Iraq in the name of the caliphs, who still had spiritual-juridical authority, was a military commander with the title of Amir al-Umara (Prince of Princes).

In 935 until 969, a new Turkish dynasty, the Ikhshidids, arose in Egypt at Fostat (old Cairo), founded by Muhammad ibn-Tughj. In 939, he received from the Abbasid Caliph Al-Radi the old Iranian royal title of Ikhshid (Prince). In 941 he added Syria and Palestine to his quasi-independent state. Near the end of the three-decade Ikhshidid dynasty which dominated Palestine (941-970), an Abyssinian eunuch, Abu al-Misk Kafur (musky camphor), a former black slave, became the *de jure* ruler of the Ikhshidid domains (966-968). He had previously been the de facto ruler during the reign of the two sons who succeeded their father, Muhammad the Ikhshid.

In 969, the Ikhshidid dynasty in Egypt was overthrown by the invading Fatimids from Tunisia, where, sixty years earlier (909), they had founded a dynasty under Sa'id ibn-Husayn who reigned as Ubaydullah (Ubayd-Allah) al-Mahdi, an adherent of the Isma'ilite sect of Shi'ite Islam. Ubaydullah claimed to be a descendant of Fatima, the daughter of Muhammad, hence the name of the dynasty, also called Maghariba (the "Westerners"). However, that genealogical claim was rejected by the enemies of the Fatimids and by several Moslem historians, though others upheld it.

In Berber Tunisia, the Fatimids had established their first capital at Kairouan (al-Kayrawan) and later at al-Mahdiyah, on the Mediterranean coast. In planning the conquest of Egypt, the Fatimid caliph al-Mu'izz and his supreme commander Jawhar benefited greatly from the advice given them by an apostate Jew, Ya'qub ibn Killis, who actually drew up the plans for the Fatimid conquest in 969.[14] A year later, the Fatimids extended their rule to Palestine, which continued for one century until 1071, with minor interludes of Qarmatian[15] and Bedouin rule. It was during the early part of their rule in Palestine that the Byzantine Emperors, John I Tzimisces and his successor Basil II, made a final attempt to regain the country for their empire, penetrating as far as Beisan (Beth-Sh'an) in 975 before retreating.

Under Fatimid rule, Palestine was governed from their new capital of Cairo, the name of a newly-built quarter of Fostat, which the Fatimids constructed immediately after conquering Egypt. The ranks of the Fatimid army consisted

---

[13] *Ibid.*, pp. 466-467.

[14] Moshe Gil, *A History of Palestine 634-1099*, Columbia University Press (paperback edition, 1977), p. 335. Ibn-Killis was later appointed vizier to Caliph al-Aziz, the son and successor of al-Mu'izz.

[15] The Qarmatians were an offshoot of the Isma'il sect of Shi'a named after its Iraqi founder, Hamdan Qarmat. They captured Palestine except for the coastal fortresses in 971 and remained in control of the country for 3 years, before being driven out by Fatimid troops. They later regained authority for a few months but were finally vanquished in 977.

of Berbers and native Egyptians or Arabicized Copts.[16] They were supplemented by imported Turkish, Circassian and Sudanese (Negro) mercenary troops who, in a later time, became the ruling class in Egypt.[17] In 1071, the Fatimids lost control of Palestine, except for the Coastal Plain, to the Seljuk Turks, briefly regaining the country for an additional ten months (in 1098-1099), just prior to the Crusader takeover.

The Seljuks were Turkish nomads coming from the Kirghiz steppes of Western Turkestan, a region in Central Asia corresponding to the present-day independent states of Turkmenistan, Uzbekistan, Tadjikistan and Kyrgyzstan, as well as the southern portion of Kazakhstan. They were the ruling family of the Oghuz (Ghuzz) Turkmen (Turkoman) tribal confederation, which also included the Osmanlis (Ottomans). By 1055, the Seljuks, as noted above, had taken control of Iran and Iraq from the Persian Buyids, governing the Abbasid state from their capital of Isfahan in central Iran, with the title of Sultan. In 1071, their leader, Sultan Alp-Arslan, decisively defeated the Byzantine army at the Battle of Manzikert (now in Eastern Turkey) under Emperor Romanus IV (Diogenes), which resulted in the Seljuk conquest of almost all of Anatolia. In the same year Alp-Arslan's general Atsiz invaded Palestine and destroyed Fatimid rule in the country by first capturing Ramla followed by Jerusalem in 1073.[18] Malik-Shah, who reigned as Sultan of the Abbasid empire after Alp-Arslan's death in c1073, gave Palestine to his brother Tutush. The Seljuks governed most of Palestine until 1098, when the Fatimids momentarily regained the country as previously noted. The latter were displaced by the Crusaders who ruled Palestine or various parts of it for a period of two centuries (1099-1291) until the fall of their last capital, Acre, to the Mamluk sultan, al-Ashraf.

Crusader rule was originally centered in Jerusalem (1099-1187) which became the name of the Latin Kingdom in the Holy Land. The kingdom was also interestingly known by two other names: the Kingdom of David and the Kingdom of Israel, both of which evoked the memorable Biblical epoch of Jewish rule. At its height the Kingdom of Jerusalem extended as far north as Beirut and embraced important parts of Transjordan, including Bashan, Gilead and all of Moab (designated as Le Crac or Kerak) up to Eilat. The establishment of several Crusader states in the Middle East was modeled upon the feudal system then in vogue in Western Europe. This made the Kingdom of Jerusalem the overlord or suzerain of lesser fiefs or lands which were ruled as separate states, consisting of the County of Tripoli, the Principality of Antioch and the County of Edessa. This overlordship or suzerainty was more nominal than real.

In 1171, the Fatimid caliphate in Egypt was overthrown by the Kurdish warrior, Yusuf ibn-Ayyub, popularly known as Saladin (Salah-ad-Din: the Righteousness

---

[16] Gil, *op. cit.*, p. 337 and Hitti, *op. cit.*, p. 625.

[17] Hitti, *op. cit.*, p. 620.

[18] Gil, *op. cit.*, p. 410; Parkes, *op. cit.*, p. 100.

of the Faith). This marked the beginning of the Ayyubid sultanate that ruled Egypt until the Mamluk takeover in 1250. After the battle of Hittin (Hattin), near Tiberias, in July 1187 and the crushing defeat of the Christian Frankish army of Guy de Lusignan, the King of Jerusalem, Ayyubid rule was extended to all of Palestine over the next four years, except for Tyre which remained in Crusader hands under the Italian Crusader, Conrad, Marquis of Montferrat. Tyre briefly became the new Crusader center until 1191 when the capital became Acre after the Crusader re-capture of that city. Acre fell in a siege laid by English, French and German troops in the Third Crusade (1189-92), preached by Pope Gregory VIII. The siege was led by three monarchs: Richard I the Lionhearted, King of England, Philip II (Philip Augustus), King of France, and Guy de Lusignan, the deposed Crusader King of Jerusalem. Frederick I, known as Frederick Barbarossa (Italian for "Red Beard"), Holy Roman Emperor, King of Germany and Italy, was also part of the Third Crusade's Royal Alliance, but he drowned in Cilicia on the way to Palestine.

As the result of a treaty concluded in September 1192 between King Richard and Saladin, the Crusader state was restored in Palestine along the coast between Jaffa and Tyre, though not in Jerusalem, where, however, Christians were given the right of free access to the Holy Sepulchre, the supposed site of Jesus' tomb. Acre, the new Crusader capital, was turned over to the Knights Hospitalers, a military and religious Order of the Hospital of St. John of Jerusalem, sometimes called the Knights of St. John, hence the French name of Saint Jean d'Acre for this port city. There was later a period of renewed Crusader rule in Jerusalem under Frederick II (1229-1244), the Holy Roman Emperor and King of Germany and Sicily, whose kingdom in Palestine was destroyed in 1244 by the Khwarizmian (Seljuk) Turks, who came from what is today Uzbekistan.[19]

A most noteworthy event of Saladin's rule was the proclamation[20] he issued in 1190, inviting Jews from all over the world to settle again in Jerusalem, from where they had been excluded during its occupation by the Crusaders. This proclamation can be viewed in retrospect as a specific recognition of the historical connection of the Jewish People with Jerusalem and the Land of Israel as a whole. In this sense, it may be compared with other proclamations of this kind, that also encouraged a Jewish return to their ancestral homeland and

---

[19] Frederick II, who led the Sixth Crusade to Palestine, had himself crowned King of Jerusalem in 1229, upon concluding a treaty with the Ayyubid Sultan of Egypt, al-Malik al-Kamil, which transferred Jerusalem to the Crusaders (excluding the Temple area which remained in Moslem hands), as well as Nazareth and other towns. The kingdom consisted of two enclaves – Jerusalem and Nazareth, which were connected to the coastal region by corridors passing through Ramla and Acre respectively.

[20] This proclamation was recorded in the writings of the Spanish-born Hebrew poet and translator, Judah al-Harizi. See his major work, Sefer Tahkemoni ("The Wise One"?), completed after 1220, in the scholarly edition prepared by Armand (Aaron) Kaminka (1899), pp. 214-215, 353, cited in *Encyclopaedia Judaica* (1971), Vol. 9, column 1417; Vol. 10, column 730; Vol. 2, column 627.

sacred places, particularly those of Cyrus, Napoleon and Balfour. As a result of Saladin's proclamation, a Jewish community was indeed renewed in Jerusalem by an influx of Jews from other towns in the country, as well as from France and North Africa. However, the events of 1229 (the Crusader re-appearance in Jerusalem) and 1244 (the Khwarizmian devastation) caused the demise of this community.

Turkish dynastic rule over Palestine was then resumed from Egypt when military slaves, called the Mamluks in Arabic, usurped power from the Egyptian Ayyubid sultans (1250), and spread their rule to Palestine a decade later by routing the Mongols at the battle of Ain Jalut (Spring of Goliath) in 1260.[21] The Mamluks also crushed the last remnants of Crusader rule in the country. Their conquest of Palestine was directed by Baybars I, a former Turkish slave who became the fourth Mamluk sultan after murdering his predecessor, Qutuz (Kotuz). He is considered to be the real founder of the Mamluk dynasty, known as "the Alexander of his age and the pillar of faith".[22] Mamluk rule of Palestine lasted for 256 years (1260-1516), until they were defeated by the Ottoman Turks.

The "slave" rulers of Egypt are customarily divided into two separate dynasties, the Bahri sultans (1250-1382) and the Burji sultans (1382-1517). The Bahri Mamluks were chiefly Turks and Mongols, while the Burji Mamluks were chiefly Circassians, a Moslem people from the Caucasus, whom the Russians called Cherkess.

The name Bahri is derived from the fact that the Turkish and Mongol bodyguard of the last effective ruler of the Ayyubid dynasty, al-Salih (1239, 1245-1249), had their barracks on an isle in the Nile River, from where they overthrew the Ayyubids. The word "bahri" (from "bahr", meaning "river" in Arabic) thus denotes the "river" origin of the Turkish-Mongol Mamluk dynasty.

The Burji Circassian Mamluk sultans were former slaves who had been garrisoned in the tower (called "burj" in Arabic, whence their name) of a citadel. All told, there were twenty-four Bahri and twenty-three Burji sultans who ruled Egypt, Syria and Palestine, reigning on the average less than seven years each, until they were overthrown by the Ottoman Sultan Selim I.

The Ottoman conquest of Palestine in 1516 and of Egypt in 1517 ushered in

---

[21] Ain Jalut is today called En-Harod, located at the northern foot of Mt. Gilboa, in the valley of Jezreel (Plain of Esdraelon). From Byzantine times, there was a belief that Ain Jalut was the sight of the famous encounter between David and Goliath. However, the prevailing view is that their encounter took place in the Valley of Elah (*'Emek Ha-elah*), the Valley of the Oak or Terebinth (I Sam 17:2, 19) identified with Wadi es-Sant, 18 kilometers southwest of Jerusalem.

[22] Hitti, *op. cit.*, p. 656. Baybars was a ruthless leader. He executed the entire Crusader garrison at Safed in 1266, after they had surrendered on condition that their lives would be spared. He committed an even worse atrocity two years later at Antioch when 16,000 were slaughtered at his command and 100,000 enslaved.

a period of near-continuous Turkish rule lasting four centuries until the British victory in 1917. The Ottoman Empire reached its zenith under Sultan Sulayman (or Suleiman) the Magnificent, whom the Jews called King Solomon, "not only because of his name but also because of his wisdom and legislative activities".[23] In 1538 he ordered the building of a wall around the present-day Old City of Jerusalem in order to protect its inhabitants against marauding Bedouins.[24] Outside the immediate concern of Palestine but of great world impact, he had even tried unsuccessfully in 1529 to capture Vienna, the capital of the Hapsburg Empire which in a later period became the Austro-Hungarian Monarchy. A second attempt was made under Mehmet IV in 1683, with the same result.

The only significant interruption of Ottoman rule over Palestine came when Muhammad Ali (Mehmet Ali), the Viceroy of Egypt, who was allied with France, rebelled against the authority of the Sublime Porte under Sultan Mahmud II and launched a successful invasion of Palestine and Syria (1831-1833) led by his eldest son, Ibrahim Pasha. Ibrahim then took over the reins of government of both regions. The nine-year interlude of Egyptian rule which followed (1832-1841) was a turning-point in the history of the Middle East, because it foreshadowed the collapse of the Ottoman Empire less than a century later. Under Ibrahim the Land of Israel was ruled as a single administrative district, the northern border of which reached as far as Sidon. His rule was abruptly ended when Britain and Austria intervened militarily on Turkey's side – Britain sent a naval force commanded by Charles Napier who captured Beirut and Acre in 1840 – and forced Ibrahim's return to Egypt. Britain acted so forcefully in pursuit of the foreign policy of Lord Palmerston (Henry John Temple) to preserve the tottering Ottoman Empire because it feared the ambitions of both Russia and France in the region in the event of the empire's disintegration.

It was during these stormy days that Palmerston, acting under the strong influence of Lord Shaftesbury,[25] then called Lord Ashley (Anthony Ashley

[23] *Encyclopaedia Judaica* (1971), Vol. 15, column 503.

[24] *Encyclopaedia Judaica* (1971), Vol. 9, column 1426-1427. The planner-engineer of the wall deviated in certain places from the accepted city contours by, for example, leaving Mount Zion outside the wall. This deviation led to his execution, according to a traditional story.

[25] The 7th Earl of Shaftesbury was a long-serving Member of Parliament (1826-1851), a prominent social reformer who initiated important legislation to aid the downtrodden and correct the ills of English society, but above all an Evangelical, who based his life on the literal acceptance of the Bible, particularly the New Testament prophecy of the Second Advent, an event which could not take place without the prior return of the Jews to the Land of Israel and their conversion to Christianity. To foster the realization of the Second Advent, he prepared detailed plans for the settlement of Jews in Palestine, which he wanted to be done under the auspices of the Anglican Church and the British Government in order to create an Anglican Israel. It was Lord Shaftesbury who convinced Lord Palmerston to whom he was related by marriage to have the British Ambassador at Constantinople, Lord Ponsonby, approach the Turkish Sultan to advise him

Cooper), initiated a policy for the restoration of the Jewish People to Palestine. Lord Palmerston, the Foreign Secretary in the Whig government of Prime Minister Lord Melbourne (William Lamb), instructed the British Ambassador at Constantinople, Lord Ponsonby, to make representations to the new Sultan, Abd Al-Majid (Abdulmecid), to allow the Jewish resettlement of Palestine. In a letter to Ponsonby dated August 11, 1840, Palmerston wrote:[26]

> There exists at the present time among the Jews dispersed over Europe, a strong notion that the time is approaching when their nation is to return to Palestine: and consequently their wish to go thither has become more keen, and their thoughts have been bent more intently than before upon the means of realizing their wish. It would be of manifest importance to the Sultan to encourage the Jews to return and to settle in Palestine because the wealth which they would bring with them would increase the resources of the Sultan's dominions; and the Jewish people, if returning under the sanction and protection and at the invitation of the Sultan, would be a check upon any future evil designs of Mehemet Ali or his successor… I have to instruct Your Excellency strongly to recommend [to the Turkish government] to hold out every just encouragement to the Jews of Europe to return to Palestine.

Lord Palmerston's letter to his ambassador is extraordinary since in urging Turkey to allow the return of Jews to Palestine, he pursued an initiative embodying the chief tenet of Zionism several decades before the movement was actually founded. Palmerston's idea of resettling Jews in their ancient land meant that he was thinking of re-establishing a Jewish State. This is confirmed in an article that appeared in the *The Globe* newspaper, a semi-official organ of the Foreign Office.[27] Palmerston again wrote to Ponsonby on February 17, 1841, instructing him to speak with the Sultan on the subject of allowing Jews to settle in Palestine. British influence with Ottoman Turkey was then at an all-time high after Britain had led the campaign to oust Muhammad Ali's army from Syria and Palestine, restoring these countries to the Sultan's rule. However, Palmerston's idea about a Jewish restoration in Palestine met with

---

that he should encourage the Jews of Europe to return to Palestine, which would also be for the Sultan's own benefit. He was also the President of the London Society for Promoting Christianity among the Jews, which he used as a platform to promote his evangelical ideas concerning the restoration of ancient Israel.

[26] Barbara W. Tuchman, *Bible and Sword : England and Palestine from the Bronze Age to Balfour* (1956), New York University Press, p. 113. See also The Jews in Palestine 1800-1882, by Tudor Parfitt, The Royal Historical Society, The Boydell Press (1987), p. 121.

[27] Franz Kobler, The Vision Was There, published for the World Jewish Congress, British Section, by Lincolns-Prager (Publishers) Ltd., London (1956), p. 62.

strong opposition from Britain's other allies, particularly Russia. As a result, the subject was not mentioned in a treaty these countries signed with Turkey on July 15, 1840, styled the "(London) Treaty for the Pacification of the Levant".

To encourage Jewish immigration to Palestine, Palmerston proposed that security for them be provided by the British for a period of twenty years. Britain had already appointed a consul, William Tanner Young[28], in Jerusalem in March 1838, becoming the first European power to do so. He had instructions from Palmerston "to afford British protection to the Jews generally" as part of his consular duty.[29] On April 21, 1841, Palmerston sent a circular letter to all British Consuls stationed in the Turkish Empire, informing them that

> The British Government feels an interest in the welfare of the Jews in general, and is anxious that they should be protected from oppression; and that the Porte has promised to afford them protection, and will certainly attend to any representations which Her Majesty's Ambassador at Constantinople may make to it in these matters.[30]

Palmerston's efforts to encourage the Jewish resettlement of Palestine did not achieve their purpose at the time – the Sultan had no sympathy for the idea, and Palmerston was soon swept out of office with the defeat of the Whig government, replaced at the Foreign Office by Lord Aberdeen (George Hamilton Gordon) in the Conservative government of Prime Minister Lord Robert Peel. The new Foreign Secretary showed a marked disdain for the Jewish resettlement project of Palestine advocated by his predecessor. Nevertheless, these first steps by Palmerston laid the groundwork for a future British policy even if it was not always diligently pursued, that would eventually culminate seven and a half decades later in the famous Balfour Declaration of November 2, 1917. What Palmerston and the government he represented did, can also be seen as an early British affirmation of the historical connection of the Jewish People with Palestine and their national rights to the country. As part of the envisaged "restoration of ancient Israel", an Anglican and Lutheran bishopric was established in Jerusalem, that also had the enthusiastic support of the Protestant King of Prussia, Frederick William IV. The first Anglican bishop appointed to this office by Palmerston on the advice of Lord Shaftesbury was a converted Jew, Michael Solomon Alexander. If Palestine had been thought of then as an Arab country, rather than a Jewish one, based on the fact that its population at the time was mainly Arab, no British statesman, parliamentarian, diplomat or church figure in the nineteenth century would have ever advocated the Jewish return to Zion, as did Palmerston, Lord Shaftesbury, James Finn, British Consul in Jerusalem (1845-1862), and the Reverend Alexander McCaul,

---

[28] Officially at first a vice-consul, 1838-41, then a consul, 1841-45.

[29] Kobler, *op. cit.*, pp. 59-60.

[30] Tudor Parfitt, *op. cit.*, pp. 132-133.

Professor of Hebrew at King's College, London. The latter, affectionately called by Lord Shaftesbury "Rabbi McCaul", wrote a work in 1835 entitled *New Testament Evidence that the Jews are to be restored to the Land of Israel.*

One of the notable proponents of Jewish national regeneration in Palestine under British auspices was Colonel Charles Henry Churchill, a former British army officer who in 1841 was the British Consul in Syria. He wrote a letter[31] to Sir Moses Montefiore on June 14, 1841 advocating that Jews commence an "agitation", as he put it," to resume their [political] existence as a people" in Palestine, with the aid of the European Powers. If this task was undertaken by the Jewish People, he predicted that they would attain in the end "the sovereignty of at least Palestine".

In a second letter dated August 15, 1842, Churchill formed the opinion that for the Jews to recover their ancient country or to regain a footing in Palestine, it could only be as subjects of the Sublime Porte and for that purpose they needed to enlist the Five Great Powers (Britain, France, Russia, Austria and Prussia) to convince the Sultan to allow the Jews to colonize Palestine under the protection of the Great Powers. The Jews would be given internal autonomy to regulate their own affairs but would be subject to a payment of taxation to the Porte. Churchill attached a written proposal to his letter in which he declared that "Judea" should become "once more a refuge and resting-place" for Jews scattered throughout the world.

As a first step to realize his plan, he proposed that an application be made by the Jews of England and Europe to the British Government, addressed to Foreign Secretary Lord Aberdeen, to send out to Syria "a fit and proper person to watch over the interests of the Jews" residing in Syria and Palestine. Churchill told Montefiore that the plan he proposed would bring an "incalculable benefit" to the Jewish nation. He ended his letter by saying[32]:

> ...God has put into my heart the desire to serve His ancient people... I have discharged a duty imposed on me by my conscience...

After some delay, Montefiore referred Churchill's two letters to the Board of Deputies of British Jews, over which he presided as President. This body, however, refused to take any initiative of its own to implement Churchill's visionary proposal. It adopted a resolution dated November 8, 1842 to inform Churchill that it was precluded from originating any measures to carry out his benevolent views, but added that it had no doubts that if the Jews of other countries were to entertain this proposal, the Jews of Great Britain "would be

---

[31] Lucien Wolf, *Notes on the Diplomatic History of the Jewish Question*, printed for the Jewish Historical Society of England by Spottiswoode, Ballantyne & Co., Ltd., London (1919), p. 119 ff.

[32] *Op. cit.*,p. 123.

ready and desirous to contribute… their most zealous support".[33]

The reticence of British Jewish leaders to be more receptive to the heartfelt appeal of Colonel Churchill for the national restoration of the Jews to Palestine was a sad example of their short-sightedness and indifference, and indicated their assimilationist proclivities (proud Englishmen of the Mosaic persuasion) – with the exception of Sir Moses Montefiore. Had it been otherwise, a brighter future for the Jews of the world might have been made possible long before the Holocaust took place in Europe. The Jews of Europe would then have had an assured "refuge and resting-place" to escape the horrors inflicted by Hitler, had Colonel Churchill's wise advice been followed. It was also ironic that the movement to restore Jews to their ancient homeland was largely preached in England in the 19th century before the advent of Theodor Herzl not by Jews themselves but by sympathetic Christians such as Charles Henry Churchill.

Another English Christian who saw the importance of establishing Jewish settlement in the Land of Israel was Colonel George Gawler, a former governor of South Australia. He propagated his views in a series of pamphlets he wrote on the subject beginning in 1845. He accompanied Sir Moses Montefiore on a trip to the country in 1849 and tried to persuade him to start large-scale agricultural settlement immediately. However, while Montefiore did express general support for this idea even before[34] Gawler had proposed it to him, no extensive organized colonization was in fact undertaken though Montefiore did finance several new agricultural settlements, as well as several new suburbs in Jerusalem.

The son of George Gawler, John Cox Gawler, also took up the cause of Jewish settlement and he, too, published a plan in 1874 for the settlement of Eretz-Israel, which aroused great interest in Jerusalem and led directly, four years later, to the founding of Petah Tikva.

One other important English supporter of the return of the Jewish People to Eretz-Israel was Laurence Oliphant. In 1878, he decided to submit a plan to the Sultan for large-scale Jewish settlement in Palestine that won the support of Prime Minister Benjamin Disraeli (Lord Beaconsfield) and Foreign Secretary Lord Salisbury, as well the French Foreign Minister, William Henry Waddington. Oliphant thought the best place to begin Jewish settlement was in the Gilead region of Transjordan. His plan, had it been acted upon, would have likely led ultimately to the early establishment of a Jewish State. However, the Ottoman Sultan, Abdul-Hamid II, suspecting a British Government intrigue, rejected Oliphant's plan, even though it had been approved by the Turkish Cabinet.

---

[33] *Op. cit.*, p. 123.

[34] In 1839, Sir Moses Montefiore met with Muhannad (Mehmet) Ali, ruler of Egypt, Palestine and Syria to obtain his approval for the Jewish colonization of Palestine and to form a bank to finance this project. Ali was supportive of Montefiore's proposal, but the project never materialized after Egypt had, because of the intervention of most of the Great Powers, ceased to be the ruler of Palestine in 1841, which now reverted to the rule of the Sultan.

The rivalry among the five Great European Powers for the control of Ottoman territories, including Palestine and Syria, was known as the Eastern Question. As a result of this rivalry, a dispute broke out in 1853 between Russia and France over who was to be the Guardian of the Holy Places in the Land of Israel or to act as the protector of the Orthodox Christians in the Ottoman Empire. This was a primary cause of the Crimean War. France, Britain, Sardinia and the Ottoman Empire allied themselves against Russia in this War which came to a negotiated end at the Congress of Paris (1856) with the signing of the Treaty of Paris (March 30, 1856). By this time, the fortunes of Turkey were sinking so low it was being called the "sick man of Europe".

As the Ottoman Empire weakened and its eventual break-up was foreseen, there emerged for the first time just prior to the opening of the Congress of Berlin in 1878 open talk of a revived Jewish State being established in Palestine. The Congress was called to revise the 1878 peace treaty between Russia and the Ottoman Empire (Treaty of San Stefano), which gave Russia a dominant position in the Balkans, to the great dismay of Great Britain and Austria-Hungary. It was attended by the leaders of all the Great Powers of Europe and presided over by the first Chancellor of the Empire of the Germans (the Iron Chancellor), Prince Otto von Bismarck. A Jewish group, hoping to emulate the achievement of the Balkan peoples of Montenegro, Serbia, Roumania and Bulgaria, who gained independence or autonomy from Turkey, submitted to Bismarck and British Prime Minister Benjamin Disraeli (Lord Beaconsfield) an anonymous memorandum written in German advocating the re-establishment of a Jewish monarchy under a constitutional regime. The memorandum, originally thought by some to have been authored by Disraeli, was later proved to have been written by the renowned Russian Hebrew poet and journalist, Judah Leib (Leon) Gordon,[35] a strong exponent of the Haskala Movement (the Enlightenment). The high-ranking statesmen at the Congress never in fact discussed this bold Jewish initiative, but the memorandum was officially listed in the protocol of Congress documents. It did, however, provoke discussion in the English press before the Congress assembled.[36]

In light of the foregoing historical synopsis since the Arab conquest, we can conclude that the five Turkish dynasties that ruled Palestine (Tulunid, Ikhshidid, Seljuk, Bahri Mamluk and Ottoman) did so for no less than six centuries, considerably more than double the time of Arab dynastic rule of Palestine which lasted only two and a half centuries. If six centuries of Turkish rule did

[35] Gordon's writings on Jewish national revival served as a principal source for the spiritual Zionism of Ahad-Ha'Am, who in his introduction to *Al Parashat Derakhim* (At the Crossroads, 1895) acknowledged his indebtedness to Gordon. It was Gordon who first adopted the Biblical call – *O House of Jacob, come and let us go* – to further the Jewish movement of Enlightenment and rapprochement to Europe, a call which later became the model of the first Bilu pioneers.

[36] *Encyclopaedia Judaica* (1971), Vol. 4, columns 656-657; Vol. 6, column 107.

not make Palestine a Turkish homeland, then a fortiori two and a half centuries of Arab rule did not convert it into an Arab homeland. Thus it is plainly absurd to call Palestine an Arab country.

Even Egypt, itself under foreign subjugation until the establishment of the Tulunid dynasty (878), never claimed national rights over Palestine despite having ruled the country for some five centuries between 878 and 1517.

Arabs in general are fond of making an inexact comparison between restored Jewish rule over the Land of Israel in the modern age and the Crusader rule which spanned two centuries, in order to foretell the eventual disappearance of the State of Israel. However, this comparison actually applies to their own rule of Palestine which lasted only half a century more than the Crusader states. The Arabs, who predated the Crusaders by about four and a half centuries, were also invaders and despoilers of the Land of Israel who imposed foreign rule upon the majority Byzantine and native Jewish population. They had no more right to claim Palestine as their homeland than the French-speaking Crusaders, in setting up an alien kingdom in a country that they and the Arabs both knew belonged eternally to the Jewish People by virtue of the Patriarchal Covenant, first made with Abraham and then confirmed with Isaac and Jacob. The fall of the Crusaders was as inevitable an event as the fall of the Arabs and all other occupiers of the Jewish country who presumed to rule another nation's country and patrimony. Their fall was, moreover, foreordained in Scripture and Jewish belief.

The Arabs of Palestine are a diverse group of many races. The word "Arab" when used in the context of the Land of Israel is a very imprecise term and basically covers most of the Arabic-speaking gentile residents of the country which the Hebrew language refers to as nochrim or aliens. Insofar as Palestine is concerned, the modern connotation of what an Arab is, is neither racial nor ethnic, but solely linguistic. Those who speak Arabic as their mother tongue, whether Moslem or Christian, are deemed to be Arabs, regardless of their national origin. It is only this linguistic aspect which can explain how the Byzantine population of Palestine which was non-Arab to begin with in the 7th century gradually evolved into an Arab one over the following centuries. The same kind of change of identity or assimilative process – this time that of Turkification – would probably have happened in Palestine as it did elsewhere, particularly in Anatolia, had the Ottoman Turkish conquerors imposed Turkish instead of Arabic as the compulsory language of the country at the outset of their rule in 1516.[37] That was however never done, so the existing population

[37] See the article on "Turks" in the *Columbia Encyclopedia*, Sixth Edition (2000), p. 2905. The writer of that article observes: "The wide differences in physical appearance and culture among the Uigurs of China, the Uzbeks of Central Asia, and the Osmanlis of Turkey (to cite random instances) make it impossible to speak of Turks as an ethnic or racial group. Although Islam is the religion of the majority of Turks, its importance came relatively late. The most significant unifying link among the Turks is the very close relation of their languages, which are marked by great regularity of pattern and clarity of structure. It is probable that many

remained "Arab", rather than becoming "Turkish".

The racial composition of the Arabs of the Land of Israel comprise many different groups. Among them are all the foreign peoples who once conquered Palestine over the centuries, ranging from the Romans and Byzantines, to the Arabs from Arabia, and all the other immigrants to the country in the wake of the Turkish, Egyptian and British invasions and occupations, a process that continued unhampered until the establishment of the State of Israel. The Arabs of the Land of Israel are thus a diverse and mixed population of Arabic-speaking gentiles in which elements of the whole panoply of Asian, European and African peoples are to be found. The result is that the "Arabs" are today basically an amalgam of races and ethnic groups and are not ethnically pure Arabs from Arabia, as this term would indicate.

In his book published in 1944, entitled *Justice For My People*, Dr. Ernst Frankenstein calculated that 75% of the Arab population of Palestine at that time were either immigrants themselves or descendants of immigrants who arrived in Palestine mainly after 1882, coinciding with the development of modern Jewish settlement which made the country more attractive for Moslem and Arabic-speaking newcomers. Among those who settled in Palestine were Bosnians, Turkomans and Circassians whom the Ottoman Turkish authorities had encouraged to do so.[38]

None of the foreign Arabic-speaking gentiles living in the Land of Israel today are descended from the indigenous inhabitants who lived there prior to the first Jewish Exile, except those who may possibly trace their lineage to converted Jews, of which there were undoubtedly some, but whose actual number can only be speculative. The Arab claim of ownership of the Jewish country based on their alleged historical connection with it dating from the Canaanite period is completely spurious, which no serious historian who is neither Arab nor Muslim has accepted. This absurd claim was made for only one purpose, to show that the Arabs who today pose as "Palestinians" antedated the Jewish presence in the land of Canaan that became the Land of Israel. However, there was no Arab nation living in the land of Canaan in the second millennium B.C.E., otherwise they would most likely have been mentioned in the Pentateuch (the five books of Moses), in the period from Abraham to the death of Moses.[39]

---

peoples who were unrelated to the original Turks adopted either wholly or in part their speech and social organization".

[38] Ernst Frankenstein, *Justice For My People*, Dial Press, New York (1944), pp. 128-130. He cites the quotation of Lloyd George from his book (*The Truth about the Peace Treaties*, Vol. II, p. 1127), based on a statement by Lord Alfred Milner: "colonies of Turkomans, Circassians, Kurds and other savage men had been planted about to hold the country in subjection."

[39] An Arab in this period of history was a nomad from the Arabian peninsula, excluding the areas adjoining it, such as Moab, Edom, the Negev and Sinai. Not all nomads were Arabs, since the early Israelites also led a nomadic existence for two generations, until they finally settled down to the sedentary life of Egypt and then in the Promised Land after the Exodus. Neither the Ishmaelites nor the

During the two-century Crusader period of rule in Palestine, most of the non-Christian inhabitants, whether Jews or Arabs, were either killed or left the country. More human slaughter followed each succeeding change of regime. The present racial mix of peoples comprising the Arabs of the Land of Israel, the so-called "Palestinians", mainly dates from the last two centuries, which hardly makes them the aboriginal inhabitants as they falsely claim to be. During most of the 19th century, their number varied between 200,000 and 300,000. Their population swelled in the 20th century by huge illegal immigration and a high birth rate accompanied by a sharp decline in the mortality rate.

The Arab claim of dispossession is equally fallacious. The people who today call themselves "Palestinians" were never a recognized nation in history, which could be "dispossessed". This happened only to the indigenous Jews of the country who were exiled from it twice. The Arabs, on the other hand, were among the invaders and conquerors, who dispossessed the Jews of the country during their ascendancy in Palestine and also "turned a fruitful land into a desert by their avarice and misgovernment".[40] Furthermore, according to Professor Ya'akov Meron:[41]

> The extent of waste land in Judea and Samaria is very large. In 1935 it was observed that "[a] very large part of the area of Palestine is mewat [i.e., waste land]... The proximity of the desert exposed Palestine, as well as the rest of the Fertile Crescent, to harassment and devastation by the desert Bedouins. In Galilee no fewer than 460 deserted villages were found over an area of 4,000 square miles... The area worst hit by the desertion of villages was the Negev. Archaeologists have noted that the cultivated areas had begun to shrink in the Negev in the 7th century, i.e., with the Arab conquest. Therefore, the decreasing cultivated area was a phenomenon which began with the Arab conquest and the penetration of the Bedouins. This process continued long after the Arab conquest.

Jews under Arab and Moslem rule suffered severe discrimination and degradation from the time of the Umayyad Caliph Umar II (ruled 717-720). They were governed by a series of decrees and regulations contained in the Covenant of Omar, which gave them an inferior legal status in their own country, as compared to Moslems. These caliphal measures placed Jews in the category of *dhimmis*, which forced them to pay a burdensome poll tax (*jizya*),

---

Midianites or Amalekites were therefore Arabs, since their places of wandering were not in Arabia proper in the pentateuchal period, and no Arab nation left its mark on history at that time.

[40] Parkes, *op. cit.*, p. 208.

[41] Ya'akov Meron, "Waste Land (Mewat) in Judea and Samaria", *Boston College International and Comparative Law Review,* Volume IV, No. 1, Spring 1981, at pp. 32-33.

to wear distinctive yellow clothes or a yellow badge and to be subject to other restrictions, as well as being under an overall threat of forcible conversion to Islam.

It is true that the Arabs who overran the Christian Byzantine Empire were displaced during the Crusader period, but that cannot qualify as a genuine dispossession, since they were not the rightful owners of the land as they amazingly claim to be, contrary to both Biblical and post-Biblical historical evidence. To overcome this inconvenient evidence, Moslem Arab writers, historians and exegetes have, ever since the Koran was composed, "amended" particular Biblical narratives to show that they, rather than the Jews, are the true inheritors of the Promised Land and were therefore justified in bringing it under the sway of Islam.

Many who admit the fact that Palestine is not an Arab homeland argue nonetheless that it is still an Islamic country that is sacred to all Moslems in the world, because they have ruled it almost continuously from 634 to 1917, except for the Crusader interregnum, a total span of close to twelve centuries. However, if length of time is the criterion to determine whether Palestine is a Jewish or Moslem country, then Moslem rule, although admittedly of long duration, was still less than Jewish rule in Palestine which existed in one form or another, either as an independent state or vested with internal autonomy, for a period of approximately 14 centuries, from the time of Moses to the Roman subjugation of Judea in the year 70. In addition, the Jews generally formed in the succeeding five centuries either the dominant or a substantial element in the population of the country, enjoying religious autonomy until the Arab conquest in the seventh century. The Jewish People can thus point to a continuous settlement in the Land of Israel for almost two thousand years prior to the Moslem takeover of the country. It may also be noted that even after Arab rule began in 634, the Jews in the country outnumbered Moslems for another century or so.

Another noteworthy feature in comparing Jewish rule with Moslem rule is that when the land was governed by Jews, it was either an independent country in its own right, without being part of a larger state, or enjoyed internal autonomy. By contrast, Palestine alone never existed as an independent Moslem or Arab state in any period up to the present day, but was always part of a larger Islamic entity and subject to its control. This alone suffices to prove that Palestine or the Land of Israel can only be considered a Jewish country by historical, geopolitical, religious or ethnic/national criteria.

If additional proof of this point is needed, recourse may be had to several Koranic verses which confirm that the Holy Land belongs to none other than the Jewish People. The most important of these verses is found in Sura (Chapter) 5 of the Koran[42], verses 20 and 21, which read as follows, according to the literal translation made by Professor Khaleel Mohammed, an observant

[42] The Arabic rendering of the word spelled *Koran* in English is *Qur'an*, hereafter denoted by the letter Q.

Moslem scholar trained in Islamic Law:[43]

> And remember when Moses said to his people: "O my people! Remember the favours of your Lord that He has bestowed upon you, as He has made prophets and kings from among you, and has given to you that which has never been given to anyone amongst the nations. Enter then, my people, the *Holy Land, that God has written for you*, and turn not back, or you will suffer." (emphasis added).

The words "has written" in the phrase "that God has written for you" as translated from the Arabic KaTaBa in the above text, Q5:20-21, are of supreme importance, notes Professor Mohammed, in conveying the meaning of these two verses:[44]

> This [Arabic] word has definite theological connotations: in Islam, as in Jewish belief, it conveys the idea of decisiveness and finality, e.g., in "written Torah" as opposed to "oral Torah". In the approximately 22 instances in the Qur'an where this action is attributed to God (directly *kataba* or indirectly *kutiba*), it likewise conveys the idea of decisiveness, finality and immutability. One such example is the verse (Q2:183) used by Muslims to indicate that the Ramadan fast is compulsory: *Kutiba alaykum al-siyaam*... literally, "written upon you is the fast" – but understood to mean "obligatory upon you is the fast".

In his remarkable manuscript, Professor Mohammed cites the views of several famous Moslem exegetes who have interpreted the meaning of Q5:20-21 containing the words "that [which] God has written for you". One such exegete was Ibn Kathir (d. 1373), who "explained *kataba* in terms that would have pleased the most ardent Zionists:[45]

> 'That which God has written for you', i.e., that which God has promised to you by the words of your father Israel as the inheritance of those among you who believe."

Another exegete, six centuries earlier, who expounded on the meaning of the foregoing Koranic verses concerning the Land of Israel, was Muqatil b.

[43] The English translation of Q5:20-21 is included in an 18-page manuscript written by Prof. Khaleel Mohammed of San Diego State University, Department of Religious Studies, entitled: "For Whom the Holy Land? A Qur'anic Answer". This text was delivered as a lecture at the Jerusalem Summit held on Nov. 30, 2004, at the King David Hotel, Jerusalem. See p. 3 of the manuscript.

[44] *Op. cit.*, p. 4.

[45] *Op. cit.*, p. 5.

Sulayman (d. 767). Professor Mohammed summarizes Muqatil's thoughts on the subject:[46]

> *Kataba* means 'ordered', i.e., Moses was saying to the Israelites: Enter the Holy Land as God has ordered you to do. Muqatil even defines the Holy Land as Jericho, in the land of Jordan as well as Palestine. But more importantly, Muqatil b. Sulayman states: Do not retreat from that land, or you will be losers. This is because God said to Abraham, when he was in the Holy Land, "Verily, this land in which you now stand will be an inheritance for your son after you."

The term *Holy Land* (in Arabic: *al-ard al-muqaddasa*) as used in Q5:20-21 was defined by Abu Ja'far al-Tabari (d. 922), "Islam's most famous exegete", as follows:[47]

> (1) Sinai and the surrounding area;
> (2) Greater Syria;
> (3) Jericho;
> (4) Damascus, Palestine [west of the Jordan River] and some of [present-day] Jordan.

As to Jerusalem, Professor Mohammed states:[48]

> Muhammad had no dreams of making Jerusalem part of the Islamic polity; such an undertaking, given its importance, would certainly have been mentioned in the Qur'an, and Islam would not have been deemed complete without reference to it... When *hadith* started being circulated, with Jerusalem in the hands of the Muslims, any tradition that could justify its possession was sought after or created... And sometime after Jerusalem fell into Muslim hands in 638, it would seem that Muslims saw the room for extension of the spiritual claim to Abraham as one involving the land itself... Certainly there are verses of polemic against Jews in the Qur'an, but these verses clearly have nothing to do with the Land of Israel, for Moses, in the Qur'an, is clearly identified as coming to the tribe of Israel, and advocating on their behalf (Q7:105). In Q5:20-21, he addresses them as "My tribe", exhorting them to enter the Holy Land. There is therefore no substance to the argument that somehow, since Muslims respect all the Biblical prophets, this in any way makes them the new inheritors of the Temple site in Jerusalem or any part of Israel.

[46] *Op. cit.*, p. 7.

[47] *Op. cit.*, p. 5

[48] *Op. cit.*, pp. 8-9.

> The shallowness of this argument is also evidenced by the fact that when this land was wrested from the Byzantines by the Muslim armies in 638, its first capital was Lod (Lydda)... it would seem that the early Muslims were keenly aware of the Qur'anic teaching that Israel (including, obviously, Jerusalem) is a holy land to the Jews – as evidenced by the traditions that show Umar, after initially agreeing to the Christian request to ban Jews from Jerusalem, later relented and decreed that the city should be opened to the Jews. The stories of Umar's journeying to Jerusalem and consulting Ka'b al-Ahbar [a Yemenite Jew who converted to Islam] about the site of the temple seem to be, as pointed out by [Shlomo Dov] Goitein, to be *pious ficitions*. The purpose of such narratives, as in the case of the hadith dictating that one should journey to the Masjid al-Aqsa, seem to create authority through back-projection of sayings to respected early personalities.

In light of Q5:20-21, as well as other Koranic verses cited by Professor Mohammed (Q7:137; 10:93; 17:104; 21:71, 81), which reinforce what is said in Q5:20-21, it is not at all surprising that he refers jocularly to the Koran, read on its own without the refraction of the *hadith*,[49] as "a very right-wing Zionist document". Indeed, in the view of Professor Mohammed, the Koran, the most authentic source of the Islamic heritage, corroborates the most fundamental tenet of Zionism, namely, that "Israel is the specific land for the Jewish People". In this matter, the Koran stands in stark contrast to the *hadith*. The latter represents Islam's oral tradition which, Professor Mohammed notes, is "putatively attributed to Muhammad". According to Professor Mohammed,[50]

> The *Hadith*... can never be mistaken for anything remotely Zionist: the land of Israel is Muslim territory to be wrested from the accursed Jews in a brutal and bloody eschatological battle.

Inasmuch as the Koran is clearly of a superior nature to the *hadith* regarding the Land of Israel and its true owner, all Moslems who rely on the Judeophobic *hadith* to virulently oppose Zionism or who deliberately or ignorantly misinterpret the above-cited Koranic verses and call for the destruction of the Jewish State are in flagrant opposition to the basic teachings of Muhammad contained in the Koran.

One argument employed by Moslems who wish to deny the validity or applicability of the "Zionist" verses in the Koran is to say that the Jews of today

[49] The *hadith* is reputedly a collection of the sayings and opinions of Muhammad, his actions and ways of behaviour, his virtues and his tacit approval of what was said or done in his presence, all of which are called in Arabic the *sunna* or traditions of the Prophet. These traditions also include the sayings and deeds of the companions of Muhammad.

[50] *Op. cit.*, p. 2.

are not the true descendants of the ancient Israelites. Such denial, however, is not compatible with the fact that from the time the Twelve Tribes of Israel became a unified nation ensconced in the Land of Israel, an unbroken chain has existed linking Jews of all generations to the enduring belief in the Laws handed down by Moses, as expounded in the Pentateuch. This link has been broken only for those Jews who have apostatized and/or lost their identity. The surviving Jews of today are therefore without doubt the true descendants of the Israelites.

For devout Moslems it is a tenet of their religion that once a country has come under Islamic rule, it must forever remain so. Since Palestine falls into this category, it is the duty of Moslems to restore it to Islam by waging a holy war known as jihad. It is for this reason that Israel can never be accepted as a legitimate state, because it contradicts Islamic theology which divides the world between *dar es-salaam* (the House of Peace, i.e., the zone under Islamic domination) and *dar el-harb* (the House of War, i.e., the territory under non-Islamic control). This concept was not applied to Spain or, for that matter, to Greece and other Balkan countries formerly under Islamic rule, simply because it was impossible to re-conquer them. Consequently, a whole new classification had to be created by Moslem theologians to distinguish former Moslem-ruled countries which had ceased to be so and for which there existed no immediate prospect of re-imposing such rule, a classification known as *dar es-sulh* (the Zone of Truce or Temporary Peace). In the case of the Land of Israel, however, different and more favourable conditions prevail. The country is completely surrounded by other Moslem states, which makes it an inviting target for re-conquest and subjugation.

In any event, all Moslem arguments asserting that Palestine is part of the Islamic world are irrelevant to the question of the national and political rights of the Jewish People to the country under international law. When the Principal Allied Powers in April 1920 divided up the Middle East Empire of the Ottoman Turks at the San Remo Peace Conference, they did so not on the basis of religion or on the duration of foreign occupation, but rather on their recognition of the nationality and historical claims of different peoples who merited independence, either in the near term, as foreseen in the cases of Mesopotamia and Syria, or more gradually, in regard to Palestine as a Jewish State. In the case of the Hedjaz, which subsequently became part of what is today Saudi Arabia, it had already declared its independence on October 30, 1916 and was accorded recognition as one of the small powers at the 1919 Paris Peace Conference. The same principle of national self-determination, independent of religion, was applied in the cases of the Serbs, Czechs, Slovaks, Poles, Lithuanians, Estonians, Latvians, Finns and others that followed the disintegration of the Austro-Hungarian Empire and the collapse of Russia and Germany in World War I. Though religion was not a determining factor in recognizing these new states that arose in Asia and Europe as a result of World War I, protection for the rights of religious and linguistic minorities was expressly provided for in the various Minorities

Treaties and international instruments drawn up at the Peace Conferences or subsequently, as well as in the constitutions of some of these states.

An absurd situation has arisen today in regard to Arab or "Palestinian" or Moslem claims to Palestine and the Land of Israel, which is not present in the parallel cases cited above. In those cases no claims were made by a foreign invader and a non-indigenous population settled in a country not its own, while in the unique case of Palestine, the claims of Arabs who brazenly assert the rights of the indigenous population have been almost universally accepted. Even less understandably, the national and political rights of the Jewish People to the country, that were recognized by international law in 1920, have been mocked, degraded, ignored or simply forgotten. Added to this incongruity has been the switch of national identities evoked by the term "Palestinian" which is now used to denote a fictitious nation when formerly it was an alternate and widely-used term for the Jews of Palestine. This switch has been accompanied by repeated illegal attempts by the United Nations, joined by Russia, the European Union and even the United States, to transfer those very same rights belonging to the Jewish People to foreign Arabs who have infiltrated into the ancient Land of the Jews over the centuries and now claim ownership over it under the patently false slogan of "Palestine for the Palestinians".

In the case of the Arab/"Palestinian"/Moslem claims to Palestine and the Land of Israel, fiction has replaced fact to a degree once impossible to imagine. No one can any longer distinguish truth from falsity unless one is consciously aware of the historical and legal facts and intricacies of the situation and is not led astray by tendentious lies presented unblinkingly by Arabs and their allies and then publicized by sympathetic, ignorant or "morally equivalent" journalists and broadcasters who parrot their fables without question and even add libels of their own to denigrate the Jewish State. The confusion of the true national and legal rights of the Jewish People to the Land of Israel, particularly as regards Judea, Samaria and Gaza, with the invented claims of the "Palestinians", must end some day, not by honouring those fantastic and unfounded Arab claims, which has been the direction taken, even by the Government of Israel ever since the time of Menachem Begin and Yitzhak Rabin, but by repudiating the gross lies that have supported those claims and upholding the historical and legal truth that is not so difficult to ascertain.

*Section Five*

# Conclusion

*Chapter 19*

# Remedial Steps to Preserve Jewish Legal Rights and Title of Sovereignty over the Land of Israel and Block Arab Attempts at Usurpation

*The author herewith proposes a series of remedial steps that need to be taken by the Knesset and Government of Israel, some now and others in the future, when it will be propitious and timely, in order to reaffirm and clarify the legal rights and title of sovereignty of the Jewish People over the Land of Israel, and also to put an end to ongoing Arab attempts to usurp them.*

## *Step 1*

To immediately scrap the "Oslo Peace Process" which illegally recognizes the national and political rights to the Land of Israel of a motley Arabic-speaking gentile people whose avowed aim is to destroy the Jewish State. That means that the Government of Israel must formally declare null and void all agreements[1] it made since August 20, 1993 with the Palestine Liberation Organization, a criminal and terrorist organization, and retract its conditional acceptance of

[1] The author, beginning in October 1993, has written extensively on the illegal Israel-PLO agreements and was the first to call for the establishment of a State Commission of Inquiry to investigate the illegalities and criminal conduct involved in the making of these agreements and to indict and prosecute those responsible. See some of the following articles:

1) *HaMasa uMatan 'im Ashaf – Hafarat Hok*, published in *Hatzofe* newspaper, November 5, 1993, page 4, and in English under the title: "PLO Negotiations and Violation of the Law", The Jewish Press, Nov. 5, 1993, p. 4;

2) *Heskem Israel-Ashaf – Bilti Hukki Ba'alil*, published by *Nativ, A Journal of Politics and the Arts*, January 1994, page 15;

3) *HaHeskemim bein Israel l'Ashaf bir'i shel Hukkei HaMedina, Nativ*, July 1996, page 42;

4) Booklet containing a series of reprinted articles, entitled *Bilti Hukki Ba'alil*, published by the Sanhedrin Institute.

the Road Map Peace Plan or any derivative thereof. This illegal plan concocted by the U.S. State Department was then approved by the so-called Quartet: the USA, Russia, the European Union and the U.N. to force Israel back to the armistice "Auschwitz" lines that existed prior to the Six-Day War. This plan envisions the end of Israel's alleged occupation of Judea, Samaria and Gaza and the establishment of a new Arab state in these regions.

To push Israel and the Palestine Liberation Organization into a new peace agreement based on the provisions of the Road Map Peace Plan, President George W. Bush convened the Annapolis Conference. He announced that a Joint Understanding had been reached on November 27, 2007 under which the parties were "to immediately launch good-faith bilateral negotiations in order to conclude a peace treaty, resolving all outstanding issues, including all cores issues without exception, as specified in previous agreements." One of these core issues to be negotiated was undoubtedly the status of Jerusalem, but Prime Minister Ehud Olmert, to prevent the fall of his government, denied that this subject was on the negotiating table, even though the Arab side affirmed it was indeed being discussed. The Joint Understanding also affirmed that the parties will "immediately implement their respective obligations under the performance-based road map to a permanent two-state solution to the Israel-Palestinian conflict". The reference to "obligations" is highly misleading since, as previously noted, the Road Map Peace Plan is not a binding international agrement, but only a plan or policy which was never fully accepted by Israel. The most disturbing aspect of the Joint Understanding is that it assigns a monitoring role to the United States to judge the compliance of both sides with the road map. This is a new pressure tactic the U.S. will wield to try to bring about the establishment of an illegal Arab state in Judea, Samaria and Gaza, which President Bush and Secretary of State Condoleezza Rice naively believe, despite the evidence of persistent Arab violence and Islamic ideology, will live side by side with Israel in peace and security. The Joint Understanding accepted by Israel also constitutes an impairment of Israeli sovereignty over the Land of Israel contrary to article 97 (a) of the Penal Law, since Israel will henceforth be subject to whatever the American "monitor" judges it must do to implement the alleged "obligations" of the Road Map, even if the monitor's judgement overlooks the 14 reservations which Israel appended to the Road Map.

## *Step 2*

To evict the falsely denominated "Palestinian Authority" and its entire leadership from the Jewish country and annul all of its illegal enactments that masquerade as "laws". There will be no end to terrorist violence in Israel so long as this criminal offshoot of the Palestine Liberation Organization created by the Declaration of Principles continues to operate freely in the Land of Israel. The same should be implemented in regard to the "Hamas" terrorist organization which has assumed power in Gaza, and any other group practicing terrorism and seeking the destruction of the Jewish State.

## *Step 3*

To exercise its sovereignty, already existing under international law, over all those parts of Judea and Samaria it still retains by incorporating these regions into the borders of the Jewish State through the application of Israeli law, jurisdiction and administration under present Israeli constitutional legislation. This was legally required to be done in June 1967, by virtue of the constitutional law known as the Area of Jurisdiction and Powers Ordinance enacted on September 16, 1948 by the Provisional State Council and promulgated on September 22, 1948, but made retroactive to May 15, 1948, the date on which the Jewish State was reborn. This law, sometimes called Ben-Gurion's law, was used by Prime Minister David Ben-Gurion in his capacity as Defense Minister of the State to annex areas of the Jewish National Home and Land of Israel recaptured beyond the frontiers demarcated in the U.N. Partition Plan of November 29, 1947.

However, the National Unity Government of Levi Eshkol did not apply Ben-Gurion's law aiming to bring all such areas freed in the Six-Day War within the framework of the State. It decided instead, almost three weeks after the end of the Six-Day War, to draft an amendment to an existing law, Section 11B of the Law and Administration Ordinance, that was enacted by the Knesset on June 27, 1967 and promulgated the next day.[2] This amendment to the law, non-existent on June 7, 1967, when Judea and Samaria were repossessed and liberated by the IDF, gave the Government a choice whether or not to incorporate these areas of the Land of Israel into the State, while Ben-Gurion's law left no choice as to what had to be done once the Minister of Defense *defined* in a proclamation that a particular area of the Land of Israel was being held by Israel's Army. The step of defining the additional areas of the Land of Israel held by the IDF was a prerequisite before any announcement or proclamation could be made to the inhabitants of the affected areas that the IDF had assumed control there. The Minister of Defense had no discretion in the matter. He was obligated to define the areas held by the IDF, otherwise no local resident, let alone Israelis and the rest of the world, would have known that the Israeli army had imposed a military government over those areas, thus replacing the previous ruler. The obligatory nature of the law is apparent from the fact that without a proclamation of this kind, the directives that were to be issued by the Military Commander to maintain proper administration, security and public order, in the IDF-held areas including, for instance, the imposition of a curfew, could not be expected to be heeded by the local population unless the Minister of Defence had acted in strict accordance with the Ordinance formulated by the Ben-Gurion Government. An appropriate proclamation was thus needed to avoid the chaos of a legal vacuum.

---

[2] See the author's work on this important subject, *A Petition to Annul the Interim Agreement*, Policy Paper 77, published by the Ariel Center for Policy Research (ACPR), Sha'arei Tikva, January 1999, p. 10-28; 35-67.

It is true that international law does not absolutely require the issuance of a proclamation, as soon as the territory of a foreign state is occupied by a hostile army, though it is customary for this to be done.[3] However, the situation is entirely different under Israeli constitutional law for areas of the Land of Israel liberated by the Israel Defense Forces that cannot be labeled "occupied territories" under international law. The Area of Jurisdiction and Powers Ordinance was enacted for the sole purpose of recovering for the Jewish State those lands that had been recognized as integral parts of the Jewish National Home under international law in 1920 and that had always been considered the patrimony of the Jewish People under Jewish law (*halakha*). If the IDF liberated various areas of the Land of Israel and no proclamation had been issued under the aforesaid Ordinance, then the purpose of the law would have been defeated and the law left with neither meaning nor effect. Moreover, if the Minister of Defense did not issue a proclamation defining the IDF-held areas, this would have meant that the Jewish People, represented by the State of Israel, had no sovereign right to the liberated areas and would have been required in due course to restore these areas to the Arab states that had illegally occupied them in 1948, a requirement that negated the underlying assumption of the Ordinance that they belonged to the Jewish People. To avoid these consequences, it was therefore incumbent upon the Minister of Defense to issue a proclamation under the Ordinance to define the areas of the Land of Israel taken over by the IDF as soon as this occurred. This was the way the Ordinance was actually interpreted and implemented throughout the War of Independence in 1948. It seems logical to conclude that it was the obligatory nature of the Ordinance that prompted the Eshkol Government in 1967, shortly after the end of the Six-Day War, to devise an alternative law (Section 11B of the Law and Administration Ordinance), to give the Government a choice in deciding whether or not to incorporate into the State the areas of the Land of Israel liberated in that war.

The area so *defined* in the proclamation meant that any law applying to the whole of the State of Israel would thereafter also apply to that *defined* area and thus such area would automatically be incorporated into the State. This procedure was adopted by Defense Minister Ben-Gurion on September 2, 1948 when he issued Proclamation No. 1 of the Israel Defense Forces Government in the Land of Israel, hereafter "the Land of Israel Proclamation", that had attached to it an illustrative map of the Land of Israel indicating by red lines the precise extent of the areas held by the IDF, which he signed and dated. On the same date and bearing the same title as Proclamation No. 1, Ben-Gurion issued Proclamation No. 2, in which he appointed a military governor for the held

[3] See article by Meir Shamgar, former President of the Supreme Court of Israel, entitled "Legal Concepts and Problems of the Israeli Military Government – The Initial Stage", in the book he edited, *Military Government in the Territories Administered by Israel 1967-1980, The Legal Aspects,* Hemed Press 1982, reprinted 1988, Vol. 1, p. 14.

areas referred to in Proclamation No. 1 and its accompanying map.[4]

The Land of Israel Proclamation established the precedent or basic norm upon which the structure of Israeli rule was to be erected in any part of the Land of Israel repossessed or liberated by the IDF. It applied the law of the State to the repossessed area in accordance with the stipulation in Section 2 of the Proclamation, rather than international law relating to belligerent occupation. It was only because of this stipulation that Beersheba, Nazareth, Ramle, Lod, Ashdod (Isdud), Ashkelon (Majdal), Eilat and other places that were not yet part of the State on May 15, 1948, were automatically incorporated into its boundaries as soon as the IDF effectively held them, as confirmed and denoted on a map of Eretz-Israel or simply by the application of Israeli law to the IDF-held area, in the event that no map was used for this purpose.

These IDF-held areas of the Land of Israel were not considered "occupied territories", even though they extended beyond the U.N. Partition lines, because they were part and parcel of the Jewish National Home and the Land of Israel, as recognized under international law as early as 1920. Moreover, there was no recognized Arab sovereign over any of the IDF-held areas in 1948 that had previously been part of an Arab state, which ruled out the possible applicability of the Hague Regulations or any other international convention. It is certain that if any part of Judea and Samaria had been repossessed by the IDF in the War of Independence, the Land of Israel Proclamation used for Beersheba, Nazareth, etc. would have mandated the application of Israeli law to that part, as is clear even from a cursory reading of it. This Proclamation was definitely part of the existing constitutional law when the IDF liberated Judea and Samaria on June 7, 1967 and should have been applied at that time. It can still be invoked today since substantial parts of the Land of Israel remain under Arab rule and await liberation by the IDF! This conclusion is apparent from the language used in the open-ended Land of Israel Proclamation where it states in both Sections 1 and 5 the following:

> 1. *Interpretation*: The term "held areas"[5] (quotation marks in the original text) – *shtahim muhzakim* – means all the areas in the Land of Israel included within the boundaries of the areas delineated in red, on the map of Land of Israel signed by me,[6] bearing the date of

[4] The Military Governor appointed by Defense Minister David Ben-Gurion to head the IDF government in the held areas of the Land of Israel was Major-General Elimelech Avner (Zelikovich). See *Itton Rishmi* (Official Gazette), Special Issue, 29th of Av, 5708 (September 3, 1948), no. 19, p. 115.

[5] "Held areas" – a term found in the literature – otherwise referred to by the present writer as "repossessed" areas.

[6] The pronoun "me" as used in the Interpretation section of the Land of Israel Proclamation (Section 1) does not mean that it applied only during the time that David Ben-Gurion was Minister of Defense. This proclamation, which is legally classified as a regulation issued on behalf of the Government of Israel, cannot

today, the 28th of Av, 5708 (September 2, 1948), or *on any other map replacing it* (emphasis added) which will be signed by me and delineated as mentioned above.

5. *Validity of Proclamation*: This proclamation shall be deemed to be in force in all respects as from midnight on the night of the Sabbath, the 6th of Iyar, 5708 (May 15, 1948); however, in respect of those parts of the held areas the possession of which passed to the Israel Defence Forces *afterwards* (emphasis added), this proclamation shall be in force only from that date.

In regard to Section 5 of the Land of Israel Proclamation, it is important to note that it refers to only one proclamation which was intended to cover all past or future territorial acquisitions in Eretz-Israel or Palestine on whatever date, apart from the area of Jerusalem and its environs. It did not matter if these acquisitions were made prior to September 2, 1948 (the actual date of the Land of Israel Proclamation) or afterwards. Once the Proclamation was duly promulgated in the Official Gazette, no further publication was required therein, if and when additional areas of the land came into the possession of the IDF after September 2, 1948, as indicated by the language of section 5 of the Proclamation.

In regard to Jerusalem, which has always required special treatment, there was a separate proclamation that was issued a month before, on August 2, 1948, formally called Proclamation No. 1 of the Israel Defence Forces Government in Jerusalem, hereafter "the Jerusalem Proclamation". This proclamation also had an illustrative map attached to it. As in the case of the Land of Israel Proclamation, the Jerusalem Proclamation applied the law of the State to the area of Jerusalem and its environs, held by the IDF in 1948 and was followed up by Proclamation No. 2, which appointed a military governor over this area.[7]

The Land of Israel Proclamation could, as noted above, also have been used on June 7, 1967, when the IDF repossessed Judea and Samaria. All that had to be done in this respect was to define the area recaptured by the IDF, by simply drawing red lines on a map of the Land of Israel and having this map signed and dated by the Minister of Defense, replacing Ben-Gurion's original map, as provided for in the Proclamation itself, and, at the same time, invoking Section

---

be interpreted as being personal in nature, limited only to him, unless specifically stated to be so. Therefore, the word "me" simply refers to the Minister of Defense at the time the Land of Israel Proclamation was proclaimed and promulgated, but it could have been invoked by any later Minister of Defense who succeeded Ben-Gurion. The same explanation applies to the Jerusalem Proclamation of August 2, 1948.

[7] The Military Governor for the IDF Government in the held area of Jerusalem was Dr. Dov (Bernard) Joseph. See *Itton Rishmi*, Special Issue, 26th of Tammuz 5708 (August 2, 1948), no. 12, p.66.

2 thereof to apply the law of the State to the area so defined on the map. This procedure did not preclude the issuing of an entirely new proclamation under the Area of Jurisdiction and Powers Ordinance accompanied by an appropriate map, had the Government chosen to do so. But in the absence of any new proclamation, the original one of September 2, 1948 should have been implemented whenever the IDF liberated additional areas of the Land of Israel not yet included in the borders of the State. Indeed, it cannot be gainsaid that if a new proclamation had not been issued on June 7, 1967, illegally applying international law to Judea and Samaria when the IDF entered the region and assumed control, then the existing Israeli constitutional law would automatically have applied, i.e., the Land of Israel Proclamation, and this entire region would have thus immediately become part of the State, without further ado. Furthermore, what applied to the territory covered by the provisions of the Land of Israel Proclamation applied no less to Jordanian-occupied eastern Jerusalem that came within the scope of the Jerusalem Proclamation.

A careful analysis of the Area of Jurisdiction and Powers Ordinance of September 16, 1948 reveals that this law incorporates within its provisions the Land of Israel Proclamation issued two weeks earlier on September 2, 1948, because this Ordinance was made retroactive to May 15, 1948, as was also the case with the Land of Israel Proclamation. This Ordinance also incorporated within its provisions the Jerusalem Proclamation issued even earlier, on August 2, 1948, having the same retroactive application as the Land of Israel Proclamation. Therefore, the word "proclamation" as used in sections 1 and 2 of the Ordinance can only be interpreted as referring to both these Proclamations. The use of similar language in all three documents (the Ordinance and the two Proclamations) regarding the application of Israeli law to IDF-held areas of Eretz-Israel indicates the existence of a definite link between them. The two proclamations and the law under which they were retroactively deemed to have been issued marked an official end to the Jewish Agency's acceptance of the U.N. General Assembly Partition Resolution of November 29, 1947.

The extreme irony of the situation was that the Military Commander of Judea and Samaria – Brigadier-General Chaim Herzog, the future President of the State – did in fact issue two military proclamations on June 7, 1967 *defining* the precise area of the Land of Israel being held by the IDF where military government was imposed, though this was done by descriptive words, rather than by an illustrative map, the method employed by Ben-Gurion. The first one concerned the assumption of power by the IDF in what was simply called "the region". However, it was the second Proclamation that actually defined the area involved as "the region of the West Bank" and stated that "the law that is in force in the region today (June 7, 1967) remains in force". This was a clear reference to the law of the Hashemite Kingdom of Jordan as if it was sovereign Jordanian land that had been occupied by the IDF, a mis-application of international law by the Eshkol Government, which should have been apparent at the time. What was highly unusual and illegal was that the 1967 Proclamations issued by Herzog acting on superior orders from the Government did not follow the aforesaid guiding and binding precedent of 1948, even though the land in question at both times was indisputably the Land of Israel, that matched in a general sense the definition of a "held area" contained in the Land of Israel Proclamation, without however marking the held area on a map. Instead of Herzog's proclamations being based on the Area of Jurisdiction and Powers Ordinance, as required by it, they were unlawfully based on the Hague Regulations of 1907, specifically articles 42 and 43 thereof. *This procedure followed by the Military Commander was tantamount to having official proclamations issued by the wrong party under the wrong source of law to apply the wrong law, a triple error committed simultaneously in total disregard for the correct legal procedure.* To comply with the constitutional law in force on June 7, 1967 and still in force (Ben-Gurion's law and the two aforementioned proclamations of 1948 have never been repealed and coexist with Section 11B), the June 7, 1967 Proclamations affecting Judea and Samaria should have been issued not by the IDF Military Commander but by the Minister of Defense, not under the Hague Regulations of 1907 governing occupied territories, but under the Area of Jurisdiction and Powers Ordinance concerning liberated areas of the Land of Israel, and last but not least, not for the purpose of continuing in force the law of the Kingdom of Jordan, but to apply the law of the State of Israel. *This egregious and monumental violation of Israeli law and the triple error it entailed has never been corrected, nor even discussed or acknowledged by Israel's legal elite.* The Government of Israel chose this short-sighted course to keep the option of "peace" open and to avoid increasing the Arab population of the State, which were considerations outside the realm of law and could have been resolved by other means. The non-observance of the existing constitutional law in June 1967 was the folly and root of all the trouble Israel faces today in the battle to preserve Jewish rights to the Land of Israel under the Rule of Law. Had the Eshkol Government done what it was legally obligated to do, no one, apart from the Arab states and their close supporters, would have dared call the ancestral Jewish lands liberated in the Six-Day War by the IDF "occupied territories" subject, after the end of active hostilities, to the laws of war embodied principally in the Hague Regulations and the Fourth Geneva Convention.

It is tragic to record that the Land of Israel Proclamation, so diligently and comprehensively applied by Ben-Gurion in 1948 as a means for annexing non-State parts of the Land of Israel restored to the Jewish People by the IDF, was simply forgotten or ignored in 1967, and has been forgotten or ignored ever since. As a direct result, the course of Israeli history, politics and law from 1967 to the present day has been radically different from what it should normally have been. The uncritical acceptance or lack of protest by any respected Israeli jurist in 1967 and in the ensuing decades against the issuance of the aforementioned military proclamations by Brigadier-General Herzog for Judea and Samaria that applied international law (i.e., the Hague Regulations and also the Fourth Geneva Convention) instead of Israeli law, as well as those proclamations issued for

Gaza, the Golan and Sinai, is not only deeply shameful and scandalous, but also exposes an amazing ignorance of Israel's legal rights and title of sovereignty to the whole of the Land of Israel and Palestine under both international law and Israeli constitutional law. The Arabs of the country and the neighboring Arab states could not have asked for a better gift from Israel's legal authorities while, conversely, it was a betrayal of the Jewish-Zionist cause by those who ought to have known better.

The Herzog Proclamations led to the birth of the erroneous concept that the combined region of Judea and Samaria (as well as Gaza, the Golan Heights and Sinai) was truly "occupied territory", governed by the rules of war, dictated by international law. By acting on this fallacious premise, Israel shot itself in the foot, greatly undermining its legal case for retaining these regions of the Jewish National Home and Land of Israel, as evidenced by its complete withdrawal from Sinai and Gaza and partial withdrawal from about two-fifths of Judea and Samaria. The damage has been catastrophic and never-ending, paving the way for foreign intervention and the eventual entry of the Palestine Liberation Organization into Judea, Samaria and Gaza to set up its own administration known as the "Palestinian Authority". It is too late to undo the damage inflicted by Israel on itself, but Israel can still abrogate the illegally-drafted military proclamations still in force in regard to those parts of Judea and Samaria remaining under its control, abolish the military regime set up there, and apply Israeli law rather than foreign law in those areas. If this is done, then the constitutional law and legal norm that prevailed in 1948 during the War of Independence will be restored to its proper place in Israel's legal system, as originally intended by Ben-Gurion.

It is bizarre that Justice Moshe Landau, the former President of the Supreme Court, in a 1979 judgment when he was then Deputy-President, declared that[8] "the basic norm upon which the structure of Israeli rule in Judea and Samaria was erected is still today, as I have said, the norm of military government and not the application of Israeli law that entails sovereignty". In making this pronouncement, Justice Landau believed wrongly that the norm of military government automatically excluded the application of Israeli law and sovereignty. He was apparently unaware of the fact that in 1948, Ben-Gurion created and repeatedly implemented the norm (as in the cases of Beersheba, Nazareth etc.) that Israeli law and sovereignty were to be applied over all areas of the Land of Israel repossessed by the IDF, even though these areas were placed under military government. It was this norm that should legally have been invoked in deciding the question of which law to apply to the territories

[8] Dwaikat v. Government of Israel (Elon Moreh case), HCJ 390/79: (1980) Supreme Court Judgments, Vol. 34 part I, at p. 12. The English translation of this case appears in Appendix A: Selected Judgments of the Supreme Court of Israel, in: *Military Government in the Territories Administered by Israel 1967-1980, The Legal Aspects,* edited by Meir Shamgar, pp. 404 ff. The above quotation by Justice Moshe Landau is found on p. 417.

liberated in the Six-Day War. The only person in June 1967 who recognized the necessity of applying this norm was the then-M.K. Eliezer Shostak of the Free Center Party, who impatiently called for the issuance of a new proclamation under the Area of Jurisdiction and Powers Ordinance, a call ridiculed at the time by the Government and curtly dismissed.

The alleged norm cited by Justice Landau ignored the legal structure that had been in place for the Land of Israel between 1948 and 1967 that naturally included Judea and Samaria. His failure to recognize the earlier norm dating back to the rebirth of the State was an inversion of Israel's rights to Judea and Samaria and also changed completely the legal reality created by Ben-Gurion. The Landau norm was a severe deviation from the Ben-Gurion norm as expressed in the Land of Israel and Jerusalem Proclamations[9] that recouped for the Jewish State lands that rightfully belonged to it but which the U.N. "generously" but illegally recommended for inclusion in a new Arab state, contrary to Article 5 of the Mandate for Palestine that was still in force at the time of the Partition Resolution. The adoption of the Landau norm was a legal travesty that paved the way to the grave situation Israel now finds itself in.

## *Step 4*

In the one instance where Israel has extended its law, jurisdiction and administration under Section 11B of the Law and Administration Ordinance, in regard to the eastern portions of the now-unified City of Jerusalem, it has strangely allowed the *waqf*, the Islamic Religious Trust, to maintain an ironclad grip over the entire Temple Mount. Under the law known as the "Protection of the Holy Places Law" that came into force on June 28, 1967, the Minister for Religious Affairs, acting in the name of the Government of Israel, was made responsible for the administration of all holy places in the State of Israel including reunified Jerusalem. Under the Basic Law: Jerusalem, Capital of Israel, promulgated on August 5, 1980, there is an identical provision for the protection of the Holy Places. Yet, in practice, the Government of Israel, through its designated Minister, does not administer the Temple Mount but has illegally transferred this responsibility to the *waqf*, now controlled by the PLO that has no legal right to operate in Jerusalem. The Government must take over the external administration of the Temple Mount and allow access to it by Jewish worshipers. Since this is not being done by the Government under current administrative arrangements, the right of access to the Temple Mount must be firmly anchored in a new Knesset law enacted for that express purpose. The Islamic *waqf*, provided it acts independently of the PLO and in conformity

---

[9] The scope of the Land of Israel Proclamation of September 2, 1948, as well as the meaning to be attached to Ben-Gurion's law, the Area of Jurisdiction and Powers Ordinance, is further discussed by the author in the booklet entitled *The Howard Grief Eretz-Israel Letters to Meir Shamgar 2005-2007 on Eretz-Israel and Israeli Constitutional Law,* edited by Yoel Lerner and published by the Office for Israeli Constitutional Law, May 2007.

with the laws of the State, can continue its internal administration only for the mosque and other Islamic buildings already located on the site prior to the Six-Day War, but it should not be allowed to administer the overall site itself, to restrict Jewish access thereto either for prayer or archeological excavation and study. Furthermore, the *waqf* should not be allowed to engage in illegal construction of any kind on the site, and if it does do so, the *waqf* officials who ordered the construction work should be duly prosecuted and prevented from entering the Temple Mount.

## *Step 5*

The 1980 Basic Law: Jerusalem, Capital of Israel provides for a united Jerusalem and an amendment to that law, adopted by the Knesset on November 27, 2000, prohibits the transfer of authority[10] over any part of the united city to a foreign entity, state or administrative body. Despite the clear intent of this law to prevent the division of Jerusalem, this has not deterred the Government of Israel, under two different Prime Ministers, in particular Ehud Barak of the Labour Party (1999-2001) and Ehud Olmert of the Kadima Party (from 2005; publication pending, still in office), from entering into negotiations with the "Palestinian Authority" to act in direct violation of this Basic Law – dividing Jerusalem by surrendering Arab-populated neighborhoods to the "Palestinian Authority". Such negotiations are in effect an attempt, in the legal sense of this term, to circumvent the existing law, an attempt which in criminal law would be equivalent to a conspiracy to perpetrate the crime. Negotiations the aim of which is to transfer jurisdiction (i.e., sovereignty) over any area of Jerusalem to a foreign entity could certainly be viewed as a crime under article 97(a) and (b) of the Penal Law, since it exposes an intention to withdraw Israel's sovereignty over the area to be transferred. Such negotiations are also a concrete act or, if carried out over a period of time, a series of acts calculated to bring about the transfer or impairment of Israel's sovereignty over its capital city. Negotiations of this type have been the chosen tactic of those on the Israeli political Left to achieve what the law specifically prohibits. This method has been successful because the Attorney-General and the Supreme Court of Israel have refused to intervene to prevent illegal negotiations from taking place on the ground that any agreement resulting from these negotiations will in any event be brought for approval before the Knesset which then will have the opportunity to adopt or reject the negotiated agreement.

This deviation from the norm could be tolerated were the legislature truly independent of the executive branch of government, as it is in the United States. There, under the federal system of constitutional government with separate elective processes for the various branches of government as part of its "checks and balances" to prevent tyrannical rule, the Executive and Legislative branches

---

[10] The Hebrew word *samkhut* may also be translated as "jurisdiction" or "power" in the context of this Basic Law.

of government are truly independent of one another. But that is not the case in a parliamentary democracy such as Israel, where the Government can simply have the Knesset approve of whatever action it proposes to take. Thus, if the Government decides contrary to the existing law to divide Jerusalem into Jewish and Arab sections, and negotiates an agreement to this effect, the Government of the day which, as a rule, controls the Knesset – otherwise, it could not survive as a Government – would not encounter any difficulty in getting this illegal agreement approved automatically by the Knesset which invariably has a majority of members supporting the Government.

What the Government is really doing when it conducts negotiations to divide Jerusalem illegally and then seeks confirmation of its action by the Knesset, which it is likely to obtain, is an inversion of the correct procedure. To abide by the law as it stands, the law must first be amended before negotiations can be conducted. The inverse procedure makes a mockery of the provisions of the current Basic Law on Jerusalem, as well as the penal law, since what is prohibited becomes permissible by the expedient of "negotiations", clearly constituting a circumvention of the stipulations of the law or standing in open defiance of it.

It is true that no law is unalterable, not even a constitutional or basic law, and any law can be amended by the will of the legislature acting in concert with the government. It is also true that discussions may be held within the Cabinet to amend or repeal an existing law. However, so long as the basic law on Jerusalem is not amended, it must not be subverted by negotiations to accomplish what the law forbids. Otherwise, the Rule of Law has no meaning and the government stands, as it were, above the Law.

To ensure that such negotiations are not undertaken while the law remains unaltered, the existing law on Jerusalem should be further amended to state that it is not only illegal to transfer any authority or jurisdiction over Jerusalem or any part thereof to a foreign entity, such as the "Palestinian Authority", it is also illegal for negotiations to be conducted or contacts made for that very purpose. The same restrictions should apply to the Golan Heights and to any other part of the Land of Israel falling under the *de jure* sovereignty of the State of Israel, as the agent and assignee of the Jewish People.

## Step 6

In conjunction with incorporating Judea, Samaria and Gaza into the State borders, as discussed *supra*, the Government of Israel must close down the operations of all Arab refugee "camps" situated there, run by the United Nations Relief and Works Agency for Palestine Refugees in the Near East, known by its initials UNRWA. This agency, like its parent body – the United Nations, has been used as a weapon to defame Israel by the coterie of Arab and Moslem states ever since the creation of UNRWA by U.N. General Assembly Resolution 302 (IV) of December 8, 1949, which directed it "to carry out in collaboration with local governments the direct relief and works programmes as recommended by the Economic Survey Mission." UNRWA has not helped to solve or bring to an end the problems of those Arabs who fled what became the State of Israel in 1948 and the rest of Cisjordan in 1967, but, on the contrary, has exacerbated and perpetuated those problems. Arabs who had the status of refugees in 1948 still have the same status today, along with millions more of their descendants. According to Moshe Efrat, who in 1993 produced a discussion paper on "The Palestinian Refugees",[11] the number of original refugees as of June 1990 was estimated to be only 15-20 percent of the total refugee population, and that percentage has continuously declined since then. This means that most of the so-called "refugees" of today are already three or four generations removed from those truly classified as refugees in 1948, who either fled the State of Israel or chose to remain in "refugee camps" located either in the rest of Mandated Palestine, i.e., Judea, Samaria and Gaza, or in neighboring Arab countries. The condition of being a refugee, sustained indefinitely as protected economic wards of the United Nations, is not meant to be a permanent aspect of life. Yet, this is what prevails today, *inter alia*, in the Gaza Strip where up to 80% of the Arab population is supported by UNRWA or other international relief organizations.

The Arabs of the Land of Israel are not the only displaced persons of the twentieth century. Over one hundred million people have become refugees either because of war or expulsion, or to escape persecution. Some notable examples were Russians who fled the Revolution of 1917, Armenian and Greek refugees who fled from Turkey early in the twentieth century, Jews fleeing Hitler's persecution, millions of displaced persons created by World War II, Hindu and Moslem refugees following the partition of the Indian sub-continent, refugees from the Korean War, from wars in Southeast Asia (Vietnam and Cambodia), in Africa, and from the break-up of Yugoslavia. Most of these refugees found new homes and started new lives in countries outside their native lands, particularly 869,000 Jews[12] who were forced to leave Arab countries between 1948 and 1967 and for whom no equivalent of UNRWA was ever established. The only refugee situation that was never ended or diminished but rather expanded with time was the one of Arab refugees, despite the fact that the actual number displaced by war in 1948 was relatively small, no more than 540,000 according to official UNRWA figures or slightly higher according to several other estimates. This is

---

[11] Moshe Efrat's discussion paper is mentioned by Professor Ya'akov Meron, in his article "The Expulsion of Jews from Arab Countries", in: *The Forgotten Millions,* ed. by Malka Hillel Shulewitz, published by Continuum, paperback, London (2000), p. 123, n. 121. As to the total original refugee population, see p. 124 of Meron's article, n. 135, and the authorities therein cited.

[12] The figure of 869,000 comes from the number of Jews who left 10 Arab countries (Morocco, Algeria, Tunisia, Libya, Egypt, Lebanon, Syria, Iraq, Yemen and Aden) between 1948 and 1967 and settled in Israel, Europe and the Americas. Of this number, almost 609,000 sought refuge in Israel while a further 260,000 went to other lands. See the 1996 Annual Report of the Central Bureau of Statistics, Israel and The Forgotten Millions, *op. cit.*, pp. 138-139.

considerably less than the 869,000 Jews displaced from Arab states. The original number of Arab refugees has skyrocketed to over 4 million today, because of UNRWA's irregular and dubious practice of conferring refugee status upon all descendants of the original refugees and converting them in effect into freeloading, unproductive wards of the U.N. This arrangement has created a perpetual and unnecessary burden on the world organization, that also benefits not only the so-called refugees, but also the large U.N. staff appointed to deal with them, whose salaries are thereby justified and their own careers enhanced. UNRWA's mode of operation is not followed by the other U.N. agency that cares for the world's other refugees, the Office of the United Nations High Commissioner for Refugees (UNHCR) established in January 1951 to replace the International Refugee Organization (IRO). In contrast to UNRWA, UNHCR seeks permanent solutions to refugee problems, not their indefinite prolongation. The only way to end the Palestine refugee travesty is for the State of Israel to evict UNRWA from Judea, Samaria and Gaza, take control of the so-called refugee camps and then gradually phase them out of existence. At the same time, it should urge the USA, the biggest donor to UNRWA, to cut off its huge financial support of this agency. There is no justification for UNRWA to continue its unnecessary activities on behalf of people who should have long ago been rehabilitated and made responsible for their own fate, instead of enjoying gratuitous U.N. handouts on a regular basis and becoming what can only be termed professional refugees. In fact, the U.N. General Assembly Resolution that created UNRWA on December 8, 1949 foresaw the day "when international assistance for relief and work projects is no longer available" for "Palestine refugees", but this assistance has continued unabated ever since – with no end in sight. It is ironic to speak of the "plight" of Palestine refugees in Judea, Samaria, Gaza and elsewhere when their standard of living is actually higher than that of the surrounding Arab population, who do not have the same access to free health care, educational facilities, welfare payments and other benefits provided by UNRWA. Once UNRWA is shut down, at least in Cisjordan, and deprived of American funds, the refugee scandal will disappear for the benefit of all parties concerned.

## *Step 7*

To elect a Prime Minister for the State of Israel infused with the spirit of Judaism and Zionism, and sustained by the knowledge of Jewish legal rights and title of sovereignty to the whole country, especially Judea, Samaria, Gaza and the Golan. Such a person will need to have the courage to assert and act upon those rights and at the same time be able to withstand unrelenting American and European pressure to recognize Arab or so-called "Palestinian" claims to the Land of Israel. No present or past leader who has concluded, implemented or endorsed any agreement with the Palestine Liberation Organization or entered into negotiations with the "Palestinian Authority" in regard to the Road Map

Peace Plan or similar initiative would be acceptable to lead the Jewish Nation. The same applies to any politician who preaches Israel's unilateral withdrawal or disengagement from any area of the Jewish National Home or does or intends to do any act calculated to bring this about.

## *Step 8*

To prosecute under the Criminal Code all current and past government leaders who while in office committed or who evinced an intention to commit treason, in regard to giving up sovereign areas of the Jewish country or impairing its sovereignty. In this regard, no honour should be bestowed upon the memory of Yitzhak Rabin who as Prime Minister endorsed the criminal process of giving up substantial areas of the Jewish National Home to a terrorist organization, the Palestine Liberation Organization, and of the Golan Heights to Syria, two acts which recklessly endangered the security of the State and, in the case of the PLO, has caused the deaths of about one thousand five hundred Israelis since 1993 and many thousands wounded and maimed. State prosecution should not be limited to indicting political leaders. It should be extended to academics and journalists who wrongly believe they have an unfettered legal right to advocate the illegal cession of sovereign territories that belong to the Jewish People and the State of Israel. Israel has more traitors of this kind than any other country in the world. The treasured right called freedom of expression is not a license to advocate the crime of treason or any other crime. None other than Supreme Court President Aharon Barak stated in the case of Rabbi Meir Kahane and the Kach Movement versus the Broadcasting Authority and others (H.C. 399/85; 41[3] P.D. 255), that "freedom of expression did not mean unbridled license", neither did it mean "freedom to break the law". Thus, any group, body or individual who illegally advocates by public appeals, articles, petitions and private "peace" initiatives and the like, the redivision of united Jerusalem, placing the Temple Mount under Arab "sovereignty", or the surrender of any other areas of the Land of Israel and the Jewish National Home presently under Israel's rule – should be duly prosecuted. This will apply in particular to those Israeli citizens or residents who call openly for diplomatic intervention by the United States, the United Nations and the European Union to press Israel to cede so-called "occupied" Jewish patrimonial lands including parts of united Jerusalem on pain of economic, cultural or academic sanctions. These are acts of treason calculated to impair or bring about the surrender of Israel's sovereignty over its capital city, Jerusalem, as well as Judea, Samaria and Gaza by placing them under the illegal rule of the Palestine Liberation Organization in plain violation of Articles 97(a), 97(b) and 100 of the Penal Code. By the same token, it is an act of treason to publicly advocate the surrender of the Golan Heights to Syria, unless done within the parameters of Cabinet and legislative debate. Treason by anyone, no matter what his or her status, must not be tolerated and, if necessary, stricter laws should be enacted to make that crystal-clear. The lack of enforcement of the laws of treason, which is the responsibility of the Attorney-General, has allowed the biggest violators in the past decades to get away scot free with their criminal conduct. The Government of Israel must therefore appoint an Attorney-General who will not hesitate to enforce the laws regarding the impairment of sovereignty or integrity of the State and the Jewish National Home by implication, thereby giving teeth to the laws against criminal treason and deterring anybody so inclined.

## *Step 9*

The Penal Code of Israel at present contains no specific provision for the crime of attempted *politicide* that occurs when a domestic or foreign group or any member thereof attempts, threatens, conspires to commit or commits any act of violence whose purpose is to bring about the destruction of the State of Israel or to encourage the Jewish populace to leave their homeland. Politicide can be distinguished from the crime of Genocide in that the former is directed at bringing about the destruction of a state, while the latter refers to the commission of various acts, the intent of which is "to destroy, in whole or part, a national, ethnical, racial or religious group".[13] Individuals or members of a group who are convicted of directly participating in the crime of Politicide would be liable to a mandatory death penalty or to life imprisonment and/or deportation. In this context it should be noted that the Penal Code does contain a provision (Article 98) defining the crime of a person who assists an enemy to bring about military action against the State, but this provision is neither broad enough nor sufficiently explicit to cover the crime of politicide. Article 98 of the Penal Code should therefore be amended and given extraterritorial applicability to enable Israel to prosecute any accused person who has engaged in activity of this type. This provision is absolutely necessary in light of the many bombings, shootings, mortar and rocket attacks as well as acts of sabotage perpetrated by Arab terrorists belonging to such groups as Fatah, Tanzim, Al-Aqsa Martyrs Brigades, Hamas and Islamic Jihad who operate inside areas of the Land of Israel controlled by the "Palestinian Authority", sometimes with accomplices in the State of Israel. Their acts of terrorism and politicide have resulted in mass casualties of ordinary Israelis (or the threat of same) on city streets, on buses, at shopping centers, restaurants, places of entertainment, in halls of celebration and even in the inner sanctum of private homes. Spokesmen for these Arab groups always claim that their members are "only resisting the occupation" when in fact they are striving to destroy the Israeli polity. The application of the death penalty or life imprisonment in those cases would be justified as an effective deterrent to prevent further acts of politicide. It would send a very strong message to all those who plan to attack Jews in their state and homeland,

[13] See the Convention on the Punishment and the Prevention of the Crime of Genocide, passed as U.N. General Assembly Resolution 260A (III) of December 9, 1948.

that they will be duly punished for their unforgivable and heinous crimes.

The crime of attempted politicide is also to be attributed to foreign leaders such as the President of the Islamic Republic of Iran, Mahmoud Ahmadinejad, who have threatened the State of Israel with annihilation, a threat potentially very serious if Iran succeeds in acquiring or developing nuclear weapons, as it at present aims to do. In this regard, the Iranian President is not the first Moslem to make public statements threatening to "wipe Israel off the map". In the run-up to the Six-Day War that erupted on June 5, 1967, Arab rulers, public officials and radio-stations in Cairo, Damascus and Baghdad voiced similar sentiments. Those who threaten to destroy the Jewish State should be brought to understand that they themselves are liable to be apprehended and rendered accountable to the Jewish People in an Israeli court-of-law, as was Adolf Eichmann in 1961.

## *Step 10*

To refrain from using language that not only fosters the legally non-existent Arab "rights" to the Land of Israel and the Jewish National Home, but also impugns or denies altogether the Jewish rights to the country. This would include avoiding the use of such inaccurate and misleading terms as "Palestinians" or the "Palestinian People" to refer to the Arabic-speaking gentile population living in the Land of Israel, since that term was reserved for Palestinian Jewry in pre-State Israel. The term "Palestinian" may be legitimately used only in reference to the period of the Mandate where it denoted the status of citizenship under the Churchill White Paper of June 3, 1922 and not of nationhood for persons who lived in the Mandated State of Palestine. There were therefore no "Palestinians" in a national sense. The current meaning, that of a "Palestinian" nation, given to this term as the result of a clever and successful PLO propaganda campaign that changed its meaning, represents the antithesis or inversion of the accepted 1922 White Paper meaning.

Other terms to be avoided include the illogical expression of "setting up a Palestinian State", since Israel is by definition the only legal Palestinian State under international law as determined in the immediate post-World War I period, which declared all of Palestine to be the Jewish National Home. In this connection it is plainly ridiculous to say that Jews "occupy" "Palestinian lands" in violation of international law and that any areas of it under Israel's rule are "occupied territories". That kind of illogical language gives substances to the myth that a sovereign Arab state of Palestine once existed before Israel "occupied" it in 1948. The use of such language is a self-denial of Jewish legal rights and title of sovereignty over the Land of Israel.

In light of the self-defeating practice in Israel itself of using pro-Arab designations for those areas of the Jewish National Home liberated in the Six-Day War of June 5-10, 1967, a practice that was especially prevalent when the Labour Party held power, it is important to pass a new law that will make it a punishable crime for anyone to use the false and accusatory term "occupied territories" for Judea, Samaria and Gaza, as well as the Golan Heights, which denies and mocks Israel's sovereign rights to those regions. Referring to them by that term is the equivalent of saying they are "foreign territories" which belong to another state that holds sovereignty over them. If that were really true, then all Jewish settlements built on occupied territories would indeed be illegal under international law. The fact that this term reflects a complete untruth when used in relation to Judea, Samaria, Gaza and the Golan and moreover tarnishes Israel as an international lawbreaker, thereby causing the state grave damage to its world standing, makes anyone who uses this term guilty either of criminal libel or of sedition against the State of Israel, as defined in Israel's Penal Code – Article 136(1): "to bring into hatred or contempt or to excite disaffection [= disloyalty] against the State..." It is Israel's presumed "occupation" of "occupied territories" which has impelled hundreds of rebellious soldiers to justify their refusal to serve there. Some politicians and journalists have even classified Israel's alleged occupation of Judea, Samaria and Gaza as the epitome of "terrorism". In light of the widespread use of this term in Israel, a remedy is urgently needed to combat this injurious libel on the State of Israel, and that can only be the enactment of a new law or Penal Code amendment to spell out in explicit terms that Judea, Samaria and Gaza are not occupied territories and that describing them as such constitutes a criminal offense against the State itself. This law should also clarify that the two instruments of international law most cited against Israel's presence in these regions, namely the Fourth Geneva Convention of 1949 and the Hague Regulations of 1907, are inapplicable to any area of the Jewish National Home. On the other hand, it should also enunciate the exact "international law" which is applicable to those areas, namely, those instruments of international law which are the foundation of modern Israel's existence, that recognized the acquired Jewish rights to all of the Jewish National Home as originally recorded in Article 22 of the Covenant of the League of Nations, founded on the Smuts Resolution, as well as the San Remo Resolution, the Mandate for Palestine and the Franco-British Boundary Convention of December 23, 1920. While these international documents have indeed run their course, the legal rights of the Jewish People derived from them remain in full force as confirmed by Article 70 (1)(b) of the 1969 Vienna Convention on the Law of Treaties, which codified what was already customary international law. During the last several years, especially since the illegal establishment of the "Palestinian Authority", frequent use has been made of the term "international law" as if it were a magic incantation to indict or castigate Israel. It is time Israel took the appropriate legal action to counter this abuse by properly defining what the true "international law" is as it applies to the Land of Israel and the Jewish National Home.

## *Step 11*

A new Basic Law or an amendment to an upgraded Law of Return should also be enacted by the Knesset, specifically allowing for the establishment and expansion of Jewish settlements anywhere in the Jewish National Home, especially in the liberated areas of Cisjordan. This law is definitely needed to put an end to the constant refrain heard from every anti-nationalist quarter in Israel and every ignoramus or Jew-hater abroad, that Israeli settlements in Judea, Samaria and Gaza are illegal under "international law" or even, in the American view, "obstacles to peace". They are not illegal, as is evident from Articles 6 and 11 of the Mandate for Palestine and the aforementioned Article 70 (1)(b) of the Vienna Convention on the Law of Treaties which embodies the principle of acquired rights surviving even after the execution of the treaty or international agreement that established them. Articles 6 and 11 are still part of the law of the State of Israel by virtue of Section 11 of the Law and Administration Ordinance and three Supreme Court decisions, rendered in the early years of the State, which overturned the untenable British judicial doctrine that the 28 articles of the Mandate were not part of the law of Palestine, unless they had been specifically incorporated in the domestic legislation of the country. An updated law on settlements which replicates the words in Article 6 of the Mandate requiring the Government to encourage "close settlement by Jews on the land", accompanied by any necessary changes to be made in the land system for this purpose, should be legislated by the Knesset. The reference to the word "land" in this context can only mean the Land of Israel, not merely the State of Israel. Conversely, the uprooting or dismantling of Israeli settlements established with government approval anywhere in the Land of Israel should be expressly prohibited under the treason provisions of the penal law. Had such a law been in existence in August 2005, Prime Minister Ariel Sharon's Unilateral Disengagement Plan that uprooted over a score of settlements in Gaza and Northern Samaria would never have been implemented.

The geographical term "Land of Israel" should also be defined in the broadest manner, to include all areas historically, geographically, economically and strategically part of it, even those not presently in possession of the State of Israel, but which one day may be, if and when favourable circumstances arise. The proposed law should stipulate that any person or body in Israel, whether Israeli or non-Israeli, who publicly calls for the uprooting of Government-authorized Israeli settlements is guilty of a crime punishable by fine or imprisonment. Furthermore, any person who accuses Israel of committing a "war crime" for building such settlements in what are falsely alleged to be "occupied territories" will be duly prosecuted either for criminal libel, sedition or treason.

In an erudite Law Review article,[14] Professor Ya'akov Meron has pointed out that ever since Israel re-conquered Judea and Samaria on June 6, 1967, in the Six-Day War, all settlements which were duly authorized by the competent authority (the Military Governor) and established on ownerless waste land not in anybody's possession, over which Jordan had no recognized legal title, are perfectly legal whether viewed from the perspective of the prevailing local law or that of international law. Article 6 of the Mandate preserved the distinction

[14] See Professor Ya'akov Meron's article in the *Boston College International Comparative Law Review,* Volume IV, no. 1, Spring 1981.

existing in the old Ottoman Land Law between *state lands* and *waste lands* not required for public purposes, a distinction which remains applicable in Judea and Samaria so long as Israeli law, jurisdiction and administration are not extended to these areas. State lands, as mentioned in the Mandate and Ottoman legislation, referred to land under the ownership of the State which the Turks called *miri* land, an abbreviated reference to land belonging to the Amir (*Amiri*) or Sultan.

By contrast, waste land meant dead land (*mewat*) or vacant (*khali*) land not in the possession of anyone by title-deed nor in public use, consisting of uncultivated or undeveloped land such as mountains, rocky places, stony fields, grazing grounds, sand dunes, swamps and marshes. Parcels of such land could be legally acquired under Ottoman law through an act of appropriation by an individual or corporate entity including the State for the purpose of vivification or cultivation. Inasmuch as most of the land in Judea, Samaria and formerly Gaza on which Israeli settlements were established since 1967, were either State-owned land or waste land that laid idle with no legal owner, this land could be appropriated by Jewish settlers with the leave of the Military Governor to allow for its vivification. No legal objection thus existed concerning the legality of these settlements according to the local law presently in force. Professor Meron's perspicacious analysis and conclusions convinced the then-U.S. President Jimmy Carter and his antagonistic State Department to stop their repeated attacks on Israel's "illegal" settlements in Judea and Samaria, and no U.S. president ever since has used this patently unjust description. However, the U.S. still regards these settlements as "obstacles to peace" reflecting a pro-Arab policy that openly insults and negates the legal rights of Israeli Jews to their homeland that was formerly under Arab occupation. As many others have pointed out, the settlements are in fact obstacles to war, necessary for the security of the State in deterring Arab attacks. They also secure the Land of Israel for the benefit of the Jewish People as a whole, in fulfillment of its national destiny.

## *Step 12*

Diplomatic steps should be taken by Israel to remind each of the Principal Allied and Associated Powers of World War I, Great Britain, France, Italy, Japan and the United States, that they are estopped from denying the legal rights of the Jewish People and its title of sovereignty over the entire Land of Israel, by virtue of their recognition of these rights in the global political and legal settlement concluded after World War I. To the counter-argument that sovereign states can, at any time, make new decisions or agreements to revoke previous ones, this would not apply to the case where the original decision or agreement was duly executed and produced a viable entity with acquired rights or created a new legal situation.

To take one example where a sovereign state is debarred from further interference with the acquired rights of another state it was instrumental in establishing, the case of Canada can be cited as illustrative of this principle.

In 1867, the U.K. Parliament enacted the British North America Act, which created the federal state of Canada with different powers assigned to the central government and the individual provinces. Once Canada was created and subsequently became independent, it could no longer be abolished as a state by the unilateral decision of the U.K. Parliament, nor could the latter make any amendments to the existing legal structure of Canada on its own initiative unless asked to do so by the Government of Canada.[15] By the same token, the legal rights and title of sovereignty conferred on the Jewish People over Palestine and the Land of Israel under international law in 1920 by virtue of the San Remo Resolution which created Palestine as the Jewish National Home and subsequently the Jewish State of Israel cannot be abrogated or amended by any new international decision or agreement unless Israel legally consents. Any action taken by the original parties or third parties to divest the Jewish People of its acquired rights to any part of the Jewish National Home, even those parts currently outside the boundaries of the State, would be contrary to authentic international law governed by the doctrine of estoppel. Estoppel would apply in particular to all the major Western powers who decide to take sanctions against Israel for its establishment of Israeli settlements in Judea, Samaria and Gaza or who espouse a new Arab state in those regions. In the specific case of the United States, American supporters of Israel could even seek the passage of an appropriate Congressional Resolution to reaffirm the very rights of the Jewish People vis-à-vis Palestine which the U.S. recognized in the 1924 Anglo-American Convention respecting the Mandate for Palestine, proclaimed by President Calvin Coolidge, and the earlier 1922 Lodge-Fish Joint Resolution of Congress signed by President Warren Gamaliel Harding. Even if such a resolution were non-binding, unless it took the form of a Joint Resolution signed by the President, as it originally did, in contrast to a Concurrent Resolution which does not require the President's signature, it would still have important evidentiary effect to further substantiate the fact that American recognition of Jewish legal rights over Palestine in 1922 and 1924 remains unchanged and ingrained in U.S. law even today, inasmuch as such recognition was never legally revoked by an Act of Congress or a supplanting treaty. In this context, it is imperative to remember that in both of the aforementioned documents (the Treaty and the Joint Resolution) the United States recognized the whole of Palestine, not 1/3, 1/4 or 1/8 of Palestine, as the future independent Jewish State, therein referred to as the Jewish National Home. These documents did not recognize the rights of a fictitious people known as the "Palestinians" or their presumed right to create a new Arab state in Judea, Samaria and Gaza, as President George W. Bush has advocated in a new precedent-setting Presidential policy, which violates the aforementioned Treaty and Joint Resolution, and should therefore

[15] A status formalized by the Statute of Westminster of 1931. This is a prime example of the existence of built-in limitations on the principle of the "supremacy of Parliament", which in theory empowers the latter to repeal any legislation previously enacted, but in practice is inappropriate and beyond its actual power.

be considered illegal under both U.S. law and international law. In the event that diplomacy or other efforts in Congress prove futile, legal proceedings founded on violations of international acts and agreements that laid the basis of the Jewish State of Israel should be initiated by the Government of Israel or, in default thereof, by Israeli citizens or legally constituted bodies in the domestic courts of the former Principal Allied and Associated Powers, especially in the more objective United States courts, where the best chance of success lies. The purpose of these actions would be to reaffirm Israel's legal rights and title of sovereignty over the Jewish National Home and to block all attempts to transfer those rights to foreign gentile Arabs calling themselves "Palestinians". In this regard, a reference case with the same purpose in mind should even be filed in the Supreme Court of Israel.

To allow for such a reference case, the present law governing the jurisdiction of Israeli courts ought to be amended to enable the Government of Israel, the Knesset or even the Attorney-General to seek an advisory opinion from the Supreme Court on issues of a constitutional nature, including questions of Jewish rights to the Land of Israel and the violation thereof by foreign entities. This law should also enable the Government of Israel, the Knesset or the Attorney-General or, in default, any private citizen or group of citizens to sue such foreign states or entities in the courts of Israel for their refusal to recognize Jewish rights to the Land of Israel that they had previously acknowledged in binding international instruments, and which they now deny.

In addition, a lawsuit should be brought against the European Union for refusing to recognize Israel's legal rights and title of sovereignty over what it vociferously and repeatedly trumpets as the "occupied territories" and for recognizing those of the Arabic-speaking gentiles of the Land of Israel, who were never granted or acknowledged as having the national and political rights in Palestine enjoyed by the Jewish People under international law. As part of its illegal policy, the European Union discriminates against Israeli-made goods and produce originating from Jewish settlements in Judea, Samaria, Gaza and the Golan by imposing an extra duty or import tax on such goods and produce on the specious ground that they are located in territories not legally belonging to the State of Israel and not part of it. Without an iota of legal justification it denounces these settlements as a violation of international law, despite Articles 6 and 11 of the Mandate for Palestine and the 1920 Boundary Convention between Britain and France which places all of Cisjordan, including the so-called "occupied territories", within the scope of the Jewish National Home. Furthermore, the EU supports the establishment of an illegal Palestinian State in favour of the Arab population in the heart and cradle of the Jewish National Home. It provides the Palestinian Authority with large sums of money for which there is no proper accounting and thereby helps to sustain a corrupt and terrorist entity prejudicial to Israel's rights to the Land of Israel and the security of its citizens. A legal action against the European Union might awaken the memory of Britain, France and Italy that they cannot retract their official recognition of Palestine as the Jewish National Home and future state encompassing all of western Palestine when they accepted the San Remo Resolution of April 25, 1920 and voted to confirm the Mandate on July 24, 1922 without at the same time destroying the legal foundation on which the State of Israel was built under international law, as well as the foundations of Syria and Iraq. For their retrogression and betrayal of the Jewish People signified by their scandalous attempt to revoke the national rights of the Jewish People to Judea, Samaria and Gaza, the European Union must be brought to account in a court of law. By its pro-Arab and anti-Israel policies, Europe is adding a new layer of infamy to its monstrous record of persecution and hatred of the Jewish People over the last millennium and more.

Outdoing even the European Union in its innate hostility to Israel is the United Nations Organization which is used as a pawn by three score Arab and Moslem states who by sheer weight of numbers keep the alleged "Palestine problem" continuously on the agenda of the General Assembly and various other agencies of the Organization. The U.N. has routinely denounced Israel in many dozens of blatantly illegal resolutions on the Middle East and established pro-Arab "Palestinian" bodies, such as the "Division of Palestinian Rights" and the absurd "Committee on the Exercise of the Inalienable Rights of the Palestinian People". Moreover, it has illegally given recognition to a fictitious entity known as "Palestine" by a series of steps beginning on November 22, 1974, when the General Assembly granted "observer status" to the "Palestine Liberation Organization". This allowed the latter to participate in the sessions and work of the General Assembly in the capacity of observer and to participate likewise in all international conferences convened under the auspices of the General Assembly or other U.N. organs. The status of the PLO was further upgraded by the U.N. on December 15, 1988 when, following the proclamation of the "State of Palestine" issued by the "Palestine National Council" a month earlier (November 15, 1988) in Algiers, the General Assembly in a new resolution decided that the designation "Palestine" should be used in place of the designation "Palestine Liberation Organization" in the United Nations system. Moreover, the General Assembly disregarded the fact that the "State of Palestine" does not qualify as a state under the Montevideo Convention of December 26, 1934 which, in Article 1, enumerates the qualifications of a state:

> The state as a person of international law should possess the following qualifications: (a) a permanent population; (b) a defined territory; (c) government; and (d) capacity to enter into relations with the other states.

At the time the "State of Palestine" allegedly came into existence in November 1988, it had none of the foregoing attributes of a state. As of now, the "State of Palestine" is still a fiction, even though the "Palestinian Authority" created under the Declaration of Principles of August-September 1993 now rules substantial parts of Judea, Samaria and Gaza, but still has no "defined territory" or capacity to enter into relations with other states. It is also a matter of debate whether or not there is a functioning "government" in effective control of territory and population. In any case, the General Assembly Resolution of December 15, 1988 was in clear violation of Article 4 of the U.N. Charter which limits membership in the U.N. to "peace-loving states".

Compounding its illegal action in recognizing the "State of Palestine", the General Assembly subsequently passed other resolutions, particularly one on July 7, 1998 giving "Palestine" additional rights and privileges theretofore reserved only for member-states of the U.N. or, in some exceptional cases, to non-member-states such as the Vatican and Switzerland (before the latter joined the U.N.), both of which possessed the qualifications of a state as defined in the above-mentioned Montevideo Convention. Among these new rights and privileges bestowed upon "Palestine" were "the right to participate in the general debate of the General Assembly" and, most importantly, "the right to *co-sponsor* draft resolutions and decisions on Palestinian and Middle East issues" (emphasis added) which however could only be put to a vote upon request from a Member State. Not being a Member State, but rather a so-called "observer State" for which category no provision is explicitly made in the U.N. Charter or in the corpus of international law, "Palestine" still did not have the right to vote or to put forward candidates. The seating of the unqualified, falsely-denominated "State of Palestine" demonstrates the astounding extent to which the U.N. goes to do the bidding of Arab states in their continuous struggle against the existence of the State of Israel. The U.N. has now become the most convenient international forum for Arab and Moslem diplomats to engage in Israel-bashing and to spread vicious anti-Semitism at no apparent cost to themselves, but on the contrary, with the approval of the conniving European Union and most of its member states.

All of the foregoing resolutions are not only illegal, but in flagrant contradiction to the national and political rights of the Jewish People over Palestine that were recognized by the U.N.'s predecessor, the League of Nations, when it confirmed the Mandate for Palestine on July 24, 1922, and which were generally upheld by the Permanent Mandates Commission at several sessions it devoted to Palestine during the 1920s and 1930s. The League of Nations never recognized the existence of a "Palestinian People" holding *a priori* rights of any kind over Palestine. Neither the League Council nor the Permanent Mandates Commission would ever have imagined that Judea, Samaria and Gaza were territories occupied by Israel under the Hague Regulations of 1907 or the subsequent Fourth Geneva Convention of 1949, as the United Nations holds to be the case today in total disregard of the acquired rights and title of sovereignty of the Jewish People over Palestine, since devolved upon the State of Israel. That would have been considered a laughable and absurd idea at total variance with the global political and legal settlement worked out by the Principal Allied and Associated Powers at the Paris and San Remo Peace Conferences of 1919 and 1920. Under that settlement, Palestine meant the Jewish National Home, not associated in any way with the yet-to-be-invented nation of "Palestinians". Hence "Palestinian land" is truly "Jewish land", rather than "Arab land", as is so commonly misrepresented today.

In light of the U.N.'s appalling record of passing illegal resolutions on the subject of "Palestine" and its implicit repudiation of Jewish legal rights and title of sovereignty to the Land of Israel, as manifested in its unwarranted demands for the establishment of an illegal Arab state in Cisjordan which would grant self-determination to a fake nation, the State of Israel has excellent grounds for suing the United Nations in an appropriate legal forum, to obtain injunctive and other relief. Specifically, Israel can demand that the General Assembly expunge its illegal resolutions granting recognition and quasi-membership status to the nonexistent "State of Palestine" and that it cease and desist from its wholesale violations of Jewish legal rights and title of sovereignty to the Land of Israel. It is time to take vigorous counter-measures to end the U.N.'s bullying of Israel under Arab-Moslem prodding and, if nothing else succeeds, to withdraw from the world body and expel all its agencies and personnel from the Land of Israel.

## *Step 13*

Another Basic Law should be enacted to define the State of Israel as the State of the Jewish People based upon the values and norms transmitted by Jewish religious law (halakha), history and Zionism, but the intention of the law should not be the creation of a theocratic form of government. This defining characteristic of the state has always been and remains the true reason for the re-constitution of the State of Israel, and should therefore be duly acknowledged in a separate Basic Law. The State of Israel should also be defined as a democracy, having representative and responsible government chosen by Jewish electors and other loyal citizens of the Jewish State who have undertaken to uphold all the laws of Israel as a Jewish State, recognize its predominantly Jewish nature and refrain from engaging in acts of treason, sedition, terrorism or incitement or other hostile acts such as anti-Israel celebrations of nakba or Land Day. In the case of the nakba commemoration, this constitutes in effect a direct repudiation of the existence of the State of Israel or a call for its eventual destruction and should therefore be outlawed. Those who nonetheless commemorate nakba should be liable to the loss of their Israeli citizenship. Unlike the precedent of the Weimar Republic which tolerated the unchecked rise of National Socialism under Adolf Hitler, attacks on the very existence of the Jewish State of Israel should be considered beyond the pale. Furthermore, no political parties which advocate Arab national rights in the Jewish State as a collectivity or entitled minority should be allowed to run for the Knesset, because such goals undermine the purpose of the Jewish State which recognizes only Jewish national rights to the exclusion of those of any other nation. All non-Jewish citizens of the Jewish State are entitled to enjoy full civil and religious rights. Non-Jews should be inducted into the Israel Defense Forces or be required to perform national service as a binding obligation of citizenship. If they refuse, they will automatically lose their citizenship and be subject to deportation. On the other hand, Jews who similarly refuse would face imprisonment, rather than denaturalization, since otherwise the Law of Return would be contravened. In the event of a conflict between the tenets of a Jewish State and the norms of democracy under this Basic Law, the former must prevail in order to preserve the Jewish character of the State. This was, in fact, the official understanding or unstated policy during the embryonic period of the Mandate. If democracy had been the primary consideration or most-cherished value in Mandated Palestine, the Arabs who at first greatly outnumbered the Jews would have used their dominant position to prevent the emergence of a Jewish State. The Basic Law defining a Jewish State should not be subject to any change without the support of a minimum of eighty Knesset members in two successive Knessets.

To inculcate a strong national consciousness and love of the Land of Israel, all streams of the educational system should feature mandatory courses on its history, covering all periods as recounted in the Bible, in the writings of Josephus Flavius (whose Hebrew name was Yosef ben Mattityahu Ha-Cohen) and in other ancient texts, with special stress on the formative periods of the Patriarchs and the Judges and the First and Second Temple periods, followed by the 1800-year Exile and culminating in the development of political Zionism. With such knowledge gained by Jewish students, it is less likely they would later on in life want to surrender any part of the precious patrimony of the Land of Israel for any reason whatsoever. The knowledge and glory of Jewish history will undoubtedly be an inspiration for all Israeli Jews. It should not be an arcane preserve only for scholars of the subject, but also be the living heritage of every Jew who lives in the State.

To make the State more accurately reflect its proud Jewish national character, ancient Hebrew names for the cities and towns of the Land of Israel should be officially restored by the Government, replacing the names given by past Gentile conquerors who ruled the country. This change should be extended even to the renaming of streets, except in those instances where the persons to be honoured, such as the admirable Arthur James Balfour, David Lloyd George, Lord Palmerston, Richard Meinertzhagen and Herbert Sidebotham, were stalwart supporters of the restoration of the Jewish State. Those streets named for Christian personages who do not fall into this elect category, such as King George V and General Edmund Allenby, should have their names changed. Nor should a Jewish personage like Herbert Samuel, who did so much to prevent the re-emergence of a Jewish State especially by hindering Jewish immigration, be accorded any honour by having streets or squares named after him.

One disturbing phenomenon of the present-day Jewish State, apparent to all who live near a mosque located in nearby Jewish-populated areas or holy sites, especially in the Old City of Jerusalem, is the unpleasant blaring of the muezzin's call to prayer over a booming loudspeaker. This public crier does that five times a day, beginning before dawn and ending at sunset. No other religion engages in this kind of unacceptable practice in the Jewish State. Jews who go to a synagogue to pray in the morning (*shaharit*), afternoon (*minha*) and evening (*'arvit* or *ma'ariv*) are not urged to do so by a rabbi using a megaphone. To do so would unnecessarily disturb the peace of every other citizen who does not attend a synagogue. This religious intrusion would not be tolerated in the United States, Canada or Europe, nor should it be permitted in Israel.

## *Step 14*

The State of Israel must formally make known in an official publication or document the legal rights and title of sovereignty which it inherited from the Jewish People over all of the Land of Israel, including all the historical and geographical areas that were either illegally excluded from Mandated Palestine or were subsequently removed through boundary agreements or acts of partition. That will be the best way to dispel the abysmal ignorance of everyone in the world, Jews and gentiles alike, especially among Government leaders and public officials, as to just exactly what those rights are, how they originated and were recognized under international law and why they continue to remain in force down to the present day, despite numerous illegal actions to rescind, obscure or disregard them altogether. It does not matter that not all these precious rights can be exercised at present by Israel. What is important is to lucidly reveal all the rights of the Jewish People to their national, ancestral and patriarchal homeland in an official publication of the State of Israel that can be relied upon, when the proper occasion arises one day in the future, to allow for the exercise of all those immutable rights.

A Government document of this kind will be the answer to all foreign and domestic critics who pretend that Jewish legal rights and title of sovereignty to all of Palestine and the Land of Israel either do not exist or are vested in the Arabs of the country, qua "Palestinians". It will shatter the prevailing amnesia concerning such rights and title.

During the Mandate period the British Government frequently issued statements of policy, official reports or documents which greatly undermined or denied exclusive Jewish national and political rights to Palestine and upheld unfounded Arab claims. The Jewish Agency for Palestine did indeed prepare and submit to the British very good replies and memoranda, but they did not go far enough to assert and substantiate the Jewish legal case to the whole country under international law, with special emphasis on the San Remo Resolution as the watershed event. It remains for the State of Israel to do so in a definitive and official manner, without any qualifications, compromises or apologetics. The present time is especially important because of renewed American and international attempts to terminate Israel's so-called "occupation" and "settlement activity" in Judea, Samaria and Gaza and to create a new Arab state in Western Palestine, as set out currently in the Road Map Peace Plan and previously in the Mitchell Committee Report, the Saudi and Arab Peace Initiatives, the speech by U.S. Secretary of State Colin Powell on November 19, 2001, in Louisville, Kentucky, and the address by President George W. Bush on June 24, 2002, *inter alia.* In his address, President Bush had the temerity to cite a verse from the Book of Deuteronomy (chapter 30, verse 19),[16] for the purpose of denouncing Israel's "occupation" and "settlement activity" in what he called the "occupied territories". He was apparently unaware that the chapter of the Bible from which he quoted has God promising the very same "occupied territories" to the Israelites and their descendants if they keep His commandments. President Bush's plan, in effect, is a repudiation of God's covenant with the Jewish People to give them eternal possession of the Land of Israel, including the "occupied territories". Bush's strange use of the Bible to suit the perverse needs of American foreign policy is the classic case of taking something out of context to change its meaning where the context connotes the very opposite of what has been alleged. The President's support for a "viable, credible [Arab] Palestinian state" is a mortal threat to the State of Israel, as well as being contrary to U.S. law and to authentic international law. It is only the abysmal and blissful ignorance of high-level American politicians and anti-Israel State Department officials concerning Israel's legal rights and title of sovereignty over all areas and regions of the Jewish homeland that allows them so easily to deplore Israel's "untenable occupation" and "settlement activity".

It is therefore imperative that a formal document be urgently prepared and published by the Government of Israel to rectify a public relations disaster depicting the State of Israel as being in violation of international law regarding its presence in Judea, Samaria and Gaza. Such a document must cogently show the falsity and baseless nature of the entire Arab case for a new, utterly unnecessary Arab state, that is bizarrely now being called "Palestine", to be established in Cisjordan. Arabs do not lack self-determination, as evidenced by the existence of twenty-one states, and Palestine was never created in 1920 to fulfil that purpose. Palestine is and has always been the Jewish National Home and there is no reason to further subdivide it. An acute awareness of Jewish legal rights and title of sovereignty over the entire Land of Israel is the sine qua non for preserving them for the benefit of future generations of the Jewish People and for preventing them from being usurped by Arab pretenders in whatever guise they adopt. It should also serve to overcome the gross ignorance of foreign government leaders and officials in the United States, Canada and Europe as well as members of the foreign media.

Foreign critics and Israeli politicians who assert that Jewish national rights to Judea, Samaria and Gaza have lapsed or, in any event, are doubtful because

---

[16] Moses, speaking as God's prophet, told the Children of Israel as they were about to cross the Jordan and enter the Promised Land, urging them to keep God's commandments: 'I call heaven and earth as witnesses. Before you I have placed life and death, the blessing and the curse. You must choose life, so that you and your descendants will survive".

Israel has never annexed these areas to the State – are mistaken. If their logic was consistent and were adopted, they would never object, as they always do, to Israel's annexation of eastern Jerusalem formerly under Jordan's illegal occupation or to its annexation of the Golan Heights. More important is the countervailing fact that Israeli constitutional law has, since the founding of the State in 1948, provided for the incorporation into the State of all areas of the Land of Israel outside its borders coming into the effective possession of the Israel Defense Forces. This is still the law in force, though the Government of Israel, for extra-legal reasons, has until now decided not to carry out further annexations of the Land in order to leave the door open for possible peace with the Arab states; nor did the Government wish to increase to a considerable extent the Arab population of the State of Israel. The failure to annex, however, does not nullify Israel's rights to all parts of the Land since, as noted *supra,* these rights are imprescriptible, indefeasible and inalienable so long as the Jewish People survives as a distinct nation. If it were otherwise, international law would never have recognized the right of the Jewish People to reconstruct their long-defunct state despite its non-existence for nineteen centuries. It is therefore immaterial that these rights are not always exercised in practice, even over lengthy periods of time.

The future steps that need to be taken to overcome Arab lies and fantasies and to restore to the bosom of the Jewish People those areas of the Land of Israel in foreign possession are clear enough. An additional important step, that of the transfer of the Arab population to other Arab countries in accordance with precedents established under international law, is discussed in the next chapter. If such steps are not eventually taken at the appropriate time by the State of Israel, then it does indeed face the de facto loss for a very long time of ancestral Jewish lands that were the wellspring of the glorious Jewish heritage dating from the days of the Bible. Jews who live today are therefore obligated to do everything necessary to ensure that all of the precious and sacred Land of Israel remains in Jewish hands forever.

*Chapter 20*

# Population Transfer

All Arabs, wherever they may live in the Land of Israel, not only in the State itself, but also in Judea, Samaria and Gaza, who are unwilling to swear allegiance to the Jewish State or who support, engage in, abet or incite terrorist activities and violence against Jews respectively, should be transferred and resettled in other Arab and Moslem countries in as orderly and humane a manner as possible, in conformity with international law. This may appear to be an unrealistic and extreme solution to those unaware of the history of population exchange or transfer, but it was the natural and most practical solution adopted to resolve several major, on-going and intractable disputes in international relations in the 20th century. Not all cases of population transfer were indeed sanctioned by international law; among those European examples that were, the following can be cited:

1. The Greek-Bulgarian population exchange, under the Convention of Neuilly of 1919;
2. The Greek-Turkish population exchange, under the Convention of Lausanne of 1923;
3. The expulsion of ethnic Germans from East Prussia, Pomerania, Brandenburg east of the Oder-Neisse Rivers, Silesia, Sudetenland and other parts of Europe under the Potsdam Agreement of 1945;
4. The expulsion of Finns from the Karelian Isthmus and other territory ceded to Russia under the Treaty of Paris of 1947.

Pursuant to the Treaty of Neuilly between Bulgaria and the Principal Allied and Associated Powers (Britain, France, Italy, Japan and the U.S.) joined by several minor Powers, a separate agreement was made, called the Convention of Neuilly, providing for a reciprocal emigration of the Greek minority from Bulgaria and the Bulgarian minority from Greece. According to the authors of the Convention, this was done to ensure peace and stability in the Balkans and to free them from endemic ethnic strife.

The Greek-Bulgarian population exchange was followed by a much larger one involving Greeks and Turks living in each other's territory. The basic cause for the transplantation of the Greek and Turkish populations was the great existing enmity between the two communities that was further exacerbated by the Greek invasion and occupation of Smyrna[1] in Western Anatolia on May 15, 1919. The Greek takeover of this important commercial city and chief port with its mixed population of Turks and Greeks, each of whom claimed to be a majority, stirred up powerful emotions amongst the Turkish masses throughout Anatolia against the Greek population and what it negatively portended for the survival of an independent Turkey after the post-World War I dismemberment of the Ottoman Empire. The Greek invasion was carried out over a year before the signing of the Treaty of Sèvres on August 10, 1920, whose provisions anticipated a Greek administration both of Smyrna and the territory adjacent to the city (Article 69) that, in all probability, would have led to full Greek sovereignty after the lapse of five years from the coming-into-force of the Peace Treaty (Article 83). To roll back the consequences of the Greek invasion and block the implementation of the Treaty provisions regarding Smyrna, a government of national defence was set up at Angora (Ankara) under the leadership of Mustapha Kemal. Both sides then prepared for war, which broke out in 1921.

A contemporary description of the prevailing state of affairs was given by the famous English historian, Arnold Joseph Toynbee (Professor of Byzantine History, London University) who wrote the following account foreshadowing the imminent separation of the two ethnic and religious communities in Anatolia:[2]

> If this fresh war had not broken out, the Smyrna zone would almost certainly have become a Greek 'reservation', whether that was the Allied intention or no. By gentle or by violent pressure the Turkish population in the zone would have been squeezed out, while, on the other hand, the Greek village-shopkeepers and urban merchants, professional men and artisans from all the rest of Anatolia would have been herded into it, with the result of bringing economic ruin to both these sets of enforced emigrants, and of undermining the prosperity of the entire country. In the light of what actually happened, however, such a *denouement* would have been relatively a happy one. By June 1922 it had become probable that, wherever the frontiers might eventually be drawn, some such inter-migration of minorities would have to be arranged. The inconclusive military operations had degenerated into a war of extermination, and feeling on both sides had been so much embittered that it was hardly credible that Greek and Turkish elements

[1] Smyrna was the Greek name of the city presently called Izmir, its Turkish name.

[2] *A History of the Peace Conference of Paris*, edited by Harold W. V. Temperley, Volume VI, Chapter 1, Part II, p. 73, Oxford University Press (first published in 1924, reprinted in 1969). See the article by A.J. Toynbee entitled "The Non-Arab Territories of the Ottoman Empire since the Armistice of the 30th October 1918", pp. 41-117.

> could continue to live together in the same towns and villages, as they had done in the past.

The military stalemate between Greek and Turkish forces suddenly ended on August 26, 1922 when a Turkish counter-offensive caused the complete collapse of the Greek army. The Turks regained Smyrna and by the middle of September, every Greek soldier still alive on the Anatolian mainland was either taken prisoner or driven out. No military action was taken by Britain or the other Allied Powers (chiefly France and Italy) to save the day for Greece or to preserve the Treaty of Sèvres from dissolution, though Britain, which had a small detachment of troops in the town of Chanak, on the Asiatic shore of the Dardanelles, did threaten to halt the Turkish advance into the neutral "Zone of the Straits". This almost led to war with the Kemalist forces before the two sides agreed to negotiate the future of the Zone and of Thrace, thus putting an end to what became known as "the Chanak Crisis". A new Armistice Convention was signed at Mudania on October 11, 1922 by General Charles Harrington on behalf of the Allied Powers and his Turkish counterpart, Ismet Pasha (later Inonu, a future Prime Minister and President of Turkey) on behalf of the Angora government. Greece acceded to the Mudania Convention three days later at the precise time the Convention went into effect. A peace conference was then convened to negotiate a new settlement, which resulted in the replacement of the Treaty of Sèvres by the Treaty of Lausanne.

With the end of the Greco-Turkish War (1921-1922), serious consequences ensued for the Greek minority in Anatolia. Many fled the area with the departing Greek troops or were ruthlessly expelled by the victorious Turks. To normalize the chaotic situation, a separate Convention (called the Convention Concerning the Exchange of Greek and Turkish Populations) was negotiated by the Greek and Turkish Governments at Lausanne (in addition to the Treaty of Lausanne) and signed on January 23, 1923, resulting in the *compulsory* and formal exchange of their respective nationals, an already accomplished fact for nearly all the Greek minorities that had formerly lived in Turkey. It is interesting to note that what is today often called "transfer" or other terms such as "repatriation", "relocation", "resettlement", etc. was simply and more fittingly described in the Convention as an "exchange of populations" between Greece and Turkey.

Article 1 of the Convention provided as follows:

> As from the 1st May, 1923, there shall take place a *compulsory* exchange of Turkish nationals of the Greek Orthodox religion established in Turkish territory, and of Greek nationals of the Moslem religion established in Greek territory (emphasis added).
>
> These persons shall not return to live in Turkey or Greece respectively without the authorisation of the Turkish Government or of the Greek Government respectively.

The population exchange provided for in Article 1 did not apply to the Greek inhabitants of Constantinople nor to the Moslem inhabitants of Western Thrace. The exchange was made retroactive (by Article 3 of the Lausanne Convention) to a period ten years earlier (October 18, 1912) to include those who had already left the Greek and Turkish territories. It is significant that both Turks and Greeks lost the nationality of the country they left and acquired that of the country of their destination (under Article 7 of the Convention). As a pioneer agreement involving a large-scale population exchange between warring enemies, the Lausanne Convention still serves as a model today under international law of what ought to have been done in the case of the Arab-Jewish population exchange which began during Israel's War of Independence between the end of November 1947 and July 1949 and what may need to be done in the future between Israel and the neighbouring Arab states.

The person who initiated the idea for the exchange of populations between Greece and Turkey was Fridtjof Nansen, the Norwegian statesman and humanitarian who had earlier achieved international fame as an Arctic explorer trying to reach the North Pole. Appointed in 1921 as High Commissioner for Refugees on behalf of the League of Nations, he received the Nobel Peace Prize the following year for the work he did to help refugees, as well as for his previous service to famine-stricken Russia and aiding the repatriation of World War I prisoners. The exchange of populations was executed under the supervision of a Mixed Commission of seven members, two from each side and three neutral members chosen by the Council of the League of Nations from among nationals of Powers which did not take part in the war of 1914-1918. The Commission was always under neutral chairmanship. The numbers involved in the intermigration were quite high for the period. Approximately 1.5 million Greeks living in Asia Minor were repatriated to Greece and approximately 800,000 Turks (Moslems) living in Greece and Bulgaria were resettled in Turkey.[3]

The Palestine Royal Commission Report, which has been hailed as the most important and impressive document produced in the Mandate period, lavished great praise on the population exchange between Greece and Turkey, calling it an act of high statesmanship and a bold decision for the sake of peace. It saw the whole operation of removing the Greek minority from Turkey and the Turkish minority from Greece as the "clean cut out [of an] ulcer" that had been a "constant irritant". It recommended the same surgical procedure to be carried out in Palestine:[4]

---

[3] See separate articles on Greece and Turkey in the *Columbia Encyclopedia* (6th edition), edited by Paul Lagasse, Columbia University Press (2000), p. 1179 and p. 2903. The numbers reported in the Palestine Royal Commission Report of 1937 were lower: 1,300,000 Greeks and 400,000 Turks.

[4] Palestine Royal Commission Report, reproduced in *The Rise of Israel*, Vol. 24, Document 2, pp. 410-11.

> If as a result, it is clear that a substantial amount of land could be made available for the re-settlement of Arabs living in the Jewish area, the most strenuous efforts should be made to obtain *an agreement for the exchange of land and population.* The provision of new land would bring the position in Palestine and Transjordan closer to what it was in 1923 in Turkey and Greece, and the number of people involved would be very much smaller. *In view of the present antagonism between the races and of the manifest advantage to both of them of reducing the opportunities of future friction to the utmost*, it is to be hoped that the Arab and the Jewish leaders might show the *same high statesmanship* as that of the Turks and the Greeks and make *the same bold decision for the sake of peace* (emphasis added).

The Peel Commission, as the Palestine Royal Commission was generally known, came, after serious study, to the inevitable and logical conclusion that a Jewish State could only be realistically established – at the time of its Report dated June 22, 1937 – if the large number of Arabs then living in the area of the projected Jewish State were transferred to the area of the projected Arab State. An agreement would be made for this purpose between the parties concerned. The transfer of the Arab population was subject to the condition that a substantial amount of land could be made available for the re-settlement of Arabs living in the Jewish area to be granted independence. To this end, the Peel Commission looked to Transjordan, Beersheba and the Jordan Valley as areas where "the execution of large-scale plans for irrigation, water-storage and development would make provision for a much larger population than exists there at the present time."[5] It recommended that as a last resort the exchange of land and population between the two states be made *compulsory*, if it could not be done on a voluntary basis. It suggested the transfer of about 225,000 Arabs from the Jewish to the Arab State. The number of Jews to be transferred from the area designated for Arab independence, some 1,250, was insignificant.

The official reaction of the British Government to the Arab transfer proposal was given by the Colonial Secretary, William Ormsby-Gore (Lord Harlech), when he appeared before the Permanent Mandates Commission at a meeting held on August 13, 1937. He said that the Mandatory Power did not accept the proposal for compulsory transfer contained in the report of the Royal Commission, but did approve voluntary transfer. He gave the following answer to a question put to him on the subject by Mlle. Valentine Dannevig of Norway, a member of the Permanent Mandates Commission from 1928-1940:[6]

> Mlle. Dannevig: Was there any hope that Arabs would wish to leave

[5] *Ibid.*, p. 411.

[6] Minutes of 32nd (Extraordinary) Session Held at Geneva from July 30th to August 18th 1937. Reprinted in *The Rise of Israel*, Vol. 25, Document 4, p. 271.

> the Jewish State, where they would have a better chance of livelihood than as settlers in a poor country, which would have to be developed with all the toil and difficulty which fell to the lot of settlers in a new country?
>
> Mr. Ormsby-Gore: As to transfer, [he] quite agreed that, if it were a case of moving the Arabs long distances to a strange country, transfer would indeed be difficult. *But these people had not hitherto regarded themselves as "Palestinians"* (quotation marks in the original), *but as part of Syria as a whole, as part of the Arab world. They would be going literally only a comparatively few miles away to a people with the same language, the same civilization, the same religion; and therefore the problem of transfer geographically and practically was easier even than the interchanges of Greeks and Turks between Asia Minor and the Balkans.* He was quite satisfied that not all the Arabs would wish to leave the Jewish State: some would realize that they would have opportunities in the Jewish State. But that some would want to leave on grounds of sentiment, he equally had no doubt; and if homesteads were provided and land was prepared for their reception not too far from their existing homes, he was confident that many would make use of that opportunity. *It would be one of the first duties of the Mandatory Power, if the League approved of its proceeding with that plan, to make an intensive survey of Transjordan with a view to ascertaining how much it would cost, and where such homesteads could be provided* (emphasis added).

The British Government in November 1938 shelved the partition plan of the Peel Commission dividing Palestine into two states, Jewish and Arab, after the four-member Woodhead Commission, officially called the Palestine Partition Commission, under Sir John Woodhead investigated the technical feasibility of that plan and found it could not recommend any boundaries "which will afford a reasonable prospect of the eventual establishment of self-supporting Arab and Jewish States." The shelving of the Peel Partition Plan also meant the end of the proposed Arab transfer plan that was an integral part of it.

However, new political support for the idea of Arab population transfer arose in 1944 from a surprising quarter – the British Labour Party, while it was part of the Churchill Coalition Cabinet, a year before it was to form the next British Government in late July 1945. Without consulting any representatives of the Labour Zionist Movement and on his own initiative, Hugh Dalton, then considered the most likely choice for Foreign Secretary in a strictly Labour Government (though in fact he never assumed that position), drafted a proposal on Palestine in January of that year which advocated the mass immigration of Jews accompanied by the mass emigration of Arabs. His proposal was accepted by the National Executive Committee of the British Labour Party and then presented as a resolution to the Annual Conference held in December of the same year in London, where it was duly adopted as part of the party election platform without any general protest. The resolution, introduced by Deputy Prime Minister (in Churchill's War Cabinet) and leader of the Labour Party, shortly-to-be Prime Minister, Clement Richard Attlee, read as follows:[7]

> Palestine. Here we are halted halfway, irresolute between conflicting policies. But there is surely neither hope nor meaning in a Jewish National Home unless we are prepared to let the Jews, if they wish, enter this tiny land in *such numbers as to become a majority*. There was a strong case for this before the War. There is an irresistible case now, after the unspeakable atrocities of the cold and calculated German Nazi plan to kill all Jews in Europe. Here, too, in Palestine surely is a case on human grounds to promote a stable settlement, for *transfer of population. Let the Arabs be encouraged to move out as the Jews move in.* Let them be compensated handsomely for their land, and their settlement elsewhere be carefully organized and generously financed. The Arabs have many wide territories of their own; they must not claim to exclude the Jews from this small area of Palestine, less than the size of Wales. *Indeed, we should re-examine also the possibility of extending the present Palestinian boundaries, by agreement with Egypt, Syria or Transjordan.* Moreover, we should seek to win the full sympathy and support both of the American and Russian Governments for the execution of this Palestinian Policy (italics supplied in Professor Joseph Gorny's extract of the Labour Party Resolution).

The above resolution on Palestine committed the Labour Party to supporting Zionist aspirations, by opening the doors of Palestine – that were to be closed after 1944 under the illegal 1939 MacDonald White Paper – to greatly increased Jewish immigration and to the establishment of a Jewish State. The Labour Party and its leader not only approved a transfer of the Arab population from Palestine to other "many wide territories of their own", but even considered extending the boundaries of Palestine, especially to adjacent Transjordan and possibly to parts of Egypt and Syria. In this regard, the historian Martin Gilbert[8] has mentioned that Attlee proposed, at a luncheon meeting held at Chequers on October 25, 1943, hosted by Prime Minister Churchill and attended by Weizmann, that "something should be done" about allowing the Jews to settle in Transjordan. Churchill commented that Attlee's proposal "was a good idea" and, later on in their conversation, added that both the Negev and Transjordan

---

[7] Joseph Gorny, *The British Labour Movement and Zionism, 1917-1948*, published by Frank Cass and Co., Ltd., London (1983), pp. 178-179.

[8] Martin Gilbert, *Churchill & The Jews*, Simon & Schuster UK Ltd, Pocket Books, p. 204. See also: "Weizmann's Report of the Prime Minister's Luncheon Party", found in *The Letters and Papers of Chaim Weizmann,* Vol. II, Series B, editor Barnet Litvinoff, Transaction Books (1984), Paper No. 71, October 25, 1943, p. 523 ff.

"might be part of the future Jewish State".[9] Churchill's opinion on Transjordan seems to have been an amazing turnabout from the position he had adopted two decades earlier (1921-1922) when, as Colonial Secretary, he initiated the separation of this territory from the Jewish National Home. In the case of Attlee, the latter completely reversed all the pro-Zionist sentiments he had espoused in his talk with Weizmann at the aforementioned luncheon gathering, upon becoming Prime Minister in July 1945.

It might have been expected that the Labour Party Resolution, "the most explicitly pro-Zionist pronouncement by any British political body since the Balfour Declaration", according to Professor Joseph Gorny, would have brought great satisfaction to the Labour Zionist leaders, but serious reservations were immediately expressed when they first learnt about its content. Moshe Sharett (then Moshe Shertok) explained why at a meeting of the Mapai Central Committee (May 8, 1944):[10]

> *We had grave doubts on the transfer issue, which were not necessarily aroused by the content of this clause.* When I came to England, this was one of the issues which was being broached. It was revived with great vigour, not on Jewish initiative but through non-Jewish logic. They said: one of two things – either nothing can be done, or, if it can, *if Palestine is to be given to the Jews, it must be given wholly; in that case the Arabs must be removed.* This theory reached us from various sources. One of these was [Hugh] Dalton and [Philip John] Noel-Baker. I had an argument on this question with Noel-Baker… he said, why can't Arabs be transferred out of Palestine? We will give them one hundred million pounds to settle elsewhere etc. *I said that this would be possible only in the final stage. It could not be the beginning of the solution or a precondition.* If one links the overall solution to transfer of Arabs, then this transfer becomes the *conditio sine qua non.* In other words, without transfer of Arabs there is no absorptive capacity. Such a transfer would be an almost impossible task, but it would be easy to arrive at the conclusion that the country has no absorptive capacity and that policy cannot be changed, and that would be the outcome (emphasis added).

As appears from the foregoing quotation, Sharett did not actually oppose in principle the transfer of Arabs out of Palestine. He thought that transfer, being a mere question of correct timing, was a possibility that could come about by agreement only in the final stage of the solution of the Palestine question after the establishment of a Jewish State. This was also his actual view on the subject a year before Dalton drafted his proposal, when he told a Zionist Executive meeting held in London on January 16, 1943 in regard to the Philby

[9] Gilbert, *op. cit.*, p. 205.

[10] Gorny, *op. cit.*, pp. 181-182.

Plan (discussed immediately below), as recorded in the short minutes of the meeting:[11]

> Mr. Shertok said that transfer could only come by agreement. He did not envisage prior agreement to large-scale Jewish immigration, or to the creation of a Jewish State, though they would work for such an agreement. British experts were of opinion that the Arabs would acquiesce to a large Yishuv [the Jewish community in Mandated Palestine] and to a Jewish State after its establishment; it was then that transfer might become a possibility; but he did not think the two things would come about simultaneously.

The Labour Zionist leaders (principally Moshe Sharrett and Berl Locker, then political adviser to the Zionist Executive in London), who did not feel comfortable with the passage of so pro-Zionist a resolution by the British Labour Party, soon discovered that their concern was premature and completely unnecessary. After coming to power in the July 1945 election, the British Labour Government, under Prime Minister Attlee and Foreign Secretary Ernest Bevin, repudiated all the promises the Labour Party had made to the Jewish People in the election campaign with regard to the Jewish National Home, specifically, the party's promise to allow Jews to enter Palestine "in such numbers as to become a majority" while simultaneously encouraging the Arabs "to move out as the Jews move in", thus paving the way for a Jewish State. Rather than facilitate Jewish immigration to Palestine, including Transjordan, Attlee and Bevin adopted a one-sided pro-Arab policy and maliciously barred the entry of 100,000 Jewish Holocaust survivors who were then languishing in Displaced Persons camps in the British and American zones of defeated Germany. The Labour Party promise of establishing a Jewish State was shelved. There would be no further talk about the 1944 Labour Party Resolution and the cogent argument it had advanced for transferring the Arab population out of Palestine. Instead, the new Labour Government decided to adhere to the infamous and illegal 1939 White Paper adopted by the pre-war Conservative Government of Neville Chamberlain. Thus Labour's sympathy and identification with the sufferings of the Jewish People in the Holocaust and with Zionist aspirations, which Professor Gorny cites as the motivation for the Labour Party Resolution, proved to be no more than a mirage or ephemeral in nature.

It is very instructive to note that the plan to move Arabs out of Palestine to various Arab states was endorsed by three British officials who were considered among the most fervent supporters of the Arab cause. These were T.E. Lawrence, a close friend and adviser to Emir Feisal ibn Hussein during the years 1916-1921, Gertrude Bell, Oriental scholar and Secretary to the High Commissioner of Iraq, 1917-1920 and especially Harry St. John Bridger Philby,

[11] *The Rise of Israel*, Vol. 32, Document 20, p. 170.

an Arabic-Islamic scholar and author who was a lifetime friend and adviser of the Wahhabi leader of the ultra-orthodox Sunni Muslim movement, Abdul-Aziz Ibn Saud. The latter became the ruler of Nejd (or Najd) in central Arabia in 1902 upon the capture of Riyadh. He later took the title of Sultan of Nejd and its Dependencies 1921-1931, King of the Hedjaz since 1926, and finally King of Saudi Arabia, 1932-1953, a span of over 50 years. In 1932, the regions of Hedjaz, Nejd and oil-rich Al-Hasa (in the eastern part of the country) were combined to form the Kingdom of Saudi Arabia. The region of Asir on the Arabian coast of the Red Sea, between Yemen and the Hedjaz, was annexed a year later.

The approval of T.E. Lawrence and Gertrude Bell for a plan of Arab emigration from Palestine to Egypt, Syria and Mesopotamia was noted in the minutes of a meeting on March 21, 1919, of the British delegation to the Paris Peace Conference held to discuss the Zionist proposals presented by Chaim Weizmann to the Conference on February 27, 1919.[12]

As for St. John Philby, a deeply-committed advocate of the Arabian cause led by Ibn Saud, who held the opinion that "the Jews have not a shadow of legal or historical right to go to Palestine",[13] he nevertheless proposed a plan to Weizmann and Lewis Bernstein Namier, Professor of Modern History at Manchester University, on September 28, 1939, at a luncheon meeting at London's Athenaeum to effect a settlement of outstanding Jewish-Arab issues over Palestine involving a *quid pro quo* that he believed would be beneficial to both sides. The plan drew a positive reaction from Weizmann and Namier. The three met again at the same place a week later, on October 6, 1939, this time joined by Moshe Sharett and Philby's son, Kim Philby, who later achieved notoriety as a Soviet spy. According to St. John Philby's account given in his book *Arabian Jubilee*[14], the plan he conceived won "the cordial approval of both Dr. Weizmann and Dr. Moshe Shertok". Philby's account is corroborated by no less a distinguished figure than the historian Professor Namier, who kept a record of the discussions that took place on October 6, 1939 between Philby, Weizmann, Sharett and himself. Namier recorded Philby's proposal at the discussion:[15]

> Philby's idea was that Western Palestine should be handed over completely to the Jews, clear of the Arab population except for a 'Vatican City' in the old city of Jerusalem. In return the Jews should try

---

[12] *Ibid.*, Vol. 10, Document 60, p. 224.

[13] H.STJ.B. Philby, *Arabian Jubilee*, Robert Hale Limited, London (1952), p. 219.

[14] This name celebrated the fifty years of absolute rule of the Wahhabi monarch in Arabia.

[15] *The Letters and Papers of Chaim Weizmann* (1984), Volume II, Series B, Document 42 "Plan for Cooperation with Ibn Saud", London, October 6, 1939, pp. 371-373.

> to secure for the Arabs national unity and independence as, according to him, was promised in the McMahon-Hussein Correspondence; moreover, extensive financial help should be given to the Arabs by the Jews. Such unity could be achieved under Ibn Saud alone. Philby envisages in the first place the handing over to Saudi Arabia of Syria and various small states on the Red Sea [a reference to Yemen and adjoining territories in South Arabia]... Philby thought that if all Arab states were granted full independence, a proper settlement would be reached.

Professor Namier also recorded the reactions of both Weizmann and Sharett to the Philby Plan:

> Dr. Weizmann said that when in America he expected to see President Roosevelt and to gain his support for some big scheme of such a character... Philby was quite frank about the financial difficulties of Ibn Saud, increased as they are by the stoppage of pilgrimages [to Mecca] during the war. He suggested the sum of £20,000,000 for Ibn Saud in case the scheme was carried out in full. Shertok [Sharett] suggested that part at least of that sum should be used for development in connection with the transfer of the Palestine Arabs to other Arab countries... Philby entirely agreed that such a subsidy would have to be distributed over a number of years, and paid, to a very large extent, in the form of goods.

The following agreement was reached with the Zionist leaders, as recounted by Philby in his book:[16]

> They agreed to use all their influence with the British and American Governments with a view to their accepting and implementing the pact, while I was authorized to inform Ibn Saud of its provisions and to endeavour to secure his goodwill in anticipation of the *démarche* to be made in due course by the two Governments concerned.

St. John Philby left England to return to Arabia where he met Ibn Saud on January 8, 1940 at Riyadh, the capital city of Saudi Arabia, and communicated the details of his plan. The essence of the plan was later divulged to Prime Minister Churchill on November 3, 1941 by his private secretary, John Miller Martin, after a meeting he had held with St. John Philby at Weizmann's behest. Martin's note to Churchill explained the plan as follows:[17]

---

[16] Philby, *op. cit.*, p. 213.

[17] *The Rise of Israel*, Vol. 32, Document 19, p. 159.

> Dr. Weizmann asked me to see Mr. St. John Philby, as the latter could give information regarding Ibn Saud's attitude towards the Palestine question of which Dr. Weizmann wished you to know in view of your remarks before his departure for the United States this summer.
>
> I saw Mr. Philby today. He explained that he felt that *there was no hope of ever settling the Palestine question on the lines of persuading Jews and Arabs to live happily together in one State and he had therefore come to the conclusion that the only solution was to give the Jews the whole of Palestine* (i.e., west of the Jordan). He returned to Arabia shortly after the outbreak of war and early in 1940 discussed the matter with *Ibn Saud. The latter was ready to agree to give Palestine to the Jews on condition that as quid pro quo he received control over all the remaining Arab countries.* It would also be part of the bargain that the Zionists should pay him a subvention of several million pounds (probably partly in kind, the products of Palestine industry), to be applied, in part, to financing a transfer of Arab population from the Jewish State. On this point Mr. Philby suggested that the transfer would be substantially reduced if the Jews could be persuaded to accept the excision of part of northern Palestine (containing some quarter of a million Arabs), which would naturally go with Syria: they might be compensated if the Egyptians would agree to give up Sinai.
>
> *Asked about the attitude of the other Arab countries, Mr. Philby said he thought they would readily accept a settlement under Wahhabi suzerainty. Abdullah, in Trans-Jordan, was of course an exception*; but, in spite of his record of loyalty, his opposition would have to be overcome. Trans-Jordan would naturally be embodied in the territories under direct Saudi-Arabian administration, while Syria and Iraq would probably retain their separate Governments, possibly under Ibn Saud's sons. Special arrangements would be required as regards Jerusalem.
>
> *Ibn Saud had been particularly anxious that the matter should not be publicly discussed* and had rebuked Mr. Philby for mentioning it (after their conversation) to one of his principal Ministers (emphasis added).

Weizmann kept his promise to Philby, that he would approach the British and American Governments to try to obtain their acceptance of his plan. According to Philby, who, during 1939, had "many contacts" with Weizmann, the latter discussed the idea with Churchill on December 17, 1939 while he was serving as the First Lord of the Admiralty in the Chamberlain War Cabinet.[18] However, there is no record of their discussion of the Philby plan in Weizmann's published letters and papers, nor in his autobiography *Trial and*

[18] Philby, *op. cit.*, pp. 208, 211.

*Error*,[19] possibly to keep the whole matter strictly secret, in accordance with Ibn Saud's admonition to St. John Philby.

Weizmann then departed to the United States for three months, where he met President Roosevelt for the first time on February 8, 1940 in the presence of Lord Lothian (Philip Henry Kerr), British Ambassador to the U.S. (1939-40) and former Private Secretary to David Lloyd George (1916-21). There is no doubt that Weizmann had the Arab transfer plan in mind as one of the topics to be discussed with Roosevelt, for only two days before the audience with the President, he dispatched a letter to Philby in Jidda to inquire if he was proceeding further with the proposal they had talked about on October 6, 1939. The details of the initial Weizmann-Roosevelt conversation concerning the plan to move the Arabs out of Palestine are, as in the case of the earlier Churchill interview, not specifically recorded in Weizmann's letters and papers. However, despite Weizmann's denial, there is a definite allusion to the Churchill plan in the following exchange of remarks between the American President and Weizmann:[20]

> The President asked: 'What about the Arabs? Can't that be settled with a little *baksheesh*?' Dr. Weizmann said it wasn't as simple as all that. Of course *they would compensate the Arabs in a reasonable way for anything they got, but there were other factors appertaining to a settlement.* One result of the disturbances had been, he thought, to bring much nearer the possibility of an arrangement with their Arab neighbours: despite a campaign of violence conducted under the most favourable auspices, the latter had completely failed in their efforts to dislodge the Jews. That was a fact which was likely to have a fundamental effect on future relations with the Arabs. Already there were signs – he was not going to exaggerate them, but they were unmistakable – that *the Arabs* were realising this failure, and *were casting around to see if they could not arrive at some modus vivendi* (emphasis added)....

The fact that Weizmann in his conversation with Roosevelt referred to a possible settlement with the Arabs, under which the Jews would compensate them for anything they got, is an indication that he did indeed discuss the Philby Plan with President Roosevelt. In this context, it should be noted that Philby, Namier, Sharett and Weizmann all used the word "settlement" in referring to the Philby Plan.

Among the Zionist leaders in London with whom Philby discussed his plan was, as already noted, Professor Namier, then serving as the political adviser

[19] C. Weizmann, *Trial and Error, the Autobiography of Chaim Weizmann*, Harper & Brothers, New York, p. 418.

[20] *The Letters and Papers of Chaim Weizmann*, (1984) Volume II, Series B, Document 46 "Roosevelt's Optimism", p. 394.

to the Jewish Agency Executive. He worked closely with Weizmann and was a convinced proponent of the Philby Plan. He was especially attracted by the idea of Arab transfer from Western Palestine to other Arab countries to secure the Jewish State. He made the following remarks to several members of the Zionist Executive at a meeting in London on January 16, 1943 convened to discuss the Philby scheme and the constitution of the Jewish State, as recorded in the minutes of that meeting:[21]

> …now that the Arabs were losing their nuisance value, should they not press for a statement by the Prime Minister and President Roosevelt on the lines of the Philby Scheme?…
>
> Professor Namier said he assumed that what they wanted was clear in everybody's mind: it was Palestine as a Jewish State. The question was what to do with the Arabs, and the interim period. There were, of course, many matters of detail; what was fundamental was to make room for mass immigration and provide facilities for the building up of a State….
>
> Professor Namier said he was in favour of establishing a Jewish State immediately…
>
> Professor Namier said that to him transfer was the most essential thing. He realized the difficulties, and that it would be more difficult to move peasants than townspeople…. the whole question of transfer would be discussed on a much larger scale after the war. [Eduard] Benes [who headed a provisional Czechoslovakian Government-in-Exile in London] told him that the question of transfer was gaining ground amongst statesmen here [in London].

At a meeting held in Washington on January 19, 1943 with Wallace Murray, the anti-Zionist Head of the Near East Division of the U.S. State Department (1929-1945) and other officials to discuss the Palestine question and its solution with the possible aid of Ibn Saud, Weizmann informed the Americans of what Churchill had told him, as recounted by Dr. Nahum Goldmann who was present at the meeting:[22]

> …Dr. Weizmann used this opportunity to tell them about Churchill's idea, – that Churchill will see us through, – and he also mentioned the cable received from Churchill on the anniversary of the Balfour Declaration which clearly indicates that the Prime Minister considers

[21] *The Rise of Israel*, Volume 32, Document 20, pp. 166-170.

[22] *The Rise of Israel,* Vol. 32, Document 22, p. 176 ff. The heading of this document is: Conversations with State Department Officials as related by Dr. Nahum Goldmann to Meyer W. Weisgal, Stenographically recorded by BJS Wardman, Park Hotel, Washington, January 19, 1943.

> the present position as unsatisfactory; that *Churchill had said he had a plan based on Ibn Saoud*, and Weizmann felt it would be a very good idea, but we could not do anything about it unless the United States and Britain would act as intermediaries and support the Zionist policy before the Arab world… (emphasis added)

To a question posed by Mr. Murray of what Dr. Weizmann thought of exploring the possibilities of the Churchill Plan with Ibn Saud, Dr. Weizmann replied:

> He would be delighted to do so and that he had said the same thing to Churchill; that he wanted to do it. Murray interjected that Philby always over-estimated his influence with Ibn Saoud. Dr. Weizmann continued that if he would take the initiative, it would have to be done after the United States and Great Britain paved the way for such conversations.
>
> Murray, turning to [Nahum] Goldmann, said, "What is your feeling about this?" Goldmann replied that he fully agreed with Dr. Weizmann and stressed the necessity of creating, as a prerequisite, a sympathetic atmosphere by the United States and Great Britain. Otherwise, he though the mission would be too difficult to carry through… Before the Zionists go to see him, he [Ibn Saud], must know that this country and Great Britain want this mission to be a success.

To Paul Alling, a State Department official who also participated in the foregoing discussions, Weizmann, in reply to a question from him concerning the basis of an understanding with Ibn Saud, stated:[23]

> …if Ibn Saud were to be recognized as overlord of the Arab world, he must recognize that Palestine is the home of the Jewish People. But then, Dr. Weizmann repeated again, the condition is that the United States and Great Britain must pave the way for such a mission. Alling said, "Would you be willing to take it up with your Government?" and Dr. Weizmann said, "I would be happy to do it, but I think it would be more effective if you, the United States, would take it up first." It was indicated that they might explore the situation.

In summing up the discussion with Wallace Murray and Paul Alling, Weizmann noted:[24]

---

[23] *Ibid.*, pp. 176 ff.

[24] *Ibid.*, p. 178.

> …the only concrete proposal was the idea about Ibn Saoud. "We would like to explore it," he said, "but it is necessary for you to pave the way with Great Britain." Dr. Weizmann also said that he would take it up with the President with whom he had already talked about rubber and Palestine, and it would be very helpful if Mr. Murray and his colleagues would explore the situation; also that we had given him just an outline; that we should have to give more details and we shall certainly meet again when Mr. Shertok [Sharett] comes here.

The plan Churchill had in mind, mentioned by Weizmann in his discussions with Murray and Alling, had been conveyed to Weizmann at a meeting at 10 Downing Street on March 12, 1941. Churchill explained that a settlement regarding Palestine could possibly be reached with Ibn Saud, then the most powerful Arab leader in the world, to take effect once the war was over. Under Churchill's plan, Ibn Saud would become "the Lord of the Arab countries – the boss of bosses", provided he settled with Weizmann. It would then be up to Weizmann to obtain the best conditions. In light of Weizmann's previous contacts with St. John Philby, these conditions could only mean that Palestine, west of the Jordan, would be established as a Jewish State, in conjunction with the transfer of the Arab population to other Arab states. In his autobiography,[25] Weizmann linked Churchill's plan to that of Philby, saying they "fitted together" or coincided with one another. He also stated in his autobiography that he only learnt of the Philby plan "a few months before" his meeting with Churchill which Weizmann said took place on March 11, 1942, but which actually occurred on March 12, 1941, a year and a day earlier. This is confirmed by a letter dated March 15, 1941 which Weizmann wrote to his close friend, the industrialist Sigmund Gestetner, containing a record of Churchill's reaction when he and Weizmann met on March 12, 1941.[26] This chronological misstating of events by Weizmann surprised St. John Philby, who commented about Weizmann's memory lapse in his book *Arabian Jubilee*:[27]

> …there are several indisputable facts within my knowledge, to say nothing of their being on record in my diaries, which suggest that, perhaps for mere convenience of handling, he has chosen to group them [i.e., these indisputable facts] round the dramatic incident of his interview with Mr. Churchill in March 1942 [Philby here reproduces Weizmann's error of the date of his meeting with Churchill].

---

[25] Weizmann, *Trial And Error, The Autobiography of Chaim Weizmann*, pp. 427-433.

[26] *The Letters and Papers of Chaim Weizmann*, Vol XX, Series A, editor Michael J. Cohen, Letter No. 129, To Sigmund Gestetner, London, March 15, 1941, p. 125. See also Gilbert, *op. cit.* p. 182.

[27] Philby, *op. cit.*, p. 207-208.

It appears from St. John Philby's account that for reasons of his own, Weizmann, because of embarrassment, reticence or outright deception, preferred in 1949, when his autobiography was published, to conceal his "cordial approval"[28] of the Philby Plan, as Philby termed it, a plan which Weizmann had linked to the Churchill Plan. By 1949, it was no longer politically correct to advocate the transfer of people from one country to another in light of the experience that befell the Jews of Europe at the hands of the Nazi German authorities. Weizmann's claim that he was "rather dazed" when Churchill mentioned his own plan of Arab transfer to him at their meeting on March 12, 1941, elicited a reproving response from Philby:[29]

> ...Dr. Weizmann's description of the incident [episode] in question is somewhat disingenuous, and so hedged in by reticences that one may wonder whether it was really worth while referring to the matter at all, unless the whole story could be told, if only to remove the aura of mystery that now shrouds a perfectly straightforward proposition which eventually came to nothing.

In comparing the separate accounts of the Philby/Churchill plans, as related by Weizmann and Philby respectively, it certainly seems that Weizmann evaded the truth of the matter, while Philby's account was accurate and reliable, as demonstrated by the documentary record adduced above. This is further confirmed in a note of a conversation between Weizmann and Colonial Secretary Lord Moyne (Walter Edward Guinness), dated July 28, 1941, on record at the Weizmann Archives (Rehovot, Israel). During this meeting, Weizmann expressed his opinion of the Philby scheme:[30]

> Dr. Weizmann told [Lord Moyne] what the Prime Minister [Churchill] said to him before his departure to the States [March 12, 1941]. Lord Moyne said that Ibn Saud was a fine man, but he had written some letters which were hostile to Zionist aspirations in Palestine. Dr. Weizmann replied that such an attitude was meant for public consumption; he thought Ibn Saud was a man with whom discussion was possible. He then told Lord Moyne of their talks with Philby [an apparent reference to the September-October 1939 talks between Weizmann, Sharett, Namier and Philby]. He told Lord Moyne that he believed that the Jews would be willing to advance between fifteen and twenty million pounds to Ibn Saud for development purposes. Lord Moyne had said that some Arabs would

[28] Philby, *op. cit.*, p. 213.

[29] Philby, *op. cit.*, p. 206.

[30] *The Rise of Israel*, Vol. 32, Document 14, p. 127: Note of an Interview with Lord Moyne, July 28, 1941.

> have to be transferred, and wondered whether this could be done without bloodshed. Dr. Weizmann said that it could be done if Britain and America talked frankly to the Arabs; they should tell them that they had received 97 cents to the dollar, and that that ought to satisfy them. Lord Moyne said that if transfer were to take place, he would like it to be done without friction.

There appears to be no doubt from the foregoing note of the Weizmann-Lord Moyne discussion read in conjunction with Namier's report of Weizmann's previous meetings with Philby in September-October 1939 and Weizmann's own letter to Gestetner of March 15, 1941, and finally his discussions with State Department officials in 1943, including Sumner Welles (see *infra*), that Weizmann viewed the Philby Plan as a viable proposition that he wholeheartedly supported and believed feasible if the American and British governments jointly exercised their influence to persuade King Ibn Saud to accept it. It also appears from the foregoing documentary record that Weizmann was well acquainted with the details of the Philby Plan, contrary to what he alleged in his autobiography, that he had known about the Philby Plan only "a few months before" his talk with Churchill in March "1942" and was "rather dazed" by it.

That a similarity did exist between the Churchill plan and the Philby Plan, as Weizmann correctly inferred, can be deduced from the fact that Churchill was well aware of the Philby Plan before he discussed his own with Weizmann, having, as already noted, been told about the earlier Philby Plan by Weizmann himself on December 17, 1939 (according to Philby's account). Then, as also already noted, Philby himself met with Churchill's private secretary, John Miller Martin, on November 3, 1941 to provide Churchill with full details of his plan. The similarity of the two plans meant that Churchill apparently approved the idea of Arab transfer in order to establish a Jewish State, if a settlement could be worked out with Ibn Saud, even though there exists no express written record of that specific provision of his plan. However, the fact that Churchill had committed himself[31] to Weizmann to securing the establishment of a future Jewish State after the war ended necessarily implied the transfer of the Arab population from Palestine as an ancillary feature of the plan, coupled with the prospect of increased Jewish immigration. In this regard, Weizmann, who once warned[32] against the idea of mass Jewish immigration into Palestine as harmful to Zionism, now thought otherwise. He suggested in 1941 that at least three million Jews should be absorbed comparatively quickly into Palestine, an idea rejected by Prime Minister Churchill and Colonial Secretary Lord Moyne as

---

[31] Gilbert, *op. cit.*, pp. 236-238; 247.

[32] *The Letters and Papers of Chaim Weizmann,* Volume I, Series B, Editor, Barnet Litvinoff, Transaction Books (1983), Document 38, Manchester, December 9, 1917, Speech at Public Meeting, p. 160 ff.

impractical.[33]

To insure large-scale Jewish immigration, especially in light of the drastically changed circumstances of European Jewry, Weizmann, now believed that the Jews needed to exercise control over their own immigration to Palestine. This was a sharp departure from what he had thought in 1921 when he turned down Colonial Secretary Churchill's proposal to have such immigration placed under the complete control of the Zionist Organization and even that it be temporarily restricted.[34] Only with greatly increased Jewish immigration, he correctly reasoned, would Jews be able to achieve their freedom and self-government, in a state of their own, while ceasing to be a minority dependent on the will and pleasure of other nations. Further, he felt that if any Arabs did not wish to remain in a Jewish State, "every facility will be given to them for transfer to one of the many and vast Arab countries."[35]

At another meeting in the State Department on January 26, 1943 with Sumner Welles, the Undersecretary of State and a close personal friend of President Roosevelt, Weizmann covered the same range of questions as he did in his meeting with Wallace Murray and Paul Alling on January 19th. When the subject got around to Ibn Saud, Weizmann said that the policy of a Jewish Palestine would be accepted by the Arabs, excluding some who would not like it, provided "the Arabs are told that the United Nations[36] considered this policy just, and that the United Nations will see that it is carried out, and will also see that the rights of the Arabs will not be trodden upon". Weizmann also told Welles:[37]

> The position in Palestine has become serious because of incessant propaganda to which Palestine was subjected for years by the communists, nazis and fascists, and by anti-Semites of all kinds. The British have been rather apologetic and vacillating. I am sure that if things had been handled firmly in the first few years, the march of

[33] Gilbert, *op. cit.*, p. 184.

[34] See: M. Mossek, *Palestine Immigration Policy under Sir Herbert Samuel, British, Zionist and Arab Attitudes,* Frank Cass and Company Ltd. (1978), pp. 43-44.

[35] "Memorandum of Chaim Weizmann Summarizing the Proposals put forward at a meeting held at New Court (London) on September 9, 1941". In attendance besides Weizmann were David Ben-Gurion, Selig Brodetsky, Lewis B. Namier, Berl Locker, Simon Marks, Leonard J. Stein and Harry Sacher. *The Letters and Papers of Chaim Weizmann,* Volume XX, Series A, Editor Michael J. Cohen, Transaction Books (1979), Document 186. Memorandum dated September 9, 1941, pp. 200-203.

[36] The term "United Nations" was first used by President Roosevelt in 1941 as a collective name to denote the twenty-six states that were waging war against the Axis Powers headed by Germany, Italy and Japan.

[37] *The Rise of Israel*, Volume 32, Document 23, Appendix IV, p. 181.

> events would have been different. That had not been done. Proper conditions must be created now.

At this meeting, Welles proposed to Weizmann that he meet with President Roosevelt to convey his views to him, an invitation which Weizmann gladly accepted on the spot.

Weizmann relayed a written report of what he had told high-ranking officials of the U.S. State Department concerned with the Palestine question to Britain's ambassador in Washington, Viscount Halifax (Edward Frederick Lindley Wood), previously Neville Chamberlain's Foreign Secretary (1938-1940). He in turn dispatched Weizmann's report to Anthony Eden (subsequently Lord Avon), then serving as the Foreign Minister in Churchill's coalition government with the Labour Party. Eden, worried by the statements Weizmann had made, sent off a touchy note (March 3, 1943) to Prime Minister Churchill to express his concern:[38]

> Dr. Weizmann told the Ambassador [Lord Halifax] that he had opened his conversation with the State Department by making it clear that he was not proposing to say anything to the United States Government that he did not repeat to H.M. Government. In accordance with this undertaking, he has provided records of meetings which took place on the 19th January with representatives of the Middle Eastern Section of the State Department, and on the 26th January with Sumner Welles.
>
> From these records, which I enclose, you will see that *Dr. Weizmann spoke of "the Prime Minister's plan" to use Ibn Saud to bring about a Zionist solution of the Palestine problem*, and that the officials of the State Department and Mr. Welles were said to be in favour of following it up. Dr. Weizmann also told the Ambassador that you had never concealed your view that the White Paper was not necessarily the last word on the Palestine problem and that you thought that your own mind and that of the President moved along the same lines. It is not clear from the record whether Dr. Weizmann actually said this in speaking to the State Department and *Sumner Welles*, although the latter *suggested that Dr. Weizmann should see the President and put the plan to him* (emphasis added).
>
> I do not know how far Dr. Weizmann has authority to speak in your name, but I am a little worried at the danger of confusion arising in Washington. Our present Palestine policy [i.e., the 1939 White Paper] has been accepted by Parliament. I know well your personal feeling on this, but there has, I think, been no discussion suggesting that the United States Government should be approached as regards the possibility of

[38] *Ibid.*, Document 25, pp. 189-191.

> modifying it. I must also record my view that it is very unlikely that Ibn Saud would be willing to receive Dr. Weizmann to discuss the future of Palestine, or that he would agree to recommend to the Arab world any scheme remotely resembling present Zionist aspirations, which include the transformation of Palestine into a Jewish state.

In a formal reply to Eden six days later, Prime Minister Churchill confirmed that Weizmann, while having no authority to speak in his name, had accurately quoted his views, both about his plan "to use Ibn Saud to bring about a Zionist solution of the Palestine problem" and the 1939 White Paper Policy. His clarifying message to Eden read:[39]

> 1. Dr. Weizmann has no authority to speak in my name. At the same time I expressed these views to him when we met some time ago, and you have often heard them from me yourself. The great difficulty is the age of Ibn Saud. I regard all discussions on these points as premature at present and only liable to cause dissension.
>
> 2. As you know, I am irrevocably opposed to the White Paper which, as I have testified in the House, I regard as a breach of a solemn undertaking to which I was a party.

It is very ironic to note that though Churchill said he was "irrevocably opposed" to the MacDonald White Paper, he nevertheless took no steps to abolish that illegal, deleterious document during the over five years he served as Prime Minister from May 1940 to July 1945. This inaction sealed the fate of many European Jews whose only hope of escaping the impending Holocaust was to find a safe refuge in Palestine. Churchill's opposition to this White Paper was therefore hollow and of no real consequence, except for ingratiating himself with Weizmann.

Weizmann met President Roosevelt again at the White House on June 11, 1943, in the presence of Sumner Welles. Roosevelt told Weizmann that he had had a conversation with Churchill about Palestine, and they had agreed to the idea of calling together the Jews and Arabs at a conference on the future of Palestine at which they would both be present. Roosevelt responded favourably to Sumner Welles' suggestion that an envoy first be sent to Ibn Saud to prepare the ground for such a conference. Among the possible candidates mentioned for this delicate mission were St. John Philby and Harold B. Hoskins.[40] The fact that Philby's name was mentioned in this context indicated the familiarity of Weizmann, Roosevelt and Welles with the Arab transfer solution to the Palestine problem and even their acceptance of this plan. Roosevelt said he would also consult with Churchill on the matter to obtain his consent. The envoy finally

---

[39] *Ibid.*, p. 192.

[40] *The Letters and Papers of Chaim Weizmann,* Vol. XXI, No. 38, n. 1, p. 39.

selected for this sensitive task was Hoskins, a New York textile merchant born to a missionary family in Beirut. He was an active supporter of the Arab cause, associated with the American University of Beirut and unfriendly to Zionism. Weizmann did not think he was the right man to approach Ibn Saud and wrote Sumner Welles to that effect, but to no avail.

Hoskins traveled to Arabia in August 1943 and spent sixteen days in the kingdom, visiting Jidda and Riyadh. He had, unlike other high-ranking American officials, no knowledge either of Philby's Palestine Plan or of that of Prime Minister Churchill when he left Washington nor even of Roosevelt's own preference for the idea of transferring Arabs out of Palestine to ensure a Jewish State in all of Western Palestine. While in Arabia, Hoskins merely sought to sound out Ibn Saud on whether he would like to meet Dr. Weizmann. He did not present any firm offer to Ibn Saud, contrary to Philby's strong advice, nor did he pave the way for a possible Weizmann visit with the King by declaring that both the United States and Great Britain strongly recommended it. When the King realized that Hoskins had not come with a firm offer from the American President and British Prime Minister as he had fully expected in accordance with the Philby Plan, he angrily and falsely accused Weizmann of having sent Philby to him to bribe him with a payment of 20 million pounds[41] which violated his honour, patriotism and religion. Hoskins reported Ibn Saud as saying that the twenty million pounds was to be guaranteed by the United States, with the approval of President Roosevelt, a guarantee never mentioned by Weizmann nor offered by Roosevelt.[42] Hoskins came away from his Riyadh meetings with Ibn Saud with the distinct impression that Philby had overstepped his bounds with the King in formulating a plan of which the King had never approved. This, however, was a wrong impression which Philby hastened to correct as soon as he learned from Weizmann what Hoskins, then in London, had told the Zionist leader of the King's absolute refusal to meet him and also of the King's great displeasure with Philby. At the suggestion of both Weizmann and Professor Namier, Philby and Hoskins met (November 15, 1943) to discuss the latter's recent visit to King Ibn Saud. During their one-and-a-half hour meeting, Philby strongly refuted the view maintained by Hoskins that the King was "uncompromisingly hostile" to the plan he had formulated to settle the Palestine question. He enlightened Hoskins "on certain outstanding facts of the case", as he put it:[43]

> It was, I said, on January 8th, 1940 – a few days after my return to Arabia, – that I communicated "the plan" to the King. There was nothing whatever to prevent him telling me then and there that it was

---

[41] Twenty million pounds sterling in the values of 2008 would be equivalent to over 300 million pounds. Gilbert, *op. cit.*, p. 202.

[42] *The Rise of Israel*, Volume 32, Document 35, p. 234.

[43] *Ibid.*, Document 33, pp. 224-5.

> an impossible and unacceptable proposition – in which case I should have informed Dr. Weizmann accordingly and dropped the whole thing. But the King did not tell me that. He told me on the contrary that some such arrangement might be possible in appropriate future circumstances, that he would keep the matter in mind, that he would give me a definite answer at the appropriate time, that meanwhile I should not breathe a word about the matter to anyone – least of all to any Arab – and, finally, that if the proposals became the subject of public discussion with any suggestion of his approving them he would have no hesitation whatsoever in denouncing me as having no authority to commit him in the matter. I was perfectly prepared to accept that position, and the King knew that I would communicate his answer to Dr. Weizmann. He did not forbid me to do so!

With the strong conviction of a person unjustly maligned and wishing to set the record straight, St. John Philby then explained to Hoskins why his "Palestine plan" had not succeeded:[44]

> He [Colonel Hoskins] had known nothing of "the plan" until it had been mentioned to him by the King. It followed that he had not gone to the King with anything in the nature of a firm offer on the lines of "the plan" on behalf of the United States Government. A further fact, of which I was cognisant though it was not actually mentioned or discussed between us, was that he had asked the King, presumably with his Government's authority (but why?), whether he would be willing to meet Dr. Weizmann or some other Jewish leader (presumably to discuss the Palestine problem). The King had deferred his answer and, when asked for it some days later, had expressed himself in strongly unfavourable terms. He was now aware, I went on, from what I had said that the King had sworn me to complete secrecy and had warned me that he would if necessary denounce me. That was exactly what had now happened, and the deduction I drew from the whole story was as follows:
>
> The King, on hearing that he was to be visited officially by a confidential emissary of the American Government, naturally assumed that that emissary was coming to communicate to him a firm offer on the lines of "the plan". The emissary came with no such offer but merely with the suggestion that Ibn Sa'ud should meet Dr. Weizmann or some other Jewish leader, presumably for the purpose of further bargaining over Palestine. The King, fully accustomed to the tortuous ways of diplomacy, had deliberately refrained both from giving a definite answer and from expressing his opinion of Dr. Weizmann. He may

[44] *Ibid.*, pp. 227-229.

well have thought that a few days of silent incubation would produce the firm offer which he had a right to expect if "the plan" reflected the desires of the British and American Governments. But Colonel Hoskins had no firm offer to make him, and when some days later he merely asked for the King's reply to his original question about seeing Dr. Weizmann, His Majesty, realising that the American Government was concerned only to throw the whole matter open to further discussion, and realising further that "the plan" had obviously not won acceptance on the part of the two Governments concerned, allowed himself, as he occasionally does in moments of disappointment, the luxury of a fit of ill temper at the expense of Dr. Weizmann, the Jews in general and myself. It was exactly what I would have expected in the circumstances. King Ibn Sa'ud is getting very weary of the ways of western diplomacy and he, perhaps rightly, suspects that the strategic, economic and political interests of certain Great Powers debar them from making any really acceptable offer to the Arabs.

Nevertheless, as I made clear to Colonel Hoskins after our very full talk over the whole business, his account of his conversations with King Ibn Sa'ud had not in the least shaken my conviction – a conviction on which I was prepared to stake my whole reputation, which was all I had to stake as I had already sacrificed a career by my fight for Arab independence – that, *had he gone out to Arabia with President Roosevelt's firm offer made on behalf of the American and British Governments on the lines of "the plan" that offer would have been accepted.* I could only draw the rather disappointing conclusion that the British and American Governments are not prepared to make the relatively light sacrifices involved in "the plan" even to save the Jews from persecution, torture and death. If, however, I am wrong on this point the opportunity presents itself for putting the matter to the test. *If the two Governments are really desirous of an arrangement on the lines of "the plan" and are prepared to make to Ibn Sa'ud a firm offer in that sense, I am convinced that the King will accept it – but it must be a firm offer on the lines of "the plan" to be accepted or rejected as it stands, without modification or bargaining.* If, on the other hand, the two Governments do not want to make the sacrifice involved and are at the same time satisfied that Colonel Hoskins' interpretation of Ibn Sa'ud's attitude is correct, let them at least make a gesture of goodwill to the Jews and confront Ibn Sa'ud with a firm offer (on the lines of "the plan") which he will, as they are advised, turn down. I have only my own conviction to pit against the views of Colonel Hoskins, but no harm can come of putting the matter to the test. Either "the plan" is accepted or the *status quo* remains intact without prejudice to anybody. *For my part I guarantee (for what my guarantee is worth) that the suggested firm offer will be accepted if made by any reasonably intelligent person of indisputable goodwill on behalf of the two Governments concerned.* It is for those Governments now to show the

> genuineness of their goodwill they are so fond of proclaiming towards the Arabs and the Jews (emphasis added).

It is apparent from Philby's testimony that Ibn Saud seriously entertained accepting the plan he had devised for settling the Palestine question, not only when it was first broached to the King on January 8, 1940, but even subsequently, provided a firm offer regarding it was made by the two Great Powers and not prematurely divulged, in which case he would have to disavow it.[45] Under this plan Ibn Saud would have become the ruler of an Arab empire embracing all the Arab countries in Asia – Syria, Iraq, Transjordan and other small states or principalities in Arabia. The Arab residents of Cisjordan would be resettled in Ibn Saud's enlarged kingdom, thus solving the Palestine problem. In addition, substantial financial and economic aid would be provided to the Saudi monarch to facilitate the Arab population transfer from Palestine and to help him overcome the financial difficulties he was then experiencing, arising from the stoppage of pilgrimages to Mecca during the war.

The version given by Colonel Hoskins, that the King found the entire Philby scheme distasteful, is belied by the fact that Philby remained a welcome guest of the King at Riyadh or in his desert camp for six and a half months after having placed his proposal before him. Ibn Saud and his entourage even tried to dissuade Philby, who had become a Moslem in 1930, from leaving the kingdom, a decision he took on his own initiative. As an enticement for him to stay on in Arabia, the King offered Philby the gift of a newly-built house. Even after he left, he was categorically assured by the Arabian minister in London that he would be welcome back in Arabia and receive the visa required for that purpose. It must be concluded, therefore, that both Hoskins and Anthony Eden had misjudged Ibn Saud's original attitude towards the Philby Plan, wrongly depicting the King as unreservedly opposed to it, when in fact he seriously considered its merits and waited for a firm offer to be made by the United States and Britain, an offer that was never forthcoming at the proper time by a suitable emissary.

In addition to the lack of the aforesaid firm offer, Weizmann, in a letter dated January 4, 1944 to Judge Samuel Rosenman, who served as legal counsel to President Roosevelt, gave two other reasons for the failure of the Philby Plan. One was the inordinately long delay (three and a half years) from the time Philby communicated the plan to Ibn Sa'ud (January 8, 1940) to the visit of Hoskins (August 1943). The other reason, the more probable one in Weizmann's view, was the intervention of the oil companies which held important concessions in Arabia and provided the King with a considerable income. The activities of such companies in the Middle East, said Weizmann, were in his experience usually

---

[45] Ibn Saud's acceptance of the Philby Plan "in principle" is reported by Philby's wife, Dora, in a letter she wrote to Lewis Namier on February 21, 1940. *The Letters and Papers of Chaim Weizmann*, Volume XIX, Series A, letter 206, n. 2, p. 224. See also letter 254, n. 1, p. 266.

anti-Jewish.[46] However, Weizmann continued to hope that the Philby Plan could be salvaged. He also told Judge Roseman that sending Hoskins to Ibn Saud had been a serious mistake. "He came empty-handed, and quite unprepared – and he is in any event none too sympathetic."[47]

Just before his letter to Judge Roseman, Weizmann wrote Sumner Welles on December 13, 1943 with the request that [Welles] bring to the President's attention the contents of the letter [Weizmann] was then sending to Welles, who had just retired from the U.S. State Department. In his letter, Weizmann repeated all the details of the Philby Plan and the misunderstandings that had arisen later as a result of it. He also admitted, contrary to what he wrote in his autobiography, that Philby first discussed his scheme with him in the autumn of 1939 in the presence of his colleague, Mr. Namier. Then he asked him the following question:[48]

> May I put my views before you once more in special connection with Mr. Philby's scheme? It is conceived on big lines, large enough to satisfy the legitimate aspirations of Arabs and Jews, and the strategic and economic interests of the United States and Britain. In my belief, none of the problems of the Middle East can be effectively settled piecemeal, but only by treating them as a connected whole. The world is deeply interested in solving the Jewish problem, the overwhelming majority of the Jews themselves desire a Jewish Commonwealth in Palestine, and expect its establishment to normalize the position of the Jews in the Dispersion; the Arabs demand complete independence and freedom to achieve unity.
>
> If the world supports the Jews in their demand for Palestine west of the Jordan, let the Arabs concede it as a *quid pro quo* for fulfilment of their claims everywhere else. Our heritage in Palestine was cut down to the bone when Transjordan was separated in 1922. What is left is clearly a unit, and further partition of it would deprive the settlement of finality. If the whole of Western Palestine is left to us, we plan to carry out a Jordan Development Scheme suggested to us by American experts. This would also benefit the Arab land on the western bank (sic!), and facilitate transfers of population. A scheme on such large lines would be greatly helped by the backing of an outstanding personality in the Arab world such as Ibn Sa'ud. I therefore feel, in spite of Colonel Hoskins' adverse report, that, properly managed, Mr. Philby's scheme offers an approach which should not be abandoned without further exploration.

---

46 *The Rise of Israel*, Volume 32, Document 36, pp. 236-7.

47 *Ibid.*, Document 36, p. 237.

48 *Ibid.*, Document 35, pp. 234-5.

Weizmann's efforts to convince Roosevelt and Churchill to pursue the Philby Plan did not produce any concrete results in the way he desired, although each of these leaders supported the basic outlines of the plan but failed to act in the decisive and coordinated manner recommended by Philby. However, it is no coincidence that the British Labour Party in 1944, when Weizmann still nurtured a hope to bring the Philby Scheme to a stage of practical consideration despite the Hoskins' fiasco, endorsed its principal feature – the transfer of the Arab population out of Palestine. Philby called the Labour Party Plan put forth by Hugh Dalton "an echo" of his own plan.[49] Nor was it by sheer chance that President Roosevelt decided to meet Ibn Saud on his way back to the United States from the Yalta Conference in 1945, shortly before Roosevelt's death. The President had the plan for Arab transfer uppermost in his mind, a plan that he had independently conceived that was not much different in essence from the Philby Plan with whose details he was now familiar. Roosevelt's views concerning the need for Arab transfer, as well as the negative results of his February 1945 meeting with Ibn Saud, are further discussed below.

The Philby Plan as originally envisaged was dead because it had been mishandled diplomatically, by both the Americans and the British, and the proper steps that could have been taken for its eventual realization were never in fact carried out. Still, it inspired others to think along similar lines, as the best way to bring about a Jewish State in Western Palestine without partition, a step which would have violated Article 5 of the Mandate for Palestine then in force. The provision for Arab transfer, an integral feature of the Philby Plan, devised by the most pro-Arab of Englishmen and endorsed or independently formulated by other prominent, fair-minded and realistic political figures such as Roosevelt, Churchill, Dalton, Weizmann, Sharett and Namier and not rejected at the outset even by Ibn Saud, is as good a refutation as can be made of the charge often leveled today, that the idea of Arab transfer from Western Palestine is inherently anti-Arab or immoral. It is to be recalled that the plan enjoyed the support of leading advocates of the Arab cause at the time, notably St. John Philby, T. E. Lawrence and Gertrude Bell. On the contrary, weighed against the global political and legal settlement of the Middle East made after World War I, the decimation of European Jewry in the Holocaust, the absolute refusal of Arabs to genuinely accept the State of Israel and the Palestinian Arab war of terrorism presently being waged against Israel with the support of the Arab world and Iran, it was in retrospect and should be seen now and in the future as the most practical and rational solution to bring an end to continuous strife and bloodshed in the Land of Israel, and thus ensure long-term peace and security in the region. Arab transfer will also end the demographic threat to the Jewish character of the State of Israel, posed by the fast-rising Arab population.

A third precedent under international law approving a very large compulsory transfer of a settled population was provided for under the Potsdam Agreement

[49] Philby, *Arabian Jubilee*, p. 210.

(Potsdam Protocol) of August 2, 1945, concluded at a conference held in the East German city of Potsdam (near Berlin) between the Heads of Government of the U.S.S.R., the U.S. and the U.K., represented respectively by Joseph Stalin, Harry S. Truman and Clement Richard Attlee, and subsequently approved by China and France. Under this agreement, there was envisaged an "Orderly Transfer of German Populations" to Germany from Poland, Czechoslovakia and Hungary. The first paragraph of Section XII of the Potsdam Agreement stated:

> The Three Governments, having considered the question in all its aspects, recognize that *the transfer to Germany of German populations*, or elements thereof, remaining in Poland, Czechoslovakia and Hungary, *will have to be undertaken.* They agree that any transfers that take place should be effected *in an orderly and humane manner* (emphasis added).

The total number of Germans who were either expelled or evacuated from pre-war German territories, in central and eastern Europe or from lands Germany annexed in the late 1930's, together with those resettled in what was to become the Federal Republic of Germany (West Germany), was over 12 million. The breakdown of this number was as follows:[50]

> **1,950,000** from the region of East Prussia on the Baltic Coast, subsequently divided at the Yalta and Potsdam conferences between Poland and the U.S.S.R. The latter received the northern section of East Prussia, including the city of Kaliningrad, formerly Konigsberg, while the rest of East Prussia was incorporated into Poland;
>
> **1,900,000** from the former Prussian province of Pomerania extending along the Baltic Sea as well as from the Baltic area of Poland. Over the centuries control over Pomerania seesawed back and forth between Poland and Prussia. In 1919, by virtue of the Treaty of Versailles, the Polish Corridor was formed from a strip of German territory taken from West Prussia, thus separating East Prussia from the rest of Germany, while at the same time Danzig became a Free City, under the protection of the League of Nations. In 1945, at the Yalta and Potsdam Conferences, the decision was taken to transfer the larger part of Pomerania to Poland, while the area west of the Oder was incorporated into East Germany, except for Stettin, the former capital of Prussian Pomerania, which Poland also took over and renamed Szczecin.

---

[50] The Aftermath of the War in Europe, Map 1: Post-war Population Movements, *The Times Atlas of World History*, Revised Edition, edited by Geoffrey Barraclough, Hammond Incorporated, Maplewood, New Jersey (1984), pp. 274-275.

**3,250,000** from Silesia, today part of Poland and the Czech Republic. At the Potsdam Conference it was further decided that most of the territory making up the former Prussian provinces of Upper Silesia and Lower Silesia, extending on both banks of the Oder River, would be transferred to Poland. The frontier between Germany and Poland thus became the Oder-Neisse line;

**1,850,000** from Russian-occupied Germany (East Germany);

**2,900,000** from Bohemia and Moravia, today part of the Czech Republic;

**200,000** from Hungary;

**50,000** from Roumania;

**250,000** from Yugoslavia.

What was very interesting from a legal point-of-view about the Potsdam Agreement between the wartime Big Three Powers was that it was concluded without the consent of the people directly affected by the decisions taken. The millions of Germans who were to be transferred from the lands they had lived in for many centuries were not asked for their consent, nor did any state whose inhabitants were to be transferred have any voice in these fateful decisions, apart from the U.S.S.R. Germany as the state most directly affected had temporarily ceased to exist as a sovereign entity and thus had no say in the matter. The transfer of German populations was deemed necessary, particularly in Poland and Czechoslovakia, because their presence could no longer be tolerated after they had vociferously supported Hitler's territorial demands or agitated for self-determination in close alliance with Germany. No one in 1945 protested their expulsion from their places of birth because it was seen as the most appropriate solution to achieve and maintain the long-term stability and security of Europe and at the same time prevent the revival of German militarism and dreams of territorial expansion (Lebensraum) that led to the infamous Munich Pact of September 30, 1938 and the outbreak of World War II on September 1, 1939. The expulsion of ethnic Germans who received no compensation was accompanied by the annexation by Russia, Poland and Czechoslovakia of lands formerly under German rule as part of the World War II settlement determined by the Allied Powers at the Yalta and Potsdam Conferences in 1945. This expulsion differed in every respect – morally and legally – from the mass deportation of Jews from their homes to the slave labour and death camps established throughout Europe, principally in Poland and Germany. In the case of the expulsion of the Germans, it represented an act of justice and condign punishment (which some would, perhaps justifiably, characterize as "revenge") for those who supported the goals of Nazism, while, on the other hand, Germany's barbaric deportation of Jews to carry out the Final Solution plumbed the depths of man's inhumanity to man and met the definition of both a war crime and a crime against humanity in general and the Jewish People in particular.[51]

Furthermore, the legal and moral difference between the mass expulsion of Germans and the mass deportation of Jews can be seen in the Charter of the International Military Tribunal (hereafter: the Nuremberg Charter) drawn up in London on August 8, 1945 as part of an agreement between the U.S., the U.K., the U.S.S.R. and France to prosecute and punish 24 former Nazi leaders whose trials were then held at Nuremberg between November 20, 1945 and October 1, 1946.

Among the various acts defined as War Crimes in the Nuremberg Charter was Germany's deportation of the civilian population in the territories it occupied to concentration camps for purposes of slave labour not justified by military necessity, while Crimes Against Humanity included deportation of any civilian population either before or during the War.

In the case of Europe's Jews, deportation meant not only slave labour but actual extermination and genocide. By contrast, the expulsion of Germans from their previous homes was of a different and even beneficial nature, individual cases notwithstanding. Its purpose was not only their repatriation to the German fatherland, but to put an end to the conflict they had helped to provoke in the regions they had inhabited. Reinforcing this central difference was the fact that the London Agreement containing the Nuremberg Charter was signed only six days after the Potsdam Agreement was announced and by the very same states, except for the addition of France. It is obvious, therefore, that the mass expulsion or transfer of Germans to dismembered Germany authorized by the Potsdam Agreement for legitimate reasons was not a war crime or a crime against humanity, as defined in the Nuremberg Charter; otherwise, the leaders of the Allied Powers would also have been guilty of the very same crimes as the Nazi war criminals. Thus it is clear that not all expulsions or transfers of people are criminal in nature or contrary to international law. A distinction must thus be made between legally-sanctioned transfers permitted under an international treaty, agreement or statute, and illegal transfers that have no such foundation or are purely arbitrary in nature, without any just cause.

The legality of transfer depends on the reasons and circumstances of a particular case. Transfer is clearly illegal if carried out by an aggressor state

[51] The distinction between a crime against humanity and a crime against the Jewish People, though not found in international law, is, however, part of the law of the State of Israel called the Nazi and Nazi Collaborators (Punishment) Law, passed by the Knesset in 1950. This law was applied in the famous trial of Adolf Eichmann that lasted from April to December 1961. In addition to being charged with crimes against humanity, war crimes and membership in an enemy and criminal organization, Eichmann was also charged with crimes against the Jewish People. It was the link existing between the State of Israel and the Jewish People which allowed an Israel court to assume jurisdiction in the Eichmann case, even though the crimes he committed occurred outside the territory of Israel before the law had been passed and before the State had come into existence.

in a foreign country it has unlawfully occupied during a period of war, such as that which occurred when Germany illegally occupied parts of Poland, Czechoslovakia, Russia and other countries during World War II. Another factor to consider in determining the legality of a mass expulsion or transfer of people is whether the deportees/expellees are allowed to take with them their movable property without restriction or payment of an exorbitant fee and receive due compensation for any immovable property left behind.

The Potsdam Agreement is an important precedent for the case of the Arabs of the Land of Israel, whose absolute enmity towards the State of Israel is well known and well documented. If the same precedent is followed to end the conflict in Western Palestine, the consent for their transfer and repatriation to nearby Arab states is not necessary. Moreover, this solution will likely achieve peace and security in the Land of Israel in the long run, just as it did in post-wartime Europe in the case of the transfer of the German population.

It was exactly these same reasons that impelled former President Herbert Hoover in 1945 to suggest applying the Potsdam precedent to the Arabs of what was then Mandated Palestine, by moving them to Iraq, which he thought would actually benefit them and be "a method of settlement with both honour and wisdom". Their move would be facilitated by international funds paid to Iraq. Hoover's proposal was based on his vast experience with humanitarian relief operations in Europe after World War I and which he also was to direct after World War II on behalf of the U.S. Government. Here is what he said on the subject when he was interviewed by the Scripps-Howard Press on November 19, 1945:

> There is room for many more Arabs in such a development in Iraq than the total of Arabs in Palestine. The soil is more fertile. They would be among their own race which is Arab[ic-] speaking and Mohammedan. The Arab population of Palestine would be [the] gainer from better lands in exchange for their present holdings. Iraq would be the gainer for it badly needs agricultural population.
>
> Today millions of people are being moved from one land to another. If the lands were organized and homes provided, this particular movement could be made the model migration of history. It would be a solution by engineering instead of by conflict.
>
> I realize that the plan offers a challenge both to the statesmanship of the Great Powers as well as to the goodwill of all parties concerned. However, I submit it, and it does offer a method of settlement with both honour and wisdom.

Hoover's proposal was adopted by a group of nineteen distinguished

Americans[52] in April 1954, who in a submission to the President of the United States, Dwight D. Eisenhower, advanced the following solution to the Arab refugee problem as part of a permanent peace settlement:

> A. That the only feasible and constructive solution of the Arab refugee problem is through settlement in Arab countries;
> B. That for this purpose a $300 million resettlement fund should be established under United Nations auspices;
> C. That Israel should be requested to make a fair contribution to this fund by way of compensation for abandoned Arab land in Israel;
> D. That the Arab countries in recognition of their responsibility to share in resolving this problem should assign tracts of land in their territories now unpopulated or under-populated but capable of being developed to support a substantial population;
> E. That a U.N. Resettlement Agency should be established for the orderly transfer of Arab refugees and for their retraining as necessary;
> F. That the government of the United States, which has thus far supplied more than half the funds for the welfare of Arab refugees, will continue such support, earmarked for a permanent resettlement program.

In support of their view, the nineteen Americans cited the following precedents, inter alia: the Bulgarian-Turkish Exchange of 1919, the Greek-Turkish Exchange of 1923 and the Turkish Repatriation from Rumania, Bulgaria and Yugoslavia, initiated by the Kemalist government of Turkey in 1931, which in a five-year period (1935-1940) led to a total of 172,000 Turks being resettled in Turkish Thrace and Anatolia. The distinguished group of Americans believed that their proposed solution to the Palestine problem, as further elaborated in their study of the subject, would not only bring peace and avoid disaster, but that it was dictated both by compassion and realism and contrasted sharply with the demonic solution of King Saud of Saudi Arabia, the eldest son and successor to Ibn Saud, who, on January 9, 1954, called upon the Arab world to wage a *jihad* (holy war) against Israel, "uproot it just like a cancer", losing, if need be, ten million Arab lives in the process.

A fourth example of compulsory transfer of population sanctioned by a treaty under international law occurred in the case of Finland and Russia after war broke out between the two countries. Russia initiated this war, known as the Winter War, on November 30, 1939. An initial peace treaty (the Treaty of

---

[52] The group of nineteen Americans numbered among them church figures, educators, labour leaders, a former member of the Anglo-American Committee of Inquiry (Frank W. Buxton) and the Chief Justice of the Supreme Court of Utah (the Hon. James H. Wolfe). The complete list of names is found in the booklet *Security and the Middle East: The Problem and its Solution – Proposals*, published in New York City, April 1954.

Moscow) was signed on March 12, 1940, under which Finland ceded to Russia its part of the Karelian Isthmus – a land bridge connecting the two countries – including the Baltic port city of Vyborg and several border territories. This spurred Finland to ally itself with Germany to recover its territories, but after Russia invaded Finland in 1944 and defeated her, the cessions of territory previously made were confirmed in an armistice agreement and later in a new Finnish-Soviet peace treaty signed in Paris in 1947. As a result of this latter treaty, about 420,000 Finns who had lived in the Finnish region of Karelia and the other territories ceded to Russia were driven out and resettled in Finland.

In Palestine, outbreaks of Arab mob violence directed against the Jewish return to their national home have occurred ever since 1920, beginning in March of that year with armed attacks on four Jewish settlements in Upper Galilee: the village of Metulla, and the kibbutzim of Kfar Giladi, Tel Hai and Hamra. This was followed in April 1920 by severe Arab rioting in Jerusalem, in the Old City and at the lower end of Jaffa Road, which resulted in the death of several Jews and hundreds injured, accompanied by looting and rape. In the decades since that initial outburst of Arab violence, it has grown much worse. Thus it is certainly reasonable and equitable, as well as legal, based on the foregoing precedents under international law to apply the very same standards of justice invoked by the Allied Powers after World War I at the Lausanne Conference and after World War II at the Potsdam Conference and Paris Conference to bring about an orderly and as humane as possible transfer of Arabs living in the Land of Israel to other Arab countries, particularly Iraq, Syria and the states of the Arabian Peninsula. There is no validity to the baseless accusation that this kind of transfer would constitute a "war crime" under international law, as falsely alleged by the opponents of transfer.

It is true that the Fourth Geneva Convention Relative to the Protection of Civilian Persons in Time of War, of August 12, 1949, inspired undoubtedly by the aforementioned Nuremburg Charter, prohibits "individual or mass forcible transfers, or deportations of *protected persons* from occupied territory to the territory of the occupying power or to that of any other country, occupied or not, *regardless of their motive*." – Article 49, paragraph 1 of the Convention. *Protected persons* are those "who, at a given moment and in any manner whatsoever, find themselves, in case of conflict or occupation, in the hands of a Party to the conflict or Occupying Power of which they are not nationals" – Article 4 of the Convention. Though Article 49(1) uses the words *regardless of their motive* in prohibiting forcible transfers and deportations of *protected persons* from occupied territory during wartime, it was never intended to be a blanket prohibition for all forced migrations of people in every conceivable situation. As already noted, the coalition of Allied Powers of World War II at the Potsdam Conference (July 17, 1945 – August 2, 1945) sanctioned the expulsion of German nationals from what was then subjugated German territory by Poland, Czechoslovakia and Russia, and then allowed these same countries to annex the very territory from which the Germans were forcibly transferred, without anyone accusing the Allied Powers of having committed war crimes or crimes against humanity. If Article 49(1) is interpreted to apply in every conceivable situation and had already been in effect in 1945, the expulsion or transfer of all Germans would have been strictly prohibited. But that was not the purpose of Article 49(1). Rather it was aimed expressly at the Nazi program rounding up parts of the civilian population in German-occupied countries of Europe, particularly Jews, Communists and gypsies, for transport to the death camps, orders that could have had no normative legal or moral justification, *regardless of their motive*. Had the Jews living in those countries simply been expelled in a humane and orderly fashion to Palestine or to any other free country and allowed to take their property with them without expropriation or to receive proper compensation therefor, many of the six million who died in the Holocaust would have survived. In that case there would have been a more limited ground or less incentive for prosecuting German leaders and officials for the commission of war crimes against the Jewish civilian population.

Invoking Article 49(1) in favour of the Arabs of Judea, Samaria and Gaza would be ironic, since, as just noted, it was intended primarily to protect Jews and other groups targeted by the Nazis from the atrocities they faced daily in war-ravaged Europe. Applying Article 49(1) to the Arabs living in the Jewish homeland who perpetrate their own acts of murderous terrorism and war crimes against the Jewish People, reminiscent of the worst deeds of Nazism, would be repugnant to the true meaning of this Article.

In the case of Israel's entry into Judea, Samaria (June 6, 1967) and Gaza (June 5, 1967), it is even clearer that Article 49 in its entirety, indeed the whole of the Fourth Geneva Convention of which it is part, does not apply to these regions because they are not "occupied territories" falling within the definition of that term as laid down in Article 42 of the Hague Regulations of 1907. These regulations constitute an annex to the Fourth Hague Convention Respecting the Laws and Customs of War on Land. The legal question of the applicability of the Fourth Geneva Convention to these territories has been the source of great argument ever since the Israel Defense Forces restored them to the possession of the Jewish People and the State of Israel in the Six-Day War. Some analysts who have approached this question have relied only on Article 2 of the Convention to determine if it applies to Judea, Samaria and Gaza, when the actual answer is to be found by combining Article 2 with Article 6 of the Convention.

The relevant paragraphs of Article 2 read as follows:

> *In addition to the provisions which shall be implemented in peacetime, the present Convention shall apply to all cases of declared war or of any other armed conflict* which may arise between two or more of the High Contracting Parties, even if the state of war is not recognized by one of them.
>
> The Convention shall also apply to all cases of *partial or total occupation of the territory of a High Contracting Party*, even if the said occupation meets with no armed resistance (emphasis added).

The relevant paragraphs of Article 6 state:

> The present Convention shall apply from the outset of any conflict or occupation mentioned in Article 2.
>
> *In the territory of Parties to the conflict, the application of the present Convention shall cease on the general close of military operations.*
>
> *In the case of occupied territory, the application of the present Convention shall cease one year after the general close of military operations*; however, the Occupying Power shall be bound, for the duration of the occupation, to the extent that such Power exercises the functions of government in such territory, by the provisions of the following Articles of the present Convention: 1-12, 27, 29 to 34, 47, 49, 51, 52, 53, 59, 61 to 77, 143. (emphasis added).

In light of the fact that Article 2(1) of the Fourth Geneva Convention applies to all cases of *declared war* or armed conflict between two or more of the High Contracting Parties and that the states engaged in the Six-Day War were and remain parties to the Convention, there can be no doubt that at the outset of the war on June 5, 1967 until its conclusion on June 10, 1967, all the provisions of the Convention applied to each of the combatant states of Israel, Egypt, Jordan and Syria and to the territories that Israel brought under its military control as a result of the war, regardless of their legal status or sovereignty at the time and regardless of whether or not they were to be considered "occupied territories" under international law. During the war, the Convention also applied, regardless of the formalistic question of whether it represented treaty law that required incorporation into the domestic law or customary law that did not require such incorporation. The discussion here will be limited to the applicability of the Fourth Geneva Convention to Judea, Samaria and Gaza *after* June 10, 1967 when the state of active war or hostilities between Israel and the combatant Arab states terminated, even without a peace treaty.

To begin with, it is important to note that the "military operations" referred to in Article 6 of the Convention ceased altogether on June 10, 1967, in accordance with three U.N. Security Council resolutions passed during the Six-Day War demanding an immediate cease-fire.[53] This call for a cease-fire was accepted by Israel and Syria between whom active fighting was still raging on the Golan Heights. The state of war may have technically continued to exist between Israel and Syria (as well as Egypt and Jordan), but there were definitely no further military operations between them, within the meaning of Article 6 of the Convention.

Article 6 distinguishes between two kinds of territory: 1) the territory of

---

[53] The three Security Council resolutions calling for a cessation of all military activities, all of which were adopted unanimously, were: 1) Resolution No. 233 of June 6, 1967; 2) Resolution No. 234 of June 7, 1967; 3) Resolution No. 235 of June 9, 1967.

the parties to the conflict, and 2) occupied territory. In the case of the former, the application of the Fourth Geneva Convention ceases "on the general close of military operations". But in the case of the latter – "occupied territory" – the Convention continues to apply until one year after the close of military operations and even beyond that date if the Occupying Power exercises the functions of government in such territory.

Inasmuch as the Six-Day War was not fought either within the existing borders of the State of Israel, or within the borders of Jordan on the east bank of the Jordan River – the only recognized borders of the country under international law, the Convention was no longer applicable to those specific areas after the cease-fire or cessation of hostilities, except for those provisions of the Convention "which shall be implemented in peacetime". The question of the further applicability of the Convention then turns on the question of whether Judea, Samaria and Gaza were "occupied territories" belonging to the Kingdom of Jordan and/or Egypt within the meaning of both Article 6 of the Convention and Article 42 of the Hague Regulations.

Article 42 defines territory as being occupied *when the territory of the Hostile State is actually placed under the authority of a Hostile Army*. It is to be noted that the text of Article 42 refers only to "territory" in a general sense, but the heading[54] of Section III under which Article 42 appears – "Military Authority over Territory of the Hostile State" – makes it clear that the word "territory" can only be a reference to the "territory of the Hostile State", as is also evident from Article 55 of that Section, which specifically mentions various immovable properties belonging to the "hostile state". Article 42 further lays down that "the occupation extends only to the territory [of the Hostile State] where such authority has been established and can be exercised."

At the conclusion of the Six-Day War, the territories of Judea, Samaria and Gaza were indeed placed under the authority of a "Hostile Army", i.e., the Israel Defense Forces. However, these territories are not to be considered legally "under occupation", unless they actually belong to either Jordan or Egypt. It is a well-known fact that though Jordan annexed Judea and Samaria on April 24, 1950, thus rendering this region a *de facto* part of the Kingdom of Jordan (i.e., the so-called "West Bank"), this unilateral annexation was never recognized as valid under the prevailing norms of international law, inasmuch as Jordan was an aggressor state in the Israel-Arab War of 1948.[55] Thus Jordan never enjoyed sovereignty over Judea and

---

[54] In interpreting the text of a treaty or of an annex to it, such as the Hague Regulations, recourse may be had according to Article 31 of the Vienna Convention on the Law of Treaties to the context to be given to the terms of the treaty and also to the treaty's object and purpose. Based on this general rule of interpretation, the term "territory" as used in Article 42 of the Hague Regulations can only refer to the "territory of the hostile state" over which the army of the other state (i.e., the Occupying State) has assumed military authority.

[55] The principle of international law that applied to the situation was *jus ex*

Samaria, while Egypt never even claimed it over Gaza. Since neither Jordan nor Egypt (nor the fictitious "Palestinian People") were recognized sovereigns of these territories, they cannot be legally classified as "occupied". The only recognized sovereign over those territories under international law prior to the Six-Day War was the Jewish People as determined by several acts of international law. The first such act was the Smuts Resolution of January 30, 1919 (the precursor of Article 22 of the League Covenant) which, in referring to the term "Palestine", must be interpreted in conjunction with the Balfour Declaration of November 2, 1917, the Lloyd George-Clemenceau Agreement of December 1, 1918 and the Weizmann-Feisal Agreement of January 3, 1919. It is thus evident that "Palestine" is a reference to the Jewish People and not to the local Arab inhabitants of the country. The other acts of international law that confirm the Jewish legal title to Palestine are the San Remo Resolution of April 25, 1920, the Mandate for Palestine of July 24, 1922, the Franco-British Boundary Convention of December 3, 1920 and the Anglo-American Convention Respecting the Mandate for Palestine of December 3, 1924. Since Israel, therefore, did not occupy the territory of a previous foreign sovereign, but only re-possessed the territory that the Principal Allied Powers of World War I had resolved was to be part and parcel of the Jewish National Home, as subsequently confirmed by the League of Nations, the Fourth Geneva Convention was not applicable to Israel's rule over Judea, Samaria and Gaza. Accordingly, it is absolutely false to assert that Judea, Samaria and Gaza are "occupied Palestinian territory", "occupied Arab territory" or simply "occupied territory" as claimed in many U.N. General Assembly and Security Council resolutions as well as by the Palestine Liberation Organization, the Palestinian Authority, the Arab League states, other governments and self-servingly, by the International Committee of the Red Cross.[56] Furthermore, when the Six-Day

*injuria non oritur* [a right does not arise from a wrong]. Even the Council of the Arab League refused to recognize the Jordanian annexation of Judea and Samaria, and four states – Egypt, Saudi Arabia, Syria and Lebanon – voted to expel Jordan for violating the League's anti-annexation resolution of April 13, 1950.

[56] The International Committee of the Red Cross (ICRC) principally formulated the four 1949 Geneva Conventions that were approved at a Diplomatic Conference for the Establishment of International Conventions for the Protection of the Victims of War, held in Geneva from April 21 to August 12, 1949. The ICRC has a special position in the implementation of these Conventions, charged with providing relief and affording protection for members of armed forces who are wounded, sick or shipwrecked; prisoners of war; and civilian persons in time of war (see, for example, Articles 3(2), 63 and 142 of Geneva Convention IV). Under the erroneous assumption of the ICRC that Judea, Samaria and Gaza are indeed "occupied territories", the Government of Israel permits it to operate freely in these parts of the Land of Israel and the Jewish National Home. It is not without irony that the man who founded the International Red Cross, Jean Henri Dunant, a Swiss Protestant philanthropist, waged an unsuccessful campaign for the settlement of Jews in Palestine during the 1860s, even going so far as to establish an association for that very purpose. Herzl recognized Dunant's unique

War broke out on June 5, 1967, there was no state in existence called "Palestine" whose territory could be considered "occupied" under international law, nor is there any such state even today, though if the Government of Israel continues to pursue the "two-state vision" of U.S. President George W. Bush, this state may yet emerge.

Despite the fact that Israel never occupied the sovereign territory of another Arab state or people, within the meaning of the Fourth Geneva Convention and the Hague Regulations, it has been falsely branded as an occupier of "Arab land". This accusation has no basis in law but has persisted because of the false belief that has been nurtured since 1969 by the United Nations and the Arab States as well as the PLO, that Israel has conquered the national homeland of another people, the "Palestinians" who inhabit the non-existent state of "Palestine". To dispel these falsehoods, it need only be remembered that Mandated Palestine was created in April, 1920 at the San Remo Peace Conference for the express purpose of the future independent state of the Jewish People, not for an imaginary people called "Palestinians", whose existence as a separate nation was unknown during the whole period of the Mandate, especially to the Arabs themselves. Since Palestine was intended to be the Jewish National Home, the State of Israel, which inherited the national rights of the Jewish People to the country, can never be seen as the occupier of land that was specifically reserved for Jews and rightfully belongs, as a result, to Israel. It is only by ignoring these indisputable facts that the cry is incessantly raised that the "occupation" must end. Sadly, Israel itself was in large measure responsible for allowing this false conception to take root, when during the Six-Day War it made the fateful decision to apply the laws of war to the liberated Jewish territories rather than the corpus of its own law, thus failing to incorporate those territories into the Jewish State. This convinced world public opinion, especially that of American and European leaders, that Israel is indeed an occupier of foreign lands. To rectify this terrible mistake, which also violated existing Israeli constitutional law, Israel should not only strongly contest the allegation of "occupation" as baseless, but also pass legislation affirming Israel's national rights to all areas of the Land of Israel and making it a criminal offense to describe its presence and status in any part of the land as "occupation".[57] This will then prevent Israel's Supreme Court and most academic jurists in Israel's institutions of higher learning from further spreading this insidious libel, as they have incredibly done up to now, to the acclaim of those who favour the re-partition of the Land of

efforts to promote Jewish settlement by referring to him as a Christian Zionist in his closing speech at the First Zionist Congress in 1897 in the Swiss city of Basle.

[57] The Knesset on July 15, 2003 took an initial step in this direction when it passed, by a margin of 26 to 8, a resolution submitted by Gideon Sa'ar that read as follows: "...the Knesset affirms that the territories of Judea and Samaria are not occupied territories, either historically or from the standpoint of international law, and not according to the diplomatic accords signed by Israel...".

Israel.

In consequence of the fact that Judea, Samaria and Gaza are not occupied territories under Israel's rule, but rather liberated Jewish territory, the Arabs living there are not *protected persons* under the provisions of the Fourth Geneva Convention. Hence they can be legally transferred or repatriated to other countries in accordance with the rules and precedents of international law established in the Conventions of Neuilly (1919) and Lausanne (1923), the Potsdam Agreement (1945) and the Finnish-Russian peace treaty (the 1947 Treaty of Paris). The resettlement of the Arab population should preferably be done through a treaty or agreement with a neighboring Arab country or countries, but if that proves impossible, it can still be effected by Israeli legislation, following the guidelines established by international law in 1919, 1923, 1945 and 1947.

The legal situation with respect to transfer or repatriation has not been materially changed by the Rome Statute of the International Criminal Court drafted and signed at Rome on July 17, 1998. According to Article 5.1 of the Statute, the International Criminal Court will have jurisdiction with respect to the following crimes: the crime of genocide, crimes against humanity, war crimes and the crime of aggression. One of the crimes against humanity is "deportation or forcible transfer of population", which the Statute defines in Article 7.2(d) as "forced displacement of the persons concerned by expulsion or other coercive acts from the area in which they are lawfully present, without grounds permitted under international law". Among the war crimes listed by the Statute in Article 8 are "unlawful deportation or transfer" [specifically Article 8.2(a)(vii)] and "the transfer, directly or indirectly by the Occupying Power of parts of its own civilian population into the territory it occupies, or the deportation or transfer of all or parts of the population of the occupied territory within or outside this territory" [specifically Article 8.2(b)(viii)].

As regards the deportation or forcible transfer of population, it should be noted that Article 7.2(d), when read conversely, does not necessarily consider such an act to be a crime, specifically in those cases where there actually exist "grounds permitted under international law". One of those grounds has to be the demonstrated irreconcilability over a considerable period of time of two ethnic or national groups vying for supremacy in the same territory to which only one has a recognized legal right under international law. Prolonged and violent irreconcilability, as was demonstrated by the twelve million former German inhabitants of areas now part of Poland, Czechoslovakia, Russia, etc., is a recognized ground for separating warring or hostile populations in a given state.[58] In the case of Palestine, there has been incessant fighting between Arabs and Jews ever since the Jews were subjected to Arab rioting and violence immediately preceding the adoption of the San Remo Resolution of April 25, 1920 confirming the right of the Jewish People to Palestine. The evidence is thus

[58] The same analogy exists in civil law, where a marriage that has irretrievably broken down is a sufficient ground for granting divorce.

compelling that this constant strife can only be eliminated and the Jewish right to Palestine secured by the transfer of most of the Arab population to nearby Arab lands in accordance with the grounds permitted under international law, as laid out in the Potsdam Agreement of 1945 and the Lausanne Convention of 1923 and as alluded to in the Rome Statute itself.

In reference to the war crime of unlawful deportation or transfer which, under Article 8.2(a)(vii) of the Rome Statute, is defined as one of the "grave breaches of the Geneva Conventions of August 12, 1949", this article of the Statute does not apply to Israel's position in Judea, Samaria and Gaza, because, as repeatedly noted, these regions are part of the Jewish National Home and Land of Israel, rather than occupied territories as defined or embodied in the Hague Regulations and Fourth Geneva Convention. Moreover, the transfer of Arabs from Judea, Samaria and Gaza would not constitute a war crime under this article because they or their descendants are not citizens of the State of Israel which has a sovereign right to these areas and can therefore deport all aliens therefrom, no matter how long these Arabs have resided in the land, so long as it is done in an orderly and humane manner. The transfer of the Arabs can also be justified because of their acts of terrorism or support of same against the Jewish State, which they endeavour to destroy and replace with an Arab state.

By the same token and contrary to widespread belief, Israel is not bound either by the so-called "anti-settlement provision" in Article 8.2(b)(viii). That provision contains a two-fold prohibition. On the one hand, it prohibits the transfer of parts of the civilian population of the Occupying Power to the occupied territory, inspired by Article 49(6) of the Fourth Geneva Convention, while, on the other hand, it also prohibits, in imitation of Article 49(1) of the Convention, the transfer or deportation of the inhabitants of the occupied territory, either within or outside it. The Rome Statute considers both kinds of transfer as "serious violations of the laws and customs applicable in international armed conflict, within the established framework of international law". This formulation of the laws and customs of war governing occupied territories was initiated by Egypt for the express purpose of branding Israeli settlements in Judea, Samaria and Gaza as war crimes under international law, even though the word "settlements" is not expressly mentioned therein. At first glance, it may seem that Egypt is succeeding in its ploy to have Israel indicted for committing war crimes. However, to gain a proper perspective and understanding of the matter, Article 8.2(b)(viii) of the Rome Statute must be weighed against Articles 6 and 11 of the Mandate for Palestine, which established a right of Jewish, hence Israeli, settlement anywhere in the Jewish National Home, particularly in the very areas where such settlements would be considered a war crime if the Egyptian interpretation proved correct. In addition, the right to continue to build settlements has been preserved by the principle of acquired legal rights which do not expire with the termination of the treaty or international instrument that gave birth to such rights, a principle subsequently enshrined in Article 70(1)(b) of the Vienna Convention on the Law of Treaties. The Jewish/Israeli right to erect settlements in the Land of Israel or former Mandated Palestine is also preserved in the Law of Return enacted by the Knesset of Israel on July 5, 1950. Furthermore, as already pointed out in the previous chapter and relying upon the scholarly work of the late renowned jurist, Professor Ya'akov Meron of Jerusalem, all the Israeli settlements established on ownerless waste lands, known in the Ottoman Turkish land system as *mewat* land, located in Judea, Samaria or Gaza, are perfectly legal under the local law prevailing there, which continued to remain in force even after Israel re-took control of these areas in the Six-Day War. Such was the case, for instance, for the score of settlements that Israel built on the arid sand dunes in the southern end of the Gaza Strip, in Gush Katif that were dismantled by the Israeli Government in August 2005. These facts regarding the legality of Israeli settlements in all of the Land of Israel under Israel's jurisdiction should conclusively rule out the application of the Rome Statute to Israeli settlements in these regions, since not only are such settlements sanctioned by international law and also by the municipal or domestic law, the land on which they are established cannot be considered "occupied territory". The false impression that the Rome Statute applies to Judea, Samaria and Gaza is one which Israel itself, as already noted, ironically and insanely nurtures whenever its political leaders, government officials, as well as Supreme Court judges and academic jurists refer to the areas of the Jewish National Home as "occupied" or "governed by the laws of belligerent occupation". This is an additional reason for stating that the Eshkol National Unity Government erred grievously in not incorporating these regions into the borders of the State of Israel in the immediate aftermath of the Six-Day War.

The word "transfer" widely used in Israel since the late 1980s to denote the removal of Arabs from the Land of Israel to an Arab country is more accurately described by one of the following terms: repatriation, resettlement, relocation or exchange of populations. "Transfer" in the legal sense, as used in the domestic law of several Western countries, generally refers to something inanimate being transferred, particularly property or land conveyed in a legal deed. Until 1945, this term was not generally used for moving people from one country to another carried out under the provisions of a treaty or other agreement, but now this word has gained widespread acceptance ever since it was used, first in the Potsdam Agreement (1945), later in the Fourth Geneva Convention (1949) and lastly in the Rome Statute (1998). The term "transfer" is not explicitly defined in the Potsdam Agreement, but is used synonymously with the term "expulsion", specifically in regard to the expulsion of German populations from the countries of their birth and domicile to Germany. In the Fourth Geneva Convention, it connotes the deportation of a person living in occupied territory who is not a national or citizen of the Occupying Power, from the occupied territory to the territory of the Occupying Power or to that of any other country, occupied or not. The definition of "transfer" was more strictly defined in the Rome Statute where it means, as pointed out above, "forced displacement of the persons concerned by expulsion or other coercive acts from the area in which they are lawfully present, without grounds permitted under international law". In this context, "transfer" simply means unlawful expulsion or deportation either to a different country or to a different region within the same country, irrespective of whether the territory is occupied or not. A specific example of a forced internal displacement of a settled population from one region to another in the same country without the loss of citizenship of the displaced persons occurred in Cyprus in July 1974 during the Turkish invasion and occupation of over 30% of the island when about 200,000 Greek Cypriots were transferred against their will from Turkish-populated areas to Greek-populated areas. An internal displacement that is coercive in nature but which does not involve a military attack by one state against another was implemented by the Government of Israel in August 2005 under Prime Minister Sharon's Unilateral Disengagement Plan approved in principle by a split Cabinet vote on June 6, 2004 after being rejected earlier in a Likud party referendum on May 2, 2004. To carry out this plan, Israeli soldiers evacuated about 9,000 Jews living in twenty-one settlements in Gush Katif and the rest of the region of Gaza as well as those in four settlements in Northern Samaria, to other parts of the Land of Israel. The settlements themselves were destroyed. Legally, it is likely that the execution of the plan fitted the definition of an illegal transfer under the Rome Statute. However, since this kind of transfer was carried out by the home government of those who were transferred and did not involve a military attack by a foreign state against Israel, it did not constitute a "crime against humanity" as defined in Article 7(1) of the Rome Statute.

Insofar as the laws of the State of Israel are concerned, the forced transfer or ouster of Jews from Gaza and Samaria was illegal. In the first instance, it violated Section 1 of the 1950 Law of Return which confirms the pre-existing right of "every Jew... *to come to this land [country]* as an *oleh* [immigrant]". The right referred to in Section 1 is called the "Right of Return" and it applies not only to the State of Israel but to all regions of the Land of Israel, as is evidenced by the use of the Hebrew word *eretz* (in the form *artza*, meaning "to the land") rather than *medina* ("state") to describe the destination of the *oleh*. The distinction between these two terms which indicates the scope of application of the Law of Return was made in the Law itself, as well as in the Explanatory Note when the bill was first presented to the Knesset on June 27, 1950. If the Right of Return had only been limited to the State, the Law when enacted should have used the term *medina* instead of *eretz*. The law enacted by the Knesset on February 16, 2005 to implement the Unilateral Disengagement Plan and the orders issued thereunder were unconstitutional because they contradicted the most fundamental right of the Jewish People, enshrined in the Law of Return, to immigrate to and settle anywhere in the Land of Israel under the State's effective control. This right existed, according to Israel's first Prime Minister, David Ben-Gurion, even before the State came into existence.

The uprooting of Israeli settlements in the Land of Israel in conjunction with the forced transfer of Jews from Gaza and Northern Samaria was a serious violation of the rights of the Jewish People derived from Article 6 of the Mandate for Palestine, which obliged the Administration of Palestine to encourage "close settlement by Jews on the land, including State lands and waste lands not required for public purposes", as further amplified in Article 11 of the Mandate which requires the Government to promote "the close settlement and intensive cultivation of the land". These rights are still in force in the State of Israel by virtue of Article 11 of the Law and Administration Ordinance,[59] with the necessary change that the Government of Israel now replaces the Administration of Palestine as the ruling body. The application of the rights derived from Article 6 today clearly means that the Government of Israel is, as in the case of the Law of Return, prohibited by its own constitutional law from uprooting authorized settlements in the Land of Israel.

The Jewish right of return and of settlement in the Land of Israel is not only embodied in the Law of Return and Article 6 of the Mandate, it is also expressly referred to in the Proclamation of Independence of the State of Israel, which declares in its opening paragraphs that "Eretz-Israel was the birthplace of the Jewish People... [who] never ceased to pray and hope for their return to it and for the restoration in it of their political freedom". Furthermore, in dismantling 25 settlement in Gaza and Northern Samaria, the Government of Israel not only violated the Law of Return, the Jewish rights inherited from the Mandate for Palestine and the Proclamation of Independence, it also impaired the sovereignty of the Jewish State over the Land of Israel in direct violation of Article 97 of the Penal Code, dealing with the crime of treason.

In contrast to the uprooting of Jews from legally established settlements, the transfer of Arabs from the Land of Israel would be legal if regulated by state law or executed in accordance with past precedents under international law. The framework of Israeli law can thus be invoked to regulate the transfer of large numbers of the Arab population in any part of the Land of Israel who have plotted, engaged in or supported acts of terrorism and violence against the people of Israel in order to destroy the State and drive out its Jewish inhabitants. Those who support these acts, including Israeli Arabs, should be denied the right to continue to live in the Land of Israel. Deportation or transfer of Israeli Arabs can also be legally justified if they refuse to swear allegiance to the Jewish State or to perform national service if a law is passed to that effect. However, as regards the Arabs of Judea, Samaria and Gaza, this should follow rather than precede the incorporation of these regions into the State to avoid the accusation that Israel has no right to do so as an "Occupying Power", even though Israel

---

[59] Article 11 of the Law and Administration Ordinance states: "The law which existed in Palestine on the 5th of Iyar, 5708 (May 14, 1948) shall remain in force, insofar as there is nothing therein repugnant to this Ordinance, or to the other laws which may be enacted by or on behalf of the Provisional Council of State and subject to such modifications as may result from the establishment of the State and its authorities."

does not fall into this category. Once this is done, then those who commit treason by supporting enemy and criminal organizations intent on destroying the State can be deported or transferred without any legal objection (cf. above, the case of the Germans expelled in the aftermath of World War II).

The converse of Arab resettlement from the Land of Israel should also be borne in mind, namely the repatriation of Jews in the Exile to the Land of Israel. That, too, at various times was considered unrealistic. The name given to Jewish repatriation is not "transfer", but rather *aliya* (immigration) or *kibbutz galuyot* (the Ingathering of the Exiles), which was the chief means for achieving the establishment of the Jewish State. It is still one of the aims and requirements of Zionism for strengthening the State of Israel as set out in the Jerusalem Program, adopted originally by the Twenty-Third Zionist Congress in 1951 and reformulated by the Twenty-Seventh Congress of 1968. If the "transfer" of Jews to Israel is seen as a positive step, there is no reason not to conclude that a similar "transfer" of Arabs to Arab countries outside the Land of Israel can be equally beneficial for them. Jewish immigration and Arab emigration do in fact complement one another. It will end the friction and the state of perpetual conflict between Arabs and Jews in the Land of Israel. As demonstrated conclusively by the accumulated evidence of almost a century of hostility and fighting, the two nations cannot peacefully coexist at all in the same land. In this regard, transfer and the exchange of populations has been decisive to the success of the Jewish State. The transfer of Jews from foreign countries, including many Arab and Moslem countries, to the Land of Israel during the 20th century rebuilt the Jewish State. On the other hand, the past exodus and future transfer of Arabs from the Land of Israel has ensured and will continue to ensure the State's permanency in peace.

The expulsion of non-Jews from the Land of Israel goes back to the events recorded in the Bible. Explicit instructions were given to Moses by God to relay to the Israelites as they were about to cross into the Land of Canaan[60] from their place of encampment east of the Jordan at Abel Shittim (or Shittin) opposite Jericho to forewarn them of what they had to do to ensure their permanent and trouble-free possession of the Promised Land. God's injunction is given in the

---

[60] There is no single geographical definition of the Land of Canaan in the Bible. According to the *Encyclopedic Dictionary of the Bible*, by Louis F. Hartman, McGraw-Hill Book Company, Inc. (1963), p. 343, Canaan "is used at times in a general sense for the whole inhabited region between Mesopotamia and Egypt (Gen 11:31; 12:5) [i.e., encompassing all of Palestine and Syria], or at least the whole region where the Patriarchs lived (Exodus 6:4), and at times, in the limited sense, only of the land west of the Jordan (Genesis 13:12; Numbers 32:30-32), but usually it refers merely to the Promised Land, in a general way". After the Israelite conquest of the Land of Canaan under Joshua bin Nun, the land was thenceforth known as the Land of Israel, and in the Second Temple Period as Judea in its broad usage, until the Romans artificially renamed the Jewish country, i.e., Judea, after the Philistines, who at the time of this renaming in the second century had already disappeared as a separate nation hundreds of years before.

Book of Numbers (Be-Midbar), chapter 33, verses 50-56:[61]

> And the Lord spoke to Moses in the Plains of Moab by the Jordan at Jericho, saying: "Speak to the Children of Israel, and say to them: 'When you cross the Jordan into the Land of Canaan, then *you shall drive out all the inhabitants of the land from before you,* and destroy all their figured stones, and destroy all their molten images and demolish all their high places. And you shall drive out the inhabitants of land and dwell therein; *since it is to you that I have given the land to possess....* But *if you do not drive out the inhabitants of the land from before you, then those who remain shall be thorns in your eyes and pricks in your sides, and they shall harass you in the land wherein you dwell. And it shall come to pass that as I thought to do to them, so will I do to you'* " (emphasis added).

The significance of these verses is twofold. First, peace will never reign in the Land of Canaan (Land of Israel) that was about to be conquered and settled by the Israelites until all the previous inhabitants were first expelled. Second, if not all these inhabitants were expelled by the Israelites, as enjoined by God, then the Israelites themselves would suffer the very fate that God had intended for the Canaanites.

An even harsher commandment, though of somewhat narrower application is given to the Israelites in the Book of Deuteronomy (*Devarim*) in chapter 7, verses 1-2:[62]

> When the Lord your God brings you into the land you are entering to possess it, He shall cast out many nations before you – the Hittites, the Girgashites, the Amorites, the Canaanites, the Perizzites, the Hivites and the Jebusites – seven nations greater and mightier than you. When the Lord your God delivers them up before you and you smite them, then *you shall utterly destroy them*; you shall make no covenant with them nor show them any mercy; neither shall you intermarry with them: do not give your daughters to their sons and do not take their daughters for your sons.... (emphasis added).

In the Deuteronomic verses, the Israelites are forewarned that after the seven Canaanite nations are uprooted and defeated in battle, they must not make any treaty with them but utterly destroy them. The inhabitants of the Land of Canaan in the days of Moses and Joshua were composed of diverse ethnic nations, including among them the Hittites (Hethites), Amorites, Girgashites,

---

[61] See *The Holy Scriptures according to the Masoretic Text*, Volume I, The Jewish Publication Society of America (1955), p. 410-411. Archaic English phraseology has been replaced by more modern phrases.

[62] *Ibid.*, p. 438-439. Archaic English phraseology has been replaced.

Hivites, Jebusites and others, most of whom were Semitic-speaking. Despite their ethnic diversity, it is stated in Genesis (10:6; 15:19) and First Chronicles (1:8, 13-16) that the nations mentioned above by name all had a common eponymous ancestor, Canaan, who was the fourth son of Ham and grandson of Noah. This was the reason they all bore the generic name "Canaanites", though the same term is sometimes also used to specify only one among the seven nations that comprised the Canaanite family. Their expulsion from the Land and destruction was justified according to the Book of Deuteronomy (9:4-6) because of their persistent wickedness over a long period and not because of the virtue of the Israelites. An additional reason was God's desire to keep the oath He had sworn to the Patriarchs, Abraham, Isaac and Jacob. The expulsion of the Canaanites brought relative quiet within the land, but the divine decree was not fully carried out immediately, since strong pockets of Canaanites continued to live among the Israelites several centuries more, until they were eventually absorbed into the Israelite nation. Those who inhabited the large coastal cities in the North, off the Mediterranean Sea (e.g. Tyre, Sidon, Gebal [Byblos]) were later known as the Phoenicians.

In comparing the two injunctions, the one in the Book of Numbers is seen to be broader in scope since it refers to *all* inhabitants of the land who the Lord said were to be driven out from the Land of Canaan, whereas the injunction in Deuteronomy refers only to the seven Canaanite nations. One interpretation of the injunction in Numbers is that it remains valid for all time, since it is an order that includes within its meaning not only the inhabitants of that day, over three thousand years ago, but also applies to the non-Jewish inhabitants of the Land at any time since. In contrast, once the Divine commands were fulfilled as regards the seven Canaanite nations, the injunction in Deuteronomy had no further application. This is confirmed by the fact that the Canaanites have long ceased to exist as separate or recognized nations.

Modern Arabs have falsely claimed to be the descendants of the ancient Canaanites to prove that they preceded the Israelites historically as the aboriginal inhabitants of the land. An undated letter sent by Ibn Saud to Churchill, shown to him on May 2, 1945 claimed that the Canaanites were "an Arab tribe" from whom the Israelite leader Joshua, the successor of Moses, had captured the land.[63] If this absurd Arab claim of Canaanite descent were literally true, then, as some have argued, the biblical injunction in the Book of Numbers would be applicable to them.

There is indeed a striking parallel between the situation that existed when the Israelites entered the Land of Canaan and when the Jews of the late 19th century started to return to their ancient homeland. In each case, the Israelites of yore and the Jews of today had to fight battles and wars to secure their rights to the Promised Land/the Jewish National Home against the settled population who were deeply antagonistic to them. If the Biblical precedent in Numbers is

[63] Gilbert, *op. cit.*, p. 237.

adhered to, most of the Arabs presently residing in the Land of Israel will be eventually transferred, otherwise, as the Bible predicts, and is already evident in unfolding events, "those who remain shall be thorns in the eyes and pricks in the sides" of the Jews, and even worse, the latter will themselves be driven out of the land.

The Biblical warning has apparently proven prophetic in the words of an Islamic Movement leader in Israel, Sheikh Kamal Khatib, who is reported to have made the following statement on May 9, 2008 at Kafr Kanna, a village in the Galilee near Nazareth:[64]

> ...in 1948, we were 150,000 Palestinians, and today we are but 1,300,000 thorns in [the Israelis'] sides and rocks on their chests... we are here to stay, like the [olive] oil of the Galilee, the grapes of the Galilee and the Jaffa orange... You speak of expulsion and transfer. You can murder and imprison us – there will not be a second "Nakba". There will not be tents, there will not be refugees. This is our decision – this land is our land whether we live on it with honour or we die on it as martyrs.

Apart from the Biblical precedent, other grounds exist for the eventual transfer of Arabs from the Land of Israel. The majority of Arabs have, demonstrably, for a long time adamantly refused to co-exist peacefully with Jews or to accept the permanent establishment of a Jewish State. Article 6[65] of the Palestinian National Covenant, as amended in July 1968, requires the eventual expulsion or uprooting of all Jews from the Land of Israel, who arrived after the "Zionist invasion". This radical provision of the Covenant, if ever realized, would mean the extinction of the Jewish State of Israel and the compulsory expulsion of several millions of Jews now living in their homeland, since these Jews are nothing more than "invaders" of Arab land. The beginning of the "Zionist invasion" which is dated by Arab spokesman either to 1917, the year of the Balfour Declaration, or even earlier, to 1882 when the first organized group of Jewish immigrants began to arrive under the impetus of the Bilu program. In the Arab mind, a "liberated Palestine" means the purification or ethnic cleansing of the land of its alien Jewish population, since only that would ensure the Arab character of the country[66] and facilitate the return of "the Palestinian refugees".

Arab antagonism to the return of Jews to their ancestral homeland has persisted unabated ever since March 1920 when Arab soldiers and marauding

---

[64] *Jerusalem Post*, Sunday, May 11, 2008.

[65] Article 6 of the Palestinian National Covenant reads as follows: "The Jews who had normally resided in Palestine until the beginning of the Zionist invasion will be considered Palestinians."

[66] Y. Harkabi, *The Palestinian Covenant and its Meaning*, Valentine, Mitchell (1979), p. 47.

Bedouin attacked four Jewish settlements in Upper Galilee, culminating in bloody riots in Jerusalem in April 1920, which coincided with Passover and Easter as well as the Moslem festival of Nebi Moussa (Prophet Moses). Even after the Jewish State was reconstituted, the local Arabs, in conjunction with the surrounding Arab States, have tried to destroy and expel most of its Jewish citizens. The Arabs have never come to terms with the fact that Palestine was created for the sole purpose of making it the Jewish National Home, belonging exclusively to the Jewish People. The transfer of the Arab population to a nearby Arab country (or countries) is a necessity to prevent present and future conflict between Jews and Arabs. It is also a necessity to prevent the Jews from being overwhelmed by an expanding hostile Arab population that threatens the Jewish character of the State.

The first person to advocate or realize the necessity of resettling the Arabs of Palestine in other Arab countries was the celebrated English Jewish author, Israel Zangwill, in an article[67] he wrote in 1919. He had formerly been active in the Zionist Movement and its spokesman in Britain when Theodor Herzl was alive. He was held in high esteem by Herzl who called him a genius. Zangwill left the movement in 1905 after the Seventh Zionist Congress rejected the East Africa (Uganda) proposal to establish a temporary Jewish settlement under a Jewish governor and a Jewish administration in the British territory, that would serve as a way-station to Palestine, or as Max Nordau put it, a Nachtasyl (shelter for the night). He rejoined the ranks of Zionism when the British Government issued the Balfour Declaration (November 2, 1917), believing it would pave the way for a Jewish State as envisioned by Herzl. However, Zangwill became disillusioned with the way the official Zionist leadership under the sway of Weizmann interpreted the Balfour Declaration as presented in the Zionist proposals submitted to the Principal Allied and Associated Powers at the Paris Peace Conference of 1919. He criticized these proposals for allowing the predominant Arab population to remain in place, while the Jews who were then outnumbered by a ratio of about 1 to 6 would "crawl into a corner of its own like a leper colony…"[68] For Zangwill, this conception of Palestine was "neither Jewish, nor National, nor a Home". To rectify this unfavourable situation and build up a model state having a Jewish majority – though not a totality – he urged the gradual resettlement of Palestine's Arabs in the adjoining territories which had just been liberated from the yoke of the Ottoman Empire. The Arabs would receive reasonable compensation for the expropriation of their privately-owned land, which would be nationalized for purposes of the projected Jewish State. Zangwill was denounced and ridiculed at the time by Weizmann and his

[67] Zangwill's article entitled "Before the Peace Conference" appeared in the journal Asia (February 1919), pp. 105 ff. A synopsis of his views on Arab resettlement is found in the book *Palestine: A Study of Jewish, Arab and British Policies*, published for the ESCO Foundation for Palestine, Inc., Yale University Press (1947), Vol. I, pp. 158-159.

[68] *Ibid.*

inner circle, but ironically, twenty years later, a variation of Zangwill's plan for Arab resettlement was embraced by Weizmann, Sharett and Namier, as the practical solution for solving the Palestine question, when it was proposed to them by Harry St. John Philby. Adding to the irony of the situation was the fact that during the twenty years that had elapsed since Zangwill had first published his thoughts on the need for Arab resettlement, the British, in administering the Mandate for Palestine, did the very opposite of what he had recommended to secure the establishment of the Jewish National Home and of the Jewish State. Instead of their resettlement, the British, from the time they began their rule in Palestine, allowed large numbers of Arabs to flow into the country unhampered thus doubling the original Arab population, while, at the same time, placing tight controls on Jewish immigration, contrary to Article 6 of the Mandate.

In retrospect, had the wise advice of Zangwill been followed in 1919 and serious action taken to implement his scheme on Arab resettlement and to forestall illegal Arab immigration from neighbouring lands into Palestine, the Jewish State could have been achieved much sooner, possibly without the war of 1948. Israel today would have been spared the bloodshed and violence it faces daily from hostile Arabs inside the Jewish National Home who pretentiously claim the land as their very own. Finally, it should be noted that the Philby Plan for Arab transfer was merely an updated rendition of the Zangwill proposal.

A 20th century precedent already exists in Palestine itself for implementing the idea of Arab transfer. This precedent involves the former German Christian community which on the eve of World War II numbered about 2,000 people whose roots in Palestine went back to 1868 when they established their first settlements. They were subdivided into three religious groups: 1350 Templers (Templars), led by Christoph Hoffmann, 450 Protestants and 200 Catholics.[69] They founded four rural settlements comprising Sarona, today a part of Tel-Aviv where the Kirya (site of the present day Israeli Ministry of Defense) is situated; Wilhelma, in the Lydda plain, named after the Kaiser; and two villages called Waldheim and Bethlehem in the Lower Galilee in the northwestern Jezreel Valley. These were supplemented by three urban or suburban quarters in Jerusalem, Jaffa and Haifa that came to be known as "the German colonies". During the Arab disturbances in 1936-1939, the Galilean villages harboured

[69] These figures were given in a memorandum submitted by the Jewish Agency in London to the British Government on May 22, 1945. It is printed in *The Jewish Case Before the Anglo-American Committee of Inquiry on Palestine, as presented by the Jewish Agency for Palestine*, Hyperion Press, Inc., Westport, Connecticut, pp. 326-330. The Templers were members of a Pietist Protestant sect founded in Wurttemberg, Germany in the mid-19th century who were expelled from the Lutheran Church in 1858. They advocated a return to early Christianity and the establishment of urban and rural settlements in Palestine. For this purpose they established a "Temple Society" under the name of Tempelgesellschaft, whence their name in English – "Templers". See articles in the *Encyclopedia Of Zionism And Israel* (1971), Volume 2, p. 1106 and the *Encyclopaedia Judaica* (1971), Vol. 15, column 994.

Arab terrorists, serving at times as bases for their operations, and the villagers even instructed them on how to carry out acts of terrorism against the Yishuv (the Jewish community of Mandated Palestine). The German settlements became enthusiastic centers of Nazi activity in the Middle East. Some young Germans in Palestine joined elite units commissioned to exterminate the Jews in Europe, called the SS or *Schutzstaffel.* The complete identification of the Palestinian Germans with Nazi Germany led to their internment, both in Palestine and abroad. Their pro-Nazi sympathies drew a fierce reaction from the Jewish Agency for Palestine. In a letter addressed to the High Commissioner on June 4, 1945, its second highest ranking representative, Moshe Sharett, who became Israel's second Prime Minister, demanded the entire evacuation of the Palestinian German Colony. This letter was also presented in evidence to the Anglo-American Committee of Inquiry, with a covering letter dated March 25, 1946. An excerpt from Sharett's original letter to the High Commissioner follows:

> It is not for the Jewish Agency to stress the dangers from the British point of view involved in the continuance in Palestine *of this vehemently hostile element.* The Jewish Agency, however, feels it its duty to give emphatic expression to Jewish feeling on this subject. Jews in Palestine feel utterly unable to contemplate the return to their country or the resumption of free residence in it of *this community of Jew-haters.* It appears to them inconceivable, after millions of their brethren were exterminated by the Nazis and their henchmen with the tacit approval of the mass of the German people, that here in the very land of the Jewish National Home, Nazi Germans, as fanatical as any of those who perpetrated the horrors in Europe, should be allowed to re-establish themselves in so close and revolting proximity to Jewish settlements and quarters and outrage the feelings of every Jew who meets them. The Jewish Agency cannot believe that H.M.G. should desire to subject the Jews of Palestine to so violent a provocation and to create in Palestine this new source of grave trouble and possible bloodshed.
>
> It is therefore the earnest submission of the Jewish Agency that the former German residents of Palestine who are now in Germany or elsewhere abroad should not be allowed to return to Palestine; that the Germans still in Palestine, presumably all in internment, should be evacuated to Germany – in short, that the *German colony in Palestine should be wound up and their fatherland be called upon to make room for its loyal and worthy sons and daughters deported from a country where their presence,* because of Germany's own misdeeds, *has become an intolerable anomaly* (emphasis added).

Further on in the same letter, Sharett said that "the evacuation and transfer" of the Palestinian German Nazis "from the country of the Jewish National Home" to their fatherland in Germany was "an absolute and imperative necessity". Though the German population in Palestine was very tiny compared to the millions of Arabs now living in the Land of Israel, the same principle and underlying rationale which justified its expulsion also holds true today for the vast majority of the Arab population which supports violence and acts of terror against Jews in their National Home. Their unbounded hatred of the State of Israel is no different in kind and degree from that exhibited by Palestinian Germans towards the Jews of Mandated Palestine and therefore the very same remedy used in regard to them should also be adopted in the case of the vehemently hostile Arabs of the Land of Israel, to be carried out within the framework of both Israeli and international law to eradicate the "source of great trouble and bloodshed" representing "an intolerable anomaly".

As already noted above, a strong proponent for expelling Arabs from Palestine was none other than the most important American political figure in the twentieth century, President Franklin Delano Roosevelt, who confided his thoughts on the matter to two of his close aides: Henry Morgenthau, Jr., Secretary of the Treasury from 1934 until 1945, and Edward Reilly Stettinius, Jr., Undersecretary of State in 1943-44 and Secretary of State from November 1944 to June 1945, succeeding Cordell Hull in the latter position. Roosevelt based his position on the overriding fact that Palestine had been promised to the Jews in the Balfour Declaration, which for him was justification enough for the entire Arab population of Palestine to be evacuated to a nearby Arab land. In 1938 he told Secretary of State Cordell Hull:[70]

> I was at Versailles [i.e., the Paris Peace Conference], and I know that the British made no secret of the fact they promised Palestine to the Jews. Why are they now reneging on their promise?

Roosevelt's conviction that Palestine was meant exclusively for the Jews inspired him to draw up his own plan to transfer hundreds of thousands of the country's Arabs to Iraq, financed by a large loan of about 300 million dollars, one third of which was to be put up by Britain and France, one third by the United States and the rest by wealthy Jews of the Western democracies.[71] This plan was quite similar to the Philby Plan but it was independently conceived and circulated several months before Philby made his own scheme known to Weizmann on September 28, 1939. Roosevelt discussed his plan early in 1939 with such prominent Jewish figures as Supreme Court Justice, Louis Dembitz

---

[70] *Israel in the Mind of America*, by Peter Grose, Alfred A. Knopf (1984), p. 134.

[71] Peter Grose, *op. cit.*, p. 138.

Brandeis,[72] and Conservative Rabbi Solomon Goldman,[73] President of the Zionist Organization of America. He also met twice with British representatives to appraise them of what he had in mind, but they did not believe the Arabs would move from Palestine, financial inducement notwithstanding.[74] However, Roosevelt continued to believe in the plan he had formulated despite the negative British reaction. He told his Zionist friends that "as soon as he was somewhat relieved from the pressure of other affairs, he might try to tackle the job," and as the author Peter Grose adds, "solve the problem by his own personal statesmanship".

In 1942, Roosevelt spoke about his Arab resettlement plan to Treasury Secretary Morgenthau, who diligently recorded what the President said in his diaries:[75]

> What I think I will do is this. First, I would call Palestine a religious country. Then I would leave Jerusalem the way it is and have it run by the Orthodox Greek Catholic Church, the Protestants and the Jews – have a joint committee run it... I actually would put a barbed wire around Palestine, and I would begin to move the Arabs out... I would provide land for the Arabs in some other part of the Middle East... Each time we move out an Arab we would bring in another Jewish family... But I don't want to bring in more than they can economically support... It would be an independent nation just like any other

---

[72] Among the Zionist leaders who saw the resettlement of Arabs as a way to end the Palestine problem which resulted in intermittent Arab riots against the Yishuv (Jewish community) was Louis Dembitz Brandeis, the most outstanding figure in the history of American Zionism and the first Jew to be appointed to the U.S. Supreme Court. See Edward Alexander's review of the book written by Rafael Medoff, *Zionism and the Arabs: An American-Jewish Dilemma, 1898-1948*, Praeger Publishers, Westport, CT (1997) – where he writes: "While Brandeis was offering scholarships to young Arabs, he was privately encouraging his colleagues to explore the possibility of resettling them outside Palestine". His review appeared in the Jewish monthly, *Midstream*, May/June 1998, p. 40.

[73] *The Letters and Papers of Chaim Weizmann*, Vol. XIX, Series A, Letter 52, "To Solomon Goldman, Chicago, April 28, 1939", pp. 53-56. A copy of Goldman's letter to Ben-Gurion dated April 6, 1939 (in Hebrew) was sent to Weizmann by Ben-Gurion. The letter gave details of Goldman's interview with President Roosevelt, who in the context of an overall solution raised the possibility of the transfer of hundreds of thousands of Palestine Arabs to Iraq. Peter Grose, in his book *Israel in the Mind of America*, states that FDR's plan to transfer Arabs was also the subject of a letter from [Nahum] Goldmann to Weizmann, June 20, 1939. Grose, *op. cit.*, p. 330. This letter is found in the Central Zionist Archives, S25/237b.

[74] Peter Grose, *op. cit.*, pp. 138-139.

[75] *Ibid.*, p. 140. The citation for FDR's 1942 comments in Peter Grose's book is: John Morton Blum, *From the Morgenthau Diaries, Years of War, 1941-45*, Boston: Houghton Mifflin, 1967, ch. 5, p. 208.

> nation… Naturally, if there are 90% Jews, the Jews would dominate the government… There are lots of places to which you could move the Arabs. All you have to do is drill a well, because there is this large underground water supply, and we can move the Arabs to places where they can really live…

Collaborating evidence of Roosevelt's vision for Palestine is provided by Secretary Stettinius's diary, in an entry he made on November 10, 1944 where he recorded the President's remarkably forthright statement:[76]

> Palestine should be for the Jews and no Arabs should be in it. He has definite ideas on the subject… It should be exclusive Jewish territory.

To accomplish the goal of making Palestine "exclusive Jewish territory", Roosevelt believed that:[77]

> the Arabs must be moved out of Palestine, whether they like it or not; whether by means of "baksheesh" or resettlement fund, a political deal with Arab nationalism or a barbed-wire fence…

The foregoing testimonies of President Roosevelt's position on Palestine, uttered privately in relaxed conversations with two leading and trusted officials serving in his Administration, who had no reason to misrepresent his actual words, are not only crystal-clear in meaning but very important for understanding today what may need to be done to preserve the Jewish State from its Arab enemies who are implacably opposed to its existence and have already demonstrated that they will stop at nothing to destroy it. In his candid statements, Roosevelt swept away all the false talk about Arab "rights" to Palestine that the British Government of Neville Chamberlain had invented in the 1939 White Paper to appease the Arabs and dissuade them from further supporting the Axis Powers of Germany, Italy and Japan in World War II. To bring about a Jewish State, Roosevelt firmly believed that if it were to be established as originally intended by the progenitors of the Balfour Declaration, David Lloyd George and Arthur James Balfour, most if not all of the Arabs would have to leave Palestine and be duly compensated. To keep the Arabs out of the country and to ensure it "should be exclusive Jewish territory", he even foresaw the necessity of erecting

[76] *The Diaries of Edward R. Stettinius, Jr., 1943-1946* (New York: New Viewpoints, 1975), p. 170, cited in Peter Grose's book, p. 147. See also "The President versus the Diplomats", contained in the book *The End of the Palestine Mandate*, edited by Wm. Roger Louis and Robert W. Stookey, published by I.B. Tauris and Co. Ltd., London, England (1986), p. 37.

[77] Grose, *op. cit.*, p. 147.

a barbed-wire fence around its perimeter. Roosevelt earnestly thought that a deal could be brokered under his prodding and guidance with the principal Arab leader of the day, Ibn-Saud, King of Saudi Arabia. In that respect he had overestimated his power of personal persuasion with Ibn Saud, who though originally amenable to the Philby Plan, had by the year 1945 rejected such plans altogether – too much time had elapsed for them to be still relevant for him. Thus, when Roosevelt met the Arab desert king aboard an American cruiser, the "Quincy", docked in the Great Bitter Lake, midway through the Suez Canal on his way home from a conference with Josef Stalin and Churchill at the Crimean resort of Yalta in February 1945, the King adamantly refused all overtures to favourably discuss the matter of Palestine with him. The King is reported to have told the President:[78]

> The Arabs and the Jews could never cooperate, neither in Palestine nor in any other country… The Arabs would choose to die rather than yield their lands to the Jews.

In an extemporaneous remark to Congress "that sent shivers through the American Jewish community and puzzled even his own advisers", according to Peter Grose, the President said:[79]

> On the problem of Arabia, I learned more about that whole problem – the Moslem problem, the Jewish problem – by talking with Ibn Saud for five minutes than I could have learned in the exchange of two or three dozen letters.

Roosevelt's change of position became clear when he informed Judge Joseph Proskauer, then President of the American Jewish Committee and himself an opponent of the establishment of a Jewish State, that "Jewish statehood was absolutely out of the question under present circumstances".[80]

Roosevelt's talk with Ibn Saud ended any hope that he could make a deal with the Saudi monarch over Palestine as he previously believed. According to the secret American account of their meeting, the President assured Ibn Saud that:[81]

> He would do nothing to assist the Jews against the Arabs and would make no move hostile to the Arab people, nor would his government

[78] Grose, *op. cit.*, p. 152. Grose's source is *FRUS*, 1945, Vol. VIII, pp. 2-3. See also: Gilbert, *op. cit.*, p. 232.

[79] Grose, *op. cit.*, p. 154; Gilbert, *op. cit.*, p. 234.

[80] Grose, *op. cit.*, p. 155.

[81] Gilbert, *op. cit.*, p. 233.

> change its policy [on] Palestine without full and prior consultation with both Jews and Arabs.

Roosevelt reiterated his commitment to Ibn-Saud in a letter dated April 5, 1945, that he would take no action as President which might prove hostile to the Arab people,[82] thus violating the spirit and intent of Article 5 of the Mandate that proscribed foreign Arab intervention in the internal affairs of Palestine.

There was no mention in the secret American report that Roosevelt even raised the plan he had independently conceived in 1939 to solve the Palestine problem by resettling the Arabs of Mandated Palestine in Iraq in order to create an independent Jewish state. However, to counter the bad impression Roosevelt left by his fawning remarks about Ibn Saud and his apparent *vŏlte-face* on Palestine, he met Rabbi Stephen Samuel Wise and told him that he still believed in the establishment of a Jewish State and that the Arabs would ultimately have to be overruled and a solution imposed by the United Nations.

Three days after Roosevelt's meeting with Ibn Saud, Churchill too met the Saudi monarch at Fayyum, Egypt to seek a settlement between the Jews and Arabs on Palestine. According to the War Cabinet Minutes, he pleaded the case of the Jews but did not achieve the result he desired.[83] Churchill and Roosevelt thus suffered similar disillusionment at the hands of Ibn Saud.

Despite having utterly failed in his meeting with Ibn Saud to gain from him any degree of acceptance of Zionism, Roosevelt was not mistaken in his earlier, outspoken view as to what should eventually be done in regard to the resettlement of the Arabs of Palestine in nearby Arab lands. If Arabs and Jews could never cooperate, as the King said, and if Arabs were unalterably opposed to Jewish immigration to Palestine, as he also stated, then it should be well understood that the two peoples could not amicably co-exist, and there would always be unbridgeable conflict between them, unless there was a mutual separation, exactly as Roosevelt had proposed in his plan for Arab transfer, and the erection of a barbed wire fence around Palestine. Subsequent events have vindicated Roosevelt's original views, which he expressed to Morgenthau and Stettinius, even though few today are brave enough to acknowledge he was right. There have been several Arab-Israeli wars since the Jewish State was established on May 15, 1948, because of steadfast Arab refusal to accept the existence of a Jewish State in their midst. Peace treaties Israel made with Egypt in 1979 and Jordan in 1994 seem to have changed the situation superficially, but on a government-to-government level little has really changed in regard to Arab aversion towards Israel, an aversion which also exists in the general population of these two Arab states. Their hatred of the Jewish State is fueled by Moslem

---

[82] Gilbert, *op. cit.*, p. 234. See also: *Palestine, A Study of Jewish, Arab and British Policies*, Esco Foundation for Palestine, Inc., Yale University Press, Volume Two, p. 1189.

[83] Gilbert, *op. cit.*, p. 235.

seminaries (*madrasas*), schools and universities, as well as in the media. Arab and Islamic terrorism continues unabated even after the Palestine Liberation Organization foreswore its use against Israel on September 9, 1993, in return for which Israel officially recognized the organization as the representative of the so-called Palestinian people. This should make it abundantly clear to neutral or unbiased observers, as it was for Roosevelt before his death on April 12, 1945, that his vision for a Jewish State with few Arabs inside it was the correct one. The opposite vision propounded by President George W. Bush of a divided or shared Cisjordanian Palestine with Jewish and Arab states living side by side in "peace" with each other is a fantasy. Rather than peace, the projected Arab state will likely become a hotbed of terrorism and irredentism. The two-state solution is thus a certain recipe for disaster that will only weaken Israel and do nothing to remove the inbred, all-consuming Arab and Moslem hatred for the Jewish State based on religious dogma and nationalist strivings to recapture the rest of what they consider to be "Arab land". Bush's two-state vision will, therefore, make Israel an inviting target for a renewed Arab assault to destroy the Jewish State.

President Roosevelt was being more truthful and far-sighted than the Jewish and Zionist leaders he consulted, who never previously advocated what he did or were simply afraid of asserting it – that Palestine should ultimately become a Jewish State in the sense that Chaim Weizmann once imagined in 1919 at the Paris Peace Conference: "as Jewish as England is English", an expression first uttered by the pro-Zionist British journalist, Herbert Sidebotham. This idea of a predominately Jewish Palestine was subsequently discarded by Weizmann who, during the 1930s, became a proponent of Jewish parity with the Arabs, and after the release of the Peel Commission Report – of the partition of Western Palestine, contrary to his earlier belief. It was only when he learnt of the parallel Roosevelt and Philby Plans that he adopted the concept of Arab population transfer rather than parity and partition but concealed his approval of it from the general public. By the time of Roosevelt's ascendancy as U.S. President, most Zionist leaders had already accepted the dismal prospect of having a large Arab minority in the Jewish State, despite the great danger this constituted.

An outstanding exception to the feeble Zionist response to the Arab menace threatening to overwhelm the Yishuv in the 1930s was Berl Katznelson of the Labour Zionist Movement who ranked with David Ben-Gurion among its most distinguished figures. One of his most devoted disciples, who knew him well, Ephraim Ben Haim of Kibbutz Givat Haim Me'uhedet, has described him impressively:[84]

> Berl was the conscience, the compass and the teacher of the historic Labour Movement.

---

[84] Letter to the author, dated 22.6.03. A moving portrait of Berl Katznelson's extraordinary life, written by Ephraim Ben-Haim, appears in the March 1998 issue of *Nativ Journal*, pp. 84-88, entitled "*Ha-Moreshet Ha-Haya shel Berl Katznelson*" (The Living Heritage of Berl Katznelson).

Katznelson discussed the question of Arab population transfer in an article he wrote in August 1937 while attending the Twentieth Zionist Congress in Zurich, Switzerland, entitled *Darkhei Mediniutenu* ("Our Policy Courses"). The article was prompted by the release of the Peel Commission Report a month before the Congress convened, one of whose recommendations concerned the *compulsory* transfer of the Arab population out of the proposed Jewish State in a tiny area of Palestine of little more than 2,500 square miles representing about 20% of the area of Western Palestine, comprising all of Galilee, the Jezreel Valley and part of the coastal plain. The proposed Arab state to co-exist with the Jewish one covered the rest of Western Palestine (about 75%), including Judea, Samaria and the Negev including Gaza, except for a British enclave under permanent mandate embracing Jerusalem and Bethlehem with a corridor to the sea at Jaffa, and Nazareth. An additional feature of the Peel Partition Plan was that the Arab state was to be united with Transjordan, which is the reason why Emir Abdullah favoured it. Katznelson did not hide his view about the merits of population transfer. He wrote:[85]

> The question of population transfer raises controversy amongst us: is it permissible or forbidden? My conscience is completely clear over this: a distant neighbour is better than a near-by enemy. They [the Arabs] will not lose by their being transferred, and we – certainly not. In the final analysis, *this is, politically speaking, a resettlement measure for the benefit of both sides*. I have long since thought that *this is the best of solutions* and in the days of the [Arab] rioting, I felt more and more convinced that *this development must come about some day*. However, it is not acceptable that the transfer "out of the Land of Israel" means to the environs of Shechem. I have believed and I still believe that they will move in the future to Syria and Iraq.
>
> Another question is what the realistic chances of that happening are. I am under the impression that England will not compel them to move and will leave it [to be settled] between the two states [i.e., the Jewish and Arab states recommended in the Peel Partition Plan of 1937]. Will the Arab state want to compromise with us on this, will it find that this does not conflict with its patriotism or its dream of irredenta? – It is too early to discuss this now.
>
> On the other hand, we should not be deluded by dreams, as if we will both carry out the evacuation [resettlement] and also have the possibility of peaceful [Jewish] settlement in the neighbouring country. It is impossible to come [to the negotiating table] with a proposal for Arab population transfer to Transjordan and also for our own settling there (translated from the Hebrew with emphasis added).

[85] Berl Katznelson, *Writings*, Vol. 12, "Our Policy Courses", Zurich (August 1937), p. 361.

No one at the time would have ever accused the great Berl Katznelson, "the teacher of the [Labour Zionist] movement and its leader and warrior", as Yitzhak Tabenkin eulogized him, of being immoral or racist or anti-Arab for suggesting that the Arabs of Palestine be transferred to Iraq or Syria, rather than Transjordan. Ben-Gurion, too, showered the highest praise on Katznelson, calling him "the greatest and most important individual in the group (ha'ari she-bahavura), the teacher of a generation… the brain, the conscience and the voice of the movement…, a polymath… trustworthy … a shining example to all who came after him"[86].Those who toss the most derogatory epithets at others who advocate what Katznelson called "the best of solutions" which, he said, "must come about some day", and huffily dismiss that solution as Nazi-like, fascist, barbaric, racist or undemocratic do not wish to see the simple wisdom of this policy, espoused unreservedly by Katznelson. This policy is made necessary by unrestrained Arab antipathy to the Jewish State, which permeates most of the Arab population in the Land of Israel. If this solution to the Palestine problem was not immoral or racist for Berl Katznelson when it was being widely debated in 1937, it is not immoral or racist today when Arabs still pose the very same existential threat to the survival of the Jewish State and its legal rights and title of sovereignty over the Land of Israel.

It is strange that among certain politicians, journalists and academics who so sanctimoniously denounce the proposed transfer of Arabs from the Land of Israel as pure evil, are the very ones who advocate that same solution in reverse – for the quarter-million Jews who now live in Judea, and Samaria, whom they feel should be "repatriated" to pre-1967 Israel. This exposes the sharp inconsistency of their position as well as their hypocrisy. They vociferously oppose the transfer of Arabs from these ancestral Jewish lands because, if implemented, it would mean that Israel would not have to relinquish them to the Arabs, as they insist must be done to achieve what they erroneously believe will be peace. Arab transfer thus provides the fitting answer to the question Israeli minimalists and defeatists always smugly pose: what alternative is there to surrendering these territories for demographic reasons and for the preservation of the Jewish character of the State? The undisguised intention of these appeasers is to stifle or put out of bounds of reasonable discourse the only natural, common-sense solution to the growing demographic problem. It is also not without humour that most of the same people who adamantly insist on Israeli withdrawal to preserve the Jewish character of the State are themselves remote from the teachings of Judaism which shape that very character. It is time to expose the basic hypocrisy and fallacy of their argument which *a priori* rejects the best solution to preserve both the Jewish character of the State as well as Jewish legal rights to all parts of the National Home.

Some other good-intentioned Jews make a wrongful comparison with the Nazi era and the Holocaust to oppose any suggestion of Arab resettlement. The

---

[86] Tabenkin's and Ben-Gurion's encomiums of Katznelson are found in Ephraim Ben Haim's article, *op. cit.*, p. 84.

very mention of this idea puts them in a state of apoplectic frenzy. This reaction is misplaced and misguided because it falsely associates transfer and resettlement with the horrors of the Holocaust, when that is hardly the case. What the Nazis of Germany did was not expulsion *per se*, but the deliberate extermination of Jews as part of their diabolical Final Solution. That should not be the defining reason to say that all transfer and resettlement is wrong at all times and in all instances. The advisability of transfer depends on the circumstances of a given case. It was indeed an unqualified evil when perpetrated by the Nazis against the Jews for the purpose of extermination. It was also evil in ancient times when Jews were expelled from their homeland by the Assyrians, Babylonians and Romans respectively to ensure foreign hegemony. In the medieval period, Jews were also expelled for religious reasons from England by Edward I (1290) and from Spain (1492) by Ferdinand and Isabella, among several notorious examples in Europe. However, in other cases, transfer or resettlement has proved to be a morally defensible and effective solution that has resolved otherwise intractable national conflicts in the 20th century, specifically those involving Greece with Turkey and Bulgaria, Germany with the U.S.S.R., Poland and Czechoslovakia, India with Pakistan and even more recently in the aforementioned dispute over Cyprus between Greece and Turkey. On the flip-side of the coin, it should not be forgotten that the mass transfer of Jews from Europe to their ancient homeland was the solution of Zionism prior to the Holocaust to free millions from their miserable plight and enable them to begin a new life of hope and achievement.

Furthermore, Jews who had lived in Arab countries for many centuries, in some cases over a thousand years before the advent of Islam, were deliberately driven out by the governments of these countries, both before and after the establishment of the Jewish State in 1948. The reason for their expulsion was not because they had engaged in violence or terrorism or were disloyal to the Arab State they lived in. It was also not because the expulsion of Jews was a retaliatory act for the exodus of Arab refugees from Palestine, since the expulsion plan was conceived before there were any such refugees. In the words of Professor Ya'akov Meron,[87]

> ...this expulsion plan was announced publicly and very formally

---

[87] The most succinct and scholarly treatment of the subject of the expulsion of Jews from Arab countries at the time of Israel's rebirth, both before and after, depicted against its historical background and legal framework, is to be found in an article written by Professor Ya'akov Meron, "The Expulsion of the Jews from the Arab Countries: the Palestinians' Attitude towards It and their Claims", in: *The Forgotten Millions* (edited by Malka Hillel Shulewitz), published by Continuum, London (paperback edition), 2000, Part 2, pp. 83-125. The remarks of Prof. Meron quoted above are found on p. 85 of his article. See also pp. 87, 89, 91 and 105-107 concerning the reasons attributed to the mass expulsion of Jews from Arab states.

> by Heykal Pasha [an Egyptian delegate to the U.N. in 1947] some four months *before* the mass departure of 540,000 Arabs (according to UNRWA) from those areas in Palestine where the State of Israel was to be established. According to a reputable Arab source, '[t]he Arabs held their ground throughout the period from November 1947 to March 1948. Until the first of March not a single Arab village had been vacated by its inhabitants and the number of people leaving the mixed towns was insignificant'. If the expulsion of Jews from Arab countries was carried out as some sort of retaliation, then, according to Heykal Pasha, it was in reaction to the U.N. Resolution of 29 November 1947 regarding the partition of Palestine. Later, after the defeat of the invading Arab armies, the expulsion plan was presented as retaliation for Israel's victory, an event with which the Jews then in the Arab lands had no connection.
>
> Additional evidence of coordination by the Arab states behind the expulsion of Jews from their territories is seen in the meeting in Beirut of senior diplomats from all the Arab states, a report of which appeared in the Syrian newspaper *Al-Kifah* on 28 March 1949, where it was stated that '[i]f Israel should oppose the return of the Arab refugees to their homes, the Arab governments will expel the Jews living in their countries'. This new motive for the expulsion was certainly designed to serve the political ends as well as the propaganda needs of the Arab states at the time. Whatever the motive, the expulsion programme of which Heykal Pasha gave notice on 24 November 1947 remained on the agenda on 28 March 1949. Thereafter, the events occurring in each of the Arab states that participated in the expulsion programme became increasingly important.

Disregarding the lies concocted by the spokesmen for the Arab League states to explain the reasons behind the mass expulsion plan of the Jews, it is apparent that one of the principal reasons the Jews were expelled was simply because they were perceived as being naturally sympathetic to Zionism and acting as a fifth column for the Jewish State by the mere fact that they were Jews. Another likely reason in the case of Iraq was that the expulsion of the Jews would enable the government to expropriate their property and wealth. A third reason was to exact vengeance for the Arab defeat in the war against the newborn State of Israel.

As to the number of Jews expelled or forced to leave Arab lands because of intolerable conditions, the Tribunal Relating to the Claims of Jews from Arab Lands presided over by Justice Arthur J. Goldberg found that there were altogether approximately 800,000 Jews who left after the War of 1948-1949 and subsequent wars, of which approximately 600,000 settled in Israel.[88] However,

[88] *The Forgotten Millions, op. cit.*, Appendix 1, pp. 208-209.

these figures slightly underestimate the actual numbers of Jews expelled from Arab lands.[89]

The Jewish expulsion from Arab League countries was a clear denial of their human rights and completely unjustified from any point of view. Jews hailing from these countries had been peaceful and law-abiding, loyal citizens, when they were caught up in the vortex of the Arab-Jewish struggle over Palestine, without any fault on their part, a struggle which in any case had been initiated by the Arab states themselves, who vociferously and steadfastly opposed the existence of a Jewish State in their midst. Among the Arab and Moslem countries who expelled their Jewish citizens or made life so unbearable for them to continue to live where they had always lived were Yemen and Aden; Saudi Arabia – which had a Jewish population in the region of Najran; Iraq – which in 1947 had a population of about 150,000 Jews; Syria, Lebanon, Egypt, Libya, Tunisia, Algeria and Morocco.[90] Jordan, when it became independent in 1946, had no Jewish minority and thus no Jews to expel. To its credit, Jordan actually opposed the wholesale expulsion of Jews from Iraq as proposed by its Prime Minister, Nuri Sa'id, at a meeting with the Jordanian Prime Minister, Samir El-Rifa'i, that took place in early 1949 in the British Embassy in Amman.[91]

In contrast to the non-violent, law-abiding and loyal behaviour of Jews in Arab countries, most of the Arabs who lived in the Land of Israel allied themselves unreservedly with the Arab states which aggressively attacked the Jews of the country with the intention of utterly destroying their fledgling State, as they publicly announced. They happily assisted the enemy in every way they could, providing manpower to swell the ranks of Arab armies and engaging in widespread acts of indiscriminate violence, sabotage and murder. This situation of internal Arab violence and lawlessness directed against the Jewish State has persisted to the present day, notwithstanding efforts made in recent years by different governments of Israel to come to a compromise resolution of the conflict with the Arabs in the Land of Israel. By their uncompromisingly hostile attitude, the latter have forfeited any claim they may have had to remain in the Land of Israel, the National Home of the Jewish People, that belongs exclusively to the Jews under international law as formulated, as we have seen, in various international agreements concluded after World War I. The intense Arab hatred of Israel and their unflagging desire to overthrow or strangle the

---

[89] For the actual figures, see above Chapter XIX.

[90] See map showing the number of Jewish refugees to Israel from Arab lands in *The Forgotten Millions, op. cit.*, p. 138.

[91] Meron, *op. cit.*, pp. 87-88 and n. 36, quoting the account given in the Memoirs of Sir Alec Kirkbride, the British ambassador in Amman from 1947 to 1951, who was present at the meeting between Iraqi Prime Minister Nuri Sa'id and Jordanian Prime Minister Samir el-Rafa'i. Nuri Sa'id proposed dumping a convoy of Iraqi Jews at the Jordanian-Israeli frontier and then forcing them to cross over into Israel. The Jordanian Prime Minister denounced this Iraqi proposal as a crime. King Abdullah, too, opposed Nuri Sa'id's expulsion plan.

Jewish State either by violent means or by flooding the country with millions of Arabs under an imaginary "right of return" justifies their resettlement outside the country. Israel cannot be expected to always remain passive in the light of such intolerable Arab behaviour which no other state in the world would accept without resorting to an overwhelmingly forceful response. The most natural step is to remove the existing menace to the security and well-being of the Jewish State and its citizens, and thereby secure its continued existence as a Jewish State against those who would destroy it from within. That means, without doubt, the transfer of the Arabs who, under the rules of elementary justice and equity, should be directed to those Arab countries that expelled practically all their Jews.[92] If that is not done, the Jews of Israel will find themselves under constant threat of losing their own homeland to the local Arabs. The transfer of the latter can be seen as a continuing mutual exchange of populations between the Arab states and Israel that was brought about not only by the former, but also by their brethren in the Land of Israel. This *de facto* exchange of populations has in the past and will in the future prevent Israel from becoming the twenty-second Arab state and also ensure eventual peace by removing the very cause of strife.

Another view about Arab population transfer that is frequently heard is that, whatever its merits, it is altogether unrealistic or impractical and therefore cannot be implemented. Those who hold this view also add that the United States and the rest of the world would never allow such transfer to take place. This view is not supported by past precedents of population exchange that have occurred in the twentieth century, and either enjoyed American or world approval or, at least, did not precipitate the intervention of third parties. In any event, Israel is not legally bound by what other states think should or should not be done for preserving its legal rights and vital interests. Israel is already severely censored in international forums where Arab and Moslem states predominate, as well as in the anti-Semitic media. One more criticism will not hurt its standing in any essential respect and should not deter it from taking necessary steps for its well-being or survival that may run afoul of international consensus at any given moment. Nor should the specter of a war-crimes trial at the Hague, a threat often raised by falsely moralistic Israelis to silence proponents of Arab population transfer, deter the Government of Israel from effecting this panacea. None of the Allied leaders were accused or prosecuted for "war crimes" after World War II when over 12,000,000 Germans were either expelled or voluntarily left their native lands in Europe to go to West Germany. Nor did this happen in any other case of population transfer in the twentieth century. Far from being exceptional, the transfer of a foreign settled population is as old as the hills. It occurred as long ago as three and a half millennia in ancient Egypt at the end of the Middle Kingdom and the start of the New Kingdom, during the 18th Dynasty when the founder of the dynasty, Amasis I (also called Ahmose),

[92] Meron, *op. cit.*, p. 101.

and his successors expelled from Egypt all the foreign Hyksos, a people of apparently mixed Semitic origin, who had several centuries before infiltrated from Western Asia, seized the kingship of the country, and controlled Egypt for about a century between approximately 1655 and 1570 (1550) B.C.E.

Moreover, world circumstances are constantly changing, either for better or for worse. What is unrealistic one day becomes realistic on the morrow. An example is the radical change in opinion that occurred after September 11, 2001 when nearly 3,000 people lost their lives in a stunning terrorist attack on the New York site of the World Trade Center. Prior to that date, no one expected that the United States would ever invade Afghanistan to topple the Taliban, the Islamic fundamentalists in power who provided a safe haven for terrorists, or to invade Iraq and overthrow the cruel dictator Saddam Hussein, who had governed the country with an iron grip for three decades. Reality is a dynamic phenomenon, more so in the Land of Israel than in other countries. It must not be assumed that the conditions that presently prevail – constant friction, violence and bloodshed perpetrated by Arabs against Jews – will forever be endured by the long-suffering people of Israel without the Government one day acting to eradicate those conditions in an all-out war against the perpetrators and those in the general Arab population who support them. Various polls taken over the past several years to measure Arab public opinion have shown that support for armed struggle against Israel is nearly universal among Arabs in Judea, Samaria and Gaza and widespread among Arabs in the State of Israel. The suicide-bombers who wreak death and destruction in the Land of Israel are acclaimed as heroes and martyrs (in Arabic: *shuhada*) for the "liberation of Palestine from the Jews". Nor is it realistic to assume that the Arab demographic threat to Israel shall always be a Sword of Damocles hanging over Israel's head without corrective measures being taken to eliminate that threat. In these circumstances where the irrefutable evidence of almost a century of constant enmity and violence between Arabs and Jews conclusively proves that there is no practical possibility for peaceful coexistence, the only viable solution is a permanent separation of the two communities. To think otherwise is to be incurably naive or suicidal. Such separation can only be achieved by the transfer of the Arabs because of the unassailable fact that Palestine was created in 1920 to be the Jewish, not Arab, National Home after more than 1800 years had elapsed since the destruction of the State of Judea in the year 70 C.E.

The State of Israel came into existence only after a valiant fifty-year struggle to overcome British betrayal and enormous hardship during which the Jewish People suffered the incalculable loss of a third of its sons and daughters, many of whom would undoubtedly have emigrated to Palestine, had the British authorities permitted their entry before or during World War II, as they were legally obliged to do. Now that Israel exists as a flourishing Jewish State and is no longer defenseless, it should not be expected to forfeit its legal right to Judea, Samaria and Gaza, regions which were always part of the Jewish National Home, to a fictitious nation that has no equivalent right to them. Equally, the world should not expect Israel to remain passive and commit suicide by becoming a minority in its own homeland and allowing non-Jews to take over the reins of government under the banner of democracy. It must be made clear to the U.S. and the rest of the world that there will be no further Arab takeover of precious Jewish land in any region of the Jewish National Home for any reason, nor any Israeli withdrawal to narrow borders that presage the destruction of the Jewish State. What must take place at a propitious moment in the future is a relocation of the Arab population from the Land of Israel to Arab or other countries, in accordance with past international legal precedents. That alone is certain to end endemic Arab terrorism and violence within the country, remove the Arab demographic threat once and for all and also bring eventual peace to the Middle East, however long it may take.

# Appendices

*Appendix I*

# Summary Table of Sovereignty over Eretz-Israel[1] from 1516 to the Present Day under International Law and Jewish Law (*halakha*)[2]

| PERIOD | Holder of *de jure* sovereignty under modern international law | Holder of *de jure* sovereignty under Jewish Law (*halakha*) | Foreign Occupier/ Ruler or Holder of attributes of sovereignty or of *de facto* sovereignty |
|---|---|---|---|
| Ottoman 1516 – January 30, 1919 | The Ottoman Empire (Turkey)[3] | Jewish People | The Ottoman Empire over the entire country |
| Principal Allied Powers January 30, 1919 –April 24, 1920 | Principal Allied Powers[4] | Jewish People | Principal Allied Powers over the entire country |
| Mandate for Palestine April 25, 1920 – May 14-15, 1948 | Jewish People | Jewish People | Great Britain over the entire country[5] |
| Third Jewish Commonwealth Established on May 15, 1948 | State of Israel[6] | State of Israel | State of Israel over the parts of the country under effective rule[7, 8, 9] |

[1] Eretz-Israel, the Land of Israel, also known *inter alia* as the Land of Judah and Israel, the Land of Zion, Judea, Palestine, and the Holy Land, consists of the following regions, based on historical, geographical and religious grounds: Cisjordan, Transjordan, southern Lebanon up to the bend of the Litani River; Bashan or Hauran, including the Golan, north of the Yarmuk River; as well as at least half of the Sinai Peninsula.

[2] Jewish Law or *halakha* presumes that the Jewish People, the descendants of the

Israelites (or Children of Israel) were given the Land of Israel by God, the Master of the World, as recorded in the Patriarchal Covenant and also in Leviticus 25:18, where it is stated that the Jews, provided they obey God's laws and observe His judgments and practice them, shall dwell in the Land in safety and consequently enjoy full possession of it.

[3] During the 400-year period of Ottoman Turkish rule over Eretz-Israel, international law, as opposed to Jewish Law, considered that *de jure* sovereignty vested in the Imperial Ottoman Empire, while Jewish sovereignty, based on the historical connection of the Jewish People with the Land, was dormant or in abeyance, but subject to revival, as indeed took place when the Balfour Declaration was adopted by the Principal Allied Powers of World War I (Great Britain, France, Italy and Japan), in recognition of the Jewish right to the country in its entirety. To put the Balfour Declaration into effect and achieve its purpose of re-establishing the Jewish State and homeland – the Allies chose Britain to govern Mandated Palestine at the San Remo Peace Conference on April 24-25, 1920.

[4] The Principal Allied Powers consisted of the wartime alliance of Britain, France, Italy and Japan. When Britain conquered Palestine in 1917-1918 in the Great War, it did so not in its name but in the name of the Principal Allied Powers. On January 30, 1919 these Powers, together with the United States, the Associated Power, definitively decided, during a meeting of the Council of Ten (Supreme Council) at the Paris Peace Conference, that neither Palestine nor the other subjugated Ottoman Empire Middle Eastern territories would be returned to Turkey. It was further decided that none of the subjugated territories constituting the Fertile Crescent or Levant would be annexed, but rather placed under the newly-conceived Mandates System, in accordance with the Smuts Resolution, the precursor of Article 22 of the Covenant of the League of Nations, as devised by its principal author, General Jan Christiaan Smuts. The consequence of these decisions was that Turkey had permanently lost its sovereignty over Palestine and the other non-Anatolian territories in the Middle East. Sovereignty over them now briefly vested in the Principal Allied Powers as the collective disposing agent until final decisions were made at the Peace Conference as to their ultimate disposition. Upon the Allied adoption of the Balfour Declaration at the San Remo Peace Conference on April 24, 1920 as the criterion for the governing of the mandated territory of Palestine in conjunction with Article 22 of the Covenant, *de jure* sovereignty was devolved upon the Jewish People, though attributes of sovereignty were to be exercised by the Mandatory Power, the whole as embodied in the San Remo Resolution of April 25, 1920.

[5] Until 1946, when Great Britain illegally granted Transjordan independence; ever since, *de facto* sovereignty over the territory east of the Jordan River has been vested in what has become the Hashemite Kingdom of Jordan. Israel in turn recognized Jordan's sovereignty, territorial integrity and political independence in a treaty concluded on October 26, 1994, contrary to the principles and assumptions inherent in Israeli constitutional law and *halakha*, that no part of the Land of Israel, even when under foreign rule, should ever be officially recognized as belonging to a foreign state.

[6] Upon the Declaration of the Establishment of the State of Israel on May 14, 1948, that took effect on May 15, 1948, *de jure* sovereignty over the Land of Israel was devolved from the Jewish People to the State of Israel, as the agent and assignee of the Jewish People. The State of Israel also exercised *de facto* sovereignty over those parts of the Land of Israel which came under its effective rule as a consequence of the United Nations General Assembly Partition

Resolution 181(II) of November 29, 1947 and the ensuing War of Independence, 1947-1949.

[7] Other parts of the Land of Israel – under illegal foreign occupation by Syria, Lebanon, Jordan, Egypt and the "Palestinian Authority". Regarding the Sinai Peninsula, Israel recognized the alleged "resumption" of Egypt's "full sovereignty" over this territory in a peace treaty concluded on March 26, 1979 that created an international boundary between the two countries described as permanent, recognized and inviolable. Egypt, however, had never enjoyed sovereignty over the entire Sinai Peninsula prior to that date, except for a territorial wedge in the northwestern corner of the peninsula, extending from El-Arish to Suez. In any case, Israel had a right to retain the Sinai within its borders, since Sinai was historically and geographically linked to the Land of Israel and has great religious significance for the Jewish People. The whole of Sinai never constituted an historical or internal part of Egypt though it was ruled by Egypt at various times as a result of conquest. Until 1906, the central portion of Sinai lay within the Independent Sanjak of Jerusalem, i.e., what was unofficially called "Turkish Palestine". However, from 1906 onwards, Sinai was detached from this Sanjak under British pressure to safeguard the Suez Canal and was henceforth administered by British-controlled Egypt on behalf of the Ottoman Empire which was legally still the sovereign territory of Sinai. By virtue of Article 132 of the Treaty of Sèvres, Sinai was ceded by Turkey to the Principal Allied Powers and thereafter fell under joint Egyptian-British administration until the termination of the British protectorate over Egypt, whereupon Egypt became the sole administrator of Sinai. Egypt in effect inherited the entire Sinai as a legacy of British imperialism, transforming its legal right of administration into an alleged right of sovereignty, as the Mandate period drew to a close. The irony is that while Egypt vociferously denounced the evils of imperialism, it gladly embraced the great benefit – Sinai – it received gratis from the hated British imperialists. To make matters even worse from the perspective of Jewish legal rights, the Egypt-Israel Peace Treaty sanctioned by Menachem Begin then wrongly conferred international legitimacy on Egypt's pretended right of sovereignty which, as noted above, it had never previously enjoyed. For Israel, this treaty represented an illegal surrender of its patrimony, thus making it an illegal surrender of Sinai by Israel to Egypt, thus making the treaty illegal from the perspective of Israeli constitutional and criminal law, as well as *halakha*.

[8] Syria rules most of Biblical Bashan or former Turkish Hauran that rightfully belongs to the Jewish National Home under the historical or biblical formula for determining the boundaries of Palestine.

[9] All of the area that is today Southern Lebanon extending from Israel's northern border to the southern bank of the Litani River is an extension of Upper Galilee and also rightfully belongs to the Jewish National Home under the historical or biblical formula.

*Appendix II*

# The Historical Origin of the Name "Palestine" and Related Regional Terms

To better understand the fraudulent usage of the name of "Palestinians" now attached to an Arabic-speaking medley of Gentiles in the Land of Israel, it is necessary to explore the historical origin of the name "Palestine", from earliest times until the modern day. The legal meaning of "Palestinian" in the Mandate period has been discussed in Chapter 16 of this book. The discussion here deals with the historical use and evolution of this and related regional terms, with concluding remarks on its modern-day usage.

The geographical term "Palestine" and its derivative "Palestinian" are derived originally from either the Egyptian speech form *prst* or from the cognate Hebrew root of the words *p'lisha* ("invasion") and *pol'shim* ("invaders"). In this context "Palestine" resembles "Philistia" in that both are linguistic corruptions of the Hebrew *P'leshet*, named for the *Pelishtim* or "Philistines", one of the six "sea peoples" who invaded the coastal area of the Land of Israel in several waves of attack and devastation during the second half of the second millenium before the common era, after which they established permanent bases of settlement. The *Pelishtim* are believed by many scholars to have originated from the coastlands and islands of the northern and eastern Mediterranean and the Aegean Sea, particularly from *Kaphtor* which these scholars understand to be a reference to the island of Crete (*Kretim* in Hebrew). The Israelites,[1] who were settled further east in the interior of the country, called the coastal strip occupied by the invading Philistines *Gelilot Peleshet* or simply *Peleshet*, a geographical term which later was corrupted by non-Hebrew speakers into "Philistia", which in turn eventually evolved through Greek and Latin into "Palestine".[2] The expression

[1] The national appellation "Israelites" derives from the Biblical text (Genesis 32:29) recounting the struggle between the Patriarch Jacob and an unidentifed heavenly being at Peniel (Penuel) in which Jacob was renamed "Israel". This was later reinforced by a vision Jacob experienced at Beth-El (Genesis 35:10), in which God appeared to him and informed him that from then on he would also be called Israel. Henceforth all Jacob's descendants were called "Israelites", literally "the Children of Israel". Prior to these divine revelations, the families of the Patriarchs were known as "Hebrews", a designation that continued to be used even afterwards, interchangeably with Israelites. A further development saw the alternative name "Jew" (*yehudi*) being used as a synonym for both "Israelite" and "Hebrew", after the northern Kingdom of Israel was destroyed by Assyria in 721 B.C.E. and only the Kingdom of Judah remained as the national center. The earliest reference to the People of Israel in an extra-biblical source dates from the time of the Egyptian Pharaoh Merneptah, c. 1225 B.C.E., whose victory stele reads: "Israel is desolate; it has no seed left".

[2] The name of Palestine which derived from Philistia and the earlier Hebrew

*Eretz-Israel* (originally short for *Eretz-Bene-Israel*, Land of the Children of Israel, as first used in the Book of Joshua [11:22]) denoted only the land actually settled by the Israelites, and "not to the whole country as a single geographical entity within its natural boundaries".[3]

The Philistines are mentioned in the first book of the Torah (Genesis 10:14) in connection with the list of Noah's descendants, from whom all the nations of the world are said to have emerged. Included in the table of nations are the Pathrusim and the Kasluhim, who were the forebears of the Philistines.[4]

In the time of the Patriarchs, Abraham and Isaac encountered on their journeys in Canaan a king by the name of Abimelech, who lived and ruled in the ancient city of Gerar, in the southern Negev between Gaza and Beersheba, in an area known as the Land of the *Pelishtim*. When the Exodus of the Israelites from Egypt occurred, the Philistines were already settled in the coastal strip (i.e., in the northwestern corner of the Sinai Peninsula) between Egypt and Gaza, which is why the Israelites made a detour inland to avoid "the way of the land of the Philistines" (Exodus 13:17). In the 12th century B.C.E., a new influx of the Sea Peoples arrived in the Land of Israel. Along their trail of attack from their Aegean homeland, they are reported to have destroyed the Hittite Empire centered in Anatolia and to have conducted invasions of Egypt during the reigns of Merneptah (c. 1224-1214 B.C.E.) and Ramses III (c. 1198-1167 B.C.E.) which ended in their defeat. One group known as the *Tjeker* (Sicilians?) settled on the coast of Palestine, south of Mount Carmel, with their principal city at Dor. Another group, the Philistines, closely related to them settled further south along the coast from Jaffa to Gaza, where they established a pentapolis or confederacy of five cities: Gaza, Ashkelon, Ashdod, Ekron and Gath, and extended their area of settlement as far east as the Judean *Shephela* (the lowland region leading up to the Judean hills or mountains).

The aggressive expansion of the Philistines led to constant warfare with the Israelites during the period of the Judges, which lasted, according to different scholarly estimates from two hundred to as much as 400 years from the death of Joshua to the judgeship of Samuel and the establishment of the Israelite

---

name of Peleshet may be compared in terms of evolution with another northwest Semitic name, that of Carthage. The original name of the North African city, near modern Tunis, was *Qart-Hadsha* ("new city") established by the Phoenicians, which was the Greek name of a Canaanite people who lived in Tyre and Sidon and other places in present-day Lebanon. The native name of Qart-Hadsha was rendered in Latin as Carthago or Cartago which in turn gave us Carthage.

[3] See the entry in *Encyclopaedia Judaica* (1971), "Land of Israel, Geographical Survey", written by Abraham J. Brawer, Vol. 9, cols. 108 ff. See also the introduction written by Gideon Biger in the book entitled *The Land that Became Israel*, edited by Ruth Kark, the Magnes Press, Jerusalem, published in the U.S. and the U.K. by Yale University Press (1990), p. 9.

[4] The Table of Nations is shown graphically in a book entitled *The Living Torah*, by Rabbi Aryeh Kaplan, Maznaim Publishing Corporation, Brooklyn, New York (1981), p. 43.

Monarchy. The Philistines drove out the tribe of Dan from the coastal plain, where it is believed to have settled in addition to the northern part of the *Shephela* (in the Valley of Sorek), overcoming the heroic exploits of the tribe's hero, Samson. The Danites migrated northwards to the sources of the Jordan River and captured the city of Laish (Leshem), which they renamed Dan. It was not until the time of King David, in the period of the United Monarchy, that the Philistines were finally subdued. From the Biblical accounts, it is known that David took a select number of Philistine mercenary troops to be part of his foreign bodyguard under the command of Benaiah, son of Jehoiada. They were known by the joint names of *K'rethites* (or *C'reithites*) and *P'lethites*, a clear indicatation of their place of origin, Kaphtor or Crete.

In the Second Temple Period, from c. 515 B.C.E. to 70 C.E., the entire area of Jewish habitation in the Land of Israel was officially called by several variations of the name of *Yehuda* (Judah). At times the Land of Judah comprised all of the Land of Israel, while at other times only a reduced area. Thus in the era of Persian rule, the Aramaic name of the Jewish region was Yehud, a tiny district in a larger province designated as the fifth satrapy of *Avar-Nahara* "beyond the [Euphrates] river" that encompassed all of Eretz-Israel, as well as Syria and Phoenicia. In the Hellenistic Period, when the land came under Ptolemaic and Seleucid governance, the name used by Greek speakers for the same area was *Iouda* or *Ioudaia*. However, the official designation of Judea was not always used by Greek classical writers when referring to this land. Some Greeks who were more familiar with the coastal area where the Philistines lived but not well acquainted with the Judean interior applied the name of Palestine to the whole of the Jewish country. This usage was inexact and unofficial. In this context, the fifth century B.C.E. Greek historian Herodotus, called the Father of History, first mentioned the name "Palestine" as an adjective, in the form "the Philistine Syria", a term which was subsequently shortened to *Palaistine*, converting the adjective into a proper noun. Others who used the name "Palestine" in the same loose sense in the classical Greek period were the fourth-century B.C.E. philosopher Aristotle, who referred to the Dead Sea as being in Palestine, and 2nd century B.C.E. antiquarian, Polemon of Ilium (Troy), who in referring to the Exodus mentioned "the country called Syria Palaestina, not far from Arabia".[5]

When Rome emerged as the dominant power of the known world, the Latin name of *Judaea* came into official use. Both the Greek and Latin terms for the Land of Judah meant "the Jewish country", which directly acknowledged the historical Jewish association with this territory and Jewish rights thereto.

During the entire period of the Second Temple, the name of Palestine was never used in an official sense to describe any part of Judea which, at the time of Herod's rule (37-4 B.C.E.), encompassed practically all of the Land of Israel, including Gaza and the coastal cities (except Ashkelon and Dor), Galilee, Samaria, Golan and parts of Transjordan inhabited by Jews. This is

---

[5] See article by Professor Louis H. Feldman, "Some Observations on the Name of Palestine", *Hebrew Union College Annual*, Volume LXI (1990), p. 6.

substantiated by Yeshiva University Professor of Classics and Literature, Louis H. Feldman, who writes: "The exclusive official usage of the name of Judea as distinct from Palestine was evidenced by Roman writings and inscriptions in letters, military documents and diplomas, in the ornaments of triumph and in coins which bore the legends of *Iudaea, Iudaea Capta* 'Judea captured' and *Iudaea Devicta* 'Judea exiled'."[6]

It is interesting to note that neither in the Hebrew Bible nor in the Christian Scriptures does the term Palestine occur. It did appear twice in the English Authorized Version, but as pointed out by Professor Bernard Lewis, this was a mistranslation for Philistia, an error later corrected in the New English Bible.[7] In the New Testament, the name Judea is used in both a narrow and a broad sense. In the narrow sense, it denoted only one part of the Land of Israel, as distinct from Samaria, Galilee, Perea and Idumea. In the wider sense, it meant the whole territory inhabited by the Jewish People.

The official terminology used in regard to Judea changed after the suppression of the Bar Kochba rebellion in 135 C.E., when Hadrian, the Roman Emperor, seeking to erase the name of Judea from the historical and geographical consciousness of the world and any trace of Jewish sovereignty, joined the territory of Judea to the province of Syria, which then took the name of *Syria Palaestina*, i.e., "Philistine Syria", as originally used by Herodotus in the fifth century B.C.E. After destroying Jerusalem and then rebuilding it, the capital city of the Jews was renamed Aelia Capitolina.[8] These changes in nomenclature were based on Hadrian's personal knowledge of the situation in Judea, for he had governed Syria in 114 before he was made emperor in 117, and had also visited both Syria and Judea in 129-130. He showed complete contempt for the Jewish People by issuing a decree denying the right of any Jew, on pain of death, to come near Jerusalem or its environs, "so that not even from a distance could [the Jewish nation] see its ancestral home".[9] He also issued wicked edicts reminiscent of those issued by the Seleucid monarch of Syria, Antiochus IV Epiphanes, prohibiting the study of Torah and the practice of Judaism, including circumcision and making their observance capital offenses. These edicts were repealed by his successor, Antoninus Pius (ruled 138-161). A temple to Jupiter Capitolinus and an equestrian statue of Hadrian were erected on Jerusalem's Temple Mount.

Despite the name changes decreed by Hadrian, that of Judea continued to be used in literary sources for several centuries afterwards, as attested to by the

---

[6] Feldman, *op. cit.*, pp. 7-9.

[7] "The Palestinians and the PLO: A Historical Approach", Bernard Lewis, *Commentary*, January 1975, p. 32.

[8] The new Roman name given by Hadrian to Jerusalem, Aelia Capitolina, honoured both himself (his full name was Publius Aelius Hadrianus) and also the supreme deity of the Roman pantheon, Jupiter Capitolinus. The Temple of Jupiter was situated on the Capitoline Hill at Rome.

[9] Feldman, *op. cit.*, p. 21.

writings of the 2nd century Greek physician Galen, the contemporary Roman philosopher Celsus, the 2nd-3rd century Roman historian and administrator Dio Cassius, the 3rd-4th century Church historian Eusebius of Caesarea, the 4th century Roman historians Festus and Eutropius, the 4th-5th century Hebrew-speaking Christian scholar St. Jerome, the 5th century Carthaginian Latin writer Martianus Capella and others.[10] Hadrian's linguistic manipulations showed the psychological and legal importance he attached to the naming of a country. People who lived in Judea after 135 C.E. were now, regardless of their ancestry, officially deemed to be Syrians, rather than Judeans or Jews. They were in any case not called Palestinians, reflecting the fact that there was no known nation by that name. The implication of Hadrian's name changes was that Judea was no longer the land of the Jews, nor Jerusalem their holy city. However, this implication was artificial since the name of Syria Palestina or simply Palestine still carried the Hebrew root and origin of the word *Peleshet*, which the Romans rendered as *Palasta.*[11] Moreover, Jerusalem remained the object of Jewish yearning for eventual restoration and Jews continued to approach and visit the city, especially on the 9th of Av, despite Hadrian's decree. The renaming of Judea as Palestine was also artificial because the Philistines themselves had already lost their independence to Assyrian, Egyptian and finally Babylonian conquerors about six centuries earlier. Then in the ensuing centuries, under Persian and Hellenistic rule, they disappeared from the stage of world history as a separate, identifiable people, which made the official Roman usage of the name of Palestine to be pointless, except as an act of hostility against the Jewish People. The Philistines had merged with the general Canaanite and Phoenician (Sidonian) populations and had become completely Hellenized and submerged within the Greek-speaking culture.

Later, the Romans separated Palestine from the province of Syria. In 284, the Roman emperor Diocletian annexed to Palestine the province of Arabia first formed in 106 encompassing the Negev and Transjordan, but in 358 the Negev and southern Transjordan were detached and renamed *Palaestine Salutaris.*[12] Over a century later, in 425, the rest of Palestine was divided into two additional provinces: *Palaestina Prima* "First Palestine" and *Palaestina Secunda* "Second Palestine", while the name of *Palaestina Salutaris* was changed to *Palaestina Tertia* "Third Palestine".

After the Arabs conquered the country between 634 and 644 (Byzantine-ruled Jerusalem fell in 638), the Roman administrative division was maintained, but the names of the three geographical units were changed and referred to as

---

[10] Feldman, *op. cit.*, pp. 17-18.

[11] Gideon Biger, *op. cit.,* p. 14.

[12] Ruth Kark (ed.), *The Land that Became Israel, Studies in Historical Geography*, Magnus Press, Hebrew University of Jerusalem (1990). See article by Gideon Biger, "The Name and Boundaries of Eretz-Israel (Palestine) as Reflections of Stages in its History", p. 14.

military districts (*junds*), rather than provinces.[13] The name *Filastin* designated the former area of Palaestina Prima, and the name of *Urdunn* or Jordan was used for Palaestina Secunda. Each of these two districts embraced significant areas of Transjordan. Palaestina Tertia ceased to exist as an independent unit and most of the territory that it formerly comprised (the Negev and southern Transjordan) was joined with Sinai and known in Arabic as *Tiha Bani Israil* – the area of the wandering of the children of Israel – or *Tiha* for short. At times, it was combined administratively with *Jund Filastin*. Both districts, *Filastin* and *Urdunn*, were incorporated into the large geographic unit of Syria or *Ash-Shams* (in Arabic).[14]

In the Crusader period and thereafter, until the time of the Egyptian invasion and conquest of Palestine and Syria in 1831-1832, the name of Palestine was no longer used officially to designate any part of the Land of Israel. Then, under Ibrahim Pasha, the stepson of the Governor of Egypt, Muhammad Ali, ruling Palestine in his stepfather's name, the region of Palestine was constituted as a separate administrative district within a wider area that also included Syria. Upon the restoration of Ottoman rule in 1840, new administrative changes were introduced and the official use of the name of Palestine was discontinued. Beginning in 1864, "Jerusalem" became a separate and independent *sanjak* under the direct supervision of the central government in Constantinople (later called Istanbul). This *sanjak* encompassed the core area of Palestine including the cities of Jerusalem, Hebron, Jaffa and Gaza, as well as a central section of Sinai extending from El-Arish to Suez and from Suez to Taba. The unofficial name of the Sanjak of Jerusalem was "Palestine" (or "Turkish Palestine"), though the name preferred by Jews was Eretz Israel. Another name that was also used was the Holy Land and sometimes even the name of Judea.

In 1897, the delegates at the First Zionist Congress at Basle ironically chose Palestine as the name of the Home for the Jewish People to be secured by public law, because of its widespread usage in the Christian world. That name received official sanction at the San Remo Peace Conference on April 24, 1920 when the Balfour Declaration was officially adopted by the Principal Allied Powers of Britain, France, Italy and Japan for the purpose of creating the mandated state

---

[13] The Arab conquest of Palestine began with an invasion ordered by the first caliph, Abu-Bakr, who had succeeded Muhammad upon his death on June 8, 632. The country was then part of the Byzantine Empire governed from Constantinople (Byzantium) by Emperor Heraclius (610-641). Just prior to the Arab invasion, Persia had occupied Palestine for fourteen years (614-628). The first decisive battle in the Arab-Byzantine War took place on July 30, 634. For detailed treatment of the Arab conquest of Palestine, see the book by Moshe Gil, *A History of Palestine, 634-1099*, translated from the Hebrew by Ethel Broido, Cambridge University Press (1992). The original Hebrew edition was published in 1983. A revised paperback edition was published in 1997. See Chapter 1, sections [59] to [73], pp. 45-60, in the paperback edition.

[14] All the above information concerning the Arab administrative divisions of Palestine is from the work of Gideon Biger, *op. cit.*, p. 16.

of Palestine, known also as the Jewish National Home. Jews who went to live in Palestine were called "Palestinians" during the whole period of modern Zionist settlement, both pre-dating the Mandate and while it was in force. The original appellation "Palestinians" for Jews who had settled in Palestine in the latter part of the 19th century and the first half of the 20th may seem strange today in light of its widespread, plagiarized usage by Arabs since 1969 to designate an alleged Palestinian nation, that no one had heard of before, but it was the common though unofficial national designation for Jews prior to May 15, 1948 when the State of Israel was established and Jews became Israelis instead of Palestinians.

The use of the name "Palestinians" for Jews in the pre-State period was acknowledged even by Arab leaders. When the Palestine Royal Commission visited Amman in March 1937, the Chairman, Lord William Peel, was handed a memorandum from Emir Abdullah, in which it was stated:[15]

> The Mandatory Power, in the opinion of the Arabs, has been extremely partial in protecting the interests of the Jews, whom it called Palestinians by force and gave them Palestine Citizenship when they were far away in their respective countries and before their feet touched or their eyes saw Palestine, whether they were Poles, Russians or of other countries.

By associating the name "Palestinians" with Jews from Poland, Russia and other countries, Abdullah intimated that he did not consider it appropriate for Arabs. Significantly, he made no direct connection between the Arabs of Palestine and the ancient Philistines – saying only that the Jews fought the latter "from whom they wrenched a portion of the land on which they settled for a limited period".[16] Rather, he connected the Arabs with the Amalekites and the Hyksos Kings by citing Arab historians of old who said that Palestine was the dwelling place of these two groups of peoples. However, any Arab connection with either of them was unlikely.

The Amalekites, a hereditary and irreconcilable enemy of the Jews from the time of Moses and Joshua, who inhabited the Negev and Sinai Desert, and for a time, the land of Ephraim – a large part of present-day Samaria (Judges 12:15), had disappeared as a distinct national group in the days of King Hezekiah (c. 726-697 B.C.E.; alternatively, c. 716-687 B.C.E.). According to the Bible (I Chronicles 4:43), the sons of Shim'on (Simeon) slaughtered the remnant of the Amalekites. Hence the Arabs, who did not at that time exist as a nation in its own right, could not have been descended from them. In fact, the Bible (Genesis 36:10-16) traces the descent of the Amalekites from Esau, the brother of Jacob, considering them a branch of the Edomites and relating them to that

---

[15] *The Rise of Israel,* Vol. 13, Document 20, p. 142.

[16] *Ibid.,* p. 136.

people. The latter do not seem to have had any ethnic connection whatever with the future Arab nation. Quite the opposite, since the Edomites were driven out of what had become their homeland east of the *'Araba* and south of *Wadi Zered* to the Gulf of Eilat by various desert tribes. They were replaced by the Nabateans in the territory that was formerly theirs and where they had lived for many centuries. The Edomites moved westward, reestablishing themselves in Southern Judea including Hebron. In 126 B.C.E., Edom, in its new venue, was conquered by the Hasmonean, John (Johanan) Hyrcanus, the independent ruler of Judea and High Priest, who forced the Edomites to convert to Judaism, thus making them an inseparable part of the Jewish People. The Edomites or Idumeans, as they were called in the "New Testament", had a lasting impact on the future course of events in Judea, for out of their ranks rose two important figures, Antipater II (Antipas) who for a time was the *de facto* ruler of the whole of Judea, and his son Herod who became its king. The incorporation of the Edomites into the Jewish People meant that the Amalekites could be seen not as an ancestor of the Arabs, as Abdullah claimed, but ironically as possibly having a most remote kinship to the Jewish People. This possibility can also be derived from a biblical verse (Judges 5:14): "Out of Ephraim came they whose root is in Amalek".

In regard to the Hyksos, who ruled Egypt for about a century and a half – sometime between 1720 (or 1710) and 1550 B.C.E. – they were apparently a heterogeneous group of different Asiatic peoples, among whom were Canaanites, Amorites and perhaps the Hurrians or Horites.[17] There could not have been any Arabs from the Arabian peninsula in this group, since they did not live in Canaan when the Hyksos invaded and occupied Egypt. The name "Hyksos" is a Greek term apparently derived from an Egyptian phrase meaning "ruler of foreign lands". To equate "Palestinians" or "Arabs" with Canaanites as their spokespersons shamelessly do today is to fictionalize the study of history

---

[17] In a 1971 article in the *Encyclopedia Judaica* on the Hyksos, written by Alan Richard Schulman, Assistant Professor of Ancient History, Queens College of the City University of New York, Schulman notes that Josephus Flavius identified the Hyksos as the Patriarchal Jews, equating their appearance in Egypt with the Joseph story in Genesis and their subsequent expulsion with the Biblical account of Exodus. Schulman dismisses this fascinating interpretation by Josephus and declares: "There is no warrant either in the Bible or outside it for equating the Hyksos with the later Hebrews, although it is not impossible that some of the latter may have been ultimately descended from some of the Hyksos". Schulman calls the Hyksos a mixture of Semites and Hurrians. The latter were a non-Semitic people inhabiting the kingdom of Mitanni in Northern Mesopotamia who penetrated into Canaan and Seir (Edom). In the Bible they are called Horites. The Hurrians have been identified by some scholars with the Hivites, one of the seven nations residing in Canaan at the time of the Israelite conquest. See separate articles about the Hurrians and Hyksos in *Encyclopaedia Judaica* (1971), Volume 8, columns 1116ff and column 1142 ff. See also separate articles about them found in the Encyclopedic Dictionary of the Bible, by Louis F. Hartman, McGraw –Hill Book Company, Inc, New York (1963), pp. 1042-1043.

in order to show they preceded the settlement of the Israelites in the country.

In referring to the Arab conquest of Palestine (634-644) Abdullah misstated or, more accurately, rewrote the country's history when he told the Peel Royal Commission in 1937:[18]

> The Arabs *regained* the country from the Romans (sic; an obvious reference to the Byzantines) and remained in possession thereof, uninterruptedly, until the present day.

His use of the word "regained" indicated prior Arab dominion over Palestine, but there is no evidence for that except possibly for the regions of Transjordan and the Negev based on the unproven assumption that the Nabateans who ruled these areas were Arabs, as alleged in the writings of the 1st century B.C.E. Sicilian historian Diodorus Siculus and the translated versions (not the original texts) of the writings of 1st century C.E. Jewish historian Josephus Flavius (Yoseph ben Mattityahu HaKohen). This widely-held assumption is not necessarily correct. The language of the Nabateans was not Arabic but Aramaic, verifiable from the inscriptions they wrote in that language. This indicates they may have had a distinct tribal identity not as Arabs, but as Nabateans, which is what they called themselves. They were centered in ancient Edom whose capital city was Petra (a Greek translation for the rose-red rock found there), identified by some with Biblical Sela (the Hebrew equivalent of "rock"). From there they spread northwards and westwards. They flourished as an independent kingdom from the fourth century B.C.E. to the year 106 C.E., when their land was conquered during the reign of 2nd century Roman emperor Trajan, who annexed it to the Roman Empire and renamed it the province of Arabia (Arabia *Petraea*), which consisted of present-day Jordan. The designation of Arabia for the lands once known as Edom, Moab, Gilead and Bashan may indicate that the Arabs lived there, too, in addition to Jews and various Greek-speaking groups, but it was a Roman practice to obliterate the memory of those peoples they defeated by attaching a foreign name to the land, as they did in the second century when they re-named Judea "Palestine".

During the period of Nabatean rule and settlement in Transjordan and the Negev, there was no Arab nation as such in existence – it emerged only in the 7th century with the founding of Islam. Until then, the term "Arab" was used in two senses: first, it referred to nomadic tent-dwellers who lived in the deserts of Arabia and rode camels. They were described as Bedouin[19] as opposed to

---

[18] *The Rise of Israel,* Vol. 13, Document 20, p. 136.

[19] According to the orientalist, Shlomo Dov Goitein, of the Hebrew University of Jerusalem (Institute of Oriental Studies), and a Professor of Arabic at the University of Pennsylvania, the word *bedou* in Arabic means "outside", and it thus refers to persons who "lived far out in the desert, where alone good camels can be raised". See his book, *Jews and Arabs: Their Contacts Through the Ages*, Schocken Books, New York,

townspeople who engaged in commerce and other urban occupations and farmers who tilled the soil and raised crops. A second meaning of the term "Arab" was geographic, since it denoted from earliest times any person who came from one of the districts or regions of the Arabian peninsula (Sabea or Sheba, Dedan, Regma, etc.). In the Persian period of world rule, it denoted a resident of the province (satrapy) of Arabia, i.e., the Arabian Peninsula. In the days of the Roman Empire, from Trajan onwards, it denoted a resident of the province of Arabia which, as stated above, was actually in present-day Transjordan rather than in the Arabian Peninsula.

Using these two meanings of the term "Arab" as a guide, the Nabateans could hardly be considered Arabs. They were neither nomads once they had settled down in towns and cities, whatever their earlier status may have been, nor inhabitants of a land known as Arabia at the time of their existence as an independent kingdom. They were traders and skilled artisans, engineers, architects and farmers. Confusion over their ethnic identity arises because, as already noted, the Romans renamed their land "Arabia" early in the 2nd century C.E., after ending their political independence. As a result, all those who lived in what was previously Nabatea but now was officially designated as "Arabia" were henceforth known as Arabs. Similarly, Jews who had lived in Judea, after Hadrian made it part of the Roman province of Syria, were no longer Jews or Judeans but Syrians. This deception failed in the case of the Jews who preserved their national identity, but succeeded in the case of the Nabateans who passed out of history with the advent of Islam in the 7th century.

The Nabateans are also identified as Arabs because many of their names and local deities seemed to have been of Arabic origin and there were also a few grammatical similarities between their language and Arabic (e.g., the definite article *al* and the plural ending *o*). This, however, cannot be considered conclusive or incontrovertible evidence of their true identity since it is known that the names of people and the use of language may be common to or shared by more than one national group. During the Second Temple period, for instance, the later Hasmonean monarchs adopted Greek names, as did some of the High Priests, which did not make them Greeks. The same phenomenon of Jews adopting Greek names and language appeared in the Diaspora. It is therefore not certain, even though the belief is widespread, to what degree the Nabateans were truly Arabs.

The practice now current among numerous scholars and writers of branding many ancient peoples as "Arabs", such as the Nabateans, despite their sedentary and highly-developed mode of life, has been extended even to the people of Israel. Various scholars from the 18th century to the present day have theorized that Israel was nothing but an Arab tribe which emerged from the Arabian desert. The noted orientalist and Biblical scholar, Shlomo Dov Goitein, dismissed this theory as not being corroborated by a single historical record. According to

---

paperback edition 1964, p. 26.

Goitein, "it is a mere theory derived by a false analogy from the conquest of the Middle East by the Muslim Arabs".[20] To buttress his counter-argument, he cites the great difference in the way of life between the camel-breeding Bedouins in Arabia as recounted in later Arab literature and the agriculture-centered life of the Israelites as evidenced by the Bible.

Though Goitein ably refutes the false hypothesis that the people of Israel were an Arab tribe and that Abraham was a typical Arab sheikh, who, according to Muhammad, was the presumed physical ancestor of the Arabs and the founder of Islam, he nevertheless accepts the general belief that the Nabateans had originally been an Arab people who spoke the Aramaic language. The latter was the *lingua franca* throughout the Middle East before it was superceded by Greek and much later, Arabic. However, the written records are not extensive enough to corroborate that belief, nor is it confirmed by their style of life. The same may be said for another alleged Arab people, the inhabitants of Palmyra (Tadmor) located in the central Syrian desert (200 km. northeast of Damascus), who are described as Arabs although they used an Aramaic script and language, just like the Nabateans. The kingdom of Palmyra briefly ruled over Palestine in the second half of the 3rd century. Its queen, Zenobia (267-273), celebrated in Arab legends as a great heroine, is reputed by two church patriarchs (St. Athanasius, 298-373; Photius, 820-891) to have been Jewish, though other scholars strongly reject this assertion.

In his memorandum, as already noted above, never once did Abdullah call his fellow Arabs in Western Palestine by the name of Palestinians. He referred to them constantly as Arabs only and equated them to the Arabs of the neighbouring countries:[21]

> When I say the Arabs and refer particularly to the Arabs in Palestine, I do not overlook their brethren in neighbouring countries, including the farthest boundaries of Arab kingdoms and principalities (Emirates).

Abdullah's repeated references to the Arabic-speaking inhabitants of Palestine as Arabs, rather than "Palestinians", carries great weight because he was one of their chief defenders and was the ruler of Transjordan. However, it must be noted that Abdullah apparently, for a brief period near the end of his life, underwent a change of mind concerning the use of the related terms "Palestine" and "Palestinian" after his military forces, called the Arab Legion and commanded by John Bagot Glubb Pasha, captured Judea and Samaria in the 1948 war with the just-declared Jewish State. He toyed with the idea of renaming his enlarged kingdom "Palestine", but in the end his British advisers convinced him not to do so. Instead he decided in March 1950 to officially call

---

[20] Goitein, *op. cit.*, p. 23.

[21] *Ibid.*, Vol. 13, Document 20, p. 134.

his kingdom "Jordan", a name that had already been unofficially used since May 25, 1946, when the Legislative Council took the oath of allegiance to "His Majesty the King of the Hashemite Kingdom of Jordan", two months after Britain and Transjordan concluded a treaty of alliance under which Britain recognized Transjordan "as a fully independent state and his Highness, the Amir, as the sovereign thereof".[22] Had Abdullah's kingdom been renamed "Palestine" instead of "Jordan", then all its inhabitants would have thenceforth been known as "Palestinians", rather than "Jordanians", representing a complete turn-around of his original view as expressed in his testimony to the Peel Royal Commission. It would also have been clear to all that Jordan had always been a constituent part of Palestine, until it was illegally detached by Britain in 1946, just prior to the termination of the British Mandate over Palestine in 1948.

During the brief two-year period when Abdullah's younger brother, Feisal, ruled Syria and Transjordan with British support (October 5, 1918-July 25, 1920), the Arabs of Palestine thought of themselves as part of the people of Syria, living in its southern portion. In this context they were Syrians, not Arabs, as Cherki Ganem, a Syrian expatriate living in Paris, told the Supreme Council of the Paris Peace Conference in February 1919 on behalf of the delegation he headed, called *Le Comite Centrale Syrien*. It was only after Feisal's ouster from Syria by French forces that some Arabs of Palestine, egged on by British agitators in the local Administration, began to clamour for its independence as a separate country detached from the Jewish National Home and to claim a new Palestinian Arab identity.

The name of "Southern Syria" for Palestine as used by the Arabs was in fact not so surprising, because at one time in the nineteenth century, Syria was in fact the name of the large Turkish *vilayet* or province covering all of Palestine, including Jerusalem. The *vilayet* of Syria was later reduced in size to exclude the area west of the Jordan River. However, even after these administrative changes took place, "Syria", a geographical term widely used by Moslems, still remained the unofficial name to describe comprehensively a vague geographical area which included the two *vilayet*s of Syria and Beirut, part of the *vilayet* of Aleppo, the Province of Lebanon and the independent *sanjak* of Jerusalem.[23]

The name of Syria is not mentioned in the masoretic text of the Bible, though it occurs in the Septuagint and Vulgate versions for rendering the Hebrew term *Aram*. It is a name which originated with the Greeks – Herodotus was the first to mention it – who used it to distinguish two separate regions of the country, Northern Syria, which they called "Syria of Mesopotamia", and Southern Syria, which was labeled "Coele Syria" or "Hollow Syria", that was later extended in

---

[22] Uriel Dann, *Studies in the History of Transjordan, 1920-1949: The Making of a State,* Westview Press / Boulder, Colorado and London (1984), p. 14.

[23] *Report on the McMahon-Hussein Correspondence*, March 16, 1937, Command 5974, Annex A, paragraph 3, page 12 (an Arab memorandum signed by George Antonius), and Annex B, paragraph 20, p. 25 (a British memorandum prepared by Lord Frederic Herbert Maugham, Lord High Chancellor of England).

the Hellenistic period to also include Cisjordanian Palestine and Transjordan. Syria is the shortened form of Assyria and was the name applied to the land ruled by the Seleucids, that was later converted into the Roman province of Syria. The Arabs called the country by the name of Esh-Sham, or "The Left", because in their expansive thinking it is at the northern or north-western end of the Arabian Peninsula. The southern side of it they called El-Yemen, or "The Right".[24] The Ottoman Turks had a different name for Syria, using the designation of Suristan or Arabustan.[25]

Arab use of the name "Syria" to also indicate the country of Palestine, in the period just prior to the start of the Mandate, can be seen in the letter sent by Emir Feisal, the future King of Iraq, acting then as the spokesman for the Arab national movement, to Felix Frankfurter representing the Zionist Movement at the Paris Peace Conference of 1919. Feisal told the future American Supreme Court Justice, just after he had signed an agreement with Weizmann recognizing the Balfour Declaration, that "there is room *in Syria* for us both". This general Moslem usage designating geographical "Syria" as one unified territory including Palestine disregarded the distinction between Syria and Palestine that was already widely current at the time of this letter. Both the 1915 De Bunsen Report and the 1916 Sykes-Picot Treaty had distinguished "Palestine" from "Syria", even before the Balfour Declaration was issued.

During the entire twenty-eight year period of the Mandate for Palestine (1920-1948) under British rule, it was very clear to everyone who exactly the "Palestinians" and the "Arabs" were and what the difference between them was. The Jews who lived in Mandated Palestine were called the "Palestinians" and accepted this designation for themselves, as is evident by the way they attached that name to all their national bodies, cultural organizations and commercial enterprises. On the other hand, the Arabs scornfully rejected the same designation for themselves, as clearly shown by Emir (later King) Abdullah's testimony to the Peel Royal Commission cited above, as well as statements issued or policies pursued (notably, the Greater Syria policy) by other prominent Arab spokesmen such as George Antonius, Professor Philip K. Hitti and Ahmed Shukeiri. The reason for their rejection of this designation was easily explainable. They knew that Palestine and the Jewish National Home were created for each other by the Principal Allied Powers of World War I and were thus inextricably linked. To be a Palestinian in the time of the Mandate was, in effect, to be Jewish, and for this reason most local Arabs refused to be called "Palestinians", which in any event was a non-Arabic name of likely Hebrew origin.

---

[24] See *The Historical Geography of the Holy Land* by George Adam Smith, 17th edition, Hodder and Stoughton, London (First edition: 1894), pp. 3-4.

[25] See the introduction written by Lt.-Col. Lawrence Martin, Geographer of the Institute of Politics, in Volume 1 of *The Treaties of Peace, 1919-1923*, published by the Carnegie Endowment for International Peace, New York (1924), p. xxxviii. Martin bases his information on the book *Arab Asia*, by Dana, published by the American Press, Beirut, 1922, p. 23.

In order not to limit the meaning of "Palestinians" to the Jews of Palestine only, the British Mandatory Government, as a concession to Arabs, Armenians, and other ethnic groups in the country, who were either Moslems or Christians, extended Palestinian nationality to include them also by the expedient of defining nationality to mean citizenship rather than membership in a specific nation – which was the other meaning of "nationality". Palestinian nationality, in the legal sense, now applied to all inhabitants, regardless of religion or ethnic origin. Despite this new interpretation for Palestinian nationality, Jews had a preferential status in law to become Palestinian citizens, for under the terms of the Mandate, their immigration to Palestine was to be "facilitated". Article 7 of the Mandate stated:

> The Administration of Palestine shall be responsible for enacting a nationality law. There shall be included in this law provisions framed so as to *facilitate* the acquisition of Palestinian citizenship by Jews who take up their permanent residence in Palestine (emphasis added).

No similar provision existed for facilitating Palestinian citizenship for Arabs living outside the borders of Palestine. This was iron-clad evidence that all of Palestine was designed to be the Jewish National Home and illustrated the close association between the name "Palestinians" and the Jews of the land who, during the Mandate period, were the proud bearers of that name. This identification with the name "Palestinian" was for the most part absent from the Arab community.

It is important to recall this information from those days because it has a direct bearing today on the question of who possesses the legal rights to Palestine under international law. These rights, including the title of sovereignty, were granted to the Jewish People, in effect to the Jews of the world who took up their permanent residence in Palestine and then exercised these rights first as "Palestinians" and then as "Israelis", after a long and arduous struggle for an internationally recognized charter to reconstruct the Jewish National Home. Had Theodor Herzl and his successors not striven for a renewed independent Jewish State, there would have been neither a mandate nor a country called Palestine nor any people holding Palestinian citizenship or nationality. None of the legal rights to the country were granted to a nation called "Arabs", "Palestinian Arabs" or Arabs whose descendants today call themselves "Palestinians".

The situation has become greatly confused because now that the local Arabs do call themselves by the name which formerly identified the Jews of Mandated Palestine, the false belief has been engendered and gained wide acceptance that the rights then granted to the Jewish People under international law were in fact granted to another people, the so-called [Arab] "Palestinians".

Though the nation of "Palestinians" is a pure fiction, it is an extremely valuable Arab propaganda tool against the State of Israel. Its main benefit for the Arabs is to convince millions of uninformed people unaware of the true legal facts and history of Palestine of the falsehood that Jews have "stolen" Palestine from the indigenous "Palestinians", a people that in fact has no historical existence and is a recent invention aimed at deluding the rest of the world that "Palestine" belongs to them.

Inasmuch as the Arab world has conspired to illegally deprive Jews of their rights to Palestine by artifice, fraud and deceit, especially through the misuse of the appellation "Palestinians", they have committed a serious crime unique in world history – that of "identity theft". This crime may be defined as appropriating the use of someone else's national identity – in the case of the Israeli Jews, its national identity during the Mandate period – to gain rights and benefits that do not rightfully or legally belong to them. The Jews of the State of Israel are the victims of this "identity theft" that has caused and continues to cause incalculable damage to their own rights, security and reputation. In the new guise of "Palestinians", the Arabs have succeeded in confusing the entire world and made it seem that Jews, rather than the Arabs, are usurpers of the Promised Land, the Land of Israel, and Zion.

The Arab penchant for lying and fabrication has reached such outrageous proportions, that it has become urgent to wage a ceaseless counter-campaign against the illegal and fraudulent usage of the designation "Palestinian". No Israeli Jew should passively accept this identity fraud, as has been the case up till now, nor for that matter any honest Gentile. World acceptance of the term "Palestinians" for the Arabs of the Land of Israel must be blamed not only on Arab League propaganda and deceitful anti-Israeli United Nations resolutions and reports issued in the 1970s, but also on top Labour Party and Likud leaders, particularly Arieh "Lova" Eliav, former Labour Party Secretary-General, who in his 1972 book *Land of the Hart* said they were "a distinctive people among the Arab peoples", having the same national-historical rights to Palestine as the Jews; Menachem Begin, the first Likud Prime Minister of Israel, who recognized the "legitimate rights of the Palestinian people and their just requirements" at Camp David in September 1978; and Shim'on Peres, the Labour Party former chairman, who in April 1986 announced that the "Palestinians are a people" after having previously recognized their legitimate rights on behalf of the Israel Labour Party. This culminated in the disastrous and illegal Israel-PLO Accords, which irresponsibly gave explicit recognition to the so-called "Palestinian people" and brought immense satisfaction to Yasser Arafat and his fellow-schemers against the Jewish State. Israeli political leaders have never realized the deleterious legal consequences their acceptance of this concept of "Palestinian nationhood" would have on Jewish national rights, not only in regard to Judea, Samaria and Gaza, but even to the State of Israel in its present narrow borders. By their ignoring these foreseeable consequences and the ensuing confusion, the rights originally secured for the Jewish People to Palestine in 1919, 1920 and 1922 have now become, in the eyes of many, the rights of [Arab] "Palestinians", particularly the right of self-determination, that was never meant for them.

The outstanding exception to this reckless recognition of the "Palestinian people" was Prime Minister Golda Meir who stoutly refused to accept the claim of false nationhood after being told all her life by Arab nationalists that there was no such thing as a "Palestinian people" in regard to Arabs. They were in fact nothing but a segment of the larger Arab nation. When the term "Palestinians" came into vogue after she became Prime Minister in 1969, she saw it as a new Arab tactic or a public-relations gimmick in their continuous campaign to liquidate Jewish national independence. It was then that the Arab refugees were suddenly transmuted into the "Palestinian people" whose goal was to regain a lost "homeland" according to their pretensions. The result of this transmutation was to change entirely the context of the Arab-Jewish Question from one of 21 Arab states fighting against the lone Jewish State to one of parity between two warring peoples, that of Israeli Jews and that of [Arab] "Palestinians", with the latter being seen as the underdog meriting world sympathy and recognition while the former was the conqueror or occupier of the land supposedly belonging to the "poor Palestinians".

The false designation "Palestinians" was at the same time extended to all the local Arabs in Judea, Samaria and Gaza. This created the present artificial distinction between the Arabs of Israel and the "Palestinians" in the other parts of the Land, although this distinction is now gradually eroding and all are becoming "Palestinians". Had Golda Meir's wise advice been heeded by her successors, the State of Israel would not be in the embarrassing and precarious position it is in today after unashamedly recognizing the alleged rights of the "Palestinian people" to most of Judea, Samaria and Gaza, a recognition contrary to historical fact, law and Zionism.

If Arabs who now designate themselves as "Palestinians" can assume the identity of Palestinian Jews as the "true Palestinians" and claim their rights, as they do today, then heritage, history and international law count for nothing and can be plagiarized at will. The State of Israel should therefore reverse its position regarding the recognition of the "Palestinian people", since it is a lethal threat both to the unity of the Land of Israel and to the Jewish State itself. Israel should take all necessary diplomatic and legal steps to combat the crime of "Palestinian identity theft" to protect and preserve its legal rights to the entire country. The establishment of a "Palestinian state" can only signify the complete success of false Arab propaganda and solidify the invented concept of a "Palestinian people". If nothing is done now or in the near future to expose and defeat this greatest of hoaxes, the identity fraud and injury to Jewish legal rights to the Land of Israel or former Mandated Palestine might become irreparable.

*Appendix III*

# Correspondence With Professor Yuval Ne'eman

1. Letter dated May 4, 2001 sent by Howard Grief to Prof. Yuval Ne'eman dealing with the concept of unallocated territories in reference to Judea, Samaria and Gaza;

2. Letter dated March 21, 2004 sent by Howard Grief to Prof. Yuval Ne'eman on the question of sovereignty over Palestine and the legal case of the Jewish People to its entire homeland;

3. Letter dated June 30, 2004 from Prof. Yuval Ne'eman (translated from the Hebrew) to Arieh Stav concerning the book by Attorney Howard Grief, The Rights of the Jewish People to the Land of Israel under International Law;

4. Letter dated December 12, 2004 sent by Howard Grief to Prof. Yuval Ne'eman concerning how the author's approach to various legal questions differs from that of other jurists;

5. Letter dated January 24, 2006 to Prof. Efraim Inbar of the Besa Center on the publication of the book The Borders of Israel under International Law by Attorney Howard Grief (translated from the Hebrew). Author's note: the new title of the book was suggested by Professor Ne'eman.

6. Letter dated March 27, 2006 from Prof. Yuval Ne'eman to Prof. Efraim Inbar enclosing documents pertaining to the book.

7. Letter dated May 17, 2006 sent by Howard Grief to Mrs. Matilda Elron concerning the untimely demise of Prof. Ne'eman.

**Howard Grief**
**Attorney and Notary**
**13/2 David Goitein St.,**
**Pisgat Ze'ev Mizrah, Jerusalem 97782**
**Tel. (Fax) : 972-2-656-0085**

Jerusalem תובב"א
11 Iyar, 5761
May 4, 2001

Prof. Yuval Ne'eman,
6 Ehud Street,
Zahala
Tel Aviv 69936

Dear Yuval,

Please find enclosed a copy of a letter I sent to my friend, Dr. Paul S. Riebenfeld, concerning the term "unallocated territories" in regard to Judea, Samaria and Gaza. Paul took umbrage at my reference to him in a letter I sent to Joel Carmichael, Editor of Midstream, in which I stated that he formerly used this expression to describe the legal status of Judea, Samaria and Gaza. I provided him with documentary evidence to support my statement that he had indeed described these areas during the greater part of the 1980's as "unallocated territories" which he now finds to be inexact terminology. May I say without undue modesty on my part that I first pointed out to him this blatant error in terminology which he originally coined and then later retracted, though not before his friend Prof. Eugene V. Rostow had already succeeded in spreading that usage around the world through his own writings, separate and apart from Paul's work.

Riebenfeld, whom I know quite well, once told me that Rostow, whom I never had the pleasure of meeting, never wrote anything for publication about Judea, Samaria and Gaza and their status under international law from the time the two of them first met in 1974, without Rostow checking his written material with Paul beforehand.

The term "unallocated territories" or its slight variation "unalloted territories" of the Mandate for Palestine with reference to Judea, Samaria and Gaza, stems from an earlier term, namely, the legal concept of the "sovereignty vacuum" which is alleged to exist in those three regions of the Land of Israel. This concept was originally used by four prominent Jewish jurists in the year or two after the Six Day War of June 1967 to describe the legal status of Judea, Samaria and Gaza under international law. These jurists were Julius Stone, Yehuda Blum, Elihu Lauterpacht and Stephen Schwebel. It was perhaps natural for them, though certainly not correct, to theorize that these areas of the Land of Israel were ownerless (*res nullius*) because, on the one hand, neither Jordan nor Egypt had any valid legal title to these territories under international law, while on the other hand, Israel asserted no legal right of ownership for itself immediately after their re-possession by the IDF on behalf of the Jewish People in the Six-Day War.

Israeli constitutional law, specifically the Area of Jurisdiction and Powers Ordinance of September 22, 1948, made retroactive to May 15, 1948, and in a more general sense, the Law of Return of July 1950, whose application extends to the whole Land of Israel, required their immediate incorporation into the State of Israel, but Prime Minister Eshkol and his National Unity Government ignored the existence and expectations of these two laws. This policy, not to apply the existing law but to implement instead the Hague Rules and Regulations of 1907 as well as the Fourth Geneva Convention of 1949 (i.e., the laws of war), even though on a voluntary basis, was concurred in inexplicably by the legal advisers of the Eshkol Government or perhaps done at their behest, most notably Meir Shamgar, then the Military Advocate-General who subsequently became Attorney-General of Israel and President of the Supreme Court of Israel.

Another opportunity to annex these areas was missed by that supposedly great champion of Eretz-Israel, Menahem Begin, when he finally came to power in 1977. Surprisingly, instead of practicing what he had preached for the previous 30 years and doing what our constitutional law itself mandated, Begin acted out of character, in a bizarre and inconceivable manner, when he devised his 26 point program to establish "Self-Rule for Palestinian Arabs", the residents of Judea, Samaria and Gaza, which he announced to the Knesset on December 28, 1977.

The key provision of the plan in regard to the question of sovereignty over these areas was Article 24 which read as follows:

> 24. Israel stands by its right and its claim of sovereignty to Judea, Samaria and the Gaza district. In the knowledge that other claims exist, it proposes for the sake of the agreement and the peace, that the question of sovereignty in these areas be left open.

To my mind, it was contradictory for Begin to use both the words "right" and "claim" in the same context as he foolishly did. Either Israel had a legal right of sovereignty or only a claim, but not both at the same time. In any event, by leaving the question of sovereignty "open", he was only asserting a claim of sovereignty and not declaring an existing right of sovereignty. His use of the word "right" was really nothing more than a bargaining or talking point, rather than an actual right founded in law, otherwise he would never have said the question of sovereignty was being left open.

Begin carried his plan a step further at the Camp David Conference held between September 5 and September 17, 1978. He now substituted more ambiguous phraseology for deciding the question of sovereignty. That was the new term of "final status" in connection with Judea, Samaria and Gaza, which would be negotiated and determined after a transitional period of five years. The proposed agreement on the "final status" and the "transitional arrangements" that would be made prior to a final status agreement conveyed a clear message to the world that sovereignty over these territories was still an open matter subject to future negotiations between the concerned parties and not a restored or pre-existing right held by Israel under international law, nor even, for that matter, under Israeli constitutional law. Moreover, he took leave of his senses when he agreed at the Camp David Conference to put the final decision on the question of sovereignty in the hands of the local Arab inhabitants, whose elected representatives would vote on whether or not the final status agreement that was reached in negotiations was acceptable to them. This procedure to determine the final status (i.e., the sovereignty) of Judea, Samaria and Gaza was not only an act of unimaginable folly by the erstwhile champion of Jewish rights over these integral parts of our homeland, but from a legal perspective, it was an act of outright treason. There is no other true way to characterize what Begin did, which may also explain at least in part, why he became a broken and reclusive man in the last ten years of his life, cut off from reality and unable to write his dreamed-of book on the reborn glory of the Jewish People in their own state after the hell of the Holocaust.

By its nature and wording, the Camp David Framework Agreement as regards Judea, Samaria and Gaza assumed the existence of a "sovereignty vacuum" in those areas which would be filled upon the making of peace by and between the four concerned parties of Israel, Egypt, Jordan and the local Arabs living there.

Aharon Barak was then the Attorney-General of Israel, and Begin spoke about him in rapturous terms. Barak played a major role in helping to draft the Camp David Framework Agreement for Peace in the Middle East, and it is a safe bet to assume that Begin's position on the whole question of sovereignty over Judea, Samaria and Gaza followed Barak's absurd advice, in conjunction, of course, with the advice of others (Moshe Dayan, Ezer Weizmann and Dr. Meir Rosenne, the legal adviser to the Foreign Ministry) who were also present at that fateful conference.

It was a short terminological step ("mis-step" is a more accurate word) from the theory of the sovereignty-vacuum to the new thesis of their being "unallocated territories" of the Mandate for Palestine which was propounded not long afterwards by Riebenfeld and Rostow working in tandem, undoubtedly influenced by the developments at the Camp David Conference and the positions taken earlier by the four Jewish jurists named above.

Rostow used this very inaccurate phrase in the title of a paper he prepared in March 1980 on "Palestinian Self-Determination: Possible Futures for the Unallocated Territories of the Palestine Mandate" (see *Yale Studies in World Public Order*, Volume 5, with the back-date of Spring 1979, Number 2). Riebenfeld followed suit with his own contribution in the "American Zionist" magazine, where he made extensive use of this ill-chosen term, as you can read in my enclosed letter sent to him.

The use of inexact terminology, specifically the worlds "sovereignty-vacuum" and then "unallocated territories" by erudite Jewish jurists did tremendous and continuing damage to Israel's legal rights and title to all of the Land of Israel, most of all to Judea, Samaria and Gaza. This wrongful usage was, in fact, a complete negation of those very legal rights and title which the State of Israel had inherited from the Jewish People to whom they had been granted unreservedly under international law by the all-important San Remo Resolution of April 25, 1920, in application of the right of self-determination under Article 22 of the Treaty of Versailles, as later embodied in the Mandate for Palestine.

Rostow had the impudence to lump together UN Security Council Resolution 242 of November 22, 1967 as further elaborated by Resolution 338 of October 22, 1973 with the provisions and principles of the Mandate for Palestine. These different acts are mutually exclusive and not complementary at all. They differ fundamentally in their legal nature since these two resolutions have no force of law (Rostow considered them "binding", nevertheless) while the terms of the Mandate for Palestine were part of recognized international law from the time it was first established and conferred upon Great Britain (April 25, 1920). Resolution 242 spoke of "occupied territories", which Rostow said was the status accorded to Judea, Samaria and Gaza in that resolution, together with the Sinai and Golan Heights. The Mandate for Palestine, on the other hand, deemed these territories (excluding Sinai) to be part of the Jewish National Home having the boundaries demarcated in the Franco-British Boundary Convention of December 23, 1920. To say that Resolution

242 and the Mandate for Palestine are in any way compatible, as Rostow does, is to exhibit such gross ignorance of the meaning of the Mandate for Palestine as to make one wonder how Rostow could even write and lecture about such an important subject or parade himself as an expert on the question.

To show Rostow's linking of the Mandate with UN Resolutions 242 and 338, I quote from his article in *Yale Studies in World Public Order* (page 168) where he says:

> Legally, politically and strategically, the obvious solution to the Palestinian problem is peace between Israel and Jordan in accordance with Resolutions 242 and 338. Such a settlement could take many forms. But peaceful settlement is the only way to end the problem of Palestine in ways which satisfy the terms of the Mandate and of the Security Council Resolutions which have sought to carry out its principles.

In the same study, Rostow described the legal status of Judea, Samaria and Gaza as follows (pages 158-59):

> Like the South West African Mandate, the Palestine Mandate survived the termination of the Mandate administration as a trust under Article 80 (of the U.N. Charter). In Palestine, Israel and Jordan already exist as states and only the Gaza Strip and the West Bank remain as unallocated parts of the Mandate.

He reiterated this, by saying (p. 160):

> The Israeli view is that while the 1907 Hague Convention and the 1949 Geneva Convention apply to the Israeli occupation of the Golan Heights and the Sinai, which are Syrian or Egyptian territory in the contemplation of international law, they do not apply to the Israeli occupation of the West Bank and the Gaza Strip, which have not been recognized as parts of any state, but are still unallocated territories of the Palestine Mandate.

In further elaboration of this point, in which he also alludes to the applicability of Resolution 242 he wrote (p. 153):

> ...Thus the West Bank and Gaza Strip are not "Arab" territories in the legal sense, but territories of the Mandate which have never been recognized as belonging to Israel or to Jordan... Moreover, for reasons which remain compelling, Security Council Resolution 242 prescribes that Israel is under no obligation to withdraw from the West Bank or the Gaza Strip until Jordan makes peace.

From all of the above quotations, it emerges that Rostow has made a jumble of the legal status of Judea, Samaria and Gaza. He does not realize as he should have that Judea, Samaria and Gaza were in fact recognized as belonging to the Jewish People (and hence to the State of Israel which is subsumed under the words "Jewish People") under the very Mandate for Palestine he cites. Nor does he realize as he should have that Judea, Samaria and Gaza were indeed specifically allocated to the Jewish People at San Remo and Sèvres, and then fully incorporated into the borders of Mandated Palestine as integral parts of the Jewish National Home. Nor does he further realize, as he should have, that Israel representing the Jewish People has absolutely no obligation – in any legal sense under international law by virtue of the rights it inherited under the Mandate for Palestine – to withdraw from any of its sovereign territories including Judea, Samaria and Gaza, even where there exists a state of peace.

Rostow has been depicted as a great friend and supporter of Israel's cause. However, you would never know that from the above quotations. A friend and supporter should not say or imply that Israel will need eventually to withdraw from the alleged "occupied territories" of Judea, Samaria and Gaza – even if that would result in "secure and recognized boundaries" as provided for in Resolution 242 – which are in truth not occupied territories in international law, as is now universally believed. He also should not have given widespread currency to the mistaken idea that Judea, Samaria and Gaza are unallocated territories which he misleadingly asserts are still "trust territories" governed by Article 80 of the UN Charter, a notion which can also be traced back to Riebenfeld. If that were really so, the UN could then legitimately intervene in a forceful manner under the persistent prodding of twenty-one Arab states in the affairs of Judea, Samaria and Gaza to the great benefit of the Palestine Liberation Organization.

Rostow pretended to be a great legal expert on the question of Israel's true legal position in Judea, Samaria and Gaza, and many in Israel acclaimed him as such, not realizing the great damage and danger his position augured for Israel's unassailable rights over these territories, rights – I may add – that should have been proclaimed and implemented and not made the subject of any negotiations. Unfortunately, Rostow's appalling legal approach was the one actually adopted, with modifications, by the Government of Israel in the secret Oslo talks with the Palestine Liberation Organization, whereby Israel agreed to withdraw from most of Judea, Samaria and Gaza and to accept an eventual so-called "Palestinian State" which would be set up there in return for "peace", except that instead of Jordan, the other party was now the PLO. I do not mean to say that the Rabin and Peres Governments took their cue directly from Rostow. Rabin or Peres may not have even been aware that they were subconsciously following Rostow's legal approach in ceding great parts of Judea, Samaria and Gaza to the PLO for "peace". But Joel Singer, their young legal adviser who drafted the original Israel-PLO agreements, was certainly aware of Rostow's ideas or those of all the other Jewish jurists who had considered the question of the legal status of Judea, Samaria and Gaza under international law, without any of them ever coming to the right and proper conclusions.

That is why today we have the great disaster of dealing with the PLO in our own backyard. What a terrible legacy these jurists, including their Israeli counterparts, have left the poor Jews of Israel who must now contend with Arafat and his gangster rule in the Land of Israel. To state the unvarnished truth, it was their legal thinking and concepts that provided all the justification that was needed for Israel's withdrawal from Judea, Samaria and Gaza. They should have known better that these areas were not occupied territories under international law as far as Israel was concerned, that they were also not governed by UN Resolutions 242 and 338, that there never existed any sovereignty vacuum over them to be filled by Arab Gentiles, and, finally, that there were no unallocated territories of the Mandate for Palestine that had not already formed part of the Jewish National Home under international law.

Sincerely,

**Howard**

P.S. – I am deeply sorry to inform you that after composing this letter and before it could be sent to you, I learnt of the passing away of my very dear friend and mentor, Dr. Paul Reibenfeld. He was someone with whom I had close contact over the past twenty years and admired very much, even though, as you know, I came to different legal conclusions than his own concerning Israel's legal rights to all of the Land of Israel.

**Howard Grief**
**Attorney and Notary**
**13/2 David Goitein St.,**
**Pisgat Ze'ev Mizrah, Jerusalem 97782 Israel**
**Tel. (Fax) : 972-2-656-0085**

---

Jerusalem תובב״א
28 Adar 5764
March 21, 2004

Prof. Yuval Ne'eman,
Professor Emeritus of Physics, TAU,
Chairman, Israel Space Agency,
6 Ehud Street,
Tel Aviv 69936

Dear Yuval,

I was very happy to meet with you on March 17th at your office, to present you with the manuscript I have written on the Legal Rights and Title of Sovereignty of the Jewish People to the Land of Israel and Palestine under International Law. I have spent two and a half years composing this manuscript and hope that once published it will become a chief source of reference on the subject dealt with, the espousal in clear terms of our exclusive national and political rights to all of Palestine and the Land of Israel. The legal case of the Jewish People to its undivided homeland under international law has never been, to my mind, properly adduced by any jurist in the way it should have been – in a coherent, organized and irrefutable fashion, without apology or compromise of any sort. I base my legal analysis and conclusions solely on the primary documents of international law (the San Remo Resolution, the Mandate for Palestine, the Franco-British Boundary Convention, the Anglo-American Convention on Palestine respecting the Mandate for Palestine), as well as on British archival material and the minutes of the Paris and San Remo Peace Conferences of 1919 and 1920 that reveal the true intentions of the Principal Allied and Associated Powers in crafting a global political and legal settlement for the disposition of the non-Turkish lands of the Ottoman Empire.

To recapitulate the core point of the book: it concerns the question of sovereignty over the whole of Palestine and the Land of Israel. I have discussed this question in two separate chapters of the book. I reject the traditional date given for Turkey's loss of sovereignty, namely the date of the signing of the Treaty of Lausanne on July 24, 1923, or on the date of its ratification on August 6, 1924. I have concluded that the real date is January 30, 1919 when the Mandates System was first approved by the Council of Ten at the Paris Peace Conference attended by British Prime Minister David Lloyd George, U.S. President Woodrow Wilson and other Allied leaders. It was decided at this Conference that the non-Turkish territories in the Middle East would not be returned to the Ottoman Empire, but governed as mandated states leading to full independence (Palestine, Mesopotamia and Syria) under the newly created Mandates System of government that ruled out any idea of annexation by the Principal Allied Powers of World War I. The decision taken on January 30, 1919 is known as the Smuts Resolution, after Jan Christiaan Smuts, the South African statesman and principal formulator of the Mandates System, that

2

shortly thereafter became Article 22 of the Covenant of the League of Nations found in the first part of the Treaty of Versailles and in all the other peace treaties concluded in 1919 and 1920 (the Treaty of St. Germain with Austria, the Treaty of Trianon with Hungary, the Treaty of Neuilly with Bulgaria and the Treaty of Sèvres with Turkey).

During the interim period from January 30, 1919 until the creation of the new mandated states of Palestine, Mesopotamia and Syria on April 24-25, 1920, at the San Remo Peace Conference, sovereignty was temporarily vested in the four-member coalition of Principal Allied Powers (Britain, France, Italy and Japan) who jointly had the power and the right, as the victors in the war against the Ottoman Empire, to dispose of these non-Turkish territories. The only reason Palestine was created on April 24, 1920 was to implement the purpose of the Balfour Declaration – to establish in Palestine a national home for the Jewish People, which also gave effect – as stated explicitly in the San Remo Resolution and Mandate – to the provisions of Article 22 of the Covenant of the League of Nations. This meant that the right of self-determination in regard to Palestine, a right implicit in Article 22, was reserved exclusively for the Jewish People. It was never the intention of the Supreme Council of the Principal Allied Powers that Palestine or any part of it be also made the Arab national home, despite the fact that its population then was overwhelmingly Arab, except for Jerusalem which had a Jewish majority. The word "home" was a mere euphemism for a Jewish State, and it applied to the whole country.

Since Palestine was meant to be a Jewish State from the very beginning, *de jure* sovereignty was thus vested in the Jewish People. It was not vested in Britain, which, though exercising the attributes of sovereignty, did not have the status of a sovereign but only that of a Mandatory, a trustee and a tutor in a combined manner. Nor was it vested in the League of Nations, whose function was to supervise the Mandatory's implementation of the Mandate for Palestine with no sovereign powers or rights of its own to this territory. Nor did sovereignty vest any longer in the Principal Allied Powers, after the global political and legal settlement was made in 1919 and 1920. This coalition of wartime powers ceased to exist after the signing of the Treaty of Sèvres on August 10, 1920. The Principal Allied Powers may be compared in a legal sense to a testator making a will who bequeaths a legacy and then forever disappears from the scene upon his death.

There is not one jurist who has ever adduced the point that the Jewish People gained legal sovereignty over all of Palestine on April 24, 1920 when Palestine was officially created and recognized as the future independent Jewish State. Palestine was from the very outset a Jewish State in the making, a process which lasted from April 24, 1920 to May 14, 1948, though the British did everything to prevent the realization of this state during most of the Mandate period.

The term "Palestine" as originally understood in the San Remo Resolution of April 25, 1920 included all of the various historical regions of the country, extending east and west of the Jordan, north and south of the Yarmuk, in accordance with the biblical formula, "from Dan to Beersheba", which meant all areas *settled* by the Twelve Tribes of Israel in the First and Second Temple Periods, or concerning which there was a real historical connection. David Lloyd George, who adopted this formula as the British standard for the delineation of Palestine's boundaries and convinced the three other Principal Allied Powers as well to accept it, relied on the maps of the Scottish scholar and ordained church minister, George Adam Smith, in his book and

3

atlas on the "Historical Geography of the Holy Land", to determine what those borders should be, especially in regard to the northern and northeastern borders of Palestine. However, in the final delineation of the boundaries in 1920 and 1922, the Israelite-settled area of the Tribe of ʽAsher embracing what is today Southern Lebanon up to the Litani river was omitted, as was also the area of Bashan, which had been inhabited by half of the Tribe of Menasseh. During the 100-year period of Herodian-Judean rule, including that of Herod's son Herod Philip, his grandson Agrippa I and his great-grandson Agrippa II, Bashan was divided into four parts which were populated by both Jews and non-Jews: (a) the Golan including Mount Hermon, (b) Batanea lying east of the Golan, (c) Trachonitis, the easternmost part of Bashan, and (d) Auranitis, south of Batanea and Trachonitis. These areas were omitted from Palestine and the Jewish National Home, due to France's stubborn adherence to the *illegal* Sykes-Picot Treaty of May 9 and 16, 1916, accompanied by strong anti-Semitic overtones. Another region not included was Sinai, which was, as you have always said to me, part of the Land of Israel, at least in regard to half of the peninsula.

In our hour-long discussion on March 17$^{th}$, you referred to my work as the continuation of what Dr. Paul Riebenfeld and Prof. Eugene Rostow started. With all due respect to my good friend and mentor Paul Riebenfeld, whom I always held in high regard, he never posited the fact that the Jewish People held sovereignty over what he originally called, in 1982 and thereafter, the "unallocated territories" of Judea, Samaria and Gaza. I personally told him in 1988, in reaction to this self-defeating terminology, that these territories had, on the contrary, already been allocated to the Jewish People. He later altered his view to say that these regions of the Jewish National Home had indeed been allocated for the purpose of Jewish settlement, but he never linked this point with the concept of sovereignty.

In regard to Prof. Eugene Rostow, he always maintained that Judea, Samaria and Gaza were "unallocated parts" of the Mandate with no existing sovereign. He also considered them "occupied territories" subject to the provisions of UN Security Council Resolution 242, though he also believed that giving up Sinai to Egypt fulfilled the demands of Resolution 242. If Rostow's view is correct, then what I wrote on the same subject is completely wrong. However, Rostow's knowledge of the Mandate for Palestine was superficial and of recent origin, imparted to him by Paul Riebenfeld, a relationship between them that began after Rostow wrote a piece in a 1973 issue of Commentary. In that article, Rostow revealed an amazing lack of knowledge in being unaware of the fact that Transjordan had been part of the Mandate for Palestine, which prompted Paul to contact him to inform him of this elementary fact. I have the actual correspondence between Riebenfeld and Rostow to prove what I say – copies of which Paul gave to me and which I also remitted to Shmuel Katz when he visited Montreal in 1984. Katz at first did not believe what I told him about Rostow's heavy reliance on Riebenfeld, but he changed his mind after I sent him by mail copies of their correspondence and then wrote a column on the subject in the Jerusalem Post. In sum, I do not think my own work on Jewish legal rights bears any relationship at all to what Rostow wrongly stated in his many articles, except in regard to the matter of Jewish settlements in Judea, Samaria and Gaza which he correctly asserted are legal under international law.

My work may be considered a continuation to a certain extent of Paul's work, though, as I say, he never explored the question of sovereignty or analyzed all the key documents of international law as I have done or drew the conclusions that

4

should have been drawn about exclusive Jewish legal rights over Palestine and the Land of Israel.

Despite this failing, I sincerely admired Paul for pursuing the idea that Transjordan is Palestine, as is certainly Cisjordan and the State of Israel and all the diverse parts of Palestine included today in Lebanon, Syria and Egypt. However, Paul concentrated only on Transjordan and what he called a "boundary dispute" between the State of Israel and the Hashemite Kingdom of Jordan. I go much further than seeing the Arab conflict with Israel as a mere "boundary dispute". The accumulated evidence of a century or more proves there is undying Arab hatred for the revival of Jewish statehood in any part of Palestine, that has nothing to do with a boundary dispute.

The Arabs of Jordan, the Lebanese, the Syrians and the Egyptians are occupying various regions of our historical land, and one day we must get it all back, whatever the reality is today. My book, I dare say, provides the juridical basis for establishing the legal rights of the Jewish People to those areas of Eretz-Israel presently under Arab occupation, including those controlled by the so-called "Palestinian Authority". We do not have to accept the British-French boundary delineation of the Jewish National Home and Jewish State as final and immutable. Nor do we have to accept the invention of a fictitious "Palestinian people" who claim "Palestine" for themselves.

I do not expect you to endorse everything I have written in the manuscript, but I do hope you will find my legal analysis and conclusions on our rights to the whole Land of Israel under international law to be well-based, logical and convincing. I am very grateful and honoured that you will take your valuable time to read my manuscript. This work which I have presented to you is also a measure of your own past encouragement in getting me started on this project when I worked for you as a legal adviser on Eretz-Israel under international law at the Ministry of Energy and Infrastructure throughout all of 1991 and January 1992. Your confidence in my work has served as a spur for me to continue to elucidate the Jewish legal case which is applicable to all parts of our country, and not merely to the areas included in the State. I am more indebted to you than to any other person for seeing the potential and the necessity of what I have undertaken.

Your introduction to my book will carry very great weight with the one person who will be most instrumental in ensuring that it is published, a reference, of course, to Arieh Stav, and it will also be very helpful in exposing the book to the general public and thereby furthering the cause of Eretz-Israel, which we both wholeheartedly believe in. I have no doubt that your admirers in Israel far exceed any detractors you may have, even if not everyone knows about all your tremendous contributions to the State of Israel in matters of defense, nuclear physics, space and politics. Your introduction to my work will thus be an invaluable gift that will make me forever grateful.

In warmest esteem and friendship and wishing you good health,

**Howard**

Yuval Ne'eman
Professor Emeritus of Physics, TAU
Chairman, Israel Space Agency
(Ministry of Science)

30 June 2004
YN - 5143

To: Mr. Arieh Stav,
Editor-in-Chief,
Nativ Journal and Publisher

Fax: 9063905

Dear Arieh,

Re: The Book by Attorney Howard Grief,
"The Rights of the Jewish People to the Land of Israel under International Law"

This letter is intended to express my full and enthusiastic support of the proposal to publish the above-mentioned book by Attorney Howard Grief under the imprint of the publishing house "Nativ" and/or, as the case may be, in conjunction with other publishers who have a prestigious reputation in the spheres of political policy, security and law. I see in the book being considered an extremely valuable life's work that fills a dangerous vacuum in the arsenal of weapons required to defend ourselves against the massive and ceaseless efforts – on the part of the Arab States and with the support of European elements – to delegitimize completely both Zionism and the State of Israel.

The texts that deal with international law can be divided into two kinds:

= academic texts which seek to deepen and broaden the legal infrastructure that is made up of various agreements and treaties – in a field where there was no exact codification of the law, as exists in most other legal fields.

= a discussion of a defined subject, as in the matter under consideration, and here it is possible to find a jumble of texts that bring to mind, in part, commercial or political manifestos and propaganda, and few are the texts with an approach that measures up to academic standards. This is not particularly surprising because (and perhaps in contrast to the exact sciences) the entire practical legal field is located on the narrow edges between statutory law, as drafted by the legislator, and the particulars of the event being discussed. The role of the attorney is to serve the interests of his client [the one who hired him], rather than to search for the complete truth.

On the subject of our rights to the land, what are mainly known are the "studies" and arguments of Professors Eugene Rostow (and to some extent that of his brother Walter) and Paul Riebenfeld. These two were active principally at the time of the discussions that followed the Six-Day War of 1967 and [their work] centered around the UN Resolutions of that year, by seizing on the play on words between the French and English versions [of Security Council Resolution 242] ("withdrawal from territories" as opposed to "withdrawal from the territories"). The principal part of their work related to the subject of Judea, Samaria and Gaza, both adopting a minimalistic approach that suited the moment, and as regards the basic issue, the quarrel was one between the borders of 1947 [for the proposed Jewish State] and those of 1948 [when the borders expanded beyond the UN lines as a result of the War of Independence]. This, too, was the point of the emphasis that the Arabs put on the term "legitimacy" concerning the rights of the "Palestinians"... On our part, an enormous gap was

2

created between "our rights" that derived from history going back to the period of the Bible as well as the archaeological findings etc. and our "current" rights, dating only from 1947 or 1948.

Howard Grief first carried out an academic study until he found the most fitting answer. For about 400 years, the Ottoman Empire ruled over all the Balkans, the Middle East and North Africa. The struggle for the liberation of those areas began in the Balkan lands at the beginning of the nineteenth century and ended in 1913. In the First World War, the job [of liberation] was completed and Turkey was reduced to the Anatolian Peninsula. All of this was contained in the San Remo Agreement of April 1920. The fact that it was precisely at that place and time that Iraq, Syria, Lebanon and the states of the Arabian Peninsula obtained [thanks to the victory of the Principal Allied Powers over the Central Powers] the very same liberation from the Ottoman yoke strengthens the approach of Grief who presents the proof for the inclusion of Palestine [i.e., the Jewish People] in the list of beneficiaries in regard to the "settlement [or disposition] of the inheritance of the Ottoman Empire." Grief has found the true and most effectual lever for our basic case, and I am convinced that his approach deserves to be utilized [in presenting our case to the world].

The question of language arises here. It is clear that the text should be published in English for the sake of precision in wording – but it is [also] needed in Hebrew to convince our own public.

In summary – I am convinced that there is great importance in the publication of this manuscript [text] and I will be happy to write a fitting introduction to it (if I am asked to do so).

Cordially yours,

Yuval Ne'eman

**Howard Grief**
**Attorney and Notary**
**13/2 David Goitein St.,**
**Pisgat Ze'ev Mizrah, Jerusalem 97782 Israel**
**Tel. (Fax) : 972-2-656-0085**

---

Jerusalem תובב״א
29 Kislev 5765
December 12, 2004

Prof. Yuval Ne'eman,
Professor Emeritus of Physics, TAU,
6 Ehud Street,
Tel Aviv 69936
E-mail: matildae@tauex.tau.ac.il

Dear Yuval,

As mentioned in our telephone conversation of Wednesday night, December 8, 2004, I would very much appreciate a letter from you to be presented to the Ariel Center for Policy Research and its Director, Arie Stav, and his Steering Committee of seven professors who will be meeting in about 10 days to decide on the publication of my manuscript. It is a matter of urgency to receive this letter before the meeting.

As to why my manuscript should be published, I submit the following comments. It offers a comprehensive and systematic legal treatment – I believe the first of its kind – of Jewish national and political rights to all of the Land of Israel based on the primary legal documents and international agreements that emerged during and after World War I, that led to the dismemberment of the Ottoman Turkish Empire and the creation of new states in the Middle East. My work is also based to some extent on British archival sources that I obtained just before coming to Israel (1989) from London's Public Record Office. The legal course of events is followed up to the present day.

Israel's legal foundation cannot be understood unless one begins at the correct departure point. That point is not the UN Partition Resolution of November 29, 1947, but the San Remo Resolution of April 25, 1920. That is when the Turkish Empire was carved up and Palestine was officially created and allotted exclusively to the Jewish People, i.e., the Jews of the world represented by the Zionist Organization. The most important part of my book is the first section which deals with the Origin of the Legal Title. The core part of my argument is that the Jewish People were vested with *de jure* sovereignty as soon as the Balfour Declaration was approved by the Principal Allied Powers (Britain, France, Italy and Japan) on April 24, 1920 at the San Remo Peace Conference as the basis for creating Palestine as a Jewish State. That represents my original thesis and analysis – which you yourself referred to in your article in Global Affairs (see p. 85 of your article).

In fact, during the entire Mandate period, it was a hotly debated issue amongst jurists of the world as to who actually possessed sovereignty over mandated territories of which there were three classes (A, B and C). A vast legal literature exists on the subject, but no final and decisive answer was ever given to this question. Some thought that it lay with the Principal Allied Powers; others with the

Mandatory Power; or with the League of Nations; or jointly with the first two or three of the above. Still others thought it was vested in the inhabitants of the mandated territories; or finally, that it was suspended while the Mandate was in force and hence was not vested in any of the above. In the case of Palestine, which was a unique Mandate (the Jews were not then the principal inhabitants of Palestine), I have given a definitive answer that rings true. The conclusion I have arrived at is that sovereignty over Palestine was originally vested during an interim phase (January 30, 1919 to April 24, 1920) in the Principal Allied Powers as a collective entity, following Turkey's defeat and subjugation in World War I. The Four Powers then devolved it upon the Jewish People at the San Remo Peace Conference. However, during the Mandatory's rule of Palestine, sovereignty in a de facto sense was exercised not by the Jews, but by the British. I have buttressed my answer with actual dates as to when Turkey lost sovereignty, when it was gained by the quartet of the Principal Allied Powers, and when it devolved in a *de jure* sense upon the Jewish People, all of which is based on my analysis of the primary documents and international agreements. I have conclusively shown that Britain was the de facto ruler exercising the prerogatives or attributes of sovereignty, but not the de jure sovereign – based on Article 1 of the Mandate for Palestine. That, I believe, is an important contribution to law never before made by anyone. My dear friend, Dr. Paul Riebenfeld, once told me that no one before me advanced this explanation of Jewish sovereignty over all of Palestine.

The general approach of modern jurists (post-1967), particularly that of Prof. Eugene Rostow, Prof. Julius Stone and Dr. Paul Riebenfeld among others, was that the question of sovereignty over Judea, Samaria and Gaza had never been resolved. This was wrong! I looked at the question of sovereignty over Palestine and the Land of Israel as a whole, and not as regards particular regions of Palestine or the Land of Israel. When Britain, France, Italy and Japan created Palestine, they did not divide the country into its component parts and say that the Jews would get only certain parts of the country while the rest would be given to Arabs. Palestine was created as an indivisible whole, exclusively for the Jewish National Home. That is why Palestine was synonymous with the Jewish homeland and why the term "Palestinians" was used as a synonym for Jews only from 1920 to 1948, until the State of Israel was created.

My approach to the question of sovereignty thus differs radically from others in that I say it was decided in 1920 at the San Remo Peace Conference and does not have to be decided again today. The latter approach was unfortunately adopted by Prime Minister Menahem Begin when he said that sovereignty was still an "open" question to be decided at final peace negotiations to determine the "final status" of Judea, Samaria and Gaza. Even though jurists like Prof. Yehuda Blum and others argued that we had the "best claim" to sovereignty, that was a mistaken approach because it negated or simply forgot the global legal and political settlement made at the San Remo Peace Conference on April 24-25, 1920. The Blum approach, although it appears pro-Israel, is a losing approach, because it opened up the possibility (which is exactly what happened!) for the Arabs to claim national rights in Palestine based on the fact that they are "Palestinians" who are the indigenous inhabitants, despite the fact that Palestine did not officially exist as a state before April 24, 1920. My approach is the best one because it shows that Palestine was created for one purpose only: to be the Jewish National Home and not the Arab or "Palestinian" national home.

3

One final point on Blum's approach. He said there was "no reversioner" in regard to Judea, Samaria and Gaza in a famous article that appeared in the April 1968 issue of the Israel Law Review. That is completely mistaken. The missing reversioner always existed. It was not the Arab inhabitants of Palestine, but the Jewish People, the national beneficiary of the Mandate, which by definition includes the State of Israel, based on the 1920 settlement.

I also approach the Balfour Declaration in a different way from other jurists, especially Leonard Stein. In his classical work on the Balfour Declaration, he stated that it is ambiguous and was progressively weakened by succeeding drafts. I cite the British Cabinet minutes of October 31, 1917 to show there was no ambiguity or watering-down. The Jewish National Home meant a state, and the words "in Palestine" were not meant to partition the country, an impression that was later and unjustifiably conveyed by Ahad Ha'Am, Herbert Samuel and Winston Churchill. The Balfour Declaration was at the outset (in 1917) a policy of the British Government, but in April 1920, at San Remo, it became part of international law that was inserted into the Treaty of Sèvres four months later and subsequently in the three opening recitals of the Preamble of the Mandate for Palestine. The Balfour Declaration thus evolved from being originally a political document into a legal document, contrary to Stein's assertion that it never had legal effect.

My approach is that I use all the supporting documents and international agreements to make the Jewish legal case for the whole of Palestine and the Land of Israel. Those documents include the 1919 Versailles Treaty establishing the Mandates system, the Smuts Resolution, the San Remo Resolution, the Treaty of Sèvres, the Mandate for Palestine, the Franco-British Boundary Convention of 1920 and the U.S.-U.K. Treaty of December 3, 1924 respecting the Mandate for Palestine. I also use the 1969 Vienna Convention on the Law of Treaties to show that the Jewish People and State of Israel never lost their national and political rights to all of Palestine, even after the expiry of the Mandate and the proclamation of the State. Some of those documents are never mentioned by jurists who deal with the question of Palestine, in particular the Smuts Resolution of January 30, 1919 (the precursor of Article 22 of the Covenant of the League of Nations contained in the Treaty of Versailles), which expressly mentions Palestine, a reference to the Jewish People, in regard to self-determination, along with Mesopotamia, Syria and other countries. This resolution has been completely forgotten in the debate about who is entitled to Palestine. The 1920 Boundary Convention which formally included a good part of Transjordan within the boundaries of Palestine is also never mentioned by writers discussing the Jewish and Arab arguments over who has rights to Palestine. During the negotiations that produced the Boundary Convention (Treaty!), it was assumed by both Britain and France that Palestine and the Jewish National Home were one and the same territorial entity, and that Palestine was not destined for Arab rule. In this connection, Transjordan, Judea, Samaria and Gaza were all part of the Jewish National Home. In determining our rights to Palestine, it is simply amazing that this Boundary Convention is never cited.

My approach to the question of rights to Palestine parallels that of Justice Louis Dembitz Brandeis. At the end of the San Remo Conference he believed that the legal and political debate over Palestine was over. We received the Charter that Herzl had diligently sought in the talks he had with the Ottoman Sultan and European statesmen. Weizmann, on the other hand, believed that the political struggle (including the legal struggle) was just beginning. Weizmann did not recognize the

4

fact that we already received the all-important legal charter at San Remo and that we had to act decisively thereafter in trying to set up a Jewish Government. None other than the anti-Zionist British Foreign Minister, George Nathaniel Curzon, referred to the San Remo Resolution as the Magna Carta of the Jewish People regarding Palestine. Weizmann squandered the great opportunity that presented itself and let the British backtrack on the legal rights conferred on us. In this sense, he contributed to the White Paper of 1939 which denied our rights altogether.

You mentioned that my approach is historical. I would dispute that. My approach is legally oriented, based on the primary documents and international agreements indicated above. Naturally, I also deal with the historical aspects for two reasons. The historical connection is one of the components of the Jewish legal title. Second, the Arabs of Palestine have used their distortion of history to show they preceded the Jews and are the indigenous inhabitants of the country. That is why I needed to write a chapter on history to refute their mendacious claims.

Another important difference in approach to other jurists is my dismissal of the Partition Resolution of November 29, 1947 and UN Security Council Resolution of November 22, 1967 as not being relevant to the legal case of the Jewish People and the State of Israel in regard to the whole country. The Partition Resolution lacked all legal validity and did not confer legal rights on anyone. I take Prof. Yoram Dinstein to task on this point. This Resolution not only did not confer rights on the Jewish People, it denied our rights to 7/8 of the country (or whatever the actual figure is; Weizmann said in 1947 we were getting only 1/8 of the original Palestine under the UNSCOP Plan). If we base any argument on the Partition Resolution, as Dinstein did, we have defeated ourselves because we ignore our true rights under the 1920 settlement. The Arabs of Palestine originally rejected the validity of the Partition Resolution, but lo and behold! They now use it to claim Judea, Samaria and Gaza, representing what they say is only 22% of Palestine – omitting Transjordan from the equation. Prof. Dinstein was one of those law professors who, in the early 1970s, made the legal arguments for Jordan's rights in Judea and Samaria, based on the Partition Resolution that has now been taken up by the so-called "Palestinians" and all the nations of the world, including our supposed friend, President George W. Bush. Shimon Peres justifies the "Oslo Peace Process" by quoting the supposed fact that Arafat accepted only 22% of the territory of Palestine, while we are getting the lion's share.

As to UN Resolution 242, the approach of Eugene Rostow, Paul Riebenfeld and other jurists has done us immense harm. It is downright silly to base our legal case to all regions of Eretz-Israel on whether or not the definite article "the" preceded the word "territories" in the sentence calling for "withdrawal of Israeli armed forces from territories occupied in the recent conflict", or whether it was deliberately omitted, as used in the English and French texts of the Resolution. Our legal case is not dependent at all on this Resolution, as Rostow made it out to be. It is actually irrelevant to our legal case. United Nations Resolutions – even those of the Security Council – have nothing to do with our legal rights that were secured back in 1920, long before the UN came into being and long before U.N. Resolution 242 was adopted. Rostow's approach undermines our rights and diminishes the importance of the primary documents and international agreements that I rely on in setting forth Israel's legal case. Rostow made his reputation on interpreting UN Resolution 242 in a way that he thought benefited Israel – he actually characterized Judea, Samaria, Gaza, Sinai and the Golan as "occupied territories" under this resolution. That, as you

5

can see, is a far cry from the approach I have adopted. Shmuel Katz once called Rostow "illustrious" in promoting Rostow's approach. I call his approach self-defeating for our legal cause. Incidentally, Shmuel Katz has recently adopted my approach in stating in an article in the Jerusalem Post that Judea, Samaria and Gaza were allocated to us under the Mandate. He never stated that before when he wrote many columns in the Jerusalem Post in the 1970s and 1980s. Nor did he mention this in the several books he has written. I specifically mentioned this fact to Katz in the last letter I sent him about three years ago, in which I enclosed copies of the correspondence I had had with Dr. Paul Riebenfeld on this matter, in which I chided Riebenfeld for formulating the concept of unallocated territories which he then passed on to Rostow.

Still another approach I have adopted concerning the legal status of Judea, Samaria and Gaza differs from that of other jurists. I consider it utterly wrong and irrelevant to apply the laws of war, i.e., the Hague Regulations of 1907 and the Fourth Geneva Convention of 1949 to the aforementioned territories that were recognized in 1920 as being integral parts of the Jewish National Home. A full understanding of what transpired in 1920 thus makes absurd the notion that Judea, Samaria and Gaza are truly governed by the laws of war. Yet, in splendid ignorance of the 1920 boundary settlement, most of the foreign jurists in the world today, those in Europe and the United States as well as our own Supreme Court, rely on the laws of war in deciding the question of what our rights are to Judea, Samaria and Gaza. Justice Aharon Barak did exactly that in the case dealing with the Security Fence in Judea and Samaria. The International Court of Justice used the same approach in the ridiculous judgment it rendered declaring the security fence to be illegal under international law. The responsibility for citing the laws of war as the guiding criterion for determining our rights to Judea, Samaria and Gaza lies with Justice Meir Shamgar, the former President of the Supreme Court and former Advocate-General of the IDF at the time of the Six-Day War, who also later served as Attorney-General. Instead of advising the Eshkol Government at the conclusion of that war to immediately incorporate the re-possessed regions of the Land of Israel into the boundaries of the State, based on the rights we inherited under international law as well as under our own constitutional laws on the subject, he advised that the laws of war be applied. That is how Judea, Samaria and Gaza came to be called "occupied territories" and Israel an "Occupying Power" under Articles 42 and 43 of the Hague Regulations. The Eshkol Government accepted Shamgar's extremely bad advice and we have been paying the full price for this mistake ever since. Our true legal position in Yesha is of course not based on the laws of war. This is a complete travesty, but it is the near universal approach of Israeli academic jurists today and of everyone else in the world, thanks to Shamgar and those who accepted his legal approach. We have, by our own folly, ignored our legal rights to Yesha. My work corrects this negation of our rights.

In regard to our rights under international law that existed at the outset of the Mandate period, the question has arisen whether those rights survived the expiry of the Mandate and the establishment of the State of Israel. The Rostow-Riebenfeld approach, adopted recently by Prof. Eliav Shochetman, is that they survived by virtue of Article 80 of the UN Charter. That article was to serve a temporary purpose, to preserve the rights of both the Jewish People and the Mandatory (i.e., His Britannic Majesty) during an interim period from the end of the Mandate up to the time a trusteeship agreement was concluded. Article 80 was not a permanent international guarantee of the rights of the Jewish People since if a new trusteeship agreement had been concluded and approved by the UN General Assembly, those rights could have been altered in the agreement. Since no trusteeship agreement for Palestine was ever made, Article 80 is now of limited value. It is still useful in preventing the alteration of Jewish legal rights to the Land of Israel by the UN itself, but not as regards the recognition of the rights of the Jewish People vis-à-vis other nations, particularly the U.S. and U.K. Therefore, my approach on the matter is to rely on the principle of acquired legal rights (codified in Article 70[1][b] of the Vienna Convention on the Law of Treaties) and on the doctrine of estoppel to challenge American and British infringement of our rights which they had previously recognized. No one but myself has coherently presented this argument against those states and organizations that support the establishment of a new Arab state in Western Palestine under the Road Map. I believe it is the right legal argument and that Article 80 is a weak reed to rely on, except, as already noted, as regards the actions of the UN itself that intentionally deny our rights to Eretz-Israel.

One more difference I may allude to is my approach to what constitutes the Land of Israel. Most jurists limit the Land of Israel to either Cisjordan or, at best, to Cisjordan and Transjordan south of the Yarmuk. I also include Southern Lebanon up to the bend of the Litani River and Transjordan north of the Yarmuk, i.e., Bashan, as well as at least half of Sinai. We have rights to the entire Land of Israel, including those parts presently in the hands of Lebanon, Syria, Jordan and Egypt. Our rights to those areas still exist even though they are unexercisable. The peace treaties made with Egypt and Jordan are illegal to the extent that we have surrendered our national rights to our national patrimony (the fertile part of Transjordan re the State of Jordan and the Sinai Peninsula re the State of Egypt).

I believe my book presents irrefutable evidence that all of the Land of Israel belongs to the Jewish People and State of Israel based only on relevant legal documents. There is no apology and no compromise in my position. I do not concede any rights to a fictitious people known today as "Palestinians", who are simply Arabs who have adopted a new identity to support their false claim to Palestine. I believe there should be no negotiations with anyone over our legal rights to Palestine and that the so-called "Palestinian Authority" that now illegally governs part of Cisjordan should be disbanded and driven out of our country. My position may seem extreme, but I believe it is the right one. We must take the steps I advocate in the conclusion of my work, otherwise we will be overthrown and overrun by Arab usurpers of the Jewish homeland.

I do not claim that my book exhausts everything to be said about our rights to the Land of Israel. But I believe it is the most comprehensive and unique treatment ever written on the subject.

Sincerely,

Howard

P.S. I have tried to show at your request the principal differences between my approach to Israel's legal case and the approaches taken by others. I believe I have covered the chief differences, though there may also be others which do not instantly come to mind. Based on what I have read, Brandeis would have been an excellent leader of the Zionist Movement, compared to the weak and vacillating Weizmann who never really understood the strength of our legal case. Nor did his chief legal adviser, Leonard Stein. Brandeis did understand our case, but left active service in

7

the Zionist Organization in 1920 after a bitter dispute with Weizmann, whom he called a liar and untrustworthy (if memory serves me correctly). Details of the Brandeis-Weizmann dispute are hardly known and not even reported in Zionist annals. I do not agree with all the opinions held by Brandeis (he was an admirer of Israeli socialists and did not like Jabotinsky), but he was on the whole a man of giant stature, with tremendous talents, who was greatly esteemed by the eminent Arthur James Balfour, the greatest Christian supporter of Zionism, to whom we owe a lot.

P.P.S. I am thinking of changing the title of my book to: The Legal Foundation and Borders of Israel under International Law. This accords well with the title you mentioned in your article in Global Affairs (see p. 83, n. 12, as well as p. 85, n. 14 of your article).

**Yuval Ne'eman**
**Professor Emeritus of Physics, TAU**
Chairman, Israel Space Agency
(Ministry of Science)

**יובל נאמן**
**פרופסור אמריטוס לפיסיקה, אוניברסיטת תל-אביב**
סוכנות החלל הישראלית
(משרד המדע)

January 24, 2006
24 Tevet 5766
6075 – יג

Prof. Efraim Inbar,
BESA Center
Bar-Ilan University
Ramat-Gan

Dear Efraim,

Re: **Publication of the book "The Borders of Israel under International Law"**
**By Attorney Howard Grief**

**Howard Grief**
**The Rights of the Jewish People to the Land of Israel**
**Under International Law** [provisional title]

I told you some time ago about Howard Grief, a Jewish attorney from Canada (Tom Hecht knows him well) who immigrated to Israel in 1990. In Canada, he was an active Zionist, took an interest in international law and in the question of the borders of the State and the strength of the legal argument regarding them. I invited him to do his year of articling ("stage") in the Office of the Legal Adviser of the Ministry of Energy and Infrastructure [I was then the Minister and I did my best to strengthen our grip on the "infrastructure of infrastructures", the land of the Homeland], and I encouraged him to pursue a serious project – constructing the Israeli legal argument to the various parts of the country. Up until now, there have been two people who explored the issue: Prof. Eugene Rostow and Dr. Paul Riebenfeld. From the very beginning, Rostow looked for a minimalist compromise and Riebenfeld did not go into it in depth. In my opinion, the argument is important even if we were intending to make concessions, for it is then possible to show the other side or, for that matter, the world, how great our concession is. After all, they argue: "You occupied territory that does not belong to you – evacuate it", and we will be able to say: "Legally, it is ours, but in the interest of peace with our neighbours etc. we are ready to make concessions". How much more important if we do not want to make concessions... Years have elapsed and he has completed the task. As the basis for the entire case, he anchored it upon the San Remo Agreements, where the Ottoman Empire was carved up [and ceased to exist]. I have tried a number of his arguments in debates, and they are quite effective.

At the time we agreed with Arieh Stav [Director of the Ariel Center for Policy Research and Editor of the Nativ Journal] that the book would be published by his organization, but now his situation has deteriorated financially and he cannot undertake it, without an outside financier. Would you be willing to take the book and publish it in your publishing house?

If you want to examine the book and/or speak with Grief – please do so through me and through my office. The man is lying ill in Jerusalem and undergoes dialysis. His telephone number is 02-6560085. Mine at home is 03-6492515 and at the office: 03-6409579.

Hoping you find my proposal of interest and with warm regards,

Yuval Ne'eman

**Tel-Aviv University, Ramat Aviv 69978, Israel Tel: 972-3-640-9580, Faz: 972-3-642-4264,**
**E-mail: matildae@tauex.tau.ac.il**

**NOTE:** This letter is an accurate English translation of the original letter in Hebrew sent by Professor Yuval Ne'eman to Professor Efraim Inbar.

**Yuval Ne'eman**
**Professor Emeritus of Physics, TAU**
Chairman, Israel Space Agency
(Ministry of Science)

**יובל נאמן**
**פרופסור אמריטוס לפיסיקה, אוניברסיטת תל-אביב**
סוכנות החלל הישראלית
(משרד המדע)

March 27, 2006
26 Adar 5766
6104 – ינ

Prof. Efraim Inbar,
BESA Center
Bar-Ilan University
Ramat-Gan

Dear Efraim,

Re: **Howard Grief's Book on the Borders of Israel under International Law**

Further to my letter of January 24, 2006 and our telephone conversation concerning the aforementioned subject, I am forwarding for your consideration a number of documents that will make it possible for you to make an orderly presentation of the proposal to the publishing house of Bar-Ilan University. If you need a letter of endorsement from me regarding the publication of the book, I would be glad to furnish it. You can also make use of my aforementioned letter (dated January 24, 2006).

The documents submitted herein include:

1. A precis of the book (in both English and Hebrew);
2. Table of Contents;
3. A legal assessment written by Dr. Ya'akov Meron who represented the Justice Ministry in this field for thirty years.

The book consists of about 600 pages and I will be able to provide it the moment the need arises.

Please let me know if any additional material is required.

Sincerely,

Yuval Ne'eman

**NOTE:** This letter is an accurate English translation of the original letter in Hebrew sent by Professor Yuval Ne'eman to Professor Efraim inbar.

**Howard Grief**
**Attorney and Notary**
**13/2 David Goitein St.,**
**Pisgat Ze'ev Mizrah, Jerusalem 97782 Israel**
**Tel. (Fax) : 972-2-656-0085**

---

Jerusalem תובב״א
19 Iyar, 5766
May 17, 2006

Mrs. Matilda Elron
C/o The Office of Professor Yuval Ne'eman
Tel Aviv University,
Ramat Aviv 69978

E-mail: matildae@tauex.tau.ac.il

Dear Matilda,

The tragic death of Yuval has left all of us in great mourning, with a deep hole in our hearts that can never be filled.

Yuval was unique and incomparable, and in my humble opinion the greatest Israeli of my lifetime – whom I had the honour to serve. His contributions to Israel's Defence and to Science were immeasurable and without equal.

As you know, I was very close with Yuval, and he was helping me with the publication of my book pertaining to the Rights of the Jewish People to the Land of Israel under International Law. For this purpose, he was in direct communication with Professor Efraim Inbar of Bar-Ilan University and the Begin-Sadat Center for Strategic Studies.

Yuval told me shortly before his death that he had written Professor Inbar urging publication of the book through his good offices and was awaiting a reply from him.

I would appreciate it very much if either you, Ronit or Haya can send me a copy of Yuval's letter (or letters) to Professor Inbar concerning my book. This will facilitate possible progress to be made in the book's publication. Yuval's support for me in this matter was and still is invaluable.

Thanking you for your kind co-operation,

Sincerely,

**Howard Grief**

## *Appendix IV*
# Juridical Assessment

*Juridical assessment of the book given on October 6, 2005 by the late Dr. Ya'akov Meron, formerly the Adviser on the Law of Arab Countries in the Ministry of Justice and Professor of Moslem Law.*

In my capacity as lector, I, the undersigned, Dr. Ya'akov Meron of Jerusalem, Israel, have read the entire manuscript of *The Legal Foundation and Borders of Israel under International Law*, and herewith is my assessment:

*The Legal Foundation and Borders of Israel under International Law* by Howard Grief is a forceful and erudite pleading for the respecting of the letter and spirit of the law, not only Israeli law but also the international law that came into existence in the wake of World War I. This law, now largely forgotten or neglected, is still relevant today in regard to the status and borders of the Land of Israel. The author makes a thorough analysis of the international documents which recognized the rights of the Jewish People to the land of their ancestors, most significantly the San Remo Resolution on Palestine, agreed to by the victorious Allies at the Peace Conference of April 1920.

The main points discussed in this book include:

The whittling down of the rights of the Jewish People which began between the two World Wars continues to our day. The principal judicial organ of the United Nations, the International Court of Justice, has decried the security fence erected by Israel in Judea and Samaria (called "West Bank" in Jordanian law). The learned judges of this tribunal did not know that Article 6 of the Mandate for Palestine states explicitly that "State lands and waste lands" are reserved for "close settlement by Jews". The security fence is therefore being built on land under the sovereignty of the State of Israel. The question to be asked is: why did the tribunal decry the security fence?

1. The severing of "Transjordania" from Palestine at Winston Churchill's March 1921 Conference in Cairo and Jerusalem, and Herbert Samuel's disloyal role in the making of this decision.

2. The author does not spare the legal authorities of his own country, Israel. The cities of Nazareth, Ramla, Lod, Beersheba, Ashkelon, Ashdod and Eilat among others were incorporated into the State of Israel under the 1948 Area of Jurisdiction and Powers Ordinance enacted by the Ben-Gurion Government without arousing international criticism of any significance. This Ordinance was totally ignored in June 1967 when Israel took possession of additional parts of the Land of Israel. The door has thereby been opened to a multitude of baseless accusations raised against Israel by malevolent elements, on both the foreign and domestic fronts.

The author is a seasoned scholar who has practiced law as an attorney for over twenty years in Canada and now in Jerusalem.

The publication of this book will be of enormous benefit and importance to the State of Israel.

Dr. YA'AKOV MERON

Formerly: The Adviser on the Law of Arab Countries at the Ministry of Justice, Jerusalem, Israel; Professor of Moslem Law in: the Faculties of Law of Jerusalem and Tel-Aviv and the School of Law of the College of Administration; Member of the Israeli delegation to the Peace Treaty negotiations with Egypt. Elected member of the **Société de Législation Comparée** in Paris.

Jerusalem, the eve of 4 Tishri 5766 (6.10.2005)

*Appendix V*

# Correspondence with Mr. Joel Carmichael, Editor of *Midstream*.

1. Letter dated April 20, 1999 from Howard Grief to Mr. Joel Carmichael
2. Letter dated May 4, 1999 from Joel Carmichael to Howard Grief
3. Letter dated November 26, 2000 from Howard Grief to Joel Carmichael
4. Letter dated January 20, 2001 from Joel Carmichael to Howard Grief
5. Letter dated January 30, 2001 from Howard Grief to Joel Carmichael
6. Letter dated February 27, 2001 from Joel Carmichael to Howard Grief
7. Letter dated May 30, 2001 from Howard Grief to Joel Carmichael
8. Article on "Jewish Legal Rights and Title to the Land of Israel and Palestine", dated April 9, 2001, sent to Joel Carmichael

Howard Grief, Attorney and Notary
13/2 David Goitein Street
Pisgat Ze'ev Mizrah
97782 Jerusalem, Israel
Telephone: (02)656-0085

Jerusalem
April 22, 1999

Mr. Joel Carmichael
Editor of Midstream
110 East 59th Street, 4th Floor
New York, NY 10022

Dear Sir,

Mr. Elliott A. Green personally gave me a copy of his article entitled *International Law: Israel and Jerusalem* (Midstream, February/March 1999). I am very much distressed that Mr. Green, a supposed friend of mine since 1990, has seen fit for a second time, despite a previous strong admonition not to do so, **to borrow without proper attribution** the principal conclusion of my research work and original analysis on the real meaning of the decision taken at the San Remo Conference on Palestine (April 25, 1920). He has, moreover, falsely attributed this conclusion to himself or to others and used it as the basis for his whole article. I find this act all the more grave since what he wrote in his article represents the central point or thesis of what I intend to enunciate and explore in a projected book dealing with sovereignty and Jewish rights to the Land of Israel. Mr. Green is well aware of my intention. Yet he has chosen to write a partial summary of my work and expose its chief point before I could do so myself in a professional and organised manner, as an attorney and jurist, who has studied this question during the last two decades.

I refer specifically to Mr. Green's statement that "international law has recognised Jewish rights to sovereignty over the Land of Israel…" based on the San Remo Decision. This conclusion is found nowhere in the existing literature on the subject except for the kind reference made by Prof. Yuval Ne'eman in regard to my own work (see his article in Global Affairs, *How to Save 'the Peace Process'*, Fall 1992, pages 83 and 85). It was never asserted by any advocate of Zionism, past or present, nor by the Jewish Agency in submitting its memoranda to various British commissions and committees of enquiry or to the United Nations prior to the realisation of Jewish statehood. The conclusion that Jewish sovereignty over all of the country was recognised under international law from the date of the San Remo Resolution on Palestine is one I reached on my own after very careful study and analysis of all the texts of the relevant agreements and treaties made pursuant to the peace settlement imposed on the defeated Ottoman Turkish Empire by the Principal Allied Powers (Britain, France, Italy and Japan) at the end of World War I. Under this settlement, the Ottoman Empire was dissolved and its far-flung territories and provinces located in Asia and Africa were given over to other nations and peoples who inhabited those territories which were thenceforth governed either as mandated territories under the newly established Mandate System or otherwise as protectorates until the stage of independence. Turkey itself, after the final peace treaty, was reduced to the limits of Anatolia and eastern Thrace and several Aegean islands in the eastern Mediterranean.

The San Remo Conference was attended by the highest-ranking British, French and Italian officials. On the British side were Prime Minister David Lloyd George and his new Foreign Minister, Lord George Nathaniel Curzon, who had replaced Arthur James Balfour in whose name the Declaration of November 2, 1917 was issued. On the French side were Prime Minister Alexandre Millerand, who also served as Foreign Minister, and the secretary-general of the Ministry of Foreign Affairs, Philippe Berthelot. The host of the conference, Italy, was represented by its Prime Minister Francesco Nitti, who actively participated in the discussions. Also present was the Japanese Ambassador to Rome. The American Government sent its Ambassador to join the meeting as an observer, who reported back to President Wilson. It was these Allied leaders who decided at San Remo that Palestine would be exclusively reserved for the benefit of the Jewish People, where their national home would be

2

reconstituted under British auspices in accordance with the provisions of Article 22 of the League of Nations Covenant pertaining to Mandates and Trusts.

In his article, Mr. Green misstates what was decided at San Remo, as far as the public record was concerned. In the various decisions made and announced at the time, no mention was made of granting sovereignty to the Jewish People over the new political and juridical entity of Palestine, though that was the actual effect and consequence of what was done, as I have concluded from my study on this subject. Nor were the borders of Palestine agreed upon by the Principal Allied Powers, not even the borders Mr. Green describes, particularly the northern border embracing the Golan. This question was indeed brought up, but it was decided that the boundaries would be determined at a later stage.

The only territorial guideline that was accepted by both the British and French Prime Ministers at the conference was the biblical formula of "Dan to Beersheba", which was to be supplemented by the interpretation offered by George Adam Smith, a Scottish scholar of the Bible and geography of Palestine, who had prepared an Atlas in 1915 showing what the borders of ancient Israel were. This guideline and interpretation meant that the borders of Mandated Palestine would follow the borders of **historical Palestine,** when Jewish independence reigned. This was further confirmed by the insertion in the Preamble of the mandate of the following statement (the third recital of the Preamble): "recognition has thereby been given to the **historical connection** of the Jewish People with Palestine and to the grounds for **reconstituting** their national home in their country". The problem afterwards was to ascertain exactly what constituted ancient Israel or Judea, which led to intensive, acrimonious and lengthy debate between the French and British negotiators, with the Zionist claims (in regard to the Litani and the Hauran) being supported by President Wilson but not realised when the borders were finally determined.

All that was formally announced by the Supreme Council of the Principal Allied Powers at the termination of their debate on the mandated territories was that Great Britain would be allotted separate mandates for Palestine and Mesopotamia (the name used for the country before it was changed to Iraq), while France would receive the mandate for Syria, which included Lebanon before its detachment. The announcement also made clear that the Mandate for Palestine was being granted to Britain for the sole purpose of putting into effect the Balfour Declaration as originally issued by the British Government on November 2, 1917, to establish a national home for the Jewish People in Palestine. That "home", despite subsequent British denials, subterfuges and outright repudiation in 1939, meant a Jewish State in all of Palestine on both sides of the Jordan River.

The question of the locus of sovereignty over mandated or trust territories has continuously perplexed international jurists since the Mandate system came into being. With regard to Palestine and other mandated territories, it was never conclusively settled in whom the right of sovereignty was vested after the Ottoman Empire ceased to be the sovereign under international law. Was it, for instance, the Mandatory, the League of Nations, the Principal Allied Powers, the local inhabitants of the mandated territory or any combination of these? Or, perhaps, was there a suspension or temporary abrogation of sovereignty during the period of the Mandate, where no entity held exclusive title of sovereignty? Based on my own detailed study, I came to the conclusion that *de jure* sovereignty under international law vis-à-vis the mandated territory of Palestine could only have been exclusively vested in the Jewish People or World Jewry, though *de facto* rule was in the hands of the Mandatory, since the Jews alone were the national beneficiary of the Mandate for Palestine, in whose favour the Mandate was expressly created and no other nation had conferred upon its members the same unassailable legal right to emigrate to, settle and develop the mandated territory even though the majority of its inhabitants were then Arabs, subject only to the condition that the civil and religious rights of the existing non-Jewish communities would not be prejudiced.

I have stated this conclusion on sovereignty as regards Mandated Palestine in various newspaper articles I have written and communicated it to many persons during the last decade. The natural consequence of this conclusion was that Judea, Samaria and Gaza, as well as Trans-Jordan and the Golan, have always been a part of the *de jure* sovereign Jewish National Home (i.e., the embryonic Jewish State) under international law regardless of the fact that these regions also came under the foreign rule of Arab states afterwards whether by partition or conquest.

My conclusion on sovereignty as regards Mandated Palestine and the legal relationship between the State of Israel and those other areas of the Land of Israel not included in the borders of the State of

3

Israel is in sharp contradistinction to the position of all jurists who, since the Six Day War, have asserted that a "sovereignty vacuum" or void exists presently in Judea, Samaria and Gaza, which they believe constitute the "unallocated" territories of the Mandate for Palestine. Among the chief proponents of this position have been Prof. Eugene Rostow and my distinguished friend, Dr. Paul Riebenfeld of New York. Prof. Rostow, while correctly stating that these regions are not "Arab" (quotations in the original), also remarks incorrectly that they have never been recognised as belonging to Israel (i.e., the Jewish People), as if the San Remo Peace Conference never happened (see his article in *Yale Studies in World Public Order*, Vol. 5, Spring 1979, Number 2, p.153 ff). He also wrongly believes that the Mandate is still in force in what he calls Israel's "occupied areas", failing to properly or clearly distinguish between the termination of the Mandate for Palestine on May 14, 1948 which is an indisputable fact and the rights of the Jewish People derived from the Mandate, which, of course, still exist both under international law and Israeli constitutional law. It is very strange indeed that Prof. Rostow uses the language of the rules of war, namely "occupation" and "military occupant" to describe Israel's standing and status.

Another noted jurist, Prof. Julius Stone, while favourably treating Israel's position, also concluded that Israel is a lawful "belligerent occupant" in Judea, Samaria and Gaza (see his book, *Israel and Palestine: Assault on the Law of Nations*, pp. 115-123). However, he contrasted that status with Jordan's and Egypt's position of holding these areas as a result of unlawful aggression which gave them no rights whatsoever under international law. What is noteworthy about Prof. Stone's analysis is that he was the very first international jurist to mention the rule of *jus ex injuria non oritur* (no legal right can arise from a wrong) as being applicable to Jordanian occupation of Judea and Samaria and the Egyptian occupation of Gaza (see his article, *The Middle East Under Cease-Fire*, October 1967). He was also the first to suggest the absence of a reversionary state holding legitimate title over these territories which had been ousted from them, as required by the laws of war in order to constitute "occupation" though he did so in less specific language than Prof. Yehuda Blum did a year after Prof. Stone's analysis first appeared (*The Missing Reversioner: Reflections on the Status of Judea and Samaria*, Israel Law Review 279 [1968]). The position of Stone and Blum was the same as that officially adopted by Israel immediately after the Six Day War, namely that it could remain in possession of the territories, as a lawful occupant, until the conclusion of peace treaties and the determination of their final status. The defect in their position was that they knew of no Jewish title of sovereignty under international law flowing from the San Remo Resolution on Palestine.

Most of the jurists who have dealt with the legal status of these territories all believed that Israel, while not enjoying actual sovereignty, had the best claim to it, in a relative sense. This argument appeared to bolster Israel's case against the charge that it was illegally occupying Arab territories, but in fact undermined and weakened it and also obscured Israel's true status in the territories. For if Israel had only a claim to make and not an absolute or exclusive right to sovereignty, so did the Arabs. This type of thinking which was a legacy of the abortive U.N. Partition Plan of November 29, 1947, which provided for Jewish and Arab States in western Palestine, led eventually to Camp David and Oslo and the loss of Jewish rights in practice over substantial parts of these territories.

In my writings I have posited the view that Israel is already vested with *de jure* and *de facto* sovereignty wherever it has effective possession of any area of the Land of Israel. In the absence of possession, it has only *de jure* sovereignty. Mr. Green in his article falsely attributes my view on the Jewish right of sovereignty over all of former mandated Palestine which I related to him on countless occasions in the past, to what he found afterwards in a legal memorandum prepared in 1947 by a group of seven eminent judges and attorneys, under the chairmanship of Justice Simon Rifkind, which also included two Appeal Court Judges, Jerome Frank and Stanley Fuld, as well as Abe Fortas, who later became a judge of the U.S. Supreme Court (It is published under the title, *The Basic Equities of the Palestine Problem*, Amo Press, 1977). This memorandum ably and persuasively sets out the legal case for Jewish statehood and exposes the true meaning of the important provisions of the Mandate for Palestine as well as official British casuistry in frustrating and subverting that meaning. It was drawn up as a lawyer's brief for the Washington law firm of Thurmond Arnold, Abe Fortas and Paul Porter to support and accompany a Petition to the U.S. State Department asking for Government help to bring to the doorstep of the International Court of Justice for final resolution, a case launched by Judge Bernard Rosenblatt in the Courts of Palestine against the validity of the Land Transfer regulations of 1940 based upon the 1939 White Paper. These regulations not only forbade Jews from acquiring land in most of Palestine, but also denied the rights of American citizens, such as Rosenblatt, also to purchase land located in restricted zones in Palestine, if they were Jews, contrary to the Anglo-American Convention

4

on Palestine of December 3, 1924. The case had earlier been rejected on tortuous and untenable grounds by both the Privy Council in London and the Palestine Supreme Court. The Petition was duly filed by Abe Fortas, but the State Department declined to intervene after the case became moot when the U.N. General Assembly accepted the proposed Partition Plan of the U.N. Special Committee on Palestine which placed the land in question owned by Rosenblatt within the Jewish State, outside the scope of the land ordinance.

This memorandum, though of a very high quality and of a comprehensive nature, says nothing about any Jewish right of sovereignty over Palestine dating from the San Remo Peace Conference as attributed to it by Mr. Green in a somewhat oblique fashion. It did refer to what is commonly known about the San Remo decision on Palestine quoting the explanation given by the Colonial Secretary, the Duke of Devonshire, in a 1923 address to the House of Lords.

Mr. Green admitted to me that he has not even read this memorandum except for a few pages. He will therefore be disappointed to find out that the learned authors of the memorandum favoured entrusting the Old City of Jerusalem, containing the Holy Places, to the custody of an international trustee, a prospect which he rightly attacks in his article. These jurists sincerely believed that the Partition Plan to create separate Jewish and Arab states was a reasonably fair solution to what they termed the "Palestine Problem" and would lessen Arab hostility, agitation and incitement. They were naive in believing that the Arabs would not vigorously oppose a Jewish state "within adequate boundaries" which they thought should also include Western Galilee and the new city of Jerusalem.

In seeking to defend himself against my accusation that he borrowed the central thesis of my work without any proper attribution, Mr. Green informed me that the Jewish right of sovereignty over the entire land of Israel is well known to everyone. In actual fact the very opposite is true.

Had the question of Jewish sovereignty over Judea, Samaria and Gaza under international law been as well known as Mr. Green pretends to believe, the Government of Israel would have surely annexed them in the aftermath of the Six Day War when they came under Jewish rule for the first time since the Roman period. But, amazingly enough, the Government of Israel treated them as "occupied territories" subject to the strictures of the Hague Rules and Regulations of 1907, even though it did so voluntarily and by choice and not because of any legal obligation to do so.

Had Jewish or Israeli sovereignty over Judea, Samaria and Gaza been recognized or properly understood, Prime Minister Begin would have never thought of leaving the question of sovereignty over these territories "open" to negotiations, as he did at the Camp David Conference which was exemplified in the Framework Agreement for Peace in the Middle East based on his earlier 26-point autonomy plan presented to the Knesset on December 28, 1977. Begin even did the unthinkable. He lent his support to the notion that the "final status" (i.e., sovereignty) of these historical areas of the Land of Israel should be determined by negotiations conducted between Israel, Jordan, Egypt and the elected representatives of the local Arab inhabitants. The agreement reached by the four parties conducting the negotiations would then need the additional approval for the second time of the elected representatives of the Arab inhabitants by means of a vote. This procedure, if followed, would have inevitably led to the recognition of Arab "sovereignty" over Judea, Samaria and Gaza rather than an affirmation of Jewish sovereignty. It was an act of gross stupidity to expect any other outcome, as Shmuel Katz has made amply clear in his book *The Hollow Peace*. It should also be noted that Israeli constitutional law and Halacha, for that matter, both assume that sovereignty over the entire Land of Israel can only be held legally by the Jewish People and not by a non-Jewish entity whose status will always be that of an occupier. It can be rightfully wondered how Begin, the champion of an undivided Israel all his life, came to approve such a bizarre agreement.

For the answer, we need look no farther than the person who was at his side at Camp David as his chief legal adviser, Mr. Aaron Barak, then the Attorney-General of the State of Israel, and now President of Israel's highest tribunal. Israeli attorneys who have pleaded cases before Judge Barak in the Supreme Court will not be surprised by his neutral or indifferent stance on Jewish sovereignty over all the Land of Israel, as reflected in the dreadful agreement he helped to draft at Camp David. Of all the jurists who should have known better, in extolling Israel's legal case to the outside world, he apparently did not realize or even conceive of the possibility that Israel may already be the *de jure* and *de facto* sovereign over Judea, Samaria and Gaza and therefore it is illegal and unconstitutional under Israeli law to surrender any part of this territory.

5

Finally, had the Government of Israel recognized the sovereignty of the State of Israel over all parts of the Jewish Homeland in its effective possession, it would never have dared, so flagrantly and illegally, to cede any land whatsoever to the "Palestine Liberation Organization" which the penal law of the State of Israel still classifies as an enemy and criminal organization.

My own view on Israel's sovereignty over Judea, Samaria and Gaza has been set forth in a Petition a colleague and I submitted to the Supreme Court of Israel in May, 1996 on behalf of eight prominent Israeli public figures, in order to annul the Interim Agreement with the PLO. The arguments presented in the Petition remain valid despite the fact that the Court dismissed it on procedural grounds because it would not adjudicate what it considered to be a political matter outside its jurisdiction. This petition has now been published as a policy paper by the Ariel Center for Policy Research.

In his article, Mr. Green does not explain why or how sovereignty over Palestine devolved on the Jewish People under international law, as a consequence of the San Remo Resolution on Palestine. He fails to mention the Treaty of Sèvres, signed on August 10, 1920 which incorporates the actual resolution itself in Article 95 of the Treaty and represents the authoritative intention of the Principal Allied Powers to appoint a Mandatory who would reconstitute Palestine as the Jewish National Home and then, by fostering its political, administrative and economic development, convert it into an independent Jewish State.

Furthermore, no mention is made by Mr. Green of the Treaty of Lausanne, ratified on September 28, 1923, which replaced the Treaty of Sèvres after Mustafa Kemal Ataturk assumed power in Turkey, deposed the last ruling Sultan (Muhammad VI) and repudiated those provisions of the earlier treaty which were completely unacceptable to the new nationalist regime. Those were the provisions which had placed most of Eastern Thrace (excluding Constantinople) and Smyrna (Izmir) under Greek administration – they reverted to Turkey under the new treaty as did the zone of the Dardanelles and the Bosphorus Straits which under the Treaty of Sèvres had not only been internationalized and demilitarized, which continued to be the case, but had also removed this zone from Turkish control. In addition, the provisions relating to an independent Armenian republic in northeastern Anatolia were dropped as was the plan for an autonomous or independent Kurdistan in southeastern Anatolia and northern Iraq. With regard to Palestine, Turkey agreed that the settlement then still being worked out by the Principal Allied Powers as regards its future, would not be disturbed. It renounced all rights and title over those territories situated outside its new frontiers.

It is also indicative of his writing that Mr. Green avoids any reference to the Covenant of the League of Nations which is especially important in understanding the question of sovereignty over mandated territories.

Lastly, he does not treat in any substantive way the Mandate for Palestine which also embodied the San Remo Resolution in the opening recitals of the Preamble. Its inclusion in the Mandate made that resolution a part of binding international law. This meant that the irrevocable rights conferred on the Jewish People under the Mandate could not be changed thereafter even when the Mandate had ended and an independent Jewish State had been proclaimed. This is a result of the legal principal of estoppel which barred those nations or states that had previously recognized Jewish rights (in effect, all members of the League of Nations plus the United States separately) from denying those rights in the future. For the same reason, it is unnecessary to rely on Article 80 of the U.N. Charter to secure Jewish rights under the Mandate.

The San Remo Resolution on Palestine is truly the defining legal moment for international recognition of Jewish rights of sovereignty over the entire country. According to Lord Curzon, it represented the "Magna Carta of the Zionists" (Letter to Prime Minister Lloyd George, October 20, 1920, F.O. 800/156 reproduced in *The Rise of Israel*, vol. 12, p. 306). It is a pity that this pivotal subject in all its legal subtleties and complexities is conveyed in Midstream magazine by a person who is not an expert in international law nor even an attorney by profession. I also find it doubly disconcerting to see my own original work and research being appropriated by a writer and translator who has only a smattering and second-hand knowledge about the whole subject of Jewish legal rights to the whole land of Israel under international law.

I do thank Mr. Green for his direct reference to me as one of his sources for his article (see footnote 3) but that hardly compensates for crediting my work on the significance of San Remo either to himself or

6

to others. A thorough or even cursory examination of his other sources cited in his article (the Rifkind Memorandum, Eugene Rostow and Julius Stone) will substantiate the fact that they actually disprove rather than confirm Mr. Green's opinion that international law recognized Jewish sovereignty over the Land of Israel based on the San Remo Resolution. The only source for his saying that comes from knowledge he gleaned from the undersigned attorney and not from his own research or analysis.

One final remark. In 1991, I prepared a paper for Professor Yuval Ne'eman, Israel's premier scientist, when he was the Minister of Engery and Infrastructure (1990-92) in the Shamir Government, outlining the Jewish legal case to all of the Land of Israel and showing how Britain betrayed the Mandate and international trust it had received. I was privileged to serve as his legal counsel on this question. With his blessing and encouragement, I intend to expand this unpublished paper into a full-length book. Unfortunately, his early departure from the ministry necessitated by the Tehiya party's withdrawal from the Government, followed by a complete change of Government in July 1992, prevented the realization of the project I had seriously embarked upon and wanted very much to complete. In addition, I could not finish the project because of lack of funding for the amount of time required to continue the work. However, I am still hopeful that one day it will be done.

Yours truly,

Howard Grief

Cc Mr. Elliott Green

# MIDSTREAM

A Monthly Jewish Review

110 East 59th Street, New York, N.Y. 10022 * Phone (212) 339-6040 * Fax (212) 318-6176

4 May 1999

Dear Mr. Grief,

I am most impressed by the analysis, dated April 22, that I have just received.

I am somewhat bewildered by one thing: the whole thing sounds as though nothing fundamental were settled.

Can that be so?

What can the Israeli authorities still do?

I see Paul Riebenfeld occasionally; he speaks with a remarkably current passion, but I seldom see what his personal intention is.

It would suit me, to be sure, journalistically, but I feel perplexed by what the first step for MIDSTREAM would be, especially in view of the deep confusion about the "Peace Process."

I should appreciate a word from you about the "polemical" situation, so to speak.

I have the impression that the "Palestinian People" goes back to only 1967, when Golda Meir heard of it for the first time and instantly poohpoohed it, Harkavy – the Arabist, not his brother – instantly accepted the invention, perhaps the most successful political act in history depending on a single word: "I don't care why someone calls himself a 'Palestinian,' what interests me is that he does."

I look forward to a word from you.

Most cordially,

Joel Carmichael, Editor

Howard Grief, Attorney and Notary
13/2 David Gotein Street
Pisgat Ze'ev Mizrah
97782 Jerusalem, Israel
Telephone: (02)656-0085

Jerusalem,
November 26, 2000

Mr. Joel Carmichael, Editor
Midstream Review
110 East 59th Street,
New York, NY 10022
U.S.A.

Dear Mr. Carmichael,

As I previously informed you, your letter dated May 4, 1999 arrived when I was in New York to visit my ailing sister, Elizabeth, who most sadly has since passed away.

I always meant to give you a substantive reply to the questions you raised in your kind letter to me, but unfortunately things always got deferred. Now I wish to remedy that act of omission.

I am very gratified that my first letter to you, dated April 22, 1999, impressed you. The information contained in that letter will one day, I hope, be greatly expanded and included in a projected book to explain how sovereignty over the Land of Israel and/or Palestine in its full dimensions was devolved upon the Jewish People under international law in the aftermath of World War I.

You write that you are bewildered because the whole thing regarding the Jewish-Arab Question sounds as though nothing fundamental was ever settled. This is where appearances and reality do differ. In fact, everything concerning the fate of the non-Turkish parts of the former Ottoman Empire was indeed settled by the decisions taken at San Remo, Sèvres and Lausanne 77 to 80 years ago, excluding consideration of the Turkish-Greek aspect of the settlement as well as the Armenian and Kurdish proposals which did not directly affect the fate of Palestine and the other newly freed, predominantly Arabic-speaking, territories in the Near East previously under Turkish dominion. But then along came George Nathaniel Curzon, Herbert Samuel and Winston Churchill and what was definitively settled at San Remo and Sèvres as regards the mandated territory of Palestine was completely disrupted by their intrigues and actions.

The Balfour Declaration and the Mandate for Palestine were clear enough: a Jewish State would be established in all of the historical land of Jewish Palestine, i.e., the Land of Israel under the Mandate and trust granted to Great Britain by the Principal Allied Powers consisting of Britain itself, France, Italy and Japan. However, Curzon, the British Foreign Secretary and previous to that a Viceroy of India, detested (this is not too strong a word) that eventuality. So he and his team at the Foreign Office attempted to whittle down the provisions of the Mandate for Palestine which had clearly enunciated the intention to establish a Jewish State in the whole country of the mandated territory. He and his team conspired to change many of the original provisions of the Draft Mandate that were approved by Arthur James Balfour when he was the Foreign Secretary in charge of overseeing the actual drafting of the Mandate for Palestine.

Despite Curzon's best attempts to prevent a Jewish state from being seen as the real and most important objective of the Mandate for Palestine, he did not fully succeed. That job was left to Herbert Samuel and Winston Churchill, who were put in charge of Palestine's affairs, when jurisdiction over colonies and mandated territories was taken away from the Foreign Office and transferred to the Colonial Office early in 1921.

The nefarious work begun by Curzon was ironically taken over and completed by the erstwhile Zionist, Herbert Samuel, who just before his appointment as British High Commissioner in

2

Palestine worked closely with Chaim Weizmann in the Zionist Organization and helped to prepare the Zionist proposals submitted to the Paris Peace Conference of 1919. Samuel's subsequent undermining of what was the true intent of the Mandate for Palestine was recorded in the anti-Zionist "Churchill White Paper" of June 3, 1922, which he wrote with the blessing and connivance of Winston Churchill, then the Secretary of State for the Colonies, and which was accepted under ominous circumstances by the official Zionist leadership just prior to its release.

It was this White Paper of June 3, 1922 which was a turning point which caused all the future difficulties in Palestine and wrecked the original plan for establishing an independent Jewish State under British tutelage. The reason is simple enough. After publication of this White Paper, all British Governments which followed over the years implemented not the actual terms of the Mandate for Palestine but the interpretation or policy contained in the White Paper as to what the British responsibility and role was to be under the Mandate. The latter required a Jewish State, while the Churchill White Paper negated it, despite Churchill's false claim that such a state was not precluded, made fourteen years later in his testimony before the Peel Royal Commission. His White Paper also elevated Arab pretensions and aspirations to such an extent that everything thereafter became muddled and unclear, subject to continuous disputes as to what was really intended by the Mandate for Palestine.

So you no longer have to be bewildered. As stated above, the "whole thing" was originally settled by the Principal Allied Powers, in the document which encapsulated the Mandate for Palestine, but that document of cardinal importance was scuttled in practice or circumvented by the British during the entire period of the Mandate (1920-1948).

Your second query was what can the Israeli authorities still do. The answer is to first learn what the rights granted to the Jewish People under international law were (i.e., under the San Remo Resolution adopting the Balfour Declaration on April 25, 1920 and its projected implementation in the Mandate for Palestine), and then appreciate how true international law was perverted and sabotaged by the British. This is extremely important because everyone today cites "international law" in favour of a fictitious nation called the "Palestinians" whose land is being "occupied" by the Jewish nation of Israel which is highly ironic and even laughable in view of the fact that this land that is called "occupied" was always meant under Articles 6 and 11 of the Mandate for Palestine to be "closely settled" not by Gentile Arabs, but by the Jews of the world who would become Palestinian and then Israeli Jews in the course of time. What true international law is on the subject is neither discussed nor exposed nor really known by hardly anyone.

Next, the Israeli authorities must act according to what that law truly presupposes, namely, a Jewish State in the whole Land of Israel, including both sides of the Jordan. Present circumstances, of course, do not allow for the fulfillment of all Jewish rights to our country, particularly as regards those parts of Transjordan which consist of the Land of Israel such as Gilead and Bashan, but we should never renounce those rights, which, lamentably, is exactly what has been done illegally by the Government and Knesset of Israel in concluding and approving a peace treaty with Jordan.

It is safe to assume that the foregoing advice will never be acted upon so long as there is an anti-nationalist Labour party and other "peace parties" who advocate a spurious peace, instead of believing in and fighting for the integrity and non-partition of the Land of Israel. Sadly, the same may even be said about the Likud party in its present configuration, because it has abandoned the ideology and spirit of what the original Herut Party once advocated in the 1950s and 1960s, namely, an indivisible Land of Israel.

Only a future Government of Israel infused with the proper Jewish nationalist and religious spirit, knowledge and pride can change what is today a murky and forlorn situation.

As for what can be done actually now, Israel must –

[1] immediately scrap the "Oslo Peace Process" which, incredibly, recognizes the national and political rights of a motley Gentile people to substantial parts of the Land of Israel;

[2] evict the so-called and falsely-denominated "Palestinian Authority" and its entire leadership from the Jewish country, and

[3] annex or incorporate all of Judea, Samaria and Gaza into the Jewish State;

[4] All Arabs who do not profess loyalty to the Jewish State must leave the country and be resettled in other Moslem countries, just as happened between the Greeks and the Turks after World War I;

[5] No Arab parties professing national and collective rights for Arabs should be allowed to sit in the Knesset.

The Moslems who live in the Land of Israel are not the indigenous inhabitants, as they falsely claim to be. They are mainly foreign Gentiles, all of whom are of mixed ancestry (including some of Jewish descent who were forcibly converted in centuries past). These foreign Gentiles (in Hebrew: *nochrim*) have no national rights to the Land of Israel and/or Palestine. They have boldly appropriated, without any right to do so, the name of "Palestinians" for themselves, though, as you yourself have written, there is no such nation and have also removed this name from its Jewish and Zionist context under the Mandate. Their claims are totally invented and are deliberately imitative of genuine Jewish national rights which exist for no other nation in the Land of Israel, but which are now impugned under a false perception or reading of international law.

As regards your perplexed feeling as to what steps Midstream can take to end the deep confusion about the "peace process", I would suggest that more articles be published which unequivocally denounce what is the most dangerous and suicidal course for Israel to follow: a Government policy which illegally transfers precious parts of the Jewish homeland to an implacable enemy bent on destroying the State and which has allowed that enemy to create foreign rule and the rudiments of a state and army in our country, led by gangs of bloody terrorists and murderers, as we see only too well today. Conversely, Midstream should not feature any laudatory pieces about those Israeli leaders who are responsible for bringing about an impossible situation which causes the "deep confusion" you refer to.

I hope the foregoing provides you with some food for thought on the "polemical" situation, as you called it.

During the 20 days or so I was in New York, I met Dr. Paul Riebenfeld several times. He is one of the two mentors I had about the Arab-Jewish Question, the other being Shmuel Katz. Paul is a storehouse of knowledge about the Mandate for Palestine with a sharp and keen wit. I learned much from him, but learned even more from my own research and analysis. With all due respect to a great man I admire very much, Paul could have done a lot more for the Jewish legal case, had he come to live in Israel when the State was being created and developed during the last five decades. He would have been a formidable personality in Israel and perhaps even risen to a position of leadership at some point or other. But what is certain, his profound knowledge could have helped Israel to blaze a different legal trail, away from the paths of those Israeli jurists who were either ignorant of Jewish legal rights to the whole country (on both sides of the Jordan) or who deliberately refused to recognize or acknowledge them. Instead of that happening, as it should have, Israel has been weighed down and encumbered by anti-Zionist and ill-founded judgments rendered by such legal luminaries as Moshe Landau and Meir Shamgar, both of whom are former Presidents of the Israeli Supreme Court, and especially by the current President of the Court, Aharon Barak.

I still intend to write a book on what the exclusive Jewish national legal rights to the Land of Israel are, but for this project I require financial backing because it would take me at least two years and perhaps more to complete it. If as a practical measure, you can find someone who can provide such backing, I would be eternally grateful.

One final note. My "friend", in a very loose sense, Mr. Elliott Green, has just had an article published in Midstream in the September-October 2000 issue, entitled "The Land of Israel and Jerusalem in 1900". As has happened before, I am chagrined and irritated by his lack of attribution of his source in regard to all his references to 1) San Remo; 2) the Jewish National Home; 3) the date and circumstances under which Palestine under the Mandate was officially designated as a separate territory. A copy of my letter to him is enclosed, which I wrote in order to re-assert or protect my rights to my own research and original conclusions, for the time to come when I can write the book about Israel's legal position as described above.

4

I also enclose a copy of my position paper which I wrote for the Ariel Center for Policy Research, entitled, "The Illegality of the Sharm-e-Sheikh Memorandum under Israeli Law", as well as an earlier work of mine, "Why Israel Needs an Independent Counsel".

Sincerely,

**Howard Grief**

# MIDSTREAM

A Monthly Jewish Review

110 East 59th Street, New York, N.Y. 10022 * Phone (212) 339-6040 * Fax (212) 318-6176

20 Jan 01

Dear Mr. Grief,

Forgive my delay in responding to your letter of 26 Nov.

I found your letter a masterpiece of condensation; I am not particularly familiar with the doubtless numerous formulations of this piece of recent history, but I should be surprised if your own formulation can be excelled.

Might I print the whole of your letter of 26 Nov as an article in MIDSTREAM?

Does it require any other material at all?

If you think it sensible, I should like to make it the leading article in some soon-to-be publishing number.

Please let me know if that would suit you. If you would like to make any changes let me know that, too.

Most cordially,

(sgd.) Joel Carmichael, Editor

Howard Grief
**Attorney and Notary**
**13/2 David Goitein St.,**
**Pisgat Ze'ev Mizrah, Jerusalem 97782**
**Tel. (Fax): 972-2-656-0085**

Jerusalem,
January 30, 2001

Mr. Joel Carmichael, Editor
Midstream
633 Third Avenue, 21st floor,
New York, NY 10017

Dear Mr. Carmichael,

It was with a feeling of great happiness and pride, that I read your letter of January 20, 2001, which was inadvertently dated Nov. 20, 2001.

I have spent the last 20 years studying Israel's legal case to the whole Land of Israel under international law, with special emphasis on the period of the Mandate for Palestine that began on April 25, 1920, the date of the San Remo Resolution granting a Mandate to Great Britain to establish the Jewish National Home and which ended with the Declaration for the Establishment of the State of Israel on May 14, 1948.

In the last ten years, I have buttressed my knowledge of the Mandate Period with a corresponding study of Israeli constitutional law as it relates in particular to the Land of Israel. Your remarks to me concerning the formulation of my position on the Arab-Jewish Question are very much appreciated.

I approve without any reservation your request to print the whole of my letter dated November 26, 2000, as an article in Midstream and to make it the leading article in some forthcoming issue, as you further suggest. You may also make use of any supplementary material which I sent you at your own discretion.

I can of course present my legal analysis and conclusions in a much longer and detailed format. But that will be done in the projected book I intend to write one day on the Jewish legal case to the Land of Israel, about which I have accumulated thousands of pages of personal notes. I therefore see no need to make any changes or additions in the letters and material I already sent you, which can stand on their own as an independent contribution, in summary form.

The only change that should be made for the purpose of publication of my letter as an article, apart from any editorial changes you yourself may wish to make, concerns the reference to the San Remo Resolution of April 25, 1920 on Palestine. To emphasize the great importance of the Resolution, it should be uniformly spelled with a capital letter "R".

I express my sincere thanks for allowing my letter to be published in Midstream. This will enable a wider audience to better know the actual legal rights of the Jewish People to all of the Land of Israel, under the original international law that prevailed when the Mandate for Palestine was first approved by the Principal Allied Powers at the San Remo Peace Conference. What is important is that these same rights were never **legally** altered as opposed to *de facto* changes, and therefore continue to remain in full force from the viewpoint of law and theory to this very day, despite numerous attempt and moves to sabotage, ignore, discard or forfeit those rights over the succeeding years, not only by the acts and statements of Great Britain, the United States, and the United Nations, but regretfully and amazingly enough by

2

the very party which was meant to enjoy and exercise those rights, namely, the State of Israel acting through various Labour and Likud Governments. Even worse, the Supreme Court of Israel has aided and abetted this disgraceful process of renunciation by various judgments it has rendered during the past three decades, which failed altogether to enunciate or recognize Jewish rights over areas it falsely assumed and even designated to be under legal "occupation" by virtue of international law. The result of this abject failure has led to the present cession of precious Jewish territories to the enemy known as the "Palestine Liberation Organization".

That in short is the sad situation we are faced with today, which has now become unbearable, with war being waged against us by the PLO to obtain even more Jewish territory.

I hope to make a dent or at least an impression in correcting this gross injustice and travesty of events. That is why I am especially pleased by your positive and kind response to my earlier letters.

Respectfully,

**Howard Grief**

**MIDSTREAM**

A Monthly Jewish Review

110 East 59th Street, New York, N.Y. 10022 * Phone (212) 339-6040 * Fax (212) 318-6176

27 Feb 01

Dear Mr. Grief,

I was much impressed by your masterpiece of condensation in your letter of 26 Nov.

It seems to me that you sum up the entire problem of, so to speak, identity (of Israel's basic claim) in the last para on p.1 and the first half of p.2.

It seems to me further that it would be most enlightening, politically, i.e., argumentatively, if you could present both of them together, with the requisite modifications, so as to make it clear that what had been at the outset a clear statement of Zionist interest was simply overwhelmed by later indecisiveness, political intrigue etc.

I was about to try my hand at it myself but it seemed obvious that it would be much easier for you and would be possible to use it at once as an explanatory banner, so to speak, in all further discussions.

At present the basic discussion, so to speak, of the subject makes it possible for enemies of Israel to sound plausible even though the map makes it obvious that without the land claimed by Israel the "Arabs" in general are holding lands equal to twice the area of the USA (I've never seen this written anywhere).

Most cordially,

(sgd.) Joel Carmichael, Ed.

Howard Grief
**Attorney and Notary**
**13/2 David Goitein St.,**
**Pisgat Ze'ev Mizrah, Jerusalem 97782**
**Tel. (Fax): 972-2-656-0085**

Jerusalem, May 30, 2001

Mr. Joel Carmichael, Editor
Midstream
633 Third Avenue,, 21st floor,
New York, NY 10017
U.S.A.

Dear Mr. Carmichael,

Further to our telephone conversation on Wednesday, May 30th, and in accordance with your direct advice to me, I am re-submitting the article I sent you on April 9, 2001, for publication in Midstream, entitled "Jewish Legal Rights and Title to the Land of Israel and Palestine", which you said you apparently did not receive. The article was sent to you be registered mail together with a letter.

I would appreciate it very much if you acknowledge receipt of this present letter and the enclosed article. I also send you over again my earlier letter of April 9, 2001.

I look forward to hearing from you.

Yours very sincerely,

**Howard Grief**

Jerusalem, April 9, 2001

## *Jewish Legal Rights and Title to the Land of Israel and Palestine*

- Howard Grief -

The legal title of the Jewish People to the mandated territory of Palestine in all of its historical parts and dimensions was first recognized under international law on April 24-25, 1920 by a Decision taken at the San Remo Peace Conference by the Supreme Council of the Principal Allied Powers to entrust Palestine to Great Britain under the Mandates System for the purpose of establishing a national home for the exclusive benefit of the Jewish People, in accordance with the terms of the Balfour Declaration of November 2, 1917.

The Supreme Council of the Allies was made up of the top political leaders and officials of Great Britain, France, Italy and Japan, and it was they in their meeting in the Italian resort city who decided the future fate of all the Asiatic territories which, as a consequence of World War I, had ceased to be under the sovereignty of the Ottoman Turkish Empire which formerly governed them.

These territories included the entire area then called the Fertile Crescent, which originally comprised Palestine, Syria and Mesopotamia (whose name later became Iraq) as separate countries, before any substantive changes were made to their boundaries. At the San Remo Peace Conference, it was decided that all three countries, whose exact borders had not yet been delineated, would be administered by Mandatories under the newly-created Mandates System, established by the Treaty of Versailles of June 28, 1919. The Mandates System did not come into being until the ratification of this Treaty on January 10, 1920. It was established simultaneously with the League of Nations whose duty it was to supervise the observance of individual mandates through a body called the Permanent Mandates Commission which reported to the Council of the League of Nations for that purpose. The actual terms of those mandates and the powers exercised by the Mandatory were to be in each case explicitly defined and confirmed by the Council of the League unless previously agreed upon by the Members of the League, in accordance with Article 22 (8) of the Covenant of the League of Nations.

British determination and influence in the wartime group of nations officially called the Principal Allied Powers in relation to Turkey excluded other areas under former Ottoman rule in Asia from being part of the new system of mandatory government, particularly the Hedjaz and the whole Arabian Peninsula.

This was the global political and legal settlement that was made after World War I, that conferred enormous benefits to the Arabic-speaking world. The Arabs received the lion's share of the territories that formerly belonged to Turkey. As a result of this munificence they hold today lands equal to twice the area of the USA, as the Editor of Midstream, Mr. Joel Carmichael, has keenly observed in a letter to the author.

Other peoples who were originally included in this settlement fared badly. Kurds and Armenians were supposed to get their own autonomous homelands or states, and the Assyro-Chaldeans, who were a Christian community centered in Mosul, were also promised protection and safeguards for their rights. However, in the final outcome, none of the promises made to them were fulfilled, because their claims and aspirations, although explicitly recognized by the Allies in the abortive Treaty of Sèvres, were subsequently discarded by both the British and French who turned over their designated areas to the complete control of both Arabs and Turks who then cruelly deprived them of their vested national rights and status within those areas.

When the settlement and division of land was devised at the San Remo Peace Conference, it was clear to all concerned parties, Arab and Jew alike and to all European, American and Japanese statesmen, that Palestine, within its historical frontiers according to the biblical formula, from Dan to Beersheba, but which still needed to be marked out in a separate agreement, was exclusively reserved for the benefit of the Jewish People all over the world, of which only a fraction then actually lived in the ancient Jewish country. What this obviously meant to one and all was an eventual independent Jewish State in all of the historical territory of Palestine.

Jewish legal rights and title to all of historical Palestine, including Transjordan and Golan, whose association with the Jewish People goes back to the earliest days of Jewish history, was indeed then formally recognized in the Franco-British Boundary Convention of December 23, 1920, even though no specific words were used to that effect but was well understood by the parties, both from the negotiations that were conducted prior to the conclusion of the Convention in consultation with Zionist leaders who pressed the British to obtain the best possible frontiers for the Jewish National Home, and from the reference to the Mandate for Palestine contained in the Convention itself. Some parts of historical Palestine were not included in the final boundaries assigned to Mandated Palestine, especially in the north and northeast, as well as the Sinai Peninsula in the south.

Jewish legal rights and title to the country of Palestine were founded on three basic pillars which comprised the following sources of support:

1. The historical connection of the Jewish People with Palestine in its entirety. Without this acknowledgment of the country's storied Jewish past, there would have been no Mandate and no Jewish National Home. The historical connection dated back to the Israelite period as described in the Bible, to the Hasmonean restoration and to the Herodian era and also, in general, to the unbroken chain of links which Jews of every

generation had always maintained with the Land of Israel from the very first days of the Patriarchs, Abraham, Isaac and Jacob, right up to the present day, embracing a continuous history of approximately 3800 years.

2. The right enshrined in Article 22 of the Treaty of Versailles which provided for national independence or self-determination for those peoples, inhabitants and communities living in the colonies and territories formerly under Turkish and German sovereignty. This principle of self-determination was also adopted for the benefit of the Jewish People by the Principal Allied Powers when they created the Mandates System even though the vast majority of Jews did not live in any of the territories described in Article 22 of the Treaty of Versailles that were destined for eventual independence. That was the most unique element of the Mandate for Palestine, different from all other Mandates that were conferred, where the local inhabitants were designated the beneficiary of the Mandate. Article 22 was placed in the First Part of the Treaty of Versailles, dealing with the Covenant of the League of Nations, which emphasized its special importance. The same was done in all the other Peace Treaties that were concluded after World War I, including the unratified Treaty of Sèvres with the Sublime Porte that was signed on August 10, 1920.
3. The right of the Jewish People to reconstitute their State of olden times in accordance with the Balfour Declaration of November 2, 1917, as adopted by the Principal Allied Powers on April 24, 1920 at the San Remo Peace Conference. The Balfour Declaration was a declaration of sympathy with Jewish Zionist aspirations as stated in the brief letter sent by Foreign Secretary Arthur James Balfour on behalf of the British Government to Lord Lionel Walter Rothschild which contained the text of the famous Declaration. It viewed with favour "the establishment in Palestine of a national home for the Jewish People" and the Government of Prime Minister David Lloyd George pledged itself "to use their best endeavours to facilitate the achievement of this object". This pledge was subsequently transformed into a binding obligation under Article 2 of the Mandate for Palestine and also by the wording used in the Preamble of that document. The British Government was thereafter responsible for putting into effect the Balfour Declaration under international law and for establishing the Jewish National Home in Palestine.

The "home" referred to in the Declaration was a euphemistic term for "state" already used 20 years earlier by the Jewish leaders attending the World Zionist Congress convoked by Theodor Herzl and held at Basle, Switzerland, in August 1897, so as not to offend Turkish sensibilities on the projected loss of Palestine from their recognized sovereign domains under international law. The word "national" was later appended to the word "home" by the long-time Zionist leader, Nahum Sokolow, while participating in the drafting of the Balfour Declaration with British officials. The addition of this word was to make it even clearer what the ultimate goal of the Zionist Organization was, on behalf of the scattered Jewish People. Strangely, what was evident by the words "national home" then became muddled by the originator of the term, Sokolow himself, who, in a display of inane and unnecessary deception, wrote in the introduction to his two-volume monumental work, **History of Zionism**, published in 1919, that the word "home" as used in the Basle Program of 1897, did not mean the creation of an independent "Jewish State", which was an interpretation he attributed to anti-Zionists who were opposed to the revival of the Jewish People as an independent nation in its ancestral homeland. This denial of the term's true meaning was contrary to what both Balfour and Lloyd-George themselves stated, both at the time the Balfour Declaration was approved by the War Cabinet and in the years afterwards. It was also contrary to President Wilson's own pronouncement on the subject, influenced by the great American Supreme Court Justice, Louis Dembitz Brandeis, both of whom had a major role in the approval of the Balfour Declaration. The matter became further confused by Ahad Ha'Am, the pompous pseudonym used by Asher Ginsberg, who stated erroneously in a deliberate trouble-provoking exegesis that the words "in Palestine" did not mean that the whole country of Palestine would become the Jewish National Home. Furthermore, he declared that Palestine was also the national home of the Arabs who deserved the same national rights as the Jews were obtaining in ruling the country they both shared.

As a result of Sokolow's and Ginsberg's astounding misrepresentations which created serious impediments on the way to Jewish independence, it thereafter became easy for succeeding British Governments to exploit their false interpretation of the Balfour Declaration and to change the policy embedded in the Declaration to the great detriment of the Jewish National Home.

Despite British backtracking, the Balfour Declaration did become in any case an act of international law of supreme importance to the cause of Zionism, when it was officially adopted by the Principal Allied Powers at the San Remo Peace Conference. It is without doubt the linch-pin or essential foundation of all Jewish legal rights to Palestine under international law, upon which everything else depended. It was the exclusive basis for the implementation of the Mandate for Palestine. It may be said without exaggeration that almost every article of the Mandate for Palestine was only an extension or elaboration of what the Balfour Declaration was meant to be in actual practice, including those provisions not ostensibly thought to be dealing with the establishment of the Jewish National Home.

The foregoing three components of the Jewish legal title to

Palestine were then integrated into one comprehensive international instrument, the Mandate for Palestine, which thereafter became the primary cited source for Jewish legal rights to the re-constituted Jewish National Home that was called Palestine in English, a name in common usage in the world outside Ottoman Turkey, that was originally chosen by the Zionist leaders in formulating the Basle Program of 1897, and rendered into Hebrew as *Eretz Yisrael,* the Land of Israel.

These rights were included specifically in the first three recitals of the Preamble of the Mandate Charter, each one of the recitals being of great importance in itself. Recital One refers to Article 22 of the Covenant of the League of Nations, which leads back to Part I of both the Treaty of Versailles and the Treaty of Sèvres. Recital Two refers to the Balfour Declaration that was adopted by the Principal Allied Powers at the San Remo Peace Conference – the San Remo Resolution – which, four months later, was transformed into Article 95 of the Treaty of Sèvres. Recital Three then mentions the historical connection of the Jewish People with Palestine and it also organically links together all three components of the Jewish legal title when it further states that “recognition has *thereby* been given... to the *grounds* for *reconstituting* their national home in that country”. The word *thereby*, together with the plural rendition of the word *grounds,* provide the connecting thread for all three recitals. Furthermore, the word *reconstituting*, as used here, is a direct reference to the State of Judea, since the only country with which there was an historical connection by the Jewish People was Judea before its name was changed to Palestine by the second century Roman Emperor Hadrian. The word *Judea* in Greek and Latin actually connotes “the Jewish country”, further evidence of the Jewish historical connection.

The instrument containing the Mandate for Palestine is thus the final locus or resting place of Jewish legal rights to all of Palestine. However, it should be remembered, that although the Mandate for Palestine is also of the greatest importance for asserting these rights, it is not the starting-point of Jewish sovereignty over all of Palestine. That was on April 24-25, 1920, the exact date when Great Britain was appointed the Mandatory and entrusted with a Mandate to implement the Balfour Declaration for the benefit of the Jewish People, who were defined as World Jewry, rather than the Jews of Palestine. It was then that Article 22 of the League of Nations Covenant became intertwined and integrated with the Balfour Declaration which together devolved *de jure* sovereignty over Palestine on the Jewish People, while granting Britain the right to exercise the attributes of sovereignty to reconstruct the Jewish National Home and State.

This constituted official recognition under international law of Jewish legal rights and title to all of Palestine, which has never since been altered by any other binding act or instrument of international law that has also met the test of legality.

In this regard, it is worthwhile to assess the argument that Jewish legal rights and title to the whole country including Judea, Samaria and Gaza, ceased to be in force with the end of the Mandate for Palestine. This argument is wrong not only for the reason that the U.N. Partition Resolution of November 29, 1947 failed to be accepted at the relevant time by the concerned Arab parties, including the local Arab inhabitants, and was in any case only a recommendation that was not self-executing. There is a more fundamental reason, relating to the doctrine of estoppel, why Jewish legal rights and title over all of Palestine continued after the end of Mandate; this doctrine is applicable both in international law as well as in the municipal or internal law of nations. It affects three distinct groups or parties. First, all the members of the League of Nations, over fifty in number, are debarred by virtue of this doctrine from denying what they had previously assented to, at the time the Mandate for Palestine was confirmed by the League, i.e., that the country in its entirety including Judea, Samaria and Gaza was exclusively reserved for the Jewish People for the purpose of setting up its national home or state.

Second, the doctrine of estoppel also applies with even greater force to the United States, which had specifically accepted all the terms of the Mandate for Palestine in a treaty it signed with Great Britain on December 3, 1924. The ratification of this treaty advised by the U.S. Senate and signed and proclaimed by the President had the additional legal effect of making the Mandate for Palestine and the Balfour Declaration, its breath and essence, part of the domestic law of the country. This is a fact of enormous importance, which has been conveniently forgotten today by the American Government that wrongly calls legally established Israeli settlements in Judea, Samaria and Gaza, "obstacles to peace", and whose expansion it considers “inflammatory and provocative”. By its previous approval of the treaty, the U.S. is legally estopped from denouncing or taking any action against Israeli settlement activity in the Land of Israel.

Finally, the doctrine of estoppel applies with equal validity to all Arab states whose own creation under international law derived from the very same global political and legal settlement made by the Principal Allied Powers at San Remo and Sèvres which led to the establishment of the Jewish State. The Arabs cannot gleefully accept national rights accorded them under this settlement while at the same time denying them to the Jewish People. By doing this, they are engaging in blind and willful disobedience of international law, which is also plainly irrational.

One additional note related to this matter is that it is unnecessary to base the continuation of Jewish legal rights and title to all of former Palestine on Article 80 of the U.N. Charter. This provision was designed as an interim measure until the new trusteeship system set up by the Charter could replace the Mandates System and take full effect. Once the Jewish State came into existence and was recognized, Article 80 ceased to apply to Palestine, since the country could no longer be placed under the trusteeship system by means of a trusteeship agreement. However, this article can still be invoked against the U.N. itself to prevent this organization from altering the national and political rights of the Jewish People to the entire country or to award those rights to any other nation.

Unfortunately what was clearly established in regard to Jewish legal rights and title to all of Palestine under international law both by the San Remo Resolution on Palestine and the Mandate for Palestine became almost immediately obscured and undermined by new events and developments. This process began with the overthrow of the Turkish Sultanate by revolutionary armed forces led by Mustafa Kemal, later called Kemal Ataturk.

After taking complete control of the Turkish Government, Ataturk refused to accede to the loss of any Turkish territories in Anatolia, as called for in the Treaty of Sèvres. These territories included Greek-speaking Smyrna and its surroundings, Cilicia or Little Armenia and the Kurdish-inhabited parts of southeastern Anatolia. His sweeping military triumphs forced the scrapping of the Treaty of Sèvres which was replaced by the Treaty of Lausanne on July 24, 1923, ratified a year later on August 6, 1924. This development did not directly affect the San Remo Resolution on Palestine nor the status of the newly emergent countries detached from the Ottoman Empire that became the Arab states of today. The damage done was of another order.

The various provisions of the Treaty of Sèvres which had clearly set out the new legal structure for Palestine and that of Syria and Mesopotamia in an unambiguous way were not repeated in the Treaty of Lausanne, but simply omitted altogether, replaced by a vague clause (Article 16) lacking the detail of the earlier treaty. This article referred only to the future of territories "being settled or to be settled by the parties concerned" among which was Palestine and over which Turkey again renounced all rights and title, as it had done previously when the Sultan's representatives signed the Treaty of Sèvres.

The change in regime in Turkey thus clouded the legal picture for Palestine in particular since the clear-cut provisions in the Treaty of Sèvres which applied to Palestine, leaving no doubt about Jewish legal rights and title to it and the all-important date of their inception under international law stemming from the San Remo Resolution, were no longer there.

As a result, many renowned jurists have wrongly maintained that Turkey only lost its sovereignty over Palestine and the rest of the Fertile Crescent when it agreed to the Treaty of Lausanne of 1923. However, the Treaty of Versailles of 1919, also recognized by Kemal's Turkey, expressly rebuts that incorrect contention, as does the first recital in the Preamble of the Mandate for Palestine as well as Turkey's earlier acceptance of Wilson's Fourteen Points, delivered in an address to the U.S. Congress on January 8, 1918. The twelfth point of that program dealt specifically with Turkey presaging the limitation of Turkish sovereignty to "the Turkish portions of the... Ottoman Empire". In any event, the provisions of the Treaty of Sèvres still have great evidentiary value despite its non-ratification, to show what the Principal Allied Powers actually had in mind when they adopted the Balfour Declaration in conjunction with Article 22 of the League Covenant as the only legal basis for the implementation of the Mandate for Palestine. The Treaty of Sèvres also remained valid as an inter-Allied Four Powers agreement regarding Palestine.

The changes produced by Ataturk's rise to power were also accompanied by a sudden American intervention in the involved process then underway to confirm all the new mandates that were allotted to Mandatories under the Mandates System. The United States unexpectedly insisted on receiving for itself as well as for its nationals the same rights and benefits that were being given to all members of the League of Nations and their nationals, which would have been granted to them in any event. This new demand unduly held up the pending confirmation of the Mandate for Palestine that had already been submitted by Balfour on behalf of the British Government to the Council of the League of Nations on December 6, 1920, and was on the verge of being acted upon.

The American maneuver produced very deleterious effects for Jewish legal rights and title to all of Palestine. Not only did it prevent the immediate confirmation of the Mandate for Palestine by the Council of the League of Nations, but, more importantly, the irritating delay gave more time to the British Government to manipulate the provisions of the Mandate for Palestine that had already gone through numerous drafts under the guiding hand of the British Foreign Minister. The American Government never acknowledged the damage their unnecessary demands caused the Jewish National Home, even if done unwittingly.

The damage done soon became evident enough. Thanks to the unwelcome American intrusion, the British deviously sneaked in a new provision into the Mandate, that of Article 25, using as a lame excuse Abdullah's threatened advance into Syria to protest his brother's eviction by the French, which had no chance of succeeding but amounted to mere bluster and feigned action. This additional provision to the Mandate for Palestine provided for a different administration of Transjordan from the rest of Palestine west of the Jordan River that led over the course of time, by various illegal steps additionally taken by the British to the complete loss of Transjordan from the Jewish National Home. The loss of that territory, once considered absolutely essential even by Chaim Weizmann and Nahum Sokolow for Palestine's future economic prosperity, deprived Palestine of a great reserve of land that was intended for Jewish settlement and development, as in the olden days when Jewish life flourished there.

The British engaged in other shady maneuvers and artifices whose combined effect was to distort the true legal meaning of the Mandate for Palestine and put in doubt Jewish legal rights and title to the whole country.

The author of this article served as a legal adviser to Professor

Yuval Ne'eman in international law matters affecting the status of the Land of Israel, at the time the latter was Minister of Energy and Infrastructure in the Shamir Government (1990-92). He presented a research paper to the Minister in which he detailed some of the methods or devices employed by Britain to falsify the explicit provisions of the Mandate for Palestine that were meant to secure the establishment of the Jewish National Home and hence the Jewish State.

However, these methods or devices were so skillfully contrived and artfully executed, they fooled most people at the time. And because they were also based on Zionist antecedents provided by the likes of Nahum Sokolow and Asher Ginsberg and supported to a certain extent by the statements of Chaim Weizmann himself, the British were able to get away with their brazen undermining of the Jewish National Home until it became obvious what they had done. By that time, it was already too late to do anything to reform the situation and execute the Mandate according to its original true meaning. The British methods or devices included the following acts of sabotage of the Jewish National Home:

1. Changing the meaning of the words "the establishment in Palestine of a national home for the Jewish People" to connote not the establishment of an independent Jewish State, but rather a cultural or spiritual center, as earlier advocated by both Ahad Ha'Am and Nahum Sokolow.
2. Misrepresenting the Mandatory's solemn obligations under the Mandate to include not only obligations in favour of the Jewish People, but also undertakings of equal weight designed to satisfy Arab aspirations for self-government in Palestine. In truth, there were no British obligations towards Arabs, in a national or collective political sense, which were contained in the Mandate for Palestine, since their claims for nationhood had already been amply satisfied in the neighbouring countries. It is true that the Mandate contained a specific provision making Arabic an official language, but since that was also done for English, it can in no way be deduced that Arab national rights were recognized under that provision alone.
3. Introducing the illegal principle of partition into the Mandate Agreement, which was expressly forbidden by Article 5 of the text of the Mandate. Here the British showed great ingenuity, using all their brilliant grammatical skills to find a mother lode of new meaning from the simple phrase "in Palestine". They turned what was an innocuous expression originally used by the Zionists in the Basle Program of 1897 into a weapon to cut down the size of the Jewish National Home, which was always meant to cover the entire territory comprising historical Palestine.
4. Administering Palestine in such a way as to bring about

the establishment of an independent Arab Government for Palestine, which was, of course, the complete opposite of what was required to be done under the Mandate's provisions. This British policy of converting a Jewish Palestine into an Arab Palestine reached its outrageous apex in the infamous White Paper of May 17, 1939, presented by Colonial Secretary Malcolm Macdonald on behalf of the British Government led by Prime Minister Neville Chamberlain. That constituted an unrivaled act of diabolical treachery that will be remembered for all time because it prevented the rescue of millions of Jews trapped in the Holocaust who could have found refuge in Palestine, had the British truly implemented the Mandate as they were legally required to do.

5. Instituting various restrictions on the entry of Jews into Palestine, despite Britains' solemn international obligation to facilitate Jewish immigration to make possible the creation of an eventual independent Jewish State. These restrictions imposed by Britain were justified by a concept not found in the Mandate, the economic absorptive capacity of the country. The inevitable result was to prevent Jews from becoming a majority of the population of Palestine in as short a period as possible, as originally visualized in the San Remo Resolution and Articles 2 and 6 of the Mandate. Conversely and ironically, the British authorities allowed hundreds of thousands of Arabs to cross over illegally into Cisjordanian Palestine, especially from Syria and Transjordan, thus doubling the size of the local Arab population and frustrating the aim of a *de facto* Jewish State.

Those British figures who were chiefly responsible for tearing asunder the definitive peace settlement reached at San Remo and Sèvres and concomitantly with obfuscating Jewish legal rights and title to all of Mandated Palestine are among the most revered personages in British and Zionist history, specifically George Nathaniel Curzon, Herbert Samuel and Winston Churchill.

Curzon was a leading member in Prime Minister Lloyd George's War Cabinet, who became Foreign Secretary upon the retirement of Arthur James Balfour. He was placed in charge of Palestine's affairs during the critical formative period of the Mandate when it was in the midst of being drafted. He displayed a very negative attitude to the task he was assigned. He detested (and this is not too strong a word) the whole idea of creating a Jewish State and did his utmost to weaken its legal basis and to slow it down. He was ably aided by his officials who were much less hostile to Jewish aspirations, notable among whom were Eric Graham Forbes Adam, Robert Vansittart and Hubert Young. What Curzon managed to do was to detrimentally change many of the original clear-cut provisions of the Mandate for Palestine designed to secure its establishment as a

Jewish State, which had already been approved earlier by Balfour when he was in charge of overseeing the actual drafting of the Mandate for Palestine.

Despite Curzon's best attempts to prevent a Jewish state from being seen as the real and most important objective of the Mandate for Palestine, he did not fully succeed. That job was left to two others, Herbert Samuel and Winston Churchill, who were put in charge of Palestine's affairs, when jurisdiction over colonies and mandated territories was taken away from the Foreign Office and transferred to the Colonial Office early in 1921.

The nefarious work begun by Curzon was ironically taken over and completed by the erstwhile Zionist, Herbert Samuel, who just before his appointment as British High Commissioner in Palestine worked closely with Chaim Weizmann in the Zionist Organization and helped to prepare the Zionist proposals submitted to the Paris Peace Conference of 1919. Samuel's subsequent undermining of what was the true intent of the Mandate for Palestine was recorded in the anti-Zionist "Churchill White Paper" of June 3, 1922, which he wrote with the blessing and connivance of Winston Churchill, then the Secretary of State for the Colonies, and which was accepted under ominous circumstances by the official Zionist leadership just prior to its release.

It was this White Paper of June 3, 1922 which was a turning point which caused all the future difficulties in Palestine and wrecked the original plan for establishing an independent Jewish State under British tutelage. The reason is simple enough. After publication of this White Paper, all British Governments which followed over the years implemented not the actual terms of the Mandate for Palestine but the interpretation or policy contained in the White Paper as to what the British responsibility and role was to be under the Mandate. The latter required a Jewish State, while the Churchill White Paper negated it, despite Churchill's false claim that such a state was not precluded, made fourteen years later in his testimony before the Peel Royal Commission. His White Paper also elevated Arab pretensions and aspirations to such an extent that everything thereafter became muddled and unclear, subject to continuous disputes as to what was really intended by the Mandate for Palestine.

The British circumvention of the Mandate for Palestine continued apace during the entire period of civilian Mandatory rule, which lasted from July 1, 1920 to May 14, 1948.

The question now arises in light of what occurred in the past just what Israel can do today to rectify the British legacy of betrayal and the consequent widespread ignorance surrounding Jewish legal rights and title to all of former Palestine. The answer is to first learn what the rights granted to the Jewish People under international law were (i.e., under the San Remo Resolution adopting the Balfour Declaration on April 24, 1920 and its projected implementation in the Mandate for Palestine, conferred on Britain the following day), and then appreciate how true international law was perverted and sabotaged by the British. This is extremely important because everyone today cites "international law" in favour of a fictitious nation called the "Palestinians" whose land is being "occupied" by the Jewish nation of Israel which is highly ironic and even laughable in view of the fact that this land that is called "occupied" was always meant under Articles 6 and 11 of the Mandate for Palestine to be "closely settled" not by Gentile Arabs, but by the Jews of the world who would become Palestinian and then Israeli Jews in the course of time. What true international law is on the subject is neither discussed nor exposed nor really known by hardly anyone.

Next, Israel must act according to what that law truly presupposes, namely a Jewish State in the whole Land of Israel, including both sides of the Jordan. Present circumstances, of course, do not allow for the fulfillment of all Jewish rights to the country, particularly as regards those parts of Transjordan which comprise the Land of Israel such as Gilead and Bashan, but those rights should never be renounced, which, lamentably, is exactly what has been done illegally by the Government and Knesset of Israel in concluding and approving a peace treaty with Jordan.

It is safe to assume that the foregoing advice will never be acted upon so long as there is an anti-nationalist Labour party and other "peace parties" who advocate a spurious peace, instead of believing in and fighting for the integrity and non-partition of the Land of Israel. Sadly, the same may even be said about the Likud party in its present configuration, because it has abandoned the ideology and spirit of what the original Herut Party once advocated in the 1950's and 1960's, namely an indivisible Land of Israel. While no one should denigrate the cause of true peace, no country in the history of the world ever voluntarily divested itself of important parts of its legally recognized ancestral homeland, for the sake of this goal. Neither should the State of Israel.

Only a future Government of Israel infused with the proper Jewish nationalist and religious spirit, knowledge and pride can change what is today a murky and forlorn situation.

As for what can be done actually now, Israel must –

[1] immediately scrap the "Oslo Peace Process" which, incredibly, recognizes the national and political rights of a motley Gentile people to substantial parts of the Land of Israel;

[2] evict the so-called and falsely-denominated "Palestinian Authority" and its entire leadership from the Jewish country, and

[3] annex or incorporate all of Judea, Samaria and Gaza into the Jewish State;

[4] All Arabs who do not profess loyalty to the Jewish State must leave the country and be re-settled in other Moslem countries, just as happened between the Greeks and the Turks after World War I;

[5] No Arab parties professing national and collective political rights for Arabs in the Jewish country should be allowed to sit in the Knesset.

The Moslems who live in the Land of Israel are not the indigenous inhabitants, as they falsely claim to be. They are mainly foreign Gentiles, all of whom are of mixed ancestry, including some of Jewish descent who were forcibly converted in centuries past. These foreign Gentiles (in Hebrew: *nochrim*) have no national rights to the Land of Israel and/or Palestine. They have boldly appropriated, without any right to do so, the name of "Palestinians" for themselves, though there is no such nation and have also removed this name from its Jewish and Zionist context under the Mandate. Their claims are totally invented and are deliberately imitative of genuine Jewish national rights which exist for no other nation in the Land of Israel, but which are now impugned under a false perception or reading of international law.

The future steps that need to be taken to restore all of the Jewish country to its sovereign owner, the Jewish People, are now clear enough.

It is fervently hoped that the day is not far off that Israel will finally abandon what has been the most dangerous and suicidal course for a Jewish government to ever have followed: a policy which illegally transfers integral parts of the Jewish homeland to an implacable enemy bent on destroying the State and which has allowed that enemy to create foreign rule and the rudiments of a state and army in the very midst of the Jewish country, led by gangs of bloody terrorists and murderers as seen only too well today.

# Index

## A

## C

### K

***L***



***M***

### *T*

## U



## V

### W



### Y



### Z